LITTLE, BROWN AND COMPANY

Law School Casebook Series

The Employment Relation and the Law. Edited by BENJAMIN AARON, Professor of Law and Director, Institute of Industrial Relations, University of California at Los Angeles

Federal Income Taxation. WILLIAM D. ANDREWS, Professor of Law, Harvard University

Antitrust Analysis: Problems, Text, Cases. PHILLIP AREEDA, Professor of Law, Harvard University

Land Transfer and Finance. ALLAN AXELROD, Professor of Law, Rutgers University, CURTIS J. BERGER, Professor of Law, Columbia University, and QUINTIN JOHNSTONE, Justus S. Hotchkiss Professor of Law, Yale University

Land Ownership and Use: Cases, Statutes, and Other Materials. CURTIS J. BERGER, Professor of Law, Columbia University

International Law: Cases and Materials. Third Edition. WILLIAM W. BISHOP, JR., Edwin M. Dickinson Professor of Law, University of Michigan

Federal Income, Estate and Gift Taxation. Third Edition. BORIS I. BITTKER, Southmayd Professor of Law, Yale University

Materials on Reorganization, Recapitalization and Insolvency. WALTER J. BLUM, Professor of Law, University of Chicago, and STANLEY A. KAPLAN, Professor of Law, University of Chicago

Jurisdiction and Judgments: Cases and Statutes. WILLIAM WIRT BLUME, Professor of Law, University of California, Hastings College of Law, and CHARLES W. JOINER, Dean and Professor of Law, Wayne State University

Pleading and Joinder: Cases and Statutes. WILLIAM WIRT BLUME, Professor of Law, University of California, Hastings College of Law, and JOHN W. REED, Professor of Law, University of Michigan

Civil Procedure: Cases and Comments on the Process of Adjudication. PAUL D. CARRINGTON, Professor of Law, University of Michigan

Estate Planning. Third Edition. A. JAMES CASNER, Weld Professor of Law, Harvard University

Cases and Text on Property. Second Edition. A. JAMES CASNER, Weld Professor of Law, Harvard University, and W. BARTON LEACH, Story Professor of Law, Emeritus, Harvard University

International Legal Process. ABRAM CHAYES, Professor of Law, Harvard University, THOMAS EHRLICH, Professor of Law, Stanford University, and ANDREAS F. LOWENFELD, Professor of Law, New York University

Cases and Materials on Debtor and Creditor. VERN COUNTRYMAN, Professor of Law, Harvard University

The Lawyer in Modern Society. VERN COUNTRYMAN, Professor of Law, Harvard University, and TED FINMAN, Professor of Law, University of Wisconsin

Law, Medicine and Forensic Science. WILLIAM J. CURRAN, Frances Glessner Lee Professor of Legal Medicine, Harvard Medical School, Harvard School of Public Health, and E. DONALD SHAPIRO, Director, Practising Law Institute, Adjunct Professor of Law, New York University

Trade Regulation: Cases and Materials. FRANK ELKOURI, Professor of Law, University of Oklahoma

Political and Civil Rights in the United States. Third Edition. THOMAS I. EMERSON, Lines Professor of Law, Yale University, DAVID HABER, Professor of Law, Rutgers University, and NORMAN DORSEN, Professor of Law and Director, Arthur Garfield Hays Civil Liberties Program, New York University

Cases and Materials on Family Law. CALEB FOOTE, Professor of Law and Criminology, University of California at Berkeley, ROBERT J. LEVY, Professor of Law, University of Minnesota, and FRANK E. A. SANDER, Professor of Law, Harvard University

Constitutional Law: Cases and Other Problems. Third Edition. PAUL A. FREUND, Carl M. Loeb University Professor, Harvard University, ARTHUR E. SUTHERLAND, Bussey Professor of Law, Emeritus, Harvard University, MARK DE WOLFE HOWE, late Charles Warren Professor of American Legal History, Harvard University, and ERNEST J. BROWN, Langdell Professor of Law, Harvard University

Cases and Materials on Corporations. ALEXANDER H. FREY, Algernon Sidney Biddle Professor of Law, Emeritus, University of Pennsylvania, C. ROBERT MORRIS, JR., Professor of Law, University of Minnesota, and JESSE CHOPER, Professor of Law, University of California at Berkeley

Cases and Materials on Torts. Second Edition. CHARLES O. GREGORY, John B. Minor Professor of Law, Emeritus, University of Virginia, and HARRY KALVEN, JR., Professor of Law, University of Chicago

Land-Use Planning: A Casebook on the Use, Misuse, and Re-use of Urban Land. CHARLES M. HAAR, Professor of Law, Harvard University

Administrative Law: Cases and Materials. Third Edition. LOUIS L. JAFFE, Byrne Professor of Administrative Law, Harvard University, and NATHANIEL L. NATHANSON, Frederic P. Vose Professor of Law, Northwestern University

Criminal Law and Its Processes: Cases and Materials. Second Edition. SANFORD H. KADISH, Professor of Law, University of California at Berkeley, and MONRAD G. PAULSEN, Dean and John B. Minor Professor of Law, University of Virginia

Constitutional Law: Cases and Materials. Third Edition. PAUL G. KAUPER, Henry M. Butzel Professor of Law, University of Michigan

Contracts: Cases and Materials. Second Edition. FRIEDRICH KESSLER, Professor of Law, University of California at Berkeley, and GRANT GILMORE, Harry A. Bigelow Professor of Law, University of Chicago

Basic Business Associations: Cases, Text and Problems. ELVIN R. LATTY, Dean Emeritus and William R. Perkins Professor of Law, Duke University, and GEORGE T. FRAMPTON, Professor of Law and Vice-Chancellor for Campus Affairs, University of Illinois

Cases and Text on the Law of Wills. Second Edition, 1960 Revision. W. BARTON LEACH, Story Professor of Law, Emeritus, Harvard University

Labor Law: Cases, Materials, and Problems. BERNARD D. MELTZER, Professor of Law, University of Chicago

Commercial Transactions: Cases and Materials. SOIA MENTSCHIKOFF, Professor of Law, University of Chicago

Legislation: Cases and Materials. FRANK C. NEWMAN, Professor of Law, University of California at Berkeley, and STANLEY S. SURREY, Jeremiah Smith, Jr., Professor of Law, Harvard University

Family Law: Cases and Materials. MORRIS PLOSCOWE, Adjunct Associate Professor of Law, New York University, and DORIS JONAS FREED, of the New York and Maryland Bars

State and Local Government Law. SHO SATO, Professor of Law, University of California at Berkeley, and ARVO VAN ALSTYNE, Professor of Law, University of Utah

Problems and Materials on Decedents' Estates and Trusts. EUGENE F. SCOLES, Dean and Professor of Law, University of Oregon, and EDWARD C. HALBACH, JR., Dean and Professor of Law, University of California at Berkeley

Cases and Other Materials on Civil Procedure. AUSTIN WAKEMAN SCOTT, Dane Professor of Law, Emeritus, Harvard University, and ROBERT B. KENT, Professor of Law, Boston University

Select Cases and Other Authorities on the Law of Trusts. AUSTIN WAKEMAN SCOTT, Dane Professor of Law, Emeritus, Harvard University, and AUSTIN WAKEMAN SCOTT, JR., late Professor of Law, University of Colorado

The Civil Law System: Cases and Materials for the Comparative Study of Law. ARTHUR TAYLOR VON MEHREN, Professor of Law, Harvard University

The Law of Multistate Problems: Cases and Materials on Conflict of Laws. ARTHUR TAYLOR VON MEHREN, Professor of Law, Harvard University, and DONALD THEODORE TRAUTMAN, Professor of Law, Harvard University

Labor Relations and the Law. Third Edition. THE LABOR LAW GROUP TRUST Under the Editorship of JERRE WILLIAMS, Rex G. and Edna Heflin Baker Professor of Constitutional Law, University of Texas, and Others

Cases on Contracts. SAMUEL WILLISTON, late Dane Professor of Law, Harvard University, Revised Sixth Edition by WILLIAM T. LAUBE, A. F. and May T. Morrison Professor of Law, University of California at Berkeley

Federal Income Taxation of Business Enterprise. BERNARD WOLFMAN, Dean and Professor of Law, University of Pennsylvania

Law School Textbook Series

Public Law Perspectives on a Private Law Problem: Auto Compensation Plans. WALTER J. BLUM, Professor of Law, University of Chicago, and HARRY KALVEN, JR., Professor of Law, University of Chicago

American Civil Procedure. WILLIAM WIRT BLUME, Professor of Law, University of California, Hastings College of Law

Readings in Jurisprudence and Legal Philosophy. MORRIS R. COHEN, late Professor of Law, City College of New York, and FELIX S. COHEN, late Visiting Professor of Law, City College of New York, and Visiting Lecturer, Yale University

The Elements of Law. THOMAS E. DAVITT, S.J., Professor of Jurisprudence, Marquette University

Handbook of Modern Equity. Second Edition. WILLIAM Q. DE FUNIAK, Visiting Professor of Law, McGeorge School of Law, University of the Pacific

The Fundamentals of Legal Drafting. F. REED DICKERSON, Professor of Law, University of Indiana (Bloomington)

The Growth of American Law: The Law Makers. JAMES WILLARD HURST, Vilas Professor of Law, University of Wisconsin

Judicial Control of Administrative Action. Abridged Student Edition. LOUIS L. JAFFE, Byrne Professor of Administrative Law, Harvard University

Civil Procedure. FLEMING JAMES, JR., Sterling Professor of Law, Yale University

Trial Tactics and Methods. ROBERT E. KEETON, Professor of Law, Harvard University

Securities Regulation. Student Edition. LOUIS LOSS, William Nelson Cromwell Professor of Law, Harvard University

A Concise History of the Common Law. Fifth Edition. THEODORE F. T. PLUCKNETT, Late Professor of Legal History in the University of London

Effective Legal Research. Third Edition. MILES O. PRICE, late Professor of Law and Law Librarian, Columbia University, and HARRY BITNER, Professor of Law and Law Librarian, Cornell University

Scott's Abridgment of The Law of Trusts. AUSTIN WAKEMAN SCOTT, Dane Professor of Law, Emeritus, Harvard University

Handbook of Law Study. FERDINAND FAIRFAX STONE, W. R. Irby Professor of Law and Director of Institute of Comparative Law, Tulane University

Federal Income Taxation

of

Business Enterprise

BERNARD WOLFMAN

DEAN AND PROFESSOR OF LAW
UNIVERSITY OF PENNSYLVANIA

LITTLE, BROWN AND COMPANY
Boston   Toronto

LIBRARY OF CONGRESS CATALOG CARD NO. 72-87782

58U1-8/71

Published simultaneously in Canada
by Little, Brown & Company (Canada) Limited

PRINTED IN THE UNITED STATES OF AMERICA

To
Zelda Wolfman

Preface

This book grew from teaching materials and a temporary edition developed for advanced course work in federal income taxation. It assumes the background of a basic federal income tax course covering the pervasive issues pertinent to both corporate and non-corporate taxpayers.

The book's principal vehicle is Subchapter C of the Internal Revenue Code of 1954, which gives rise to most of the federal income tax questions affecting corporations and their investors. Every case and ruling presented will require attention to the applicable provisions of the Code and Treasury Regulations.

Part I of the book (Chapters 1 through 4) is the core. It addresses the tax issues of common concern to both publicly and closely held corporations and their investors. The materials in this part are designed for a three-semester-hour offering.

In the main, Part II (Chapters 5 through 9) exposes some of the problems special to closely held enterprises. It is less detailed than Part I. Chapter 5 introduces partnership taxation, intended to illustrate some of the structural questions and to provide a basis for comparison with the tax treatment of corporations under Subchapter C and Subchapter S of the Code. Chapter 9 is less concerned with closely held business. It presents some of the peculiar tax issues posed by the fact of corporate fiction.

Part II is designed for a two-semester-hour course, although both parts can be adapted to a single four-semester-hour course. The book can also serve as a resource for seminar-centered problem solving and research. See B. Wolfman, A Seminar in Counseling—Tax Conscious Planning of Corporate Transactions, 16 J. Legal Ed. 181 (1963), for a description of a seminar format for the study of corporate income taxation.

Tax lawyers, particularly those who deal with corporate tax problems, often seek advance rulings from the Internal Revenue Service before advising their clients to enter important business transactions. Part A of the Appendix contains material designed to introduce the student to rulings procedure. Part B of the Appendix reproduces problems which have been used in planning seminars and in examinations. They are presented as possible research tools, for discussion, and for study and review by students on their own.

The division of the book into chapters and the order of the chapters reflect my personal pedagogic scheme and my sense of how best to present a complex body of law with a thematic underpinning. But there is no magic to the ordering of the chapters, no clearly right place to begin. Although for me it has been useful to start with the corporation income tax (Chapter 1), others may prefer to begin with problems of incorporation (Chapter 3), or to introduce the course with tax-free reorganizations (Chapter 4).

Liberties have been taken. Footnotes in the cases have been omitted freely, often without renumbering those that remain. Citations to the Internal Revenue Code of 1954 have been substituted for provisions of earlier statutes where substitution seemed helpful. Brackets will indicate this change. Where the original statutory language is important, it is preserved; sometimes the corresponding provision of current law is indicated for comparative purposes.

This is a *casebook*.* My experience suggests that the case method, with its painstaking concern for judicial extrapolation of the statute, is more likely than other methods to guide students to the points of inquiry and understanding which make for a broad perspective, a sense of organic legal development, and a critical, even skeptical, view of accepted policy and dogma.

I am grateful to my students at Pennsylvania. Those teachers helped me in the preparation of both my early teaching materials and the temporary edition of this casebook published in 1969. The comments and criticisms of students and professors at Pennsylvania and elsewhere helped me produce this permanent edition.

Bernard Wolfman

Philadelphia
June, 1971

*CCH Federal Taxation—Current Cases and Comment provides up-to-date developments with appropriate cross-references to this casebook. For textual treatment of corporate income taxation, see B. Bittker and J. Eustice, Federal Income Taxation of Corporations and Shareholders (3d ed. 1971) and D. Kahn, Basic Corporate Taxation (1970). For a text on federal income taxation generally, see J. Chommie, The Law of Federal Income Taxation (Hornbook Series 1968).

Summary of Contents

Table of Contents

PART II

Table of Cases

Italic type indicates principal cases.

xix

Table of Internal Revenue Rulings and Procedures

Italic type indicates principal rulings and procedures.

Miscellaneous Authorities

PART I

1 | The Corporation Income Tax

I. HISTORY AND RATE STRUCTURE

Congress has imposed a tax on the income of corporations without interruption since 1909. An earlier federal tax on corporate income imposed in 1894 fell with the tax on individual incomes in Pollock v. Farmers' Loan & Trust Co., 158 U.S. 601 (1895). The constitutionality of the 1909 corporate impost was sustained in Flint v. Stone Tracy Co., 220 U.S. 107 (1911), as an "indirect" or "excise" tax, not requiring apportionment, on the corporation's "exercise of the privilege" of engaging in business as a corporation. The federal income tax enacted during the Civil War treated corporate income as the income of its shareholders and taxed the individual shareholders accordingly. Today partnership income is treated as the income of the partners and taxed to them, but corporate income is taxed to the corporation, and its shareholders are taxed only on the dividends which the corporation distributes to them.

Because corporations may not ordinarily deduct from their income the dividends they pay to their shareholders, corporate income is said to be subject in general to a "double tax," to a tax at the corporate level and then, when and if the income is distributed to shareholders, to a tax as income in the hands of the shareholders.

The tax on corporations is imposed by §11 of the Internal Revenue Code of 1954. It consists of a "normal tax" of 22 per cent of taxable income and a "surtax" of 26 per cent. The first $25,000 of taxable income is exempt from the surtax. This means that corporations whose taxable incomes exceed $25,000 pay a tax equal to 48 per cent of their taxable income less $6500 (26% x $25,000). Corporations whose incomes do not exceed $25,000 pay a tax of 22 per cent. Although the jump in rate effective once a corporation's taxable income exceeds $25,000 is substantial, and it introduces a degree of graduation into the overall corporate rate structure, the degree of graduation is modest by comparison with the progression of rates applicable under the individual income tax. The Tax Reform Act of 1969 imposed a "minimum tax" of 10 per cent on items of "tax preference" (§§56-58), applicable for the most part to corporations as to other taxpayers.

Corporate tax rates have fluctuated widely since Congress imposed a one per cent tax on corporate income in excess of $5000 in 1909. As recently as 1963 the corporate rate on income over $25,000 was 52 per cent, and the rate applicable to income up to $25,000 was 30 per cent. During wartime Congress has sometimes imposed corporate excess profits taxes which exacted taxes at very high rates on the income remaining after imposition of the ordinary corporate tax to the extent that it exceeded the income of a specified prewar period or exceeded a "normal" return on invested capital.

Today the corporate income tax produces about 25 per cent of federal revenues, with approximately 1,250,000 corporate returns being filed. (The individual income tax produces about 40 per cent of federal revenues, with approximately 68 million individual returns being filed.)

The so-called "double tax" on corporate income is relieved to a degree by the provisions of §116 which permit all noncorporate shareholders to exclude from their income $100 of dividend income each year. Corporate shareholders may be entitled to a more liberal "dividends received deduction" (§243). Creditors of a corporation must include the interest they receive in their income without the benefit of any exclusion or credit, but the corporate debtor (like an individual debtor) is permitted by §163 to deduct all interest paid. The fact that corporations may deduct interest but not dividends has an effect on the extent to which corporations seek debt rather than equity capital.

There are a number of special types of corporations which the Code treats specially, some tax-exempt like the University of Pennsylvania, others, like insurance companies, taxable under special formulae (Subchapter L of the Code). This chapter is concerned with the ordinary business corporation whose taxable income is subject to tax under §11.

II. THE CORPORATION'S INCOME — ITS SPECIAL ASPECTS

"Taxable income" is the base on which the corporation income tax is levied. For the most part "taxable income" is computed for the corporation as it is for the individual businessman. The makeup of gross income and the allowable business deductions are substantially the same for corporations and businessmen. The so-called personal deductions, dependency exemptions, and the standard deduction are not allowed to corporations. The charitable deduction is available, but with limitations and conditions that are unique to corporations.

Some transactions which are peculiar to corporations have generated problems in determining a corporation's gross income that do not arise in the case of an individual. Others have generated unique problems as to deductions. As the materials in this part of the chapter will illustrate, these transactions ordinarily involve dealings between the corporations and its present or prospective investors.

A. *"GROSS INCOME"*

1. *Distribution of Assets "In Kind"*

a. TO SHAREHOLDERS — §§311, 336

GENERAL UTILITIES & OPERATING CO. v. HELVERING
296 U.S. 200 (1935),
rev'g 74 F.2d 972 (4th Cir. 1935)

Mr. Justice McReynolds delivered the opinion of the Court. January 1st, 1927, petitioner — General Utilities, a Delaware corporation — acquired 20,000 shares (one-half of total outstanding) common stock Islands Edison Company, for which it paid $2,000. Gillet & Company owned the remainder.

During January, 1928, Whetstone, President of Southern Cities Utilities Company, contemplated acquisition by his company of all Islands Edison common stock. He discussed the matter with Lucas, petitioner's president, also with Gillet & Company. The latter concern agreed to sell its holdings upon terms acceptable to all. But Lucas pointed out that the shares which his company held could only be purchased after distribution of them among stockholders, since a sale by it would subject the realized profit to taxation, and when the proceeds passed to the stockholders there would be further exaction. Lucas had no power to sell, but he, Gillet and Whetstone were in accord concerning the terms and conditions under which purchase of all the stock might become possible — "it being understood and agreed between them that petitioner would make distribution of the stock of the Islands Edison Company to its stockholders and that counsel would prepare a written agreement embodying the terms and conditions of the said sale, agreement to be submitted for approval to the stockholders of the Islands Edison Company after the distribution of said stock by the petitioner."

Petitioner's directors, March 22, 1928, considered the disposition of the Islands Edison shares. Officers reported they were worth $1,122,500, and recommended an appreciation on the books to that figure. Thereupon a resolution directed this change; also "that a dividend in the amount of $1,071,426.25 be and it is hereby declared on the Common Stock of this Company payable in Common Stock of The Islands Edison Company at a valuation of $56.12½ a share, out of the surplus of the Company arising from the appreciation in the value of the Common Stock of The Islands Edison Company held by this Company, viz., $1,120,500.00, the payment of the dividend to be made by the delivery to the stockholders of this Company, pro rata, of certificates for the Common Stock of The Islands Edison Company held by this Company at the rate of two shares of such stock for each share of Company Stock of this Corporation."

Accordingly, 19,090 shares were distributed amongst petitioner's thirty-three stockholders and proper transfers to them were made upon the issuing corporation's books. It retained 910 shares.

After this transfer, all holders of Islands Edison stock, sold to Southern Cities Utilities Company at $56.12½ per share. Petitioner realized $46,346.30 net profit on 910 shares and this was duly returned for taxation. There was no report of gain upon the 19,090 shares distributed to stockholders.

The Commissioner of Internal Revenue declared a taxable gain upon distribution of the stock in payment of the dividend declared March 22nd, and made the questioned deficiency assessment. Seeking redetermination by the Board of Tax Appeals, petitioner alleged, "The Commissioner of Internal Revenue has erroneously held that the petitioner corporation made a profit of $1,069,517.25 by distributing to its own stockholders certain capital stock of another corporation which it had theretofore owned." And it asked a ruling that no taxable gain resulted from the appreciation upon its books and subsequent distribution of the shares. Answering, the Commissioner denied that his action was erroneous, but advanced no new basis of support. A stipulation concerning the facts followed; and upon this and the pleadings, the Board heard the cause.

It found "The respondent has determined a deficiency in income tax in the amount of $128,342.07 for the calendar year 1928. The only question presented in this proceeding for redetermination is whether petitioner realized taxable gain in declaring a dividend and paying it in the stock of another company at an agreed value per share, which value was in excess of the cost of the stock to petitioner." Also, "On March 26, 1928, the stockholders of the Islands Edison Company (one of which was petitioner, owning 910 shares) and the Southern Cities Utilities Company, entered into a written contract of sale of the Islands Edison Company stock. At no time did petitioner agree with Whetstone or the Southern Cities Utilities Company, verbally or in writing, to make sale to him or to the Southern Cities Utilities Company of any of said stock except the aforesaid 910 shares of the Islands Edison Company."

The opinion recites — The Commissioner's "theory is that upon the declaration of the dividend on March 22, 1928, petitioner became indebted to its stockholders in the amount of $1,071,426.25, and that the discharge of that liability by the delivery of property costing less than the amount of the debt constituted income, citing United States v. Kirby Lumber Co., 284 U.S. 1." "The intent of the directors of petitioner was to declare a dividend payable in Islands Edison stock; their intent was expressed in that way in the resolution formally adopted; and the dividend was paid in the way intended and declared. We so construe the transaction, and on authority of First Utah Savings Bank, supra [17 B.T.A. 804; aff'd, 60 App. D.C. 307; 53 F.(2d) 919 (1931)], we hold that the declaration and payment of the dividend resulted in no taxable income."

The Commissioner asked the Circuit Court of Appeals, 4th Circuit, to review the Board's determination. He alleged, "The only question to be decided is whether the petitioner [taxpayer] realized taxable income in declaring a dividend and paying it in stock of another company at an agreed value per share, which value was in excess of the cost of the stock."

The court stated: "There are two grounds upon which the petitioner urges that the action of the Board of Tax Appeals was wrong: First, that the dividend declared was in effect a cash dividend and that the respondent realized a taxable income by the distribution of the Islands Edison Company stock to its stockholders equal to the difference between the amount of the dividend declared and the cost of the stock; second, that the sale made of the Islands Edison Company stock was in reality a sale by the respondent (with all the terms agreed upon before the declaration of the dividend), through its stockholders who were virtually acting as agents of the respondent, the real vendor."

Upon the first ground, it sustained the Board. Concerning the second, it held that, although not raised before the Board, the point should be ruled upon. "When we come to consider the sale of the stock of the Islands Edison Company, we cannot escape the conclusion that the transaction was deliberately planned and carried out for the sole purpose of escaping taxation. The purchaser was found by the officers of the respondent; the exact terms of the sale as finally consummated were agreed to by the same officers; the purchaser of the stock stated that the delivery of all the stock was essential and that the delivery of a part thereof would not suffice; the details were worked out for the express and admitted purpose of avoiding the payment of the tax and for the reason that the attorneys for the respondent had advised that, unless some such plan was adopted, the tax would have to be paid; and a written agreement was to be prepared by counsel for the respondent which was to be submitted to the stockholders — all this without the stockholders, or any of them, who were ostensibly making the sale, being informed, advised, or consulted. Such admitted facts plainly constituted a plan, not to use the harsher terms of scheme, artifice or conspiracy, to evade the payment of the tax. For the purposes of this decision, it is not necessary to consider whether such a course as is here shown constituted a fraud, it is sufficient if we conclude that the object was to evade the payment of a tax justly due the government.

"The sale of the stock in question was, in substance, made by the respondent company, through the stockholders as agents or conduits through whom the transfer of the title was effected. The stockholders, even in their character as agents, had little or no option in the matter and in no sense exercised any independent judgment. They automatically ratified the agreement prepared and submitted to them."

A judgment of reversal followed.

Both tribunals below rightly decided that petitioner derived no taxable gain from the distribution among its stockholders of the Islands Edison shares as a dividend. This was no sale; assets were not used to discharge indebtedness.

The second ground of objection, although sustained by the court, was not presented to or ruled upon by the Board. The petition for review relied wholly upon the first point; and, in the circumstances, we think the court should have considered no other. Always a taxpayer is entitled to know with fair certainty the basis of the claim against him. Stipulations concerning facts and any other evidence properly are accommodated to issues adequately raised.

Recently (April, 1935) this court pointed out: "The Court of Appeals is without power on review of proceedings of the Board of Tax Appeals to make any findings of fact." "The function of the court is to decide whether the correct rule of law was applied to the facts found; and whether there was substantial evidence before the Board to support the findings made." "If the Board has failed to make an essential finding and the record on review is insufficient to provide the basis for a final determination, the proper procedure is to remand the case for further proceedings before the Board." "And the same procedure is appropriate even when the findings omitted by the Board might be supplied from examination of the records." Helvering v. Rankin, 295 U.S. 123, 131, 132.

Here the court undertook to decide a question not properly raised. Also it made an inference of fact directly in conflict with the stipulation of the parties and the findings, for which we think the record affords no support whatever. To remand the cause for further findings would be futile. The Board could not properly find anything which would assist the Commissioner's cause.

The judgment of the court below must be reversed. The action of the Board of Tax Appeals is approved.

Reversed.

NOTE

1. On procedural grounds the Supreme Court rejected the Government's argument that the shareholder's sale of the stock should be attributed to the corporation. Implicit in the Government's contention was the twofold proposition that a sale by a corporation triggers realization of gain, but that absent a sale (and an "amount realized") by the corporation there is no realization. Ten years later the Government succeeded in an "attribution of sale" approach in Commissioner v. Court Holding Co., page 20 infra.

The Supreme Court rejected on its merits the Government's contention that distribution of the stock was the equivalent of a sale in that it satisfied a corporate debt which the corporation owed to its shareholders as a result of the dividend declaration. The Board of Tax Appeals and the Court of Appeals had also rejected this contention. The Supreme Court (page 7 supra) said "this was no sale; assets were not used to discharge indebtedness." Why is "sale" so crucial? Was there no "indebtedness," or was it that assets were not used to "discharge" it?

The Supreme Court's opinion ignored a third contention advanced by the Government. The Government argued that "in making it available to its own stockholders the corporation is realizing the appreciation, and nothing more is necessary. It . . . is incomprehensible how a corporation can distribute to its stockholders something which it has not itself received." Brief for Commissioner at 18-19, Commissioner v. Court Holding Co., 324 U.S. 331 (1945). In essence the Government contended that the distribution of the stock, if not a "sale," was nevertheless a "disposition," and that in distributing the appreciation to its shareholders the "amount" was "realized." §1001(a). The Court's failure to deal with this contention is not explained. The Government's failure to raise the argument in either of the lower courts may be the reason. Nevertheless, the *General Utilities* decision is widely regarded as standing for the proposition that a corporation realizes no income (or loss) on the distribution of appreciated (or depreciated) assets to its shareholders. For many years the Regulations had stated that a liquidating distribution of appreciated (or depreciated) property does not trigger a realization of gain (or loss) (Treas. Reg. 118, §39.22(a)-20 (1939 Code)), and *General Utilities* seemed to many to confirm that "rule" in the case of nonliquidating distributions by operating corporations. (In tax parlance a corporation is "liquidating" when it distributes its assets to its shareholders in retirement of their stock. Liquidation does not connote the conversion of non-cash assets into cash.)

2. Under the *General Utilities* doctrine, if a corporation owns a marketable asset with an adjusted basis of $10,000 and a fair market value of $20,000, if it wishes its shareholders to have $20,000, and if neither the corporation nor the shareholders want the asset, the corporation may be well advised to distribute the asset to the individual shareholders as tenants-in-common. They will be able to sell it for cash without incurring any individual income tax liability different from the liability that would have attended a cash dividend. (The shareholders would ordinarily include the asset in their income at its fair market value, §301(b)(1)(A), and the basis of the asset in the shareholders' hands would be its fair market value, §301(d)(1). When they sell the asset at that value their cash and tax will be the same as they would have been if the dividend had been paid in cash.) The tax posture of a corporate shareholder receiving a dividend-in-kind differs from that of a non-corporate distributee. See §§301(b)(1)(B) and (d)(2). (The taxation of corporate distributees will be discussed on page 75 infra. The taxation of noncorporate distributees will be discussed in Chapter 2.)

3. Why had the Commissioner conceded in the Regulations that no corporate gain or loss was to be recognized in liquidating distributions? On what basis might the tax treatment of interim distributions by an ongoing corporation be differentiated? Ought they be differentiated? Might the Commissioner have fared better in *General Utilities* if he had first revoked the provisions of the Regulations as to liquidating distributions and then had promulgated one that asserted that any distribution of an asset to its shareholders would result in corporate realization of gain or loss to the same extent as in a sale? Should he have done so after *General Utilities*? Would such a provision have been valid after that decision? Bear in mind that, despite the *General Utilities* doctrine as it came to be, the Supreme Court ignored the Government's third argument. Would it have been reasonable for the Treasury to seek a statutory reversal of *General Utilities* as to gain but not as to loss? Is there a reasonable basis for treating loss in an interim distribution differently from loss in a liquidating distribution, at least in the case of closely held corporations? See §§267(a)(1) and (b)(2).

4. After the *General Utilities* decision the Government placed renewed emphasis on form. In cases where a dividend declaration called merely for the distribution of an asset, the Government did not assert that a corporate realization had occurred when the asset was distributed. Where the dividend resolution

spoke in terms of a dollar amount, distribution of an appreciated asset in payment of the dividend frequently brought forth a claim of realization on a "satisfaction of debt" theory. It was the Commissioner's position that *General Utilities* had not disturbed cases like Bacon-McMillan Veneer Co., 20 B.T.A. 556 (1930), in which such claims had been sustained. The apparent importance of the form of the dividend declaration was dramatized in Natural Gasoline Corp. v. Commissioner, 219 F.2d 682 (10th Cir. 1955), where the issue turned on the deftness and clarity of the language used in the dividend resolution. Reversing the Tax Court, the Court of Appeals accepted the taxpayer's interpretation of the unsophisticated language of its directors.

5. Tax lawyers expected that the general revision of the Internal Revenue Code in 1954 would clarify this area of the law, and it did. Many thought the revision would clarify it by overruling *General Utilities*; it did not. Sections 311 and 336 were the legislative response.

Ordinarily gain or loss that is not recognized at a particular time is deferred for recognition at a later date. Through continuity of basis (e.g., §§1031(d) and 1034(e)), the gain or loss will probably have tax impact at a later date. When §§311(a) and 336 provide that "no gain or loss shall be recognized . . . ," what do they mean?

6. Both §§311 and 336 refer to §453(d) as an exception to their general rule of nonrecognition. Why this exception? Subsections (b) and (c) of §311 contain additional exceptions which do not encumber §336. Why were these additional exceptions provided in §311? Why were they not provided in §336?

7(a) A corporation borrows $100,000. To secure its obligation it gives a mortgage on its plant. The plant has an adjusted basis of $75,000 and a fair market value of $125,000. What is the tax consequence to the corporation when it distributes the plant, subject to the mortgage, as a dividend to its sole shareholder? Suppose prior to distribution the fair market value of the plant has dropped from $125,000 to $50,000, with adjustments for depreciation reducing its basis to $60,000. What are the tax consequences to the corporation when it distributes the plant, subject to the mortgage? Suppose the basis had been reduced to $45,000?

(b) The aggregate basis of all the assets of a corporation is $500,000, and they are subject to a one million dollar mortgage, the corporation's only liability. What are the tax consequences to the corporation when, in liquidation, it distributes its assets, subject to the mortgage, to its sole shareholder? Should it matter that at the time of distribution the corporation's gross assets were worth one million dollars? $400,000? In the latter case, if the mortgagee had foreclosed prior to distribution to the shareholder, what would the tax consequences to the corporation have been?

(c) In each of the foregoing cases what would the tax consequences to the corporation have been if, instead of distributing its assets to its shareholders, it had sold them for their fair market value? How might such transactions have been arranged where the mortgage liability exceeded the value of the assets? Would it be relevant to know whether the corporation's liability for the mortgage debt was limited to the mortgaged property? Why?

WILLIAMSON v. UNITED STATES
292 F.2d 524 (Ct. Cl. 1961)

JONES, Chief Judge. This is an action brought to recover a sum which was paid under protest as an assessed deficiency in Federal income taxes for the period November 1, 1954, to August 22, 1955. The deficiency was assessed against the plaintiff as transferee of the assets of the Williamson Well Service, Inc. The parties are agreed on the facts. The plaintiff has moved for judgment on the pleadings; the defendant has filed a cross motion to dismiss. The question presented is whether a cash method corporation which is presently entitled to receive income for services rendered can escape taxation through liquidation whereby in advance of payment it gives away to its stockholders the right to receive this income.

The plaintiff, J. C. Williamson, organized the corporation, Williamson Well Service, Inc., under the laws of the State of Texas on January 2, 1953. The corporation was engaged in the business of servicing oil and gas wells. Its services were performed on a contract basis; it derived all of its income from these services, and it did not engage in any other business. The corporation maintained no inventories and leased most of the fixed assets used in the business.

The corporation kept its books on the cash receipts and disbursements method of accounting and reported its income and expenses on that basis for Federal income tax purposes. Except for the corporation's failure to include in its final return as taxable income certain accounts receivable of $192,052.08 the Commissioner of Internal Revenue never objected to the corporation's method of accounting or method of reporting its income for Federal income tax purposes.

On July 25, 1955, the plaintiff, as sole stockholder, duly authorized the liquidation and dissolution of the corporation. Under the terms of the liquidation, the plaintiff received all of the corporate properties, including accounts receivable of $192,052.08, in consideration for all of the corporate stock held by him. The accounts receivable of $192,052.08 evidenced amounts due the corporation, but not paid, for services rendered by the corporation in full performance of various well-servicing contracts prior to the date of distribution. The corporation was dissolved on August 22, 1955.

Following the dissolution, the plaintiff collected all but $2,089.47 of the accounts receivable assigned to him. The plaintiff did not perform any services individually for the debtors who paid the distributed accounts.

In the corporation's final income tax return none of the accounts receivable was reported as income, although undoubtedly the expenses of performing the contracts from which the accounts receivable arose were taken as deductions. Upon audit of the corporation's final tax return covering the period November 1, 1954, to August 22, 1955, the Commissioner increased the corporation's income for the final period by the amount of $192,052.08. In making his ruling, the Commissioner relied upon §446 of the Internal Revenue Code of 1954, 26 U.S.C. (I.R.C. 1954) §446, which provides that if the taxpayer's method of accounting "does not clearly reflect income, the computation of taxable income shall be made under such method as, in the opinion of the Secretary or his delegate, does clearly reflect income." Plaintiff paid the Commissioner's asserted deficiency plus interest thereon as transferee of the corporation.

In the individual income tax return filed by the plaintiff and his wife for the calendar year 1955 showing his gain on the liquidation and dissolution of the corporation, the plaintiff included the accounts receivable of $192,052.08 at face value among the assets he received in exchange for his capital stock.

On June 24, 1958, the plaintiff, as transferee of the corporation, filed a timely claim for refund with the Commissioner. The claim was disallowed in full and this suit was filed.

Through the years, transfers of money and property between related corporations or between corporations and individual stockholders have produced an entire series of tax problems for the courts and the Congress. When these transfers take the form of dividends in kinds and when subsequent to distribution the property is sold or otherwise converted into money by the stockholders the problems and the solutions become highly complex. Twice in recent years the Supreme Court has addressed itself to one aspect of the general problem in determining whether sales of corporate assets following distribution should realistically be attributed to the stockholders or to the corporation. Commissioner of Internal Revenue v. Court Holding Co., 1945, 324 U.S. 331, 65 S. Ct. 707, 89 L. Ed. 981; United States v. Cumberland Public Service Co., 1950, 338 U.S. 451, 70 S. Ct. 280, 94 L. Ed. 251 affirming 1949, 83 F. Supp. 843, 113 Ct. Cl. 460. Other courts have tested completed dividend transactions under the "business purpose" doctrine of Gregory v. Helvering, 1935, 293 U.S. 465, 55 S. Ct. 266, 79 L. Ed. 596, when it appeared that distributions of property were sham transactions made only to avoid taxes. Commissioner of Internal Revenue v. Transport Trading & Terminal Corp., 2 Cir., 1949, 176 F.2d 570. This court has decided related problems. . . .

The question presented by the case at bar is yet another aspect of the over-all problem, the question being whether the fact of liquidation prior to the actual collection of the accounts receivable prevents their being realized by and taxed to the corporation even though the corporation itself earned the money and fully perfected its right to receive the money prior to liquidation.

The resolution of this problem must start with the decision of the Supreme Court in General Utilities & Operating Co. v. United States, 1935, 296 U.S. 200, 56 S. Ct. 185, 80 L. Ed. 154, a case which concerned the distribution by a corporation of appreciated stock as a dividend in kind to its stockholders. Relying on United States v. Kirby Lumber Co., 1931, 284 U.S. 1, 52 S. Ct. 4, 76 L. Ed. 131, the Commissioner declared a taxable gain to the utility corporation upon the distribution of the stock in payment of a dividend. The Commissioner's theory was that the declaration of the dividend created an indebtedness of the corporation to its stockholders and the discharge of that liability by the delivery of property costing less than the amount of the debt constituted income to the corporation. The Board of Tax Appeals and the Court of Appeals upheld the Commissioner. The Supreme Court reversed, stating that the corporation had neither sold assets, discharged an indebtedness, nor realized taxable gain on the distribution among its stockholders of the appreciated stock as a dividend. The case was generally thought to stand for the proposition that no gain or loss is realized by a corporation on the distribution of property as a dividend.

Thereafter, in Helvering v. Horst, 1940, 311 U.S. 112, 61 S. Ct. 144, 85 L. Ed. 75, the Supreme Court was confronted with the situation where an individual had detached interest coupons from some negotiable bonds shortly before their due date and had given them to his son. The donee in the same year collected the coupons at maturity. The Commissioner ruled that the interest coupons were taxable to the *donor* in the year when paid even though the donor kept his books on the cash receipts basis and had never received the interest payments in cash. The Supreme Court upheld the Commissioner and reiterated the famous horticultural aphorism of Justice Holmes from Lucas v. Earl, 1930, 281 U.S. 111, 50 S. Ct. 241, 74 L. Ed. 731, to the effect that "the fruit is not to be attributed to a different tree from that on which it grew." The Court in *Horst* said that the "power to dispose of income is the equivalent of ownership of it. The exercise of that power to procure the payment of income to another is the enjoyment and hence the realization of the income by him who exercises it." Furthermore, the *"dominant purpose of the revenue laws is the taxation of income to those who earn or otherwise create the right to receive it" and this purpose cannot "be escaped by 'anticipatory arrangements . . . however skilfully devised' to prevent the income from vesting even for a second in the donor."* [Emphasis supplied.] [311 U.S. at pages 118, 119, 120, 61 S. Ct. at page 147.]

The Commissioner seized upon the *Horst* doctrine as a means of limiting the application of the *General Utilities* rule. In Commissioner of Internal Revenue v. First State Bank of Stratford, 5 Cir., 1948, 168 F.2d 1004, 7 A.L.R.2d 738, a bank, prior to 1942, had charged off certain notes as worthless, the deductions producing a tax benefit. When it appeared in 1942 that the notes would be paid, the bank declared a dividend in kind of the notes and assigned them to its stockholders. The Commissioner successfully included in the bank's income for 1942 the amounts collected by the stockholders during the year on the notes. The court held that the dividend, in effect, represented an anticipatory assignment of potential income since the notes when collected would have been ordinary income to the bank. The court said:

> "The avoidance of taxes may be perfectly legitimate, but it cannot be done by the anticipatory assignment of notes representing income, as a dividend in kind, and the subsequent collection of said notes by the assignees. . . .
>
> "The distinction between General Utilities v. Helvering, [296 U.S. 200, 56 S. Ct. 185, 80 L. Ed. 154 (1935)], and this case lies in the difference in the character of the respective properties distributed as dividends in kind; one represented a capital asset, the other represents income. In the former, the fruit was on the tree; in the latter, the tree itself represents fruit of prior years that was not taxed. . . ." 168 F.2d at page 1009.

It was against this background of litigation that the Congress passed §§311 and 336 of the 1954 Internal Revenue Code. Section 311(a) is as follows:

"§311. Taxability of corporation on distribution

"(a) *General rule.* — Except as provided in subsections (b) and (c) of this section and section 453(d), no gain or loss shall be recognized to a corporation on the distribution, with respect to its stock, of —

"(1) its stock (or rights to acquire its stock), or

"(2) property." . . .

This section appears to state flatly that except as provided for in certain subsections with which we are not here concerned, a dividend distribution cannot result in gain or loss to the corporation. But the Senate Finance Committee emphatically qualified this position as follows:

"Your committee does not intend, however, through subsection (a), to alter existing law in the case of distributions of property, which has appreciated or depreciated in value, where such distributions are made to persons other than shareholders or are made to shareholders in a capacity other than that of a shareholder. . . . *Likewise your committee does not intend to change existing law with respect to attribution of income of shareholders to their corporation as exemplified for example in the case of Commissioner v. First State Bank of Stratford (168 F.2d 1004, cert. den. 335 U.S. 867, 69 S. Ct. 137 [93 L. Ed. 412])."* [Italics supplied.] Sen. Rep. No. 1622, 83d Cong., 2d Sess. 247 (1954), U.S. Code Cong. and Adm. News 1954, p. 4884.

Section 311, however, does not govern the instant case directly because the Congress passed a companion section, §336, which related more specifically to corporate distributions in partial or complete liquidation. It is as follows:

"§336. General rule

"Except as provided in section 453(d) (relating to disposition of installment obligations), no gain or loss shall be recognized to a corporation on the distribution of property in partial or complete liquidation." 26 U.S.C. (I.R.C. 1954) §336.

The committee reports accompanying §336 do not state the committee's position on the applicability of the *Bank of Stratford* rule in interpreting this section. But §§311 and 336 of the Code correspond to §§311 and 336 of the House Bill as amended by the Senate, and the Senate derived these sections by splitting up one section, §308, of the original House Bill. See Sen. Rep. No. 1622, supra, at 247 and 258; and H.R. Rep. No. 1337, 83d Cong., 2d Sess. A90, A91 (1954). It is obvious from a reading of these sections together that they are designed to be parallel provisions, and we think they should be interpreted consistently.

The problem then finally resolves itself into the question of whether the distribution of the accounts receivable by the corporation was an anticipatory assignment *and* a realization of income within the scope of the decisions in *Bank of Stratford* and *Horst.* A careful study of the decisional law, which includes precedents of this court, compels us to answer this question in the affirmative.

In the recent case of Telephone Directory Advertising Co. v. United States,

142 F. Supp. 884, 135 Ct. Cl. 670, the plaintiff on the accrual method of accounting was the advertising broker for a large telephone company. Advertisers were billed by the telephone company and were required to pay a certain amount per month for each month in which their advertisement appeared in the telephone directory. The telephone company paid the plaintiff commissions limited to amounts collected from advertisers. The telephone company had exclusive control over the length of time a directory was outstanding and the estimated life of a directory was frequently extended or cut back as needs arose. At the end of each month a directory was outstanding, the plaintiff accrued on its books the monthly portions of the commissions it was entitled to receive from the telephone company. In 1950, the plaintiff was completely dissolved and all of its assets were distributed to its shareholders as a liquidating dividend. We held that the monies paid by the telephone company to the plaintiff's shareholders, as transferees of the plaintiff's assets, after liquidation were not taxable to the plaintiff corporation. Our decision was based on the fact that the plaintiff did *not* have a fixed and determined right to receive these commissions on the date of its dissolution. The plaintiff did not realize the income because it was not in existence either when the right to the income first accrued or when it was paid.

The distinctions between the *Telephone Directory* case and the instant case are apparent. The Williamson Corporation had a fixed right to future income on the date of its dissolution. It alone had earned the income; it had done everything necessary to perfect its right to the income; the money was due and owing the corporation on the date of dissolution.

In Rudco Oil & Gas Co. v. United States, 82 F. Supp. 746, 113 Ct. Cl. 206, decided by this court in 1949, an accrual method corporation was the lessee in a number of oil and gas leases under which it was producing and selling oil. The corporation declared a dividend out of earnings and in satisfaction of this dividend transferred to its only two shareholders (husband and wife) partial interests in a number of producing oil and gas leases. The transfer was for such length of time as would be required to pay the shareholders a stated sum of money out of the production receipts of each lease. At the end of a stated time the leases reverted back to the corporation. In a unanimous decision we held that the dividend in kind paid by the corporation was an assignment of anticipated corporate income made only to avoid taxes to the corporation and did not affect the corporation's liability for tax on the income. To the same effect see United States v. Joliet & Chicago R. Co., 1942, 315 U.S. 44, 62 S. Ct. 442, 86 L. Ed. 658; Jud Plumbing & Heating, Inc. v. Commissioner of Internal Revenue, 5 Cir., 1946, 153 F.2d 681; Standard Paving Co. v. Commissioner of Internal Revenue, 10 Cir., 190 F.2d 330, certiorari denied 1951, 342 U.S. 860, 72 S. Ct. 87, 96 L. Ed. 647; United States v. Lynch, 9 Cir., 1951, 192 F.2d 718, certiorari denied 1952, 343 U.S. 934, 72 S. Ct. 770, 96 L. Ed. 1342; Floyd v. Scofield, 5 Cir., 1952, 193 F.2d 594; . . . Cf. Family Record Plan, Inc. v. Commissioner, [36 T.C. 305 (1961), aff'd, 309 F.2d 208 (9th Cir. 1962), cert. denied, 373 U.S. 910 (1963)].

Plaintiff would distinguish these cases on the grounds that involve mainly *accrual* method corporations which had transferred rights to future income as *ordinary* dividends, whereas the Williamson Corporation was a *cash* method taxpayer and its assignment of accounts receivable was a *liquidating* dividend. We see no merit in these distinctions.

As we stated above, we believe that both §§311 and 336 of the Code must be given consistent interpretations and that they are both subject to the *Bank of Stratford* rule. In cases as the one at bar, ordinary and liquidating dividends are to be treated alike. Furthermore, *Jud Plumbing, Standard Paving, Scofield, . . .* cited above, held the payment of liquidating dividends to be realizations of income to the corporations involved. We note particularly the case of Floyd v. Scofield, supra, because it contained the important factors present in the instant case, a cash method taxpayer and a distribution of accounts receivable as liquidating dividends. The Fifth Circuit Court of Appeals reached the same conclusion in that case that we reach now.

The differences in accounting methods noted by the plaintiff among the other cases are not significant either, although the problem before us now is outlined more strikingly with a cash method taxpayer. In any case the outcome hinges upon whether there had been a realization of income by the distributing corporation. It is fundamental that all economic gain is not taxable income and that it is the realization of income that is the taxable event. But the law contemplates that there is some point at which all income which has accrued, in the sense of having been fully earned, will be realized and taxable to him who earned it regardless of the accounting method involved. An acceptable accounting method should simply indicate this point logically and consistently.

Under the accrual method, income is held to be realized when there arises in the taxpayer a fixed and unconditional right to receive it. Continental Tie & Lumber Co. v. United States, 1931, 52 F.2d 1045, 72 Ct. Cl. 595, affirmed 1932, 286 U.S. 290, 52 S. Ct. 529, 76 L. Ed. 1111. Under the cash method of accounting the realization of income is usually deemed to occur when payment is actually received by the taxpayer. "But the decisions and regulations have consistently recognized that receipt in cash or property is not the only characteristic of realization of income to a taxpayer on the cash receipts basis. Where the taxpayer does not receive payment of income in money or property realization may occur when the last step is taken by which he obtains the fruition of the economic gain which has already accrued to him." Helvering v. Horst, 1940, 311 U.S. 112, at page 115, 61 S. Ct. 144, at page 146, 85 L. Ed. 75.

When the Williamson corporation paid the dividend to the plaintiff it obtained the fruition of the economic gain which had accrued to it upon the performance of the well services; it realized income. Paying the dividend was the enjoyment of its income. A body corporate can be said to enjoy its income in no other way. *First [State] Bank of Stratford,* supra.

Finally, the plaintiff says that if it should be determined that the Commissioner was authorized to adjust the corporation's final return to show the accounts receivable as income, then the Commissioner must also set off against this sum the amount of the accounts receivable outstanding at the beginning of the final tax year which were collected during that year. The plaintiff's theory is that the Commissioner by his action placed the corporation on the accrual basis for the last year and, therefore, accounts outstanding at the beginning of that year which were collected during that year belong to the prior year's income and are not properly includible in the final tax return. The plaintiff did not present this contention to the Commissioner in his claim for refund; he mentioned it for the first time in the amended petition and briefs addressed to this court. This amended petition was filed more than 2 years after the payment of the tax deficiency. There is little doubt that this claim was not timely made. United States v. Andrews, 1938, 302 U.S. 517, 58 S. Ct. 315, 82 L. Ed. 398; Real Estate-Land Title & Trust Co. v. United States, 1940, 309 U.S. 13, 60 S. Ct. 371, 84 L. Ed. 542; First National Bank of Montgomery, Executor of the Estate of Algernon Blair v. United States, Ct. Cl., 280 F.2d 818. In any event, the Commissioner's adjustment did not necessarily put the corporation on the accrual basis, but merely affected the accounting treatment of one item in order clearly to reflect the realization by the corporation of earned income. In our view the adjustment by the Commissioner in this case has no direct relation to accounts outstanding from prior years or cash collected on these accounts during the final year of the corporation's existence. The same argument which plaintiff makes here was made and rejected in Carter v. Commissioner, 1947, 9 T.C. 364, affirmed 2 Cir., 1948, 170 F.2d 911.

The record indicates that $2,089.47 of accounts owing to the corporation on the date of its dissolution were uncollectible, yet these accounts were taxed to the corporation by the Commissioner. The corporation is not subject to tax on this amount. If and to the extent a tax on this amount has been assessed and paid, the plaintiff, as tranferee of the corporation, is entitled to a refund. To this extent plaintiff's motion is granted and judgment to that effect will be entered, with the amount of recovery to be determined pursuant to Rule 38(c), 28 U.S.C. In all other respects defendant's motion is granted and plaintiff's petition will be dismissed.

It is so ordered.

DURFEE, LARAMORE, MADDEN and WHITAKER, Judges, concur.

NOTE

1. As the Court in *Williamson* indicates, the Senate Finance Committee did not regard §311 as adversely affecting the result in Commissioner v. First State Bank of Stratford, 168 F.2d 1004 (5th Cir.), cert. denied, 335 U.S. 867 (1948). Why was that result to be preserved? When should a court treat the stated exceptions to a statutory rule, like those in §§311(b) and (c), as the exclusive exceptions? Would the result in *Williamson* have been different in the absence of the Finance Committee's Report? See Comment, The Imputed Sale and Anticipatory Assignment of Income Doctrines: Their Effect on IRC §§311 and 336, 15 Buffalo L. Rev. 154 (1965); B. Bittker, Stock Dividends, Distributions in Kind, Redemptions and Liquidations Under the 1954 Code, 1955 So. Calif. Tax Inst. 349.

2. A corporation distributes to its shareholder, either as an interim dividend or in liquidation, a building with fair market value of $100,000 and an adjusted basis

of $50,000. The cost of the building had been $80,000, but straight line depreciation deductions for which there had been tax benefit reduced the basis to $50,000. Would *First State Bank of Stratford* and *Williamson* imply corporate realization at the time of distribution to the extent of the depreciation deductions? Would the result be different if the building had been fully depreciated prior to distribution? Does §1250 affect the result? Does the mere presence in the Code of §§1245 and 1250 affect the result?

3. Reconsider the questions in Note 6, page 10 supra in light of the Court's statement in *Williamson* as to the "parallel" positions of §§311 and 336, pages 13-14 supra. Does this mean that subsections (b) and (c) of §311 limit §336, or does it mean only that the judicially created limitations on the rules of nonrecognition are to be applied to both sections? What inferences different from those drawn by the Court might one derive from the splitting of the single section proposed in the House Bill into §§311 and 336?

4. Why is the avoidance of the corporate tax legitimate as to appreciation in marketable securities but illegitimate as to notes previously charged off or as to accounts receivable for services rendered by a cash basis taxpayer or for apples grown in the taxpayer's orchard (United States v. Lynch, 192 F.2d 718 (9th Cir.), cert. denied, 343 U.S. 934 (1952))? As to marketable securities — would it matter that the corporation was a dealer in those securities and that the corporation "knew" its shareholders planned to sell them upon receipt? Should it matter? The *Lynch* opinion speaks to these types of questions. Is it persuasive?

5. Prior to enactment of the Tax Reform Act of 1969 a corporation's use of appreciated property (such as marketable securities) to purchase (redeem) all or part of its outstanding stock was treated generally as a "distribution [of property] with respect to [the distributing corporation's] stock." See Treas. Reg. §1.311-1(a). For the Treasury's effort at limiting the generality of that interpretation of the statute, see Treas. Reg. §1.311(e)(1) and (2), especially Ex. (2). Would a corporate dealer in securities have recognition if it used marketable securities to redeem the stock of one of its shareholders? What administrative problems are presented in light of Treas. Reg. §1.311(e)(1)? Is Treas. Reg. §1.311-1(a) reasonable insofar as it deals with redemptions? See D. Watts, Recognition of Gain or Loss to a Corporation on a Distribution of Property in Exchange for Its Own Stock, 22 Tax Lawyer 161 (1968).

The Tax Reform Act of 1969 added subsection (d) to §311 of the Code. Its principal effect is to recognize gain to a corporation when it distributes appreciated property in redemption of its outstanding stock. The new rule of recognition is inapplicable, however, in several specified redemption situations, the two most important of which are the redemption of all the stock of a 10 per cent or more shareholder and the complete or partial liquidation of a corporation.

The Senate had proposed that gain be recognized in all redemption transactions. The House had proposed nothing. Section 311(d) emerged from the conference committee and was enacted as a compromise, modifying the accepted interpretation of prior law set forth in Treas. Reg. §1.311-1(a). Why do you think §311 was repealed only as to redemptions, and why was the repeal made applicable to some but not all redemptions? Should §311 be repealed in its entirety? Should it be restored to its pre-1969 Act scope? Or what?

Section 311(a) covers only a corporation's distributions "with respect to its stock." A corporation's use of appreciated property to pay a debt (not one created by a dividend resolution) results in a realization of the gain. Why are distributions to creditors differentiated from those to shareholders? Ought the differentiation persist in the case of distributions to long-term bondholders? Should distributions to preferred stockholders be treated like distributions to common stockholders or to bondholders?

6. Section 311(a)(2) exempts gain on a corporation's distribution of its own stock "with respect to its stock." For example, if a corporation bought its own shares on the market for $10.00 a share and later, when they were worth $20.00 a share, distributed them as a dividend, the gain would not be taxed. This rule is not derived necessarily from *General Utilities*. Critics of §§311 and 336 in general would probably not want this rule overturned. The concept of corporate gain in a corporation's dealing in its own shares is treated in connection with §1032, page 73 infra.

7. *General Utilities* and §§311 and 336, despite their exceptions, statutory and otherwise, tend to treat a corporation more favorably if it distributes appreciated property to its shareholders than if it sells and distributes the proceeds. This difference in treatment is responsible for substantial tax planning by corporations and their lawyers and for a host of complex transactions and Code provisions designed to deal with them. As you proceed through the rest of this chapter, consider what problems and complexities would have been avoided, and whether for better or worse, if *General Utilities* had been decided for the Government (on which theory?) or had been overturned instead of codified in 1954. See Lewis, A Proposed New Treatment for Corporate Distributions and Sales in Liquidation, in 3 Tax Revision Compendium 1643 (House Ways and Means Comm. 1959).

b. TO CREDITORS AND OTHERS

As stated in Note 5, page 18 supra, §§311 and 336 are applicable only to distributions made to shareholders. If Corporation X owes $1000 to a creditor for supplies and pays that debt by delivering an A.T.&T. bond worth $1000 with a basis of $900, this is treated as a taxable exchange, and there is a recognized gain of $100. If the creditor were a bondholder holding a matured 50-year Corporation X bond, just as in the case of the trade creditor the payment-in-kind would be treated as a taxable exchange, with the $100 gain recognized.

If Corporation X has a valued employee to whom it wishes to give a $500 Christmas bonus, will Corporation X have recognized gain if it delivers shares of General Motors stock which are now worth $500 but which cost Corporation X $250? Why? What will be the amount of Corporation X's deduction under §162? (For the result if Corporation X had distributed stock in Corporation X, see Rev. Rul. 62-217, 1962-2 Cum. Bull. 59, page 101 infra.)

If you concluded in your answers to the questions posed in Note 5, page 18 supra, that distributions of appreciated assets to shareholders should not be differentiated from distributions to creditors (at least long-term creditors), how should they be treated? Why? If you believe they should be treated differently, are you satisfied with the treatment under current law? Why? If not, what do you propose?

c. TO CREDITOR-SHAREHOLDER — §332(c)

Assume that Corporation P owns 100 per cent of the outstanding stock of Corporation S, that S owes P $100,000, and that P liquidates S (i.e., causes S to distribute all of its assets to P in retirement of P's stock in S). Prior to the enactment of §332(c) , if S had an asset worth $100,000 with an adjusted basis of $80,000, S would be charged with $20,000 of income if distribution of that asset could be viewed as payment in satisfaction of the indebtedness. I.T. 4109, 1952-2 Cum. Bull. 138. (Appreciated assets used to retire stock would not result in recognition because of the rule codified in §336.) The result in the case of inter-corporate indebtedness could have been avoided if, prior to the liquidation, the subsidiary had discharged the debt with cash or the parent had contributed the debt to the subsidiary's capital. Since the result could be avoided so easily by mere formal changes, and since the difference in treatment of stock and debt seemed too extreme in the case of parent and subsidiary, §332(c) was enacted in 1954 to provide for nonrecognition where the parent meets the 80 per cent stock ownership requirement provided in §332(b).

There is no statutory counterpart to §332(c) for the case of corporate indebtedness owing to a noncorporate shareholder, even one owning 100 per cent of the debtor corporation's stock. Should there be? Why?

2. *Sale and Purchase of Assets*

a. IMPUTATION OF GAIN

COMMISSIONER v. COURT HOLDING CO.
324 U.S. 331 (1945), rev'g 143 F.2d 823 (5th Cir. 1944)

Mr. Justice BLACK delivered the opinion of the Court. An apartment house, which was the sole asset of the respondent corporation, was transferred in the form of a liquidating dividend to the corporation's two shareholders. They in turn formally conveyed it to a purchaser who had originally negotiated for the purchase from the corporation. The question is whether the Circuit Court of Appeals properly reversed the Tax Court's conclusion that the corporation was taxable under §[61] of the Internal Revenue Code[3] for the gain which accrued from the sale. The answer depends upon whether the findings of the Tax Court that the whole trans-

---

[3]Profits from the sale of property are taxable as income under §[61] of the Internal Revenue Code . . . . The Treasury Regulations have long provided that gains accruing from the sales of a corporation's assets, in whole or in part, constitute income to it, but that a corporation realizes no taxable gain by a mere distribution of its assets in kind, in partial or in complete liquidation, however much they may have appreciated in value since acquisition. §§19.22(a)-19, 19.22(a)-21, Treasury Regulations 103. [1939 Code.]

action showed a sale by the corporation rather than by the stockholders were final and binding upon the Circuit Court of Appeals.

It is unnecessary to set out in detail the evidence introduced before the Tax Court or its findings. Despite conflicting evidence, the following findings of the Tax Court are supported by the record:

The respondent corporation was organized in 1934 solely to buy and hold the apartment building which was the only property ever owned by it. All of its outstanding stock was owned by Minnie Miller and her husband. Between October 1, 1939 and February, 1940, while the corporation still had legal title to the property, negotiations for its sale took place. These negotiations were between the corporation and the lessees of the property, together with a sister and brother-in-law. An oral agreement was reached as to the terms and conditions of sale, and on February 22, 1940, the parties met to reduce the agreement to writing. The purchaser was then advised by the corporation's attorney that the sale could not be consummated because it would result in the imposition of a large income tax on the corporation. The next day, the corporation declared a "liquidating dividend," which involved complete liquidation of its assets, and surrender of all outstanding stock. Mrs. Miller and her husband surrendered their stock, and the building was deeded to them. A sale contract was then drawn, naming the Millers individually as vendors, and the lessees' sister as vendee, which embodied substantially the same terms and conditions previously agreed upon. One thousand dollars, which a month and a half earlier had been paid to the corporation by the lessees, was applied in part payment of the purchase price. Three days later, the property was conveyed to the lessees' sister.

The Tax Court concluded from these facts that, despite the declaration of a "liquidating dividend" followed by the transfers of legal title, the corporation had not abandoned the sales negotiations; that these were mere formalities designed "to make the transaction appear to be other than what it was" in order to avoid tax liability. The Circuit Court of Appeals drawing different inferences from the record, held that the corporation had "called off" the sale, and treated the stockholders' sale as unrelated to the prior negotiations.

There was evidence to support the findings of the Tax Court, and its findings must therefore be accepted by the courts. Dobson v. Commissioner, 320 U.S. 489; Commissioner v. Heininger, 320 U.S. 467; Commissioner v. Scottish American Investment Co., 323 U.S. 119. On the basis of these findings, the Tax Court was justified in attributing the gain from the sale to respondent corporation. The incidence of taxation depends upon the substance of a transaction. The tax consequences which arise from gains from a sale of property are not finally to be determined solely by the means employed to transfer legal title. Rather, the transaction must be viewed as a whole, and each step, from the commencement of negotiations to the consummation of the sale, is relevant. A sale by one person cannot be transformed for tax purposes into a sale by another by using the latter as a conduit through which to pass title. To permit the true nature of a transaction to be disguised by mere formalisms, which exist solely to alter tax liabilities, would seriously impair the effective administration of the tax policies of Congress.

It is urged that respondent corporation never executed a written agreement, and that an oral agreement to sell land cannot be enforced in Florida because of the Statute of Frauds, Comp. Gen. Laws of Florida, 1927, vol. 3, §5779. But the fact that respondent corporation itself never executed a written contract is unimportant, since the Tax Court found from the facts of the entire transaction that the executed sale was in substance the sale of the corporation. The decision of the Circuit Court of Appeals is reversed, and that of the Tax Court affirmed.

It is so ordered.

UNITED STATES v. CUMBERLAND PUBLIC SERVICE CO.
338 U.S. 451 (1950), aff'g 83 F. Supp. 843 (Ct. Cl. 1949)

Mr. Justice BLACK delivered the opinion of the Court. A corporation selling its physical properties is taxed on capital gains resulting from the sale. There is no corporate tax, however, on distribution of assets in kind to shareholders as part of a genuine liquidation.[2] The respondent corporation transferred property to its shareholders as a liquidating dividend in kind. The shareholders transferred it to a purchaser. The question is whether, despite contrary findings by the Court of Claims, this record requires a holding that the transaction was in fact a sale by the corporation subjecting the corporation to a capital gains tax.

Details of the transaction are as follows. The respondent, a closely held corporation, was long engaged in the business of generating and distributing electric power in three Kentucky counties. In 1936 a local cooperative began to distribute Tennessee Valley Authority power in the area served by respondent. It soon became obvious that respondent's Diesel-generated power could not compete with TVA power, which respondent had been unable to obtain. Respondent's shareholders, realizing that the corporation must get out of the power business unless it obtained TVA power, accordingly offered to sell all the corporate stock to the cooperative, which was receiving such power. The cooperative refused to buy the stock, but countered with an offer to buy from the corporation its transmission and distribution equipment. The corporation rejected the offer because it would have been compelled to pay a heavy capital gains tax. At the same time the shareholders, desiring to save payment of the corporate capital gains tax, offered to acquire the transmission and distribution equipment and then sell to the cooperative. The cooperative accepted. The corporation transferred the transmission and distribution systems to its shareholders in partial liquidation. The remaining assets were sold and the corporation dissolved. The shareholders then executed the previously contemplated sale to the cooperative.

Upon this sale by the shareholders, the Commissioner assessed and collected a $17,000 tax from the corporation on the theory that the shareholders had been used

---

[2] ". . . No gain or loss is realized by a corporation from the mere distribution of its assets in kind in partial or complete liquidation, however they may have appreciated or depreciated in value since their acquisition. . . ." Treas. Reg. 103, §19.22(a)-21. [1939 Code.]

as a mere conduit for effectuating what was really a corporate sale. Respondent corporation brought this action to recover the amount of the tax. The Court of Claims found that the method by which the stockholders disposed of the properties was avowedly chosen in order to reduce taxes, but that the liquidation and dissolution genuinely ended the corporation's activities and existence. The court also found that at no time did the corporation plan to make the sale itself. Accordingly it found as a fact that the sale was made by the shareholders rather than the corporation, and entered judgment for respondent. One judge dissented, believing that our opinion in Commissioner v. Court Holding Co., 324 U.S. 331, required a finding that the sale had been made by the corporation. Certiorari was granted, 338 U.S. 846, to clear up doubts arising out of the *Court Holding Co.* case.

Our *Court Holding Co.* decision rested on findings of fact by the Tax Court that a sale had been made and gains realized by the taxpayer corporation. There the corporation had negotiated for the sale of its assets and had reached an oral agreement of sale. When the tax consequences of the corporate sale were belatedly recognized, the corporation purported to "call off" the sale at the last minute and distributed the physical properties in kind to the stockholders. They promptly conveyed these properties to the same persons who had negotiated with the corporation. The terms of purchase were substantially those of the previous oral agreement. One thousand dollars already paid to the corporation was applied as part payment of the purchase price. The Tax Court found that the corporation never really abandoned its sales negotiations, that it never did dissolve, and that the sole purpose of the so-called liquidation was to disguise a corporate sale through use of mere formalisms in order to avoid tax liability. The Circuit Court of Appeals took a different view of the evidence. In this Court the Government contended that whether a liquidation distribution was genuine or merely a sham was traditionally a question of fact. We agreed with this contention, and reinstated the Tax Court's findings and judgment. Discussing the evidence which supported the findings of fact, we went on to say that "the incidence of taxation depends upon the substance of a transaction" regardless of "mere formalisms," and that taxes on a corporate sale cannot be avoided by using the shareholders as a "conduit through which to pass title."

This language does not mean that a corporation can be taxed even when the sale has been made by its stockholders following a genuine liquidation and dissolution.[3] While the distinction between sales by a corporation as compared with distribution in kind followed by shareholder sales may be particularly shadowy and artificial when the corporation is closely held, Congress has chosen to recognize such a distinction for tax purposes. The corporate tax is thus aimed primarily at the profits

---

[3]What we said in the *Court Holding Co.* case was an approval of the action of the Tax Court in looking beyond the papers executed by the corporation and shareholders in order to determine whether the sale there had actually been made by the corporation. We were but emphasizing the established principle that in resolving such questions as who made a sale, fact-finding tribunals in tax cases can consider motives, intent, and conduct in addition to what appears in written instruments used by parties to control rights as among themselves. See, e.g., Helvering v. Clifford, 309 U.S. 331, 335-337; Commissioner v. Tower, 327 U.S. 280.

of a going concern. This is true despite the fact that gains realized from corporate sales are taxed, perhaps to prevent tax evasions, even where the cash proceeds are at once distributed in liquidation.[4] But Congress has imposed no tax on liquidating distributions in kind or on dissolution, whatever may be the motive for such liquidation. Consequently, a corporation may liquidate or dissolve without subjecting itself to the corporate gains tax, even though a primary motive is to avoid the burden of corporate taxation.

Here, on the basis of adequate subsidiary findings, the Court of Claims has found that the sale in question was made by the stockholders rather than the corporation. The Government's argument that the shareholders acted as a mere "conduit" for a sale by respondent corporation must fall before this finding. The subsidiary finding that a major motive of the shareholders was to reduce taxes does not bar this conclusion. Whatever the motive and however relevant it may be in determining whether the transaction was real or a sham, sales of physical properties by shareholders following a genuine liquidation distribution cannot be attributed to the corporation for tax purposes.

The oddities in tax consequences that emerge from the tax provisions here controlling appear to be inherent in the present tax pattern. For a corporation is taxed if it sells all its physical properties and distributes the cash proceeds as liquidating dividends, yet is not taxed if that property is distributed in kind and is then sold by the shareholders. In both instances the interest of the shareholders in the business has been transferred to the purchaser. Again, if these stockholders had succeeded in their original effort to sell all their stock, their interest would have been transferred to the purchasers just as effectively. Yet on such a transaction the corporation would have realized no taxable gain.

Congress having determined that different tax consequences shall flow from different methods by which the shareholders of a closely held corporation may dispose of corporate property, we accept its mandate. It is for the trial court, upon consideration of an entire transaction, to determine the factual category in which a particular transaction belongs. Here as in the *Court Holding Co.* case we accept the ultimate findings of fact of the trial tribunal. Accordingly the judgment of the Court of Claims is

Affirmed.

Mr. Justice DOUGLAS took no part in the consideration or decision of this case.

NOTE

1. Would you have expected the Tax Court to draw the same conclusions from the evidence in *Cumberland* as the Court of Claims did? Why? What

[4]It has also been held that where corporate liquidations are effected through trustees or agents, gains from sales are taxable to the corporation as though it were a going concern. See, e.g., First National Bank [of Greeley] v. United States, 86 F.2d 938, 941; Treas. Reg. 103, §19.22(a)-21. [1939 Code.]

evidence in *Cumberland* led the Court of Claims to reach a conclusion different from the one the Tax Court reached in *Court Holding Co.*? In the context of the two cases, in what sense is the inquiry as to who made the sale a factual one? What guidance did the Supreme Court provide for trial courts charged with determining "the factual category in which a particular transaction belongs," supra?

2. If *General Utilities* had been decided for the Government (on which theory?), might *Court Holding Co.* and *Cumberland* have arisen anyhow? The Supreme Court did not cite *General Utilities* in either case. Why not? In *Cumberland* the Court said that the "corporate tax . . . aimed primarily at the profits of a going concern," page 23 supra. *Court Holding Co.* did not involve a "going concern"; *General Utilities* did. In *Court Holding Co.* the corporate tax was imposed; in *General Utilities* it was not. Does the *Cumberland* opinion imply that thereafter trial courts should be less willing to impute an apparent shareholder sale to the corporation when it follows a liquidation than when it follows an interim dividend? Why?

3. After *Cumberland* there was little certainty, but the lower courts rarely imputed to the corporation a postliquidating shareholder sale despite preliquidation negotiations by corporate management as long as the contract for sale was executed by the shareholders after the liquidation had been effected. See, e.g., St. Louis Union Trust Co. v. Finnegan, 197 F.2d 565 (8th Cir. 1952); Merkra Holding Co., 27 T.C. 82 (1956).

4. Assume corporate assets were worth one million dollars and that their basis to the corporation was $500,000. Assume, too, that the sole shareholder had a basis for his stock of $500,000. If the shareholder sold the assets for one million dollars following liquidation and *Court Holding Co.* were applicable, what would the total tax on the transactions be? What would the total tax be if, under *Cumberland,* the sale were not imputed to the corporation?

5. If the shareholder in the above hypothetical had sold all his stock for one million dollars, the tax result to him would have been the same as in a case where the corporation had first liquidated and he then had sold the assets, as long as *Cumberland* prevented imputation of the sale to the corporation. In Dallas Downtown Development Company v. Commissioner, 12 T.C. 114 (1949), however, the Commissioner argued that despite a formal sale of stock by the shareholders the corporation had in effect sold its assets and then had distributed the proceeds of sale to its shareholders. He failed in that contention, as he had earlier in Steubenville Bridge Co. v. Commissioner, 11 T.C. 789 (1948). Should he have succeeded?

6. If assets are sold, either by the corporation (directly or by imputation) or by its shareholders, the buyer's cost for the assets would ordinarily constitute their new basis under §1012. If stock is sold the buyer would have a cost basis in the stock (a nondepreciable asset) but not in the underlying corporate assets. Under some circumstances, however, a buyer of stock may be permitted to ascribe the cost basis of the stock to the underlying corporate assets. See §334(b)(2) and pages 62-67 infra.

See W. Cary, The Effect of Taxation on Selling Out a Corporate Business for Cash, 45 Ill. L. Rev. 423 (1950).

b. EXEMPTION OF GAIN — §337

CITY BANK OF WASHINGTON v. COMMISSIONER
38 T.C. 713 (1962)

MULRONEY, Judge: The respondent determined deficiences in the petitioner's income tax for the year 1956 in the amount of $117,753.72 and for the taxable period January 1, 1959, to May 29, 1959, in the amount of $258,838.57. The year 1956 is here involved solely because of respondent's disallowance of a net operating loss carryback to that year from 1959. The issues are (1) whether the loss realized by petitioner in the sale of certain United States Treasury obligations is to be recognized, which turns upon whether the sale took place before or after petitioner's adoption of a plan of liquidation under section 337 of the Internal Revenue Code of 1954, and (2) whether a gross receipts tax assessed by the District of Columbia on the gain realized by petitioner on the sale of its assets after the adoption of a plan of liquidation under section 337 is an expense relating to exempt income which is not deductible under section 265.

Findings of Fact

Some of the facts were stipulated and they are herein included by this reference.

The City Bank of Washington, hereinafter called City Bank or petitioner, is a corporation organized under the laws of Virginia. Its Federal income tax returns for the periods here involved were filed with the district director of internal revenue for the district of Baltimore, Maryland. Except for its concluding fiscal year, City Bank was on a calendar year and it used an accrual method of accounting in maintaining its books of account and in preparing its tax returns.

For many years the City Bank carried on a banking business in the District of Columbia, under the banking laws of said District. Since the close of business on May 29, 1959, City Bank has conducted no business except that incident to its liquidation.

American Security and Trust Company, hereinafter called American Security, is a corporation originally chartered under the laws of Virginia in 1889 and reincorporated in 1890 under the banking laws of the District of Columbia, where it has carried on a banking business at all times material herein. American Security Corporation, hereinafter called the affiliate, is a corporation organized in 1957 under the District of Columbia Business Corporation Act. The stockholders of American Security hold the stock of the affiliate in the same proportions. At all times material herein the affiliate has carried on general business operations in the District of Columbia, primarily in the financial, but nonbanking, field. Robert C. Baker is president of both American Security and the affiliate.

From time to time prior to March 17, 1959, representatives of American Security and the affiliate and representatives of City Bank discussed the possibility of combining American Security and City Bank. American Security desired the combination in order to broaden its base and improve its competitive position in the District of Columbia. At the same time representatives of City Bank were conducting similar discussions with representatives of the Riggs National Bank of Washington, D.C., and this fact was known to the representative of American Security and affiliate. On March 17, 1959, a meeting was held in the offices of Robert C. Baker which, in addition to Baker, was attended by Clarence F. Burton, chairman of the board of directors of City Bank; John C. Pyles, Jr., president of City Bank; Robert G. Merrick, a majority stockholder of City Bank, and William F. Kelly, counsel for City Bank. Burton, Pyles, Merrick, and Kelly together owned or controlled 16,506 shares of the 26,000 shares of outstanding stock of City Bank. In the course of the meeting, Baker, speaking for American Security and the affiliate, stated that American Security and affiliate were prepared to purchase the stock of City Bank upon a basis which would net the City Bank stockholders $325 per share. Burton, Pyles, Merrick, and Kelly expressed their willingness to accept such an offer and stated that they would recommend its acceptance by the other stockholders of City Bank.

On March 19, 1959, Baker and Thomas D. Carson, vice president of American Security, together with counsel, met with Deputy Comptrollers of the Currency to explain the proposed program for the acquisition of the stock and assets of City Bank, the liquidation of City Bank, and the assumption of its liabilities, and to request expeditious action by the office of the Comptroller of the Currency on such program.

In a letter dated March 20, 1959, and addressed to Burton and Pyles (City Bank), Baker confirmed that, subject to the approval of the boards of directors of American Security and the affiliate, affiliate would offer to promptly purchase all of the 26,000 outstanding shares of City Bank at $325 per share net to each stockholder on certain enumerated terms and conditions. Six stockholders of City Bank affixed their signatures to the letter under the legend "Agreed," committing a total of 17,573 shares of City Bank stock to the proposal.

On March 24, 1959, American Security filed an application with the Comptroller of the Currency for consent to purchase the assets and assume the liabilities of City Bank. On March 24, 1959, the boards of directors of American Security and the affiliate adopted resolutions at special meetings approving the plan to purchase the assets and assume the liabilities of City Bank and authorized certain of their respective officers to take necessary steps for putting the program into effect.

On March 25, 1959, City Bank, American Security, and the affiliate executed a "Basic Memorandum Agreement" which provided that American Security and the affiliate would enter into agreements to purchase all of the assets of City Bank for $8,450,000 and assume all of its liabilities as promptly as possible after the approval of the Comptroller of the Currency had been obtained. The basic agreement further provided that the affiliate would make an offer to purchase all of the 26,000 shares of City Bank stock at a net price of $325 per share.

On April 6, 1959, City Bank and American Security executed a "Purchase and Assumption Agreement" covering the sale of City Bank's banking assets to American Security and the assumption by American Security of the liabilities of City Bank. The agreement provided, in part, as follows:

"WHEREAS, Seller [City Bank] intends to cease the transaction of the business for which it was organized and thereafter proceed with the voluntary liquidation of its assets, and dissolution; and . . . .

"EIGHTH: Seller agrees that immediately after the closing date it will proceed to complete its liquidation by distributing its assets and thereupon dissolve. . . .

"TENTH: The closing date shall be the close of business of the day on which Seller shall cease to do business preparatory to its liquidation and dissolution, such date to be fixed by the stockholders of Seller.

"ELEVENTH: This agreement is subject to the approval of the Plan of Voluntary Dissolution and Complete Liquidation of Seller by a vote of holders of two-thirds (2/3rds) of its stock, and is further subject to the prior approval by the Comptroller of the Currency and his prior consent to the establishment and operation by Purchaser of branch banks at the present locations of Seller."

On April 6, 1959, City Bank and the affiliate executed a similar "Purchase and Assumption Agreement" covering the sale of City Bank's nonbanking assets to the affiliate. The aggregate price to be paid by American Security and the affiliate to City Bank for its assets was $8,450,000 which would give each stockholder of City Bank $325 for each share.

On April 1, 1959, and on April 9, 1959, the Antitrust Division of the Department of Justice requested certain information from American Security about the proposed acquisition of City Bank, and the requested information was supplied to the Department of Justice on April 20, 1959, and April 28, 1959.

Between April 2, 1959, and April 10, 1959, the affiliate purchased 20,500 shares of City Bank from numerous shareholders at a price of $325 per share. In order to finance such purchases in part the affiliate borrowed $6,361,000 from the Guaranty Trust Company of New York. Between April 10, 1959, and May 27, 1959, Alex. Brown and Sons, a firm dealing in securities, purchased 5,277 shares of City Bank stock from numerous stockholders at $325 per share pursuant to an underwriting agreement which had been executed on March 31, 1959.

On May 19, 1959, American Security and the affiliate executed an agreement under which American Security agreed to pay $4,400,170 of the total amount paid for the City Bank assets and the affiliate agreed to pay $4,049,830, such decision being based upon the agreed relative value of the banking and nonbanking assets of City Bank.

On May 26, 1959, the Comptroller of the Currency, in a letter to American Security, consented to the takeover of City Bank, giving as one condition for his approval "That all bonds and securities of the selling bank will be set up on the books of your bank at the market price on the effective date of the takeover." The Comptroller also stated that "It is understood that the proposed purchase of assets and assumption of liabilities of The City Bank of Washington, by your bank, will be presented to the shareholders of The City Bank for ratification on May 29, 1959, and if approved, the proposal will be consummated shortly thereafter."

On May 26, 1959, the portfolio of City Bank included certain United States Treasury bonds and notes which were currently being quoted at less than their cost to City Bank. On that date Baker (president of American Security) and Burton (chairman of the board of City Bank), upon being informed that the letter of approval of Comptroller of the Currency was being dispatched, and of the substance of its contents, consulted with each other and agreed that City Bank should forthwith sell said United States Treasury bonds and notes. Burton immediately arranged for such sale to be made through the Guaranty Trust Company of New York. On that same day the Guaranty Trust Company sold nine issues of United States Treasury bonds and notes for a total sales price of $14,286,081.25. Eight of the issues were sold for a loss and one issue was sold at a gain ($31.25). The net loss realized upon the sale of these nine issues was $583,543.36. Seven issues of United States Treasury obligations were held by City Bank at the close of business on May 26, 1959, and the basis of such obligations held by City Bank was identical to, or lower than, their fair market value or redemption value.

A special meeting of the stockholders of City Bank was called on May 7, 1959, adjourned to May 22, 1959, reconvened on May 22, 1959, and again adjourned to May 29, 1959. At the special meeting held on May 29, 1959, the City Bank stockholders approved the sale of the City Bank assets to American Security and the affiliate and the assumption of the City Bank liabilities by American Security. The stockholders also adopted at the May 29, 1959, meeting a resolution for the voluntary liquidation of City Bank and for the creation of a liquidating committee. The resolutions adopted by the stockholders at the May 29, 1959, meeting stated, in part, as follows:

"Resolution No. 1.

"STOCKHOLDER RESOLUTION APPROVING PLAN FOR THE SALE BY THE CITY BANK OF ITS ASSETS TO AMERICAN SECURITY AND TRUST COMPANY AND AMERICAN SECURITY CORPORATION, AND THE ASSUMPTION OF ITS LIABILITIES BY AMERICAN SECURITY AND TRUST COMPANY

"WHEREAS, the Board of Directors of this Bank by resolution dated March 24, 1959, approved a Basic Memorandum Agreement with American Security and Trust Company (hereinafter called American Security) and American Security Corporation (hereinafter called Affiliate) pursuant to which it was agreed, subject to certain specified conditions, that American Security and Affiliate would enter into Purchase and Assumption Agreements with this Bank providing for the purchase of all the assets of this Bank by American Security and Affiliate and the assumption of all of the liabilities of this Bank by American Security, such purchase to be for a price which will give to each stockholder of this Bank $325 for each share held (i.e., aggregate net price of $8,450,000); and

"WHEREAS, such Purchase and Assumption Agreements were entered into on April 6, 1959 and are subject to the condition, among others, that stockholders of this Bank holding at least two-thirds (2/3rds) of its outstanding stock should first approve of the plan for the liquidation (dissolution) of this Bank as the basis for the purchase of its assets and the assumption of its liabilities;

"NOW, THEREFORE,

"(1) Approval is hereby given to the aforesaid Purchase and Assumption Agreements between this Bank and American Security and between this Bank and Affiliate whereby American Security and Affiliate will purchase all the assets of this Bank and American Security will assume all of its liabilities for a price which will give to each stockholder of this Bank $325 for each share held; and

"(2) Approval is hereby given to the plan of voluntary dissolution and complete liquidation of this Bank as proposed at this meeting with the understanding that such liquidation shall be completed within one year of the date hereof.

"Resolution No. 2.

STOCKHOLDER RESOLUTION FOR VOLUNTARY LIQUIDATION

"RESOLVED, That The City Bank of Washington be placed in voluntary liquidation (or dissolution), pursuant to law, to take effect at 2:00 P.M. (E.D.T.), May 29, 1959; and

"That C. F. Burton, Thomas D. Carson, and Chester B. Sellner be appointed Liquidating Committee of said Bank to serve under the general supervision of the Board of Directors of said Bank.

"Resolution No. 3.

STOCKHOLDER RESOLUTION REGARDING LIQUIDATING COMMITTEE

"RESOLVED:

"(1) That the Liquidating Committee of this Bank, heretofore appointed, shall be responsible for all liquidating (dissolution) activities of the Bank, and be authorized, either personally or by delegates (including officers of the Bank) duly appointed by such Committee, to execute all necessary deeds and other legal documents, sign checks and otherwise act for the Bank in liquidation;

"(2) That any and all action of the Liquidating Committee, taken with the concurrence of any two members thereof, shall constitute the authoritative action of the Liquidating Committee; . . .

"Resolution No. 4.

STOCKHOLDER RESOLUTION FOR SALE OF ASSETS AND
DISSOLUTION UNDER VIRGINIA LAW

"WHEREAS, the Board of Directors of this Bank on March 24, 1959, adopted a resolution recommending that the property and assets of the corporation be sold to American Security and Trust Company and American Security Corporation, and that the corporation be dissolved (or liquidated), and directing that the questions of such sale and dissolution be submitted to a vote at a special meeting of stockholders; and

"WHEREAS, a special meeting of stockholders was thereafter called for May 7, 1959, and duly adjourned to May 29, 1959, and due notice of such special meeting, stating that its purpose is to consider the advisability of such sale and dissolution, was on April 10, 1959, given to each stockholder of record;

"NOW, THEREFORE, BE IT RESOLVED

"(1) Such proposed sale of this corporation's assets to American Security and Trust Company and American Security Corporation is hereby authorized and approved, on the terms and conditions and for the consideration heretofore fixed and agreed to by the Board of Directors, as set forth in the Purchase and Assumption Agreements dated April 6, 1959, with American Security and Trust Company and American Security Corporation, or with such modifications thereof as may be agreed to by the Board of Directors.

"(2) Such proposed dissolution of this corporation is hereby approved, which dissolution shall be conducted by the Liquidating Committee designated for such purpose under the general supervision of the Board of Directors and with the full assistance of all the officers of the corporation necessary or available for such purpose; and such officers are hereby authorized to execute and verify the corporation's statement of intent to dissolve and its articles of dissolution, and to take such other and further action as the Liquidating Committee and the Board of Directors shall deem necessary or appropriate to complete the liquidation and dissolution of this corporation."

On May 29, 1959, after the meeting of the City Bank stockholders, American Security accepted an assignment of the banking assets of City Bank and assumed its liabilities, and paid City Bank the sum of $4,921,000. On the same date, after the meeting of the City Bank stockholders, the affiliate accepted an assignment of the nonbanking assets of City Bank and paid City Bank the sum of $3,529,000. In order to raise the funds for such payment, and for other purposes, the affiliate borrowed $3,750,000 from the Guaranty Trust Company of New York.

On May 29, 1959, the liquidating committee of City Bank approved a 100-per cent liquidating dividend amounting to $325 per share payable forthwith to the City Bank stockholders. As of the close of business on May 29, 1959, the 26,000 shares of City Bank stock were held as follows: The affiliate, 20,500 shares; Alex. Brown and Sons, 5,277 shares; and 39 miscellaneous shareholders, 223 shares. Beginning May 29, 1959, the liquidating committee paid to the City Bank stockholders who had duly deposited their shares, $325 per share. On May 29, 1959, the affiliate in such manner received $6,662,500, and on the same date the affiliate paid $6,361,000 to the Guaranty Trust Company of New York in repayment of the amounts borrowed by the affiliate in April 1959 to finance its purchases of City Bank stock.

On May 29, 1959, City Bank sent a statement of intent to dissolve to the State Corporation Commission of Virginia, and on June 16, 1959, filed articles of dissolution with the State Corporation Commission, which approved them on June 19, 1959.

By December 31, 1959, the liquidation of City Bank had been completed, except for the payment of the liquidating distribution of $325 per share in respect of 36 shares of City Bank stock whose owners had not presented the same for payment.

At all times material herein, it was the intention and purpose of the managements of American Security and the affiliate, provided that the affiliate could acquire the requisite number of shares of the stock of City Bank, and further provided that no other circumstances or events intervened to thwart such intention and purpose, to cause the liquidation of City Bank to be effected; to cause the banking assets of City Bank to be purchased by American Security; to cause the nonbanking assets of City Bank to be purchased by the affiliate; and to cause the liabilities of City Bank to be assumed by American Security. At no time material herein was it the intention or purpose of the managements of American Security or the affiliate, to permit or cause City Bank to be operated indefinitely as a separate banking institution unless circumstances or events intervened which would make such separate operation necessary or desirable. At all times material herein, it was the intention and purpose of the managements of American Security and the affiliate that, if circumstances or events intervened which would make separate operation of City Bank necessary or desirable, the affiliate would hold the stock of City Bank as an investment.

The District of Columbia determined that City Bank realized a gain of $3,867,500 from the sale of its assets to American Security and to the affiliate and that the so-called gross receipts tax on such gain was $154,700, which was duly paid. City Bank claimed this amount as a deduction in its Federal income tax return for the period ended May 29, 1959. Respondent disallowed the deduction in full.

In its Federal income tax return for the period ended May 29, 1959, City Bank claimed a deduction in the amount of $583,543.36 sustained in the sale of certain of its United States Treasury obligations on May 26, 1959. This loss deduction was claimed under section 582(c), which permits banks to deduct such losses as ordinary losses. Respondent disallowed this loss deduction with the following explanation: "(c) The net loss on sale of U.S. Treasury Bonds claimed on your amended final return in the amount of $583,543.36 is disallowed for the reason that the sale of the bonds qualifies for nonrecognition of gain or loss for Federal tax purposes within the provisions of Section 337 of the Internal Revenue Code of 1954."

Opinion

This first issue we must decide is whether the loss of $583,543.36 realized by petitioner on the sale of its United States Treasury obligations on May 26, 1959, falls within the nonrecognition provisions of section 337. This turns upon the date of adoption by the corporation of a plan of liquidation, which is the heart of the dispute between the parties. City Bank contends that this date is May 29, 1959, when, at a special meeting of the City Bank stockholders, a plan of complete liquidation was adopted. Respondent argues that "all of the facts and circumstances in the instant case clearly indicate that the plan of liquidation was adopted on or before May 26, 1959."

The avowed purpose of Congress in enacting section 337 was to introduce some certainty in an area where existing court decisions had created disagreements between taxing authorities and taxpayers as to whether sales were made by the corporation or the shareholders depending upon whether such sales were before or after the adoption of a plan of liquidation. S. Rept. No. 1622, 83d Cong., 2d Sess., p. 49. The Senate Finance Committee explained the new section as follows at page 258 of its report:

> "Section 337 corresponds in function to section 333 of the House bill and concerns the problems raised by the decisions in Commissioner v. Court Holding Company, 324 U.S. 451 [331], and U.S. v. Cumberland Public Service Co., 338 U.S. 341 [451], and the numerous related cases. These decisions involve the question of whether the corporation or the shareholder effected a sale of property in connection with the liquidation of the corporation. Under the decision in *Cumberland Public Service Co.*, supra, it is indicated that in the case of a distribution of property in liquidation of a corporation followed by its sale made in fact by its shareholders, a single tax is imposed at the shareholder level. Where the shareholders in fact did not effect the sale, tax is imposed both at the corporate and at the shareholder level. Accordingly, under present law the tax consequences arising from sales made in the course of liquidations may depend primarily upon the formal manner in which the transactions are arranged. Your committee intends in section 337 to provide a definitive rule which will eliminate the present uncertainties. . . ."

Petitioner readily concedes that a tax advantage was deliberately sought. It sold the bonds it was holding at a book loss because it had substantial income for the first 5 months of 1959 and the bond market was low, and it anticipated the adoption of a plan of liquidation under section 337 that would end its tax year. It had to sell them before adopting the plan of liquidation in order to have the loss recognized.[3]

Respondent's argument seems to be that if a corporation, by shareholder resolution, adopts a plan of complete liquidation, the real date it adopted the plan of liquidation, for the purposes of section 337, is somehow moved back to a date when the adoption of the plan in the near future became likely or even virtually certain.

Respondent's approach would hardly make for certainty. It is to be noted the statute also makes the date of the adoption of the plan important in that such adoption starts the running of the 12-month period within which liquidation distribution must be made. On brief respondent candidly admits that "In cases in which the date of adoption of the plan of liquidation is to be determined from all of the facts and circumstances, it is often difficult to pinpoint the exact date of adoption." In fact, respondent makes no attempt to pinpoint such date here but in his brief lists some eight "facts and circumstances" which he contends show "in-

---

[3]Under a special statutory provision (sec. 582) applicable only to banks net capital losses attributable to sales or exchanges of bonds or other evidences of indebtedness are allowed in full against other income.

escapably" that the plan of liquidation was in existence on May 26, 1959. Some of these events took place as early as March 24, 1959, when the board of directors of American Security adopted a resolution which approved the program of acquiring the assets of City Bank and also indicated that City Bank would be liquidated. Certainly this alone would not mean that the plan of liquidation was adopted at that early date, yet it would be as logical to pick that date as it would be to select any of the other seven "facts and circumstances" as the date of adoption of such a plan.

These "facts and circumstances" do nothing more than show that the parties were intending eventually to adopt a plan of liquidation for City Bank. They add nothing for it has been stipulated that "At all times material herein, it was the intention and purpose of the managements of American Security and the Affiliate, provided that the Affiliate could acquire the requisite number of shares of the stock of City Bank, and further provided that no other circumstances or events intervened to thwart such intention and purpose, to cause the liquidation of City Bank to be effected; . . . ." The general intention to liquidate is not the adoption of a plan of liquidation.

We can thus agree that on May 26, 1959, when City Bank sold a portion of its United States Treasury obligations at a loss, it did so in anticipation that the City Bank shareholders would in the future adopt a plan of complete liquidation. But this is immaterial for purposes of section 337. In Virginia Ice & Freezing Corporation, 30 T.C. 1251, the taxpayer sold a portion of its assets at a loss on October 1 and 4, 1954, and its shareholders did not adopt a plan of complete liquidation until October 22, 1954. We rejected respondent's argument that the directors' anticipation on October 1 and 4, when the assets were sold, that the shareholders would ultimately adopt a plan of liquidation constituted an informal adoption of a plan of liquidation.

Respondent cites Mountain Water Co. of La Crescenta, 35 T.C. 418, in support of his position. But that case is clearly distinguishable since the stockholders there never adopted a resolution for a plan of liquidation and, at most, all the stockholders did was consent to the dissolution of the corporation. Absent such formal action, it was necessary for this Court to examine all the facts and circumstances to determine whether or not a plan of liquidation did in fact exist. The other cases cited by respondent are similarly distinguishable.

We hold that City Bank is entitled to a loss deduction of $583,543.36 in its taxable period ending May 29, 1959, realized from the sale of United States Government obligations on May 26, 1959. See sec. 582(c).

The next issue is whether City Bank is entitled to deduct the District of Columbia gross receipts tax imposed on the gain realized from the sale of City Bank's assets, which gain is not recognized under section 337 for Federal income tax purposes. A similar issue was before this Court in Bertha Gassie McDonald, 36 T.C. 1108, [aff'd, 320 F.2d 109 (5th Cir. 1963)], where we held that Louisiana State income taxes imposed on gains from the sale of assets which were entitled to nonrecognition under section 337 were deductible by the taxpayer. The same result was reached in Hawaiian Trust Company, Limited v. United States, 291 F.2d 761. These cases are controlling here. We decide this issue for the petitioner.

Decision will be entered under Rule 50.

NOTE

1. If City Bank had sold its Treasury obligations at a gain do you think the Commissioner would have contended successfully that the plan of complete liquidation had not been adopted prior to May 29, 1959? See Treas. Reg. §1.337-2(b).

2. Is §337 a sensible legislative response to the problems posed by *Court Holding Co.* (page 20 supra) and *Cumberland* (page 22 supra)? What other techniques might have been employed, given the concurrent enactment of §§311 and 336? If the principles underlying §§311 and 336 had been reversed would there have been a *Court Holding Co. — Cumberland* issue for which a §337 would have been thought necessary? Why?

3. What is meant by the phrase "no gain or loss shall be recognized," as it is used in §337? Compare the use of that phrase in §337 and §§311 and 336 with its use in §1031. How do the uses differ?

4. Should the deduction of the District of Columbia gross receipts tax have been denied under §265(1)? Why? After losing the issue in Commissioner v. Universal Leaf Tobacco Co., 318 F.2d 658 (4th Cir. 1963), and in Commissioner v. McDonald, 320 F.2d 109 (5th Cir. 1963), the Commissioner conceded the point. Rev. Rul. 63-233, 1963-2 Cum. Bull. 113. Should he have continued to press in an effort to develop a conflict among the Circuits and thus lay the way for Supreme Court review? Does the answer depend only on whether the Commissioner was "right" on the merits, or might it depend on other issues of tax administration? What might such issues be? If the Commissioner is convinced he is "right" and cannot secure Supreme Court review (or does not wish to), when ought he seek a legislative remedy? On the merits of the substantive issue under the existing statute, see 110 U. Pa. L. Rev. 451 (1962).

BLOOMINGTON HOTEL CO. v. UNITED STATES
65-1 U.S. Tax Cas. ¶9283 (S.D. Ill. Jan. 7, 1965)

Poos, District Judge.

Afternoon Session

THE COURT: Ladies and gentlemen of the Jury: This is a suit for the recovery of taxes paid, allegedly in excess of that which was legally due, and paid under protest at the time. The suit is brought by the Bloomington Hotel Company, an Illinois corporation. It is alleged by the Plaintiff, Bloomington Hotel Company, that the board of directors and the holders of more than two-thirds of the stock of the Bloomington Hotel Company adopted a plan to sell the assets of the corporation and distribute the proceeds, and to liquidate the corporation within twelve months, pursuant to Section 337A of Title 26 of the United States Code.

It is further alleged that following the adoption of a plan of liquidation the assets were sold and the proceeds distributed to the shareholders, less amounts retained to meet taxes.

Defendant denies that the Plaintiff, Bloomington Hotel Company, adopted a plan of complete liquidation between the dates of November 28th, 1961 and December 29, 1961. This denial places the burden of proof upon the Plaintiff to establish the right of recovery by a preponderance of the evidence.

Section 337A of Title 26 of the United States Code is substantially as follows: Section 337: Gain or loss on sales or exchanges in connection with certain liquidations. A: General rule. If: (1) A corporation adopts a plan of complete liquidation on or after June 22nd, 1954; and (2) Within the twelve month period beginning on the date of the adoption of such plan all of the assets of the corporation are distributed in complete liquidation, less assets retained to meet claims; there can be no gain or loss — .Then no gain or loss shall be recognized to such corporation from the sale or exchange by it of property within such twelve month period.

You are instructed that the adoption of a plan of liquidation in compliance with Section 337 does not require the adoption of a formal resolution of liquidation by the directors or stockholders.

You are instructed that in determining whether a plan of liquidation was adopted for purposes of Section 337 you are not to be concerned with State law requirements for dissolution.

You are instructed that a plan of liquidation for purposes of Section 337 is the method of putting into effect an intention or proposal to liquidate.

You are instructed that there are no requirements under the Internal Revenue Code that all the stockholders of Bloomington Hotel Company be present and vote at a stated meeting on a complete plan of liquidation.

You are further instructed that Dana Rollins, Harry Riddle, and Frank Haupert, as executor of the O. A. McClintock estate, had the power to legally adopt a plan of complete liquidation of the Bloomington Hotel Company, without all the stockholders of that company being present at such meeting; nor was it a legal necessity that all stockholders of the Bloomington Hotel Company be personally notified or notified in writing that such a meeting would be held to vote on the plan of liquidation. . . .

Now that you have heard the evidence and the arguments of Counsel, the time has come to instruct you as to the law governing this case. . . .

The Commissioner of Internal Revenue has made the determination that a plan of complete liquidation was not adopted by the Plaintiff.

I instruct you as a matter of law that this determination of the Commissioner of Internal Revenue is presumed to be correct. This does not mean that you are required to follow the Commissioner's determination, but it does mean that the

Plaintiff, the Bloomington Hotel Company, has the burden of proving that the Commissioner was wrong, by a preponderance of the evidence.

To establish by a preponderance of the evidence means to prove that something is more likely so than not so. In other words, a preponderance of the evidence means such evidence, as when considered and compared with that opposed to it, has more convincing force and produces in your minds belief that what is sought to be proved is more likely true than not true.

Now where the evidence is equally balanced, and you are unable to determine in your minds on which side the scale should come down, then the Plaintiff has failed to carry its burden, and the Court instructs you that you must bring in a verdict for the Defendant, the United States of America. . . .

Ladies and gentlemen of the Jury, the task before you is to find the date or dates upon which the Plaintiff, Bloomington Hotel Company, adopted a plan of complete liquidation. My job will be to define what constitutes an adoption by the Bloomington Hotel Company of a plan of complete liquidation. Your job will be to find upon what date or dates the Bloomington Hotel Company took the action that constitutes adoption as I have defined it.

I instruct you that you must accept the definition of what constitutes adoption of a plan of complete liquidation as I give it to you, and it would be a violation of your sworn duty to disregard my definition.

Now two terms have been used a great deal in this case, one is liquidation, and one is dissolution.

I instruct you that on the date a corporation elects to dissolve, it also elects to liquidate. Liquidation is that part of the dissolution process whereby the assets of the corporation are collected, the debts of the corporation paid, and the remaining assets distributed to the shareholders.

By complete liquidation we mean that all the assets of a corporation are distributed to the shareholders of the corporation, the shareholders give up their stock. In other words, complete liquidation is the process of distributing the assets to the shareholders.

In a case — in the case before us, the liquidation of Bloomington Hotel Corporation is the distribution to shareholders of the money received from the sale of the Illinois Hotel building, in exchange for the surrender of the Bloomington Hotel Company stock by its shareholders.

You are instructed that the liquidation of a corporation is the process of winding up its affairs by realizing upon its assets, paying its debts, and distributing the remaining assets to its shareholders. It differs from normal operation for incurring profit in that it ordinarily results in the winding up of the corporation affairs, and there must be a manifest intention to liquidate, a continuing purpose to terminate its affairs and to dissolve the corporation, and its activities must be directed and confined thereto.

As you know by now, a corporation acts in one of three ways: It acts by its officers; it acts by its directors; and it acts by its shareholders. The law of the State of Illinois sets forth certain corporate acts and determines which of the three groups shall exercise them on behalf of the corporation. For example, the law of the State of Illinois gives the power to declare dividends to the board of directors, and the law of the State of Illinois gives the power to elect directors to the stockholders. Thus, the power to act for the corporation is parceled out, some to the directors, and some to the shareholders.

Authorizing the distribution of the assets of a corporation to its shareholders in complete liquidation is a corporate act. The law of the State of Illinois gives the shareholders the power to act for the corporation in authorizing distribution in complete liquidation. This corporate act of authorizing complete liquidation is accomplished by the shareholders of two-thirds of the shares electing to dissolve. When the shareholders have elected to dissolve, the corporation may then stop its business, collect its assets, pay its debts, distribute its remaining assets to its shareholders in complete liquidation, and go out of business. Prior to such an election, the corporation has not acted to authorize distribution in complete liquidation to its shareholders.

A corporation may sell its assets and continue in business. If such — in such a case, it chooses to take the proceeds of the sale and go into a new business.

However, if a corporation does not wish to continue in business after a sale of its assets, the shareholders may vote to distribute those assets to themselves. In such a case, two-thirds of all outstanding shares and the shareholders who own them must meet for the purpose of authorizing the winding up of the corporate affairs, the payment of the corporate debts, and the distribution of the remaining assets to the shareholders.

I instruct you that the resolutions passed by the board of directors on November 28, 1961 do not alone constitute adoption by the Bloomington Hotel Company of a plan of complete liquidation, but this resolution — but these resolutions may be taken into consideration together with all the other evidence in the case and all reasonable inferences that may be drawn, in determining whether or not a plan of complete liquidation was, in fact, adopted by the corporation.

You are further instructed that if you believe the directors and holders of more than two-thirds of the shares of the stock of Bloomington Hotel Company met prior to the sale, on or about November 28, 1961, and not later than December 29, 1961, at which time the directors and holders of more than two-thirds of its shares voted to liquidate the corporation within one year, then such may be considered together with all the other facts and circumstances in the evidence, together with all reasonable inferences that may be drawn therefrom, to determine whether or not a plan was, in fact, adopted.

A plan of complete liquidation is not adopted by Plaintiff, Bloomington Hotel Company, by the fact that less than the holders of sixty-six and two-thirds per cent of the shares forms the intention to liquidate the corporation. But if the owners of sixty-six and two-thirds per cent of all outstanding stock formed the intention to liquidate the corporation and adopted a plan of complete liquidation, this fact may be taken into consideration together with all other facts and circumstances in the evidence, and all reasonable inferences that may be drawn therefrom, to determine whether or not a plan to liquidate and distribute the assets was, in fact, adopted.

A plan of complete liquidation is not adopted by Plaintiff, Bloomington Hotel

Company, at the time that the major shareholders find themselves in agreement that the corporation should be liquidated, but this fact may be taken into consideration with all the evidence in the case, and all reasonable inferences that may be drawn therefrom, in determining whether or not a plan of complete liquidation was adopted by the corporation.

A plan of complete liquidation of the Plaintiff, Bloomington Hotel Company, is not adopted by the fact that the major shareholders came to an understanding that a liquidation should take place, but this fact may be taken into consideration with all the other evidence in the case and all reasonable inferences that may be drawn therefrom in determining whether or not a plan of complete liquidation was, in fact, adopted by the corporation.

A plan of complete liquidation is not adopted by Bloomington Hotel Company by a binding agreement among the holders of more than two-thirds of the common stock outstanding and the vote — and to vote their shares in favor of liquidation of Bloomington Hotel Company, but this fact may be taken into consideration with all the other evidence in the case, with all reasonable inferences that may be drawn therefrom, in determining whether or not a complete liquidation plan was, in fact, adopted.

A plan of complete liquidation is adopted when a resolution approving the distribution of all the assets of the corporation, in redemption of all of its stock, is passed by its shareholders. But the fact that such a resolution was adopted on January 11th, 1962 is not conclusive of this fact, but such fact may be taken into consideration with all the other evidence in the case and all reasonable inferences that may be drawn therefrom in determining whether or not a plan of complete liquidation was, in fact, adopted prior thereto.

Now, ladies and gentlemen, in this case you're going to have to do two things. One is, you're having submitted to you a special interrogatory, and the special interrogatory is this: The Court instructs the Jury that your verdict will be an answer to a written question, pursuant to Rule 49A of the Federal Rules of Civil Procedure. The question is: Has the Plaintiff, Bloomington Hotel Company, proven by a preponderance of the evidence that it adopted a plan of complete liquidation between the dates of November 28th and December the 29th, 1961? Answer, yes or no, inserting in the blank space what you so find, and then signing this special interrogatory.

Then, in addition to that, you have to find a verdict either in favor of the Plaintiff or in favor of the Defendant. If you find that the answer to the question is yes, then you, as the Jury, may use this form of verdict in — may use this form in reaching your verdict: We, the Jury, find the issues in favor of the Plaintiff. In the event that your answer to the special interrogatory is no, then the form of your verdict may be: We, the Jury, find the issues in favor of the Defendant. . . .

You can take the Jury out.

(Whereupon the Jury retired to consider of its verdict.)

Verdict

Has the plaintiff, Bloomington Hotel Company proven by a preponderance of the evidence, that it adopted a plan of complete liquidation between the dates of November 28th and December 29th, 1961? Answer. Yes.

We, the Jury find the issues in favor of the Plaintiff.

NOTE

1. Is a jury an appropriate body to resolve the "factual" issues involved in cases like *Bloomington Hotel* and *City Bank of Washington*? Is it clear that the issue in *Bloomington Hotel* could not have been decided as a question of law?

2. Corporation M distributes all of its assets to its shareholders in complete liquidation. The shareholders then sell the assets to B Corporation under terms negotiated by Corporation M's management prior to liquidation. If the Commissioner contends successfully that, under the *Court Holding Co.* doctrine, the shareholders' sale is imputable to Corporation M, will §337 prevent taxation of its gain? Why?

3. What is a "sale or exchange" to which the immunity of §337 attaches? As to involuntary conversions, see Rev. Rul. 64-100, 1964-1 Cum. Bull. 130. Despite the existence of a "plan of complete liquidation" and a "sale or exchange," §337(c) denies the benefits of §337(a) to collapsible corporations (Chapter 2, pages 249-278 infra), some liquidations under §332 (Chapter 4) and liquidations under §333 (Chapter 2, pages 154-248 infra). With respect to some aspects of §§337(c) and 332, see Note 1, page 51 infra.

4. Corporation X sells all its assets at a profit after adopting a §337 plan and distributes the proceeds within 12 months of the adoption.

(a) X pays its lawyers a $20,000 fee for handling the sale of its assets in the course of its complete liquidation. Is the fee deductible from ordinary corporate income? Compare, e.g., Lanrao, Inc. v. United States, 422 F.2d 481 (6th Cir. 1970), aff'g per curiam 288 F. Supp. 464 (E.D. Tenn. 1968) (no deduction allowed), and United States v. Morton, 387 F.2d 441 (8th Cir. 1968) (no deduction allowed), with United States v. Mountain States Mixed Feed Co., 365 F.2d 244 (10th Cir. 1966) (deduction allowed). How would you resolve the conflict? Why? See Note, 21 Vand. L. Rev. 571 (1968).

(b) Is it reasonable for the Commissioner to continue litigating the deductibility of the legal fees after he has conceded the deductibility of the state tax (Note 4, page 35 supra)? Why?

5. The sale referred to in §337(a) may be an "installment sale" as defined in §453(b) (if made after the adoption of the plan of complete liquidation, §337(b)(1) (C)). The purpose of §453 generally is to permit delay in the payment of tax on profit from a sale until the time when the seller receives actual payment. Hence, unless a seller receives more than 30 per cent of the sale price in the taxable year of sale, he pays tax only on the portion of the installment received which his gross profit bears to the total contract price. See §453(a)(1). The Tax Reform Act of 1969 has narrowed the scope of the installment sale provision by the addition of subsection (3) to §453(b). It provides that certain corporate or governmental debt

instruments are to be treated like cash. Such debt will be included as payments in determining whether payments in the taxable year of sale exceed 30 per cent of the selling price. Congress concluded that §453 went beyond its basic purpose when it permitted a seller who received marketable debt instruments which he could easily convert into cash to defer his tax.

It should be noted, however, that whereas the §453 installment sale is very useful in many business transactions, its benefit is severely limited when employed in conjunction with a §337 sale and liquidation, and this was and is true wholly apart from the 1969 amendment. When the installment sale debt instrument is distributed to the liquidating corporation's shareholders, there is no recognition of gain at the corporate level (see §453(d)(4)(B)), but the shareholders must recognize gain under §331 on the full fair market value of all assets distributed, including the installment debt. Thus, they will receive payments from the purchaser of the assets in the future, but they are liable for their entire tax (usually long-term capital gain under §331) in the year the corporation distributes in liquidation. Section 311 is studied in some detail in Chapter 2, but it is mentioned here because its reach limits §337 transactions to those where there is no objection to immediate payment of the shareholders' tax. Where the seller wants tax deferral under §453, he must sell his stock and then avoid — if he can — the limitations added in 1969 by the enactment of §453(b)(3).

WALTHAM NETOCO THEATRES, INC. v. COMMISSIONER
49 T.C. 399 (1968)

TANNENWALD, Judge: Respondent determined a deficiency in petitioner's corporate income tax in the amount of $37,457.37 for the taxable year 1959. The sole issue for our consideration is whether the gain derived from a sale of all the stock in petitioner's wholly owned subsidiary should be taxable to petitioner.

Findings of Fact

Some of the facts have been stipulated and are found accordingly.

Petitioner Waltham Netoco Theatres, Inc. (sometimes hereinafter referred to as Waltham), had its principal place of business in Boston, Mass., at the time of the filing of the petition herein. It timely filed its Federal income tax return for the taxable year with the district director of internal revenue, Boston, Mass.

American Theatres Corp., Inc. (hereinafter referred to as American) owned all the stock of Pilgrim Theatres Corp. (hereinafter referred to as Pilgrim), which, either directly or through subsidiaries, owned all or a majority of the outstanding shares of stock of numerous other corporations, including petitioner herein. The principal business of American, Pilgrim, petitioner, and the other affiliated corporations (hereinafter sometimes collectively referred to as the American Group) was the management and operation of motion-picture theaters. American provided management services to each of its affiliates pursuant to individual written management agreements.

Throughout 1959, the outstanding stock of petitioner was held as follows:

Pilgrim	501	shares class A
Anna V. Doyle	31	shares class B
Mary A. Kelleher	31	shares class B
James H. Doyle, Jr.	32	shares class B
South Boston Theatre Co.	125	shares class B
Harold E. Gordon	$83\frac{1}{3}$	shares class B
Ellis L. Gordon	$83\frac{1}{3}$	shares class B
Sidney Gordon	$83\frac{1}{3}$	shares class B
Marie L. Doyle	31	shares class B
Total shares	1,001	

The holders of class A stock were entitled to elect three members of the five-member board of directors, the remaining two being elected by class B stockholders. Otherwise, the rights of class A and class B stock were equal, share for share. During the time relevant herein, none of petitioner's stockholders owned any shares or were otherwise interested in American.

During 1958 and at least until June 30, 1959, the principal business of petitioner was the operation of two motion-picture theaters. One of its assets was all of the issued and outstanding stock of Massachusetts Enterprises, Inc., whose sole asset was a parcel of unimproved real estate, which it had originally acquired in 1954 for the purpose of constructing a drive-in theater. Because of a general decline in the motion-picture business in addition to various financial and zoning problems, such purpose was never accomplished. By 1959, the value of the land had increased substantially above its original cost. Legal title to the land was held in the name of a nominee for Massachusetts Enterprises.

During the period in question, the following offices were held by the designated persons in American, Pilgrim, Massachusetts Enterprises, petitioner, and all of the affiliated corporations:

President	Samuel Pinanski
Treasurer	Edward S. Canter
Assistant treasurer	Robert Foster
Clerk	Benjamin A. Trussman

The salary of Edward S. Canter was paid entirely by American.

As of January 1959, Pilgrim had outstanding defaulted financial obligations in the amount of approximately $3 million to the First National Bank of Boston. In addition, certain Pilgrim subsidiaries were indebted to the same bank in an aggregate amount of more than $400,000. All of these debts were secured by mortgages on property of Pilgrim or its subsidiaries. Pursuant to discussion with officers of First National, it was orally agreed that if Pilgrim could make a cash payment of approximately $300,000, the bank would write down the total indebtedness to approximately $1,400,000 and would also reduce the interest rate on such amount. In order to raise the $300,000 essential to this proposed refinancing, the management of American and Pilgrim anticipated raising $150,000 from the American stockholders and utilizing $65,000 already on deposit representing the proceeds from earlier sales of certain theater properties of the American Group. It was hoped that the balance could be derived from the proceeds of the sale of the real estate owned by Massachusetts Enterprises.

As early as January 1958, the real estate was listed with the brokerage firm of R. M. Bradley & Co., Inc. (hereinafter referred to as Bradley) through Fred F. Stockwell, the firm's vice president. Efforts to sell the land were handled by Canter on behalf of the seller and Bradley as broker for the seller, with all of the latter's correspondence being addressed to Canter at American.

Prior to the listing with Bradley, Canter had had conversations with Harold Gordon, one of petitioner's minority stockholders. Canter understood that Gordon also represented the other minority stockholders. Gordon had often expressed the desire of the minority stockholders to get some cash dividends from petitioner and was desirous that the land be sold.

After discussing the matter with Gordon, Canter authorized Bradley to quote a price for the land of $250,000. For the remainder of 1958 and the early part of 1959, the land remained unsold. In March 1959, Stockwell began negotiations for the sale of the land with Clevite Transistor Products Corp. (hereinafter referred to as Clevite). Clevite expressed a definite interest in the land.

In a letter dated March 31, 1959, from Stockwell to Canter, the former transmitted an offer on behalf of Clevite to pay $3,000 for a 60-day option to purchase the land for $200,000, contingent upon a rezoning of the 10 residential acres. Upon receipt of this offer, Canter consulted further with Gordon, and they agreed to make a counteroffer to close the deal for a price of $200,000 net after Bradley's commission — i.e., a purchase price of $214,300. In the early part of April 1959, Stockwell advised Canter that Clevite had accepted this counterproposal. At no time prior to April 1959 had Canter ever mentioned, either in his discussions or in other communications with Stockwell, the name of petitioner or Massachusetts Enterprises. Neither Stockwell nor Clevite appeared to have any knowledge of the relationship of either the petitioner or of Massachusetts Enterprises to the land.

Having learned through Stockwell that Clevite was agreeable to his proposal, Canter turned the matter over to Mr. George P. Davis of Nutter, McClennen & Fish, counsel to the American Group, and asked him to prepare the necessary papers. Prior to that time, no one having any connection with American, Pilgrim, or the petitioner had discussed with counsel any aspect of the transaction.

On April 27, 1959, an agreement for the sale of all of the stock of Massachusetts Enterprises was entered into between each of the shareholders of petitioner, including Pilgrim, and Clevite. Canter signed the agreement on behalf of Pilgrim. The agreement was contingent on rezoning the land. This was accomplished early in June 1959.

The reason for handling the above transaction as a sale of stock by petitioner's shareholders was to realize for Pilgrim the maximum net amount possible after taxes for use in the proposed bank refinancing.

On June 30, 1959, a special meeting of the board of directors of petitioner was held. At this meeting, the directors agreed to cancel an outstanding indebtedness of Massachusetts Enterprises to petitioner and treat the same as a contribution to the capital of the subsidiary. In addition, the directors declared a dividend of all of the stock of Massachusetts Enterprises "payable this day to stockholders of record on the date of this meeting, in equal proportions according to the number of shares held by such stockholders."

Also on June 30, 1959, subsequent to the above declaration of a dividend, all of the stockholders of petitioner endorsed their respective shares of Massachusetts Enterprises to Clevite. After the closing, Bradley rendered, directly to the stockholders of petitioner, its bill for services in connection with arranging the sale. The bill was paid by a check of Nutter, McClennen & Fish out of the proceeds of the sale.

As the holder of 501 shares of the outstanding stock of the petitioner, Pilgrim received $97,282.48 as its share of the net proceeds from the sale. Of this amount, $90,000 was paid to the bank for application against Pilgrim's indebtedness to it, the balance being used to reduce another debt of Pilgrim. Subsequent to the Clevite sale, a written refinancing agreement incorporating the previous oral understanding was entered into between Pilgrim and the bank. Pursuant to this agreement, Pilgrim made up the balance of the $300,000 required cash payment from the $65,000 proceeds of earlier property sales and $145,000 provided by the stockholders of American.

On its Federal income tax return for 1959, petitioner reported a net loss of $12,517.36 (including a $5,603.73 operating loss carryover from 1958). No gain was reported with regard to the sale of the stock in Massachusetts Enterprises.

Opinion

The precise issue arises in the context of section 311(a) of the Internal Revenue Code of 1954. In pertinent part and except for certain circumstances not relevant herein, that section provides that "no gain or loss shall be recognized to a corporation on the distribution, with respect to its stock, of . . . property." Petitioner contends that, since the instant situation does not fall within any of the exceptions to section 311(a), that section operates as an iron curtain against taxability, and any inquiry as to the applicability of Commissioner v. Court Holding Co., 324 U.S. 331 (1945), and United States v. Cumberland Pub. Serv. Co., 338 U.S. 451 (1950), is improper. Alternatively, petitioner asserts that, in any event, the subsequent sale of the distributed stock was made independently by and on behalf of petitioner's shareholders, thus falling under the umbrella of *Cumberland*. Respondent counters that the sale was in reality made by petitioner pursuant to a prearranged plan, which was totally lacking in substance and had as its sole purpose the avoidance of a tax at the corporate level. He therefore claims that *Court Holding Co.* applies and relies heavily upon his own regulations which provide that "the proceeds of the sale of property in form made by a shareholder receiving such property in kind from the corporation may be imputed to the corporation *if, in fact, the corporation made the sale.*" See 1.311-1(a), Income Tax Regs. (Emphasis added.)

We deal first with the assertion that the principles of *Court Holding* and *Cumberland* do not apply to the instant case and that section 311(a) standing alone governs. Concededly, at the time the 1954 Code was enacted, Congress did not look with favor upon the fine distinctions developed by the courts in applying these two cases and, as a consequence, incorporated section 337 into the Code.[2] See H. Rept. No. 1337, 83d Cong., 2d Sess., pp. 38, A106 (1954); S. Rept. No. 1622, 83d Cong., 2d Sess., pp. 48, 258 (1954). Section 337 was a specific legislative elaboration on section 336, which provides that generally "no gain or loss shall be recognized to a corporation on the distribution of property in partial or complete liquidation." No similar elaboration was engrafted upon section 311(a), although the statutory language used is substantially identical to that of section 336. Moreover, at the time of the enactment of section 311(a), Congress clearly indicated that existing case law, imposing a tax at the corporate level in situations involving distributions in kind, was to remain intact, except, of course, where section 337 was applicable. See H. Rept. No. 1337, supra at A108; S. Rept. No. 1622, supra at 247; Mintz and Plumb, "Dividends in Kind — The Thunderbolts and the New Look," 10 Tax L. Rev. 41, 45, fn.22. Consequently, it has been held that the courts remain free to apply the nonstatutory rules enunciated by the decided cases, including not only assignment of income situations such as was involved in Commissioner v. First State Bank [of Stratford], 168 F.2d 1004 (C.A. 5, 1948), but those encompassed by *Court Holding* and *Cumberland* as well. Wood Harmon Corporation v. United States, 311 F.2d 918, 924 (C.A. 2, 1963); A.B.C.D. Lands, Inc., 41 T.C. 840, 847 (1964). See generally Bittker and Eustice, Federal Income Taxation of Corporations and Shareholders, 176-185 (2d ed. 1966); Mintz and Plumb, supra at 44-48.

In view of the foregoing, we are satisfied that the principles of *Court Holding* and *Cumberland* retain their vitality in the area of section 311(a) (see Williamson v. United States, 292 F.2d 524, 530-531 (Ct. Cl. 1961)), althtough it may be that, in situations where the safe harbor of *Cumberland* would be available, the taxpayer will face another barrier (see pp. 405-406 infra). We recognize that, in the context of these two decisions, it can be argued that the formalities of handling a particular transaction assume a disproportionate importance and that a premium is placed on consulting one's lawyer early enough in the game. Certainly the necessary distinctions "may be particularly shadowy and artificial when the corporation is closely held." See United States v. Cumberland Pub. Serv. Co., 338 U.S. at 454-455. But, in light of the applicable legislative history and case law, we conceive it to be our function herein first to consider the circumstances surrounding the sale of the Massachusetts Enterprises stock in light of the tests enunciated in *Court Holding* and *Cumberland*.

There is no real dispute as to the relevant underlying facts herein. The initial objective was to sell the land owned by Massachusetts Enterprises and the negotiations were all carried on in that context. Nothing in the record before us indicates that the conversations between Canter and Gordon, representing the other shareholders of petitioner, encompassed anything but the desire of all concerned to sell the land as a means of obtaining cash. All of the discussions between, and actions by, Canter and the broker fit a pattern of negotiations at the corporate level. There

---

[2]Sec. 337, which by its terms is limited to complete liquidations, has no application herein.

was never any break in the negotiations. They were active and continuous right up until the moment that the deal with Clevite had been made and the matter had been turned over to the lawyers for the preparation of the legal documents. It was not until after that point in time that a sale at the noncorporate level by petitioner's shareholders was suggested.

Petitioner seeks to avoid the application of *Court Holding* herein by seizing on the fact that the negotiations were in respect of a sale of the land and never in respect of the sale of the stock; that the multiple capacity of Canter provided a legitimate cover for the identity of the seller which was never revealed during the negotiations; and that, in the end, it was the stock of Massachusetts Enterprises which was actually sold. Petitioner may not thus utilize the "hidden ball" play with a screened ball carrier at the expense of the Federal fisc. That the stock of Massachusetts Enterprises was substituted for the land at the last minute does not detract from the fact that the sale herein was never conceived and negotiated as a sale *by the shareholders of petitioner*. Cf. Merkra Holding Co., 27 T.C. 82 (1956); Doyle Hosiery Corporation, 17 T.C. 641 (1951). The presence of substantial negotiations on behalf of the shareholders, not to mention the fact that the corporation expressly refused to sell the asset at the corporate level, was the distinguishing feature in *Cumberland*. The absence of this element, namely, independent negotiations at the noncorporate level, is the essential weakness of petitioner's position herein.

We cannot accept petitioner's premise that, because there were no negotiations with respect to the sale of the Massachusetts Enterprises stock, the sale must be considered as having been made by petitioner's shareholders. We think that, in order to claim the protection of *Cumberland,* it was incumbent on petitioner to show that the sale was independently negotiated on behalf of its shareholders. Petitioner having failed so to do, we see no reason to disturb respondent's determination that the gain on the sale should be taxable to the entity, i.e., the petitioner, who owned the asset throughout the negotiations and up to the very day of actual transfer to the purchaser. In this connection, we note that the dividend in kind of the stock of Massachusetts Enterprises was not distributed until the day of its prearranged transfer to Clevite. In short, whether we consider the sale itself as having been made by petitioner, or simply that the negotiations had been sufficiently finalized prior to the distribution in kind to warrant attributing the gain to petitioner, we hold that it is taxable on the gain from the sale under the principles of *Court Holding* and *Cumberland*.

We are not unmindful of the language in some decisions that the protection of *Cumberland* may not be available to nonliquidating distributions in kind by an ongoing corporation and that the corporation may be held taxable simply on the ground that there was a tax-motivated preconceived plan. E.g., United States v. Lynch, 192 F.2d 718 (C.A. 9, 1951); Commissioner v. Transport Trad. & Term. Corp., 176 F.2d 570 (C.A. 2, 1949); A.B.C.D. Lands, Inc., supra; but see Diggs v. Commissioner, 281 F.2d 326 (C.A. 2, 1960). See also Bittker and Eustice, supra at 182; Mintz and Plumb, supra at 46-48; Bierman, "Corporate Distributions of Appreciated and Depreciated Property: Gain or Loss to the Distributor," 8th Ann.

N.Y.U. Tax Inst. 792 (1950); Comment, "The Imputed Sale and Anticipatory Assignment of Income Doctrines: Their Effect on I.R.C. Sections 311, 1336," 15 Buffalo L. Rev. 154 (1966). Although the difficulties of applying the distinctions of *Court Holding* and *Cumberland* might be avoided if we were to adopt the broader concept suggested with respect to nonliquidating distributions, we would then be faced with equal, if not greater, difficulties in deciding the relative importance of other factors, such as the character of the assets involved, the effect of a distribution clearly in partial liquidation, the presence or absence of a prior commitment of the shareholders to sell the distributed assets or of an expectation of sale by the shareholders, and the impact of an exclusively or predominant tax-avoidance motivation. Particularly since the actual facts of the above-cited cases do not require the more general rationale found in the opinions, we see no point in exploring such wider horizons until we are compelled to do so. None of the foregoing cases prohibits the application of *Court Holding* and it is that decision which is the foundation of our conclusion herein.

Decision will be entered for the respondent.

WALTHAM NETOCO THEATRES, INC. v. COMMISSIONER
401 F.2d 333 (1st Cir. 1968)

Before ALDRICH, Chief Judge, McENTEE and COFFIN, Circuit Judges.

McENTEE, Circuit Judge. The question raised by this petition for review is whether the Tax Court erred in holding that the gain derived from a sale of all the stock in petitioner's wholly owned subsidiary was taxable to petitioner. There is no dispute as to the relevant underlying facts. Only the Tax Court's conclusions are questioned. . . .

. . . The total amount paid by the purchaser for these shares was the same as the amount that had been agreed upon orally as the purchase price for the land.[2]

In petitioner's income tax return for 1959 no gain was reported with regard to the sale of stock. Then as now it took the position that this was a sale by the stockholders, not the petitioner. The Tax Court upheld the Commissioner of Internal Revenue in rejecting that contention. The basic question of who *in reality* was the seller in this transaction is a question of fact. In Commissioner v. Court Holding Co., 324 U.S. 331, 334 (1945), the Court said:

"The incidence of taxation depends upon the substance of a transaction. The tax consequences which arise from gains from a sale of property are not finally to be determined solely by the means employed to transfer legal title. Rather, the transaction must be viewed as a whole, and each step, from the commencement of negotiations to the consummation of the sale, is relevant. A sale by one person cannot be transformed for tax purposes

[2] The total purchase price was $214,300 of which $14,300 represented the real estate broker's commission. Pilgrim's share of the proceeds was some $97,000.

into a sale by another by using the latter as a conduit through which to pass title. To permit the true nature of a transaction to be disguised by mere formalisms, which exist solely to alter tax liabilities, would seriously impair the effective administration of the tax policies of Congress."

Our function is to review the record of the Tax Court to see if there is sufficient evidence to warrant its findings. Commissioner v. Duberstein, 363 U.S. 278 (1960); Palmer v. Commissioner, 354 F.2d 974, 975 (1st Cir. 1965). As stated in United States v. Cumberland Public Service Co., 338 U.S. 451, 456 (1950), a case upon which the petitioner relies, "It is for the trial court, upon consideration of an entire transaction, to determine the factual category in which a particular transaction belongs."

In the instant case the Tax Court found, among other things, that the initial objective of this transaction "was to sell the land owned by Massachusetts Enterprises and the negotiations were all carried on in that context." The evidence shows that from the beginning all the negotiations were for the sale of the real estate and were carried on by Canter acting for American. It was in this capacity that Canter originally listed the real estate for sale, retained the broker, negotiated the terms and conditions of the sale and reached an oral agreement with Clevite in mid April for the sale of the real estate. Also, it is undisputed that the expense of advertising this real estate for sale was incurred at the corporate level. The record shows that after the oral agreement of sale was reached Canter, acting for American, consulted the attorneys for the corporate group for the purpose of having the papers drawn. It was only after that consultation that the sale by petitioner's stockholders was suggested. By that time, however, the deal with Clevite for the sale of the real estate had been struck and only the formalities of the transaction remained.

Petitioner claims that the sale of the distributed stock, as detailed above, brings the case within the holding in United States v. Cumberland Public Service Co., supra. But this would be true only if the sale were the result of independent and active negotiations by its stockholders with Clevite. We think there is sufficient evidence in the record to support the Tax Court's finding and conclusion that the transaction in question was a sale on the corporate rather than on the stockholder level and that the gain derived therefrom is taxable to the petitioner. See Commissioner v. Court Holding Co., supra.

The decision of the Tax Court is affirmed.

NOTE

1. Both the Tax Court and the Court of Appeals in *Waltham Netoco Theatres, Inc.* accept as a "fact" that it was the real estate of Massachusetts Enterprises that was the real subject of the sale and purchase. Yet the Commissioner, on the basis of that "fact," contended successfully that the taxpayer sold the stock of Massachusetts Enterprises. Based on that "fact" and *Court Holding Company* doctrine, should not the gain on the imputed sale of the real estate have been taxed to Massachusetts Enter-

prises? How does "the deal with Clevite for the sale of the real estate" (page 48 supra) justify taxing the taxpayer with gain on an allegedly imputed sale by it of its stock in Massachusetts Enterprises?

2. Section 337 applies only to complete liquidations. If a corporation distributes part, but not all, of its assets, and its shareholders then sell them, the *Court Holding* vs. *Cumberland* issue persists. What precautions should a corporate lawyer take to avoid the application of *Court Holding* in the case of a partial (less than complete) liquidation? Should §337 be amended to apply to partial liquidations? Why? Should §337 be retained in the Code? In its present form? Why? (For some of the tax consequences to shareholders in complete and partial liquidations see Chapter 2, pages 154-248 infra.)

FAMILY RECORD PLAN, INC. v. COMMISSIONER
309 F.2d 208 (9th Cir. 1962), cert. denied, 373 U.S. 910 (1963)

Before HAMLEY, MERRILL and DUNIWAY, Circuit Judges.

DUNIWAY, Circuit Judge. In this petition to review decisions of the Tax Court, the problem presented is strikingly similar to that dealt with by us in Commissioner of Internal Revenue v. Kuckenberg, 309 F.2d 202, decided October 11, 1962.

Family Record Plan, Incorporated (dissolved), here referred to as Transferor, and Family Record Plan, Incorporated (formerly F.R.P., Inc.), here referred to as Transferee, are the petitioners. There is no substantial dispute as to the material facts.

The period in question is the tax year of Transferor, September 1, 1954 to February 28, 1955. It had for some years been in the business of selling to members of the public the right (represented by a certificate and embodied in a written contract) to have portrait photographs taken at stated intervals, free, by a studio in the customers' vicinity, and an album in which to mount the photographs so taken. A small down payment (usually $5.00 or $10.00) was made, and the balance was payable, usually at $5.00 per month, over a period, the length of which depended upon which of two types of contracts was used. The maximum contract period was nine months. Transferor carried no stock of albums; it ordered an album from the manufacturer, to be shipped direct to the customer, and this was done, as to each customer, when at least $10.00 had been paid, the cost of the album to Transferor being less than that amount. Transferor had written agreements with a large number of studios whereby the studio agreed to take the pictures and supply one copy to the customer, without cost for the first copy either to Transferor or to the customer. Each customer's contract designated a studio. Once the customer got the album, Transferor's sole remaining responsibility was to designate another studio if the named studio did not perform, or if the customer moved, or, if there were no available studio, to enlarge, retouch, print and return to the customer, a picture from a negative furnished by the customer. There is no showing that Transferor was called upon to perform any of these obligations in connection with any contract assigned, as hereafter described.

Transferee was organized for the purpose of buying the stock of Transferor, liquidating it, and continuing the business. The stockholders of Transferee had no connection with those of Transferor. On October 25, 1954, Transferee bought all of the stock for $1,120,000. It allocated $800,000 of the price on its books to the cost of the accounts receivable then owned by Transferor, such accounts representing payments owing to Transferor from its customers. After October 25, Transferor was a wholly owned subsidiary of Transferee.

On December 10, 1954, the board of directors of Transferor adopted a plan of complete liquidation, and Transferee, as sole stockholder, consented. The plan required that Transferor cease business, which it did (except as hereafter indicated), and it duly filed the required information return with the Commissioner of Internal Revenue. The plan contemplated sale of "all or any part of the assets" of Transferor. Winding up was to be completed not later than November 30, 1955.

On December 17, 1954, Transferor sold its contracts with its customers, by written agreement, to one Smith and wife. The agreement covered all outstanding contracts, there being about 49,000 with an unpaid balance of $1,390,331.91, including about 9,000 delinquent accounts in the hands of collection agencies with an unpaid balance of $319,801.77. The Smiths did not undertake to perform the contracts; all that they got was the right to the collections. The sale was without recourse. The purchase price was $800,000, payable $200,000 down and the balance in installments, with the final payment due not later than September 1, 1955. The Smiths' obligation to pay was unconditional. Transferor was appointed agent of the Smiths to collect, the agency being irrevocable until the price was paid or until September 1, 1955, and all collections (net) were to be applied on the price. In fact, Transferor's collections resulted in full payment by April 19, 1955.

Meanwhile, by February 28, 1955, Transferor was fully wound up and dissolved, and all of its assets, including the contract with the Smiths, were assigned to Transferee. The transfer of the Smith contract was made as of December 30, 1954. Of the collections on the customer contracts, $225,000 was paid to Transferor, and $575,000 was paid, all after January 1, 1955, to Transferee. It is stipulated, however, that if any gain on the sale of the accounts "is recognized to transferor for federal income tax purposes, the amount of the gain to be included in income for the period September 1, 1954, to February 28, 1955, would be $800,000.00."

Both Transferor and Transferee were on the cash basis of accounting. In its final income tax return, Transferor did not include any part of the $800,000 in its income. The Commissioner included all of it, and the Tax Court affirmed the Commissioner. Transferee is in the proceeding solely as a transferee; its liability for tax on its own income is not here involved.

As in *Kuckenberg*, supra, the taxpayers' contention is that the sale of the contracts was a sale of "property" within the meaning of section 337 of the Internal Revenue Code (26 U.S.C. §337) and that therefore no gain or loss to Transferor is recognized for income tax purposes. The Tax Court held that the sale was not a sale of "property," but a sale of "installment obligations" within the meaning of section 337(b). We do not pass upon this question, but expressly leave it undecided, because we think the decision correct for the reasons stated in *Kuckenberg*. We think that here, as there, the Commissioner was entitled, as he asserted before the Tax Court, in the exercise of his authority under section 446(b) (26 U.S.C. §446(b)), to disregard Transferor's cash basis of accounting and to require computation by a method that would clearly reflect income. Essentially, what was "sold" was a right to receive income generated by Transferor in the regular course of its business, and nothing more, and receipt of $800,000 for that right was the receipt of income.

If the Tax Court was right in its conclusions, we should affirm, even if we think that it applied wrong legal reasons. (Boe v. Commissioner, 9 Cir., 1962, 307 F.2d 339). In this case, the Tax Court gave taxpayers ample opportunity to present additional evidence as to the application of section 446(b). None was offered. The question, as in *Boe*, is not what are the facts, but what are the legal rules applicable to the facts?

Petitioners also assert that the decision is contrary to the provisions of section 334(b)(2) of the Internal Revenue Code (26 U.S.C. §334(b)(2)). There is nothing in the point. That section deals solely with the "basis," for capital gains purposes, of property received by Transferee, and not at all with the liability of Transferor for tax upon its own income, which is the sole question before us.

Affirmed.

NOTE

1. Section 332 applied to the liquidation of Transferor into Transferee, but subparagraph (B), and not subparagraph (A), of §337(c)(2) described the transaction. As a result, there was no literal bar to the application of §337(a). (In general, §337(c) results in recognition of the gain on sale in circumstances where, as a result of §332, the liquidating distribution would not be taxable to the shareholder. The theme seems to be to eliminate the corporate tax only if the liquidating distribution is taxable to the shareholders, and §332 ordinarily makes a liquidating distribution tax-free to certain corporate shareholders. Although the liquidation of Transferor into Transferee would be tax-free to Transferee under §332, the applicability of §337(a) is preserved because of the dominant policy implied in §344(b)(2) (pages 57-67 infra) which is preserved by §337(c)(2)(B). Section 332 is discussed in Chapter 4 infra.)

2. Why was the Commissioner entitled to disregard the Transferor's cash basis method of accounting? Were the contracts sold to Smith "property" within the meaning of §337(b)? The Tax Court answered that question in the negative. Why? Inventory is not "property" unless sold in the fashion described in §337(b)(2). Why is inventory first excluded from the "property" concept and then, under certain circumstances, included? Should the contracts in *Family Record* have been classified as "installment obligations"? Why? See Coast Coil Company, 50 T.C. 528 (1968), aff'd per curiam, 422 F.2d 402 (9th Cir. 1970). Why does §337(b) deal with "installment obligations" as it does?

COMMISSIONER v. ANDERS
414 F.2d 1283 (10th Cir. 1969), rev'g 48 T.C. 815 (1967),
cert. denied, 396 U.S. 958 (1970)

Before PICKETT, Senior Circuit Judge, and HICKEY and HOLLOWAY, Circuit Judges.

HOLLOWAY, Circuit Judge. This petition for review challenges the decision against the Government by the Tax Court in Anders v. Commissioner, 48 T.C. 815 (1967).

The issue involved is whether the amount received for rental items of apparel, towels and the like in a sale of corporate assets preceding a complete liquidation was a gain from the sale of property within the provisions of §337 of the Internal Revenue Code of 1954 for non-recognition of gain to the corporation where the cost of such items had been fully expensed when they were purchased, or whether such gain was taxable as ordinary income to the corporation under tax benefit principles. The Government contends that due to the tax benefit obtained when the charges to expense accounts were made, the gain should be treated as ordinary income. The taxpayer[1] maintains that tax benefit principles do not apply and that there was only a gain from the sale of property within the non-recognition provisions of §337 on liquidations. The tax Court sustained the taxpayer's position.

The undisputed facts show the following. Service Industrial Cleaners, Inc., (Service) was a Kansas corporation engaged in the business of providing a rental service of laundered towels, seat covers, wiping and dusting materials, coveralls, coats, shirts and other items of apparel. The items had a useful life of 12 to 18 months or somewhat longer depending on the use made of them. Service also carried on a general cleaning and laundering business for such items owned by others and an industrial laundry business. For Federal income tax purposes Service charged the full cost of the rental items described to expense accounts when purchased. At the end of its tax years the expense accounts were credited with the cost of items not placed in service during the year. The expensed replacement cost of the rental items ran about $200,000 annually. There is no dispute as to the propriety of these charges.

In May, 1961, respondent Anders, owner of the stock of Service directly or through nominees, made an agreement for the sale of the business and properties of Service. On May 12 Service's directors and stockholders passed resolutions approving the terms of sale and adopting a plan of complete liquidation pursuant to §337. On May 16 Service executed a written agreement of sale with the individuals purchasing the business who were acting in behalf of a newly formed Kansas corporation also known as Service Industrial Cleaners, Inc., through which purchasers desired to carry on the business. On May 22 and 23 the rental items in question and substantially all of Service's assets were sold to the purchasers. Compliance by Service with the requirements of §337 for such complete liquidations is not disputed.

In the terms of sale Service agreed with the purchasers on specific consideration to be paid for the inventory of rental items in question and also specified consideration to be paid for furniture, realty, goodwill and accounts receivable. For the purposes of this opinion it is sufficient to note that Service reported a gain of $446,601 from the sale of all such property and claimed non-recognition of the gain under §337. This gain included $233,000 received for the rental items in use whose cost had been fully expensed giving them a zero basis. It is this gain from disposition of the rental items in use which the Government says should be taxed as ordinary income due to tax benefits obtained when the cost of the rental items was

---

[1]It is undisputed that respondent Anders as a stockholder received distributions in excess of the deficiency asserted against the corporation and would be liable as transferee if the corporation is liable for the deficiency.

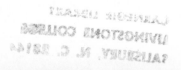

charged to expense on purchase. The tax return of Service in issue was on an accrual basis.

The Government position essentially is that §337 carries the same exceptions and limitations applicable to capital gains treatment under the Code generally, which is shown by similar definitions of property in §337 and of capital assets in §1221 and other statutory provisions;[2] that such exceptions include decisions imposing ordinary income taxation under the tax benefit rule where an amount deducted from gross income in one year is recovered in a later year; that under these principles the proceeds from the disposition of the rental items should be treated as ordinary income against which the expense of purchasing the items was charged; and that where there is no gain representing appreciation in value there is no basis for affording the transaction treatment as a gain entitled to non-recognition under §337.

The taxpayer's position in substance is that there was a sale of items constituting property within the broad definition of that term in §337 and not covered by its specified exclusions; that the tax benefit cases are of limited application, those involving anticipatory assignment of income and others relied on by the Government being inapposite; and that, in any event, the deductions taken by Service on purchase of the rental items were in the nature of depreciation deductions and not subject to recapture.

In rejecting the Government's contentions the Tax Court stated:

> "Assuming, for the purposes of this case, that the amount in question represents the recovery of expenses previously deducted from gross income by the corporation and that such recovered amount would be taxable to the corporation in the year of recovery under other circumstances, it is nevertheless gain which resulted to the corporation from the sale of all its assets pursuant to a plan of complete liquidation and is nonrecognizable *to the corporation* under the provisions of section 337" (48 T.C. at 820-821)

We do not interpret §337 as having the special effect on this transaction which the Tax Court finds. If "under other circumstances" (i.e., the sale of the rental items in question without a §337 liquidation) the tax benefit rule and similar principles would have made the proceeds from the sale of such property taxable as ordinary income, they should also be taxable as ordinary income here. In §337 Congress dealt with the problem of taxation on gain to both corporation and its stockholders where a sale of assets and subsequent liquidation occur, arising from the decisions in Commissioner v. Court Holding Co., 324 U.S. 331, 65 S. Ct. 707, 89 L. Ed. 981 (1945), and United States v. Cumberland Public Service Co., 338 U.S. 451, 70 S. Ct. 280, 94 L. Ed. 251 (1950). And the means employed was to provide for non-recognition of the gain to the corporation on the sale of property (as de-

---

[2] . . . The Government also relies on §111 of the 1954 Code which imposed certain restrictions on application of the tax benefit rule. This provision is said to evidence legislative approval of decisions fashioning the rule. Reference is also made to a ruling which denied treatment as a non-recognizable gain in a §337 liquidation involving the sale of coal, plumbing supplies and small tools. See Rev. Rul. 61-214, 1961-2 Cum. Bull. 60.

fined in §337) by it before its liquidation. The statute used a definition of property in §337 parallel to that of assets in §1221 of the 1954 Code.[4] Moreover, there is no provision in the statute showing an intent to alter or bar the application in cases under §337 of tax benefit principles fashioned under other provisions of the Code. Therefore, we conclude that tax benefit principles are applicable here as under other statutory provisions and that §337 intended no disregard of them in liquidation cases. See Citizens Federal Savings & Loan Association of Cleveland v. United States, 290 F.2d 932, 154 Ct. Cl. 305 (1961), and West Seattle National Bank of Seattle v. Commissioner, 288 F.2d 47 (9th Cir. 1961).

We turn to a consideration of this case under tax benefiit principles. The rental items in question had a zero basis and their cost had been fully expensed on purchase by Service in its Federal income tax returns and deductions were taken therefor by Service. In similar circumstances a recovery of property by the taxpayer was treated as recoupment of prior charitable deductions and as taxable income. Alice Phelan Sullivan Corporation v. United States, 381 F.2d 399, 402, 180 Ct. Cl. 659 (1967). In view of Service's charging the full cost of the rental items to expense, the " . . . increment realized in this area over and beyond adjusted basis does not then represent any gain in capital or asset value." West Seattle National Bank of Seattle v. Commissioner, supra, 288 F.2d at 49. The *West Seattle* case involved the transfer of loans receivable at face value with recoupment thereby affected of prior bad debt charges. We conclude that the logic of tax benefit principles applies here, despite various distinctions suggested between Service's case and existing tax benefit decisions. Under such principles the proceeds of the rental items should properly be treated as recoupment of the expense charges. . . .

The taxpayer maintains that such principles may not apply since the rental items in question come literally within the general meaning of property in §337. Thus, it is argued, on disposition of the rental items the proceeds must be treated as a gain from the sale of property. We do not agree. The fact that a transaction involves disposition of property does not compel treatment of the proceeds as gain from such a transfer. Commissioner v. Gillette Motor Co., 364 U.S. 130, 134, 80 S. Ct. 1497, 4 L. Ed. 2d 1617 (1960); . . . Instead, we conclude that tax benefit principles call for treatment of the proceeds not as gain from the sale of property, but as ordinary income which was deducted on its purchase.

The taxpayer contends further that the expense charges were the same as depreciation which is not subject to recapture, and that the proceeds of the rental items should be treated as gain from a sale above a depreciated basis at zero, relying on Fribourg Navigation Co., Inc. v. Commissioner, 383 U.S. 272, 86 S. Ct. 862, 15 L. Ed. 2d 751 (1966).[7] However the *Fribourg* case emphasizes that such treatment follows the use of the depreciation method of tax accounting dealing with wear and tear or gradual expiration of the useful life of the property. Id. at 276, 86 S. Ct.

---

[4]See Pridemark v. Commissioner . . . , 345 F.2d at 45, and Merchants National Bank of Mobile v. Commissioner, 199 F.2d 657 (5th Cir. 1952), applying the tax benefit rule and denying capital gains treatment under the predecessor to §1221.

[7]In view of 26 U.S.C.A. §1245, this argument seems foreclosed for dispositions occurring in taxable years beginning after December 31, 1962, and involving depreciation deductions taken after December 31, 1961.

862; West Seattle National Bank of Seattle v. Commissioner, supra, 288 F.2d at 49. While some comparisons may be drawn between depreciation and the charges to expense made by Service at purchase of the rental items, we conclude that in substance the methods are not the same. By charging to expense the full cost of the rental items at purchase and not capitalizing them, there was no real depreciation method employed coming within the *Fribourg* case so as to qualify the disposition of the rental items for treatment as gain from a sale above a depreciated basis. There was no realization of appreciation in value entitled to such treatment. Commissioner v. Gillette Motor Co., supra, 364 U.S. at 134, 80 S. Ct. 1497; Citizens Federal Savings & Loan Association of Cleveland v. United States, supra, 290 F.2d at 936.

As the taxpayer says, the controversy is not clearly decided by any of these cases. However, the recoupment of the charges involved here reasonably comes within the tax benefit principles and similar cases, and §337 does not alter or bar their application. In these circumstances we do not believe that treatment as a non-recognizable gain was intended by Congress.

The decision is reversed.

Order Denying Petition For Rehearing

We have considered the petition for rehearing and conclude that it raises no material new issue. These comments are made due to Service's contentions, among others, that the opinion was based on reference to an incorrect regulation and that it did not discuss a pertinent alternative theory.

It is argued that the expensing of the cost of the rental items was not made under §1.162-3 of the Treasury Regulations on Income Tax dealing with the "Cost of Materials" as originally stated in the opinion. Instead, the taxpayer refers to the statement in the opinion of the Tax Court that: "Respondent has not questioned the propriety of expensing the rental items when purchased, or the fact that they were not inventoried. See sec. 446(a) and (c), I.R.C. 1954; sec. 1.446-1 (c)(iv), Income Tax Regs.; sec. 471, I.R.C. 1954; sec 1.471-1, Income Tax Regs." 48 T.C. at 823. §1.162-3 was cited by the Government brief, but we find no record proof that it was the regulation relied on by Service. The regulations cited by the Tax Court have general provisions on inventories and for use of the cash method for expense accounts by an accrual method taxpayer (which Service was) and others which do apply. We therefore consider what effect the applicability of the regulations cited by the Tax Court may have.

We note that the Tax Court findings, 48 T.C. at 816-818, in substance re-stated the following stipulation of the parties:

"6. For Federal income tax purposes Service charged to its expense accounts when purchased the cost of the items used in conducting the aforesaid rental service business. At the end of each taxable year the expense accounts were credited with the costs of the ending inventory of items which had not been placed in service at the end of such taxable year. In the sale of the business to Buyer, hereinafter referred to in paragraph 8 hereof, the sum of $233,000 of the consideration paid was allocated for the items in use."

We have considered the stipulation, the Tax Court findings to the same effect, the related facts and all the cited regulations. Accepting the proposition that Treasury Regulation §1.162-3 was not the basis of the taxpayer's expense charges, the result is the same. In any event the cost of the rental items was fully expensed at purchase and tax deductions therefor taken. The regulation permitting the deductions is not controlling. Therefore, as stated in the opinion, we conclude that under tax benefit principles the proceeds received for the rental items should properly be treated as recoupment of the prior deductions and as taxable income.

It is also contended that an alternative theory of the taxpayer was not considered. The argument is that if the rental items are not treated as property under §337(b), then they are entitled to treatment as stock in trade or other property includible in inventory under §337(b)(2). It is said that since the items were sold to one person in one transaction the taxpayer is still entitled to nonrecognition of the gain under §337(a).

The theory does not strengthen Service's position. We dealt with the contention that the rental items come literally within the general meaning of property in §337. As the opinion stated, we conclude that the fact that a transaction involves the disposition of property within the meaning of §337 does not compel treatment of the proceeds from it as gain from a transfer of the property. The same reasoning applies if the property is treated as within the meaning of §337(b)(2). Where the cost of the property was fully expensed and deducted for tax purposes, tax benefit principles reasonably call for treatment of the proceeds as recoupment of the prior charges and ordinary income. By §337 Congress showed no intention to discard such principles.

The opinion is corrected by substituted pages 2, 3 and 8 to omit reference to Treasury Regulation §1.162-3. We also omit a statement, which followed one made in the Tax Court opinion, that the parties agreed that the rental items were not stock in trade, et cetera. This is done to show that the taxpayer has asserted the alternative theory under §337(b)(2), discussed above.

We conclude that neither the grounds discussed above nor others urged warrant a rehearing or altering the decision. The petition for rehearing is denied.

NOTE

1. Does the *Anders* decision mesh with the statute? Why is "tax benefit" from depreciation conceived as something different from "tax benefit" derived from an immediate writeoff? Compare Ricketts, The Tax Benefit, Recoveries and Sales of Property Under Section 337, 9 Wm. and Mary L. Rev. 476 (1967).

Corporation M's sale of assets following the adoption of its plan of complete liquidation includes a supply of small tools which it had expensed, machinery purchased in 1963 which it had been depreciating on an accelerated basis, and the purchase money obligation of the purchaser of a plant it had sold in 1960, gain on which it has been reporting on the "deferred-payment" (Treas. Reg. §1.453-6) method. Would §337(a) prevent taxation of the gain attributable to those assets if

Corporation M distributed all of its assets within the required twelve months? What is the relevance of §1245?

2. For more detailed treatment of some of the issues posed in this section of the casebook see Lyon, Ordinary Income May Arise in Section 337 Sales Under the Assignment of Income Doctrine, 16 J. Taxation 2 (1962); Gardner, The Impact of Sections 1245 and 1250 on Corporate Liquidations, 17 U. Fla. L. Rev. 58 (1964); B. Bittker and J. Eustice, Federal Income Taxation of Corporations and Shareholders 392-408 (2d ed. 1966).

c. COMPUTATION OF GAIN — QUESTION OF BASIS — §§1012, 334(b)(1) AND (b)(2)

UNITED STATES v. GENERAL GEOPHYSICAL CO.
296 F.2d 86 (5th Cir. 1961), cert. denied, 369 U.S. 849 (1962)

Before RIVES and WISDOM, Circuit Judges, and DAWKINS, JR., District Judge.

WISDOM, Circuit Judge. February 25, 1954 General Geophysical Company, the taxpayer, transferred certain depreciable assets having a tax basis of $169,290 and a market value of $746,525 to two of its major stockholders in the redemption of their stock. Later that day the taxpayer reacquired the same assets from the former stockholders in exchange for corporate notes in the amount of $746,525. In its 1954 income tax return the corporation claimed depreciation deductions using as the cost basis the market value of the assets at the time of the transaction. The sole question this litigation presents is whether the corporation's reacquisition of the assets stepped up the basis. We hold that it did not and reverse the decision below.

Earl W. Johnson founded General Geophysical Company in 1933 to engage in oil exploration, and managed its operations until his sudden death in 1953. At his death his estate, his wife, his mother, and a friend Paul L. Davis owned 77% of the corporation's total stock and 94% of its voting shares. The major portion of the remaining shares was owned by Chester Sappington, T. O. Hall, and Albert B. Gruff, who were also officers in the corporation. The Johnson stock was community property: half belonged to the widow and the other half was held by the Second National Bank of Houston as executor and trustee for Johnson's estate. The testimony shows that the bank and Mrs. Johnson soon realized that neither of them could contribute anything of value to running the corporate business, and that they should not attempt it. They realized also that if the corporation were liquidated and its properties sold, they would receive less than the value of their stock in a going concern. Sappington, Hall, and Grubb believed that they could run the corporation successfully and if so, they should receive its future profits. Accordingly, the corporation agreed to retire the stock held by the bank, the two Mrs. Johnsons, and Davis. After long negotiations the parties settled on a valuation of the stock at $245 a share, payable partly in cash and partly in notes. The attorney for the retiring stockholders advised against this proposal for fear that it would leave the stockholders without sufficient protection in case the corporation should be forced into bankruptcy. He based this legitimate business fear on Robinson v. Wangemann, 5 Cir., 1935, 75 F.2d 756, 758, which holds that when a former shareholder owns notes of a bankrupt corporation, received in the redemption of his stock, he "cannot be permitted to share with the other unsecured creditors in the distribution of the assets of the bankrupt estate." To avoid exposure to this risk, the stockholders proposed that the Johnson stock be retired in exchange for cash and corporate property having a market value equal to that of the stock. The redemption was carried out in accordance with this proposal. A few hours later, the corporation repurchased the property for corporate notes, giving the former stockholders a mortgage on certain of its properties.

Witnesses for the taxpayer insisted that there was no agreement between the corporation and the stockholders to reexchange the corporate properties transferred to the stockholders in the redemption of their shares. The trial judge so found, and it seems clear that there was no legally binding agreement to that effect. The attorney for the stockholders did testify, however, that he had discussed the possibility of such a resale and before February 25, 1954 had prepared the documents for a resale in case that was decided upon after the initial transfer.

Under Section 1012 of the Internal Revenue Code of 1954, 26 U.S.C.A. §1012, "the basis of property shall be the cost of such property." This requires a determination of when the taxpayer acquired the property and the price he paid for it. Our decision depends on whether or not the transactions in question created an interruption in the ownership of the property, producing a new basis on its reacquisition. The Government asserts that we should disregard the form of the transfer and recognize that the substance of the transactions was a redemption of the corporate stock for cash and notes, leaving the ownership and basis of the depreciable assets undisturbed. The taxpayer answers that there was no fraud or subterfuge in these transactions, that the stockholders acquired complete and unfettered ownership of the properties, and that the trial judge's finding of two separate and independent transactions cannot be overturned on appeal.

The solution of hard tax cases requires something more than the easy generalization that the substance rather than the form of a transaction is determinative of its tax effect, since in numerous situations the form by which a transaction is effected does influence or control its tax consequences. This generalization does, however, reflect the truth that courts will, on occasion, look beyond the superficial formalities of a transaction to determine the proper tax treatment.

In the landmark case of Gregory v. Helvering, 1935, 293 U.S. 465, 55 S. Ct. 266, 79 L. Ed. 596, the Supreme Court refused to give effect to corporate transactions which complied precisely with the formal requirements for nontaxable corporate reorganizations, on the ground that the transactions had served no function other than that of a contrivance to bail out corporate earnings to the sole shareholder at capital gains tax rates. In Commissioner v. Court Holding Co., 1945, 324 U.S. 331, 65 S. Ct. 707, 89 L. Ed. 981, the Supreme Court taxed a corporation on the gain from the sale of an apartment house notwithstanding a transfer of the house to the corporation's two shareholders before the sale, since it found that the transfer was made solely to set in a more favorable tax form a sale which in reality was made by the corporation. Similarly, in Helvering v. Clifford, 1940, 309 U.S. 331, 60 S. Ct. 554, 84 L. Ed. 788, the Supreme Court taxed a trust grantor on the income of the trust property since the formal transfer of the property by the grantor was lacking in substance. The Court found that the dilution in his control seemed insignificant and immaterial and that "since the husband retains control over the investment, he has rather complete assurance that the trust will not effect any substantial change in his economic position." 309 U.S. at pages 335-336, 60 S. Ct. at page 557. . . . Each case must be decided on its own merits by examining the form and substance of the transactions and the purpose of the relevant tax provisions to determine whether recognition of the form of the transaction would defeat the statutory purpose.

The case at bar presents an unusual tax question created by the conjunction of two parts of the tax code not frequently brought together by a single transaction: the provisions governing basis and capital gains, and the rule that no gain is recognized by a corporation when it distributes property with respect to its stock. The basis of property is determined by its cost; when the property is sold the owner realizes a taxable gain equal to the difference between the basis and the proceeds received in the sale. There is no danger that a taxpayer could effect an artificial sale and repurchase to raise the basis of appreciated property, since such a transaction would subject him to a tax on the step-up in the basis. There are, therefore, no provisions to prevent tax avoidance by such a device, and the question whether a transfer and reacquisition should be recognized as independent transactions creating tax consequences would generally affect only the *timing* of the imposition of a tax rather than its *amount*. The twist here comes from the fact that the corporation did not incur a tax on the difference between basis and current market value when it transferred the assets to its shareholders in redemption of their stock. Section 311(a) of the Code, 26 U.S.C.A. §311(a), provides that "no gain or loss shall be recognized to a corporation on the distribution, with respect to its stock, of . . . property." This provision is expressly made applicable to stock redemption distributions by the Treasury Regulations.[2] The rule may be easily justified by the fact that when a corporation transfers appreciated property to its shareholders, as a dividend or in exchange for their shares, the gain created by the appreciation has not accrued to the corporation and should not be taxed to it.[3]

A new horizon of tax avoidance opportunities would be opened by allowing

---

[2]Treas. Reg. 1.311-1(a) (1955).

[3]If the corporation in effect does realize the gain by handling the sale of the property after its distribution to the shareholders, the gain probably would be attributed to the corporation. See United States v. Lynch, 9 Cir., 1951, 192 F.2d 718, certiorari denied 1952, 343 U.S. 934, 72 S. Ct. 770, 96 L. Ed. 1342; Commissioner v. Transport Trading & Terminal Corp., 2 Cir., 1949, 176 F.2d 570, certiorari denied 1950, 338 U.S. 955, 70 S. Ct. 493, 94 L. Ed. 589. These cases were decided before enactment of Section 311, but since that section is largely a codification of the rule laid down by General Utilities & Operating Co. v. Helvering, 1935, 296 U.S. 200, 56 S. Ct. 185, 80 L. Ed. 154, which did precede these cases their validity is probably not undercut by the statute. Mintz and Plumb, Dividends in Kind — The Thunderbolts and the New Look, 10 Tax L. Rev. 41, 45-48 (1954). See generally Raum, Dividends in Kind: Their Tax Aspects, 63 Harv. L. Rev. 593 (1950).

The tax treatment of the corporation making a stock redemption is of course not to be confused with the taxation of the shareholders, a field bursting with difficult problems. . . .

a stepped-up basis to result from the transaction here effected. Corporations would be enabled without difficulty to raise the basis of their assets whenever it fell below the market value by transferring the assets to shareholders by a dividend or stock redemption and then buying back the same assets for the cash that they otherwise would have distributed directly. Since market values are often pushed up by inflation and the basis is frequently reduced under the liberal depreciation rules far faster than the assets actually depreciate, this possibility would have enormous practical significance. These tax avoidance implications do not constitute a license to courts to distort the laws or to write in new provisions; they do mean that we should guard against giving force to a purported transfer which gives off an unmistakably hollow sound when it is tapped. It is a hollow sound for tax purposes; here, we are not concerned with business purposes or the legal effectiveness of the transaction under the law of Texas. Under the tax law, it is of course open to a corporation making a dividend distribution or a stock redemption to distribute appreciated assets rather than cash and to use its cash to purchase similar assets for replacement at a stepped-up basis. Such transactions are however limited by their costs. Moreover, in such a case it would be clear that the corporation had disposed of its former assets and acquired new ones. When, however, a corporation contends that it stepped up the basis by transferring assets to its shareholders and then reacquiring them, we must scrutinize the transactions to make sure that the alleged divestiture did occur. The transactions should be recognized as creating an interruption in the ownership of the assets sufficient to produce a new basis *only* when the corporation has made a clear and distinct severance of its ownership prior to the reacquisition.

The facts of these transactions will not support a holding that the corporation had terminated its ownership for these purposes. It parted with bare legal title to the property for a few short hours. It made no physical delivery of any of the assets. Its control and use of the property were never interrupted. Even the surrender of its legal title was made under circumstances creating a strong expectation that it would be returned shortly. True, the stockholders may have had complete legal freedom to refuse to resell the assets to the corporation, but there was almost no likelihood that they would do so. It was a foregone conclusion that they would resell the assets to someone, since the very reason for the original redemption was that the stockholders did not wish to continue ownership of the assets and management of the business. And since the assets were already integrated into the operations of the taxpayer and represented 47% of its assets,[4] the taxpayer was the logical, and as a practical matter, the only possible purchaser. That the stockholders had already drawn up papers for the resale, in case they decided to make one, undoubtedly strengthened the confidence with which the taxpayer could look forward to the reacquisition of the properties. There was never the whisper of a suggestion that the company was to cut down on its operation, as would be inevitable if it permanently parted with 47% of its assets, including three rigs. The most that can

---

[4]The assets transferred were valued by the parties at $746,525. At the rate of $245 per share, that total would represent 3047 shares, or slightly over 47% of the 6461 shares then outstanding.

be said is that the taxpayer gave to the bank and Mrs. Johnson the power to divest it of its ownership of certain properties; they held that power for a few hours and then returned it. The transactions, from the corporation's standpoint, were more like an option than a sale, and the option expired quickly without having been exercised.

The taxpayer asserts that the transactions were prompted by a valid business purpose and were effected without a motive of tax avoidance. We accept these assertions, which are supported by the trial judge's findings, as true. They lend support to the taxpayer's case, but they do not control the disposition of the case. Intent often is relevant in questions of taxation, particularly where the bona fides of a transaction is called into question, but in most cases tax treatment depends on what was done, not why it was done. And our decision in this case rests not on the motivation of the transactions in question but rather on our conclusion that the admitted facts of the two transfers preclude a finding of a sufficient hiatus in the corporate ownership of the assets to justify bestowal of a new basis on them after the reacquisition.[5]

To determine the basis of the assets we look backward to ascertain when the corporation acquired them. We note the transactions here in question, but we can scarcely say that the corporation's ownership dates from that occasion. These transactions, whatever their effect on other legal questions, did not create an interruption in the ownership sufficient to produce a new basis. The basis must be found from the original purchase price and the adjustments made to it. The district court's findings may be correct; his conclusions are in error.

The judgment is
Reversed.

On Petition for Rehearing

PER CURIAM. The petition for rehearing in this case expresses strongly the petitioner's conviction that this Court failed to recognize the bona fides of the transaction. In denying this petition we wish, again, to make clear that we did not base the decision on a lack of good faith in the parties to the transaction. It is true that we said, "we should guard against giving force to a purported transfer which gives off an unmistakably hollow sound when it is tapped." But this statement was set off (in the same sentence) against the other extreme: "These tax avoidance implications do not constitute a license to courts to distort the laws or to write in new provisions." Throughout the opinion we were careful to say that our decision was not based on any lack of good faith in the parties to the transaction, and that we did not pass on the legal effect of the transaction outside of the tax frame of reference. We do not question the integrity of the parties or suggest that there was any flim-flam. We do not doubt the business purposes of the transaction. The decision does not purport to question the effectiveness of the transaction in protecting the stockholders against the holding in Robinson v. Wangeman, 5 Cir., 1935,

---

[5]If these transactions could not have been explained by valid nontax reasons, they obviously would have been only a subterfuge which could not have been effective to change the basis of the assets. . . .

75 F.2d 756. But we hold and reaffirm that *for tax purposes* there was not a sufficient severance of the corporation's ownership over the assets for the transaction to create the tax consequence that when the corporation reacquired the assets it took them with a stepped-up basis. The transaction is analogous to a *Clifford* trust, valid under state law but ineffective *for tax purposes* to remove the trust income from the settlor's taxable income. Helvering v. Clifford, 1940, 309 U.S. 331, 60 S. Ct. 554, 84 L. Ed. 788. It is ordered that the petition for rehearing filed in the above styled and numbered cause be, and the same is hereby

Denied.

NOTE

The court said (page 58 supra) that its "decision depends on whether or not the transactions in question created an interruption in the ownership of the property. . . ." What is the source of the court's premise? Is it a fair premise for determining "cost" under §1012? The court also said (page 59 supra) that the "twist [in this case] comes from the fact that the corporation did not incur a tax on the difference between basis and current market value when it transferred the assets to its shareholders in redemption of their stock. Section 311(a) . . . ."

Consider this case: Corporation M would like to step up the $500,000 basis of its manufacturing plant (building, not land) to its one million dollar value in order to increase its depreciation deductions. It would also like to increase its cash position. It therefore sells its plant to a bank for one million dollars in cash and immediately thereafter buys it back, paying for it with its ten-year, 8 per cent note, secured by a first mortgage on the plant and the land under it. As taxpayer's counsel, what would you argue to the Fifth Circuit as your principal basis for distinguishing *General Geophysical*? What additional facts would you like to find in the record to buttress your position? What would you expect that court to decide was Corporation M's basis? Why?

KIMBELL-DIAMOND MILLING CO. v. COMMISSIONER
14 T.C. 74 (1950), aff'd per curiam, 187 F.2d 718 (5th Cir. 1950), cert. denied, 342 U.S. 827 (1951)

BLACK, Judge: This proceeding involves deficiencies in income, declared value excess profits, and excess profits taxes for the fiscal years ended May 31, 1945 and 1946 . . . . The deficiencies are primarily due to respondent's reduction of petitioner's basis in assets acquired by it in December, 1942, through the liquidation of another corporation known as Whaley Mill & Elevator Co. (sometimes hereinafter referred to as Whaley). By reason of this reduction respondent has adjusted petitioner's allowable depreciation and its excess profits tax credit based on equity invested capital. By appropriate assignments of error petitioner contests these adjustments. Other adjustments which respondent made have been conceded.

This leaves for our consideration the determination of petitioner's basis in the assets acquired from Whaley.

The facts have been stipulated and are adopted as our findings of fact. They may be summarized as follows:

Petitioner is a Texas corporation, engaged primarily in the business of milling, processing, and selling grain products, and has its principal office in Fort Worth, Texas. Petitioner maintained its books and records and filed its corporation tax returns on an accrual basis for fiscal years ended May 31 of each year. For the years ended May 31, 1945 and 1946, its returns were filed with the collector of internal revenue for the second collection district of Texas.

On or about August 13, 1942, petitioner sustained a fire casualty at its Wolfe City, Texas, plant which resulted in the destruction of its mill property at that location. The assets so destroyed . . . [had an aggregate adjusted basis of $18,921.90]. . . . This property was covered by insurance, and on or about November 14, 1942, petitioner collected insurance in the amount of $124,551.10 ($118,200.16 as a reimbursement for the loss sustained by the fire and $6,350.94 as a premium refund). On December 26, 1942, petitioner's directors approved the transaction set forth in the minutes below:

"THAT, WHEREAS, on or about August 1, 1942, the flour mill and milling plant of Kimbell-Diamond Milling Company located at Wolfe City, Texas was destroyed by fire; and

"WHEREAS, Kimbell-Diamond Milling Company collected from the insurance companies carrying the insurance on the said destroyed properties the sum of $125,000.00 as indemnification for the loss sustained, which said insurance proceeds were by the proper officers of this corporation promptly deposited in a special account in the Fort Worth National Bank of Fort Worth, Texas, where they have since been kept intact in order to have the same available for replacing, as nearly as might be, the destroyed properties; and

"WHEREAS, it has at all times been the intention and desire of Kimbell-Diamond Milling Company to replace its burned mill either by constructing a new mill or by purchasing facilities of substantially similar kind and use; and

"WHEREAS, due to existing building restrictions and other causes, it has been found impractical and impossible to replace the destroyed facilities by new construction, but it has come to the attention of the officers of this corporation that the stock of Whaley Mill & Elevator Company, a Texas corporation, which, among its other assets, owns physical properties substantially comparable to the destroyed Wolfe City Milling plant, can be purchased;

"NOW, THEREFORE, BE IT RESOLVED:

"1. That the proper officers of Kimbell-Diamond Milling Company be, and they are hereby, authorized, empowered and directed to purchase the entire authorized, issued and outstanding capital stock of Whaley Mill

& Elevator Company, a Texas corporation, consisting of 4,000 shares of the face or par value of $100.00 per share, for a sum not in excess of $210,000.00; that payment for the said stock of Whaley Mill & Elevator Company be made, to the extent possible, from the insurance proceeds deposited in a special account in the Fort Worth National Bank, and that the balance of the agreed consideration for the stock of Whaley Mill & Elevator Company be paid out of the general funds of Kimbell-Diamond Milling Company.

"2. That as soon as practicable after the purchase of the Whaley Mill & Elevator Company stock hereby authorized has been consummated, all necessary steps be taken to completely liquidate the said corporation by transferring its entire assets, particularly its mill and milling equipment, to Kimbell-Diamond Milling Company in cancellation and redemption of the entire issued and outstanding capital stock of Whaley Mill & Elevator Company, and that the charter of said corporation be forthwith surrendered and cancelled."

On December 26, 1942, petitioner acquired 100 per cent of the stock of Whaley Mill & Elevator Co. of Gainesville, Texas, paying therefor $210,000 in cash which payment, to the extent of $118,200.16, was made with the insurance proceeds received by petitioner as a result of the fire on or about August 13, 1942.

On December 29, 1942, the stockholders of Whaley assented to the dissolution and distribution of assets thereof. On the same date an "Agreement and Program of Complete Liquidation" was entered into between petitioner and Whaley, which provided, inter alia:

"THAT, WHEREAS, KIMBELL-DIAMOND owns the entire authorized issued and outstanding capital stock of WHALEY, consisting of 4000 shares of a par value of $100.00 per share, which said stock was acquired by KIMBELL-DIAMOND primarily for the purpose of enabling it to secure possession and ownership of the flour mill and milling plant owned by WHALEY, the parties herewith agree that the said mill and milling plant shall forthwith be conveyed to KIMBELL-DIAMOND by WHALEY under the following program for the complete liquidation of WHALEY viz.:

"(1) KIMBELL-DIAMOND shall cause the 4000 shares of the capital stock of WHALEY owned by it to be surrendered to WHALEY for cancellation and retirement, whereupon WHALEY shall forthwith convey, transfer and assign unto KIMBELL-DIAMOND all property of every kind and character owned or claimed by it, particularly its flour mill and milling plant, located at Gainesville, Texas, and all machinery and equipment appurtenant thereto, or used in connection therewith, in full and complete liquidation of all of the outstanding stock of WHALEY. The aforesaid distribution in complete liquidation shall be fully consummated by not later than midnight, December 31, 1942.

"(2) When the entire assets of every kind and character, owned by WHALEY, have been transferred to KIMBELL-DIAMOND in full and complete liquidation of the capital stock of WHALEY, owned by KIMBELL-DIAMOND,

WHALEY shall forthwith make application to the Secretary of State of the State of Texas for its dissolution as a corporation and surrender its corporate charter."

On December 31, 1942, the Secretary of State of the State of Texas certified that the Whaley Mill & Elevator Co. was dissolved as of that date. . . .

There is no dispute that the petitioner's adjusted basis in its depreciable assets which were destroyed by fire was $18,921.90; nor that the depreciable assets which it received from Whaley had an adjusted basis in the hands of Whaley of $139,521.62. Petitioner, in the years herein involved, proceeded under the theory that it was entitled to Whaley's basis. Respondent takes the position that petitioner's cost is its basis in the assets acquired from Whaley. . . . The petitioner does not controvert the allocation of cost made by respondent to the various assets acquired from Whaley, both depreciable and nondepreciable property. As to the depreciable assets purchased to replace those involuntarily converted, respondent contends that petitioner's basis is limited by [§1033(c)] of the Internal Revenue Code. . . .

. . . Petitioner argues that the acquisition of Whaley's assets and the subsequent liquidation of Whaley brings petitioner within the provisions of [§332] and, therefore, by reason of [§334(b)(1)*] petitioner's basis in these assets is the same as the basis in Whaley's hands. In so contending, petitioner asks that we treat the acquisition of Whaley's stock and the subsequent liquidation of Whaley as separate transactions. It is well settled that the incidence of taxation depends upon the substance of a transaction. Commissioner v. Court Holding Co., 324 U.S. 331. It is inescapable from petitioner's minutes set out above and from the "Agreement and Program of Complete Liquidation" entered into between petitioner and Whaley, that the only intention petitioner ever had was to acquire Whaley's assets.

We think that this proceeding is governed by the principles of Commissioner v. Ashland Oil & Refining Co., 99 Fed. (2d) 588, certiorari denied, 306 U.S. 661. In that case the stock was retained for almost a year before liquidation. Ruling on the question of whether the stock or the assets of the corporation were purchased, the court stated:

> "The question remains, however, whether if the entire transaction, whatever its form, was essentially in intent, purpose and result, a purchase by Swiss of property, its several steps may be treated separately and each be given an effect for tax purposes as though each constituted a distinct transaction. . . . And without regard to whether the result is imposition or relief from taxation, the courts have recognized that where the essential nature of a transaction is the acquisition of property, it will be viewed as a whole, and closely related steps will not be separated either at the instance of the taxpayer or the taxing authority. Prairie Oil & Gas Co. v. Motter, 10 Cir., 66 F.2d 309; Tulsa Tribune Co. v. Commissioner, 10 Cir., 58 F.2d 937, 940; Ahles Realty Corp. v. Commissioner, 2 Cir., 71 F.2d 150; Helvering v. Security Savings Bank, 4 Cir., 72 F.2d 874. . . ."

See also Koppers Coal Co., 6 T.C. 1209 and cases there cited.

*There was no counterpart to §334(b)(2) in the 1939 Code. — Ed.

We hold that the purchase of Whaley's stock and its subsequent liquidation must be considered as one transaction, namely, the purchase of Whaley's assets which was petitioner's sole intention. This was not a reorganization within [§332], and petitioner's basis in these assets, both depreciable and nondepreciable, is, therefore, its cost, or $110,721.74 ($18,921.90, the basis of petitioner's assets destroyed by fire plus $91,799.84, the amount expended over the insurance proceeds). Since petitioner does not controvert respondent's allocation of cost to the individual assets acquired from Whaley, both depreciable and nondepreciable, respondent's allocation is sustained. . . .

Decision will be entered for the respondent.

. . . Reviewed by the Court.

NOTE

1. Ordinarily, when a parent corporation liquidates a subsidiary, the parent has no recognized gain or loss (§322; Chapter 4 infra), and the parent takes the subsidiary's assets at their basis in the subsidiary's hands (§334(b)(1)). This basis rule differs from the more usual one, which prescribes that a transferor in a tax-free transaction preserve the basis of the assets surrendered. Compare, e.g., §§1031(d) and 1033(c). Application of the more usual rule in *Kimbell-Diamond* would have meant that the subsidiary's assets would take a new basis equal to the basis of the stock the taxpayer owned in Whaley. That basis was substantially less than the basis available by operation of §334(b)(1). The Commissioner contended successfully, however, that the taxpayer should be deemed to have bought the assets of Whaley, and not its stock, and thus the taxpayer's basis for the assets was its cost and not the basis of the assets in Whaley's hands. Although this was a victory for the Commissioner, many taxpayers used the "doctrine" of *Kimbell-Diamond* to step up the basis of a newly acquired subsidiary's assets to the stock cost (where the latter was higher), doing so by carefully building a record to show that assets — not stock — had really been desired and by liquidating the subsidiary into the parent corporation promptly after its purchase of the subsidiary's stock.

2. *Kimbell-Diamond* led to great uncertainty. It was impossible to be sure when a taxpayer would succeed in bringing its apparent purchase of stock within the doctrine. Where a taxpayer wished to avoid application of the doctrine, however, it could readily do so by delaying the liquidation until a considerable period after the purchase of its stock had elapsed. To bring certainty to this area, Congress in 1954 added subsection (b)(2) to §334. The net effect of the enactment of §§336, 337 and 334(b)(2) is to permit all the assets of a corporation (or all of its stock) to be sold to a buying corporation with no tax on asset appreciation at the corporate level, despite the fact that the buying corporation may use its cost as the new basis of the assets. Is this desirable legislative policy? Why?

3(a) What are the practical circumstances that might lead the shareholders of a corporation to insist on selling their stock rather than to have their corporation sell assets (with or without the umbrella of §337)? Consider particularly (but not exclusively) the position of the shareholders if they are to receive their purchase price over an extended period and would like to pay their capital gains tax on the installment method under §453. A shareholder receiving a liquidating distribution from a corporation must ordinarily recognize his gain (or loss). Section 331(a); Chapter 2, pages 154-248 infra. A shareholder who sells his stock must ordinarily recognize his gain (or loss). Section 1001(a).

(b) What are the practical circumstances that might lead a buying corporation to prefer (1) to purchase assets or (2) to purchase stock?

4(a) M Corporation acquires 100 per cent of the outstanding stock of X Corporation from X's shareholders, in exchange for which M Corporation issues shares of its own voting stock. (That transaction is "reorganization" under §368(a)(1)(B) and, as a result, the basis of the X Corporation stock in the hands of M Corporation is the same as that basis was in the hands of X Corporation's former shareholders.*) Within a few days after M Corporation acquires the X Corporation stock, the latter is completely liquidated. How must M Corporation determine the basis of the assets it received from X Corporation? Why?

(b) N Corporation purchases for cash 100 per cent of the stock of A Corporation, whose only asset is 100 per cent of the stock of B Corporation. Section 334(b)(3) was amended in 1966 to facilitate arrangements whereby N Corporation might acquire direct ownership of B Corporation's assets with their basis determined under §334(b)(2). In the absence of the amendment (the last sentence of subsection (3)), what advice would you have given N Corporation to accomplish its objectives? Why?

(c) X Corporation wants to buy the assets of the A Corporation, which operates a radio station. Since government regulations would result in a substantial delay, X Corporation buys 100 per cent of the stock of A Corporation, intending to liquidate A Corporation as soon as governmental authorities permit. Final authority is not granted until two years and one week after the stock purchase was effected. Within 48 hours thereafter, A Corporation is liquidated. May X Corporation determine the basis of the assets it has acquired from A Corporation by reference to the price it paid for the A Corporation stock? Why?

5. See M. Lewis, Cost-of-Stock Basis for Assets Received from Acquired Corporation, 19 U. Miami L. Rev. 159 (1964); H. Mansfield, The *Kimbell-Diamond* Situation: Basis to the Purchaser in Connection with Liquidation, 13 N.Y.U. Inst. on Fed. Tax. 623 (1955).

AMERICAN POTASH & CHEMICAL CORP. v. UNITED STATES
399 F.2d 194 (Ct. Cl. 1968)

On Defendant's Motion for Summary Judgment

Before Cowen, Chief Judge, and Laramore, Durfee, Davis, Collins, Skelton,* and Nichols, Judges.

*Section 362(b).

LARAMORE, Judge. This is a corporate income tax refund case. The Commissioner of Internal Revenue reduced the amount of a depreciation deduction taken by plaintiff, American Potash & Chemical Corporation (hereinafter referred to as Potash) in each of the four fiscal years which followed July 1, 1956. The only issue before the court is the determination of the basis of depreciable assets upon which the deduction is based. Taxpayer argues that a cost basis is appropriate, and defendant contends that a carryover basis is required. Defendant has moved for summary judgment.

The facts are not in dispute. Taxpayer is engaged in the production and sale of industrial and agricultural chemicals. Between September 1954 and November 1955, Potash acquired all of the outstanding stock of Western Electrochemical Company (hereinafter referred to as Wecco) in exchange for 66,662 shares of its voting stock and $466.12 in cash paid for fractional shares.[1]

Between September 28, 1954 and November 3, 1954, Potash acquired 48 percent of the Wecco stock in exchange for 33,367 shares of Potash plus $466.12 in cash. On November 30, 1955 Potash acquired the remaining 52 percent of Wecco stock in exchange for 33,295 shares of Potash.

Potash made two separate offers to purchase all of the Wecco stock. In August, 1954 it offered each Wecco stockholder one share of Potash (selling at approximately $60 per share) for 6.5 shares of Wecco. For shares not evenly divisible by 6.5 it offered $9.23 per Wecco share (on the basis of $60 per Potash share). That offer expired on November 18, 1954, and some 52 percent of Wecco shareholders did not accept it.

In November, 1955 Potash again approached the Wecco shareholders with a new offer of one Potash share (now selling at $90 per share) for seven shares of Wecco. There were no fractional shares involved. The remaining 52 percent shareholders accepted this offer, and Potash acquired complete ownership.

Plaintiff admits that both of these stock acquisitions were to further its ultimate purpose — obtaining the Wecco assets — and that if it could not have obtained the remaining 52 percent ownership it would have sold the 48 percent interest acquired in 1954.

Potash did not acquire either 80 percent of the total combined voting power of all voting stock or 80 percent of the total number of shares of all other classes of stock during any 12-month period between September 1954 and November 1955.

For seven months, from December 1, 1955 to June 30, 1956, Wecco was operated by Potash. During that period taxpayer advanced $646,293 to Wecco for working capital and other miscellaneous current operating needs. On June 30, 1956, Wecco

---

[1]The purchases involved were as follows:

Date acquired	Shares acquired	Consideration paid	
		Potash stock	Cash
9/20/54	191,074	29,392	$239.98
9/28/54	450	69	13.84
10/28/54	24,625	3,785	207.69
11/3/54	787	121	4.61
11/30/55	233,064	33,295	......
Total	450,000	66,662	$466.12

was completely liquidated and all of its assets were distributed to (and its liabilities were assumed by) Potash. The fair market value of the assets distributed to Potash was $10,843,023. The liabilities assumed were $4,934,448 which, together with the $646,293 advanced, totaled $5,580,741 in liabilities.

For 1957, 1958, and 1959 and 1960 fiscal tax years Potash computed its depreciation deduction for the depreciable assets received from Wecco on an adjusted basis of $7,085,551. This was its "cost" of the depreciable assets. That "cost" included the value of the 66,662 shares transferred in acquiring Wecco stock, the liabilities assumed on the liquidation and the cash advanced during the seven months that it operated Wecco. Immediately prior to the liquidation Wecco's basis in these assets was $3,788, 779.

On audit of Potash's 1956 and 1957 tax returns the Internal Revenue Service determined that the correct basis of these assets was $3,788,779, the basis in the hands of Wecco prior to the liquidation. Taxpayer's adjusted basis was reduced by $3,296,772 and, accordingly, its yearly depreciation deduction was reduced by $100,843 per year. Taxpayer paid the 1957 deficiency on May 19, 1961. It adjusted its 1958, 1959 and 1960 tax returns, and the increased tax was included in the taxes paid for those years. . . .

For the purpose of this motion, both plaintiff and defendant agree that the stock acquisition of Wecco and its liquidation were undertaken for the purpose of obtaining the Wecco assets, i.e., plaintiff purchased the stock to reach the assets.

I.

The government, in support of its motion for summary judgment, argues that, as a matter of law, a carryover basis is required because either the entire transaction was a reorganization under section 368(a)(1)(C) of the Internal Revenue Code of 1954, 68A Stat. 120, or alternatively, if the stock acquisition can be separated from the liquidation, the assets received in the liquidation are subject to a carryover basis under section 332 and 334 as assets received by a parent (Potash) in the process of liquidating its wholly-owned subsidiary (Wecco). Plaintiff argues that the transaction cannot be termed a reorganization and that the liquidation transaction, separately considered, is excepted from the application of sections 332 and 334 by the doctrine enunciated in Kimbell-Diamond Milling Co. v. Commissioner, 14 T.C. 74 (1950), affirmed per curiam, 187 F.2d 718 (5th Cir. 1951), cert. denied, 342 U.S. 827, which remains viable and was not pre-empted by the enactment of section 334(b)(2), the legislative exception to the general rule of section 334(b)(1).

We will consider each of defendant's alternative arguments separately. We find that the facts do not establish that this transaction was a reorganization, and that the *Kimbell-Diamond* doctrine has not been preempted by the enactment of section 334(b)(2). . . .

[The portion of the opinion dealing with the government's contentions that the transaction was a §368(a)(1)(C) reorganization which produced a carryover basis under §362(b) is omitted here, but is reproduced at page 550 infra.]

III.

Defendant argues, alternatively, that plaintiff cannot employ a section 1012 cost basis for the depreciable assets even if the transaction is not a reorganization because Potash, on June 30, 1956, adopted a plan of complete liquidation for its subsidiary Wecco. Under these circumstances the assets of Wecco were received by Potash as a distribution in complete liquidation of its wholly-owned subsidiary and, therefore, under sections 332(a) and 334 a carryover basis is required.

The basis of assets received in a complete liquidation is determined by section 334(b)(1). The general rule provides that when a parent corporation liquidates its subsidiary in the process of a non-taxable liquidation, the basis of the property acquired by the parent is the same as the basis in the hands of the subsidiary. This is the carryover basis that defendant argues is applicable.

The exception to this general rule is section 334(b)(2), enacted in 1954, which provides that the basis for the assets received in liquidation shall be the same as the basis of the stock of the subsidiary which is held by the parent. The parent corporation's basis for the subsidiary's stock is generally its cost of the stock, and that amount becomes the basis of the assets. The basis of the assets in the hands of the subsidiary is not carried over to the parent.

On its fact it would seem that section 334(b)(1) is applicable and that the transaction does not meet the specific requirements of section 334(b)(2) because Potash did not acquire the requisite amount of stock within a 12-month period. Taxpayer argues, however, that a parent-subsidiary relationship was never created, and that section 334 is inapplicable because throughout the entire 14-month period of acquisition its only purpose and intent was to acquire the assets of Wecco. It argues that the basic doctrine of *Kimbell-Diamond Milling Co.,* supra, is applicable, and that it has not been pre-empted by the enactment of section 334(b)(2).

We will decide only the question whether the *Kimbell-Diamond* doctrine has been pre-empted by section 334(b)(2). We find that it has not and, therefore, return this case to a trial commissioner for further proceedings to determine if it is applicable to the particular facts of this case.

In pre-1954 Code years the statute required a carryover basis for assets received in complete liquidation of a company. This created a difference between the basis for assets which were purchased directly (where a cost basis would be applicable) and assets received in liquidation of a company whose stock was acquired only for the purpose of permitting the acquiring company to liquidate and reach assets which were otherwise unobtainable (a carryover basis was required).

To equate the direct purchase of assets with the indirect acquisition of assets by a purchase of stock, the *Kimbell-Diamond* doctrine was promulgated as an exception to the general rule that a carryover basis is required when a corporation is completely liquidated.

In the *Kimbell-Diamond* case, the government argued that if stock is purchased and the subsidiary thereby acquired is liquidated as part of one unified plan to obtain assets, a purchase of assets (and not stock) has "in reality" taken place and the interim step — liquidation — will not be given tax significance. The taxpayer had purchased stock of another company for cash. Several days later the acquired subsidiary was liquidated and its assets distributed to the parent. The court found that the transaction was *not a reorganization* and concluded that: ". . . [T]he purchase of . . . [the acquired company's] stock and its subsequent liquidation must be considered as one transaction, namely, the purchase of . . . assets which was petitioner's sole intention. [14 T.C. at 80.]"

The step-transaction doctrine developed as part of the broader tax concept that substance should prevail over form. Its application, originally, was as a judicial exception to a statutory general rule that a carryover basis was required for assets received in liquidation. . . .

Neither party disputes the inapplicability of section 334(b)(2). Defendant argues that it is reasonable to conclude that Congress enacted the precise requirements of section 334(b)(2) in an attempt to eliminate further resort to the judicial doctrine of *Kimbell-Diamond* with its attendant problems of determining a taxpayer's subjective intent when it acquired the stock of the corporation which it later liquidated. Defendant argues that the exclusive mechanism for obtaining an exception from the carryover rules of section 334(b)(1) is qualification under section 334(b)(2). Plaintiff argues that the basic doctrine of *Kimbell-Diamond* remains viable and is applicable. The question before us is whether Congress intended to pre-empt the subsequent use of the step-transaction doctrine by enacting section 334(b)(2). We find that it did not intend to eliminate the *Kimbell-Diamond* doctrine.

There is no instance in the legislative history where Congress states either that section 334(b)(2) is the exclusive exception to the carryover rule, or that the *Kimbell-Diamond* rule is superseded or, on the other hand, that it is viable.

Obviously Congress intended to inject some degree of certainty into an area of the tax law previously occupied by problems of proving that a taxpayer had the requisite intent. It is not a necessary conclusion therefrom that Congress intended, by establishing an objective route for obtaining a cost basis without the need for proving an intent to acquire assets, to prohibit both the government and taxpayers from further resort to proof of a subjective intent to obtain the assets (without complying with the precise objective tests of section 334(b)(2)).

This issue has never before been litigated, and the tax commentary authorities are divided over it.[14] Our examination of the relevant (albeit limited) legislative history reinforces our conclusion that *Kimbell-Diamond* is not "dead." The House Report on the 1954 Code, H. Rep. No. 1337, 83rd Cong., 2d Sess. 38 (1954) reads: ". . . under the bill a shareholder will in general be permitted to receive the purchase

[14]See: Cohen, Gelberg, Surrey, Tarleau & Warren, Corporate Liquidations Under the Internal Revenue Code of 1954, 55 Colum. L. Rev. 37 (1955); Goldman, The C Reorganization, 19 Tax L. Rev. 31 (1963); Freling, What is New in Subchapter C: The Service's Current Ruling Policy, 23 N.Y.U. Institute on Federal Taxation 421 (1965); Bittker and Eustice, Federal Income Taxation of Corporations and Shareholders (2d Ed.) 524; Mansfield, The Kimbell-Diamond Situation: Basis to the Purchaser in Connection with Liquidation, 13 N.Y.U. Institute on Federal Taxation 623 (1955); Rabkin and Johnson, Federal Income, Gift and Estate Taxation (1966) §23.11(4); 3 Mertens, Law of Federal Income Taxation (Rev.) §20.161; Schwartz, Acquisition of Stock of Another Corporation in Order to Acquire Assets, 1957 So. Cal. Tax Institute 45, 65-66; Brookes, Corporate Liquidations, 1960 So. Cal. Tax Institute 233.

price for his stock as his basis for the assets distributed to him in liquidation irrespective of the assets' cost to the corporation. In this respect *the principle of Kimbell-Diamond Milling Co.,* [187 F.2d 718] is effectuated. [Emphasis supplied.]"

The Senate Report, however [S. Rep. No. 1622, 83d Cong., 2d Sess. (1954)], modified the original House proposal and limited the scope of the section to corporate situations where a corporation purchases the stock of another corporation and within two years after the purchase adopts a plan of liquidation. The House proposal would have made the cost-of-stock basis rule applicable to all taxpayers, both individuals and corporations.

The Senate concluded that its substitute provision "effectuates principles *derived* from *Kimbell-Diamond Milling Co.,* supra." S. Rep., supra, pp. 38, A109. The principle of section 334(b)(2) is *derived* from the broader, more general rule of *Kimbell-Diamond*. It is a precise, narrow and objective application of the broader doctrine.

There is no indication that a taxpayer is, by virtue of the precise rule of section 334(b)(2) to be afforded an opportunity to choose between a carryover and a cost basis. The House Report would seem to indicate that a cost basis should be applicable in all situations where a stock purchase is followed by a liquidation, and both are part of one plan. If the statute is the only route for avoiding a carryover basis, a taxpayer can, with relative ease, choose either to comply with the statute or not to comply. There is no indication that the basis of assets acquired in these transactions is an elective matter. Compliance with the statute would result in a cost basis; non-compliance would yield a carryover basis. It would seem preferable, from the government's point of view, to retain the basic step-transaction approach to achieve substance over form in a situation where a taxpayer, possessed of the requisite subjective intent, deliberately avoids the statute.

The *Kimbell-Diamond* doctrine, without question, remains viable for *individual* taxpayers because section 334(b)(2) is applicable only to corporate taxpayers. We cannot conclude that Congress intended to differentiate between corporate and individual taxpayers and permit the use of the judicial *Kimbell-Diamond* doctrine by an individual who has acquired stock during a period in excess of 12 months, and to deny its application to a corporate taxpayer under the same circumstances. There is nothing in the legislative history to indicate that this anomaly was intended. In the absence of some specific direction that *Kimbell-Diamond* is no longer viable, we find that it has not been pre-empted by section 334(b)(2).

Moreover, where Congress intends to modify or to change an existing judicial rule, it generally makes some statements of its purpose for enacting a particular statute. . . .

In discussing section 337, the Senate Report noted, at p. 258: ". . . the problems raised by the decision in Commissioner v. Court Holding Company, 324 U.S. 331 and United States v. Cumberland Public Service Co., 338 U.S. 451 . . . . Your committee intends in section 337 to provide a definitive rule which will eliminate present uncertainties."

In enacting section 1223, the Senate Report, at page 432, states: "This will change prospectively the rule laid down in Commissioner v. Gracey, (159 F.2d 324) . . . ."

Numerous similar examples are present throughout the Code. (See: section

1232 where the decision in Lurie v. Commissioner, 156 F.2d 436 (9th Cir. 1946) was specifically overruled (S. Rep., supra, at 433); section 1304, where the decision in Hofferbert v. Marshall, 200 F.2d 648 (4th Cir. 1952) was overruled (S. Rep., supra, at 447)). A comparable statement in the legislative history of section 334(b)(2) is conspicuously absent.

We cannot infer that Congress had any intent other than to establish a precise rule under which a taxpayer could proceed, assured that the cost basis of its stock acquired to obtain the assets would become the basis of the assets when they were received in the subsequent liquidation. We conclude that the *Kimbell-Diamond* doctrine has not been pre-empted.

There remain at issue, therefore, questions involving the presence, or absence, of the factual circumstances wherein the *Kimbell-Diamond* doctrine has been, or should be, applied. In general, it has been deemed applicable when an acquiring corporation planned from beginning to end (and had a subjective intent) to acquire assets of another corporation and, to obtain the assets, it either chose, or was required, to purchase the stock of that other corporation and liquidate. The stock purchase is an interim, transitory step in what is deemed a single unified purchase of assets. We note, but do not now decide, the possible effect of Potash operating Wecco as a subsidiary for seven months and the tax consequences, if any, of a liquidation which is preceded by an exchange of stock for stock rather than a purchase of stock. Defendant's motion for summary judgment is denied. The case is returned to the trial commissioner for further proceedings in accordance with this opinion, to make findings of fact and a recommended conclusion of law on whether the *Kimbell-Diamond* doctrine applies to the facts of this case, and if not, if it should be extended to include this transaction, and to decide the case accordingly.

NOTE

1. The acquiring corporation's cash outlay was small. The step-up in basis, without payment of corporate tax, was great. Should the law permit this result? Why? See the court's treatment of the reorganization issue at page 550 infra.

2. Is the court correct in preserving the *Kimbell-Diamond* doctrine after enactment of §334(b)(2)? Why? See Note, Tax-Free Liquidation of a Subsidiary: Resurrection of the *Kimbell-Diamond* Doctrine, 54 Cornell L. Rev. 286 (1969).

3. *Receipt of Capital*

a. EQUITY — §§118, 1032

Section 1032, added to the Code in 1954, has a broad sweep. It makes it clear that a corporation does not have income upon the receipt of payment for its own stock, whether the stock was newly issued or treasury stock.

Prior to the 1954 Code the following type of case presented a problem. Corporation **M** buys on the open market 1000 shares of its own common stock at $90 per share. The acquired shares are held as treasury stock. Subsequently, when the market in M stock goes up, Corporation M sells in the open market 2000 shares of its own stock at $125 per share. Of the shares it sells, 1000 were newly issued and 1000 were the shares it had purchased at $90 per share. The Commissioner might have contended that as to the treasury shares the corporation had a recognized gain of $35 per share. Treas. Reg. 118, §39.22(a)-15(b) (1939 Code) provided that, although a corporation had no recognized gain or loss on receipt of payment for newly issued shares, irrespective of the relationship of the amount paid to the shares' par of stated value, ". . . if a corporation deals in its own shares as it might in the shares of another corporation, the resulting gain or loss is to be computed in the same manner as though the corporation were dealing in the shares of another." Would that provision have justified the Commissioner's position as to Corporation M? Why? See Penn-Texas Corp. v. United States, 308 F.2d 575 (Ct. Cl. 1962).

Section 1032 represents a conscious effort to eliminate the pre-1954 Code distinction sometimes existing between payments received for treasury shares and payments received for newly issued shares. Does §1032 represent wise legislative policy? Why? In arriving at your answers consider the case of Corporation M. Ought it to be taxed on its treasury share transactions? Why?

Contributions to the capital of a corporation have not been treated as income to the corporation when made by shareholders. Contributions made by nonshareholders have presented more difficult problems, both as to the income question and as to the question of the basis of property contributed in kind or acquired with contributed cash. See, e.g., Detroit Edison Co. v. Commissioner, 319 U.S. 98 (1943); Brown Shoe Co. v. Commissioner, 339 U.S. 583 (1950); Edwards v. Cuba Railroad Co., 268 U.S. 628 (1925). Section 118, enacted in 1954, is a large umbrella, covering both shareholder and nonshareholder contributions, but the crucial interpretive issue that remains is whether the money or other property received by a corporation constitutes a "contribution." Consider this case: X Corporation is the tenant under a ten-year lease of property which the Y Corporation wishes to occupy. The landlord is willing to lease to Y Corporation if X Corporation agrees. Y Corporation thereupon agrees with X Corporation "to make a contribution to its capital" of $100,000 if X Corporation surrenders its lease. X Corporation does so and receives $100,000 from Y Corporation. Does X Corporation have income in the transaction? Why? See Treas. Reg. §1.118-1.

What is the basis of property (other than cash) received by a corporation in exchange for its stock where the transferor is in "control" of the corporation within the meaning of §§351 and 368(c)? (As to §351 generally, see Chapter 3 infra.) What is the basis where a "controlling" shareholder makes a contribution to capital and does not receive stock in exchange? What is the result where the contributing shareholder in each of those cases is not in "control"? What is the basis where a contribution to capital is made by a nonshareholder who receives no stock in exchange? What is the basis of property purchased by a corporation with money contributed by a nonshareholder who receives no stock in exchange? See §362 and Treas. Reg. §1.1032-1(d). See Note, Taxation of Nonshareholder Contributions to Corporate Capital, 82 Harv. L. Rev. 619 (1969).

Corporation N issues treasury stock to A as a bonus for his valuable services. The shares cost Corporation N $100 per share and are worth $200 per share when delivered to A. Does Corporation N have income? Why? As to whether it has a deduction, see Rev. Rul. 62-217, page 101 infra. As to the tax consequences to A, see Chapter 4, pages 446-460 infra. See generally B. Bittker and J. Eustice, Federal Income Taxation of Corporations and Shareholders, 105-112 (2d ed. 1966).

b. DEBT

When a corporation issues instruments of debt — e.g., notes, bonds, debentures — the money or other property it receives in exchange therefor is not income. Just as "borrowed money" is not treated as income in the case of an individual, so borrowed money is not regarded as income in the case of a corporation. Is it likely that an issue has arisen in connection with a corporation's resale of its bonds for a price higher than the price it paid to buy them on the open market? Why?

4. *Receipt of a Dividend* — §§243, 301(b)(1)(B)

Section 301(c)(1) requires that the "portion of [a corporate] distribution which is a dividend (as defined in §316) . . ." be "included in gross income." The "portion of a distribution" that is not a dividend is first applied against the basis of the shareholder's stock, and after the basis is exhausted the excess of the distribution is treated as "gain from the sale or exchange" of the stock. Section 301(c)(2) and (3); see §301(a).

Section 301(b)(1) provides that (1) in the case of a noncorporate recipient of a distribution, the "amount of any distribution" shall be the amount of cash plus the fair market value of other property received and (2) in the case of corporate recipients, the "amount of any distribution" is the amount of cash received plus the lesser of (a) the fair market value of other property received or (b) (in general) the adjusted basis of that other property in the hands of the distributing corporation.

Why is the amount of a dividend-in-kind to a corporate shareholder generally limited to its basis in the distributing corporation's hands when that basis is lower than fair market value? Before answering that question note the provisions of §243 and consider why a "dividends received" deduction is allowed. Does the coexistence of §§311 and 243 help answer the first question posed in this paragraph? Why? What problems do you think led to the enactment of §301(b)(1)(B)(ii)?

Corporation S, a Pennsylvania corporation, distributes to its parent, Corporation P, a dividend consisting of 1000 shares of General Motors common stock. The shares had an adjusted basis of $50 per share in Corporation S's hands and are worth $85 per share at the time of distribution. What are the tax consequences of the distribution to Corporation S and to Corporation P? Why? When Corporation P, one year after receipt, sells the stock for $90 per share, what will the tax conseqences be? Why? See §301(d). How would each of the tax consequences be varied if the General Motors stock had been subject to a $30 per share liability which Corporation P assumed?

5. *Reduction of Outstanding Capital*

a.   DEBT — §§108, 1017

UNITED STATES v. KIRBY LUMBER CO.
284 U.S. 1 (1931), rev'g 44 F.2d 885 (Ct. Cl. 1930)

Mr. Justice HOLMES delivered the opinion of the Court.

In July, 1923, the plaintiff, the Kirby Lumber Company, issued its own bonds for $12,126,800 for which it received their par value. Later in the same year it purchased in the open market some of the same bonds at less than par, the difference of price being $137,521.30. The question is whether this difference is a taxable gain or income of the plaintiff for the year 1923. By [§61] gross income includes "gains or profits and income derived from any source whatever," and by the Treasury Regulations . . . that have been in force through repeated reenactments, "If the corporation purchases and retires any of such bonds at a price less than the issuing price or face value, the excess of the issuing price or face value over the purchase price is gain or income for the taxable year." . . . We see no reason why the Regulations should not be accepted as a correct statement of the law.

In Bowers v. Kerbaugh-Empire Co., 271 U.S. 170, the defendant in error owned the stock of another company that had borrowed money repayable in marks or their equivalent for an enterprise that failed. At the time of payment the marks had fallen in value, which so far as it went was a gain for the defendant in error, and it was contended by the plaintiff in error that the gain was taxable income. But the transaction as a whole was a loss, and the contention was denied. Here there was no shrinkage of assets and the taxpayer made a clear gain. As a result of its dealings it made available $137,521.30 assets previously offset by the obligation of bonds now extinct. We see nothing to be gained by the discussion of judicial definitions. The defendant in error has realized within the year an accession to income, if we take words in their plain popular meaning, as they should be taken here. Burnet v. Sanford & Brooks Co., 282 U.S. 359, 364.

Judgment reversed.

NOTE

1. If the taxpayer in *Kirby Lumber Co.* had purchased its bonds at a discount today what might it do to avoid the immediate recognition of gain? See §§108 and 1017.

2. If shareholders are also creditors of a corporation and they reduce or cancel the indebtedness, does the corporation have income? Why? Does it matter whether the shareholders held the corporate debt in proportion to their stockholdings and whether they all agreed to a proportionate debt reduction or cancellation? Why?

See Treas. Reg. §1.61-12(a). Does the shareholders' reason for cancelling the debt matter? Compare Utilities & Industries Corp., 41 T.C. 888 (1964), with Helvering v. Jane Holding Corp., 109 F.2d 933 (8th Cir. 1940), cert. denied, 310 U.S. 653 (1940).

b. EQUITY

Corporation M issued its $100 par value preferred stock for $100 per share. Years later, the stock is selling at $85 per share in the open market. Sensing a bargain, Corporation M, acting at the direction of its Board which is controlled by a share-holder who owns 40 per cent of the outstanding stock, offers to buy at $90 per share all of its stock that is tendered. Twenty per cent of the outstanding stock is tendered, for which Corporation M pays the offered price. Upon delivery of the shares the acquired stock is cancelled, and Corporation M reduces its authorized and outstanding capital by the par value of the shares. Does Corporation M realize income in the transaction? Why? Cf. J. A. Maurer, Inc., 30 T.C. 1273 (1958). See E. Sanders, Debt Cancellation — Without Realization of Income, 1959 So. Calif. Tax Inst. 565.

B. *DEDUCTIONS*

1. *Distributions of Property (Including Cash)*

a. DIVIDEND vs. INTEREST

FIN HAY REALTY CO. v. UNITED STATES
398 F.2d 694 (3d Cir. 1968)

Before HASTIE, Chief Judge, FREEDMAN and VAN DUSEN, Circuit Judges.

FREEDMAN, Circuit Judge. We are presented in this case with the recurrent problem whether funds paid to a close corporation by its shareholders were additional contributions to capital or loans on which the corporation's payment of interest was deductible under §163 of the Internal Revenue Code of 1954.[1]

The problem necessarily calls for an evaluation of the facts, which we therefore detail.

Fin Hay Realty Co., the taxpayer, was organized on February 14, 1934, by Frank L. Finlaw and J. Louis Hay. Each of them contributed $10,000 for which he received one-half of the corporation's stock and at the same time each advanced an additional $15,000 for which the corporation issued to him its unsecured promissory note payable on demand and bearing interest at the rate of six per cent per annum. The corporation immediately purchased an apartment house in Newark, New Jersey, for $39,000 in cash. About a month later the two shareholders each advanced an additional $35,000 to the corporation in return for six per cent demand promissory notes and the next day the corporation purchased two apartment buildings in East

---

[1]Section 163(a) provides: "There shall be allowed as a deduction all interest paid or accrued within the taxable year on indebtedness."

Orange, New Jersey, for which it paid $75,000 in cash and gave the seller a six per cent, five year purchase money mortgage for the balance of $100,000.

Three years later, in October, 1937, the corporation created a new mortgage on all three properties and from the proceeds paid off the old mortgage on the East Orange property, which had been partially amortized. The new mortgage was for a five year term in the amount of $82,000 with interest at four and one-half per cent. In the following three years each of the shareholders advanced an additional $3,000 to the corporation, bringing the total advanced by each shareholder to $53,000, in addition to their acknowledged stock subscriptions of $10,000 each.

Finlaw died in 1941 and his stock and notes passed to his two daughters in equal shares. A year later the mortgage, which was about to fall due, was extended for a further period of five years interest at four per cent. From the record it appears that it was subsequently extended until 1951.[3] In 1949 Hay died and in 1951 his executor requested the retirement of his stock and the payment of his notes. The corporation thereupon refinanced its real estate for $125,000 and sold one of the buildings. With the net proceeds it paid Hay's estate $24,000 in redemption of his stock and $53,000 in retirement of his notes.[4] Finlaw's daughters then became and still remain the sole shareholders of the corporation.

Thereafter the corporation continued to pay and deduct interest on Finlaw's notes, now held by his two daughters. In 1962 the Internal Revenue Service for the first time declared the payments on the notes not allowable as interest deductions and disallowed them for the tax years 1959 and 1960. The corporation thereupon repaid a total of $6,000 on account of the outstanding notes and in the following year after refinancing the mortgage on its real estate repaid the balance of $47,000. A short time later the Internal Revenue Service disallowed the interest deductions for the years 1961 and 1962. When the corporation failed to obtain refunds it brought this refund action in the district court. After a nonjury trial the court denied the claims and entered judgment for the United States. 261 F. Supp. 823 (D.N.J. 1967). From this judgment the corporation appeals.

This case arose in a factual setting where it is the corporation which is the party concerned that its obligations be deemed to represent a debt and not a stock interest. In the long run in cases of this kind it is also important to the shareholder that his advance be deemed a loan rather than a capital contribution, for in such a case his receipt of repayment may be treated as the retirement of a loan rather than a taxable dividend.[6] There are other instances in which it is in the shareholder's interest that his advance to the corporation be considered a debt rather than an increase

---

[3] The corporation's tax returns returns show a continuing decline in the principal of the debt until that year.

[4] The record is fragmentary and provides no clear basis from which to reconstruct the events of 1951. It may perhaps be inferred from it that Hay's estate received the total of $77,000 solely for the redemption of his stock and that the notes of $53,000 were retired either from the proceeds of the sale of real estate or in some other manner during the same year. In such event the total paid in redemption of Hay's stock and the retirement of his notes would be $130,000 rather than $77,000.

[6] The partial retirement of an equity interest may be considered as essentially equivalent to a dividend under §302, while the repayment of even a debt whose principal has appreciated is taxed only as a capital gain under §1232.

in his equity. A loss resulting from the worthlessness of stock is a capital loss under §165(g), whereas a bad debt may be treated as an ordinary loss if it qualifies as a business bad debt under §166. Similarly, it is only if a taxpayer receives debt obligations of a controlled corporation[7] that he can avoid the provision for nonrecognition of gains or losses on transfers of property to such a corporation under §351.[8] These advantages in having the funds entrusted to a corporation treated as corporate obligations instead of contributions to capital have required the courts to look beyond the literal terms in which the parties have cast the transaction in order to determine its substantive nature.

In attempting to deal with this problem courts and commentators have isolated a number of criteria by which to judge the true nature of an investment which is in form a debt: (1) the intent of the parties; (2) the identity between creditors and shareholders; (3) the extent of participation in management by the holder of the instrument; (4) the ability of the corporation to obtain funds from outside sources; (5) the "thinness" of the capital structure in relation to debt; (6) the risk involved; (7) the formal indicia of the arrangement; (8) the relative position of the obligees as to other creditors regarding the payment of interest and principal; (9) the voting power of the holder of the instrument; (10) the provision of a fixed rate of interest; (11) a contingency on the obligation to repay; (12) the source of the interest payments; (13) the presence or absence of a fixed maturity date; (14) a provision for redemption by the corporation; (15) a provision for redemption at the option of the holder; and (16) the timing of the advance with reference to the organization of the corporation.[9]

While the Internal Revenue Code of 1954 was under consideration, and after its adoption, Congress sought to identify the criteria which would determine whether an investment represents a debt or equity, but these and similar efforts have not found acceptance.[10] It still remains true that neither any single criterion nor any

[7]While not all debt obligations qualify for the desired tax treatment, equity interests can never qualify.

[8]A taxpayer might wish to avoid §351 when he transfers depreciated property to the corporation and seeks to recognize the loss immediately and also when the transferred property is to be resold by the corporation but will not qualify for capital gains treatment in the hands of the corporation.

[9]See J. S. Biritz Construction Co. v. Commissioner of Internal Revenue, 387 F.2d 451 (8 Cir. 1967); Tomlinson v. 1661 Corporation, 377 F.2d 291 (5 Cir. 1967); Smith v. Commissioner of Internal Revenue, 370 F.2d 178 (6 Cir. 1966); Gilbert v. Commissioner of Internal Revenue, 262 F.2d 512 (2 Cir. 1959); 4A Mertens, Law of Federal Income Taxation, §§26.10a, 26.10c (1966).

[10]The original House version of the 1954 Code, H.R. 8300, 83d Cong., 2d Sess., contained a provision, §312, which distinguished between "securities", "participating stock", and "nonparticipating stock". Only payments with regard to "securities" were deductible by the corporation as interest. See proposed §275. "Securities" were defined as unconditional obligations to pay a sum certain with an unconditional interest requirement not dependent on corporate earnings. The Senate rejected the proposed classification on the ground that it was inflexible. See S. Rep. No. 1622, 83d Cong., 2d Sess., 1954-3 U.S.C. Cong. & Admin. News 4621, 4673.

A similar list of determinants was proposed in 1957 by an advisory group to a subcommittee of the House Committee on Ways and Means, but was not acted upon. [See Advisory Group on Subchapter C of the Internal Revenue Code, Report on Corporate Distributions and Adjustments, in Hearings on Topics Pertaining to the General Revision of the Internal Revenue Code Before the Committee on Ways and Means, House of Representatives, 85th Cong., 2d Sess., pt. 3, at 2516 (1958); cf. Subchapter C, Advisory Group Proposed Amendments, id. at 2468. — Ed.]

series of criteria can provide a conclusive answer in the kaleidoscopic circumstances which individual cases present. See John Kelley Co. v. Commissioner of Internal Revenue, 326 U.S. 521, 530, 66 S. Ct. 299, 90 L. Ed. 278 (1946).

The various factors which have been identified in the cases are only aids in answering the ultimate question whether the investment, analyzed in terms of its economic reality, constitutes risk capital entirely subject to the fortunes of the corporate venture or represents a strict debtor-creditor relationship.[11] Since there is often an element of risk in a loan, just as there is an element of risk in an equity interest, the conflicting elements do not end at a clear line in all cases.

In a corporation which has numerous shareholders with varying interests, the arm's-length relationship between the corporation and a shareholder who supplies funds to it inevitably results in a transaction whose form mirrors its substance. Where the corporation is closely held, however, and the same persons occupy both sides of the bargaining table, form does not necessarily correspond to the intrinsic economic nature of the transaction, for the parties may mold it at their will with no countervailing pull. This is particularly so where a shareholder can have the funds he advances to a corporation treated as corporate obligations instead of contributions to capital without affecting his proportionate equity interest. Labels, which are perhaps the best expression of the subjective intention of parties to a transaction, thus lose their meaningfulness.

To seek economic reality in objective terms of course disregards the personal interest which a shareholder may have in the welfare of the corporation in which he is a dominant force. But an objective standard is one imposed by the very fact of his dominant position and is much fairer than one which would presumptively construe all such transactions against the shareholder's interest. Under an objective test of economic reality it is useful to compare the form which a similar transaction would have taken had it been between the corporation and an outside lender, and if the shareholder's advance is far more speculative than what an outsider would make, it is obviously a loan in name only.

In the present case all the formal indicia of an obligation were meticulously made to appear. The corporation, however, was the complete creature of the two shareholders who had the power to create whatever appearance would be of tax benefit to them despite the economic reality of the transaction. Each shareholder owned an equal proportion of stock and was making an equal additional contribution, so that whether Finlaw and Hay designated any part of their additional contributions as debt or as stock would not dilute their proportionate equity interests. There was no restriction because of the possible excessive debt structure, for the corporation had been created to acquire real estate and had no outside creditors except mortgagees who, of course, would have no concern for general creditors be-

---

In 1954 the American Law Institute embodied such a test in §x500 of its draft income tax statute. See ALI Federal Tax Project, Income Tax Problems of Corporations and Shareholders 396 (1958).

[11]See Bittker & Eustice, Federal Income Taxation of Corporations and Shareholders, §4.04, at 127 (2d ed. 1966); Stone, Debt-Equity Distinctions in the Tax Treatment of the Corporation and Its Shareholders, 42 Tulane L. Rev. 251, 253-62 (1968).

cause they had priority in the security of the real estate. The position of the mortgagees also rendered of no significance the possible subordination of the notes to other debts of the corporation, a matter which in some cases this Court has deemed significant.[12]

The shareholders here, moreover, lacked one of the principal advantages of creditors. Although the corporation issued demand notes for the advances, nevertheless, as the court below found, it could not have repaid them for a number of years. The economic reality was that the corporation used the proceeds of the notes to purchase its original assets, and the advances represented a long term commitment dependent on the future value of the real estate and the ability of the corporation to sell or refinance it. Only because such an entwining of interest existed between the two shareholders and the corporation, so different from the arm's-length relationship between a corporation and an outside creditor, were they willing to invest in the notes and allow them to go unpaid for so many years while the corporation continued to enjoy the advantages of uninterrupted ownership of its real estate.

It is true that real estate values rose steadily with a consequent improvement in the mortgage market, so that looking back the investment now appears to have been a good one. As events unfolded, the corporation reached a point at which it could have repaid the notes through refinancing, but this does not obliterate the uncontradicted testimony that in 1934 it was impossible to obtain any outside mortgage financing for real estate of this kind except through the device of a purchase money mortgage taken back by the seller.

It is argued that the rate of interest at six per cent per annum was far more than the shareholders could have obtained from other investments. This argument, however, is self-defeating, for it implies that the shareholders would damage their own corporation by an overcharge for interest. There was, moreover, enough objective evidence to neutralize this contention. The outside mortgage obtained at the time the corporation purchased the East Orange property bore interest at the rate of six per cent even though the mortgagee was protected by an equity in excess of forty per cent of the value of the property.[14] In any event, to compare the six per cent interest rate of the notes with other 1934 rates ignores the most salient feature of the notes — their risk. It is difficult to escape the inference that a prudent outside businessman would not have risked his capital in six per cent unsecured demand notes in Fin Hay Realty Co. in 1934. The evidence therefore amply justifies the conclusion of the district court that the form which the parties gave to their transaction did not match its economic reality.

It is argued that even if the advances may be deemed to have been contributions to capital when they were originally made in 1934, a decisive change occurred when the original shareholder, Finlaw, died and his heirs continued to hold the notes without demanding payment. This, it is said could be construed as a decision to

[12]See P. M. Finance Corp. v. Commissioner, 302 F.2d 786 (3 Cir. 1962); General Alloy Casting Co. v. Commissioner of Internal Revenue, 345 F.2d 794 (3 Cir. 1965), aff'g per curiam 23 CCH T.C. Mem. 887 (1964).

[14]The corporation purchased the property for $175,000 and the sellers took back a purchase money mortgage of $100,000.

reinvest, and if by 1941 the notes were sufficiently secure to be considered bona fide debt, they should now be so treated for tax purposes. Such a conclusion, however, does not inevitably follow. Indeed, the weight of the circumstances leads to the opposite conclusion.

First, there is nothing in the record to indicate that the corporation could have readily raised the cash with which to pay off Finlaw's notes on his death in 1941. When Hay, the other shareholder, died in 1949 and his executor two years later requested the retirement of his interest, the corporation in order to carry this out sold one of its properties and refinanced the others. Again, when in 1963 the corporation paid off the notes held by Finlaw's daughters after the Internal Revenue Service had disallowed the interest deductions for 1961 and 1962 it again refinanced its real estate. There is nothing in the record which would sustain a finding that the corporation could have readily undertaken a similar financing in 1941, when Finlaw died even if we assume that the corporation was able to undertake the appropriate refinancing ten years later to liquidate Hay's interest. Moreover, there was no objective evidence to indicate that in 1941 Finlaw's daughters viewed the notes as changed in character or in security, or indeed that they viewed the stock and notes as separate and distinct investments. To indulge in a theoretical conversion of equity contributions into a debt obligation in 1941 when Finlaw died would be to ignore what such a conversion might have entailed. For Finlaw's estate might then have been chargeable with the receipt of dividends at the time the equity was redeemed and converted into a debt. To recognize retrospectively such a change in the character of the obligation would be to assume a conclusion with consequences unfavorable to the parties, which they themselves never acknowledged.

The burden was on the taxpayer to prove that the determination by the Internal Revenue Service that the advances represented capital contributions was incorrect. The district court was justified in holding that the taxpayer had not met this burden.

This judgment of the district court will be affirmed.

VAN DUSEN, Circuit Judge (dissenting). I respectfully dissent on the ground that the "entire evidence," in light of appellate court decision discussing the often-presented problem of corporate debt versus equity, does not permit the conclusion reached by the District Court.[1]

When the parties holding debt of the taxpayer corporation have a formal debt obligation and it is clear that all parties intended the investment to take the form of debt, a series of considerations such as those mentioned by the District Court

---

[1]As to the determination of the trial court that payments were not "interest paid . . . on indebtedness" (26 U.S.C. §163), this court has stated: ". . . it is well-settled that such findings are 'in the nature of an ultimate finding of fact and since such finding is but a legal inference from other facts it is subject to review free of the restraining impact of the so-called "clearly erroneous" rule applicable to ordinary findings of fact by the trial court. . . .'" Kaltreider v. Commissioner of Internal Revenue, 255 F.2d 833, 837 (3rd Cir. 1958). Although listed under legal conclusions by the District Court, this determination is similar to the "findings" referred to in *Kaltreider.* See, also, Soles v. Franzblau, 352 F.2d 47, 50 (3rd Cir. 1965). Moreover, regardless of the characterization of the District Court's findings, I am "left with the definite and firm conviction that a mistake has been committed" by the trial court on the record in this case. Diamond Bros. Company v. C.I.R., 322 F.2d 725, 731, n.9 (3rd Cir. 1963), quoting from United States v. United States Gypsum Co., 333 U.S. 364, 395 (1948).

should be used to determine whether the form and intent should be disregarded for federal tax purposes. Tomlinson v. 1661 Corporation, 337 F.2d 291 (5th Cir. 1967);[2] J. S. Biritz Construction Co. v. C.I.R., 387 F.2d 451, 455-56 (8th Cir. 1967). As I read the District Court's opinion, the focus was entirely on inferring "the intent of the taxpayer's only two stockholders" at the time the debt was created. To that end, the District Court drew certain inferences which are largely immaterial to the proper decision, and which are clearly erroneous in light of the stipulated facts and uncontroverted evidence.

Whether or not the corporate taxpayer is entitled to an interest deduction turns in this case on the "real nature of the transaction in question" or on whether "the degree of risk may be said to be reasonably equivalent to that which equity capital would bear had an investor, under similar circumstances, made the advances . . . ." Diamond Bros. Company v. C.I.R., 322 F.2d 725, 732 (3rd Cir. 1963); Tomlinson v. 1661 Corporation, supra, at 295. When this test is used, the entire history of the corporate taxpayer becomes relevant and a focus solely on the year of incorporation or investment of the debt is not sufficient.

Turning within this framework to the facts, the record does not justify the conclusion that the form of the debt should be disregarded for purposes of federal taxation. The debt was evidenced by written notes, carried 6% interest which was paid every year, and was not subordinated in any way to similar debt of general creditors. It was carried on the corporate books and tax returns as debt, being payable on demand, it was always listed as a debt maturing in less than one year,[10] and on Mr. Finlaw's estate tax return was listed as promissory notes payable on demand.[11]

---

[2]The panel which decided *Tomlinson* included Senior Circuit Judge Maris of this court. The corporate taxpayer seeking to deduct interest payments was engaged in the construction, owning and operation of a certain office building, an economic activity quite similar to that of the corporate taxpayer in this case except that construction of real estate arguably increases the "risk" involved in the enterprise. *Tomlinson* relied heavily on United States v. Snyder Brothers Company, 367 F.2d 980 (5th Cir. 1966), in which the Fifth Circuit adopted with approval the conceptual analysis of Kraft Foods Company v. Commissioner of Internal Revenue, 232 F.2d 118, 123 (2nd Cir., 1956). This carefully reasoned Second Circuit decision suggested that the relevant inquiry for courts seeking to define "indebtedness' under 26 U.S.C. §163 should turn initially on whether the alleged debt is a "hybrid," partaking of certain characteristics of traditional corporate equity as well as characteristics of debt, or whether the alleged debt is in form entirely debt and intended to be such. See, also, Gloucester Ice & Cold Storage Co. v. C.I.R., 298 F.2d 183, 185 (1st Cir. 1962). It is noteworthy that the Third Circuit case relied on heavily by the District Court, Mullin Building Corporation v. C.I.R., 9 T.C. 350 (1957), aff'd 167 F.2d 1001 (3rd Cir. 1948), is a case of a "hybrid" investment which, although the corporate taxpayer was formed solely to hold real estate, was named "debenture preferred stock" and demanded corporate liquidation before the "debenture preferred stock" principal could be returned. Similarly, Messenger Publishing Co. v. C.I.R., P.H. Memo, T.C., ¶41.241, aff'd 168 F.2d 903 (3rd Cir. 1948), involved a hybrid named "preferred stock."

[10]Apparently the District Court regarded demand notes as having no fixed maturity, see Conclusion of Law 4. This seems incorrect since demand paper means that the debt is "mature" at the holder's option. The better characterization would seem to be that demand notes held by someone with a voice in management are a type of long-term investment. See, e.g., Taft v. C.I.R., 314 F.2d 620 (9th Cir. 1963).

[11]This consistent treatment does not, of course, estop either the Commissioner or the taxpayer any more than the decision in this case controls the tax status of repaid principal on these loans in the hands of the remaining Fin Hay shareholders. The Government may well have sought to challenge these corporate interest deductions before challenging the individuals' returns as a

The parties clearly intended the advances as debt and unfailingly treated them as such. The only testimony on the usual capitalization of real estate companies in the Newark area was that:

> "The usual capitalization is a thousand dollar investment in capital and then the rest of the monies are loaned either . . . by individuals or stockholders of the corporation to the corporation, which in turn the individuals lending the money expect a return for their loans. . . .
>
> "[Of the real estate corporations that] I have dealt with, at least ninety-five per cent and more have had a thousand capitalization and, of course, loans from the various lenders would depend upon the size of the transaction, monies that were required."

On this record, Conclusions of Law 3-8 as worded are not justified. The District Court placed heavy reliance on the fact that the stockholder's debt was in the same proportion as their equity holdings. This fact, without more, is not controlling since there is no doubt that investors can have a dual status. The inferences that "more" was involved in this case are not justified by this record. The fact that the loans were used to begin the corporate life and buy the income-producing assets must be placed in proper perspective. Without any basis in the record, the District Court assumed that the loans were advanced to prevent a sudden corporate deficit that was created by the Wainwright Street property investment's unexpectedly requiring more funds than the corporation had. Real estate cases, however, and uncontroverted testimony in this case show that corporations owning and operating buildings frequently and traditionally borrow the substantial part of money needed to secure their principal assets and that this was contemplated by a corporate resolution passed in the month of organization at the original directors' meeting. Cases denying the validity of debt because it is contemporaneously advanced with the start of corporate life generally involve other industries or a partnership becoming a corporation.

The loans were denied debt status because there was no intent to seek repayment within a "reasonable time," because the corporation had no retirement provision (or fund) for the principal and because the debt had no maturity date (Conclusions 3 and 4). To the contrary, demand notes have a maturity date at the discretion of the holder (or of his transferee when the notes are freely negotiable, as were the Fin Hay notes). And failure to transfer the notes or demand payment is irrelevant when, as here, the evidence shows that the 6% rate made the debt a good investment. In addition, when a corporation holds appreciating real estate and contemplates recourse to refinancing, the lack of a sinking fund assumes little, if any, significance. There was no evidence and no discussion of what constitutes a "reasonable time" for refraining from making a demand on such a promissory note.

The loans were also found to be equity because redemption was expected only

---

matter of tactics, but this, and the question of the tax consequences of the liquidation of the remaining loans in 1962-1963, should not influence the decision in the present case, see Budd Company v. United States, 252 F.2d 456, 458 (3rd Cir. 1957).

out of future earnings or surplus and because they were unsecured and subordinate to prior secured loans (Conclusions 6 and 8). To the contrary, the evidence shows that the parties contemplated redemption out of "refinancing" as well if a demand were made when surplus was deficient; and this in fact was what happened in 1951 and 1962-1963.[18] Corporate debt does not become equity because it is contemplated that principal will be retired by refinancing. In addition, a review of the "subordination" cases shows that there was no "subordination" in this case as that term is used in other cases where the challenged debt was subordinated to all other debt of similar type or otherwise subordinated by agreement.

The District Court also placed emphasis on the fact that at the end of 1935 the shareholders' salaries were accrued but unpaid in the amount of $2400 and that in 1938 through 1940 the shareholders advanced an additional $6000 as loans. The corporate tax returns and books, however, show that the salaries could have been paid at the end of 1935 from $4,340.21 in cash on deposit,[20] and that during the period of the additional loans of $6000 the shareholders received $6800 in dividends from the corporation.[21] These additional facts, unexplained by the District Court, negate the implication that Fin Hay Realty Company was in serious financial trouble at the outset of its existence, at least to any such degree that all the challenged loans were made "at a risk" similar to that of venture capital.[22] It is noted, in addition, that by 1938, when the original purchase money mortgage was re-financed, $18,000 of principal had been paid.

[18]The Hay interests were bought out entirely in 1951, apparently after arm's-length dealing with his executor. After study of the tax returns and corporate books introduced as exhibits, the cash events of 1951 seem to be as follows (figures rounded off):

A.	Refinance, new mortgage of	$124,000.	
B.	Pay Hay notes	53,000.	
	Balance		$ 71,000.
C.	Sell Wainwright Street		79,000.
	Balance		$150,000.
D.	Expenses — cost of sale	$ 3,000.	
	Capital Gains tax	10,000.	
	Pay off old mortgage	40,000.	53,000.
	Balance		$ 97,000.
E.	Redeem Hay stock		77,000.
	Balance		$ 20,000.

The 1952 return lists the $20,000 as invested in "S. & L. Assn." As can be seen, even though the sale proceeds were used to pay off the old mortgage, more than enough money was available from the refinancing to pay off the notes and the mortgage. Similarly, the 1963 re-mortgaging gave net mortgage proceeds of approximately $210,000 for paying $47,000 of the remaining $53,000 in notes ($6,000 was apparently paid for out of earnings).

[20]Even with the subsequent payment of these salaries, the 1936 salaries of $4000, and a $1600 dividend for 1936, the 1936 year-end cash balance improved to $5,657.13. It does not appear that the corporation had to maintain such large cash balances; subsequent tax returns show several lower year-end totals: 1937 — $158.29; 1939 — $536.98; 1940 — $2,532.93.

[21]Thus the stockholders received $800 more than they loaned during the period 1938-1940. These dividends were paid continuously from 1936 through 1952, a total of $26,000.00.

[22]See, for instance, the factors of "risk" noted in Gilbert v. C.I.R., 262 F.2d 512, 514 (2nd Cir. 1959).

Although appellate decisions on the debt-equity problem constantly reiterate the maxim that each instance of definition turns on the particular facts of each case, a reading of many of these cases, including all those cited above, indicates two rather distinct conclusions concerning the assessment of the severity of the "risk" attached to alleged debt transactions. First, when the problem of definition arises under 26 U.S.C. §§165, 166 (worthless stock, bad debt), the risk of failure has already been realized and the party seeking to minimize the degree of such risk must show more "factors" than otherwise clearly argue for a debt classification. Secondly, regardless of the end purpose for defining indebtedness, fewer factors need be present (such as subordination, no interest, etc.) to allow a conclusion of "equity" when, as a matter of common knowledge, the economic enterprise has a higher chance of commercial failure. Consequently, few cases (and particularly few where taxpayers holding formal debt lose) deny debt status or even raise the question where the enterprise risk, as in this case, involves the mere holding and operation of real estate. As the risks increase, involving in addition construction of the real estate, or non-real estate operations subject to more immediate risk-creating problems of marketing, labor, advertisement, supplies, etc., the frequency of cases challenging debt and of decisions finding equity increase. The uncontradicted testimony (without finding of lack of credibility) of the universal practice in the Newark area in conformity to the course followed by taxpayer . . . is entitled to consideration. Also, the subsequent successful history of this corporate taxpayer cannot be disregarded and militates strongly against denying an interest deduction on this record. The Fin Hay Realty Co. did not go bankrupt, was not unable to refinance or extend its purchase money mortgage due in 1939, and has never failed to meet a demanded purchase of the notes.

On this record, these loans were bona fide loans, "at risk" in this enterprise in no different way than any debt investment is "at risk" for a general creditor[23] of a real estate holding and operating corporation. The District Court pointedly took judicial notice, both of the bargain real estate purchases possible in 1934 and of the steadily rising real estate values in Essex County, New Jersey. Subsequent refinancings by the taxpayer, as well as the entire course of its history, demonstrate that this investment in this particular venture was not a "risk capital" investment of the type that should compel disregarding the clear intent of the parties and form of the transaction. Two recent "real estate" decisions (involving, moreover, construction as well as holding of real estate) suggest the proper result for the present case. As stated in Tomlinson v. 1661 Corporation, supra, at 300:

> "We cannot, by manipulation of tax law, preclude the parties from exercising sound business judgment in obtaining needed investment funds at the most favorable rate possible, whether it be a commercial loan, or, more likely and as is the case here, a loan from private interested sources with sufficient faith in the success of the venture and their ultimate repayment to delete or minimize the 'risk factor' in their rate of return."

[23]The interest paid reflects to a certain extent the risk involved, Tomlinson v. 1661 Corporation, supra, at 300, and the 6% rate does not appear to be sufficiently low to suggest that in this case a substantial amount of risk was unreflected in the interest rate and, hence, the notes must be equity investment.

Similarly, in J. S. Biritz Construction Co. v. C.I.R., supra, at 459, the court said:

> "There is actually no evidence that this was not a loan, was not intended to be a loan, or that Biritz actually intended to make a capital investment rather than a loan.
>
> "We think the Tax Court has painted with too broad a brush in limiting the permissible activities of an entrepreneur in personally financing his business. Financing embraces both equity and debt transactions and we do not think the courts should enunciate a rule of law that a sole stockholder may not loan money or transfer assets to a corporation in a loan transaction. If this is to be the law, Congress should so declare it. We feel the controlling principle should be that any transaction which is intrinsically clear upon its face should be accorded its legal due unless the transaction is a mere sham or subterfuge set up solely or principally for tax-avoidance purposes."

I would reverse and enter judgment for the corporate taxpayer.

NOTE

1. The debt vs. equity problem raised in *Fin Hay Realty* is not a new one. The Supreme Court faced the issue in two companion cases, John Kelley Co. v. Commissioner, and Talbot Mills v. Commissioner, 326 U.S. 521 (1946). Whether the corporations in those cases could deduct "interest" payments depended upon the classification of the "hybrid" securities on which the payments had been made. The instruments in *John Kelley Co.* were 20-year, 8 per cent, noncumulative income debenture bonds, some of which were issued to the shareholders (all members of a family group) in exchange for stock and others of which had been sold to these shareholders for cash. Payment of the interest was conditioned on sufficient net income to meet the obligation. Although the debentures were subordinated to all other creditors, they contained acceleration provisions in the event of defaults. The terms of the indenture excluded the holders from management. The Tax Court had held that the payments were interest on indebtedness, deductible under §163; the Court of Appeals for the Seventh Circuit reversed.

In the companion case (*Talbot Mills*) 25-year registered notes were issued to the shareholders — once again a family group — in exchange for four-fifths of their stock. The annual interest was not to exceed 10 per cent nor to be less than 2 per cent; it was computed by a formula that took into account the annual earnings of the corporation. Although the interest could be deferred until maturity when "necessary by reason of the condition of the corporation," it was cumulative, and dividends could not be paid until interest arrearages were met. The corporation's right to mortgage its real property was limited, and the board of directors was given power to subordinate the notes. Emphasizing the fluctuating payments and the fact that all the notes were issued in exchange for stock, the Tax Court had distinguished its decision in *Kelley,* holding the payments to be dividends; the First Circuit affirmed.

After hearing both cases together, the Supreme Court held that the debt vs. equity issue was, under the *Dobson* (320 U.S. 489 (1943)) doctrine, one for the Tax Court to resolve. Stating that no one characteristic could be decisive, the Supreme Court directed affirmance of the Tax Court's very nearly inconsistent holdings.

In light of the Supreme Court's deference the factors deemed significant by the Tax Court in *Kelley* and *Talbot Mills* became the seeds for the growth of "tests" to distinguish debt from equity. The Tax Court's seeming reliance on the formal structure of ordinary debt instruments soon led most taxpayers to abandon hybrid securities and to adopt formal, fixed interest, fixed maturity, unconditional debt instruments; it is around these formal debt instruments that most of today's battles are fought.

2. One of the important early tests was the so-called "debt to equity" ratio. The Supreme Court had cautioned against an "obviously excessive debt structure" (326 U.S. at 526), but since the 4:1 ratio of debt to equity in *Talbot Mills* had not been labelled "obviously excessive," many tax planners concluded that 4:1 was a "safe" ratio. The courts held that interest was deductible in a number of cases where the ratio was less than 4:1; the Commissioner's acquiescences seemed to confirm the margin of safety. See, e.g., Gazette Telegraph Co., 19 T.C. 692 (1953) (acq.), aff'd on other grounds, 209 F.2d 926 (10th Cir. 1954); Ruspyn Corp., 18 T.C. 769 (1952) (acq.); Cleveland Adolph Mayer Realty Corp., 6 T.C. 730 (1946) (acq.).

Concurrently, capital structures with high debt to equity ratios were struck down. See, e.g., Alfred R. Bachrack, 18 T.C. 479 (1952), aff'd per curiam, 205 F.2d 151 (2d Cir. 1953); Isidor Dobkin, 15 T.C. 31 (1950), aff'd per curiam, 192 F.2d 392 (2d Cir. 1951); Mullin Bldg. Corp., 9 T.C. 350 (1947), aff'd per curiam, 167 F.2d 1001 (3d Cir. 1948). For a compilation of the cases in tabular form with their ratios computed, see M. Caplin, The Caloric Count of a Thin Corporation, 17 N.Y.U. Inst. on Fed. Tax. 771, 43 Marq. L. Rev. 31 (1959).

The great reliance placed on the debt to equity ratio received a jarring blow in Gooding Amusement Co., 23 T.C. 408 (1954), aff'd, 236 F.2d 159 (6th Cir. 1956), where formal debt instruments were classified as equity despite a ratio of 1:1. The court held the "real intention" of the parties was never to enforce the notes or otherwise to assert the rights of bona fide creditors.

Although in *Gooding* itself equity classification was the result, that case ironically paved the way for debt classification in cases where a high debt to equity ratio existed. Since the ratio was no longer talismanic, taxpayers with increasing frequency urged the courts to ignore it just as the Commissioner had done in *Gooding*. Where sufficient justification was found, the courts passed over a high debt to equity ratio and ruled in favor of the taxpayers. See Arthur M. Rosenthal, 24 CCH Tax Ct. Mem. 1373 (1965) (14:1 ratio not significant in view of substantial cash invested and fact that notes were issued for property which corporation could have rented instead of buying — a "non-essential" asset); Charles E. Curry, 43 T.C. 667 (1965) (see page 304 infra) (30:1 ratio not unreasonable in light of substantial disproportion between holdings of stock and notes, substantial cash contribution, and commercially reasonable indenture terms); Royalty Service Corp. v. United States, 178 F. Supp. 216 (D. Mont. 1959) (50,000:1 "temporary" ratio at inception of corporation; five years later ratio was 1:1 or 2.25:1 depending on method of computation).

Several courts have abandoned the ratio test entirely. See Gloucester Ice & Cold Storage Co. v. Commissioner, 298 F.2d 183, 185 (1st Cir. 1962); Rowan v. United States, 219 F.2d 51, 55 (5th Cir. 1955).

3. Some of the justifications for ignoring the debt to equity ratio have assumed the status of independent tests.

(a) Whether "substantial capital" had been contributed has become an important question. See, e.g., Sheldon Tauber, 24 T.C. 179 (1955). In Murphy Logging Co. v. United States, 378 F.2d 222 (9th Cir. 1967), a corporation with a debt to equity ratio of 160:1 was permitted to deduct interest payments on loans where the shareholders "contributed" their ability to procure contracts and "their own integrity and reputation for getting things done."

(b) Whether debt and equity are held pro rata by the shareholders has also become an important question. Pro rata holdings have been a formidable barrier when not insuperable to taxpayer successes. See Gilbert v. Commissioner, 248 F.2d 399 (2d Cir. 1957). Conversely, disproportionate holdings may be helpful to the taxpayer (see Leach Corp., 30 T.C. 563 (1958)), although they may not be a guarantee of success. See P. M. Finance Corp. v. Commissioner, 302 F.2d 786 (3d Cir. 1962). Might "disproportion" lead to no more than the conclusion that the corporation "had issued disproportionate amounts of common and preferred stock"? See The Colony, Inc. v. Commissioner, 26 T.C. 30, 43 (1956), aff'd on other grounds, 244 F.2d 75 (6th Cir. 1957), rev'd on other grounds, 357 U.S. 28 (1958). As to alleged indebtedness owing to a corporation's sole shareholder, see, e.g., Alma deB. Spreckles, 8 CCH Tax Ct. Mem. 1113 (1949), and Maloney v. Spencer, 172 F.2d 638 (9th Cir. 1949), instances in which the debt classification was sustained. Many "sole shareholders" are easier targets for the opposite result.

4. May loans granted by a nonshareholder be classified as equity, preferred stock, for example? See Foresun, Inc. v. Commissioner, 348 F.2d 1006 (6th Cir. 1965) (lender related to shareholders); Motel Co. v. Commissioner, 340 F.2d 445 (2d Cir. 1965) (lender related to shareholders); Merlo Builders, 23 CCH Tax Ct. Mem. 185 (1964) (lender unrelated to shareholders).

5. How would you articulate a test to help distinguish debt from equity? Recent cases emphasize the question whether the funds were placed at the "risk of the business." See Schine Chain Theaters, 22 CCH Tax Ct. Mem. 488 (1963), aff'd, 331 F.2d 849 (2d Cir. 1964). Is that an adequate test? Why? In the case of shareholder loans, would you approve of a test which asks whether an outside lending institution would have advanced funds subject to the same conditions as the advances made by the shareholders? Why?

6. Should the initial characterization of a debt instrument as equity continue after the instrument is sold by the shareholder-creditor to a nonshareholder? See Texoma Supply Co., 17 CCH Tax Ct. Mem. 147 (1958). Might "debt" become "equity" when the debt instrument is sold by the creditor to a shareholder whose investment in stock is small vis-à-vis his investment in debt? See Edwards v. Commissioner, page 91 infra. Compare Jewell Ridge Coal Corp., 21 CCH Tax Ct. Mem. 1048 (1962), aff'd, 318 F.2d 695 (4th Cir. 1963).

7. Three shareholders form a new corporation, contributing $1500 to its capital.

Then a bank lends $240,000 to the corporation but does so only because the individual shareholders guarantee the loan. May the corporation deduct the interest paid to the bank? See Murphy Logging Co. v. United States, 239 F. Supp. 794 (D. Ore. 1965), rev'd, 378 F.2d 222 (9th Cir. 1967). You should read both the District Court's and the Court of Appeals' opinions. Compare General Alloy Casting Co., 23 CCH Tax Ct. Mem. 887 (1964), aff'd per curiam, 345 F.2d 794 (3d Cir. 1965), where the deductibility of interest on a shareholder-guaranteed bank loan went unchallenged notwithstanding the fact that the deductibility of alleged interest payments on a direct $200,000 "loan" from shareholders was denied. See also Fors Farms, Inc., 66-1 U.S. Tax Cas. ¶9206 (W.D. Wash. 1966).

See B. Bittker, Thin Capitalization: Some Current Questions, 34 Taxes 830, 834-835 (1956), reprinted with minor revisions, 10 U. Fla. L. Rev. 25, 35-37 (1957); D. Holzman, The Current Trend in Guaranty Cases: An Impetus to Thin-Incorporation? 11 Tax L. Rev. 29, 47-48 (1955).

If, as current law dictates, the corporate tax impact of interest payments is to be different from that of dividends, should there be a statutory definition of "debt" and "equity"? How would you draft a provision distinguishing those terms for the purposes of the interest deduction under §163? Why? For views on the desirability of precise statutory definitions compare S. Brown, An Approach to Subchapter C, 3 Tax Revision Compendium 1619 (House Ways and Means Comm. 1959), with S. Surrey, Income Tax Problems of Corporations and Shareholders: American Law Institute Tax Project — American Bar Association Committee Study on Legislative Revision, 14 Tax L. Rev. 1, 43-48 (1958). Although §312(c) of the House version of the 1954 Code reflected an effort to provide a definition of debt, the Senate rejected the effort. See S. Rep. No. 1662, 83rd Cong., 2d Sess. 42 (1954).

Ought the corporate income tax treat "interest" differently from "dividends"? Why? If they were to be treated identically, should they both be deductible or nondeductible? Why? See B. Bittker and J. Eustice, Federal Income Taxation of Corporations and Shareholders 119-120 (2d ed. 1966); H. Groves, Production, Jobs and Taxes 25-27 (1944); G. Lent, Bond Interest Deduction and the Federal Corporation Income Tax, 2 Natl. Tax J. 131 (1949).

Section 247 provides that a public utility may deduct the dividends it pays on certain of its preferred stock. Why?

8. The classification of an investment as "debt" or "equity" has direct tax significance to the investor, apart from the question whether the corporation has made a deductible interest payment or a nondeductible dividend payment. In the investor's case the classification of an investment as "equity" as opposed to "debt" has relatively minor impact insofar as his taxibility on the alleged "interest" payment is concerned. When the alleged "debt" is repaid, however, its classification as "equity" would have major impact. If the investment proves worthless the tax deduction will be of greater tax benefit usually if the "debt" stands up as such and is not classified as stock. Why might Finlaw's estate in *Fin Hay Realty* have been "chargeable with the receipt of dividends" if the equity had been treated as redeemed and converted into debt (page 82 supra)?

In footnote 8 of the majority opinion (page 79 supra) in *Fin Hay Realty* the Court indicates that debt (not constituting a "security") may be issued to one wishing to avoid §351 in order to secure recognition of a loss. It is likely that a loss will be recognized to a controlling shareholder even if a particular property transfer avoids §351? Consider the breadth and impact of §267(a)(1) and (b)(2).

Might a transferee corporation wish to avoid §351 only if, as footnote 8 implies, it will not be entitled to capital gains treatment when it sells the property? Why?

The sentence of text in the majority opinion at footnotes 7 and 8 (page 79 supra) does not mean, as it seems to say, that a taxpayer can avoid §351 only by receiving debt in a controlled corporation. It probably was intended to point out that if a transferor is in control (as defined in §368(c)), then he can avoid §351 only by receiving debt (not constituting a "security") in exchange for the transferred property.

9. For a thoroughgoing survey of the law prior to §385, see W. Goldstein, Corporate Indebtedness to Shareholders: "Thin Capitalization" and Related Problems, 16 Tax L. Rev. 1 (1960). The Commissioner's handling of the problem in the context of an advance ruling involving "registered subordinated debentures" of a New York Stock Exchange company is reflected in Rev. Rul. 68-54, 1968-1 Cum. Bull. 69.

10. The Tax Reform Act of 1969 added §385 to the Code. It is intended to give the Treasury a firmer hand in dealing with the debt vs. equity question and also to provide a basis for prediction for taxpayers who must plan. It remains to be seen whether either objective will be achieved.

Section 279, also added to the Code by the 1969 Act, disallows interest due on corporate debt issued in connection with particular types of corporate acquisitions. The Code creates the term "corporate acquisition indebtedness" for this purpose. Seemingly intended to discourage acquisitions of businesses by large corporations which are financed significantly through debt, the interest deduction is disallowed where the debt, although accepted generally as debt and not equity, has certain of the characteristics of equity.

In cases covered by §267, interest will be disallowed because of the relationship of the particular creditor and debtor, although the debt may be unassailably debt and not equity.

EDWARDS v. COMMISSIONER
415 F.2d 578 (10th Cir. 1969), rev'g 50 T.C. 220 (1968)

Before Murrah, Chief Judge, and Lewis and Holloway, Circuit Judges.

Lewis, Circuit Judge. This joint petition brought by taxpayers pursuant to 26 U.S.C. §7482 seeks review of a decision of the Tax Court of the United States, 50 T.C. 220, wherein that court, with five judges dissenting, determined that certain income received by petitioning taxpayers during the years 1962, 1963, and 1964 should be taxed as ordinary dividend income pursuant to 26 U.S.C. §§301 and 316, rather than as capital gains within the purview of 26 U.S.C. §1232. A deficiency in the sum of $21,058.24 was assessed against petitioners Edwards and the sum of $19,821.00 against petitioners Disler. The evidentiary background facts of the transaction premising the controversy are detailed in the opinions of the Tax Court, but the determinative issue on review may be brought into focus by summary.

In 1958, Edwards and Disler organized the Disler Engineering Corporation (Disler) for the purpose of manufacturing and selling heat exchangers. Disler operated on leased land in Sand Springs, Oklahoma, and prospered greatly. Gross sales increased from $72,000 in 1958 to $1,266,212.85 in 1962. Since the location of Disler was inadequate to allow expansion, the company in 1961 began looking for a new location.

Another company, Birmingham Steel & Supply, Inc. (Birmingham) was also located on leased land in Sand Springs. This company was wholly owned by Ovid Birmingham and was engaged in the fabrication of structural steel including parts for heat exchangers. Birmingham Steel was not then prospering and had incurred substantial losses in 1959, 1960, and 1961, although in prior years the company had enjoyed continued success. At the invitation of one Stainer, attorney for and secretary of Birmingham, Disler was invited to inspect the Birmingham property as a prospective purchaser.

On June 12, 1962, Edwards and Disler did inspect the Birmingham property and upon Stainer's inquiry as to what the "whole place" was worth Edwards replied that he would appraise it at $75,000. At that time Edwards knew nothing of the financial condition of Birmingham. Two days later Stainer advised Edwards that the "offer" was accepted. Edwards responded that his appraisal of the physical facilities was not intended as an offer but that he would consider making a firm offer after he was given an opportunity to examine the Birmingham corporate records including the balance sheet. Thereafter, Birmingham furnished the following abbreviated financial statement:

ESTIMATED CONDITION OF BIRMINGHAM STEEL & SUPPLY, INC.
SUBJECT TO AUDIT

LIABILITIES:	
Vouchers Payable	$65,526.00
Accrued Payroll	6,712.44
Accrued Withholding & Social Security T4	2,661.17
Chattel Mortgage on Machinery & Equipment	581.99
Notes Payable — National Bank of Tulsa — secured by accounts receivable	20,417.58
TOTAL LIABILITIES	$95,899.18
ASSETS:	
Current Assets:	
Cash	$ 3,923.93
Accounts Receivable Less Reserve for Bad Debts	37,727.75
Inventory	110,000.00
TOTAL CURRENT ASSETS	$151,651.68
Fixed Assets:	
Machinery, equipment, Tools, Furniture, Fixtures, etc. — Book Value Dec. 31, 1961	93,041.30
TOTAL ASSETS	$244,692.98

After considering this financial statement, taxpayers concluded that they would be willing to pay $75,000 for all the Birmingham stock and letters of intent were prepared stating:

> This letter will confirm our offer to purchase from you all of the outstanding stock issued by Birmingham Steel & Supply, Inc., an Oklahoma corporation, for the purchase price of $75,000.00, and this letter may be used as a letter of intent for said purchase. It is understood and agreed, however, that this purchase is subject to the approximate correctness of an estimated financial statement of said Corporation which was issued by you, said statement listing total liabilities in the approximate amount of $95,899.18, total current assets in the approximate amount of $151,651.68, and total fixed assets in the approximate amount of $93,041.30, and further realizing there might be a slight difference, either plus or minus, to said accounts.

After preparation of the letter of intent but before execution, a Disler accountant discovered that the Birmingham financial statement did not reflect six outstanding promissory notes payable to Ovid Birmingham in the total amount of $241,904.82. The letters of intent were then amended by adding a handwritten final sentence providing for the assignment of the notes to taxpayers and, as amended, were executed. Thereafter a formal contract of purchase was executed by the parties wherein the purchase price of $75,000 was allocated, $5,000 to the stock of Birmingham Steel and $70,000 to the Ovid Birmingham notes. The contract was prepared by Stainer, the Birmingham attorney.[2]

After taking over Birmingham, taxpayers continued to operate that company as a separate entity and without any addition to capital soon turned what had been an

[2]Pertinent parts of the contract provided:

WHEREAS, Seller is the owner of all of the outstanding shares of stock issued by Birmingham Steel & Supply, Inc., an Oklahoma corporation, and Promissory Notes executed by Birmingham Steel & Supply, Inc. to Seller, and whereas, Seller desires to sell said shares of stock in said Corporation and said Promissory Notes executed by said Corporation to the Seller, and whereas Purchaser desires to purchase said shares of stock and said Promissory Notes.

NOW, therefore, in consideration of the covenants and agreements hereinafter set forth, it is mutually agreed between the parties thereto as follows:

1. Seller agrees to sell to Purchaser all of the outstanding shares of stock issued by Birmingham Steel & Supply, Inc., an Oklahoma corporation, the same being four thousand one hundred two (4,102) shares of common stock, said shares being issued by Certificates Number One (1) through Twenty-four (24) inclusive, and all of the Promissory Notes executed by Birmingham Steel & Supply, Inc. to Seller, said Notes to be indorsed without recourse; that the consideration to be received by the Seller from the Purchaser for said shares of stock and said Promissory Notes shall be as follows: Five Thousand Dollars ($5,000.00) for all of the shares of stock issued by Birmingham Steel & Supply, Inc., and Seventy Thousand Dollars ($70,000.00) for all of the Promissory Notes executed by Birmingham Steel & Supply, Inc., to Seller, said Notes to be indorsed without recourse; that the consideration shall be paid by the Purchaser to the Seller as follows: . . .

2. Purchaser agrees to pay Seller the amount of Five Thousand Dollars ($5,000.00) for the outstanding shares of stock issued by Birmingham Steel & Supply, Inc., and Seventy Thousand Dollars ($70,000.00) for all of the Promissory Notes executed by Birmingham Steel & Supply, Inc., to Seller, said Notes to be indorsed over to Purchaser by Seller without recourse . . . .

unprofitable enterprise back into a money-making venture. Beginning in 1962, earnings from Birmingham were paid to taxpayers to be applied on the notes. Edwards and Disler each received $10,952.41 in 1962; $50,000 in 1963; $15,000 in 1964; and by 1966 the notes were paid in full. For tax purposes, taxpayers treated such payments as first a return of capital and thereafter as long-term capital gains. The Commissioner classified the payments as the equivalent of dividends taxable as ordinary income and this controversy was thus born.

The initial issue that was presented to the Tax Court was whether the subject notes when held by Ovid Birmingham constituted a valid corporate indebtedness of the Birmingham company to him. The Tax Court determined that the notes did constitute a valid and bona fide corporate debt, and that determination is not now disputed by the Commissioner. The Tax Court further determined that the "promissory notes in issue constituted valid indebtedness of Birmingham Steel in the hands of Ovid Birmingham but did not retain such character when purchased by petitioners." Although this determination is labeled as an "ultimate finding of fact," it obviously is a result reached by legal reasoning springing from evidentiary facts and the inferences to be drawn therefrom. As in Commissioner v. Duberstein, 363 U.S. 278, [289] . . . where the determinative issue involved gift or income, "primary weight in this area must be given to the conclusions of the trier of fact. . . ." This we do and also accept the basic facts from which the legal reasoning of the majority opinion of the Tax Court springs to the conclusion that the subject notes, for tax purposes, immediately changed nature when acquired by taxpayers from a genuine corporate indebtedness to a contribution to capital. The heart of the majority opinion is premised on the continuing consideration of $75,000 present throughout the negotiations and the initial and continuing desire of taxpayers to obtain the physical assets of Birmingham. All other circumstances of the transaction are set aside as pure form and it is said to "hold otherwise would be to exalt form over substance." We disagree and believe the decision of the Tax Court clearly exalts a legal fiction over both the form and substance of the parties' transaction.

It is of course true that the contractual form of a transaction cannot control the imposition of tax liability when the realities of the transaction show that form does not represent a bona fide and actual agreement. But it is equally true that the form of a contract is the considered and chosen method of expressing the substance of contractual agreements between parties and the dignity of contractual right cannot be judicially set aside simply because a tax benefit results either by design or accident. Form, absent exceptional circumstances, reflects substance. We do not find present in this case any of the traditional exceptional circumstances that justify the piercing of form to impose an exceptional tax liability. This is not a "thin capitalization" case as in Jewell Ridge Coal Corp. v. Commissioner, 4 Cir., 318 F.2d 695. After acquisition, Birmingham was operated on its original capital and the sufficiency of that capital, aided by competent management, restored to the profit column what had once been a successful company.[4] Nor is this a case such as Covey Investment Co. v. United

---

[4]The distinction between *Jewell* and the case at bar is distinguished both factually and legally in the dissenting opinion of Judge Featherston. See 50 T.C. 220 at 232-233. We agree with his analysis.

States, 10 Cir., 377 F.2d 403, where long overdue notes were never treated as recognizable indebtedness. In the instant case, repayment followed the corporate ability to repay. Neither the fact that the combined contract value attributed to the stock and notes equaled the original value assigned by taxpayers to the stock alone, nor the fact that the principal purpose of the contract, as far as taxpayers were concerned was to procure needed physical assets supports the court's inference that irrespective of the contract provisions to the contrary, the notes had no independent significance.[5] The significance of the notes to taxpayers is borne out by the court's ruling that the notes in the hands of Ovid Birmingham constituted a valid outstanding corporate indebtedness. Had Mr. Birmingham retained the notes for himself or assigned them to some third person, he or that third person could have "forced" the corporation to honor the indebtedness to the personal monetary detriment of taxpayers as controlling shareholders of the Disler Company. Certain it is that the value of the stock to taxpayers was materially affected by the discovery of this large outstanding debt and that they were entitled to take this debt into account when contracting for the purchase of the corporate stock.[6] This is exactly what they did when, after learning of the existence of the notes, they procured an agreement to assign the notes and when they signed the contract which allocated the purchase price between the stock and the notes. The fact that in this admitted arms-length transaction the combined purchase price of the notes and stock, either by chance or by design, happens to be identical to that originally offered for the corporate facilities, and later for the stock of the corporation, in no way negates the importance of the notes in the hands of taxpayers. Rather it is safe to assume that if a satisfactory arrangement respecting the notes had not been worked out, taxpayers would have rescinded, and justifiably so, their offer to buy the stock. The notes representing a corporate indebtedness of over $241,000 constituted a liability that taxpayers could ill afford to ignore and the assignment of the notes, as opposed to their cancellation, was the means chosen by the contracting parties to deal with said factor. Both buyer Edwards and seller Ovid Birmingham testified that the negotiations centered around the assignment of the notes and that there was never any discussion about the cancellation thereof.

When applicable statutory laws do not prevent a shareholder of a given corporation from also becoming a creditor of that corporation and where the transaction creating the debtor-creditor relationship is not a sham or subterfuge, the terms of

[5]Although rejecting the majority view that the notes constituted a contribution to capital, Judge Withey concurred in the result in the Tax Court on the theory that no investment consideration was paid by taxpayers for the notes. See id. at 230. We think this approach is also negatived by the total circumstances of the transaction.

[6]Even though the purchase of the stock did enable taxpayers to achieve their principal objective in obtaining assets admittedly needed for expansion of their controlled corporation, the transaction cannot be classified as a mere purchase of corporate assets. The fact that upon obtaining the corporate stock taxpayers did not liquidate the corporation in order to reach the corporate assets, but rather kept it alive as a separate and distinct corporation, clearly distinguishes the subject case from Kimbell-Diamond Milling Co. v. Commissioner, 5 Cir., 187 F.2d 718, cert. denied, 342 U.S. 827, 72 S. Ct. 50, 96 L. Ed. 626, and cases related to it. In this regard, it is important to note that Ovid Birmingham testified he would have been willing to sell the assets independent of the company's stock, which shows that if taxpayers' interest, as finalized, was in fact limited to the corporate assets, they could have accomplished this purpose without also purchasing the stock.

the transaction must be honored by the court. J. S. Biritz Const. Co. v. Commissioner, 8 Cir., 387 F.2d 451; Nassau Lens Co. v. Commissioner, 2 Cir., 308 F.2d 39. There is no evidence of a sham or subterfuge in the subject case. Rather taxpayers as the dissent below states "merely took the capital financial structure as they found it"; and the fact that the nature of the transaction enables appellants to take advantage of the favorable provision of §1232 is not by itself sufficient cause to disregard the form of the transaction. *Nassau Lens,* supra. The totality of the circumstances leading to the execution of the subject contract allows no different inferences to be drawn as to the substance of the transaction than if the parties had arrived at their final agreement in the orthodox method of offer and acceptance after full disclosure and knowledge of the financial structure of Birmingham. Had the latter procedure occurred, we can conceive of no reason to permissibly infer that form did not reflect substance. Taxpayers not only took the financial structure of Birmingham as they found it but they proceeded to operate it as they found it, albeit more competently, and paid its debt as they found them.

The petition to review is granted and the decision of the Tax Court is reversed.

HOLLOWAY, Circuit Judge (dissenting): I respectfully dissent. To me the decision of the Tax Court is based, as it states, on an ultimate finding of fact. The finding was that although the notes constituted valid outstanding indebtedness in the hands of Mr. Birmingham, they ". . . did not retain such character when purchased by petitioners." 50 T.C. at 226. The question whether the transaction resulted in the notes' representing equity investment or corporate debt is one ". . . leading to findings of ultimate fact." . . .

The majority opinion and that of the Tax Court state the facts in detail. The Tax Court found that the notes constituted bona fide debt in the hands of Mr. Birmingham. However, the petitioners set out to invest $75,000 to obtain the property. This was attempted by an offer in that amount for the stock alone after some examination of the books. As first drawn the letter of intent showed that the petitioners did not then contemplate obtaining assignment of the notes, whose existence was unknown. And the entire purchase price — which remained the same in the final agreement — was only a portion of the face amount of the notes. While the majority opinion here persuasively points to facts supporting its view, the ultimate finding of fact by the Tax Court on the entire record was not clearly erroneous. To me the case is one that does turn on a fact question and one where we cannot say that the Tax Court finding was clearly erroneous. In such circumstances the finding is binding. 26 U.S.C.A. §7482(a); Commissioner v. Duberstein, 363 U.S. 278, . . . (1960). For these reasons I would not disturb the decision of the Tax Court.

NOTE

The Tenth Circuit rejected the lower court's view that debt in the hands of the original creditor-shareholder might become equity in the hands of a transferee. Is such a view untenable? Is such a view necessarily inconsistent with the refusal of the Third Circuit in *Fin Hay Realty,* page 77 supra, to find a conversion from equity to debt when Finlaw died?

b. DIVIDEND vs. BUSINESS EXPENSE

A closely held corporation may incur an expense which it seeks to deduct under §162 but which the Commissioner will disallow because it benefits the shareholders personally and is not meaningful in terms of the corporation's conduct of its business or income producing activities. Such expenses are frequently called "constructive" or "disguised" dividends. (Disallowance of the deduction is often accompanied by the taxation of the payment to the shareholders as a dividend. See page 152 infra.) See, e.g., American Properties, Inc. v. Commissioner, 262 F.2d 150 (9th Cir. 1958), in which the court sustained the disallowance of a corporate payment for the construction and upkeep of a boat which bore a direct relationship to the shareholder's hobby but none to the corporation's business. On what grounds would you expect a corporation to claim the right to a §162 deduction of the payments made to cover the expenses of the wedding of the majority shareholder's daughter? See Haverhill Shoe Novelty Co., 15 T.C. 517 (1950); cf. Warren Brekke, 40 T.C. 789 (1963) (corporate payments not actually for the use of property despite the tag of "rent"). But see Sanitary Farm's Dairy, Inc., 25 T.C. 463 (1955) (acq.) (costs of an African safari allowed). The latter case was part of the Treasury's weaponry in its battle to secure the 1962 amendments which comprise §274.

What of a corporate payment that is of little significance to the corporation's business activity, but benefits only some, but not all, of its shareholders? Can it be disallowed? Can it be characterized as a dividend? Cf. Paramount-Richards Theatres, Inc. v. Commissioner, 153 F.2d 602 (5th Cir. 1946). Compare the situation involving an alleged interest payment where the "debt" is not held by an avowed shareholder (page 89 supra).

As to alleged "salary" that may be disallowed as a dividend, see Treas. Reg. §1.162-7(b)(1); S. Brodsky, What Is Reasonable Compensation? 14 Tul. Inst. on Fed. Tax. 389 (1965). As to accrued salary owing to a cash basis employee-shareholder owning more than 50 per cent in value of the corporation's stock, see §§267(a)(1) and (b)(2).

c. DIVIDEND vs. PURCHASE

Corporation M purchased a yacht and a seashore residence. The yacht is used half the time to entertain corporate customers and half the time for the pleasure of the sole shareholder and his family. The seashore residence is used exclusively for the pleasure of the shareholder and his family. What are the tax consequences to Corporation M of the purchases it has made? What are the tax consequences to the shareholder? See page 152 infra.

d. RETIREMENT OF SHARES vs. BUSINESS EXPENSE

FIVE STAR MFG. CO. v. COMMISSIONER
355 F.2d 724 (5th Cir. 1966)

Before JONES and WISDOM, Circuit Judges, and BREWSTER, District Judge.

WARREN L. JONES, Circuit Judge: . . . In 1949, Andrew L. Freeman of Grand Forks, North Dakota, procured a patent on an automobile heater known as the Freeman Headbolt Heater. In 1950 Freeman, by a patent license agreement, gave to W. S. Kincade and H. E. Smith, Jr., the exclusive right to manufacture, use and sell the patented heater within the United States, its territories and dependencies, for the term of the patent and any renewal thereof, for a consideration of $80,000, plus royalties of five percent of the price of heaters sold with a minimum royalty of $10,000 per year. Kincade and Smith transferred to the petitioner, Five Star Manufacturing Company, an exclusive ten year license to manufacture the heater for a consideration of $80,000, payment to Kincade and Smith of ten percent of the selling price of all heaters in excess of $200,000 per year, and the discharge of the obligations under the Freeman agreement including the royalty payments to him. Kincade and Smith were equal owners of the stock of Five Star, and they and their wives were its directors.

During 1950 Five Star commenced manufacturing the Freeman heater. From the beginning of the operation until April 20, 1952, royalties were regularly paid to Freeman. After that date and during all times here pertinent, no royalties were paid to Freeman. Smith drew heavily from Five Star's treasury, and by early 1954, his withdrawals for salary, expenses and money borrowed amounted to over $350,000. At that time Five Star held Smith's promissory notes in the amount of $88,000. In April of 1954, Freeman brought suit against Smith, Kincade and Five Star for unpaid royalties and attached most of Five Star's assets. The court gave Freeman a judgment and cancelled the patent licensing agreement which Freeman had given to Kincade and Smith and which they had leased or assigned to Five Star. Kincade paid a part of the judgment and gave Freeman satisfactory assurances that the balance would be paid. Freeman made a new agreement with Kincade which provided for a licensing of the patent on substantially the same terms as the prior arrangement. Freeman was unwilling to enter into any arrangement in which Smith was a participant as a stockholder of a corporation or otherwise.

Five Star made an unsuccessful demand on Smith for the payment of his indebtedness. He countered by a suit seeking, among other things, a receivership for Five Star. Cross-complaints and counterclaims were filed. A judgment was entered on May 5, 1954 for Five Star against Smith for the net amount of $56,715.43. Kincade was given a judgment against Five Star for $296,723.21. Salary claims of Smith and Kincade against Five Star were not adjudicated. The court refused to put Five Star in receivership and for its reason commented in these terms:

"If there were any creditors or innocent stockholders of this corporation,

I would unhesitatingly put it in receivership, with orders to the receiver to proceed, in so far as possible, to make the directors disgorge for their benefits. I find no one, however, in that category. The only creditor of any consequence [Kincade] is not here complaining and seems to be well on the way toward protecting himself in litigation now pending. . . .

"The court finds that, if there is to be salvation for The Five Star Manufacturing Company, it will have to come from the use of Mr. Kincade's personal credit, his know-how in this business and his energy and business ability, and that to hamper this use by the appointment of a receiver would be absolutely fatal to the future of the corporation and could mean only liquidation, disastrous to all concerned, and, therefore, the prayer for a receivership is denied."

Smith's stock was put up for sale and the only bid was $40,000 offered by Five Star. Smith opposed confirmation of the sale on the ground of inadequacy of price and guaranteed a bid of $48,000 for the stock. A resale was ordered, and upon the second offering the only bid was of $56,000 made by Five Star. The bid was accepted, the sale was confirmed. Smith v. Kincade, 5th Cir. 1956, 232 F.2d 306. The acquisition of the stock was set up on the books of Five Star at $56,000 and that amount was credited against Smith. Efforts to collect further sums from Smith were unsuccessful. He had no assets from which payment of any of the remainder of the obligation could be realized.

Five Star attempted to borrow money from its bank and the bank refused to make the loan. To provide it with funds Kincade borrowed money and advanced them to Five Star. During the year ending June 30, 1953, Five Star reported net income for income tax purposes of $24,714.72, and for the year ending June 30, 1954, its return showed a net loss of $168,167.51. . . .

At the time of the judicial sale of the Smith stock, two-thirds of the Finished Goods Inventory was under the attachment made at the behest of Freeman. The license to manufacture and sell under the Freeman patent had been cancelled. Five Star had neither the right to sell nor goods which could have been sold. It had no working capital and no credit. It had obligations which could not have been paid from the assets upon a liquidation which would have been inevitable if Smith had not been removed from the scene. As intimated by the district court, the future of the company, at the time of the sale, depended upon Kincade, his credit, his know-how, energy and business ability. It also depended upon Freeman's willingness to allow Five Star to continue in business under Kincade's management and backing but only if Smith was out of the picture. Had Smith remained as the owner of fifty percent of the stock of Five Star, its liquidation was inevitable, and in the event of its liquidation there could have been no realization for stockholders. With the removal of Smith, with the management and credit of Kincade, and with the cooperation of Freeman, there was a chance for survival.

To be deductible as a business expense, the payment must be both ordinary and necessary. It seems unquestionable that the payment to Smith to terminate his interest in Five Star was a necessary expense. Whether it was an ordinary expense depends upon the nature of the transaction. Even though it may arise in a situation unlikely to ever recur, an expense will be regarded as ordinary if it is of a kind that would be common or frequent in the type of business involved. Deputy v. duPont, 308 U.S. 488, 60 S. Ct. 363, 84 L. Ed. 416; Welch v. Helvering, 290 U.S. 111, 54 S. Ct. 8, 78 L. Ed. 212; Campbell v. Fields, 5th Cir. 1956, 229 F.2d 197. It can scarcely be held that the payment to Smith was for the acquisition of a capital asset, but rather one which would permit Five Star again to use assets for income production by freeing its management from unwarranted fetters. Allen v. Selig, 5th Cir. 1952, 200 F.2d 487; Campbell v. Fields, supra; Helvering v. Community Bond & Mortgage Corporation, 2d Cir. 1935, 74 F.2d 727. Illustrative of the principle is Hogg v. Allen, M.D. Ga. 1952, 105 F. Supp. 12, aff. sub. nom. Edwards v. Hogg, 5th Cir. 1954, 214 F.2d 640, where it was held that the loss from the sale of shares of stock purchased by a partnership in a wholesale whiskey business for the purpose of acquiring whiskey procurement rights attached to the stock was deductible as an ordinary and necessary business expense. In a similar situation the Tax Court has held that the loss resulting from the purchase of debentures of a supplier made to insure preferential treatment was a deductible expense. Tulane Hardwood Lumber Co. v. Commissioner, 24 T.C. 1146.

Concluding, as we do, that the payment for the Smith stock was deductible as an ordinary and necessary business expense, we find it unnecessary to decide the question as to the value of the stock.

The decision of the Tax Court is reversed and the cause is remanded for further proceedings.

Reversed and remanded.

NOTE

1. Corporation M had operating income of $100,000 in 1966. Just before the end of that year, the state in which it did business enacted a tax on corporations doing business within the state in 1967, the tax to be measured by 1966 income. To avoid the imposition, on December 31, 1966, Corporation M distributed all its assets to its shareholders in complete liquidation of the corporation, and thereafter the business was conducted by the former shareholders as partners. The assets, net of liabilities, were worth one million dollars. Was the net worth of Corporation M's assets deductible against its 1966 operating income under §162, and was the excess available as a net operating loss carryback under §172? Why? What would the Fifth Circuit be likely to hold and say in such a case? Cf. Coca-Cola Co. v. Commissioner, 369 F.2d 913 (8th Cir. 1966). How would the Fifth Circuit decide that case? Why?

2. How would you have decided *Five Star Mfg. Co.?* Why? Do you expect the Commissioner and courts other than the Fifth Circuit to follow the decision in that case? Why?

3. What is the function of §162 in the context of the corporate income tax?

What should be the corporate tax significance of a payment made for good business reasons in retirement of some or all of the paying corporation's outstanding stock? Why?

e. INCORPORATION EXPENSE

Prior to the enactment of §248 in 1954, a corporation's organizational expenses (e.g., lawyers' fees, fees to the State upon filing of Articles of Incorporation, etc.) were not deductible under §162 because they were regarded as capital expenditures. If the corporation did not have a limited life, the intangible assets the expenditures produced were treated as having an indefinite life, and so no amortization was permitted under §167. Ultimately, on complete liquidation of the corporation, a loss might be allowed under §165(a).

Section 248 authorizes corporations to elect ratable amortization of their organizational expenses over any period selected as long as it is not less than 60 months. When and how is an election made? When must the period for amortization begin? See §248; Treas. Reg. §1.248-1.

Should organizational expenses be deductible in full when incurred or paid? Should they not be deductible at all? Not until liquidation? Is the approach of §248 sensible? Why?

See J. Pinhorn, Organizational Expenses: Helping the Corporation to Increase Its Deduction, 3 Taxation for Accountants 170 (July-Aug. 1968).

2. *Distributions of Stock*

a. TO PAY AN EXPENSE

Compensation — *§§162, 421.* Corporation M pays a reasonable bonus to one of its salesmen by issuing to him Corporation M common stock having a fair market value of $5000. What are the tax consequences to Corporation M? What is the authority for your conclusion? Would the result be different if the salesman were also the sole shareholder? Why?

REVENUE RULING 62-217
1962-2 Cum. Bull. 59

A corporation distributed shares of its treasury stock to its employees as compensation for services rendered. The cost basis of the treasury stock to the corporation was less than its fair market value on the date of the distribution to the employees. In filing its Federal income tax return for the taxable year, the corporation deducted the fair market value of the stock on the date of the distribution as a business expense.

In accordance with the nonrecognition of gain or loss provisions of section 1032(a) of the Internal Revenue Code of 1954 and section 1.1032-1(a) of the Income Tax Regulations, relating to the receipt by a corporation of money or other property in exchange for its own stock (including a transfer of shares as compensation for services), the corporation did not report gain upon the distribution of treasury stock.

Held, the fair market value of the treasury stock on the date of the distribution is deductible as a business expense in accordance with the provisions of section 162(a) of the Code. The nonrecognition of gain or loss provisions of section 1032(a) of the Code have no effect upon a business expense deduction that is otherwise allowable under section 162(a) of the Code.

NOTE

Is Rev. Rul. 62-217 correct in its holding as to the business expense deduction? Why? Consider the §1032 aspect of the ruling in connection with the materials on pages 73-75 supra.

Corporation X grants its executives options to buy from it Corporation X common stock at $10 per share. At the time of the grant the stock is worth $10 a share. Two years later, when one of the executives exercises the option, the stock is worth $15 per share. What is the tax consequence to Corporation X? Why? See §421(a)(2) and the Regulations thereunder. If you require more facts to answer these questions, what are they?

Salary due to sole shareholder-employees is deducted in the year accrued by an accrual basis corporation and is paid in a subsequent year by issuance of the corporation's stock. Assume that §267 is inapplicable. What is the tax consequence to the corporation when the stock is issued? Why? See *Fender Sales*, page 446 infra.

§§*162, 163*. Corporation N, a manufacturing company, orders raw materials from its supplier and is billed in the amount of $10,000. Wishing to conserve cash, Corporation N offers to satisfy the bill by issuing shares of its common stock fairly valued at $11,000, although the shares are not readily marketable because of a thin market. The supplier accepts the stock. What are the tax consequences to Corporation N? Why?

Under your conception of an ideal corporate income tax, in what circumstances should a corporation be entitled to a §162 deduction upon the issuance of its own shares? Why?

b. TO BUY AN ASSET — §§1032, 1012, 362, 334

Corporation A uses Treasury shares worth $50,000 (acquired a year earlier for $40,000) to purchase needed machinery. What are the tax consequences to Corporation A at the time of purchase? Why? What is Corporation A's basis in the machinery? Why?

If Corporation A purchased stock in Corporation Z, paying for it with its own common stock, there would be no immediate tax consequence to Corporation A. Section 1032. The basis of the Z stock acquired (or the assets acquired from Corporation X after its liquidation into Corporation A) would depend in part on whether the acquisition was a "reorganization" as defined in §368(a). See Chapter 4 infra.

c. TO ACQUIRE CASH — §§162, 1032

Newly issued stock distributed in exchange for cash equal to the stock's value gives rise to no corporate deduction. What is the result if a valued employee is permitted to buy stock worth $10,000 for $8000? Why? Compare page 101 supra. If the corporation had used Treasury stock which had cost it $8000 would the result be different? Why? See pages 73-75 supra.

d. TO PAY A DIVIDEND

Corporation M pays its common shareholders dividends consisting of ten shares of newly issued Corporation M common stock for each share of stock held. What are the tax consequences to Corporation M? Why? As to the consequences to the shareholders see Chapter 4, pages 403-460 infra.

III. THE INCIDENCE OF THE CORPORATION INCOME TAX

J. PECHMAN, FEDERAL TAX POLICY*
111-116 (rev. ed. 1971)

There is no more controversial issue in taxation than the question: *Who bears the corporation income tax?* On this question, economists and businessmen alike differ among themselves. The following quotations are representative of these divergent views:

> "The initial or short-run incidence of the corporate income tax seems to be largely on corporations and their stockholders. . . . There seems to be little foundation for the belief that a large part of the corporate tax comes out of wages or is passed on to consumers in the same way that a selective excise [tax] tends to be shifted to buyers." (Richard Goode, The Corporation Income Tax, John Wiley, 1951, pp. 71-72.)

> ". . . the corporation profits tax is almost entirely shifted; the government simply uses the corporation as a tax collector." (Kenneth E. Boulding, The Organizational Revolution, Harper and Brothers, 1953, p. 277.)

> "Corporate taxes are simply costs, and the method of their assessment does not change this fact. Costs must be paid by the public in prices, and corporate taxes are thus, in effect, concealed sales taxes." (Enders M. Voorhees,

*Published by the Brookings Institution. Reprinted by permission. First edition reviewed, B. Wolfman, 76 Yale L.J. 1036 (1967). — ED.

chairman of Finance Committee, U.S. Steel Corporation, address before the Controllers' Institute of America, New York, Sept. 21, 1943.)

"The observation is frequently made that because in the long run the [corporate] tax tends to be included in the price of the product, it is to this extent borne by consumers. This observation misconstrues the nature of the tax. Fundamentally, it is a tax on a factor of production: corporate equity capital." (Arnold C. Harberger, "The Corporation Income Tax: An Empirical Appraisal," Tax Revision Compendium, House Ways and Means Committee, Vol. 1, 1959, p. 241.)

". . . an increase in the [corporate] tax is shifted fully through short-run adjustments to prevent a decline in the net rate of return [on corporate investment], and . . . these adjustments are maintained subsequently." (Marian Krzyzaniak and Richard A. Musgrave, The Shifting of the Corporation Income Tax, Johns Hopkins Press, 1963, p. 65.)

Unfortunately, economics has not yet provided a scientific basis for accepting or rejecting one side or the other. This section presents the logic of each view and summarizes the evidence.

The Shifting Mechanism

One reason for the sharply divergent views is that the opponents frequently do not refer to the same type of shifting. It is important to distinguish between short- and long-run shifting and the mechanisms through which they operate. The "short run" is defined by economists as a period that is too short for firms to adjust their capital to changing demand and supply conditions. The "long run" is a period in which capital can be adjusted.

Short Run. The classical view in economics is that the corporation income tax cannot be shifted in the short run. The argument is as follows: all business firms, whether they are competitive or monopolistic, seek to maximize net profits. This maximum occurs when output and prices are set at the point where the cost of producing an additional unit is exactly equal to the additional revenue obtained from the sale of that unit. In the short run, a corporation income tax should make no difference in this decision. The output and price that maximized the firm's profits before the tax will continue to maximize profits after the tax is imposed. (This follows from simple arithmetic. If a series of figures is reduced by the same percentage, the figure that was highest before will still be the highest after the percentage reduction is made.)

The argument against this view is that today's markets are characterized neither by perfect competition nor by monopoly; instead, they show considerable imperfection and mutual interdependence or oligopoly. In such markets, business firms may set their prices at the level that covers their full costs *plus* a margin for profits. Alternatively, the firms are described as aiming at an after-tax target rate of return on invested capital. Under the cost-plus behavior, the firm treats the tax as an element of cost and raises its price to recover the tax. Similarly, if the firm's objective is the after-tax target rate of return, imposition of a tax or an increase in the tax rate — by reducing the rate of return on invested capital — will have to be accounted for in making output and price decisions. To preserve the target rate of return, the tax must be shifted forward to consumers or backward to the workers, or be shifted partly forward and partly backward.

It is also argued that the economists' models are irrelevant in most markets where one or a few large firms exercise a substantial degree of leadership. In such markets, efficient producers raise their prices to recover the tax, and the tax merely forms an "umbrella" that permits less efficient or marginal producers to survive.

When business managers are asked about their pricing policies, they often say that they shift the corporation income tax. However, there is little evidence to support this position. Economists have debated whether firms actually behave in this way, but they have not reached a consensus.

Even if this behavior on the part of business firms is accepted, some doubts must be expressed about their ability to shift fully the corporation income tax in the short run. In the first place, the tax depends on the outcome of business operations during an entire year. The businessman can only guess the ratio of the tax to his gross receipts, and it is hard to conceive of his setting a price that would recover the precise amount of tax he will eventually pay. (If shifting were possible, there would be some instances of firms shifting more than 100 percent of the tax, but few economists believe that overshifting does in fact occur.)

Second, the businessman knows that if he should attempt to recover the corporation income tax through higher prices (or lower wages), other firms would not necessarily do the same. Some firms make no profit and thus pay no tax; among other firms, the ratio of tax to gross receipts differs. In multiproduct firms, the producer has very little basis for judging the ratio of tax to gross receipts for each product. All these possibilities increase the uncertainty of response by other firms and make the attempt to shift part or all of the corporation income tax hazardous.

Long Run. Unless it is shifted in the short run to consumers or wage earners, or both, the corporation income tax influences investment in the long run by reducing the rate of return on corporate equity. The tax may discourage the use of capital altogether or encourage investment in debt-intensive industries (for example, real estate) and unincorporated enterprises. The result is a smaller supply of corporate products, unless the reduction in equity investment is offset by an increase in borrowing.

The incidence of the corporation income tax depends on whether the tax is or is not shifted in the short run. Short-run shifting means that net after-tax rates of return are maintained at the levels prevailing before the tax; the burden of the tax falls on consumers or wage earners. If the tax is not shifted in the short run, net after-tax rates of return are depressed, and the amount of corporate investment is reduced. After-tax rates of return tend to be equalized with those in the noncorporate sector, but in the process, corporate capital and output will have been permanently reduced. Thus, in the absence of short-run shifting, the burden of the tax falls on the owners of capital.

The Evidence

The evidence on the incidence of the corporation income tax is inconclusive. The data do not permit a clear determination of the factors affecting price and wage decisions: different authors examining the same set of facts have come to diametrically opposite conclusions.

With respect to the long run, there is evidence first that unincorporated business has not grown at the expense of incorporated business. Corporations accounted for 58 percent of the national income originating in the business sector in 1929, 61 percent in 1948, and 68 percent in 1969 (Figure 5-1). Much of the increase comes from the relative decline of industries, particularly farming, in which corporations are not important; but, even in the rest of the economy, there is no indication of a shift away from the corporate form of organization. The advantages of doing business in the corporate form far outweigh whatever deterrent effects the corporation tax might have on corporate investment.

Beyond this, the data are conflicting. On the one hand, rates of return reported

FIGURE 5-1

PERCENTAGE OF BUSINESS INCOME ORIGINATING
IN THE CORPORATE SECTOR, 1929-69[a]

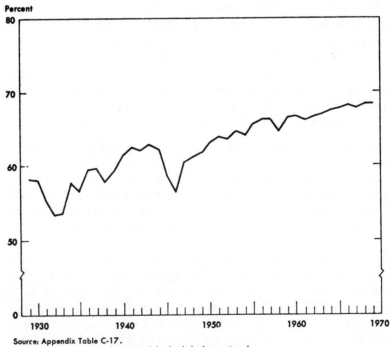

Source: Appendix Table C-17.
[a] Business income is national income originating in business enterprises.

Source: Appendix Table C-17.
[a]Business income is national income originating in business enterprises.

by corporations after tax were slightly higher in the 1950s and 1960s than in the late 1920s, when the corporation income tax was much lower. After-tax rates of return on equity capital in manufacturing were 7.8 percent in 1927-29, 8.8 percent in 1953-56, 6.9 percent in 1957-61, and 9.6 percent in 1964-67. On total capital (equity plus debt), the returns were 7.8 percent, 8.0 percent, 6.5 percent, and 8.7 percent, respectively (Table 5-1).* Before-tax rates of return were 70 to 100 percent higher in the 1960s than in the late 1920s.

On the other hand, the share of property income before tax (profits, interest, and capital consumption allowances) in corporate gross product changed little over the same period (Figure 5-2). Thus, corporations have been able to increase their before-tax profits enough to avoid a reduction in the after-tax return, without increasing their share of income in the corporate sector. These observations suggest that corporations have not increased rates of return before tax by marking up prices or by lowering wages, but by making more efficient use of their capital. However, what might have occurred in the absence of the tax is unknown, and thus its long-run effect remains unclear.

FIGURE 5-2

PROPERTY INCOME SHARE IN CORPORATE GROSS PRODUCT
LESS INDIRECT TAXES, 1922-29 AND 1948-69[a]

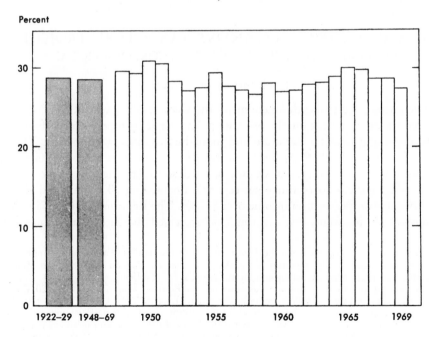

Sources: 1922-29: Worksheets of U.S. Department of Commerce, Office of Business Economics; 1948-69: Appendix Table C-17.

[a]Property income includes corporate profits before tax and inventory valuation adjustment, net interest, and corporate capital consumption allowances.

*Table 5-1 appears on page 108 infra. — ED.

TABLE 5-1

RATES OF RETURN AND DEBT-CAPITAL RATIO,

MANUFACTURING CORPORATIONS, SELECTED YEARS, 1927-67

(In percentages)

Item	1927-29	1936-39	1953-56	1957-61	1964-67
Return on equity[a]					
Before tax	8.8	7.8	18.4	14.1	17.8
After tax	7.8	6.4	8.8	6.9	9.6
Return on total capital[ab]					
Before tax	8.7	7.3	15.6	12.2	14.9
After tax	7.8	6.2	8.0	6.5	8.7
Ratio of debt to total capital[c]	15.2	15.0	19.0	20.5	25.1
General corporation tax rate[d]	12.2	17.0	52.0	52.0	48.5

Source: Appendix Tables A-3 and C-18.

[a]Equity and debt capital are averages of book values for the beginning and end of the year.

[b]Profits plus interest paid as a percentage of total capital.

[c]End of year.

[d]Statutory rate of federal corporation income tax applicable to large corporations (average of annual figures).

C. GALVIN, THE SUBSTANTIVE TAX REFORM PROJECT: PRELIMINARY FINDINGS ON THE CORPORATE TAX*

I. History of the Project

Even before the sixteenth amendment, the Corporation Excise Tax of 1909 had provided for an excise tax on all corporations measured by a percentage of income.[1] In the beginning rates on corporate and individual incomes were modest. The corporate rate under the 1909 Act was one per cent on incomes over $5,000. During subsequent years rates progressed steadily upward, so that by the time of the Revenue Act of 1951 a normal tax of thirty per cent was imposed on all income and an additional twenty-two per cent on income over $25,000. The Revenue Act of 1964 reduced the normal tax to twenty-two per cent and increased the surtax on incomes over

*This paper is abstracted from the book: Studies in Substantive Tax Reform, published in December 1968, under the sponsorship of the American Bar Foundation and Southern Methodist University. . . . [Reprinted by permission from 22 Sw. L.J. 717 (1968). — ED.]

[1]The constitutionality of this tax was sustained in Flint v. Stone Tracy Co., 220 U.S. 107 (1911). The court refused to follow Pollock v. Farmers' Loan & Trust Co., 157 U.S. 429 (1895) which had declared the income tax imposed by the Wilson Tariff Act of 1894 unconstitutional: "Within the category of indirect taxation, as we shall have further occasion to show, is embraced a tax upon business done in a corporate capacity, which is the subject-matter of the tax imposed in the act under consideration. The *Pollock Case* construed the tax there levied as direct, because it was imposed upon property simply because of its ownership. In the present case the tax is not payable unless there be a carrying on or doing of business in the designated capacity, and this is made the occasion for the tax, measured by the standard prescribed. The difference between the acts is not merely nominal, but rests upon substantial differences between the mere ownership of property and the actual doing of business in a certain way." 220 U.S. at 150.

$25,000 to twenty-six per cent. In addition to the corporate income tax, excess profits taxes were imposed during World War I, World War II, and the Korean War.

With respect to individual incomes, a normal tax of one per cent and a surtax rate of one per cent progressing to six per cent were imposed under the 1913 Act. In World War I the surtax rate progressed to sixty-five per cent at the top. Normal tax and surtax rates were reduced in the Twenties, the surtax rate at the highest bracket being twenty per cent for the years 1925 to 1931. Both normal and surtax rates were increased in the Thirties to finance the social and economic legislation of the New Deal Era and increased further in the Forties to finance World War II, with a normal tax of three per cent and a top surtax rate of ninety-one per cent.[2] Some reductions were made for the years 1946 to 1950, but higher rates were restored to finance the Korean War; rates thereafter remained substantially high until the reductions effected in 1964.

Until the Forties, individual and corporate rates were not high enough to cause any profound concern about the income tax. Following World War II, however, individuals and business organizations evinced greater concern about the tax. Although economists had been writing about different kinds of taxes for a number of years, it was not until the post-World War II period that legal scholars began to give any significant attention to the subject. Indeed, prior to World War II, only a few law schools offered a separate course in federal taxation, and the offering of multiple courses in taxation in the curricula of law schools did not emerge generally until the late Forties and early Fifties. The two disciplines, law and economics, went their separate ways. Economists wrote on the shifting and incidence of taxes, the effect of different kinds of taxes on allocation of resources, and the development of economic models in which the tax factor was significant. Legal scholars were largely concerned with technical analysis of tax rules and critiques of the tax impact on various business and investment patterns. The emphasis in economic writing was on macro-economic analysis; in legal writing the emphasis was on the application of the law to particular transactional patterns. In the Fifties the Joint Committee on the Economic Report and the House Committee on Ways and Means inaugurated multidisciplinary discussions on tax policy for the future.[3] These efforts constituted the first major broad scale consideration of tax reform.

It was against this background that the Section of Taxation of the American Bar Association undertook a major effort in substantive tax reform in 1962. A Special Committee on Substantive Tax Reform was organized to consider fundamental changes in federal tax policy. This was the first time that a group of private practi-

---

[2]Historically, there have been two income taxes: a normal tax and a surtax. The normal tax was generally a flat rate, and the surtax, a progressive rate, relatively much higher than the normal tax. In 1954 Congress combined the two into a single rate table but interest on certain obligations of the United States was exempted from normal tax. Therefore Int. Rev. Code of 1954, §1(c) provides for a calculation of the tax in these cases by eliminating the 3% normal tax.

[3]See, e.g., Hearings on General Revenue Revision Before the Comm. on Ways and Means, 85th Cong., 2d Sess. (1958); House Comm. on Ways and Means, 86th Cong., 1st Sess., Tax Revision Compendium (3 vols.) (Comm. Print 1960); House Comm. on Ways and Means, 86th Cong., 1st Sess., Panel Discussions on Income Tax Revision (Comm. Print 1960); Joint Comm. on the Economic Report, 84th Cong., 1st Sess., Federal Tax Policy for Economic Growth and Stability (Comm. Print 1956).

tioners had undertaken such a project.[4] By early 1964, the committee had delineated nineteen items for particular study and requested the Treasury Department to supply certain statistical data with respect to them.[5] The committee was aware that these items were only a beginning, but it believed that the data would provide important insights into the general problem and suggest further areas of exploration. As a trial run the committee proposed an individual income tax rate schedule of ten to forty per cent and a corporate rate of forty per cent.

After extensive work in the development of analyses on various assumptions, the committee concluded that a group of lawyers working as volunteers on a professional project could not hope to gather all the relevant data and make the necessary detailed research without a full-time staff.[6] Accordingly, appropriate recommendations were made through the Section of Taxation to the Board of Governors of the American Bar Association, and, as a result, a special committee was organized to present the project to the American Bar Foundation under the directorship of Arthur B. Willis, Esq., of the Los Angeles Bar.[7] The Foundation in early 1967 agreed to sponsor a pilot, or demonstration, project.

Dr. Benjamin Okner, formerly associate professor of economics at Ohio State University, served during the summer of 1967 as principal investigator and then accepted a position on the staff of The Brookings Institution.[8] Thereafter, the American Bar Foundation, in cooperation with Southern Methodist University, continued the project under Mr. Willis's direction with Doctors David J. and Attiat Ott of the Department of Economics of Southern Methodist University, as principal investigators. Also contributing to the project were Professor Robert A. Bernstein and this author of the School of Law of Southern Methodist University, and Messrs. Gary A. Robbins, Robert W. Tinney, and J. Scott Turner, graduate student assistants to the Doctors Ott. A comprehensive report of the project will appear in the American Bar Foundation-Southern Methodist University publication: Studies in Substantive Tax Reform. The Foundation's declination to give further support to the project is regrettable in view of the excellent working team which Mr. Willis had assembled. However, the comprehensive report may induce others to continue this most necessary research, the results of which affect the economic welfare of the entire nation.

[4]See Report of the Board of Governors, 88 ABA Rep. 468-70 (1963); Resolutions on Substantive Tax Reform, 16 ABA Tax Section Ann. Rep. 4-5 (1963). See also Galvin, Tax Reform — What? Again?, 17 Sw. L.J. 203 (1963).

[5]Report of the Special Comm. on Substantive Tax Reform, 17 ABA Tax Section Ann. Rep. 277, 282 (1964).

[6]The Committee emphasized that it took no position with respect to any area of inquiry. Nevertheless, various groups objected strenuously to the work of the Committee. See Galvin, More on Boris Bittker and the Comprehensive Tax Base: The Practicalities of Tax Reform and the ABA's CSTR, 81 Harv. L. Rev. 1016 (1968); Galvin, Progress in Substantive Tax Reform; Work of the American Bar Association; Treasury Studies; What Tax Practitioners Can Do, U. So. Cal. 1965 Tax Inst. 1; Willis, A New Approach to Substantive Tax Reform: A Lawyer's Views, U. So. Cal. 1968 Tax Inst. 845; Report of the Special Committee on Substantive Tax Reform, 21 ABA Tax. Section Ann. Rep. 734 (1968).

[7]Report of the Special Comm. on Substantive Tax Reform, 90 ABA Rep. 555 (1965).

[8]For Okner's economic and statistical analysis of proposals for changes in the income tax, see B. Okner, Income Distribution and the Federal Income Tax 77-81 (1966).

II. Summary of Principal Findings

Economists frequently allude to a concept of income consistent with what is known as the Haig-Simons definition; that is, between two points of time, income consists of net accretions to wealth, or power of consumption, plus the value of transfers of wealth and the market value of rights exercised in consumption.[9] In developing two models of a broadened tax base (BTB₁ and BTB₂) the Otts applied the Haig-Simons definition using such data as could be analyzed and programmed on the computer within the limits of time and resources available. Their major findings are summarized in Table 1.

TABLE I

SUMMARY OF EFFECTS OF BASE BROADENING ON THE TAX BASE;
A COMPARISON OF THE ALTERNATIVE TAX BASES
(BTB₁ AND BTB₂)

Item	BTB_1	BTB_2
1. Old Tax Base (billions of dollars)	230.4	230.4
2. New Tax Base (billions of dollars)	481.6	501.3
3. Change in Tax Base (billions of dollars)	251.2	270.9*
a. State and local bonds interest	1.1	1.1
b. Interest on life insurance	1.7	1.7
c. Employer's contribution to and interest on profit sharing and pension plans	7.0	7.0
d. 1. Partnership treatment of corporate profits	44.1	—
2. Dividends plus capital gains (realized and unrealized) on corporate stock	—	58.6
e. Deductions and exemptions	179.5	179.5
f. Realized capital gains as ordinary income	11.2	—
g. Old Age Insurance benefits	3.6	3.6
h. Social Security survivors' benefits	.2	.2
i. Imputed rent	—	28.7
j. Unemployment compensation	2.2	2.2
k. Sick pay	.6	.6

*The sum of items a. through k. equals $283.2 billion under BTB₂. Items e. and i. were calculated separately and, in each calculation, mortgage interest on homes ($6.4 billion) and real estate taxes on homes ($5.9 billion) were treated as nondeductible items. Therefore, the total of $12.3 billion must be eliminated from either item e. or item i. The resultant addition to base is $270.9 billion ($283.2 — 12.3 billion).

The major differences in BTB₁ and BTB₂ are that BTB₁ excludes imputed rent and attributes corporate profits to the shareholders as partnership income, whereas

[9]H. Simons, Personal Income Taxation 61-62, 206 (1938); Haig, The Concept of Income — Economic and Legal Aspects, in The Federal Income Tax 7 (R. Haig ed. 1921). The principle of the Haig-Simons definition has been adopted by the Canadian Royal Commission on Taxation. 3 Report of the Royal Comm'n on Taxation (Canada) 39 (1966).

BTB₂ includes imputed rent on owner-occupied dwellings, "grosses up" dividends as if there were no corporate tax, and includes the full amount of capital gains, realized and unrealized, on corporate stock.[10] The Otts used 1965 tax rates on 1964 revenues as obtained from the Tax File, a carefully selected group of 100,000 individual income tax returns for 1964.[11]

Table 2 reflects that a flat, or proportional, rate of 14.4 per cent on BTB₁ and

TABLE 2

COMPARISON OF THE TAX REVENUE EFFECTS
OF ALTERNATIVE BROAD TAX BASES

Item	BTB_1	BTB_2
1. Estimated Tax Revenue From Application of 1965 Tax Rates to 1964 Brookings Tax File (Before Tax Revision), plus Actual 1964 Tax Revenue From the Corporate Income Tax (billions of dollars)	69.7	69.7
2. Tax Revenue From BTB at 1965 Tax Rates (after revision) (billions of dollars)	113.3	126.4
3. Flat Tax Rate Needed to Raise Amount in 1[13]	14.4%	13.9%

13.9 per cent on BTB₂ would produce the same revenue collected in 1964 under the progressive rate structure then in effect.[12] These results become even more dramatic when one realizes that there are several major base-broadening items not taken into account in the Otts' calculations. Thus, in a major continuing project the base would be further broadened by the addition of (1) gifts, devises, and inheritances,[14] (2) gains on exchanges not recognized under present rules such as like-kind and reorganization exchanges, (3) unrealized appreciation in all property values,[15] (4) conversion of

---

[10]Assume that a taxpayer owns a share of stock in which his cost, or basis is $100, that this share of the corporate earnings before corporate taxes with respect to this stock is $200, that the corporate tax is 50%, and that the corporate dividend distribution attributable to this share is $50. Under the calculations for BTB₂, the shareholder's dividend is "grossed up" as if there were no corporate tax, that is, by an additional $50 and the increase in the share value is also added to the shareholder's income. Thus, this method has approximately the same effect as the partnership treatment because it eliminates the tax at the corporate level and taxes the shareholder on dividends received on a gross-up basis plus the change in value of his stock.

[11]Four tapes have been prepared for the years 1960, 1962, 1964, and 1966. The Otts used the 1964 tape as the 1966 tape has become available only recently. The 100,000 returns were selected out of 65 million filed. Some information which does not appear on the returns had to be gleaned from other sources and programmed with the information appearing on the tape.

[12]The 14.4% rate is the result of using the tax base of $481.6 billion of BTB₁ and dividing into the actual individual and corporate income tax revenue of $69.7 billion. The 13.9% rate is determined by dividing BTB₂ of $501.3 billion into $69.7 billion.

[13]See note 12 supra.

[14]Bittker estimates that transfers of wealth by death in 1953 amounted to $23.3 billion. Bittker, A "Comprehensive Tax Base" as a Goal of Income Tax Reform, 80 Harv. L. Rev. 925, 945 (1967).

[15]It has been estimated that the inclusion of appreciation on publicly held stock (not all stock or all assets) as ordinary income would have increased the individual income tax yield in 1965 by at least $15 to $26 billion. Slawson, Taxing as Ordinary Income the Appreciation of Publicly Held Stock, 76 Yale L.J. 623, 631-32 (1967). The Otts have calculated that in 1964 the addiction to taxable base by including unrealized appreciation would be about $35 billion. They did not break this figure out separately to obtain the effect on revenue in AGI classes.

LIFO inventories to FIFO, (5) imputed rent on taxpayer occupancy or use of properties other than dwellings, (6) unreported income,[16] and so on. Without the recognition of these items, both BTB₁ and BTB₂ tend to have a bias against service-related income. What is significant from the Otts' preliminary findings is that a rate of twelve to fourteen per cent is possible under one of the broadest possible bases. A rate so low would provide opportunities for simplification, equity, and ease of administration and thereby eliminate much of the social cost incurred under the present system.

III. Taxation of the Corporate Income Stream

The Otts proceeded on the assumption that the choice of organizational form should not be influenced by a more onerous tax burden on one form as compared with others. It is contended that those who pool their capital to operate a business should have the same after-tax effect on the business profits irrespective of whether they operate in general partnership, limited partnership, pool, syndicate, corporation, or some other form of business association. A contrary argument is that the limited-liability feature of corporate operation permits the amassing of capital to form the industrial giants of modern American business, and, therefore, this feature is properly susceptible to some surcharge.[17] The study proceeded on the assumption that if the double taxation of the corporate income stream should be eliminated, several desirable mechanisms could be used: (1) The entire corporate income could be attributed to the shareholders on a partnership basis similar to the pattern of present Subchapter S. (2) The corporate income could be subject to tax at a rate equal to, say, the highest individual income tax-rate; and as income is distributed, the shareholder would "gross up" his dividend receipt by the amount of tax paid at the corporate level on his share of corporate earnings and claim a credit for the tax thus withheld. This technique is similar to that now applied in the case of withholding on wages and salaries and foreign taxes paid at the source on corporate distributions.[18] (3) The corporation could claim a deduction for dividends paid. (4) The dividends, once

---

[16]In 1959 Surrey noted that unreported income might be as high as $26.5 billion. Surrey, The Federal Income Tax Base for Individuals, in House Committee on Ways and Means, 86th Cong., 1st Sess., 1 Tax Revision Compendium of Papers on Broadening the Tax Base 1, 11 (Comm. Print 1959).

[17]See R. Goode, The Corporation Income Tax 24-40 (1951).

[18]The gross-up-and-credit method is explained in Willis, Comments and Observations by the Project Director, in Studies in Substantive Tax Reform (1968):

"Under the full credit concept, individuals receiving dividends whose marginal tax rate was less than the corporate tax rate would receive a refund. Thus, assuming an individual whose marginal tax rate on his dividend income was 20 per cent and assuming a corporate tax rate of 48 per cent, he would receive a refund (or a credit against income tax owed on other income) of 28 per cent of his grossed-up dividend income. On $520 of actual dividend income, he would receive a refund (or its equivalent) of $280, computed as follows:

"Actual dividend income	$ 520
"Dividend income after gross-up for 48% corporate tax	$1,000
"Tax payable on $1,000 of grossed-up dividend income (marginal rate of 20%)	$ 200
"Credit for corporate tax (at 485)	$ 480
"Net tax or (refund)	$ (280)

"Thus, the low bracket taxpayer in this example really would receive $800 ($520 plus $280) of tax free income. What capital gain treatment can possibly be that good!"

taxed at the corporate level, would be excluded from the shareholder's gross income, a technique presently recognized to a limited extent in the case of the $100 dividend exclusion. Taking into account the revenue costs resulting from these methods and the argument, alluded to above, that some differential in tax cost may be justified for the corporate operation, the Otts then explored one modification — the constrained credit — a device which does not eliminate all the double tax on the corporate income stream.[19]

Table 3 is an analysis of the partnership treatment of corporate income.[20] Under

TABLE 3

PARTNERSHIP TREATMENT OF CORPORATE INCOME

(millions of dollars)

Adjusted Gross Income Class	Amount Imputed		Change in Tax Revenue from Imputation		Change in Tax Revenue after Removing Imputation from BTB
0- 600	208		50		59
600- 1500	509		81		96
1500- 3000	1,598	23%	285	12%	342
3000- 5000	2,495		533		641
5000- 7000	2,168	50%	539	33%	627
7000- 10000	3,557		1,008		1,161
10000- 15000	4,931		1,586		1,814
15000- 20000	3,917		1,503		1,708
20000- 25000	2,423		1,025		1,160
25000- 50000	7,809		4,049		4,379
50000-100000	6,193		3,847		4,025
100000-500000	5,985		4,122		4,178
500000-over	2,341		1,638		1,639
Total	44,134		20,265		21,830

the partnership treatment approximately twenty-three per cent of the imputed income occurs in brackets from $0-10,000 and these brackets account for approximately twelve

[19]The constrained credit would limit the credit allowed for the corporate tax by the taxpayer-recipient's actual tax computed at his marginal tax rate on his grossed-up dividend income. Thus, in the example given in note 10 supra, the constrained credit would be $200, computed as follows:

Actual dividend income	$ 520
Dividend income after gross-up for 48% corporate tax	$1,000
Tax payable on $1,000 of grossed-up dividend income, assuming the marginal rate to be 20%	$ 200
Credit for corporate tax, limited to tax paid on dividend	$ 200
Refund	-0-

[20]Table 3 is typical of many similar tables relating to the analysis of base broadening items. The Otts devised an ingenious method of presenting as to each base broadening item the tax revenue by AGI classes as if the particular item were the *only* item added to the base and the difference in tax revenue if *all* base broadening items were considered and the particular item was "peeled off."

per cent of the added revenue. Similarly, approximately fifty per cent of the imputed income occurs in brackets from $0-25,000 and these brackets account for approximately thirty-three per cent of the added revenue. These figures belie the contention that the partnership treatment would soak the rich.

Professor Bernstein in his comments on the Otts' findings has considered the partnership treatment as "probably unworkable, and possibly unconstitutional, as applied to large publicly-held corporations."[21] The administrative problems are formidable. The stockholder of a large corporation would have to account for his aliquot share of corporate income, and unless the corporation distributed sufficient cash, he would have the problem of seeking funds from other sources to meet the tax liability. Other problems would include the determination of the date the share of earnings would be allocated, the burden of record-keeping imposed on the stockholder, the handling of adjustments to corporate income of prior years, the calculation of the allocable share of income in cases in which there are several classes of stock with varying rights in corporate earnings, and the treatment of shareholder recipients who under present rules are tax-exempt.[22]

TABLE 4

REVENUE EFFECTS OF GROSS-UP AND FULL CREDIT
OF DIVIDENDS, 1964
(millions of dollars)
(zero shifting)
(no change in dividends)

Adjusted Gross Income Class	*Change in Tax Revenue*
0- 600	- 41.0
600- 1500	- 102.0
1500- 3000	- 327.3
3000- 5000	- 504.0
5000- 7000	- 418.2
7000- 10000	- 660.0
10000- 15000	- 877.7
15000- 20000	- 666.0
20000- 25000	- 392.1
25000- 50000	-1,091.4
50000-100000	- 682.3
100000-500000	- 512.3
500000-over	- 185.8
Total	-6,460.1

Table 4 reflects the results of the "gross-up-and-credit" method, pursuant to which the tax withheld at the corporate level would be added to the recipient-shareholder's

[21]Bernstein, Some Legal Consideration in Substantive Tax Reform Proposals, in Studies in Substantive Tax Reform (1968).
[22]Id.

income and credited to his tax liability. It is assumed that (1) the corporate tax is not shifted, and that (2) dividend distributions remain unaffected. With respect to these two qualifiers, some comment should be made. In an economy of monopolistic competition the corporate managers may shift the tax to the consumers in price or to one of the production factors — labor, land, capital — in reduction of cost. If the corporate tax is susceptible of 100 per cent shifting, the effect on shareholders is the same as if there were no tax.[23] The shifting effect may be illustrated by the following example. Assume a selling price of $200, costs of $100, a net income of $100, and a corporate tax of fifty per cent which is not shifted, shifted fifty per cent, and shifted one hundred per cent.

	Col. 1 No tax	Col. 2 No shifting	Col. 3 50% shifting	Col. 4 100% shifting
Price	$200	$200	$233.3	$300
Cost	100	100	100	100
Pre-tax net income	100	100	133.3	200
Corporate tax	—	50	66.6	100
After-tax net income distributed	100	50	66.6	100
Gross-up	100	100	100	100
Credit	—	50	33.3	—

In column 1 it is assumed that there is no corporate tax and all profits are distributed. In column 2, if no part of the tax is shifted, or stated otherwise, if the shareholders bear all the corporate tax, then the shareholders are entitled to a full gross-up and credit to place themselves in the same position as if no corporate tax were imposed. In column 3 it is assumed that the corporate managers are able to make a price adjustment to shift the tax to the consumer. In such case, only half the corporate tax is borne by the shareholders; therefore, the gross-up and credit equals half the tax.[24] In column 4, there is complete shifting of the tax through price adjustment; therefore, no gross-up and credit is applied.

Table 5 reflects the effect of changes in dividend policy assuming the gross-up and credit would impel an increase in dividends. Even with a fifty per cent and one hundred per cent increase in dividends, the revenue effects are not significantly

[23]R. Goode, The Corporation Income Tax 44 (1951).

[24]The Otts used the formula $P = \dfrac{P^1}{1-St}$ where P is the pre-tax corporate net income, P^1 is the corporate net income if there were no tax, t is the tax, and S is the shifting parameter. M. Krzyzaniak & R. Musgrave, The Shifting of the Corporate Income Tax: An Empirical Study of Its Short-Run Effects upon the Rate of Returns 11-12 (1963). As an example, suppose that the corporate tax rate, t, is equal to 50%, the corporate net income if there were no tax, P^1, is $100, and the corporation can shift 50% of the tax. Assume that all corporate income after taxes is distributed. Then $P = \dfrac{100}{1-.50 \times .50}$, or P = $133. Thus, the corporate managers will make a price adjustment or reduce costs to increase pre-tax net income by $33. This is illustrated in col. 3.

TABLE 5

REVENUE EFFECTS OF GROSS-UP AND FULL CREDIT
OF DIVIDENDS, 1964
(millions of dollars)
(zero shifting)

Adjusted Gross Income Class	No Change in Dividends	50% Rise in Dividends	100% Rise in Dividends
0- 600	- 41.0	- 54.1	- 65.1
600- 1500	- 102.0	- 144.1	- 184.8
1500- 3000	- 327.3	- 455.0	- 576.1
3000- 5000	- 504.0	- 685.2	- 847.6
5000- 7000	- 418.2	- 555.5	- 672.2
7000- 10000	- 660.0	- 849.5	-1,003.6
10000- 15000	- 877.7	-1,089.3	-1,251.3
15000- 20000	- 666.0	- 773.9	- 834.5
20000- 25000	- 392.1	- 432.6	- 445.4
25000- 50000	-1,091.4	-1,015.5	- 858.9
50000-100000	- 682.3	- 443.8	- 164.3
100000-500000	- 512.3	- 165.7	187.9
500000-over	- 185.8	- 44.4	97.1
Total	-6,460.1	-6,708.5	-6,618.7

different.[25] This is an important revelation, for if a change in corporate tax policy which would induce larger dividend distributions should have a serious effect either for or against the fisc, such change in policy would have to be approached warily.[26] This, however, seems not to be the case from the Otts' findings. In the long run, of course, the gross-up-and-credit method tends to approach, but never reaches, the same result as the partnership method; that is, if all corporate earnings were distributed, then, assuming no shifting, all taxes would be grossed up and credited at the shareho'der level.[27]

As has been mentioned above, the revenue implications of a full gross-up and credit suggested some compromise proposal. Assuming that dividends received were

[25]In the lower adjusted gross income groups the increase in dividends causes an increase in the tax revenue loss because the tax credit is greater than the marginal tax rate which the individual pays on dividend income. The trend changes in the $15-20,000 group because the marginal tax rate is approximately equal to the corporate rate; increases in tax revenue in these brackets are almost entirely offset by the tax credit. In the highest brackets, the increases in dividends are not entirely offset by the credit, and as the dividend income is doubled in these brackets, the credit factor becomes a smaller percentage of the tax on the dividend.

This offsetting of the effect on the lower income groups against that experienced in the higher income groups also explains why the revenue loss, assuming a 50% rise in dividends, is about the same as the revenue loss, assuming a 100% rise in dividends.

[26]Brittain notes that if 1929 income tax rates had been in effect in 1947 the payout ratio would have been 40 percentage points higher and dividends would have been 112% higher than they were in 1947. J. Brittain, Corporate Dividend Policy 205 (1966).

[27]If the dividend-profits ratio were 1, then all corporate profits would be taxed at the stockholder-recipients' respective tax rates.

grossed up by the amount of the tax paid at the corporate level, the Otts then determined the revenue implications of constraining, or restricting, the credit so that a taxpayer would claim the credit against his tax but could not claim a refund. The constrained credit may be criticized as working haphazardly on individuals and thereby producing inequities. Thus, two individuals, each with the same salary, and each with the same dividend income, but one having an unexpected loss in some extraneous transaction, would have different tax consequences as to dividends. One would receive the full credit; the other, after deducting his loss, might produce a much reduced tax liability which would limit the dividends-received credit. Table 6

TABLE 6

REVENUE EFFECT OF GROSS-UP AND CONSTRAINED
CREDIT OF DIVIDENDS, 1964
(millions of dollars)
(zero shifting)
(no changes in dividends)

Adjusted Gross Income Class	*Change in Tax Revenue*
0- 600	- 8.2
600- 1500	- 14.3
1500- 3000	- 52.6
3000- 5000	- 89.8
5000- 7000	- 77.1
7000- 10000	- 131.6
10000- 15000	- 193.2
15000- 20000	- 185.2
20000- 25000	- 122.8
25000- 50000	- 498.3
50000-100000	- 521.1
100000-500000	- 506.5
500000-over	- 185.7
Total	-2,586.5

is the result of this study. Note that the revenue loss under the constrained credit is $2.586 billion as contrasted with $6.460 billion under the full credit. Table 7 is the result of the constrained credit assuming a fifty per cent and a one hundred per cent rise in dividends respectively.

Table 8 compares the two methods — gross-up and full credit and gross-up and constrained credit — with a complete exclusion of dividend income from the taxable base of individuals. In adjusted gross income (AGI) classes $0-5000 the "full credit" accounts for fifteen per cent of the revenue loss, the constrained credit for 6.4 per cent of the revenue loss, and the dividend exclusion, 1.7 per cent of the revenue loss.[28]

---

[28]The gross-up-and-full-credit will produce refunds in the lower brackets, because the taxpayers' marginal rates are less than the corporate tax rate. When the credit is constrained, the refunds in the lower brackets are eliminated so that these brackets do not contribute as much to the

TABLE 7

REVENUE EFFECT OF GROSS-UP AND CONSTRAINED
CREDIT OF DIVIDENDS, 1964
(millions of dollars)
(zero shifting)

Adjusted Gross Income Class	No Change in Dividends	50% Rise in Dividends	100% Rise in Dividends
0- 600	- 8.2	- 9.5	- 10.3
600- 1500	- 14.3	- 15.0	- 15.5
1500- 3000	- 52.6	- 54.4	- 56.1
3000- 5000	- 89.8	- 91.4	- 92.8
5000- 7000	- 77.1	- 74.1	- 71.0
7000- 10000	- 131.6	- 123.1	-114.3
10000- 15000	- 193.2	- 171.4	-148.8
15000- 20000	- 185.2	- 163.6	-137.3
20000- 25000	- 122.8	- 102.2	- 70.7
25000- 50000	- 498.3	- 368.3	-184.3
50000-100000	- 521.1	- 309.8	- 45.5
100000-500000	- 506.5	- 162.5	190.1
500000-over	- 185.7	- 44.4	97.1
Total	-2,586.5	-1,689.5	-659.6

The AGI brackets of $25,000 and above would account for thirty-eight per cent of the revenue loss under the full credit, sixty-six per cent under the constrained credit, and seventy-three per cent under the dividend exclusion. Allowing a deduction to the corporation for dividends distributed, the revenue loss is the same as the gross-up and full credit. These significantly different allocations of effect among AGI classes require a more intensive analysis in order to provide the basis for policy choices.

As was noted earlier, BTB₂ also assumes that sales of corporate stock and unrealized appreciation in stock at the end of the year would be included in full as part of the taxable base. Thus, the $58.6 billion of added base consists of $35 billion in net unrealized increments in stock value, $11.2 billion of previously nonincluded capital gains on stock sales, and $12.4 billion of grossed up dividends.

IV. Influence on Corporate Managers and Shareholders

All the tabulations previously described relate to first-order effects; thus, in each case the assumption has been that the actions of corporate managers in the money market remain the same. Any major study in substantive tax reform would have to consider second-order and third-order effects in response to fundamental changes

---

overall loss in revenue as is the case with the full credit. In the case of the 100% dividend exclusion there is neither a grossing-up factor nor a refund or credit factor in the lower brackets so that the contribution to the overall revenue loss from these brackets is relatively smaller than in either of the other two methods.

[29]For a recent analysis of second-order and third-order effects of present tax policy, see R. Barlow, H. Brazier & J. Morgan, Economic Behavior of the Affluent 151-71 (1966).

TABLE 8

REVENUE EFFECTS OF ALTERNATIVE TAX TREATMENTS
OF DIVIDENDS: GROSS-UP AND FULL CREDIT, GROSS-UP
AND CONSTRAINED CREDIT, AND 100% DIVIDEND EXCLUSION
(millions of dollars)
(zero shifting)
(no changes in dividends)

Adjusted Gross Income Class	Gross-Up and Full Credit		Gross-Up and Constrained Credit		100% Dividend Exclusion	
0- 600	- 41.0	⎱	- 8.2	⎱	0.0	⎱
600- 1500	- 102.0		- 14.3		- .3	
1500- 3000	- 327.3	15%	- 52.6	6.4%	- 6.7	1.7%
3000- 5000	- 504.0	⎰	- 89.8	⎰	- 34.8	⎰
5000- 7000	- 418.2		- 77.1		- 56.9	
7000- 10000	- 660.0		- 131.6		- 95.8	
10000- 15000	- 877.7		- 193.2		- 179.5	
15000- 20000	- 666.0		- 185.2		- 176.6	
20000- 25000	- 392.1		- 122.8		- 136.3	
25000- 50000	-1,091.4	⎱	- 498.3	⎱	- 513.1	⎱
50000-100000	- 682.3		- 521.1		- 573.6	
100000-500000	- 512.3	38%	- 506.5	66%	- 531.8	73%
500000-over	- 185.8	⎰	- 185.7	⎰	- 131.4	⎰
Total	-6,460.1		-2,586.5		-2,436.8	

in corporate tax policy.[29] All of the methods described would probably have the effect of impelling greater distributions of corporate earnings than at present. Growth companies would tend to distribute earnings and then resort to the money market for new capital. If dividends were nontaxable, or if the shareholder could look forward to credits for taxes paid at the corporate level, he would probably withdraw funds from interest-bearing securities in favor of stock investments. Thus, there would be a tendency to cause a flight from savings and loan and similar accounts. On the other hand, the treatment of realized and unrealized capital gains as part of the taxable base would have countervailing effects on the attractiveness of the stock market investments. The reallocation of resources against the background of such fundamental changes in tax policy would have to be carefully analyzed in a long range project.

Of special significance would be the effect on closely held corporations. At present, these corporations tend to pay as large salaries as possible to officer-stockholders and little or no dividends. The threat of section 531[30] taxes often impels the owners to sell to or to exchange stock with larger, listed, companies in order to bail out accumulated earnings at capital gains and to achieve estate liquidity. Under the various mechanisms described herein, the complex statutory provisions, regulations, rulings, and problems of administration and compliance relating to unreasonable accumula-

[30]Int. Rev. Code of 1954, §531.

tions of earnings,[31] personal holding companies,[32] collapsible corporations,[33] redemptions of stock,[34] and the like, could be reduced to a minimum or eliminated altogether.

All of the foregoing considerations relating to effects on corporate managers and shareholders must be considered in light of substantial reduction in rates. If substantive tax reform means anything, it must mean drastic reduction in rates. Whether it be a flat rate of, say, ten to fifteen per cent, or a graduated rate from, say, five to thirty-five per cent, one cannot speculate on effects as the tax law *is* but as it *may come to be.* In making critical judgments about proposals, one finds it difficult not to look at them in the perspective of the present law, whereas personal motivations, interactions in the economy, and choices of business and investment activity would be quite different under a system of lower rates and a substantially broadened base.

V. The Report of the Royal Commission on Taxation

No discussion of the subject of substantive tax reform would be complete without reference to the recently published major study of the Canadian tax system (the Carter report).[35] There, much of the same rhetoric is employed to urge basic reform in tax policy. A broadened tax base conforming to the Haig-Simons definition, lower rates, and elimination of the double tax on corporate income, are included in the multi-volume report. With respect to the corporate tax, a so-called full-integration system was proposed as follows:

"1. The income of Canadian corporations should be subject to a flat rate of tax of approximately 50 per cent.

"2. Individuals and families should be subject to progressive rates of tax with a top marginal rate of 50 per cent.

"3. The tax base of the resident shareholder should include the corporate income paid or allocated to him, 'grossed-up' for the corporation tax paid.

"4. The resident shareholder should receive credit against his personal income tax liabilities for the full amount of the corporation tax paid in respect of the after-tax corporate income paid or allocated to him, with a refund if the credit exceeded the liability.

"5. Realized gains or losses on corporate shares should be included in income and taxed at full progressive rates.

"6. The corporation should be allowed to allocate after-tax corporate income to shareholders without having to pay cash dividends.

"7. The cost basis of shares should be increased when the corporation allocated retained corporate earnings to shareholders, so that share gains resulting from the retention of earnings that had been taxed to the shareholder would not be taxed again to the shareholder when realized."[36]

---

[31]Id.
[32]Id. §541.
[33]Id. §341.
[34]Id. §§302, 337, 346.
[35]Report of the Royal Comm'n on Taxation (Canada) (6 vols.) (1966).
[36]4 Report of the Royal Comm'n on Taxation (Canada) 7 (1966).

It should be noted that the above proposals combine a gross-up-and-credit mechanism with an optional Subchapter S treatment; that is, after the gross-up and credit is applied to dividends received, the board of directors might allocate *retained* earnings on the partnership basis.

VI. Conclusion

The Substantive Tax Reform Project is a demonstration of the kind of research that must and ultimately will be carried forward by someone. It is my hope, of course, that lawyers will assume the leadership in this work as they have in other areas where efficiency and effectiveness of the laws were at stake. Lawyers have the skill and training to assemble and analyze facts, drawing upon the skills of other disciplines. Nor is this the kind of project that can be done by half-measures. The Canadians spent millions on the Carter report and certainly this country could do no less. The computer provides an invaluable new component in inter-disciplinary research. Data can be arranged in numerous patterns using a variety of assumptions and sub-assumptions not heretofore feasible or practicable.

In no area of inquiry is the need for careful critical analysis more important than that of the corporate tax. Whatever choice of policy is made as to the corporate tax will have profound significance on American industry and the incentives to the formation of capital in this country.

2 | The Individual Income Tax — Corporate Distributions and Dispositions of Investor Interests (Not in Reorganization)

I. HISTORY — RATE STRUCTURE — CORRELATION WITH CORPORATION INCOME TAX

From 1913 to 1954, the personal income tax consisted of two parts, a "normal" tax and an "additional" tax.

The personal income tax act of 1913 exempted dividends from normal tax. Both the tax rate on corporate income and the normal rate on personal income were set at 1 percent; thus, for distributed earnings, the corporate tax operated as a withholding feature of the personal levy.* This treatment continued through 1918, as increases in the personal normal rate were matched by increases in the corporate rate. [Author's footnote: "With these exceptions: a corporate rate greater than the personal normal rate in 1917, and greater than the rate applicable to the first $4000 of normal tax income in 1918."] But from 1919 on, the corporate rate exceeded the personal normal rate and thus the corporate tax became, in part, a separate and distinct levy on distributed corporate earnings. The rate gap widened gradually until 1936 when the bridge between the two taxes was removed completely by the abolition of the dividend exemption. A return to something like the 1919-36 procedure was instituted by the Internal Revenue Code of 1954 in the form of a tax credit based on dividends received. But here, too, a substantial gap exists between the personal income tax credit and the rate of corporate tax. Therefore, since 1919, the distributed earnings of corporate enterprises have been treated differently from the other sources of income for Federal income-tax purposes: from 1919 to 1936, because the corporate rate was higher than the personal normal rate; from 1936 through 1953, because corporate earnings were taxed at the corporate level when earned with no allowance at the personal level when distributed; and from 1954 on, because the per-

---

*The personal income tax consisted of both a "normal" and an "additional" tax from 1913 to 1954. Dividends were not exempted from the additional tax. — Ed.

sonal income-tax relief accorded distributed earnings falls short of the corporate tax rate.*

In 1954 Congress had approached the taxation of dividends in two ways. First, an individual shareholder was permitted to exclude $50 of dividends from his gross income. In addition, he was permitted (subject to limitations) to credit against his tax liability 4 per cent of his dividends received in excess of the exclusion.

In the tax message that led to the Revenue Act of 1964, President Kennedy called for repeal of both the exclusion and the credit. Congress responded by repealing the credit and increasing the exclusion to $100.

Although there has been Congressional vacillation over the years as to the extent to which corporate earnings are to be subjected to both a corporate and an individual tax, Congress has imposed a "double tax" on distributed earnings since 1913.

The taxation of dividends is not dependent alone on the statutory word "income." The Code is explicit in providing that "dividends" are includable in a taxpayer's gross income. §§61(a)(7) and 301(c)(1). As defined in §316(a), a "dividend" for income tax purposes is "any distribution of property made by a corporation to its shareholders (1) out of its earnings and profits accumulated after February 28, 1913, or (2) out of its earnings and profits" of the current taxable year. A distribution which does not constitute a "dividend" as defined is treated as a tax-free return of capital to the extent of the taxpayer's basis in his stock (§301(c)(2)), but to the extent that the distribution exceeds the taxpayer's basis, the excess is treated as "gain from the sale or exchange of" his stock (§301(c)(3)(A)). Usually, but not always, the gain taxable as a result of §301(c)(3)(A) is a capital gain, long-term if the stock has been held for more than six months. If the taxpayer is a securities dealer or if the corporation is a "collapsible" corporation (see page 249 infra), the gain may not be capital. If a non-dividend distribution that exceeds the taxpayer's basis in his stock happens to be "out of increase in value accrued before March 1, 1913," the gain will be tax-exempt (§301(c)(3)(B)).

The concept of "earnings and profits" is a crucial one within the present tax structure. In many respects it is similar to, and sometimes — but only sometimes — identical with, "earned surplus" or "retained earnings" as those terms are normally used in corporate accounting. One situation in which the "earned surplus" figure on a corporation's balance sheet may not be reflective of the accumulated earnings and profits occurs when the corporation has distributed a dividend in its own stock, thereby capitalizing all or part of its "earned surplus." Despite the reduction in "earned surplus," there is no reduction in the corporation's earnings and profits, since no corporate assets have been distributed.

Although §312 describes the impact on "earnings and profits" which results from various transactions, the Code itself does not define the term "earnings and profits." The process of definition has been left to a common-law type of evolvement and, in part, to the Treasury. See Treas. Reg. §1.312-6. It is important to recognize

---

*D. Holland, Differential Taxation and Tax Relief, 3 Tax Revision Compendium 1551, 1552 (House Ways and Means Comm. 1959).

that the concept of a corporation's "earnings and profits" is not relevant to the corporation's income tax liability. Its relevance is in determining whether a corporate distribution constitutes dividend income to the shareholders within the definition of "dividend" in §316(a).

The statute did not always limit taxation to "earnings and profits" accumulated after March 1, 1913. See Lynch v. Hornby, 247 U.S. 339, 344 (1918), in which the Supreme Court said:

> Dividends are the appropriate fruit of stock ownership, are commonly reckoned as income, and are expended as such by the stockholder without regard to whether they are declared from the most recent earnings, or from a surplus accumulated from the earnings of the past, or are based upon the increased value of the property of the corporation. The stockholder is, in the ordinary case, a different entity from the corporation, and Congress was at liberty to treat the dividends as coming to him ab extra, and as constituting a part of his income when they came to hand.
>
> Hence we construe the provisions of the Act that "the net income of a taxable person, shall include gains, profits, and income derived from . . . interest, rent, dividends, . . . or gains or profits and income derived from any source whatever" as including . . . all dividends declared and paid in the ordinary course of business by a corporation to its stockholders after the taking effect of the Act (March 1, 1913), whether from current earnings, or from the accumulated surplus made up of past earnings or increase in value of corporate assets, notwithstanding it accrued to the corporation in whole or in part prior to March 1, 1913.

Before the *Hornby* decision came down Congress amended the statute prospectively to define "the term 'dividends' . . . [as] any distribution made or ordered to be made by a corporation . . . out of its earnings or profits accrued since March first, nineteen hundred and thirteen." In 1936 the law was amended again, this time to broaden the source for dividends to include current earnings even if there are no accumulated earnings and profits (i.e., the "nimble dividend").

The first four cases that follow this Introduction deal with the definitional aspect of "earnings and profits" and some of the controversy that arises in the effort to compute "earnings and profits" and to determine the tax impact when the "earnings and profits" are inadequate to justify the classification of a distribution as a "dividend."

II. CORPORATE DISTRIBUTIONS OF PROPERTY (INCLUDING CASH)

A. *DISTRIBUTIONS*

1. *Earnings and Profits*

BANGOR & AROOSTOOK R.R. v. COMMISSIONER
193 F.2d 827 (1st Cir. 1951), cert. denied, 343 U.S. 934 (1952)

Before MAGRUDER, Chief Judge, and WOODBURY and HARTIGAN, Circuit Judges.

MAGRUDER, Chief Judge. Bangor and Aroostook Railroad Company petitions for review of a decision of the Tax Court of the United States determining that there is a deficiency in petitioner's excess profits tax in the sum of $3,677.45 for the calendar year 1943.

The applicable statute is the Excess Profits Act of 1940, 54 Stat. 975; Internal Revenue Code §710 et seq., 26 U.S.C.A. §710 et seq. Speaking generally, the "excess profits credit" is the statutory measure of normal profits exempt from the excess profits tax; the credit is deducted from the "excess profits net income" to obtain the "adjusted excess profits net income" upon which the tax is laid. The excess profits credit could be computed in either of two ways, by the average earnings method, I.R.C. §713, or by the invested capital method, I.R.C. §714. Petitioner elected the latter method, under which eight per cent of its "invested capital" became its excess profits credit. One component entering into the calculation of the "invested capital" was the "accumulated earnings and profits as of the beginning of such taxable year" I.R.C. §718(a)(4).

In 1942 petitioner purchased in the open market for retirement and cancellation certain of its bonds of an aggregate par value of $634,000. The total purchase price was $497,553.30; and the difference between these two sums, or $136,446.70, is referred to hereinafter as petitioner's "bond profit" for the calendar year 1942. It is undisputed that this bond profit was realized income within the general definition of I.R.C. §22(a), 26 U.S.C.A. §22(a).* United States v. Kirby Lumber Co., 1931, 284 U.S. 1, 52 S. Ct. 4, 76 L. Ed. 131; Commissioner of Internal Revenue v. Jacobson, 1949, 336 U.S. 28, 69 S. Ct. 358, 93 L. Ed. 477. Petitioner would have been taxable upon the whole amount of the bond profit in 1942, except for the fact that it elected to take advantage of the option provided under I.R.C. §[108] and §[1017] and thus was permitted to exclude the bond profit from the computation of its normal tax net income and surtax net income in its return for 1942.

Notwithstanding this treatment of the bond profit in its 1942 return, petitioner

*Section 61(a) is the 1954 Code counterpart of §22(a) of the 1939 Code, but §22(a) did not have the equivalent of §61(a)(12). — ED.

sought to diminish its excess profits tax for the calendar year 1943 by including $136,446.70, or the whole amount of the so-called bond profit, in the item "accumulated earnings and profits" as of January 1, 1943. Such inclusion enhanced the figure for petitioner's "invested capital" and its "excess profits credit", with a resultant reduction in petitioner's excess profits tax for 1943. The Tax Court ruled that the bond profit, not having been "recognized" though "realized" in 1942, should be excluded from "accumulated earnings and profits" as of January 1, 1943. This exclusion produced the deficiency found in the decision now under review.

We think the ruling of the Tax Court was correct. In view of the full and careful opinion by Judge Raum, concurred in without dissent by the whole court, our own discussion will be briefer than otherwise might have been appropriate.

It is important to observe the distinction between (1) income which is exempt from tax and (2) income which, though "realized" in a constitutional sense and thus within the power of Congress to tax, is not at the outset "recognized", the incidence of the tax being merely postponed.

As to (1), exempt income, such for instance as interest on tax-free bonds, if income of this sort is to be taken into "earnings or profits", the only logical time to do so is when the income is realized. It is so provided by regulation. Section [1.312-6(b)] on the subject of corporate dividends out of "earnings or profits", states that among the items "entering into the computation of corporate earnings or profits for a particular period are all income exempted by statute, income not taxable by the Federal Government under the Constitution, as well as all items includible in gross income under section [61] or corresponding provisions of prior Revenue Acts . . . . Interest on State bonds and certain other obligations, although not taxable when received by a corporation, is taxable to the same extent as other dividends when distributed to shareholders in the form of dividends."

It is not in express terms provided that tax-exempt income, when realized, is also taken into "accumulated earnings and profits" under I.R.C. §718(a)(4). That term is not defined in the Code. But §35.718-2 of Reg. 112 refers back to §[312] of the Code and the regulations prescribed thereunder, and states that in general "the concept of 'accumulated earnings and profits' for the purpose of the excess profits tax is the same as for the purpose of the income tax. . . ." . . . The clear inference from the regulations that truly exempted income may be carried into "accumulated earnings and profits", is evidently in accordance with the congressional purpose. . . . If therefore a corporation receives during a given year income which is exempt from taxation, such as interest on tax-free bonds, and such income is left in the business to be available as working capital, it is reasonable and proper that such income, though not taxable to the corporation receiving it, should be included in the item "accumulated earnings and profits" as of the beginning of the following year, §718 (a)(4) of the Code, in the computation of the corporation's excess profits tax for that year.

But as to (2), income which, though "realized", is not at the outset "recognized", the problem is quite different. This concept in perhaps its most familiar instances appears in [the nonrecognition provisions of the Code]. The thought behind the nonrecognition provisions . . . is that, in certain transactions involving "the sale or exchange of property", though a gain may have been realized in a constitutional sense, it is unfair or inappropriate to tax the gain at the outset in view of the fact that in a popular and economic sense there has been a mere change in the form of ownership and the taxpayer has not yet really "cashed in" on the more or less theoretical gain. As expressed by the Supreme Court in Commissioner of Internal Revenue v. Wheeler, 1945, 324 U.S. 542, 546, 65 S. Ct. 799, 802, 89 L. Ed. 1166: "Congress has determined that in certain types of transaction the economic changes are not definitive enough to be given tax consequences, and has clearly provided that gains and losses on such transactions shall not be recognized for income-tax liability but shall be taken account of later. . . . *It is sensible to carry through the theory in determining the tax effect of such transactions on earnings and profits.*" [Italics added.]

In Commissioner of Internal Revenue v. F. J. Young Corp., 1939, 103 F.2d 137, the third circuit had held that a gain which resulted from a tax-free exchange of securities under §[351] of the Revenue Act of 1928 must be considered "earnings or profits" out of which a "dividend" might be declared within the meaning of §[316] of the Act. But the court ignored or overlooked a provision of Art. 115-3 of Reg. 94 . . . [Treas. Reg. §1.312-6(b)] which explicitly stated: "Gains and losses within the purview of §[1002] *or corresponding provisions of prior Acts* are brought into the earnings and profits at the time and to the extent such gains and losses are recognized under that section." [Italics added.] . . . In Commissioner of Internal Revenue v. Wheeler, 1945, 324 U.S. 542, 65 S. Ct. 799, supra, the Supreme Court expressly upheld the regulation as a reasonable and valid exercise of the rule-making power. It follows that Commissioner of Internal Revenue v. F. J. Young Corp., supra, and cases like it, cannot be taken as authorities in support of the position urged by the taxpayer in the case at bar.

Congress itself has indicated approval of the foregoing regulation by writing it expressly into the law. Section [312(f) provides:] "Gain or loss so realized shall increase or decrease the earnings and profits to, but not beyond, the extent to which such a realized gain or loss was recognized in computing net income under the law applicable to the year in which such sale or disposition was made." This evidently was regarded as not a change in existing law but only in the nature of a clarifying amendment. The House committee stated that the provision of [§312(f)] merely enacted the rule which had been applied by the Treasury under existing law. It was pointed out that while taxpayers generally had concurred in the Treasury rule, the Board of Tax Appeals and some court decisions, mentioning specifically Commissioner of Internal Revenue v. F. J. Young Corp., 3 Cir., 103 F.2d 137, had followed the contrary theory "that gain or loss, even though not recognized in computing net income, nevertheless affects earnings and profits." The report further stated: "The purpose of this amendment is to clarify the law with respect to what constitutes earnings and profits of a corporation. This is important not only for the purpose of determining whether distributions are taxable dividends but also in determining equity invested capital for excess-profits-tax purposes." H.R. Rep. No. 2894, 76th Cong., 3d Sess., p. 41.

It is true enough that the result reached here by the Tax Court is not directly commanded by §[312(f)] of the Code, for that subsection by its terms deals with the delayed recognition of gain or loss realized from the "sale or other disposition of property by a corporation", whereas the nonrecognized gain in the present case resulted from the taxpayer's reacquisition of its own bonds. But it does not follow that the underlined principle exemplified by the specific instances covered by the literal language of §[312(f)] should not be applied in other analogous nonrecognition situations. . . .

Congress sought in §[312(f)] to "clarify" the law in particular instances where the law had been muddied by court decisions like Commissioner of Internal Revenue v. F. J. Young Corp., 3 Cir., 1939, 103 F.2d 137. But when §[312(f)] was enacted, there had been no similar court decisions dealing with the effect on earnings and profits of gains from the discharge of indebtedness realized but not at the same time recognized; so that particular problem did not receive the attention of Congress when §[312(f)] was in process of enactment. The Tax Court properly observed in the case at bar: "Surely, by taking pains to make certain that unrecognized gains or losses from sales or other dispositions of property would not be reflected in earnings and profits, Congress could not have intended thereby to produce a different result with respect to other unrecognized gains or losses, merely by failing to mention them."

The underlying principle, of which §[312(f)] is but an illustration, is that "earnings and profits" must be computed on the same basis as that employed in computing income subject to the income tax; in other words, that gains ought to be reflected in earnings and profits at the time they are "recognized" and taken into account for income tax purposes. See Commissioner of Internal Revenue v. South Texas Lumber Co., 1948, 333 U.S. 496, 68 S. Ct. 695, 92 L. Ed. 831. That case held that a corporate taxpayer which filed its income and excess profits tax return on the accrual basis, but elected to report income from certain installment sales on the installment basis as authorized by §[453] . . . , may not, in computing its excess profits tax credit, include in the "accumulated earnings and profits" component of its "invested capital" the unreported profits from such installment sales. The Court pointed out, 333 U.S. at page 505, 68 S. Ct. at page 701: "The congressional reports on §[312(f)] do not provide support for the idea that gains not included in taxable income under the taxpayer's method of accounting may nevertheless be considered 'realized' and 'recognized' for computing tax adjustments or deductions so long as they might have entered into such computations under a different method of accounting."

We think it clear that an analogous situation is presented in the case at bar. The taxpayer having technically realized its so-called bond profit in 1942, elected under an optional method of accounting permitted by the statute to postpone recognition of such gain and to exclude the amount thereof from its gross income reported for 1942. It cannot then shift its method of accounting, and treat that gain as both realized and recognized in 1942, for the purpose of enhancing a deduction (the excess profits credit) used in the computation of its excess profits tax liability for 1943.

The rule in United States v. Kirby Lumber Co., 1931, 284 U.S. 1, 52 S. Ct. 4, 76 L. Ed. 131, has been criticized both on theoretical and practical grounds, and doubtless in many cases it worked a hardship. Congress took account of these criticisms in 1939, when it amended the Internal Revenue Code by adding [§108]. . . .

It appears, then, that when the provision of §[108] for delayed recognition of gain is compared with the . . . delayed recognition situations, the . . . sections stem from a common legislative conviction that it is fairer not to impose the income tax forthwith upon the theoretical gains realized from certain transactions, but to postpone the recognition of the gain, and the incidence of the tax, until the occurrence of an economically more significant event.

. . . The Commissioner, in auditing the taxpayer's 1942 return, reduced the basis of its depreciable property pursuant to the applicable regulations under §[1017]. As a result, the taxpayer's depreciation deduction for 1942 was reduced in the amount of $1,736.69. This adjustment correspondingly increased the taxpayer's taxable income for 1942. Such increased income in the sum of $1,736.69 was therefore added by the Commissioner to the taxpayer's "accumulated earnings and profits" as of January 1, 1943, for the purpose of computing the taxpayer's excess profits credit in determining the excess profits tax for 1943. The Commissioner and the Tax Court agree that, to that extent, the bond profit having been reflected in 1942 income should be reflected also in the item of accumulated earnings and profits as of January 1, 1943. The taxpayer's basis having been reduced, by command of the statute, depreciation to be taken by the taxpayer for income tax purposes in the succeeding years will necessarily be lower, and taxable gains correspondingly higher; and as the bond profit is thus gradually recognized and reflected in income, it will at the same time be reflected in earnings and profits. If and when the taxpayer sells the property the basis of which has thus been reduced, the whole of the bond profit will have been recognized and reflected both in income and in earnings and profits. . . . Such treatment of the bond profit seems to be clearly required by the statute and the applicable regulations. It would necessarily follow that the Tax Court properly rejected the taxpayer's contention that the whole amount of the bond profit should be taken into "accumulated earnings and profits" as of January 1, 1943; for otherwise, the bond profit would be doing double duty in reducing taxpayer's excess profits tax liability for 1943 and subsequent years. . . .

The decision of the Tax Court is affirmed.

NOTE

1. In January 1965, Corporation Y is formed, and it has no earnings for that year. In 1966, Y loses $10,000. In 1967, Y earns $10,000. What is the tax consequence to the shareholders if a dividend is declared at the end of 1966? At the beginning of 1967? See §316(a). Is the difference in result appropriate? Why?

2. X Corporation distributes to its shareholders as a dividend a building with an adjusted basis of $50,000 and a fair market value of $100,000. What impact does that distribution have on the corporation's earnings and profits? Why? Would the result be the same if the building were an "inventory" item in the corporation's hands? Why? In answering these questions and those in Note 3, see the Regulations under §312.

3. Corporation M computes its taxable income with the benefit of percentage depletion. Its taxable income for 1966 so computed is $225,000. On a cost depletion basis its taxable income would be $250,000. By what sum (approximately) is the corporation's earnings and profits account increased as a result of the year's operations?

4. X Corporation's current and accumulated earnings and profits aggregate $100,000. The corporation makes a pro rata distribution to its shareholders (all individuals) of (a) assets having a basis of $80,000, (b) assets having a basis of $100,000. In both (a) and (b) the assets have a fair market value of $150,000. What is the aggregate total amount that may be included in the gross income of the shareholders in (a)? In (b)? See Treas. Reg. §1.316-1(a)(3), Ex. For judicial resolution of the problem under the 1939 Code, see Commissioner v. Hirshon Trust, 213 F.2d 523 (2d Cir.), cert. denied, 348 U.S. 861 (1954); Commissioner v. Godley's Estate, 213 F.2d 529 (3d Cir.), cert. denied, 348 U.S. 862 (1954). See generally, as to this problem and its history, B. Bittker and J. Eustice, Federal Income Taxation of Corporations and Shareholders 185-188 (2d ed. 1966).

5. If a corporate shareholder received the aggregate distributions in the Note 4 problems, what would be the amount of its gross income in (a)? In (b)? What is your authority?

6. Should tax-deferred income (such as that involved in *Bangor & Aroostook R.R.*) augment the earnings and profits account for purposes of §316(a) only as and if it becomes recognized? Why?

7. Corporation X, owning stock in Corporation Y, receives a distribution from Corporation Y which was not taxable as a dividend. What is the impact on Corporation X's earnings and profits? What happens to the basis of the stock Corporation X holds in Corporation Y? See §312(f)(2).

8. Mr. Able buys ten shares of Corporation Z's stock on September 30, 1966. On October 1, 1966, a dividend is declared to all Z shareholders. What will determine the income tax consequence to Able? Why? Ought a shareholder be required to treat a distribution as a dividend if the covering earnings and profits all antedate his stock purchase and if his stock basis exceeds the amount of his distribution? See United States v. Phellis, 257 U.S. 156, 171-172 (1922); T. Powell, Income from Corporate Dividends, 35 Harv. L. Rev. 363 (1922). Ought distributions by an ongoing corporation be treated as dividends, whether or not there are earnings or profits to cover? See W. Andrews, "Out of Its Earnings and Profits": Some Reflections on the Taxation of Dividends, 69 Harv. L. Rev. 1403 (1956). For extensive treatment of the problems of "earnings and profits," see H. Rudick, "Dividends" and "Earnings or Profits" Under the Income Tax Law: Corporate Non-Liquidating Distributions, 89 U. Pa. L. Rev. 865 (1941); A. Albrecht, "Dividends" and "Earnings or Profits," 7 Tax L. Rev. 157 (1952); H. Zarky and A. Biblin, The Role of Earnings and Profits in the Tax Law, 1966 So. Calif. Tax Inst. 145, 145-174; and B. Bittker and J. Eustice, Federal Income Taxation of Corporations and Shareholders 148-162 (2d ed. 1966).

9. X, the sole shareholder of Corporation Y, withdraws sums from the Corporation in 1960. The Corporation and X characterize the withdrawals as loans. Thereafter the Commissioner contends successfully that the withdrawals were dividends.

In determining whether a 1970 distribution is a dividend, are accumulated earnings and profits reduced by the 1960 withdrawals? Suppose the withdrawals were really dividends, but the Commissioner awakened to the fact after the statute of limitations barred deficiency assessments for the year 1960? See Jacob M. Kaplan, 43 T.C. 580 (1965); H. Korbel, Recent Developments in the Earnings and Profits Area: "Past Errors" and "Deficit Carryovers," 43 Taxes 494 (1965). See generally Rev. Proc. 65-10, 1965-1 Cum. Bull. 738, modified by Rev. Proc. 67-12, 1967-1 Cum. Bull. 589, issued by the Commissioner "to provide stockholders more certainty as to the taxable status of distributions."

MEYER v. COMMISSIONER
383 F.2d 883 (8th Cir. 1967)

Before VAN OOSTERHOUT, BLACKMUN and MEHAFFY, Circuit Judges.

BLACKMUN, Circuit Judge. Section 395 of the Bankruptcy Act, as amended, 11 U.S.C. §795, is part of Chapter 11 relating to Arrangements. It provides (with exceptions not applicable here) that no taxable income shall be deemed to have been realized by a debtor by reason of a modification or cancellation of indebtedness in a Chapter 11 proceeding.[1] This rule, of course, is repeated in the income tax regulations. Treas. Regs. §1.61-12(b)(1)(ii). For the corporation-debtor-taxpayer which has had an Arrangement confirmed under Chapter 11, this is all probably clear enough.

What, however, is the effect of that adjustment of indebtedness upon the debtor corporation's earnings and profits? The answer to this question becomes important when, subsequent to court confirmation of the Arrangement, the corporation makes a distribution. The nature of that distribution (as income or as capital) in the hands of the receiving shareholder obviously has a direct income tax consequence for that shareholder. This is the primary issue before us here. Despite the fact that §395, and the corresponding §§268, 520, and 679 of the Bankruptcy Act, 11 U.S.C. §§668, 920, and 1079, have been on the statute books for almost thirty years, this may be an issue of first impression.

The taxpayers are Leon R. Meyer and Lucile H. Meyer. They are husband and wife. The taxable year involved is the calendar year 1959. The Meyers filed separate income tax returns for that year on the cash basis.

[1]"§795. Taxes; income or profit from modification of indebtedness

"Except as provided in section 796 of this title, no income or profit, taxable under any law of the United States or of any State now in force or which may hereafter be enacted, shall, in respect to the adjustment of the indebtedness of a debtor in a proceeding under this chapter, be deemed to have accrued to or to have been realized by a debtor or a corporation organized or made use of for effectuating an arrangement under this chapter by reason of a modification in or cancellation in whole or in part of any such indebtedness in a proceeding under this chapter: *Provided, however,* That if it shall be made to appear that the arrangement had for one of its principal purposes the evasion of any income tax, the exemption provided by this section shall be disallowed."

Similar and corresponding provisions are §§268, 520, and 679 of the Bankruptcy Act, 11 U.S.C. §§668, 920, and 1079, which are respectively, parts of Chapters 10, 12, and 13 having to do with Corporate Reorganizations, Real Property Arrangements, and Wage Earners' Plans. Sections 395, 268, 520, and 679 were all added by the Chandler Act of June 22, 1938.

The controversy centers on Lucile's tax. The Commissioner, by his 90-day letters, proposed deficiencies of $17,402.09 and $40,101.55 in Lucile's and Leon's respective 1959 taxes. The Tax Court, in a decision not reviewed by the full court, determined deficiencies of $16,149.16 and $1,918.02, respectively. Lucile petitions for review. Leon does not. The Commissioner, however, has filed a petition in Leon's case as a protective step against the possibility that the decision in Lucile's appeal is adverse to the Commissioner on a theory of constructive receipt on behalf of Leon.

The two cases are thus interdependent. They were consolidated for trial in the Tax Court. We consider them together here.

The Tax Court's findings and opinion are reported as Leon H. Meyer, 46 T.C. 65 (1966).

The facts are complicated. They are set forth in great detail at pp. 68-81 of 46 T.C., to which we made general reference. They need not all be repeated here. We outline those particularly pertinent for our review.

1. For a time prior to July 31, 1946, Leon and Lucile were equal partners in a jewelry business known as Meyer Jewelry Co., in Kansas City, Missouri.[2]

2. In 1946 the Meyers incorporated this business, with the same name, under Missouri law. All the partnership assets, except a small amount of cash, were transferred to the corporation in exchange for its assumption of the partnership liabilities and its issuance to Leon and Lucile, equally, of its $100 par Class A voting capital stock and its $50,000, face value, 10-year promissory notes. The assets so transferred had aggregate carrying values of $315,899.22. The liabilities so assumed amounted to $206,399.22. The corporation kept its books on the basis of the fiscal year ended June 30.

3. In 1947 these promissory notes of the corporation were exchanged by the Meyers at face value without accrued interest for $100 par Class B voting shares of the corporation. The Class B shares possessed annual dividend priority and were subject to redemption at par. This exchange capitalized the corporation's theretofore existing liabilities to Leon and Lucile and improved its statement for credit purposes.

4. No dividends were paid by the corporation on any of its outstanding shares during its fiscal years 1946-1958 inclusive.

5. By 1956 the corporation was in financial difficulty. An involuntary bankruptcy petition was filed against it on May 31 of that year. The corporation, as debtor, then proposed a Chapter 11 Arrangement with its unsecured creditors. This Arrangement called for (a) the contribution by Leon of $25,000 to the corporation as additional working capital; (b) a loan of $100,000 to the corporation from a Kansas City bank, the loan to be guaranteed individually by Leon and partially by others, and to require principal payments of $10,000 in six months and $5,000 per quarter thereafter; (c) the issuance by the corporation to Leon of 250 additional shares of its Class B stock; and (d) the payment of expenses and specified debts in full and all other debts only to the extent of 30%.

---

[2]For further background see Meyer Jewelry Co., 3 B.T.A. 1319 (1926), and Meyer v. United States, 121 F. Supp. 898 . . . (1954), cert. denied 348 U.S. 929 . . . .

6. The agreement with the Kansas City bank for its loan to the corporation provided that, in order to secure Leon's guaranty, Leon and Lucile were to pledge with the bank most of the corporation's issued and outstanding shares which they then held. Leon, in order to raise his $25,000 contribution, cashed in a life insurance policy on his life, on which Lucile was the beneficiary, and borrowed $15,000 from the same bank. This loan was secured by 798 shares of Thiokol Corp., which had a then fair market value of about $30,000.

7. The adjustment in the corporation's debts, as proposed by the Arrangement, amounted to $189,785.42. Of this amount, $74,886.84 served to reduce the corporation's income tax bases in its retained assets, as required by §396 of the Act, 11 U.S.C. §796.

8. In anticipation of the Arrangement, the corporation's accountant set up an account, designated "Contributed Capital", on the corporation's books and credited that account in the amount of $178,211.16. This was the amount of the debts so discharged, less certain items. Also, the corporation's assets were appraised and their carrying values were brought into line with their then lower fair market values.

9. The proposed Arrangement was accepted by creditors to the extent required by the Act and on July 3, 1956, it was confirmed by the district court. Payment of claims was effected shortly thereafter.

10. In September 1958, by appropriate corporate action, the respective rights of the Class A and Class B shares were made identical.

11. In December 1958 and February 1959 Lucile effected gifts of certain shares of the corporation to the Meyers' son, Louis S. Meyer, to their son-in-law, Richard C. Burstein, and to Jack Becker, an officer but not related. Thereafter Lucile owned only 40 Class A shares and 250 Class B shares.

12. Meanwhile, the 798 shares of Thiokol stock which Leon had pledged to the bank as collateral for his $15,000 note had grown to 1,848 shares through stock dividends, splits and exercises of rights. In addition, the Thiokol stock had greatly increased in value.

13. By April 1959 a plan was evolved aimed at the elimination both of the corporation's indebtedness (by then reduced to $50,000) to the bank and of Lucile's investment in the corporation. This was made feasible by the substantial increase in the value of Leon's Thiokol stock. The plan was effectuated in April and May by (a) Leon's making a capital contribution to the corporation of 700 of his collateralized 1,848 shares of Thiokol; (b) the corporation's authorizing the sale of the shares so contributed; (c) the bank's releasing to a broker certificates for 700 shares with appropriately executed stock powers; (d) the issuance of new certificates in the broker's name for those shares; (e) the sale of 638 of the shares by the broker on the New York Stock Exchange for the account of the corporation; (f) the corporation's receipt of $81,328.17 for the 638 shares; (g) the corporation's use of $50,000 thereof to pay the balance of its note to the bank; (h) the corporation's payment of the $31,328.17 remainder in two checks to Lucile; and (i) the corporation's placing this $31,328.17 on its books as a debit in an account receivable from Lucile, it being the intent of the parties that these payments to Lucile were to be in ultimate redemption of Lucile's stock in the corporation. These steps were followed by (j)

Lucile's delivery of her stock for redemption late in the summer of 1959; (k) an agreement by the parties (reached after June 30, 1959) that Lucile's stock was redeemed at par ($29,000) rather than at its greater book value ($37,337.50) as of June 30, 1959; and (l) the corporation's crediting the account receivable from Lucile to the extent of $29,000 and debiting its capital stock accounts in the same amount as of December 31, 1959.

14. The $2,328.17 difference, between the $31,328.17 and the $29,000 figures, was continued, with other very minor items, in the corporation's account receivable from Lucile. The record does not show that this balance was ever paid.

15. This left 62 shares of the 700 which had been transferred from Leon. Of these, 32 were reissued in Leon's name. The other 30 were transferred, at Leon's direction, half to Louis S. Meyer and his wife as joint tenants, and half to Richard C. Burstein and his wife as joint tenants. The corporation's books reflect no account receivable from Leon with respect to these 62 shares and he made no payment to the corporation on account of them.

16. Leon was president and a director of the corporation. Throughout its fiscal years 1959-62, inclusive, Lucile was vice-president of the corporation and received a salary.

17. Lucile's income tax basis in her stock in the corporation was $29,000.

18. Lucile and Leon maintained two joint checking accounts. On one of these, Lucile's name appeared first and the statements for this account were sent to her. On the other, Leon's name appeared first and the statements for that account were sent to him. The two checks issued by the corporation to Lucile for its shares were deposited in the first of these accounts. Leon's $15,000 note to the bank was paid by a check drawn on this account by Lucile. Lucile drew other checks on the account payable to Leon or utilized for his obligations or expenses.

19. The corporation's earned surplus on June 30, 1955, as shown on its federal income tax return for fiscal 1955, was $21,970.23. Its returns for succeeding fiscal years showed taxable loss or income as follows:

Fiscal year 1956, loss of	($132,582.37)
Fiscal year 1957, loss of	(16,147.89)
Fiscal year 1958, loss of	(69,914.20)
Fiscal year 1959, income of	66,007.10
Fiscal year 1960, income of	2,492.13

The 1959 income includes, and results from, reported gain of $81,228.17 on the sale of the 638 shares of Thiokol stock. The 1956 loss includes the write-down in inventory.

20. In its fiscal years 1955-60, inclusive, the corporation made charitable contributions somewhat in excess of the amounts allowed as income tax deductions. Although these excesses were not deductible, they served to reduce earnings. Thus the corporation's actual net income for fiscal 1960, when adjusted downward for its excess contributions in that year, was $2,117.13.

21. For present purposes and *apart* from the effect, if any, upon earnings of the debt adjustment in the Arrangement, it suffices to say that, as of the end of fiscal

1959, the corporation had a sizeable accumulated deficit in earnings and profits. If, however, earnings were increased by the excess of the Arrangement's debt adjustment, the corporation possessed accumulated earnings from which dividends of $31,328.17 could be paid in fiscal 1960.

The Commissioner, in his 90-day letter to Lucile, included the $31,328.17 paid by the corporation to Lucile as taxable income to her for her taxable year 1959 on the theory that this was dividend income to her. It is this inclusion which produces the deficiency in Lucile's tax now in controversy. In his 90-day letter to Leon the Commissioner included, among other adjustment, a like amount of dividend income to Leon. This was on the theory that Lucile's receipt was on Leon's behalf. The item of course, if it is income at all, cannot be income to both taxpayers.

The Tax Court held that the payments made to Lucile in the corporation's fiscal year 1960 were essentially equivalent to a dividend to her in calendar 1959, within the meaning of §302(b)(1) of the Internal Revenue Code of 1954, 26 U.S.C. §302(b)(1); that the adjustment of the corporation's indebtedness in its 1956 Arrangement, to the extent the reduction exceeded the statutorily required reduction in bases of the corporation's assets, generated earnings and profits for the corporation; and that the entire distribution to Lucile in 1959 was a dividend includable, under Code's §301(c)(1), in her gross income. It also held that no part of the distribution was taxable to Leon.

Thus our basic question is whether the $31,328.17 is income under §301(c)(1). If the answer to this question should be in the affirmative, we would have the additional question whether that income is taxable to Lucile or to Leon.

We pass, for the moment, our consideration of the intricate issue of dividend equivalency and proceed directly to what we regard as the threshhold question and the heart of the matter, namely, whether the corporation in fiscal 1960 possessed earnings and profits (other than the current fiscal year's net income) from which a dividend, as defined in §316(a)(1), includable in the recipient's gross income, could be paid.

Section 301 of the 1954 Code governs the taxation of distributions of property by a corporation to its shareholders. Section 301(c)(1) provides that that portion of a corporate distribution which is a dividend shall be included in gross income. Section 316(a) provides that the term "dividend" means any distribution of property to shareholders out of either accumulated or current earnings and profits. Section 312 has some concern with the computation of a corporation's earnings and profits. Nowhere in the Code, however, are corporate earnings and profits specifically defined. The regulations would fill this gap at least partially. Treas. Regs. §1.312-6(b) brings into the computation of corporate earnings all exempt and nontaxable income and all items includable in gross income under §61.

It has long been said that income may be realized by a taxpayer upon the cancellation of indebtedness and the amount canceled is then to be included in gross income. §61(a)(12) of the 1954 Code; Treas. Regs. §1.61-12(a). See United States v. Kirby Lumber Co., 284 U.S. 1, 52 S. Ct. 4, 76 L. Ed. 131 (1931). But, as we have noted, §395 of the Bankruptcy Act provides an exception to this rule when it states that "no income or profit, taxable under any law of the United States . . . shall, in respect to the adjustment of the indebtedness of a debtor in a proceeding under this chapter, be deemed to have accrued to or to have been realized by a debtor . . . by reason of a modification in or cancellation in whole or in part of any such indebtedness" in an Arrangement proceeding. The question, therefore, is whether, although the debt cancellation resulted in no generation of taxable income for the corporation, it nevertheless still effected the creation of earnings and profits for the corporation.

The Commissioner asserts that this aspect of the case is controlled by the First Circuit's decision in Bangor & A.R.R. v. Commissioner, 193 F.2d 827 (1 Cir. 1951), cert. denied 343 U.S. 934, 72 S. Ct. 770, 96 L. Ed. 1342, affirming the Tax Court's decision reported at 16 T.C. 578 (1951). This was an excess profits tax case. At issue was the amount of the taxpayer's excess profits tax credit for 1943. In 1942 the taxpayer purchased some of its outstanding bonds on the open market at prices less than their face value. It was said, 193 F.2d p. 828, that "It is undisputed that this bond profit was realized income within the general definition of the" 1939 Code, and that the taxpayer "would have been taxable upon the whole amount of the bond profit in 1942" except for its exercise of an option, available to it under §22(b)(9) and §113(b)(3) of the 1939 Code and the applicable regulations, to exclude such profit from gross income and, instead, to reduce by the amount thereof, the bases of property it held. The taxpayer thus properly excluded the bond profit from normal tax and surtax net income for 1942. It sought, however, to add the profit to its earnings and profits as of the beginning of 1943. The effect of so doing would increase its invested capital and excess profits credit and thereby serve to reduce its excess profits tax for 1943. The Tax Court and the First Circuit ruled that the bond profit, although realized in 1942, was, by the exercise of the option, not then recognized and was to be excluded from the computation of earnings and profits for excess profits tax purposes.

The First Circuit drew the distinction between exempt income, on the one hand, and income which is realized but not recognized, on the other. As to exempt income, it said, p. 829 of 193 F.2d, that "the only logical time" to take it into earnings and profits is when it is realized; that the concept of accumulated earnings and profits for the purpose of the excess profits tax was the same as that for the income tax; and that, therefore, exempt income which is received and left in the business as working capital is to be included in earnings and profits for excess profits tax purposes. But, as to realized but not recognized income, the court said, pp. 829-30, "the problem is quite different." Here Congress has determined that "the economic changes are not definitive enough to be given tax consequences" but are to "be taken account of later." The addition, by the Second Revenue Act of 1940, of §115(1) of the 1939 Code relating to the effect on earnings and profits of nonrecognized gains was thought to be only a clarifying amendment and not one effecting a change in existing law. The court said, p. 831, that the underlying principle is that earnings and profits must be computed on the same basis as that employed in computing income subject to the income tax, that is, that gains are to be reflected in earnings when they are recognized.

To the same effect is Alabama By-Products Corp. v. United States, 137 F. Supp. 252 (N.D. Ala. 1955), aff'd 228 F.2d 958 (5 Cir. 1956).

We are inclined to the view that this First Circuit case is not controlling here. It was not a bankruptcy situation. It dealt with what concededly was income realized by the taxpayer or, as Judge Raum of the Tax Court described it, p. 580 of 16 T.C., the taxpayer "realized a taxable gain." The emphasis was on this realization of income. The Meyer corporation, instead, by the specific provisions of §395, realized no income by the Arrangement. The First Circuit taxpayer had an option, and utilized it, to avoid income taxation in 1942 on its then concededly realized and otherwise taxable income and to apply the amount thereof in the reduction of bases of assets held, thus merely postponing the income tax consequence, to what the court regarded as "an economically more significant event." Existing income and its allocation present an issue very different from that of statutorily declared absence of income. It is the latter with which we are here concerned.

We conclude that, under all the facts of the present case, the adjustment of the corporation's debts in its Arrangement did not result in the creation of earnings and profits for the corporation, with the dividend consequences which would otherwise ensue. We base this conclusion upon:

1. The specific and emphatic denial in §395 of the Bankruptcy Act that by the Arrangement's debt adjustment "no income or profit, taxable under any law . . . shall . . . be deemed to have accrued to or to have been realized by a debtor . . . ." This is a flat statutory nullification of any theory of income receipt. It is a positive denial, not a mere deferral of the tax recognition of realized income. And, for what the observation may be worth, the nullification applies to profit as well as to income.

2. The Chandler Act of 1938 was enacted after the 1931 decision in United States v. Kirby Lumber Co., supra. Thus, §395 of the Bankruptcy Act and, indeed, the parallel §§268, 520 and 679 of that Act, all came into being after *Kirby Lumber*. This chronology supplies and supports an inference that these new and added sections of the Bankruptcy Act, denying the accrual or realization of income to a debtor by an adjustment of its indebtedness, were adopted to overcome any possible adverse implication in the *Kirby* decision and others like it.

3. Claridge Apartments Co. v. Commissioner, 323 U.S. 141, 65 S. Ct. 172, 89 L. Ed. 139 (1944), seems to make this clear. That case concerned §§268 and 270 of the Act; these are those sections of the Corporate Reorganizations chapter corresponding to §§395 and 396. The Supreme Court referred to the *Kirby* case and the uncertainty which surrounded the question as to the realization of income from the adjustment of indebtedness. It noted "the conflicting pulls of policy involved in the revenue acts and in the bankruptcy legislation." It stated that §268 "had no other object, and there was no other occasion for its being, than to free Chapter X reorganizations from the tax deterrents, including tax uncertainties, imposed by the existing revenue act provisions." It said that "One who followed the procedure could be assured he would not thereby run into tax consequences which would be worse than the economic illness requiring that cure." See pp. 146-52 of 323 U.S., 65 S. Ct. pp. 177-178. This language and this approach, it seems to us, are equally applicable to §395. See 2 Mertens, Law of Federal Income Taxation (1961 revision), §11.23.

4. The conviction that Congress, by its enactment of the Arrangements chapter of the Bankruptcy Act, meant to provide a means for the preservation of a going business which otherwise, because of overwhelming debt burden, would disappear

from the economic scene, and that Congress, as a part of its aim and purpose, meant to avoid the deterrent effect of all adverse income tax consequences which otherwise might be conceived and which, if theoretically valid, would discourage the use of the Arrangement device. See Claridge Apartments Co. v. Commissioner, supra, p. 149 of 323 U.S., 65 S. Ct. 172, and Commissioner v. Motor Mart Trust, 156 F.2d 122, 125 (1 Cir. 1946).

5. The conviction that such congressional purpose was not confined to the corporate debtor's own income tax situation but extended to the debtor's accounting for all proper tax purposes. We do not read a partial limitation into §395.

6. The conviction that the confirmation of the Arrangement did not and could not serve to create earnings and profits in the Meyer corporation out of its preexisting earnings deficit. The *Kirby Lumber* rule is not absolute and applicable to all debt adjustments. See, for example, Helvering v. American Dental Co., 318 U.S. 322, 63 S. Ct. 577, 87 L. Ed. 785 (1943). Compare Commissioner v. Jacobson, 336 U.S. 28, 69 S. Ct. 358, 93 L. Ed. 477 (1949). Furthermore, the *Kirby* rule has no direct application here for the Meyer corporation did not acquire its own obligations at a discount.

7. The feeling that the First Circuit case supports rather than stands against Lucile's position. The court there stated, 193 F.2d p. 831, that the underlying principle is that earnings and profits must be computed on the same basis as that employed in computing income subject to the income tax. If this is so, and the debt adjustment is not realized income, it should not constitute earnings and profits. See Commissioner v. Wheeler, 324 U.S. 542, 547, 65 S. Ct. 799, 89 L. Ed. 1166 (1945).

8. The Supreme Court has typified §§268 and 270 of the Bankruptcy Act as "essentially reorganization provisions" and as "essentially tax relief provisions," and has said that their primary object and function "were to provide tax relief for parties undertaking reorganization and to prevent the clogging effects of the existing tax laws upon the cooperation of the Chandler Act." Claridge Apartments Co. v. Commissioner, supra, footnote 35, p. 163 of 323 U.S., 65 S. Ct. 172, 184. See Commissioner v. Motor Mart Trust, supra, p. 126 of 156 F.2d. What the Supreme Court said of §§268 and 270 must have application to §§395 and 396. The emphasis, therefore, is on tax relief and the proper effectuation of the Bankruptcy Act, rather than upon the raising of revenue. This being so, we give priority to the bankruptcy purpose.

9. Long ago, the Supreme Court defined income, for income tax purposes, "as the gain derived from capital, from labor, or from both combined." Eisner v. Macomber, 252 U.S. 189, 207, 40 S. Ct. 189, 193, 64 L. Ed. 521 (1920). Further, Treas. Reg. §1.61-12(b) referring to discharge of indebtedness, speaks in terms of the "realization" of income and states that "income is not realized" by a reduction of indebtedness in an Arrangement. This is a flat disqualification on the plateau of non-realization.

10. We draw no contrary inference from the fact that §396 requires the decrease of basis of the corporation's property for the debt adjustment but not beyond the property's fair market value as of the date of the order confirming the Arrangement. The argument is that the statutory requirement of basis adjustment carries an implication that, to the extent the debt decrease exceeds the basis decrease, it must constitute earnings to the corporation. The fair market value limitation upon the basis adjust-

ment requirement was added to the statute in 1940. Its omission in 1938 in the corresponding section in Chapter 10 has been characterized by the Supreme Court as "a plain blunder" which made the cure "worse than the disease." Claridge Apartments Co. v. Commissioner, supra, p. 151 of 323 U.S., 65 S. Ct. 172. Because Congress chose to adjust basis and thus to lessen available depreciation deductions and to afford an opportunity for the realization of greater capital gain when the asset is eventually disposed of, does not, it seems to us, imply that the excess debt adjustment over basis adjustment equates with corporate earnings forthwith. The statute certainly does not so provide or impose any such condition. We might expect to find the statute specific if the legislative intent had been to that effect. And the technical creation of immediate earnings strikes us as being an even more vivid example of the cure being worse than the disease than was afforded in the *Claridge Apartments* situation by the mere possibility of "higher taxes resulting in later years from the absence of any depreciation base and in case of sale of the property acquired." P. 151 of 323 U.S., 65 S. Ct. p. 179. We revert to §395's provision that "no income or profit taxable under any law . . . shall, in respect to the adjustment of the indebtedness of a debtor in a proceeding under this chapter, be deemed . . . to have been realized by a debtor. . . ."

11. This situation, we think, differs from the one where a corporation receives what clearly is income but which is statutorily exempt. The usual example is interest on state or municipal bonds or on some of the older government bonds. Income of this kind, although exempt to the corporation for purposes of the federal income tax, nevertheless constitutes earnings and is a source of taxable distributions. See, generally, 1 Mertens, Law of Federal Income Taxation (1962 revision) §9.32. That treatise observes, "Presumably, however, the receipt must have the characteristics of income to be included in earnings and profits." Debt adjustment, as we have noted, in some circumstances may have the characteristic of income but in other circumstances it does not. Where our governing statute is so positive in its denial of "income or profit" we place the present situation in the latter category.

We therefore conclude that the bankruptcy accounting for the corporation did not serve to create earnings and profits for it.

This leaves for determination the subsidiary question whether the existence of fiscal 1960 net earnings of $2,117.13 in the corporation resulted in taxable income to Lucile in that amount under §§302(b)(1) and 301(c)(1). This depends upon whether the distribution to her was essentially equivalent to a dividend. . . . [The Court's brief discussion and acceptance of the Tax Court's conclusion that the distribution was essentially equivalent to a dividend is omitted.]

In view of the Commissioner's approach to Leon's case and his characterization of the petition for review as one filed merely for the purpose of protecting the revenue, we do not disturb the Tax Court's determination there.

The Tax Court's decision in Leon's case, No. 18,531, is affirmed. Its decision in Lucile's case, No. 18,480, is vacated and that case is remanded for a redetermination of the deficiency in tax for the calendar year 1959 in accord with the views herein expressed.

NOTE

1. Suppose Corporation X's only income in 1966 is the interest it receives on its municipal bond holdings. X receives $10,000 in interest and distributes $10,000 to its shareholders. Do the shareholders have dividend income? What is the effect of §103? How is the result in this case distinguishable from the result in *Meyer*? Will the corporation in either of these cases ever recognize income? Compare *Bangor & Aroostook R.R.*, page 126 supra. In *Meyer* the court gave §395 of the Bankruptcy Act a scope that provides tax relief not only to the bankrupt corporation but also to the shareholders who receive distributions from the corporation. Is this a wise or compelled result?

2. In *Luckman*, 50 T.C. 619 (1968), a corporation had granted "restricted stock options" under §421 to employees who exercised the options at prices below the market value of the stock. The Tax Court held that under §421(a)(3) there was no deductible expense for the corporation and so no reduction in earnings and profits. The Seventh Circuit reversed, 418 F.2d 281 (1969). Is the Tax Court or Seventh Circuit the more persuasive? Why?

a. RELEVANCE AND COMPUTATION

JOSEPH B. FERGUSON v. COMMISSIONER
47 T.C. 11 (1966)

Hoyt, Judge: . . . . [The taxpayer was the sole shareholder in a corporation called "444," which was on the cash basis. In 1959 it expended $75,000 which the Commissioner characterized as a "constructive dividend" to the taxpayer. As of the beginning of 1959, 444 had a deficit in its earnings and profits account. Its current earnings in 1959 were sufficient to cover the "constructive dividend" unless, as taxpayer contended, the current earnings and profits account were to be charged with 444's income tax liability for 1959. The Commissioner contended that the corporate tax liability was an improper charge for two reasons: the tax had not been paid during the year 1959, and 444 was on the cash basis.]

. . . We have found as an ultimate fact that 444 was on the cash basis in 1959 and so we hold.

This holding brings us face-to-face with one of the classic unresolved problems in the area of earnings and profits: Are current year's earnings and profits of a cash basis corporation reduced by Federal income tax on current year's income although such tax is not paid until the following year (or years)? The regulations under section 312, I.R.C. 1954, provide (in sec. 1.312-6):

"(a) In determining the amount of earnings and profits (whether of the taxable year, or accumulated since February 28, 1913, or accumulated before

March 1, 1913) due consideration must be given to the facts, and, while mere bookkeeping entries increasing or decreasing surplus will not be conclusive, the amount of the earnings and profits in any case will be dependent upon the method of accounting properly employed in computing taxable income (or net income, as the case may be). For instance, a corporation keeping its books and filing its income tax returns under subchapter E, chapter 1 of the Code, on the cash receipts and disbursements basis may not use the accrual basis in determining earnings and profits; . . ."

Despite the unambiguous language of this regulation, the courts have had considerable difficulty coping with the effect of Federal income taxes on the earnings and profits of a cash basis corporation.[3] Leading text writers have noted the split of authority which exists in the cases today. Bittker, Federal Income Taxation of Corporations and Shareholders 145, fn. 9; Surrey and Warren, Federal Income Taxation 1238 (1960). This Court has played an integral role in the turbulent history of this problem, a history which must be reviewed and understood in order to adequately analyze and decide the issue in this particular case.

This question was first decided in Hadden v. Commissioner, 49 F.2d 709 (C.A. 2, 1931), in which it was held that earnings and profits of a cash basis corporation *are* reduced by income tax on current year's income. Our first encounter with the problem arose in M. H. Alworth Trust, 46 B.T.A. 1045 (1942), revd. 136 F.2d 812 (C.A. 8, 1943), certiorari denied 320 U.S. 784, in which we held that earnings and profits *are* reduced. We relied on the *Hadden* case but did not discuss it. Our decision was based upon corporate law and accounting concepts of dividends and impairment of capital. We reasoned that earnings and profits must take into account "outstanding liabilities" or else a distribution would leave such liabilities "as a charge on capital, regardless of the method by which the corporation keeps its books and to the extent thereof the distribution would impair capital and would not be a dividend." (46 B.T.A. at 1048). The language used was broad enough to cover all accrued liabilities — not just income taxes.

The decision in *Alworth* was reviewed by the Eighth Circuit, Helvering v. Alworth Trust, 136 F.2d 812 (C.A. 8, 1943), which rejected our reliance on corporate and accounting principles. The Court of Appeals pointed out that the *Hadden* case suffered from a marked lack of reasoning to support its result and that the tax rules prescribed by the internal revenue laws regarding dividends do not necessarily conform to standard corporate law concepts; that a distribution may be taxable as a dividend under the tax law even though the corporation making the distribution may have been barred by local corporate statutes (by reason of capital impairment, etc.) from distributing earnings. It was held that it would be an unwarranted extension of the tax statute to require that earnings and profits must be reduced by Federal taxes for the current year of a cash basis corporation.

This Court has followed the rule of the Eighth Circuit in *Alworth* in subsequent

---

[3]Although no one ever seems to have questioned the regulation insofar as it prohibits the reduction of earnings and profits of a cash basis corporation by accrued expenses *other than Federal income taxes* (and penalties related thereto).

cases in which we have considered the issue. Paulina duPont Dean, 9 T.C. 256 (1947), acq. 1947-2 C.B. 2, appeal dismissed nolle prosequi (C.A. 3, 1949); United Mercantile Agencies, Inc., 23 T.C. 1105 (1955).[4] Our opinion in United Mercantile Agencies, Inc., supra, was reversed by the Sixth Circuit sub. nom. Drybrough v. Commissioner, 238 F.2d 735 (C.A. 6, 1956), and the *Drybrough* case has become established as the leading case taking what is generally regarded as the polar position to *Alworth*. The reversal of our opinion in *United Mercantile* by *Drybrough* has been followed in Thompson v. United States, 214 F. Supp. 97 (N.D. Ohio 1962); and Demmon v. United States, 321 F.2d 203 (C.A. 7, 1963).[5]

There can be no quarrel with the fact that current year's earnings and profits are not necessarily synonymous with current year's taxable income. For example, interest received on tax-exempt bonds is not included in taxable income, yet must be included in earnings and profits, sec. 1.312-6(b), Income Tax Regs.; the reduction of earnings and profits for depletion is limited to depletion computed on the cost method even though the deduction from taxable income may be based on the more liberal percentage method. Ibid. sec. 1.312-6(c)(1). This absence of synonymity between earnings and profits and taxable income has been emphasized by the cases which adhere to the *Drybrough* view. Thus, one of the principal arguments raised has been: Since earnings and profits are determined for another purpose and are not necessarily the same as taxable income, there is no good reason why a strict cash basis must be adhered to for earnings and profits purposes even though the cash basis is used in accounting for taxable income.

This position is correct only in that there is no statute or inescapable rule of logic which *requires* strict adherence to the cash basis for earnings and profits purposes. However, there *is* a long-standing regulation which establishes such a requirement, sec. 1.312-6(a), Income Tax Regs., such a regulation has a sound basis in administrative policy and there are no persuasive reasons why any departure from the cash basis used for reporting income *should be* permitted for purposes of computing earnings and profits and why the Commissioner's regulations should be ignored.

The rationale which appears to underlie *Drybrough* and its progeny is traceable all the way back to the Board of Tax Appeal's opinion in *Alworth,* which was subsequently reversed in the Eighth Circuit. On page 739 of 238 F.2d, the court in *Drybrough* expressly states that it is persuaded by the reasoning of the Board in *Alworth*. After being reversed in *Alworth,* this Court has consistently followed the reversal, and we see no reason why we should not adhere to the same view here. The quoted regulations have been in existence for many years and should be upheld.

We hold that the current earnings and profits of 444, a cash basis taxpayer, for

[4]See also Newark Amusement Corporation, T.C. Memo. 1960-137, in which we relied on the regulations, followed *Alworth* and distinguished *Drybrough,* observing that *Drybrough* did not specifically disagree with *Alworth*. Estate of John H. Wheeler, 1 T.C. 640 (1943), reversed without discussion of this point, 143 F.2d 162 (C.A. 9, 1944), revd. 324 U.S. 542 (1945), in which we followed our original decision in *Alworth,* was decided before our holding in *Alworth* was reversed by the Eighth Circuit.

[5]The *Demmon* case is discussed in 19 J. Taxation 263 (1963). See also "Tax Consequences of Shareholder Diversions in Close Corporations," 21 Tax L. Rev. 223 (1966), for a general discussion of the issue and all of the cases.

the year 1959 are not to be reduced by any unpaid 1959 Federal income tax liability of 444. Helvering v. Alworth Trust, supra; Paulina duPont Dean, supra. Sec. 1.312-6(a), Income Tax Regs. Hence, the petitioner is chargeable with constructive dividend income. . . .

NOTE

1. A corporation incurs fraud penalties which are disallowed as deductions for income tax purposes on "public policy" grounds. Do the penalties, when accrued or paid, reduce earnings and profits? Estate of Esther M. Stein, 25 T.C. 940, 965-967 (1956).

2. Corporation Y, a subsidiary of Corporation X, pays Corporation X a $1000 dividend. As a result of §243 Corporation X's taxable income is increased by $150. What is the effect on Corporation X's earnings and profits? Are more facts needed? See R. M. Weyerhaeuser, 33 B.T.A. 594, 597 (1935). Compare H. Zarky and A. Biblin, The Role of Earnings and Profits in the Tax Law, 1966 So. Calif. Tax Inst. 145, 154.

b. EFFECT OF "INADEQUACY"

DiZENZO v. COMMISSIONER
348 F.2d 122 (2d Cir. 1965)

Before LUMBARD, Chief Judge, and SMITH and KAUFMAN, Circuit Judges.

LUMBARD, Chief Judge. Patsy DiZenzo and his wife appeal from that portion of a Tax Court decision which held them liable for additional taxes on their joint returns for 1946 through 1948. The issues on this appeal stem from the Tax Court's finding that Patsy DiZenzo diverted to his own use, but did not report on the appellants' tax returns, a part of the income of Patsy Frank, Inc. ("Patsy Frank"), a corporation controlled by him and engaged in general masonry and carpentry work in Bridgeport, Connecticut. Patsy DiZenzo owned 98 per cent of its stock; the balance was owned by his wife and son.

The appellants do not dispute that substantial amounts were diverted from Patsy Frank. However, they . . . contend that the court erred in holding that the entire amount should be treated as ordinary income to them without regard to whether Patsy Frank then had earnings and profits equal to the diversions.

. . . Section 115(d)* of the Internal Revenue Code of 1939 provides, so far as relevant here, that

> "any distribution made by a corporation to its shareholders . . . [which] is not a dividend . . . shall be applied against and reduce the adjusted basis of the stock provided in section 113, and if in excess of such basis, such excess

*Section 301(c)(2) and (3) are the 1954 Code counterparts. — ED.

shall be taxable in the same manner as a gain from the sale or exchange of property."

And §[316(a)] defines a corporate dividend as

"any distribution made by a corporation to its shareholders . . . (1) out of its earnings or profits accumulated after February 28, 1913, or (2) out of the earnings or profits of the taxable year . . . without regard to the amount of the earnings and profits at the time the distribution was made."

If [§§301(c)(1) and 316(a)] control, the amount of taxes due on the amounts diverted from Patsy Frank depends on whether or not the diversions exceed the corporation's earnings and profits and, if so, on the appellants' basis in their stock. The Tax Court, however, held that [these sections do] not control under the circumstances of this case. The controlling principle, according to the Tax Court, is "that amounts of corporate funds diverted by the dominant stockholder of a corporation constitute income to him regardless of whether they might be treated as a constructive dividend, and that taxability to the stockholder need not turn upon the existence of corporate earnings and profits." Or, restating the principle, . . . such amounts are to be treated under the general definition of gross income, §[61(a)], and not under the special provision for corporation distributions . . . .

We think that the Tax Court's interpretation is in error and that [§§301 and 316(a)] do control. We are not here dealing with sums stolen or embezzled by a taxpayer. There has been no suggestion that the diversions in this case were improper as a matter of corporate law, and no reason appears why they cannot properly be described as "distribution[s] made by a corporation to its shareholders." We are of course aware that statutory history and purposes may give special meanings to the language of the tax code. But the government has not shown that the ordinary meaning of the language of [§§301 and 316(a) is] inadequate in this instance.

The interpretation for which the government contends is of comparatively recent origin. As recently as 1960, the government itself was contending in a case similar to this that the amounts diverted constituted constructive dividends. Federbush v. Commissioner of Internal Revenue, 34 T.C. 740, 754 (1960), aff'd per curiam, 325 F.2d 1 (2 Cir. 1964). The government's present interpretation . . . seems to have first appeared in the reported cases in Davis v. United States, 226 F.2d 331, 334 (6 Cir. 1955), cert. denied, 350 U.S. 965, 76 S. Ct. 432, 100 L. Ed. 838 (1956), where it was accepted by the court. The Sixth Circuit later seemed to disavow *Davis* so far as civil cases are concerned, Drybrough v. Commissioner of Internal Revenue, 6 Cir., 238 F.2d 735, 737 (1956), but now has accepted the government's interpretation for both civil and criminal cases, Weir v. Commissioner of Internal Revenue, 6 Cir., 283 F.2d 675, 684 (1960). This interpretation may also have been accepted by the Third Circuit in United States v. Goldberg, D.C., 330 F.2d 30, 38, cert. denied, 377 U.S. 953, 84 S. Ct. 1630, 12 L. Ed. 2d 497 (1964), although the issue was not there squarely presented.

On the other hand, the government's view has been expressly rejected by the Eighth Circuit, Simon v. Commissioner of Internal Revenue, 8 Cir., 248 F.2d 869, 873 (1957), and decisions of the Fifth and Seventh Circuits tend in the same direction.

Bernstein v. United States, 234 F.2d 475, 482 (5 Cir.), cert. denied, 352 U.S. 915, 77 S. Ct. 213, 1 L. Ed. 2d 122 (1956); Demmon v. United States, 321 F.2d 203 (7 Cir. 1963). This court has not previously passed on the question; although diversions similar to those in this case were involved in Federbush v. Commissioner of Internal Revenue, supra, the government there argued that they constituted constructive dividends, and the Commissioner treated them as ordinary income only to the extent that he found that the corporation had earnings and profits. 34 T.C. at 754.

The case against the government's interpretation was well stated by the Eighth Circuit in Simon v. Commissioner of Internal Revenue:

"The corporate distribution here was made with the knowledge of the stock-holders and was acquiesced in by them. The corporation is liable for a substantial tax upon the diverted income it failed to report. Further tax will be collected from taxpayers under the constructive dividend theory. Fraudulent tax dealings should not be encouraged. Criminal penalties are provided for tax evasion, and fraud and delinquency penalties are assessed upon taxes due when the circumstances warrant. The Government should be allowed to collect all tax and penalties authorized by law, but it is not our function to expand tax liability to fields not covered by statute. We find nothing in the Tax Court's opinion to indicate that the diverted sums represented salary or any other recognized ordinary income. We believe that the only way that the diverted income already taxed to the corporation can be taxed to the individual taxpayers is by the treatment of such diversions as dividends and corporate distributions." 248 F.2d at 876-877.

The government has in this case pointed to the difficulty of reconstructing the earnings and profits of Patsy Frank in view of the corporation's hopelessly inadequate books and records. The answer to this problem is not to give a special meaning to the language of [§§301 and 316(a)] however, but rather to place the burden on the individual taxpayers to establish that the corporation did *not* have earnings and profits equal to the amounts diverted. See Lash v. Commissioner of Internal Revenue, 15 T.C.M. 453, 460 (1956), rev'd in part on other grounds, 245 F.2d 20 (1 Cir. 1957). We have no doubt that on the present record the Tax Court could properly have found that the appellants failed to establish that the accumulated earnings and profits of Patsy Frank did not equal the amounts which they diverted. The Tax Court made no findings in this respect, however, and the record is not so clear as to permit us to hold as a matter of law that the appellants failed to sustain this burden. This issue therefore must be left for disposition on remand.

The judgment of the Tax Court is reversed in part, and the case is remanded for additional findings.

NOTE

Corporation M, an accrual basis taxpayer, has an accumulated and a current deficit in earnings and profits. Its sales manager, who owns 10 per cent of the corporation's stock, pockets directly a customer's $10,000 payment for previously billed merchandise. The payment does not go through the corporation's bank account or books, and no other shareholder or corporate officer knows of the payment. Does the sales manager have $10,000 in ordinary income? Why? What is the impact of James v. United States, 366 U.S. 213 (1961), in this context? Would the result be different if the sales manager's wife owned 90 per cent of the stock? Why? Would the result be different if the sales manager (with no wife) owned 50 per cent of the stock? Ninety per cent of the stock? Why?

2. Constructive Dividends

a. DIVIDEND vs. CORPORATE INVESTMENT

PRUNIER v. COMMISSIONER
248 F.2d 818 (1st Cir. 1957)

Before MAGRUDER, Chief Judge, and WOODBURY and HARTIGAN, Circuit Judges.

MAGRUDER, Chief Judge. There is now before us a joint petition for review of two decisions of the Tax Court entered on April 12, 1957 — one determining that there is a deficiency in income tax of Henry E. Prunier and wife for the taxable year 1950 in the amount of $1,080.88, the other determining that there is a deficiency in income tax of Joseph E. Prunier and wife for the same taxable year in the amount of $1,348.98. The Tax Court (three judges dissenting) thus sustained a determination by the Commissioner that certain premiums paid by the corporation J. S. Prunier & Sons, Inc., on insurance policies on the lives of Henry and Joseph Prunier constituted taxable income to the taxpayers under the general language of §[61(a)].

Of the 450 shares of stock of J. S. Prunier & Sons, Inc., outstanding, Henry Prunier and his brother Joseph each owned one half or 225 shares until late in 1950, when it was voted at a stockholders' meeting that the two brothers would transfer five shares each to their cousin Irene M. Prunier, clerk of the corporation, who also served as the corporation's bookkeeper. Henry held the offices of president and treasurer, and Joseph was vice-president of the corporation.

As not infrequently happens in these closely held family corporations, the corporate books and records were kept in so sketchy and messy a fashion as to make it difficult to determine what was corporate action and what was the individual action of the two dominant stockholders.

Beginning in 1942 and running up to and including 1950, the brothers took out a total of eight life insurance policies. Four were purchased by Henry on his own life, naming his brother Joseph as beneficiary, in a total face amount of $45,000. Four were taken out by Joseph on his own life, naming his brother Henry as beneficiary, in a total amount of $45,000.

During the taxable year 1950 there was nothing in the terms of the policies, nor in the endorsements thereon, to indicate that the corporation had become their beneficial owner. Some question having been raised by the taxing authorities about this, it appears that at various dates in 1952 (which was subsequent to the tax year in question) endorsements were placed on each of the eight policies naming the corporation J. S. Prunier & Sons, Inc., beneficiary, but inexplicably containing the reservation, in all eight policies, of a right in Henry to change the beneficiary.

From at least as far back as 1946 the corporation has paid the premiums due on the various policies. It was testified on behalf of the taxpayers, and found as a fact by the Tax Court, as follows:

"When the policies were written, Henry and Joseph informed the agent of the substance of the written agreements which the policies were intended to carry out. They intended that in the event of the death of either the corporation should be the owner of the proceeds of the policies on the life of the deceased party for a single specific purpose, namely, use the proceeds to purchase the stock interest of the deceased party in the corporation at a price agreed upon by them prior to the death of either."

The tax treatment given to these transactions by the corporation was consistent with this found intention of the parties. Thus, in the agreed stipulation of facts the following statements appear:

"The corporation did not claim a deduction for the premiums paid on the above-mentioned insurance policies on its income tax return for the taxable year 1959, but did include the amount thereof in the adjustment made to surplus on Schedule M of its said return as follows:

" '8. Insurance premiums paid on the life of any officer or employee where the corporation is directly or indirectly a beneficiary . . . $8,081.44.'

"Similar adjustments were made by the corporation on its income tax returns for the taxable years 1946 and 1949, inclusive, for the premiums paid on those of the above-mentioned policies in effect during those years."

The aforesaid understanding that the corporation was to become the owner of the policies was first reflected on the books of the corporation, sometime toward the end of 1946, by the following entry in the minute book of the corporation describing a meeting of the directors:

"It is understood and agreed that any policies that Henry E. Prunier has on Joseph E. Prunier and any policies that Joseph E. Prunier has on Henry E. Prunier shall go to the corporation in the event of the death of either of them and this money is to be used by the corporation to buy out the interest of the party that dies.

"These policies are the ones that the corporation pays the premiums on.

"This will apply to any policies that may be bought in the future.

"(s) Henry E. Prunier
"(s) Joseph E. Prunier

"Witness
"(s) Irene M. Prunier"

A further corporate record appeared as Petitioners' Exhibit No. 2, reading:

"A special meeting of the stockholders and directors of J. S. Prunier & Sons, Inc., was held at the office of the corporation, on *Thursday, November* 2, 1950 at 7:30 P.M.

"On motion duly made and seconded, the following was proposed and agreed upon and made part of the by-laws:

"It was agreed by and between *Joseph E. Prunier, Vice-President* and *Henry E. Prunier, President* and *Treasurer* and present stockholders that the fair value of the Corporation stock is *One Hundred and Ten Thousand Dollars* ($110,000.00), and it is their desire that this be the value used should a stockholder sever his connection with the corporation, or in the event of death of either that the corporation will purchase the interest of the deceased party at said value, with the insurance money.

"It was also voted, at said meeting that both Joseph E. and Henry E. Prunier would issue each *five* of their shares to *Irene M. Prunier, Clerk*.

"In witness whereof they have executed this agreement, on this *third* day of *November* 1950.

"(s) Joseph E. Prunier
"*Vice-Pres.*
"(s) Henry E. Prunier
"*President & Treas.*

"Witness
"(s) Omer E. Prunier"

Petitioners place their reliance upon the settled ruling that where a corporation is the beneficiary and owner of a policy of insurance on the life of an employee or stockholder, the payment of premiums by the corporation does not constitute income to the insured individual. Casale v. Commissioner, 2 Cir., 1957, 247 F.2d 440. . . .

On the other hand, the Commissioner thinks the present case falls within the equally settled ruling that where a corporate employee or stockholder, or someone related to him, is beneficiary, and not the corporation, on a policy of life insurance on such employee or stockholder, payment of the premiums on such policy by the corporation constitutes income to the insured individual. Paramount-Richards Theatres, Inc. v. Commissioner, 5 Cir., 1946, 153 F.2d 602. . . .

We think the present case is more nearly like the type of case relied upon by petitioners. Despite the informality of the transactions, it seems to us that, in view of the facts in the record and of the findings by the Tax Court, the corporation would have been held to be the beneficial owner of the eight insurance policies under controlling Massachusetts law, and thus could have obtained the help of a court of equity to recover the proceeds of the insurance policies if one of the brothers had died in 1950. . . . We suspect also that in that event the corporation, on some theory of "ratification" or of "adoption", would have been held contractually bound to apply the proceeds of the policies to buy out the stock interest of the deceased stockholder, and that the deceased stockholder's legal representative would have been contractually bound to sell. . . .

Whether the corporation would have been legally obliged to continue paying the premiums in 1950 we do not need to say. The fact is that the corporation did pay the premiums. Also we do not have to decide what would have been the respective legal obligations of the parties, and what would have been the tax consequences, if one of the insured brothers had died in 1950. The fact is that neither brother died in 1950, and so far as appears both are still alive. It is sufficient for the purposes of the present case to say that neither brother realized any taxable gain in 1950 from the payment of the life insurance premiums by the corporation.

We do not understand that the majority of the Tax Court reached the conclusion they did on any notion of "disregarding the corporation fiction". Human beings take advantage of laws permitting incorporation because they think it will be economically advantageous to them individually. That is so whether the corporation is a "closely held" company owned by two stockholders, or one having two thousand stockholders. In a loose manner of speaking, it can be said that any corporate gain is a benefit, indirectly, to the stockholders, so that if a corporation becomes the beneficial owner of insurance policies, the stockholders receive the benefit thereof. Of course this argument proves too much, for it would lead to the conclusion that profits made by a corporation in its business are automatically taxable income to the stockholders. This is contrary to the taxation scheme of the Internal Revenue Code. And the government is only contending in this case that it was the payment of premiums by the corporation which constituted income to the insured employees and stockholders, which in itself is a recognition of the corporation as a separate legal entity.

The gist of the Tax Court's argument is contained in the following excerpt from the majority opinion:

> "In view of what has been said above, it appears that if Joseph or Henry had died during the taxable year, the corporation would not have been enriched by receiving the proceeds from insurance policies on the life of the deceased and using them to purchase stock he had owned in the corporation. The corporation's indebtedness to creditors would have remained undiminished, and while the corporation would have eliminated at least the greater part of the deceased's ownership interest in it, represented by his stock, the proportional interest of the surviving stockholder, or stockholders, thereby would have been greatly increased. In this situation and since the record does not otherwise indicate any benefit which might flow to the corporation from the purchase of a deceased insured's stock interest, we conclude that during the taxable year the corporation was neither the beneficial owner nor the beneficiary of the insurance policies on the lives of Joseph and Henry involved here."

Certainly the fact that the corporation may have been contractually bound to apply any proceeds of the policies, had they matured in 1950, to buy out the stock interest of a deceased stockholder, does not mean that the corporation would not have been "enriched" by collecting the face amount of the policies. All that would then have been involved would have been a change in the form of the assets from cash to treasury stock. We have hitherto pointed out the limited utility of the concept of corporate purpose as distinguished from stockholder purpose. See Lewis v. Commissioner, 1 Cir., 1949, 176 F.2d 646, 649-650. But if it were necessary to look for a corporate business purpose in the present case, we could refer to the arguments in Mannheimer & Friedman, "Stock-Retirement Agreements," 28 Taxes 423, 425 (1950), as follows:

> "Even while the decedent is still alive, the agreement and insurance benefit the corporation because they tend to stabilize the corporation's business. If the bank knows about the agreement, it may well be inclined to extend credit more liberally to the corporation because the possibility of inexperienced shareholders injecting themselves into the management is eliminated. If the key employees are informed of the agreement, it will be an inducement to them to remain with the corporation because they realize that the continuation of the business in the hands of the survivor is assured — and with it their jobs.
>
> "If there is no stock-retirement agreement when the decedent dies, often his family will ask a high price for his stock, or demand dividends without regard to the needs of the corporation, or even press for dissolution. So far as the survivor is concerned, he may very well be unwilling to work indirectly for the benefit of his former 'partner's' family or directly with the second husband of his former 'partner's' widow."

In the present case the government has not made any real effort to controvert the argument that under the Massachusetts decisions a court of equity would treat the corporation as the equitable owner of the policies of insurance. That being so, and having in mind the statutory scheme whereby the corporation J. S. Prunier & Sons, Inc., is dealt with as a separate legal entity and a separate taxable unit, and disregarding the loose sense in which it could be said that a benefit to J. S. Prunier & Sons, Inc., is a benefit to its controlling stockholders, it is sufficiently evident that the payment of premiums by the corporation in 1950 did not constitute, in that taxable year, reportable income to Henry and Joseph Prunier. See generally, Casale v. Commissioner, 2 Cir., 1957, 247 F.2d 440. What will happen when one of the brothers dies is not before us.

A judgment will be entered vacating the decisions of the Tax Court and remanding the case to that Court for further proceedings not inconsistent with this opinion.

NOTE

If a corporation owns an insurance policy on the life of a principal shareholder and designates (revocably) the shareholder's estate as the beneficiary, what is the tax consequence to the estate when the proceeds are paid to the insured's estate after he dies? Why? The answer given in Ducros v. Commissioner, 272 F.2d 49 (6th Cir. 1959), is one which the Commissioner has announced he will not follow. Rev. Rul. 61-134, 1961-2 Cum. Bull. 250.

If a corporation makes an irrevocable designation of its shareholder-insured's estate as beneficiary, would premium payments made after the designation constitute dividends? Why?

See W. Goldstein, Tax Aspects of Corporate Business Use of Life Insurance, 18 Tax L. Rev. 133 (1963); J. Sneed, A Defense of the Tax Court's Result in *Prunier* and *Casale,* 43 Cornell L.Q. 339 (1958).

b. DIVIDEND vs. INTEREST OR "UNREASONABLE EXPENSE" — §116

In John L. Ashby, 50 T.C. 409 (1968), the Tax Court held that the corporate taxpayer was not entitled to deduct club and entertainment expenses or depreciation, maintenance and repairs on a boat which it owned. The corporation failed to prove error in the amount of entertainment expense the Commissioner had allowed and failed to prove the club or boat was used primarily for business, as required by §274. The Commissioner also sought to tax the majority shareholder with the disallowed expenses as a dividend. The court sustained the Commissioner in full as to the entertainment and club items. As to the boat, however, the shareholder was taxed only on 48/68ths of the costs involved, since the court found that only that percentage of the boat use benefitted the individual. The "primary" use rule of §274 does not prevent allocation as to the individual shareholder, although it may require disallowance in full as to the corporation.

In general, as the Tax Court said in *Ashby,* 50 T.C. at 417, "[i]t is well established that any expenditure made by a corporation for the personal benefit of its stockholders or the making available of corporate-owned facilities to stockholders for their personal benefit may result in the receipt by the stockholders of constructive dividends. See Challenge Manufacturing Co., 37 T.C. 650 [(1962)], and cases cited therein."

If an expense is disallowed to the corporate taxpayer as "unreasonable," as in the case of excessive salary to a sole shareholder, is it to be taxed to the recipient as a "dividend" in all cases? Why? What is the impact on earnings and profits of a disallowed corporate expense taxed to a shareholder as a dividend? Why? Does it make any difference to the individual whether a disallowed corporate expense is taxed to him as a dividend or as salary? Consider §116.

3. *Waiver of Dividend*

REVENUE PROCEDURE 67-14
1967-1 Cum. Bull. 591

§1. *Purpose.*

The purpose of this Revenue Procedure is to specify the conditions which must be present before the Internal Revenue Service will consider issuing a ruling on a proposed waiver of dividends transaction.

§2. *Background.*

The Service has published two Revenue Rulings involving a waiver by a majority stockholder of his right to future undeclared dividends.

.01 Revenue Ruling 45, C.B. 1953-1, 178, described a fact situation under which no family or direct business relationship existed between the majority and minority stockholders, and the waiver was executed for a valid business purpose. The Revenue Ruling concluded that any dividend payments to the minority stockholders would not result in income to the waiving stockholder.

.02 On the other hand, Revenue Ruling 56-431, C.B. 1956-2, 171, involved a waiver by a majority stockholder whose relatives owned 25 percent of the stock of the corporation. Because of the existence of the significant family interest, the alleged business purpose was considered incidental and the waiver was considered as having been executed primarily for the benefit of the related stockholders. The Revenue Ruling concluded that the waiving stockholder would be taxed on the increased distribution to the related stockholders resulting from the waiver.

.03 Revenue Ruling 65-256, C.B. 1965-2, 85, although not involving an explicit waiver of dividends, did involve a merger under the terms of which the majority stockholder of one of the corporations agreed to accept a separate class of stock in the successor corporation subject to certain dividend limitations. In that ruling, members of the majority stockholder's family owned only 0.06 percent of the total capital stock of the surviving corporation and there were bona fide business reasons for the majority stockholder's acceptance of a class of stock with dividend restrictions. The ruling concluded that the majority stockholder would not be in constructive receipt of income when dividends are paid on a second class of stock.

§3. *Requests for Rulings.*

Based upon the Revenue Rulings described above, the Service will consider a request for a ruling on a proposed waiver of dividends transaction under the following conditions:

.01 A bona fide business reason must exist for the proposed waiver of dividends.

.02 The relatives of the stockholder proposing to waive his right to future dividends must not be in a position to receive more than 20 percent of the total dividends distributed to the nonwaiving shareholders. For this purpose the relatives of a waiving stockholder include his brother and sister (whether by the whole or half blood), spouse, ancestors, and lineal descendants, the spouses of his brothers and sisters (whether by the whole or half blood) and the spouses of his lineal descendants.

.03 A ruling issued on a proposed waiver of dividends transaction will clearly indicate that the ruling will no longer be applicable if any change in the stock ownership during the waiver period enables nonwaiving relatives to receive more than 20 percent of a dividend, unless the change occurs because of death.

.04 A ruling issued on a proposed waiver of dividends transaction will not be effective for a period longer than three years from the date of the ruling.

.05 A request for a ruling on a proposed waiver of dividends transaction must be submitted to the National Office in accordance with Revenue Procedure 67-1 [1967-1 Cum. Bull. 544].

NOTE

What is meant by a "bona fide business reason" in the context of a dividend waiver? What is an example of such a "business reason"? On what theory is a "waived" dividend taxed to a shareholder who does not receive an actual distribution? Why is family relationship with other shareholders relevant? If shareholders neglect to "waive" before receipt, may they return a dividend distribution and be free of tax on the dividend if they could have waived on a tax-free basis before the distribution? Why?

Suppose a corporation declares a pro rata dividend on November 1, 1968, payable on January 10, 1969, to shareholders of record on December 30, 1968. On December 30, 1968, all shareholders ask the Board of Directors to rescind the dividend declaration and the Board does so. Do the shareholders have income and, if so, when? Why? Would your answer be different if the shareholders made their request and the Board acted on January 5, 1969? On January 10, 1969? Why?

B. *DISTRIBUTIONS IN RETIREMENT OF INVESTOR INTEREST*

1. *Liquidating Distributions and Redemptions*

a. COMPLETE LIQUIDATIONS — §§331, 333

COMMISSIONER v. CARTER
170 F.2d 911 (2d Cir. 1948)

Before L. Hand, Chief Judge, and Swan and Chase, Circuit Judges.

Swan, Circuit Judge. This appeal presents the question whether income received by the taxpayer in 1943 is taxable as long-term capital gain, as the Tax Court ruled, or as ordinary income as the Commissioner contends. The facts are not in dispute. The taxpayer, Mrs. Carter, had owned for ten years all the stock of a corporation which was dissolved on December 31, 1942. Upon its dissolution all of its assets were distributed to her in kind, subject to all its liabilities which she assumed. In the distribution she received property having a fair market value exceeding by about $20,000 the cost basis of her stock, and she reported such excess as a capital gain in her 1942 return and paid the tax thereon. In the corporate liquidation she also received 32 oil brokerage contracts which the parties stipulated had no ascertainable fair market value when distributed. Each contract provided for payment to the corporation of commissions on future deliveries of oil by a named seller to a named buyer. The contracts required no additional services to be performed by the corporation or its distributee, and the future commissions were conditioned on contingencies which made uncertain the amount and time of payment. In 1943 the taxpayer collected commissions of $34,992.20 under these contracts. She reported this sum as a long-term capital gain; the Commissioner determined it to be ordinary income. The Tax Court held it taxable as capital gain. The correctness of this decision is the sole question presented by the Commissioner's appeal.

Mrs. Carter's stock was a "capital asset" as defined by [§1221]. In exchange for her stock, she received the assets of the corporation upon its dissolution. The tax consequences of such a transaction are controlled by [§331(a)(1) which calls for liquidating distribution to be "treated as in full payment in exchange for stock," §1001(a) which defines gain or loss as the spread between "adjusted basis" and "amount realized," §1001(b) which defines "amount realized" as "the sum of any money received plus the fair market value of . . . property . . . received," and §1002 which provides that all gain or loss is to be recognized unless otherwise provided in the statute]. . . . From the foregoing statutory provisions, it is obvious that if the oil brokerage contracts distributed to the taxpayer had then had a "fair market value," such value would have increased correspondingly the "amount realized" by her in exchange for her stock and would have been taxable as long-term capital gain, not as ordinary income. Boudreau v. Commissioner of Internal Revenue, 5 Cir., 134 F.2d 360; Fleming v. Commissioner of Internal Revenue, 5 Cir., 153 F.2d 361. The question presented by the present appeal is whether a different result is required when contract obligations having no ascertainable fair market value are distributed in liquidation of a corporation and collections thereunder are made by the distributee in later years.

In answering this question in the negative, the Tax Court relied primarily upon Burnet v. Logan, 283 U.S. 404, 51 S. Ct. 550, 75 L. Ed. 1143. . . .*

The Commissioner argues that the *Logan* case is inapplicable because there the taxpayer had not recovered the cost basis of her stock while here she had. The Tax Court thought the distinction immaterial. We agree. The Supreme Court spoke of the annual payments as constituting "profit" after the seller's capital investment should be returned. Until such return it cannot be known whether gain or loss will result from a sale; thereafter it becomes certain that future payments will result in gain. No reason is apparent for taxing them as ordinary income. As this court said in Commissioner of Internal Revenue v. Hopkinson, 2 Cir., 126 F.2d 406, 410, "payments received by the seller after his basis had been extinguished would have been taxable to him as capital gains from the sale of the property," citing Burnet v. Logan as authority.

The Commissioner also urges that the *Logan* case is distinguishable because it dealt with a sale of stock rather than exchange of stock for assets distributed in a corporate liquidation. This contention is answered by White v. United States, 305 U.S. 281, 288, 59 S. Ct. 179, 83 L. Ed. 172, and Helvering v. Chester N. Weaver

---

*Burnet v. Logan involved a year when capital gains and ordinary income were taxed at the same rate. — Ed.

Co., 305 U.S. 293, 295, 59 S. Ct. 185, 83 L. Ed. 180, where the court held that the recognition required . . . of gains and losses on liquidations must for purposes of computation of the tax, be taken to be the same as that accorded to gains and losses on sales of property.* Consequently we agree with the Tax Court's ruling that the principle of the *Logan* case is applicable to a corporate liquidation where stock is exchanged in part for contracts having no ascertainable market value, and that future collections under such contracts are taxable as capital gain in the year when received if the distributee has previously recovered the cost basis for the stock.

The Commissioner's argument that such collections are analogous to the receipt of interest or rent upon bonds or real estate distributed in a corporate liquidation overlooks a significant distinction. Payment of interest or rent does not impair the value of the bond or real estate since each remains as a capital asset regardless of the number of payments. See Helvering v. Manhattan Life Ins. Co., 2 Cir., 71 F.2d 292, 293. But with respect to the oil brokerage contracts, under which no additional services were to be rendered by the payee, each payment decreases their value until, with the final payment it will be completely exhausted; and, if the payments be treated as income, the distributee has no way to recoup his capital investment, since concededly he has no economic interest in the oil producing properties and therefore no right to depletion deductions.[2] Hence to consider the brokerage payments as ordinary income would produce a most unjust result and one quite unlike the result which follows the distribution of bonds or real estate in a corporate liquidation.

For the foregoing reasons we think the decision of the Tax Court correct. It is affirmed.

NOTE

1. In Rev. Rul. 58-402, 1958-2 Cum. Bull. 15, the Service reviewed *Carter, Burnet v. Logan*, 283 U.S. 404 (1931), and other cases and concluded that it "will continue to require valuation of contracts and claims to receive indefinite amounts of income, such as those acquired with respect to stock in liquidation of a corporation, except in rare and extraordinary cases." Why? What is a "rare and extraordinary" case in this context? Under what circumstances might it be to the taxpayer's advantage to have a "contracts right" distribution in liquidation valued at time of liquidation?

---

*See cross-reference provisions of §331(c). — ED.

[2]It is true, in the case at bar, the taxpayer had no capital investment in the brokerage contracts because from other assets distributed she had already recovered the cost basis of her stock and the oil brokerage contracts had no ascertainable fair market value. But the Commissioner's analogy argument would be equally applicable if the brokerage contracts had been the only corporate assets distributed and it had been possible to ascribe to them a fair market value of $21,000. In that case, the distributee's capital investment in the brokerage contracts would have been $20,000, the cost basis of her stock being $1,000. She would be entitled to recover her capital investment before she could be charged with receiving either gain or ordinary income, and the only source of recovery would be the payments which would ultimately exhaust the value of the contracts. Hence the answer given above to the analogy argument is apposite.

2. Suppose Mr. Baker forms a corporation of which he is the sole shareholder, making an initial contribution to capital of $50,000. The corporation is very successful and in three years has retained earnings and profits of $450,000. Baker liquidates the corporation, distributing all the assets to himself in one liquidating distribution. What are the tax consequences to Baker? See §331. What are the arguable justifications for §331? For a contrary rule?

3. In *Carter*, what would the result have been if the brokerage contracts had had an ascertainable fair market value of $10 in 1942?

4. See T. Farer, Corporate Liquidations: Transmuting Ordinary Income into Capital Gains, 75 Harv. L. Rev. 527 (1962). See B. Bittker and J. Eustice, Complete Liquidations and Related Problems, 26 Tax L. Rev. 191 (1971).

COMMISSIONER v. DOERING
335 F.2d 738 (2d Cir. 1964)

Before WATERMAN, FRIENDLY, and HAYS, Circuit Judges.

FRIENDLY, Circuit Judge. The Commissioner of Internal Revenue invites us to reverse a decision of the full Tax Court, 39 T.C. 647 (1963), permitting the taxpayer to deduct $6,760 of legal fees and related expenses as an ordinary and necessary expense paid or incurred "for the production or collection of income" under §212(1) of the Internal Revenue Code of 1954. We must decline the invitation.

The taxpayer, Otto C. Doering, Jr., had long owned stock, ultimately 20%, of Argosy Pictures Corporation, which was engaged in producing motion pictures. In 1950 Argosy contracted with Republic Pictures Corporation for the latter to distribute and exhibit three pictures which Argosy was to produce; Argosy was to receive a specified portion of Republic's profits from distribution and exhibition. Argosy completed the pictures by the end of 1952. A dispute as to the amount payable by Republic shortly ensued. Over a three-year period Argosy paid substantial fees and disbursements to the attorneys representing it in the dispute. An accounting firm thought Argosy was entitled to $1,000,000 more than Republic had remitted; Republic contended it had overpaid.

In January, 1956, Argosy was dissolved. Each stockholder received his share of its cash, $12,822.05 in Doering's case, and of the claim against Republic. It is stipulated that the claim against Republic had no ascertainable market value when Argosy was dissolved. The former stockholders retained the same law firm that had represented Argosy to effect collection from Republic; in order to meet anticipated legal expenses, they deposited the cash they received with Bankers Trust Company, which was also to act as agent to receive and disburse any recovery. Negotiations conducted by the attorneys led to Republic's paying $540,000 in final settlement in December, 1956. Bankers Trust Company credited Doering, on his 20% share, with $108,000, which it paid over to him after deducting $6,360 and $400 to cover his portion of the fees for legal and banking services.

Doering's 1956 return reported the excess of $120,822.05 over the basis of his stock as proceeds from the sale or exchange of a long-term capital asset, I.R.C.,

§§331(a)(1), 1001, 1002, 1011, 1012, taxable at 25% under the "alternative tax" of §1201(b). He deducted the amounts he had paid the attorneys and the Trust Company as "ordinary and necessary expenses . . . for the production or collection of income" under §212(1). The Commissioner disallowed the deduction, asserting that because, under the rule of C.I.R. v. Carter, 170 F.2d 911 (2 Cir. 1948) and Westover v. Smith, 173 F.2d 90 (9 Cir. 1949), cf. Burnet v. Logan, 283 U.S. 404, 51 S. Ct. 550, 75 L. Ed. 1143 (1931), the amount collected by Doering from Republic was taxable at the rate applicable to long-term capital gains, the fees were capital in nature and should be subtracted from the gross amount received for the stock. The Tax Court sustained the taxpayer, four judges dissenting.

"Collection of income" would seem to have been the precise purpose for which the fees were paid. Argosy's claim against Republic did not arise from the sale of a capital asset but from the grant of the right to distribute and exhibit its films. The Commissioner concedes that Argosy's receipts from Republic were taxable as ordinary income and that its legal expenses in effectuating collection were "ordinary and necessary expenses paid or incurred in carrying on its trade or business" under §162 and its predecessor. If Argosy had remained in business through 1956, the very legal fees here at issue would thus have been deductible under §162. If at the outset Argosy had paid the attorneys a lump sum for all the work to be done in achieving a final disposition of the claim, that also would have been deductible under §162, even though, as a result of the subsequent dissolution, the avails all went to the stockholders; assuming that Argosy had offsetting income, the economic impact of the legal fees here at issue thus would have been only 48% of the sum paid. More important, counsel for the Commissioner admitted at the argument that, had Doering's claim been susceptible of valuation at the time of liquidation, any excess subsequently realized by virtue of further negotiation or litigation would be taxable as ordinary income and the legal fees would be deductible under §212(1). No different conclusion with respect to the tax status of the legal fees is warranted by the fact that in this case "where the property distributed on liquidation has no ascertainable fair market value, the transaction is held open for tax purposes, and subsequent payments, being treated as part of the liquidation, are taxed as capital gains." Campagna v. United States, 290 F.2d 682, 684 (2 Cir. 1961).

What is critical under the statute is what the stockholders were trying to get, not the rate at which Congress chose to tax what they got . . . . To be sure, the Commissioner is right that the word "income" in §212(1) is not to be given a wholly literal reading. If a taxpayer sells securities or other capital assets, §212(1) does not permit him to deduct expenses of sale even though the sale produces a gain which constitutes "gross income," §61(a)(3), Davis v. C.I.R., 151 F.2d 441 (8 Cir. 1945), cert. denied, 327 U.S. 783, 66 S. Ct. 682, 90 L. Ed. 1010 (1946) — any more than the provision for deduction of business expenses had permitted a similar deduction, Spreckels v. C.I.R., 315 U.S. 626, 62 S. Ct. 777, 86 L. Ed. 1073 (1942); Isaac G. Johnson & Co. v. United States, 149 F.2d 851 (2 Cir. 1945). Similarly, the allowance in §212(2) of a deduction for expenses paid or incurred "for the management, conservation, or maintenance of property held for the production of income," did not oust the established rule requiring capitalization of expenditures in defense of the title to property . . . . But neither of these principles carries the day for the Commissioner in this case. The only disposition of a capital asset here was the exchange of Doering's stock in Argosy for a share of the company's assets; the further payments from Republic were eligible for the alternative tax of §1201(b), not because they represented the sale or exchange of a capital asset but because their collection constituted part of the "gain from the sale or other disposition," I.R.C. §1001(a), of Doering's stock.

Munson v. McGinnes, 283 F.2d 338 (3 Cir.), cert. denied, 364 U.S. 880, 81 S. Ct. 171, 5 L. Ed. 2d 103 (1960), followed in Spangler v. C.I.R., 323 F.2d 913, 921 (9 Cir. 1963), much relied on by the Commissioner, does not assist him. The Third Circuit there concluded that legal expenses incurred by a seller in avoiding a sale induced by the buyer's fraud and obtaining a higher price was "the kind of selling expense which must be capitalized," since the problem was still "to reach mutually satisfactory or binding terms of sale." 283 F.2d at 335. Judge Hastie carefully differentiated true cases of "collection" of income; on that basis he distinguished Naylor v. C.I.R., 203 F.2d 346 (5 Cir. 1953), which held that legal fees incurred in collecting the amount claimed to be due under a contract of sale qualified for deduction under the predecessor of §212(1), even though the sale was of a capital asset. Doering naturally relies on *Naylor* but neither he nor we need go so far; we leave open whether we should follow that decision on facts such as were there presented. The decision of this Court in Isaac G. Johnson & Co. v. United States, supra, 149 F.2d 851, relied upon by our dissenting brother, went upon the ground that the expenses there in question were "incident to a sale of a capital asset." See footnote 4, p. 852. Neither of these ingredients is present here.

It is quite true that for taxpayers whose income attains the brackets attracting rates considerably above 25%, the result reached by the Tax Court makes the economic bite of the expenses much softer than if these were required to be deducted from the receipts. But it is equally true that the position urged by the Commissioner could produce a seemingly unjustified difference in result between a case like the present and one where a corporation had paid the legal fees before the distribution; and concentration of attention on the tax benefit of deductions may sometimes obscure that what the taxpayer would truly have liked was not to have to make the payment at all. In any event it is not appropriate for courts to deny benefits to which taxpayers are entitled under a normal reading of the words used by Congress in the absence of clear evidence of contrary Congressional purpose . . . . We find nothing to indicate that Congress meant to eliminate from §212 expenses coming within the ordinary meaning of the language save those, such as expenses of purchasing and selling, in defense of title, and other capital expenditures (e.g., for improvements), which had long been banned under §162 and its predecessors. In fact the legislative history is rather unfavorable to the Commissioner's position. The Committee Reports on the bill adding what has become §212 stated that "The term 'income' . . . is not confined to recurring income but applies as well to gain from the disposition of property." 77th Cong. 2d Sess., H.R. Rep. No. 2333, 75, S. Rep. No. 1631, 87 (1942). Consistent with this the Regulations, §1.212-1(b), say that when the section speaks of "income", it "is not confined to recurring income but applies as well to gains from the disposition of property" and gives as an example the purchase of defaulted bonds "with the expectation of realizing capital gain on their resale, even though no current yield thereon is anticipated." The Regulations do rule out "(k) Expenses paid or incurred in defending title to property . . . ," and "(n) Capital expenditures . . . ," but Doering's payments do not fall under these rubrics.

Affirmed.

HAYS, Circuit Judge (dissenting): The majority opinion rests on the language of the statute. " 'Collection of income' would seem to have been the precise purpose for which the fees were paid." But the attitude of assurance conveyed by this resort to literalism is considerably shaken when we examine the authorities. The majority opinion itself concedes that "income" "is not to be given a wholly literal reading," citing cases in which §212(1) was not applied to expenditures for the "collection of income." . . .

In fact the only authority cited for the majority's position is Naylor v. C.I.R., 203 F.2d 346 (5th Cir. 1953), a decision, the soundness of which is questioned in Spangler v. C.I.R., 323 F.2d 913, 919-20 n.15 (9th Cir. 1963), which is characterized by Mertens as "questionable" (4 Mertens, Law of Federal Income Taxation §25A. 12 fn. 40 (1960 revision)), and about which the majority leaves open the question as to whether this court would follow it on its facts.

The majority is sure that the transaction here in question must be charaterized for the purpose of §212(1) as the collection of income because the amount collected would have been income if Argosy had not been liquidated and its assets distributed. But Argosy *was* liquidated and the payment to the taxpayer was in fact a part of the distribution of its assets. As the government says in its Brief "not only was the capital transaction open when the contested expenses were incurred, but they also had their origin in the liquidation exchange and were an essential incident to that transaction."

The conclusion that the legal expenses must be capitalized is vividly emphasized by the hypothetical situation set forth by Judge Raum's dissent in the Tax Court:

> "If, for example, the expenses herein were $70,000, we would have the strange result that at most only $54,000 would be reportable as income (one-half of the $108,000 proceeds, by reason of the capital gains provisions) whereas a deduction of $70,000 would be allowable under the Court's decision. Thus, a transaction actually producing a net profit would appear on the return as a net loss."

Surely we are not compelled to read the statute in a way that will produce so bizarre a result.

If it were well established by judicial construction of Section 212(1) that an ordinary deduction could be taken for legal expenses incurred in factual circumstances such as those before this court, we should of course hesitate to introduce uncertainty into the tax law by reaching a contrary result. But the court is presented here with a unique situation and prior decisions dealing with similar circumstances are sharply in conflict . . . .

The decision of this circuit that is closest in point is Isaac G. Johnson & Co. v. United States, 149 F.2d 851 (2d Cir. 1945), which held that legal expenses in a condemnation proceeding must be capitalized. Accord, Williams v. Burnet, 61 App. D.C. 181, 59 F.2d 357 (1932). Under state law title vested in the state upon the initiation of the condemnation proceedings; the subsequent litigation was concerned only with determining the amount of compensation required under the standard of fair market value. This decision is patently antithetical to Naylor v. C.I.R., supra. In both the "sale" had been consummated and all that remained was to settle a dispute concerning the "sales" price — "book value" in one case, "fair market value" in the other. That is also the situation in the present case, the dispute being over what constitutes the "profits" of Republic in which Argosy was to share.

The controlling principle in this case is that stated in Towanda Textiles, Inc. v. United States, [180 F. Supp. 373]: "For many years it has been recognized that fees incurred in realizing a capital gain must be deducted from the gross amount received to arrive at the net gain for tax purposes." 180 F. Supp. at 377. That principle, which was the foundation of this court's decision in Isaac G. Johnson & Co. v. United States, supra, requires us to rule for the Commissioner in this case.

I would reverse the decision of the Tax Court.

NOTE

What function does the concept of a "deduction" serve in the scheme of the income tax? With whose opinion, Judge Friendly's or Judge Hays', does that concept fit best? Is the majority or the dissent "right" under the statute? Why?

WALES v. COMMISSIONER
50 T.C. 399 (1968)

FORRESTER, Judge: . . . . Some concessions have been made as to 1961, and the only question now remaining is whether petitioners have shown their election to liquidate their wholly owned corporation under section 333 of the Internal Revenue Code to be invalid.

It is stipulated that in the event respondent's position is sustained on this issue, the deficiency for the taxable year 1961 will be as determined by the respondent for that year. In the event the petitioners' position is sustained, it is stipulated that the deficiency will be $9,493.09.

Findings of Fact

Some of the facts have been stipulated and are so found.

The petitioners, Harold and Dorothy Wales, . . . individually and jointly, have held all of the outstanding stock of the Harmack Grain Company (hereinafter sometimes referred to as Harmack) at all relevant times. This company was engaged in the grain storage and grain merchandising business and as of May 23, 1960, it elected to be taxed as a small business corporation under subchapter S of the Internal Revenue Code (sections 1371-1378).

On November 18, 1960, the petitioners filed an instrument dated November 15, 1960, with the State of Colorado. It bears the caption "Voluntary Dissolution of Harmack Grain Co. by Consent of Shareholders" and is identified in the stipulation as "A statement of intent to dissolve." It is reproduced below:

VOLUNTARY DISSOLUTION OF
HARMACK GRAIN CO.
BY
CONSENT OF SHAREHOLDERS

KNOW ALL MEN BY THESE PRESENTS That we, H. O. Wales and Dorothy Wales, being all of the shareholders of Harmack Grain Co. of Cheyenne Wells, Colorado, hereby and by these presents make our statement of intent to dissolve the said corporation and set forth the following information . . . .

Pursuant to this instrument, petitioners filed the following "Articles of Dissolution" with the Department of State of Colorado on February 16, 1961:

ARTICLES OF DISSOLUTION
OF
HARMACK GRAIN COMPANY

Pursuant to the provisions of the Colorado Corporation Act, the undersigned corporation adopts the following Articles of Dissolution for the purpose of dissolving the corporation.

FIRST: The name of the corporation is Harmack Grain Company, Cheyenne Wells, Colorado.

SECOND: A statement of intent to dissolve the corporation was filed in the office of the Secretary of State of the State of Colorado on November 18, 1960.

THIRD: All debts, obligations and liabilities of the corporation have been paid and discharged, or adequate provision has been made therefor.

FOURTH: All remaining property and assets of the corporation have been distributed among its shareholders, in accordance with their respective rights and interests.

FIFTH: There are no suits pending against the corporation in any court in respect of which adequate provision has not been made for the satisfaction of any judgment, order, or decree which may be entered against it. . . .

On March 3, 1961, the Secretary of State of the State of Colorado issued the Certificate of Dissolution of the Harmack Grain Company: . . .

On March 17, 1961, Form 966 was mailed to the district director of internal revenue in Denver on behalf of Harmack by Harold Wales. The form is titled "Return of Information Under Section 6043 of the Internal Revenue Code of 1954 to be Filed by Corporations within 30 Days After Adoption of Resolution or Plan of Dissolution, or Complete or Partial Liquidation." The form recited that Harmack corporation had adopted a plan of "dissolution, or complete or partial liquidation" as of February 16, 1961. Attached to this form were two Forms 964 signed by Harold Wales and Dorothy Wales respectively, which forms recited that the person signing same elected to have each and every share of capital stock in Harmack taxed in accordance with section 333 of the Internal Revenue Code. The forms recited that all property owned by the corporation was to be transferred in the month of March 1961. These documents were received by the district director on March 20, 1961.

On Harmack's income tax return for the fiscal year ended April 30, 1961, there was a footnote reciting that the stockholders elected to liquidate under section 333 of the Internal Revenue Code of 1954. Attached to the return was the following document:

Special Meeting of the Stockholders of
Harmack Grain Company
Cheyenne Wells, Colorado

A special meeting of the stockholders of Harmack Grain Company was held in Cheyenne Wells, Colorado, upon due notice and call, on the 16th day of February, 1961, for the purpose of liquidation of said corporation.

All stockholders being present in person, namely Dorothy Wales and H. O. Wales, representing 850 shares of stock, the meeting having been called to order by the President, the minutes of the previous meeting having been read and approved, upon motion duly made, seconded and unanimously carried, the resolution was adopted:

"Whereas the Harmack Grain Company is in the process of being dissolved as a Corporation, and

"Whereas a plan of liquidation should be adopted for the distribution of the assets of said Corporation, now, therefore,

"Be it Resolved that the following plan of liquidation be and the same is hereby adopted and approved, to-wit:

"1. All of the assets of the Corporation shall be assigned, transferred and conveyed to the stockholders of said Corporation jointly, each to own an undivided interest therein in the proportion that his or her stock bears to the total amount of stock issued and outstanding.

"2. Said distribution shall be made within 20 days of the date of the adoption of this resolution in exchange for the stock owned by such stockholders, which stock shall be surrendered to the Secretary of the Corporation and cancelled forthwith." . . .

On their joint income tax return for the calendar year 1961 petitioners reported as long-term capital gain amounts received by them which resulted from the liquidation distributions from Harmack. In his statutory notice of deficiency, respondent determined that such amounts were ordinary income (dividends) to the petitioners under section 333(e) of the Internal Revenue Code.

Ultimate Finding of Fact

Petitioners failed in their attempt to become "Qualified Electing Shareholders" of Harmack Grain Company under the provisions of sections 333(c) and (d) of the Internal Revenue Code.

Opinion

This case presents the narrow factual question whether Harmack's plan of liquidation was adopted on February 16, 1961, as contended by respondent, or on November 18, 1960, as is contended by petitioners. This depends upon the narrow combined question of law and fact as to whether the November 1960 activities of Harmack amounted to the adoption of a "plan of liquidation."

Sections 333(c) and (d) of the Code provide that in order to become a "qualified electing shareholder," a shareholder *must* file his written election within 30 days after the date of adoption of "the plan of liquidation."

Neither party contests that in the instant case the petitioners' attempted elections on Forms 964 were timely if February 16, 1961, is the date of the adoption of the plan, but were out of time if the plan was adopted on November 18, 1960.

Petitioners urge other and alternative grounds for avoidance of their attempted elections which we need not, and do not consider.

In this case it is apparent that petitioners misconceived the meaning and effect of a liquidation of their wholly owned corporation under the provisions of Code Section 333. On their joint income tax return for 1961 they showed their liquidation distributions from Harmack as long-term capital gains in contravention to the requirements of section 333(e)(1). Respondent's determination treated the requisite portion of such distributions as dividends under that section. Petitioners now realize that their attempted elections were to their disadvantage and seek to avoid them.

The instant case presents an essentially identical question as was presented to us in Frank T. Shull, 34 T.C. 533 (1960), reversed and remanded 291 F.2d 680 (C.A. 4, 1961). In *Shull* the taxpayers, sole owners of a corporation, filed a consent to dissolution with the Virginia State Corporation Commission on March 27, 1952. Subsequently they filed an election to be taxed under section 112(b)(7) of the 1939 Code (now section 333), and stated that they had formally adopted a plan of liquidation on March 31, 1952. The election was filed within 30 days of March 31, but more than 30 days after March 27. Subsequently, the taxpayers realized that their election was to their disadvantage and contended that their election was invalid, because they had actually adopted a plan of liquidation on March 27.

As in the instant case, the Commissioner contended that their election did conform to the requirements of (now) section 333.

When the issue was presented to us, we found that no plan of liquidation was adopted when the shareholder consents to dissolution were obtained because the consents were "no more than a unanimous vote to accomplish dissolution," and a vote to dissolve was not the equivalent of an adoption of a plan of liquidation. Our holding in *Shull* amounted in effect to a requirement that the "plan of liquidation" specified in the statute be a completely detailed and definitive plan.

There is no definition of the term "plan of liquidation" in section 333. The term appears in a number of other sections in both the 1939 and 1954 Codes, but none of them afford a definition of the term. Cf. sections 337, 332, and 346 of the 1954 Code and 112(b)(6), 112(b)(7) and (prior to its amendment in 1942) 115(c) of the 1939 Code.

Since deciding *Shull* we have departed from the views expressed therein. In Mountain Water Co. of La Crescenta, 35 T.C. 418 (1960) we said (pp. 426-427):

> "We think it is clear from the evidence in this case that a plan of liquidation was adopted by petitioner on April 25, 1955, when the directors decided to accept the condemnation award without appeal and in fact accepted a check for the net amount thereof. Prior to that date the directors had recognized the probability that all the operating assets of the company would be taken by the county water district and the purpose for existence of the company would cease; and it is apparent that the *consensus of opinion* was that if the condemnation was successful, the proceeds from the involuntary sale should be distributed in liquidation. But in view of the reluctance of the stockholders to sell without a fight, no final decision was made until the meeting of April 25, 1955. When the decision to accept the award was made at that meeting, the plan of liquidation was put into effect even though no formal resolution of liquidation or dissolution was adopted. Obtaining the consent of the stockholders to dissolve the company and the subsequent adoption of a resolution of dissolution at the directors meeting on June 7, 1955, [the date contended for by respondent] was only one of the formal steps taken in carrying out the plan of liquidation. . . . [Emphasis supplied.]"

Similarly, in Alameda Realty Corporation, 42 T.C. 273 (1964), we said (p. 281):

> "Raymond and Irma (the sole stockholders and directors of Alameda) decided to accept the offer and take the money received by Alameda from the sale of the building for their own use. The facts show that this decision was made on or shortly prior to October 6, 1955, when Alameda entered into the contract to sell the Finance Building. The facts further show that the Finance Building was Alameda's only operating asset. After Alameda had sold the Finance Building, its only asset other than debts due it by Raymond and Irma, was money and Raymond and Irma withdrew this money for their personal use as they planned to do when they agreed to have Alameda sell the building. These facts show a plan of liquidation and distribution of assets. . . ."

Thus in these two cases we have held: (1) that the acceptance of a condemnation award coupled with a "consensus of opinion" to liquidate, and (2) that the sale of the only operating asset of a corporation, were each sufficient to evidence the adoption of a "plan of liquidation." Certainly neither case is factually as strong as is the case where the corporation's shareholders have taken action to come under a state statute committing the company to liquidation under a plan therein set forth.

Prior to *Shull* we had held repeatedly that no formal plan of liquidation was necessary. . . .

In reversing us in *Shull,* 291 F.2d 680 (C.A. 4, 1961), the Circuit Court held that when written consents to dissolution were signed and filed by the shareholders, a written plan of liquidation was effectively adopted. That court pointed out that under the Code of Virginia, upon filing a written consent to dissolution by the shareholders of a corporation, a certificate of dissolution was caused to be issued and the corporation was officially dissolved. Thereafter the corporation had a limited existence for the purpose of settling the corporate affairs, selling and conveying its property and dividing its assets among its stockholders in final liquidation. In addition, by statute, the business of the corporation could no longer be continued.

Under those circumstances, the Court found that the corporation in that case was clearly in a status of liquidation under a plan of liquidation. The shareholders had "stripped from the corporation its old clothes and placed upon it the shroud of liquidation. Since they had acted deliberately, they would hardly be heard to say they had no plan to do what they had done."

In holding the plan to be one envisioned by Congress in enacting (now) section 333, the Court pointed out at 682-683:

"There is nothing in §112(b)(7) [now 333] which requires that a plan of liquidation must be in writing or in any particular form.

"Paragraph (A) [now (a)] simply provides that if liquidation occurs within one calendar month, the distribution in complete liquidation will result in limited recognition of gain to electing shareholders with respect to the shares they own at the time of the adoption of the plan of liquidation.

"Paragraph (D) [now (d)] provides that the election must be filed within thirty days after the adoption of the plan of liquidation, but nowhere does §112(b)(7) [now 333] purport to declare how a plan of liquidation is to be adopted or how its adoption is to be evidenced.

"Paragraph (C) [now (c)] does provide that the election of an individual shall be ineffective unless stockholders having not less than eighty per cent of the total combined voting value of all classes of stock entitled to vote on the adoption of the plan of liquidation make similar elections, but this conditional limitation upon the right of stockholders to make an election does not import into Paragraph (A) a requirement that the plan shall have been adopted at an open stockholders' meeting called for that purpose or suggest that the unanimous written consent of all stockholders to a plan of liquidation is not an effective adoption of the plan within the meaning of §112(b)(7).

"It appears, therefore, that when the two stockholders who owned the entire outstanding stock of the corporation signed and filed their written consent to its dissolution under the provisions of Virginia's laws a written plan of liquidation was effectively adopted. The Certificate of Dissolution, which then issued, and Virginia's statutes fully authorized the directors to do everything necessary to accomplish the liquidation of the corporation without further action by the stockholders."

In conclusion, the Court stated at 684-685:

"Unquestionably, whether a plan of liquidation has or has not been adopted is a question of fact ordinarily for the Tax Court. When the stockholders acted deliberately, however, and had gone so far in the actual execution of a plan of liquidation as to dissolve the corporation and terminate its existence for all purposes other than liquidation, we find no escape from the conclusion that a plan of liquidation had been adopted. If subsequently, the stockholders in a formal way declared their intention to do what they already had done, the declaration was of no controlling significance."

In the instant case, petitioners entered into an agreement to dissolve their wholly owned corporation and filed the agreement with the State of Colorado. Thereafter they complied with the Colorado statutes providing for dissolution and eventually received a certificate of dissolution from the state.

Under Colorado law, . . . a corporation filing a statement of intent to dissolve was required to cease normal business operations, proceed to wind up its affairs, and distribute all assets to its shareholders after making provision for its obligations. These provisions are substantially identical to the provisions of the Virginia statute which controlled *Shull.* . . .

When petitioners' statement was filed with the State of Colorado . . . the Colorado statutes . . . not only set forth the manner of liquidation but prohibited the corporation from all other activity. When the petitioners, as sole shareholders, filed their intent to dissolve, they affirmatively committed themselves to follow those provisions. And we find, as the Fourth Circuit found in *Shull,* that that type of commitment was sufficient to constitute the adoption of a plan of liquidation.

Certainly under the reasoning of the decided cases, there would have been no doubt that a plan of liquidation existed had the statement of intent to dissolve stated a course of liquidation identical to the Colorado statutes. The fact that the statutory provisions bound the petitioners by operation of law at the time of filing, rather than through formal adoption by them of a compatible plan, does not change the fact that the petitioners agreed to carry out liquidation in a specific manner.

We note further that section 333(a)(1) merely requires that the liquidation be in pursuance of a plan of liquidation — nothing more. Such language is in contrast to that in section 332(b)(3), which refers to liquidation of subsidiaries, where the provision requires a "plan of liquidation under which the transfer of all the property under the liquidation is to be completed within 3 years from the close of the taxable year during which is made the first of the series of distributions under the plan." It seems clear that had Congress wished the plan of liquidation to be as explicit in section 333 as in 332(b)(3), it would have used language as explicit as that in 332(b)(3).

Under the Colorado statutes, dissolution is delayed until a final distribution is made, while in Virginia it occurs immediately after filing a consent to dissolve. However, this distinction does not alter the fact that in both states, when the respective declarations of intent to dissolve are filed, there is shown an intent to proceed to liquidate a corporation in a prescribed manner. In each state the duties of the directors of a corporation to effect the final distribution of a corporation's assets are substantially identical.

Therefore, we recognize the identity between this case and *Shull,* and follow the Court of Appeals therein.

Having found that a plan of liquidation was adopted on November 18, 1960, we find that no election to liquidate under section 333 was timely filed within 30 days of that time; thus petitioners' election to liquidate under that section was invalid. We therefore adopt the stipulation of the parties that petitioners' tax liability for 1961 is $9,493.09 and in that amount.

Reviewed by the Court.

Decision will be entered in accordance with the foregoing opinion.

DRENNEN, J., concurs in the result.

NOTE

1. Should a shareholder's gain on liquidation be recognized at all and, if so, to what extent? Why? If it should be recognized, how should it be taxed? Why? Should a shareholder be taxed to the extent of his allocable share of earnings and profits even if he has no gain, and if so, how? Why? Should a shareholder's loss be recognized on complete liquidation? Why? See §267(a)(1). The scheme of taxation reflected in §331(a)(1) has been the law for many years, but it has not always been the law.

2. Section 334(a) provides for a "fair market value" basis for assets received by a shareholder in a liquidation in which gain or loss is recognized under §331. If you were to provide for nonrecognition to any extent, would you follow the approach of §334(c) in your accompanying basis provision? Why?

3. What do you perceive to be the policy underlying §333? To what extent do you agree with it? Why? Why should "money," "stock," and "securities" produce the result provided in §333(e)(2)?

4. Why do you think §333(a)(2) requires a distribution within "some one calendar month"? If a plan is adopted within the meaning of §333(a)(1) on October 28, if the parties wish to complete the liquidation as soon as possible and if it will take at least five consecutive days to distribute all the assets, what would you advise the parties to do to make sure that the shareholders receive the benefits of §333? Why?

5. Section 332 provides for the nonrecognition of a parent corporation's gain on the liquidation of its subsidiary in particularized circumstances. Functionally, an intercorporate liquidation (at least where the shareholder corporation is in control of the subsidiary) may be very similar to a merger. For that reason, §332 will be studied with "reorganizations." See Chapter 4, page 460 infra.

6. Is the court's approach in *Wales* consistent with that in The City Bank of Washington, 38 T.C. 713 (1962), page 26 supra? Should it be?

7. See J. McGaffey, The Deferral of Gain in One-Month Liquidations, 19 Tax L. Rev. 327 (1964); G. Bickford, Special Liquidations Other than Under Section 337, 13 W. Res. L. Rev. 265, 265-269 (1962); B. Bittker and J. Eustice, Federal Income Taxation of Corporations and Shareholders 354-364 (2d ed. 1966).

b. REDEMPTIONS — §§302, 304, 301, 318, 303

(i) COMPLETE TERMINATION OF INTEREST

MATHIS v. COMMISSIONER
47 T.C. 248 (1966), Acq. 1967-1 Cum. Bull. 2

Hoyt, Judge: . . . The questions here presented are whether the petitioners received dividend income on certain shares of preferred stock of the Krispy Kreme Doughnut Corp., and if so, whether the failure of the petitioners to file Federal income tax returns reporting such distributions was due to reasonable cause and not to willful neglect.

Findings of Fact

The facts have been fully stipulated. The stipulation of facts and exhibits referred to therein are incorporated herein by this reference.

Oscar L. Mathis, hereinafter referred to as the decedent, died intestate on February 22, 1960, while a resident of Kentucky. Josie L. Mathis, widow of the decedent, was appointed administratrix of the decedent's estate. Josie L. Mathis filed a joint individual income tax return for 1960 for herself and her deceased husband with the district director of internal revenue at Louisville, Ky. No income tax return by or on behalf of the Estate of Oscar L. Mathis, deceased, was filed for 1960. Josie L. Mathis did not file income tax returns for 1961 and 1962.

The Krispy Kreme Doughnut Corp., hereinafter referred to as Krispy Kreme, a North Carolina corporation with principal offices at Winston-Salem, had two issues of stock prior to and during October 1960, neither of which was listed on any major stock exchange. One issue consisted of 16,314 shares of Class A common, and the other consisted of 2,088 shares of 6-percent cumulative preferred with a par value of $100 per share.

The decedent's estate included 380 shares of preferred stock and 1,880 shares of common stock of Krispy Kreme. The decedent's stock ownership constituted 18.20 percent of the preferred stock and 11.52 percent of the common stock. The decedent acquired 250 shares of Krispy Kreme preferred stock on June 10, 1947 and 130 shares of the preferred stock on November 20, 1948. Prior to January 1, 1960, Krispy Kreme had never formally declared, or actually paid, a dividend on the preferred stock. Krispy Kreme did not formally declare a dividend on the preferred stock while the decedent or his estate was an owner.

The decedent owed Krispy Kreme $51,555.61 with accrued interest at the time of his death. This debt was represented by a note dated July 23, 1959, issued in the face amount of $64,000. The principal amount had been reduced by seven installment payments. As security for this note, decedent had pledged and delivered 940 shares of common stock and 380 shares of preferred stock to Krispy Kreme.

The decedent's estate had insufficient funds to pay the Krispy Kreme debt which was in default. Therefore, the administratrix of the estate entered into negotiations with Krispy Kreme to work out an arrangement, satisfactory to both parties, under which the debt could be discharged. On October 21, 1960, an agreement was ultimately executed. . . . [The court's recital of the contract is omitted. — Ed.]

Pursuant to the terms of the contract between the administratrix and the company, she sold 1880 shares of Krispy Kreme common stock to the corporation accepting in payment therefor 620 shares of preferred stock and a credit of $49,860 against decedent's debt to Krispy Kreme. The balance of $2,486.14 due on decedent's debt to Krispy Kreme was to be paid by the estate out of the cash payment hereinafter mentioned due under the contract. Krispy Kreme in turn agreed to purchase the estate's total of 1,000 shares of preferred stock for $132,630. This total consideration was to be paid as follows: $26,130 in cash upon the signing of the contract, $6,500 in monthly installments of $500 each for 13 months, and a final payment of $100,000 due on or before September 30, 1961. At Krispy Kreme's option, final payment could be delayed until May 1, 1962, but in this event Krispy Kreme would be required to pay an additional consideration of $500 per month during the extended period.

Krispy Kreme paid the administratrix the sum of $26,130 in October of 1960 upon the signing of the contract which was dated October 21, 1960; the administratrix delivered 1880 shares of common stock to Krispy Kreme and Krispy Kreme in turn delivered 1,000 shares of preferred stock to the administratrix. In addition Krispy Kreme made monthly payments of $500 each to the administratrix which totaled $2,000, $6,000, and $2,000 for the years 1960, 1961, and 1962, respectively. The administratrix delivered 1,000 shares of Krispy Kreme preferred stock to the First National Bank of Winston-Salem in accordance with an escrow agreement made on October 24, 1960, pursuant to the terms of the contract above specified. On May 1, 1962, Krispy Kreme paid the sum of $100,000 to the escrow agent and upon receipt thereof the escrow agent paid said sum over to the administratrix and delivered the 1,000 shares of Krispy Kreme preferred stock to Krispy Kreme.

The articles of incorporation of Krispy Kreme provide that no dividends are to be paid to holders of its common stock until all accrued dividends owed the preferred stockholders have been paid. Krispy Kreme's corporate charter provides that upon dissolution of the corporation, the preferred stock shall be repaid its par value, together with all accumulated and unpaid dividends, before any amount is paid on the common stock; and, after such payment, the preferred stock shall not further share in the assets of the corporation. The preferred shares of stock in Krispy Kreme had no voting rights.

During the years 1960, 1961, and 1962, respectively, Josie L. Mathis, as administratrix, distributed to herself as an heir a portion of the monthly payments made by

Krispy Kreme under the settlement contract in the amounts of $2,050, $3,000, and $1,000.

Decedent's estate reported and paid estate taxes on the value of its shares in Krispy Kreme, which value was reported as follows: 380 shares preferred, $70,630; 1,800 shares common, $111,860.

No federal fiduciary income tax return was filed on behalf of the decedent's estate for 1960, 1961, or 1962.

The decedent was the uncle of Vernon Rudolph, president of Krispy Kreme, and of two other employees of Krispy Kreme. Josie L. Mathis had no blood relationship with anyone connected with Krispy Kreme. The decedent, his wife, and their children had no other close relationship to any of Krispy Kreme's stockholders.

The respondent assessed deficiencies based on his determination that the decedent's estate received dividend income as a result of the distributions made by Krispy Kreme with respect to the preferred stock owned by decedent's estate during 1960, 1961, and 1962, and as provided for in the contractual agreement relating to the purchase of the stock by Krispy Kreme. Total dividends were determined to be $36,130, and this was the total amount received by the administratrix on the preferred stock prior to the final payment of $100,000. The deficiency notice adjustments increased the estate's taxable income for 1960 by dividends in the amount of $28,130. For the same year the joint income tax liability of the Estate of Oscar L. Mathis, deceased, and Josie L. Mathis was increased by adding dividend income of $2,000 to the taxable income disclosed by the joint return filed. In the explanation of adjustment contained in the respondent's determination it was stated that the amount of $2,050 received by Josie Mathis in 1960 as distributions from the Estate of Oscar L. Mathis, deceased, constitutes taxable income. After deduction of the dividend exclusion in the amount of $50, additional income of $2,000 was added to the income disclosed by the return filed.

For the years 1961 and 1962 it was determined that Josie L. Mathis received dividend income in the respective amounts of $3,000 and $1,000, such amounts being dividend income distributed from the Estate of Oscar L. Mathis, deceased, in those years. Decedent's estate was allowed a deduction in the deficiency computation for 1960 for distributions made to beneficiaries.

Ultimate Findings of Fact

All of the payments made by Krispy Kreme pursuant to its agreement dated October 21, 1960, were part of and steps in an integrated plan to effect a complete redemption of the preferred stock in question; they were all distributions in part or full payment in exchange for the stock redeemed which resulted in a complete termination of the petitioners' interest in the corporation.

Opinion

Respondent contends that the decedent's estate received accumulated and current dividends on Krispy Kreme preferred stock in the amount of $36,130. Section 316 provides that the term "dividend" means any distribution of property made by a corporation to its shareholders out of its earnings and profits. Dividends are included in gross income under section 61(a)(7).

Petitioners contend that the $36,130 in issue here constituted installment payments made under the purchase contract relating to Krispy Kreme stock owned by the decedent's estate. If these payments qualify under section 302(a) as distributions in redemption of all of the Krispy Kreme preferred stock owned by the decedent's estate, the distributions will be considered as part or full payment in exchange for the stock. In such a case, therefore, the transaction would be accorded capital gains treatment rather than dividend treatment.

Respondent concedes that the purchase of the 1,000 shares of preferred stock by Krispy Kreme on May 1, 1962, qualifies as a redemption within the provisions of section 302(a), and that the gain realized is taxable at capital gains rates. However, respondent maintains that the purchase price of the preferred stock was $100,000, the amount paid on May 1, 1962. He argues that all amounts received under the terms of the contractual agreement between Krispy Kreme and the decedent's estate from the time of its execution until May 1, 1962, were dividends and therefore not part of the overall purchase price of the preferred stock.

Respondent contends that the contractual agreement fixed the price of the preferred stock at $100,000 plus the amount of accrued dividends owed at the date of redemption. He concludes that since no dividends were owned on May 1, 1962, only $100,000 was paid and this amount represented the true purchase price. Respondent places reliance on certain factors to bolster his argument.

The decedent's estate reported the value of the 380 shares of preferred stock owned at the date of death as $70,630, or approximately $185 per share. This valuation was the estimated fair market value of the stock as of the date of death. See sec. 2031. Petitioners state that this value was determined by subtracting $62,000, the contract price placed upon the 620 preferred shares issued for the redeemed common, from the minimum redemption price for all 1,000 shares of preferred which was $132,630. It is petitioner's position that the 1,000 shares were redeemed for $136,130, or $136.13 per share.

Respondent explains the differing values by stating that the fair market value of preferred stock depends largely on the amount of the accrued dividends. Thus it is argued that the value of the preferred shares might have been $185 per share at the date of death because of accrued dividends, but the fair market value would drop to $100 per share if all the dividends were paid.

It is respondent's view that the parties to the contractual agreement recognized that the price to be paid for the preferred shares when they were finally redeemed would depend on the amount of accrued dividends. Respondent concludes from his analysis that dividends in arrears on the 380 shares of preferred stock owned by decedent at his death were paid upon execution of the purchase agreement. He then argues that Krispy Kreme thereafter made monthly dividend payments on all 1,000 shares and held an option to purchase the preferred stock for $100,000 any time after October 21, 1960, but not later than May 1, 1962.

The evidence of record has convinced us that $36,130 of the $136,130 received under the preferred stock redemption agreement actually was measured by an allowance for accrued and unpaid dividends, although no formal declaration of dividends had ever occurred. However, this does not mean that the $36,130 should be treated as ordinary dividend income. On the contrary, accrued dividends on preferred stock paid in connection with a stock redemption are properly treated as part of the payment in exchange for the stock. See G.C.M. 5180, VII-2 C.B. 110. The decisive question, therefore, is whether the $36,130 here involved should be considered to have been paid in part payment for the preferred stock in connection with a stock redemption.

While conceding that the sale of the preferred shares was in complete redemption, respondent contends that the initial and installment payments were dividends and the final payment was the true redemption price. The problem with his argument is that it fails to distinguish an obligation arising under a purchase contract from an intangible right to dividends which have never been declared. At the time the redemption contract was executed, Krispy Kreme had no obligation to pay dividends which had theoretically accrued on the preferred stock. While it is true that owners of the preferred stock would be entitled to accrued dividends before dividends could be paid on the common stock or before distributions could be made to common shareholders upon dissolution of the corporation, this does not support the existence of a presently enforceable right to receive accrued dividends in a certain dollar amount on the date the purchase contract was executed. Therefore, we see no reason to segregate the receipt of $36,130 from the redemption of the preferred shares based upon the foregoing reasoning of respondent.

Respondent's final argument for treatment of the $36,130 as ordinary dividend income focuses upon the terms of the purchase agreement. It is contended that the sale of the preferred stock did not occur until May 1, 1962, with the payment of $100,000, since the agreement was only an agreement to purchase which did not pass title to the stock. Relying on Warren National Bank, Executor, 22 B.T.A. 759 (1931), affd. 61 F.2d 325 (C.A. 3, 1932), respondent maintains that under the agreement, Krispy Kreme had the choice of tendering the $100,000 to the escrow agent and purchasing the stock, or not tendering the $100,000, in which case no sale would occur and the escrow agent would return the stock to the decedent's estate. It is further maintained that the payments of $36,130 were made prior to the passage of title and could not be returned regardless of whether Krispy Kreme later purchased the stock. Payments on the preferred stock should therefore have constituted dividends when made and this characterization should not change whether or not Krispy Kreme later purchased the stock. Merrill C. Gilmore, 25 T.C. 1321 (1956).

Respondent emphasizes the lack of penalties if either party had refused to honor the purchase agreement for the preferrd stock. There was no need for penalties, according to respondent, since neither party would lose because of nonperformance. The decedent's estate would still own the stock and Krispy Kreme would have had to pay the accrued dividends someday.

We find respondent's interpretation of the purchase agreement unrealistic. He would have us construe it as essentially an option to purchase exercisable no later than May 1, 1962, at a price of $100,000, and a reciprocal option to sell at that price. This theory ignores the express terms of the purchase agreement. Krispy Kreme was specifically obligated to purchase all 1,000 shares of preferred stock, with the final payment being due no later than May 1, 1962. The decedent's estate placed the stock in escrow with the understanding that the ultimate transfer would occur upon Krispy Kreme's compliance with the terms of the agreement, and final performance was to occur no later than May 1, 1962.

The fact that title to the preferred stock did not pass upon execution of the purchase agreement does not preclude the existence of a binding redemption contract. Respondent's reliance upon the *Warren National Bank* case is misplaced. There, the question was whether the initial payment on a sales contract was taxable in the year made, or in the year the contract became binding. The existence of a sales contract was found to be contingent upon the buyer gaining approval of a public service commission. It was held that there was no payment on the sale until the contingency was removed during the following year.

The purchase agreement in this case contained no contingencies and was thus absolutely binding on both buyer and seller. The absence of penalty provisions would not eliminate a cause of action for breach of contract upon nonperformance by either party. The decedent's estate could not have kept the payments made under the agreement and refused to convey the stock when the final payment was tendered.

It is our opinion that the $36,130 received under the purchase agreement prior to May 1, 1962, was received in connection with a redemption which qualifies under section 302(b)(3) as a complete termination of a shareholder's interest. Viewing the entire transaction as a whole, it seems that the only distinction between this redemption and the normal redemption of stock which qualifies under section 302(b)(3) is the presence of installment payments. The statute contains no prohibition against payment of the redemption price on an installment basis. At the time the purchase agreement was executed, both parties became bound to effectuate a complete redemption of all the preferred stock owned by the decedent's estate by a certain date and for a maximum price.

A complete termination of the shareholder's interest in the Krispy Kreme stock did occur in accordance with the purchase agreement. We are not persuaded that petitioners should be denied the favorable tax treatment provided by section 302 (b)(3) for installment payments received under a binding redemption contract. Although the purchase agreement was more complicated than necessary to accomplish the goal of redeeming all the Krispy Kreme stock held by the decedent's estate at the time of death, such purpose was clearly the bona fide intent of the parties.

After considering all the pertinent facts and not being conclusively bound by the form in which parties to an agreement clothe their arrangement, we have made a determination of the realities of the transaction. See Carl L. Danielson, 44 T.C. 549 (1965). We hold, therefore, that the $36,130 did not constitute dividend income because it was received in connection with a redemption qualifying under section 302(b)(3), and it constituted part of the price paid for the 1,000 shares of preferred stock. We are not willing to fragmentize this transaction as respondent would have us do. Petitioners' evidence is convincing that the redemption has been piloted to the safe harbor provided by sections 302(a) and 302(b)(3)....

Petitioners have conceded upon brief that their basis for computing gain on transfer of the 1,000 shares of preferred stock was $132,630 and this minimum redemption price was also utilized in the estate tax return. Therefore, petitioners recognize that a long-term capital gains tax is owed on the difference between this basis and the total amount received for the shares, $136,130, the difference constituting a gain of $3,500. The gain would be taxable to the decedent's estate in the year received, 1962, but this year is not before us with respect to the estate. However, petitioner Josie L. Mathis is taxable under section 691 for the amount of the gain distributed to her in 1962, and her tax deficiency for 1962 is before us. The deficiencies will be determined accordingly . . . . To reflect all necessary adjustments —

Decisions will be entered under Rule 50.

NOTE

1. A buys a $1000, 6 per cent corporate bond at par. More than six months after the purchase, between interest dates, A, a cash basis taxpayer, sells the bond to B for a lump sum equal to par plus accrued interest. What are A's tax consequences? Why? See Treas. Reg. §1.61-7(d); Charles T. Fisher, 19 T.C. 384 (1952), aff'd, 209 F.2d 513 (6th Cir.), cert. denied, 347 U.S. 1014 (1954). Cf. Jaglom v. Commissioner, 303 F.2d 847 (2d Cir. 1962) (bond with defaulted interest purchased "flat"; on resale, sale price allocable to interest accrued since taxpayer's purchase).

2(a) A corporate bond bearing 6 per cent interest, issued in 1966 for its $1000 face value, changes hands in the market. B buys it on the open market for $900. More than six months thereafter the corporation retires the bond, paying B $1000 plus accrued interest of $30. What is the tax consequence to B? What is your authority?

(b) Corporation M in 1966 issued a face amount $1000 bond, due 1980, bearing interest at 6 per cent, for $900. A buys the bond in 1970 in the open market for $850. In 1980 the corporation retired the bond, paying A $1000 plus $30 accrued interest. What is the tax consequence to A? Why? See §1232.

3. Should the tax treatment on the sale or retirement of preferred stock with cumulative dividend arrearages differ from that accorded bonds with defaulted interest? Why?

4. If beneficiaries of the Mathis estate had owned 90 per cent of the remaining stock in the corporation, might the result in the case have been different? Why? Consider the effect of §318.

(ii) INCOMPLETE TERMINATION OF INTEREST

LEWIS v. COMMISSIONER
47 T.C. 129 (1966)

TANNENWALD, Judge: The respondent determined deficiencies in petitioners' income tax in the amounts of $1,596.87 for 1959, $1,701.45 for 1960, and $1,703.52 for

1961. The only question remaining is whether the proceeds of a redemption of stock shall be treated as capital gain or as a dividend. All other adjustments have been settled by stipulation and will be reflected in a Rule 50 computation.

Findings of Fact

Some of the facts are stipulated and are found accordingly.

Perry S. Lewis and Esther Lewis are husband and wife residing in Crawfordsville, Ind. They filed joint income tax returns on a cash basis with the district director of internal revenue at Indianapolis, Ind., for the taxable years 1959, 1960, and 1961. Any reference herein to "petitioner" shall be deemed to mean Perry S. Lewis.

Petitioner entered the retail automobile business in 1910 and purchased the Ford agency at Crawfordsville, Ind., in 1926. He operated it as a sole proprietorship until 1950, when it was incorporated as Perry Lewis Co., Inc. (hereinafter referred to as the corporation).

Petitioner at all pertinent times understood that Ford Motor Co., because the retail automotive business was highly competitive, was very much interested in having its dealers acquire and keep young blood and young people in the active management of their businesses.

Petitioner likewise planned that his sons would come into the business and one day acquire it from him. John and Perry, petitioner's sons, began working full time in the business about 1946. They were joined by Gene, their youngest brother, after he graduated from college in 1952.

After World War II, the petitioner constantly reduced his role in the active conduct of the business. From 1950 to 1956, petitioner was president and a director, but his services to the corporation were on a diminished scale, consisting for the most part of consulting with his sons and giving them advice regarding the business.

In 1950 when the corporation was organized, the petitioner owned all of the stock. It was his intent to dispose of his stock to his sons at such times as they were able to purchase it. By July 1956, petitioner owned 495 shares, Gene owned 1 share, and John owned the remaining 504 shares.[1]

The petitioner acquired and began to operate a farm in 1941. In 1956, he decided to dispose of all of his interest in the corporation and devote himself to farming. At that time, petitioner was 69 years old.

In June 1956, petitioner offered to sell his 495 shares to the corporation at $100 per share, which was their approximate book value. At special meetings of the board of directors and of the shareholders, held on June 28, 1956, petitioner's offer was accepted. The directors also granted to Gene the right to purchase from the corporation from time to time a maximum of 250 of the shares to be acquired from petitioner at book value at the time of each purchase.[2]

---

[1] John had purchased some of his shares from his brother Perry, but the record does not disclose how many shares. Nor does the record disclose how his brother Perry acquired such shares, nor how John acquired his other shares.

[2] The record does not disclose whether Gene in fact purchased any shares, although Schedule M of the corporation's Federal income tax returns for 1957 through 1961 shows an item entitled "Gain on Treas. Stock" which, in all probability, represents an adjustment arising out of sales of shares to Gene.

On July 1, 1956, petitioner entered into an agreement with the corporation which provided that the latter would purchase all of his stock for $49,500. The corporation was to pay petitioner $500 per month with interest at 5 percent per annum on the unpaid balance, with a right in the corporation to pay more than the required monthly amounts. At the end of each year, the total payments to principal were to be calculated and petitioner was required to deliver the number of shares paid for at the rate of $100 per share. The petitioner retained the right to vote any of the shares not paid for and delivered to the purchaser. The agreement provided that the certificates representing petitioner's shares were to be endorsed with a legend referring to the sale of the shares. Following this transaction, there was no basic change in the day-to-day business operations of the corporation.

Commencing July 1, 1956, petitioner's salary of $1,000 per month was discontinued. He resigned as president and was elected vice president of the corporation on June 11, 1956. He retained this position and his position on the board of directors through all of the taxable years in question.[3] After July 1, 1956, petitioner neither performed any services for the corporation nor actively exercised any powers as vice president or director.[4] Petitioner attended informal meetings of the board of directors but did not participate in any of the deliberations. The business was operated solely by John and Gene, although petitioner from time to time inquired generally how business was progressing.

On May 6, 1958, a major medical plan covering the officers of the corporation was considered at a special meeting of the board of directors, and the officers of the corporation were authorized to acquire an appropriate insurance policy.

The corporation has never paid a dividend and had accumulated earnings and profits at the end of 1956 in the amounts of $42,163.41; in 1959, $62,263.82; in 1960, $77,648.15; and in 1961, $86,711.60.

After the respondent had begun an audit of petitioner's income tax returns, petitioner mailed a document dated June 5, 1963, purporting to be an agreement under section 302(c)(2)(A)(iii) of the Internal Revenue Code of 1954. Petitioner requested that such document be attached to his 1961 income tax return, but respondent rejected it on the grounds that it was not filed in duplicate and should have contained an agreement to notify the district director of any reacquisition within 10 years from December 31, 1961, instead of July 1, 1956, the date used by petitioner in the document.

In each of the taxable years in issue, 1959, 1960, and 1961, petitioner received principal payments of $10,000 and in exchange delivered 100 shares of stock at the close of each year. In addition to the payments of principal, petitioner received interest payments of $1,394.16 in 1959, $882.00 in 1960, and $351.21 in 1961, which he

---

[3]Petitioner was also elected treasurer at the June 11, 1956 board meeting. While the record does not affirmatively disclose when petitioner ceased to hold that office, we think it can be fairly inferred from the testimony, and we therefore conclude, that this occurred prior to the taxable years involved.

[4]Petitioner's inactivity is further evidenced by the fact that, although the minutes of a meeting of the board of directors on May 6, 1958, recite that all directors were present and, by signing the minutes, waived notice, petitioner did not in fact sign the minutes but John and Gene did.

separately reported on his tax returns for those years. Petitioner's final delivery of 100 shares in 1961 completely terminated his actual stock ownership in the corporation. Petitioner's basis for his shares in 1956 was $61.20 per share, and, as of January 1, 1959, he had an unrecovered cost basis of $18,360 for 300 shares.

The payments received by petitioner in payment for his shares during the taxable years in question were not essentially equivalent to a dividend.

Opinion

Once again we are faced with the troublesome question whether a distribution by a corporation to a shareholder is "essentially equivalent to a dividend" within the meaning of section 302(b)(1). A finding of nondividend equivalency would dispose of the case and make unnecessary a determination as to whether there was a complete redemption within the meaning of section 302(b)(3) and the subsidiary question whether petitioner complied with the requirements of section 302(c). . . .

At the outset, we emphasize that this case involves a situation where the taxpayer was both a *minority* shareholder and an active participant in the business and that, leaving aside the attribution rules, the transaction herein resulted in the complete termination of such active participation and shareholder interest. We believe that the numerous cases, involving only a partial redemption and where the taxpayer was a *majority* shareholder and it was apparent that he continued in a position of control, are clearly distinguishable.

The fact that petitioner did not immediately surrender all of his stock, but rather did so over a period of 5 years, is not an impediment to the application of section 302(b)(1) if the partial redemptions were but steps in a single transaction. In Re Lukens' Estate, 246 F.2d 403 (C.A. 3, 1957), reversing 26 T.C. 900 (1956); Jackson Howell, 26 T.C. 846 (1956), affd. 247 F.2d 156 (C.A. 9, 1957); Carter Tiffany, 16 T.C. 1443 (1951), acq. 1957-1 C.B. 5. An examination of the record convinces us that this was in fact the case. Without contradiction, petitioner testified that it was his long-held intention to retire from the business and allow his sons to purchase it. His conduct for the past 26 years confirms and supports this testimony. Both the provisions of the agreement with the corporation and the conduct of the parties in adhering to its terms convince us that this transaction must be considered in its entirety.

It is clear that, even if there was not a complete redemption under section 302 (b)(3) because of petitioner's alleged failure to comply with the provisions of section 302(c), petitioner is not precluded from claiming the benefits of section 302(b)(1). See sec. 302(b)(5). As the report of the Senate Committee on Finance at the time of the enactment of the Internal Revenue Code of 1954 states —

> "in general under . . . [sec. 302(b)] your committee intends to incorporate into the bill existing law as to whether or not a reduction is essentially equivalent to a dividend under section 115(g)(1) of the 1939 Code, and *in addition* to provide three definite standards in order to provide certainty in specific instances. [Emphasis added. S. Rept. No. 1622, 83d Cong., 2d Sess., p. 233 (1954).]"

Thus, any implication from the failure to qualify under the "safe harbor" of section 302(b)(3) is clearly negated. By the same token, the mere fact that, without regard to the attribution rules, complete termination of a shareholder's interest is contemplated or accomplished does not automatically insure protection under the dividend equivalency test of section 302(b)(1). To hold otherwise would make meaningless the specific requirements of sections 302(b)(3) and 302(c). Indeed, it is in this latter regard that the attribution rules have an impact and inhibit the applicability of the cases decided under the 1939 Code. See Bradbury v. Commissioner, 298 F.2d 111, 116 (C.A. 1, 1962), affirming a Memorandum Opinion of this Court; Estate of Arthur H. Squier, 35 T.C. 950, 955 (1961), acq. 1961-2 C.B. 5; Thomas G. Lewis, 35 T.C. 71, 75-76 (1960).

Turning to the question whether the distributions herein were "essentially equivalent to a dividend" under section 302(b)(1), we recognize that the inquiry is a factual one. S. Rept. No. 1622, 83d Cong., 2d Sess., pp. 233-234 (1954). Under such circumstances, it is difficult, if not impossible, to prescribe any set of rules which is susceptible of computerized application. Indeed, the problem of dividend equivalency has had a gremlinesque quality which has endowed it with "as many colors as Joseph's coat." Cf. Weible v. United States, 244 F.2d 158, 163 (C.A. 9, 1957). See Henry McK. Haserot, 46 T.C. 864 (1966): "The colors of the cloth of dividend equivalency are not completely fast." We must recognize that no two cases are exactly alike and that, at best, we can only hope to provide, in any given case, a modest degree of guidance in a "landscape of shifting sands." Cf. Wingate E. Underhill, 45 T.C. 489, 492 (1966).

We think that "the indispensable first step [in determining dividend equivalency] is whether the redemption of stock has caused a meaningful change in the position of the shareholder with relation to his corporation and the other shareholders." See Bradbury v. Commissioner, supra at 116. Obviously where one ceases to be a shareholder, there is such a change in position. But, as we have previously pointed out, something more must be present in order to synthesize the provisions of section 302(b)(1) with those of sections 302(b)(3) and 302(c). There must be some raison d'être for the redemption reasonably related to business exigencies and not founded upon the personal whims of the taxpayer or, in the case of a closely held corporation, upon the machinations of other shareholders whose shares would be attributable to him. Compare Sorem v. Commissioner, 334 F.2d 275 (C.A. 10, 1964), reversing 40 T.C. 206 (1963), Estate of Arthur H. Squier, supra, and John A. Decker, 32 T.C. 326 (1959), affirmed per curiam 286 F.2d 427 (C.A. 6, 1960), with Tabery v. Commissioner, 354 F.2d 422 (C.A. 9, 1965), affirming a Memorandum Opinion of this Court, and Leon R. Meyer, 46 T.C. 65 (1966), on appeal (C.A. 8, June 15, 1966). In short, there must be a business purpose.

In this instant case, the petitioner was well along in years. His desire to retire from the business made sense, not only personally and businesswise but also because of the pressures of an independent third party, the Ford Motor Co. Obviously, petitioner's case would have been stronger if these pressures had included a demand that he relinquish ownership as well as withdraw from active management, but there is no suggestion that the position of the Ford Motor Co. was not in fact bona fide, and we think that petitioner's broad rather than literal interpretation of Ford's position was not unreasonable. Petitioner did withdraw from both ownership and management except for formal but inactive retention of his position as an officer and director. Not only did his sons, who had worked with him for several years, succeed to the ownership of the business but they independently took over active management and clearly were not just fronts for petitioner. Finally, there is not a shred of testimony which suggests that the transaction herein was motivated to the slighest degree, either in conception or execution, by reasons of tax avoidance.[7]

Against this background, we see no need to dissect the differences between corporate and shareholder business purpose which have so often troubled the courts. See Kerr v. Commissioner, 326 F.2d 225 (C.A. 9, 1964), affirming 38 T.C. 723 (1962), certiorari denied 377 U.S. 963; Parshelsky's Estate v. Commissioner, 303 F.2d 14, 21 (C.A. 2, 1962), reversing 34 T.C. 946 (1960); Ballenger v. United States, 301 F.2d 192, 198 (C.A. 4, 1962). We hold that, under the limited circumstances herein, there was a "conspicuous countervailing consideration" of business purpose sufficient "to dispel the aura of dividend equivalence." See Bradbury v. Commissioner, supra at 117.

In view of this conclusion, we do not reach the question whether the nominal retention of an officership or directorship violates the provisions of section 302(c)(2) (A)(i). In this connection, we note that petitioner's continuation as vice president of the corporation, even though inactive, would presumably have qualified him to participate in the major medical policy which the corporation's board of directors authorized to be procured. (The record is silent as to whether any such plan was in fact established.) Furthermore, there is an indication that petitioner ceased to be an officer and director in February 1962 — a matter of weeks after he received the last payment for his stock. At the very least, this raises the suspicion that his continuation in these posts, while he was receiving payments, had some significance.

Nor do we need to decide whether the agreement which petitioner sought to file with the respondent met the requirements of section 302(c)(2)(A)(iii) and, in particular, whether the 10-year period specified therein ran from July 1, 1956, or December 31, 1961. Cf. Georgie S. Cary, 41 T.C. 214 (1963); Pearce v. United States, 226 F. Supp. 702 (W.D.N.Y. 1964); Van Keppel v. United States, 206 F. Supp. 42 (D. Kans. 1962); Archbold v. United States, 201 F. Supp. 329 (D.N.J. 1962), affirmed per curiam 311 F.2d 228 (C.A. 3, 1963).

Reviewed by the Court.

Decision will be entered under Rule 50.

SIMPSON, J., concurring: Although I agree with the result reached by the majority, I cannot agree with the reasoning by which it concludes that the distributions in this case were not essentially equivalent to dividends. The Court, I believe, fails

---

[7]We recognize that the lack of a dividend history and the presence of accumulated earnings and profits is sometimes pointed to as an element in determining dividend equivalency. See, e.g., Thomas Kerr, 38 T.C. 723, 730 (1962), affd. 326 F.2d 225 (C.A. 9, 1964), certiorari denied 377 U.S. 963 (1964); John A. Decker, 32 T.C. 326, 331 (1959), affirmed per curiam 286 F.2d 427 (C.A. 6, 1960). But, in fact, this element is little more than a guidepost in determining the bona fides of the asserted business purpose and the absence of a tax-avoidance motive. . . .

to give full effect to the attribution rules and fails to apply properly the tests which have been established for determining when a distribution is essentially equivalent to a dividend.

In this case, we have an individual, who owned 49.5 percent of the stock of a corporation and whose sons owned the remaining stock of the corporation, arranging to have his stock redeemed by the corporation. It may be that if this redemption had occurred before the enactment of the Internal Revenue Code of 1954, the redemption would have been treated as a sale. However, section 302(c)(1) of the 1954 Code provides that the attribution rules of section 318 shall be applied for purposes of section 302. Accordingly, in determining whether this redemption is to be treated as essentially equivalent to a dividend, we must look at it as if the distribution had been made to an individual who owned all of the stock of the corporation. In other cases, this Court has recognized that the attribution rules are now applicable in determining whether a redemption is to be treated as a dividend, Thomas G. Lewis, 35 T.C. 71 (1960); Ralph L. Humphrey, 39 T.C. 199 (1962), but in this case, the Court refuses to give full effect to those attribution rules.

The majority recognizes that the mere fact that the petitioner wishes to retire from the business is not a sufficient reason to treat the redemption as a sale; yet, the Court finds that there was a business purpose for the redemption, when, in fact, none was established in the record. All that this record shows is that the petitioner believed that the Ford Motor Co. wanted younger people to manage the dealership. However, the petitioner was not at the time of this redemption engaged in the active management of the business, and we were not given any reason why he needed to redeem his stock in order to transfer management into younger hands.

Though I disagree with the reasoning of the majority, I agree with the result because I have concluded that there was a waiver of the attribution rules under section 302(c)(2) and a complete termination of the petitioner's interest within the meaning of section 302(b)(3). I agree with the majority that the several redemptions of the petitioner's stock should be treated as a single redemption terminating his actual ownership in the corporation. Yet, the question remains as to whether he has met the conditions of section 302(c)(2) so as to waive the application of the attribution rules.

I cannot agree with the respondent's contention that petitioner's position as director and vice president, subsequent to the redemption, violates the condition of section 302(c)(2)(A)(i). I am convinced that petitioner performed no services as an officer or director after June 1956. Even the informal and infrequent consultations which he rendered to the company prior to that time were discontinued after he signed the contract selling his shares to the corporation. Thus, in no way did he serve the corporation or direct its affairs. Moreover, the petitioner was paid no compensation as an officer or director subsequent to the sale.[1] His $1,000-per-month salary as president was terminated at the time of the sale of his shares and termination of his interest and activities. Hence, he did not benefit from the activities of

[1] I certainly cannot find compensation in the fact that the directors once decided to buy a medical policy for the officers when the record does not show that a policy was purchased or whether it covered the petitioner.

the corporation in any way other than to receive the payments for the redemption of his stock. Cf. Leon R. Meyer, 46 T.C. 65 (1966), on appeal (C.A. 8, June 15, 1966); Rev. Rul. 59-119, 1959-1 C.B. 68.

As I read section 302(c)(2)(A)(i), it does not provide that every officer or director shall be treated as having retained an interest in a corporation. It provides merely that a retained interest *may* include an interest as an officer or director, but it does not require us to find that every officer or director has retained an interest. The purpose of section 302(c)(2) is to provide that when there is a bona fide severance of the shareholder's interest, he will receive capital gains treatment. On the other hand, although there is no direct judicial authority or statement in the legislative history of section 302(c)(2), I believe that Congress did not intend us to hold that an officer or director who performs no duties, receives no compensation, and exercises no influence has retained an interest in the corporation. It is a fair inference from the section as a whole and from its legislative history that Congress was concerned with the situation in which there was a nominal transfer of stock in a family corporation, although the transferor continued to control the corporation and benefit by its operations. Immediately after the enactment of the 1954 Code, it was recognized that section 302(c)(2)(A)(i) did not prohibit office holding per se, but was concerned with a retained financial stake in the corporation, such as a profit-sharing plan, or in the creation of an ostensible sale that really changed nothing so far as corporate management was concerned. Finally, I believe that form should not be placed above substance, that in substance this petitioner did not retain an interest in the corporation, and that accordingly he has met the condition of section 302(c)(2)(A)(i).[4]

As an additional reason for holding section 302(c)(2) inapplicable, the respondent has argued that the agreement required by section 302(c)(2)(A)(iii) has not been filed, but I do not agree with this argument. In support of this argument, the respondent contends that the agreement was not filed in accordance with the regulations in that it was not filed in duplicate and was not filed timely. These regulations provide:

"Sec. 1.302-4 Termination of shareholder's interest.

"(a) The agreement specified in section 302(c)(2)(A)(iii) shall be in the form of a separate statement in duplicate signed by the distributee and attached to his return timely filed for the year in which the distribution described in section 302(b)(3) occurs. The agreement shall recite that the distributee has not acquired any interest in the corporation (as described in section 302(c)(2)(A)(i)) since such distribution, and that he agrees to notify the district director for the internal revenue district in which such return is filed of any acquisition of such an interest in the corporation within 30 days after such acquisition if such acquisition occurs within 10 years from the date of such distribution."

---

[4]The majority opinion states that the record contains an indication that petitioner resigned his positions in 1962 and that such an indication gives rise to a suspicion that his offices had significance. I can see other explanations of this resignation, if it occurred, and consequently do not attach much significance to it.

In an opinion reviewed by the Court, this Court held that the requirements of section 302(c)(2)(A)(iii) are procedural and directory and compliance with the regulations is not a mandatory condition for the application of section 302(c)(2)(A). Georgie S. Cary, 41 T.C. 214 (1963), nonacq. 1964-2 C.B. 8. In the *Cary* case, the Court ascertained that section 302(c)(2)(A)(iii) was added by the Senate primarily to enable the respondent to require the distributee to maintain records fully identifying the amount of tax payable had the redemption been treated as a dividend. In that case, the Court held that a substantial compliance with the Code was all that is necessary — it is not necessary to comply literally with all the rules of the regulations. If the distributee fully reports his income from the distribution, he may comply with the Code by filing an agreement when his inadvertence is brought to his attention, even at a time when his returns are being audited. Van Keppel v. United States, 206 F. Supp. 42 (D. Kans. 1962), affd. 321 F.2d 717 (C.A. 10, 1963). I believe that the petitioner substantially complied with the requirements of section 302(c)(2)(A)(iii). Rejection of petitioner's agreement because it did not accompany the return, because it was not in duplicate, or because the return was not timely was an abuse of discretion. Pearce v. United States, 226 F. Supp. 702 (W.D.N.Y. 1964).

Respondent has also asserted that Petitioner's agreement is improper because it should have promised to notify the district director of any reacquisition within 10 years commencing on December 31, 1961. Petitioner's tendered agreement specified July 1, 1956, as the date for the beginning of the 10-year period. However, I cannot find that petitioner's agreement was inconsistent with the Code or with respondent's regulations. The regulations make no provision expressly for distributions which occur in more than 1 taxable year. I do not understand the existing regulations to require the filing of an agreement every year. In this case, the petitioner treated the redemption as occurring on July 1, 1956, and treated the 10-year period as beginning to run after that date; for purposes of preparing and filing the agreement, I think that this is not an unreasonable interpretation of the regulations.

Accordingly, I would find that the terms of section 302(c)(2) were met, and the stock owned by the petitioner's sons should not be attributed to the petitioner for the purpose of section 302(b)(3). I am aware that section 302(b)(2)(B)(ii) might apply to this case and require us to apply the stock attribution rules. Indeed, the facts presented suggest that there may have been a disposition of the type described in that provision. However, the respondent has not argued that such a disposition occurred, and the record shows clearly that the parties did not consider that provision to be an issue in this case.

Therefore, I would limit the holding in this case to a decision for the petitioner under section 302(b)(3).

ATKINS, J., agrees with this concurring opinion.

NOTE

1. In *Lewis,* did Judge Tannenwald essentially ignore the attribution of ownership provisions of §318(a)(1), or did he conclude that despite them the distribu-

tion was within §302(b)(1)? Would either be justified? Why? See Treas. Reg. §1.302-2(b).

2. Was Judge Simpson's treatment of §302(c)(2)(A)(i) in the context of the facts of *Lewis* correct? Why? Does his handling of the §302(c)(2)(A)(iii) problem comport with the Congressional purpose and concern? What were Congress' purpose and concern?

LEVIN v. COMMISSIONER
385 F.2d 521 (2d Cir. 1967)

Before Moore, Smith and Kaufman, Circuit Judges.

Kaufman, Circuit Judge: The perils of acting without competent tax advice are demonstrated anew, if further evidence be needed, by this petition to review a decision of the Tax Court, 47 T.C. 258 (1966), holding that distributions in 1960, 1961, 1962, and 1963 to the taxpayer in redemption of her stock in a family corporation were "essentially equivalent to a dividend" within the meaning of section 302(b)(1) of the Internal Revenue Code of 1954, and hence taxable at ordinary rates.[2] We affirm the decision of the Tax Court.

The evidence, as found by the Tax Court,[3] established that Mrs. Levin's family corporation, the Connecticut Novelty Corporation, Inc., commenced operations as a partnership between her husband and her brother, Joseph Levine. In its early years the business centered on the wholesale distribution of "fireworks," but it shifted exclusively to retail jewelry after the state prohibited their use in 1951. Taxpayer succeeded to her husband's interest in the business upon his death in 1940. Thereafter, her brother Joseph came to live with her and her son Jerome, and became a "second father" to him. She relied heavily on Joseph's advice in business matters.

Following incorporation of the business in 1948, its 1300 outstanding single class common shares were held as follows: Joseph Levine, 650 shares; Mrs. Levin, 649 shares; Jerome Levin, 1 share.[4] The three stockholders also constituted the board of directors and officers of the corporation until Joseph Levine's death in April 1962, when Jerome's wife became a director. Taxpayer was secretary and treasurer until 1959, when she limited her office in the company to secretary.

Jerome was employed full time in the business since graduating from high

---

[2]The Tax Court found deficiencies in income taxes due of $1,015.22 in 1960, $1,037.74 in 1961, $970.04 in 1962, and $2,783.44 in 1963.

[3]The facts were largely stipulated. The only significant factual dispute is whether a shift in control over the corporation actually occurred as a result of the redemption. In the view we take of the case, it is unnecessary to decide this question; nor need we consider whether, as taxpayer urges, the clearly erroneous rule has any application to §302(b)(1) cases. Compare Himmel v. Commissioner, 338 F.2d 815, 816 (2d Cir. 1964), Northup v. United States, 240 F.2d 304, 307 (2d Cir. 1957) with Towers v. Commissioner, 247 F.2d 233, 235-236 (2d Cir. 1957), cert. denied, 355 U.S. 914 (1958), Kirschenbaum v. Commissioner, 155 F.2d 23 (2d Cir.), cert. denied, 329 U.S. 726 (1946). See generally 1 Mertens, Law of Federal Income Taxation, §9.100, p. 212, nn.47.1 and 47.2 (Oliver ed. 1962).

[4]Jerome paid no consideration for his one share.

school in 1944. In 1957 he contemplated marriage and discussed his status in the company with his mother and uncle in order to learn "where he stood" in the business. He insisted on this so that if it became necessary he could embark on another career while still young. Thereafter, Joseph and the taxpayer agreed to give him a greater participation in the business ownership and management. As a result the existing stock was cancelled and 1300 new shares of common stock were issued and distributed in this manner: Joseph, 485 shares; taxpayer, 484 shares; Jerome, 331 shares. Jerome gave no consideration for the 330 additional shares.

Within a few years Jerome sought outright ownership of the business and to retire his uncle and mother. But he desired to accomplish this by a method which would make provision for them during the balance of their lives. Accordingly, on January 19, 1960, a plan was devised whereby the corporation would redeem the stock of taxpayer and Joseph at $200 per share. Pursuant to this plan Joseph and taxpayer executed identical agreements with the corporation. She was to receive $7000 per year without interest beginning April 1, 1960 until $96,800[5] was paid. Upon default the unpaid balance would become due upon the "seller's" election. As an alternative, the corporation was given the option to pay the entire or any part of the purchase price at any time. After the plan was consummated, Jerome conducted the business with "a greater freedom of action." But out of "respect and sentiment," as we are told, Joseph and taxpayer were retained as directors and officers of the corporation.

Coincidentally, the taxpayer and Joseph became eligible for social security benefits. But, they continued to perform services for the corporation and to receive salaries while at the same time taxpayer accepted a cut in her salary to $1200 per year, the maximum amount then permitted to be earned without a reduction in her social security benefits. See 42 U.S.C. §403 (1964 ed.).

The dispute before us arises from taxpayer's treatment of the $7000 payments. In the taxable years in question, 1960 through 1963, she reported the compensation from the corporation under the 1960 agreement as long-term capital gains.[6] The Commissioner treated the payments as essentially equivalent to dividends and accordingly determined deficiencies for all the years in question.[7]

I

The difference between a stock redemption that is essentially equivalent to a dividend and one that is not is grounded on a long history in the tax law. The distinction was essential because without it the tax on dividends at ordinary income rates could easily be defeated by the simple expedient of issuing more stock to the shareholders, who then would "sell" back their new shares to the corporation. It would then be asserted that the proceeds of this alleged sale were taxable at capital gains

---

[5]This was computed by multiplying the number of shares taxpayer actually owned, 484, by the purchase price per share, $200.

[6]She reported her cost as $100 per share, one-half the sales price.

[7]The Commissioner also treated as essentially equivalent to dividends credits which the corporation allowed taxpayer against her obligation to pay for a cottage transferred to her in 1962. The Tax Court's valuation of this cottage at $19,000 is not challenged here.

rates because they represented proceeds from the "sale" of a capital asset. To eliminate this patent loophole, Congress early provided that such distributions would receive capital gain treatment only if they were "not essentially equivalent to a dividend." See generally 1 Mertens, Law of Federal Income Taxation §9.99 (Oliver ed. 1962).

But this simplistic formula created more problems than it solved for the courts were then called upon to answer the elusive question as to when a distribution was or was not "essentially equivalent to a dividend." At first it was generally believed that, in view of its history, the provision was aimed only at distributions motivated by a tax avoidance purpose. Accordingly, if a distribution served a "business purpose," the courts held it was not essentially equivalent to a dividend. This rationale was becoming increasingly difficult to apply, however, and it came to its demise in 1945 when, in interpreting an analogous statutory provision, the Supreme Court ruled that motive had little relevancy. The Court then adopted a more objective "net effect" test, under which the question of dividend equivalency depended on whether the distribution in redemption of stock had the same economic effect as a distribution of a dividend would have had. Commissioner v. Estate of Bedford, 325 U.S. 283, 65 S. Ct. 1157, 89 L. Ed. 1611 (1945).[8] In time this test also proved ephemeral; some courts developed many criteria to determine the "net effect" of a distribution,[9] while in determining "net effect" we differed and relied primarily on changes in "basic rights of ownership."[10] However, most cases have been resolved on their own facts and circumstances.[11]

Until 1954 the "not essentially equivalent to a dividend" test, with all its perplexing problems, had been the sole statutory guide in this area. But the draftsmen of the 1954 Internal Revenue Code, faced with "the morass created by the decisions,"[12] attempted to clarify the standards and thus to make more precise the dividing line between stock redemptions that qualified for capital gains treatment and those that did not by adding objective tests, see §302(b)(2)-(4), and rules defining constructive ownership, see §318.

Since the "not essentially equivalent to a dividend" test is no longer applied in a vacuum, it is impossible to interpret it without examining the statutory scheme of which it is now a part. Section 302(a) provides that a stock redemption[13] shall be

---

[8]We recognized in Kirschenbaum v. Commissioner, 155 F.2d 23 (2d Cir.), cert. denied, 329 U.S. 726, 67 S. Ct. 75, 91 L. Ed. 628 (1946), that our earlier cases had been overruled as a result of *Bedford.*

[9]Numerous criteria are listed in 1 Mertens §9.100, at 214-15. See, e.g., Ferro v. Commissioner, 242 F.2d 838, 841 (3d Cir. 1957).

[10]See, e.g., Himmel v. Commissioner, 338 F.2d 815, 817 (2d Cir. 1964).

[11]See, e.g., Ferro v. Commissioner, 242 F.2d 838, 841 (3d Cir. 1957). See generally 1 Mertens §§9.99-9.100.

[12]Ballenger v. United States, 301 F.2d 192, 196 (4th Cir. 1962).

[13]Section 317(b) defines redemption for purposes of §§301-395 as a corporation's acquisition in its stock from a shareholder in exchange for property, whether or not the stock is cancelled, retired, or held as a treasury stock. This definition settled the question whether there could be dividend equivalence if the redeemed stock was held as treasury stock rather than being cancelled. See Kirschenbaum v. Commissioner, 155 F.2d 23, 25 (2d Cir.), cert. denied, 329 U.S. 726, 67 S. Ct. 75, 91 L. Ed. 628 (1946).

treated as an "exchange" if it falls into any one of the categories of §302(b).[14] These categories are: (1) a redemption that is "not essentially equivalent to a dividend" under §302(b)(1); (2) a "substantially disproportionate" redemption under § 302(b) (2); (3) a complete redemption terminating the shareholder's interest in the corporation under §302(b)(3).[15] Section 302(b)(2) contains an exact mathematical formula to determine whether the disproportion is "substantial." The test in §302(b)(3) is not mathematical, but it is stated with equal clarity. The shareholder must redeem all of his actually and constructively owned stock to qualify for capital gain treatment under this provision, and §302(c)(2) provides that if certain clear-cut conditions are met the family attribution rules of §318(a) will not apply in determining whether the shareholder has disposed of all his stock.

Mrs. Levin concedes that she fails to meet the requirements of either §302(b)(2) or §302(b)(3),[16] and so she relies on §302(b)(1).[17] Our task of interpretation and reasoned elaboration cannot be adequately performed if we examine each provision as if it existed in a vacuum. The Code draftsmen hopefully expected that the preciseness of the tests set out in the new provisions, §302(b)(2) and §302(b)(3), would serve to relieve the pressure on the "not essentially equivalent to a dividend" test re-enacted as §302(b)(1). The new requirements, if carefully observed, provided safe harbors for taxpayers seeking capital gain treatment. As a result, their enactment permitted more accurate and long range tax planning.

The legislative history of §302(b)(1) supports the view that it was designed to play a modest role in the statutory scheme. As originally passed by the House of Representatives, no provision was made for the "not essentially equivalent to a dividend" test; reliance was placed entirely on provisions similar to §302(b)(2) and §302(b)(3). Thereafter the Senate Finance Committee added §302(b)(1) and explained its action as follows:[18]

> "While the House bill set forth definite conditions under which stock may be redeemed at capital-gain rates, these rules appeared unnecessarily restrictive, particularly in the case of redemptions of preferred stock which might be called by the corporation without the shareholder having any control over when the redemption may take place. Accordingly, your committee follows existing law by reinserting the general language indicating that a redemption shall be treated as a distribution in part or full payment in exchange for stock if the redemption is not essentially equivalent to a dividend."

[14]A redemption that does not fall within one of these categories is treated, by virtue of §302(d), as a distribution under §301, i.e., as a dividend to the extent of current and post 1913 earnings and profits.

[15]A fourth category deals with the redemption of the stock of certain railroad corporations under §302(b)(4).

[16]Taxpayer fails to meet the test of §302(b)(3) because she remained a director, an officer, and an employee of the corporation after the redemption. Moreover, she failed to file the proper notification with the Secretary of the Treasury.

[17]In determining whether the redemption satisfies §302(b)(1), we are directed by §302(b)(5) not to take into account that the redemption fails to meet the requirements of §302(b)(2) or §302(b)(3); but a discussion and understanding of these provisions are useful in interpreting §302(b)(1).

[18]S. Rep. No. 1622, 83rd Cong., 2d Sess., 44-5 (1954).

As a leading commentator observed, "It is not easy to give §302(b)(1) an expansive construction in view of this indication that its major function was the narrow one of immunizing redemptions of minority holdings of preferred stock."[19]

II.

The 1954 Code also adopted a number of constructive ownership rules that provided for the attribution of stock owned by one person or legal entity to another. These provisions overruled the prior case law which unrealistically had not viewed the family as a unit unless other family members were "dummy stockholders." Lukens v. Commissioner, 246 F.2d 403, 407-408 (3d Cir. 1957). By providing a "reasonable rule of thumb,"[20] these rules reduced the difficulties necessarily involved in determining in each case the extent of actual control in a family corporation, in which informal influence over relatives, often impossible of proof, was more important than formal control through voting rights based on actual stock ownership. Like §302(b)(2) and §302(b)(3), these rules represented an attempt to make the law more predictable, and thereby to serve as aids to the tax or estate planner.

Section 318(a), the family attribution rule applicable here, provides in relevant part:

> "*General rule.* — For purposes of those provisions of this subchapter [§§301-395] to which the rules contained in this section are expressly made applicable —
> "(1) *Members of family.* —
> "(A) *In general.* — An individual shall be considered as owning the stock owned, directly or indirectly, by or for — . . .
> "(ii) his children . . . ."

In this case, then, the taxpayer must be deemed the owner of her son's shares since §302(c)(1) provides in part: "section 318(a) shall apply in determining the ownership of stock for purposes of this section."[21]

III.

Taxpayer argues that the family attribution rules should not be determinative in this §302(b)(1) case. But the definitive language of the statute gives her small comfort despite the three cases upon which she relies so heavily.

In Perry S. Lewis, 47 T.C. 129 (1966), the Tax Court ignored the stock attribution rules in deciding a §302(b)(1) case. Lewis and his sons owned an automobile

---

[19]Bittker & Eustice, Federal Income Taxation of Corporations and Shareholders (2d ed.) 291.

[20]Bittker & Eustice, op. cit., 288.

[21]Although some commentators have argued that the attribution rules are not applicable to §302(b)(1) because it does not expressly refer to the "ownership" of stock, Bittker & Eustice, op. cit., 292, correctly point out that it is reasonable to apply the attribution rules whenever ownership of stock is relevant, whether by statutory direction or otherwise. Indeed, the Treasury Regulations initially made the application of the attribution rules to §302(b)(1) mandatory, 19 Fed. Reg. 8240 (1954), although they now provide only that the attribution rules "must be considered," Treas. Regs. §1.302-2(b), thus allowing some play in the joints for cases hereinafter discussed, e.g., situations involving family estrangement.

dealer franchise, and Lewis' shares were redeemed after the automobile manufacturer put heavy pressure on older men like Lewis to yield franchises to younger men. Lewis severed all relations with the corporation other than remaining as an apparently honorary director and officer. The Tax Court held that distributions to Lewis over a period of five years in exchange for his stock were not essentially equivalent to a dividend, because the stock redemption served a substantial "business purpose." While the majority ignored altogether the family attribution rules, Judge Simpson, in a separate concurrence, pointed out that they required that Lewis be treated as owning his sons' shares, and hence as owning 100% of the corporation's outstanding stock. He concurred, however, on the ground that there was a complete termination of Lewis' interest in the corporation which satisfied §302(b)(3). *Lewis* does not aid the taxpayer[22] because this court has not looked with favor upon the "business purpose" test.[23] Even if we were to consider it, the Tax Court failed to articulate any reason for ignoring §318. But, taxpayer argues that the Tax Court in *Lewis* simply considered the "bona fides" of the change in ownership with special care because of the attribution rules, and suggests we do the same. We have already stated that the core of the changes made by the 1954 Code in this not uncommon reticulate fashion for a tax statute was to shift from uncertainty and impreciseness to objective tests; "tax administration would be severely handicapped if the rules applied only as presumptions . . ." Ringel, Surrey & Warren, Attribution of Stock Ownership in the Internal Revenue Code, 72 Harv. L. Rev. 209 (1958). Acceptance of taxpayer's argument would eviscerate the attribution rules and all that Congress hoped to achieve thereby.

Mrs. Levin also refers us to the footnote dictum in Ballenger v. United States, 301 F.2d 192, 199 (4th Cir. 1962), indicating that some commentators have "suggested that the attribution rules should not be too literally applied to §302(b)(1)." It is interesting, however, that the attribution rules were applied in *Ballenger*, and the quoted dictum lends feeble support to taxpayer's claim that the attribution rules should be ignored here as they were in *Lewis.*

Finally, taxpayer relies on another footnote observation in Himmel v. Commissioner, 338 F.2d 815, 820 (2d Cir. 1964) [page 195 infra], stating that "[w]e think it quite proper to be aware of the effect of a distribution on significant corporate interest without strict regard to the attribution rules." The reliance is misplaced. In *Himmel* we *applied* the attribution rules in determining that if there had been a dividend on the common stock rather than a redemption of the non-voting cumulative preferred taxpayer *constructively* would have received significantly *less* than he did as a result of the redemption. This alteration in rights to earnings was "substantial enough in itself to bar treatment of the redemption as 'essentially equivalent to a dividend.' In no other case has a comparable difference apparently been considered otherwise." Himmel, at 818. In the case before us, if there had been $14,000 annual dividends (the amount of the annual distributions to taxpayer and Joseph) instead of a stock redemption, taxpayer would have received constructively about

[22]Of course the concurring opinion in *Lewis* does not support taxpayer's position here, because she makes no claim that there was a complete redemption under §302(b)(3).

[23]See McGinty v. Commissioner, 325 F.2d 820 (2d Cir. 1963).

$8,778[24] or *more* than she received from the stock redemption. The Tax Court correctly stated that the comparative dividend test is designed to test "whether the distributions *equal or exceed* the amounts that would be received as a cash dividend," and that accordingly *Himmel* "is not analogous."

Moreover, *Himmel* involved a corporation with three classes of stock which were not held proportionately. This situation created "additional and more difficult problems;"[25] compliance with §302(b)(3) was impossible,[26] and immediate compliance with §302(b)(3) was impractical.[27] By contrast, in the present case taxpayer easily could have complied with §302(b)(3) by simply resigning as a director, officer, and employee of the corporation and notifying the Secretary of the Treasury.[28] She simply could not have her cake and eat it too.

We do not hold that there may not be cases in which strict application of the attribution rules may be inappropriate. In addition to the preferred stock situations referred to in the Senate Report quoted supra, family estrangement may render the application of the family attribution rules unwise. See Bittker, The Taxation of Stock Redemptions and Partial Liquidations, 44 Cornell L.Q. 299, 324 (1959); Moore, Dividend Equivalency — Taxation of Distributions in Redemption of Stock, 19 Tax L. Rev. 249, 252-55 (1964). But in the case before us taxpayer has offered no valid reason for ignoring the family attribution rules, and we perceive none.

IV.

Accordingly, we must attribute Jerome's shares to his mother. As a result, before the redemption she constructively owned her 484 shares and her son's 331 shares, or about 63 per cent of the 1300 outstanding shares. After the redemption she still constructively owned her son's shares. Thus, after the redemption of the stock owned by her and her brother, by the rule of attribution she became the constructive owner of 100 per cent of the outstanding stock. It is apparent therefore that her constructive ownership actually increased as a result of the redemptions. As the Tax Court said, this "is most unlike a sale." For when a taxpayer's (constructive) ownership decreases by a significant amount, we are justified in concluding that a substantial reduction in taxpayer's interest in the corporation has occurred warranting capital gain treatment as a sale or exchange. But when only a small reduction in control occurs, the distribution has been held to be essentially equivalent to a dividend; a fortiori, when no reduction, but rather an increase, in control occurs, taxpayer has not parted with anything justifying capital gain treatment.

The Tax Court correctly noted that in this case control in the sense of access to corporate benefits was more important than any legal right to direct the destiny of the corporation. In reality, taxpayer's benefits from the corporation changed little as a

---

[24]Taxpayer actually owned 37.2 per cent of the stock, and constructively owned another 25.5 per cent (Jerome's), or 62.7 per cent in all; 62.7 per cent of $14,000 is $8,778.

[25]Himmel, supra 338 F.2d at 818.

[26]The test of §302(b)(2) depends on a reduction in the amount of voting stock held; in *Himmel*, non-voting stock was redeemed.

[27]The corporation lacked the funds to redeem all the taxpayer's stock.

[28]See §302(c)(2)(A). In addition, taxpayer would have had to satisfy the requirement of the last sentence of §302(c)(2)(B).

result of the redemption. Before 1960 she received a salary of $7800 per year; after 1960 she received $8200 per year, composed of annual distributions of $7000 and salary of $1200. While in form taxpayer redeemed her stock, in substance she parted with nothing justifying capital gain treatment.[29]

The judgment is affirmed.

NOTE

Review your responses to the questions posed in the Note on page 183 supra. Are they the same in light of the *Levin* opinion? Do you agree with the result and the opinion in *Levin?* Why?

HIMMEL v. COMMISSIONER
338 F.2d 815 (2d Cir. 1964)

Before MOORE, SMITH and KAUFMAN, Circuit Judges.

MOORE, Circuit Judge. Isidore and Lillian Himmel (collectively referred to as the taxpayer) petition for review of a decision of the Tax Court, 41 T.C. 62 (1963), upholding the Commissioner of Internal Revenue's determination of deficiency in taxpayer's income tax for the years 1957 and 1958 in the amount of $2,346.11 and $3,287.45, respectively. In both years, taxpayer received from the H. A. Leed Co. in redemption of certain shares of stock held by him, payments which he did not report in his tax returns for those years. The Commissioner and the Tax Court found the payments to be essentially equivalent to dividends, which, under the Internal Revenue Code of 1954, Section 302, should have been treated as ordinary income. We disagree with that finding and, accordingly, reverse the judgment.

Whether a redemption "is 'essentially equivalent to' a dividend, involving as it does application of a statutory rule to found facts, is a question of law. . . ."[2]

In 1946 taxpayer with Leonard Goldfarb and Edward G. Schenfield incorporated the H. A. Leed Co. to process aluminum. The original capital was $8,100 and each shareholder received 27 shares of $100 par common stock. Taxpayer was president until early 1956. From the beginning until late 1948 taxpayer made advances to the company which were carried on the books as "Loans Payable." He expected to be repaid when the company was able to do so. In a recapitalization in late 1948 to improve the company's credit position, each shareholder received 5 more shares of common in cancellation of $500 notes to each. Taxpayer also received 266 shares of $100 par Class A 2% cumulative nonvoting preferred and 110 shares of $100 par

---

[29]We reject as without merit taxpayer's argument that our holding imposes a tax on her gross receipts in violation of Art. I, §9, Cl. 4 of the Constitution, which forbids "direct" taxes except in proportion to the census. Her basis does no disappear; it simply is transferred to her son. See Treas. Regs. §1.302-2(c).

[2]Though equivalence depends upon the facts, see Treas. Reg. §1.302-2(b), it is not itself a fact.

Class B 2% cumulative voting preferred, in cancellation of the then outstanding indebtedness to him of $37,600. Both classes of preferred stock were created at that time and both were redeemable, but the Class B stock could not be redeemed until all the Class A stock had been redeemed. In 1950 taxpayer gave his 32 shares of common to his two sons, 16 to each. In 1954 on the death of Schenfield, the company purchased his 32 shares from his estate. By corporate action in February 1956 a special account was set up into which $3,000 per year was to be deposited solely for the retirement of the company's outstanding preferred stock of the total par value of $37,600. In late 1956 the shareholders voted to redeem 50 shares of Class A at par and the taxpayer agreed to waive all accrued but unpaid dividends on the redeemed shares. Similar provision was made for redemption at taxpayer's death and for other redemptions during taxpayer's life. In January 1957, 50 shares of Class A were redeemed for $5,000, and in 1958 70 shares of Class A were redeemed for $7,000. No dividends had been paid through December 31, 1958, and in both 1957 and 1958 earnings and profits exceeded the amounts distributed.

Distributions of property by a corporation to a shareholder to the extent they are made out of earnings and profits, section 316, are generally to be included in the gross income of the shareholder. Section 301(a), (c). The ordinary income tax rates would thus be applicable. However, if a corporation redeems its stock, section 317(b), the redemption may be treated as a distribution in part or in full payment in exchange for the stock, section 302(a), thus subjecting the distribution to tax only in the event of capital gains. But this preferential treatment may be availed of only in certain circumstances, one of which is that "the redemption is not essentially equivalent to a dividend." Sections 302(b)(1), 302(d). Primarily the problem is to determine and apply the appropriate tests of dividend equivalence. But the relevance of each of the possible criteria depends largely upon the particular capital structure-distribution pattern.

Ownership of stock can involve three important rights: (1) to vote, and thereby exercise control, (2) to participate in current earnings and accumulated surplus, and (3) to share in net assets on liquidation. Ownership of common stock generally involves all of these. Ownership of preferred stock generally involves the last two, but only to limited extents, unless otherwise provided. Payments to a shareholder with respect to his stock can be of three general sorts: (1) distribution of earnings and profits which effects no change in basic relationships between the shareholder and either the corporation or the other shareholders — i.e., a dividend; (2) payments to a shareholder by a third party in exchange for ownership of the stock and its attendant rights, which accordingly eliminates or contracts pro tanto the shareholder's rights — i.e., a sale; and (3) payments to a shareholder by the corporation in exchange for ownership of the stock. With the last, which can often formally be called a redemption, the effect on the shareholder's basic rights vis-à-vis the corporation and other shareholders depends upon many facts. It is possible for such a transaction to resemble, exactly or substantially, either a dividend or a sale. For tax purposes the payment is considered ordinary income if, by its "net effect," it is "essentially equivalent to a dividend."

The hallmarks of a dividend, then, are pro rata distribution of earnings and profits *and* no change in basic shareholder relationships. Too frequently the inquiry in §302(b) cases does not keep this sufficiently in mind. Existence of a pro rata distribution may be determined by comparing the patterns of distribution to see whether the shareholders received the same amount as they would have received had the total distribution been a dividend on the common stock outstanding. But, aside from a single-shareholder corporation, it is not enough merely that the taxpayer received the same amount as he would have received with a dividend, for that could be the result of a sale of some stock to a third party. Rather, pro rata distribution indicates also, at least in a one-class capital structure, the extent to which — if any — the basic rights of ownership have been affected. Where there is only common those rights would exist in proportion to shares held. Therefore, quite often the net effect of a distribution may adequately be gauged by determining what would have been the pattern with a dividend.[4]

Additional and more difficult problems are raised when a corporation has more than one class of stock. The additional class will often be a preferred, which typically has no voting rights, has preferential though limited rights to participate in earnings, and has rights to share in liquidation only to the extent of capital contributed, and perhaps accrued but unpaid dividends. Redemption of some preferred stock consequently may cause different changes in a shareholder's total rights than would redemption of common. Even more is this so when the preferred and common are not held in the same proportions by the same shareholders. Shares of different classes should therefore not casually be lumped together. For example, redemption of a nonvoting preferred can have no effect on relative voting rights, and can never meet the "substantially disproportionate" tests of section 302(b)(2). Rights to earnings will depend upon the exact preference given the preferred, e.g., whether it participates beyond its dividend, whether the dividend is cumulative, etc. Rights on liquidation may vary similarly.

These problems are all well illustrated by this case. In the two years in question, taxpayer received from the corporation $5,000 and $7,000, in redemption of 50 and 70 of the 266 shares of Class A nonvoting preferred, all held by him. Other shareholders received nothing. Had the same funds been distributed as a dividend on the 64 shares of common outstanding, Goldfarb would have received $2,500 and $3,500 and taxpayer would actually have received nothing, as he held no common. However, by dint of the attribution rules, section 318(a)(1)(A)(ii), he would be deemed to have owned his sons' shares and therefore to have received the $2,500 and $3,500 actually received by them. Thus he would have received 50% of what he actually did receive.

---

[4]In stressing the importance of the "substantially pro rata" test, we are not unmindful of the more specific provision of §302(b)(2). The pro rata test, quite assuredly, developed under §115(g) whose only provision was for distributions "essentially equivalent to a dividend." While the 1954 revision added specific "safe harbors" for redemptions that completely terminate a shareholder's interest in the corporation, §302(b)(3), and for distributions that are substantially disproportionate according to certain precise quantitative standards, §302(b)(2), it also kept the 1939 Code provision for distributions not "essentially equivalent to a dividend." Moreover, it stated that failure to meet any one of the more specific tests should not be taken into account in applying he old test. §302(b)(5). And since 302(b)(2) is keyed only to changes in voting power, it is obvious that without 302(b)(1) a substantially disproportionate redemption of nonvoting stock could never qualify for capital gain treatment.

Even if the funds had first gone to pay accumulated but unpaid dividends on the two classes of preferred, taxpayer would have received, according to the Commissioner's calculations, only 82.5% of what he actually did receive.[5]

With a multi-class capitalization, the amount of a hypothetical dividend that would have been received can reflect the shareholder's right to participate in current and accumulated earnings, though it is a less accurate index of the effects on voting power or rights on liquidation. Here, an alteration in rights to earnings of 17.5% (waiver of dividends) or 50% (nonwaiver of dividends) is substantial enough in itself to bar treatment of the redemption as "essentially equivalent to a dividend." In no other case has a comparable difference apparently been considered otherwise. For example, "no equivalency" was found in the following cases. In Northup v. United States, [137 F. Supp. 268], the three taxpayers involved in the case received aggregately 41.6% of a redemption of preferred, though they would have received 66.6% of a dividend on the common — a difference of 25%. Several of the shareholders there held only preferred or only common, and those holding both held them in different proportions. See Northup v. United States, 137 F. Supp. 268, 269 (D. Conn. 1955). In Cobb v. Callan Court Co., 274 F.2d 532 (5th Cir. 1960), the major shareholder received 50% of a redemption payment and two others each received 25%, though the shares of a dividend would have been 67%: 15%: 15% — differences of 17% and 10%. In Arthur H. Squier, 35 T.C. 950 (1961), taxpayer received 100% of the redemption, though he would have received only 63.3% of a dividend — a difference of 36.7%. In Abraham Frisch, 18 CCH Tax Ct. Mem. 358 (1959), taxpayers received 88.3% and 11.7%, respectively, on redemption, though they would have received 66.7% and 33.3% of a dividend — a difference of 21.6%. And just recently in Sorem v. Commissioner, 334 F.2d 275 (10th Cir. 1964), taxpayers each received 50% of the redemption, though they would have been deemed to have received 43.77% and 37.91% of a dividend — a difference of 6.23% and 12.09%. We need not consider whether the same conclusion would follow if the difference were only 7%, see Friend v. United States, 226 F. Supp. 814 (D. Mass. 1964),* or 8.7%, see Bradbury v. Commissioner, 298 F.2d 111 (1st Cir. 1962).

The Tax Court acknowledged the difference in result between the distribution here and a dividend but thought it unimportant because taxpayer was "the owner of such a heavy percentage of the distributing corporation's stock. . . ." 41 T.C. at 71. But the cases relied on by the Tax Court are very different from the one before us. In *Bradbury* only 8.7% of the distribution would have gone to the other shareholders were it a dividend, and 91.3% of all shares were considered owned by the taxpayer. Moreover, even without attribution taxpayer was the controlling shareholder. And in Keefe v. Cote, 213 F.2d 651 (1st Cir. 1954), taxpayer owned over 99% of all shares and would have received all of any dividend save a fraction of 1%. Indeed, there a "legitimate business purpose" was found adequate to bar dividend equivalency. Lastly, in both cases only common stock existed so that all essential shareholder relationships existed pro rata with dividend rights.

[5]We do not consider what might have been the proper tax treatment for the amount of dividends actually waived as neither party raised the issue.

*Aff'd, 345 F.2d 761 (1st Cir. 1965). — ED.

The Tax Court also stressed the fact that the redemption effected no change in voting power. Of course, this could be relevant if only common stock existed; but where nonvoting stock exists redemption even of all of it cannot affect voting power. Since nonvoting preferred was redeemed here we do not think such weight should have been given to the absence of any change in voting power. However, were voting shares redeemed we think that the Tax Court's lumping together of common and voting preferred would have been justifiable, if only to gauge the impact on voting power.

However, the Tax Court also stressed the fact that taxpayer's total ownership of all shares was reduced only 2.74% by the redemption, a change not thought substantial. But this figure was obtained by lumping together all shares outstanding — common, voting preferred, and nonvoting preferred. We think that such a figure is not particularly helpful. It cannot stand in the abstract, but must be related to some significant aspect of the complex of shareholder rights. The Tax Court did not indicate any such relationship and we are not convinced that necessarily there is any in a corporation having several differently defined classes of stock. The figure does not relate to voting power. It does not relate to rights to share in earnings. It might be thought to relate to rights on liquidation, but it does not accurately do that either.

Taxpayer urges us to consider the changes in relative shares of net worth attributable to each shareholder. Some courts have looked to these changes in book value of a shareholder's total holdings in order to assess the effect of the distribution on liquidation rights. See, e.g., Abraham Frisch, supra. We agree that it is a proper inquiry. The test has not been extensively developed, however, perhaps because relatively few of the cases have involved even two classes of stock, and none that we have found has involved three classes, as are present here. Of course with only one class there is no need to turn to a net worth test since liquidation rights, like the other basic shareholder rights, will exist in direct proportion to shares held.

Taxpayer asserts, and the Commissioner did not contend otherwise, that the effect of the distributions was to reduce his share of net worth from 62% to 57% — a difference of 5%. We cannot say that this difference is so insubstantial as to make the redemptions "essentially equivalent to a dividend." To place the changes in context we note that with redemption of the last shares held by taxpayer — either in one complete redemption or as the culmination of a series the last of which would perforce be a "complete" redemption — his sons' shares would no longer be attributed to him since on these facts his interest in the company would be terminated. Sections 302(b)(3), 302(c)(2). Prior to any redemption, the preferred itself represented only 22% of the net worth as of December 31, 1957. Thus, for taxpayer, the maximum possible share of net worth that could be affected by a redemption was 22%, not the 62% attributed to him through section 318. A change of 5% should be compared with this lesser figure.[7]

_____

[7] We think it quite proper to be aware of the effect of a distribution on significant corporate interests without strict regard to the attribution rules. Cf. Moore, Dividend Equivalency — Taxation of Distributions in Redemption of Stock, 19 Tax L. Rev. 249, 252-55 (1964); Note, Stock Redemptions from Close Family Corporations Under Section 302, 47 Minn. L. Rev. 853, 867-70 (1963).

In fact, taxpayer would also have us support our conclusion by finding, contrary to the Tax Court, that the redemptions were part of an overall plan to terminate his interest in the corporation. However, we do not feel compelled to reach the question. The parties also dispute whether the initial advances by taxpayer constituted debt or equity capital. Cf. 1964 Wis. L. Rev. 331. Given our view of the case, it makes no difference and we do not decide the question.

. The decision of the Tax Court is reversed.

NOTE

What is the significance of the "comparative dividend" test in determining dividend equivalency? Review *Levin* and *Himmel*. Which is the preferable test, "net effect" or "comparative dividend"? Why? Must they be mutually exclusive? Are the courts consistent in their application of the "comparative dividend" test? Is a shareholder more likely to have dividend income if the redemption proceeds provide him with more or with less than an outright dividend distribution would give him? Why?

UNITED STATES v. DAVIS
397 U.S. 301 (1970), rev'g 408 F.2d 1139 (6th Cir. 1969)

Mr. Justice MARSHALL delivered the opinion of the Court. In 1945, taxpayer and E. B. Bradley organized a corporation. In exchange for property transferred to the new company, Bradley received 500 shares of common stock, and taxpayer and his wife similarly each received 250 such shares. Shortly thereafter, taxpayer made an additional contribution to the corporation, purchasing 1,000 shares of preferred stock at a par value of $25 per share.

The purpose of this latter transaction was to increase the company's working capital and thereby to qualify for a loan previously negotiated through the Reconstruction Finance Corporation. It was understood that the corporation would redeem the preferred stock when the RFC loan had been repaid. Although in the interim taxpayer bought Bradley's 500 shares and divided them between his son and daughter, the total capitalization of the company remained the same until 1963. That year, after the loan was fully repaid and in accordance with the original understanding, the company redeemed taxpayer's preferred stock.

In his 1963 personal income tax return taxpayer did not report the $25,000 received by him upon the redemption of his preferred stock as income. Rather, taxpayer considered the redemption as a sale of his preferred stock to the company — a capital gains transaction under §302 of the Internal Revenue Code of 1954 resulting in no tax since taxpayer's basis in the stock equaled the amount he received for it. The Commissioner of Internal Revenue, however, did not approve this tax treatment. According to the Commissioner, the redemption of taxpayer's stock was essentially equivalent to a dividend and was thus taxable as ordinary income under §§301 and 316 of the Code. Taxpayer paid the resulting deficiency and brought this suit for a refund. The District Court ruled in his favor, 274 F. Supp. 466 (D.C.M.D. Tenn. 1967), and on appeal the Court of Appeals affirmed. 408 F.2d 1139 (C.A. 6th Cir. 1969).

The Court of Appeals held that the $25,000 received by taxpayer was "not essentially equivalent to a dividend" within the meaning of that phrase in §302(b)(1) of the Code because the redemption was the final step in a course of action that had a legitimate business (as opposed to a tax avoidance) purpose. That holding represents only one of a variety of treatments accorded similar transactions under §302(b)(1) in the circuit courts of appeals.[2] We granted certiorari, 396 U.S. 815 (1969), in order to resolve this recurring tax question involving stock redemptions by closely held corporations. We reverse.

I

The Internal Revenue Code of 1954 provides generally in §§301 and 316 for the tax treatment of distributions by a corporation to its shareholders; under those provisions, a distribution is includable in a taxpayer's gross income as a dividend out of earnings and profits to the extent such earnings exist.[3] There are exceptions to the application of these general provisions, however, and among them are those found in §302 involving certain distributions for redeemed stock. The basic question in this case is whether the $25,000 distribution by the corporation to taxpayer falls under that section — more specifically, whether its legitimate business motivation qualifies the distribution under §302(b)(1) of the Code. Preliminarily, however, we must consider the relationship between §302(b)(1) and the rules regarding the attribution of stock ownership found in §318(a) of the Code.

Under subsection (a) of §302, a distribution is treated as "payment in exchange for the stock," thus qualifying for capital gains rather than ordinary income treatment, if the conditions contained in any one of the four paragraphs of subsection (b) are met. In addition to paragraph (1)'s "not essentially equivalent to a dividend" test, capital gains treatment is available where (2) the taxpayer's voting strength is substantially diminished, (3) his interest in the company is completely terminated, or (4) certain railroad stock is redeemed. Paragraph (4) is not involved here, and taxpayer admits that paragraphs (2) and (3) do not apply. Moreover, taxpayer agrees

---

[2] Only the Second Circuit has unequivocally adopted the Commissioner's view and held irrelevant the motivation of the redemption. See Levin v. Commissioner, 385 F.2d 521 (1967); Hasbrook v. United States, 343 F.2d 811 (1965). The First Circuit, however, seems almost to have come to that conclusion, too. Compare Wiseman v. United States, 371 F.2d 816 (1967), with Bradbury v. Commissioner, 298 F.2d 111 (1962).

The other courts of appeals that have passed on the question are apparently willing to give at least some weight under §302(b)(1) to the business motivation of a distribution and redemption. See, e.g., Commissioner v. Berenbaum, 369 F.2d 337 (C.A. 10th Cir. 1966); Kerr v. Commissioner, 326 F.2d 225 (C.A. 9th Cir. 1964); Ballenger v. United States, 301 F.2d 192 (C.A. 4th Cir. 1962); Heman v. Commissioner, 283 F.2d 227 (C.A. 8th Cir. 1960); United States v. Fewell, 255 F.2d 496 (C.A. 5th Cir. 1958). See also Neff v. United States, 157 Ct. Cl. 322, 305 F.2d 455 (1962). Even among those courts that consider business purpose, however, it is generally required that the business purpose be related, not to the issuance of the stock, but to the redemption of it. See Commissioner v. Berenbaum, supra; Ballenger v. United States, supra.

[3] . . . Taxpayer makes no contention that the corporation did not have $25,000 in accumulated earnings and profits.

that for the purposes of §§302(b)(2) and (3) the attribution rules of §318(a) apply and he is considered to own the 750 outstanding shares of common stock held by his wife and children in addition to the 250 shares in his own name.[4]

Taxpayer, however, argues that the attribution rules do not apply in considering whether a distribution is essentially equivalent to a dividend under §302(b)(1). According to taxpayer, he should thus be considered to own only 25 percent of the corporation's common stock, and the distribution would then qualify under §302(b)(1) since it was not pro rata or proportionate to his stock interest, the fundamental test of dividend equivalency. See Treas. Reg. 1.302-2(b). However, the plain language of the statute compels rejection of the argument. In subsection (c) of §302, the attribution rules are made specifically applicable "in determining the ownership of stock for purposes of this section." Applying this language, both courts below held that §318(a) applies to all of §302, including §302(b)(1) — a view in accord with the decisions of the other courts of appeals, a longstanding treasury regulation,[6] and the opinion of the leading commentators.

Against this weight of authority, taxpayer argues that the result under paragraph (1) should be different because there is no explicit reference to stock ownership as there is in paragraphs (2) and (3). Neither that fact, however, nor the purpose and history of §302(b)(1) support taxpayer's argument. The attribution rules — designed to provide a clear answer to what would otherwise be a difficult tax question — formed part of the tax bill that was subsequently enacted as the 1954 Code. As is discussed further, infra, the bill as passed by the House of Representatives contained no provision comparable to §302(b)(1). When that provision was added in the Senate, no purpose was evidenced to restrict the applicability of §318(a). Rather, the attribution rules continued to be made specifically applicable to the entire section, and we believe that Congress intended that they be taken into account wherever ownership of stock was relevant.

Indeed, it was necessary that the attribution rules apply to §302(b)(1) unless they were to be effectively eliminated from consideration with regard to §§302(b)(2) and (3) also. For if a transaction failed to qualify under one of those sections solely because of the attribution rules, it would according to taxpayer's argument nonetheless qualify under §302(b)(1). We cannot agree that Congress intended so to nullify its explicit directive. We conclude, therefore, that the attribution rules of §318(a) do apply; and, for the purposes of deciding whether a distribution is "not essentially equivalent to a dividend" under §302(b)(1), taxpayer must be deemed the owner of all 1,000 shares of the company's common stock.

II

After application of the stock ownership attribution rules, this case viewed most simply involves a sole stockholder who causes part of his shares to be redeemed by the corporation. We conclude that such a redemption is always "essentially equiv-

---

[4]. . . §318(b) the rules contained in subsection (a) are made specifically applicable to "section 302 (relating to redemption of stock)."
[6]See Treas. Reg. 1.302-2(b).

alent to a dividend" within the meaning of that phrase in §302(b)(1)[8] and therefore do not reach the Government's alternative argument that in any event the distribution should not on the facts of this case qualify for capital gains treatment.[9]

The predecessor of §302(b)(1) came into the tax law as §201(d) of the Revenue Act of 1921, 42 Stat. 228:

> "A stock dividend shall not be subject to tax but if after the distribution of any such dividend the corporation proceeds to cancel or redeem its stock at such time and in such manner as to make the distribution and cancellation or redemption essentially equivalent to the distribution of a taxable dividend, the amount received in redemption or cancellation of the stock shall be treated as a taxable dividend . . . ."

Enacted in response to this court's decision that pro rata stock dividends do not constitute taxable income, Eisner v. Macomber, 252 U.S. 189 (1920), the provision had the obvious purpose of preventing a corporation from avoiding dividend tax treatment by distributing earnings to its shareholders in two transactions — a pro rata stock dividend followed by a pro rata redemption — that would have the same economic consequences as a simple dividend. Congress, however, soon recognized that even without a prior stock dividend essentially the same result could be affected whereby any corporation, "especially one which has only a few stockholders, might be able to make a distribution to its stockholders which would have the same effect as a taxable dividend." H.R. Rep. No. 1, 69th Cong., 1st Sess., 5. In order to cover this situation, the law was amended to apply "(whether or not such stock was issued as a stock dividend)" whenever a distribution in redemption of stock was made "at such time and in such manner" that it was essentially equivalent to a taxable dividend. Revenue Act of 1926, §201(g), 44 Stat. 11.

This provision of the 1926 Act was carried forward in each subsequent revenue act and finally became §115(g)(1) of the Internal Revenue Code of 1939. Unfortunately, however, the policies encompassed within the general language of §115(g)(1) and its predecessors were not clear, and there resulted much confusion in the tax law. At first, courts assumed that the provision was aimed at tax avoidance schemes and sought only to determine whether such a scheme existed. See, e.g., Commissioner v. Quackenbos, 78 F.2d 156 (C.A. 2d Cir. 1935). Although later the emphasis changed and the focus was more on the effect of the distribution, many courts continued to find that distributions otherwise like a dividend were not "essentially equivalent" if, for example, they were motivated by a sufficiently strong nontax business purpose. See cases cited n.2, supra. There was general disagreement, however, about what would qualify as such a purpose, and the result was a case-by-case deter-

---

[8] Of course, this just means that a distribution in redemption to a sole shareholder will be treated under the general provisions of §301, and it will only be taxed as a dividend under §316 to the extent that there are earnings and profits.

[9] The Government argues that even if business purpose were relevant under §302(b)(1), the business purpose present here related only to the original investment and not at all to the necessity for redemption. See cases cited, n.2, supra. Under either view, taxpayer does not lose his basis in the preferred stock. Under Treas. Reg. 1.302-2(c) that basis is applied to taxpayers' common stock.

mination with each case decided "on the basis of the particular facts of the transaction in question." Bains v. United States, 153 Ct. Cl. 599, 603, 289 F.2d 644, 646 (1961).

By the time of the general revision resulting in the Internal Revenue Code of 1954, the draftsmen were faced with what has aptly been described as "the morass created by the decisions." Ballenger v. United States, 301 F.2d 192, 196 (C.A. 4th Cir. 1962). In an effort to eliminate "the considerable confusion which exists in this area" and thereby to facilitate tax planning, H.R. Rep. No. 1337, 83d Cong., 2d Sess., 35, the authors of the new Code sought to provide objective tests to govern the tax consequences of stock redemptions. Thus, the tax bill passed by the House of Representatives contained no "essentially equivalent" language. Rather, it provided for "safe harbors" where capital gains treatment would be accorded to corporate redemptions that met the conditions now found in §§302(b)(2) and (3) of the Code.

It was in the Senate Finance Committee's consideration of the tax bill that §302 (b)(1) was added, and Congress thereby provided that capital gains treatment should be available "if the redemption is not essentially equivalent to a dividend." Taxpayer argues that the purpose was to continue "existing law," and there is support in the legislative history that §302(b)(1) reverted "in part" or "in general" to the "essentially equivalent" provision of §115(g)(1) of the 1939 Code. According to the Government, even under the old law it would have been improper for the Court of Appeals to rely on "a business purpose for the redemption" and "an absence of the proscribed tax avoidance purpose to bail out dividends at favorable tax rates." See Northup v. United States, 240 F.2d 304, 307 (C.A. 2d Cir. 1957); Smith v. United States, 121 F.2d 692, 695 (C.A. 3d Cir. 1941); cf. Commissioner v. Estate of Bedford, 325 U.S. 283 (1945). However, we need not decide that question, for we find from the history of the 1954 revisions and the purpose of §302(b)(1) that Congress intended more than merely to re-enact the prior law.

In explaining the reason for adding the "essentially equivalent" test, the Senate Committee stated that the House provisions "appeared unnecessarily restrictive, particularly, in the case of redemptions of preferred stock which might be called by the corporation without the shareholder having any control over when the redemption may take place." S. Rep. No. 1622, 83d Cong., 2d Sess., 44. This explanation gives no indication that the purpose behind the redemption should affect the result.[10] Rather, in its more detailed technical evaluation of §302(b)(1), the Senate Committee reported as follows:

> "The test intended to be incorporated in the interpretation of paragraph (1) is in general that currently employed under section 115(g)(1) of the 1939 Code. Your committee further intends that in applying this test for the future that the inquiry will be devoted solely to the question of whether or not the transaction by its nature may properly be characterized as a sale of

---

[10]See Bittker & Eustice, [Federal Income Taxation of Corporations and Shareholders], at 291: "It is not easy to give §302(b)(1) an expansive construction in view of this indication that its major function was the narrow one of immunizing redemptions of minority holdings of preferred stock."

stock by the redeeming shareholder to the corporation. For this purpose the presence or absence of earnings and profits of the corporation is not material. Example: X, the sole shareholder of a corporation having no earnings or profits causes the corporation to redeem half of its stock. Paragraph (1) does not apply to such redemption notwithstanding the absence of earnings and profits." S. Rep. No. 1622, supra, at 234.

The intended scope of §302(b)(1) as revealed by this legislative history is certainly not free from doubt. However, we agree with the Government that by making the sole inquiry relevant for the future the narrow one whether the redemption could be characterized as a sale, Congress was apparently rejecting past court decisions that had also considered factors indicating the presence or absence of a tax-avoidance motive.[11] At least that is the implication of the example given. Congress clearly mandated that pro rata distributions be treated under the general rules laid down in §§301 and 316 rather than under §302, and nothing suggests that there should be a different result if there were a "business purpose" for the redemption. Indeed, just the opposite inference must be drawn since there would not likely be a tax-avoidance purpose in a situation where there were no earnings or profits. We conclude that the Court of Appeals was therefore wrong in looking for a business purpose and considering it in deciding whether the redemption was equivalent to a dividend. Rather, we agree with the Court of Appeals for the Second Circuit that "the business purpose of a transaction is irrelevant in determining dividend equivalence" under §302(b)(1). Hasbrook v. United States, 343 F.2d 811, 814 (1965).

Taxpayer strongly argues that to treat the redemption involved here as essentially equivalent to a dividend is to elevate form over substance. Thus, taxpayer argues, had he not bought Bradley's shares or had he made a subordinated loan to the company instead of buying preferred stock, he could have gotten back his $25,000 with favorable tax treatment. However, the difference between form and substance in the tax law is largely problematical, and taxpayer's complaints have little to do with whether a business purpose is relevant under §302(b)(1). It was clearly proper for Congress to treat distributions generally as taxable dividends when made out of earnings and profits and then to prevent avoidance of that result without regard to motivation where the distribution is in exchange for redeemed stock.

We conclude that that is what Congress did when enacting §302(b)(1). If a corporation distributes property as a simple dividend, the effect is to transfer the property from the company to its shareholders without a change in the relative economic interests or rights of the stockholders. Where a redemption has that same

---

[11]This rejection is confirmed by the Committee's acceptance of the House treatment of distributions involving corporate contractions — a factor present in many of the earlier "business purpose" redemptions. In describing its action, the Committee stated as follows:

"Your committee, as did the House bill, separates into their significant elements the kind of transactions now incoherently aggregated in the definition of a partial liquidation. Those distributions which may have capital-gain characteristics *because they are not made pro rata* among the various shareholders would be subjected, at the shareholder level, to the separate tests described in [§§301 to 318]. On the other hand, those distributions characterized by what happens solely at the corporate level by reason of the assets distributed would be included as within the concept of a partial liquidation." S. Rep. No. 1622, supra, at 49. (Emphasis added.)

effect, it cannot be said to have satisfied the "not essentially equivalent to a dividend" requirement of §302(b)(1). Rather, to qualify for preferred treatment under that section, a redemption must result in a meaningful reduction of the shareholder's proportionate interest in the corporation. Clearly, taxpayer here, who (after application of the attribution rules) was the sole shareholder of the corporation both before and after the redemption, did not qualify under this test. The decision of the Court of Appeals must therefore be reversed and the case remanded to the District Court for dismissal of the complaint.

It is so ordered.

Mr. Justice Douglas, with whom The Chief Justice and Mr. Justice Brennan concur, dissenting.

I agree with the District Court, 274 F. Supp. 466, and with the Court of Appeals, 408 F.2d 1139, that respondent's contribution of working capital in the amount of $25,000 in exchange for 1,000 shares of preferred stock with a par value of $25 was made in order for the corporation to obtain a loan from the RFC and that the preferred stock was to be redeemed when the loan was repaid. For the reasons stated by the two lower courts, this redemption was not "essentially equivalent to a dividend," for the bona fide business purpose of the redemption belies the payment of a dividend. As stated by the Court of Appeals:

> "Although closely-held corporations call for close scrutiny under the tax law, we will not, under the facts and circumstances of this case, allow mechanical attribution rules to transform a legitimate corporate transaction into a tax avoidance scheme." 408 F.2d, at 1143-1144.

When the Court holds it was a dividend, it effectively cancels §302(b)(1) from the Code. This result is not a matter of conjecture, for the Court says that in case of closely held or one-man corporations a redemption of stock is "always" equivalent to a dividend. I would leave such revision to the Congress.

NOTE

In light of *Davis*, what would you now expect in the results and opinions in cases such as *Lewis*, page 175 supra; *Levin*, page 184 supra; and *Himmel*, page 191 supra?

COMMISSIONER v. ESTATE OF ANTRIM
395 F.2d 430 (4th Cir. 1968)

Before Haynsworth, Chief Judge, Winter, Circuit Judge, and Merhige, District Judge.

Winter, Circuit Judge: In Estate of Joseph L. Antrim, Jr., Deceased, et al. [26 T.C.M. 320 (1967)], a redemption of preferred stock was held entitled to capital gains treatment under §302(b)(1) of the Internal Revenue Code of 1954. 26 U.S.C.A. §302(b)(1). The Tax Court's decision that the distribution was "not essentially equivalent to a dividend," within the meaning of the Code, proceeded primarily from its findings that "the redemption was substantially disproportionate with regard to the common stockholders and it thus lacked an important dividend characteristic, that of prorata distribution of earnings and profits among holders of the common stock." Id. The government challenges the correctness of this conclusion in this appeal.

In Ballenger v. United States, 301 F.2d 192 (4 Cir. 1962), we had occasion to consider a similar question, and we approved resort to the test of dividend equivalence employed by the Tax Court in this case. In *Ballenger* we noted the existence of two lines of decisions — the "net effect" test, under which a court hypothesizes the declaration of dividend, instead of the redemption of stock, in "the same amount" (Id., p. 196) as the redemption and determines, from the standpoint of each stockholder-taxpayer, if the results from the hypothetical dividend and the actual redemption are essentially the same; and what may be called the "net effect, plus" test, under which the "net effect" test is employed together with a further consideration, namely, whether there are legitimate business purposes for the redmption. Under the "net effect" test, dissimilarity, or substantial disproportion, usually results in a taxpayer-stockholder's being afforded capital gains treatment;[1] under the "net effect, plus" test similarity, or substantial proration, does not operate to deny capital gains treatment if a legitimate business purpose for the redemption is proved. It was unnecessary for us in *Ballenger* to choose between the lines of authority, and we declined to do so. Likewise, we find it unnecessary to make a choice in the instant case.

The government does not question the propriety of resort to the strict "net effect" test in these cases. Its claim is that the test was misapplied. Analysis of its claim requires a consideration of the facts:

Stripped of unessentials, the facts are that C. W. Antrim & Sons, Inc. (the "corporation") concluded to redeem its 800 shares of 6% cumulative, non-voting preferred stock. As of October 1, 1959, the date of redemption, the preferred stock was redeemable, in toto, at $100 per share plus accumulated dividends. At the time of the redemption, the preferred stock, and all of the corporation's issued common stock, was owned by the following persons, who received the following amounts, exclusive of dividends:

	Common Stock Shares	%	Preferred Stock Shares	%	Distribution in Redemption
Joseph L. Antrim, Jr.	5,333	66⅔	120	15	$12,000
Richard H. Cardwell, Jr.	2,667	33⅓	20	2½	2,000
Annie Belle T. Cardwell			20	2½	2,000
Nora Lee Antrim			640	80	64,000
Total Shares	8,000		800		

[1] Under this test, a taxpayer-stockholder may still be entitled to capital gains treatment even though the redemption is prorata with the hypothetical dividend if, as a result of the redemption, he incurs a detriment vis-à-vis other stockholders in such matters as liquidation rights. Himmel v. Commissioner, 338 F.2d 815 (2 Cir. 1965).

The tax consequences of the distribution to Joseph L. Antrim, Jr. and to Richard H. Cardwell, Jr. for the year 1959 are in issue. Since Joseph L. Antrim, Jr. has died, the litigation is carried on by his estate. Since Richard H. Cardwell, Jr. and Annie Belle T. Cardwell are husband and wife, and since they filed a joint return for 1959, both are parties to the litigation. Additionally, §318(a)(1)(A)(i) of the Code, 26 U.S.C.A. §318(a)(1)(A)(i), require that, inter alia, for the purpose of determining capital gains treatment of a stock redemption, Richard H. Cardwell, Jr. shall be considered as owning the stock owned by his wife, Annie Belle T. Cardwell. The distribution to Nora Lee Antrim is not in issue because that distribution fits into the §302(b)(3) "safe harbor" provision, of the Code. 26 U.S.C.A. §302(b)(3).[2]

To determine whether the redemption was essentially equivalent to a dividend, the Tax Court hypothesized a dividend in the aggregate amount of $80,000 on the corporation's common stock and determined that the taxpayers would receive the amounts (in round figures) which bore the relationship to the amounts which they received as a result of the redemption, as shown in the following table:

	Distribution in Redemption	Distribution of Hypothetical Dividend
Joseph L. Antrim, Jr.	$12,000	$53,333
Richard J. Cardwell, Jr.	4,000[3]	26,666

To avoid the manifest disparity between the amounts that the taxpayers received in redemption and what they would have received if the same amount were distributed as a dividend on common stock, the Commissioner argues that the only proper comparison is between the distribution of $80,000 in redemption of preferred stock and $16,000 in payment of a dividend on common stock. Short of the comparison he urges, the Commissioner concedes that the distributions to the taxpayers were not comparable, and that he cannot prevail; but, he argues, in postulating a hypothetical dividend, stockholders who own common stock are the only ones to whom dividend equivalence can be an issue and, hence, the amounts distributed in redemption of preferred stock to shareholders who own only preferred stock must be eliminated in fixing the aggregate amount of the hypothetical dividend on common stock. If the Commissioner's urged adjustment of the aggregate amount of the hypothetical dividend is adopted, Joseph L. Antrim would have received (in round figures) $10,666, and Richard H. Cardwell, Jr. would have received (in round figures) $5,333, which, the Commissioner urges, are essentially equivalent to the $12,000 and $4,000 that they received respectively on redemption of the preferred stock.[4]

[2]This provision affords capital gains treatment, without more, "if the redemption is in complete redemption of all of the stock of the corporation owned by the stockholder."

[3]By virtue of . . . §318(a)(1)(A), Richard was considered to have received the $2,000 paid in redemption of preferred stock to his wife, Annie.

[4]Under this computation Antrim received $8\frac{1}{3}\%$ more and Cardwell $8\frac{1}{3}\%$ less for redemption of their preferred stock than they would have received if a dividend on common stock had been declared. The Commissioner urges that these differences are less than ones which have been held not to destroy essential equivalence, citing Bradbury v. Commissioner, 298 F.2d 111 (1 Cir. 1962); Commissioner v. Berenbaum, 369 F.2d 337 (10 Cir. 1966), and . . . §302(b)(2).

Based upon the legislative history of §302(b)(1), the Commissioner asserts that the section is intended only to benefit owners of preferred stock who own no common stock when there is a partial redemption of their preferred stock.[5] The Commissioner's argument, even if advanced,[6] has not been adopted by any court and we perceive three reasons why it should not be adopted. First, if Congress had intended to benefit only this narrowly defined class, it is reasonable to suppose that Congress would have created another specific "safe harbor" rather than to employ the general language "not essentially equivalent to a dividend." The further supposition that use of the general language was an expression of intent that §302(b)(1) have wider scope than that urged by the Commissioner is equally justified. Second, as the Commissioner candidly, albeit contradictorily, states in his brief, the concept of "dividend equivalence" has meaning only where a common stockholder is involved. Section 302(b)(1) thus, by its terms, has application broader than that contended for by the Commissioner. Third, the Commissioner's construction would have the grossly unfair consequence of disallowing capital gains treatment under all circumstances where a taxpayer owned only one share of common stock but all or a portion of his preferred stock was redeemed. While gross unfairness is not determinative of the invalidity of the construction which the Commissioner presses, it is a result to be avoided if possible.

The legislative history of §302(b)(1) and related provisions does show that Congress intended to create certain "safe harbors" (the present subsections (b)(2), (b)(3) and (b)(4) of §302); but that in the course of enactment of the legislation, Congress concluded to retain the "essentially equivalent to a dividend" provision, §302(b)(1), because the "safe harbors," standing alone, "appeared unnecessarily restrictive." S. Rep. No. 1622, 83rd Cong., 2d Sess. pp. 44-45; 3 U.S.C. Cong. & Adm. News (1954) pp. 4621, 4675. See Levin v. Commissioner, 385 F.2d 521, 524-525 (2 Cir. 1967). Significantly, however, we find nothing in that history to indicate that in those cases in which the hypothetical dividend test is appropriate, the aggregate amount of the hypothetical dividend is to be reduced by the amounts paid to stockholders who are in a "safe harbor." True, §302(b)(5) states that, if a redemption fails to qualify for a "safe harbor" berth under subsections (b)(2), (b)(3) or (b)(4), that fact shall not be considered in determining whether it "is not essentially equivalent to a dividend" under (b)(1); but such a statement, in our view, falls short of indicating that the test of dividend equivalence must be applied by disregarding amounts paid to shareholders who have available a "safe harbor." Our analysis of the legislative history and the inferences which we draw from the use by Congress of the broad language "essentially equivalent to a dividend" persuades us that the

---

[5]The §302(b)(3) "safe harbor" which would otherwise be available to him is, by its terms, available only where there is a *complete* redemption of all of his stock. We note, however, that §1.302-2(a) of the Income Tax Regulations (1968) gives, as the *only* example of a qualified §302(b)(1) redemption, the redemption of one-half of the non-voting preferred stock of a shareholder who owns no shares of any other class of stock.

[6]While the Commissioner quite strongly suggests this argument in several places in his brief, elsewhere the Commissioner advances other arguments which may be deemed either modifications thereof or alternative arguments. We deem it proper to deal with the argument at face value.

implicit and explicit statements in prior cases about the aggregate base of the hypothetical dividend are still valid.

In *Ballenger*, as we have noted, we stated that the comparative hypothetical dividend should be in "the same amount" as the distribution on redemption. While in *Ballenger* the taxpayer was the sole owner of all of the preferred and common stock, in Northup v. United States, 240 F.2d 304, 306 (2 Cir. 1957), stockholders owning 74.7% of preferred stock owned no common stock; and yet it seems clear from a reading of the opinion that application of the hypothetical dividend on common stock test was premised on the aggregate amount of dividend on common stock as being equal to the total sum distributed in redemption of preferred. Himmel v. Commissioner, supra, 338 F.2d pp. 817-819 (2 Cir. 1965), continued to look to total distribution in determining the effect of a hypothetical dividend even after enactment of the Internal Revenue Code of 1954.

The Commissioner urges us not to follow the direction to which these decisions point, and, instead, to reduce the total $80,000 redemption by the portion received by Miss Antrim ($64,000 — which the Commissioner asserts is immaterial), because her stock could have been redeemed well in advance, or well after, redemption of taxpayers' preferred stock. Basically, his position is that where common stockholders are in the picture, the question of dividend equivalence turns on their positions each to the other and not with regard to those who own no voting stock.

To this argument there are several answers. In fact, Miss Antrim's stock was not redeemed either before or after redemption of the taxpayer's preferred stock. Indeed, under the charter of the corporation, it could not have been redeemed before, unless the taxpayers waived their right of redemption, or after, unless Miss Antrim waived her right of redemption. Miss Antrim's stock was redeemed as part and parcel of a total redemption of all preferred stock, including that held by the taxpayers. This statement does not place undue emphasis on form, ignoring substance, because it is clear that in its revision of §302 Congress intended to introduce a measure of clarity into an otherwise confusing and confused area of the tax laws so that taxpayers by intelligent planning and literal compliance could achieve safe harbors and be entitled to capital gains treatment. Levin v. Commissioner, 385 F.2d 521, 525 (2 Cir. 1967). Of course, it is not a safe harbor provision which is involved here, but the legislative intent of facilitating tax planning would clearly be frustrated if every plan, regardless of its form, could be retrospectively altered by the Commissioner in determining its tax consequences.

There is a more basic flaw in the Commissioner's argument, however. Implied is the premise that in order to distribute $16,000 to themselves, taxpayers were required, or found it necessary, to distribute $80,000. Nothing could be less the fact. If the ultimate object of the transaction had been to put $16,000 into their own hands, taxpayers were at liberty to declare a dividend of $16,000 on the corporation's common stock and to provide nothing for Miss Antrim. If the ultimate object were only to distribute $80,000, taxpayers could have even declared a dividend of $80,000 on the corporation's common stock, again providing nothing for Miss Antrim. By attempting to bifurcate the distribution which did occur, the Commissioner's argument ignores the critical fact that the taxpayers received much less than they would have received had the total been devoted to the declaration of a dividend on common stock. Dividend equivalence, in our view, requires that hypothetical treatment of the *total sum* be considered.

In short, we think that the Commissioner asks us to compare apples with oranges. We find no warrant for his request in the language of §302, its legislative history, in the precedents, or in logic. We agree with the Tax Court that when the hypothetical dividend test is used the aggregate amount of the hypothetical dividend is the same as the aggregate amount distributed in redemption, irrespective of whether a portion thereof finds a "safe harbor." The decisions of the Tax Court are
    Affirmed.

NOTE

For purposes of determining dividend equivalency, should a court look to the relative interests of all the shareholders or only to those who retain an interest in the ongoing corporation? In *Antrim,* was there a substantial change in the interests inter sese of the shareholders who remained after the redemption? Do the remaining shareholders have the same, more, or less of an interest in the total corporate assets than they had before the redemption? Is this significant?

BLOCH v. UNITED STATES
261 F. Supp. 597 (S.D. Tex. 1966),
aff'd per curiam, 386 F.2d 839 (5th Cir. 1967)

[Southern Elevator and Storage Company, Inc. was a Texas corporation engaged in the operation of grain storage facilities. Immediately before the redemption here in question the corporation had 680 shares of capital stock outstanding which were owned as follows: 306 shares (45 per cent) by Bloch, the taxpayer; 306 shares (45 per cent) by Bryan; and 68 shares (10 per cent) by Harris. In order to give Parrish, the plant manager, an equity interest in the corporation, the corporation had, on June 1, 1956, adopted a resolution whereby the corporation was to redeem 15 per cent of the corporation's stock from Bloch and 15 per cent from Bryan, or 102 shares from each, which were to be held by the corporation; Parrish was given an option to buy two-thirds of this redeemed stock from the corporation, and Harris was given an option to buy one-third. The option price for both was 85 per cent of the redemption price. (This arrangement was adopted in preference to a direct sale from Bloch and Bryan to Parrish and Harris in order to enable them to purchase the stock at a lower price than Bloch and Bryan were to receive for it, while giving Parrish and Harris the benefit of the restricted stock option provisions of the Code.)]

GRAVEN, Senior District Judge. . . . 6. At a meeting of the Board of Directors of Southern on January 2, 1959, a resolution was adopted authorizing an immediate stock redemption from Bryan and Bloch of 15 percent each of their Southern stock. This was in accordance with the resolution and agreement of June 1, 1956, referred to above. Pursuant to the January 2, 1959, resolution, on January 15, 1959, Bloch and Bryan each surrendered to Southern 102 shares of stock. In connection therewith, each of them received a non-negotiable, non-interest bearing note from the corporation in the amount of $35,700, dated January 2, 1959, and payable on or before three years from that date. That sum represented a redemption price of $350 per share, which was determined in accordance with the corporation's resolution of June 1, 1956, heretofore set out.

Southern paid the following amounts to Bloch on the dates indicated in satisfaction of the $35,700 note: $2,700 on April 28, 1960; $1,487.50 on February 3, 1961; $9,371.25 on February 24, 1961; and the remaining $22,141.25 on September 30, 1961. The note held by Bryan was fully paid not later than October 23, 1961.

In his 1960 and 1961 income tax returns Bloch reported the payments above set forth as capital gains. The Internal Revenue Service assessed the deficiency taxes based upon the contention that those payments constituted dividends, taxable as ordinary income. It is the character of those payments to Bloch that is in controversy herein.

7. On January 15, 1959, Bloch and Bryan each surrendered to Southern his certificate for 306 shares of stock and each received a new certificate for 204 shares. The remaining 204 shares were cancelled in redemption by the secretary of the corporation and affixed to the corporate stock records as redeemed shares. Those 204 shares were then held in the corporate treasury for sale pursuant to the option contract to Parrish and Harris until paid for by the optionees. The resolution of January 2, 1959, heretofore noted, had granted Parrish and Harris an option for five years to purchase the redeemed stock at a price of $297.50 per share. Parrish and Harris exercised their options and redeemed shares were issued to them as paid for by them at various intervals subsequent to the redemption of the shares by the corporation. Reissue of the redeemed shares was made as follows:

Price Paid to Corporation	Optionee	Date of Payment	Number of Treasury Shares Purchased
$ 1,487.50	Parrish	2/ 4/61	5
1,487.50	Harris	2/ 4/61	5
18,742.50	Harris	2/24/61	63
38,972.50	Parrish	10/23/61	131
$60,690.00			204

... On May 15, 1956, Bryan, Bloch, Harris and Parrish entered into a partnership to engage in the business of buying, selling, and factoring grain and other products. That partnership will be referred to in more detail later on.

8. It was heretofore noted that the hub of this controversy is whether the stock redemption distributions made by Southern to the taxpayer in 1960 and 1961 should be taxed as ordinary income or as capital gains. In that connection, it is necessary to consider certain statutory provisions and regulations. Section 316(a), Ttile 26 U.S.C.A., sets out the general rule or proposition that distributions by a corporation

to its shareholders out of either current earnings and profits or earnings and profits accumulated since February 28, 1913, are dividends. Section 301(c)(1), Title 26 U.S.C.A., provides the further general rule that dividend distributions are taxable to the recipient as ordinary income unless they come within certain exceptions. Some of these exceptions are found in Section 302, Title 26 U.S.C.A., pertaining to distributions in redemption of stock. Section 302(a) provides that if the transaction constitutes a stock redemption within the definition of Section 302(b), it will be treated as in part or full payment in exchange for the stock and will qualify for capital gains treatment. Section 302(b) sets out four categories of stock redemption transactions, each of which will qualify for capital gains treatment. Since the parties agree that two of these four categories are not material under the facts of this case, only the two which the taxpayer contends do apply will be examined. Thus the pertinent points of Section 302 for purposes of this case are [§§302(b)(1) and (2)]. . . . In the application of the provisions of Section 302 to the facts of this case, Section 318(a), Title 26 U.S.C.A., must also be considered since Section 302(c)(1) provides that in determining the ownership of stock for purpose of application of the provisions of Section 302(b) to the facts of a particular case, the attribution rules of Section 318(a) are pertinent. . . .

It will be noted that [§§302(b)(1) and (2)] characterize two types of transactions, either of which will qualify as a capital gains redemption. The first type of transaction is set forth in Subsection (b)(1), i.e., where the redemption is not essentially equivalent to a dividend. The other type of transaction is set forth in Subsection (b)(2), i.e., where the distribution is substantially disproportionate within the meaning of the Section. The parties are in controversy as to whether the redemption in this case falls into either of those categories. The issue as to the matter of the redemption in question being substantially disproportionate will first be considered.

Under the provisions of Section 302 relating to disproportionate distributions, a taxpayer is required to meet two tests, both of which are arithmetical in character. Those tests are as follows:

> "(1) Immediately after the redemption, the taxpayer must own less than 50 percent of the total combined voting power of all classes of stock entitled to vote, and
>
> "(2) Immediately after the redemption, the portion of the corporation's voting stock then owned by the taxpayer must be less than 80 percent of the portion of the stock owned by him before the redemption."

To state these tests another way, after the redemption a taxpayer must own less than 50 percent of the voting stock of the corporation, and the redemption must have reduced the ratio of his voting stock to the total corporate voting stock to an amount less than 80 percent of such ratio before the redemption.

It was heretofore noted that there were originally 680 shares of Southern voting stock, of which the taxpayer owned 306 shares. It was also heretofore noted that on January 15, 1959, the taxpayer and Bryan each surrendered his certificate for 306 shares and each was reissued a certificate for 204 shares. The 102 shares surrendered by each were surrendered for the purpose of carrying out the option agreements with Parrish and Harris. If these 204 shares were to be considered as not constituting voting stock of the corporation, then the voting stock consisted of 486* shares. It is clear that whether the voting stock is considered as being 680 shares or 486 shares, the taxpayer meets what will be referred to for convenience as the 50 percent test. The parties are not in controversy as to the taxpayer meeting that test. They are in controversy as to whether the taxpayer meets what will be referred to for convenience as the 80 percent test. That controversy revolves, in part, around whether the 204 shares surrendered by the taxpayer and Bryan and held in the treasury for the purpose of meeting the stock purchase options of Parrish and Harris shall be considered as voting stock for the purpose of applying the 80 percent test. The Government contends that those shares are not to be so considered. The taxpayer contends that they are to be so considered. The provisions of Section 302(b)(2) noted above make reference to the "voting stock" or "voting power" of the corporation. Treasury Regulations Section 1.302-3(a) relating thereto provides that the stock to be considered is that "which is issued and outstanding in the hands of the shareholders." Southern was a Texas corporation. A reference to Texas law is made by the taxpayer in his main brief in which he states: "Texas law would not permit the issuance of the shares to Parrish and Harris in exchange for Notes. Therefore the shares were held in the Corporate treasury until paid for in compliance with the law. . . ." It appears that the stock in question was held in the corporate treasury until paid for. The pretrial stipulation of facts reflects that Parrish and Harris participated in corporate dividends only as to the issued shares. The taxpayer relies strongly on the case of Sorem v. Commissioner of Internal Revenue (10th Cir. 1964), 334 F.2d 275, in which a similar question is involved. The Court in that case held that for purposes of applying the constructive ownership or attribution rules of Section 318, employees who held stock options must be considered as owning the stock for which they held options. Under the holding of that case, the shares held in the corporate treasury by Southern for the purpose of meeting the options held by Parrish and Harris would be considered as owned by them in connection with the matter of the taxpayer meeting the 80 percent test. The provisions of Regulations Section 1.318-3(c), when coupled with those of Regulations Section 1.302-3(a), noted above, might be interpreted as requiring a different conclusion. Because of another feature, it is not necessary for the Court to decide whether the holding of the *Sorem* case should or should not be followed. However, if in this case this Court was squarely presented with the question as to whether the holding of the *Sorem* case should or should not be followed, it would be reluctant to follow such holding. It would seem that it would be highly questionable that stock held in the treasury of a corporation which might be issued or might never be issued depending upon whether the optionees of such stock would or would not exercise their options could not properly be considered as being owned by the optionees for the purpose of applying the attribution rules under Section 318.

However, assuming, as contended by the taxpayer, that Parrish and Harris are to be regarded as the owners of the 204 shares of stock in question, there comes into

*476? — ED.

focus Section 318, heretofore set out and referred to by the parties as the constructive ownership or attribution statute. A portion of that statute pertinent to the facts in this case has since been repealed,* but was in effect during the period of time here involved. It was heretofore noted that in 1956 Bloch, Bryan, Parrish and Harris had entered into a partnership. Because of some confusion and conflict in the briefs as to that partnership, it seems appropriate to set out a portion of the pretrial stipulation of facts relating to such partnership, as follows:

"14. On May 15, 1956, B. F. Bryan, William H. Bloch, Lee Orr Harris, and William R. Parrish entered into a partnership to engage in the business of brokering, factoring, and buying and selling grain and other products, the profits to be divided equally by said partners as to the first $10,000.00 of net partnership profits and with profits in excess of $10,000.00 to be distributed as follows: 40 percent to B. F. Bryan and 20 percent each to William H. Bloch, Lee Orr Harris and William R. Parrish. Losses were to be divided equally. The partnership made a profit in each and every year of its operation. The partnership actively began conduct of business in late June 1956."

The partnership was known as the Southern Elevator Grain Company. It continued to carry on its business operations through July 1961, when it was dissolved, apparently because of dissension between B. F. Bryan and the other partners. The interest of the parties did not change during the existence of the partnership.

Under the provisions of the attribution statute (Section 318) then in effect, stock owned by a partner is deemed to be owned by the partnership, and stock owned by the partnership (including that which it is deemed to own because a partner actually owns it) is deemed to be owned by the partners in their partnership proportions. If, as the taxpayer contends, Parrish and Harris were the owners of the 204 shares of option stock, under the provisions of Section 302(b)(2) it is manifest that they were also to be considered the owners of it under Section 318(a)(2), which is specifically made applicable to Section 302.

If the 680 shares are to be considered as the shares of stock outstanding both before and after redemption, it is then necessary to determine the ownership percentage in the light of the attribution statute. Before the redemption, the taxpayer owned 306 shares in his own right and constructively owned 93.5 shares through the partnership. The total percentage owned (399.5/680) was 58.75 percent. After the redemption, he owned 204 shares in his own right and constructively owned 119 shares through the partnership. The total percentage owned (323/680) was 47.5 percent. The after-redemption ownership was 80.8+ percent of the before-redemption ownership (47.5 to 58.75). Thus the taxpayer does not meet the 80 percent test.

The above conclusions result from application of the constructive ownership rules to the partnership situation, as follows. The ownership of the partnership shares before the redemption was as follows: Bryan's 306 shares and Harris' 68 shares, totalling 374 shares, are deemed to be owned by the partnership and are, in turn, deemed owned to the extent of one-fourth, or 93.5 shares, by the taxpayer as a part-

*See §318(a)(5)(C), which was not part of the statute during the years involved. — Ed.

ner to that extent. The ownership of the partnership shares after the redemption was as follows: Bryan's 204 shares, Parrish's 136 shares and Harris' 136 shares, totalling 476 shares, are deemed to be owned by the partnership and are, in turn, deemed owned to the extent of one-fourth, or 119 shares, by the taxpayer as a partner. The partnership was apparently somewhat related to Southern because of its personnel and business activities. However, in order for Section 318 to be applicable it is not necessary that the partnership be engaged in activities similar to that of the corporation involved.

If the 204 shares of stock held in the treasury are not regarded as voting stock, then the situation would be as follows: prior to the redemption the taxpayer owned 306 shares of the 680 shares outstanding, or 45 percent, and after the redemption he will have owned 204 shares of the 476 shares outstanding, or 42.8 percent. The 42.8 percent ownership percentage after redemption is substantially more than 80 percent of the 45 percent ownership percentage before redemption (being 95+ percent), so the taxpayer would also fail to meet the 80 percent test under this assumption of facts.

By way of summary, it can be stated that if the 204 shares held in the treasury of Southern are to be regarded as not outstanding stock, then the taxpayer would not meet the 80 percent test irrespective of constructive ownership or attribution rules. If those 204 shares are to be regarded as outstanding, then the taxpayer fails to meet the 80 percent test because of the applicability of the attribution statute (Section 318). . . .

9. The next matter for consideration is whether the stock redemption distributions to the taxpayer were within the scope of Section 302(b)(1). As heretofore set out, that Section provides that a redemption is entitled to capital gains treatment "if the redemption is not essentially equivalent to a dividend." Several related issues are involved in a consideration of this question. These have to do with the adequacy of the corporate earnings and profits, whether the claims for refund properly raised such issue, and the proper time at which to measure corporate earnings and profits for purposes of applying the provisions of Section 302(b)(1) to the facts of this case. The taxpayer contends that at the pertinent time in question the corporate earnings and profits were not adequate to cover the redemption distributions. In connection with this contention the Government asserts that the taxpayer did not properly raise such issue in his claims for refund. . . . [The Court decided this issue in the taxpayer's favor.]

The next issue for consideration is whether the corporate earnings and profits and accumulated surplus were adequate to cover the redemption disbursements. This is the subject of vigorous controversy. Considerable evidence was presented on this issue and it was discussed at some length in the briefs. It involves a number of questions. The first question is the proper time to measure the adequacy of corporate earnings and profits. The parties are in agreement that the redemption occurred on January 15, 1959. The parties are also in agreement that the cash disbursements by Southern to the taxpayer took place in 1960 and 1961 when the corporate non-interest bearing note given by Southern to the taxpayer was paid. Both parties seem to be in agreement that the 1960 and 1961 corporate distributions should be taxed to him in those years, i.e., the years of receipt, rather than in 1959 when he received the corporate note. The taxpayer reported the disbursements in his 1960 and 1961 income tax returns and he claimed a refund of the taxes involved for those same years. The taxpayer contends that although the tax impact of the redemption distributions should fall in the years of receipt, the proper point in time for the purpose of measuring the adequacy of corporate earnings and profits on the dividend issue shall have been on January 15, 1959, when the redemption occurred. The taxpayer cites in support of this last contention the case of Estate of James T. Moore, Tax Court Memo Decision 1961-257. That case does not support his contention. It had to do with when a redemption actually occurred and not when corporate earnings or profits are to be measured. In urging his position on this point the taxpayer seems to assume that the distribution occurred on January 15, 1959, when he was placed in possession of a non-negotiable, non-interest paying note not due for three years. It appears to be well settled that the date of the payment of a note rather than the date of delivery of the note is the dividend date. Emil Stein (1942), 46 B.T.A. 135; Estate of Joseph Nitto (1949), 13 T.C. 858, 867. The Court is of the view and holds that the time payments were made on the note is the proper time for measuring corporate earnings and profits for dividend purposes. . . .

[The court found that there were adequate earnings and profits. It then went on to hold that the distribution was essentially equivalent to a dividend. It held first that there was not a bona fide corporate purpose for casting the transaction in the form of a redemption, since the purpose was to give the sellers a greater amount for their stock than the buyers would have to pay for it, while giving the buyers certain tax benefits. It then relied on the following factors to find dividend equivalency: there were adequate earnings profits for a dividend in the amount of the distributions; the taxpayer's position vis-à-vis the corporation was not substantially altered by the transaction since he remained a minority stockholder; and the transaction was not part of a contraction of the business. The fact that the distribution was not pro rata was not sufficient to negate the finding of dividend equivalency.

The Commissioner's deficiency assessment with respect to the distributions was upheld.]*

NOTE

What does §318(a)(5)(C) accomplish? If it had been applicable to the years involved in this case would it have affected the result? Why?

PROBLEMS

The following problems relate to the preceding six cases and to §§302 and 318 generally:

*In its brief per curiam opinion of affirmance the Fifth Circuit embraced the district court's decision, but said, "it is unnecessary to adopt the opinion of the district court . . . ." 386 F.2d 839. — ED.

1. Husband (H) and Wife (W) each own 50 per cent of the outstanding stock of Corporation C. The parties wish C to redeem all of H's stock for an amount of cash equal to the stock's fair market value. What facts must you know and what must you advise be done as conditions to your giving an opinion that the redemption will be within §302(b)(3)?

2. The facts are the same as in Problem 1, except that H wishes to retain at least a minimal stock interest. Can you suggest the redemption of a sufficient percentage of his shares to permit the redemption to qualify under §302(b)(2)?

3. The facts are the same as in Problem 1, except that H and W also own 50 per cent each of Corporation B. Will your opinion as to the applicability of §302 (b)(3) on the redemption of H's stock in C have to be altered? What would have been your answer prior to the adoption of §318(a)(5)(C) in 1964? Would the result in *Bloch* have been different if §318(a)(5)(C) had been applicable?

4. H owns 50 per cent of the stock in Corporation M. A trust of which W is sole beneficiary owns the remaining 50 per cent. Is it possible for a redemption of all of the M stock held by the trust to qualify under §302(b)(3)? Why? Cf. Rev. Rul. 59-233, 1959-2 Cum. Bull. 106. What probable concerns led the Commissioner to take the position set forth in that ruling? Is the ruling correct? Why?

5. X owns all (100 shares) of the stock of Corporation N. Corporation N redeems 50 of X's shares under circumstances making the distribution essentially equivalent to a dividend. X's basis for his stock was $100 per share. Five years after the redemption X sells his remaining 50 shares for $50,000. What is his gain on the sale? Why?

6. If a corporation without earnings and profits redeems part of a shareholder's stock under circumstances that make the distribution "essentially equivalent to a dividend," might the tax consequences differ from those that would attend a distribution that was not "essentially equivalent to a dividend"? Consider, inter alia, the question whether the basis of the redeemed shares remains identified with those shares or whether the shareholder's aggregate basis for all his shares is to be allocated. If allocated, how? Why?

7. Brother (B) and Sister (S) each owned 50 per cent of the stock of P Corporation. S died, bequeathing $10,000 in cash to B. Corporation P wishes to redeem the stock held by S's estate for its fair market value of $500,000. S's estate as a whole is worth $1 million. Except as to the bequest to B, colleges and universities are the sole beneficiaries of S's estate. May the redemption qualify under §302(b)(3)? Why? See Treas. Regs. §1.318-3(a). Cf. Estate of Webber v. United States, 404 F.2d 411 (6th Cir. 1968), aff'g 263 F. Supp. 703 (E.D. Ky. 1967).

8. Under the 1939 Code redemptions were not subject to attribution of ownership rules. Given a Congressional purpose to make family and financial relationships relevant, how would you have written what is now §318? Given the Congressional view that "essential equivalence" was not a definite enough test to stand by itself, how would you have written what is now §302?

9. See W. Goldstein, Stock Redemptions and the Attribution Rules, 27 N.Y.U. Inst. on Fed. Tax. 793 (1969); L. Brown, Selected Problems in Stock Redemption, 1959 So. Calif. Tax Inst. 171; B. Wolfman, Some of the Attribution-of-Ownership

Problems Involved in the Redemption of Stock Under the 1954 Code, 33 Taxes 382 (1955); B. Bittker and J. Eustice, Federal Income Taxation of Corporations and Shareholders 272-294 (2d ed. 1966).

(iii) REDEMPTIONS RELATED TO INTER-SHAREHOLDER TRANSFERS

COMMISSIONER v. ROBERTS
203 F.2d 304 (4th Cir. 1953), rev'g 17 T.C. 1415 (1952)

Before PARKER, Chief Judge, and SOPER and DOBIE, Circuit Judges.

DOBIE, Circuit Judge. This is a petition by the Commissioner of Internal Revenue to review a decision of the Tax Court of the United States. The Tax Court held that the distribution in connection with the redemption of the stock of the corporation, *under the circumstances of this case*, was not essentially equivalent to, and not taxable as, the distributions of a dividend under [§§302(b)(1) and 302(d)] of the Internal Revenue Code. We think the decision of the Tax Court was clearly erroneous. It must, therefore, be reversed.

We quote the applicable provisions of the Internal Revenue Code and Treasury Regulations: . . .

> "The question whether a distribution in connection with a cancellation or redemption of stock is essentially equivalent to the distribution of a taxable dividend depends upon the circumstances of each case. A cancellation or redemption by a corporation of a portion of its stock pro rata among all the shareholders will generally be considered as effecting a distribution essentially equivalent to a dividend distribution to the extent of the earnings and profits accumulated after February 28, 1913. On the other hand, a cancellation or redemption by a corporation of all of the stock of a particular shareholder, so that the shareholder ceases to be interested in the affairs of the corporation, does not effect a distribution of a taxable dividend. A bona fide distribution in complete cancellation or redemption of all of the stock of a corporation, or one of a series of bona fide distributions in complete cancellation or redemption of all of the stock of a corporation, is not essentially equivalent to the distribution of a taxable dividend. If a distribution is made pursuant to a corporate resolution reciting that the distribution is made in liquidation of the corporation, and the corporation is completely liquidated and dissolved within one year after the distribution, the distribution will not be considered essentially equivalent to the distribution of a taxable dividend; in all other cases the facts and circumstances should be reported to the Commissioner for his determination whether the distribution, or any part thereof, is essentially equivalent to the distribution of a taxable dividend." [Treas. Reg. 111, §29.115-9.]

There is little or no dispute about the facts of this case. In March 1932, John T.

Roberts, hereinafter called taxpayer, and his brother transferred to a newly created corporation all of the assets of a wholesale plumbing and heating supply business, theretofore conducted by them in partnership, in exchange for all of the stock of the corporation, consisting of 2,000 shares of common stock, par value $100 each. Fifteen hundred shares were issued to taxpayer, who continued to hold them through the taxable year 1944 here involved. Five hundred shares were issued to taxpayer's brother. Taxpayer's brother died in October 1943, and by his last will made a specific bequest to taxpayer of any shares of stock of the corporation owned by him at the time of his death. Pursuant to an order of the probate court, the executor of the brother's will transferred to taxpayer stock certificates for the 500 shares of the corporation's stock which the brother had owned. These 500 shares were valued for estate tax purposes at $92,000. . . .

On January 1, 1944, total assets amounted to approximately $414,000 (including cash of $160,000 and United States obligations of $96,000), and the earned surplus amounted to approximately $170,000. As of December 31, 1944 (that is, after the distribution in redemption of stock here involved), the corporation's balance sheets showed assets of $320,000 (including cash of $60,000 and United States obligations of $106,000) and an earned surplus of $135,000.

The corporation paid a dividend of $4 a share in 1934; $16 in 1935; $8 in each year 1936 through 1940; $6 in 1941; and no dividends in 1942 and 1943. In 1944, after the stock redemption hereinafter mentioned, a dividend of $2 was distributed. In 1944 taxpayer also was paid a salary of $27,900 by the corporation as its president.

On December 26, 1944, at a special meeting of the corporation's board of directors, on motion of taxpayer, it was resolved that the corporation purchase from taxpayer for $92,000 the 500 shares of stock which taxpayer had acquired by bequest from his brother, and that the capital stock of the corporation be reduced to 1,500 shares, par value $100. On the same day, a special meeting of the stockholders (namely, taxpayer, for he then owned all the shares of stock in this corporation,) approved; the transaction was completed; and an amendment to the certificate of incorporation was executed which was later approved by the State Tax Commission. Taxpayer never considered selling his shares to anyone but the corporation because he wanted to keep the stock in the family.

The taxpayer did not report the transaction in controversy on his return, and the Commissioner determined a deficiency on the ground that the amount of $92,000 paid by the corporation was taxable as a dividend.

The Tax Court specifically found that the earnings and profits of the corporation prior to and during 1944 were accumulated for no definite purpose; that the operations of the corporation were not impaired by reason of the transaction in controversy, and that the corporation had never followed a policy of contraction of business; that the corporation's financial position on December 26, 1944, permitted of a dividend of $92,000, and that the corporation continued in the same business in subsequent years.

The Tax Court further found that the payment of the $92,000 to taxpayer by the corporation in the taxable year was a distribution in complete cancellation and redemption of all of that portion of the corporation's stock bequeathed by taxpayer's brother, constituting a partial liquidation, and not the essential equivalent of the distribution of a taxable dividend.

We cannot agree with the holding of the Tax Court that, as of the time of the stock redemption, the stock acquired by taxpayer which was redeemed, must be regarded as the stock of the brother. This runs absolutely counter to reality. This stock had been the brother's; but, months before the redemption, taxpayer's title to this stock had been completely perfected. . . .

The vital thing here, as we see it, is that, by the redemption of this stock, the *essential relation* of the taxpayer to the corporation was not, in any practical aspect, changed. Before the redemption, he was the sole stockholder in the corporation; after the redemption, he was still the sole stockholder. Of what real consequence was it that before the redemption his sole ownership was divided into 2,000 shares, and after the redemption, this same sole ownership was divided into 1,500 shares: He owned the whole corporation before the redemption; after the redemption, he was still the sole owner.

Here, then, we find a single individual owning all the corporate stock. . . . The corporation had on hand a large and unnecessary accumulation of cash, representing "earnings or profits accumulated after February 28, 1913." . . . The corporation did not then intend to liquidate or to contract its business. . . . The redemption served no business purpose of the corporation; it was motivated entirely by the personal considerations of taxpayer. . . . The net effect of the redemption was clearly to distribute to taxpayer the corporate earnings just as if a cash dividend had been declared. . . . Indeed, it is difficult to imagine a more ideal set-up for the application of [§§302(b) (1) and 302(d)] than the facts involved in the instant case.

The cases of Flinn v. Commissioner, 37 B.T.A. 1085 and Tiffany v. Commissioner, 16 T.C. 1443, cited by the Tax Court are clearly not in point. There, the corporations purchased all of the stock of a particular stockholder, when there were still other stockholders; here, the corporation merely purchased part of the stock of its sole stockholder. There, the relationship of the stockholder to the corporation was radically changed by the redemption from stockholder to mere ex-stockholder; here, as we have pointed out, there was no such change for, both before and after the redemption taxpayer was and remained the sole stockholder of the corporation.

The ultimate question of whether, in a particular case, [§§302(b)(1) and 302(d) do or do] not apply, is usually held to be a question of fact. . . .

The Regulations, which have been in effect for many years, provide in part that a redemption by a corporation of a portion of its stock pro rata among all the shareholders would generally be considered as effecting a distribution essentially equivalent to a dividend distribution to the extent of the earnings and profits accumulated after February 28, 1913. That provision of the Regulations is fully met in this case, and likewise other factors which have sometimes been held relevant are also present here.

It might be noted that while dividends were paid by the corporation here prior to 1942, no dividends were paid by the corporation in 1942, 1943, or 1944 prior to redemption, though the corporate earnings in all these years were quite substantial.

Any conclusion other than that which we have reached readily shows how easily the tactics of the taxpayer here could be used as a means of tax evasion. A prosperous corporation, for example, with a single stockholder, earns large sums of money, available for, and which should be paid out as, dividends. This sole stockholder siphons off this money (as was done in the instant case) to himself by selling a portion of his stock to the corporation at a price per share which will just cover these earnings. Surely, this is a redemption "essentially equivalent to the distribution of a taxable dividend." Congress must have had just such a situation in mind when it enacted [§§302(b)(1) and 302(d)]. . . .

The decision of the Tax Court of the United States is reversed and the case is remanded with directions to enter a decision in favor of the Commissioner.

Reversed and remanded with directions.

NOTE

What would the tax consequences have been to the estate and to the taxpayer if, in *Roberts,* (1) the decedent's will had made a bequest of the cash value of the shares, not the shares themselves, (2) the corporation had redeemed the shares in the estate's hands, and (3) the estate turned over to the taxpayer the cash proceeds? Would the result be different if the estate had paid the taxpayer the cash bequest and then had the stock redeemed in its hands? In answering these questions consider §§302(b)(3), 318, 1014 and 102(a). See Treas. Reg. §1.318-3(a).

HOLSEY v. COMMISSIONER
258 F.2d 865 (3d Cir. 1958), rev'g 28 T.C. 962 (1957)

Before MARIS, GOODRICH and McLAUGHLIN, Circuit Judges.

MARIS, Circuit Judge. This is a petition to review a decision of the Tax Court. The petitioners, husband and wife, filed a joint return and the case involves their income tax liability for the year 1951. The income in controversy is that of the husband alone, however, and he will accordingly be referred to as the taxpayer. The facts as found by the Tax Court, some of which were stipulated, may be summarized as follows:

J. R. Holsey Sales Company, a New Jersey corporation, was organized on April 28, 1936, as an Oldsmobile dealership. Taxpayer has been president and a director of the company since its organization. Only 20 shares were issued out of the 2,500 shares of no par value stock authorized; these 20 shares were issued to Greenville Auto Sales Company, a Chevrolet dealership, in exchange for all of the latter's right, title, and interest to the Oldsmobile franchise and other assets with respect to the franchise which had been owned and operated by the Greenville Company. The 20 shares issued were assigned a value of $11,000. Taxpayer's father, Charles V. Holsey, in 1936, owned more than two-thirds of the outstanding stock of the Greenville Company, and taxpayer was vice-president and a director of that corporation.

On April 30, 1936, taxpayer acquired from the Greenville Company an option to purchase 50% of the outstanding shares of the Holsey Company for $11,000, and a further option to purchase, within ten years after the exercise of the first option, all the remaining shares for a sum to be agreed upon. The Greenville Company owned all of the outstanding stock of the Holsey Company from its organization in 1936 until November, 1939, when taxpayer exercised his first option and purchased 50% of the outstanding stock of the Holsey Company for $11,000.

On June 28, 1946, the further option in favor of taxpayer was revised. Under the terms of the revised option, taxpayer was granted the right to purchase the remaining outstanding shares of the Holsey Company at any time up to and including June 28, 1951, for $80,000. The revised option was in favor of taxpayer individually and was not assignable by him to anyone other than a corporation in which he owned not less than 50% of the voting stock. On the date of the revision of this option, taxpayer's father owned 76% of the stock of the Greenville Company and taxpayer was a vice-president and director of that corporation. On April 28, 1948, the Holsey Company declared a 3-for-1 stock dividend and the common stock was allocated a value of $750 per share. This stock dividend increased the outstanding stock to 80 shares which was held in equal amounts by taxpayer and the Greenville Company.

On January 19, 1951, taxpayer assigned his revised option to the Holsey Company; on the same date the Holsey Company exercised the option and paid the Greenville Company $80,000 for the stock held by it. This transaction resulted in taxpayer becoming the owner of 100% of the outstanding stock of the Holsey Company. In his income tax return for the year 1951, taxpayer gave no effect to this transaction.

The principal officers and only directors of the Holsey Company from April 28, 1936, to December 31, 1951, were taxpayer, his brother, Charles D. Holsey, and their father, Charles V. Holsey. On January 19, 1951, when the revised option was exercised, the earned surplus of the Holsey Company was in excess of $300,000.

The Oldsmobile franchise, under which the Holsey Company operated, was a yearly contract entered into by the Corporation and the manufacturer in reliance upon the personal qualifications and representations of taxpayer as an individual. It was the manufacturer's policy to have its dealers own all of the stock in dealership organizations.

The Commissioner determined that the effect of the transaction of January 19, 1951, wherein the Holsey Company paid $80,000 to the Greenville Company for 50% of the outstanding stock of the Holsey Company, constituted a dividend to taxpayer, the remaining stockholder. The Commissioner therefore asserted a deficiency against taxpayer in the sum of $41,385.34. The Tax Court sustained the Commissioner. 28 T.C. 962.

The question presented for decision in this case is whether the Tax Court erred in holding that the payment by the Holsey Company of $80,000 to the Greenville Company for the purchase from that company of its stock in the Holsey Company was essentially equivalent to the distribution of a taxable dividend to the taxpayer, the remaining stockholder of the Holsey Company. To determine that question we must begin with the applicable statute . . . .

It will be observed that section [316(a)] defines a dividend as a distribution made by a corporation "to its shareholders". Accordingly unless a distribution which is sought to be taxed to a stockholder as a dividend is made to him or for his benefit it may not be regarded as either a dividend or the legal equivalent of a dividend. Here the distribution was made to the Greenville Company, not to the taxpayer. This the Government, of course, concedes but urges that it was made for the benefit of the taxpayer. It is true that it has been held that a distribution by a corporation in redemption of stock which the taxpayer stockholder has a contractual obligation to purchase is essentially the equivalent of a dividend to him since it operates to discharge his obligation. . . . But where, as here, the taxpayer was never under any legal obligation to purchase the stock held by the other stockholder, the Greenville Company, having merely an option to purchase which he did not exercise but instead assigned to the Holsey Company, the distribution did not discharge any obligation of his and did not benefit him in any direct sense.

It is, of course, true that the taxpayer was benefited indirectly by the distribution. The value of his own stock was increased, since the redemption was for less than book value, and he became sole stockholder. But these benefits operated only to increase the value of the taxpayer's stock holdings; they could not give rise to taxable income within the meaning of the Sixteenth Amendment until the corporation makes a distribution to the taxpayer or his stock is sold. Eisner v. Macomber, 1920, 252 U.S. 189, 40 S. Ct. 189, 64 L. Ed. 521; Schmitt v. Commissioner of Internal Revenue, 3 Cir., 1954, 208 F.2d 819. In the latter case in a somewhat similar connection this court said (p. 821):

> "During these years when Wolverine was buying its own shares it, of course, was subject to income tax as a corporation. Mrs. Green was subject to tax on whatever profit she made by the sale of these shares to the corporation. But what happened to warrant imposing a tax upon Schmitt and Lehren? If one owns a piece of real estate and, because of its favorable location in a city, the land becomes increasingly valuable over a period of years, the owner is not subject to income taxation upon the annual increase in value. In the same way, if a man owns shares in a corporation which gradually become more valuable through the years he is not taxed because of the increase in value even though he is richer at the end of each year than he was at the end of the year before. If he disposes of that which has increased, of course he must pay tax upon his profit. All of this is hornbook law of taxation; nobody denies it."

We think that the principle thus stated is equally applicable here. Indeed the Tax Court itself has so held in essentially similar cases. . . .

The question whether payments made by a corporation in the acquisition and redemption of its stock are essentially equivalent to the distribution of a taxable dividend has been often before the courts and certain criteria have been enunciated. The most significant of these is said to be whether the distribution leaves the proportionate interests of the stockholders unchanged as occurs when a true dividend is paid. Ferro v. Commissioner of Internal Revenue, 3 Cir., 1957, 242 F.2d 838, 841. The application of that criterion to the facts of this case compels the conclusion that in the absence of a direct pecuniary benefit to the taxpayer the Tax Court erred in holding the distribution in question taxable to him. For in his case prior to the distribution the taxpayer and the Greenville Company each had a 50% interest in the Holsey Company whereas after it was over the taxpayer had 100% of the outstanding stock and the Greenville Company none.

The Government urges the lack of a corporate purpose for the distribution and the taxpayer seeks to establish one. But we do not consider this point for, as we have recently held, "It is the effect of the redemption, rather than the purpose which actuated it, which controls the determination of dividend equivalence." Kessner v. Commissioner of Internal Revenue, 3 Cir., 1957, 248 F.2d 943, 944. Nor need we discuss the present position of the Government that the transaction must be treated as a sham and the purchase of the stock as having been made by the taxpayer through his alter ego, the Holsey Company. For the Tax Court made no such finding, doubtless in view of the fact that at the time the taxpayer owned only 50% of the stock and was in a minority on the board of directors. On the contrary, that court based its decision on the benefit which the distribution by the corporation to the Greenville Company conferred upon the taxpayer, which it thought gave rise to taxable income in his hands.

For the reasons stated we think that the Tax Court erred in its decision. The decision will accordingly be reversed and the cause remanded for further proceedings not inconsistent with this opinion.

McLaughlin, Circuit Judge (dissenting). I think that the net effect of the facile operation disclosed in this case amounts to the distribution of a taxable dividend to the taxpayer. I do not think that the *Schmitt* decision controls here. Quite the contrary to the *Schmitt* facts, this taxpayer himself acquired a valuable option to buy the shares and solely on the theory of a gift of the option rights would make the corporation the true purchaser. I agree with the Tax Court that "The assignment of the option contract to J. R. Holsey Sales Co. was clearly for the purpose of having that company pay the $80,000 in exercise of the option that was executed for the petitioner's personal benefit. The payment was intended to secure and did secure for petitioner exactly what it was always intended he should get if he made the payment personally, namely, all of the stock in J. R. Holsey Sales Co."

I would affirm the Tax Court decision.

NOTE

1. What is the factual difference in *Holsey* that may justify a result different from that in *Roberts,* page 215 supra? Is the factual difference sufficient, in your judgment? Why? If not, which result is preferable? Why?

2. In Rev. Rul. 58-614, 1958-2 Cum. Bull. 920, the Service announced its intention to follow the *Holsey* decision. It distinguished *Holsey* from the case in which the stock "is in reality purchased by a remaining shareholder," and for the latter type of case cited Wall v. Commissioner, 164 F.2d 462 (4th Cir. 1947), and Zipp v. Commissioner, 259 F.2d 119 (6th Cir. 1958), aff'g 28 T.C. 314 (1957). See also Rev. Rul. 59-286, 1959-2 Cum. Bull. 103.

SULLIVAN v. UNITED STATES
363 F.2d 724 (8th Cir. 1966), cert. denied, 387 U.S. 905 (1967)

Before Vogel, Chief Judge, Blackmun, Circuit Judge, and Stephenson, District Judge.

Stephenson, District Judge. This is an appeal by the taxpayer from the District Court's judgment (Sullivan v. United States, 244 F. Supp. 605 (W.D. Mo. 1965)) denying recovery for that portion of his 1956 income taxes alleged to have been assessed and collected wrongfully. The taxpayer made a timely claim for a refund. Jurisdiction exists under the provisions of 28 U.S.C. §1346(a)(1).

The facts are set out in detail in the District Court's opinion. In brief, the taxpayer Sullivan purchased the assets of an automobile dealership in Blytheville, Arkansas in 1941. He then formed a corporation to operate the dealership. The individual who became resident manager of the dealership, Loy Eich, eventually acquired 120 shares of the 300 shares of stock outstanding — the rest being owned by taxpayer Sullivan. When Eich terminated his management of the dealership in February 1948, Sullivan purchased his 120 shares of stock. Thereafter, in September, 1948, Frank Nelson became the resident manager of the dealership under an arrangement which included an agreement permitting Nelson to acquire up to forty (40) per cent of the stock and further providing for taxpayer's repurchase of said stock upon Nelson's termination of his employment. After acquiring approximately 38% of the corporation's outstanding stock, Nelson announced his intention to depart from his position in 1956 and offered to sell his stock to taxpayer Sullivan. The corporation's Board of Directors then authorized the redemption of Nelson's stock by the corporation.

The ultimate question before the District Court involved a determination of whether the payment by the corporation in redemption of Nelson's stock constituted a taxable distribution to taxpayer Sullivan, the sole remaining stockholder of the corporation. The District Court found that taxpayer Sullivan was unconditionally and primarily obligated to purchase Nelson's stock in 1956 and that said stock was purchased by the Corporation out of profits distributable as a dividend and therefore held that the taxpayer constructively received income equivalent to a dividend in the amount paid by the Corporation for said stock, ($198,334.58). Initially, an interpretation of the memorandum agreement entered into by Sullivan and Nelson at the time the latter assumed his managerial functions is necessary. The agreement contained the following provisions:

> "6. Transfer of Shares of Stock. It is understood and agreed that Sullivan is permitting Nelson to buy stock in said corporation for the purpose of giving him a working interest only, and said Nelson agrees that said shares of stock cannot and will not be mortgaged, hypothecated or transferred by him, his heirs, executor, administrator or trustee to any person other than William J. Sullivan or such person as said Sullivan directs in writing. Any such sale, delivery or transfer to any other person, firm or corporation shall

be null and void. Said Sullivan agrees that he will, within thirty (30) days after such shares have been offered for sale to him, accept the offer to sell, provided always that such shares shall be offered for sale at a price to be determined according to this contract."

"7. TERMINATION OF CONTRACT. Said Nelson agrees that if he should terminate his employment or relationship with William J. Sullivan or employment by the said corporation, and if his connection and association with the corporation should cease or be terminated by Sullivan or the majority owners of the stock of the corporation, then said Nelson agrees to sell and transfer and deliver to Sullivan at the then book value all shares of stock owned by him in the Sullivan-Nelson Chevrolet Co. . . . If said contract is terminated by Nelson or Sullivan as herein provided or by the death of Nelson, the value of the stock owned by Nelson shall be fixed and determined as set up in paragraphs four and five of this agreement. If said Nelson should die or become so disabled by injury or sickness as to become incapable of managing and operating the business, then said Sullivan shall have the immediate and exclusive rights to purchase the stock owned by Nelson or by his heirs, administrators or executors in accordance with the terms of this contract. Title so (sic) said shares of stock shall automatically rest in Sullivan upon Nelson's death and said Sullivan shall be obligated to Nelson's personal representative or representatives for the value thereof as fixed by this agreement."

On the face of the agreement it would appear that Sullivan obligated himself to purchase Nelson's stock when it was offered to him for sale. . . .

. . . The District Court was justified in concluding that Sullivan was unconditionally obligated to purchase Nelson's stock.[5]

At this juncture, the payment by the corporation to Nelson presents two basic questions: (1) Was that payment in actuality a dividend and therefore includable in Sullivan's gross income under §§61(a)(7), 316(a) and 301(c)(1) of the Internal Revenue Code? (2) If the payment is considered as a corporate redemption of stock, was the payment includable in Sullivan's gross income as being essentially equivalent to a dividend within the meaning of §302(b)(1)? This court has recognized that both questions are to be resolved as fact issues. Idol v. Commissioner of Internal Revenue, 319 F.2d 647 (8th Cir. 1963). If a finding is supported by substantial evidence on the record as a whole and is not against or induced by an erroneous view of the law, it will not be disturbed on appeal.

When an individual shareholder receives an economic benefit through a diversion of corporate earnings and profits, such a receipt may be taxed as a constructive dividend. This court set forth a criteria for determining whether a payment consti-

---

[5]The taxpayer makes an alternative argument to the effect that, even if he was unconditionally obligated to purchase Sullivan's stock, subsequent events constituted a modification or novation of that agreement. Even if this contention is accepted, the court is at a loss as to how the taxpayer is aided. The novation or modification itself would be considered as resulting in an economic benefit and possible constructive dividend taxable against Sullivan. The taxpayer would be left in essentially the same position with respect to his possible tax liability.

tutes a constructive dividend in Sachs v. Commissioner of Internal Revenue, 277 F.2d 879, 882-883 (8th Cir. 1960):

> "The motive, or expressed intent of the corporation is not determinative, and constructive dividends have been found contrary to the expressed intent of the corporation. The courts, as arbiters of the true nature of corporate payments, have consistently used as a standard the measure of receipt of economic benefit as the proper occasion for taxation." (footnote omitted)

This court has also adopted criteria for determining whether a redemption of stock is essentially equivalent to a dividend. . . . While there is no sole decisive test in this connection, the several guidelines for the determination include "whether there is a bona fide corporate business purpose, whether the action was initiated by the corporation or by the shareholders, whether there was a contraction of the business, and whether there was a substantial change in proportionate stock ownership." Idol v. Commissioner of Internal Revenue, 319 F.2d 647, 651 (8th Cir. 1963). In addition, the Court has observed that the "net effect of the transaction is at least an important consideration in determining dividend equivalency.". . .

The general net effect and the purpose of and circumstances surrounding the transaction involved herein must be carefully scrutinized to ascertain whether Sullivan received a taxable dividend. Prior to the transaction, Sullivan held approximately 62% of the shares outstanding while Nelson owned the remaining shares. As previously discussed, Sullivan was unconditionally obligated to purchase Nelson's stock if it was offered to him for sale. After the transaction was completed, the relevant facts were essentially as follows: (1) Sullivan's personal obligation had been discharged (2) Sullivan owned all of the outstanding shares of stock of the corporation (3) the corporation's assets were decreased by the amount paid to Nelson for his stock (4) Nelson's stock was held by the corporation as treasury stock. It is true that in terms of the financial worth of Sullivan's interest in the corporation, it was the same after the transaction as it was before.[7] The transaction still resulted in an economic benefit to Sullivan, however, because he was relieved of his personal obligation to purchase Nelson's stock. After careful consideration this court concludes that there was no corporate business purpose or other factor which justifies the taxpayer's position that as to him the payment must be considered a stock redemption and not the equivalent of a dividend.[9] On the facts of this case, Sullivan received a taxable dividend as the result of the corporation's purchase of Nelson's stock.

---

[7]Prior to the transfer of Nelson's stock Sullivan owned 186 shares of the 300 shares outstanding. His stock at this time was worth approximately $323,597.00. After the transfer, his 186 shares were the only outstanding stock of the corporation. Due to the corporate purchase of Nelson's stock, however, the value of the taxpayer's shares remained at approximately $323,597.00.

[9]The taxpayer has strongly urged that there was a corporate business purpose motivating the purchase of Nelson's stock because of the valuable services received from him as resident manager of the corporation. The services had already been performed, however, when the stock was purchased. Moreover, it was Sullivan, not the corporation, who was obligated to purchase the stock. Under these circumstances, the District Court properly found that the purchase was not induced by a business purpose. The net effect of the transaction further indicates that a dividend was received by the taxpayer.

This court is aware that it is often difficult to distinguish true substance from mere form. Tax law places some weight and significance on form and the choice of one alternative rather than another for achieving a desired end is often critical and may be determinative of the tax effect of a transaction. Judge Becker's opinion comprehensively deals with the evidence and the applicable law of this case. The taxpayer has failed to establish grounds for reversal. The judgment of the District Court is affirmed.

NOTE

Are *Holsey,* page 218 supra, and *Sullivan* distinguishable? Is it relevant that in *Sullivan* the taxpayer had an obligation to purchase, whereas in *Holsey* there was only an option? Why? Are *Sullivan* and the Government's position in *Sullivan* consistent with (as to the Government, justifiable in light of) Rev. Rul. 59-286, 1959-2 Cum. Bull. 103? In the latter, the surviving shareholder was obligated either to buy the decedent's stock or to vote his stock for liquidation of the corporation. By post-mortem agreement the corporation redeemed the decedent's stock at its fair market value. Despite the fact that the remaining shareholder was "personally obligated" to buy the stock and he was "relieved [of his] obligation," he was ruled not to be in receipt of a dividend since the stock was not "in reality . . . purchased by the remaining shareholder. . . ."

ZENZ v. QUINLIVAN
213 F.2d 914 (6th Cir. 1954)

Before MILLER, Circuit Judge, and GOURLEY and STARR, District Judges.

GOURLEY, District Judge. The appeal relates to the interpretation of Section [302(b)(1)] . . . and poses the question — Is a distribution of substantially all of the accumulated earnings and surplus of a corporation, which are not necessary to the conduct of the business of the corporation, in redemption of all outstanding shares of stock of said corporation owned by one person *essentially equivalent to the distribution of a taxable dividend under the Internal Revenue Code?*

The District Court answered in the affirmative and sustained a deficiency assessment by the Commissioner of Internal Revenue.

After consideration of the records, briefs and arguments of counsel for the parties, we believe the judgment should be reversed.

Under the applicable statutes and Treasury Regulations a corporation's distribution of its earned surplus out of its accumulated earnings or profits or out of the earnings or profits for the taxable year is subject to tax as an ordinary dividend, but an amount distributed by a corporation in partial liquidation shall be treated as in complete cancellation or redemption of a part of its stock and as in full payment in exchange for the stock. However, if a corporation cancels or redeems its stock at such time and in such manner as to make the distribution and cancellation or redemption in whole or in part essentially equivalent to the distribution of a taxable dividend, the amount so distributed in redemption or cancellation of the stock, to the extent that it represents a distribution of accumulated earnings or profits, shall be treated as a taxable dividend. Whether a distribution in connection with a cancellation or redemption of stock is essentially equivalent to the distribution of a taxable dividend depends upon the facts and circumstances of each case.

The question stems from the following circumstances:

Appellant is the widow of the person who was the motivating spirit behind the closed corporation which engaged in the business of excavating and laying of sewers. Through death of her husband she became the owner of all shares of stock issued by the corporation. She operated the business until remarriage, when her second husband assumed the management. As a result of a marital rift, separation, and final divorce, taxpayer sought to dispose of her company to a competitor who was anxious to eliminate competition.

Prospective buyer did not want to assume the tax liabilities which it was believed were inherent in the accumulated earnings and profits of the corporation. To avoid said profits and earnings as a source of future taxable dividends, buyer purchased part of taxpayer's stock for cash. Three weeks later, after corporate reorganization and corporate action, the corporation redeemed the balance of taxpayer's stock, purchasing the same as treasury stock which absorbed substantially all of the accumulated earnings and surplus of the corporation.

Taxpayer, in her tax return, invoked Section [302(a)] of the Internal Revenue Code . . . as constituting a cancellation or redemption by a corporation of all of the stock of a particular shareholder, and therefore was not subject to being treated as a distribution of a taxable dividend.

The District Court sustained the deficiency assessment of the Commissioner that the amount received from accumulated earnings and profits was ordinary income since the stock redeemed by the corporation was "at such time and in such manner as to make the redemption thereof essentially equivalent to the distribution of a taxable dividend" under [§§302(b)(1) and (d)] of the Code.

The District Court's findings were premised upon the view that taxpayer employed a circuitous approach in an attempt to avoid the tax consequences which would have attended the outright distribution of the surplus to the taxpayer by the declaration of a taxable dividend.

The rationale of the District Court is dedicated to piercing the external manifestations of the taxpayer's transactions in order to establish a subterfuge or sham.

Nevertheless, the general principle is well settled that a taxpayer has the legal right to decrease the amount of what otherwise would be his taxes or altogether avoid them, by means which the law permits. . . . The taxpayer's motive to avoid taxation will not establish liability if the transaction does not do so without it. . . .

The question accordingly presented is not whether the overall transaction, admittedly carried out for the purpose of avoiding taxes, actually avoided taxes which would have been incurred if the transaction had taken a different form, but whether the sale constituted a taxable dividend or the sale of a capital asset. . . .

It is a salutary fact that Section [302(a)] is an exception to Section [316] that all distributions of earnings and profits are taxable as a dividend.

The basic precept underlying the capital gains theory of taxation as distinguished from ordinary income tax is the concept that a person who has developed an enterprise in which earnings have been accumulated over a period of years should not be required to expend the ordinary income tax rate in the one year when he withdraws from his enterprise and realizes his gain.

Common logic dictates that a fair basis of measuring income is not determined upon the profits on hand in the year of liquidation but is properly attributable to each year in which the profits were gained.

We cannot concur with the legal proposition enunciated by the District Court that a corporate distribution can be essentially equivalent to a taxable dividend even though that distribution extinguishes the shareholder's interest in the corporation. To the contrary, we are satisfied that where the taxpayer effects a redemption which completely extinguishes the taxpayer's interest in the corporation, and does not retain any beneficial interest whatever, that such transaction is not the equivalent of the distribution of a taxable dividend as to him. . . .

The statutory concept of dividend is a distribution out of earnings and profits, and normally it is proportionate to shares and leaves the shareholder holding his shares as his capital investment. . . .

Complete and partial liquidations are treated for the purpose of the statute, as sales with a consequent measure of gain or loss, even though the proceeds may to some extent be derived from earnings. . . .

The use of corporate earnings or profits to purchase and make payment for all the shares of a taxpayer's holdings in a corporation is not controlling, and the question as to whether the distribution in connection with the cancellation or the redemption of said stock is essentially equivalent to the distribution of a taxable dividend under the Internal Revenue Code and Treasury Regulations must depend upon the circumstances of each case.

Since the intent of the taxpayer was to bring about a complete liquidation of her holdings and to become separated from all interest in the corporation, the conclusion is inevitable that the distribution of the earnings and profits by the corporation in payment for said stock was not made at such time and in such manner as to make the distribution and cancellation or redemption thereof essentially equivalent to the distribution of a taxable dividend.

In view of the fact that the application of [§302(b)(1) and (d)] of the Internal Revenue Code contemplate that the shareholder receiving the distribution will remain in the corporation, the circumstances of this proceeding militate against treating taxpayer's sale as a distribution of a taxable dividend.

We do not feel that a taxpayer should be penalized for exercising legal means to secure a tax advantage. The conduct of this taxpayer does not appear to contravene the purport or congressional intent of the provisions of the Internal Revenue Act which taxpayer invoked.

We conclude that under the facts and circumstances of the present case the

District Court was in error, and the taxpayer is not liable as a distributee of a taxable dividend under [§§302(b)(1) and (d)] of the Internal Revenue Code.

The decision and judgment of the District Court is reversed and the case remanded with instruction to enter judgment in accordance with this opinion.

NOTE

1. Suppose Corporation X, wholly owned by Mr. Doe, has a net worth of $1 million, allocated as follows: $600,000 in operating assets needed in the business, $200,000 in securities, and $200,000 in cash. Doe's basis in his stock is $300,000. Buyer is willing to purchase the operating assets of X, but he has only $700,000. Doe is unwilling to sell $7/10$ of the business to Buyer on the condition that Buyer will later cause X to redeem Doe's remaining shares, and Buyer is unwilling to purchase assets not within the corporate form (thus ruling out a §337 transaction). How would you design a transaction that would assure Doe a long-term capital gain of $700,000?

2. Mr. Eagle wishes to dispose of his corporation. A transaction is negotiated under which Mr. Smith purchases half of the stock for $500,000 in cash and the corporation simultaneously redeems the remaining half, paying for it with its ten-year, 6 per cent note in the face amount of $500,000 payable only out of the corporation's future income. What are the income tax consequences to Mr. Eagle? Cf. Commissioner v. Brown, 380 U.S. 563 (1965).

3. D. Rees, Tax Techniques of Bootstrap Acquisitions, 18 W. Res. L. Rev. 803 (1967); J. Sexton, Providing Security for the Outgoing Stockholder and Avoiding Tax Disadvantages to Selling and Remaining Stockholders, 24 N.Y.U. Inst. on Fed. Tax. 555, 574-589 (1966); M. Lange, Bootstrap Financing: The Redemption Technique, 18 Tax L. Rev. 323 (1963); R. Graham, Redemption Problems — The *Holsey* and *Zipp* Cases, 36 Taxes 925 (1958).

(iv) REDEMPTIONS BY RELATED CORPORATIONS — §304

1. Prior to 1950 the Commissioner was unsuccessful in his effort to treat as a distribution essentially equivalent to a dividend the purchase by a subsidiary corporation of a portion of the stock held by the shareholder of its parent corporation. See Commissioner v. John Rodman Wanamaker, Trustee, 11 T.C. 365 (1948), aff'd per curiam, 178 F.2d 10 (3d Cir. 1949). To meet this problem Congress in 1950 enacted the statutory predecessor of §304(a)(2).

2. Prior to 1954 the Commissioner was unsuccessful in his effort to treat as a distribution essentially equivalent to a dividend the purchase by Corporation A (wholly owned by X) of part of X's stock in Corporation B (wholly owned by X). See, e.g., Emma Cramer, 20 T.C. 679 (1953); Rev. Rul. 59-97, 1959-1 Cum. Bull. 684, revoking Rev. Rul. 55-15, 1955-1 Cum. Bull. 361. To meet this problem Congress in 1954 enacted §304(a)(1).

3. X owns all the stock of Corporation M which owns all the stock of Corporation N. Corporation N has no earnings and profits; Corporation M has ample

earnings and profits. Corporation N purchases one half of X's stock in M. Might dividend treatment attend the distribution? Why? What would the result be if N had ample earnings and profits and M had none? Why?

4. X owns all the stock of Corporations A and B. B purchases one half of X's stock in A. A has ample earnings and profits; B has none. Might the distribution be treated as a dividend? Why? What would the result be if A had no earnings and profits but B's were ample? Why?

5. Y owns all the stock in Corporations D and E. E buys all Y's stock in D. The distribution is treated as a dividend. What becomes of Y's basis in his D stock? Why?

6. Sections 351 and 304 may compete for dominance in some circumstances. See Haserot v. Commissioner, 46 T.C. 864 (1966), page 373 infra. See J. Marans, Section 304: The Shadowy World of Redemptions through Related Corporations, 22 Tax L. Rev. 161 (1967).

7. See T. Lefevre, How to Avoid the Pitfalls in Stock Redemptions Between Related Corporations, 22 J. Taxation 332 (1965); T. Terry, §304 of the Internal Revenue Code of 1954: Redemptions by Related Corporations, 3 Wm. and Mary L. Rev. 457 (1962); B. Bittker and J. Eustice, Federal Income Taxation of Corporations and Shareholders 300-304 (2d ed. 1966).

COYLE v. UNITED STATES
415 F.2d 488 (4th Cir. 1968), rev'g 268 F. Supp. 233 (1967)

Before SOBELOFF, CRAVEN and BUTZNER, Circuit Judges.

SOBELOFF, Circuit Judge: Our task in this tax refund case is to apply to a stipulated set of facts an unambiguous, if involved, network of statutes to determine whether the proceeds from a transfer of corporate stock are to be taxed as capital gains or ordinary income. The District Court ruled that money which the taxpayer received in exchange for the shares of a corporation he controlled to a corporation wholly owned by his sons should be treated as a capital gain. We disagree and reverse the judgment.

In 1958, taxpayer George L. Coyle, Sr. (now deceased) transferred 66 shares of Coyle & Richardson, Inc. [hereinafter referred to as C & R] to Coyle Realty Company [hereinafter referred to as Realty] for $19,800. Reporting a long term capital gain on this "sale," Coyle paid a tax computed at that rate on $9,900, which is the difference between the sale price and his basis in the stock. The Internal Revenue Service was of the view that the proceeds should be treated as a dividend and assessed the taxpayer an additional $7,181.90 plus interest. Having fully paid the assessment, taxpayer made timely claim for refund. The District Court granted the refund, but we conclude that it should be denied.

Before the transaction, the 688 outstanding shares of C & R were distributed in the following manner: taxpayer, 369; taxpayer's three sons, an aggregate of 288; taxpayer's wife, 1; O. M. Buck, 25; Julia Farley, 5.[1] Thus, taxpayer and his imme-

---

[1]Buck and Farley are unrelated to the Coyle family as far as the record shows. Their insignificant holdings in C & R play no part in this case.

diate family owned more than 95.6% of the corporation whose shares were sold. Realty, the acquiring corporation, was owned in equal parts by taxpayer's three sons, each holding 125 of the 375 outstanding shares. Although the taxpayer had once held one share of Realty, he had no stock in it when the transaction under inquiry took place.

The initial point of controversy is whether the purchase by Realty is to be treated as a sale or as a redemption. Section 304 of the Internal Revenue Code of 1954, . . . provides in pertinent part:

"(a) Treatment of certain stock purchases. —

"(1) Acquisition by related corporation. —

"[I]f (A) one or more persons are in control of each of two corporations, and (B) in return for property, one of the corporations acquires stock in the other corporation from the person . . . so in control, then . . . such property *shall be treated as a distribution in redemption* of the stock of the corporation acquiring such stock. . . ." (Emphasis added.)

Control is defined in §304(c)(1) as at least 50% of the combined voting power of all voting stock or at least 50% of the total value of all classes of stock. For purposes of determining control, §304(c)(2) specifically makes applicable the constructive ownership provisions of §318, 26 U.S.C. §318. Under that section, "an individual shall be considered as owning the stock owned, directly or indirectly, by or for . . . his children. . . ."

Thus, applying the statute literally, taxpayer was in control of both corporations and the acquisition from him by Realty of the C & R stock must be treated as a redemption. His control of C & R results from his actual ownership of 54% of its outstanding stock, not to mention the attribution to him of his sons' 40%. He had 100% control of Realty by virtue of the fact that all of his sons' stock is attributable to him. The District Court recognized and the taxpayer concedes, as he must, that a plain meaning application of Sections 304 and 318 requires this conclusion.

However, the District Court eschewed this direct approach. The court reasoned that since the taxpayer actually owned no shares in Realty, there should be no attribution to him and thus the transaction here was not one between related corporations. Its conclusion then was that the transfer should not be deemed a redemption but a simple sale entitled to long term capital gain treatment.

This interpretation of the constructive ownership rules is at war with both the language of the statute and legislative purpose of the Congress. The family attribution rules, which are specifically prescribed by the statute, were designated to create predictability for the tax planner and to obviate the necessity of a court's scrutinizing family arrangements to determine whether every family member is in fact a completely independent financial entity. An authoritative study of the subject begins: "The rules of constructive ownership rest on certain assumptions which are readily supported in the everyday conduct of affairs. . . . Tax administration would be severely handicapped if the rules applied only as presumptions. . . ." Ringel, Surrey & Warren, Attribution of Stock Ownership in the Internal Revenue Code, 72 Harv. L. Rev. 209 (1958). Yet despite the clear congressional judgment and mandate that the shares of a son are to be treated as his father's for certain limited purposes, the court below read the explicit language as no more than a presumption and then disregarded it.

The statute does not require that a person be an actual shareholder in a corporation before shares in that corporation may be attributed to him. In a recent Second Circuit case, Levin v. Commissioner, 385 F.2d 521 (1967), the court attributed 100% ownership to a mother who had redeemed all her shares of a corporation whose sole remaining shareholder was her son. Similarly, an example given in the Federal Tax Regulations unquestionably assumes that one holding no stock in a corporation may nevertheless constructively own 100% of its shares. 26 C.F.R. §1.304-2.[2] Indeed, any other construction would be untenable. Under the District Court's reading, if the taxpayer had retained at the time of the transfer his otherwise insignificant single share in Realty, then 100% of the stock of that corporation could be attributed to him. Clearly such a distinction could not have been proposed by the Congress.

Appellee urges upon us that at least one anomaly will flow from holding the instant transaction subject to §304. Subsection (a)(1) provides that the stock acquired from the person or persons in control shall be treated as a contribution to the capital of the acquiring corporation. It is asserted that since only a shareholder makes contributions to capital and since taxpayer was not an actual shareholder of Realty, the stock acquired from him cannot realistically be so treated. The short answer is that appellee's underlying premise is fallacious. Non-shareholders may and do make contributions to capital, and the Internal Revenue Code recognizes this fact. See §362(c); see also Brown Shoe Co. v. Commissioner of Internal Revenue, 339 U.S. 583 (1950). Moreover, the law requires that the stock only be "treated" for certain tax purposes as a contribution to capital by a person who is "treated" as a shareholder. Just as the transfer is directed by statute to be "treated" like a redemption when in fact the issuing corporation does not get its stock back, so this stock may be "treated" as a capital contribution even though it does not come from an actual shareholder. It should be stressed that appellee raises no specter of adverse effects from treating the shares as a capital contribution either on the non-shareholder or the corporation. The only point made is that the Code's treatment as applied here is "economically unrealistic." This is simply too thin a reed with which to bring down the clear statutory scheme.

Nor is there merit in appellee's contention that simply because the Treasury Regulations[3] and portions of the legislative history[4] speak interchangeably of the person in control as "taxpayer" or "shareholder," the section may not be applied if the person deemed in control of both corporations is not an actual shareholder in

---

[2]Example (3) in Treas. Reg. §1.304-2 reads: "Corporation X and corporation Y each have outstanding 100 shares of common stock. H, an individual, W, his wife, S, his son, and G, his grandson, each own 25 shares of stock of each corporation. H sells all of his 25 shares of corporation X to corporation Y. . . . [B]oth before and after the transaction H owned directly and constructively 100 per cent of the stock of corporation X. . . ." 26 C.F.R. §1.304-2.

[3]See, e.g., Treas. Reg. §1.304-2 which assumes that the taxpayer is an actual shareholder in the acquiring corporation.

[4]See S. Rep. No. 1622, 83d Cong. 2d Sess. (1954), 3 U.S. Code Cong. & Ad. News 4876 (1954); H. Rep. No. 1337, 83d Cong. 2d Sess. (1954), 3 U.S. Code Cong. & Ad. News 4062 (1954).

both. It is, of course, true that ordinarily the person transferring stock in a §304 case will be a shareholder in the acquiring corporation. The Regulations and Committee Reports were simply addressing themselves to the commonplace transaction. Merely because these interpretative aids do not envision an insubstantial wrinkle on the same fundamental pattern is no adequate ground for holding uncovered that which is clearly within the statute.

The instant case is significantly different from this court's earlier decision in Alvord v. Commissioner of Internal Revenue, 277 F.2d 713 (1960). There, what appeared to be mandated by the tax statute was the exact antithesis of the clear legislative design. The case before us involves two close corporations owned by the same family and a transfer by the head of that family of stock in one of the corporations to the other. This is precisely the situation which §304 was meant to govern.

Since the District Court held redemption treatment unwarranted, it did not reach the second question to which we now turn: Is the redemption here to be treated as an exchange of stock and thus subject only to a capital gains tax or is it to be treated as a dividend and taxed at ordinary income rates?

Section 302(b), 26 U.S.C. §302(b), enumerates those categories of redemptions which are to be treated as exchanges. Both sides agree that the only pertinent category in this case is the most general one, (b)(1), which provides that a redemption shall be treated as an exchange if it "is not essentially equivalent to a dividend."

Determination of dividend equivalency requires a factual inquiry into the circumstances of each case. See Ballenger v. United States of America, 301 F.2d 192 (4th Cir. 1962). Ordinarily, then, we would remand for further evidentiary hearings. However, in this case, which was submitted on stipulated facts, both the Government and the taxpayer's estate concur that no remand is necessary. For this reason, as well as the relative simplicity of the facts here, this court proceeds to adjudicate the issue of dividend equivalence.

On this question, appellee's sole contention is that a payment by a corporation to a non-shareholder may not be characterized as a dividend. With this we agree, for §316 defines a "dividend" as "any distribution of property made by a corporation to its *shareholders*" out of earnings and profits. (Emphasis added.) The rub is that §304(b)(1) specifically states: ". . . determinations as to whether the acquisition is, by reason of section 302(b), to be treated as a distribution in part or full payment in exchange for the stock shall be made by reference to the stock of the *issuing corporation*." (Emphasis added.) Thus, in determining whether this redemption was essentially equivalent to a dividend, we must focus attention upon C & R, of which taxpayer was not only a shareholder but by far the major one.[5]

Although several tests have been devised and several factors exalted in determining whether a redemption is not in essence a dividend, we think there is one overriding objective criterion — a significant modification of shareholder interests. See Moore, Dividend Equivalency — Taxation of Distribution in Redemption of

---

[5]Available earnings and profits are to be reckoned by reference to the acquiring corporation. §304(b)(2)(A). Appellee admits that Realty's earnings and profits were adequate to cover the distribution in this case.

Stock, 19 Tax L. Rev. 249 (1964). As the First Circuit has declared, ". . . we believe that the indispensable first step in making this determination is whether the redemption of stock has caused any meaningful change in the position of the shareholder with relation to his corporation and the other shareholders." Bradbury v. Commissioner of Internal Revenue, 298 F.2d 111, 116 (1962). If the taxpayer's control or ownership of the corporation is basically unaltered by the transaction, then the proceeds he has received as a result of manipulating his corporate stock must be taxed as a dividend. See Commissioner v. Berenbaum, 369 F.2d 337 (10th Cir. 1966).

In examining the respective shareholder interests of C & R before and after the transfer of stock, we must bear in mind that §302(c)(1) explicitly makes applicable to this inquiry the constructive stock ownership rules of §318. Thus, before the transfer, taxpayer is deemed to have owned not only the 369 shares of C & R actually in his name but also the 288 shares owned by his sons[8] and the one share held by his wife.[9] In all, for purposes of §302, taxpayer before the transaction owned 658 of C & R's 688 outstanding shares. After the transaction, he held only 303 shares in his own name, but in addition, of course, he also is deemed to have owned the 289 shares of his wife and sons. Moreover, the 66 shares now held by Realty must likewise be attributed to him. Section 318(a)(2)(C) provides that stock owned by a corporation will be attributed proportionally to any person owning 50% or more of the corporation. Section 304(b)(1) directs that in applying the constructive ownership rules for testing whether a redemption is an exchange or a dividend, the 50% requirement of §318(a)(2)(C) shall not be applicable. In the instant case, this means that the 66 shares held by Realty shall be attributed equally to its owners, taxpayer's sons, and under §318(a)(1)(A)(ii), these shares are attributed from the sons to the taxpayer. Consequently, after the transaction taxpayer owned 658 shares of C & R, precisely the number with which he started.

As noted in Wiseman v. United States, 371 F.2d 816, 818 (1st Cir. 1967), "the real question is what was accomplished by this transaction." The answer here is that while corporate ownership and control remained the same, taxpayer, the major shareholder, had come into possession of $19,800. This was essentially nothing but a dividend and was properly taxed as such.

One tangential difficulty arising from this disposition of the case is the proper allocation of taxpayer's basis in the 66 transferred shares. This potential problem is not before us at this time, but we note in passing that there are at least two reasonable solutions. Ordinarily, when there is an acquisition by a related corporation the controlling person is a shareholder in both, and the basis of his stock in the acquiring corporation is increased by his basis in the stock transferred by him. See Treas. Reg. 26 C.F.R. §1.304-2. In this case, since taxpayer held no shares in Realty, such an approach is not feasible. However, it would be consonant with the underlying rationale of this approach to increase pro rata the basis of the sons' shares in Realty. In Levin v. Commissioner, supra at 528 n.29, where the taxpayer had redeemed all of her shares in the corporation but had not sufficiently severed relations with it to avoid

[8]Section 318(a)(1)(A)(ii).
[9]Section 318(a)(1)(A)(i).

dividend equivalence treatment, the Court said: "Her basis does not disappear; it simply is transferred to her son." As an alternative to increasing the basis of taxpayer's sons in Realty, taxpayer's own basis in his remaining 303 shares of C & R could be augmented by his basis in the 66 transferred shares. In any event, it is clear that taxpayer's basis will not disappear.

To sum up, we construe this transaction as a redemption under §304(a) and find that this redemption was essentially equivalent to a dividend under §302(b). Therefore, we reverse the judgment of the District Court and enter judgment in favor of the Government.

Reversed.

(v) REDEMPTIONS FOLLOWING DEATH — §303

X owned all the stock in Corporation M. On X's death, his stock is worth $1 million. M redeems 30 per cent of the stock from X's estate for $300,000. If the distribution is within §303(a), what is the tax consequence to X's estate? Why? What is the tax consequence if the redemption occurs one year after death when 30 per cent of the stock is worth and is redeemed for $325,000? Why? What might the tax consequences be in each instance if §303(a) covered only $275,000 of the distribution? Why? See generally M. Meyer, Redemption of Stock in the Close Corporation to Pay Death Taxes: I.R.C. Section 303, 27 N.Y.U. Inst. on Fed. Tax. 401 (1969).

What policy objectives does the adoption of §303 probably reflect? Do you support those objectives and the §303 technique for achieving them? Why?

c. PARTIAL LIQUIDATIONS — §346

CHANDLER v. COMMISSIONER
22 T.C. 1158 (1954)

. . . The issue for decision is whether respondent correctly determined that a pro rata cash distribution in cancellation of half the stock of a corporation was made at such a time and in such manner as to be essentially equivalent to the distribution of a taxable dividend to the extent of accumulated earnings and profits within the purview of section 115(g), Internal Revenue Code of 1939.

Findings of Fact

. . . All of the petitioners were stockholders of Chandler-Singleton Company (hereinafter referred to as the Company), a Tennessee corporation organized on May 9, 1923. The capital stock of the Company consisted of 500 shares of common stock of $100 par value, all of which were outstanding until November 7, 1946. From its organization until February 28, 1946, the Company was engaged in the operation of a general department store in Maryville, Tennessee. It had a ladies' ready-to-wear department, men's department, children's department, piece goods department, and a bargain basement.

Chandler was the president and manager of the Company. At the beginning of 1944 he was in very poor health. John W. Bush was the secretary of the Company, but until 1944 he had not been particularly active in its affairs. On January 1, 1944, he became assistant manager of the Company. By profession he was a civil engineer, but at that time he was unemployed due to a change in the administration of the City of Knoxville, Tennessee. During 1944 and 1945 Chandler was sick most of the time. In his absence John W. Bush managed the department store.

John W. Bush did not like being a merchant and decided to return to engineering. In November 1945 he informed Chandler that he was resigning as manager at the end of the year. Chandler, feeling unable to manage the department store himself, decided to sell.

At a stockholders' meeting held on February 20, 1946 it was unanimously agreed that the Company should accept an offer to purchase its merchandise, furniture and fixtures, and lease. Chandler was instructed to consummate the deal. The sale was consummated and a bill of sale was executed. . . .

The Company ceased operating the department store on February 28, 1946. McArthur's Incorporated moved in that night and began operating the store the following day.

Chandler had worked hard in the department store and had no outside interest. He wanted something to do and did not want to get out of business entirely. It was planned that a ladies' ready-to-wear store would be opened by the Company to be managed by Clara T. McConnell (now Clara M. Register) who had managed the ladies' ready-to-wear department of the department store. Thirty shares of stock in the Company owned by Chandler's wife were canceled on April 5, 1946. Ten of these shares were issued to Clara McConnell on April 13, 1946, in order that she might have an interest in the Company whose store she was going to manage. A men's store, to be eventually taken over by the eldest son of John and Margaret Bush, was also contemplated. It was thought that approximately half of the assets of the Company would be needed for each of the two stores.

The charter of the Company was amended on May 18, 1946, changing the name of the Company to "Chandler's" pursuant to a resolution passed at a stockholder's meeting held on May 15, 1946.

About the first of June 1946, the Company obtained space for the ladies' ready-to-wear store about one-half block from the old department store now occupied by McArthur's Incorporated. Merchandise was purchased beginning in June; improvements were made; furniture and supplies were acquired; and the store was opened on September 23, 1946. No sales had been made by the Company between February 28, 1946, and September 23, 1946.

The ladies' ready-to-wear store was about the same size as that department in the former department store. The department store had occupied 8,000 to 9,000 square feet of floor space, had employed 10 to 20 persons, and had carried fire insurance in the amount of $65,000 on its stock and fixtures. The new store had approximately 1,800 square feet of floor space, employed 4 to 6 persons, and carried fire insurance in the amount of $10,000.

A meeting of the board of directors of the Company was held on September 28, 1946, and the minutes of said meeting read in part as follows:

"The Chairman stated that the purpose of the meeting was to consider the advisability of proposing to the stockholders an Amendment to the Charter of Incorporation so as to provide for a reduction of the number of shares of stock heretofore authorized from 500 shares of $100.00 par value to 250 shares of $100.00 par value to the end that this corporation may redeem from each share holder one-half ($\frac{1}{2}$) of the stock issued to said respective share holder paying therefor the book value of said respective shares of stock to be thus redeemed.

"WHEREUPON, Margaret Chandler Bush, introduced the following Resolution:

'BE IT RESOLVED, that application be made to the State of Tennessee for an Amendment to the Charter of Incorporation of the Company so as to provide for a reduction in the capital stock of the corporation from 500 shares of $100.00 par value to 250 shares of $100.00 par value.

'BE IT FURTHER RESOLVED that the President call a meeting of all the stockholders of the corporation to the end that said proposed amendment to the Charter be submitted to the stockholders for approval.'

A special meeting of the stockholders was held on September 28, 1946, the minutes of which read in part as follows:

"The Chairman explained that the purpose of the meeting was to authorize partial liquidation for the following reasons:

"The old business was sold and plans were developed to go back into business, operating two stores, a ladies ready-to-wear business and a men's store. The ladies ready-to-wear store has been opened and is now operating. Up to now, we have been unable to negotiate a lease for a suitable location, and, after considerable thought, it has been decided to abandon the idea of operating an exclusive men's shop and operate only the one store at the present time. It appears that requirements of the one store will be approximately one-half the capital now invested in Chandler's, Inc.

"Upon motion of Margaret Chandler Bush, seconded by J. W. Bush, and unanimously carried, the officials were authorized and instructed to redeem from each shareholder one-half of his stock, paying therefor the book value, which is approximately $269.00 per share. Therefore they are authorized to retire one-half of each shareholder's stock at $269.00 per share and are authorized to apply to the Secretary of State for reduction of the outstanding stock from 500 shares to 250 shares of $100.00 each."

On October 29, 1946, the charter of the Company was amended and its capital stock was reduced from 500 shares of $100 par value common stock, to 250 shares of $100 par value common stock. On November 7, 1946, the 500 shares of outstanding capital stock designated "Chandler-Singleton Company" were called in and canceled. Each stockholder received 1 share of stock designated "Chandler's" and

$269 in cash for each 2 shares turned in. The $269 represented the approximate book value of 1 share of Chandler-Singleton Company stock on February 28, 1946. . . .

The comparative balance sheets on December 31, 1945, on February 28, 1946, after the sale to McArthur's Incorporated, and on December 31, 1946, were as follows:

	Dec. 31, 1945	Feb. 28, 1946	Dec. 31, 1946
Assets			
Current assets:			
Cash	$ 74,486.67	$111,095.14	$16,372.69
U.S. bonds and accrued interest	34,089.20	34,089.20	....
Accounts receivable	16,195.87	....	6,028.49
Notes receivable	1,531.67	1,531.67	....
Savings and Loan Association	....	....	5,000.00
Credit balance in accounts payable	....	132.52	....
Postwar refund excess profits tax and refund bonds	9,610.85	4,124.34	....
Inventories	30,412.83	....	16,409.23
Total current assets	$166,327.09	$150,972.87	$43,810.41
Fixed assets:			
Furniture and fixtures	$ 15,465.61	....	$ 7,829.35
Bookkeeping machine	875.67	....	....
Automoblie	692.40	....	692.40
Carpet, leasehold improvements, neon signs	....	....	7,716.29
	$ 17,033.68	....	$16,238.04
Less:			
Reserve for depreciation	14,709.98	....	1,142.60
Fixed assets — net	$ 2,323.70	....	$15,095.44
Prepaid insurance	85.00	....	184.80
Total assets	$168,735.79	$150,972.87	$59,090.65
Liabilities and Net Worth			
Current liabilities:			
Accounts payable	$ 21,558.42	....	$ 5,369.34
Accrued taxes	39,570.58	$ 16,405.64	6,943.40
Total current liabilities	$ 61,129.00	$ 16,405.64	$12,312.74
Net worth:			
Capital stock — common	$ 50,000.00	$ 50,000.00	$25,000.00
Paid in surplus	6,000.00	6,000.00	3,000.00
Earned surplus	51,606.79	78,567.23	18,777.91
Total net worth	$107,606.79	$134,567.23	$46,777.91
Total liabilities and net worth	$168,735.79	$150,972.87	$59,090.65

A 10 per cent dividend totaling $5,000 was declared on September 24, 1943. The amount of cash and United States bonds possessed by the Company at the beginning of 1946 exceeded the amount required for the current operation of the business by approximately $45,000. Between January 1 and February 28, 1946, the Company's earned surplus increased by $39,460.44, out of which the Company paid dividends in the amount of $12,500. To the extent of at least $58,027.91, the excess cash possessed by the Company prior to the November 7 distribution was not created by a reduction in the amount of capital needed to operate the Company's business.

Petitioners reported the excess of the payments received over the cost of the stock in their individual income tax returns as capital gain. Respondent treated the payments, to the extent of the earned surplus of $58,027.91, as dividends and taxed them to the petitioners as ordinary income.

The acquisition and cancellation of one-half the Company's stock in 1946 was done at such a time and in such a manner as to make the distribution and cancellation essentially equivalent to the distribution of a taxable dividend to the extent of $58,027.91.

Opinion

BRUCE, Judge: Respondent contends that the Company's pro rata distribution in redemption of half its capital stock at book value was made at such a time and in such manner as to make the distribution essentially equivalent to the distribution of a taxable dividend to the extent of earnings and profits. If respondent's contention is correct the distribution to the extent of earnings and profits loses its capital gain status acquired under section 115(c) and (i) and is treated as a taxable dividend under section 115(g)[1] of the Internal Revenue Code of 1939 as it applied in 1946.[2]

A cancellation or redemption by a corporation of all of the stock of a particular shareholder has been held not to be essentially equivalent to the distribution of a taxable dividend. Cf. Carter Tiffany, 16 T.C. 1443; Zenz v. Quinlivan, (C.A. 6) 213 F.2d 914; Regs. 111, sec. 29.115-9. However, "A cancellation or redemption by a corporation of its stock pro rata among all the shareholders will generally be considered

[1]SEC. 115. DISTRIBUTIONS BY CORPORATIONS.

(g) REDEMPTION OF STOCK. — If a corporation cancels or redeems its stock (whether or not such stock was issued as a stock dividend) at such time and in such manner as to make the distribution and cancellation or redemption in whole or in part essentially equivalent to the distribution of a taxable dividend, the amount so distributed in redemption or cancellation of the stock, to the extent that it represents a distribution of earnings or profits accumulated after February 28, 1913, shall be treated as a taxable dividend.

[2]Senate Report No. 1631, 77th Cong., 2d Sess., 1942-2 C.B. 504, 591, in proposing that the Revenue Act of 1942 amend section 115(c) as described below, made the following statement regarding section 115(g):

"Under existing law the gain realized from a distribution in partial liquidation is treated, despite the provisions of section 117, as a short-term capital gain. This treatment was occasioned by the facility with which ordinary dividends may be distributed under the guise of distributions in partial liquidation, although section 115(g) makes explicit provision for the treatment of such distributions as ordinary dividends. Inequality results, however, under the existing law in the case of unquestionable bona fide redemptions of stock not equivalent in any way to the distribution of a taxable dividend. It is believed that the proper application of section 115(g) will prove adequate to prevent taxable dividends disguised as liquidations from receiving capital gain treatment. Accordingly, this section of the bill eliminates the provision requiring the gain from a partial liquidation to be treated as a short-term capital gain."

as effecting a distribution essentially equivalent to a dividend distribution to the extent of the earnings and profits accumulated after February 28, 1913." Regs. 111, sec. 29.115-9. Such a redemption of stock is generally considered equivalent to a dividend because it does not, as a practical matter, change the essential relationship between the shareholders and the corporation. Cf. Commissioner v. Roberts, (C.A. 4) 203 F.2d 304, reversing 17 T.C. 1415. But, as pointed out by the regulations, a pro rata distribution is not always "essentially equivalent to the distribution of a taxable dividend" and each case depends upon its own particular circumstances. Commissioner v. Sullivan, (C.A. 5) 210 F.2d 607, affirming John L. Sullivan, 17 T.C. 1420. The circumstances in the instant case, however, do not warrant a finding that to the extent of earnings and profits the pro rata distribution was not essentially equivalent to a taxable dividend.

Being a question of fact, the decided cases are not controlling. However, in Joseph W. Imler, 11 T.C. 836, 840, we listed some of the factors which have been considered important, viz, "the presence or absence of a real business purpose, the motives of the corporation at the time of the distribution, the size of the corporate surplus, the past dividend policy, and the presence of any special circumstances relating to the distribution." . . .

An examination of the facts reveals that the Company had a large earned surplus and an unnecessary accumulation of cash from the standpoint of business requirement, both of which could have been reduced to the extent of earnings and profits by the declaration of a true dividend. The only suggested benefit accruing to the business by the distribution in cancellation of half the stock was the elimination of a substantial amount of this excess cash. Ordinarily such cash would be disposed of by the payment of a dividend. Coupled with the fact that the stockholders' proportionate interests in the enterprise remained unchanged, these factors indicate that section 115(g) is applicable. . . .

Petitioners seek to avoid the application of section 115(g) by contending that the cash distribution and redemption of stock did not represent an artifice to disguise the payment of a dividend but was occasioned by a bona fide contraction of business with a resulting decrease in the need for capital. While important, the absence of a plan to avoid taxation is not controlling. A distribution in redemption of stock may be essentially equivalent to a taxable dividend although it does not represent an attempt to camouflage such a dividend. . . . Whether a cancellation or redemption of stock is "essentially equivalent" to a taxable dividend depends primarily upon the net effect of the distribution rather than the motives and plans of the shareholders or the corporation. . . . Moreover, we cannot find from the present record that the reduction of taxes was not the motivating factor causing the stockholders to make a distribution in redemption of stock rather than to declare a dividend to the extent of earnings and profits.

Petitioners' primary contention is that the sale of the department store and the opening of the smaller ladies' ready-to-wear store resulted in a contraction of corporate business. This is a vital factor to be considered, but a contraction of business per se does not render section 115(g) inapplicable. L. M. Lockhart, 8 T.C. 436. Furthermore, even though it is clear that there was a diminution in the size of the

Company's business, there was no contraction such as was present in Commissioner v. Sullivan, Joseph W. Imler, and L. M. Lockhart, all supra. In those cases there was a contraction of business with a corresponding reduction in the amount of capital used. Here, although the business was smaller, the amount of capital actually committed to the corporate business was not reduced accordingly. On December 31, 1945, before the sale of the department store to McArthur's Incorporated, the Company had $32,736.53 tied up in fixed assets and inventories. On December 31, 1946, after the ladies' ready-to-wear store was opened, it had $31,504.67 invested in those items. Undoubtedly the department store required larger reserves than the ladies' ready-to-wear store for purchasing inventories and carrying accounts receivable. But to the extent of earnings and profits the excess cash distributed was not created by a reduction in the amount of capital required for the operation of the business. Most of the excess cash had existed since prior to the sale of the department store and did not arise from fortuitous circumstances, as petitioners contend, but from an accumulation of earnings beyond the needs of the business. This excess could have been eliminated by the payment of a taxable dividend, and its distribution in redemption of stock was essentially equivalent to a taxable dividend.

It is true that the entire $67,250 distribution could not have been made in the form of an ordinary dividend and to some extent a redemption of stock was required. But section 115(g) applies if the distribution is only "in part" essentially equivalent to a taxable dividend, and here the distribution was essentially equivalent to a taxable dividend to the extent of earnings and profits.

Decisions will be entered for the respondent.

REVENUE RULING 67-299
1967-2 Cum. Bull. 138

Advice has been requested whether the transaction described below involves a distribution resulting from a genuine contraction of the corporate business within the meaning of section 1.346-1(a)(2) of the Income Tax Regulations.

A corporation which is engaged in the business of owning and leasing real estate adopted a plan of partial liquidation. Pursuant to the plan the corporation sold one of its operating parcels of real estate for cash. It used the sales proceeds to remodel some of its remaining parcels of real estate. Shortly thereafter, and within the same taxable year in which the plan was adopted, it distributed an amount of money equal to the sales proceeds to its shareholders in redemption of some of its stock.

Section 346(a)(2) of the Internal Revenue Code of 1954 provides that a distribution will be treated as in partial liquidation of a corporation if the distribution is not essentially equivalent to a dividend, is in redemption of a part of the stock of the corporation pursuant to a plan, and occurs within the taxable year the plan is adopted or within the succeeding taxable year. Section 1.346-1(a)(2) of the regulations states that an example of a distribution which will qualify as a partial liquidation under section 346(a)(2) of the Code is a distribution resulting from a genuine contraction of the corporate business.

In this case, the sale of one parcel of real estate was a potential contraction of the corporate business. However, the remodeling of some of the remaining property was an expansion of the corporation's business offsetting any possible contraction effected by the sale. Thus, the sale of real estate did not result in a genuine contraction of the corporate business, since the net effect of the transactions was to keep the corporate assets at the same level which existed prior to the sale.

Accordingly, the above distribution by the corporation to its shareholders does not qualify as a distribution resulting from a genuine contraction of the corporate business within the meaning of section 1.346-1(a)(2) of the regulations.

NOTE

1. What would the result in *Chandler* (page 234 supra) have been if §346 had been applicable? Why?

2. If the corporation involved in Rev. Rul. 67-299 had used excess cash to remodel the real estate it expected to retain before selling the parcel it sold, would the Service's decision have been different? Should it be different? Is Rev. Rul. 67-299 correct? Why? As to the concept of the "active conduct of a trade or business," see Chapter 4, pages 522-526 infra; Treas. Reg. §1.355-1(c); Treas. Reg. §1.346-1(c).

3. Corporation M has conducted two separate, active businesses for ten years. In a distribution qualifying as a partial liquidation under §346, Corporation M distributes the assets of one of the businesses to its shareholders pro rata. Immediately thereafter the shareholders sell the distributed assets to X pursuant to terms negotiated prior to the distribution. What might the tax consequences be to Corporation M? Why? See Treas. Reg. §1.346-3; Note 3, page 40 supra.

4. What is the significance of §346(c) and Treas. Reg. §1.346-2? If there is a distribution that would qualify under both §§346 and 302(a), and the shareholders surrendered one-half their stock in exchange for the distribution, what is the relevance of the basis of the stock they surrendered? See Treas. Reg. §1.331-1(b).

5. Do the attribution of ownership provisions of §318 apply to §346 transactions? Should they? Why?

BLASCHKA v. UNITED STATES
393 F.2d 983 (Ct. Cl. 1968)

Before Cowen, Chief Judge, and Laramore, Durfee, Davis, Collins, Skelton, and Nichols, Judges.

Opinion

Per Curiam: This case was referred to Trial Commissioner Roald A. Hogenson with directions to make findings of fact and recommendation for conclusions of law under the order of reference and Rule 57(a). The commissioner has done so in an opinion and report filed on April 19, 1967. The commissioner's findings of fact were accepted by the parties but plaintiff excepted to the commissioner's conclusions of law. The case has been submitted to the court on the briefs of the parties and oral argument of counsel.

With respect to §346(a)(2), the court puts its decision, not only on the basis stated by the trial commissioner, but also on the ground that the distribution here was "essentially equivalent to a dividend" in that there was no contraction of C & C's business. See Bittker and Eustice, Federal Income Taxation of Corporations and Shareholders (1966), Sec. 7.62, pp. 309-312.

Since the court agrees with the commissioner's opinion with deletions, his findings, and his recommended conclusion of law, as hereinafter set forth, it hereby adopts the same, as modified, and as supplemented by the preceding paragraph, as the basis for its judgment in this case. Therefore, plaintiff is not entitled to recover and the petition is dismissed.

Commissioner Hogenson's opinion, as modified by the court, is as follows:

Plaintiff has brought suit to recover income tax and deficiency interest for the year 1959 in the total amount of $74,344.38 plus interest. The sole question is whether a distribution of $115,000 to plaintiff by C. & C. Blaschka, Inc., was a dividend taxable as ordinary income or was a distribution in partial liquidation with the gain realized taxable as long-term capital gain.

The basic facts are not in dispute. Plaintiff and her husband, Carl J. Blaschka, are and were the sole stockholders in C. & C. Blaschka, Inc. (hereinafter referred to as C & C), plaintiff owning approximately 92.3 percent of the stock and her husband 7.7 percent. The Blaschkas are the executive officers of C & C and, together with their accountant, comprise the board of directors. From 1955 until 1959, both plaintiff and her husband devoted full time to the business activities of C & C.

Until July 1, 1959, C & C was engaged in the wholesaling of popularly priced gloves throughout the United States. This business requires the ability to select popular glove styles, a talent demanding ingenuity and years of experience as well as a great deal of time and travel. Plaintiff and her brother-in-law did the selecting for C & C. In addition, C & C has a wholly owned Canadian subsidiary, Max Mayer & Co., Ltd. (hereinafter called Max Mayer, Ltd.), which is engaged in the wholesale glove business in Canada. C & C keeps tight control over this Canadian corporation and makes every decision of any importance for it. In return for these services, Max Mayer, Ltd. has paid C & C since 1935 an annual "administrative fee" of 3 percent of the net sales of Max Mayer, Ltd.

In 1958, after the loss of two key employees through illness and death, C & C decided to dispose of its United States glove business. By a contract effective July 1, 1959, C & C sold this business to unrelated third parties for $646,442.31, payable in notes and preferred stock. The sale included the name Max Mayer which became the name of the new corporation to which C & C transferred all the assets.

As a result of the sale, C & C had more funds than it needed. After a number of conferences involving the Blaschkas, their accountant and their attorney, it was decided that C & C would enter the real estate rental field. To that end, C & C purchased all the outstanding stock of the Clairette Manufacturing Company, Inc. (hereinafter referred to as Clairette) from its sole stockholder, Mrs. Blaschka, plaintiff herein. Since 1955, Clairette's sole business had been the renting of a building it owned to C & C for warehouse purposes. After the sale, Clairette continued to rent the building to the purchasers of C & C's United States glove business. The transaction was consummated on September 28, 1959, with the transfer by plaintiff of the entire Clairette stock in return for $115,000. It is the tax treatment of this purchase by C & C that is in dispute.

Since plaintiff owned more than 50 percent of the outstanding stock of C & C and Clairette, this sale falls within §304 of the Internal Revenue Code of 1954. (References to the Internal Revenue Code of 1954 will hereinafter be made by section number only.) In essence §304(a)(1) provides that if a person is in control of each of two corporations, and, in return for property, one of the corporations acquires stock in the other corporation from that person, the property is treated as a distribution in redemption of the stock of the acquiring corporation. This provision was enacted in response to a series of unfavorable judicial decisions in which the Treasury attempted unsuccessfully to tax these transactions as distributions essentially equivalent to a dividend and therefore taxable as ordinary income under what is now §§301 and 302. . . .

The function of §304, then, is to complement §302. To that end, §304(b)(1) provides that such a sale is defined as a redemption of the stock of the acquiring corporation, and that for purposes of §302(b), whether such stock acquisition is to be treated as a distribution in exchange for the stock is determined by reference to the stock of the issuing corporation. See also Reg. 1.304-2(a); Ralph L. Humphrey, 39 T.C. 199, 205 (1962). The essential question is whether the distribution has affected the stockholder's proportionate interest and control in the issuing corporation, and for that reason the special rule of §304(b)(1) points to the issuing corporation to apply §304(a) to §302. S. Rep. No. 1622, 83d Cong., 2d Sess. 240 (1954); H.R. Rep. No. 1337, 83d Cong., 2d Sess., A79 (1954); 3 U.S.C. Cong. & Admn. News, pp. 4217, 4877 (1954). The stockholder's sale of his stock in one corporation to a related corporation could substantially change his interest in the issuing corporation, or on the other hand, be a change of form only, with no effect on the stockholder's actual control. Lefevre, Purchases of Stock by Related Corporations — Acquisitions or Redemptions?, 14th Ann. Tul. Tax Inst. 441, 449 (1965). Although §304(b)(2) provides that the determination of the amount, paid in the stock redemption as defined in §304(a)(1), which is a dividend shall be made solely with reference to the earnings and profits of the acquiring corporation, no mention is made of §302(b) in that paragraph, nor is there any provision in §304[2] or elsewhere in the 1954 Code, as to which corporation is to be tested to determine whether there has been a partial liquidation in a stock redemption through use of related corporations. It is significant, however, that subsection (e) of §302, by statutory cross reference, points to §331, and this together with the considerations underlying the tax treatment of partial liquidations require that a §304 stock redemption, involving the question of

---

[2]For an excellent analysis of the complexities and uncertainties of §304, with special attention to recent cases, and with recommendations for legislative and administrative clarifications, see Marans, Section 304: The Shadowy World of Redemptions Through Related Corporations, 22 N.Y.U. **Tax Law Rev.** 161 (1967).

a partial liquidation under §§331(a)(2) and 346, be tested on the level of the acquiring corporation. S. Rep. No. 1622, supra, at 49; U.S.C. Cong. & Admn. News, supra, at p. 4680. The very nature of a partial liquidation, at least as purportedly involved in this case, is a curtailment or contraction of the activities of the acquiring corporation, and the distribution to a stockholder of unneeded funds in exchange for stock in a related corporation. It is concluded that the purported partial liquidation is not to be measured by §302, but that the general rule of §304(a) — that the stock sale is to be treated as a redemption by the acquiring corporation — applies, subject, however, to the statutory definition as to what constitutes a partial liquidation under §§331 and 346 of the 1954 Code, applied to the acquiring corporation.

Thus, whether the payment of $115,000 by C & C for the stock of Clairette is a partial liquidation under §§331(a)(2) and 346 must be determined with respect to the activities of C & C. Section 346 provides three tests to determine whether a distribution is to be treated as a payment in partial liquidation. The first dealing with a series of distributions culminating in the complete liquidation of the corporation, is not applicable here since C & C has not and has no intention of completely liquidating. The second, §346(a)(2), provides that a distribution will be considered as a payment in partial liquidation if it is not essentially equivalent to a dividend and is made pursuant to a plan, the payments being made within 2 years of the adoption of the plan. The requirement that the payment be made pursuant to a plan is crucial here, since it is apparent that C & C never adopted a formal plan of partial liquidation. The third test concerns the provisions of §346(b), hereinafter discussed.

That a formal plan of liquidation is not required to qualify under §346 is clear. Fowler Hosiery Co. v. Commissioner, 36 T.C. 201, 218 (1961), aff'd, 301 F.2d 394, 397 (7th Cir. 1962). However, there must be clear evidence of an intention to liquidate if an informal plan is to be established. Oberndorfer, Partial Liquidations, N.Y.U. 13th Ann. Inst. on Fed. Tax. 637, 643 (1955). . . .

In the instant case, C & C had adopted no plan of partial liquidation, either formal or informal, when it paid $115,000 for the Clairette stock. The official minutes of C & C show that there were two special meetings of the stockholders and four special meetings of the board of directors in 1959, and no meetings of either the stockholders or the directors in 1960. Nowhere in these minutes is there any discussion or mention of a plan of partial liquidation of C & C. The corporate resolution dated September 10, 1959, which accepted Mrs. Blaschka's offer of the Clairette stock, likewise makes no mention of any partial liquidation.

Plaintiff contends, however, that the purchase of the Clairette stock was part of a plan of partial liquidation discussed and informally adopted by the directors of C & C, and that the plan was not recorded in the corporate minutes because C & C's accountant and attorney did not think it necessary. But the facts indicate otherwise. Mr. Blaschka admitted that the purchase of Clairette's stock was made only after considering the tax aspects of the transaction. To assert that legal counsel advised a partial liquidation but did not make any written record of the plan is incredulous.

This is all the more so when one considers plaintiff's Notice of Protest of the tax deficiency in controversy in this suit, a nine-page memorandum filed under oath with the Internal Revenue Service. No mention is made in that document of any partial liquidation being carried out by C & C. Furthermore, C & C stated in a memorandum sent to the Internal Revenue Service in 1961 concerning accumulated earnings tax that after its sale of the United States glove business, C & C decided to enter the industrial real estate business rather than liquidate. This is substantiated by Mr. Blaschka's testimony that the purchase of Clairette, whose sole business was the renting of a warehouse, was chosen as C & C's initial entry into this new field because the warehouse was known to be a good rentable building. In view of all this evidence, it is clear that the purchase of the Clairette stock was not pursuant to a plan of partial liquidation and the transaction cannot qualify under §346(a)(2).

Nor does it come under the so-called "safe harbor" of §346(b). Under that subsection, if a corporation has been conducting two or more separate and active businesses for at least 5 years and then ceases one of the businesses, the distribution of the assets of this ceased business or the proceeds from their sale shall be treated as a payment in partial liquidation so long as after the distribution the corporation continues to conduct actively at least one of the preexisting businesses. Just what constitutes "actively engaged in the conduct of a trade or business" for purposes of §346 is defined in §1.346-1(c) of the Regulations, by incorporation of §1.355-1(c):

> "a trade or business consists of a specific existing group of activities being carried on for the purpose of earning income or profit from only such group of activities, and the activities included in such group must include every operation which forms a part of, or a step in, the process of earning income or profit from such group. Such group of activities ordinarily must include the collection of income and the payment of expenses." [Treas. Reg. §1.355-1(c)]

Plaintiff contends the C & C's management of its wholly owned subsidiary, Max Mayer, Ltd., is a separate trade or business apart from its United States glove business, thereby qualifying the distribution of the proceeds from the sale of the United States business through the purchase of the Clairette stock as a partial liquidation.

Aside from the general definition found in the Regulation, only a few cases have considered the question of what constitutes two separate trades or businesses. What few guidelines exist are found mainly in the 16 examples contained in Reg. §1.355-1(d) and in the more than 25 rulings published by the Treasury. See McDonald, Tax Considerations in Corporate Divisions: Contraction and Liquidation, 39 Taxes (The Tax Magazine of C.C.H.) 994, 1000-1001, nn.60-63 for a complete listing of these rulings through 1961. As a result, the law has developed slowly on an ad hoc basis, with general principles not readily discernible from these factual patterns. However, common threads that run through many of these cases indicate that C & C was not engaged in the active conduct of two separate businesses in 1959.

One factor that reappears in several of the rulings is whether each business produces a substantial part of the combined income. In Rev. Rul. 57-333, 1957-2 Cum. Bull. 239, a corporation engaged in the food brokerage business also owned an adjacent vacant lot which it leased to a used car dealer. The rental received for the land for each of the last 5 years was less than 2 percent of the total gross income of the entire business. It was ruled that the rental of the lot did not constitute a separate business for purposes of §346(b), with specific mention being made that the rental income received was only a nominal portion of the total gross income. In Rev. Rul. 56-266, 1956-1 Cum. Bull. 184, a corporation operated a retail grocery chain, manufactured and distributed bakery products, and produced and distributed creamery products, as well as owned real estate which it leased to its grocery stores for a rental based on a percentage of gross sales. The real estate activities were ruled not to be a business separate and apart from the grocery business.

Again, in Rev. Rul. 57-464, 1957-2 Cum. Bull. 244, a corporation manufactured heating equipment and owned a modern factory building, an old factory building which it used for storage purposes, and three rental properties. The real estate activities did not constitute a separate business, ruled the Treasury. Once more it was pointed out that the net income received from these properties was "negligible."

Also, in three judicial decisions all holding that two separate businesses did not exist, in which the question was whether the businesses were being *actively* conducted or not, the courts in each instance made reference to the small amount of income produced and lack of adequate record-keeping usually performed in a business. Isabel A. Elliott, 32 T.C. 283, 290-291 (1959); Theodore F. Appleby, 35 T.C. 755, 761 (1961), aff'd per curiam, 296 F.2d 925 (3d Cir. 1962), cert. denied, 370 U.S. 910 (1962); Bonsall v. Commissioner, 317 F.2d 61, 64 (2d Cir. 1963). Cf. Example (16) in Reg. §1.355-1(d) involving a corporation that manufactured and sold automobiles and maintained an executive dining room for profit.[4]

That the underlying consideration running throughout these rulings was the sufficiency or insufficiency of income produced rather than some other factor can be seen in those rulings in which two separate businesses were found. Most striking is Rev. Rul. 58-164, 1958-1 Cum. Bull. 184. There, a corporation sold textile products as a commission merchant and owned a valuable building which it leased to outsiders for a substantial net rental. It was ruled that two separate businesses existed. Also, in Rev. Rul. 57-334, 1957-2 Cum. Bull. 240, a corporation rented to others three separate parcels of real estate. It was ruled that rental of one of the three buildings involved constituted a separate business since the remaining real estate accounted for only half the corporation's income. And in Rev. Rul. 56-557, 1965-2 Cum. Bull. 199, the ruling again points to the importance of the fact that the income from the challenged business was substantial, in a determination that there were two separate businesses.

Turning to the income figures in the instant case, they reflect clearly that the services performed for Max Mayer, Ltd., by C & C produced so little income as not to be a business separate and distinct from the United States glove business. In return for these services, Max Mayer, Ltd., paid C & C an "administrative fee" of 3 percent of Max Mayer, Ltd.'s net sales, a figure set in 1935 by plaintiff's uncle. From 1952 through 1958, this *gross* administrative fee was only 1 percent of C & C's *net* sales of $13,893,677.95 for that period. Furthermore, from 1935 to 1962, C & C did not even allocate on its books the expenses attributable to the work performed for Max Mayer, Ltd. — hardly the practice of a corporation in the business of managerial and finan-

---

[4]Each "Example" cited will be from Reg. 1.355-1(d).

cial services. Cf. Isabel A. Elliott, supra; Theodore F. Appleby, supra; Bonsall v. Commissioner, supra. Since 1962, the Canadian authorities have required C & C to submit a detailed statement of the specific charges for its services to Max Mayer, Ltd. In 1962, out of a total administrative fee of $24,784.05, C & C earned a profit of only $751.96, or a return of approximately 3 percent. Projecting this profit margin back over the period from 1952 through 1958, C & C's total profits from administrative fees were approximately $4,261, or 1.5 percent of C & C's total net profits before taxes of $283,622 for that period. Such negligible amounts hardly meet the requirement included in Regulation §1.346-1(c) that the activities be carried on "for the purpose of earning income or profit." Treas. Reg. §1.355-1(c), supra.

The Regulations and Treasury Rulings, also, seem to require some form of separation of control and supervision to find separate businesses. In Rev. Rul. 58-54, 1958-1 Cum. Bull. 181, a corporation operated a soft drink bottling and distributing business. All the bottling was done at the main plant although it was distributed through facilities located in four different localities. The Treasury ruled that the distributing facilities did not constitute a separate business or businesses "despite some geographical differences in warehouse locations. They all formed part of one integrated business wherein the product was manufactured in one place, although distributed through several warehouse points." 1958-1 Cum. Bull. 181 at 182.

Rev. Rul. 56-451, 1956-2 Cum. Bull. 208 involved a corporation which published four trade magazines. The metal working magazine had its own editorial staff and advertising space salesmen, who devoted their entire time to this magazine. This publication had separate offices in the same building as the others and kept separate books. The only employees it shared with the others were the general officers of the corporation and certain clerical and production employees. The three other magazines served the electrical industry. The Treasury ruled that the metal working magazine was a separate business.

The Regulations provide still another example. Taxpayer corporation owns and operates two men's retail clothing stores, one in the city and one in the suburbs. The manager of each store directs its operations and makes the necessary purchases. No common warehouse is maintained. Under these circumstances the Regulations state that the activities of each store constitute a trade or business, evidently on the grounds of separate control and operation. (Example (10).)

In short, Max Mayer, Ltd., is a separate and distinct business from C & C in corporate form, but otherwise only in a geographical sense. There is some indication in the Regulations that geographical separation is enough. In Example (8), a corporation which manufactures ice cream at plants in two states is said to operate a trade or business in each state. To the same effect are Examples (13), (14), and (15). Just how these Examples relate to Example (10) supra, where geographical separation existed but where other factors were specifically mentioned, is not clear. Moreover, there is Rev. Rul. 57-190, 1957-1 Cum. Bull. 121. The facts there involved a corporation which sold and serviced cars, carrying on its operations in two buildings located some distance apart in the same city. The Treasury ruled that the separate locations were not sufficient to create separate businesses.

Thus, geographical separation by itself is of questionable significance. Also, all of the above-mentioned Examples (where apparently geographical separation was sufficient) are distinguishable from the instant case. Each Example involved a manufacturing business, manufacturing its products at several locations. Each plant was a viable entity, capable of producing the product from beginning to end. In spite of its separate corporate entity, Max Mayer, Ltd., was in no way viable by itself. Rather did it depend upon the decision of C & C for what it sold and how it sold. Before the Clairette stock sale, plaintiff owned 100 percent of the Clairette stock and 92.3 percent of the C & C stock, and C & C owned 100 percent of Max Mayer, Ltd. This control of all three corporations becomes absolute when the husband's 7.7 percent share of C & C is added. The circumstances strongly infer that in reality the "stock redemption" was equivalent to the declaration of a dividend, especially in view of the large accumulation of earned surplus by the redeeming corporation. When this factor is considered with the negligible amount of income and profits realized, the conclusion is that the management services provided by C & C to Max Mayer, Ltd., were not an "active trade or business" separate and apart from its own operations.

Therefore, the purchase of the Clairette stock by C & C was not a distribution in partial liquidation. The sum of $115,000 is deemed to be paid out of C & C's earnings and profits and taxable at ordinary income rates as a dividend pursuant to §§302 and 301(c)(1). Plaintiff's petition for a refund should be dismissed.

NOTE

Should §331(a)(2) and §346 be part of the Code? What justification is there for capital gains treatment for a distribution that does not meet the requirements of §302(a)? What is the relevance of corporate business contraction in deciding at the Congressional level whether a distribution should receive capital gains treatment? See J. Chommie, Section 346(a)(2): The Contraction Theory, 11 Tax. L. Rev. 407 (1956); F. Schoettle, Section 346 of the Internal Revenue Code: A Legislative Enigma, 109 U. Pa. L. Rev. 944 (1961). See also J. McGaffey and B. Garmer, III, Factors That Will Today Prove a Distribution Was Made in Partial Liquidation, 31 J. Taxation 204 (1969); R. Schlossberg, Confusion Between Partial Liquidations and Redemptions Often Clouds Tax Planning, 22 J. Taxation 152 (1965).

2. *Debt Retirement vs. Dividend or Redemption of Stock*

If a sole shareholder lends money to his corporation and that corporation repays the loan, what is the tax consequence to the shareholder? Suppose the loan is properly regarded as equity. What might the tax consequences be? Why?

Reread *Edwards,* page 91 supra, and review the "thinness" issues posed in the materials in Chapter 1 at pages 87-91 supra.

III. COLLAPSIBLE CORPORATIONS

A. *THE "COMMON LAW"*

O'BRIEN v. COMMISSIONER
25 T.C. 376 (1955)

. . . The respondent determined the deficiencies herein on alternative theories. He first determined that Terneen Productions, Inc., was not a bona fide corporation for Federal tax purposes and that all sums received by petitioners Pat and Eloise T. O'Brien, Phil L. and Gladys Ryan, and Graydon B. Howe from Columbia Pictures Corporation under a distribution contract between it and Terneen were taxable to such recipients as ordinary income rather than as capital gains. The first issue is, therefore, whether the respondent erred in that determination. If he did, he determined, in the alternative, that Terneen was a bona fide corporation but that its liquidation in August 1944, and its subsequent dissolution in November 1944, were without substance and should not be recognized for Federal tax purposes. On this theory, he determined that the sums which the O'Briens, Ryans, and Graydon B. Howe received from Columbia during the years in issue were income of Terneen, taxable to it, and that the above-named petitioners were liable as its transferees for the deficiencies which he determined against Terneen for the years 1944 to 1947, inclusive. The second issue is whether he erred in this determination and in determining penalties for Terneen's failure to file tax returns for such years.

On their income tax returns for 1947, the O'Briens and the Ryans reported as ordinary income the sums received from Columbia during that year, which were in excess of the amount which they had reported in 1944 as the fair market value of all assets received by them as the stockholders of Terneen. They now claim that such sums should have been reported as additional capital gains and claim an overpayment of taxes for the year 1947. This issue is whether the sums which the petitioners received in excess of the reported fair market value of the assets of Terneen upon its liquidation were properly reportable by them as ordinary income or as capital gains. . . .

Findings of Fact

. . . Early in 1943, Phil L. Ryan read a story in the Saturday Evening Post, entitled "Pile Buck," which he believed would make a good motion picture. He discussed the story with Pat O'Brien, who agreed that he would like to play the leading role in a motion picture based on the story. Ryan and O'Brien wanted to produce an independent motion picture and toward that end they, together with two attorneys, organized Terneen on June 30, 1943.

The first meeting of Terneen's incorporators was held on July 8, 1943. They elected themselves as the permanent directors of the corporation, and were also its officers. Ryan was president and O'Brien was vice-president. On July 28, 1943, the Commissioner of Corporations of California issued a permit to Terneen authorizing it to sell 1,250 of its shares of stock at $10 per share. On August 9, 1943, Terneen issued 625 shares to Pat O'Brien, 500 shares to Phil Ryan, and 125 shares to Graydon B. Howe. The shareholders paid $10 per share for the stock and the proceeds in the amount of $12,500 were deposited by Terneen in its bank account on August 23, 1943.

The independent production of motion pictures by actors and directors was common during the years here in issue. The financing of such productions was often handled by forming a corporation which entered into a distribution agreement with one of the major motion picture companies; that company agreed to provide its facilities for the production of the proposed picture and agreed to distribute it when completed; and on the strength of such agreements and with a mortgage on the completed film, banks would lend up to 60 per cent of the proposed budget of the picture. Terneen followed the above-described pattern in producing the picture here in question.

On July 1, 1943, it entered into a production distribution agreement with Columbia Pictures Corporation (hereinafter referred to as Columbia) whereby Terneen was to produce a motion picture based on the story "Pile Buck." Columbia had exclusive distribution rights to the picture and agreed to distribute the picture throughout the world upon its completion. The agreement specifically provided that Columbia was in no way acting in a fiduciary capacity with respect to any moneys which it collected from the distribution of the picture and that it had the right to commingle such funds with its own moneys. The agreement provided that Columbia would make its facilities and credits available for the production of the proposed motion picture; that it would finance the proposed budget for the picture up to 40 per cent, or more, if bank financing was not available; and that it would repay any of Terneen's bank loans directly out of the proceeds realized from distribution of the motion picture. For the services which it agreed to perform, Columbia was to receive a distribution fee of 25 per cent of the gross revenue from the picture while being reimbursed for all cash advances and credits to Terneen; and Columbia, after it had recouped such advances and credits and repaid any bank loans, was to share equally with Terneen the remaining proceeds from the picture.

Terneen employed Phil Ryan as the producer of the motion picture at a salary of $25,000 and employed Pat O'Brien as the principal star for the sum of $25,000. Eddie Sutherland was employed as the director of the picture at a salary of $30,000. Between December 1943 and February 1944, Terneen arranged for and signed contracts for the balance of the cast which consisted of 21 actors and actresses and 4 stand-ins. On February 7, 1944, Terneen borrowed $314,000 from the Bank of America to finance the production of the motion picture. The loan was secured by a mortgage of its rights and properties in the picture. Terneen procured workmen's compensation insurance from Lumberman Mutual Casualty Company for its employees. It likewise applied for and received an employer's identification number from the United States Treasury. It withheld from the wages of its employees the amounts required under the Federal Contribution Act and withholding tax statutes and made returns and payment of the taxes so withheld. Unsecured personal property taxes were assessed against Terneen by the Los Angeles tax assessor. Terneen paid such taxes in the amount of $4,793.96 on July 18, 1944.

The motion picture was completed and released for distribution under the title of "Secret Command" late in July 1944. On August 4, 1944, Terneen borrowed $35,000 from Columbia; and, after deducting withholding taxes, paid the balance of such sum to Pat O'Brien and Phil Ryan for salary due them.

On August 9, 1944, a special stockholders' meeting of Terneen was held, at which it was unanimously decided to wind up and dissolve the corporation. A resolution to that effect was passed and notice thereof given to Columbia and to the Bank of America on that date. A certificate of election to wind up and dissolve was filed with the secretary of state of California on August 11, 1944, and a copy thereof was certified by the secretary of state and filed in the office of the Los Angeles county clerk on August 14, 1944.

At the meeting on August 9th, the stockholders surrendered their certificates of stock for which they received Terneen's assignment of all of its right, title, and interest in the motion picture "Secret Command," in proportion to their stockholdings. Such assignment was subject to the Bank of America loan and to the claims of Columbia. On August 31, 1944, $6,238.46 remained in Terneen's bank account. On that date, such sum was distributed to the stockholders in proportion to their interest in the corporation. On October 25, 1944, the franchise tax commissioner of California issued a tax clearance for Terneen. On November 2, 1944, a certificate of dissolution was filed in the office of the secretary of state, and a copy thereof, certified by the secretary of state, was filed on November 6, 1944, in the office of the Los Angeles county clerk, Los Angeles, California. On November 18, 1944, Terneen filed a final income tax return for the fiscal period January 1 to November 6, 1944.

On their income tax returns for 1944, the O'Briens, Phil L. Ryan and Graydon B. Howe reported the fair market value of Terneen's right, title, and interest in "Secret Command" to be $150,000 and reported the difference in such sum (plus cash received) and the cost basis of their stock as a capital gain and paid the tax thereon. Ryan had many years experience in the sales and distribution of motion pictures. The estimate of the fair market value of Terneen's interest in "Secret Command" was made by him from detailed information of the receipts of the picture during its first weeks of showing and from other additional information from which an accurate appraisal of expected gross receipts of the picture could be made.

On their returns for 1947, the O'Briens and Ryans reported the amounts received from Columbia in excess of the fair market value of Terneen's assets as ordinary income but now contend that such sums should have been reported as additional capital gains. They claimed a refund of taxes paid for that year.

Terneen ceased doing business, liquidated and commenced dissolution on August 9, 1944. The fair market value of its right, title, and interest in the motion picture "Secret Command," on August 9, 1944, was $150,000. . . .

Opinion

Rice, Judge: The substance of the respondent's determination of deficiencies here is that Terneen was a "collapsible corporation" as that term is known in the law of Federal taxation. Had Terneen's shareholders realized the gains in question on or after January 1, 1950, the taxability of such gains as ordinary income or as capital gains would be determined pursuant to specific statutory standards. . . . [In § 341], Congress provided that the gain from the sale or exchange of stock of a collapsible corporation should be taxed as ordinary income. It defined a collapsible corporation as a corporation formed for the production of property, with a view to the sale or exchange of its stock by its shareholders, in liquidation or otherwise, prior to the realization by the corporation of a substantial part of the net income which would be derived from its production of property. We, of course, do not decide whether the gains here in question, had they been realized after January 1, 1950, would be taxable as ordinary income under the provisions of section [341].

The reports of the House Ways and Means Committee and the Senate Finance Committee indicate that Congress was fully aware that so-called collapsible corporations were in widespread use in the motion picture industry. Congress further recognized that no such corporation had, at that time, been before the courts. Hence, section 212(b) of the 1950 Act provided that the courts were free to decide, with no inference being drawn from the enactment of such subsection, whether the gains arising from the sale or exchange of stock of an alleged collapsible corporation prior to January 1, 1950, were taxable as ordinary income or as capital gains.

A case with facts almost identical to those here was decided by the United States District Court for the Southern District of California — Herbert v. Riddell, 103 F. Supp. 369 (S.D., Cal., 1952). In that case, the Government argued that the gains realized by the stockholders of an alleged collapsible corporation, after its dissolution and assignment of its assets to them, were taxable as ordinary income on the same theories the respondent advanced here. The District Court rejected the Government's arguments and held that the gains there in question were taxable as capital gains. The petitioners here, of course, rely on that case. We think that conclusion was correct.

The respondent's determination of the deficiencies here is predicated on what he believes to be strong equitable considerations in his favor. While solicitude for the revenue may sometimes be an appealing basis on which to decide a particular tax case, it is often a treacherous one. And here, irrespective of what equitable arguments might be advanced in support of the respondent's position, we think it clear that his determination has no support in law.

The deficiencies in Docket Nos. 46372, 46373, 46375, 46376, and 46379 were determined on the theory that Terneen was not a bona fide corporation for Federal tax purposes. The respondent, however, did not argue that theory on brief, and we assume he now deems it to be without merit. Nor need we belabor that question. Suffice it to say, that the facts as set forth in our findings show clearly that Terneen was a bona fide corporation until August 1944, when it ceased doing business, liquidated, and commenced dissolution. Cf. Gregory v. Helvering, 293 U.S. 465 (1935); and Higgins v. Smith, 308 U.S. 473 (1940).

The respondent's alternative determination that Terneen did not dissolve for Federal tax purposes in 1944 is based on two arguments. His first argument is predicated on the holdings of such cases as: United States v. Joliet & Chicago R. Co., 315 U.S. 44 (1942); Helvering v. Horst, 311 U.S. 112 (1940); Helvering v. Eubank, 311 U.S. 122 (1940); and Lucas v. Earl, 281 U.S. 111 (1930). Those cases, of course, stand for the proposition that the one to whom income is truly attributable cannot escape the tax thereon by anticipatory assignments or other artificial devices which channel the actual receipt of the income directly into the hands of others. The respondent places particular emphasis on the *Joliet & Chicago R. Co.* case. An examination of the holding therein will serve as well as any other to demonstrate the error of the respondent's position. In that case, the Joliet & Chicago Railroad Company transferred all of its assets to a second railway company under an agreement whereby the second company agreed to pay Joliet stockholders a dividend. Joliet sought to escape tax liability by arguing that it had ceased doing business and that the dividends received by its stockholders were, in fact, paid by the second railway company and constituted income of the stockholders only. The Supreme Court rejected those arguments and held that Joliet was first taxable on the total amount of the dividends ultimately paid to its stockholders. The significant distinction between the *Joliet & Chicago R. Co.* case, as well as the other similar above-cited anticipatory assignment cases, and the case before us here, is that in each of those cases the taxpayer to whom the income was truly attributable was still in existence at the time the income was received by the assignees. Here, Terneen was not in existence when the income in question arose, the income came from property owned by individuals and Terneen, therefore, cannot be liable for taxes on such income.

The second argument which the respondent advances for disregarding Terneen's corporate dissolution in 1944 is predicated on the basis of the holding of Commissioner v. Court Holding Co., 324 U.S. 331 (1945). In that case, the Supreme Court held that a corporation could not negotiate for the sale of its property and then transfer the property to its stockholders and dissolve; thus permitting them to receive the purchase price for the property and itself escape taxation. The doctrine of the *Court Holding Co.* case is confined to the facts on which it was decided. United States v. Cumberland Pub. Serv. Co., 338 U.S. 451 (1950). It obviously is not applicable to the facts here because Terneen did not arrange for the sale of anything. It did not pass on to its stockholders, upon its dissolution, a substantially completed contract for the sale of its assets. It assigned to them only its right, title, and interest in the film "Secret Command," which was subject to the distribution agreement signed more than a year previously with Columbia. While the stockholders expected to realize a profit on the assets transferred to them, there was no assurance that they would do so. Columbia agreed only to distribute the picture; it did not agree to buy it.

We think the respondent clearly erred in disregarding Terneen's liquidation in 1944 and in determining deficiencies in taxes and penalties against it for that and subsequent years, and in determining deficiencies against the individual petitioners here as its transferees. United States v. Horschel, 205 F.2d 646 (C.A. 9, 1953); Herbert v. Riddell, supra.

The third issue is whether the sums which the O'Briens and the Ryans received from Columbia in 1947, which sums were in excess of the fair market value of

Terneen's assets as reported by them in 1944, were taxable as ordinary income or as additional capital gains. On their returns for 1947, they reported such excess as ordinary income; but, upon the respondent's determination of the deficiencies herein, they claim such sums should have been reported as additional capital gains. In support of their position they cite Westover v. Smith, 173 F.2d 90 (C.A. 9, 1949); and Susan J. Carter, 9 T.C. 364 (1947), affd. 170 F.2d 911 (C.A. 2, 1948).

The respondent argues that those cases are distinguishable on their facts from the one here; and, in support of his argument that the excess sums in question here were ordinary income, cites an unreported opinion of the United States District Court for the Southern District of California — Lewin v. Westover, decided October 29, 1953.[6] On facts similar to those here, the District Court there concluded that the taxpayer should have reported similar excess sums as ordinary income.

We agree with the respondent that Westover v. Smith, supra, and Susan J. Carter, supra, are not applicable to the facts here. In those cases, corporate stockholders received contractual obligations having no fair market value upon the dissolution of the corporation. In the *Smith* case, the contractual obligation was for royalty payments and in the *Carter* case for oil brokerage commissions. The courts said that collections on those obligations in years after the dissolution of the corporations, constituted capital gains because the dissolution of the corporations was not a closed transaction for tax purposes with respect to assets which had no fair market value on the date of dissolution.

Here, the interest in the film which Terneen's stockholders received had a readily ascertainable fair market value at the time Terneen dissolved. The distribution of the assets was a closed transaction for Federal tax purposes. Hence, the amounts in excess of such fair market value, which the petitioners received in 1947, were properly reported by them as ordinary income, since their basis in the asset had been recovered by that time. . . .

NOTE

Might the Commissioner have argued tenably that Terneen Productions, Inc. should be required to accrue income upon liquidation in order to reflect its income properly? See *Family Record Plan, Inc.,* page 49 supra.

B. *SECTION 341*

1. *General Impact*

BRAUNSTEIN v. COMMISSIONER
374 U.S. 65 (1963), aff'g 305 F.2d 949 (2d Cir. 1962)

Mr. Justice HARLAN delivered the opinion of the Court. This case involves the applicability of the "collapsible corporation" provisions of the federal income tax

[6]53-2 U.S.T.C. par. 9619, 45 A.F.T.R. 944.

laws which, during the period relevant here, were set forth in [§341]. . . . These provisions require that under certain circumstances, gain from the sale of stock which would otherwise be considered as long-term capital gain, and accordingly taxed at a maximum rate of 25%, must be reported as ordinary income.

The three taxpayers who are petitioners here became associated in 1938 and have since participated in a number of construction projects, usually through corporations in which the stock was equally divided. In 1948 the petitioners received a commitment from the Federal Housing Administration to insure loans for the construction of a multiple-dwelling apartment project in Queens County, New York. Two corporations were formed to carry out this project, and each petitioner was issued one-third of the stock in each corporation. After the costs of construction had been paid, the corporations each had an unused amount of mortgage loan funds remaining, and in 1950 the petitioners sold their stock at a profit, receiving as part of the sale transaction distributions from the corporations which included the unused funds. The petitioners reported the excess of the amounts received over their bases in the stock as long-term capital gains of $313,854.17 each.[3]

The Commissioner asserted a deficiency, treating the gain as ordinary income on the ground that the corporations were "collapsible" within the meaning of §[341]. The Tax Court sustained the Commissioner, 36 T.C. 22, and the Court of Appeals affirmed the Tax Court, 305 F.2d 949, holding that (1) the taxpayers had the requisite "view" during construction of the property . . . ; (2) more than 70% of the gain realized by the taxpayers was attributable to the constructed property . . . ; and (3) §[341] applies even if the constructed buildings would have produced capital gain on a sale by the taxpayers had no corporations been formed. This last holding was in response to an argument by the taxpayers based on a theory similar to that adopted by the Court of Appeals for the Fifth Circuit in United States v. Ivey, 294 F.2d 799. In view of the conflict between the decision below and that in *Ivey* on this point, we granted certiorari, 371 U.S. 933, stating that the grant was limited to the following question:

> "Whether Section [341] of the Internal Revenue Code of [1954] which provides that gain 'from the sale or exchange . . . of stock of a collapsible corporation' is taxable as ordinary income rather than capital gain, is inapplicable in circumstances where the stockholders would have been entitled to capital gains treatment had they conducted the enterprise in their individual capacities without utilizing a corporation."

Briefly summarized, petitioners' argument runs as follows: As the legislative history shows, the collapsible corporation provisions of the code were designed to close a loophole through which some persons had been able to convert ordinary income into long-term capital gain by use of the corporate form. For example, in the case of an individual who constructed a property which he held primarily for sale to customers in the ordinary course of his trade or business, any gain from the

---

[3]The parties have agreed that the distributions from the corporations and the amounts received directly from the buyers of the stock may be considered together, as if the entire amount had been received from the buyers.

sale of the asset would be ordinary income; but if that same individual were to form a corporation to construct the property, intending to sell his stock on the completion of construction, it was at least arguable prior to the enactment of §[341] that the proceeds of the ultimate sale of the stock were entitled to capital-gains treatment. It was this and similar devices that §[341] was designed to frustrate, but it was *not* intended to have the inequitable effect of converting into ordinary income what would properly have been a capital gain prior to its enactment even in the absence of any corporate form. Thus, it is argued, the phrase "gain attributable to such property," as used in §[341(b)(1)(B)], must apply only to profit that would have constituted ordinary income if a corporation had not been utilized, for only in such cases is the corporation made to serve as a device for tax avoidance. In the present case, neither the corporation nor the individual petitioners were in the trade or business of selling apartment buildings, and thus the corporations were not used to convert ordinary income into capital gain and the provisions of §[341] are inapplicable.[5]

We have concluded that petitioners' contentions must be rejected. Their argument is wholly inconsistent with the plain meaning of the language of §[341], and we find nothing in the purpose of the statute, as indicated by its legislative history, to warrant any departure from that meaning in this case.

I

As to the language used, §[341] defines a collapsible corporation as embracing one formed or availed of principally for the manufacture, construction, or production of property with a view to (1) the sale or exchange of stock prior to the realization by the corporation of a substantial part of the net income from the property *and* (2) the realization "of gain attributable to such property." The section is then expressly made inapplicable to gain realized during any year "unless more than 70 per centum of such gain is attributable to the property so manufactured, constructed, or produced." If used in their ordinary meaning, the word "gain" in these contexts simply refers to the excess of proceeds over cost or basis, and the phrase "attributable to" merely confines consideration to that gain caused or generated by the property in question. With these definitions, the section makes eminent sense, since the terms operate to limit its application to cases in which the corporation was availed of with a view to profiting from the constructed property by a sale or exchange of stock soon after completion of construction *and* in which a substantial part of the profit from the sale or exchange of stock in a given year was in fact generated by such property.

There is nothing in the language or structure of the section to demand or even justify reading into these provisions the *additional* requirement that the taxpayer must in fact have been using the corporate form as a device to convert ordinary income into capital gain. If a corporation owns but one asset, and the shareholders sell their stock at a profit resulting from an increase in the value of the asset, they

---

[5]The Government has assumed for purposes of its argument here, but does not concede, that petitioners would have been entitled to capital-gains treatment had they conducted the enterprise without utilizing a corporation.

have "gain attributable to" that asset in the natural meaning of the phrase regardless of their desire, or lack of desire, to avoid the bite of federal income taxes.

II

Nor is there anything in the legislative history that would lead us to depart from the plain meaning of the statute as petitioners would have us do. There can of course be no question that the purpose of §[341] was, as petitioners contend, to close a loophole that Congress feared could be used to convert ordinary income into capital gain. See H.R. Rep. No. 2319, 81st Cong., 2d Sess.; S. Rep. No. 2375, 81st Cong., 2d Sess. But the crucial point for present purposes is that the *method* chosen to close this loophole was to establish a carefully and elaborately defined category of transactions in which what might otherwise be a capital gain would have to be treated as ordinary income. There is no indication whatever of any congressional desire to have the Commissioner or the courts make a determination in each case as to whether the use of the corporation was for tax avoidance. Indeed, the drawing of certain arbitrary lines not here involved — such as making the section inapplicable to any shareholder owning 10% or less of the stock or to any gain realized more than three years after the completion of construction — tends to refute any such indication. It is our understanding, in other words, that Congress intended to define what is believed to be a tax avoidance device rather than to leave the presence or absence of tax avoidance elements for decision on a case-to-case basis.

We are reinforced in this conclusion by the practical difficulties — indeed the impossibilities — of considering without more legislative guidance than is furnished by §[341] whether there has in fact been "conversion" of ordinary income into capital gains in a particular case. For example, if we were to inquire whether or not the profit would have been ordinary income had an enterprise been individually owned, would we treat each taxpaying shareholder differently and look only to *his* trade or business or would we consider the matter in terms of the trade or business of *any* or at least a substantial number of shareholders? There is simply no basis in the statute for a judicial resolution of this question, and indeed when Congress addressed itself to the problem in 1958, it approved an intricate formulation falling between these two extremes.[6]

As a further example, what if the individual in question is not himself engaged in any trade or business but owns stock in varying amounts in a number of corporate ventures other than the one before the court? Do we pierce *each* of the corporate veils, regardless of the extent and share of the individual's investment, and charge him with being in the trade or business of each such corporation? Again, there is no basis for a rational judicial answer; the judgment is essentially a legislative one and in the 1958 amendments Congress enacted a specific provision designed to deal with this matter, that is far too complex to be summarized here.[7]

These examples should suffice to demonstrate the point: The question whether there has in fact been a "conversion" of ordinary income in a particular case is far

[6]Int. Rev. Code, 1954, §341(e), added by the Technical Amendments Act of 1958, §20(a), 72 Stat. 1615.
[7]Int. Rev. Code, 1954, §341(e)(1)(C).

easier to state than to answer, and involves a number of thorny issues that may not appear on the surface.[8] We find no basis in either the terms or the history of §[341] for concluding that Congress intended the Commissioner and the courts to enter this thicket and to arrive at ad hoc determinations for every taxpayer. Accordingly, the judgments below must be

Affirmed.

Mr. Justice DOUGLAS dissents.

NOTE

1. In *Braunstein* the Court intimates that Congress was worried principally about the conversion of ordinary income into capital gains through the use of a collapsible corporation. Do you agree? In 1964 Congress added §341(f) to the Code. Is there a Congressional worry concerning avoidance of the corporate tax? Is there a confluence of worries or just an ambiguous or undefined state of worry? Should there be a worry? If so, what? How should it be met? Why?

2. Justice Harlan makes reference to the 1958 amendment adding §341(e). What is its purpose and effect? Why was §341(f) thought necessary in 1964?

2. *"Substantial Part"*

COMMISSIONER v. KELLEY
293 F.2d 904 (5th Cir. 1961)

Before TUTTLE, Chief Judge, and RIVES and WISDOM, Circuit Judges.

WISDOM, Circuit Judge. The tax definition of a "collapsible corporation" illustrates again that the "difficulties of so-called interpretation arise when the legislature had no meaning at all; when the question which is raised on the statute never occurred to" the legislature. In the matter now before us our difficulties come from the certainty of the general congressional purpose in enacting Section [341] of the Internal Revenue Code . . . and the uncertainty of the meaning to be extracted from language of the section that is, perhaps, Janus-faced. It seems hardly possible that Congress could have considered the specific question the *Kelley-Waltman* cases raise.

In the *Kelley-Waltman* cases on appeal from the Tax Court this Court must determine the meaning of the term *"a substantial part"* as that term is used in Section [341] . . . . This section defines a collapsible corporation as one "formed or

---

[8]The Government has emphasized in its argument here that the present case involves a particularly "blatant" conversion of ordinary income because by charging the corporations only for the out-of-pocket costs of construction "petitioners contributed their services to create a valuable property for the corporation[s] and then realized upon that value by selling their stock." Thus, the Government concludes, the petitioners claim as capital gain "what ought to have been (and, in an arm's-length transaction, would have been) taxed as compensation for services."

availed of . . . with a view to the sale or exchange of stock by its shareholders . . . prior to realization by the corporation . . . of a substantial part of the net income to be derived[4] from [its] property, and the realization by such shareholders of gain attributable to such property". If Island Shores, Inc., the corporation in question here, was a collapsible corporation in 1952, Kelley and Waltman, the taxpayers (stockholders), should have reported the gain from the sale of their stock as ordinary income; they reported it as a capital gain.

Section [341] has been said to confront the Court with the necessity of choosing one of two conflicting meanings, each of which may be defended on grammatical and semantic grounds.[6] Does "a substantial part" mean the part already realized or does it mean the part not yet realized? After this choice is made, the Court must then determine how much is "substantial"?

There is no dispute over the facts.[7] In 1952 Island Shores had realized one-third

---

[4]In determining the "income to be derived" the total net income which will eventually be derived from the property is estimated as of the date of the sale, exchange, or distribution — assuming that there had been no sale, exchange, or distribution. See Rose Sidney, 1958, 30 T.C. 1155, affirmed 2 Cir., 1960, 273 F.2d 928. This is consistent with the statutory language, "net income to be derived from such property"; but there is a serious question whether the phrase "to be derived" refers only to the value of the assets at the sale or liquidation. In this case there is no dispute over the Tax Court finding that Island Shores had realized one-third of its anticipated total net income.

[6]"The clause 'prior to the realization . . . of a substantial part of the net income to be derived from such property' can conceivably be given either of two meanings. The first, which is probably intended, would interpret the provision to mean that a substantial part of the total net income must be realized before the sale or liquidation. The second, also grammatically correct, would interpret the provision to mean that no substantial part of the total net income remains to be derived from the property at the time of the sale or liquidation. The committee reports do not make clear which of these interpretations is intended. As in the case of the statute itself, the numerous general statements in the Regulations using the phrase 'income to be derived' can be read both ways, although probably it will be more readily assumed that they refer to the part of the income realized before the sale or exchange." McLean, Collapsible Corporation, 67 Harv. L. Rev. 55, 67 fn. 18 (1953).

[7]In April 1950 the taxpayers formed Island Shores, Inc., a Florida corporation, to buy and subdivide a tract of land on Estero Island, a short distance from Fort Myers, Florida. The corporation purchased the tract for $150,000 and spent about $30,500 on improvements. Before closing the purchase, the taxpayers submitted plans to the Federal Housing Authority to obtain FHA-guaranteed financing for a subdivision and a hotel. Later, they learned that they could not meet FHA standards unless they made costly improvements to raise the ground level of the island a minimum of four or five feet and to build a sea-wall. They attempted to find private financing to construct a hotel on the site but were unsuccessful. In December 1950 the corporation began selling lots, and during the following months it sold about one-third of the land. In May 1950 Waltman, the principal shareholder, announced that because of his wife's poor health he would have to go to another climate for a considerable period of time and that he was considering a permanent move to another area; the Waltmans spent the summer of 1951 in Colorado because of Mrs. Waltman's poor health. In October 1951 five of the shareholders, who were directors and owners of fifty per cent of the stock, sold their stock to the corporation. After the withdrawal of these shareholders Waltman owned five-sixths of the stock and Kelley one-sixth. The following month a syndicate offered to buy all of the land still owned by the corporation. Waltman and Kelley decided to sell. Accordingly, they transferred the stock to the purchasers for $192,666 and liquidated the corporation.

The taxpayers made three contentions before the Tax Court: (1) that they did not at any time have any intention of forming or availing of the corporation with a view of collapsing it. (2) that they sold their stock in 1952 as a result of circumstances arising after the purchase and development of the corporation and therefore, under Regulation [341-2(a)(3)], [§341] is inap-

of the total net income it might expect to derive from its property. The Tax Court held that the definition of a collapsible corporation looks to the income already realized and that one-third is a substantial part; that Island Shores, therefore, was not a collapsible corporation in 1952. We agree. Unfortunately, this result falls short of accomplishing the full objective of the statute[8] but, required to choose between two possible constructions, we feel compelled to give effect to the one that more naturally conveys the ordinary meaning of the words as they are written in the statute.

I

The collapsible corporation is a brain child of resourceful tax advisors to the motion picture and the construction industries. By using corporate trappings tax-payers, before 1950, were able to cloak a single venture or short-term project with the appearance of a long-term investment; for example, a corporation would be organized to produce a single picture, the director and actors would receive stock instead of salaries, and the stock would be sold or the corporation liquidated as soon as the picture was made. Congressional committee reports describe the collapsible corporation as "a device whereby one or more individuals attempt to convert the profits from their participation in a project from income taxable at ordinary rates [20 per cent to 91 per cent for individuals and from 30 per cent to 52 per cent for corporations] to a long-term capital gain taxable only at a rate of 25 per cent".[10]

---

plicable; (3) that the corporation is not within the statutory definition of a collapsible corporation. The Tax Court found it unnecessary to decide the first two contentions as do we.

[8]Commentators usually condemn the section. Two well-known authorities write, for example: "Section [341] is a patchwork of interlaced problems of interpretations. For recurring obscurities of meaning it is hard to surpass. Neither well conceived nor well drafted, it is replete with vague concepts and obscure or faulty phraseology". DeWind and Anthoine, Collapsible Corporations, 56 Col. L. Rev. 475, 534 (1956). But as the court observed in Levenson v. United States, D.C.N.D. Ala. 1957, 157 F. Supp. 244, 250: "It ill becomes this court to criticize the language employed by the Congress in drafting a Revenue Act. It is quite easy to observe after the event has occurred that in lieu of 'substantial' the Congress might have employed a percentage to express its true meaning. However, this court has been impressed time and again more often with the excellence of legislative draftsmanship than with its deficiencies."

[10]H. Rep. No. 2319, 81st Cong., 2d Sess. 96 (1950-2 Cum. Bull. 380, 449); S. Rep. No. 2375, 81st Cong., 2d Sess., 88 (1950-2 Cum. Bull. 483, 546); 1950 U.S. Code Cong. Serv. pp. 3099, 3145, 3232. See similar statements in President Truman's message to Congress, January 23, 1950, H. Doc. No. 451; Hearings before Committee on Ways and Means on Revenue Revision of 1950, 81st Cong., 2d Sess. 2, 5 (1950); and see the statement of Secretary Snyder, id., at 7, 20. See particularly Honaker Drilling, Inc. v. Koehler, D.C. Kan. 1960, 190 F. Supp. 287, 292.

As originally conceived, the device called for the formation of a temporary corporation to construct or to produce one property. The stockholders, after holding the stock more than six months but before the corporation realized any considerable income, would sell their stock taking a long-term capital gain. The purchaser could then liquidate the corporation at no tax cost to him, taking as a basis for the corporate property the price he paid for the stock. If instead of selling their stock, the shareholders liquidated the corporation, a subsequent sale of the property acquired resulted in no additional tax because the basis of the property in the shareholders' hands was the fair market value at the time of distribution. Taking advantage of this loophole in the tax laws, prior to 1950, it was not uncommon for taxpayers to form a corporation to produce a single motion picture. After completing the picture, but before realizing any income, the incorporators would liquidate the corporation or sell their stock. In exchange for their stock the shareholders would receive undivided interests in the assets, and pay a capital gains tax on the

The problem before Congress was how to prevent taxpayers' conversion of ordinary income into capital gain through the use and abuse of the corporate form. Congress attacked the problem on the shareholder level, not on the corporate level; Section [341] defines a collapsible corporation and denies long-term capital gain treatment when the shareholders sell their stock in such a corporation or liquidate the corporation. The policy of the law is to require realization of income at the corporate level but to visit the sins of collapsibility on the shareholders by converting all of their gain into ordinary income. The resulting uncertainty over the meaning of Section [341] makes the solution somewhat less than wholly successful.

As the Commissioner sees it, the test of collapsibility is whether a substantial part of the total net income remains to be realized *after* the date of the taxpayers' sale of stock. Here, according to the Commissioner, since two-thirds of Island Shores' income had not been realized, the sale occurred "prior to the realization by the corporation of a substantial part of the total net income to be realized". According to the taxpayers, one-third is a substantial part and since they sold their stock *after* a substantial part of the total net income had been realized the sale did not occur prior to the realization of a substantial part. The grit in the oil is that *a* substantial part has already been realized, but *a* substantial part remains to be realized, leaving "plenty of life in the collapsible corporation device".[12]

For authority, the Commissioner relies on two cases: Abbott v. Commissioner, 3 Cir., 1958, 258 F.2d 537, affirming 1957, 28 T.C. 795 and Payne v. Commissioner, 5 Cir., 1959, 268 F.2d 617, affirming 1958, 30 T.C. 1044.

In *Abbott*, 258 F.2d 537, 542, the Court said:

> "Petitioners make a final contention that Leland was not a collapsible corporation because it had already realized a 'substantial part' of the net income to be derived from the property. The corporation realized $23,472.75 profit from the sale of land in 1949. Petitioners' profit on liquidation was $191,876.45, or a total profit of $215,349.20. It is argued that the profit in 1949 is 10.84% of the total profit and was therefore a 'substantial part' of it."
>
> "The real question posed by the statute, however, is not whether a substantial part of the total profit was realized prior to dissolution, but rather whether that part of the total profit realized *after* dissolution was substantial. This was the test correctly applied by the Tax Court in making its finding that the dissolution took place before a substantial part (nearly 90%) of the total profit was realized."

The Third Circuit's interpretation of the Tax Court's decision in *Abbott* was a surprise to the majority of the Tax Court in the instant case.[13] Judge Kern, writing

---

difference between the cost of the stock and the fair market value of their undivided interests in the property at the time of liquidation. The entire proceeds from distributing the motion picture would be treated as a tax free return of capital. The same tax-saving device was often used by building contractors in the construction of a subdivision or a large apartment house.

[12]Bittker, Federal Income Taxation of Corporations and Shareholders 307 (1959).

[13]It was a surprise to most of the legal commentators. "This [the court's approach in *Abbott*] is an approach for which no precedent exists. Legislative history [Sen. Rep. No. 7375, 81st Cong. 2d Sess. 89 (1950) and H. R. Rep. No. 2319, 81st Cong. 2d Sess. 97 (1950)], the statute itself, the

for the majority, pointed out, in a carefully reasoned opinion: "With all due deference to the Court of Appeals for the Third Circuit, we were not aware that we made the finding and applied the test referred to in the above question." Judge Kern said that in *Abbott* the Tax Court simply held, inferentially, that 10.8 per cent, already realized at the date of liquidation, was not a substantial part:[14]

> "[In *Abbott*] we were concerned with the question of whether 'only the property actually sold by the corporation can be regarded as giving rise to the income from the transaction' or whether the enhancements in value to the property arising from commitments made by the corporation but carried out by the stockholders after its dissolution could also be considered. Having resolved this question, we found as a conclusion of fact that '[w]hen Leland [the corporation] distributed the land to petitioners [the stockholders], it had not realized a substantial part of the net income to be derived from the property.' In that case the 'part of the net income to be derived from the property' which had been realized by Leland at the time of its dissolution was approximately 10 per cent of such income. Therefore, we inferentially held in that case that 10 per cent of the net income to be derived from the property was not a substantial part thereof." 1960, 32 T.C. 135.

Expressly rejecting the view imputed to it,[15] the Tax Court found that "the question

---

Regulations [Reg. §1.341-5(c)(2)], and existing case law all indicate that the 'substantial realization' referred to in the collapsible definition must take place at the corporate level." Weithorn, Collapsible Corporations: 1960 Status, 19 N.Y.U. Tax Inst. 593, 603 (1961). "In view of the attitude of the Service, the Congressional purpose, and the understanding of the tax bar, the *Abbott* case is shocking." Axelrad, Recent Developments in Collapsible Corporations, 36 Taxes 893, 895 (1958). "Until the appellate decision in *Abbott,* 3 Cir., 1958, 258 F.2d 537, nearly everyone had assumed, apparently, that a corporation would not meet the collapsible definition if, at the time of the sale or distribution, it had already realized a substantial part of the income expected to be derived from its property. This construction is the obvious one that would be derived from a reading of the statute, and there is nothing contrary in the Regulations or Congressional Committee Reports." Ryan, Payne, Kelley, Other Recent Cases, Add New Uncertainty to Collapsible Provisions, 12 Journ. of Taxation 71 (1960).

Informal rulings issued prior to the spring of 1956 interpreted "substantial part" as referring to the realized income. Axelrad, Tax Advantages and Pitfalls in Collapsible Corporations and Partnerships, 34 Taxes 841 (1956); Axelrad, Recent Developments in Collapsible Corporations, 36 Taxes 893 (1958). In the only clear reference in the Regulations, U.S. Treas. Reg. 111, §29.117-11 (1953), Example 4 refers to the sale of the stock at a date when the corporation "has realized" a substantial part of the net income to be derived from each of its productions except the last.

[14]Cf. "The court of appeals' statement that its test, that 'substantial part' refers to the unrealized portion, was applied by the Tax Court is questionable. The Tax Court's view that a substantial part had not been realized is fully consistent with the conclusion that 10.84 per cent was not itself substantial. . . ."Axelrad, Recent Developments in Collapsible Corporations, 36 Taxes 893, 895 (1958). "The result in [*Abbott*] where only 10 per cent of the profit was realized before liquidation can be easily defended; but it is difficult to find support in the statute for its theory that a substantial amount of *unrealized* income is fatal." Bittker, Federal Income Taxation of Corporations and Shareholders 306 (1959).

[15]Five judges on the Tax Court dissented. Judge Opper, author of the dissenting opinion in *Kelley,* wrote the Tax Court opinion in *Abbott.* In his short dissenting opinion in *Kelley,* Judge Opper said: "[T]he only appellate court which has spoken, clearly views the critical words as meaning the opposite of what is now being accepted. Abbott v. Commissioner, (C.A. 3) 258 F.2d 537, affirming 28 T.C. 795. And this was not a reversal of a Tax Court opinion but its affirmance. Cf. Arthur L. Lawrence, 27 T.C. 713, revd. (C.A. 9) 258 F.2d 562." The dissent relies on the

to be decided is whether the *realized* income is a substantial part of the net income to be derived.[16] . . . [T]here may be two (or more) substantial parts of a whole, and therefore a finding that the unrealized part of such net income is substantial does not preclude a finding that the realized part of such net income is substantial".

The Commission relies also on certain language of this Court in Payne v. Commissioner, 5 Cir., 1959, 268 F.2d 617, 622, affirming 1958, 30 T.C. 1044. We there stated that "the Tax Court could properly find on the record that a substantial part of the income of the corporations remained to be realized over the 35 remaining years of their expected life".[17] The questions before us in *Payne* are not before us here. The basic question there was whether the plan of stock redemption had been established at the time the corporation was formed; there was no consideration of the question here presented. The taxpayers and the Commissioner took it for granted that the corporation would not be deemed collapsible unless the distribution was made before the corporation had realized any substantial portion of its income, and the Tax Court decision was based on the finding that no substantial portion of income had been realized. Although the language of the *Payne* opinion when taken by itself may tend to suggest the interpretation of the statutory phrase "a substantial part" here urged by the Commissioner, its more natural meaning when viewed in context is that it was intended simply to affirm the findings of the Tax Court, that the earnings of the corporation at the time of the distribution did not constitute "a substantial part". In short, neither *Payne* nor *Abbott* is controlling here.

In Levenson v. United States, D.C. Ala. 1957, 157 F. Supp. 244, the only case in which the interpretation of "a substantial part" was clearly posed for decision, the district court looked to the already realized portion of the income as determinative of the question. In *Levenson* a corporation was formed in July 1953 to carry on a business conducted by a partnership. The partnership assigned to the corporation a contract to purchase 3,495 trailers. By February 15, 1954, the corporation had sold 1,795 trailers, thereby realizing 51.37 per cent of the entire net income to be derived from the 3,495 trailers. February 15, 1954, the taxpayers sold all their stock, and four days later the buyers liquidated the corporation. The court concluded that the 51.37 per cent already realized constituted a substantial part of the net income to be derived from all of the corporate property and, accordingly, held that the corporation was not collapsible. *Levenson,* therefore, plugs the loophole just about halfway. The Commissioner did not appeal.

---

general legislative purpose to preclude transformation of "substantial" amounts of ordinary income into capital gains. The dissent also questions whether the legislative purpose can be fulfilled if anything less than fifty per cent of the total net income should be considered as being a substantial part of the whole.

[16]Judge Kern cited Rose Sidney, 1958, 30 T.C. 1155, affirmed 2 Cir. 1960, 273 F.2d 928, in which the Tax Court said: "In determining what is 'a substantial part of the net income to be derived from such property' we must consider the relationship between net income realized prior to the corporations to the distributions and the whole of the net income which may be reasonably anticipated to be derived from such property."

[17]If this statement in *Payne* is to be taken as literally as the Commissioner takes it, a corporation would be collapsible even though it had realized all the total net income to be derived from its property. This is contrary to the Regulations, which treat the *actual* realization, not the *intended* realization as controlling. See Rev. Rul. 58-241, 1958-1 CB 179; Rev. Rul. 56-104, 1956-1 CB 178; Rev. Rul. 56-50, 1956-1 CB 174; Reg. §1.341-2(a)(4) and Reg. §1.341-5(c)(2).

The weakness in the Commissioner's argument is the assumption that there can be only one substantial part of a whole. There is no logical or legal basis for this assumption. There were certainly two substantial parts of a whole in *Levenson*. Unquestionably there would be two substantial parts if each were fifty per cent of the whole. The brief for the Commissioner states: "Specifically, the issue is whether this two-thirds portion constituted *the* 'substantial part of the net income to be derived from the property'." But Section [341] does not use the definite article "the" in referring to "substantial part". The statute does not require that *the* substantial part be realized or that substantially all of the total income be realized or that the part unrealized be insubstantial in relation to the part realized, in order for a corporation to escape collapsibility. It is necessary to read some such language into the statute in order to construe Section [341] as the Commissioner would have us construe it. Section [341] requires only that "*a* substantial part" be realized. The indefinite article "a" says in plain language that there may be two or more substantial parts.[18] Accepting the statute at its face value — what Congress said, not necessarily what Congress might have intended to say if this case had been presented as a specific problem for legislative resolution — when the first "substantial part" is realized, the statutory requirement is met, and it is immaterial that another substantial part remains to be realized. Mr. Justice Holmes succinctly stated the limits of judicial inquiry in such a case: "We do not inquire what the legislature meant; we ask only what the statute means." Holmes, Collected Legal Papers 207 (1920).

Courts are not captives of grammars and dictionaries. Neither are they free to ignore common usage and dictionary-tested meaning — especially in the field of tax legislation, where the necessities of the subject require technically exact language and certainty of meaning.

Still, a statutory provision must be construed in context and in harmony with the statutory purpose. There is nothing in the legislative history or in the factual setting that produced Section [341] to indicate that Congress designed the law to penalize the reasonable use of the corporate form of enterprise. The problem Congress faced was *not only* "how to prevent avoidance of ordinary tax rates by the use of the corporate vehicle but also how to do so without changing the basic scheme of corporate-shareholder taxation and without introducing excessively intricate statutory provisions". Congress was aiming at abuse of the corporate entity. The committee reports show that Section [341] was adopted in the light of problems raised by "one shot" motion pictures and one-project building corporations when stock in

---

[18]"In Webster's New International Dictionary, published in 1926, *a* is defined as 'one or any — without special emphasis on the number.' The letter *A* was derived from Anglo-Saxon *an*, 'one,' the same word as the numeral. For a long time it was used as *an* 'one,' but for reasons of euphony it lost the *n* before words beginning with the consonant sound. Gradually it lost its definite meaning of 'one' and became indefinite. It is now known as one of the indefinite articles, which may signify 'one' or 'any'. The word *any*, meaning one indifferently out of a number, goes back to Anglo-Saxon *aenig*, a variation of *an*. . . . More often *a* has the indefinite meaning, although it did originally mean 'one'" Bryant, English in the Law Courts 39 (1926). See also the definition of "one" in Partridge, Word Origins 451 (1958). Webster's New International Dictionary (1957) defined "a" as "one" or "any." The Oxford English Dictionary (1933) defines "a" as "one, same, any: the oneness or indefiniteness, being implied rather than asserted."

such corporations was sold or the corporation was dissolved, as described in Senate Report 2375, before "any" income was realized.

The legislative approach to taxing capital gains has not been distinguished for clarity or consistency. From time to time some have questioned the policy and the whole tax treatment of capital gains. Nevertheless, since 1921 our tax scheme has embraced the principle that a capital gain is not really income; that the gain from the sale of stock is a capital gain, not ordinary income. The concept of a collapsible corporation is an exception to that principle aimed at a particularly outrageous example of taxpayers' overreaching of which the instant case is not characteristic. Such an exception is in derogation of the general rule governing the sale of capital assets. The "all-or-nothing" approach of Section [341] has, in fact, certain penal implications: here, for example, there is surely some part of the gain that is properly a capital gain. It seems to us, therefore, that a court should not give such an exception a broad-brush interpretation based on, first, the court's finding that Congress intended to plug the loophole more tightly than Congress said it was plugging the loophole, then, the court's supplying appropriate verbiage in the name of legislative intent.

The effect of our holding is to leave the loophole two-thirds open to these taxpayers.[21] Section [341] as we feel we should construe it, seems therefore a poor sort of tool for plugging loopholes. But the best workman can work only with the tools he has. If Congress wants a better job done, Congress should provide a tool that will not just plug the loophole "a substantial part of the way".

II

The next step is to determine what amount constitutes a "substantial" realization. The committee reports and the statute do not hint at the definition of this term. Nor is resort to other areas satisfactory. We think that the term is a relative one. Without reading too much into the silence of Congress, it seems to us that if the test were to be mechanically applied by the use of an arbitrary percentage, Congress would have phrased the statute in terms of a percentage of the income. Not having done so, the recurring question must be resolved on the facts of each case, giving weight to the findings of the Tax Court. We have no litmus-paper test. The ordinary dictionary meaning of "substantial" is: "Considerable, in amount, value or the like; large, as a *substantial* gain" (Webster's New International Dictionary (2d Ed. unabridged 1958)); "of ample or considerable amount, quantity or dimension" (Oxford English Dictionary 1933). We agree with the Tax Court that, giving the word "substantial" its ordinary meaning, one-third constitutes a substantial part.

In summary, we hold that the term "a substantial part" in Section [341(b)(1) (A)] . . . refers to the realized, not to the unrealized, portion of the income; we hold that the one-third already realized constitutes "a substantial part" of the total net income to be derived from the property by the corporation. We affirm the decision

[21]"In private rulings the Commission has until recently followed the informal rule that, if at least 50% of the total taxable income of the property had been realized, then a 'substantial' part will be deemed to have been realized. . . ." 3B Mertens, Law of Federal Income Taxation, c. 22 p. 256 (1958). This of course is only one-sixth more than the part considered substantial in the instant case.

of the Tax Court that Island Shores, Inc., was not a collapsible corporation in 1952. The opinion of the Tax Court is hereby

Affirmed.

RIVES, Circuit Judge (dissenting). Faced with the choice of one of two conflicting meanings of Section [341], I would say that "a substantial part" has reference to the part not yet realized. That construction would carry out the overriding legislative purpose, which was to prevent transformation of ordinary income into capital gain. To concur with the majority in this case, I would have to think that Congress did not intend to close a loophole, but intended to close it only a part of the way, and to leave the loophole two-thirds open to taxpayers bent on saving taxes by the use of collapsible corporations. I cannot conceive that, in its enactment of a corrective statute, Congress intended to leave such a gaping loophole. We should adopt a rule of statutory interpretation which strikes more directly at the evil at which Congress aimed. I therefore respectfully dissent.

NOTE

Judge Wisdom states that §341 was intended to "prevent taxpayers' conversion of ordinary income into capital gain" (page 261 supra). If so, why was "substantial part" added to the statute? If Congress was concerned about the conversion of ordinary income, does it make sense to allow the taxpayer an "out" after only one third of the corporation's income has been realized?

Could Congress have meant that the corporate form would not be recognized if its only purpose was to give the taxpayer a capital gain? Might the presumption of this purpose be rebutted if the corporation had itself realized a "substantial part" of its income and had paid a tax thereon? At what point can a taxpayer be said to have sufficiently "used" the corporation for purposes other than to avoid ordinary income at the shareholder level?

Would §341 be necessary if the Government had won *General Utilities,* page 5 supra, and if §§311 and 336 had not been enacted? See J. Lewis, A Proposed New Treatment for Corporate Distributions and Sales in Liquidation, 3 Tax Revision Compendium 1643 (House Ways and Means Comm. 1959); see also Note 7, page 19 supra.

HEFT v. COMMISSIONER
294 F.2d 795 (5th Cir. 1961)

Before RIVES, CAMERON, and WISDOM, Circuit Judges.

WISDOM, Circuit Judge. The tax question for decision in this case has to do with collapsible corporations. The taxpayers, Mr. and Mrs. G. A. Heft, on their joint returns for 1952, reported long-term capital gains representing liquidation distributions from the Gulf Construction Corporation, a company wholly owned by the Hefts. The Commissioner determined that the corporation was "collapsible" under

Section [341]. . . . Accordingly, he treated the gains as ordinary income and assessed a deficiency against the taxpayers. The Tax Court sustained the Commissioner's determination. We agree.

The facts are stipulated. In 1949 G. A. Heft organized the Gulf Construction Corporation, a Louisiana corporation, and acquired all its stock for $1,000. The corporation purchased 53 unimproved lots in September 1950 and constructed a single family dwelling on each lot. Mr. Heft expected to sell each house and lot for about $7,825 to $8,800. Gulf sold sixteen of these properties before January 21, 1952. On that date the directors commenced voluntary liquidation proceedings. On the same day, Mr. Heft, as liquidator, transferred to himself 26 of the remaining properties. As liquidator, he sold the other eleven properties during the next four months. He completed liquidation October 31, 1952, by transferring to himself $11,715.61 in cash.

Under Section [341] a shareholder is taxed at ordinary income rates on gain from the sale or exchange or liquidation of stock of a collapsible corporation. The section defines a "collapsible corporation" as one "formed or availed of principally for the . . . construction . . . of property . . . with a view to [(A)] the sale or exchange of stock by its shareholders (whether in liquidation or otherwise), or a distribution to its shareholders, prior to the realization by the corporation . . . of a substantial part of the net income to be derived from such property, and [(B)] the realization by such shareholders of gain attributable to such property." It is undisputed that Gulf was "formed or availed of principally for the . . . construction . . . of property . . . with a view to" the distributions which took place. The parties agree that this case hinges on whether those distributions occurred "prior to the realization by the corporation . . . of a substantial part of the net income to be derived from such property." It is agreed that the total net income "to be derived" from the properties was $45,700. By January 21, 1952, the date of the first distribution, the corporation had realized $7,797 profit, or 17.07 per cent of the total;[2] before the final liquidation in October the corporation had realized a cumulative profit of $23,308, or 51 per cent of the total.

I

The taxpayer contends that the $7,797 profit, 17.07 per cent of the total, earned before the initial distribution was a "substantial part" of the total net income of the corporation; that selling 16 properties before liquidation removed any stigma of collapsibility.

This case requires the application of an uncertain general standard to certain, particular facts. In this Court's recent decision in Commissioner v. Kelley, August 2, 1961, 5 Cir., 293 F.2d 904, affirming the Tax Court's holding that 33 per cent was "substantial", we pointed out that "the ordinary dictionary meaning of 'substantial' is: 'Considerable, in amount, value or the like; large, as a *substantial* gain' (Webster's New International Dictionary (2d Ed. unabridged 1958)); 'of ample or considerable amount, quantity or dimension' (Oxford English Dictionary 1933)." We concluded

[2]The profit from the sales of the 16 properties was $5,092.54, or 12.86 per cent. The income from the net rent was $2,704.03. The two amount to 17.07 per cent of the total net income of $45,700 expected to be realized from the properties.

that the term "substantial" is a relative one. Its meaning rests on an implied comparison between the described subject and a larger unit, just as the expression "a substantial saving," suggests that the saving is "substantial" in comparison with the value of the item purchased. In contrast to a fixed relative term, such as twenty per cent, expressing the same proportional relationship in every context, "substantial" may indicate a certain proportion in one instance, a different proportion in another. To ascertain its meaning in any particular context one must examine the frame of reference and the purpose intended by use of the term. The taxpayers have referred to several decisions holding that portions smaller than seventeen per cent are "substantial." In none of those cases does the term "substantial" appear in the tax context in which it must be considered here.

The purpose of Section [341] is to prevent taxpayers from utilizing the corporate form as a "device whereby one or more individuals attempt to convert the profits from their participation in a project from income taxable at ordinary rates to long-term capital gain taxable only at a rate of 25 percent." See Commissioner v. Kelley. Section [341] is directed at curtailing use of this loophole. By its terms, however, it does not apply if the owners hold their stock until after a "substantial" part of the corporation's income has been realized. This restriction enables taxpayers to continue to bring a considerable part of the corporation's ordinary income through the hole in the fence to the greener pasture of capital gains treatment. In spite of the large hole in the fence, the purpose of Congress to prevent abuse of the favored treatment accorded capital gains is clear, and the statutory terms should be construed to promote that purpose. Undoubtedly seventeen per cent could in many contexts constitute a "substantial" portion, but this result is not demanded by the inherent meaning of the term, and a larger portion may appropriately be required in order to satisfy the statutory standard. The ease with which the statutory purpose might otherwise be avoided presents a strong reason for giving the term a broad rather than a narrow meaning. Considering this statutory purpose and giving weight, as we should, to the findings of the Tax Court, we hold that one-sixth of the total net income to be derived from property does not constitute a "substantial part" for purposes of determining collapsibility.

II

The taxpayers contend that even if the seventeen per cent profits earned before January 21, 1952 are not considered a "substantial part of the net income" of the corporation, Section [341] does not apply. This is on the ground that the corporation continued operations after the initial distribution and, before its termination, realized over fifty per cent of its income and paid taxes thereon. If the corporation had withheld the initial distribution until its final liquidation in October, Section [341] would not have applied. Petitioners contend that "it is the fact of realization by the corporation and not the time thereof that is important."

Unfortunately for the petitioners, the statute focuses on the timing of the transactions: the corporation is collapsible, if the exchange of stock occurs "*prior to* the realization"; the corporation must realize a "substantial part of its net income" *before* the stockholders sell or exchange their stock. The collapsibility of the corporation is determined, therefore, when the shareholders first sell or exchange stock in the corporation. Since the test is embodied in the definition of "collapsible corporation" and the statute applies indiscriminately to any gain from the sale or exchange of stock in a collapsible corporation, if an initial liquidating distribution falls within the statute all subsequent distributions also come within the ambit of the statute irrespective of whether at the time of a later distribution the corporation has earned a substantial part of its income.[6]

It may well be that shareholders who liquidate their corporation by a series of distributions may be caught under Section [341] even though most or even all of the corporation's income is eventually realized by the corporation and taxed to it, whereas by waiting until a substantial part of the income has been realized they could have avoided Section [341] and yet have acquired a major part of the corporation's property without the income attributable to it being taxed to the corporation. However, the statute is not directed at the avoidance of *corporate* income taxes. Section [341] is aimed at preventing taxpayers using a corporation to avoid individual stockholder gains from stock sales or corporate distributions from being accorded capital gain treatment. These are separate problems. Even if Section [341] applied except when one hundred per cent of the income was realized by the corporation, this would not entirely close the personal tax loophole; the corporate tax added to a capital gains tax could still be less than the regular income tax at a high bracket. To screen out the most flagrant cases abusing the favored capital gains treatment accorded to sales or exchanges of stock, Congress selected a test based on the sequence of transactions rather than a test geared to the amount of tax paid by the corporation. Under the chosen test, the statute unmistakably applies to the taxpayers in this case.

Judgment is
Affirmed.

CAMERON, Circuit Judge, concurs in the result.

RIVES, Circuit Judge (concurring specially). As stated in a brief dissent in Commissioner v. Kelley, 5 Cir., 1961, 293 F.2d 904, 914, I hold the opinion that "a substantial part," as used in Section [341] should be construed to have reference to the part not yet realized. If that is the true construction of Section [341], then it is clear that the decision of the Tax Court in the present case should be affirmed. If, however, the majority opinion in Commissioner v. Kelley, supra, is accepted, then I would still think that the decision of the Tax Court in the present case should be affirmed, but, in that event, for the reasons so well expressed in the opinion in this case by Judge Wisdom. I therefore concur specially.

NOTE

1. The same court decided both *Kelley* and *Heft*. Does the majority's reading of the statute or Judge Rives' reading more faithfully carry forward the statutory

[6]Petitioner argued that under Louisiana law the distribution did not occur until the later date when it was completed. The time of distribution, however, is governed by federal rather than state law, and the distribution was legally effective when made.

scheme? What criteria should a court use in determining whether "a substantial part" of the corporation's income has been realized?

2. See Taxation — Collapsible Corporations — Judicial Interpretation of "Substantial" Part of Net Income, 8 N.Y. Law Forum 544 (1962); W. Ryan, Prior Realization of ⅓ of Income Avoids Collapsibility, CA-5 Holds in *Kelley,* 15 J. Taxation 246 (1961).

3. *The Requisite "View"*

GLICKMAN v. COMMISSIONER
256 F.2d 108 (2d Cir. 1958)

Before CLARK, Chief Judge, and SWAN and LUMBARD, Circuit Judges.

SWAN, Circuit Judge. This petition involves deficiencies in income taxes for the calendar year 1950 of three taxpayers, Arthur, Herman and Aaron Glickman. . . .

The issue presented is whether gains realized by each of the taxpayers in 1950 are properly taxable as capital gains, as they claim, or as ordinary income, as the Tax Court held in reliance upon §117(m) of the Internal Revenue Code of 1939, as amended by §212 of the Revenue Act of 1950, 26 U.S.C.A. §117(m), which relates to "collapsible corporations."* The findings of fact and opinion of the Tax Court are reported in T.C. Memo. 1957-124.

The facts may be summarized as follows: In February 1949 the taxpayers organized a New York corporation (for brevity hereafter referred to as Mott) for the purpose of constructing an apartment project to be financed by a mortgage loan insured by the Federal Housing Administration (F.H.A.) pursuant to §608 of the National Housing Act, 12 U.S.C.A. §1743. Mott acquired vacant land in Far Rockaway, New York, at a cost of $59,000. F.H.A. issued a commitment to insure a mortgage loan to Mott, as intended mortgagee, not to exceed in amount $1,066,500 for the construction of a 126 family apartment project to be known as Bayswater Gardens. Mott obtained the money from the Manhattan Company, and the apartment project was constructed for $55,400 less than the insured mortgage loan. From the time of Mott's incorporation until the taxpayers sold their shares as hereafter mentioned, the taxpayers were the only common stockholders and the only officers and directors of Mott. In January 1950 the directors resolved to write up the value of the corporate property, so as to create a capital surplus on its books, and on January 13 Mott distributed $55,000 in cash to its common stockholders. In the distribution Arthur and Aaron received $13,750 each, and Herman $27,500. The cost basis of their stock was $500 each for Arthur and Aaron, and $1,000 for Herman. All three sold their common shares on August 1, 1950, pursuant to their May 10th contract to sell, at a price which gave Arthur and Aaron $23,411.70 each, and Herman $46,823.39. Mott was not liquidated and its present shareholders operate the project pursuant to

*Section 341 is the 1954 Code successor to §117(m) of the 1939 Code. — ED.

F.H.A. regulations and the terms of the mortgage between Mott and the Manhattan Company.

In reaching its decision that the gains realized by the taxpayers, from the cash distribution by Mott and from the sale of their stock should be taxed as ordinary income pursuant to §117(m), the Tax Court relied upon two of its own prior decisions, Burge v. Commissioner, 28 T.C. 246, and Weil v. Commissioner, 25 T.C. 809. It considered the *Glickman* cases indistinguishable from *Burge* in all material respects. *Burge* was subsequently affirmed by the Fourth Circuit, 253 F.2d 765, Judge Parker writing for the court. We are in entire agreement with Judge Parker's opinion. The *Weil* decision was affirmed by the Second Circuit in 252 F.2d 805. These two cases obviate the necessity of lengthy discussion of the petitioners' various contentions which assert that the Tax Court erred in holding Mott to be a "collapsible corporation," as defined in §117(m).[2]

One of the petitioners' contentions, Point VI of their brief, is that Mott was not a collapsible corporation "because it was not a temporary corporation used to convert ordinary income into capital gain." In support of this contention they refer to the legislative history of the section. It is true that in the discussion of the evils which the statute was intended to prevent, there is frequent mention of cases where liquidation of the corporation occurred; but, as stated by Judge Parker [253 F.2d 769], "it is clear from the committee reports that it was not intended that the legislation be limited to such cases and the act as passed in not so limited." We agree. The statute expressly refutes the idea that the corporate life must be cut short; it taxes "Gain from the sale or exchange (*whether in liquidation or otherwise*) of stock . . . ." [Emphasis added.]

In Point IV of their brief the petitioners argue that §117(m) does not apply to the cash distribution received by them on January 13, 1950. . . .

The Tax Court found that the taxpayers' intention to make the cash distribution was formed about January 1, 1950. The petitioners contend that this was too late. They argue that the requisite "view" must exist when the corporation is formed or at least when construction is begun. We agree with Judge Parker's statement in *Burge:* "It is not necessary that the 'view' exist when the corporation is formed. It is sufficient that it exist when the corporation is 'availed of' . . . ." Since the corporation may at any time during its corporate life be "availed of" for the proscribed purpose, subject, of course, to the limitations imposed by §117(m)(3), it seems surprising that the Regulations have adopted a narrower interpretation of the statute, and require the requisite view to exist "during the construction . . ." or to be "at-

---

[2]§117(m)(2)(A) defines the term as follows:

"(2) *Definitions.* —

"(A) For the purposes of this subsection, the term 'collapsible corporation' means a corporation formed or availed of principally for the manufacture, construction, or production of property, . . . or for the holding of stock in a corporation so formed or availed of, with a view to —

"(i) the sale or exchange of stock by its shareholders (whether in liquidation or otherwise), or a distribution to its shareholders, prior to the realization by the corporation manufacturing, constructing, producing . . . the property of a substantial part of the net income to be derived from such property, and

"(ii) the realization by such shareholders of gain attributable to such property."

The applicable Regulation is too long to be quoted, Treasury Regulations 111, §29.117-11.

tributable" to "circumstances which reasonably could be anticipated by the time of such . . . construction."* We are disposed to disagree with so narrow an interpretation, but whether the Regulation is valid need not be determined now. The Tax Court assumed it to be valid, and this assumption, if wrong, was unduly favorable to the petitioners. The court then found that "construction was not completed until some time after the middle of January 1950."

This finding the petitioners say is erroneous because construction was "substantially" completed by December 7, 1949 when the municipal authorities issued their final certificate of occupancy. But we agree that under the correct interpretation of the statute "construction" should be defined technically to mean all construction required to perform the contract completely.[3] Concededly something remained to be done after January 1 to complete the buildings and landscape the grounds as required by the contract. Final inspection by the F.H.A. inspector was not made until January 17, 1950. As stated by the Tax Court in the *Weil* decision at page 815: "The statute is concerned with the realization of 'net income from the property.' It aims at a situation where before substantial part of that net income has been realized, the individual stockholders take action designed to result in capital gain."

The petitioners further contend that the gains recognized on the cash distribution and the sale of stock are not within §117(m) because at least 30% of those gains was attributable to appreciation on the value of the land "apart from building construction."[4] This is far too narrow an interpretation of the statute to be accepted. As to the cash distribution the Tax Court correctly held that all of it was directly attributable to the constructed property, since it was paid out of the funds advanced to Mott on the F.H.A. mortgage. The petitioners say that the Tax Court found as a fact that the "value of the land alone, at $1 per square foot, totaled $120,945." The entire statement from which the quotation is taken appears in the margin.[5] We think the petitioners have misinterpreted the court's statement. It made no finding that the land was worth $1 per square foot apart from the constructed building. Nor did Mott itself so treat the land value; its tax return for 1950 put down the land at cost, $59,000, and ascribed the increase in value of its property to "building fixtures and equipment."

The final contention asserts that even if the cash distribution is deemed to fall within §117(m) the gain on the stock sale is not taxable under that section. The petitioners concede that a literal reading of subdivision (2)(A) would support the Tax Court's result but urge that the distribution and the stock sale should be tested separately. We agree with the Tax Court's view that the cash distribution brought Mott within the statutory definition. The statute contains no provision relieving a corporation from its "collapsible" status once an event has occurred which brings it

---

*See Treas. Reg. §1.341-2(a)(3). — Ed.

[3]See discussion in Weil v. Commissioner, 28 T.C. 809.

[4]The 30% limitation is imposed by subdivision (3)(B) of §117(m).

[5]"Early in January 1950, in answer to Herman's inquiry his accountant reported that if a recognized appraisal showed that improvements made were worth more than cost, Mott could distribute cash to its shareholders. Herman requested that a real estate firm make an immediate appraisal which on January 10, 1950 valued the land and buildings at $1,249,431. The value of the land alone, at $1 per square foot, total $120,945."

within that definition. Although at first glance so literal an application might seem unfair, it is perfectly consistent with the purpose of the statute to tax as normal income all gains received before the realization of a substantial portion of the net income to be derived from the property. And if, subsequent to a condemned distribution, but prior to a stock sale, the corporation realizes a substantial part of the net income, a court should have no difficulty in holding §117(m) inapplicable to such transaction.*

We see no error in decision. It is affirmed.

NOTE

What is the purpose of the three-year period required in §341(d)(3)? If the requisite "view" has been formed before construction is completed, will the limitations of §341(d)(3) ever be available to the taxpayer? Is goodwill "property . . . manufactured, constructed, produced or purchased . . ." within the meaning of §341(d)(2)? If so, when is the production of goodwill completed for purposes of the three-year period in §341(d)(3)? See generally C. Nordberg, Jr., "Collapsible" Corporations and the "View," 40 Taxes 372 (1962).

COMMISSIONER v. LOWERY
335 F.2d 680 (3d Cir. 1964)

Before KALODNER, STALEY and HASTIE, Circuit Judges.

KALODNER, Circuit Judge. The issue presented is whether gains realized by the taxpayer in 1951 and 1952 from the sale of his stock in two corporations, Parkway House, Inc. ("Parkway") and Raleigh Construction Company ("Raleigh") were taxable as ordinary income pursuant to section [341] . . . , relating to collapsible corporations.

The stipulated facts, found by the Tax Court, may be summarized as follows:

Taxpayer's principal occupation is that of a "Builder". In 1949 he had been associated with E. J. Frankel ("Frankel") in the building of an apartment project in Collingswood, New Jersey. Frankel had supervised the actual construction of that project and taxpayer had arranged for the Federal Housing Administration ("FHA") commitment. Thereafter, in January, 1950, Frankel was instrumental in organizing Parkway for the purpose of constructing a luxury apartment house in Philadelphia, and because of his earlier successful association with taxpayer he permitted taxpayer to participate in this project. On October 18, 1950, taxpayer purchased for $750 a 30% interest in Parkway, receiving 75 shares of $10 par value stock out of the corporation's authorized capital of 250 shares. Parkway was initially financed by means of a conventional mortgage and taxpayer's special ability and knowledge with respect to FHA mortgages was not required.

---

*What is the significance of this sentence? Compare Part II of the opinion in *Heft*, page 268 supra. Which provides the more persuasive interpretation? Why? — ED.

After the actual construction of the project was approximately 50% completed, Frankel determined that certain improvements in the building were desirable, including complete air-conditioning. He advised taxpayer that the project would cost approximately $700,000 more than the invested capital and mortgage proceeds and an additional investment on the part of the shareholders would therefore be required. Taxpayer was not in a position to advance the additional funds, nor did he desire to do so. Frankel then informed taxpayer that he had contacted two people who were willing to advance a portion of the needed funds on the condition that they obtain an equity interest in the corporation. On August 29, 1951, at about the time the project was 50% complete, taxpayer sold his 75 shares in Parkway for $45,000. Frankel did not sell his interest in Parkway. On his 1951 income tax return taxpayer reported $44,250 gain on the sale of his stock as long-term capital gain.

About one month after the organization of Parkway, Raleigh was organized under the laws of New Jersey with an authorized capital of 100 shares of no par value common stock for the purpose of constructing the Warwick Apartments, another luxury apartment development. All of the authorized shares of Raleigh were issued for $10 per share as follows:

Shareholder	No. of Shares	Percent
S. J. Lowery	40	40
E. J. Frankel	40	40
Frank Steinberg	13	13
Nate Margolin	7	7

At the time of Raleigh's incorporation, the shareholders also organized a subsidiary corporation known as Raleigh, Inc., which owned the project (Warwick Apartments), and all the stock of Raleigh, Inc., was owned by Raleigh.

Taxpayer successfully undertook to obtain an FHA insurance commitment for this project. Construction loans totalling $2,489,000 were obtained from the Irving Trust Co. of New York, although, as a condition to advancing this sum, the shareholders were required to execute an FHA indemnity agreement of approximately $235,000 to insure compliance with the requirements of the building loan agreement. Construction of the project was begun in the early part of 1950 and it was substantially completed by July, 1951, at a cost of about $2,755,274. The excess cost over construction loans and invested capital was approximately $265,374.

Frankel advised the shareholders that because of the excess cost additional funds would be needed. Although the corporation attempted to secure additional bank loans, it was only successful in obtaining $100,000 from this source. Taxpayer thereupon advised Frankel that he was unable to advance any additional funds to the corporation.

Sometime in August of 1951, Frankel informed taxpayer that Morris Hassel ("Hassel") would be willing to advance the needed funds provided he received a substantial interest in Raleigh. After a meeting with Hassel, it was agreed that taxpayer would receive $151,500 for his shares.

On October 23, 1951, all the shareholders of Raleigh, including taxpayer, entered into an agreement the purpose of which was to give Frankel and Hassel each a 43% interest and Steinberg a 14% nonvoting interest. Hassel thereupon advanced $360,000 to the corporation and received a corporate note as security. On the same date taxpayer borrowed $140,000 from Raleigh at 4% interest, giving his 40 shares of stock as security. On January 31, 1952, Raleigh purchased taxpayer's shares for the $151,500 previously agreed to by cancelling the $140,000 loan and paying him $9,981.17, the difference between the agreed purchase price and the $140,000 loan together with interest of $1,518.83. Raleigh also agreed to indemnify taxpayer in case of any loss due to taxpayer's previous endorsement of the construction loans.

Taxpayer reported $149,981.17 gain on the sale of his stock in Raleigh in his 1952 return as long-term capital gain. At the time of the stock sale Raleigh and its wholly owned subsidiary, Raleigh, Inc., had realized gross income of approximately $300,000, of which more than $250,000 represented rental income from apartment leases, although the combined income tax return of the two corporations indicated a loss in excess of $100,000, more than $80,000 of which was attributable to depreciation.

Frankel retained his interest in Raleigh for more than three years.

The Tax Court found "Neither corporation was availed of 'with a view to' the action described in section [341(b)(1)], by those owning a majority of the stock and controlling its policies" and, that "Neither corporation was collapsible or was in fact ever collapsed." It held that "section [341] was not intended to apply where, as here, a minority stockholder is compelled, because of circumstances over which he had no control, to dispose of his investment in a corporation which is thereafter continued in operation by the majority stockholders", and "Accordingly, . . . neither Parkway nor Raleigh was a collapsible corporation within the meaning of section [341]," and thus the taxpayer had correctly reported his profits from the sale of his corporate stock holdings as capital gains. 39 T.C. 959, 969-970 (1963).

The Tax Court did not determine whether taxpayer, at the time he sold his stock, "did so 'with a view to' the action proscribed by section [341(b)(1)]," stating on that score that it was unnecessary to make such a determination "in view of our disposition of the issue relating to the sale of his stock . . . as a minority stockholder." 39 T.C. 970.

Section [341] was added to the revenue laws . . . to frustrate use of the "collapsible" corporation device to convert ordinary income into long-term capital gain.[3] It provides that gain from the sale or exchange of stock of a "collapsible" corporation, which, but for section [341] would be taxed as gain from the sale of a capital asset, must be taxed as ordinary income. The section defines a "collapsible" corporation as a corporation "formed or availed of" for the construction or production of property, or for the holding of stock in such a corporation, "with a view to" (1) the sale or exchange of stock by its owners, or a distribution to them, prior to the realization by the corporation of a substantial part of the net income to be derived from such property, and (2) the realization by such shareholders of gains attributable to

---

[3]Braunstein v. Commissioner, 374 U.S. 65, 71, 83 S. Ct. 1663, 10 L. Ed. 2d 757 (1963).

such property. The "view" with which a corporation is used must be a view entertained at the time of such use.[4]

In the instant case the Commissioner urges that the Tax Court erred both in considering the "view" of those controlling Parkway and Raleigh, and in failing to determine the "view" of the taxpayer.

He further contends (1) section [341] applies to any stockholder who owns ten per cent or more of the stock of a corporation and sells his shares, irrespective of whether he controls the policies of the corporation; (2) assuming arguendo (as the Tax Court held) that the statute is inapplicable to a selling stockholder who is not in a position to control the corporation's policies, that "the Tax Court erred in holding that taxpayer was not one of several selling shareholders who could collectively determine the policies of the corporation"; and (3) "the taxpayer must have had the 'view' required by the statute" since "he must have contemplated the mid-construction sale of his stock as one of the possible alternatives if the need for additional funds in fact materialized."

We find it unnecessary to discuss the Commissioner's contentions that the Tax Court premised its decision on the issue of corporate control and the "view" of those exercising such control and that it applied improper standards of law in reaching it. The Tax Court made the fact-finding that the taxpayer was compelled to sell because of circumstances beyond his control, and, since we cannot say that it was clearly erroneous, it precludes a finding that the taxpayer acted with the "view" proscribed by section [341(b)(1)].

We are of the opinion that section [341] contemplates a freedom of choice in reaching a decision to sell stock in determining whether a shareholder had the "view" proscribed by the section, and that where a sale is compelled by circumstances beyond control the "view" does not exist.

Our view is in accord with that recently expressed by the Second Circuit in Commissioner v. Solow, 333 F.2d 76, decided June 9, 1964. There the taxpayer, who with one Sarner shared equal ownership of stock of a corporation which was engaged in the construction of apartment houses, sold to Sarner when the latter threatened to ruin him unless he did so.

In affirming the Tax Court's decision that the corporation was not a collapsible one the Second Circuit said:

> ". . . it is clear the section does not contemplate a ruling that the necessary view may be present under circumstances where a shareholder, with no previous design or thought to sell his stock, reluctantly agrees to sell because he must. Where individual stockholder action, as opposed to action directed by the corporation itself, is sought to be used as a basis for characterizing a corporation collapsible as to the acting shareholder, that shareholder must at least have been possessed of some reasonable degree of free choice in determining whether to act. A shareholder suddenly ordered to sell under threat of financial ruin, by one reasonably in a position to make good on

[4]Jacobson v. Commissioner, 281 F.2d 703, 705 (3 Cir. 1960).

the threat, is certainly possessed of no greater degree of free choice than a shareholder who must sell because of sudden illness, see Shilowitz v. United States, 221 F. Supp. 179 (D.N.J. 1963), Temkin v. Commissioner, 35 T.C. 906 (1961), and he is possessed of even less freedom of choice than a shareholder who feels he is required to sell to obtain funds to cover the cost of separate business ventures which require financing, see Riley v. Commissioner, 35 T.C. 848 (1961)."

Like the taxpayer in *Solow* who was forced to dispose of his stock in order to avoid financial ruin, and the taxpayer in *Shilowitz* whose heart attack made sale of his corporate interest imperative, the taxpayer here was compelled to sell his stock by events beyond his control. His free choice in determining whether to retain or dispose of his shares was effectively foreclosed by the requirements of Parkway and Raleigh for additional capital investment. Thus, the "view to sale", required by section [341(b)(1)], was not present. Lacking that element, neither Parkway nor Raleigh could be deemed "collapsible".

For the reasons stated the decision of the Tax Court will be affirmed.

NOTE

1. Did the taxpayer in *Lowery* have another argument that he might have made? See Treas. Reg. §1.341-1. What is the significance of the reference in Treas. Reg. §1.341-1 to an "actual" sale or exchange of stock?

2. Ten men form Corporation X for the purpose of developing an industrial park. After two years of operations the property has appreciated greatly in value, but there still remains much land which can be developed profitably. Several of the shareholders want to diversify their holdings, however, and they suggest that X "go public" by having each of the ten shareholders sell 25 per cent of the stock each holds. If the stock is sold, what will be the tax consequences to the ten shareholders? Can such a result be avoided? See §§341(e) and (f).

Suppose a large, growth-minded corporation (Y) offers to purchase all the stock of X in exchange for its own voting stock. Assume such a transaction would come under §368(a)(1)(B), and thus no gain would be recognized to the shareholders of X under §354(a)(1). See Chapter 4 infra. Does this present a collapsible corporation loophole which should be redressed? Why? What will be the shareholders' tax consequences when they subsequently sell their Y stock? What will be Y's basis in its X stock? What will be Y's basis in the assets of X if it liquidates X under §332 promptly after acquisition? See §§334(b)(1), (2) and (3). When the shareholders dispose of their newly acquired Y stock, will they have capital gain or ordinary income? What must you know to answer this? If capital gain, does this present a §341 loophole? Why?

3. See R. Eifler, Recent Developments in Collapsible Corporations, 27 N.Y.U. Inst. on Fed. Tax. 857 (1969); F. Peel, Collapsible Corporations, 24 N.Y.U. Inst. on

Fed. Tax. 1179 (1966); D. Malouf and D. McLane, Collapsible Corporations — Section 341 of the Internal Revenue Code of 1954, 20 Sw. L.J. 748 (1966); W. Goldstein, Section 341(d) and (e) — A Journey into Never-Never Land, 10 Vill. L. Rev. 215 (1965); J. Hall, The Consenting Collapsible Corporation — Section 341(f) of the Internal Revenue Code of 1954, 12 U.C.L.A.L. Rev. 1365 (1965); B. Bittker and J. Eustice, Federal Income Taxation of Corporations and Shareholders 416-448 (2d ed. 1966).

3 | Incorporation of Assets

I. INTRODUCTION

Assume that Smith owns and operates a successful retail furniture business in unincorporated form. Assume, too, that his business assets are reflected below:

	Adjusted Basis	Fair Market Value
Cash	$ 20,000	$ 20,000
Inventory	150,000	190,000
Accounts Receivable	20,000	20,000
Fixed Assets	25,000	35,000
Goodwill	ZERO	50,000
	$215,000	$315,000

If Smith transfers those assets to a corporation in exchange for all of its authorized capital stock, his $100,000 gain (asset appreciation) will be "realized" (§1001(b)), but it will not be "recognized" (§351(a)). If Smith had effected the transfer prior to the Revenue Act of 1921, his gain would have been both "realized" and "recognized." Prior to that Act, therefore, his taxable income in the year of incorporation would have included the appreciation in the assets which he continued to own in corporate form. By the same process, if his assets had depreciated below their adjusted basis, his realized loss on incorporation prior to the Revenue Act of 1921 would have been recognized (absent a provision such as §267). The Revenue Act of 1921, as with all subsequent enactments inclusive of the current §351(a), provided for nonrecognition of the loss.

Section 351 and its predecessor provisions dating to 1921 are grounded on the thesis that taxation (or deduction of a loss) ought not to occur "where in a popular and economic sense there has been a mere change in the form of ownership and the taxpayer has not really 'cashed in' on the theoretical gain, or closed out a losing venture." Portland Oil Co. v. Commissioner, 109 F.2d 479, 488 (1st Cir. 1940). See also S. Rep. No. 275, 67th Cong., 1st Sess., 1939-1 Cum. Bull. (part 2), 181, 188-189. The thesis is so well accepted that even the depreciation recapture provisions of §§1245 and 1250 yield generally to the nonrecognition command of §351. See §§1245(b)(3) and 1250(d)(3).

Incorporation of the assets of sole proprietorships, partnerships and previously unaffiliated investors is a workaday occurrence in the world of commerce and for the lawyer. Usually the proposed incorporation transaction and §351 mesh well. Nonrecognition is the result. There are many situations, however, in which only painstaking care will bring a transaction within §351. In fewer, but nevertheless important, situations the tax lawyer wants to avoid §351; i.e., he wants recognition. Here it is his role to tailor the proposed transaction to escape the reach of §351. That section is not operative only when the taxpayer elects to have it apply, in contrast to provisions such as §§453 and 1033. If a transaction fits within §351, there is nonrecognition irrespective of the taxpayer's wishes. The language of the Code and Regulations and the history of their application present a host of intricate questions. This chapter will deal with a number of them.

Recognition (or not) of the transferor's gain is only one aspect of an incorporation transaction. If all the gain is recognized the transferor's basis for the stock he receives is its fair market value ("tax cost") under §1012. If §351 covers and provides for nonrecognition, the transferor's basis for his stock is determined under §358. The transferee corporation realizes no gain when it issues its stock for assets (§1032), but its basis for the assets received will be determined under §1012 if the transferor recognizes all his gain, and under §362(a) if he does not. If the transferor receives not only stock and securities but cash as well, he may have partial recognition. The measure of recognition and determination of basis for transferor and transferee become more complex in that case. By its terms §351 applies if the transferor receives "stock or securities" in exchange for his property. It is not always simple to resolve the question whether a debt instrument is a "security" or something else, and some doubt has been raised as to whether §351 applies if only securities (no stock) are issued.

If §351 governs a transaction the "holding period" of the stock or securities received by the transferor will be determined under §1223(1), and the corporation's "holding period" for the property it receives will be determined under §1223(2). "Tacking" occurs in both cases.

Sometimes a corporation may be the transferor, transferring all or part of its assets to another corporation. Section 351 may apply, as in the case of a noncorporate transferor, and §361 (involving "reorganizations," to be studied in Chapter 4, page 402 infra) may also apply.

Section 351(d) and the first parenthetical clause in §351(a) were added to the Code in 1966 as a response to an ingenious development and a lively administrative controversy involving newly organized, widely held, mutual fund-type investment companies. To what kind of transactions do you think these provisions are addressed? Why? See M. Chirelstein, Tax Pooling and Tax Postponement — The Capital Exchange Funds, 75 Yale L.J. 183 (1965). Treas. Reg. §1.351-1(c) is the Treasury's interpretation of the 1966 legislation.

As with a number of other nonrecognition provisions, §351 may be inapplicable to gain (not loss) on a transfer to a foreign corporation. See §367. In addition, a special tax may apply to such a transfer. See §§1491 and 1492. This book does not delve into problems peculiar to foreign corporations, but a few of the problems on incorporation are touched at the end of this chapter.

Before approaching the knotty tax problems, you should give thought to some of the mechanics of incorporation. How does one incorporate his real estate, his lathe, his accounts receivable, his goodwill? How are stocks and bonds "issued"? What docu-

ments are required, to whom are they delivered, and what assents and acknowledg-
ments are necessary? Do not refer to "incorporating a man's business" without knowing
exactly how it is accomplished. Livery of seisin is rare today, and it was never effective
as to a furniture man's goodwill.

See generally J. Sobeloff, Tax Problems of an Initial Public Offering, 58 Geo. L.J.
1063 (1970); T. White, III, Sleepers That Travel With Section 351 Transfers, 56
Va. L. Rev. 37 (1970); G. Baldwin, Section 351 of the Internal Revenue Code and
"Midstream" Incorporations, 38 U. Cin. L. Rev. 96 (1969); E. Benjamin, Jr., Prob-
lems in Transition from Sole Proprietorship to Corporation, 26 N.Y.U. Inst. on Fed.
Tax. 791 (1968); S. Weiss, Problems in the Tax-Free Incorporation of a Business, 48
Ind. L.J. 666 (1966); B. Bittker and J. Eustice, Federal Income Taxation of Corpo-
rations and Shareholders 64-117 (2d ed. 1966).

II. RECEIPT OF STOCK OR SECURITIES IN EXCHANGE —
TAX IMPACT ON INVESTOR — §351

A. *QUESTIONS OF "CONTROL"*

1. *Timing and the "Group"*

AMERICAN BANTAM CAR CO. v. COMMISSIONER
11 T.C. 397 (1948), aff'd per curiam, 177 F.2d 513 (3d Cir. 1949),
cert. denied, 339 U.S. 920 (1950)

[In August 1935, A, B and C (hereinafter called the associates) acquired the assets
of the defunct American Austin Car Co. by purchase from its liquidating trustees. They
paid $5000 in cash; the assets were subject to liabilities of $219,099.83. In May 1936, they
decided to form the American Bantam Car Co., the petitioner in this case. Under the
plan the associates were to transfer the American Austin assets, subject to the existing
liabilities, and $500 in cash to the petitioner in exchange for 300,000 shares of the latter's
no par common stock; 90,000 shares of the petitioner's preference stock were to be
offered to the public through underwriters. If the underwriters were successful in disposing of the stock they were to receive from the associates 100,000 shares of the common
stock in addition to their regular underwriting commissions. All of the interested
parties agreed orally to the substance of this plan on June 2, 1936, but no formal written
contract was entered into at that time. On the same date petitioner was incorporated
with an authorized capital stock of 700,000 shares, consisting of 100,000 shares of $10 par
value preferred stock and 600,000 shares of no par common stock. The holders of the
preferred stock were entitled to three votes for each share held, and the holders of the
common were entitled to one vote per share. On June 3, 1936, the associates transferred
the American Austin assets, subject to the aforementioned liabilities, and $500 in cash
to the petitioner, and the latter issued 300,000 shares of the common stock to the
associates in accordance with their proportionate interests in the assets and money.

An appraisal made of the American Austin assets at that time indicated that they were worth $840,800.

On June 8, 1936, petitioner executed a written agreement with the underwriters for the sale of 90,000 shares of its preferred stock to the public. A selling schedule was established under which the stock was to be disposed of in varying amounts over a period of one year. At the same time the associates and the underwriters executed a written contract under which the former were to transfer a total of 100,000 shares of the petitioner's common stock to the latter as they sold the preferred stock. To facilitate the transfer the associates placed all of the common stock held by them in the custody of a bank. The bank was to hold the common shares until the preferred stock was completely sold; then the common was to be returned to the associates, and they were to deliver 100,000 shares to the underwriters. By October 1937, the underwriters had sold 83,618 shares of the preferred to the public, and at that time they received 87,900 shares of the common from the associates pursuant to the agreement. The underwriters, within one month, sold 1008 shares of the common to the public.

For the taxable years 1936 through 1941 the petitioner used $145,000 as its basis for the depreciation of the American Austin assets. In 1942 and 1943, when petitioner showed profit from war production, it used $840,800 as the basis for those assets. The Commissioner contended that the assets had been received in a tax-free exchange and that their basis to the petitioner depended upon their basis in the hands of the associates.]

HILL, Judge: This case requires the determination of the proper basis for the Austin assets acquired by petitioner on June 3, 1936, in exchange for stock. We must decide whether under the facts here section [362(a)] requires petitioner, in computing deductions for depreciation, to take as the basis of the assets so acquired the basis thereof in the hands of the transferors. This section is applicable if the exchange by which petitioner received the Austin assets was one in which gain or loss is not recognized under the provisions of section [351(a)]. . . . We therefore must first consider whether, when the associates turned over the Austin assets to petitioner, subject to liabilities of $219,099.83, plus $500 in cash, and in return petitioner issued to the associates 300,000 shares of its no par common stock, all the requirements of section [351(a)] were satisfied.

At the outset it should be noted that the statute requires for a nontaxable exchange that the property turned over by the transferors be "solely" in exchange for stock or securities of the transferee corporation. The transferors in the instant case actually received from petitioner upon the exchange only 300,000 shares of common stock. Thus, the statutory requirement is met unless it can be said the transferors indirectly received "other property or money" by virtue of the fact the petitioner acquired the transferred property subject to liabilities. Section [357(a)] . . . specifically states that such an acquisition of property subject to liability shall not be considered as "other property or money" received by the transferors. It is clear that a definite business purpose motivated this transaction. Therefore such acquisition by the petitioner does not prevent the exchange from being within the provisions of section [351(a)] and the transferors in exchange for their property did receive "solely" stock from the corporation.

It has been held that money turned over to the transferee corporation by the transferors does not prevent a tax-free exchange, for it is includible within the term "property" in section [351(a)]. [G.C.M. 24415, 1944 Cum. Bull. 219]; Haliburton v. Commissioner, 78 Fed. (2d) 265. Therefore, the $500 transfer of cash to petitioner by the associates comes within the terms of section [351(a)].

The first major test of a tax-free exchange under section [351(a)] is whether the transferors have "control" of the corporation immediately after the exchange. Section [368(c)] . . . defines "control":

"As used in this section the term 'control' means the ownership of stock possessing at least 80 per centum of the total combined voting power of all classes of stock entitled to vote and at least 80 per centum of the total number of shares of all other classes of stock of the corporation."

The first question, then, is whether the associates had such "control" over the petitioner immediately after the exchange on June 3, 1936. Prima facie, when the various steps taken to organize the new corporation and transfer assets to it are considered separately, the associates did have "control" of the petitioner immediately after the exchange within the statutory definition of the word. We think that from June 3 to June 8, 1936, they owned 100 per cent of all the issued stock, and from June 8, 1936, until October 1937 they owned stock possessing at least 80 per cent of the total combined voting power of all classes of stock. On June 3, 1936, the associates were issued absolutely and unconditionally 300,000 shares of no par common stock. The resolution of the board of directors of petitioner accepting the associates' offer of the Austin assets attached no strings whatsoever to the issuance of the stock to them. It is true that on June 2, 1936, petitioner had an authorized capital stock of 700,000 shares, 600,000 common shares and 100,000 preferred shares, but in determining control only stock actually issued is considered. Louangel Holding Corporation v. Anderson, 9 Fed. Supp. 550. On June 8 no other common stock had been issued, and a contract regarding possible future assignment of those 300,000 shares already issued was not entered into before that date. No preferred stock had been issued on June 3, nor was a contract for its sale provided until June 8. The statutory words "immediately after the exchange" require control for no longer period; in fact, momentary control is sufficient. Evans Products Co., 29 B.T.A. 992. Certainly, therefore, the associates had absolute control over the corporation from June 3 to June 8, 1936, due to their complete ownership of all outstanding stock.

It is true that, by virtue of their agreement with the associates on June 8, 1936, the underwriters did at that time acquire the right to earn shares of the common stock issued to the associates by the sale of certain percentages of preferred stock, but the ownership of the 300,000 shares remained in the associates until such sales were completed. It is significant to note that this agreement stated that the associates were the owners of the 300,000 shares. On August 16, 1936, the associates deposited all their shares in escrow with the Butler County National Bank & Trust Co., but they only surrendered possession by the terms of their agreement with the bank and retained all other attributes of ownership.

During all of 1936 the associates retained ownership over the 300,000 shares of common stock and during that interval the underwriters sold only 14,757 shares of preferred stock, which did not entitle them to any common stock under the agreement of June 8, 1936. The corporation's bylaws provided that each share of preferred stock should have 3 votes, while each share of common stock should have 1 vote. Therefore, at the end of 1936, out of 344,271 possible stock votes, the total combined voting power of all outstanding stock, the associates owned 300,000, or over 80 per cent. It was not until October 1937, when the underwriter Grant* received 87,900 shares of the associates' common stock in fulfillment of the underwriting agreement, that the associates lost "control" of petitioner within the statutory definition of the word. Retention of "control" for such a duration of time satisfies the governing provision of section [351(a)].

Petitioner, however, contends that the series of steps organizing the new corporation, transferring assets to it, and arranging for the sale of its preference stock must be considered as parts of the integrated plan formulated in May 1936, and, therefore, considered as parts of a single transaction. It argues that this unified transaction started on June 2, 1936, when petitioner was incorporated, and ended in October 1937, when the public offering of the preferred stock by the underwriters ceased and Grant was awarded 87,900 shares of common stock; that the transfer of common stock to Grant in 1937 was the final step of an indivisible operation and must be viewed concurrently with the preceding steps. On this theory the associates did not obtain control of petitioner, for on consummation of this final step in the general plan the associates had only 212,100 shares of common stock, while Grant had 86,892 shares and the public had 1,008 and there were 83,618 shares of outstanding preferred stock owned by the public. The 212,100 stock votes held by the associates in October 1937 fell shy of the required 80 per cent to give the requisite control.

In determining whether a series of steps are to be treated as a single indivisible transaction or should retain their separate entity, the courts use a variety of tests. Paul, Selected Studies in Federal Taxation, 2d series, pp. 200-254. Among the factors considered are the intent of the parties, the time element, and the pragmatic test of the ultimate result. An important test is that of mutual interdependence. Were the steps so interdependent that the legal relations created by one transaction would have been fruitless without a completion of the series?

Using these tests as a basis for their decisions the courts in Hazeltine Corporation v. Commissioner, 89 Fed. (2d) 513, and Bassick v. Commissioner, 85 Fed. (2d) 8, treated the series of steps involved in each case as parts of a unified transaction and therefore determined that the transferors of assets to the new corporation did not acquire the requisite control. An analysis of the fact situations involved shows salient distinguishing features from the present facts. In each of the above cases there was a written contract prior both to the organization of the new corporation and the exchange of assets for stock which bound the transferors unconditionally to assign part of the stock acquired to third parties after the exchange. Thus, at the moment of the exchange the recipient of the stock did not own it, but held it subject to a binding contractual obligation to transfer a portion. The court in each case thought that the incorporation and exchange would never have been agreed upon without the supplemental agreement turning over stock to a third party. In such situations it is logical for the courts to say that the

---

*The factual statement uses the word *underwriters*, while the court's opinion refers to Grant. — ED.

exchange and the subsequent transfer are part of one and the same transaction, so that the transferor never actually owned the shares he later assigned.

A close examination of the facts surrounding the exchange in the present case makes it clear that the exchange of assets for stock and the subsequent transfer of a portion of that stock to Grant therein involved should not be considered part of the same transaction so as to deprive the associates of "control" immediately after the exchange. The facts are distinguishable from those existing in the *Hazeltine* and *Bassick* cases on three grounds. First, there was no written contract prior to the exchange binding the associates to transfer stock to the underwriters. At the most, there was an informal oral understanding of a general plan contemplating the organization of a new corporation, the exchange of assets for stock, and marketing of preferred stock of the new corporation to the public. A written contract providing for the transfer of shares from the associates to the underwriters did not come until five days after the exchange. Secondly, when the transfer of shares to the underwriters was embodied specifically in a formal contract, the underwriters received no absolute right to ownership of the common stock, but only when, as, and if, certain percentages of preferred stock were sold. How clearly contingent was the nature of their rights is illustrated by the fact that only one underwriter, Grant, met the terms of the agreement and became entitled to any shares. Thirdly, the necessity of placing the 300,000 shares in escrow with a bank is indicative of complete ownership of such stock by the associates following the exchange.

The standard required by the courts to enable them to say that a series of steps are interdependent and thus should be viewed as a single transaction do not exist here. It is true that all the steps may have been contemplated under the same general plan of May 1936; yet the contemplated arrangement for the sale of preferred stock to the public was entirely secondary and supplemental to the principal goal of the plan — to organize the new corporation and exchange its stock for the Austin assets. The understanding with the underwriters for disposing of the preferred stock, however important, was not a sine qua non in the general plan, without which no other step would have been taken. While the incorporation and exchange of assets would have been purposeless one without the other, yet both would have been carried out even though the contemplated·method of marketing the preferred stock might fail. The very fact that in the contracts of June 8, 1936, the associates retained the right to cancel the marketing order and, consequently the underwriters' means to own common stock issued to the associates, refutes the proprosition that the legal relations resulting from the steps of organizing the corporation and transferring assets to it would have been fruitless without the sale of the preferred stock in the manner contemplated.

Finally, to say that the separate steps should be viewed as one transaction so that ownership of 87,900 shares never passed to the associates has the disadvantage of inferring that the interested parties intended to suspend ownership of 300,000 shares from June 3, 1936, until such time as the underwriters definitely did or did not earn the right to such shares — as it turned out, until October 1937. It is much more logical to say that ownership of all 300,000 shares rested in the associates until the conditions precedent had been fulfilled by the underwriters, and that when the associates turned over the stock to Grant they were exercising their rights of ownership acquired on June 3, 1936. To allow petitioner's contention is to permit a 15-month time lag after the exchange before determining "control immediately after the exchange." Such a proposition defeats the very language of the statute.

A review of decisions encountering this problem under section [351(a)] shows that courts have determined control of the new corporation remained with the transferors of assets following the exchange under circumstances less favorable than in the present case. . . .

Thus we conclude that in the present case the exchange of assets for stock between the associates and petitioner on June 3, 1936, was a separate completed transaction, distinct from the subsequent transfer of common stock to Grant, so that the associates were in control of petitioner immediately after the exchange within the provisions of section [351(a)]. . . .

What then is the basis for depreciation purposes of property acquired by a corporation by a tax-free exchange under section [351(a)]? Section [362(a)] of the code specifically answers this question. The basis is the same as it would be in the hands of the transferor. In the instant case the basis of the Austin assets in the hands of the associates was the cost of those assets to them. They paid $5,000 cash and received the property subject to liabilities of $219,099.83. Thus the basis in their hands was $224,099.83. Therefore, the basis for the Austin assets to the petitioner is also $224,099.83, as contended by the respondent.

Reviewed by the Court.

Decision will be entered under Rule 50.

LEECH, J., concurring: In my judgment the various steps outlined in the majority opinion were integrated parts of a single plan rather than independent undertakings. The fact that the plan was not reduced to writing is unimportant, since it was carried out as orally agreed upon. The record, in my opinion, is insufficient to establish that the corporation agreed to pay or paid more for the assets it acquired than the price at which the transferors purchased them. Hence, the basis to the corporation would be the same as found by the majority. Therefore, I concur only in the result.

NOTE

1. A partnership with appreciated assets is interested in expansion. Accordingly, the partners transfer all their assets to a corporation in exchange for stock. Upon receipt of the stock, pursuant to prior plan, they sell 30 per cent of the stock to an underwriter who distributes the stock to the public the same day. Do the partners recognize gain in the amount of the unrealized appreciation of the assets when they form the corporation? Why?

2. Mr. Fox owns a sole proprietorship, the assets of which have substantially appreciated in value since he purchased it. Because he wishes to bring his son into the business, he incorporates under a firm commitment to give 30 per cent of the stock to his son immediately. His son has given nothing in return for the stock. Does Fox recognize any income? Why? Would the result be different if there were no firm commitment to his son, but only an understanding that the son would eventually join the the business? Why?

3. Mr. Good incorporates his business with the expectation that he will immediately sell 30 per cent of the stock to Mr. Howard. Does Good recognize gain on incorporation? What if Good had made a commitment to sell 30 per cent to Howard simultaneously with the incorporation? What if Good had sold Howard a 30 per cent interest in the business before incorporation and then Good and Howard had transferred the assets to the corporation for 70 per cent and 30 per cent of the stock respectively? Cf. Fahs v. Florida Machine and Foundry Co., 168 F.2d 957 (5th Cir. 1948).

4. Suppose A contributes $100,000 in appreciated property in return for 100 per cent of the non-voting preferred stock of Corporation Z, and B contributes $900,000 in cash for 100 per cent of the voting common stock. Does A recognize gain? Why?

5. See B. Bittker and J. Eustice, Federal Income Taxation of Corporations and Shareholders 89-94 (2d ed. 1966); J. Rabkin and M. Johnson, Federal Income, Gift and Estate Taxation §31.02 (1970).

2. *Effect of "Services"*

MAILLOUX v. COMMISSIONER
320 F.2d 60 (5th Cir. 1963)

Before RIVES, JONES and BROWN, Circuit Judges.

JONES, Circuit Judge. The petitioners bring to the Court for review a decision of the Tax Court finding income tax deficiencies against them. Joint returns had been filed. Only the husbands, Melvin Mailloux and Robert R. Foley, were participants in the transactions giving rise to the finding of tax liability, and they will be referred to as the taxpayers.

Critchell Parsons was the principal promoter of of Rocky Mountain Uranium Corporation. It was incorporated on May 3, 1954. Transfers of uranium mining claims to the corporation were made or agreed upon in exchange for 1,450,000 shares of the stock of the corporation of the par value of ten cents per share, and the stock was issued on May 18, 1954. Of this stock, 900,000 shares were issued to Parsons. Each of the taxpayers received, on May 18, 1954, 120,000 shares of the stock by a transfer from Parsons out of the 900,000 shares which had been issued to him. The taxpayers were to receive ten per cent of the proceeds of stock sales made prior to a public offering of the stock. The sales were to be at 50 cents a share. The taxpayers received $12,000 from this commission arrangement. The stock was transferred under an agreement that the taxpayers would make no sales without Parsons' approval. This restriction was to permit Parsons to prevent depressing the price by overselling the market. During 1954 Mailloux sold 23,650 shares and Foley sold 24,375 shares. These sales were made at various prices which averaged something over a dollar a share. In the latter part of 1954, some transactions and adjustments between Parsons and the taxpayers were made which resulted in his obtaining and retaining some of their stock certificates. Before the end of the year Parsons and the taxpayers had a disagreement which arose from the failure, which Parsons attributed to the taxpayers, to procure approval from the Securities and Exchange Commission and the Texas Securities Commission of a public offering of the stock. Parsons directed the transfer agent not to make transfers of the taxpayers' certificates. They sued to establish their ownership. The litigation was compromised and settled in 1956. The taxpayers sold a part of their remaining stock in 1956 for ten cents a share and the rest in 1957 for five cents a share.

In their 1954 returns the taxpayers did not report any income on account of the receipt of the stock. The Commissioner made a determination that the stock was compensation for services, and that it had a value of fifty cents a share. A tax deficiency was proposed. The Tax Court, in a memorandum opinion, sustained the Commissioner.

Two questions are presented by the taxpayers' petition for review. The contention is made that the stock was received by the taxpayers in a tax-free exchange for property under 26 U.S.C.A. (I.R.C. 1954) §351. If there was no tax-free exchange and the stock was received for services, the taxpayers contend that it had no market value when received or, in the alternative, the value did not exceed ten cents a share, or at the most, an amount in excess of what they received for it.

Although the taxpayers claimed, and supported the claim with their testimony, that they had an interest in uranium claims which were conveyed to the corporation for shares of its stock, the testimony of Parsons is to the contrary. He testified that they had no interest in the claims. The Tax Court found against the taxpayers on this controverted fact issue, and its findings that the stock was for services and not for property are supported by evidence.

The Tax Court, in fixing the value of the stock, reviewed the sales made by the taxpayers, by Parsons, and by the corporation, and found that the stock, at the time it was transferred to the taxpayers, had a value of not less than fifty cents a share. There was ample evidence before the Tax Court to sustain this finding of the value of the stock issued to the taxpayers unless, as the taxpayers assert, the effect of the restrictive agreement was such as to reduce the value of their stock to an amount less than fifty cents a share. The Tax Court concluded that such restrictions as may have existed had no bearing upon the fair market value of the stock at the time the taxpayers received it. Where a stock is of a highly speculative quality and the terms of a restrictive agreement make a sale impossible, it may be that no fair market value can be attributed to it. Helvering v. Tex-Penn Oil Co., 300 U.S. 481, 57 S. Ct. 569, 81 L. Ed. 755. But where there is no absolute prohibition against a sale, a restriction may reduce but does not destroy fair market value. Trinity Corporation v. Commissioner, 5th Cir., 1942, 127 F.2d 604, cert. den. 317 U.S. 651, 63 S. Ct. 47, 87 L. Ed. 524; Kirby v. Commissioner, 5th Cir., 1939, 102 F.2d 115; ABC Realty Co. v. Commissioner, 8th Cir., 1961, 295 F.2d 98; Goldwasser v. Commissioner, 47 B.T.A. 445, aff. Goldwasser v. Nunon, 2 Cir., 142 F.2d 556; Mertens, Law of Federal Income Taxation §59.20.

We do not think it can be said that where the holder of a highly speculative stock — and speculative Rocky Mountain Uranium Corporation surely was — can carry it into the market place only at the indulgence of another, the fair market value of the stock is the same as it would be if the dominion of the holder was free and unfettered. Parsons prevented the taxpayers from selling a portion of their stock from December 1954 for nearly a year and a half. In December 1954 the national market for the stock was around $3 per share. When the taxpayers were able to sell they realized five and ten cents a share. The inability of the taxpayers to sell between December 1954 and May 1956 may not have been occasioned by the exercise of Parsons' right under the restrictive agreement, but the result would have been no more disastrous if the exercise of the right had been the cause of the inability to sell.

We think the Tax Court should have recognized the effect of impairing the market value of the stock and given effect to that impairment in the ascertainment of fair market value. To permit it to do so, its decision will be reversed and the cause remanded for further proceedings.

Reversed and remanded.

NOTE

1. The facts as set forth in the Fifth Circuit's opinion in *Mailloux* may not be entirely clear. On May 18, 1954, the corporation issued a total of 1,450,000 shares to a group of people from whom, in exchange for the shares, the corporation received rights in certain mining claims. Those shares at that time represented 100 per cent of the corporation's outstanding stock. Parsons, principal promoter in the group, received 900,000 of the shares. The taxpayers, Mailloux and Foley, did not receive shares directly from the corporation. On May 18, 1954, however, they each received 120,000 shares from Parsons, these coming out of his 900,000 shares, The Tax Court held that the shares which the taxpayers received constituted ordinary income to them in 1954, valuing the shares at 50 cents each. See the more complete factual statement at 20 CCH Tax Ct. Mem. 942 (1961).

2. If the taxpayers had received 150,000 shares each what tax impact might that have had on Parsons? Why? If, by prearrangement, Parsons had delivered 150,000 shares to Mailloux for his services and 150,000 shares to Foley for cash equal to fair market value, what might the tax impact on Parsons have been? Why?

3. If, upon incorporation of X Corporation, A transfers appreciated assets in exchange for the corporation's entire issue of nonvoting preferred stock and B pays cash for the corporation's entire issue of common stock, what is the tax impact on A? If B had received his common stock for services the tax impact on both A and B would have been quite different. Why should that be so as to A? As to B? Review your response to the problem in Note 4, page 287 supra. See D. Herwitz, Allocation of Stock Between Services and Capital in the Organization of a Close Corporation, 75 Harv. L. Rev. 1098 (1962).

3. *Classification of Stock and Computation — §368(c)*

For §351(a) to operate the transferors of the incorporated assets must be "in control" of the transferee corporation immediately after they effect the exchange. Section 368(c), defining "control," requires the transferors to own stock with at least (1) 80 per cent of the total combined voting power of all classes of stock entitled to vote, and (2) 80 per cent of the total number of shares of all other classes of outstanding stock.

When is stock with "voting power" "entitled to vote"? Cf. §§302(b)(2)(B) and 334(b)(2)(B). Does the "entitled to vote" concept add anything to the "voting power" concept? Cf. §1504(a)(1). Is stock which is not "entitled to vote" different from "nonvoting stock" (§1504(a))? There is no clear-cut answer to these questions, and they arise only infrequently. The language differences may represent only a difference in expression of the same ideas, enacted at different times without regard to earlier modes of expression. It is generally accepted that stock has "voting power" and is "entitled to vote" only when it entitles its owner to vote for directors in ordinary course. Stock that permits such voting only after a contingency occurs (e.g., preferred which is permitted to vote only after dividends are in default) probably becomes "entitled to vote" only after the contingency has occurred. Cf. Treas. Reg. §1.302-3(a)(3).

Suppose Mr. T, a transferor, receives 100 per cent of a corporation's common (voting) stock in exchange for appreciated property; 10,000 shares of the Class A, 6 per cent nonvoting preferred, $1.00 par, for cash of $10,000; and 1000 shares of the Class B, 7 per cent nonvoting preferred, $5.00 par, for cash of $5000. He has received all of the authorized Class A preferred and half of the authorized Class B preferred. The other half of the authorized Class B preferred (1000 shares) is issued to Mr. E in exchange for services worth $5000. Is Mr. T "in control"? Why? See Rev. Rul. 59-259, 1959-2 Cum. Bull. 115.

B. *"STOCK," "SECURITIES" AND/OR SOMETHING ELSE*

1. *Definitional Criteria — Effect of Total Absence*

BURR OAKS CORP. v. COMMISSIONER
43 T.C. 635 (1965), aff'd, 365 F.2d 24 (7th Cir. 1966), cert. denied,
385 U.S. 1007 (1967)

FAY, Judge. Respondent, pursuant to a statutory notice of deficiency, determined deficiencies in the income tax of petitioner Burr Oaks Corp. for its taxable years ended September 30, 1958, 1959, and 1960, in the respective amounts of $15,067.26, $52,595.26, and $16,602.61. With regard to the various individual petitioners, respondent determined the following deficiencies in their respective income taxes:

Docket No.	Petitioners	Taxable year ended Dec.31 —	Deficiency
4772-62	A. Aaron and Rosella Elkind	1958	$ 499.32
		1959	35,520.49
		1960	1,778.90
1581-63	Harold A. and Fannie G. Watkins	1959	30,386.55
1583-63	Maurice and Esther Leah Ritz	1959	37,702.90

Petitioner Burr Oaks Corp. will hereinafter be referred to as the petitioner, and petitioners A. Aaron Elkind, Harold A. Watkins, and Maurice Ritz will hereinafter sometimes be referred to respectively as Elkind, Watkins, and Ritz, or as the individual petitioners.

The only question remaining to be determined insofar as petitioner is concerned as its correct basis in certain unimproved real estate transferred to it by Elkind, Watkins, and Ritz. In order to make this determination, we must first decide whether the transfer by Elkind, Watkins, and Ritz to petitioner constituted a valid sale or a contribution to capital. In the event we find it to be the latter, we must further determine whether it constitutes a transfer to a controlled corporation within the meaning of section 351.

Insofar as petitioners Elkind, Watkins, and Ritz are concerned, we must determine whether certain amounts received by them during 1959 from petitioner were taxable as ordinary income, rather than as long-term capital gain.

Findings of Fact

. . . Petitioner is a corporation formed under the laws of the State of Wisconsin. It maintains its books of account and files its Federal income tax returns on the basis of an accrual method of accounting and a fiscal year ended September 30. . . . [The individual petitioners filed their returns on the basis of a calendar year and the cash method of accounting.]

Elkind, at all times relevant hereto, has been engaged in various aspects of real estate development, with primary emphasis on the development of tracts of one-family houses. These various endeavors were generally conducted through corporations in which Elkind or members of his family were majority stockholders. Elkind also has made a number of investments in real estate, including raw land as well as improved property producing rental income.

Ritz, at all times relevant hereto, was a certified public accountant and the senior partner of an accounting firm of which Elkind was a client. Ritz had made various investments in improved and unimproved real estate prior to the years in issue herein, primarily as a result of opportunities which he came across in connection with his accounting practice.

At all times relevant hereto, Watkins was the president and principal stockholder of a corporation engaged in the manufacture and sale of slippers and other types of casual footwear. Watkins, also, had made several investments in real property over the years, primarily in improved properties producing rental income.

Elkind, Watkins, and Ritz have, at least upon one occasion other than that involved herein, jointly invested in a relatively large tract of unimproved real estate. Thus, on June 4, 1953, they purchased for the sum of $70,124.15 a tract of undeveloped land located just outside the city of Madison, Wis. These individuals held that property (hereinafter referred to as the Gay Farm) jointly until April 20, 1954, at which time is was sold to one of Elkind's development corporations for the sum of $149,650.79. That corporation subdivided the property into 353 lots, constructed one-family homes thereon, and made substantial profits totaling approximately $500,000 upon their sale.

In the fall of 1954 Elkind came across the opportunity to purchase a similar piece of property, this time a tract of land of approximately 70 acres, also located near the outskirts of the city of Madison and theretofore used as a golf course. This property will hereinafter sometimes be referred to as the Burr Oaks property.

Elkind, in December of the same year, contacted Ritz and Watkins in regard to their participation with him in the purchase of that land. Watkins and Ritz agreed to join him in the acquisition upon the understanding that each of them would obtain a one-third interest therein. On December 7 of that year, Elkind tendered to the owner of said property a written offer to purchase the property for the sum of $100,000. The offer provided that $10,000 of the purchase price was payable at the time of acceptance, $10,000 on February 15, 1955, $5,000 on April 1, 1955, with payments of $5,000 due quarterly thereafter until the final balance was paid. The offer was accepted on December 8, 1954.

From the time they acquired the Burr Oaks property through the summer of 1957 Elkind, Watkins, and Ritz attempted to develop said property as a shopping center site or as an industrial park. In furtherance of this plan, they purchased in 1955 an additional 80 feet of frontage on an adjoining thoroughfare for the purpose of providing better access to the Burr Oaks property in the event of its commercial development. This 80 feet of frontage will hereinafter be referred to as the Brinkman property. Their efforts to develop the Burr Oaks property for commercial purposes, however, proved fruitless.

Sometime during 1957 Elkind became convinced that their plans to develop the Burr Oaks property as a shopping center or an industrial park would not materialize. Contemplating that one of his corporations might purchase the property for purposes of subdivision or development, Elkind requested two of his business associates to investigate the zoning and platting possibilities of the Burr Oaks property. On March 11, 1957, a petition was filed with the City Council of Madison, Wis., to change the zoning of the Burr Oaks property from residential A (single-family dwellings) to residential A2 and B (two-family and four-family dwellings) and commercial A and B.

Elkind then proposed to Watkins and Ritz that the three of them sell the Burr Oaks property to one of Elkind's real estate corporations, as they had done with the Gay Farm property. Watkins and Ritz, recalling the substantial profits made by Elkind's corporation after they had sold the Gay Farm property to it, rejected this proposal. Ritz suggested that the three of them transfer the Burr Oaks property to a corporation which they would form for the purpose of subdividing, developing, and selling the property; that the shareholders thereof would be comprised of his two brothers and the wives of Watkins and Elkind; and that in return for the transfer of the land, the corporation would issue promissory notes to Elkind, Watkins, and Ritz. It was agreed that they would follow Ritz' suggestions.

On September 9, 1957, the City Council of Madison approved a preliminary plat incorporating the zoning proposed for the property in the aforementioned petition filed on March 11, 1957. The land as platted contained 89 lots zoned for single-family dwellings (residential A); 65 lots zoned for four-family apartments (residential B); 110 lots zoned for multiple-family apartments (residential C); 1 site zoned for commercial use; and 1 site zoned for a school. This zoning received final approval from the Madison City Council on November 25, 1957.

Petitioner was incorporated on October 8, 1957, for the purpose of (1) acquiring the Burr Oaks property from Elkind, Watkins, and Ritz; (2) developing and subdividing said property; and (3) selling improved lots therefrom to customers. At the time petitioner was formed, the Burr Oaks property was completely unimproved. Elkind, Watkins, and Ritz were aware of a local ordinance pursuant to which owners of unimproved land could request the city of Madison to make improvements thereon such as streets, sewers, water, and sidewalks. The city would make these improvements and assess the costs incurred in connection therewith against the property. However, it was realized that the cost of some of the improvements to be made, such as grading and supplying crushed stone, would have to be borne directly by the developers. The total cost of such improvements, as estimated by petitioner, was in the amount of $107,243.33.

It was determined by Ritz, Watkins, and Elkind that petitioner's initial capital would be $4,500.

Petitioner issued a total of 450 shares of its common stock to a group composed of Elkind's wife, Watkins' wife, and Ritz' brothers, Philip and Erwin, for an aggregate consideration of $4,500. Elkind's wife received 150 shares of the stock; Watkins' wife also received 150 shares; and Philip and Erwin Ritz each received 75 shares. The record does not indicate the exact date when this stock was issued. Philip and Erwin Ritz paid for their stock by their respective checks, each in the amount of $750 and dated October 9, 1957, Watkins' wife paid for her stock by a check in the amount of $1,500 dated October 14, 1957. Each of the above-mentioned four persons received from petitioner a receipt dated November 1, 1957, evidencing their payment for the stock. At all times relevant hereto, petitioner's stockholders of record and officers and directors were as follows:

Shareholder	Number of shares held	Officers	Position held	Directors
Rosella Elkind		Watkins	President.	Watkins.
(Elkind's wife).....	150	Philip M. Ritz ...	Vice	Ritz.
Fannie G. Watkins		Rosella Elkind ...	president.	Elkind.
(Watkins' wife)....	150		Secretary-	Fannie G.
Philip M. Ritz			treasurer.	Watkins.
(Ritz' brother)......	75			Philip M. Ritz.
Erwin M. Ritz				Rosella Elkind.
(Ritz' brother)......	75			

... On November 1, 1957, Elkind, Watkins, and Ritz transferred their respective interests in the Burr Oaks property to petitioner. In consideration for this transfer, petitioner assumed the remaining unpaid balance for the property, namely $30,000, and issued to each of Elkind, Watkins, and Ritz what purported on the face thereof to be a promissory note in the principal amount of $110,000. Each of the notes recited that it bore interest at the rate of 6 per cent and that it was payable 2 years after the making thereof. The $30,000 obligation for the Burr Oaks property to its original owner, assumed by petitioner from Elkind, Watkins, and Ritz, was entered on petitioner's books under an account captioned "Mortgage Payable." An additional account was set up under the title "Land Contract Payable" in the amount of $330,000 to represent the alleged promissory notes. At the time Elkind, Watkins, and Ritz transferred the Burr Oaks property to petitioner, the fair market value of said property was substantially less than $360,000. The property was not worth more than $165,000 at that time.

Although at the time Elkind, Watkins, and Ritz transferred their interests in said property to petitioner they hoped that petitioner's business would be successful, petitioner's prospects were uncertain. The nature of their investment can best be described by the term "speculative."

Shortly after its incorporation, petitioner found that it did not have sufficient funds on hand with which to commence operations. Therefore, on November 30, 1957, it borrowed $15,000 from Elkind. On February 28, 1958, Elkind loaned petitioner an additional $10,000. These loans, together with interest thereon in the amount of $1,859.78, were repaid on June 30, 1959.

None of petitioner's stockholders of record, namely Watkins' and Elkind's respective wives and Ritz' brothers, took any active interest in the management of petitioner. In fact, none of them had any real idea of the nature of petitioner's business, other than some vague notion that it was engaged in "real estate" in some way or other.

Watkins and Ritz hired Albert McGinnes to manage petitioner. His work included the supervision of the platting, development, and subdivision of the land, as well as taking charge of advertising and sales. McGinnes had known and worked for Elkind and his various corporations for approximately 15 years prior to that time as a lawyer and real estate broker and in various other capacities. McGinnes, moreover, was the person who first interested Elkind in purchasing the Burr Oaks property and checked into the zoning and platting possibilities for the land. During the years in issue, McGinnes continued to work for various Elkind interests.

Ritz' accounting firm, Ritz, Holman & Co., kept petitioner's books and took care of its accounting work. McGinnes was required to account to Ritz, Holman & Co. for the funds which he took in and disbursed in connection with his operation of petitioner's business.

Upon a number of occasions, petitioner transferred various lots or parcels of property to Elkind, Watkins, and Ritz, either at no cost or at a price less than the amount for which such lots could have been sold to third parties. Thus, by deed dated November 3, 1958, petitioner conveyed to Elkind, Watkins, and Ritz a strip of commercial property, 70 feet by 120 feet, located in the southeast corner of the

Burr Oaks property. This property was contiguous with another piece of commercial property, the Brinkman property, which Elkind, Watkins, and Ritz had purchased when they were contemplating using Burr Oaks for a shopping center. Nothing was paid to petitioner in consideration for this transfer. The deed by which the transfer was effected purported on its face to correct an erroneous conveyance of the land to petitioner in the first place.

On November 14, 1958, petitioner sold five lots at a price of $3,000 per lot to the Leo Building Corp., which was owned and controlled by Elkind and an associate of his. On the same date petitioner sold an additional five lots for the same price to Carsons, Inc., a corporation owned by Watkins. Petitioner, on May 20, 1960, sold five more lots at $3,000 per lot to M & L Investment, Inc., a corporation in which Ritz owned a substantial interest. Each of the lots involved in these transfers was zoned residential B to accommodate four-family apartments. The evidence indicates that, at the time they were sold after having been platted, subdivided, and improved, each of these lots could have been sold to outsiders for $500 to $1,000 more than was received from the above corporations. None of petitioner's shareholders of record (Philip and Erwin Ritz, Elkind's wife, or Watkins' wife) was consulted with regard to, or knew of, any of these transfers. Nor was any such transfer authorized by a meeting of petitioner's board of directors.

Although McGinnes was in charge of petitioner's day-to-day operations, Elkind, Watkins, and Ritz controlled and dominated petitioner's affairs.

During its taxable years 1958 through 1963, inclusive, petitioner had gross receipts in the following amounts as a result of its subdivision and sale of the Burr Oaks property:

Taxable year ended Sept. 30 —	Gross sales of lots
1958	$ 86,095
1959	177,200
1960	118,625
1961	68,250
1962	49,400
1963	13,900
Total	513,470

As had been contemplated by Elkind, Watkins, and Ritz at the time of petitioner's incorporation, improvements to the Burr Oaks property, such as streets, sewers, water, and sidewalks, were made by the city of Madison. The city was to recover the cost of these improvements by special assessments against the lots, which assessments were generally payable over a period of 5 to 8 years. To the extent that installments of the special assessments came due prior to the sale of the lots, they were paid by petitioner and added to the price of the lots. To the extent the assessments had not been paid prior to the sale of the lots, they were assumed by the purchaser. Certain costs incurred in connection with the subdivision and improvement of the Burr Oaks property were borne directly by petitioner. . . .

In the latter part of 1959 Elkind, Watkins, and Ritz surrendered to petitioner the original "promissory notes" which they had received from petitioner in connection with their transfer of the Burr Oaks property. In return for the surrender of the notes, each of the individual petitioners received from petitioner a distribution of $23,000 in cash and a promissory note dated November 1, 1959, in the principal amount of $87,000. The new notes recited (1) that they were payable 1 year after the making thereof and (2) that they bore interest at the rate of 6 percent per annum. Later that same year, petitioner paid an additional $8,000 apiece to Elkind, Watkins, and Ritz. Petitioner at that time, in exchange for each of their notes in the principal amount of $87,000, issued to each of them a new promisory note in the principal amount of $79,000.

On December 29, 1959, petitioner purported to repay the outstanding balance on these "new promissory notes." At the close of business on that date petitioner had a bank balance of $5,498.88. The record does not clearly indicate how petitioner purported to repay these notes. However, the record does clearly indicate that petitioner urgently needed as working capital the $237,000 which it claims to have used to repay the three promissory notes. Theerfore, immediately after those notes were "repaid," Elkind, Watkins, and Ritz each "loaned" $79,000 to petitioner, and petitioner, in turn, issued to each of the individual petitioners a "new" 1-year promissory note dated December 31, 1959, in the principal amount of $79,000. This transaction did not represent a repayment of the alleged "promissory notes." It was merely an extension of the purported maturity date. The individual petitioners never had any intention of enforcing their "notes" against petitioner.

In addition to the foregoing, petitioner made the following distributions to each of the individual petitioners with regard to the "promissory notes":

Date of distribution	Amount paid to each of the individual petitioners
Aug. 31, 1960	$ 8,000
Jan. 31, 1961	15,000
Dec. 31, 1961	10,000

There was an aggregate balance of $138,000 outstanding upon the three "notes" at the time of the trial in this proceeding, or a total of $46,000 due upon each of saids notes.

Petitioner has not distributed any of its earnings to any of the shareholders of record.

Elkind, Watkins, and Ritz treated their transfer of the Burr Oaks property to petitioner in November 1957 as a sale. Petitioner did likewise and set up on its books a cost of $360,000 for said property. Elkind, Watkins, and Ritz, however, did not report any gain with regard to this alleged sale until 1959 when petitioner purportedly paid in full the promissory notes which it had issued to them in connection with said transfer. In their respective income tax returns for 1959, each of them reported long-term capital gain in the amount of $85,729.06 as a result of their transfer of the Burr Oaks property to petitioner in 1957.

Respondent, pursuant to separate notices of deficiency issued to Elkind, Watkins, and Ritz with respect to their taxable year ended December 31, 1959, determined that —

"the gain realized from the sale of . . . [the Burr Oaks property] in the total amount of $85,729.06 is taxable as ordinary income rather than as long-term capital gains reported on your income tax return. . . ."

Pursuant to a statutory notice of deficiency issued to petitioner with respect to its taxable years 1958 through 1960, respondent increased petitioner's taxable income for said years by an aggregate amount totaling $192,686.98. This increase was based on respondent's determination that petitioner had understated its income for those years by claiming too high a basis or cost in the land sold by it in that period. The notice of deficiency indicates that, in making his determination, respondent treated petitioner as having a basis of $100,000 in the Burr Oaks property, rather than a basis of $360,000, as petitioner had claimed.

Opinion

There are two issues to be determined in this case. These are (1) petitioner's correct basis in the Burr Oaks property and (2) the proper tax treatment of the amounts received by Elkind, Watkins, and Ritz from petitioner during 1959. In order to resolve these issues, we must classify, for tax purposes, the transaction wherein each of the individual petitioners in November 1957 (1) transferred his respective interest in the Burr Oaks property to petitioner and (2) in return therefor received an instrument purporting to be a promissory note in the principal amount of $110,000.

It is contended by Elkind, Watkins, and Ritz (1) that their transfer of the Burr Oaks property to petitioner constitutes the sale or exchange of a capital asset held in excess of 6 months; (2) that the promissory note received by each of them in return therefor represents a valid indebtedness incurred by petitioner; and (3) that the gain realized by them in connection with said transfer is properly reportable in 1959 when they allege that petitioner "paid in full" the "promissory notes" which had been issued to them.[5]

It is contended by petitioner that it purchased the Burr Oaks property from Elkin, Watkins, and Ritz at a cost of $360,000 and that such cost is its correct basis in said property.

[5]Passing over for the moment the validity of the first two parts of the individual petitioners' argument, we believe it appropriate to point out that the third part of their argument, namely, that the gain realized by them on the transfer of the Burr Oaks property was properly reportable in 1959, is incorrect. Watkins, Elkind, and Ritz at all times relevant hereto were cash basis taxpayers. When cash basis taxpayers sell property, they must include in income the fair market value of any property received in exchange therefor. This would include the fair market value of any notes received. See Pinellas Ice Co. v. Commissioner, 287 U.S. 462 (1933). The individual petitioners have not advanced any of the arguments which would enable them to avoid the applicability of this general rule. Thus, they have made no argument that the "promissory notes" received by them were of indeterminate or unascertainable value or that the notes were not received by them in payment for the land. Cf. Robert J. Dial, 24 T.C. 117 (1955); Jay A. Williams, 28 T.C. 1000 (1957); and Schlemmer v. United States, 94 F.2d 77 (C.A. 2, 1938). Nor do they contend (1) that the fair market value of the "notes" received by them was less than their respective bases in the land, cf. sec. 1.1001-1, Income Tax Regs., or (2) that the transfer was not a closed transaction, cf. Joseph Marcello, 43 T.C. 168 (1964). There is nothing in the record to show that (1) they elected to report the gain realized by them at the time of the transfer on the installment method or (2) that they were entitled to report their gain on the deferred payment sale method. See sec. 1.453-4(b)(1) and (2) and sec. 1.453-6, Income Tax Regs.

The plethora of arguments advanced by respondent in his opening statement and on brief indicates to us that the Government had some difficulty in formulating a suitable rationale under which to classify the transfer of the Burr Oaks property to petitioner. It would serve no purpose to set forth at this point the various contentions made by respondent since we believe that the transaction was not a sale, but an equity contribution.[6]

It is true that Elkind, Watkins, and Ritz attempted to cast their transfer of the Burr Oaks property to petitioner in the form of a sale. It is also true that, from a standpoint of form, the alleged promissory notes issued to the individual petitioners are clear evidences of indebtedness. However, it has often been noted in connection with similar issues, the substance of the transaction, rather than its form, is the controlling factor in the determination of the proper tax treatment to be accorded thereto. Sherwood Memorial Gardens, Inc., 42 T.C. 211 (1964), on appeal (C.A. 7, Aug. 10, 1964); 1432 Broadway Corporation, 4 T.C. 1158 (1945), affd. 160 F.2d 885 (C.A. 2, 1947). Whether a transaction such as the one we are now confronted with is in substance, as well as in form, a sale is essentially a question of fact. Gooding Amusement Co., 23 T.C. 408 (1954), affd. 236 F.2d 159 (C.A. 6, 1956), certiorari denied 352 U.S. 1031 (1957).

As we view the creditable evidence presently before us, the transfer of the Burr Oaks property to petitioner is so lacking in the essential characteristics of a sale and is replete with so many of the elements normally found in an equity contribution (cf. Emanuel N. (Manny) Kolkey, 27 T.C. 37 (1956), affd. 254 F.2d 51 (C.A. 7, 1958), and Bruce v. Knox, 180 F. Supp. 907 (D. Minn. 1960)) that it appears to us as nothing more than a shabby attempt to withdraw from petitioner, at capital gains rates, the developer's profit normally inherent in the subdivision and sale of raw acreage such as the Burr Oaks property.

This Court has been required upon numerous occasions to determine the true nature of alleged sales or transfers of assets to corporations. In the *Kolkey* case, we listed the following questions as among the relevant criteria for making such a determination:

---

[6]The statutory notices issued to the individual petitioners seem to be grounded on the theory that Elkind, Watkins, and Ritz were not entitled to report the sale of the Burr Oaks property as long-term capital gain since they were dealers. The deficiency notices did not raise any question with regard to the proper year for reporting the gain. In view of the fact that respondent, in the deficiency notice to petitioner-corporation, determined that petitioner's basis for the Burr Oaks property was the same as that of the transferors of the property, said statutory notice would seem to be based on the theory that the transfer was governed by sec. 351. This is undoubtedly what caused Elkind, Watkins, and Ritz to raise the following issue by way of amended petition: "In the alternative, in the event the basis of the . . . [Burr Oaks property] in the hands of . . . [petitioner] is determined under section 351 of the Internal Revenue Code, respondent erred in failing to determine that petitioners had no taxable gain for the year 1959 as a result of the transfer of the said real estate to . . . [petitioner]."

We have concluded that the transfer of the Burr Oaks property to petitioner was not a sale on the basis of the clear, uncontroverted facts in the record and without resort to the burden of proof. Nevertheless, we believe it appropriate to point out that the petitioners Elkind, Watkins, and Ritz, as well as the Burr Oaks Corp., have the burden of proof on this issue. For even if we were to regard the issue of whether the transfer of the property constitutes a bona fide sale as new matter insofar as Elkind, Watkins, and Ritz are concerned, they raised that question by way of their amended petition.

"Was the capital and credit structure of the new corporation realistic? What was the business purpose, if any, of organizing the new corporation? Were the noteholders the actual promoters and entrepreneurs of the new adventure? Did the noteholders bear the principal risks of loss attendant upon the adventure? Were payments of 'principal and interest' on the notes subordinated to dividends and to the claims of creditors? Did the noteholders have substantial control over the business operations; and if so, was such control reserved to them as an integral part of the plan under which the notes were issued? Was the 'price' of the properties, for which the notes were issued, disproportionate to the fair market value of such properties? Did the noteholders, when default of the notes occurred, attempt to enforce the obligations? [Emanuel N. (Manny) Kolkey, supra at 59.]"

We have set forth in our Findings of Fact, with some degree of specificity, the various factors which cause us to conclude that the transfer of the Burr Oaks property to petitioner was an equity contribution, rather than a sale. We set forth below some of the more significant factors which led us to this conclusion.

In the first place, petitioner, from the start of its existence, was not only undercapitalized, but, in fact, had no significant capitalization at all. Cf. Hoguet Real Estate Corporation, 30 T.C. 580, 598 (1958). Thus, petitioner was organized in October with a paid-in capital of $4,500. Shortly thereafter, when Elkind, Watkins, and Ritz transferred the Burr Oaks property to petitioner, its books of account reflected liabilities of $360,000. In addition, it was contemplated from the very outset of petitioner's existence that although the city of Madison would initially pay the major portion of the cost of improving the Burr Oaks property, petitioner would, nevertheless, be required to incur substantial development costs. Petitioner estimated that these costs would be in excess of $100,000.

Another factor indicating that petitioner was undercapitalized and did not have sufficient funds with which to commence business is that on November 30, 1957, less than 2 months after it was formed, it borrowed $15,000 from Elkind. On February 28, 1958, it borrowed an additional $10,000 from Elkind.

Moreover, the land transferred to petitioner by Elkind, Watkins, and Ritz was its only asset of significance and, without it, petitioner could not have engaged in business. See and compare Edward G. Janeway, 2 T.C. 197 (1943), affd. 147 F.2d 602 (C.A. 2, 1945); Aqualane Shores, Inc., 30 T.C. 519 (1958), affd. 269 F.2d 116 (C.A. 5, 1959). It was at all times contemplated by Elkind, Watkins, and Ritz that the land would remain at the risk of petitioner's business.

It is generally recognized that one of the crucial factors in determining whether the transfer of property to a thinly capitalized corporation constitutes a bona fide sale, rather than a mere contribution to capital, is the anticipated source of payment to the transferor. Gilbert v. Commissioner, 262 F.2d 512, 514 (C.A. 2, 1959), affirming a Memorandum Opinion of this Court, certiorari denied 359 U.S. 1002 (1959). If payment to the transferor is dependent solely upon the success of an untried, under-capitalized business, the prospects of which are uncertain, the transfer of property raises a strong inference that it is, in fact, an equity contribution. But cf. Miller's

Estate v. Commissioner, 239 F.2d 729, 733 (C.A. 9, 1956), reversing 24 T.C. 923 (1955); Sheldon Tauber, 24 T.C. 179, 181-182 (1955); and Ainslie Perrault, 25 T.C. 439 (1955), affirmed per curiam 244 F.2d 408 (C.A. 10, 1957), where repayment of the notes involved was dependent upon the continued success of an established business with a good earnings record and excellent future prospects.

At the time of the transfer of the Burr Oaks property to petitioner, its business prospects can only be described as speculative and uncertain. Elkind, Watkins, and Ritz realized that the only way petitioner could raise the $100,000 needed by it for improvements would be from sales of lots. It is obvious that the only hope that Elkind, Watkins, and Ritz had of obtaining repayment of the so-called promissory notes depended upon the successful development and sale of the lots in the Burr Oaks property.

Despite the fact that the respective interests of Elkind, Watkins, and Ritz in petitioner were represented by what purported on their face to be promissory notes in the principal amount of $110,000, the evidence before us indicates that it was the intent of all concerned with the affairs of petitioner that these instruments would give Elkind, Watkins, and Ritz a continuing interest in petitioner's business. The instruments issued by petitioner to Elkind, Watkins, and Ritz recited that they were to mature in 2 years from the date of issuance. However, after a review of the entire record, we believe that it was understood that no payment would be made on the notes, or would ever be demanded by Elkind, Watkins, and Ritz, which in any way would weaken or undermine petitioner's business. See Charter Wire, Inc. v. United States, 309 F.2d 878, 881 (C.A. 7, 1962). It is true that petitioner during 1959 paid $31,000 apiece to Elkind, Watkins, and Ritz with respect to their so-called promissory notes.[8] However, petitioner's history with regard to making payments on the alleged promissory notes indicates that the payments thereon came only from gains derived through the sale of lots. Moreover, the fact that there was outstanding a substantial principal balance ($46,000) on each of the notes issued to the individual petitioners even as late as the time of the trial herein indicates that the alleged notes were intended to give the individual petitioners a continuing quity interest in petitioner. See Charter Wire, Inc. v. United States, supra at 881.

The evidence clearly indicates that although Elkind, Watkins, and Ritz were not stockholders of record in petitioner, nevertheless, they completely dominated and controlled petitioner's affairs. Watkins was petitioner's president. Petitioner's board of directors consisted of Elkind, his wife, Ritz, his brother Philip, Watkins, and Watkins' wife. McGinnes, the man who ran petitioner's day-to-day affairs, had been employed by Elkind in one capacity or another for a period of at least 15 years. His activities were generally supervised by Ritz' accounting firm. After listening

[8]On brief, it is argued on behalf of the various petitioners herein that the series of exchanges of notes that occurred at the end of December 1959 between Elkind, Watkins, and Ritz, on the one hand, and petitioner, on the other, constituted a repayment by petitioner of the "unpaid principal balance" in the amount of $79,000 on each of the alleged promissory notes, followed immediately by an advance of a similar amount by each of the individual petitioners. This alleged repayment by petitioner of an aggregate of $237,000 took place at a time when petitioner's liquid assets totaled less than $5,500. It is too much to ask this Court to believe that such an obvious sham constituted a repayment of the alleged notes. Cf. Arthur L. Kniffen, 39 T.C. 553, 565-566 (1962).

to his testimony and that of Elkind, Watkins, and Ritz, we are convinced that McGinnes operated petitioner in accordance with their wishes.

Petitioner's shareholders of record consisted of Ritz' brothers Philip and Erwin, Elkind's wife, and Watkins' wife. They knew and understood little, if anything, of the nature of petitioner's business. Moreover, after listening to the testimony at the trial, it was obvious to us that they were subject to the control of Elkind, Watkins, and Ritz.

By virtue of the provision in petitioner's articles of incorporation regarding the issuance of additional shares of common stock at such prices as a majority of the board of directors should determine, Elkind, Watkins, and Ritz were in a position to appropriate to themselves (through the issuance of additional common stock at whatever price they chose) substantially all of the profits that petitioner might realize after repaying its purported indebtedness to them.

The record also indicates that in transferring the Burr Oaks property to petitioner, Elkind, Watkins, and Ritz assigned a highly inflated value to said property. Cf. Emanuel N. (Manny) Kolkey, supra at 61. The transfer of the Burr Oaks property to petitioner seems to us an integral part of a plan devised by Ritz whereby Ritz, Watkins, and Elkind could obtain an assured participation in the fruits of the development and subdivision of said property. See Bruce v. Knox, supra at 912. Watkins and Ritz both admitted that petitioner was formed in order to allow them to receive some part of the development profits. The inflation of the "sales price" to petitioner served to extend the period during which Elkind, Watkins, and Ritz could participate in petitioner's business as "creditors" and increased the amount which they could withdraw as "principal" if the venture proved successful.

These are some of the factors which led us to conclude that the promissory notes received by Elkind, Watkins, and Ritz did not represent a true indebtedness. The purported promissory notes issued to the individual petitioners in our opinion constitute preferred stock.[10] See 1432 Broadway Corporation, supra at 1166; Foresun, Inc., 41 T.C. 706, 717 (1964), on appeal (C.A. 6, Apr. 20, 1964); and Sherwood Memorial Gardens, Inc., supra at 230.

Having decided that for tax purposes the so-called promisory notes issued to Elkind, Watkins, and Ritz constitute an equity interest in petitioner, we must now determine whether the transfer of the Burr Oaks property is governed by section 351.

Section 351 deals with transfers of property to a corporation controlled by the transferor or transferors. In pertinent part that section provides:

"(a) . . . No gain or loss shall be recognized if property is transferred to a corporation by one or more persons solely in exchange for stock or securities in such corporation and immediately after the exchange such person or persons are in con-

---

[10]Although we have found the purported promissory notes to constitute equity interests in petitioner for tax purposes, we believe that the holders of those instruments occupied a preferred position vis-à-vis the holders of the common stock. In the first place, the purported promissory notes called for the payment of interest at 6 percent a year. This provision constituted a prior charge on the earnings of petitioner in favor of the holders of those instruments, not unlike a preferred dividend. Thus, we regard the purported promissory notes as preferred stock.

trol (as defined in section 368(c)) of the corporation. . . ." Section 368(c) defines "control" for purposes of section 351 as meaning "ownership of stock possessing at least 80 percent of the total combined voting power of all classes of stock entitled to vote and at least 80 percent of the total number of shares of all other classes of stock of the corporation."

In contending that section 351 does not govern the transfer of the Burr Oaks property, petitioner has presented three arguments. Two of the arguments (that the transaction was a sale and that no stock or securities were issued to the transferors of the property) have been previously considered and resolved adversely to petitioner. The third argument presented is that Elkind, Watkins, and Ritz, who transferred the Burr Oaks property to petitioner, were not, immediately after that transaction, in control of that corporation within the meaning of the term "control" as defined in section 368(c). Thus, it is contended that even if the promissory notes held by Elkind, Watkins, and Ritz constituted stock, that stock did not carry with it any voting rights. Petitioner further points out (1) that pursuant to its bylaws the right to vote was reserved exclusively to the shareholders of record, namely, Elkind's wife, Watkins' wife, and Ritz' two brothers, and (2) that, for the above reason, the transferors of the Burr Oaks property (Elkind, Watkins, and Ritz) failed to comply with the control requirements set forth in section 368(c) because they did not possess "ownership of stock possessing at least 80 percent of the total combined voting power of all classes of stock entitled to vote." There is a basic fallacy in petitioner's argument in that it is premised on the assumption that Elkind, Watkins, and Ritz were the only transferors of property to petitioner.

As we view the transaction, Elkind, Watkins, and Ritz acted together with Elkind's wife, Watkins' wife, and Ritz' two brothers in forming petitioner. The record clearly indicates that each of them transferred property to petitioner. As we have previously found, Elkind's wife, Watkins' wife, and Philip and Erwin Ritz transferred to petitioner a total of $4,500 shortly after its incorporation. It is settled law that money constitutes property for purposes of section 351. . . . In return therefor, petitioner issued to them an aggregate of 450 shares of its common stock. Shortly thereafter, Elkind, Watkins, and Ritz transferred to petitioner their respective interests in the Burr Oaks property and, in return, received what on its face purported to be promissory notes, but what we have previously determined to be preferred stock.

Although Elkind, Watkins, and Ritz may not have received their preferred stock interests in petitioner at exactly the same time as the common stock was issued to Ritz' brothers and the respective wives of Elkind and Watkins, it seems clear that the transfers of cash and the Burr Oaks property to petitioner were integral parts of a unified transaction. Camp Wolters Enterprises v. Commissioner, 230 F.2d 555, 559 (C.A. 5, 1956), affirming 22 T.C. 737 (1954), certiorari denied 352 U.S. 826 (1956). See also section 1.351-1(a)(1), Income Tax Regs., which provides:

> The phrase "immediately after the exchange" does not necessarily require simultaneous exchanges by two or more persons, but comprehends a situation where the rights of the parties have been previously defined and the execution of the agreement proceeds with an expedition consistent with orderly procedure. . . .

On the basis of the record before us, it appears to us that Elkind, Watkins, and Ritz, together with Ritz' brothers, Elkind's wife, and Watkins' wife, were in control of petitioner, as defined in section 368(c), immediately after their transfer of property to it. The fact that Elkind, Watkins, and Ritz received no common stock, which according to petitioner's articles of incorporation was the only class of stock entitled to vote, is of no significance; for there is no requirement in section 351 that each transferor receive voting stock for that section to be applicable. See Cyrus S. Eaton, 37 B.T.A. 715 (1938), which involved the transfer of property by two persons to a controlled corporation. One transferor therein received only common stock and the other received only nonvoting preferred. In commenting upon the question of control, we stated: "Inasmuch as the transferors . . . owned all of the stock of the corporation, they have the necessary control required by the statute."[11] See also Gus Russell, Inc., 36 T.C. 965 (1961).

Since the nonrecognition provisions of section 351 apply to the transfer of the Burr Oaks property to petitioner, petitioner's basis in said property is limited to $100,000, which is a carryover basis from the transferors. Sec. 362(a)(1).

Insofar as the distributions made by petitioner during 1959 to Elkind, Watkins, and Ritz are concerned, we have previously found that, to the extent they purported to be a repayment of the "promissory notes," they were a sham. The net effect of the various payments by petitioner and exchanges of notes was that petitioner distributed $31,000 apiece to Elkind, Watkins, and Ritz in 1959. To this extent, the distributions resemble a redemption of stock in that the respective interests of these three individuals in petitioner were proportionately lessened. However, we are unable to find that said distributions fit within any of the paragraphs of section 302(b). Therefore, the $31,000 distributed by petitioner to Watkins, Elkind, and Ritz is governed by section 302(d) and to the extent of petitioner's earnings and profits is to be treated as a dividend.

Decisions will be entered under Rule 50.

NOTE

What argument might have been advanced for Ritz, but not for the others, to avoid dividend treatment? Consider the scope of §318(a)(1) in answering this question. Should the argument prevail?

COMMENT, SECTION 351 TRANSFERS TO CONTROLLED CORPORATIONS: THE FORGOTTEN TERM — "SECURITIES"
114 U. Pa. L. Rev. 314 (1965)

Tax advisors dealing with a transfer of property to a controlled corporation often find themselves in a quandary, for although there have been many cases in

---

[11]This Court ultimately held that the nonrecognition provisions of sec. 112(b), I.R.C. 1939 (the predecessor of sec. 351), did not apply because the transferors failed to comply with the provisions of the "substantially proportionate" test which Congress deleted from the section when it was reenacted as sec. 351, I.R.C. 1954.

this area, no clear rule has evolved for deciding whether a given transfer is governed by the nonrecognition provisions of section 351. This situation has come about because courts generally use an analysis that forecloses consideration of an important issue raised by the statute. The Tax Court's recent handling of these cases[2] illustrates this approach and its defects.

A dispute between the Commissioner and the corporation over the latter's proper basis in the transferred property often raises the question of the applicability of section 351. If a transfer is governed by section 351, the basis to the corporation is the same basis that the property had in the hands of the transferor;[3] whereas if the transfer is not governed by section 351, the basis to the corporation is its cost.[4] When the property is depreciable, the Commissioner often disallows part of the corporation's depreciation deduction, contending that the proper basis was that of the transferor and not the cost. Charles E. Curry[5] demonstrates the advantages that can result from the exclusion of a transfer of depreciable property from section 351.[6]

In *Curry,* four adult members of a family transferred income producing real property to a corporation controlled partly by two of the transferors and partly by a related third person.[7] There had been prior negotiations with an outside party. The final terms were basically similar to those offered by the outsider. The transferors received a small cash down payment and took a first and a second mortgage on the property.[8] No restrictions were placed on the right to alienate the corporation's shares, and in fact by the time of trial one of the shareholders had transferred his shares to an unrelated third party.

Judge Forrester, in a decision reviewed by the court, rejected the Commissioner's contention that the transaction was governed by section 351, holding instead that the transfer constituted a "sale" and that section 351 does not apply to "sales." The

---

[2]E.g., Arthur M. Rosenthal, 24 CCH Tax Ct. Mem. 1373 (1965); Charles E. Curry, 43 T.C. 667 (1965), acq., 1965 Int. Rev. Bull. No. 38, at 4; Burr Oaks Corp., 43 T.C. 635 (1965).

[3]Int. Rev. Code of 1954, §362(a).

[4]See Int. Rev. Code of 1954, §1012. The cost of the property will ordinarily be the fair market value of what the corporation gives up for it. In the absence of a readily ascertainable market value for what the corporation gives up, the cost will be the fair market value of the transferred property. United States v. Davis, 370 U.S. 65, 72-73 (1962).

[5]43 T.C. 667 (1965), acq., 1965 Int. Rev. Bull. No. 38, at 4.

[6]But see Int. Rev. Code of 1954, §§1239, 1245, 1250, which mitigate the benefits gained by transferring depreciable property to a corporation at a stepped up basis.

[7]The shares before and after the transfer were apportioned as follows:

	Share of Property	Share of Corporate Stock
Father	30%	10%
Mother	30%	—
Son	20%	45%
Daughter	20%	—
Son-in-law	—	45%
	100%	100%

[8]Principal payments on the second mortgage were not scheduled to begin until the first mortgage was satisfied. In addition principal payments on the second mortgage could be waived if the cash flow from the property was not equal to the sum of cash expenses, payments on the first mortgage, capital expenditures and taxes.

effect of this decision was to allow the corporation to use a 1,400,000 dollar basis on which to take depreciation rather than the 85,000 dollar basis of the transferors.

Even when the transferred property is not depreciable, the question of the proper basis to the corporation is often disputed. In Burr Oaks Corp.,[11] three individuals who owned a tract of land with a low basis and a high market value transferred it to a new corporation they had organized. The corporation was to subdivide and improve the land and sell it in lots.[12] The stockholders of the corporation were the wives and brothers of the three transferors and had nothing to do with its operation. In payment for the land each transferor received a two year promissory note bearing six percent interest. During 1959 each received payments from the corporation on the notes. At maturity the notes were extended, and at the time of the trial still had not been paid in full.

Judge Fay, in a decision reviewed by the court, held that the transfer of the land to the corporation was a capital contribution rather than a sale and that the promissory notes given to the transferors in return represented preferred stock. He went on to hold the transaction governed by section 351, and that therefore, the corporation took the transferors' basis in the property. The corporation's taxable income was increased by the amount its basis in the property was reduced;[15] the transferors were denied capital gains treatment on the sale of the land to the corporation, and their basis for the corporate stock became the same as their basis had been in the exchanged property.[16]

A related issue often present in these cases in the proper treatment to be given the amounts paid to the transferors on the notes they were given in exchange for the transferred property. The Commissioner often disallows the corporation's interest deduction, contending that the notes represent capital contributions and the payments, dividends.[17] If the Commissioner prevails, not only is the corporation denied its deduction, but the individual transferors must pay tax on the "dividends" that they had hoped would be treated as tax free principal. This issue, commonly known as the debt-equity issue, arises in many areas of the Code and can hardly be characterized as unique to section 351 cases.[18] Its determination requires a factual evaluation of all relevant circumstances to see whether the substance of the debt instrument upholds its form.[19]

In handling these cases the courts usually fail to separate the debt-equity and nonrecognition issues. The Commissioner usually attempts to have the transfer

---

[11]43 T.C. 635 (1965).

[12]This factual situation is a common one. See, e.g., Bruce v. Knox, 180 F. Supp. 907 (D. Minn. 1960); Aqualane Shores, Inc., 30 T.C. 519 (1958), aff'd, 269 F.2d 116 (5th Cir. 1959).

[15]The corporation's basis was reduced from the claimed $360,000 to $100,000, and when all the lots have been sold its taxable income will have been increased by the $260,000 difference.

[16]Int. Rev. Code of 1954, §358(a).

[17]See, e.g., Castle Heights, Inc. v. United States, 242 F. Supp. 350 (E.D. Tenn. 1965); Bruce v. Knox, 180 F. Supp. 907 (D. Minn. 1960); Burr Oaks Corp., 43 T.C. 635 (1965).

[18]See Caplin, The Caloric Count of a Thin Incorporation, 17 N.Y.U. Inst. on Fed. Tax. 771, 811 n.198 (1959). See generally Goldstein, Corporate Indebtedness to Shareholders: "Thin Capitalization" and Related Problems, 16 Tax L. Rev. 1 (1960).

[19]See Gooding Amusement Co., 23 T.C. 408, 418 (1954), aff'd, 236 F.2d 159 (6th Cir. 1956), cert. denied, 352 U.S. 1031 (1957).

classified as a capital contribution because the corporation would then be denied both its interest deduction and a stepped up basis. If he is successful, the debt will be "stock" for purposes of section 351.[20] On the other hand, the corporation's goal is to have the transfer classified as a "sale"[21] because the courts do not apply section 351 to "sales."[22] When a court frames the issue in terms of whether a transfer is a "sale" as opposed to a "capital contribution," it is considering the debt-equity issue and the issue of the applicability of section 351 simultaneously, and is thereby foreclosing the possibility of finding the debt valid but the transaction nevertheless within section 351.

The courts rely on a number of criteria in determining whether a transfer is a "sale." When a transfer is held to be a capital contribution rather than a sale, three factors are most likely to be emphasized. The first is whether the corporation is undercapitalized. Although undercapitalization alone cannot be determinative,[23] the courts still consider it.[24]

The second factor — variously referred to as "risk of the business" or "anticipated source of payments" — concerns the source of the funds necessary to pay off the corporate debt obligations. Where the transferred property is undeveloped and constitutes the corporation's only significant asset, the payment of the notes is completely dependent upon the successful development of the property. In these cases the courts tend to view the debt obligations as representing a continuing equity interest in the transferred property.[25] In contrast, when the property already produces sufficient income to cover payments on the notes, the courts are less likely to stress this factor,[26] although theoretically the payment of the notes is dependent upon the future success of the business.

The third criterion — whether the parties intended to create a bona fide debtor-creditor relationship — is based on a judgment of whether the transferor would enforce the notes if they were not paid, even though enforcement would weaken the

[20]Burr Oaks Corp., 43 T.C. 635, 649, 651 (1965).

[21]See Charles E. Curry, 43 T.C. 667 (1965), acq., 1965 Int. Rev. Bull. No. 38, at 4; Evwalt Dev. Corp., 22 CCH Tax Ct. Mem. 220 (1963); J. I. Morgan, Inc., 30 T.C. 881 (1958), acq., 1959-1 Cum. Bull. 4; Ainslie Perrault, 25 T.C. 439 (1955), acq., 1956-1 Cum. Bull. 5.

[22]Arthur M. Rosenthal, 24 CCH Tax Ct. Mem. 1373, 1383 n.4 (1965); Charles E. Curry, supra note 21; see Evwalt Dev. Corp., supra note 21; J. I. Morgan, Inc., supra note 21; Harry F. Shannon, 29 T.C. 702 (1958); Ainslie Perrault, supra note 21.

[23]See Estate of Miller v. Commissioner, 239 F.2d 729 (9th Cir. 1956). A number of cases have held a transfer to be a sale despite a high debt-equity ratio. E.g., Sun Properties, Inc. v. United States, 220 F.2d 171 (5th Cir. 1955) (ratio of 310:1); J. I. Morgan, Inc., 30 T.C. 881 (1958), acq., 1959-1 Cum. Bull. 4 (ratio of 50:1). Compare Caplin, supra note 18, at 777-84, which tells of the complete reliance on the ratio test in the period 1946-1956.

[24]E.g., Bruce v. Knox, 180 F. Supp. 907, 912 (D. Minn. 1960); Burr Oaks Corp., 43 T.C. 635, 646 (1965); Marsan Realty Corp., 22 CCH Tax Ct. Mem. 1513, 1523 (1963).

[25]See Aqualane Shores, Inc. v. Commissioner, 269 F.2d 116 (5th Cir. 1959); Castle Heights, Inc. v. United States, 242 F. Supp. 350 (E.D. Tenn. 1965); Bruce v. Knox, supra note 24; Burr Oaks Corp., supra note 24; Daro Corp., 20 CCH Tax Ct. Mem. 1588 (1961).

[26]See Charles E. Curry, 43 T.C. 667 (1965), acq., 1965 Int. Rev. Bull. No. 38, at 4; Aqualane Shores, Inc. v. Commissioner, supra note 25, at 120 (dictum). But see Marsan Realty Corp., 22 CCH Tax Ct. Mem. 1513 (1963). For cases where the court has found a "sale," stressing that the transferred property was not at the risk of the business, see J. I. Morgan, Inc., 30 T.C. 881, 891 (1958), acq., 1959-1 Cum. Bull. 4; Warren H. Brown, 27 T.C. 27, 33 (1956), acq., 1957-2 Cum. Bull. 4.

corporation's financial position.[27] In cases where payments were missed and the transferors took no action,[28] the determination of the intent question is easier than in cases where the notes have always been paid on time. In the latter cases the court must infer the parties' intent.

When the court finds the transferors had a "valid business purpose" for "selling" rather than making a capital contribution, the transfer is likely to be excluded from section 351 regardless of what other factors are present.[29] For example, the Tax Court found a valid business purpose where the transferor sold equipment to the corporation because a capital contribution in return for stock would have greatly diluted the equity interests of his two business partners and held that section 351 did not apply.[30] In other cases where a "sale" is upheld the court is likely to stress the intent of the parties to make a "sale."[31]

Although these criteria are relevant to deciding the debt-equity issue, by themselves they are not suited for determining the applicability of section 351 to a given transfer. To begin with, they do not accord with the language of the section. Of course since equity is stock within section 351, the solution of the debt-equity issue does bear to some extent upon the section 351 problem; but even where the debt is valid, the transfer may come within the section's "securities" provision. Further, the debt-equity criteria do not reflect the underlying policy of section 351. That policy was clearly expressed by Judge Magruder twenty-five years ago:

"It is the purpose of [section 351] . . . to save the taxpayer from an immediate recognition of a gain, or to intermit the claim of a loss, in certain transactions where gain or loss may have accrued in a constitutional sense, but where in a popular and economic sense there has been a mere change in the form of ownership and the taxpayer has not really 'cashed-in' on the theoretical gain or closed out a losing venture. . . . The transaction described in the statute lacks a distinguishing characteristic of a sale, in that, instead of the transaction having the effect of terminating or extinguishing the beneficial interests of the transferors in the transferred property, after the consummation of the transaction the transferors continue to be beneficially interested in the transferred property and have dominion over it by virtue of their control of the new corporate owner of it."[32]

---

[27]Gooding Amusement Co., 23 T.C. 408, 418 (1954), aff'd, 236 F.2d 159 (6th Cir. 1956), cert. denied, 352 U.S. 1031 (1957).

[28]See Marsan Realty Corp., 22 CCH Tax Ct. Mem. 1513 (1963); cf. R. M. Gunn, 25 T.C. 424 (1955), aff'd per curiam sub nom. Perrault v. Commissioner, 244 F.2d 408 (10th Cir.), cert. denied, 355 U.S. 830 (1957). In *Gunn* when the Commissioner asserted that the payments on the "notes" were really dividends the corporation stopped making payments in order to avoid further tax if it lost the case. The court noted this stoppage in finding an intent not to enforce payment of the notes.

[29]See Estate of Miller v. Commissioner, 239 F.2d 729 (9th Cir. 1956), reversing 24 T.C. 923 (1955) (to continue business after impending death of one of three partners); Warren H. Brown, 27 T.C. 27 (1956), acq., 1957-2 Cum. Bull. 4 (to settle dispute over expansion between two partners).

[30]J. I. Morgan, Inc., 30 T.C. 881 (1958), acq., 1959-1 Cum. Bull. 4.

[31]See Evwalt Dev. Corp., 22 CCH Tax Ct. Mem. 220 (1963); Harry F. Shannon, 29 T.C. 702 (1958).

[32]Portland Oil Co. v. Commissioner, 109 F.2d 479, 488 (1st Cir.) (quoting American Com-

The legislative history[33] and other cases[34] accord with this expression of the section's policy.

The determination of the "sale" issue does not and can not answer the question of the applicability of section 351. Its use by the courts, therefore, is improper. Its effect is to foreclose consideration of an important issue raised by the statutory language: Whether the transfer was made "in exchange for stock or securities" of the corporation.

In Campbell v. Carter Foundation Prod. Co.[35] the Fifth Circuit considered the debt-equity and section 351 issues separately. In that case a tax exempt foundation transferred income-producing property to a corporation of which it was the sole stockholder for the purpose of avoiding the tax on unrelated business income.[36] In return for the property the foundation received a small cash payment and eleven promissory notes which matured over the following five years. Deciding the debt-equity issue first, the court found the corporate notes to represent valid indebtedness and the interest paid thereon to be deductible. The court then proceeded to consider whether section 351 was applicable, stating the issue as "whether businessmen acting with all honor and sincerity have, or have not, set up a transaction which tax law regards as 'stock' or 'securities.'" The court then concluded that even though there was a valid business reason for the transfer, no rearrangement of beneficial ownership had taken place, and in the final analysis economic ownership remained the same. It therefore found the transfer to be within section 351 even though the debt was valid. In addition to separating the two issues, the court avoided the use of the term "sale" and its tendency to divert the court's attention from the proper issue.

If, like *Carter,* the courts did not use the "sale" analysis, they would have to decide whether valid debt instruments were "securities" for purposes of section 351. Although the term "securities" is not defined in section 351, it has the same meaning there that it has under the reorganization provisions of the Code.[40]

The scope of that meaning was first outlined in Pinellas Ice & Cold Storage Co. v. Commissioner[41] where the Supreme Court held that short term notes were not "securities" on the theory that the notes were equivalent to cash and that the tax free organization provision did not apply to cash transactions. Even though this holding is arguably wrong,[43] it seems to be well embedded in the tax law.

---

press & Warehouse Co. v. Bender, 70 F.2d 655, 657 (5th Cir. 1934)), cert. denied, 310 U.S. 650 (1940).

[33]See S. Rep. No. 275, 67th Cong., 1st Sess. 11 (1921), in 1939-1 Cum Bull. 188-89. The 1954 Code made no change in the basic purpose of the section. See H.R. Rep. No. 1337, 83d Cong., 2d Sess. A116 (1954).

[34]Cf. Jordan Marsh Co. v. Commissioner, 269 F.2d 453, 456 (2d Cir. 1959); Trenton Cotton Oil Co. v. Commissioner, 147 F.2d 33, 36 (6th Cir. 1945); Clyde Bacon, Inc., 4 T.C. 1107, 1117 (1945).

[35]322 F.2d 827 (5th Cir. 1963).

[36]Int. Rev. Code of 1954, §512.

[40]Lloyd-Smith v. Commissioner, 116 F.2d 642, 644 (2d Cir. 1941); Camp Wolters Enterprises, Inc., 22 T.C. 737, 751 (1954), aff'd, 230 F.2d 555 (5th Cir.), cert. denied, 352 U.S. 826 (1956). For the reorganization provisions, see Int. Rev. Code of 1954, §§354-95.

[41]287 U.S. 462 (1933).

[43]See Griswold, "Securities" and "Continuity of Interest," 58 Harv. L. Rev. 705, 706-12, 718-

From *Pinellas* two separate tests developed for deciding whether a given instrument was a "security"—its term and its name. The importance of the term of the instrument follows naturally from the rationale of *Pinellas*. The rule of thumb was that instruments payable in five years or less did not qualify as "securities" while those for ten years or more qualified.[45] The Commissioner's position was that notes of less than four years did not qualify as "securities."[46] However, that ruling was withdrawn[47] in line with his new policy of not issuing advance rulings on whether debt instruments are "stock" or "securities" for purposes of section 351.[48]

The second factor relied on by the courts was the name given to the debt instrument by the parties. It was thought that "notes" did not qualify as "securities."[49] The dichotomy between notes on the one hand and bonds and debentures on the other had little basis in the case decisions.[50] The distinction is fortunately no longer used by the courts.[51] One kind of instrument in which the name may remain important is the "installment sales contract." The Tax Court in Warren H. Brown[52] held that a contract calling for ten annual installments with interest on the unpaid balance was not a "security" because "the installment contract in question was not intended to insure the partners a continued participation in the business of the transferee corporation, but was intended rather to effect a termination of such continuing interest." The decision does not seem to be valid. There are no economic differences between a long term installment sales agreement and a formal long term corporate debenture that should lead to different tax consequences under section 351. The holders of both instruments will have a "continuing interest" in the affairs of the corporation for the duration of the term. The only difference is the amount of the interest and that is not relevant to defining "securities." Furthermore, under the court's theory, no debt that was being amortized could qualify as a "security" regardless of the length of its term. In any event, *Brown* is the only case holding installment sales contracts not to be "securities."

The current test used by the courts was announced by the Tax Court in Camp Wolters Enterprises, Inc.[54] where five to nine year subordinated notes were held to be "securities" within section 351:

---

25 (1945). Griswold also states that the decision has led the courts to restrict unduly the scope of the term "securities." Id. at 719.

[45]See Camp Wolters Enterprises, Inc., 22 T.C. 737, 751 (1954); Bittker, Federal Income Taxation of Corporations and Shareholders 82 (1959); Comment, 16 U. Miami L. Rev. 434, 445 (1962).

[46]Rev. Rul. 56-303, 1956-2 Cum. Bull. 193.

[47]Rev. Rul. 63-28, 1963-1 Cum. Bull. 76.

[48]Rev. Proc. 62-32, §4.015, 1962-2 Cum Bull. 527, 532.

[49]See Griswold, supra note 43, at 719; Weiss, Notes as Securities Within Section 112(b)(3), 26 Taxes 228 (1948).

[50]See id. at 228-20. Compare L & E Stirn, Inc. v. Commissioner, 107 F.2d 390 (2d Cir. 1939) (bonds held not to be securities), with Burnham v. Commissioner, 86 F.2d 776 (7th Cir.), cert. denied, 300 U.S. 683 (1936) (notes held to be securities).

[51]See Camp Wolters Enterprises, Inc., 22 T.C. 737, 750-51 (1954). Bittker questions the need for any formal instrument in a close corporation, contending that the corporation's promise on open account has the same meaning to the shareholder as a bond or note. Bittker, op. cit. supra note 45, at 104.

[52]27 T.C. 27 (1956), acq., 1957-2 Cum. Bull. 4.

[54]22 T.C. 773 (1954).

"The test . . . is not a mechanical determination of the time period of the note. Though time is an important factor, the controlling consideration is an over-all evaluation of the nature of the debt, degree of participation and continuing interest in the business, the extent of proprietary interest compared with the similarity of the note to a cash payment, the purposes of the advances, etc."

Since the courts so rarely reach the "securities" issue, and since the only case since *Camp Wolters* to consider it thoroughly was the incorrectly decided *Brown* case, it is not clear how the test will operate as compared to the term test. It is probable that the new test will treat short term debt of the *Pinellas* type and long term debt in the same manner as before. The holding in *Camp Wolters* suggests that debt falling within these two extremes will more likely be classified as "securities" under the new test than they were under the old term test.

This general test will probably be used to decide most of the cases that arise. However, other factors may be employed in solving specific problems as, for example, where an individual[56] transfers property to a corporation of which he is the sole share-holder in exchange for debt instruments of the corporation. On these facts the court in the *Carter* case[57] held the transfer to be within section 351 without specifying whether the notes were "stock" or "securities." Although the court's finding that the debt was valid seems to indicate that the notes were "securities," its express refusal to categorize them at all may mean that it was not concerned about an exact classification. This would not be inexplicable, since the policy of section 351 applies to all cases where, because the transferor is the sole shareholder of the corporation, it is impossible to have a shift in beneficial ownership.

The beneficial ownership test, however, works only in cases like *Carter* where it is literally impossible to have a change in beneficial ownership.[60] Otherwise, the reasoning behind its application would become circular, since the extent of beneficial ownership is measured by ownership of "stock" or "securities": section 351 is inapplicable only if there is a genuine rearrangement of beneficial interest, but there is a genuine rearrangement of beneficial ownership only if the notes are not "securities." Thus in *Curry*, when the Tax Court held section 351 inapplicable because of the disproportion between stock and note ownership, it held by implication that the notes were not "securities." The issue the court said it did not have to decide was therefore the key to the correctness of its decision.

There were two promissory notes issued by the transferee corporation to the transferors in *Curry*. The first was for ten years, secured by a first mortgage and provided for equal semi-annual principal payments plus interest on the unpaid balance. The second note, secured by a second mortgage, required semi-annual interest payments on the unpaid balance with principal payments to start in the

---

[56]The transferor-shareholder could also be a group. See Arthur M. Rosenthal, 24 CCH Tax Ct. Mem. 1373 (1965).

[57]Campbell v. Carter Foundation Prod. Co., 322 F.2d 827 (5th Cir. 1963).

[60]*Curry* would have been such a case except that the court found as a fact that the parties, despite their family relationship, had dealt with each other at "arms length." Charles E. Curry, 43 T.C. 667, 687 (1965), acq., 1965 Int. Rev. Bull. No. 38, at 4.

eleventh year and to continue for ten years in equal annual installments. There was also a waiver clause on second mortgage principal payments under certain circumstances.

Considering the twenty year length of the second note, the absence of principal payments for ten years, and the waiver clause, the note should be classified as a "security."[66] The first mortgage note is harder to classify. On its face it is very similar to the installment sales contract which *Brown* held not to be a "security." But even assuming that *Brown* is right, *Curry* is distinguishable because the continued subordination of payments to other expenditures tends to show that the instrument evidenced a "continuing interest" in the corporation's business.

Curry illustrates the danger the "sale" analysis presents to the proper handling of section 351 cases. In that case the "sale" approach led to the wrong result. These problems could be avoided if the courts would consider the cases in light of the issues raised by the statutory language of section 351 rather than by looking for a "sale."

STEVENS PASS, INC. v. COMMISSIONER
48 T.C. 532 (1967)

FAY, Judge. . . . The parties have stipulated as to certain items raised in the statutory notice of deficiency so that [one of] the issues remaining for determination [is] as follows:

(1) Whether, upon the liquidation of its subsidiary, petitioner was entitled to the step-up in the basis of depreciable assets pursuant to section 334(b)(2) of the Internal Revenue Code of 1954. . . .

Findings of Fact

. . . Petitioner, Stevens Pass, Inc., is a Washington corporation which was organized on September 29, 1960. Its principal office at the date of filing the petition was located at Stevens Pass, Washington. Since December 1, 1960, petitioner has operated the ski area at Stevens Pass. Petitioner, an accrual basis taxpayer, computed its income on the basis of a fiscal year ending September 30. . . .

Petitioner is the survivor by merger, under the laws of the State of Washington, with Stevens Pass Company, Inc. (hereinafter referred to as the old company), on December 1, 1960.

The old company was organized in 1946 to operate the ski facilities and area at Stevens Pass, Washington. In 1960 the authorized capital of the old company consisted of 100 shares of Class A voting common stock and 33⅓ shares of Class B nonvoting common stock. The Class A and Class B stocks share in the earnings and capital on the basis of two-thirds to Class A and one-third to Class B. The total authorized and issued shares of the old company on November 30, 1960, were owned as follows:

[66]See Camp Wolters Enterprises, Inc., 22 T.C. 737, 751 (1954).

Name	Class A	Class B
Donald G. Adams*	50	0
Bruce Kehr*	50	0
John H. Caley	0	$33\frac{1}{3}$

*By agreements dated June 16, 1948, and September 15, 1948, between Adams and Kehr, Adams had 51 percent voting control of the old company.

Sometime during the spring of 1960 an irreparable dispute arose between Donald G. Adams (hereinafter referred to as Adams) and Bruce Kehr (hereinafter referred to as Kehr). It was determined that the dispute could not be settled unless one or the other sold his stock in the old company. However, no agreement was reached that was satisfactory to both parties. Thereafter, Adams, Kehr, and John H. Caley (hereinafter referred to as Caley) attempted to interest outside investors in acquiring stock in a new corporation to be formed to acquire the stock of the old company and then to dissolve it.

On June 10, 1960, Adams, Kehr, and Caley offered to sell all of their shares in the old company to Loren D. Prescott, an agent for undisclosed principals, for the sum of $650,000. Contemporaneously with the execution of the offer to sell, they executed an agreement among themselves concerning the division of the $650,000 sales proceeds as follows: Adams, $250,000; Kehr, $200,000; and Caley, $200,000. This latter agreement also called for the transfer by Kehr of his stock ($33\frac{1}{3}$ shares) in a corporation known as Trams, Inc., to Adams for the sum of $4,800.

On or about June 30, 1960, a prospectus relevant to the financial condition of the old company was prepared and circulated to various potential investors. The prospectus proposed that a new company (petitioner) be formed to purchase all the shares of the old company and then dissolve it.

On September 2, 1960, a subscription account was set up for investment in petitioner. The subscribers, amount subscribed, and date subscribed were as follows:

Date	Name	Units Subscribed*
Aug. 30, 1960	Melvin R. Whitman	4
Sept. 1, 1960	Mel S. Johnston	3
Sept. 6, 1960	Donald P. Christianson	4
Sept. 8, 1960	Miles W. Tippery	4
Sept. 27, 1960	John M. Shiach	$1\frac{1}{3}$
Sept. 27, 1960	Bernard J. Goiney	$1\frac{1}{3}$
Sept. 27, 1960	Homer V. Hartzell	$1\frac{1}{3}$
Oct. 13, 1960	Reider Tanner	1
Nov. 2, 1960	Vernon O. Lundmark	1
		21

*A unit consisted of 10 shares of no par common stock at $250 per share and one $2,500, 20-year, 6-percent debenture at par for a total investment of $5,000.

The subscribers deposited 10 percent of the subscription price into escrow at a bank located in Seattle, Washington.

On September 9, 1960, the offer to sell made by Adams, Kehr, and Caley was accepted. On September 29, 1960, petitioner was organized. On October 22, 1960, petitioner's stock certificate book reflects the issuance of 400 shares of its no par common stock to the following individuals for a total of $100,000.

Certificate No.	Name	Shares
1	Miles W. or Nellie Tippery	40
2	Bruce Kehr	120*
3	John H. Caley	80
4	Reider Tanner	10
5	Melvin R. Whitman	40
6	Mel S. Johnston	30
7	Vernon O. Lundmark	10
8	Donald P. Christianson	20*
9	John M. Shiach	13.33
10	Homer V. Hartzell	13.33
11	Bernard J. Goiney	13.33
12	Mel S. Johnston	10
		400

*Ten of the shares issued in the name of Bruce Kehr are subject to a trust agreement as the property of Christianson and are held by Kehr as security for a loan of $5,000 made by him to Christianson to enable the latter to purchase an investment unit in petitioner.

On November 4, 1960, petitioner entered into a written agreement with Adams, Kehr, and Caley to purchase their shares in the old company for the sum of $650,000, payment to be made as follows:

"(a) $10,000 upon execution of this agreement
"(b) $178,500 on closing the transaction
"(c) The balance of $461,500 payable in ten equal annual installments of $46,150, plus interest at 5 percent on the declining balance from the date of closing and payable on or before June 30 of each succeeding year beginning with 1961."

This agreement was closed in Seattle, Washington, on November 30, 1960.

In December 1960, petitioner issued 6-percent, 20-year debenture bonds in registered form in the total amount of $100,000. The debentures were dated October 22, 1960, and were issued to the following individuals:

Name	Amount
Miles W. or Nellie Tippery	$ 10,000.00
Bruce Kehr	30,000.00*
John H. Caley	20,000.00
Melvin R. Whitman	10,000.00
Donald P. Christianson	5,000.00*
Vernon O. Lundmark	2,500.00
Reider Tanner	2,500.00
John M. Shiach	3,333.33
Bernard J. Goiney	3,333.33
Homer V. Hartzell	3,333.33
Mel S. Johnston	10,000.00
	$100,000.00

*Of the debentures issued to Kehr, the amount of $2,500 is subject to a trust agreement as the property of Donald Christianson and is held by Kehr as security for a loan of $5,000 by him to Christianson.

On December 1, 1960, the old company and petitioner, through appropriate Board of Directors' and shareholders' action, entered into a joint plan of merger and agreement of merger, whereupon the old company, the wholly-owned subsidiary of petitioner, was liquidated pursuant to section 332, and the assets subject to the liabilities were transferred to petitioner.

On December 1, 1960, the old company had assets with a book value of $245,-504.83 and liabilities of $125,946.59. Petitioner included the assets received on liquidation at a cost of $775,946.59 (the total of the cost of the stock, $650,000, and the amount of the liabilities assumed, $125,946.59) pursuant to section 334(b)(2). The increase in the book value of assets on the merger was $530,381.76.

The allocation of the step-up in basis is made on the basis of the net fair market values of the assets received (fair market value less applicable liabilities). Petitioner, therefore, estimated the net fair market values of the tram equipment and the other assets and allocated the $650,000 purchase price of the stock to them. Petitioner determined that the old company had had no goodwill and that certain special use permits were without fair market value. It, therefore, did not allocate any portion of the step-up in basis to either item. . . .

Respondent, in his statutory notice of deficiency, determined that section 344(b)(2) was inapplicable in determining the basis of the assets in question and that the basis should be determined under section 334(b)(1). . . .

Opinion

The first issue for determination is whether petitioner may properly compute under section 334(b)(2) the basis of assets received in the liquidation of its wholly owned subsidiary pursuant to section 332. Respondent contends that petitioner must compute the basis of the assets received under section 334(b)(1). . . .

The crux of the present dispute is whether petitioner acquired the stock of the old company by "purchase" as defined by section 334(b)(3). Petitioner contends that it acquired the stock of the old company by the purchase and sale contract closed on November 30, 1960. Respondent at trial took the position that the transfer came within the language of subsection 3(C) of section 334(b). He has, however, failed to pursue this theory[5] and, on brief, argues that the shares acquired from Kehr and Caley were in fact acquired by petitioner in a transaction to which section 351 applied and that the exchange, therefore, falls within subsection 3(B) of section 334(b). The rationale of respondent's contention is that the transaction should be viewed as an exchange by Kehr and Caley of cash and their shares of stock in the old company for stock and debentures in petitioner, plus a cash down payment (an amount unrelated to the cash given by Kehr and Caley) and a 10-year installment obligation. Respondent then states that the cash down payment received should be netted against the cash paid in for the stock and debentures of the petitioner. He further states that the "control" requirement of section 351 is satisfied since the outside investors contributed cash, in effect, simultaneously with the transfer by Kehr and Caley so that they all may be considered as one transferor group.

We cannot agree.

Though at first blush respondent's argument appears to have some merit, on closer inspection we are of the opinion that respondent's position requires an unwarranted extension of the scope of the nonrecognition provisions of section 351. This is the same contention respondent urged us to adopt in the case of Charles E. Curry, 43 T.C. 667 (1965). We declined to do so then, and we decline to do so now. The factual pattern of the *Curry* case is strikingly similar to the case before us. In *Curry,* a family group composed of Charles F. Curry and his wife (Janet), Charles E. Curry, and Carolyn Elbel (daughter of Charles F. and Janet), owned undivided interests in a building, as follows:

> Charles F. and Janet Curry 60%
> Charles E. Curry 20%
> Carolyn Elbel 20%

This group transferred their building to a corporation formed to purchase it for cash and notes. The shares in the purchasing corporation were held as follows:

> Charles E. Curry 45%
> Donald Elbel (Carolyn's husband) 45%
> Charles F. Curry 10%

The corporation took as its basis for depreciation, its cost. Respondent, however, contended that since the transaction should be properly characterized as a section 351 transfer (he argued that the notes were in fact securities), the basis to the purchasing corporation should be the transferor's basis as provided in section 362. We held that section 351 was inapplicable and stated that —

> "If respondent's position were adopted, section 351 would apply even where an unrelated third party was the stockholder of the corporation. As-

[5]In any event, we are of the opinion that section 334(b)(3)(C) has no application to the factual situation before us. Respondent has urged in his opening statement that Kehr and Caley be treated collectively as one person in order to apply section 318. We can find no authority for such a premise.

sume, for example, a transaction identical to that involved in the instant case except that A.T. & T. was the sole shareholder of [the purchasing corporation]. We cannot believe that Congress intended nonrecognition of gain in such a case. Indeed, respondent would undoubtedly be quick to obejct if taxpayers tried to prevent recognition by such a device. Yet it is clear that, in a sale effected in this manner, the transfers of cash for stock and property for notes are interdependent steps of a single plan. It is not a ground for distinction that two of the stockholders in the instant case were also transferors of realty, since we have found the parties were capable of independent action and intended a bona fide sale.[6] [43 T.C. at 697]"

It is our opinion that this statement is equally applicable to the facts before us. We do not believe that this is a proper situation for the application of section 351.

The case of Houck v. Hinds, 215 F.2d 673 (C.A. 10, 1954), which is respondent's sole citation of authority for his contention, is readily distinguishable from the case at bar. In Houck v. Hinds, the members of a partnership sold its assets to a newly formed corporation organized by a third party for installment notes. The third party was unable to interest others in the venture, and members of the partnership then purchased his shares and suscribed for the balance of the corporate shares. The net effect was that the members of the partnership now owned the corporate shares and the corporation's installment notes in the same proportion as their old partnership interests. The Tenth Circuit held that what had occurred was the mere incorporation of the partnership in that the shares were held by the same persons and in the same proportions as the partnership interests.

The case at bar is distinguishable on its facts. We can hardly ignore the facts that, whereas in Houck v. Hinds the ownership remained exactly the same throughout, in this case Adams' 50-percent ownership disappeared, Kehr's 50-percent common-stock interest was reduced to less than 30 percent, Caley's 100-percent nonvoting-stock interest was changed to a 20-percent voting interest, and finally that over 50 percent of the petitioner-corporation is owned by persons who possessed no interest whatever in the old company.

We therefore hold that section 351 is inapplicable and that petitioner may properly compute the basis for the assets received under section 334(b)(2). . . .

NYE v. COMMISSIONER
50 T.C. 203 (1968)

Featherston, Judge. All issues presented for decision arise from the creation of a corporation, Delta Sheet Metal & Air Conditioning, Inc. (sometimes referred to herein as "corporation") and the transfer thereto of assets of a partnership composed of petitioners, Dale Thornton and George Nye. The issues to be decided are as follows:

---

[6]The instant case, like the case of Charles E. Curry, 43 T.C. 667 (1965), unquestionably involves an arm's-length transaction. . . .

1. Whether the transaction whereby the partnership assets were transferred to the corporation falls within the provisions of Code section 351. Our resolution of this issue is also dispositive of the following subsidiary issues: (a) Whether payments on the principal of a note for $73,889.30 are taxable to Thornton and Nye as capital gain or as dividends; (b) whether interest payments on the note are deductible by the corporation and taxable as such to Thornton and Nye; and (c) whether the corporation takes the partnership's basis as its basis for the transferred assets.

[The second issue is omitted.]

Findings of Fact

Some of the facts are stipulated and are found accordingly.

George A. Nye and Myrtle E. Nye[4] are husband and wife, and residing in Northridge, California, at the time their petition was filed. . . .

Dale Thornton and Lucille M. Thornton are husband and wife and resided in Sepulveda, California, at the time their petition was filed. . . .

Delta Sheet Metal & Air Conditioning, Inc. is a corporation formed under the laws of the State of California. . . .

On or about September 1, 1954, Thornton and Nye, as equal partners, formed a partnership, Delta Sheet Metal Company (sometimes referred to herein as "partnership") to engage in the business of operating a sheet metal shop and doing sheet metal contracting. In 1961, Thornton and Nye decided to expand their business. They consulted their attorney and, for various reasons including limiting their presonal liability, decided to form a corporation through which their business would be conducted. The corporation was formed on October 10, 1961, to succeed the partnership in the operation of the sheet metal business. It had authorized stock consisting of 2,000 shares of $100 par value common stock.

On October 31, 1961, a check in the amount of $4,000 was drawn on the partnership bank account and made payable to the corporation and the corporation later issued a total of 40 shares of its common stock to Thornton and Nye. No other stock was outstanding during the periods relevant to this proceeding. On October 31, 1961, another check in the amount of $10,000 representing a loan was drawn on the account of the partnership and made payable to the corporation. . . .

On November 1, 1961, all assets of the partnership, except cash in bank and accounts receivable, were transferred to the corporation pursuant to an "agreement" and "amendment to agreement" signed by Thornton and Nye as "Sellers" and, on behalf of the corporation, as "Buyer." The agreement transferred the physical assets of the partnership as well as intangibles, including goodwill, to the corporation. The recited consideration was $177,179.30, which consisted of $3,290 cash designated for inventory; a $73,889.30 promissory note designated for the transfer of the tangible and intangible assets of the partnership (other than inventory, cash, and accounts

---

[4]The individual tax liabilities grow out of the activities of individual petitioners Dale Thornton and George A. Nye (sometimes referred to herein as Thornton and Nye); their spouses are parties only by virtue of joint returns. The term "petitioners" as used herein refers to the corporation, Delta Sheet Metal & Air Conditioning, Inc., and Thornton and Nye, unless otherwise indicated.

receivable); and a $100,000 promissory note designated for a covenant not to compete. . . .

. . . The value of the business as a going concern and of its goodwill was substantial, but no part of the recited consideration was allocated to them.

On November 1, 1961, the corporation executed an unsecured promissory note payable to Thornton and Nye in the amount of $73,889.30, with interest of 6 percent per annum. The note was payable in annual installments of $7,388.93, or more, plus interest, the first payment to become due "on or before" December 31, 1962. The corporation executed another document dated November 1, 1961, entitled "Promissory Note", calling for the corporation to pay $100,000, without interest, in annual installments of $10,000 or more, the first payment to become due December 31, 1962.

The $73,889.30 promissory note was not subordinated to claims of stockholders or other creditors, and payments of principal and interest were made annually when due. Payments of principal on the $100,000 promissory note were also made annually when due. . . .

On November 1, 1961, the first meeting of the corporation's incorporators and directors was held. Dale Thornton was elected president, and George A. Nye, vice president. They served in these capacities during the years 1962, 1963 and 1964.

On November 27, 1961, 40 shares of stock of the corporation were issued at par value in the following names:

Name	No. of Shares
Dale Thornton	20 shares
George A. Nye	20 shares

. . . Account number 408, *"Loans from stockholders and officers,"* on the books of the corporation, contains the following entries, reflecting certain loans made by Thornton and Nye to the corporation:

	Posting Reference	Dr.	Cr.	Balance
10-12-61	CR 1	. . . . .	1,000	. . . . .
10-31-61	CR 1	. . . . .	10,000	. . . . .
11-15-61	CR 3	. . . . .	15,000	26,000
9-10-62	CD 30	26,000	. . . . .	–0–
12-11-62	CR 25	. . . . .	20,000	. . . . .
9-30-63	CR 44	. . . . .	15,000	. . . . .
12-12-63	CR 51	. . . . .	25,000	60,000
5-12-65	CD 126	20,000	. . . . .	40,000

The loans made in 1961 were non-interestbearing and unsecured. The loans made in 1962 and 1963 were unsecured and bore interest at the rate of 6 percent per annum.

The business continued to prosper following its transfer to the corporation. The partnership return for 1961 discloses sales of $471,918.72 and net income of $84,941.26.[5]

---

[5]The partnership used the calendar year for reporting income for tax purposes. The transfer of assets from the partnership to the corporation occurred on November 1, 1961. The partnership did not file its return for 1961 on the basis of a "short" taxable year but continued in existence for

The corporate tax returns for the fiscal years ending September 30, 1962, 1963 and 1964 show net sales of $501,832.58, $574,839.58 and $503,264.65, respectively. The corporate tax return for the fiscal year ending September 30, 1962, the first taxable year of the corporation, shows taxable income of $66,615.83. This figure is unadjusted for interest, . . . [and] depreciation . . . which are in dispute. . . .

Ultimate Findings of Fact

The transaction whereby the partnership assets were transferred to the corporation was not a bona fide sale of assets to the corporation by Thornton and Nye or by the partnership. Rather it was part of a larger transaction whereby the individual partners transferred cash and assets to the corporation in exchange for stock and a promissory note in the amount of $73,889.30. The promissory note in the amount of $73,889.30 was a security within the meaning of section 351 and constituted bona fide indebtedness of the corporation. . . .

Opinion

On October 10, 1961, Dale Thornton and George Nye, partners in an air conditioning contracting business, organized a corporation, Delta Sheet Metal & Air Conditioning, Inc., to take over their partnership business. Thereafter, on October 31, 1961, Thornton and Nye caused the partnership to transfer $4,000 in cash to the corporation and the corporation subsequently issued to Thornton and Nye 40 shares of $100 par value common stock. The next day, November 1, 1961, Thornton and Nye executed an agreement and an amendment thereto whereby they transferred and purportedly sold the assets of the partnership (excluding cash and accounts receivable) to the corporation for $3,290 cash, stated to have been paid for inventory, and a 10-year, interest-bearing installment promissory note of $73,889.30, stated to have been given for the remaining tangible and intangible assets of the partnership.*

Respondent contends that the transfer of cash and partnership assets were both contributions of capital to the corporation under section 351 and the $73,889.30 note was evidence of an equity interest in the corporation in the nature of stock with the following tax results: (1) The payments of the principal of the note were dividend income to Thornton and Nye, as were the interest payments; (2) the corporation was not entitled to deductions for the interest payments; and, (3) the corporation, under Code section 362, took the partnership's basis for the transferred assets.

Petitioners contend that Thornton and Nye created the corporation with a cash capital contribution of $4,000 and then in a separate transaction sold the partnership assets to the corporation. They contend that the $73,889.30 note was not "stock" but evidence of bona fide indebtedness of the corporation and that the transaction produced the following tax results: (1) The payments of the principal of the note, to the

---

the purpose of collecting accounts receivable which were retained and also to collect payments on the notes executed by the corporation. The sales figure in the 1961 partnership return reflected sales only through October 31, 1961.

*The $100,000 received by Thornton and Nye for the covenant not to compete is ordinary income to them. See Commissioner v. Danielson, 378 F.2d 771 (3d Cir. 1967); and Comment, The *Danielson* Rule on the Tax Consequences of a Covenant Not to Compete, 116 U. Pa. L. Rev. 517 (1968). — Ed.

extent they exceed basis, were taxable to Thornton and Nye as capital gain; (2) the interest payments on the note were taxable to Thornton and Nye as interest and were deductible as such by the corporation; and, (3) the corporation took as its basis for the transferred assets the purchase price of $73,889.30 as allocated among the transferred assets in the November 1, 1961 agreement.

All the tax adjustments in dispute depend upon whether section 351 should be applied and, if so, how it should be applied. Recognizing that each case presenting this recurring set of problems turns on its own facts, we have concluded that the partnership's transfers of cash and business assets fall within section 351, as contended by respondent. However, petitioners correctly contend that the $73,889.30 note was not stock but evidence of indebtedness and, under the decided cases, the note was, in our opinion, a "security" within the meaning of the section.[7] . . .

Section 351 provides that no "gain or loss shall be recognized if property is transferred to a corporation . . . by one or more persons solely in exchange for stock or securities in such corporation" and immediately after the exchange such person or persons are in "control" of the corporation. Provisions similar to section 351 have been in the tax law since 1921. H. Rept. No. 350, 67th Cong., 1st Sess. (1921), p. 10; S. Rept. No. 275, 67th Cong., 1st Sess. (1921), p. 11. Their purpose is to permit business readjustments without immediate tax consequences. Helvering v. Cement Investors, 316 U.S. 527, 533 (1942). In some cases they work to the advantage of the taxpayer and in others to his disadvantage. They are not optional, however, and apply regardless of the intent of the transferors. . . .

Here, in a transaction carried out pursuant to a preconceived plan, cash and business assets were transferred to the corporation by Thornton and Nye. Property includes money, so the fact that cash as well as business assets was transferred does not prevent the applicability of the section. Halliburton v. Commissioner, 78 F.2d 265 (C.A. 9, 1935); George M. Holstein, III, 23 T.C. 923 (1955). In exchange for such property, Thornton and Nye admittedly received stock and a note which, we conclude, was a security of the corporation. Immediately after the transfer Thornton and Nye were in control of the corporation. The transaction, therefore, falls squarely within section 351. . . .

To escape the applicability of section 351, petitioners contend that: (a) Thornton and Nye were not in "control" of the corporation immediately after the transaction in which the partnership assets were transferred to the corporation; (b) the transaction in which the transfer occurred was a sale, not an "exchange"; and, closely related to the second contention, (c) the $73,889.30 note was not "stock or securities" within the section.

(a) *Control.* Section 368(c) defines "control" as used in section 351 to mean "the ownership of stock possessing at least 80 percent of the total combined voting power of all classes of stock entitled to vote and at least 80 percent of the total number of shares of all other classes of stock of the corporation." Pointing to this definition, petitioners contend that Thornton and Nye, equal partners, transferred partnership

---

[7]While respondent on brief has taken the broader position that the $73,889.30 note was evidence of equity interests, rather than indebtedness, our conclusion that the note was a security within section 351 is comfortably within the language of the notices of deficiencies.

assets, which they held as tenants in partnership, to the corporation and, under California law, their wives obtained a community interest in the stock issued by the corporation, with the result that Thornton and Nye did not have the requisite 80 percent control of the corporation.

The general rule of California law is that property acquired with community funds is community property and Thornton and Nye concede that they created the partnership with community funds. However, a "partner is co-owner with his partners of specific partnership property holding as a tenant in partnership" and a "partner's right in specific partnership property . . . is not community property." Cal. Corp. Code sec. 15025(1) and sec. 15025(2)(e). The community property exception in sec. 15025(2)(e) as to specific partnership assets does not apply, however, to corporate stock acquired with community funds. Such stock is community property, and a wife has an interest "present, existing and equal" to that of her husband. See Cal. Civil Code sec. 161a. Petitioners rely upon these statutes to show that Thornton and Nye, the sole transferors of the partnership assets, but owners of only a community interest in the corporate stock, lacked the requisite 80 percent control of the corporation.

In Miller Bros. Electric, Inc., [49 T.C. 446 (1968)], we considered and rejected a similar argument. Relying upon decisions of the California courts we held that there occurred either (1) a conversion of the partnership property to individual property immediately prior to the transfer to the corporation, or (2) actual or constructive receipt by the partnership of the stock prior to its distribution to the individuals. In either case the control requirements of section 351 were met. We adhere to those views.

(b) *Sale v. Exchange.* Petitioners next contend that Thornton and Nye created the corporation and purchased its stock for $4,000 cash and, as a separate transaction, later sold the partnership assets to the corporation in consideration of the $73,889.30 interest-bearing note, payable in 10 annual installments. Indeed, with the assistance of counsel they meticulously cast the transaction in the form of a sale. They emphasize that the sale price was based on the fair market value of the assets as determined through an independent appraisal and argue that they transferred no partnership assets to the corporation in exchange for stock.

Whether a transfer of property to a corporation, for purposes of Federal taxation, is a sale as distinguished from an exchange within section 351, requires consideration of all the facts. No rule of thumb applies; no single criterion determines the result; each case must be adjudicated upon its own facts. Gooding Amusement Co. v. Commissioner, 236 F.2d 159, 165 (C.A. 6, 1956), affirming 23 T.C. 408 (1954), certiorari denied 352 U.S. 1031 (1957). The burden of proving that the transfer was a sale rests with petitioners.

We are not convinced that the evidence here shows a sale. The language used in the transfer documents is, of course, to be considered, but standing alone it is not sufficient to require a portion of the transaction to be treated as a sale; substance, not form, governs. Commissioner v. Court Holding Co., 324 U.S. 331 (1945).

In our view, petitioners have provided no factual basis for their contention that the purported sale of business assets was a transaction separate from the $4,000 cash transfer. On the contrary, the evidence shows clearly that the transfers of cash and business assets and the receipt of stock and the note were inseparably related. The corporation was formed by Thornton and Nye on October 10, 1961, following conferences with their attorney. On October 31, 1961, the partnership issued a check in the amount of $4,000 in payment for 40 shares to be issued to Thornton and Nye. The next day the parties entered into an agreement transferring the partnership's assets to the corporation for cash and notes. The testimony is unmistakably clear that these steps were part of a preconceived plan developed by petitioners' attorney to change the organization of the business from partnership to corporate form. The fact that the cash was purportedly paid for stock one day and the assets transferred for the note the next confirms the oral testimony that the whole transaction was the consummation of a single plan.

Thornton and Nye testified that their reason for incorporating the business was to limit their liabilities for possible losses from a projected expansion of their operations. However, they gave no reason why the transaction was divided into two parts, the transfer of cash for stock and the purported sale of the business assets for the note. Such evidence might have confirmed that the form in which the transaction was cast was consistent with its true nature. . . . Lack of such evidence is worthy of note because it fails to negate the inference to be drawn from other facts indicating that the two parts of the transaction were inseparably related. . . . In the absence of evidence of a business reason for dividing the transaction, we conclude that a separate sale has not been shown.

(c) *Promissory note as a security under Section 351.* Our conclusion that the transaction was not a sale but an exchange within section 351 makes it necessary to determine whether the $73,889.30 promissory note was "stock" or a "security" within the meaning of section 351(a) or "other property" within the meaning of section 351(b). See Peter Raich, 46 T.C. 604 (1966). We have concluded that the note constituted a "security."

The law is now well settled that promissory notes may qualify as securities within the purview of section 351. Parkland Place Co. v. United States, 354 F.2d 916 (C.A. 5, 1966); Campbell v. Carter Foundation Production Co., 322 F.2d 827 (C.A. 5, 1963); Burnham v. Commissioner, 86 F.2d 776 (C.A. 7, 1936), affirming 33 B.T.A. 147 (1935), certiorari denied 300 U.S. 683 (1936); Baker Commodities, Inc., [48 T.C. 374 (1967)], Camp Wolters Enterprises, Inc., 22 T.C. 737 (1954), affd. 230 F.2d 555 (C.A. 5, 1956) . . . . Basic to this settled rule, however, is a requirement that the notes have a sufficiently long term to accord them an investment quality rather than the characteristics of cash.[9] The latter characteristics may disqualify short-term notes as securities. See Pinellas Ice Co. v. Commissioner, 287 U.S. 462

---

[9]Commentators view the term of a note as the single most important quality and agree that notes with a maturity of 10 years or longer may be safely termed securities. Bittker and Eustice, Federal Income Taxation of Corporations and Shareholders, Sec. 3.03 (2d Ed., 1966) states: "Notes with a five year term or less seem to be unable to qualify as 'securities,' while a term of ten years or more is apparently sufficient to bring them within the statute." See also Kaufman, "Securities Within the Tax-Free Reorganization and Exchange Provisions," 8th Ann. N.Y.U. Tax Inst. 117, 120 (1956).

(1933); Commissioner v. Sisto Financial Corp., 139 F.2d 253 (C.A. 2, 1943). The settled rule recognizes that section 351 refers to both "stock" and "securities." The section incorporates the definition of "control" contained in section 368(c) which relates only to stock and thus indicates that the control of the corporation need not be exercised through the securities.

In Camp Wolters Enterprises, Inc., . . . this Court adopted the following guide for determining whether debt instruments qualify as "securities" as that term is used in the predecessor of section 351, section 112(b)(5) of the 1939 Code:

> "The test as to whether notes are securities is not a mechanical determination of the time period of the note. Though time is an important factor, the controlling consideration is an overall evaluation of the nature of the debt, degree of participation and continuing interest in the business, the extent of proprietary interest compared with the similarity of the note to a cash payment, the purpose of the advances, etc. It is not necessary for the debt obligation to be the equivalent of stock since section 112(b)(5) specifically includes both 'stock' and 'securities.'"

An "overall evaluation" of the $73,889.30 note given to Thornton and Nye shows that it was a security within section 351. The note contained an unconditional promise to pay the holder $73,889.30 in 10 equal annual installments plus interest at the rate of 6 percent per annum. The holder of the note had the right to declare the entire balance due upon default by the maker in payments of principal or interest. If the holder was required to institute a suit to collect, he was entitled to recover attorney's fees.

The note did not evidence an isolated transaction of purchase and sale having its inception after the formation and launching of the corporation but, as we have indicated, was "an integral part of the scheme of its forming and financing"; the note and the stock ownership by Thornton and Nye "were together different forms of the assured participation in the potluck of the enterprise," for a 10-year period. . . . The properties for which the note was issued constituted a permanent contribution to the corporation, indeed virtually its sole operational assets; such properties did not represent short-term advances to be used by the corporation for temporary or current corporate needs. . . . In no sense was the note the equivalent of cash. Pinellas Ice Co. v. Commissioner, supra. Along with their stock, the note gave Thornton and Nye, the sole stockholders, a continuing investment in the enterprise. At the time the note was issued the corporation did not have sufficient liquid assets to retire it; it could have been paid only through sale of the business as a going concern. As a practical matter payment was intended to be derived from earnings. As sole stockholders and as officers Thornton and Nye had all the control necessary to assure protection of their long-term investment and payment of the note.

In sum, the 10-year $73,889.30 note was no less a security than, for example, the debt obligations which were held to fall within that category in Helvering v. Watts, 296 U.S. 387 (1935) (one to seven-year bonds); Parkland Place Co. v. United States, supra, (ten-year promissory note); Campbell v. Carter Foundation Production Co., supra, (five-year promissory note); Burnham v. Commissioner, supra, (ten-year promissory note); and Camp Wolters Enterprises, Inc. v. Commissioner, supra, (five to nine-year promissory notes).

Implicit in our conclusion that the 10-year $73,889.30 promissory note was indebtedness in the form of a security within section 351 is the rejection of respondent's broader contention that the note was in reality evidence of an equity interest, in the nature of stock. Some of the points made by respondent in support of his stock argument also support our conclusion that the note was a security. However, other factors must be considered.

As noted above, the note was in the form of a debt obligation. Its terms in no way resembled stock. Form is, of course, not determinative, but is a factor to be considered. . . .

Respondent relies primarily on four factors to show that the promissory note did not in fact constitute debt. He contends that the corporation was undercapitalized; that Thornton and Nye placed the partnership's assets at the risk of the business; that the notes were owned in the same proportion as the stock, and that the value placed on the assets was overstated.

In attacking the adequacy of the capital structure of the corporation, respondent adds to the promissory note of $73,889.30, the loans made by Thornton and Nye to the corporation of $1,000 on October 12, 1961; $10,000 on October 31, 1961, and $15,000 on November 15, 1961, and compares this total indebtedness of $99,889.30 with the $4,000 cash capital contribution in arriving at a debt-equity ratio of twenty-five to one.

As we pointed out in Burr Oaks Corp., 43 T.C. 635 (1965), affd. 365 F.2d 24 (C.A. 7, 1966), the transfer of property to a thinly capitalized corporation raises an inference that the transfer is a capital contribution. However, thin capitalization is only one of the factors from which the presence or absence of a bona fide debtor-creditor relationship may be determined, and the existence of that factor alone will not transform a valid indebtedness into equity capital. . . . The thin capitalization argument must be viewed in the light of the further principle that stockholders in creating a corporation have discretion in deciding how much of their funds or assets they care to risk in the form of capital and how much they are willing to lend as credit. . . . The problem is to ascertain the substance of what was done.

Here the partnership had operated successfully since its inception in 1954. The partnership return for the year 1961 shows sales of $471,918.72, and net income to each partner of $42,470.63, a total of $84,941.26, a sum larger than the amount of the note. The corporate returns show net sales of $501,832.58, $574,839.58 and $503,264.65, for the fiscal years ended September 30, 1962, 1963 and 1964, respectively. Looking at the net income of the partnership in 1961 of $84,941.26 and the net income of the corporation computed in like manner for its first taxable year of $132,943.72, it is clear that reasonably anticipated current earnings were sufficient to permit retirement of the $73,889.30 note. In addition, the corporation made all payments of principal and interest on the $73,889.30 promissory note when due. These facts rebut the inference raised by the high ratio of debt to capital that the note was not true indebtedness. . . .

Moreover, we perceive no reason why either the going concern value or the goodwill of the established business should not be taken into account in testing the adequacy of the corporation's capitalization. While no evidence was offered to establish precisely the going concern value of the business, the high level of income both before and after the transfer demonstrates substantial value. Murphy Logging Co. v. United States, 378 F.2d 222 (C.A. 9, 1967); . . . Such going concern value is not to be treated as merely incidental to the depreciable assets; it is, in itself, a nondepreciable intangible asset. United States v. Cornish, 348 F.2d 175 (C.A. 9, 1965). Respondent's mathematical computation of a debt-to-capital ratio ignores these factors. We believe that both the goodwill and going concern value, which were placed at the risk of the business as capital contributions, were substantial.

To support the thin capitalization argument, respondent also contends that excessive values were assigned by petitioners to the following assets transferred in exchange for the $73,889.30 promissory note:

	Petitioner's Values	Respondent's Values
Pacific Hydraulic Press Brake	$11,000	$ 4,000
Wysong Shear	8,700	6,650
Whitney Hand Brake	700	· 575
Chicago Hand Brake	1,150	125
Peddinghams Iron Works	8,900	3,750
Total	$30,450	$15,100

Respondent does not challenge the reasonableness of the values assigned to other transferred assets totaling $43,439.30.

The testimony of Thornton and Nye was undisputed that they employed an independent appraiser to give them an opinion as to the values of the transferred assets and that such values were used in computing the contract prices. Later, when a revenue agent questioned the values used, petitioners employed another appraiser, Gerald P. Cashion, whose competence was admitted by respondent. Cashion personally inspected the disputed items in March 1965, and testified that the values assigned by petitioners were the approximate values of the assets.

While it is true that Cashion estimated the values as of March 1965, nothing in the record suggests that the equipment was more valuable after $3\frac{1}{2}$ years of use than in October 1961. Respondent offered no testimony in support of a lower valuation; instead, respondent relied on book values — notoriously poor guides to fair market value. . . . We find that the values assigned in the agreements of November 1, 1961, were the approximate fair market values of the various assets on that date. In any event, the goodwill and going concern value, in the light of the business history of the enterprise, were sufficient to establish that it was adequately capitalized even if the values of some of the machinery items were overstated.

Respondent next argues that the assets were placed at the risk of the business and that the ownership of the stock and note was proportionate. We agree that Thornton and Nye assumed some risk in transferring the partnership assets to the corporation; any long-term investment in the form of a security involves some risk. Cf. Camp Wolters Enterprises, Inc. v. Commissioner, supra. But the $73,889.30

promissory note was in no way subordinated to the claims of general creditors or to the claims of shareholders. Payments on the note were made when due and there is no evidence that the parties ever intended otherwise. Petitioners no doubt expected the note to be paid from earnings, but the payment of indebtedness usually depends to a large extent upon the success of the obligor. American Processing & Sales Co. v. United States, 371 F.2d 842, 856-857 (Ct. Cl., 1967); cf. Richard Drachman, 23 T.C. 558, 562 (1958).

While it is true that the stock ownership was in the same proportion as the note, this factor is not conclusive. Campbell v. Carter Foundation Production Co., supra. It is well settled that an individual can occupy the dual relationship of stockholder and creditor whether such stockholder-creditor owns all or a mere fraction of the debtor-corporation's stock. Farley Realty Corp. v. Commissioner, 279 F.2d 701 (C.A. 2, 1960), affirming a Memorandum Opinion of this Court. The fact that Thornton and Nye each owned 50 percent of the corporation's stock and 50 percent of the note in question is not unusual since they each owned 50 percent of the assets transferred to the corporation.

Thus we find no substantial basis on which this Court could declare that the $73,889.30 note was not what it purported to be, i.e., indebtedness. This is what the petitioners intended it to be and they treated it as such. By its unambiguous terms the note created indebtedness. It was subordinated to no other claims. The business history of the enterprise demonstrates that the corporation had a capacity to pay indebtedness of this amount; indeed, the face of the note was in an amount less than the prior year's net earnings of the partnership. The facts are that the high level of earnings continued and the annual installments were paid when due. Taking into account the goodwill and going concern values of the business we think it is clear that the corporation was adequately capitalized from the beginning. The note represented a long-term investment of valuable assets and was given as an integral part of the formation, launching and financing of the corporation. We see no substantial basis for a conclusion that the note did not represent indebtedness.

In summary, the following tax results flow from our conclusions that the transaction falls within section 351[11] and the $73,889.30 note was a security: (1) Since the note was a capital asset in the hands of Thornton and Nye, payments of the principal thereof to the extent they exceed basis are taxable as long-term capital gain under section 1232(a)(1) which provides that amounts received in retirement of "bonds, debentures, notes, or certificates" shall be "considered as amounts received in exchange therefor," Baker Commodities, Inc. . . . ; (2) interest payments on the note are deductible by the corporation and taxable (as such) to Thornton and Nye; and, (3) since section 362(a) provides that, if property is acquired by a corporation in a transaction to which section 351 applies, "the basis shall be the same as it would be in the hands of the transferor," the corporation here takes the partnership's basis for the purpose of computing depreciation of the transferred assets; the step-up in basis claimed by petitioners is denied. . . .

---

[11]Viewed as a single transaction involving the transfer of cash and partnership assets for stock and the $73,889.30 note, the transaction falls within section 351(a) rather than section 351(b).

NOTE

1. A owns all the stock of Corporation X. He contributes to X a piece of real estate worth $100,000 but receives nothing in return. The basis of the real estate before transfer is $50,000. What are the tax consequences to A? To X? Why? What is the basis of the real estate in X's hands? What impact does the transfer have on the basis of A's stock? Why?

2. C, owning 90 per cent of Corporation Z, transfers to Z property worth $100,000, with a basis of $50,000, for $75,000 of stock and $75,000 cash. What are the tax consequences to C? To Z? Why?

3. See T. White, III, Sleepers That Travel With Section 351 Transfers, 56 Va. L. Rev. 37 (1970); 351 Covers "Sale" After Transfer; but Alternatives Exist, 29 J. Taxation 4 (1968); G. Fisher, The Conversion of Ordinary Income to Capital Gain by Intentionally Avoiding Section 351 of the Internal Revenue Code of 1954, 32 Mo. L. Rev. 421 (1967).

2. *Taxation of "Boot"*

a. CAPITAL GAIN OR LOSS — AMOUNT; HOLDING PERIOD

If a transferor receives not only the "stock or securities" permitted by §351(a), but "other property or money" to boot, §351(b)(2) provides for nonrecognition of loss but §351(b)(1) calls for recognition of gain (the amount realized over basis), only to the extent of the "boot" (the money plus the fair market value of the "other property" received). For example, suppose T transfers an asset with adjusted basis of $50,000 and fair market value of $100,000 to a corporation in exchange for its common stock (worth $75,000) and cash in the amount of $25,000. Assume, too, that T is "in control" after the exchange. T's realized gain is $50,000. His recognized gain, however, is $25,000, since §351(b) restricts recognition of the gain to the amount of the boot, here the cash of $25,000.

In the case put, if the asset transferred is a capital asset or a §1231 asset held for more than six months (and if §§1239, 1245 and 1250 are inapplicable), the recognized gain should be treated as a long-term capital gain (§1222).

If two assets are transferred, one at a $50,000 gain and one at a $40,000 loss, and "boot" of $30,000 is received (in addition to stock that qualifies under §351(a)), what is the tax impact? Why?

Suppose the taxpayer receives "boot" of $15,000 for an asset with a basis of $10,000 and a fair market value of $12,000. What is the tax impact on the transferor? Are you concerned with the earnings and profits account of the corporation? Why?

See B. Bittker and J. Eustice, Federal Income Taxation of Corporations and Shareholders 76-79 (2d ed. 1966); J. Rabinovitz, Allocating Boot in Section 351 Exchanges, 24 Tax L. Rev. 337 (1969).

b. NON-CAPITAL GAIN — §1239

TROTZ v. COMMISSIONER
361 F.2d 927 (10th Cir. 1966)

Before MURRAH, Chief Judge, and BREITENSTEIN and SETH, Circuit Judges.

BREITENSTEIN, Circuit Judge. . . . The issue is whether a gain on an installment sale of depreciable property by taxpayer to Trotz Construction, Inc., is taxable as a long-term capital gain. Section 1239 of the Internal Revenue Code of 1954 provides that gain on the sale of depreciable property by an individual to a corporation "more than 80 percent in value of the outstanding stock of which is owned by such individual, his spouse, and his minor children and minor grandchildren" is to be treated as ordinary income rather than capital gain.

Trotz Construction, Inc., was incorporated under New Mexico law in February, 1958. The charter authorized 400 shares of common stock with a par value of $100 per share. The corporation issued 316 shares, or 79% of the authorized stock, to the taxpayer and his wife. The remaining 84 shares, or 21% of the authorized stock, were issued to Ben F. Kelly, Jr., who was not related to the taxpayer by blood or marriage. All of the $40,000 capital of the corporation was paid by taxpayer in cash.

Taxpayer was named president of the new company. His wife was secretary-treasurer, and Kelly was vice-president. The three of them made up the board of directors. The minutes of the first meeting of the stockholders and directors fixed the amount of salary and bonus of net profits to which each would be entitled.

Kelly owed taxpayer $8,400 for the stock issued to him and executed a promissory note payable to taxpayer in this amount. The note was secured by a pledge of the stock which provided that all bonuses accruing to Kelly were to be paid to the taxpayer and applied on the indebtedness. Dividends were also payable to taxpayer but without application on the debt. Kelly also executed an agreement giving taxpayer an option to purchase his stock in the corporation at book value, excluding good will and other intangibles, in the event Kelly should die or cease to be an officer or director of the company. The corporate by-laws provided that an officer or director could be removed, with or without cause, by a vote of the majority of the stockholders.

Kelly's employment with the company began in March, 1958, and ended in December of that year when he voluntarily resigned as an officer and director because of a disagreement between him and the taxpayer. Kelly then surrendered his company stock to the taxpayer who cancelled the $8,400 note. Kelly made no payments of either principal or interest on the note.

Immediately following the organization of the company taxpayer sold substantially all of his construction equipment to the company for $183,153.33 which was the median market value as determined by three independent appraisers. The long-term gain on the sale was reported on the instalment basis in the taxpayer's income tax returns for the years 1958 and 1959.

The Tax Court did not find that the transaction between the taxpayer and Kelly was a sham. The record indicates that it was made in good faith, that Kelly was intended to have rights, and that it was voluntarily terminated by Kelly. The problem is whether taxpayer at the pertinent time owned "more than 80 per cent in value of the outstanding stock" of the company. If he did, §1239 requires that the profit is taxable as ordinary income rather than as a capital gain.

The Tax Court held that the taxpayer's "rights with respect to the stock issued to Kelly were so complete that they were tantamount to ownership by petitioner for the purposes of section 1239." One judge dissented pointing out that §1239 uses the word "owned" and that it does not mean "in effect," "tantamount to," or "in substance." We agree with the dissenting judge.

Taxpayer owned less than 80% of the stock unless the ownership of Kelly's shares is attributed to him. His rights to the Kelly stock were contract rights and were dependent on an option to purchase in the event Kelly died or ceased to be an officer and director. The Commissioner concedes that optioned stock is owned by the optioner but insists that the totality of the circumstances sustains the Tax Court decision. The argument would be impressive if the record showed sham or lack of good faith — but it does not.

On the authority of the Fourth Circuit decision in Mitchell v. Commissioner of Internal Revenue, 4 Cir., 300 F.2d 533, we held in United States v. Rothenberg, 10 Cir., 350 F.2d 319, that the term "owned" as used in §1239 did not include property beneficially owned. Although those decisions rested upon the question of attribution of ownership because of family relationship they are pertinent in their rejection of the Commissioner's contention that a qualified ownership suffices to require the application of the statute.

The argument of the Commissioner equates ownership with control and urges that, because taxpayer controlled the stock, he owned it. Parenthetically, we observe that here control of the corporation is unimportant because taxpayer and his wife owned 79% of the stock and did not need Kelly's stock to dominate corporate activities. We believe that if Congress had intended control to be the criterion rather than ownership it would have said so.

Section 1239 is a carry-over in the 1954 Code of §117(o) of the 1939 Code, and was enacted as a part of the Revenue Act of 1951. As pointed out in *Mitchell* the original version as passed in the House of Representatives denied capital gains treatment on a sale to a corporation of which 50% of the value of the stock was "owned, directly or indirectly by or for" the seller.[4] The Senate eliminated this provision.[5] After the report of a Conference Committee, the present language was adopted.[6]

To us the elimination of constructive ownership is significant. Attribution of ownership occurs only in situations of family relationship. We find nothing in the legislative history which shows a congressional intent to use the word "owned" as embracing a concept other than legal title. As pointed out in *Mitchell*,[7] "the Internal

[4] 2 U.S. Congressional and Administrative Service '51, p. 1909.
[5] Id. pp. 2041-2042.
[6] Id. p. 2135.
[7] 300 F.2d 533, 536.

Revenue Code is specific whenever tax consequences depend upon the equitable ownership of stock, as contrasted to its legal ownership."

In the case at bar the taxpayer did not have the legal title. All he had was a contract right to acquire that title. The fact that such contract right brought the legal title to him is immaterial because the operation of the contract resulted from the voluntary act of Kelly, the legal owner of the stock. The Tax Court held that the contract rights were "tantamount to ownership." In our opinion tantamount ownership is not sufficient to satisfy the statute. Stock which a taxpayer has only a contract right to acquire is not owned by him.

The Commissioner presents as an alternative position the argument that even if the taxpayer is not considered as the owner of all the outstanding stock, the stock held by him represents more than 80% in value of the outstanding stock. Although this point was argued to it, the Tax Court did not resolve the issue because of its decision on the ownership question. The phrase "in value" as used in §1239 must have an intended meaning. If the 80% determination is to be on the basis of the number of shares outstanding, no reason exists for the use of the words "in value."

The contention of the taxpayer and the amicus is that a value test may be applied only where more than one class of stock is outstanding. The answer is that the statute makes no such distinction but applies the value test without qualification to the outstanding stock of the corporation in question. The amicus says that the value test is impracticable but points to no reason why it may not be practically applied in the case at bar. The argument that a value test is not used in other provisions of the Internal Revenue Code is irrelevant. We are not going to write the words "in value" out of §1239.

We make no comment on the claim that the taxpayer in fact owned more than 80% in value of the outstanding stock. This presents a factual issue for determination in the first instance by the Tax Court. All we hold is that a numerical count of outstanding shares, in and of itself, does not determine the percentage of value.

The decision of the Tax Court is reversed and the case is remanded for a factual determination as to whether the taxpayer's shares were 80% or more in value of all outstanding shares.

Seth, Circuit Judge (dissenting). I respectfully dissent from the opinion of the majority of the court.

The record shows that the eighty-four shares of the corporation stock in question were originally issued in the name of Ben F. Kelly, Jr., and when the entire transaction is examined, that is about all that can be said about his interest in the company. The certificates on issuance were endorsed by Kelly to Trotz and were delivered to the possession of Trotz where they remained at all material times thereafter, and Trotz had the right to receive the dividends on the shares. Trotz provided all of the cash to the corporation for the issuance of the shares, including the $8,400.00 for the eighty-four shares in question. As between Trotz and Kelly this amount was treated as a loan to Kelly, who gave back a promissory note. There was however no personal liability on this note (the stock could be surrendered as payment), and the record does not indicate that any payments were made on it.

However the most significant feature of the arrangement was the fact that upon its completion, Kelly had no right to regain possession of the shares of stock as against the wishes of Trotz. The corporate bylaws made express provision for the removal of an officer or director by a majority vote (which Trotz had), and in the event Kelly was so removed Trotz had the right to have the shares reissued in his name. This could be done by giving credit on the note or by payment of the book value of the stock, not including intangibles, as determined by the board of directors. Thus as far as Trotz was concerned, he was in a position to always retain possession of the shares of stock as against the wishes of Kelly. It would seem that the conception of ownership would include the enforceability, practically and legally, of rights as to the property in question. If the transaction is so examined, it is clear that all of the effective rights were retained by Trotz.

Thus when the arrangement is examined on the before and after basis, it is apparent that Trotz gave up nothing by way of ownership in his contracting business through the incorporation and the arrangement with Kelly.

The purpose of the Act under consideration is to prevent the transfer of assets of the nature of those in question from an individual to a corporation controlled by such individual and vice versa, and thus to prevent the transfer of depreciated assets from one pocket to the other to secure tax advantages under the capital gains rates and the new base for depreciation. "Control" for the purpose of this section of the Code would appear to have been defined by Congress as the ownership of more than eighty per cent in value of the shares of the corporation, and is not corporate control in the usual sense. Congress has presumed that the taxpayer has control of shares which may be wholly owned by his spouse, by his minor children, or by his minor grandchildren. Congress has not expressed any other presumed control, and thus we are left with the question as to whether or not Congress intended by the use of the word "owned" to include control by the taxpayer over shares which are issued in the names of other persons. It would appear that the matter must be so examined in the light of "control" over the corporation or over the shares. This guide for construction should be utilized although it has been pointed out by the parties that the House version of the legislation which referred to direct or indirect ownership was eliminated from the Bill as it was finally adopted. . . .

. . . We do not have a question of attributing ownership as the term is ordinarily used nor do we have the case where the bare contract rights of the parties will determine the transaction.

In my opinion when the substance of the transaction is examined, the case falls within the intention of Congress that the transfer of depreciated assets be not permitted from one pocket to the other. For the purpose of the statute, Trotz "owned" the shares in question and Kelly had no "ownership" in them. This ownership is just as effective or more effective than the presumed control which Congress has found to exist, for example, in circumstances where the stock is owned by the grandchildren of the taxpayer, and comes within the meaning of the statute.

I would affirm the decision of the Tax Court.

TROTZ v. COMMISSIONER
26 CCH Tax Ct. Mem. 632 (1967)

FAY, Judge: This case is presently before the Court on remand from the United States Court of Appeals for the Tenth Circuit . . . . The only issue is whether the shares owned by petitioners in Trotz Construction, Inc., were 80 percent or more in value of all outstanding shares in said corporation for purposes of section 1239 of the Internal Revenue Code of 1954.

. . . Section 1239(a)(2) provides: "(a) . . . In the case of a sale . . . of property . . . (2) between an individual and a corporation more than 80 percent in value of the outstanding stock of which is owned by such individual, his spouse, . . . any gain . . . shall be considered as gain . . . which is neither a capital asset nor property described in section 1231."

In our original decision herein we held that Trotz's "rights with respect to the stock issued to Kelly were so complete that they were tantamount to ownership by petitioner [Trotz] for purposes of section 1239." The Court of Appeals for the Tenth Circuit reversed our decision on this issue on the grounds that "tantamount ownership is not sufficient to satisfy the statute" and, accordingly, Trotz did not "own" Kelly's shares for the purposes of section 1239.

In the original proceeding the respondent presented as an alternative position the argument that even if Trotz is not considered as the owner of all the outstanding stock of Construction, Inc., the stock held by him represents more than 80 percent in value of the outstanding stock. We did not resolve this contention because of our decision on the "ownership" question. The Tenth Circuit specifically made no comment on respondent's claim that Trotz in fact owned more than 80 percent in value of the outstanding stock. However, the case was remanded for a factual determination as to whether Trotz's shares were 80 percent or more in value of all outstanding stock. The Tenth Circuit stated that a "numerical count of outstanding shares, in and of itself, does not determine the percentage of value" for purposes of section 1239. Thus, under the terms of the remand, we must determine whether the value of petitioners' shares exceeded 80 percent of the value of the total outstanding stock of Construction, Inc.

Respondent contends that the total dollar value of the outstanding stock of Construction, Inc., on March 1, 1958, was $42,000 as opposed to the book value of the stock on the same date which was $40,000. Respondent bases his contention on the testimony of Robert C. Smith, respondent's expert witness.[2] Smith testified that he believed the value of the outstanding stock of Construction, Inc., was in excess of book value (1) because Construction, Inc., was a going business as of March 1, 1958, and (2) because of the "goodwill" factor attributable to Trotz's past record in the road contracting business. Respondent also maintains that petitioners' 79 percent

---

[2]Robert C. Smith worked in the credit department of the Valley National Bank from January 1955 until March 1956 doing credit analysis. Some loans were made to contractors. At the time of the trial herein Smith was employed by a brokerage firm located in Phoenix, Arizona, and a member of the New York Stock Exchange.

stock interest in Construction, Inc., had a dollar value of $38,000, or 90 percent of the total value ($42,000) that he ascribed to the corporation's outstanding stock. Once again, respondent's position is based upon the opinion of his expert witness. The two basic reasons for Smith's, and respondent's, belief that petitioners' 79 percent stock interest was worth 90 percent of the fair market value of all Construction, Inc.'s outstanding stock are (1) the factor of petitioners' control over Construction, Inc., by reason of their ownership of 79 percent of its stock, and (2) the existence of Trotz's option to purchase Kelly's stock. (Respondent adds that if the total dollar value of the outstanding stock of Construction, Inc., was $40,000, then petitioners' 79 percent stock interest had a value of $36,000, or 90 percent of the aforesaid total stock value.)

In substance respondent has based his entire argument upon the testimony of his expert witness.

Although Smith testified that he considered the factor of control to be a primary consideration in reaching his estimate as to the value of petitioners' stock in Construction, Inc., he admitted that he had no occasion to evaluate, or any experience in evaluating, the dollar value of the control factor in relation to road construction firms. Moreover, he testified on cross-examination that he had no experience whatsoever in creating a market for or dealing in the stock of small road construction firms. Smith based his opinion in the instant case upon his observation that premiums are paid for control of companies in cases *where a public market for the stock does exist.* Smith also admitted that he realized no market existed for Construction, Inc., stock.

Smith's conclusion that the factor of control enhances the value of stock in Construction, Inc., even though he admitted that no market for the stock in Construction, Inc., exists, places his expertise in this area in irremediable doubt.

The testimony of petitioners' expert witnesses was not contradicted in any respect but was, in fact, corroborated by the testimony of respondent's expert witness. Petitioners' expert witnesses, James H. Ryan[3] and John W. Jones,[4] confirmed Smith's admission that no market existed for stock in Construction, Inc., or in like companies. Although they lack experience in marketing stock, they are familiar with the market for small- and medium-sized road construction companies in New Mexico. It is clear to us from their testimony that in general (1) small- or medium-sized construction companies located in New Mexico have no "going concern" value and (2) the value of any stock in such corporations is equivalent to the value of their underlying assets, i.e., the equipment used in road construction.

Construction, Inc., lacked any transferable goodwill. Any goodwill associated with Construction, Inc., as of March 1, 1958, was personal to Trotz himself. On cross-examination Smith admitted that if Trotz severed his connection with Construction, Inc., he would not attribute any goodwill to the corporation. He stated that

[3]As of the date of the trial proceedings herein, James H. Ryan had been in the road and bridge construction business in New Mexico since 1929. He served as president and majority shareholder of a construction company since 1953, the year in which he incorporated his construction business.

[4]As of the date of the trial proceedings herein, John W. Jones had been a highway contractor for about 20 years. He conducted his road construction business in corporate form and is the majority shareholder and president of that corporation. He served for two years, 1960 and 1966, as president of the New Mexico chapter of the Associated General Contractors of America.

Construction, Inc., had no goodwill as a corporation or as a firm, apart from Trotz's personal experience and knowledge. We stated in Danco Co., 14 T.C. 276, 284 (1950): "Indeed, it has long been held that 'Ability, skill, experience, acquaintanceship, or other personal characteristics or qualifications [of an officer or employee] do not constitute good will as an item of property [to the corporate employer] nor do they exist in such form that they could be the subject of transfer.'" Moreover, in the instant cases Trotz had no contractual obligation to continue his services with Construction, Inc. In Ruth M. Cullen, 14 T.C. 368, 372 (1950), we specifically noted: "The personal ability, personality, and reputation of [the shareholder-officer] did not belong to the corporation as intangible assets, since he had no contractual obligation to continue his connection with it."

The fact that petitioners' shares represented a "control" of Construction, Inc., would not add value to such stock since a prospective purchaser of Construction, Inc.'s stock would not be interested in acquiring Construction, Inc., as a going concern but would be interested only in purchasing its underlying assets. Consequently, "control" of Construction, Inc., would not be considered of any particular value and a buyer would not pay a premium for control as one might in purchasing stock representing a controlling interest in a corporation having a going concern value.

Respondent also argues, on the basis of Smith's testimony, that Trotz's option to purchase Kelly's stock increases the value of petitioners' shares. We believe that respondent's argument is both legally and factually untenable. Initially, we note that the option was not attached to petitioners' stock in Construction, Inc., but was a separate asset owned by petitioners. They could dispose of either their stock or the option while retaining one or the other. Secondly, section 1239 speaks in terms of the value of the stock which a taxpayer owns in a specific corporation and not any other rights which that taxpayer may hold against the same corporation. Finally, we do not believe that the option herein had any particular value since Construction, Inc., (1) lacked going concern value and (2) had market value only in terms of its underlying assets.

For the reasons stated above, we find as a fact that the value of petitioners' shares in Construction, Inc., did not exceed 80 percent of the value of the total outstanding stock of Construction, Inc. Therefore, we hold for petitioners on this issue.

Decision will be entered under Rule 50.

UNITED STATES v. PARKER
376 F.2d 402 (5th Cir. 1967)

Before Gewin and Goldberg, Circuit Judges, and Spears, District Judge.

Goldberg, Circuit Judge: The protesting and unhappy taxpayers, Curtis L. Parker and his wife, Martha, owned a wholesale and retail oil and gasoline business. On April 1, 1959, Parker and B. K. Eaves, a longtime employee, formed a Louisiana corporation incorporating Parker's business. The corporation had an authorized capital stock of 1,000 shares.

Parker subscribed to 800 shares and paid for them by transferring to the corporation certain property valued at $93,400.00 to be used in the corporation's business. Eaves subscribed to the remaining 200 shares. He paid $7,500.00 cash and agreed to pay the balance of $23,350.00 over a period of 5 years.

At the first meeting of the corporation's board of directors a resolution was passed accepting Eaves's subscription. He was issued stock certificates for the amount of stock paid for at that time (64.239 shares), and the board of directors resolved that the remainder of Eaves's stock certificates would be issued as their purchase price was paid. The Articles of Incorporation included a provision stating that none of the stock of the corporation might be transferred unless the stock were first offered to the corporation at the same price offered by the proposed transferee. (If the corporation did not accept the offer, another stockholder could.)

Parker and Eaves also entered into a stockholders' agreement which provided that whenever Eaves's employment should terminate for any reason, including death, his shares would then be purchased by Parker at a price to be governed by the fair market value per share of the corporation's assets, specifically excluding good will "or any other intangible asset." The value per share was set at $116.75 for the first year of the corporation's existence (until April 1, 1960), and thereafter the price was to be set by agreement between Parker and Eaves, with arbitration if they could not agree.

The face of all stock certificates issued to Parker and Eaves carried notice of the restriction on sale created by the Articles of Incorporation. Only the stock certificates issued to Eaves carried a legend that they were subject to the Eaves-Parker buy-and-sell agreement.

Also, at the first meeting of the board of directors, Parker sold to the corporation certain other assets which were depreciable property (such as motor vehicles, furniture and fixtures, and other equipment which Parker had apparently used in the business before the incorporation) worth $95,738.70. The corporation was to pay for this property in ten annual installments with interest of 5 per cent. Parker elected to treat the sale as a capital transaction, and reported the gain from it as long term capital gain. IRC §1231.

The present suit arises because the Internal Revenue Service treated the gain as as ordinary income under IRC §1239, based upon the contention that the taxpayers owned more than 80 per cent "in value" of all outstanding stock of the corporation at the time of sale. The Service assessed deficiencies for the calendar years 1959, 1960, and 1961. Taxpayers paid the assessments under protest and sued in district court for a refund. 28 U.S.C.A. §1346(a). The district court granted summary judgment for the taxpayers, and the government appeals. We reverse.

The government makes two contentions on appeal: first, that the taxpayers owned more than 80 per cent of the outstanding stock because Eaves, at the time of sale, had "outstanding" only those shares which he had paid for and had actually been issued to him and had a mere contract to purchase the remainder. Second, the government argues that even if the full 20 per cent of the shares allotted to Eaves was "outstanding" at the time of the sale, "the restrictions placed upon those shares and their inherent limitations made them worth less per share than Parker's." We disagree with the first of the government's contentions, but agree with the second.

I.

The government argues that Eaves had a mere contract to purchase stock from the corporation, and that therefore the only "outstanding" stock which he owned at the relevant time was the 64.239 shares for which he had paid and for which certificates had been issued to him. It relies on 5 LSA-RS §12:15A.

"A. No allotment of shares for a corporation shall be made except:
"(1) Pursuant to a subscription received therefor; or
"(2) Pursuant to the declaration of a stock dividend; or
"(3) Pursuant to purchase on payment therefor."

The government insists that because Eaves had not paid for 135.761 shares, he failed to own them under §12:15A(3). The government here fails to recognize that §12:15A sets out three ways to become a shareholder. While Eaves did not qualify under §12:15A(3), he did qualify under §12:15A(1). The record shows that Eaves had subscribed for all of the 200 shares and that the corporation had accepted the subscription. It is only where there is no subscription that payment is a condition precedent to becoming an allottee.

The government next argues that because the 135.761 shares had been "allotted" but not "issued", they were not "outstanding" shares within IRC §1239. Shares are not "issued" by the corporation until they are fully paid for. But 5 LSA-RS §12:1N says in part:

"'Shareholder' means one who owns one or more shares. A subscriber becomes a shareholder upon the allotment of shares to him." . . .

. . . Eaves owned the shares subject to his obligation to pay for them. Issuance of the certificates must await full payment only because

". . . an express mandate of the Louisiana Constitution [La. Const. Art. 13, §2] prohibits the issuance of a certificate of stock 'until the shares represented thereby have been fully paid for.' Thus, the share certificate cannot be issued in payment for services yet to be rendered, or property yet to be received. This restriction is necessitated by the negotiable qualities of the certificate. It does not prevent a subscriber from immediately becoming a shareholder upon the allotment of his shares, but does prohibit the issuance of a certificate to him until the shares are fully paid for." Bennett, Louisiana Business Corporation Act of 1928, 2 La. L. Rev. 597, 616 (1940).

A man need not hold issued shares to be a stockholder; he need only have been allotted shares. Eaves had 200 shares allotted to him by the corporation, and those shares were therefore not subject to disposition by the corporation or anyone other than Eaves. We agree with the district court that shares allotted under the Louisiana Act are "outstanding" within the meaning of §1239.

II.

Section 1239 prevents capital gain treatment of a "sale or exchange" of depreciable property to a controlled corporation or a spouse. Without this section a taxpayer who had property which had been depreciated to a low basis could sell that property to a controlled corporation or spouse and pay only capital gains rates on the gain. The transferee (who is virtually identical to the transferor in the proscribed area) could then redepreciate the property, using the sale price as a new basis. The depreciation, of course, would be deducted from ordinary income. Section 1239 renders such a scheme profitless by taxing the gain on the transfer at ordinary rather than capital rates.

The issue here, of course, is whether Parker's corporation is sufficiently Parker's slave to justify invocation of §1239. We have concluded that Parker owned for purposes of §1239, exactly 80 per cent of the corporation's outstanding stock. The decisive question now is whether this 80 per cent is, under §1239, "more than 80 per cent *in value* of the outstanding stock." [italics added]

We first note what §1239 does not say. It does not use the standard of §368(c) which is invoked by §351 for transfers to a controlled corporation in exchange for that corporation's stock or securities. Control is defined by §368(c) as "ownership of stock possessing at least 80 per cent of the total combined *voting power* of all classes of stock entitled to vote and at least 80 percent of the total *number* of shares of all other classes of stock of the corporation." [italics added]

By contrast, §1239 says "more than 80 per cent *in value*." The words "in value" in §1239 must have some meaning. Trotz v. Commissioner of Internal Revenue, 10 Cir. 1966, 361 F.2d 927, 930. We cannot indulge in statutory interpretation by excision. Statutory explication may be an art, but it must not be artful. Further, we cannot say that by using "in value" Congress intended us to consider only the factors of voting power or number of shares. "If the 80% determination is to be [merely] on the basis of the number of shares outstanding, no reason exists for the use of the words 'in value'." Trotz v. Commissioner of Internal Revenue, supra, 361 F.2d at 930. Or, if number of shares and voting power were the sole indicia, Congress could have limited §1239 by using terms similar to those which §351 draws from §368(c) in an analogous situation within the Code's framework. "In value" is a broader phrase, and we think that it calls for the familiar, though difficult, process of fair market valuation. . . .

We next note that in the present case Eaves owned exactly 20 per cent of the outstanding stock, and Parker owned exactly 80 per cent. Therefore, if any fact can be found which shows that the value per share of Parker's stock exceeded by any amount, no matter how small, the value per share of Eaves's, then Parker owned more than 80 per cent in value of the outstanding stock. While it is true that Parker and Eaves owned the same class of stock, Eaves's stock was burdened with impedimenta from which Parker's stock was free. We hold that as a matter of law these impedimenta must have decreased the value per share of Eaves's stock, and as we need only show that this value per share was lower by any indeterminate amount, no matter how minuscule, than the value per share of Parker's stock, we are able to render judgment here without remand.[8]

---

[8]In this aspect the present case differs from Trotz v. Commissioner of Internal Revenue, supra. There, the taxpayer Trotz owned 79 per cent of the outstanding stock and the lesser shareholder owned 21 per cent. The Tenth Circuit remanded the case for a factual determination by the Tax

The impedimenta which depress the value spring from two sources.

A. *The restrictions on transfer of stock.* Eaves's stock was encumbered by two kinds of restrictions. First, the articles of incorporation stated that the corporation had the right of first refusal of any offer to sell to a third party. Second, Eaves's agreement with Parker stated that if Eaves left the employ of the corporation for any reason, he must sell all of his stock to Parker at a price representing the value per share of the assets, specifically excluding good will. Notice to the world of these restrictions, like the mark of Cain, was on the face of Eaves's stock certificates.

The practical effect of these restrictions was to reduce the number of opportunities for Eaves to sell or give away the stock and to place a limit (the duration of his employment) upon the period when he might hold the stock. "A commodity freely salable is obviously worth more on the market than a precisely similar commodity which cannot be freely sold." Judge Woodbury for the First Circuit in Worcester County Trust Co. v. Commissioner of Internal Revenue, 1 Cir. 1943, 134 F.2d 578, 582.

The alienability of Parker's stock was restricted only by the limitation imposed by the articles of incorporation. Whether this limitation, in the light of Parker's complete control, had any real effect on alienability we need not consider, for Eaves's stock was burdened not only by the articles but also by the extra and potent limitation of the buy-sell agreement. Even if we consider the Eaves and Parker stock as identically limited by the articles, Parker's stock was not affected by the buy-sell agreement; Eaves's was. "In our view it must be said that the restriction necessarily had a depressing effect upon the value of the stock in the market." Worcester County Trust Co., supra, 134 F.2d at 578. That such an extra limitation on alienability would depress market value to some greater extent is a well-recognized proposition: Mailloux v. Commissioner of Internal Revenue, 5 Cir. 1963, 320 F.2d 60 . . . .

B. *The lack of control.* Eaves owned only 20 per cent of the stock. This left Parker in sole control of the corporation's affairs. Parker could, without Eaves, elect and remove directors and officers, amend the articles, and promulgate by-laws. He could dissolve the corporation. 5 LSA-RS §12:54. With these powers, Parker controlled without possibility of challenge the entire operation from the smallest detail to the largest. He exercised so much power that the corporation was his alter ego, or his slave. This is the situation at which §1239 aims.

Any purchaser of Eaves's stock would not be buying any degree of control over the corporation. The voting power which technically inhered in Eaves's stock was in reality worthless; Parker owned all of the real voting stock.

We hold that this disability which inhered in Eaves's stock reduced its value per share below that of Parker's stock as a matter of law. . . .

"Even absent any contemplated change in management, control increases the value of an investment by protecting it. The power to change the manage-

---

Court of whether any difference between the values per share of the large and small blocks brought Trotz's holding above 80 per cent in value. In contrast, in the present case any extra value per share in Parker's stock will bring his holding above 80 per cent in value. No determination is needed of how much more per share Parker's stock is worth.

ment, even while unexercised, protects the investor with control against an abrupt change by someone else and against a gradual deterioration of the incumbent management, Therefore, in a sense, controlling shares are inherently worth more than noncontrolling shares for reasons relating solely to investment value. When control is diffused, the same reasoning establishes, to a lesser degree, that shares enabling their holder to participate in control are worth more than those that do not. This is the strangest part of any argument against a broad reading of [Perlman v. Feldmann, 2 Cir. 1955, 219 F.2d 173, cert. denied, 349 U.S. 952 (1955)]. It is the kernel of truth in the assertion that a premium paid for controlling shares only shows that controlling shares are inherently worth more than minority shares." Andrews, The Stockholder's Right to Equal Opportunity in the Sale of Shares, 78 Harvard L. Rev. 505, 526 (1965).[9]

. . . We reiterate that in the present case it is sufficient for the rendering of judgment to note that the restriction on Eaves's stock and its minority qualities combine to have some depressing effect, no matter how small, on its value per share. We hold, therefore, that Parker owned more than 80 per cent in value of the corporation's stock, and that any gain on the sale of the depreciable property was properly taxed at ordinary rates. We render judgment for the government.

Reversed and rendered.

NOTE

See J. Kendrick, Definition of "Eighty Per Cent in Value" Under Section 1239, 21 Sw. L.J. 565 (1967); P. Monte, Determination of Related Parties: A Critical Discussion of the Value Test Prescribed in the Internal Revenue Code, 9 B.C. Ind. & Com. L. Rev. 171 (1967); R. Greene and R. Hobbet, I.R.S. Says Section 1239 Applies to Sales Between 80%-Controlled Corporations, 30 J. Taxation 291 (1968); R. Mankoff, *Parker* Decision Creates a New Problem for Tax Planners, 45 Taxes 522 (1967).

3. Effect of Liabilities — §357

SIMON v. COMMISSIONER
285 F.2d 422 (3d Cir. 1960)

Before GOODRICH, McLAUGHLIN and STALEY, Circuit Judges.

STALEY, Circuit Judge. Does a recognizable gain accrue to a taxpayer where pursuant to a prearranged plan he mortgages real estate and receives therefor an

---

[9]This entire article is concerned with the inherent disparity of value between controlling and noncontrolling shares. Professor Andrews proposes a remedy to allow minority shareholders to share in the premium paid for controlling stock, but that remedy is not part of the law of Louisiana; the article's call for a remedy demonstrates how real the problem is.

amount in excess of the property's adjusted basis under Section [1001(b)] . . . , and shortly thereafter transfers the property without consideration but subject to the mortgage?

The facts as found by the Tax Court, stipulated in part, may be summarized as follows:

In 1941 Joseph B. Simon, petitioner, purchased the RKO Building ("property") in Philadelphia, Pennsylvania, for $104,220.45. On September 28, 1951, he placed a mortgage on it not involving personal liability and received therefor $120,000. On December 27, 1951, the petitioners conveyed the property subject to the mortgage to Exco Corporation ("Exco"), and shortly thereafter, Exco conveyed the same property to Penn-Liberty Insurance Company ("Penn-Liberty").

The petitioners' joint income tax return for the year 1951 did not show receipt of the mortgaged proceeds or reflect in any way the conveyance of the property to Exco. The Commissioner determined that these transactions constituted a sale from which the petitioner realized a long-term capital gain in the amount of $35,108.33 for the taxable year 1951. A tax deficiency in the amount of $10,715.94 was assessed against the petitioners . . . . The Tax Court sustained the Commissioner's determination . . . .

In this court the petitioner does not assail the facts, largely stipulated, as found by the Tax Court, but only its ultimate finding that a sale took place, asserting that "there are no facts to support the Court's conclusion that a 'sale', or any other kind of taxable disposition, took place." . . .

In our evaluation of the evidence before the Tax Court to determine its persuasiveness of that court's conclusion, we are guided in part by what was said in Commissioner of Internal Revenue v. Court Holding Co., 1945, 324 U.S. 331, 334, 65 S. Ct. 707, 708, 89 L. Ed. 981:

> ". . . The incidence of taxation depends upon the substance of a transaction. The tax consequences which arise from gains from a sale of property are not finally to be determined solely by the means employed to transfer legal title. Rather, the transaction must be viewed as a whole, and each step, from the commencement of negotiations to the consummation of the sale, is relevant. A sale by one person cannot be transformed for tax purposes into a sale by another by using the latter as a conduit through which to pass title. To permit the true nature of a transaction to be disguised by mere formalisms, which exist solely to alter tax liabilities, would seriously impair the effective administration of the tax policies of Congress."

During 1951 Penn-Liberty was confronted with a deteriorating financial condition caused by substantial losses arising from claims for hurricane damage which had occurred at the end of 1950. The petitioner, Charles Denby, and the officers of Penn-Liberty discussed this situation and agreed to a plan whereby the property in question would be mortgaged and thereafter conveyed, subject to the mortgage, to Penn-Liberty to help maintain its legal reserves. The interest shown by petitioner and Denby in Penn-Liberty's plight was understandable. Petitioner was president of Exco and treasurer of Penn-Liberty, while Denby served as treasurer of Exco. Together, they owned and controlled Exco, which in turn owned Penn-Liberty.

The petitioner proceeded to execute the plan. Either because Penn-Liberty did not require a contribution equal to the full value of the property, or because the petitioner was unwilling to make a contribution for that amount, he mortgaged the property on September 28, 1951, for $120,000. The petitioner used $79,587.27 of the mortgage proceeds to satisfy two prior mortgages and pay closing costs, and reduced the principal debt to $119,098.22 by making payments thereon in November and December, 1951, retaining $40,412.73 of the proceeds.

On December 27, 1951, when the property had an adjusted basis of $82,205.17, the petitioners conveyed it to Exco, and immediately thereafter, on December 31, 1951, petitioner, as president of Exco, signed a deed conveying the same property to Penn-Liberty. In both instances the property was conveyed subject to the mortgage for a recited but never paid consideration of $100.

Petitioner testified and he here contends that he intended the conveyance to be a contribution to capital meant to improve Penn-Liberty's financial condition. He also maintains that neither that conveyance nor the placing of the mortgage and retention of part of the proceeds can constitute separately or together a taxable event. However, in determining the true nature of the transaction based on the mortgage and subsequent conveyances, the Tax Court was free to draw its own conclusion from the evidence as a whole, not being bound by the interested though uncontradicted testimony of the taxpayer. . . .

Taxpayer may very well have intended to and probably did improve Penn-Liberty's financial condition by the method employed, for at the time of the conveyance to Penn-Liberty, the property was entered on its books as an asset with an appraised value of $242,800 (less the unpaid principal on the mortgage and $471.43 accrued interest), which was well in excess of the mortgage for $120,000. It thus appears that these transactions served as a means of fulfilling petitioner's intentions while simultaneously returning to him an amount in excess of his then existing investment in the property.

It is immaterial, we think, that in financing the transaction the mortgage was negotiated for and placed by the petitioner prior to the transfer rather than by the purchaser-transferee as is the usual practice. As a matter of fact, when the petitioner gave the mortgage on September 28, 1951, he was at that time president of Exco and treasurer of Penn-Liberty, acting in pursuance of a plan agreed to by both corporations. It would certainly not be untenable to conclude that at the time petitioner gave the mortgage, he was already acting as an agent for both Exco and Penn-Liberty in securing the loan, the proceeds of which would in turn be used to purchase the property from him in his individual capacity.

The time interval between the various steps leading up to the subsequent conveyance to Penn-Liberty and the petitioner's testimony that it was a "Penn-Liberty deal" from the beginning fully support the Tax Court's conclusion that it was a single integrated transaction and constituted a sale. In fact, it seems to us that this conclusion is the only plausible one. . . .

Petitioner relies on Mendham Corp., 1947, 9 T.C. 320, and Woodsam Associates, Inc. v. Commissioner, 2 Cir., 1952, 198 F.2d 357, which we think are not in point. Neither of these cases was concerned with the tax liability of the transferor, for both involved a transfer of property to a corporation for stock under Section [351] . . . , whereby no gain or loss was to be recognized. Our conclusion also makes inapplicable Crane v. Commissioner, 1947, 331 U.S. 1, 67 S. Ct. 1047, 91 L. Ed. 1301, and Parker v. Delaney, 1 Cir., 1950, 186 F.2d 455, certiorari denied 1951, 341 U.S. 926, 71 S. Ct. 797, 95 L. Ed. 1357, where the mortgaging of the property and its subsequent disposition by the mortgagor or his successor were unrelated. The Court in *Crane* was faced solely with the question of determining the adjusted basis of real estate. Here there is no dispute as to the property's adjusted basis.

The decision of the Tax Court will be affirmed.

EASSON v. COMMISSIONER
294 F.2d 653 (9th Cir. 1961)

Before ORR, BARNES and MERRILL, Circuit Judges.

BARNES, Circuit Judge. . . . In 1952 taxpayer owned and operated an apartment house in Portland, Oregon. On June 19, 1952, taxpayer encumbered the apartment house with a $250,000 mortgage, taxpayer himself signing and assuming personal liability on the notes underlying the mortgage. In October of 1952, taxpayer formed the Envoy Apartments, an Oregon corporation, and transferred the property, subject to the mortgage, to the corporation in exchange for all of its capital stock. Taxpayer, however, remained personally liable on the notes. The Tax Court found that taxpayer had a legitimate business purpose in consummating this transaction .and that his principal purpose was not tax avoidance.

At the time of the transfer, the basis of appellant's property was $87,214.86, and its fair market value was $320,000. The principal balance of the mortgage was $247,064.01. Taxpayer and his wife, on their 1952 returns, reported no gain in connection with the transfer of the apartment to the corporation. They claimed that the transfer was tax free under §112(b)(5), Internal Revenue Code of 1939, 26 U.S.C.A. §112(b)(5).* The Commissioner, however, determined that taxpayer realized a gain on the transaction and determined further that such gain was taxable at ordinary income tax rates rather than at capital gains rates.

I. The Tax Court's Decision

The Tax Court agreed fully with neither the Commissioner nor the taxpayer. It held that only a portion of the gain should be recognized and taxed in 1952. The taxable portion, the court held, was the difference between taxpayer's basis ($87,214.86) and the principal balance on the mortgage ($247,064.01), viz. $159,849.15. . . .

Section 112(b)(5) provides that no gain or loss is to be recognized when property is transferred to a corporation solely in exchange for stock of the corporation, if immediately after the transfer, the transferor is in control of the corporation. Thus,

---

*Section 112(b)(5) of the 1939 Code is the predecessor of §351 of the 1954 Code. — ED.

at first blush, it would appear that taxpayer should prevail; he exchanged the apartment for stock of the corporation and immediately after the exchange he was in control of the corporation. He has met the requirements of §112(b)(5). But there was more to the transaction than just an exchange of an apartment house for stock. The apartment was transferred subject to a mortgage and this circumstance can, in some circumstances, alter the tax consequences of the transaction. Subsection (c) (of §112)* provides that gain will be recognized in a §112(b)(5) transaction to the extent that "boot," i.e., money or property other than stock, is received by the taxpayer. Can the transfer of encumbered property be considered as the receipt of "boot"? Section 112(k)† provides a clear answer to this question.[2] It provides that the transfer of property subject to a liability does *not* constitute the receipt of money or other property within the meaning of §112(c), and the existence of the encumbrance does not disqualify the exchange for tax-free treatment under §112(b)(5) — *unless* the purpose of the taxpayer, in this regard, was tax avoidance or was not a bona fide business purpose. The burden to establish his exemption is on the taxpayer. Here, however, the Tax Court specifically found that taxpayer was not principally motivated by considerations of tax avoidance and that he had a bona fide business purpose. Thus, taxpayer met the test of the specific provisions of §112(k); the

*Section 351(b) of the 1954 Code. — ED.

†Sections 357(a) and (b) of the 1954 Code. — ED.

[2]It reads as follows:

"(k) [as added by §213(a), Revenue Act of 1939, and amended by §121(d)(5), Revenue Act of 1943, supra] Assumption of liability not recognized. Where upon an exchange the taxpayer receives as part of the consideration property which would be permitted by subsection (b)(4), (5), or (10) of this section to be received without the recognition of gain if it were the sole consideration, and as part of the consideration another party to the exchange assumes a liability of the taxpayer or acquires from the taxpayer property subject to a liability, such assumption or acquisition shall not be considered as 'other property or money' received by the taxpayer within the meaning of subsection (c), (d), or (e) of this section and shall not prevent the exchange from being within the provisions of subsection (b)(4), (5), or (10); except that if, taking into consideration the nature of the liability and the circumstances in the light of which the arrangement for the assumption or acquisition was made, it appears that the principal purpose of the taxpayer with respect to the assumption or acquisition was a purpose to avoid Federal income tax on the exchange, or if not such purpose, was not a bona fide business purpose, such assumption or acquisition (in the amount of the liability) shall, for the purposes of this section, be considered as money received by the taxpayer upon the exchange. In any suit or proceeding where the burden is on the taxpayer to prove that such assumption or acquisition is not to be considered as money received by the taxpayer, such burden shall not be considered as sustained unless the taxpayer sustains such burden by the clear preponderance of the evidence." (26 U.S.C. 1952 ed., §112.)

Section 112(k) was enacted to avoid the holding of Walter Haase, 37 B.T.A. 948 and United States v. Hendler, 1938, 303 U.S. 564, 58 S. Ct. 655, 82 L. Ed. 1018 [Chapter 4, page 560 infra]. The latter case was described in the Congressional discussion preceding the enactment of §112(k) as overturning "what had been the uniform policy and consistent practice of the Treasury Department since" enaction.

Cong. Record, Vol. 84, and see discussion and reference to Congressional History, Petitioner's Brief, pp. 29-33. And vide, Helvering v. Southwest Consol. Corp., 1942, 315 U.S. 194, 199, 62 S. Ct. 546, 86 L. Ed. 789.

In 1954, Congress re-enacted §112(k) of the 1939 Code as §357(a) and (b) and added the present §357(c), which for the first time limits §112(k) by declaring that liabilities in excess of basis shall be considered gain. This was characterized in House Report No. 1337 as having "no counterpart under the 1939 Code." Of course, the instant case arose before the passage of §357(c).

provisions of §112(c) are, therefore, inapplicable to this transaction. It would seem, then, that the entire transaction comes within §112(b)(5), and that no gain should yet be recognized. Nevertheless, the Tax Court did not so hold.

The Tax Court noted that a statute must be construed in accordance with its purposes and must not be so interpreted as to lead to "absurd results." The purpose of §112(b)(5) is not to exempt gain from taxation but to postpone the taxable event to a later time. This postponement is effectuated by adjusting the basis of the stock which the taxpayer receives in the tax free exchange. Under §[358(a)], the basis of the stock is the basis of the property transferred, decreased, however, by the amount of money received, including for purposes of this section the amount of the mortgage, and increased by any gain recognized. Thus, unrecognized gain is retained as a potential liability by reducing the basis of taxpayer's stock.

As an example, if a taxpayer in a §112(b)(5) transaction transfers property worth $10,000 which cost him $1,000, he has an unrecognized gain of $9,000. Since his stock takes the same basis as the property transferred (viz. $1,000), he will recognize the gain when he sells the stock at a later date (presumably at $10,000). If the property transferred were subject to a $500 mortgage, taxpayer would have an additional gain of $500, the gain being currently unrecognized, however, by virtue of §112(k). This additional gain would be postponed by reducing the basis of the stock received by the taxpayer as follows: "Basis of stock received by taxpayer equals the basis of the property transferred, $1,000, less money or property received (including the amount of the mortgage), $500, plus the amount of gain currently recognized ($-0-$), viz. $500." When taxpayer sells the stock, presumably, for $10,000, he would realize and pay tax upon a gain of $9,500.

As applied to the facts of this case, the computation prescribed by §[358(a)], would result in a *negative* basis with respect to the stock acquired by taxpayer. Taxpayer's basis on the transferred property was $87,214.86; deducting from this figure the amount of the mortgage ($247,064.01) yields a basis of minus $159,849.15. Holding that property cannot have a negative basis, the court held, further, that the adjusted basis of the stock is zero. This determination, however, would permit the gain of $159,849.15 to escape taxation, unless the nonrecognition provisions of §112(b)(5) are ignored. If petitioner sold his zero basis stock for an amount that equaled the equity in the property transferred, $72,935.99 ($320,000, fair market value, less $247,064.01, mortgage), he would be taxed on that amount and nothing more. Taxpayer would, in effect, have converted the property into cash, realizing a gain of $232,785.14, but never paying a tax on $159,849.15 of it. Since the purpose of §112(b)(5) is not [to] permit a tax avoidance but only to permit postponement, it cannot, consistently with its purpose, be applied without limitation to this transaction. That portion of the gain, which if not presently recognized, will never be recognized, must be taxed now. The Tax Court thus held that $159,849.15 should be currently recognized and taxed. . . . Both the taxpayer and the Commissioner have appealed from the Tax Court's decision.

II. Appeal of Jack Easson, Taxpayer

Taxpayer contends that the Tax Court's holding does violence to the clear and unambiguous language of the code sections involved. Section 112(b)(5) states unequivocally that no gain is to be recognized when property is transferred to a corporation in exchange for stock and immediately after the exchange the transferor controls the corporation. Section 112(k) is also clear in providing that the existence of an encumbrance on property exchanged in a §112(b)(5) transaction does not deny the transferor the benefits conferred by §112(b)(5). When a statute is unambiguous, the courts may not look elsewhere for the legislative intent. . . . We believe that the Tax Court did err in failing to adhere to the unambiguous language contained in the statutes in question here. Assuredly, there is authority for departing from the literal meaning of statutory language when literal application would produce absurd results (1 Mertens, Law of Federal Income Taxation, §3.04), but here the Tax Court's interpretation is directly contrary to the language of the statute. Section 112(b)(5) says no gain shall be recognized if certain conditions are fulfilled, yet the Tax Court says gain shall be recognized even though all the conditions enumerated are fulfilled. This is judicial legislation. If absurd results occur by reason of taxing statutes honestly and correctly followed by a taxpayer, it is up to the Congress to remedy the loophole.

Taxpayer's case on this point is bolstered by the fact that the 1954 Code contains a provision specifically covering the situation presented by this case. Section 357(c) of the 1954 Code, 26 U.S.C.A. §357(c), expressly provides that if the transferred property is subject to liabilities which exceed the transferor's basis in the property then the excess is to be presently recognized as gain. (See note 2, supra.) The court below brushed this aside as a clarification of existing law and not new law (noting dicta to the contrary, however, in W. H. Weaver, 32 T.C. 411, 436). In commenting upon the general effect of the provisions contained in §357(c), the House Ways and Means Committee noted that the provisions are "not found in existing law." H.R. No. 1337 (83d Cong. 2d Sess., p. A129; U.S. Code, Congressional and Administrative News, 1954, v. 3, p. 4066). Thus the existence and history of later legislation tend to indicate that Congress "meant" precisely what it said — and no more — when it adopted §112(b)(5) of the 1939 Code.

In departing from the express language of §112(b)(5), the Tax Court relied upon the fact that a literal interpretation of the section would lead to absurd results. If no such absurd consequences are inherent in a literal application of the section, then no justification for the Tax Court's departure is established. The absurd result feared by the Tax Court was that §112(b)(5) would become an instrument of tax exemption rather than of tax deferment. This conviction stemmed from the Tax Court's belief that there could be no such legal phenomenon as a negative basis. And this is perhaps the most crucial issue in the appeal presented by the taxpayer.

Can property have a negative basis? There is little law on the subject,[3] and we

[3]For an informative and well authenticated argument in support of the recognition of a negative basis, see . . . a thesis . . . written by George Cooper, entitled "Negative Basis," dated April 20th, 1961 [75 Harv. L. Rev. 1352 (1962)], and discussing the instant case, and listing the favorable and unfavorable considerations which might establish the value of recognizing a negative basis, under certain factual conditions, and in some, but not all, cases.

As an aside, it is interesting to note that Mr. Cooper concludes that without the "suggestion"

are far from satisfied that the Tax Court's outright rejection of this concept is justifiable. Why, then, did the Tax Court conclude that property cannot have a negative basis? In footnote 8 of its opinion (Record, p. 59), the court explains:

> "It is a fundamental concept of income taxation to tax gain when its fruits are available for payment of the tax. If a negative base were allowed then recognition of gain could be deferred until a subsequent loss sale or even an abandonment, and unless taxpayer had other resources the tax would never be collected."

The Tax Court, thus, rejects the negative basis concept on the ground that it may impair the future collectibility of the tax. "We must recognize and collect the tax now, or we may never be able to do so." But such argument is equally applicable to any provision for the deferment of tax; nonrecognition of present gain with a corresponding reduction of basis creates the prospect that tax on the deferred gain may never actually be collected. This prospect is equally real, whether basis is reduced to zero, to a point above zero, or to less than zero.

Judicial hostility to a negative basis is confined to an implication that deductions from a minus basis are undesirable. Crane v. Commissioner, 1947, 331 U.S. 1, 9-10, 67 S. Ct. 1047, 91 L. Ed. 1301. . . .

There is some judicial support for the concept of negative basis in Parker v. Delaney, 1 Cir., 1950, 186 F.2d 455, 459, certiorari denied 341 U.S. 926, 71 S. Ct. 797, 95 L. Ed. 1357. There, Chief Judge Magruder in a concurring opinion offered an alternative theory to reach the result obtained by the majority, but "with less strain upon the statutory language." His computation involved the use of a negative basis.

The authority bearing on the question presented here, is, then, inconclusive. The "absurd result" which the Tax Court envisions is by no means the necessary consequence of literally applying §112(b)(5). If the mandate of §112(b)(5) is followed and none of taxpayer's gain is presently recognized, taxpayer's stock can be given a negative basis, so that all of his gain will be recognized and taxed when he sells the stock. . . .

III. Appeal by Commissioner

This brings us to the appeal by the Commissioner. The Commissioner contends that the Tax Court erred in not holding *all* of taxpayer's gain from the exchange to be presently recognizable and taxable. This is the Commissioner's primary position and his defense of the Tax Court's decision in the appeal brought by taxpayer is only an alternative position, if his position here is rejected.

The Commissioner contends that the transaction is governed by §112(c). This section, it will be recalled, provides that gain will be recognized in a §112(b)(5) transaction to the extent that "boot" (money or property other than stock) is received by taxpayer. The corporation's acquisition of the property subject to the mortgage, the Commissioner contends, constitutes the receipt by taxpayer of "boot." Since the boot

---

of §357(c) of the 1954 Code, the Tax Court would not have reached the result it did in the instant case.

so received, $247,064.01, exceeds taxpayer's gain of $232,785.14 (fair market value of the property, $320,000, less taxpayer's basis, $87,214.86), all of the gain must be recognized and taxed. Section 112(k), we have seen, precludes the result contended for by the Commissioner, but §112(k) contains an exception and it is this exception which the Commissioner relies upon now. Section 112(k) provides that

> "[if] it appears that the principal purpose of the taxpayer with respect to the assumption or acquisition was a purpose to avoid Federal income tax on the exchange, or if not such purpose, was not a bona fide business purpose, such assumption or acquisition (in the amount of the liability) shall, for the purposes of this section, be considered as money received by the taxpayer upon the exchange."

The Tax Court found, however, that taxpayer's "principal purpose in exchanging the property subject to the mortgage for all the capital stock of the new corporation was not to avoid Federal income tax on the exchange, and that he had a bona fide business purpose in so transferring the property." (Record, p. 51.) In so finding, the Commissioner contends, the Tax Court erred.

The Tax Court substantiated its ultimate findings by finding further that taxpayer desired to place himself in an extremely liquid position to take advantage of a business downturn which, he believed, would soon occur. In order to achieve this liquid position, taxpayer mortgaged his property, since he was unable to sell it despite efforts to do so. Having decided to retain the apartment for himself, taxpayer also decided to operate the property in corporate form, as he had done for twenty years. For tax reasons, taxpayer had taken the apartment out of the corporation when he had contemplated selling it. After deciding not to sell it, he desired to return it to corporate form in order to secure limited liability and convenience of management should he desire to move elsewhere and to turn the property over to a local real estate organization.

The Commissioner contends (and this is the crux of his appeal) that the Tax Court missed the point of §112(k). The "true question," missed by the Tax Court, the Commissioner contends, is whether the corporation's taking subject to the liability had some bona fide business purpose in connection with the *corporation's* business. Thus, the Commissioner contends, the question was not whether the transfer of the property subject to the liability benefited taxpayer's business interests as an investor; the issue is whether the taking-subject-to-the-liability had any purpose with respect to the business of operating the apartments as rental property. The Tax Court found no such business purpose, and, therefore, the Commissioner claims, it erred in holding that taxpayer met the test of §112(k).

We cannot go along with the Commissioner's interpretation of the statute. We believe it is erroneous. It finds little, if any, support in the case authority cited. The test suggested by the Commissioner looks to the origin of the encumbrance and to the use of the proceeds derived from it. Section 112(k), however, says nothing about the origin of the encumbrance. It says only that if a corporation "acquires from the taxpayer property subject to *a* liability such . . . acquisition shall not be considered as" boot, unless taxpayer's principal purpose regarding the acquisition is tax avoidance or not a bona fide business purpose. Nor is there anything in the section which deals with the reasons for the encumbrance, or the manner in which the mortgage proceeds are used. If there is a good business purpose for transferring the property without first removing the encumbrance, the requirements of §112(k) are satisfied. Certainly, an investor's desire to remain liquid in order to capitalize on an expected business recession is a good business reason for not discharging the mortgage. . . .

The Commissioner seeks support for his position in Bryan v. Commissioner, 4 Cir., 1960, 281 F.2d 238, certiorari denied 364 U.S. 931, 81 S. Ct. 378, 5 L. Ed. 2d 364. The facts of that case, with some simplification, may be readily stated. Taxpayer obtained construction loans of $1,643,500 to build houses. This exceeded his actual cost by $157,798.04. After building the houses taxpayer transferred them to four corporations which in exchange gave him stock and assumed the construction loan. The Tax Court and the Court of Appeals held that taxpayer, under these circumstances, received money or other property and therefore did not meet the requirements of §112(b)(5).

This case, however, provides only weak support for the Commissioner's position here. The Tax Court found in *Bryan,* as it did not find in the instant case, that taxpayer's "principal purpose with respect to the assumption of the liabilities by the four corporations was a purpose to avoid tax," and hence that it was "immaterial . . . whether such purpose might otherwise be considered not a bona fide business purpose." (W. H. Weaver, 32 T.C. 414, 434.) The court of appeals agreed that "his only purpose was to appropriate to himself a major portion of the excess funds . . .' and to do it in a form which gave him hope of avoiding federal taxes on the funds with which he enriched himself." Bryan v. Commissioner, supra, 281 F.2d at page 242. There was, therefore, no problem in determining that §112(k) did not apply.

The *Bryan* case does offer some support for the Commissioner's position in stating that the corporation's assumption of the mortgage in excess of taxpayer's basis constituted an indirect payment of cash to taxpayer. "As a cash payment, the nonrecognition sections would have no application." Ibid. These statements must, however, be considered as dicta in view of the court's holding that taxpayer did not meet the requirements of §112(k) and that therefore the assumption of the mortgage constituted the payment of "money or other property." If, on the other hand, the court had held §112(k) applicable, the statements would have been inappropriate. Section 112(k) provides, clearly, that an assumption of liability is not the payment of "other property or money," and to hold that such assumption constitutes a cash payment is a clear contradiction of the words of the statute.

The Tax Court's findings regarding taxpayer's business purpose have not, in our opinion, been shown to be clearly erroneous. And the Commissioner's assertion that taxpayer is a "highly tax conscious person" (Commissioner's brief, as petitioner, p. 28), as are many citizens these days, is certainly not sufficient to overthrow the Tax Court's further finding that taxpayer's principal motive in *this* transaction was not tax avoidance. The Tax Court fully examined the evidence regarding the exchange before concluding that taxpayer entered this transaction for bona fide business reasons and not to avoid federal taxes.

In concluding his main argument, the Commissioner says, "There is nothing theoretical about Easson's gain. The unencumbered cash is in his hand, and ought to be immediately subject to the payment of income tax." This statement, we believe, lays bare the Commissioner's basic error. The Commissioner believes that taxpayer is in a genuinely different position now than he was before the exchange. This, we believe, is not so. Before the exchange taxpayer owned an apartment house subject to a liability. After the exchange, taxpayer was the sole owner of a corporation which owned the same apartment house subject to the same liability. Where was *any* income? His stock in the corporation was worth no more than the physical asset which he owned directly before incorporation. Section 112(b)(5) was enacted to deal with this very situation — to permit business reorganizations which, realistically viewed, do not alter the taxpayer's basic position. To use the Commissioner's phraseology, "the unencumbered cash" was in taxpayer's hand as soon as taxpayer had mortgaged the apartment, but the Commissioner does not claim that the hypothecation of the building constituted a taxable event (see brief for Commissioner as respondent, p. 13). Taxpayer's transfer of his encumbered apartment house to his wholly owned corporation did not make the case obtained from the mortgaged transaction any more real or any less encumbered than it was before the transfer. It is our belief that the purpose of the tax laws will best be served by not assessing a tax against taxpayer until he realizes his gain in a transaction in which, realistically speaking, he actually changes his position.

The Commissioner's next contention applies only if the court rejects his positions both as appellee and appellant. In such event, Commissioner contends, taxpayer received dividend income (§115(a), 1954 Code, 26 U.S.C.A. §115(a)) in 1953 by virtue of the corporation's payments on the mortgage. This contention is based upon the theory that the corporation's payments discharged a legal obligation of taxpayer. While the corporation may incidentally have benefited taxpayer by reducing the mortgage, it is clear that the corporation did not thereby distribute any assets. The corporation owned the apartment subject to the mortgage and as the mortgage decreased its equity in the apartment house increased. Thus when it took money out of cash and applied that amount to the mortgage, its net worth remained constant. Its total assets were unchanged because the credit to the cash account was offset by a corresponding debit to the fixed assets account. The payments of interest on the mortgage cannot, obviously, be analyzed in this way; these payments, it would seem, did constitute income to the taxpayer who would then be entitled to take the deduction for interest paid (1 Mertens, Law of Federal Income Taxation, §9.08, p. 19, n.74). The net effect would be to deny the deduction to the corporation. This interpretation is, however, at variance with the Commissioner's own regulations and should, therefore, be rejected. 26 C.F.R. 1.163(1)(b) provides:

"Interest paid by the taxpayer on a mortgage upon real estate of which he is the legal or equitable owner, even though the taxpayer is not directly liable upon the bond or note secured by such mortgage may be deducted as interest on his indebtedness." And see Mertens, supra, §26.03.

We believe the Commissioner erred in asserting a deficiency against taxpayer based on the 1952 transaction, whereby taxpayer exchanged the apartment house for stock of Envoy Apartments. Furthermore, the Commissioner is in error in his contention that taxpayer received dividend income in 1953 by reason of mortgage and interest payments made by the corporation. We *reverse* the judgment of the Tax Court, and direct that judgment be entered in favor of taxpayer.

NOTE

1. D, owning 100 per cent of Corporation W, transfers to W property worth $100,000, with a basis in his hands of $50,000 and subject to a mortgage of $25,000, in exchange for $75,000 worth of stock. What are the tax consequences to D? To W? What is the effect on basis to D and to W? Suppose the stock were worth $125,000? That variable may require your understanding of §305, which is to be considered in Chapter 4 infra. Suppose the stock were worth $75,000, but the mortgage debt was $60,000?

2. *Easson* is the only case in which a court majority has accepted the concept of negative basis. Of what relevance is the fact that the taxpayer is not likely, after incorporation of the asset, to have to repay the obligation he incurred? Are *Simon,* page 339 supra, and *Easson* reconcilable? Is §357(c) a better or worse approach than Easson's as a matter of policy? Why? See N. Schlesinger, Negative Basis, Recognized in *Easson* as Possible, Will Arise Only Rarely, 16 J. Taxation 212 (1962); M. Berl, Disposition of Property Mortgaged in Excess of Basis, 19 N.Y.U. Inst. on Fed. Tax. 1033 (1961).

RAICH v. COMMISSIONER
46 T.C. 604 (1966)

Opinion

WITHEY, Judge: Respondent determined deficiencies in petitioners' income tax for the calendar years 1961 and 1962 in the amounts of $12,840.49 and $221.84, respectively. Petitioners have conceded some of the issues raised by their petition, leaving the following issues to be decided:

(1) Whether the transfer by petitioners in 1961 of the assets and liabilities of their sole proprietorship to their controlled corporation constituted a taxable exchange under sections 351 and 357(c) of the Internal Revenue Code of 1954.

(2) Whether petitioners' receipt from the corporation of a promissory note in the adjusted amount of $12,755.50, as partial payment for the assets and liabilities transferred to it, resulted in gain to petitioners in that amount.

All of the facts have been stipulated and are so found.

Petitioners Peter Raich and Wanda J. Raich are husband and wife residing in San Jose, Calif. For the years in question, 1961 and 1962, they filed joint Federal income tax returns with the district director at San Francisco, Calif. Petitioners filed said returns on the cash receipts and disbursements method of accounting.

Prior to January 3, 1961, petitioner Peter Raich conducted, as a sole proprietorship, a sheetrock and drywall contracting business under the name of Pete Raich Sheetrock

Taping Service. For accounting purposes, the business had as its taxable year the calendar year and operated on a cash basis method of accounting.

On or about January 3, 1961, petitioners transferred to the Pete Raich Sheetrock Taping Service, Inc. (hereinafter the corporation), and the corporation accepted all of the assets and liabilities of the sole proprietorship business previously conducted by petitioners. The transfer of the business was intended to qualify as a nontaxable exchange under the provisions of section 351 of the Internal Revenue Code of 1954. In accordance with the transfer of the business of the sole proprietorship to the corporation, the corporation received the following assets and liabilities, listed on the books and records of the transferor in the following amounts:

ASSETS

Cash		$ 1,045.40
Trade accounts receivable		77,361.66[1]
Receivables		1,833.97
Prepaid rent		125.00
Equipment	$13,626.30	
Less: Accumulated depreciation	5,378.94	8,247.36
Total		$88,613.39

LIABILITIES

Trade accounts payable	37,719.78
Notes payable	8,273.03[2]
Total	$45,992.81

[1]No amount of these receivables were reported as income on the returns of the transferor, but rather, was reported as income by the corporation in the fiscal periods in which they were collected. The petitioners personally guarteed payment of all trade receivables transferred in the exchange.

[2]Of this amount, $3,273.03 constituted a specific encumbrance on equipment transferred to the corporation. The remaining $5,000 of this item represented the unpaid balance on a bank loan.

All the trade accounts payable were in existence as of January 3, 1961, the date of the transfer. None of these accounts were deducted for income tax purposes by the transferors but were deducted by the corporation, an accrual basis taxpayer, in its initial taxable period, the short fiscal year beginning January 1, 1961, and ending May 31, 1961. The capital stock received by the petitioners from the corporation consisted of 2,500 shares of $10 par value common stock which constituted all the issued stock of the corporation. The stock received by petitioners was listed on the books and records of the corporation at a total valuation of $25,000. As additional consideration, petitioners received a short-term unsecured promissory note in the face amount of $16,280.58. The note was payable on demand and carried interest at the rate of 6 percent per annum. Because of uncollectible accounts receivable in the amount of $3,525.08, whose collection had been guaranteed by petitioners, the face amount of the demand note was reduced by an equal amount, to $12,755.50. The balance of the note was reduced, by payment thereon, to $4,150.54 by the close of the corporation's fiscal period ended May 31, 1961. It was further reduced to $1,780.51 by the close of the corporation's fiscal year ended May 31, 1962, and was paid off in full by the close of the corporation's fiscal year ended May 31, 1964.

Issue 1

The principal issue is whether the transfer of petitioners' sole proprietorship to their wholly owned corporation constituted a nontaxable exchange pursuant to section 351, or constituted a taxable event under section 357(c). Both parties agree that the transfer qualifies as a section 351 exchange. The parties disagree with respect to the applicability of section 357(c).

Section 351(a) provides that where property is transferred to a corporation solely in exchange for stock or securities of such corporation and immediately after the exchange the transferor is in control of the corporation, no gain or loss shall be recognized on the exchange. However, section 351(d)(1) provides that where another party to the exchange assumes a liability or acquires property subject to a liability, reference shall be made to section 357. Section 357(c)(1) provides that in a section 351 exchange —

> "if the sum of the amount of the liabilities assumed, plus the amount of the liabilities to which the property is subject, exceeds the total of the *adjusted basis* of the property transferred pursuant to such exchange, then such excess shall be considered as a gain from the sale or exchange of a capital asset or of property which is not a capital asset, as the case may be. [Emphasis supplied.]"

Respondent contends that, under the facts in the instant case, a section 357(c) computation is required since the liabilities assumed by the corporate transferee, $45,992.81,[4] exceeds the "adjusted basis" of the property transferred to it, $11,251.73.[5] Under section 357(c), petitioners would thus incur a tax on the excess of liabilities assumed over property transferred in the amount of $34,741.08. In determining the adjusted basis of the property transferred to the corporation pursuant to section 357(c), respondent failed to include trade accounts receivable valued on the books of the transferor sole proprietorship at $77,361.66, on the ground that since the transferor's sole proprietorship was operated on a cash basis method of accounting, accounts receivable held by it had an "adjusted basis" of zero. Respondent thus takes the position that when the accounts receivable were transferred to the corporation, they retained their basis of zero in a section 357(c) computation.

Petitioners, on the other hand, contend that Congress intended section 357(c) to apply to a section 351 exchange only if the liabilities assumed by the corporate transferee exceed, not only the "adjusted basis of the property transferred," but also the book value of that property. Thus, since the liabilities assumed did not exceed the book value of the property transferred in this case, they contend section 357(c) should not apply. They contend in the alternative that assuming section 357(c) was intended to apply to the type of transaction presented by the instant case, the trade accounts

---

[4]The liabilities transferred consisted of trade accounts payable in the amount of $37,719.78, and notes payable in the amount of $8,273.03.

[5]Respondent included the following assets in this total: cash, $1,045.40; accounts receivable, $1,833.97; prepaid rent, $125; and equipment, $8,247.36. Excluded from the total were trade accounts receivable, valued on the books of petitioners' sole proprietorship at $77,361.66.

receivable had a basis, for purposes of section 357(c), at least equal to the amount of the trade accounts payable assumed by the corporate transferee, $37,719.78.

These contentions thus require a determination as to whether a section 357(c) computation is required under the facts in question and if so, whether the accounts receivable of a cash basis transferor, when transferred to its wholly owned corporation under a section 351 exchange, are includable in the "adjusted basis of the property transferred" as these words are used in section 357(c).

Prior to the Revenue Act of 1921, property received on any exchange was treated, to the extent of its fair market value, as the equivalent of cash received for the purpose of determining gain or loss. This principle was applied to an exchange of property for the stock of the transferor's controlled corporation since the corporation was treated as an entity separate from the transferor. Because such taxation seriously interfered with necessary business adjustments, Congress enacted section 202(c)(3) of the 1921 Act to permit business reorganizations without recognition of gain at the time of transfer. Section 202(c)(3) was reenacted as section 112(b)(5) of the 1928 Act which ultimately became section 351(a) of the 1954 Code. Thus, since 1921, Congress has provided for the nonrecognition of gain or loss resulting from the transfer of property to a controlled corporation solely in exchange for its stock or securities.

In section 351(e)(1), however, Congress provided that where, as the result of a section 351 transaction, a party other than the transferor assumes a liability or acquires property subject to a liability, reference shall be made to section 357. Subsection (a) of section 357 provides that where the transferor's liabilities are assumed by another party to the exchange, such assumption shall not prevent the transferor from benefiting from the nonrecognition provisions of section 351.[6] However, under subsection (c) of section 357, if the liability assumed by the corporate transferee exceeds the adjusted basis of the property transferred, the excess is taxable as gain to the transferor.

A literal interpretation of sections 351(d)(1) and 357(c) compels the application of section 357(c) to the transaction in question. If, as the respondent contends, the trade accounts receivable in the hands of petitioners' sole proprietorship had an adjusted basis of zero at the time of their transfer to the corporation, the liabilities assumed by the corporate transferee ($45,992.81) would exceed the adjusted basis of the transferor's property ($11,251.73) by the amount of $34,741.08, which amount, under section 357(c), must be recognized as gain to petitioners.

Petitioners contend, however, that section 357(c) should not be applied to the reorganization in question. They argue that Congress did not intend for that provision to apply to a situation, like that in the instant case, where the book value of the assets transferred exceeds the liabilities assumed and where the transferor receives no economic benefit or gain from such assumption. In support of their "gain" theory,

---

[6]Sec. 357(a)'s predecessor, sec. 112(k) of the 1939 Code, was enacted to nullify the result caused by United States v. Hendler, 303 U.S. 564 (1938) [see Chapter 4, page 560 infra]. In *Hendler,* the Supreme Court construed sec. 112(b)(5) of the 1939 Code, the predecessor of sec. 351(a), to mean that if any amount of a taxpayer's liabilities were assumed and paid by the transferee corporation in what was otherwise a tax-free reorganization, then gain was to be recognized to the full extent of such assumption and payment.

petitioners rely on the case of N. F. Testor, 40 T.C. 273 (1963), affd. 327 F.2d 788 (C.A. 7, 1964). We agree with petitioners that in the *Testor* case the transferor was economically benefited by the corporate assumption of his liabilities since the liabilities assumed by the corporate transferee exceeded not only the adjusted basis of the assets transferred but likewise exceeded their book value. We cannot agree, however, that because those facts existed in *Testor,* we are now required to limit the application of section 357(c) only to those cases where such facts exist.

Petitioners further attempt to bolster their "gain" theory by pointing out that the examples cited by both the House and Senate Committee reports to illustrate the application of section 357(c) involved a situation where the transferor would have received a present financial windfall if no tax were imposed at the point of transfer. The example referred to by petitioners is as follows:

> "Thus, if an individual transfers, under section 351, property having a basis in his hands of $20,000, but subject to a mortgage of $50,000, to a corporation controlled by him, such individual would be subject to tax with respect to $30,000, the excess of the amount of liability over the adjusted basis of the property in the hands of the transferor. . . ." [7]

While the foregoing example involves a situation where the transferor would reap economic gain if a tax were not imposed at the point of transfer, we do not understand that Congress, in using that example, intended to limit the application of section 357(c) only to identical fact situations. We must assume that if Congress had so intended to limit this section, it would have employed the necessary language. Finding nothing in the language of section 357(c) or in the legislative history of the 1954 Code to indicate any congressional intent to so limit the application of this provision, we must reject petitioners' argument and hold that a computation under section 357(c) is required by the facts in this case.

Section 357(c), which has no legislative counterpart under the 1939 Code, was first enacted in 1954 and provides that the gain to be recognized to the transferor from a section 351 exchange is the amount by which the liabilities assumed exceed the adjusted basis of the property transferred. If, as respondent contends, the trade accounts receivable are to be given a zero basis, then the amount of the trade receivables, $77,361.66, is not includable within the "adjusted basis of the property transferred" as that phrase is used in section 357(c). Such an interpretation of the statute would render petitioners liable for a tax on the gain resulting from the exchange in the amount determined by respondent, $34,741.08. To counter the effect of such a result, petitioners present the novel argument that in making a section 357(c) computation, the accounts receivable must be given an adjusted basis at least equal to the amount of the accounts payable assumed by the corporate transferee, or $37,719.78. If we were to accept this argument, the adjusted basis of the property transferred to the corporation would be $48,971.51.[8] Since this amount exceeds the total liabilities assumed by

[7] S. Rept. No. 1622, to accompany H.R. 8300 (Pub. L. 591), 83d Cong., 2d Sess., p. 270 (1954); H. Rept. No. 1337, to accompany H.R. 8300 (Pub. L. 591), 83d Cong., 2d sess., p. A129 (1954). The pertinent Treasury regulation, sec. 1.357-2(a), Income Tax Regs., contains a similar example.

[8] The adjusted basis of the property transferred, excluding trade accounts receivable, is $11,251.73 (fn. 7, supra). If the trade accounts receivable are given a basis of $37,719.78, then the adjusted basis of all property transferred would be the total of these two figures, or $48,971.51.

the corporate transferee, i.e., $45,992.81, no tax would be imposed under a section 357(c) computation.

Petitioners attempt to support this argument by the following syllogism: Under section 1012, the basis of property is its cost; the cost of the trade accounts receivable transferred equals the amount of the trade accounts payable ($37,719.78); therefore, the basis of the receivables is equal to the amount of the payables, or $37,719.78. The weakness in this argument stems from the fact that petitioners have failed to show that the cost of the receivables equals the amount of the payables. Their entire argument on this point appears in their brief, at page 22, as follows:

> "An examination of the cost of the accounts receivable transferred to the corporation indicates that most of them were encumbered by liens which were in the amount of the accounts payable transferred. Under the California Civil Code the mechanic's liens filed against petitioners would require that any payment of the accounts receivable transferred would be encumbered and would be immediately payable to the suppliers or other lien claimants. The only benefit to the owner of the receivables would be the net profit after payment of the payables. If petitioners are to be taxed in any amount, it should only be the net profit."

While petitioners above state that most of the receivables were encumbered by liens which were in the amount of the payables transferred, the record nowhere supports such a statement. On the contrary, the parties have specifically stipulated that "All of such trade accounts payable were on open account and none of them specifically encumbered any of the transferred assets." Neither are we satisfied, as petitioners' unsupported statement above assumes, that under the California mechanic's lien law the accounts receivable transferred represent the sole source from which mechanic's liens incurred in petitioners' sole proprietorship business would be satisfied. We conclude that since the accounts receivable transferred did not have a basis equal to the amount of the accounts payable transferred, petitioners' theory must be rejected.

Accounts receivable in the hands of a cash basis taxpayer have a basis of zero.[9] Similarly, when an individual or partnership reporting income on the cash receipts and disbursements method transfers accounts receivable to a corporation, the receivables have a zero basis to the corporate transferee. Helvering v. Cement Investors, 316 U.S. 527 (1942); Ezo Products Co., 37 T.C. 385 (1961); P. A. Birren & Son v. Commissioner, 116 F.2d 718 (C.A. 7, 1940), affirming a Memorandum Opinion of this Court. This result is specifically required by section 362(a) which provides, in substance, that property acquired by a corporation in a section 351 exchange retains the same basis as it had in the hands of the transferor. Thus, the trade accounts receivable, both in the hands of petitioners' sole proprietorship and in the transferee corporation, had a basis of zero. The fact that the receivables had a book value of $77,361.66 at the time of the transfer is irrelevant to the disposition of this issue since the pertinent language of section 357(c) speaks only in terms of the "adjusted basis" of the property transferred. Inasmuch as this language is clear and unambiguous, we will not disturb its obvious meaning. We therefore hold that as a

[9]See P. A. Birren & Son v. Commissioner, 116 F.2d 718, 720 (C.A. 7, 1940).

result of the section 351 exchange, petitioners incurred a gain under section 357(c) of $34,741.08. Whether this gain is to be taxed as ordinary income or as capital gain depends upon the nature of the individual assets transferred.[10]

As we stated in Andrew W. Monaghan, 40 T.C. 680, 687 (1963):

"The sale of a going business operated as a proprietorship has long been considered as a sale of the separate business assets for purposes of ascertaining whether profit results in capital gain or ordinary income. Williams v. Mc-Gowan, 152 F.2d 570 (C.A. 2); Ernest A. Watson, 15 T.C. 800, affd. 197 F.2d 56, affd. 345 U.S. 544, rehearing denied 345 U.S. 1003; Rev. Rul. 55-79, 1955-1 C.B. 370, . . ."

In the instant case, petitioners transferred the following assets to their wholly owned corporation: Cash, trade accounts receivable, receivables, prepaid rent, and equipment (less accumulated depreciation). Accounts receivable are specifically excluded from the definition of a capital asset by section 1221(4). The equipment, being a depreciable asset in the hands of the transferee corporation, is likewise denied capital asset treatment under section 1239. Since cash is generally disposed of at face value, and petitioners make no contention to the contrary, its transfer in the instant case resulted in neither gain nor loss. Williams v. McGowan, 152 F.2d 570, 572 (C.A. 2, 1945). Similarly, prepaid rent is generally transferred at face value, resulting in no gain or loss. We therefore hold that the gain received by petitioners pursuant to section 357(c) is taxable as ordinary income.

In applying section 357(c) to the facts herein, we are not unmindful that the result reached may conflct with the well established intent of Congress to foster tax-free business reorganizations. However, in the absence of a clearly expressed congressional intent, we decline to adopt a construction of section 357(c) which is supported neither by its language nor its legislative history.

Issue 2

As the result of the transfer of petitioners' sole proprietorship to their wholly owned corporation, they received, in addition to the entire capital stock of the corporation, an unsecured promissory note. Whether this note is to be treated as debt or equity constitutes the basis of this issue. The problem arises from the different tax treatment accorded the promissory note depending upon its proper characterization. If, at the time of its issuance, the note constituted "equity" in the corporation, as petitioners contend, it can be characterized as a "security" of the corporation and thereby avoid tax consequences pursuant to the nonrecognition provisions of subsection (a) of section 351. That subsection provides in effect that no tax consequences attach to a section 351 transaction if the consideration received by the transferor from the corporation consists solely of "stock or securities of such corporation." On the other hand, subsection (b) of section 351 provides that if the transferor receives, in addition to corporate stock or securities, "other property or money," gain to the transferor is to be recognized to the amount of the fair market value of such "other

---

[10]Sec. 357(c)(1) specifically requires such a determination by providing that "such excess [of liabilities assumed over property transferred] shall be considered as a gain from the sale or exchange of a capital asset or of property which is not a capital asset, as the case may be."

property." Thus, if the promissory note constituted corporate debt, as respondent contends, it would fall within the meaning of "other property" under section 351(b), causing petitioners to incur a tax on its fair market value.

The note in question was a short-term unsecured promissory note in the original amount of $16,280.58, payable on demand and bearing interest at the rate of 6 percent per annum. The face amount of the note was reduced to $12,755.50 to reflect uncollectible trade accounts receivable in the amount of $3,525.08.[11] The note was paid off by the corporation as follows:

Date	Balance of note
Jan. 3, 1961	$12,755.50
May 31, 1961	4,150.54
May 31, 1962	1,780.51
May 31, 1964	0

Whether the note in question is a "security" under section 351(a) or "other property" under section 351(b) depends upon the particular facts surrounding its issuance. In Camp Wolters Enterprises, Inc., 22 T.C. 737 (1954), affd. 230 F.2d 555 (C.A. 5, 1956), we were met with the same question under section 351's predecessor, sec. 112(b)(5), I.R.C. 1939. We there adopted, at page 751, the following guide for resolving this issue:

> "The test as to whether notes are securities is not a mechanical determination of the time period of the note. Though time is an important factor, the controlling consideration is an over-all evaluation of the nature of the debt, degree of participation and continuing interest in the business, the extent of proprietary interest compared with the similarity of the note to a cash payment, the purpose of the advances, etc. It is not necessary for the debt obligation to be the equivalent of stock since section 112(b)(5) specifically includes both 'stock' and 'securities.' "

The fact that the note in question was payable on demand argues strongly against its constituting a corporate "security." Pacific Public Service Co., 4 T.C. 742, 748 (1945), affd. 154 F.2d 713 (C.A. 9, 1946); Sisto Financial Corporation, 47 B.T.A 425, 429 (1942), affd. 139 F.2d 253 (C.A. 2, 1943). The balance due on the note was substantially reduced within 17 months of its issuance and completely paid off in less than 3½ years from its issuance. Such rapid payment is inconsistent with the proposition that the note was intended to represent a proprietary interest in the corporation. On the above facts and case authority, we hold that when the corporation issued the note in question, petitioners received "other property" within the meaning of section 351(b), causing them to incur gain in the amount of the note's book value, $12,755.50, taxable as ordinary income.

Decision will be entered for the respondent.*

---

[11]In transferring the trade accounts receivable of their sole proprietorship to the corporation, petitioners personally guaranteed payment of the receivables. When receivables in the amount of $3,525.08 became uncollectible, that amount was deducted from the face amount of the note.

*The taxpayer's appeal to the Ninth Circuit was dismissed by agreement of the parties as a result of a compromise settlement. — Ed.

COMMENT, SECTION 357(c) AND THE
CASH BASIS TAXPAYER
115 U. Pa. L. Rev. 1154 (1967)

In a typical incorporation, an individual might transfer the assets and liabilities of a going business to a corporation in exchange for its capital stock. Since the inception of the income tax, Congress has struggled with the problem of how such a transfer should be treated for tax purposes. Prior to the enactment of the Revenue Act of 1921,[1] if an individual transferred assets to a corporation and received stock in exchange, he was taxed to the extent that the fair market value of the stock exceeded his basis in the assets.[2] Recognizing that such a procedure would seriously impede necessary incorporations,[3] Congress provided in section 202 of the Revenue Act of 1921 that no gain or loss would be realized by the transferor when he conveyed assets to the corporation so long as he was in control of the corporation after the transfer.[4]

Section 202 was reenacted without major modification in section 112(b)(5) of the 1939 Internal Revenue Code.[5] Several important facets of this complex problem still required clarification, however. Under section 112(c)(1), if the transferor received from the corporation "property or money" other than stock or securities in the corporation, he would be taxed to the extent the fair market value of that "other property or money" exceeded his basis in the assets transferred to the corporation.[6] This provision left an important question unanswered: if the corporation assumed a

---

[1] Revenue Act of 1921, ch. 136, 42 Stat. 227.

[2] "When property is exchanged for other property, the property received in exchange shall for the purposes of determining gain or loss be treated as the equivalent of cash to the amount of its fair market value, if any; but when in connection with the reorganization, merger, or consolidation of a corporation a person receives in place of stock or securities owned by him new stock or securities of no greater aggregate par or face value, no gain or loss shall be deemed to occur from the exchange . . . ." Revenue Act of 1918, ch. 18, §202(b), 40 Stat. 1060.

[3] "Under existing law 'when property is exchanged for other property, the property received in exchange shall, for the purpose of determining gain or loss, be treated as the equivalent of cash to the amount of its fair market value, if any . . . .' Probably no part of the present income tax law has been productive of so much uncertainty or has more seriously interfered with necessary business readjustments." S. Rep. No. 275, 67th Cong., 1st Sess. 11 (1921).

[4] Section 202 provided in part:
"(c) For the purposes of this title, on an exchange of property, real, personal or mixed, for any other such property, no gain or loss shall be recognized unless the property received in exchange has a readily realizable market value; but even if the property received in exchange has a readily realizable market value, no gain or loss shall be recognized —
"(3) When (A) a person transfers any property, real, personal or mixed, to a corporation, and immediately after the transfer is in control of such corporation . . . ." Revenue Act of 1921, ch. 136, 42 Stat. 230.

[5] "No gain or loss shall be recognized if property is transferred to a corporation by one or more persons solely in exchange for stock or securities in such corporation, and immediately after the exchange such person or persons are in control of the corporation . . . ." Int. Rev. Code of 1939, ch. 1, §112(b)(5), 53 Stat. 37 (now Int. Rev. Code of 1954, §351(a)).

[6] "If an exchange would be within the provisions of subsection (b) . . . (5) . . . if it were not for the fact that the property received in exchange consists not only of property permitted by such paragraph . . . to be received without the recognition of gain, but also of other property or money, then the gain, if any to the recipient shall be recognized, but in an amount not in excess of the sum of such money and the fair market value of such other property." Int. Rev. Code of 1939, ch. 1, §112(c)(1), 53 Stat. 39 (now Int. Rev. Code of 1954, §351(b)).

debt of the transferor, did such an assumption constitute "other property or money" so that the transferor would be taxed to the extent of the assumption? The Supreme Court's opinion in United States v. Hendler[7] answered this question in the affirmative:

> The transaction . . . under which the Borden Company assumed and paid the debt and obligation of the Hendler Company is to be regarded in substance as though the $534,297.40 had been paid directly to the Hendler Company. . . . Its gain was as real and substantial as if the money had been paid it and then paid over by it to its creditors. The discharge of liability by the payment of the Hendler Company's indebtedness constituted income to the Hendler Company and is to be treated as such.[8]

In a typical incorporation of an existing business, the transferor does not liquidate his liabilities before conveying his assets to the corporation. Realizing, therefore, that the *Hendler* result could defeat the purpose of section 112(b)(5),[9] Congress added section 112(k) to the Code. The new section provided that the assumption of a liability by the corporation was not "other property or money" unless it appeared either that the transferor's purpose in having the corporation assume the debt was tax avoidance or that the transaction was not a bona fide business deal.[10] The courts interpreted section 112(k) as overruling the *Hendler* result,[11] and this section was subsequently reenacted without major change in sections 357(a) and (b) of the 1954 Code.[12] A third provision was added to section 357, however, which had no prede-

---

[7]303 U.S. 564 (1938). *Hendler* arose under section 112(c)(1) of the Revenue Act of 1928, ch. 852, 45 Stat. 817. Section 112(c)(1) was reenacted without major change in section 112(c)(1) of the Internal Revenue Code of 1939. See Walter F. Haass, 37 B.T.A. 948 (1938); Brons Hotel, Inc., 34 B.T.A. 376 (1936).

[8]303 U.S. at 566.

[9]"The recent Supreme Court case of United States v. Hendler . . . has been broadly interpreted to require that, if a taxpayer's liabilities are assumed by another party in what is otherwise a tax-free reorganization, gain is recognized to the extent of the assumption. In typical transactions changing the form or entity of a business it is not customary to liquidate the liabilities of the business and such liabilities are almost invariably assumed by the corporation which continues the business. Your committee therefore believes that such a broad interpretation as is indicated above will largely nullify the provisions of existing law which postpone the recognition of gain in such cases. . . ." H.R. Rep. No. 855, 76th Cong., 1st Sess. 19 (1939).

[10]"Where upon an exchange the taxpayer receives as part of the consideration property which would be permitted by subsection (b) . . . (5) . . . to be received without the recognition of gain if it were the sole consideration, and as part of the consideration another party to the exchange assumes a liability of the taxpayer or acquires from the taxpayer property subject to a liability, such assumption or acquisition shall not be considered as 'other property or money' received by the taxpayer within the meaning of subsection (c) . . . ; except that if, taking into consideration the nature of the liability and the circumstances in the light of which the arrangement for the assumption or acquisition was made, it appears that the principal purpose of the taxpayer with respect to the assumption or acquisition was a purpose to avoid Federal income tax on the exchange, or, if not such purpose, was not a bona fide business purpose, such assumption or acquisition (in the amount of the liability) shall, for the purposes of this section, be considered as money received by the taxpayer upon the exchange. . . ." Int. Rev. Code of 1939, §112(k), added by Revenue Act of 1939, ch. 247, §213(a), 53 Stat. 870.

[11]See, e.g., Helvering v. Taylor, 128 F.2d 885 (2d Cir. 1942).

[12]"(a) General Rule — Except as provided in subsections (b) and (c), if —

"(1) the taxpayer receives property which would be permitted to be received under section

cessor in the 1939 Code. Subsection (c) provides that if the sum of the liabilities assumed by the corporation plus the sum of the liabilities to which the transferred assets are subject, exceed the total adjusted basis of the assets transferred, then the transferor will be taxed on the difference.[13] The committee reports dealing with the new subsection fail to specify Congress' reason for adding to the earlier provisions.[14] Therefore, in order to understand what problem the new subsection was intended to cure, it is necessary to examine the difficulty which arose under section 112(k).

Mortgaged Property

The situation arising most frequently in cases involving the assumption of liabilities is the transfer of mortgaged property. In Crane v. Commissioner,[15] the taxpayer was devised a parcel of land and a building with an outstanding mortgage of $255,000.[16] Some years later she sold the building and land for $3,000 subject to the

---

351 . . . without the recognition of gain if it were the sole consideration, and (2) as part of the consideration, another party to the exchange assumes a liability of the taxpayer, or acquires from the taxpayer property subject to a liability, then such assumption or acquisition shall not be treated as money or other property . . . ." Int. Rev. Code of 1954, §357(a).

For cases interpreting this subsection and its predecessor, §112(k), see, e.g., Jewell v. United States, 330 F.2d 761 (9th Cir. 1964); Edwards Motor Transit Co., 23 CCH Tax Ct. Mem. 1968 (1964).

"(b) Tax Avoidance Purpose —

"(1) In General — If, taking into consideration the nature of the liability and the circumstances in the light of which the arrangement for the assumption or acquisition was made, it appears that the principal purpose of the taxpayer with respect to the assumption or acquisition described in subsection (a) —

"(A) was a purpose to avoid Federal income tax on the exchange, or

"(B) if not such purpose, was not a bona fide business purpose,

then such assumption or acquisition (in the total amount of the liability assumed or acquired pursuant to such exchange) shall, for purposes of section 351 . . . be considered by the taxpayer on the exchange. . . ." Int. Rev. Code of 1954, §357(b).

For cases interpreting this subsection and its predecessor, §112(k), see, e.g., Campbell v. Wheeler, 342 F.2d 837 (5th Cir. 1965); Bryan v. Commissioner, 281 F.2d 238 (4th Cir. 1960), cert. denied, 364 U.S. 931 (1961); W. H. B. Simpson, 43 T.C. 900 (1965); F. W. Drybrough, 42 T.C. 1029 (1964); Estate of John G. Stoll, 38 T.C. 223 (1962). See Hertz, Getting Property into and out of the Corporation, N.Y.U. 21st Inst. on Fed. Tax 347, 352-53 (1963); Levitan, How to Reduce the Amount of Equity Capital Invested in Controlled Corporations, 21 J. Taxation 214, 216 (1964).

[13]"(c) Liabilities in Excess of Basis —

"(1) In General — In the case of an exchange —

"(A) to which section 351 applies . . . if the sum of the amount of the liabilities assumed, plus the amount of the liabilities to which the property is subject, exceeds the total of the adjusted basis of the property transferred pursuant to such exchange, then such excess shall be considered as a gain from the sale or exchange of a capital asset or of property which is not a capital asset, as the case may be.

"(2) Exceptions — Paragraph (1) shall not apply to any exchange to which —

"(A) subsection (b)(1) of this section applies . . . ." Int. Rev. Code of 1954, §357(c).

For cases interpreting this subsection, see, e.g., Testor v. Commissioner, 327 F.2d 788 (7th Cir. 1964); Arthur L. Kniffen, 39 T.C. 533 (1962); Peter W. DeFelice, 25 CCH Tax Ct. Mem. 835 (1966). See notes 49, 50 infra and accompanying text.

[14]H.R. Rep. No. 1337, 83d Cong., 2d Sess. A129 (1954); S. Rep. No. 1622, 83d Cong., 2d Sess. 270 (1954).

[15]331 U.S. 1 (1947).

[16]The entire property was subject to the mortgage of $255,000. However, for our purposes, only the value of the building is essential, since land is not a depreciable asset. Therefore, the

mortgage. The issue before the Supreme Court was whether the amount of the original mortgage should be included in the taxpayer's basis in the property and whether the outstanding mortgage assumed by the purchaser should be included in the amount the taxpayer realized on the sale. The taxpayer maintained that since she was not personally liable on the mortgage, her gain on the sale was limited to the cash she actually received. The Court, however, held that the amount of the original mortgage was included in her basis in the property[17] and that the outstanding mortgage assumed by the purchaser was included in the amount she realized on the sale. Furthermore, the Court held that her basis in the property had to be reduced by the sum of the depreciation deductions she had taken on the building while she owned the property.[18] Upon subtracting this adjusted basis from the amount realized, the Court found her taxable gain to be $24,000.[19]

Three years later, when faced with a fact situation similar to that presented in *Crane*,[20] the First Circuit, in Parker v. Delaney,[21] followed the Supreme Court's

---

discussion below pertains only to the value of the building and the figures are adjusted to exclude the value of the land. The figures below have been rounded off.

[17]Since the taxpayer received the property from a decedent, the basis of the property in her hands was its fair market value at the date of her husband's death. Int. Rev. Code of 1954, §1014(a). If the taxpayer had purchased the property, her basis in the property would have been cost. Int. Rev. Code of 1954, §1012. See Parker v. Delaney, 186 F.2d 455, 458 (1st Cir. 1950), cert. denied, 341 U.S. 926 (1951).

[18]Although the Court emphasized that the mortgage was not a personal obligation of the taxpayer, subsequent decisions have not relied on this distinction, and the rule now seems well established that depreciation deductions will reduce the taxpayer's original basis regardless of whether or not he is personally liable on the mortgage.

[19]Rounding off the figures in *Crane* and disregarding the value of the land, the transaction was as follows:

Sale Price — Amount of mortgage	$201,000	
Boot for Building	2,000	
Total amount realized on sale		$203,000
Original basis in building	$207,000	
Minus: Depreciation deductions	28,000	
Minus: Adjusted basis		$179,000
Taxable gain		$ 24,000

Boot is defined as cash or non-qualifying property received by the taxpayer in addition to the qualifying property which he received without incurring a taxable gain in the section 351 exchange. Bittker, Federal Income, Estate and Gift Taxation 470 (3d ed. 1965).

The total boot received in the sale of the property was $3000. Since we are concerned solely with the sale of the building, we have allotted $2000 of the boot to the building and the remaining $1000 to the land.

For a critique of the *Crane* case, see Adams, Exploring the Outer Boundaries of the *Crane* Doctrine: An Imaginary Supreme Court Opinion, 21 Tax L. Rev. 159 (1966).

[20]The taxpayer made arrangements with two banks to take over and manage four apartment houses held by the banks after foreclosures. In each case a straw party gave the bank a note secured by a first mortgage on the property and then gave the taxpayer a second mortgage on each of the properties. The first mortgage liens totaled $273,000. During the period in which the taxpayer managed the properties, he paid $14,000 on the mortgages and deducted $45,000 for depreciation. In 1945 the mortgages were in default and the banks took the properties back. The court held that the taxpayer realized a taxable gain of $31,000 on the foreclosure. The taxpayer's original basis in the properties, $273,000, was reduced by the amount of the depreciation deductions,

approach in computing the taxpayer's gain on the transfer. In a concurring opinion,[22] Judge Magruder suggested an alternative approach which has come to be known as the negative basis doctrine. Judge Magruder argued that since the taxpayer incurred no out-of-pocket expenses in acquiring the mortgaged property, his original basis ought to be zero. A negative basis resulted when the depreciation deductions were subtracted from the zero basis in computing the adjusted basis.[23] Under the terms of the sale the taxpayer was relieved of the property and the obligation on the mortgage; therefore, Judge Magruder maintained, for tax purposes the amount realized on the sale was also zero. The amount realized on the sale, zero, minus the negative adjusted basis resulted in a taxable gain.[24] Although Judge Magruder arrived at the same figure as the majority, he sanctioned a doctrine which could potentially produce far different results in subsequent mortgaged property cases.[25]

A potential problem created by the *Crane* and *Parker* decisions came to the forefront in Woodsam Associates, Inc. v. Commissioner.[26] In that case the taxpayer was a corporation which had received property from a stockholder in an earlier tax-free exchange. The controversy in the case concerned the taxpayer's basis in the property, which, in turn, depended on the basis of the property in the hands of the stockholder.[27]

The stockholder had acquired the property for $300,000. After her basis in the property had been reduced to $270,000 because of depreciation deductions, she mortgaged the property for $400,000.[28] At this point she transferred the property to the corporation. The Commissioner maintained that the taxpayer's basis in the property was its original cost to the stockholder ($300,000) less the depreciation deductions.

$45,000, and increased by the sum of the payments on the mortgage, $14,000, to arrive at an adjusted basis of $242,000. On the foreclosure, the taxpayer realized $273,000, the amount of the mortgage of which he was relieved. The amount realized, $273,000, minus the adjusted basis, $242,000, resulted in the taxable gain of $31,000.

[21] 186 F.2d 455 (1950), cert. denied, 341 U.S. 926 (1951).

[22] 186 F.2d at 459.

[23] Since Judge Magruder had assigned a zero basis to the property, it may seem unusual that he had taken into account depreciation deductions in computing the taxpayer's basis at the time of sale, for technically when one has no basis, he can take no depreciation deductions. Int. Rev. Code of 1954, §167. However, the approach used by Judge Magruder is proper since in computing basis on sale, the basis of the property is reduced by the allowed or allowable depreciation deductions. Int. Rev. Code of 1954, §1016(a)(2). In Parker v. Delaney, the Commissioner had allowed $28,000 of depreciation expenses over a period of years.

[24] Amount realized on foreclosure		$ 0
Original basis in building	$ 0	
Minus: Depreciation deductions	45,000	
Plus: Mortgage payments	14,000	
Minus: Total adjusted basis		$−31,000
Taxable gain		$ 31,000

[25] See Easson v. Commissioner, 294 F.2d 653 (9th Cir. 1961).

[26] 198 F.2d 357 (2d Cir. 1952).

[27] When the corporation received the property from the stockholder it assumed her basis in the property. Int. Rev. Code of 1939, ch. 1, §113(a)(7), 53 Stat. 41 (now Int. Rev. Code of 1954, §362(b)).

[28] *Woodsam Associates* is the archetype of the negative basis problem which will be discussed at length below. The negative basis problem arises when property appreciates in value and is then mortgaged for more than the taxpayer's original basis.

The taxpayer, on the other hand, argued that the amount by which the mortgage exceeded the stockholder's adjusted basis in the property ($130,000) should have been taxable gain to her at the time of the transfer, and that the resulting stepped-up basis of $400,000 carried over to the corporation.

In deciding in favor of the Commissioner, the Second Circuit held that the stockholder never "sold or otherwise dispos[ed] of" the property within the meaning of section 1001(a),[29] and therefore a taxable event did not occur at the time of the transfer and would only occur when the property was actually sold. The mortgage did not change her basis in the property.[30]

Woodsam Associates is an excellent example of the fuzzy thinking which exists concerning the taxability of borrowed money. The crucial issue is not how the taxpayer disposes of the property but whether she realizes a gain by disposing of the property and the corresponding mortgage. Under the court's holding, the stockholder in *Woodsam Associates* realized a tax-free profit of $130,000 by mortgaging the property for more than her cost and then disposing of it along with the mortgage.[31] It is important to realize that when the taxpayer borrows money and is later relieved of the obligation to repay the loan, he has the unrestricted possession of cash which he did not have before. Therefore, at the point when the taxpayer is relieved of the obligation to repay, he realizes a gain on which he should be taxed.

In Jack L. Easson,[32] the Tax Court, when faced with an indistinguishable factual situation,[33] recognized the problem posed by the decision in *Woodsam Associates:*

> It is clear that there will not be a mere postponement of taxation, but possibly a complete tax exemption, if gain on the exchange in question is not presently recognized to the extent that the mortgage to which the transferred property was subject exceeded the petitioner's adjusted basis.[34]

Although *Easson* was decided in 1960, the events involved occurred before 1954 so that section 357(c) was not applicable. Since the court specifically found no evidence of tax avoidance or a sham exchange, the clear language of section 112(k) (now section 357(a)) would seem to indicate that there was no taxable gain. The Tax Court, however, was perplexed by the negative basis problem. If the taxpayer's

---

[29]"The gain from the sale or other disposition of property shall be the excess of the amount realized therefrom over the adjusted basis provided in section 1011 for determining gain . . . ." Int. Rev. Code of 1954, §1001(a).

[30]When an individual borrows money, he does not realize a taxable gain. 198 F.2d at 359; 1 Mertens, Federal Income Taxation §5.12, at 32, 34 (rev. ed. 1962); Spears, Mortgages in Excess of Basis, U. So. Cal. 1959 Tax Inst. 883, 885.

[31]Some writers maintain that the *Woodsam* result will lead to tax postponement, not tax avoidance. Cooper, Negative Basis, 75 Harv. L. Rev. 1352, 1355 (1962); Spears, supra note 30, at 886. However, if the stockholder in *Woodsam* never sells the stock she received in exchange for the property, she will never pay tax on the $130,000. See note 44 infra.

[32]33 T.C. 963 (1960).

[33]In 1929 the taxpayer built an apartment house. In 1952 he mortgaged the property for $250,000. Later that year he incorporated his business and transferred the property and the mortgage to the corporation. On the day of transfer his basis in the property was $87,000 and the outstanding mortgage was $247,000. The taxpayer claimed he realized no gain on the transfer.

[34]33 T.C. at 969.

original basis in the property were $87,000 and the property were mortgaged for $247,000, the taxpayer's basis in the stock received in exchange for the property would be — $159,000.[35] Citing the ancient tax maxim that property cannot have a negative basis,[36] the court concluded that the taxpayer must have realized a taxable gain of $159,000 on the exchange so that his basis in the stock upon transfer would be zero. The court looked to 357(c) as proof that the Code authorized its position. Subsection (c) was not in existence when the events of this case took place, but the court avoided that problem by saying that subsection (c) merely clarified existing law.

The Ninth Circuit reversed,[37] holding that the language of sections 112(b)(5) and 112(k) clearly indicated that there was no taxable gain on the exchange. As for the negative basis problem, the court looked to Judge Magruder's concerning opinion in *Parker* as evidence that a negative basis was a possibility. The court concluded, therefore, that the taxpayer did not realize a taxable gain on the exchange under 112(k) and that the stock he received had a basis of — $159,000. Furthermore, the legislative history of 357(c) emphasized that the subsection had no predecessor in the 1939 Code, so that the principles of that subsection were inapplicable to the facts of this case. To date the Ninth Circuit is the only court which has allowed a negative basis.[38]

The Tax Court in *Easson* was correct in realizing that 357(c) was adopted to resolve the negative basis problem which first arose in *Woodsam Associates* and later in *Easson*.[39] Admittedly, nowhere in the legislative history of subsection (c) is this purpose clearly enunciated. Nevertheless, the examples cited in the Treasury Regulations to illustrate the application of sections 357(c) and 358 indicate that negative basis was the crux of the problem that subsection (c) was intended to cure.[40] Section 358 states, in effect, that the basis of any stock or securities received in a 351 exchange is the same as that of the property transferred.[41] In example two in the regulations,

[35]Not only would the taxpayer's basis in the stock received in exchange for the property be negative, but the corporation's basis in the property would also be minus $159,000. See note 27 supra.

[36]33 T.C. at 970 & n.8. See Cooper, supra note 31, at 1353 & authorities cited n.6.

[37]Easson v. Commissioner, 294 F.2d 653 (1961).

[38]In a case arising in the Third Circuit, the Commissioner was successful in convincing the court that the taxpayer should be taxed on the difference between his adjusted basis in the property and the amount of the mortgage assumed by the corporation upon transfer. Simon v. Commissioner, 285 F.2d 422 (3d Cir. 1960). The crucial fact in that case was that the taxpayer mortgaged the property only three months before transferring it to the corporation, and the court held that, in effect, there was a sale of the property to the corporation with the corporation obtaining the necessary funds for the purchase by mortgaging the property. Id. at 425.

[39]See Advisory Group on Subchapter C of Internal Revenue Code of 1954, Revised Report to the House Subcommittee on Internal Revenue Taxation of Corporation Distributions and Adjustments, 86 Cong., 1st Sess., ser. 18, pt. 33, at 548-49 (1959); Reply Brief for Respondent, p. 5, Peter Raich, 46 T.C. 604 (1966); Cooper, supra note 31, at 1358-60; Neuhoff, Mortgaging Out and Related Problems, 1961 Wash. U.L.Q. 132, 143; Schlesinger, Negative Basis, Recognized in *Easson* as Possible, Will Arise Only Rarely, 16 J. Taxation 212, 213-14 (1962).

[40]Treas. Regs. §1.357-2 (1955), as amended, T.D. 6528, 1961-1 Cum. Bull. 79, 81-82 and §1.358-3(b) (1955).

[41]"In the case of an exchange to which section 351 . . . applies —

"(1) The basis of the property permitted to be received under such section without the recognition of gain or loss shall be the same as that of the property exchanged —

"(A) decreased by —

an individual owned property with an adjusted basis of $25,000 and a mortgage of $50,000. He transferred the property to a corporation in exchange for all of its stock. The individual realized a taxable gain of $25,000 on the exchange under 357(c), thus increasing his basis in the stock received to zero.[42] This is exactly the result the Tax Court reached in *Easson*; in effect, then, subsection (c) rejects the theory of both *Woodsam Associates* and the Court of Appeals in *Easson*.[43]

As indicated in the discussion of *Woodsam Associates*, subsection (c) is necessary to prevent tax avoidance, not merely tax postponement. In *Woodsam Associates*, the stockholder cleared a tax-free profit of $130,000 on the exchange. Whenever an individual is able to mortgage property for more than its basis and then dispose of the property along with the mortgage, he must be taxed on the difference between his basis and the amount of the mortgage at the time of the exchange. Otherwise, he may escape taxation altogether.[44] What is essential to remember is that it is the transferor, not the corporation, who has received the benefit of the mortgage; therefore, it is the transferor and not the corporation who should be taxed on the difference between the transferor's original basis and the amount of the mortgage assumed.

Since 357(c) was adopted in a milieu composed largely of mortgaged property cases, the thinking regarding such cases may have a critical bearing on how the subsection will be applied in other areas. Unfortunately, some of the conclusions resulting from this discussion may mislead courts attempting to apply subsection (c) to non-mortgage cases. First, the mortgaged property doctrine of *Crane* applies both to cash and accrual basis taxpayers. With mortgaged property there is no need to distinguish between cash and accrual basis taxpayers since they will both treat the mortgage identically for tax purposes.[45] However, other types of liabilities computed under

---

"(i) the fair market value of any other property (except money) received by the taxpayer . . .

"(B) increased by —

"(ii) the amount of gain to the taxpayer which was recognized on such exchange . . . ." Int. Rev. Code of 1954, §358(a).

[42]Int. Rev. Code of 1954, §358(a)(1)(B)(ii).

[43]This was the position argued by the taxpayer in *Woodsam*. The taxpayer maintained that the stockholder should have realized the tax on the difference between her original basis and the amount of the mortgage assumed. Had this been the case, the corporation would have assumed her stepped-up basis of $400,000 in the property under Int. Rev. Code of 1939, ch. 1, §113(a)(7), 53 Stat. 41 (now Int. Rev. Code of 1954, §362(b)). See Commissioner v. Corpus Christi Terminal Co., 126 F.2d 898 (5th Cir. 1942).

The attorney for the taxpayer has written an article on mortgaging property for more than cost. Lurie, Mortgagor's Gain on Mortgaging Property for More Than Cost Without Personal Liability, 6 Tax L. Rev. 319 (1951).

[44]Assuming that the taxpayer in *Woodsam Associates* received stock in exchange for the property, she will never pay tax on the $130,000 profit on the exchange if the value of the property depreciates below the amount of the outstanding mortgage and is subsequently forfeited. The taxpayer in this case has the unrestricted use of money with no obligation to repay. She, in effect, has received a windfall unless she is taxed on the amount of the debt at the time when she is relieved of the obligation to repay the loan. See text accompanying note 31 supra. In addition, even if the value of the property is always sufficient to satisfy the encumbrance, the taxpayer will pay no tax if she retains the stock until her death, for the basis in the stock to her devisee would be its fair market value. Int. Rev. Code of 1954, §1014(a). Cooper, supra note 31, fails to consider fully these possibilities.

[45]The acquisition of a building is a capital expenditure for which no deduction is allowed for either cash or accrual basis taxpayers. Int. Rev. Code of 1954, §263(a)(1) and Treas. Reg. §1.263(a)-2(a) (1958).

357(c) might require different treatment by the two types of taxpayers. Second, the discussion of negative basis causes one to wonder whether practitioners have arrived at a clear understanding of the tax consequences which should follow when money is borrowed and the debt thereby incurred is transferred to another taxpayer. For these reasons, it is not surprising that there has been little thought about the proper application of subsection (c) to cash basis taxpayers in non-mortgage cases.

Peter Raich

A recent opinion in the Tax Court should generate some thought concerning the proper application of subsection (c) to cash basis taxpayers.[46] In *Raich*, a cash basis taxpayer incorporated his sole proprietorship. On the day of incorporation his balance sheet showed assets of $88,613.39, including $77,361.66 of trade accounts receivable. His liabilities totaled $45,992.66, $37,719.78 of which were trade accounts payable. The taxpayer personally guaranteed payment of the accounts receivable. In exchange for these assets, the taxpayer received stock valued at $25,000 on the corporation's books and a promissory note for $16,280.58. Thus the corporation's balance sheet on the day of incorporation showed that the value of the assets transferred exceeded total liabilities and capital stock by $1,340.[47] Nevertheless, the Tax Court held that the transferor realized a gain of $34,741.08, reasoning as follows: since the taxpayer was on the cash basis, the trade accounts receivable had an adjusted basis of zero.[48] Therefore, the assets transferred were assigned a value which was $77,361.66 less than the taxpayer's evaluation, or $11,251.73. The liabilities assumed, $45,992.81, exceeded the adjusted basis of the assets by $34,741.08, thus bringing subsection (c) into play.

A handful of cases had arisen before in which accounts receivable and payable had been involved.[49] Admittedly, in each of the cases the issue did not involve the adjusted basis of the receivables.[50] Nevertheless, the Commissioner seemed content to assume that if the market value of the assets transferred was greater than the market value of the liabilities assumed, then the exchange was tax-free under 357(a). Apparently the Commissioner has reversed his position in *Raich* and will now go beyond

---

[46]Peter Raich, 46 T.C. 604 (1966).

[47]

Assets transferred		$88,613.39
Liabilities transferred	$45,992.81	
Promissory note	16,280.85	
Capital stock	25,000.00	
Total liabilities		$87,273.39
Difference		$ 1,340.00

[48]For some unexplained reason the court differentiated between the "receivables" and the "trade accounts receivable" on the taxpayer's balance sheet. The Commissioner permitted the taxpayer to include the market value of the "receivables," $1,833.97, in his adjusted basis for the assets transferred.

[49]Testor v. Commissioner, 327 F.2d 788 (7th Cir. 1964); Arthur L. Kniffen, 39 T.C. 553 (1962); Peter W. DeFelice, 25 CCH Tax Ct. Mem. 835 (1966).

[50]In *Testor*, the issue was whether subsection (c) applies if the assets are not specifically encumbered by the assets transferred. In *Kniffen*, the issue was whether the assumption of a debt owed to the corporation by the transferor was a taxable event in itself. In *DeFelice*, the court taxed the transferor on the difference between the market value of the liabilities assumed and the market value of the assets transferred.

a comparison of market values and consider whether the transferor is on the cash or accrual basis. Since the Commissioner's stand in *Raich* appears inconsistent with his earlier position, the time has come to consider the question more fully.

Before examining the technical tax aspects involved in this question, one might consider whether Raich is the type of individual who should be taxed. It is difficult to understand how he realized a "gain" by incorporating for he did not "cash out" by holding assets and transferring the corresponding obligations to another party. Since Raich personally guaranteed the accounts receivable if they proved uncollectible, he certainly transferred assets sufficient to pay the liabilities assumed by the corporation. Furthermore, this is not a case where the taxpayer incurred a debt, took a deduction for the debt, and then transferred the debt to a corporation, for, since Raich was on the cash basis, by definition he could not deduct the accounts payable until he paid them.[51] The case is also far different from *Woodsam Associates* where the stockholder enjoyed a clear cash profit of $130,000 on the exchange.[52] The court itself admits that its decision might not produce the best policy result:

> In applying section 357(c) to the facts herein, we are not unmindful that the result reached may conflict with the well established intent of Congress to foster tax-free business reorganizations. However, in the absence of a clearly expressed congressional intent, we decline to adopt a construction of section 357(c) which is supported neither by its language nor its legislative history.[53]

As indicated above, the legislative history of subsection (c) is not very helpful in interpreting the purpose behind the section.[54] Therefore, we must inquire whether the section itself is so clear that the decision in *Raich* was dictated by the language of the statute despite the poor policy result. Is the section as clear as the court implied or is this a case where the court has not considered carefully the tax consequences which should follow when a cash basis taxpayer transfers accounts receivable and payable?

The court begins by stating that since the taxpayer was on the cash basis, the accounts receivable had a basis of zero. It is important to realize that basis is a tax concept. Therefore, although the accounts receivable might have a market value of $77,361.66, for tax purposes they do have a basis of zero in the hands of a cash basis taxpayer since he has received no money for them and, more importantly, has not reported them as income.[55] The taxpayer in *Raich*, however, chose to base a major part of his attack on this issue. First, he attempted to distinguish the cases the Commissioner cited for the zero basis proposition in an effort to prove that the receivables should be valued at market cost.[56] In the alternative he maintained that even if the

---

[51]Treas. Reg. §1.446-1(c)(1)(i) (1961). An accrual basis taxpayer, on the other hand, may deduct the accounts payable in the year in which they accrue. Treas. Reg. §1.446-1(c)(1)(ii).

[52]See note 44 supra.

[53]46 T.C. at 611.

[54]See note 14 supra and accompanying text.

[55]P. A. Birren & Son v. Commissioner, 116 F.2d 718, 720 (7th Cir. 1940); Ezo Products Co., 37 T.C. 385, 393 (1961).

[56]Brief for Petitioner, pp. 8-25, Peter Raich, 46 T.C. 604 (1966). The Commissioner cited P. A. Birren & Son v. Commissioner and Ezo Products Co., supra note 55.

receivables were not valued at market, they should still offset the payables.[57] To support this contention the taxpayer tried to prove that the accounts receivable were encumbered by liens so that as soon as they were collected, the proceeds would be used to liquidate the payables. This was the stronger of his two arguments, and the court never rejected it in theory but merely held that the taxpayer had failed to prove that the receivables were actually so encumbered.[58]

To simplify the issues in *Raich,* imagine the following hypothetical case. An individual on the cash basis owns a proprietorship with $100,000 in accounts receivable as the sole asset and $50,000 in accounts payable as the only liability. If the individual decides to incorporate his proprietorship, he could conceivably do one of three things with his receivables and payables. First, he could collect the receivables, liquidate the payables, pay all income taxes and transfer the balance in cash to the corporation. As Congress noted when enacting section 112(k) of the 1939 Code to overrule the *Hendler* result, requiring such a practice would make incorporations cumbersome and difficult.[59] Therefore, the individual would probably transfer all or part of his assets and liabilities to the newly-formed corporation. In our hypothetical he might transfer either all the receivables or both the receivables and the payables.[60] In enacting section 112(k) to counteract *Hendler,* Congress recognized that if the purpose of the Internal Revenue Code is to encourage legitimate incorporations, the tax consequences of transferring all the assets and liabilities of a going business to a corporation should be no more onerous than the consequences of liquidating all the liabilities before transferring the remaining assets.[61]

In our hypothetical, if the taxpayer collects the receivables he will have $100,000 in taxable income. If he then proceeds to pay the payables, he can deduct $50,000 from his income for a net taxable gain of $50,000. Assuming that his tax rate is 50 per cent, he will have $25,000 in cash remaining after paying his tax for the year. If instead of liquidating the payables with the proceeds from the receivables, he transfers both to a corporation; under the Tax Court's reasoning in *Raich,* he will realize a taxable gain of $50,000 on the exchange since the receivables have a basis of zero and the amount of the payables is $50,000. When the taxpayer transfers the receivables and payables to a corporation, he is disadvantaged in two respects. First, after the transfer he has no money left to pay the tax which we will again assume is 50 per

---

[57]Id. at 22-24.

[58]46 T.C. at 610. The theory that if the assets are specifically encumbered by liabilities, then the transfer will be tax-free provided the liabilities are not greater in amount than the basis of the assets, is probably another holdover from the mortgaged property area. In reality, however, should it make any difference whether the assets are specifically encumbered by the liabilities transferred in the exchange? Even though the payables do not specifically encumber the receivables, the payables still are a cost of producing the receivables and therefore should be set off against them as if they specifically encumbered the receivables. This is especially true in this case since the taxpayer guaranteed payment of the receivables if they proved uncollectible. If the Tax Court in *Raich* had merely set off the payables against the receivables, it could have avoided the difficult task of deciding whether the payables were actually "liabilities" within the meaning of the statute.

[59]See note 9 supra.

[60]A fourth possibility would be to transfer only the payables to the corporation. However, since such a transfer would probably be construed as tax avoidance, the Commissioner would most likely tax the entire transaction under Section 357(b). See note 12 supra.

[61]See note 9 supra.

cent, or $25,000. Second, after he pays the tax he will obviously have no money left, whereas if he had liquidated the liabilities after collecting the receivables, he would have had $25,000 left after paying his income tax. Under the Tax Court's analysis, then, the taxpayer loses $50,000 if he transfers the assets and liabilities of his proprietorship to the corporation.

This hypothetical should cause one to wonder whether subsection (c) is as clear as the court implied. The court is correct in holding that the receivables have a basis of zero, but, as the hypothetical should indicate, the court stumbles when it considers the other side of the balance sheet. The court held that the payables in the hands of the cash basis taxpayer should be valued at their face amount of $37,719.78. It seems incongruous that the receivables had a basis of zero while the payables were valued at market. Either both might be valued at market[62] or both might be valued at zero, but to combine the two results makes neither tax nor accounting good sense.

If the court is correct in holding that the receivables have a basis of zero, then the payables must also be accounted for at zero for tax purposes.[63] Perhaps the court's thinking became snarled over the word "liabilities" in subsection (c). "Liability" has both an accounting and a tax definition. Certainly, in *Raich* the taxpayer would include an accounts payable liability of $37,719.78 on his business balance sheet. The business balance sheet, however, is not necessarily synonymous with the tax balance sheet. For tax purposes, a cash basis taxpayer has no "liabilities" until he has actually paid them and been allowed a deduction for them.[64] Thus, although it may seem artificial to say that in *Raich* the taxpayer's payables are not a liability to him, nevertheless, for tax purposes they are not until he actually pays them and receives a deduction. The situation is analogous to the receivables. The receivables do not appear on the tax balance sheet until the money is actually received and reported as income. Likewise, the payables do not appear on the tax balance sheet until they are paid and deducted.

Consider once again the hypothetical, but this time assume that the payables are valued at zero. When the taxpayer transfers the payables and receivables to the corporation, he recognizes no taxable gain. It is true that by transferring the receiv-

---

[62]It is maintained below that the payables and receivables of a cash basis taxpayer should not be valued at market but should be valued at zero. In one sense, however, it is possible to value the receivables at market. If one considers the payables as a cost of producing the receivables, then it is proper to value the receivables at market to the extent of the payables. See note 58 supra.

[63]Neither the Internal Revenue Code nor the Treasury Regulations are as precise on this point as they should be. Nevertheless, both the Code and the Regulation lend support to this conclusion. Section 1012 of the Code states that "the basis of property shall be the cost of such property . . . ." The Regulations are slightly more specific: "In general, the basis of property is the cost thereof. The cost is the amount paid for such property in cash or other property." Treas. Reg. §1.1012-1(a) (1966). The Regulations also state: "Generally, under the cash receipts and disbursements method in the computation of taxable income . . . . expenditures are to be deducted for the taxable year in which actually made." Treas. Reg. §1.446-1(c)(1)(i) (1961). Since a cash basis taxpayer has paid nothing in cash for his accounts payable and cannot deduct them until he does so, they should be valued at zero until such time as he actually does pay them.

[64]If the taxpayer in *Raich* had not incorporated and had claimed a deduction for the payables without actually paying them, the Commissioner would have disallowed the deduction because the taxpayer was on the cash basis. Treas. Reg. §1.1012-1(a) (1966); 2 Mertens, Federal Income Taxation §12.53, at 147 & n.29 (rev. ed. 1961).

ables and the payables to the corporation he has temporarily avoided paying $25,000 in federal income tax. At the same time, however, after paying the tax he does not have the $25,000 in cash remaining that he would have incurred had he kept the receivables and liquidated the payables.

This hypothetical serves to point up another inequity in the court's decision. If the payables are valued at market, no one will ever get a deduction when they are liquidated. Because the taxpayer is on the cash basis, he cannot deduct the payables since he did not pay them himself. The corporation, however, also cannot claim a deduction since when it pays the payables, it will merely be paying off an expense already recognized by another taxpayer.[65]

Consider once more the hypothetical and follow it one more step to its natural conclusion. Under section 362(b), the corporation assumes the transferor's basis in the property transferred.[66] Under the interpretation advanced above, the basis would be zero since both the receivables and the payables are valued at zero when they are transferred. The corporation will get the benefit of the $50,000 deduction for the payables, but will also have to pay tax on the $100,000 of receivables.[67]

Upon transferring the assets and liabilities to the corporation, the taxpayer received stock in the corporation. The basis of the stock in the transferor's hands is the adjusted basis of the assets transferred, or, in the hypothetical, zero.[68] Presumably, on the day of transfer the transferor could sell the stock for $50,000, the net worth of the corporation, and incur a taxable gain of $50,000. The taxpayer's taxable gain on the entire transaction is the same as if he kept the payables and used the receipts from the receivables to liquidate them, but by transferring the assets and liabilities to the corporation, he has postponed the time when he would realize that taxable gain. A transfer of accounts receivable and payable by a cash basis taxpayer to a corporation is thus a complete wash, as it should be, and the taxable gain, if any, is postponed until the taxpayer disposes of the stock he receives in exchange for the assets.

Applying the Tax Court's holding in *Raich* to this hypothetical, one can see that the taxpayer in *Raich* will eventually pay a double tax if he disposes of the stock he received in exchange for the assets of his business. The Tax Court would hold in this hypothetical that the taxpayer realized a taxable gain of $50,000 upon transferring the assets and liabilities of his business to a corporation, since the receivables have a basis of zero and the payables are valued at $50,000. Since the assets he transferred are valued at zero, the stock he receives in exchange for the assets is also valued at zero under section 358(a). The taxpayer, however, is allowed to increase his basis in the stock by the amount of the taxable gain he realized on the transfer, or $50,000 in the

---

[65]See Paul & Kalish, Transition from a Partnership to a Corporation, N.Y.U. 18th Inst. on Fed. Tax 639, 656-57 (1960); Tritt & Spencer, Current Tax Problems in Incorporation of a Going Business, U. So. Cal. 1958 Tax Inst. 71, 98-99.

[66]"If property was acquired by a corporation in connection with a reorganization to which this part applies, then the basis shall be the same as it would be in the hands of the transferor, increased in the amount of gain recognized to the transferor on such transfer. . . ." Int. Rev. Code of 1954, §362(b).

[67]See, e.g., P. A. Birren & Son, Inc. v. Commissioner, 116 F.2d 718 (7th Cir. 1940); Portland Oil Co. v. Commissioner, 109 F.2d 479 (1st Cir.), cert. denied, 310 U.S. 650 (1940).

[68]See note 41 supra.

hypothetical. Under section 358(d),[69] however, he is required to reduce his basis in the stock by the amount of the liabilities assumed by the corporation, or $50,000. This provision, in effect, offsets the credit allowed for the tax paid so that the taxpayer's basis in the stock is again reduced to zero. Consequently, when the taxpayer sells the stock he will realize another taxable gain of $50,000, or a total taxable gain of $100,000. The inequity in the Tax Court's holding is that the taxpayer is taxed twice when his debts are assumed by another party. First, he must pay a tax on the amount of the liabilities assumed when the debt is transferred. Second, he loses the credit for this tax since he must reduce his basis in the stock by the amount of the debt assumed.

At this juncture the question arises whether or not 357(c) would ever apply to accounts receivable and payable. If a cash basis taxpayer transfers only receivables and payables to a corporation, subsection (c) should not apply.[70] Consider the accrual basis taxpayer, however. Clearly, if he transfers $100,000 in accounts receivable and $50,000 in accounts payable to a corporation, he has not recognized a taxable gain.[71] This result follows naturally from the discussion above. The taxpayer has transferred sufficient assets to liquidate the liabilities assumed. Although he has been allowed a deduction for the payables since he is on the accrual method, he nevertheless also has paid tax on the receivables. In this case, the taxpayer has not realized a gain by transferring the receivables and payables to the corporation.

If the figures are reversed, however, the result is different. If an accrual basis taxpayer conveys $50,000 in receivables and $100,000 in payables, he realizes a taxable gain of $50,000 under 357(c) in order to prevent the stock received in exchange from having a negative basis. The taxpayer has, in effect, dumped a liability of $50,000 on the corporation which he will not have to pay. At the same time, he has gained a tax benefit of $50,000 since his deduction for the payables exceeded his tax on the receivables by $50,000. In such a case, it is only just that he be taxed on the transfer.

In conclusion, then, if . . . accounts receivable and payable are transferred to a corporation, a taxable event should not occur [as to them] under 357(c) unless the taxpayer is on the accrual method and the [payables are] greater in amount than the basis of the [receivables] transferred.

NOTE

In Rev. Rul. 69-442, 1969-2 Cum. Bull. 53, the Internal Revenue Service announced that it will continue to apply §357(c) to situations involving facts similar to those in *Raich* "inasmuch as such section literally applies and the legislative history clearly

---

[69]"(d) Assumption of Liability — Where, as part of the consideration to the taxpayer, another party to the exchange assumed a liability of the taxpayer or acquired from the taxpayer property subject to a liability, such assumption or acquisition (in the amount of the liability) shall, for purposes of this section, be treated as money received by the taxpayer on the exchange."

[70]This, of course, assumes that the Commissioner does not conclude that the purpose behind the transfer was tax avoidance or that the transfer was not a legitimate business deal. Int. Rev. Code of 1954, §357(b).

[71]This statement assumes that the receivables do not appreciate in value while in the hands of the taxpayer. If the taxpayer's original basis in the receivables and his basis at the time of transfer are the same, this statement is correct.

supports the application of that section under such circumstances." The Service does not describe or cite references to the "legislative history" to which it refers. The ruling concludes with the statement that "the trade accounts receivable [in *Raich*] would not have had a zero basis if the taxpayer had been on the accrual method of accounting prior to the transfer of the business under §351 of the Code." It is doubtful that the latter statement will be of much solace to the cash basis taxpayer or provide him with understanding. See T. White, III, Sleepers That Travel With Section 351 Transfers, 56 Va. L. Rev. 37 (1970); F. Burke, Jr. and S. Chisholm, Section 357: A Hidden Trap in Tax-Free Incorporations, 25 Tax L. Rev. 211 (1970).

C. BASIS OF STOCK AND SECURITIES RECEIVED AND HOLDING PERIOD

1. *Taxable Transfer — §1012*

Assume that T transfers property with adjusted basis of $10,000 and fair market value of $20,000 to X Corporation in exchange for its common stock worth $20,000. Assume, too, that T is not "in control" after the exchange. As a result, T's gain is recognized, §351 is inapplicable, and §1012 prescribes a cost ($20,000) basis for the stock which T receives.

2. *Tax-free Transfer (in Whole or in Part) — §358*

In the case put in subsection (a) supra, if T had been "in control" after the exchange, and §351(a) had applied, T's gain would not have been recognized. His basis for the stock received would have been $10,000, determined under §358(a)(1).

Assume that T had received stock worth $15,000 and cash of $5000, that he was "in control" and that his gain of $10,000 was recognized to the extent of $5000 under §351(b)(1). What is the basis of his stock? Why?

Assume that, instead of cash, T had received an A.T. & T. bond worth $5000. What would be its basis in T's hands? Why? Consider §358(a)(2); Treas. Reg. §1.358-1.

Suppose that, in a §351 transaction in which T receives stock worth $10,000 and bonds worth $15,000, the asset he transferred had had a basis of $15,000. At what basis does T hold the stock? The bonds? Why? Consider §358(b)(1); Treas. Reg. §1.358-2.

Suppose T, in a §351 transaction, transfers an asset with an adjusted basis of $50,000 and fair market value of $100,000 to X Corporation for common stock worth $75,000 plus X Corporation's assumption of a $25,000 liability which T had incurred when he purchased the asset. What is the basis for the stock in T's hands? Why? Consider §358(a)(1)(A)(ii) and (d); Treas. Reg. §1.358-3.

See J. Rabinovitz, Allocating Boot in Section 351 Exchanges, 24 Tax L. Rev. 337 (1969).

3. Holding Period — §1223(1)

If §358 determines a transferor's basis as to the stock or securities issued him by a corporation (as in a §351 transaction), his holding period for the stock or securities will ordinarily include the period during which he held the assets transferred. This rule for "tacking" and its exceptions are set forth in §1223(1).

D. *CAPITAL CONTRIBUTION (§351) vs. REDEMPTION (§304)*

HASEROT v. COMMISSIONER
46 T.C. 864 (1966), aff'd, 399 F.2d 828 (6th Cir. 1968)*

[The Haserot Company (Company) was engaged in processing food and in distributing its own products and those of the Northport Cherry Factory, Inc. (Northport) and the Gypsum Canning Co. (Gypsum). Prior to the transaction in question taxpayer, Henry McK. Haserot, owned a majority of the stock of all three companies, and Company owned the bulk of the balance of the outstanding stock of Northport and Gypsum. Taxpayer owned 18,895 of Company's 33,014 shares and had an option under his father's will to purchase the shares owned from his father's estate, 10,293 shares, for $80,484.28; taxpayer's son, Henry, owned 1023 shares, and others owned the balance of 2803 shares. In August 1956, taxpayer purchased $27,000 worth of shares from his father's estate by causing Company to issue a check in that amount to the executor, and on February 11, 1958, he purchased the balance of the shares by causing Company to issue to his order a check for $53,984.23 which he endorsed over to and delivered to the executor. Both checks were charged against taxpayer's account with Company.

Company's success was dependent in part on maintaining Northport and Gypsum as suppliers. Although the stock of all three companies had at all relevant times belonged to members of taxpayer's family, supply lines had been disrupted earlier in the companies' history because the three companies had been under the control of different family members. To avoid such difficulties of split control in the future taxpayer proposed, and Company's board of directors agreed, that Company should buy taxpayer's stock in Northport and Gypsum for $64,850 in cash and 2,432 shares of Company's authorized but unissued stock which had a fair market value of $48,637.50. Taxpayer had an aggregate adjusted basis in his Northport and Gypsum shares of $72,905.15. This transaction was consummated on February 2, 1958, Company crediting petitioner's account with the amount of the cash, and petitioner making a gift of the 2432 shares of Company stock to his son. Taxpayer omitted any reference to this transaction in his tax return.

*See page 384 infra. — Ed.

The Commissioner assessed a deficiency, charging that the cash credit received plus the fair market of the stock received constituted a dividend to taxpayer, Company having ample earnings and profits. He later withdrew his claims as to the stock but contended that the $64,850 cash constituted a dividend. Taxpayer agreed that some tax was due but argued that the cash payment should be taxed as a capital gain.]

TANNENWALD, Judge. . . . On January 27, 1964, this Court filed its findings of fact and opinion in Henry McK. Haserot, 41 T.C. 562 (1964), holding that the cash credit was capital gain and entered its decision therein under Rule 50 on April 8, 1964.

Respondent appealed the decision to the U.S. Court of Appeals for the Sixth Circuit, which, on November 3, 1965, remanded the case to this Court for a determination as to whether the transaction involved herein was "essentially equivalent to a dividend" within the meaning of sections 302(b)(1) and 301(a). In its order Commissioner v. Haserot, 355 F.2d 200 (C.A. 6, 1965), the Court of Appeals stated:

"The Tax Court did not determine if the redemption was here equivalent to a dividend . . .

"It appears to this Court, upon review, that a determination of the issue of equivalency might indeed be dispositive of the thrust of petitioner's argument on the Section 304 application to the transaction herein and that such a determination should be made. . . . As such, it should be decided initially by the Tax Court.

"This matter is hereby remanded to the Tax Court for further proceedings in accordance with the views expressed in this order. [355 F.2d at p. 201.]"

On December 7, 1965, this Court vacated the decision in Henry McK. Haserot, supra. Thereafter, on January 4, 1966, petitioner filed a motion to revive that decision. . . .

Opinion

The critical issue for our present consideration is whether the cash credited to petitioner was essentially equivalent to a dividend within the meaning of sections 302(b)(1) and 301(a). The parties agree that a finding of no dividend equivalency would be dispositive of the case.

The colors of the cloth of dividend equivalency are not completely fast. Indeed, the fabric "bleeds," madras-like, to such an extent that the decided cases have been described as a "morass" (see Ballenger v. United States, 301 F.2d 192, 196 (C.A. 4, 1962)) and the underlying statutory provisions referred to as "exasperatingly complex" (see Charles Swan, 42 T.C. 291, 297 (1964), affd. 355 F.2d 795 (C.A. 6, 1966)). Under such circumstances, we believe it would be a sterile exercise to indulge in an analysis of all the factors involved and the weight to be given to each factor.

The legislative history of section 302(b)(1) indicates that it is to be interpreted "in general" in the same manner as section 115(g) of the Internal Revenue Code of 1939 and that the inquiry is to be "factual." S. Rept. No. 1622, 83d Cong., 2d Sess., pp. 233-234 (1954).

There are two main prongs to petitioner's argument that the transaction was not essentially equivalent to a dividend within the meaning of section 302(b)(1). He asserts (a) it produced a substantial change of control at the shareholder level and (b) it was motivated by and achieved a corporate business purpose.

Respondent answers that there was no meaningful shift of stock ownership as a result of the transaction, that there was no valid corporate business purpose for the transaction, and that therefore its net effect was a dividend.

Before the transactions, the ownership of the corporations was as follows:

Northport (4,562 shares): Petitioner, 1,999; Gypsum, 1,312; Company, 1,250; others, 1.

Gypsum (6,582 shares): Petitioner, 4,486; Company, 2,022; others, 74.

Company[1] (33,014 shares): Petitioner, 18,895; petitioner's son, 1,023; estate of petitioner's father, 10,293; others, 2,803.

After the transactions, the ownership was as follows:

Northport (4,562 shares): Company, 3,249; Gypsum, 1,312; others 1.

Gypsum (6,582 shares): Company, 6,508; others, 74.

Company (35,446 shares): Petitioner, 29,188; petitioner's son, 3,455; others, 2,803.

If we look only to the shares registered in petitioner's name, his percentage of control is as follows:

	Northport percent	*Gypsum* percent	*Company* percent
Before	43.8	68.2	57.2
After	0	0	82.3

However, the Company owned shares in both Gypsum and Northport. A majority of the issued and outstanding shares of the Company were registered in petitioner's name and he therefore could dictate actions to be taken by Company with respect to its Northport and Gypsum shares. As a result, petitioner had effective control of a majority of the shares of all three corporations, as revealed by the following table:

	Northport percent	*Gypsum* percent	*Company* percent
Before	99.9	98.9	57.2
After	99.9	98.9	82.3

Finally, if we apply the attribution rules of section 318,[6] the following pattern of petitioner's control appears:

---

[1] The Haserot Co.

[6] Under the will of petitioner's father, petitioner had the choice of (a) receiving all the Company shares bequeathed to him on payment to the estate of an amount equal to certain taxes for which the estate was liable or (b) not paying the amount mentioned in (a) and receiving all of the shares *less* the number of such shares the value of which equaled such taxes. Although petitioner might not be considered a "beneficiary" of the estate for the purposes of sec. 318(a)(2)(A) with regard to the number of shares the values of which equaled the taxes, see sec. 1.318-3(a), Income Tax Regs., and sec. 643(c), he would be treated as having an option to acquire same, and ownership thereof would be attributed to him pursuant to sec. 318(a)(3). See Winthrop M. Crane III, 45 T.C. 397 [aff'd, 368 F.2d 800 (1st Cir. 1966)].

	Company percent	Gypsum percent	Northport percent
Before	91.5	96.3	96.6
After	92.1	91.1	91.8

Parenthetically, we note that petitioner disputes the attribution to him of the shares acquired from his father's estate and the shares issued to his son. He supports his position by the general assertion that "[T]his has the anomalous result of using stock acquired with cash to make the cash itself look more like a dividend." Additionally, petitioner argues that attributing ownership of Northport and Gypsum to him through his ownership of Company shares after the transaction is "unreal." In support of his contentions he relies upon Estate of Arthur H. Squier, 35 T.C. 950 (1961), acq. 1961-2 C.B. 5. The opinion in that case did contain some indication that the attribution rules would not be applied inflexibly in determining whether a redemption is essentially equivalent to a dividend. But the Court made clear that it reached the same result even after applying the attribution rules of section 318. See 35 T.C. at 955. Moreover, the Court emphasized that the redemption therein "in fact resulted in a crucial reduction of the estate's *control* over the corporation."[7] See 35 T.C. at 955-956. If we look at the reality of control herein, it is obvious that, with or without the application of the attribution rules, petitioner was at all times in a position to dominate all three corporations.

Petitioner further seeks to avoid the impact of his continuing dominant position by asserting that the transaction herein was merely a step in a plan to transfer control of the corporate complex to his son. Whatever may be the merits of this assertion in another context, it has no relevance to the instant case. The only actual change in the formal management occurred in 1960 when petitioner's son became president of the three corporations. Petitioner, in his testimony, adverted to a plan for transferring the shares he owned at his death in such a manner that his son would have majority control. Needless to say, any such plan was at all times subject to change until petitioner died and therefore may properly be disregarded. Friend v. United States, 345 F.2d 761 (C.A. 1, 1965); see Neff v. United States, 305 F.2d 455, 458 (Ct. Cl. 1962).

To confine ourselves to petitioner's limited view of the situation would be to exalt illusion over reality. We hold that under all the circumstances of this case there has not been that "meaningful change" in petitioner's shareholder position which is the "indispensable first step" to a finding of lack of dividend equivalence. Bradbury v. Commissioner, 298 F.2d 111 (C.A. 1, 1962), affirming a Memorandum Opinion of this Court; Leon R. Meyer, 46 T.C. 65 (1966), [aff'd in part, vacated and remanded in part, 383 F.2d 883 (8th Cir. 1967)]; Ralph L. Humphrey, 39 T.C. 199 (1962).

We turn to the second main prong of petitioner's position, namely, that the

---

[7]The taxpayer's direct ownership dropped from slightly over a majority (50.09 percent) to substantially less than a majority (41.27 percent). Under such circumstances the cleavage between the father's executors and members of the family which in fact existed in that case became a meaningful impediment to taxpayer's control. We note that there is no such claim of cleavage herein. The same situation existed in Herbert C. Parker, T.C. Memo. 1961-176, also relied upon by petitioner, where there was a cleavage between a father and son and where the taxpayer and his wife owned 50.3 percent of the shares before and 28.7 percent after the redemption. See also pp. 870-871, infra.

transaction herein was clothed with a corporate business purpose. We recognize that such a purpose may, under certain circumstances, constitute a "conspicuous countervailing consideration" sufficient "to dispel the aura of dividend equivalence." See Bradbury v. Commissioner, supra at 117. But it is equally true that such a purpose does not per se establish nonequivalence. See Neff v. United States, supra at 457; Charles Swan, supra, at 299.

Petitioner contends that the transaction herein had as its objectives assurance of Company control over Northport and Gypsum and preservation of Company stock ownership in active Company management. Petitioner's witnesses testified that, when petitioner's father was an active participant in the business, he did not attempt to take charge of Company's operation but did, on occasion, personally take charge of the operation of Northport and Gypsum and that this was inimical to the best interests of the corporate complex. Petitioner further suggests that there was a possibility that he might, in his later years, acquire the vices of his father in this regard. The superficiality of petitioner's blandishments are starkly revealed by the facts herein. Assuming that petitioner might have become a "chip off the old block," the record indicates that the operating difficulties allegedly created by petitioner's father occurred during the period when there was a lack of common control over the three corporations. During the period 1942 to 1951, petitioner was the president and controlling shareholder of the Company and petitioner's father was the president and controlling shareholder of Northport and Gypsum. In 1951, the essential common control was created by the resignation of petitioner's father as president of Northport and Gypsum and the transfer of his shares in those two corporations to petitioner. From and after that time, the possibility of divisive activity would seem to have disappeared. Even if we ignore (as petitioner does) the leverage of the Company over Northport and Gypsum, arising from the Company's position as a substantial and the principal creditor, common ownership by petitioner of all three corporations assured *unity of success or of failure* of operations. The 1958 transaction neither enhanced nor lessened this possibility. Indeed, if petitioner's position is sound regarding the consequence of a change from a brother-sister to a parent-subsidiary relationship, a valid business purpose could be imported into every section 304 transaction involving interrelated business operations. We doubt that Congress intended to provide such an extensive safe harbor in enacting that section.

Nor are we impressed by petitioner's assertion that the requisite business purpose existed in the alleged goal of preserving ownership of the Company in active management. Such an assertion ignores the cardinal fact that management of a corporation is in the final analysis at the mercy of the shareholders. Even assuming that it was in the best interests of the Company for the majority interest to be retained in petitioner's son or others active in its management, the instant transaction did not accomplish this objective. Petitioner could have transferred a controlling interest in the Company inter vivos or at death to persons outside this circle. Such a transfer would have resulted in the *complete* loss of control by management over the Company *and* Northport and Gypsum.[10] Under the circumstances, we cannot say that acquisition by the

[10]We have made a finding that there was some kind of an agreement requiring a holder to sell his stock if he left the Company for any reason. But we were not enlightened as to the details of the agreement or the extent to which it was applicable to petitioner. In any event, the record

Company of the Northport and Gypsum shares and "assisting" petitioner to acquire the Company shares owned by the estate of petitioner's father constituted a sufficient "conspicuous countervailing consideration." See Bradbury v. Commissioner, supra at 117.

Petitioner also seeks to sustain his position by arguing that the transaction herein was in effect only a step in the acquisition by the Company of the shares held by the estate of petitioner's father and that petitioner had more money in corporate solution after the transaction than he had prior thereto. Both of these arguments miss the mark.

The fact is that the Company did not acquire any of the shares from the estate of petitioner's father — either directly or indirectly. The petitioner acquired *and retained* the additional shares, which remained available to him for his use. Nor is it necessarily true that petitioner had more money in corporate solution as a result of the transaction. In support of this position, petitioner limits himself to the cash flow in the 1958 transaction and arrives at an alleged additional cash investment by petitioner of $16,134.28, the difference between the cash credit of $64,850 and the aggregate of $80,984.28 paid for the estate's shares. Petitioner conveniently ignores the facts that in 1956 he had received from the Company and paid to the estate $27,000 against the $80,984.28 and that he had a running account with the Company which reflected other items of advances and repayments. Moreover, immediately after the transaction herein, petitioner's account with the Company showed a *credit* balance of $13,958.95. To this extent, his additional investment was in the form of an indebtedness to him rather than a capital investment. Even if we assume that petitioner might find salvation if he in fact had more invested in the corporate solution, we cannot say that petitioner has met the threshold condition. Cf. William K. Edmister, 46 T.C. 651 (1966).

The case of John A. Decker, 32 T.C. 326 (1959), affirmed per curiam 286 F.2d 427 (C.A. 6, 1960), heavily relied upon by petitioner, is distinguishable. In that case, although the shares were initially acquired by the remaining shareholders, they were *immediately transferred by them to the corporation.* Thus, it was possible to treat the purchasing shareholders as mere agents for the corporation. See Edgar S. Idol, 38 T.C. 444, 460 (1962), affd. 319 F.2d 647 (C.A. 8, 1963). Furthermore, there was a modicum of business purpose in that it appears that the corporation acquired the shares for resale, and in fact did resell some of the shares, to their employees. Compare Fred B. Snite, 10 T.C. 523 (1948), affd. 177 F.2d 819 (C.A. 7, 1949), with Neff v. United States, supra. Finally, there was a real shift in effective control in *Decker.* Prior to the transaction therein, majority action required the agreement of *three* of the five equal shareholders; after the transaction a majority could be achieved by a combination of *two* of the remaining three principal shareholders plus the holder of one share from the minority group. Thus, the veto power of each of the three principal shareholders was significantly lessened. Indeed, this distinction indicates the fundamental weakness of petitioner's position on the issue of dividend equivalence.

---

shows that some transfers were permissible because petitioner testified that his will contained provisions for a trust of his shares.

Petitioner has made a computer-like analysis of the cases to show that the courts have held that there was no dividend equivalence even where there was a very small percentage shift in ownership. In so doing, petitioner has overlooked the fact that, although the percentage shift was small, the effect of the shift was critical. For example, as we have already pointed out (see fn. 7, supra), in Estate of Arthur H. Squier, supra, heavily relied upon by petitioner, actual ownership of the stock by the taxpayer only dropped from 50.09 percent to 41.27 percent but in fact the change was from majority to minority control. A similar analysis distinguishes Sorem v. Commissioner, 334 F.2d 275 (C.A. 10, 1964), reversing 40 T.C. 206 (1963), where the taxpayer's 50-percent *direct* ownership (and a concomitant negative control) was replaced by an indirect ownership of only 37.91 percent reflected in the ownership, *counting attributed shares,* of the stock in the parent corporation. Clearly it was no longer possible for the taxpayer to block corporate action at either parent or subsidiary level. Such a situation is a far cry from petitioner's position herein where he increased rather than decreased his percentage of ownership of the Company (which after the transaction had overwhelming control of Northport and Gypsum) and at all times had majority control by a wide margin. Cf. William K. Edmister, supra; see Wiseman v. United States, 259 F. Supp. 90 (D. Maine 1966); Charles Swan, supra at 298.

Petitioner also emphasizes the nontax pristine purity of the motivations for the transactions involved herein. But, at best, the absence of a tax avoidance motive has long since been relegated to a subsidiary ingredient in the potion of dividend equivalence. Kerr v. Commissioner, 326 F.2d 225 (C.A. 9, 1964), affirming 38 T.C. 723 (1962), certiorari denied 377 U.S. 963; cf. William K. Edmister, supra; see 1 Mertens, Law of Federal Income Taxation, sec. 9.100.

Finally, we are unimpressed by petitioner's contention that the transaction herein could have been conducted in a manner unobjectionable to respondent and tax-free to petitioner. It may well be that the same result could have been achieved by a combination of redemption by the Company of some of the shares held by the estate of petitioner's father, direct acquisition of the remaining shares by petitioner for a smaller cash payment, and an exchange of petitioner's Northport and Gypsum shares solely for Company shares. Cf. Zenz v. Quinlivan, 213 F.2d 914 (C.A. 6, 1954). But the fact of the matter is that the form and substance of the transaction herein coincided and petitioner does not contend otherwise. That a result may have different tax consequences, if brought about in another way, does not mean that the actual transaction may be disregarded. United States v. Collins, 300 F.2d 821, 825 (C.A. 1, 1962); Wiseman v. United States, supra.

On all the facts and circumstances of this case, we hold that the distribution of $64,850 to petitioner by the Company in 1958 was essentially equivalent to a dividend within the meaning of section 302(b)(1). Although the majority recognizes that this Court may have the power to review its prior decision herein and that there may be significant doubts as to its correctness (the writer's separate views on this score are appended hereto), they nevertheless are constrained to confine themselves to the specific question raised by the remand. Consequently, subject to our finding as to dividend equivalence, petitioners' motion to revive our prior decision, in accordance with the prior Rule-50 computation, is granted.

Reviewed by the Court.

Decision will be entered that there is a deficiency of $90 in petitioners' income tax for the taxable year 1958.

TANNENWALD, J., speaking separately. I do not share the reluctance of my colleagues to reconsider the question whether the fact that the transaction falls within the literal language of section 351 operates to preclude the application of section 304(a). There is no doubt that we have the power so to do, since the Court of Appeals neither expressly nor by implication ruled on this issue. Commissioner v. Lincoln Electric Co., 176 F.2d 815 (C.A. 6, 1949), certiorari denied 338 U.S. 949 (1950); see Gunn v. United States, 283 F.2d 358, 361 (C.A. 8, 1960).

. . . In reexamining our prior position, I would adopt the Supreme Court's admonition in Helvering v. Hallock, 309 U.S. 106 (1940), and conclude that we can and should reject the "doctrine of disability at self-correction."

Petitioner applies a double-barreled syllogism to reach the conclusion that section 351 applies as follows:

(a) Section 304 applies only to "sales" and not "exchanges." Moreover, if stock is acquired for property, section 304 is literally inapplicable since, under section 317(a), stock of Company is not "property." Consequently, section 351 alone controls.

(b) Even if section 317 is not operative to preclude the applicability of section 304, the transaction fits literally within both section 304 and section 351. The energizing force for section 304 is section 302. Section 302(d) provides that, "Except as otherwise provided in this subchapter" (subch. C), a redemption not falling within section 302(a) will be characterized for tax purposes under section 301. In, view of the presence of the "except" clause in section 302(d) and the absence of similar language in section 351, Congress intended that section 351 control. Moreover, section 301(a) has a similar "except" clause and this is further recognition that other sections may limit what might otherwise be characterized as dividends.

Respondent vigorously contests the logic of this syllogism, arguing that section 317 does not prevent the characterization of the instant transaction as a redemption; that section 351 applies only to exchanges; that section 351 is not one of the Code sections referred to in the "except" clauses; and that the detailed specificity of section 304 must therefore control. Finally, respondent asserts, with obvious anguish, that petitioner's reasoning would result in section 304 controlling transactions where the shareholder owned more than 50 percent but less than 80 percent of the two corporations and section 351 controlling transactions where he owned 80 percent or more, thereby creating an absurd construction of the statute — a situation which the Supreme Court has abjured. See Holy Trinity Church v. United States, 143 U.S. 457, 459 (1892).

As is usually the case, the path to be followed is not as clearcut as either petitioner or respondent would have us believe. The statutory provisions and legislative history reflect a certain ambiguity, if not outright inconsistency. But the magnitude of the challenge cannot justify a failure of response. As was stated by Lord Justice Denning in Seaford Court Estates Ltd. v. Asher, [1949] 2 K.B. 481, 499:

"It would certainly save the judges trouble if Acts of Parliament were drafted with divine prescience and perfect clarity. In the absence of it, when a defect appears, a judge cannot simply fold his hands and blame the draftsman. He must set to work on the constructive task of finding the intention of Parliament . . . . Put into homely metaphor it is this: A judge should ask himself the question: If the makers of the Act had themselves come across this ruck in the texture of it, how would they have straightened it out? He must then do as they would have done. A judge must not alter the material of which it is woven, but he can and should iron out the creases."

Petitioner's assertion that section 304 applies only to "sales," and that the instant transaction is an "exchange" and not a "sale," is fallacious. It is true that the Congressional committee reports dealing with section 304 speak in terms of "sales" without quotation marks. See H. Rept. No. 1337, 83d Cong., 2d Sess., p. A79 (1954); S. Rept. No. 1622, 83d Cong., 2d Sess., p. 239 (1954). But the word "acquisition" is used in the section itself and in other sections of the Code where clearly it encompasses a broader spectrum of transactions than "sales." Cf., e.g., secs. 269 and 357. And it is not without significance that when Congress first dealt with the category of loophole involved herein, i.e., the acquisition by a subsidiary of shares in a parent corporation, its characterization of such transactions as sales was set off with quotation marks. See H. Rept. No. 2319, 81st Cong., 2d Sess., p. 53 (1950).

Petitioner's further contention as to the impact of section 317(a) on section 304(a)(1)(B) also does not stand up. First, if Congress had intended that section 304(a) apply only if the acquisition was "solely" for property as defined by section 317(a), it could have easily inserted the term in the former section, as it did in sections 354(a)(1), 355(a)(1)(A), and 368(a)(1)(B) and (C). Second, it seems clear that the purpose of section 317(a) was to avoid treating as a distribution under section 301(a) and 302(d) the value of stock distributed by the acquiring corporation, a result which would otherwise have been required under the language of those sections.

It could be argued with equal or greater logic that, by virtue of section 317(a), the stock of the acquiring corporation (the Company herein) should be disregarded with the result that petitioner should be viewed for the purposes of section 304 as having received only a cash credit. Such a reading of the statute would obviously make the transaction herein a simple sale of the Northport and Gypsum shares, thereby precluding any possibility of applying section 351 and clearly requiring taxability of the cash credit as a dividend by virtue of the interplay of sections 304(a)(1), 302(d), and 301(a).

In view of the foregoing, I am unwilling to engage in such obvious subversion of section 304(a)(1) by reading the word "solely" into the statutory mandate.[4]

---

[4]Nor does the existence of certain lacunae in the statutory provisions as to the treatment of the acquiring corporation's stock require a different conclusion. It is true that, unlike other sections of the Code, notably secs. 354(a)(1), 355(a)(1)(A), and 356, sec. 304 does not contain any cross-reference to a section governing the treatment of the acquiring corporation's stock. Reading secs. 304(a)(1), 305(a), 307(a), and 317(a) together, it would appear that the Company would treat the Northport and Gypsum stock as a contribution to its capital, governed by sec. 362(a)(2), the distribution of Company stock to petitioner would be rendered nontaxable by sec. 305(a), and

I turn now to petitioner's assertion that, because of the phrase "except as otherwise provided" in sections 302(d) and 301(a), the instant case is controlled by section 351 rather than section 304.

The legislative history of subchapter C blurs rather than illumines the problem. Section 351 of the House version of H.R. 8300 (which in final form became the Internal Revenue Code of 1954) contained a cross reference which made it plain that cash distributions in a transaction of the type involved herein could be characterized as a dividend under section 301. Neither section 301 nor section 302 contained any "except" clauses. Under the House bill, therefore, section 301 was intended to have basket coverage. See H. Rept. No. 1337, 83d Cong., 2d Sess., pp. 39, A70 (1954). Had these provisions been finally enacted, the answer to the problem in the instant case would have been clear.

In the Senate, the provisions relating to corporate distributions were substantially recast. In so doing, the Senate evinced a desire to adopt a "less extreme approach." It was concerned that the House had used "few of the terms or concepts with which the courts . . . have become familiar over the years" and sought "to preserve the terms and concepts of existing law wherever possible." The Senate emphasized, however, that it had "not hesitated to depart from the present statute, where such departure was necessary in order to . . . preclude the use of avoidance devices which have proved successful under the existing code." See S. Rept. No. 1622, 83d Cong., 2d Sess., p. 42 (1954). It was within this context that the "except" clauses were included in sections 302(d) and 301(a).

Against this background, petitioner argues that Congress used the words "subchapter" and "chapter" in sections 302(d) and 301(a) in their literal senses and meant to except a transaction falling *literally* within *any* other section of the subchapter and chapter. His argument derives inferential support from the fact that Congress showed elsewhere in the 1954 Code that it knew how to refer specifically in other clauses to (a) "subsections" (secs. 357(a), 305(a), and 311(a)); (b) "sections" (secs. 336 and 312(a)); (c) "paragraphs" (sec. 302(c)(1)); (d) "subtitles" (sec. 316(a)); (e) "parts" (sec. 317(a)); and (f) "subchapters" (sec. 354(c)). I think, however, that petitioner's literal reading of the statute imputes a dragnet exclusion from dividend equivalence of types of distributions which Congress intended to be included. As has been pointed out, the Senate made it clear that, although its rewrite of the House version of H.R. 8300 was occasioned principally by a desire to preserve "terms and concepts of existing law," such rewrite was still directed at "the use of avoidance devices which have proved successful under the existing Code." See S. Rept. No. 1622, supra. The transfer of stock of brother-sister corporations was precisely such a device. See S. Rept. No. 1622, supra at 45-46, 239.

If petitioner's view were adopted, it would to a large degree negate the long-standing efforts to deal legislatively with problems of the type involved herein. Commencing in 1950, when the predecessor of section 304 was enacted to control

---

the basis of his Company stock would be determined under sec. 307(a). Since a transaction to which sec. 304 is applicable and which fails to meet the tests of sec. 302(b) is not treated as an exchange of stock under sec. 301(a), it follows that the transferee's stock would be treated as received in a distribution rather than an exchange and sec. 305(a) would, on its face, apply.

redemptions by a subsidiary from a parent (sec. 208 of the Revenue Act of 1950, which added sec. 115(g) to the Internal Revenue Act of 1939), Congress has shown concern for the possibilities of mischief arising from dealings between related corporations and their controlling shareholders in such corporations' stock. See H. Rept. No. 2319, supra; S. Rept. No. 2375, 81st Cong., 2d Sess., p. 81 (1950). In 1954, in order to minimize further the possibilities of mischief, it enacted section 304, which requires "brother-sister" participants to walk the tightrope of section 302(b) in order to qualify for capital gains treatment when the same person or persons control 50 per cent of each corporation.

Petitioner would have us modify the requirement of control from "fifty percent" to "fifty percent *but less than eighty percent.*" Such a result would enable an 80-percent-or-more shareholder to play fast and loose with section 304 to a degree not permitted to the holder of a lesser percentage but nevertheless majority control. The instant situation is not comparable, as petitioner suggests, to those where one receives favorable or unfavorable treatment because he owns less than a *statutorily specified* percentage of the outstanding stock, as, for example, in sections 318 and 368, as well as in sections 304 and 351. In each of those sections, Congress has consciously, for policy reasons, established a self-contained mathematical trigger to provide taxpayers with some certainty in the planning of their affairs. If Congress had specifically provided that section 351 did not apply where the transferor owned 79 percent but did apply where he owned 20 percent or that section 304(a)(1) did not apply where common control was 49 percent but did apply where it was 10 percent, we would be bound by such limits, however bizarre we might judge them to be. But it does not follow that we should *infer* such an eccentric choice for the purpose of providing a safe harbor under section 304 in situations where there is an 80 percent or more, as well as less than 50-percent ownership.

The paradox of petitioner's position is dramatized if one considers the interrelationship between section 301, on the one hand, and section 1002 on the other. If the "except" clause in the former requires us to look at other sections, the "except" clause of the latter requires us to do the same. The task of disposing of the renvoi problem thus presented is second only to that of squaring the circle. Moreover, under petitioner's interpretation, section 351 would control even where only a peppercorn of stock is issued by the acquiring corporation. Perhaps petitioner is correct when he suggests that such a result could be obviated by treating the transaction as "sham." But I see no need to expand the fertile field of argument as to what transactions are "real" or "sham," if such a course can be avoided.

Unquestionably, Congress has the power to legislate eccentrically, but I am loath to find that it has exercised this power where a reasonable basis for synthesis exists. See J. C. Penney Co. v. Commissioner, 312 F.2d 65, 68 (C.A. 2, 1962), affirming 37 T.C. 1013.[7]

---

[7]Even from the point of view of literal interpretation, the opposite result from that advanced by petitioner can be reached. Sec. 304(a)(1) specifically provides: *"For purposes of section 302 and 303* . . . [the property received] . . . *shall be treated as a distribution in redemption* of the stock of the corporation acquiring such stock. In any such case, the stock so acquired *shall be treated* as having been transferred by the person from whom acquired, and as having been received

Doubtless the statute would have been clearer if Congress had directly connected the "except" clauses by placing them immediately after the phrases "such redemption" and "a distribution." Nevertheless, I believe that the "except" clauses of section 302(d) and 301(a) relate to the terms "redemption" and "distribution" in the respective subsections and are therefore limited to the provisions dealing with such situations. Such reasoning allows the permissiveness of section 351 to yield to the preventive policy of section 304. See Kempf, "Disguised Dividends in Related Corporation Transactions," 33 U. Chi. L. Rev. 94 (1965). It best achieves the underlying legislative intent and policy and, in my opinion, more nearly reflects the manner in which Congress would have "straightened this ruck out if they had come across it."[8] See Seaford Court Estates Ltd. v. Asher, supra.

I would therefore hold that section 304(a)(1) controls.

SIMPSON, J., agrees with this separate opinion.

COMMISSIONER v. STICKNEY, EX'R OF HASEROT ESTATE
399 F.2d 828 (6th Cir. 1968)

Before PECK and COMBS, Circuit Judges, and CECIL, Senior Circuit Judge.

PECK, Circuit Judge. This is the fourth time that this case has been the subject of judicial consideration. The original determination made by the Tax Court in favor of the Taxpayer was brought before this court for review by the Commissioner of Internal Revenue. Our order of remand again resulted in a conclusion favorable to the Taxpayer, albeit by a divided Tax Court, and the Commissioner has again petitioned for review here. During the pendency of these proceedings the Taxpayer principally concerned (his wife is a party hereto solely by virtue of their filing of joint returns) died and the executor of his estate has been substituted as a party. . . .

The issue involves the tax consequences of a cash transfer to Taxpayer and of transfers of stock in three corporations, all of which were before and after the transfers controlled by the Taxpayer. . . . [Portions of the court's statement of facts are omitted because of their inclusion in the Tax Court's opinion, page 373 supra.]

Consummation of the transaction occurred February 21, 1958, when Taxpayer

---

by the corporation acquiring it, *as a contribution to the capital of such corporation.* [Emphasis added.]"

From the use of the mandatory phrase "shall be treated," it might logically be concluded that Congress had mandated that sec. 304 transactions be treated as redemptions and has therefore "otherwise provided." Under such an interpretation, resort to sec. 351 is precluded or, at most, we are left with a transaction that literally falls within two coordinate sections. In the latter case, we have no hesitancy in holding that sec. 304 controls. . . .

[8]The interpretative process is unaffected by the fact that a choice between secs. 304 and 351 produces a different treatment of other components in the type of transaction involved herein (basis of the redeemed stock under sec. 1.304-2(a), Income Tax Regs., or sec. 362(a), the treatment of an assumption of the transferor's indebtedness under sec. 304 or sec. 357, and the applicability to securities of sec. 317 or the nonrecognition provisions of sec. 351). Differences in treatment in the area of corporate distributions are not unknown where the statutory language affords no choice. Compare, for example, the treatment of "boot" in a transaction which otherwise complies with sec. 368(a)(1)(B) and in a sec. 351 transaction or a reorganization covered by sec. 354. Compare also fn. 4, supra.

transferred his shares in Northport and Gypsum to Haserot. The latter credited Taxpayer's account on its books with the value of the Northport and Gypsum stock and debited his account in the amount of the value of the 2,432 Haserot shares which were issued to Taxpayer's son as a gift from him. Stipulation in the Tax Court established that the proper amount of the credit was $113,490 and that the fair market value of the stock was $48,640. In the deficiency notice issued by Commissioner after examination and audit of Taxpayer's 1958 return his taxable income was increased $113,490, the total of the cash ($64,850) and the fair market value of Haserot stock (determined by Commissioner to be $48,640) Taxpayer received in the transaction. The Tax Court found as a fact that, "In planning the transaction, [Taxpayer] was unaware that it involved either tax problems or tax advantages. He did not consult in advance with counsel or with anyone else as to the income tax consequences of the transaction."

This case has presented difficulties at every stage of the proceedings because the transaction falls within the literal language of both Section 351 and Section 304. Although the value of the 2,432 Haserot shares issued to Taxpayer is now conceded by the Commissioner not to have constituted taxable income, the parties are in disagreement as to how the $64,850 cash payment should be returned. If Section 351 controls, the gain is to be taxed as a capital gain while if Section 304 controls it should be taxed either as a capital gain or the cash payment is to be taxed as a dividend, depending upon the relevant portions of Section 302. Stated in terms of dollars, if Section 304(a) applies (as Commissioner urges), the $64,850 is dividend income taxable at ordinary rates. If Section 351 applies (as the Tax Court held), no dividend results; rather Taxpayer's gain ($40,584.85 — $64,850 (cash) plus $48,650 (value of Haserot shares) minus $72,905.12 (basis of Northport and Gypsum stock)) is taxable as a long-term capital gain.

In its original determination (41 T.C. 562 (1964)), the Tax Court held that the cash credit was capital gain, and upon review this court remanded the case for a determination by the Tax Court as to whether the transaction was "essentially equivalent to a dividend" within the meaning of Section 302(b)(1) and 301(a) (Commissioner v. Haserot, 355 F.2d 200 (1965)). Pursuant to the remand, the Tax Court found that, "The $64,850 cash credit received by petitioner in 1958 constituted a distribution essentially equivalent to a dividend." In arguing to the contrary, Taxpayer asserts that (1) the transaction produced a substantial change of control at the shareholder level, and that (2) the transaction was motivated by and achieved a corporate business purpose.

With reference to Taxpayer's first point, it is true that if only the shares registered in his own name are taken into account his percentage of control is as follows:

	Northport	*Gypsum*	*Haserot*
Before	43.8%	68.2%	57.2%
After	0 %	0 %	82.3%

This is not, however, an accurate reflection of Taxpayer's control because of his

ownership of the majority interest in Haserot, which in turn held stock in Northport and Gypsum. The following table indicates the effective control enjoyed by
Taxpayer over all three corporations, both before and after the transaction:[2]

	Northport	Gypsum	Haserot
Before	99.9%	98.9%	57.2%
After	99.9%	98.9%	82.3%

After a review of the facts and a discussion of Taxpayer's arguments, the Tax
Court concluded: "We hold that under all the circumstances of this case there has
not been that 'meaningful change' in [Taxpayer's] shareholder position which is
the 'indispensible first step' to a finding of lack of dividend equivalents. Bradbury v.
Commissioner. . . , 298 F.2d 111 (1st Cir. 1962) . . . ."

With reference to Taxpayer's second point, Taxpayer argues that a corporate
business purpose existed sufficient to constitute . . . ". . . conspicuously countervailing
considerations to dispel the aura of dividend equivalence . . . ." See Bradbury v. Commissioner, supra, p. 117. However, such a purpose does not per se establish non-
equivalences. . . . It is Taxpayer's contention that the transaction assured Haserot
control over Northport and Gypsum and preservation of Haserot stock ownership.
The argument contends that Taxpayer might have become a "chip off the old
block" and might then have repeated the mistakes made by his father. This argument falls of its own weight when it is remembered that the operating difficulties
allegedly created by Taxpayer's father in his advancing years occurred during the
period when there was a lack of common control over the three corporations. Thereafter, the Tax Court found that Taxpayer's common ownership of all three corporations assured a unity of success or failure of their operations.

Taxpayer argued further, in connection with his second point, that a business
purpose existed in the alleged goal of preserving ownership of Haserot in active
management. We agree with the Tax Court that this argument fails to take into
account the cardinal fact that management of a corporation is in the final analysis at
the mercy of the shareholders. Following the transaction Taxpayer remained free
to transfer, either inter vivos or at death, to persons within the circle — or to stran-
gers to it. In the circumstances the Tax Court properly concluded "that acquisition
by [Haserot] of the Northport and Gypsum shares and 'assisting' petitioner to
acquire the [Haserot] shares owned by the estate of [Taxpayer's] father constituted
a sufficient 'conspicuous countervailing consideration.' See Bradbury v. Commissioner . . . , supra, at 117."

Based on its rejection of Taxpayer's arguments, and after a full discussion of them,
as hereinabove indicated the Tax Court responded to our mandate by concluding

[2]Because of the manner of Taxpayer's acquisition of Haserot stock under his father's will,
there was a dispute in the Tax Court as to the application of the attribution rules under Section
318. Such application would have increased his percentage control of Haserot (both before and
after the transaction), and slightly decreased his percentage control of Gypsum and Northport, but
a discussion of such application is omitted herefrom as immaterial to the conclusion. For different
but obvious reasons discussion is also omitted of the argument that the transaction was really a
step in Taxpayer's plan to ultimately transfer control to his son.

that the cash credit distributed to Taxpayer constituted a distribution essentially equivalent to a dividend. That holding is not clearly erroneous and is here affirmed.

The significance of this determination lies in the fact that had a finding of a lack of dividend equivalency been made Section 302(a) would have had application, and under the direction of that section the sum would be subject to treatment "as a distribution in part or full payment in exchange for stock." Equivalency having been found, and Section 302(a) having been thereby excluded from consideration, we return to the question as to whether tax liability should be determined under Section 302(a)(1) or under Section 351. The treatment provided under 304(a) is appropriate where "one or more taxpayers are in control of each of two corporations," while Section 351 treatment (by virtue of the definition contained in Section 368(c)) only becomes available where a holding of 80% of the combined voting power of stock is held. Had Taxpayer's holdings amounted to only 50% to 80% the Section 304(a) treatment would have been exclusively available, and the question therefore is whether in this instance of an exchange as distinguished from a sale the fact that when his holding passed the 80% mark the tax treatment to be accorded passed exclusively to that provided by Section 351.

In its opinion on the remand, the Tax Court specifically limited itself to a consideration of the dividend equivalency question and reached no conclusion as to whether Section 351 operates so as to preclude the application of Section 304(a). However, there is appended to the Tax Court opinion a document in which Judge Tannenwald (the author of the opinion) "speaking separately" expressed his views on the latter question. That separate opinion (in which one other judge joined) first expressed the view, not shared by a majority of his colleagues, that the Tax Court had the power to reconsider the question of the applicability of Sections 351 or 304(a). Thereafter, Judge Tannenwald reaches the conclusion that Section 304(a) rather than 351, controls. We disagree, and instead affirm the reaffirmance by a majority of the Tax Court of its original decision.

Taxpayer urges that the case fits within the provisions of Section 351, and the Commissioner's brief in this court opens with a statement of the question involved, which contains the statement that the transaction "fits within the literal terms of Section 351.". . .

In view of the agreement of the parties as to the application of this section to the factual pattern of this case it would serve no useful purpose to further labor the point, particularly since a comparison of the foregoing quotation from Section 351 and the facts clearly demonstrates the applicability. In marked contrast, if Section 304(a) also applies, that can only be determined by laboring through a labyrinth of related sections. Section 304 is not self-executing in any sense, and where it has application the tax liability can only be determined by reading other sections in pari materia. One of the sections which must be so read, and to which specific reference is made in 304, is Section 301. That section is the initial section of the chapter which contains all of the sections quoted in this opinion, and it begins with the words, "Except as otherwise provided in this Chapter . . . ." To hold that the tortured construction of Section 304(a) urged by the Commissioner causes it to fit the situation in issue is difficult, and to conclude that it is controlling is to entirely ignore the existence of the opening language of the chapter, "Except as otherwise provided in this Chapter." The only reasonable explanation for the presence of those words (we are unable to agree with the tenuous explanation offered by Commissioner) is that when another section of the chapter has application the Section 301 treatment is to be excluded; as previously indicated, this includes the Section 304(a) formula. We decline to follow the devious approach urged by the Commissioner, and conclude that Section 351 applies.

In reaching this conclusion we are not unmindful of the argument advanced by the Commissioner concerning legislative intent. As a background for this argument, he presents the illustration of a stockholder controlling two or more corporations who arranges to have one corporation purchase the stock of another for cash in order to bail out (at the cost of no more than a capital gains tax) corporate earnings which would otherwise be taxed as dividends at ordinary rates. Against this background the Commissioner urges that Congress could not have intended such bailing out practices to be denied shareholders owning control in the 50-79% bracket while they remained available to the stockholder whose control exceeded 80%. While this is concededly an oversimplification of his argument, the fact remains that the applicable section is not to be determined solely on the basis of the extent of control. The application of Section 304 is limited to sales and to sales alone. Section 351 contains no such limitation, and by its express provisions extends its application to exchanges, with which we are engaged in the present situation.

Particularly able arguments were heard in this case, and counsel stopped just short of agreeing that Commissioner was contending his construction of statutes to be correct because that was what Congress should have said. If our logic seems to support that contention it is sufficient to respond that Congress did not say it, but did utter the clearly applicable language enacted as Section 351. Had Congress intended the Section 304(a) treatment to apply to such situations as the present one that end could have been accomplished by a specific affirmative enactment, or by a negation of 351 application.

In the original opinion of the Tax Court, Judge Train stated:

> "We have no reason to believe that Congress had any intent with regard to the fact pattern in this case. However, the statements in sections 301(a) and 302(d), 'except as otherwise provided in this chapter' [or subchapter] of the Code, indicate that Congress made the policy decision that dividend treatment will result from the application of Section 302 only if no other provision in the relevant parts of the Code requires other treatment. Section 351 has no such limitation. That section is, by its terms, applicable. That section provides for tax treatment of the payment in question in a manner other than and different from the distribution treatment provided for by sections 302(d) and 301. Consequently, the very words in the latter section preclude dividend treatment in this case."

We are in accord with this determination, and accordingly affirm the decision of the Tax Court.

NOTE

1. Initially, the Commissioner treated both the cash credit and the value of the stock received as taxable dividend income to the taxpayer. Later, he withdrew the claim as to the stock. Why? Was he right in doing so within his own theory as to the primacy of §304? See §305; Chapter 4, pages 403-460 infra.

2. How would you have resolved the seeming dilemma posed by §§351 and 304 in *Haserot Estate*? How would you consider the problem from a legislative point of view? Draft your proposed legislative proposal and accompany it with a proposed report for the Ways and Means Committee to adopt.

3. See R. Greene and R. Hobbet, CA-6 Says 351 Bars Dividend Treatment Under 304, 29 J. Taxation 356 (1968); Note, Section 351 Precludes Dividend Treatment of "Boot" Paid in a Section 304 Redemption of Brother-Corporation Stock Even When The "Boot" Is Essentially Equivalent to a Dividend, 45 Texas L. Rev. 771 (1967); J. Marans, Section 304: The Shadowy World of Redemptions through Related Corporations, 22 Tax L. Rev. 161 (1967); J. Marans, Section 304: The Shadowy World Revisited, 22 Tax L. Rev. 721 (1967).

III. ISSUANCE OF STOCK OR SECURITIES — IMPACT ON CORPORATION

See Chapter 1, pages 73-75, 101-103 supra; and W. Landis, Contributions to Capital of Corporations, 24 Tax. L. Rev. 241 (1969).

IV. BASIS OF PROPERTY RECEIVED BY CORPORATION FOR STOCK OR SECURITIES

A. *TAXABLE TRANSFER — §1012*

When a corporation issues stock to a shareholder in exchange for property in circumstances which render the transaction wholly taxable to the shareholder, the corporation is treated as a purchaser of the assets and its basis is cost under §1012. See Treas. Reg. §1.1032-1(d) (last sentence).

What is a corporation's "cost" if it issues newly authorized stock in exchange for assets with a fair market value of $1000? Does it matter that the stock has a fair market value of $1050? Of $950? Of $1000? Does it matter that the stock represents a minority interest in a closely held corporation and that there is no market for the stock?

Suppose a corporation issues its ten-year, 8 per cent bond in exchange for an asset in circumstances which render the bondholder taxable on the asset appreciation. What is the corporation's basis for the asset? Why?

B. *TAX-FREE TRANSFER (IN WHOLE OR IN PART) — §362(a)*

If a corporation receives assets in a transaction to which §351 applies, the basis is governed by §362(a). See Treas. Reg. §1.1032-1(d); §1.362-1.

Suppose Corporation C issues $10,000 worth of its stock, $5000 worth of its long-term debentures, and cash of $5000 to its sole shareholder in exchange for an asset worth $20,000 which had a basis in the shareholder's hands of $10,000. What is the basis of the asset in Corporation C's hands? Why?

C. *HOLDING PERIOD — §1223(2)*

If a corporation receives property with its basis determined under §362, as in a §351 transaction, the corporation's holding period will include the period during which the property was held by the transferor. This "tacking" rule is provided in §1223(2).

V. ACCOUNTING CONTINUITY

DEARBORN GAGE CO. v. COMMISSIONER
48 T.C. 190 (1967)

TANNENWALD, Judge. Respondent determined deficiencies in petitioner's income tax for the taxable years ended November 30, 1960, 1961, and 1962 in the amounts of $32,962.47, $4,218.02, and $979.78, respectively.

Petitioner having conceded all other items in the deficiency notice, two issues remain for our consideration:

1. Was respondent entitled to require petitioner to include overhead costs in inventory values instead of deducting such costs in the year spent?

2. If so, to what extent, if any, were adjustments properly made under section 481?

Findings of Fact

[The taxpayer was incorporated on May 1, 1957. On that date it received the assets and ongoing business of a partnership in a transaction that qualified under Section 351. The taxpayer, like its predecessor partnership, engaged in manufacturing and maintained substantial inventories. From its inception the taxpayer valued its inventories under the FIFO method and included only the *direct* costs of labor and materials in its valuation. It never included indirect costs and administrative expenses (overhead). The taxpayer's predecessor partnership also excluded overhead costs in its inventory valuations but valued its inventories at the lower of cost or market.

In 1963 the Commissioner examined the taxpayer's returns for fiscal years 1960, 1961, and 1962 and determined that its ending inventories for those years should be increased to reflect overhead costs. The Commissioner made no adjustment to the 1960 opening inventory.

The Tax Court sustained the Commissioner's judgment that the taxpayer's method of accounting for inventories did not clearly reflect income and that overhead costs should be included. The taxpayer then argued that similar adjustments should be made to the predecessor partnership's inventories for the period since January 1, 1954. Such adjustments would have increased the closing inventories of the partnership on the date it transferred its assets to the taxpayer, and so the taxpayer's opening inventories on May 1, 1957 would have been higher. The Tax Court's opinion with respect to this aspect of the case follows.]

. . . Under section 481, the determination of the petitioner's liability *for the taxable year 1960* must take into account adjustments for prior taxable years to which that section applies. The process of computing these adjustments involves reconstructing petitioner's opening and closing inventories for the taxable years 1957, 1958, and 1959. Unquestionably, overhead costs must be included in petitioner's opening and closing inventories for 1958 and 1959 and the closing inventory for 1957. The critical question which we must resolve is whether such costs must be also included in opening inventory for 1957. In so doing, we must decide which of two general principles applies. The first principle requires that opening inventory be computed on the same basis as closing inventory . . . . The second principle requires that, pursuant to section 362, in a tax-free exchange such as occurred herein when the predecessor partnership transferred its assets to petitioner, the basis of the transferred assets in the hands of the latter is the same as it was in the hands of the former. In implementing this second principle it has been held that the basis of initial opening inventory in the hands of the transferee corporation should not be adjusted in order to correct for an erroneous method of accounting for that inventory by the predecessor transferor. Ezo Products Co., [37 T.C. 385 (1961)] . . . ; Frank G. Wikstrom & Sons, Inc., [20 T.C. 359 (1953)] . . . ; see Fred P. Pursell, [38 T.C. 263, 276, aff'd per curiam, 315 F.2d 629 (3rd Cir. 1963)] . . . ; but cf. Manhattan Building Co., 27 T.C. 1032 (1957), a case not involving inventories, where the taxpayer was permitted to make changes in the basis of property to take into account errors in the tax treatment of prior transactions involving the property. None of these decisions dealt with the interrelationship of the two principles but this question was discussed in Textile Apron Co., 21 T.C. 147 (1953), where we said that the principle respecting the uniform method of valuing opening and closing inventory for a given taxable year does not apply where the inventory was acquired in a tax-free exchange.

Petitioner argues that, on the basis of the agreed cumulative method utilized in computing petitioner's inventory, the refusal of respondent to make an adjustment based on overhead costs related to its opening inventory for the taxable year 1957 in effect allows respondent to tax $6,643.26 in overhead costs expensed by its predecessor during the period January 1, 1954 to April 30, 1957 and $10,087.47 in such costs thus expensed prior to January 1, 1954. Thus, petitioner insists that it is being taxed on $16,730.73 which is properly attributable to periods to which section 481 does not apply, because of the decisions that that section may only be applied to the petitioner-taxpayer and because that section, by its terms, precludes pre-1954 adjustments where a change of accounting method is made by the respondent,[9] as is the case herein.

The fact of the matter is that these asserted consequences are more apparent than real. In the first place, it can be argued that overhead costs are incurred only after inventory is acquired and that, *as to this petitioner,* there were no overhead costs in its May 1, 1967 opening inventory. See Frank G. Wikstrom & Sons, Inc., supra at p. 361. Such an approach, together with the fact that petitioner acquired the inventory through the issuance of its own shares, justifies the conclusion that petitioner is not being deprived, economically or financially, of the benefit of any actual payment in excess of its predecessor's basis. Secondly, it is not necessarily true that there are any overhead costs actually attributable to closing inventory in the hands of petitioner's predecessor which were incurred by the predecessor prior to January 1, 1954. It seems likely (and the record does not indicate otherwise) that all of the inventory acquired prior to January 1, 1954 was disposed of by the predecessor prior to April 30, 1957 so that the closing inventory on that date represented only acquisitions since January 1, 1954. Indeed, theoretically all of the inventory acquired prior to January 1, 1957 could have been disposed of by petitioner's predecessor prior to April 30, 1957 so that the closing inventory on that date included only acquisitions during the last four-month taxable period. See the lucid discussion of Judge Learned Hand as to how inventories are handled in Commissioner v. Dwyer, [203 F.2d 522 (2nd Cir. (1953))] . . . ; see also David W. Hughes, [22 T.C. 1 (1954)] . . . (Judge Opper's dissenting opinion [at page 5]).

We recognize that, if petitioner had never been formed, and the predecessor partnership had continued in business, and the issue before us involved a comparable change in the latter's method of accounting for overhead costs, respondent would have been precluded by the express provisions of section 481 from making any adjustments with respect to periods prior to January 1, 1954 and would, under the applicable decisions, have been required, in making the necessary computations, to include overhead costs both in the opening inventory and closing inventory for the taxable year 1954. Thus, petitioner — a taxpayer separate and distinct from its predecessor — appears to fare worse than its predecessor would have. We also recognize that, in point of fact, the tax benefit of the deductions for overhead costs taken by petitioner's predecessor may not have been as great as the tax burden which our rationale now requires petitioner to bear, e.g., because the partners may have been in lower tax brackets or the partnership may have operated at a loss in some of the prior years. Moreover, if the ownership of petitioner's stock had changed prior to the taxable years herein involved, the economic effect of the tax benefit would not inure to, nor would the tax burden fall upon, the same persons. But these are nothing more than some of the myriad of different consequences which may result from a change to the

[9]Section 481(a)(2) expressly permits pre-1954 adjustments only where the change of accounting method is not initiated by the respondent.

corporate form of doing business or from the acquisition of stock of a corporation rather than corporate assets.[10]. . .

We do not have before us an attempt by the respondent to impose a tax in 1960 on amounts which had previously been taxed in barred years, with double taxation the result. Cf. John Wanamaker Philadelphia, Inc. v. United States, 359 F.2d 437 (Ct. Cl. 1966). On the contrary, we are confronted with an attempt by petitioner to resist the application of section 481 and the accepted rule as to the basis of inventory acquired in a tax-free exchange in order to obtain our blessing of a double deduction. Under these circumstances and taking into account the progressive legislative design over the years to ameliorate the effects of the statute of limitations through the enactment of section 481, as well as the mitigation provisions of section 1311 et seq., we are not disposed to accept petitioner's arguments and depart from the framework established by the decided cases. To do otherwise would require us to import into section 351 exchanges a concept of continuity of taxpayers which has clearly been rejected. Joseph E. Seagram & Sons, Inc., [46 T.C. 698 (1966)]; Ezo Products Co., supra; Akron, Canton & Youngstown Railroad Co., 22 T.C. 648 (1954); Textile Apron Co., supra. We conclude, therefore, that, although section 481 is the vehicle by which respondent's adjustments are to be made, he may nevertheless, in computing those adjustments, take advantage of a rule available to him without regard to that section. Ezo Products Co., supra; Textile Apron Co., supra; Frank G. Wikstrom & Sons, Inc., supra. . . .

Decision will be entered for the respondent.

NOTE

Where language of the statute itself is not compelling, one way or the other, should a court resolve the continuity of basis question posed in *Dearborn Gage* restrictively, as the Tax Court did, or should it adopt a broader approach to continuity of basis in view of the thesis underlying §§351(a) and 362(a)(1)? Why?

If a partnership incorporates a building under §351(a), and the building had been carried on the partnership's books erroneously at a basis of $50,000 but had an actual basis of $40,000, at what basis will the corporation-transferee take the building? Why?

NASH v. UNITED STATES
398 U.S. 1 (1970), rev'g 414 F.2d 627 (5th Cir. 1969)

Mr. Justice Douglas delivered the opinion of the Court.

Petitioners were partners operating eight finance offices in Alabama. The partnership reported its income on the accrual method of accounting and instead of

---

[10]We note that, with respect to years in which a subchapter S election (see sections 1371-1378) has been made, it may be possible to confine respondent's adjustments in a case of the type involved herein to post January 1, 1954 periods. Cf. Paul H. Travis, [47 T.C. 502 (1966)]; see E. Morris Cox, [43 T.C. 448 (1965),] at p. 459.

deducting bad debts within the taxable year as permitted by §166(a) of the Internal Revenue Code of 1954 it used the reserve method of accounting as permitted by §166(c). Under the reserve method of accounting a taxpayer includes in his income the full-face amount of a receivable on its creation and adjusts at the end of each taxable year the reserve account so that it equals that portion of current accounts receivable which is estimated to become worthless in subsequent years. Any additions necessary to increase the reserve are currently deductible. When an account receivable becomes worthless during the year, the reserve account is decreased and no additional bad debt deduction is allowed. As of May 31, 1960, the partnership books showed accounts receivable of $486,853.69 and a reserve for bad debts of $73,028.05.

On June 1, 1960, petitioners formed eight new corporations and transferred the assets of the eight partnership offices, including the accounts receivable, to the corporations in exchange for shares of the corporations — a transfer which concededly provided no gain or loss under §351 of the Code.

The Commissioner determined that the partnership should have included in income the amount of the bad debt reserve ($73,028.05) applicable to the accounts receivable that had been transferred. Tax deficiencies were computed; and petitioners, having paid them, brought this suit for refunds. The District Court allowed recovery and the Court of Appeals reversed, 414 F.2d 627. We granted the petition for certiorari to resolve the conflict between the Fifth and the Ninth Circuits[1] on this question of law. 396 U.S. 1000, 90 S. Ct. 556, 24 L. Ed. 2d 492. We share the view of the Ninth Circuit and reverse the present judgment.

There is no provision of the Code that deals precisely with this question. But the Commissioner's basic premise[2] rests on the so-called tax benefit rule viz. that a recovery of an item that has produced an income tax benefit in a prior year is to be added to income in the year of recovery.[3] The Commissioner argues that that rule, applicable here, means that unused amounts in a bad debt reserve must be restored to income when the reserve is found to be no longer necessary, as it was here, when the partnerships "need" for the reserves ended with the termination of its business. Congress could make the end of "need" synonymous with "recovery" in the meaning of the tax benefit rule and make the rule read: "a bad debt reserve which has produced an income tax benefit in a prior year is to be added to income in the year when it was recovered or when its need is ended." The semantics would then be honored by the Commissioner's ruling. But we do not feel free to state the tax benefit rule in those terms in the present context. We deal with §351(a) of the Code which provides:

> "No gain or loss shall be recognized if property is transferred to a corporation by one or more persons solely in exchange for stock or securities in such corporation and immediately after the exchange such person or persons are in control . . . of the corporation."

All that petitioners received from the corporations were securities equal in value to the net worth of the accounts transferred, that is the face value less the amount of

[1] Estate of Schmidt v. Commissioner of Internal Revenue, 9 Cir., 355 F.2d 111.
[2] See Rev. Rule 62-128, 1962-2 Cum. Bull. 139.
[3] Section 111(a) . . . .

the reserve for bad debts. If, as conceded, there is no "gain" or "loss" recognized as a result of the transaction, it seems anomalous to treat the bad debt reserve as "income" to the transferor.[4]

Deduction of the reserve from the face amount of the receivables transferred conforms to the reality of the transaction, as the risk of noncollection was on the transferee. Since the reserve for purposes of this case was deemed to be reasonable and the value of the stock received upon the transfer was equal to the *net value* of the receivables, there does not seem to us to have been any "recovery." A tax benefit was received by the partnership when the bad debt reserve was originally taken as a deduction from income. There would be a double benefit to the partnership if securities were issued covering the face amount of the receivables. We do not, however, understand how there can be a "recovery" of the benefit of the bad debt reserve when the receivables are transferred less the reserve.[5] That merely perpetuates the status quo and does not tinker with it for any double benefit out of the bad debt reserve.

For these reasons, the Court of Appeals in the *Schmidt* case held that although the "need" for the reserve ended with the transfer, the end of that need did not mark a "recovery" within the meaning of the tax benefit cases, 355 F.2d, at 113. We agree and accordingly reverse the judgment below.

Reversed.

Mr. Justice BLACK and Mr. Justice STEWART, dissenting.

We agree with the reasoning of Judge Tuttle's opinion for the Court of Appeals in this case, 414 F.2d 627, and with Judge Raum's opinion for the Tax Court in Schuster v. Commissioner, 50 T.C. 98. Accordingly, we would affirm the judgment.

NOTE

How do the transferee corporations in *Nash* determine the basis of each of the accounts receivable which they acquired in the §351 transaction? The transferors in *Nash* maintained a bad debt reserve (§166(c)). May any or all of the transferee corporations charge off their bad debts as incurred (§166(a)), or must they each carry over an aliquot portion of the transferors' reserve? How should the basis of the stock received by the transferors in the §351 transaction in *Nash* reflect the accounts receivable which they transferred to the corporations? Should Justice Douglas' opinion have dealt with any of these questions? See L. Raskind, The Tax Treatment of the Reserve for Bad Debts on Incorporation: The Supreme Court Resolution in *Nash,* 31 Ohio St. L.J. 411 (1970).

---

[4]As stated in Geyer, Cornell & Newell, Inc. v. Commissioner, 6 T.C. 96, 100: "A reserve consists of entries upon books of account. It is neither an asset nor a liability. It has no existence except upon the books, and, unlike an asset or a liability, it can not be transferred to any other entity."

[5]". . . the infirmities in the accounts receivable which justify the bad debt reserve carry over to those accounts in the hands of the corporation. Presumably the amount that will ultimately be collected by the corporation will not be the gross amount of the receivables, but rather the net amount after deducting the bad debt reserve. Thus, the stock received in exchange for such accounts receivable can only be worth what the receivables themselves are worth, namely, the net collectable amount rather than the gross amount." Arent, Reallocation of Income and Expenses in Connection with Formation and Liquidation of Corporations, 40 Taxes 995, 998 (1962).

REVENUE RULING 56-256
1956-1 Cum. Bull. 129

Taxpayer, an individual, constructed a building and purchased equipment in 1954 upon which depreciation was computed on the declining balance method as prescribed in section 167(b)(2) of the Internal Revenue Code of 1954. In 1955, the taxpayer transferred the building and equipment to a newly formed corporation in a nontaxable exchange. Held, since the new corporation is a taxable entity separate from that of the individual taxpayer, it follows that the new corporation acquired property, the original use of which did not commence with it as required under section 167(c)(2) of the Code. Accordingly, under the limitations imposed by section 167(c) of the Code, the new corporation may not continue the use of the declining balance method of computing depreciation provided for in section 167(b)(2) of the Code; nor may it use the methods and rates of computing depreciation provided for in section 167(b)(3) of the Code, relating to the sum of the years-digits method, and section 167(b)(4) of the Code, relating to certain other consistent methods, with respect to the property. Depreciation on the building and equipment acquired by the corporation may be computed by using the straight line method or any other method, exclusive of those provided for in paragraphs (2), (3) and (4) of section 167(b) of the Code, which will, based upon existing operating conditions, produce a reasonable allowance therefor within the purview of section 167 of the Code. The above principle is equally applicable in cases where depreciable property is similarly transferred between other separate tax entities. However, see sections 381(a) and 381(c)(6) of the Code, relative to certain acquisitions of assets of a corporation by another corporation; and section 1.1502-46 of the Income Tax Regulations, relative to property received by a member of an affiliated group from another member of the group during a consolidated return period.

NOTE

In Rev. Rul. 67-286, 1967-2 Cum. Bull. 101, the Service reaffirmed the position announced in Rev. Rul. 56-256. In Rev. Rul. 67-286, however, the Service also held that "for purposes of section 167(c). . . , the useful life of an asset with an estimated useful life of three years or more to the taxpayer [a sole proprietor] at the time of acquisition will not be redetermined merely because the taxpayer [within three years of acquisition] incorporated the . . . business in which the asset was used [under §351]." As a result, the proprietor's election to use one of the depreciation methods permitted by §167(b)(2), (3), or (4) for the less-than-three-year period prior to incorporation was not disturbed.

VI. FOREIGN CORPORATIONS — §§367, 1491, 1492

REVENUE RULING 67-192
1967-2 Cum. Bull. 140

Advice has been requested as to the extent to which gain will be recognized on the transfer of property by a domestic corporation to its wholly owned foreign subsidiary under the circumstances presented below.

X, a domestic corporation, transferred an automobile and a piece of machinery used in its business and 1000 shares of stock of foreign corporation Y to Z, a wholly owned foreign subsidiary operating a business in Canada in exchange for additional Z stock. The automobile had a market value in excess of its adjusted basis for Federal income tax purposes, but the value of the machinery was less than its adjusted basis. The shares of Y had been purchased by X on several occasions. As a result, X's basis in some of the Y stock was greater than the fair market value of the Y stock, and X's basis in the remainder of the Y stock was less than its fair market value. Prior to the exchange, X had not, pursuant to section 367 of the Internal Revenue Code of 1954, established to the satisfaction of the Commissioner that the exchange was not in pursuance of a plan having as one of its principal purposes the avoidance of Federal income taxes.

Under section 351 of the Code no gain or loss is recognized if property is transferred to a corporation in exchange for its stock if immediately after the exchange the transferor is in control of the corporation.

Under section 367 of the Code, however, the nonrecognition provisions of section 351 of the Code are not applicable to the gains where a taxpayer has not established to the satisfaction of the Commissioner that the exchange was not in pursuance of a plan having as one of its principal purposes the avoidance of Federal income tax. Consequently, the realized gain on the transfer of the property from X to Z is recognized.

In determining the amount of gain to be recognized, each item of property transferred is considered to have been separately exchanged. See Aaron F. Williams v. McGowan, 152 F.2d 570 (1945) and United States Holding Co., 44 T.C. 323 (1965), acquiescence I.R.B. 1966-46, 5. The principle has been adopted in analogous cases decided under the predecessor of section 367 of the Code dealing with the nonrecognition of loss in the case of a sale between related parties. See, e.g., Morris Investment Corporation v. Commissioner, 156 F.2d 748 (1946), certiorari denied, 329 U.S. 788 (1946) where the separate sale or exchange principle was applied to a transaction involving shares of stock in the same corporation upon which both gain and loss were realized.

Accordingly, in determining the amount of gain recognized, each item of property transferred in the above-described transaction is to be treated as the subject of a separate exchange. Thus, the realized gain on the transfer of the automobile and the appreciated shares of Y stock is to be recognized without regard to section 351 of the Code.

Since section 367 of the Code applies only to those transactions upon which gain is realized, the loss realized on the exchange of those shares of Y stock which have a basis greater than their fair market value and the loss realized on the exchange of machinery will not be recognized under the provisions of section 351 of the Code.

NOTE

Legislation approved by the President on January 12, 1971, amended §367 to provide that in the case of transfers made after December 31, 1970, an advance ruling must be obtained to gain tax-free treatment of a capital contribution to a controlled foreign corporation, even though no stock is received for the contribution. Interpreting §367 prior to this amendment, the Second Circuit held to the contrary. Abegg v. Commissioner, 429 F.2d 1209 (2d Cir. 1970), cert. denied sub nom. Cresta Corp., 400 U.S. 1008 (1971), page 726 infra.

REVENUE PROCEDURE 68-23
1968-1 Cum. Bull. 821

Section 1. Purpose.

The purpose of this Revenue Procedure is to set forth guidelines for taxpayers and their representatives in connection with requests for advance rulings required under section 367 of the Internal Revenue Code of 1954 in respect of certain types of transactions involving foreign corporations. . . .

Sec. 3. Transactions Which Ordinarily Receive Favorable Consideration under Section 367 of the Code. . . .

.02 Section 351 of the Code. Transfer to foreign corporation controlled by transferor.

(1) Where property is transferred to a foreign corporation and such property is to be devoted by the transferee foreign corporation to the active conduct, in any foreign country, of a trade or business or is property described in the exception stated in Sec. 3.02(a)(iii) below. It is contemplated that the transferee foreign corporation, in addition to the active conduct of a trade or business, will have need for a substantial investment in fixed assets in such business or will be engaged in the purchase and sale abroad of manufactured goods.

(a) However, a favorable ruling under section 367 of the Code will not be issued for an exchange described in section 351 of the Code where the property to be transferred to the foreign corporation is one of the following kinds of property:

(i) Property described in section 1221(1) of the Code (relating to inventory or other property held for sale to customers) or section 1221(3) of the Code (relating to copyrights, etc.);

(ii) Property, such as accounts receivable or installment obligations, in respect of which income has been earned, unless the income attributable to such property has been or will be included in the gross income of the transferor for Federal income tax purposes;

(iii) Stock or securities, except that a favorable ruling under section 367 of the Code may be issued with respect to the following:

(A) Stock or securities of less developed country corporations described in section 955(c)(1) of the Code to be transferred to a controlled foreign corporation (as defined in section 957(a) of the Code) which immediately after the exchange will be a less developed country corporation holding company described in section 902(d)(2) of the Code without regard to the holding period referred to in section 1.902-4(a)(2)(i) of the regulations. This exception shall apply only on the condition that these requirements which must be met immediately after the exchange will continue to be met in the reasonably foreseeable future.

(B) Stock of a foreign corporation which immediately after the exchange is (1) controlled (within the meaning of section 368(c) of the Code) by the transferee foreign corporation and (2) meets the requirements of subsection 954(c)(4)(A)(i) and (ii) of the Code and the transferee foreign corporation is controlled (within the meaning of section 954(d)(3) of the Code) by a person or persons who immediately prior to such exchange controlled the foreign corporation whose stock is transferred. This exception shall apply only on the condition that these requirements which must be met immediately after the exchange will continue to be met in the reasonably foreseeable future.

(iv) Property to be transferred under circumstances which make it reasonable to believe that its sale or other disposition by the transferee foreign corporation is one of the principal purposes of its transfer.

(b) In addition, a favorable ruling under section 367 of the Code generally will not be issued for an exchange described in section 351 of the Code where the property to be transferred to the foreign corporation is one of the following kinds of property:

(i) Property in respect of which the transferor is a lessor or licensor at the time of transfer. The preceding clause shall not apply to property in respect of which the transferee foreign corporation is the lessee or licensee.

(ii) Property to be transferred under circumstances which make it reasonable to believe that the property transferred will be licensed or leased by the transferee foreign corporation after such transfer.

(iii) United States patents, trade-marks and similar intangibles to be used in connection with (1) conduct of a trade or business in the United States or (2) the manufacture in the United States or a foreign country of goods for sale or consumption in the United States.

(iv) Foreign patents, trade-marks and similar intangibles to be used in connection with the sale of goods manufactured in the United States.

(c) The following examples illustrate the applications of Sec. 3.02(1)(b)(iii) and Sec. 3.02(1)(b)(iv) above:

(i) X, a domestic corporation, produces a product in the United States which it sells to unrelated parties in the United States and abroad for a stated price per unit without X's trademark affixed and for a higher price per unit with X's trademark affixed. X organizes foreign corporation Y to sell the product to parties to which X had previously sold the product with X's trademark affixed and X proposes to transfer its United States and foreign trademark to Y in a transaction described in section 351 of the Code. Irrespective of the extent of or absence of any price differential, a favorable ruling under section 367 of the Code will be denied in respect of such a transfer since the principal purpose for the transfer will be considered to be the avoidance of Federal income taxes by means of the purchase and resale by Y of a product produced in the United States.

(ii) Assume the same facts as in example (i) except that X organizes foreign corporation Y to manufacture and sell the product either directly to United States consumers or to X for resale to United States consumers. Irrespective of the extent of or absence of any price differential, a favorable ruling under section 367 of the Code will be denied in respect of a transfer by X of the United States trademark to Y in a transaction described in section 351 of the Code because the principal purpose for the transfer will be considered to be the avoidance of Federal income taxes by means of the manufacture by Y of a product for sale or consumption in the United States.

(d) Where property described in Sec. 3.02(1)(a)(i) through Sec. 3.02(1)(a)(iv) and Sec. 3.02(1)(b)(i) through Sec. 3.02(1)(b)(iv) above (or other property which would not be accorded a favorable ruling under this subsection) is to be transferred to a foreign corporation in an exchange described in section 351 of the Code, and other property which is to be devoted by the transferee foreign corporation to the active conduct, in any foreign country, of a trade or business (it is contemplated that the transferee foreign corporation will have need for a substantial investment in fixed assets in such business or will be engaged in the purchase and sale abroad of manufactured goods), or is property described in the exception stated in Sec. 3.02(1)(a)(iii) above, also is to be transferred to such foreign corporation, a favorable ruling will be issued only upon the condition that the transferor agrees to include in its gross income for its taxable year in which the transfer occurs an appropriate amount to reflect realization of income or gain in respect of those transferred assets the transfer of which would not be accorded a favorable ruling under this subsection. If gain or income is required to be taken into gross income under this paragraph, the character of the income or gain shall be determined, and adjustments in basis made, as though the assets transferred by the United States transferor were acquired by the transferee foreign corporation in a taxable exchange.

(2) Where property is transferred from one foreign corporation to another foreign corporation. However, if stock of a foreign corporation is part of the property transferred see Sec. 5.02 below. . . .

Sec. 5. Other Principles and Requirements.

.01 If a proposed transaction is not carried out in accordance with a plan submitted in respect of which a favorable ruling is issued by the Service under section 367 of the Code, such favorable ruling will not make the transaction tax free. See section 1.367-1 of the regulations. If a change in plans is proposed the taxpayer may apply for a supplemental ruling that the change has no effect upon the original ruling and it remains in full force and effect.

.02 In cases in which a favorable ruling is issued under section 367 of the Code, appropriate adjustments to bases, earnings and profits, carryovers, and carrybacks, and other similar adjustments may be required. In addition, in appropriate cases not specifically mentioned in the guidelines but involving an exchange of stock of a foreign corporation within the ambit of section 367, the shareholders participating in such exchange may be required to include in their gross income, as a dividend deemed paid in money for their taxable year in which such exchange occurs, the portion of the earnings and profits, if any, of the foreign corporation properly attributable under section 1248 of the Code to such shareholders' stock in such foreign corporation which would have been includible in their gross income under section 1248 of the Code if at the time of such exchange the stock of such foreign corporation was exchanged in a taxable transaction. The preceding sentence is intended to insure that the tax under section 1248 of the Code will be imposed in any case in which failure to impose such tax may result in the permanent avoidance of such section 1248 tax in respect of post-1962 earnings and profits of a foreign corporation. . . .

NOTE

1. Clearance under §367 *in advance* of a proposed §351 transaction is mandatory if there is to be nonrecognition of gain to the transferor. Cf. Texas-Canadian Oil Corp., Ltd., 44 B.T.A. 913 (1941). Administrative procedures for protesting an adverse determination under §367 by the Director of the I.R.S. Income Tax Division are set forth in Rev. Proc. 69-12, 1969-1 Cum. Bull. 401. For a thoroughgoing analysis of the reviewability of the Commissioner's actions (and non-actions) under §367, see Note, The Availability and Reviewability of Rulings of the Internal Revenue Service, 113 U. Pa. L. Rev. 81 (1964).

2. Section 1491 has produced little revenue and little litigation. Recent stirrings are suggested, however, by Rev. Rul. 69-450, 1969-2 Cum. Bull. 168, and Rev. Rul. 70-111, 1970-1 Cum. Bull. 185.

3. See Note, page 741 infra.

4 | Reorganizations and Related Adjustments of Investor Interest

I. INTRODUCTION AND HISTORY

As a general rule, gain (or loss) is realized when an asset worth more (or less) than its adjusted basis is exchanged for another asset. In an arm's length transaction one would expect the asset received to be equal in value to the one surrendered, and the measure of the gain or loss realized would be the difference between the value of the asset received and the adjusted basis of the asset surrendered. See §1001(a) and (b); United States v. Davis, 370 U.S. 65 (1962).

Unless the Code provides otherwise, all realized gain or loss is recognized in the computation of a taxpayer's income. See §§1001(c) and 1002. In many cases, however, Congress has provided for nonrecognition, usually because the exchange has not produced an economically significant change in the nature of the taxpayer's investment or has not brought him close enough to cash or consumable goods to justify taxation in light of the pervasive doctrine which generally prohibits taxation of "unrealized" appreciation.

If a taxpayer buys a share of General Motors common stock at $50, the doctrine of unrealized appreciation prevents taxation of his "gain" even when the stock is worth $75 and the cash can be realized with a telephone call to a broker. If, pursuant to a "stock split" or a plan of recapitalization, the taxpayer exchanges his single share of General Motors common for two shares of General Motors common, each worth $37.50, his realized gain is not recognized. Section 1036(a); §§368(a)(1)(E) and 354(a)(1). But if the taxpayer instead exchanges his stock for his neighbor's Ford Motor common stock worth $75, his $25 gain is realized and recognized. If the exchange of General Motors stock for Ford Motor stock is not a privately arranged exchange between neighbors but is effected directly with Ford Motor Company as a result of a statutory merger of General Motors Company into Ford, the gain is not recognized. Sections 368(a)(1)(A) and 354(a)(1). If the plan of merger results in the taxpayer's receiving Ford stock worth $60 and cash of $15 (or a $15 Ford bond), $15 of the gain is recognized. Sections 354(a)(2), 356(a). The recognized gain may be taxable as a dividend (§356(a)(2)), although a sale to (or exchange with) the neighbor probably would produce capital gain. Transactions like these and the complex tax problems they present to corporations and their investors are the subject of this chapter.

Parts II and III of this chapter deal with stock dividends and recapitalizations, transactions in which the corporate investor's interest in his corporation is reclassified or represented in a new form. The receipt of a new stock certificate (or a bond) in addition to, or in exchange for, the investor's old certificate usually triggers the recognition problem.

For the most part, the remainder of the chapter deals with reorganizations involving more than one corporation: amalgamating reorganizations (mergers and consolidations), divisive reorganizations (spin-offs, split-offs, and split-ups), and corporate substitutions (one corporation replacing another). These types of reorganizations raise questions of recognition and basis adjustment for both the investors and one or more of the corporations involved. Ordinarily, stock dividends and recapitalizations (involving a single corporation) raise such questions only for the investor.

In Part VIII, this chapter presents issues involving the carryover of tax attributes from one corporation to another, particularly earnings and profits and net operating losses. Usually, but not always, the carryover problems will grow out of a reorganization.

Finally, as in Chapter 3, there is reference to the special problems posed when one or more of the corporations in reorganization is a foreign corporation. The income taxation of foreign corporations warrants a detailed, specialized treatment outside the scope of this book. See, e.g., B. Bittker and L. Ebb, United States Taxation of Foreign Income and Foreign Persons (2d ed. 1968); S. Roberts and W. Warren, United States Income Taxation of Foreign Corporations and Nonresident Aliens (1966).

II. STOCK DIVIDENDS — RECEIPT AND DISPOSITION

A. *TAXABILITY OF RECEIPT — HISTORY*

EISNER v. MACOMBER
252 U.S. 189 (1920)

Mr. Justice PITNEY delivered the opinion of the court. This case presents the question whether, by virtue of the Sixteenth Amendment, Congress has the power to tax, as income of the stockholder and without apportionment, a stock dividend made lawfully and in good faith against profits accumulated by the corporation since March 1, 1913.

It arises under the Revenue Act of September 8, 1916, c. 463, 39 Stat. 756, et seq., which, in our opinion . . . plainly evinces the purpose of Congress to tax stock dividends as income.[1]

---

[1]TITLE I. — INCOME TAX. Part I. — on individuals.
Sec. 2(a) That, subject only to such exemptions and deductions as are hereinafter allowed,

The facts, in outline, are as follows:

On January 1, 1916, the Standard Oil Company of California, a corporation of that State, out of an authorized capital stock of $100,000,000, had shares of stock outstanding, par value $100 each, amounting in round figures to $50,000,000. In addition, it had surplus and undivided profits invested in plant, property, and business and required for the purposes of the corporation, amounting to about $45,000,000, of which about $20,000,000 had been earned prior to March 1, 1913, the balance thereafter. In January, 1916, in order to readjust the capitalization, the board of directors decided to issue additional shares sufficient to constitute a stock dividend of 50 per cent. of the outstanding stock, and to transfer from surplus account to capital stock account an amount equivalent to such issue. Appropriate resolutions were adopted, an amount equivalent to the par value of the proposed new stock was transferred accordingly, and the new stock duly issued against it and divided among the stockholders.

Defendant in error, being the owner of 2,200 shares of the old stock, received certificates for 1,100 additional shares, of which 18.07 per cent., or 198.77 shares, par value $19,877, were treated as representing surplus earned between March 1, 1913, and January 1, 1916. She was called upon to pay, and did pay under protest, a tax imposed under the Revenue Act of 1916, based upon a supposed income of $19,877 because of the new shares; and an appeal to the Commissioner of Internal Revenue having been disallowed, she brought action against the Collector to recover the tax. In her complaint she alleged the above facts, and contended that in imposing such a tax the Revenue Act of 1916 violated Art. I, §2, cl. 3, and Art. I, §9, cl. 4, of the Constitution of the United States, requiring direct taxes to be apportioned according to population, and that the stock dividend was not income within the meaning of the Sixteenth Amendment. A general demurrer to the complaint was overruled upon the authority of Towne v. Eisner, 245 U.S. 418; and, defendant having failed to plead further, final judgment went against him. To review it, the present writ of error is prosecuted.

The case was argued at the last term, and reargued at the present term, both orally and by additional briefs.

We are constrained to hold that the judgment of the District Court must be affirmed: First, because the question at issue is controlled by Towne v. Eisner, supra; secondly, because a re-examination of the question, with the additional light thrown upon it by elaborate arguments, has confirmed the view that the underlying ground of that decision is sound, that it disposes of the question here presented, and that other fundamental considerations lead to the same result.

In Towne v. Eisner, the question was whether a stock dividend made in 1914

---

the net income of a taxable person shall include gains, profits, and income derived . . . , also from interest, rent, dividends, securities, or the transaction of any business carried on for gain or profit, or gains or profits and income derived from any source whatever: *Provided,* That the term "dividends" as used in this title shall be held to mean any distribution made or ordered to be made by a corporation, . . . out of its earnings or profits accrued since March first, nineteen hundred and thirteen, and payable to its shareholders, whether in cash or in stock of the corporation, . . . which stock dividend shall be considered income, to the amount of its cash value.

against surplus earned prior to January 1, 1913, was taxable against the stockholder under the Act of October 3, 1913, c. 16, 38 Stat. 114, 166, which provided (§B, p. 167) that net income should include "dividends," and also "gains or profits and income derived from any source whatever." Suit having been brought by a stockholder to recover the tax assessed against him by reason of the dividend, the District Court sustained a demurrer to the complaint. 242 Fed. Rep. 702. The court treated the construction of the act as inseparable from the interpretation of the Sixteenth Amendment; and, having referred to Pollock v. Farmers' Loan & Trust Co., 158 U.S. 601, and quoted the Amendment, proceeded very properly to say (p. 704): "It is manifest that the stock dividend in question cannot be reached by the Income Tax Act, and could not, even though Congress expressly declared it to be taxable as income, unless it is in fact income." It declined, however, to accede to the contention that in Gibbons v. Mahon, 136 U.S. 549, "stock dividends" had received a definition sufficiently clear to be controlling, treated the language of this court in that case as obiter dictum in respect of the matter then before it (p. 706), and examined the question as res nova, with the result stated. When the case came here, after overruling a motion to dismiss made by the Government upon the ground that the only question involved was the construction of the statute and not its constitutionality, we dealt upon the merits with the question of construction only, but disposed of it upon consideration of the essential nature of a stock dividend, disregarding the fact that the one in question was based upon surplus earnings that accrued before the Sixteenth Amendment took effect. Not only so, but we rejected the reasoning of the District Court, saying (245 U.S. 426): "Notwithstanding the thoughtful discussion that the case received below we cannot doubt that the dividend was capital as well for the purposes of the Income Tax Law as for distribution between tenant for life and remainderman. What was said by this court upon the latter question is equally true for the former. 'A stock dividend really takes nothing from the property of the corporation, and adds nothing to the interests of the shareholders. Its property is not diminished, and their interests are not increased. . . . The proportional interest of each shareholder remains the same. The only change is in the evidence which represents that interest, the new shares and the original shares together representing the same proportional interest that the original shares represented before the issue of the new ones.' Gibbons v. Mahon, 136 U.S. 549, 559, 560. In short, the corporation is no poorer and the stockholder is no richer than they were before. Logan County v. United States, 169 U.S. 255, 261. If the plaintiff gained any small advantage by the change, it certainly was not an advantage of $417,450, the sum upon which he was taxed. . . . What has happened is that the plaintiff's old certificates have been split up in effect and have diminished in value to the extent of the value of the new."

This language aptly answered not only the reasoning of the District Court but the argument of the Solicitor General in this court, which discussed the essential nature of a stock dividend. And if, for the reasons thus expressed, such a dividend is not to be regarded as "income" or "dividends" within the meaning of the Act of 1913, we are unable to see how it can be brought within the meaning of "incomes" in the Sixteenth Amendment; it being very clear that Congress intended in that act to exert its power to the extent permitted by the Amendment. In Towne v. Eisner it was not contended that any construction of the statute could make it narrower than the constitutional grant; rather the contrary.

The fact that the dividend was charged against profits earned before the Act of 1913 took effect, even before the Amendment was adopted, was neither relied upon nor alluded to in our consideration of the merits in that case. Not only so, but had we considered that a stock dividend constituted income in any true sense, it would have been held taxable under the Act of 1913 notwithstanding it was based upon profits earned before the Amendment. We ruled at the same term, in Lynch v. Hornby, 247 U.S. 339, that a cash dividend extraordinary in amount, and in Peabody v. Eisner, 247 U.S. 347, that a dividend paid in stock of another company, were taxable as income although based upon earnings that accrued before adoption of the Amendment. . . .

Therefore, Towne v. Eisner cannot be regarded as turning upon the point that the surplus accrued to the company before the act took effect and before adoption of the Amendment. And what we have quoted from the opinion in that case cannot be regarded as obiter dictum, it having furnished the entire basis for the conclusion reached. We adhere to the view then expressed, and might rest the present case there; not because that case in terms decided the constitutional question, for it did not; but because the conclusion there reached as to the essential nature of a stock dividend necessarily prevents its being regarded as income in any true sense.

Nevertheless, in view of the importance of the matter, and the fact that Congress in the Revenue Act of 1916 declared (39 Stat. 757) that a "stock dividend shall be considered income, to the amount of its cash value," we will deal at length with the constitutional question, incidentally testing the soundness of our previous conclusion.

The Sixteenth Amendment must be construed in connection with the taxing clauses of the original Constitution and the effect attributed to them before the Amendment was adopted. In Pollock v. Farmers' Loan & Trust Co., 158 U.S. 601, under the Act of August 27, 1894, c. 349, §27, 28 Stat. 509, 553, it was held that taxes upon rents and profits of real estate and upon returns from investments of personal property were in effect direct taxes upon the property from which such income arose, imposed by reason of ownership; and that Congress could not impose such taxes without apportioning them among the States according to population, as required by Art. I, §2, cl. 3, and §9, cl. 4, of the original Constitution.

Aferwards, and evidently in recognition of the limitation upon the taxing power of Congress thus determined, the Sixteenth Amendment was adopted, in words lucidly expressing the object to be accomplished: "The Congress shall have power to lay and collect taxes on incomes, from whatever source derived, without apportionment among the several States, and without regard to any census or enumeration." As repeatedly held, this did not extend the taxing power to new subjects, but merely removed the necessity which otherwise might exist for an apportionment among the States of taxes laid on income. Brushaber v. Union Pacific R.R. Co., 240 U.S. 1, 17-19; Stanton v. Baltic Mining Co., 240 U.S. 103, 112 et seq.; Peck & Co. v. Lowe, 247 U.S. 165, 172-173.

A proper regard for its genesis, as well as its very clear language, requires also that this Amendment shall not be extended by loose construction, so as to repeal or modify, except as applied to income, those provisions of the Constitution that require an apportionment according to population for direct taxes upon property, real and personal. This limitation still has an appropriate and important function, and is not to be overridden by Congress or disregarded by the courts.

In order, therefore, that the clauses cited from Article I of the Constitution may have proper force and effect, save only as modified by the Amendment, and that the latter also may have proper effect, it becomes essential to distinguish between what is and what is not "income," as the term is there used; and to apply the distinction, as cases arise, according to truth and substance, without regard to form. Congress cannot by any definition it may adopt conclude the matter, since it cannot by legislation alter the Constitution, from which alone it derives its power to legislate, and within whose limitations alone that power can be lawfully exercised.

The fundamental relation of "capital" to "income" has been much discussed by economists, the former being likened to the tree or the land, the latter to the fruit or the crop; the former depicted as a reservoir supplied from springs, the latter as the outlet stream, to be measured by its flow during a period of time. For the present purpose we require only a clear definition of the term "income," as used in common speech, in order to determine its meaning in the Amendment; and, having formed also a correct judgment as to the nature of a stock dividend, we shall find it easy to decide the matter at issue.

After examining dictionaries in common use . . . , we find little to add to the succinct definition adopted in two cases arising under the Corporation Tax Act of 1909 (Stratton's Independence v. Howbert, 231 U.S. 399, 415; Doyle v. Mitchell Bros. Co., 247 U.S. 179, 185) — "Income may be defined as the gain derived from capital, from labor, or from both combined," provided it be understood to include profit gained through a sale or conversion of capital assets, to which it was applied in the *Doyle* Case (pp. 183, 185).

Brief as it is, it indicates the characteristic and distinguishing attribute of income essential for a correct solution of the present controversy. The Government, although basing its argument upon the definition as quoted, placed chief emphasis upon the world "gain," which was extended to include a variety of meanings; while the significance of the next three words was either overlooked or misconceived. *"Derived — from — capital"; —* "the *gain — derived — from — capital,"* etc. Here we have the essential matter: *not* a gain *accruing to* capital, not a *growth* or *increment* of value *in* the investment; but a gain, a profit, something of exchangeable value *proceeding from* the property, *severed from* the capital however invested or employed, and *coming in,* being *"derived,"* that is, *received* or *drawn by* the recipient (the taxpayer) for his *separate* use, benefit and disposal; — *that* is income derived from property. Nothing else answers the description.

The same fundamental conception is clearly set forth in the Sixteenth Amendment — "incomes, *from* whatever *source derived"* — the essential thought being expressed with a conciseness and lucidity entirely in harmony with the form and style of the Constitution.

Can a stock dividend, considering its essential character, be brought within the definition? To answer this, regard must be had to the nature of a corporation and the stockholder's relation to it. We refer, of course, to a corporation such as the one in the case at bar, organized for profit, and having a capital stock divided into shares to which a nominal or par value is attributed.

Certainly the interest of the stockholder is a capital interest, and his certificates of stock are but the evidence of it. They state the number of shares to which he is entitled and indicate their par value and how the stock may be transferred. They show that he or his assignors, immediate or remote, have contributed capital to the enterprise, that he is entitled to a corresponding interest proportionate to the whole, entitled to have the property and business of the company devoted during the corporate existence to attainment of the common objects, entitled to vote at stockholders' meetings, to receive dividends out of the corporation's profits if and when declared, and, in the event of liquidation, to receive a proportionate share of the net assets, if any, remaining after paying creditors. Short of liquidation, or until dividend declared, he has no right to withdraw any part of either capital or profits from the common enterprise; on the contrary, his interest pertains not to any part, divisible or indivisible, but to the entire assets, business, and affairs of the company. Nor is it the interest of an owner in the assets themselves, since the corporation has full title, legal and equitable, to the whole. . . . If he desires to dissociate himself from the company he can do so only by disposing of his stock.

. . . The dividend normally is payable in money, under exceptional circumstances in some other divisible property; and when so paid, then only (excluding, of course, a possible advantageous sale of his stock or winding-up of the company) does the stockholder realize a profit or gain which becomes his separate property, and thus derive income from the capital that he or his predecessor has invested.

In the present case, the corporation had surplus and undivided profits invested in plant, property, and business, and required for the purposes of the corporation, amounting to about $45,000,000, in addition to outstanding capital stock of $50,000,000. In this the case is not extraordinary. The profits of a corporation, as they appear upon the balance sheet at the end of the year, need not be in the form of money on hand in excess of what is required to meet current liabilities and finance current operations of the company. Often, especially in a growing business, only a part, sometimes a small part, of the year's profits is in property capable of division; the remainder having been absorbed in the acquisition of increased plant, equipment, stock in trade, or accounts receivable, or in decrease of outstanding liabilities. When only a part is available for dividends, the balance of the year's profits is carried to the credit of undivided profits, or surplus, or some other account having like significance. If thereafter the company finds itself in funds beyond current needs it may declare dividends out of such surplus or undivided profits; otherwise it may go on for years conducting a successful business, but requiring more and more working capital because of the extension of its operations, and therefore unable to declare dividends approximating the amount of its profits. Thus the surplus may increase until it equals or even exceeds the par value of the outstanding capital stock. This may be adjusted upon the books in the mode adopted in the case at bar — by declaring a "stock dividend." This, however, is no more than a book adjustment, in essence not a dividend but rather the opposite; no part of the assets of the company is separated from the common fund, nothing distributed except paper certificates that evidence an antecedent increase in the value of the stockholder's capital interest resulting from an accumulation of profits by the company, but profits so far absorbed in the business as to render it impracticable to separate them for withdrawal and distribution. In order to make the adjustment, a charge is made against surplus account with corresponding credit to capital stock account, equal to the proposed "dividend"; the new stock is issued against this and the certificates delivered to the existing stockholders in proportion to their previous holdings. This, however, is merely bookkeeping. . . .

A "stock dividend" shows that the company's accumulated profits have been capitalized, instead of distributed to the stockholders or retained as surplus available for distribution in money or in kind should opportunity offer. Far from being a realization of profits of the stockholder, it tends rather to postpone such realization, in that the fund represented by the new stock has been transferred from surplus to capital, and no longer is available for actual distribution.

The essential and controlling fact is that the stockholder has received nothing out of the company's assets for his separate use and benefit . . . . Having regard to the very truth of the matter, to substance and not to form, he has received nothing that answers the definition of income within the meaning of the Sixteenth Amendment. . . .

It is said that a stockholder may sell the new shares acquired in the stock dividend; and so he may, if he can find a buyer. It is equally true that if he does sell, and in doing so realizes a profit, such profit, like any other, is income, and so far as it may have arisen since the Sixteenth Amendment is taxable by Congress without apportionment. The same would be true were he to sell some of his original shares at a profit. But if a shareholder sells dividend stock he necessarily disposes of a part of his capital interest, just as if he should sell a part of his old stock, either before or after the dividend. . . . A corresponding and proportionate decrease in capital interest and in voting power would befall a minority holder should he sell dividend stock; it being in the nature of things impossible for one to dispose of any part of such an issue without a proportionate disturbance of the distribution of the entire capital stock, and a like diminution of the seller's comparative voting power — that "right preservative of rights" in the control of a corporation. Yet, without selling, the shareholder, unless possessed of other resources, has not the wherewithal to pay an income tax upon the dividend stock. . . .

We have no doubt of the power or duty of a court to look through the form of the corporation and determine the question of the stockholder's right, in order to ascertain whether he has received income taxable by Congress without apportionment. But, looking through the form, we cannot disregard the essential truth disclosed; ignore the substantial difference between corporation and stockholder; treat the entire organization as unreal; look upon stockholders as partners, when they are not such; treat them as having in equity a right to a partition of the corporate assets, when they have none; and indulge the fiction that they have received and realized a share of the profits of the company which in truth they have neither received nor realized. We must treat the corporation as a substantial entity separate from the stockholder, not only because such is the practical fact but because it is only by recognizing such separateness that any dividend — even one paid in money or property — can be regarded as income of the stockholder. Did we regard corporation and stockholders as altogether identical, there would be no income except as the corporation acquired it; and while this would be taxable against the corporation as income under appropriate provisions of law, the individual stockholders could not be separately and additionally taxed with respect to their several shares even when divided, since if there were entire identity between them and the company they could not be regarded as receiving anything from it, any more than if one's money were to be removed from one pocket to another.

Conceding that the mere issue of a stock dividend makes the recipient no richer than before, the Government nevertheless contends that the new certificates measure the extent to which the gains accumulated by the corporation have made him the richer. There are two insuperable difficulties with this: In the first place, it would depend upon how long he had held the stock whether the stock dividend indicated the extent to which he had been enriched by the operations of the company; unless he had held it throughout such operations the measure would not hold true. Secondly, and more important for present purposes, enrichment through increase in value of capital investment is not income in any proper meaning of the term.

The complaint contains averments respecting the market prices of stock such as plaintiff held, based upon sales before and after the stock dividend, tending to show that the receipt of the additional shares did not substantially change the market value of her entire holdings. This tends to show that in this instance market quotations reflected intrinsic values — a thing they do not always do. But we regard the market prices of the securities as an unsafe criterion in an inquiry such as the present, when the question must be, not what will the thing sell for, but what is it in truth and in essence.

It is said there is no difference in principle between a simple stock dividend and a case where stockholders use money received as cash dividends to purchase additional stock contemporaneously issued by the corporation. But an actual cash dividend, with a real option to the stockholder either to keep the money for his own or to reinvest it in new shares, would be as far removed as possible from a true stock dividend, such as the one we have under consideration, where nothing of value is taken from the company's assets and transferred to the individual ownership of the several stockholders and thereby subjected to their disposal.

The Government's reliance upon the supposed analogy between a dividend of the corporation's own shares and one made by distributing shares owned by it in the stock of another company, calls for no comment beyond the statement that the latter distributes assets of the company among the shareholders while the former does not; and for no citation of authority except Peabody v. Eisner, 247 U.S. 347, 349-350. . . .

Upon the second argument, the Government, recognizing the force of the decision in Towne v. Eisner, supra, and virtually abandoning the contention that a stock dividend increases the interest of the stockholder or otherwise enriches him, insisted as an alternative that by the true construction of the Act of 1916 the tax is imposed not upon the stock dividend but rather upon the stockholder's share of the undivided profits previously accumulated by the corporation; the tax being levied as a matter of convenience at the time such profits become manifest through the stock dividend. If so construed, would the act be constitutional?

That Congress has power to tax shareholders upon their property interests in the stock of corporations is beyond question; and that such interests might be valued in view of the condition of the company, including its accumulated and undivided profits, is equally clear. But that this would be taxation of property because of ownership, and hence would require apportionment under the provisions of the Constitution, is settled beyond peradventure by previous decisions of this court.

The Government relies upon Collector v. Hubbard (1870), 12 Wall. 1, 17, which arose under §117 of the Act of June 30, 1864, c. 173, 13 Stat. 223, 282, providing that "the gains and profits of all companies, whether incorporated or partnership, other than the companies specified in this section, shall be included in estimating the annual gains, profits, or income of any person entitled to the same, whether divided or otherwise." The court held an individual taxable upon his proportion of the earnings of a corporation although not declared as dividends and although invested in assets not in their nature divisible. . . . In so far as this seems to uphold the right of Congress to tax without apportionment a stockholder's interest in accumulated earnings prior to dividend declared, it must be regarded as overruled by Pollock v. Farmers' Loan & Trust Co., 158 U.S. 601, 627, 628, 637. Conceding Collector v. Hubbard was inconsistent with the doctrine of that case, because it sustained a direct tax upon property not apportioned among the States, the Government nevertheless insists that the Sixteenth Amendment removed this obstacle, so that now the *Hubbard* Case is authority for the power of Congress to levy a tax on the stockholder's share in the accumulated profits of the corporation even before division by the declaration of a dividend of any kind. Manifestly this argument must be rejected, since the Amendment applies to income only, and what is called the stockholder's share in the accumulated profits of the company is capital, not income. As we have pointed out, a stockholder has no individual share in accumulated profits, nor in any particular part of the assets of the corporation, prior to dividend declared.

Thus, from every point of view, we are brought irresistibly to the conclusion that neither under the Sixteenth Amendment nor otherwise has Congress power to tax without apportionment a true stock dividend made lawfully and in good faith, or the accumulated profits behind it, as income of the stockholder. The Revenue Act of 1916, in so far as it imposes a tax upon the stockholder because of such dividend, contravenes the provisions of Article I, §2, cl. 3, and Article I, §9, cl. 4, of the Constitution, and to this extent is invalid notwithstanding the Sixteenth Amendment.

Judgment affirmed.

Mr. Justice HOLMES, dissenting. I think that Towne v. Eisner, 245 U.S. 418, was right in its reasoning and result and that on sound principles the stock dividend was not income. But it was clearly intimated in that case that the construction of the statute then before the Court might be different from that of the Constitution. 245 U.S. 425. I think that the word "incomes" in the Sixteenth Amendment should be read in "a sense most obvious to the common understanding at the time of its adoption." . . . For it was for public adoption that it was proposed. McCulloch v. Maryland, 4 Wheat. 316, 407. The known purpose of this Amendment was to get rid of nice questions as to what might be direct taxes, and I cannot doubt that most people not lawyers would suppose when they voted for it that they put a question like the present to rest. I am of opinion that the Amendment justifies the tax. See Tax Commissioner v. Putnam, 227 Massachusetts, 522, 532, 533.

Mr. Justice DAY concurs in this opinion.

Mr. Justice BRANDEIS, dissenting, delivered the following opinion, in which Mr. Justice CLARKE concurred. Financiers, with the aid of lawyers, devised long ago two different methods by which a corporation can, without increasing its indebtedness, keep for corporate purposes accumulated profits, and yet, in effect, distribute these profits among its stockholders. One method is a simple one. The capital stock is increased; the new stock is paid up with the accumulated profits; and the new shares of paid-up stock are then distributed among the stockholders pro rata as a dividend. If the stockholder prefers ready money to increasing his holding of the stock in the company, he sells the new stock received as a dividend. The other method is slightly more complicated. Arrangements are made for an increase of stock to be offered to stockholders pro rata at par and, at the same time, for the payment of a cash dividend equal to the amount which the stockholder will be required to pay to the company, if he avails himself of the right to subscribe for his pro rata of the new stock. If the stockholder takes the new stock, as is expected, he may endorse the dividend check received to the corporation and thus pay for the new stock. In order to ensure that all the new stock so offered will be taken, the price at which it is offered is fixed far below what it is believed will be its market value. If the stockholder prefers ready money to an increase of his holdings of stock, he may sell his right to take new stock pro rata, which is evidenced by an assignable instrument. In that event the purchaser of the rights repays to the corporation, as the subscription price of the new stock, an amount equal to that which it had paid as a cash dividend to the stockholder.

Both of these methods of retaining accumulated profits while in effect distributing them as a dividend had been in common use in the United States for many years prior to the adoption of the Sixteenth Amendment. They were recognized equivalents. Whether a particular corporation employed one or the other method was determined sometimes by requirements of the law under which the corporation was organized; sometimes it was determined by preferences of the individual officials of the corporation; and sometimes by stock market conditions. Whichever method was employed the resultant distribution of the new stock was commonly referred to as a stock dividend. . . .

. . . [T]he financial results to the corporation and to the stockholders of the two methods are substantially the same — unless a difference results from the application of the federal income tax law. . . .

It is conceded that if the stock dividend paid to Mrs. Macomber had been made by the more complicated method . . . , that is, issuing rights to take new stock pro rata and paying to each stockholder simultaneously a dividend in cash sufficient in amount to enable him to pay for this pro rata of new stock to be purchased — the dividend so paid to him would have been taxable as income, whether he retained the cash or whether he returned it to the corporation in payment for his pro rata of new stock. But it is contended that, because the simple method was adopted of having the new stock issued direct to the stockholders as paid-up stock, the new stock is not to be deemed income, whether she retained it or converted it into cash by sale. If such a different result can flow merely from the difference in the method pursued, it must be because Congress is without power to tax as income of the stockholder either the stock received under the latter method or the proceeds of its sale; for Congress has, by the provisions in the Revenue Act of 1916, expressly declared its purpose to make stock dividends, by whichever method paid, taxable as income. . . .

The Revenue Act of September 8, 1916, c. 463, 39 Stat. 756, 757, provided:

"That the term 'dividends' as used in this title shall be held to mean any distribution made or ordered to be made by a corporation, . . . out of its earnings or profits accrued since March first, nineteen hundred and thirteen, and payable to its shareholders, whether in cash or in stock of the corporation . . . which stock dividend shall be considered income, to the amount of its cash value."

Hitherto powers conferred upon Congress by the Constitution have been liberally construed, and have been held to extend to every means appropriate to attain the end sought. In determining the scope of the power the substance of the transaction, not its form has been regarded. . . . Is there anything in the phraseology of the Sixteenth Amendment or in the nature of corporate dividends which should lead to a departure from these rules of construction and compel this court to hold, that Congress is powerless to prevent a result so extraordinary as that here contended for by the stockholder?

First: The term "income" when applied to the investment of the stockholder in a corporation, had, before the adoption of the Sixteenth Amendment, been commonly understood to mean the returns from time to time received by the stockholder from gains or earnings of the corporation. A dividend received by a stockholder from a corporation may be either in distribution of capital assets or in distribution of profits. Whether it is the one or the other is in no way affected by the medium in which it is paid, nor by the method or means through which the particular thing distributed as a dividend was procured. If the dividend is declared payable in cash, the money with which to pay it is ordinarily taken from surplus cash in the treasury. But (if there are profits legally available for distribution and the law under which the company was incorporated so permits) the company may raise the money by discounting negotiable paper; or by selling bonds, scrip or stock of another corporation then in the treasury; or by selling its own bonds, scrip or stock then in the treasury; or by selling its own bonds, scrip or stock issued expressly for that purpose. How the money shall be raised is wholly a matter of financial management. The manner in which it is raised in no way affects the question whether the dividend received by the stockholder is income or capital; nor can it conceivably affect the question whether it is taxable as income.

Likewise whether a dividend declared payable from profits shall be paid in cash or in some other medium is also wholly a matter of financial management. If some other medium is decided upon, it is also wholly a question of financial management whether the distribution shall be, for instance, in bonds, scrip or stock of another corporation or in issues of its own. . . . If a dividend paid in securities of that nature represents a distribution of profits Congress may, of course, tax it as income of the stockholder. Is the result different where the security distributed is common stock? . . .

Second: It has been said that a dividend payable in bonds or preferred stock created for the purpose of distributing profits may be income and taxable as such, but that the case is different where the distribution is in common stock created for that purpose. Various reasons are assigned for making this distinction. One is that the proportion of the stockholder's ownership to the aggregate number of the shares of the company is not changed by the distribution. But that is equally true where the dividend is paid in its bonds or in its preferred stock. Furthermore, neither maintenance nor change in the proportionate ownership of a stockholder in a corporation has any bearing upon the question here involved. Another reason assigned is that the value of the old stock held is reduced approximately by the value of the new stock received, so that the stockholder after receipt of the stock dividend has no more than he had before it was paid. That is equally true whether the dividend be paid in cash or in other property, for instance, bonds, scrip or preferred stock of the company. The payment from profits of a large cash dividend, and even a small one, customarily lowers the then market value of stock because the undivided property represented by each share has been correspondingly reduced. The argument which appears to be most strongly urged for the stockholders is, that when a stock dividend is made, no portion of the assets of the company is thereby segregated for the stockholder. But does the issue of new bonds or of preferred stock created for use as a dividend result in any segregation of assets for the stockholder? In each case he receives a piece of paper which entitles him to certain rights in the undivided property. Clearly segregation of assets in a physical sense is not an essential of income. The year's gains of a partner are taxable as income, although there, likewise, no segregation of his share in the gains from that of his partners is had.

The objection that there has been no segregation is presented also in another form. It is argued that until there is a segregation, the stockholder cannot know whether he has really received gains; since the gains may be invested in plant or merchandise or other property and perhaps be later lost. But is not this equally true of the share of a partner in the year's profits of the firm or, indeed, of the profits of the individual who is engaged in business alone? And is it not true, also, when dividends are paid in cash? The gains of a business, whether conducted by an individual, by a firm or by a corporation, are ordinarily reinvested in large part. Many a cash dividend honestly declared as a distribution of profits, proves later to have been paid out of capital, because errors in forecast prevent correct ascertainment of values. Until a business adventure has been completely liquidated, it can never be determined with certainty whether there have been profits unless the returns have at least exceeded the capital originally invested. Business men, dealing with the problem practically, fix necessarily periods and rules for determining whether there have been net profits — that is income or gains. They protect themselves from being seriously misled by adopting a system of depreciation charges and reserves. Then, they act upon their own determination, whether profits have been made. Congress in legislating has wisely adopted their practices as its own rules of action.

Third: The Government urges that it would have been within the power of Congress to have taxed as income of the stockholder his pro rata share of undistributed profits earned, even if no stock dividend representing it had been paid. Strong reasons may be assigned for such a view. See Collector v. Hubbard, 12 Wall. 1. The undivided share of a partner in the year's undistributed profits of his firm is taxable as income of the partner, although the share in the gain is not evidenced by any action taken by the firm. Why may not the stockholder's interest in the gains of the company? The law finds no difficulty in disregarding the corporate fiction whenever that is deemed necessary to attain a just result. . . . The stockholder's interest in the property of the corporation differs, not fundamentally but in form only, from the interest of a partner in the property of the firm. There is much authority for the proposition that, under our law, a partnership or joint stock company is just as distinct and palpable an entity in the idea of the law, as distinguished from the individuals composing it, as is a corporation. No reason appears, why Congress, in legislating under a grant of power so comprehensive as that authorizing the levy of an income tax, should be limited by the particular view of the relation of the stockholder to the corporation and its property which may, in the absence of legislation, have been taken by this court. But we have no occasion to decide the question whether Congress might have taxed to the stockholder his undivided share of the corporation's earnings. For Congress has in this act limited the income tax to that share of the stockholder in the earnings which is, in effect, distributed by means of the stock dividend paid. . . .

Sixth: If stock dividends representing profits are held exempt from taxation under the Sixteenth Amendment, the owners of the most successful businesses in America will, as the facts in this case illustrate, be able to escape taxation on a large part of what is actually their income. So far as their profits are represented by stock received as dividends they will pay these taxes not upon their income but only upon the income of their income. That such a result was intended by the people of the United States when adopting the Sixteenth Amendment is inconceivable. Our sole duty is to ascertain their intent as therein expressed. In terse, comprehensive language befitting the Constitution, they empowered Congress "to lay and collect taxes on incomes, from whatever source derived." They intended to include thereby everything which by reasonable understanding can fairly be regarded as income. That stock dividends representing profits are so regarded, not only by the plain people but by investors and financiers, and by most of the courts of the country, is shown, beyond peradventure, by their acts and by their utterances. It seems to me clear, therefore, that Congress possesses the power which it exercised to make dividends representing profits, taxable as income, whether the medium in which the dividend is paid be cash or stock, and that it may define, as it has done, what dividends representing profits shall be deemed income. It surely is not clear that the enactment exceeds the power granted by the Sixteenth Amendment. And, as this court has so often said, the high prerogative of declaring an act of Congress invalid, should never be exercised except in a clear case. "It is but a decent respect due to the wisdom, the integrity and the patriotism of the legislative body, by which any law is passed, to presume in favor of its validity, until its violation of the Constitution is proved beyond all reasonable doubt." Ogden v. Saunders, 12 Wheat. 213, 270.

Mr. Justice CLARKE concurs in this opinion.

HELVERING v. GOWRAN
302 U.S. 238 (1937), rev'g 87 F.2d 125 (7th Cir.)

Mr. Justice BRANDEIS delivered the opinion of the Court. The questions for decision concern the taxation as income of a dividend in preferred stock and the proceeds received on its sale.

On June 29, 1929, the Hamilton Manufacturing Company, a Wisconsin corporation, had outstanding preferred stock of the par value of $100 a share and common stock without par value. On that day the directors declared from the surplus earnings a dividend of $14 a share on the common stock, payable on July 1, 1929, in preferred stock at its par value. Gowran, as owner of common stock, received as his dividend 533 and a fraction shares of the preferred. On or about October 1, 1929, the company acquired his preferred stock and paid him therefor, at $100 a share, $53,371.50. In his income tax return for the year Gowran did not treat this sum as taxable income, but included $27,262.72 as capital net gain on the shares received and sold, computing the gain under Articles 58 and 600 of Regulations 74, then in force. The Commissioner rejected that treatment of the matter; determined that the $53,371.50 received was income taxable under the Revenue Act of 1928, §115(g), 45 Stat. 791, 822, as a stock dividend redeemed; and assessed a deficiency of $5,831.67.

The taxpayer sought a redetermination by the Board of Tax Appeals. A division of the Board concluded, upon testimony and stipulated facts, that there had been no cancellation or redemption of the preferred stock so as to make it a taxable dividend under §115(g); that the transaction by which the company acquired it constituted a sale. The Commissioner secured a reconsideration of the case. He then contended that, under the rule declared in Commissioner of Internal Revenue v. Tillotson Mfg. Co., 76 F.(2d) 189, the stock dividend was taxable, because it had resulted in a change of Gowran's proportionate interest in the company. That contention was sustained by the Board; and, on that ground, it affirmed the Commissioner's determination of a deficiency. 32 B.T.A. 820.

The taxpayer sought a review by the Circuit Court of Appeals. The Commissioner again urged that the stock dividend was taxable; and then, for the first time, contended that, even if it was not taxable, the determination of the deficiency should be affirmed, because within the tax year the stock had been sold at its par value and, as its cost had been zero, the entire proceeds constituted income. The Court of Appeals recognized that, since the dividends in preferred stock gave to Gowran an interest different in character from that which his common stock represented, it was constitutionally taxable under Koshland v. Helvering, 298 U.S. 441; but it held that the dividend could not be taxed as income, since by §115(f) Congress had provided: "A stock dividend shall not be subject to tax." And it held further that no part of the proceeds could be taxed as income, since there was no profit on the sale, it being agreed that the fair market value of the stock, both at the date of receipt and at the date of the sale, was $100 a share. 87 F.(2d) 125.

Because of the importance of the questions presented in the administration of the revenue laws, certiorari was granted.

First. The Government contends that §115(f) should be read as prohibiting taxation only of those stock dividends which the Constitution does not permit to be taxed; and that, since by the dividend Gowran acquired an interest in the corporation essentially different from that theretofore represented by his common stock, the dividend was taxable. In support of that construction of §115(f), it is urged that Congress has in income tax legislation manifested generally its intention to use, to the full extent, its constitutional power, Helvering v. Stockholms Bank, 293 U.S. 84, 89; Douglas v. Willcuts, 296 U.S. 1, 9; that this Court holds grants of immunity from taxation should always be strictly construed, Pacific Co. v. Johnson, 285 U.S. 480, 491; and that the only reason for exempting stock dividends was to comply with the Constitution.

This preferred stock had substantially the same attributes as that involved in the *Koshland* case. There the dividend was of common stock to a preferred stockholder, it is true; but we are of opinion that under the rule there declared Congress could have taxed this stock dividend. Nevertheless, by §115(f) it enacted in 1928, as it did in earlier and later Revenue Acts, that "a stock dividend shall not be subject to tax." The prohibition is comprehensive. It is so clearly expressed as to leave no room for construction. It extends to all stock dividends. Such was the construction consistently given to it by the Treasury Department.[1] The purpose of Congress when enacting §115(f) may have been merely to comply with the requirement of the Constitution as interpreted in Eisner v. Macomber, 252 U.S. 189; and the comprehensive language in §115(f) may have been adopted in the erroneous belief that under the rule declared in that case no stock dividend could be taxed. But such facts would not justify the Court in departing from the unmistakable command embodied

---

[1]Eisner v. Macomber was decided March 8, 1920. Soon thereafter, the Treasury Department declared, in a series of Decisions and Regulations, that no stock dividend was taxable. Treas. Dec. 3052, 3 C.B. 38 (August 4, 1920); Treas. Dec. 3059, 3 C.B. 38 (August 16, 1920); Office Dec. 732, 3 C.B. 39 (October 28, 1920). Office Dec. 801, 4 C.B. 24 (January 5, 1921) provided: "A stock dividend paid in true preferred stock is exempt from tax the same as though the dividend were paid in common stock." Then followed legislation in the precise form embodied in §115(f) of the Revenue Act of 1928. See §201(d) of the Revenue Act of 1921, 42 Stat. 227, 228; §201(f) of the Revenue Act of 1924, 43 Stat. 253, 255; §201(f) of the Revenue Act of 1926, 44 Stat. 9, 11; §115(f) of the Revenue Act of 1932, 47 Stat. 169, 204; §115(f) of the Revenue Act of 1934, 48 Stat. 680, 712. Article 628 of the Regulations in force in 1928 provided: "Stock dividends. — The issuance of its own stock by a corporation as a dividend to its shareholders does not result in taxable income to such shareholders, but gain may be derived or loss sustained by the shareholders from the sale of such stock. The amount of gain derived or loss sustained from the sale of such stock, or from the sale of the stock in respect of which it is issued, shall be determined as provided in Articles 561 and 600."

Koshland v. Helvering, 298 U.S. 441, was decided May 18, 1936. On June 22, 1936, Congress, in enacting the Revenue Act of 1936, provided in §115(f): "1. General Rule — A distribution made by a corporation to its shareholders in its stock or in rights to acquire its stock shall not be treated as a dividend to the extent that it does not constitute income to the shareholder within the meaning of the Sixteenth Amendment to the Constitution." 49 Stat. 1648, 1688. See also §115(h).

in the statute. Congress declared that the preferred stock should not be taxed as a dividend.

Second. The Government contends that, even if §115(f) be construed as prohibiting taxation of the preferred stock dividend, the decision of the Board of Tax Appeals affirming the Commissioner's determination of a deficiency should be sustained, because the gain from sale of the stock within the year was taxable income and the entire proceeds must be deemed income, since the stock had cost Gowran nothing. The Circuit Court of Appeals rejected that contention. It held that there was no income, because, as stipulated, there was no difference between the value of the stock when received and its value when sold. The court likened a non-taxable stock dividend to a tax-free gift or legacy and said: "One who receives a tax-free gift and later sells it, in the absence of statute providing otherwise, is taxed upon the profit arising from the difference in its value at the time he receives it and the sale price. Similarly one who receives a tax-free bequest, when selling it, is taxed upon the profit arising from any excess of the sale price over its fair market value at the time of receipt." [p. 128] Compare Taft v. Bowers, 278 U.S. 470.

The cases are not analogous. Unlike earlier legislation, §113(a)(2) of the Revenue Act of 1928 prescribes specifically the basis for determining the gain on tax-free gifts and legacies. It provides that: "If the property was acquired by gift after December 31, 1920, the basis shall be the same as it would be in the hands of the donor or the last preceding owner by whom it was not acquired by gift." And the basis for the computation on property transmitted at death is provided for in paragraph (5). But the method of computing the income from the sale of stock dividends constitutionally taxable is not specifically provided for. Furthermore, unlike §22(b)(3), excluding from gross income the value of gifts and legacies, §115(f) cannot, in view of its history, be taken as a declaration of Congressional intent that the value of all stock dividends shall be immune from tax not only when received but also when converted into money or other property. Gain on them is, therefore, to be computed as provided in §§111 and 113, by the "excess of the amount realized" over "the cost of such property" to the taxpayer. As the cost of the preferred stock to Gowran was zero, the whole of the proceeds is taxable.

Gowran asserts that if this "basis of zero" theory is accepted, the proceeds are taxable not as determined by the Commissioner but as a capital gain at a different rate and under different regulations. This depends upon whether the preferred stock received as a dividend was a "capital asset," defined by §101(c)(8) as "property held by the taxpayer for more than two years." The record is silent as to when Gowran acquired the common stock upon which the preferred was issued as a dividend, but it may be assumed that he had held it for more than two years. For that fact is immaterial since the dividend stock had been held for only three months. Whether taxed by Congress or not, it was income, substantially equivalent for income tax purposes to cash or property, and under §115(b) was presumed to have been made "out of earnings or profits to the extent thereof, and from the most recently accumulated earnings or profits." In no sense, therefore, can it be said to have been "held" by Gowran prior to its declaration.[2] Since the proceeds were therefore not "capital

---

[2]Article 501 of Regulations 74 states that "if the taxpayer has held for more than two years

gains," they were taxable at the normal and surtax rates applicable to ordinary income.[3]. . .

Reversed.

STOCK DIVIDENDS*

A. Prior Law

Under the 1939 Code, stock dividends were taxable if the proportionate interest of the shareholder receiving the stock dividend was increased. The 1954 Code abandoned the proportionate interest test as too difficult to administer and provided that stock dividends are tax-free unless (a) any shareholder had an election to take property in lieu of stock or (b) the stock was distributed in discharge of preference dividends of the taxable year or the preceding taxable year.

A number of corporations developed plans for paying tax-free stock dividends which the Internal Revenue Service felt were abuses. Under one such plan, a corporation creates two classes of common stock which are virtually identical except that one class receives cash dividends and the other class receives stock dividends approximately equal in value to the cash dividends. The group receiving the stock dividends increases its proportionate interest in the corporation vis-à-vis the group receiving cash dividends. The result is the same as if the former group had received a cash dividend and used it to purchase additional stock in the corporation. However, under the 1954 Code such a stock dividend was apparently tax-free.

The same result can be achieved by using special or preferred stock which pays no cash dividends but is convertible into common shares, initially at a one-for-one ratio, with the ratio increasing each time a cash dividend is paid on the common shares.

A third way of reaching the same result is by using a special or preferred stock which receives cash dividends, which is convertible into common shares at one-for-one, and which has no anti-dilution protection for stock dividends paid to the common shareholders in an amount equal to the cash dividends on the preferred stock.

These three types of plans permit one group of shareholders to receive cash dividends and the other group to receive an approximately equal stock dividend which was apparently tax-free.

Another type of alleged abuse utilized special or preferred stock which paid

---

stock upon which a stock dividend has been declared, both the original and dividend shares are considered to be capital assets." But this was based upon the erroneous premise that stock dividends could not be income, and was part of an administrative scheme to apportion some of the cost of the original shares to the stock received by way of dividend. This arrangement we declared in Koshland v. Helvering, 298 U.S. 441, to be without statutory authority, and the same must be said of the Regulation involved here.

[3]See Burnet v. Harmel, 287 U.S. 103, 105-106; Helvering v. New York Trust Co., 292 U.S. 455, 463; McFeely v. Commissioner, 296 U.S. 102, 106-107.

*Excerpted from J. S. Levin, Corporate Adjustments, in A Practitioner's Guide to the Tax Reform Act of 1969 (Practising Law Inst. 1970), at 29. Reprinted by permission. — ED.

no cash dividends but was convertible into common shares at a ratio which automatically increased each year. This increase in conversion ratio was automatic and was not tied to the payment of cash dividends on the common shares. By virtue of these increases in conversion ratio the holders of this special class of stock automatically received the right to an increased proportionate interest in the corporation each year. This has the same effect as if the convertible special stock were receiving a fixed cash dividend which was being reinvested in additional convertible special stock. However, under the 1954 Code such automatic increases in conversion ratio were apparently tax-free.

Still another method for possible abuse was the issuance of a preferred stock for $100 per share which paid no cash dividends but was redeemable at a stated date for an amount in excess of $100. In effect the preferred dividends were accumulated and paid at the time of redemption. However, such a scheme might convert the preferred dividends into capital gain.

In January 1969 the Treasury finalized regulations designed to prevent some of these alleged abuses. However, there was substantial doubt as to whether the regulations were valid.

B. Changes Made By The 1969 Act

The 1969 Act closed virtually all of these alleged loopholes. It continued the general rule that stock dividends and distributions of stock rights are nontaxable but enacted five complicated exceptions. It is still clear that a corporation can distribute a tax-free dividend of common stock or preferred stock pro-rata to all holders of its common stock where there is no other class of stock outstanding. However, almost any other type of stock dividend must be examined carefully.

The first exception section 305(b)(1) merely continues the rule of the 1954 Code that if any shareholder has an election to receive property in lieu of stock, the stock dividend will be taxable to all shareholders. For this purpose, property does not include stock of the corporation.

The second exception section 305(b)(2) provides that a stock dividend is taxable if the distribution (or a series of distributions) has the result of the receipt of property by some shareholders and an increase in the proportionate interest of others. Under this rule, a distribution of stock will be taxable if there are related distributions of both stock and property and the stock is not distributed pro-rata.

This provision blocks the schemes where one class of common stock receives cash dividends and the other class receives stock dividends in an approximately equal amount. It also covers schemes designed to reach the same result, where cash dividends are paid on convertible preferred stock, stock dividends in an approximately equal amount are paid on common stock, and no anti-dilution provision protects the preferred.

Moreover, new section 305(d) provides that a holder of convertible debentures or warrants will be treated as a shareholder for this purpose. Thus, section 305(b)(2) will apply where interest is paid in cash on convertible debentures, stock dividends in an approximately equal amount are paid on common stock, and no anti-dilution provision protects the convertible debentures.

Section 305(b)(2) will also probably apply where convertible preferred receives cash dividends and the conversion ratio is reduced to compensate the common shareholders for the cash dividends which they did not receive. In such a case the common shareholders will be taxed as if they had received a constructive stock dividend, because their proportionate interest in the corporation increases. New section 305(c) gives the Treasury authority to treat a change in conversion ratio as a distribution to any shareholder whose proportionate interest is increased. Presumably the shareholders who are treated as having received a constructive dividend will increase their basis in their stock by the amount of the constructive dividend.

New section 305(c) also gives the Treasury authority to promulgate regulations stating that a redemption from one shareholder which is treated as a dividend to him under section 302(d) constitutes a constructive distribution of stock (and thus a taxable stock dividend) to the other shareholders. The legislative history makes it clear that Congress meant this provision to apply only where there are periodic small redemptions (such as an offer to redeem 2% of the stock of any shareholder who wants to receive cash) and not to an isolated redemption.

The new statute is unclear as to the result if, in a series of distributions, one class of common shares receives $2 in cash dividends and the other class of common shares receives $3 in stock dividends. It can be argued that the stock dividend should be taxed only to the extent that the other shareholders received cash and that the extra $1 of stock dividend should be tax free. On the other hand, the statute could be read as requiring the entire stock dividend to be taxed if it is part of a series of non-pro-rata distributions of both cash and stock.

Consider the possible application of this provision to a stock dividend in which cash is paid in lieu of fractional shares. Some shareholders receive stock and a small amount of property, while other shareholders receive only stock and thus increase their proportionate interest in the corporation vis-à-vis those shareholders receiving cash in lieu of fractional shares. Read literally, section 305(b)(2) might be applicable. However, Congress certainly did not intend to cover the normal cash-in-lieu-of-fractional-shares situation. Hopefully the regulations will clarify this matter. Compare the *Mills* case where the Fifth Circuit held that the payment of cash in lieu of fractional shares does not violate the solely-for-stock rule of a "B" reorganization; the Internal Revenue Service has acquiesced in this holding.

The third exception section 305(b)(3) provides that a stock dividend is taxable if the distribution (or series of distributions) has the result of the receipt of preferred stock by some common shareholders, and common stock by other common shareholders.

This provision thus covers the situation where common shareholders have a choice between receiving a dividend in either common stock or preferred stock and some take common stock while others take preferred stock. It also applies where there are two classes of common, with common stock dividends paid on one class and preferred stock dividends paid on the other class, even though, absent this provision, the preferred stock would have been section 306 stock. In these cases, the distribution is taxable with respect to the recipients of both common stock and preferred stock even though no shareholder received property. If the preferred stock is taxed upon receipt, it does not become section 306 stock.

New section 305(c) grants the Treasury authority to treat a recapitalization as a distribution. Thus it is theoretically possible for the Internal Revenue Service to argue that a recapitalization in which some common shareholders exchange part of their common stock for preferred stock falls within section 305(b)(3) on the ground that some common shareholders received preferred stock (in exchange for their common shares) and some common shareholders received a constructive distribution of common stock (since their proportionate interest in the corporation increased). However, the debate on the Senate floor indicates that section 305(b)(3) was not intended to impede any recapitalization which had a business purpose, such as reducing the equity participation of older or less active shareholders.

The next exception section 305(b)(5) provides that a distribution of convertible preferred is taxable unless the Commissioner is satisfied the result will not be that described in section 305(b)(2), that is, the receipt of property by some shareholders and stock by others. Since preferred stock is not property, this can occur only if some shareholders sell or redeem their preferred stock. The reference to section 305(b)(2) appears to have been a drafting error; the reference probably should have been to section 305(b)(3), so that a distribution of convertible preferred would be taxable if there was a plan for some shareholders to convert into common stock and others to hold the stock as preferred stock after the conversion privilege expired. The Senate Committee Report indicates that the provision was designed to apply where there is a short-term conversion privilege, such as 4 months, at a price approximately equal to the common stock price, so that some shareholders will convert and others will not, but that where the conversion privilege lasts for a long period, such as 20 years, the distribution of convertible preferred is not taxable, because the likelihood is that all of it will eventually be converted and there will be no change in proportionate interests.

The final exception section 305(b)(4) provides that a stock dividend is taxable if it constitutes a distribution with respect to preferred stock, other than an increase in the conversion ratio to take account of a stock dividend or a stock split.

This provision blocks the practice of paying accumulated preference dividends in stock, tax-free (other than those of the current and immediately prior year). It also prevents a tax-free distribution of new stock in exchange for preferred stock with dividend arrearages in a recapitalization. Since section 305(c) grants the Treasury authority to treat a recapitalization as a distribution, the stock received in payment of the dividend arrearages would be taxable.

This provision also applies to a class of special or preferred stock convertible into common stock at automatically increasing ratios, since a change in conversion ratio is treated under section 305(c) as a distribution to the shareholders whose proportionate interests are increased.

However, it appears that a class of convertible debentures with an automatically increasing conversion ratio would not be covered by section 305(b)(4). Although section 305(d) provides that the holder of a convertible debenture is treated as a shareholder for purposes of section 305, it does not provide that a convertible debenture is treated as preferred stock. And section 305(b)(4) deals with distributions with respect to preferred stock.

As I have already discussed, new section 305(c) gives the Treasury authority to issue regulations stating when a change in conversion ratio or redemption price, a difference between issue price and redemption price, a redemption taxable as a dividend under section 301, or any other transaction having a similar effect (including a recapitalization) will be treated as a distribution to those shareholders whose proportionate interest is increased. Thus, the regulations under section 305(c) may answer a lot of questions about the scope of the new statute.

The effective dates of amended section 305 are quite complicated. In general, it is applicable to distributions after January 10, 1969. However, sections 305(b)(2) and (4) do not apply to distributions on stock which was outstanding on January 10, 1969, if made before January 1, 1991 but there are several complex exceptions to this rule.

NOTE

See J. Eustice, Corporations and Corporate Investors, 25 Tax L. Rev. 509, 537-552 (1970). Temporary Regulations (§13.10) were issued on May 1, 1970 with respect to distributions of money in lieu of fractional shares under the 1969 Act. 3 CCH 1971 Stand. Fed. Tax Rep. ¶2334A. Cf. M. Chirelstein, Optional Redemptions and Optional Dividends: Taxing the Repurchase of Common Shares, 78 Yale L.J. 739 (1969).

B. EFFECT OF A DISPOSITION

1. *Before §§305 and 306*

CHAMBERLIN v. COMMISSIONER
207 F.2d 462 (6th Cir. 1953), cert. denied, 347 U.S. 918 (1954)

Before SIMONS, Chief Judge, and McALLISTER and MILLER, Circuit Judges.

MILLER, Circuit Judge. Petitioner C. P. Chamberlin seeks a review of an income tax deficiency determined by the Respondent for the calendar year 1946, and sustained by the Tax Court. In the Tax Court the proceeding was consolidated with the proceedings of five other taxpayers similarly situated, all of which proceedings involved the same factual and legal questions. The taxpayers, all of whom were stockholders of Metal Moulding Corporation, about which this litigation centers, and their respective deficiencies were as follows:

C. P. Chamberlin	$343,650.86
Grace A. Chamberlin, his wife	63,225.55
John H. Toner	19,620.37
Benjamin James Carl	7,244.29
Guy V. Schrock	9,177.83
Robert and Josephine Pierce	14,635.19

The Tax Court upheld the deficiency assessment in each proceeding. . . .

The Metal Moulding Corporation, hereinafter referred to as the Corporation, is a Michigan corporation engaged in the business of manufacturing metal mouldings and bright work trim used in the manufacture of automobiles. It was incorporated on December 2, 1924 with an authorized common capital stock of $25,000, which was increased in 1935 to $150,000, represented by 1,500 shares of $100 par value voting common stock. From 1940 until December 20, 1946, the issued and outstanding common stock totaled 1,002½ shares, of which Chamberlin and his wife together owned 83.8%. The directors of the corporation from 1940 to February 12, 1946 consisted of C. P. Chamberlin, Grace A. Chamberlin, and Edward W. Smith. On February 12, 1946, John H. Toner and Raymond H. Berry were added. On October 11, 1946, Smith died and during the remainder of 1946 the board consisted of the four remaining members. From 1940 to the end of 1946, C. P. Chamberlin was president and treasurer, John H. Toner was vice-president and general manager, and Grace Chamberlin was for various periods vice-president, assistant treasurer, and secretary. Benjamin J. Carl was assistant secretary and treasurer until February 12, 1946.

The business of the Corporation prospered, and after paying substantial cash dividends over a period of years, its balance sheet at the end of the first six months in 1946 reflected total assets of $2,488,836.53 and included in current assets $722,404.56 cash and $549,950 United States Government Bonds and notes.

On December 16, 1946, the Corporation's authorized capital stock was increased from $150,000 to $650,000, represented by 6,500 shares of $100 par value common stock. On December 20, 1946, a stock dividend was declared and distributed of five shares of common for each share of common outstanding, and the Corporation's accounts were adjusted by transferring $501,250 from earned surplus to capital account.

On December 26, 1946, the articles of incorporation were amended so as to authorize, in addition to the 6,500 shares of common stock, 8,020 shares of 4½% cumulative $100 par value preferred stock. On December 28, 1946, a stock dividend was declared of 1⅓ shares of the newly authorized preferred stock for each share of common stock outstanding, to be issued pro rata to the holders of common stock as of December 27, 1946, and the Company's accounts were adjusted by transferring $802,000 from earned surplus to capital account. The preferred stock was issued to the stockholders on the same day. Prior to the declaration of the preferred stock dividend, the Corporation at all times had only one class of stock outstanding.

On December 30, 1946, as the result of prior negotiations hereinafter referred to, all of the holders of the preferred stock, except the estate of Edward W. Smith, deceased, which owned 20 shares, signed a "Purchase Agreement," with The

Northwestern Mutual Life Insurance Company and The Lincoln National Life Insurance Company, which instrument was also endorsed by the Corporation for the purpose of making certain representations, warranties and agreements. Under the "Purchase Agreement" 4,000 shares of the preferred stock was sold to each of the two insurance companies at a cash price of $100 per share plus accrued dividends from November 1st, 1946 to date of delivery. Pursuant to the "Purchase Agreement" the holders of the preferred stock, with the exception of the estate of Edward W. Smith, delivered their stock certificates endorsed in blank to agents of the two insurance companies, who transferred to C. P. Chamberlin as agent for the stockholders funds for the amount of the purchase price, which Chamberlin distributed to the stockholders in proportion to their interests by delivery of his personal checks.

Immediately thereafter, on December 30, 1946, the insurance companies delivered the stock certificates to the Corporation for transfer. The Corporation cancelled the certificates and in lieu thereof issued its certificate dated December 30, 1946 to the Northwestern Mutual Life Insurance Company for 4,000 shares of its preferred stock and its certificate likewise dated December 30, 1946 to the Lincoln National Life Insurance Company for 4,000 shares of its preferred stock. The expenses incident to the sale of the stock, including legal fees, commissions and federal documentary stamps totaled $13,500.22, which were paid by Chamberlin, who in turn was reimbursed by the selling stockholders.

In the latter part of 1945, the Corporation's attorney and Chamberlin discussed with an investment firm in Chicago the possibility of selling an issue of preferred stock similar to the stock subsequently issued. The Corporation had such a large accumulated earned surplus it was fearful of being subjected to the surtax provided for by [§531], Internal Revenue Code, but at the same time Chamberlin, the majority stockholder, was not willing to have the Corporation distribute any substantial portion of its earned surplus as ordinary dividends because his individual income was taxable at high surtax rates. It was proposed that the issuance of a stock dividend to the stockholders and the sale of it by the stockholders would enable the stockholders to obtain accumulated earnings of the Corporation in the form of capital gains rather than as taxable dividends. The investment counselor contacted The Lincoln National Life Insurance Company of Fort Wayne, Indiana, and during October 1946, furnished the Insurance Company financial information relative to the Corporation. On November 7, 1946, a representative of the Insurance Company came to Detroit and made an inspection of the plant and properties of the Corporation. On November 20, 1946, The Lincoln National Life Insurance Company's finance committee approved the proposed issue and the purchase of one-half thereof. The Northwestern Mutual Life Insurance Company was contacted for the purpose of participating in the purchase of the preferred stock. It made a detailed investigation of the Corporation and of the terms and conditions of the proposed preferred stock issue, and about two weeks before December 30, 1946, its committee on investments approved the purchase of 4,000 shares of the preferred stock to be issued, and passed the matter over to its legal department for the conclusion of the transaction.

The preferred stock contained the following provisions among others: The holders were entitled to cumulative cash dividends at the rate of $4.50 per annum payable quarterly beginning November 1, 1946; the stock was subject to redemption on any quarterly dividend date in whole or in part at par plus specified premiums and accrued dividends; it was subject to mandatory retirement in amounts not exceeding 2,000 shares on May 1, 1948 and 1,000 on May 1st on each succeeding year, depending upon the Corporation's net earnings for the preceding year, until fully retired on May 1, 1954; in the event of certain default of dividend payments or annual retirements, the holders were entitled to elect a majority of the directors; as long as any preferred shares remained outstanding the consent of the holders of at least 75% thereof was required to validate certain actions, including changing the articles of incorporation or capital structure, the sale of the Company's property, or the incurrence of indebtedness for borrowed money in excess of a certain amount; the Corporation could not pay any cash dividend upon any stock junior to the preferred if there was any default in the payment of dividend upon and the annual retirements of the preferred, or if such dividend reduced the net working capital of the Corporation below an amount equal to 150% of the aggregate par value of all outstanding preferred, or $750,000, whichever amount was greater, or reduced the [current] assets of the Company to an amount less than 200% of current liabilities. These provisions had been discussed with the Lincoln National Life Insurance Company and some of them, at least, were included in order to satisfy the investment requirements of the two insurance companies.

No agreement of purchase and sale was entered into between any of the petitioners and either of the two insurance companies prior to the "Purchase Agreement" executed on December 30, 1946, but the stockholders and directors of the Corporation took the necessary actions to put the negotiated plan into effect, as hereinabove set out, only after the insurance companies certified their willingness to participate in the purchase, if, as, and when the preferred stock was issued on the terms and conditions prescribed by them and as set out in the Company's charter as amended on December 27, 1946.

In reporting this sale of the preferred stock in their 1946 tax returns, each of the stockholders reported his proportion of the proceeds from the sale as a net long-term capital gain from the sale of a capital asset held for more than six months, used a substituted basis as the cost basis of the preferred stock, and in determining the period the preferred stock had been held included the holding period of the common stock upon which the preferred stock dividend was declared.

The Respondent ruled that the preferred stock constituted a dividend taxable as ordinary income, and further determined that the value was the amount received on the sale of the shares against which the expenses incurred in the sale were a valid deduction. This ruling resulted in the deficiency assessments involved in these consolidated proceedings.

Before considering the ruling of the Tax Court it is well to briefly review some of the Supreme Court decisions involving the taxability of stock dividends. This is well done in Note 5, in the Tax Court's opinion, which, together with the analysis of some of the opinions and the legislative enactments applicable to the problem in Helvering v. Griffiths, 318 U.S. 371, 63 S. Ct. 636, 87 L. Ed. 843, makes a detailed restatement unnecessary in this opinion. In Towne v. Eisner, 245 U.S. 418, 38 S. Ct. 158, 62 L. Ed. 372 and Eisner v. Macomber, 252 U.S. 189, 40 S. Ct. 189, 194,

64 L. Ed. 521, the Court held that a stock dividend of common stock to the holders of the common stock was not income to the stockholder taxable by Congress under the Sixteenth Amendment, in that it did not alter the preexisting proportionate interest of any stockholder or increase the intrinsic value of his holding or of the aggregate holdings of the other stockholders as they stood before. The Court said: "The new certificates simply increase the number of the shares, with consequent dilution of the value of each share" and that a stock dividend "shows that the company's accumulated profits have been capitalized, instead of distributed to the stockholders or retained as surplus available for distribution in money or in kind should opportunity offer." In Koshland v. Helvering, 298 U.S. 441, 56 S. Ct. 767, 80 L. Ed. 1268, the Court held that a stock dividend of common stock to the holders of preferred stock was taxable income because it gave the preferred stockholder an interest different from that which his former stockholdings represented. In Helvering v. Gowran, 302 U.S. 238, 58 S. Ct. 154, 82 L. Ed. 224, the Court held that a stock dividend in preferred stock to the holders of common stock, where similar preferred stock was outstanding, was taxable income because it gave the common stockholder an interest essentially different from that theretofore represented by his common stock. In Helvering v. Griffiths, supra, the Court refused to reconsider the ruling in Eisner v. Macomber, supra, holding that legislation subsequent to that ruling did not attempt to make such stock dividends taxable. In Helvering v. Sprouse, 318 U.S. 604, 63 S. Ct. 791, 87 L. Ed. 1029, and in Strassburger v. Commissioner of Internal Revenue, 318 U.S. 604, 63 S. Ct. 791, 87 L. Ed. 1029, the Court restated the rule that in order to render a stock dividend taxable as income there must be a change brought about by the issue of shares as a dividend whereby the proportional interest of the stockholder after the distribution was essentially different from his former interest. The rule was applied to the facts in the *Strassburger* case where preferred stock was created and distributed as a stock dividend to a stockholder who owned the entire outstanding common stock, the Court holding that the preferred stock dividend did not constitute taxable income.

The Commissioner supported his assessment on the ground that although the preferred stock was issued as a non-taxable dividend, a concerted plan to sell the dividend shares was formulated prior to the distribution of such shares, which, coupled with actual sale immediately after receipt and the payment of the proceeds of sale direct to the stockholders constituted a taxable dividend to the extent of available earnings. He also took the position that the plan and the immediate sale resulted in a change in the proportional interest of the stockholders which was sufficient to exclude it from the rulings in the Supreme Court cases above referred to.

In the Tax Court the petitioner contended that under the rulings in Towne v. Eisner, supra, 245 U.S. 418, 38 S. Ct. 158, 62 L. Ed. 372; Eisner v. Macomber, supra, 252 U.S. 189; Helvering v. Griffiths, supra, 318 U.S. 371, 63 S. Ct. 636, and Strassburger v. Commissioner, supra, 318 U.S. 604, 63 S. Ct. 791, and the provisions of Sec. 115(f)(1), Internal Revenue Code, 26 U.S.C.A. §115(f)(1),* the preferred stock dividend was not income within the meaning of the Sixteenth Amendment, and ac-

*Section 115(f) was the 1939 predecessor of §305, although §305 is more detailed and, in some circumstances, differs in its impact. The 1939 Code contained no counterpart of §306. — Ed

cordingly not taxable as in the case of ordinary dividends under Sec. [61(a)] . . . .
Sec. 115(f)(1) provides: "A distribution made by a corporation to its shareholders
in its stock or in rights to acquire its stock shall not be treated as a dividend to the
extent that it does not constitute income to the shareholder within the meaning of
the Sixteenth Amendment to the Constitution."

The Tax Court held that the issue of whether the stock dividend constituted
income to the stockholders should be determined from a consideration of all the
facts and circumstances surrounding the issuance of the dividend and not by a
consideration limited to the characteristics of the stock declared as a dividend; that
each case involving a stock dividend must be decided upon its own facts and
circumstances as establishing whether the receipt of a particular kind of stock
dividend was in fact taxable; that such a decision did not rest upon matters of form
or nomenclature attending a stock dividend distribution but rather upon the real
substance of the transaction involved; that disregarding the circumstances and terms
of the issue it might be said that as a matter of form the stock dividend constituted
one which fell within the *Strassburger* case, but that considering the real substance
of the transaction it was of the opinion that the stock dividend was not in good
faith for any bona fide corporate business purpose, and that the attending circumstances and conditions under which it was issued made it the equivalent of a cash
dividend distribution out of available earnings, thus constituting ordinary taxable
income in the amount of the value of the preferred shares received. The Court also
said that the real purpose of the issuance of the preferred shares was concurrently to
place them in the hands of others not then stockholders of the Corporation, thereby
substantially altering the common stockholders' pre-existing proportionate interests
in the Corporation's net assets and thereby creating an entirely new relationship
amongst all the stockholders and the Corporation. One judge concurred in the result
without separate opinion; one judge concurred in a separate opinion which did not
concur in the reasoning of the majority opinion, and the third judge wrote a dissenting opinion.

In our opinion, the declaration and distribution of the preferred stock dividend,
considered by itself, falls clearly within the principles established in Towne v. Eisner,
supra, and Eisner v. Macomber, supra, and is controlled by the ruling in the
Strassburger case. Accordingly, as a preliminary matter, we do not agree with the
Tax Court's statement that the stock dividend is taxable because as a result of the
dividend and immediate sale thereafter it substantially altered the common stockholders' pre-existing proportional interests in the Corporation's net assets. The sale
to the insurance companies of course resulted in such a change, but the legal effect
of the dividend with respect to rights in the corporate assets is determined at the
time of its distribution, not by what the stockholders do with it after its receipt. In
Helvering v. Griffiths, supra, 318 U.S. 371, at page 394, 63 S. Ct. at page 648, 87 L. Ed.
843, the Court pointed out: "at the latest the time of receipt of the dividend is the
critical one for determining taxability." In none of the Supreme Court cases referred
to above is it suggested that events subsequent to the distribution have any bearing
on whether the stockholder's proportional interest is changed. The fact that events
occur in quick succession does not by itself change their legal effect. Biddle Avenue

Realty Corp. v. Commissioner, 6 Cir., 94 F.2d 435. It seems clear to us that if taxability exists it is not because of the change in pre-existing proportional interests caused by a later sale, but by reason of the other ground relied upon by the Tax Court, namely, that viewed in all its aspects it was a distribution of cash rather than a distribution of stock. That this is the real basis of the ruling appears from the statement in the opinion that "disregarding the circumstances and terms of the issue, it might be said as a matter of form the stock dividend constituted one which fell within the *Sprouse* and *Strassburger* cases. . . . However, . . . , not form but the real substance of the transaction is controlling."

The general principle is well settled that a taxpayer has the legal right to decrease the amount of what otherwise would be his taxes, or altogether avoid them, by means which the law permits; . . . and that the taxpayer's motive to avoid taxation will not establish liability if the transaction does not do so without it. . . .

It is equally well settled that this principle does not prevent the Government from going behind the form which the transaction takes and ascertaining the reality and genuineness of the component parts of the transaction in order to determine whether the transaction is really what it purports to be or is merely a formality without substance which for tax purposes can and should be disregarded. . . .

The question accordingly presented is not whether the overall transaction, admittedly carried out for the purpose of avoiding taxes, actually avoided taxes which would have been incurred if the transaction had taken a different form, but whether the stock dividend was a stock dividend in substance as well as in form.

No question is raised about the legality of the declaration of the dividend. Respondent does not contend that proper corporate procedure was not used in creating the preferred stock and in distributing it to the stockholders in the form of a dividend. If the transaction had stopped there we think it is clear that the dividend would not have been taxable in the hands of the stockholders. Strassburger v. Commissioner, supra. Whether the declaration of the dividend was in furtherance of any corporate business purpose or was the result of correct judgment and proper business policy on the part of the management, we believe is immaterial on this phase of the case. The Supreme Court cases in no way suggest that the taxability of a stock dividend depends on the purpose of its issuance or the good or bad judgment of the directors in capitalizing earnings instead of distributing them. The decisions are based squarely upon the proportional interest doctrine. See also Tourtelot v. Commissioner of Internal Revenue, 7 Cir., 189 F.2d 167; Wiegand v. Commissioner of Internal Revenue, 3 Cir., 194 F.2d 479. In Dreyfuss v. Manning, D.C.N.J., 44 F. Supp. 383, a stock dividend of preferred stock, declared solely for the purpose of avoiding taxes on undistributed net income, was held non-taxable, which ruling apparently was not appealed by the Commissioner. The presence or absence of a corporate business purpose may play a part in determining whether a stock dividend is a bona fide one, one in substance as well as in form, but it does not by itself change an otherwise valid dividend into an invalid one. A stock dividend, legally created and distributed, which is a dividend in substance as well as in form, does not change from a non-taxable dividend into a taxable one because of the purpose of its issuance or on account of the good or bad judgment of the directors in declaring it. Eisner v. Macomber, supra, 252 U.S. at page 211, 40 S. Ct. at page 194.

Nor is there any question about the genuineness and unconditional character of the sale of the preferred stock by the stockholders who received it to the two insurance companies. The facts show conclusively that title passed irrevocably from the stockholders to the insurance companies, and that the sellers received in cash without restriction a full consideration, the adequacy of which respondent does not question. But respondent contends that the sale of the stock following immediately upon its receipt resulted in the stockholder acquiring cash instead of stock, thus making it a taxable dividend under Secs. [61(a)] and 115(a), Internal Revenue Code. There are two answers to this contention.

A non-taxable stock dividend does not become a taxable cash dividend upon its sale by the recipient. On the contrary, it is a sale of a capital asset. Eisner v. Macomber, 252 U.S. 189, 212, 40 S. Ct. 189; Miles v. Safe Deposit & Trust Co., 259 U.S. 247, 42 S. Ct. 483, 66 L. Ed. 923. The rulings in those cases make it clear that its character as a capital asset is in no way dependent upon how long it is held by the taxpayer before its sale. In none of the Supreme Court cases referred to above, dealing with the taxability of stock dividends, was the length of the holding period considered as a factor. Obviously, if the non-taxability of a stock dividend rests solely upon the principle that it does not alter the pre-existing proportionate interest of any stock-holder or increase the intrinsic value of his holdings, the disposition of the stock dividend by the stockholder thereafter is not a factor in the determination. See also: Insull v. Commissioner, 7 Cir., 87 F.2d 648; Silas H. Burnham, 29 B.T.A. 605.

The foregoing conclusion is supported by Sec. 117(h)(5), Internal Revenue Code, 26 U.S.C.A. §117(h)(5),* which provides that for the purpose of determining whether a non-taxable stock dividend which has been sold is a long-term capital gain there shall be included in the holding period the period for which the taxpayer held the stock in the distributing corporation prior to the receipt of the stock dividend. This necessarily recognizes that a stock dividend will often be sold before the expiration of six months after its receipt, and makes no distinction between a stock dividend held one day or for any other period less than six months. Likewise, Sec. 29.113(a)(19)-1, Treasury Regulations III, in establishing the cost basis of a non-taxable stock dividend which has been sold for a gain or loss, makes no distinction between a stock dividend sold immediately after receipt and one held a long period of time before sale.

The other answer to the contention is that although the stockholder *acquired* money in the final analysis, he did not *receive* either money or property *from* the corporation. Sec. 115(a), Internal Revenue Code, in dealing with taxable dividends, defines a dividend as "any distribution *made by a corporation* to its shareholders, whether in money or in other property . . . out of its earnings or profits . . . ." (Emphasis added.) The money he received was received from the insurance companies. It was not a "distribution" by the corporation declaring the dividend, as required by the statute.

We come then to what in our opinion is the dominant and decisive issue in

*Section 1223(5) of the 1954 Code. — ED.

the case, namely, whether the stock dividend, which, by reason of its redemption feature, enabled the Corporation to ultimately distribute its earnings to its stockholders on a taxable basis materially lower than would have been the case by declaring and paying the usual cash dividend, was a bona fide one, one in substance as well as in form. As pointed out in Chisholm v. Commissioner . . . , 2 Cir., 79 F.2d 14, 15, certiorari denied Helvering v. Chisholm, 296 U.S. 641, 56 S. Ct. 174, 80 L. Ed. 456, the Court cannot ignore the legal effect of a bona fide transaction on the ground that it avoids taxes, and that "The question always is whether the transaction under scrutiny is in fact what it appears to be in form; a marriage may be a joke; a contract may be intended only to deceive others; an agreement may have a collateral defeasance. In such cases the transaction as a whole is different from its appearance." But if the transaction is actually what it purports to be it must be accepted for its legal results. There are numerous cases, some of which are pressed upon us by the respondent, where the Court, in keeping with the above principle, refused to give effect taxwise to transactions on the part of corporations because the facts and circumstances showed that the so-called corporation was one in form only, incorporated for the sole purpose of avoiding taxes and having no legitimate business purpose, masquerading under the corporate form, and accordingly not a bona fide corporation. See Gregory v. Helvering . . . , 293 U.S. 465, 55 S. Ct. 266, 79 L. Ed. 596; Higgins v. Smith . . . , 308 U.S. 473, 60 S. Ct. 355, 84 L. Ed. 406. In other cases a valid conveyance has been disregarded taxwise because the purchaser acquired no real interest in the property conveyed, was a mere conduit in passing title to another, and the conveyance was in fact a sham. See Minnesota Tea Co. v. (Helvering) Commissioner . . . , 302 U.S. 609, 58 S. Ct. 393, 82 L. Ed. 474; Griffiths v. (Helvering) Commissioner, 308 U.S. 355, 60 S. Ct. 277, 84 L. Ed. 319; Commissioner v. Court Holding Co., 324 U.S. 331, 65 S. Ct. 707, 89 L. Ed. 981. In the recent case of Bazley v. Commissioner . . . , 331 U.S. 737, 67 S. Ct. 1489, 91 L. Ed. 1782, the Court disregarded a so-called recapitalization of a corporation which would have resulted in a tax exempt distribution of its securities because the recapitalization was merely a formal paper recapitalization rather than a bona fide one contemplated by the statute. Likewise in Commissioner v. Tower . . . , 327 U.S. 280, 66 S. Ct. 532, 90 L. Ed. 670, the Court disregarded a partnership taxwise because it was a partnership merely in form and not in substance.

In our opinion, the stock dividend in this case does not fall within any of the principles discussed above. It seems clear that it was an issue of stock in substance as well as in form. According to its terms, and in the absence of a finding that it was immediately or shortly thereafter redeemed at a premium, we assume that a large portion of it has remained outstanding over a period of years with some of it still unredeemed after nearly seven years. It has been in the hands of the investing public, free of any control by the corporation over its owners, whose enforceable rights with respect to operations of the corporation would not be waived or neglected. Substantial sums have been paid in dividends. The insurance companies bought it in the regular course of their business and have held it as approved investments. For the Court to now tell them that they have been holding a sham issue of stock would be most startling and disturbing news.

It also seems clear that the insurance companies were not purchasers in form only without acquiring any real interest in the property conveyed. The character of the transaction as a bona fide investment on the part of the insurance companies is not challenged by the respondent. The element of a formal conduit without any business interest is entirely lacking.

If the transaction lacks the good faith necessary to avoid the assessment it must be because of the redemption feature of the stock, which, in the final analysis, is what ultimately permitted the distribution of the corporate earnings and is the key factor in the overall transaction. Redemption features are well known and often used in corporate financing. If the one in question was a reasonable one, not violative of the general principles of bona fide corporate financing, and acceptable to experienced bona fide investors familiar with investment fundamentals and the opportunities afforded by the investment market we fail to see how a court can properly classify the issue, by reason of the redemption feature, as lacking in good faith or as not being what it purports to be. The insurance companies, conservative, experienced investors, analyzed the stock issue very carefully, provisions were required to make it conform to sound investment requirements, and each of the two companies, acting independently of the other, purchased a very substantial amount in the regular course of their investment purchases. If the redemption feature was unreasonable or not in accord with generally accepted investment principles the stock would not have been approved as an investment and purchased by the two insurance companies. In our opinion, the redemption feature, qualified as it was with respect to premiums, amounts subject to redemption in each year, and the length of time the stock would be outstanding, together with the acceptance of the stock as an investment issue, did not destroy the bona fide quality of the issue. We cannot say that the preferred stock was not in fact what it purported to be, namely, an issue of stock in substance as well as in form. Chisholm v. Commissioner, supra.

Each case necessarily depends upon its own facts. The facts in this case show tax avoidance, and it is so conceded by petitioner. But they also show a series of legal transactions, no one of which is fictitious or so lacking in substance as to be anything different from what it purports to be. Unless we are to adopt the broad policy of holding taxable any series of transactions, the purpose and result of which is the avoidance of taxes which would otherwise accrue if handled in a different way, regardless of the legality and realities of the component parts, the tax assessed by the Commissioner was successfully avoided in the present case. We do not construe the controlling decisions as having adopted that view. United States v. Isham . . . , 17 Wall. at page 506; Gregory v. Helvering, supra, 293 U.S. at page 469, 55 S. Ct. at page 267; Commissioner v. Tower, supra, 327 U.S. at page 288, 66 S. Ct. at page 536; United States v. Cumberland Public Service Co. . . . , 338 U.S. at page 455, 70 S. Ct. at page 282 . . . .

In deciding this case it must be kept in mind that it does not involve a ruling that the profit derived from the sale of the stock dividend is or is not taxable income. Such profit is conceded to be taxable. The issue is whether it is taxable as income from a cash dividend or as income resulting from a long-term capital gain. Accordingly, it is not the usual case of total tax avoidance. Congress has adopted the policy of taxing long-term capital gains differently from ordinary income. By Sec. 115(g), Internal Revenue Code,* it has specifically excluded certain transactions with respect to stock dividends from the classification of a capital gain. The present transaction is not within the exclusion. If the profit from a transaction like the one here involved is to be taxed at the same rate as ordinary income, it should be done by appropriate legislation, not court decision.

The judgment is reversed and the case remanded to the Tax Court for proceedings consistent with the views expressed herein.

ROSENBERG v. COMMISSIONER
36 T.C. 716 (1961)

TIETJENS, Judge: The Commissioner determined deficiencies in income tax for 1952 as follows:

Petitioners	Docket No.	Deficiency
Estate of Henry A. Rosenberg and Ruth B. Rosenberg	75781	$386,481.88
Estate of Fanny B. Thalheimer and Alvin Thalheimer	75782	387,208.92
Jacob Blaustein and Hilda K. Blaustein	75783	371,305.93

The sole issue presented is whether under the circumstances here present, the proceeds realized from the sale of preferred stock in 1952 resulted in capital gain or ordinary income.

Findings of Fact

Some of the facts have been stipulated and are incorporated herein by reference.

Henry A. Rosenberg and Ruth B. Rosenberg, Alvin Thalheimer and Fanny B. Thalheimer, and Jacob Blaustein and Hilda K. Blaustein were, respectively, husband and wife in the year 1952 and each couple filed a joint income tax return for that year with the director of internal revenue at Baltimore, Maryland. . . .

American Trading and Production Corporation, hereinafter designated as Atapco, is a corporation organized in 1931 under the laws of the State of Maryland. In 1951 and 1952 Atapco was engaged in the oil industry. Its interests included the marine transportation of petroleum products and the acquisition, exploration, and development of crude oil and gas properties. Also, Atapco and the Blaustein family together owned between 25 and 30 percent of the stock of Pan American Petroleum

---

*"(g) Redemption of Stock —

(1) In General. — If a corporation cancels or redeems its stock (whether or not such stock was issued as a stock dividend) at such time and in such manner as to make the distribution and cancellation or redemption in whole or in part essentially equivalent to the distribution of a taxable dividend, the amount so distributed in redemption or cancellation of the stock, to the extent that it represents a distribution of earnings or profits accumulated after February 28, 1913, shall be treated as a taxable dividend. . . ."

Section 302 of the 1954 Code (particularly (b)(1) and (d)) is the successor to Section 115(g)(1) of the 1939 Code. — ED.

and Transport Company, the majority of which was owned by Standard Oil of Indiana. In addition, Atapco had stockholdings in the Crown Central Petroleum Corporation.

On December 26, 1951, the authorized stock of Atapco consisted of 30,000 shares of no-par common stock of which 22,000 were outstanding. These shares were held as follows:

Stockholders	*Shares*
Jacob Blaustein, trustee	5,500
Henrietta Blaustein	1,600
Jacob Blaustein	3,597
Fanny B. Thalheimer	3,917
Ruth B. Rosenberg	3,917
In treasury	3,469
	22,000

The 5,500 shares held by Jacob Blaustein, as trustee, were in trust for the benefit of his wife and their three children. Henrietta Blaustein is the mother of petitioners.

In 1951 Karl F. Steinmann, counsel for Atapco and the Blaustein family, contacted a broker in Baltimore with reference to doing some financing for Atapco. The broker referred him to the First Boston Corporation. In the late spring of 1951, Steinmann and John W. Cable who also represented Atapco and the Blausteins met with Charles Glavin, a vice president of First Boston, to discuss the financial arrangements of Atapco and its stockholders. Steinmann at that time was contemplating making a recommendation that a public market be created in the common stock of Atapco. Glavin pointed out the problems involved with making an offering of that type, such as the registration with the Securities and Exchange Commission which would include a complete disclosure, the cost and expense, as well as the substantial sacrifice in values that generally accompanies an initial offering by a company unknown to the public. The idea of creating a public market was subsequently abandoned.

Steinmann, thereafter, disclosed to Glavin that petitioners were considering replacing the outstanding common stock of Atapco with several classes of stock. Glavin was asked to advise them on the terms of a first preferred stock which would be salable by the holders thereof. The objective was to create a good-quality preferred stock which would be accepted by institutional investors. Atapco did not need additional outside capital in 1951 as it had sufficient earnings and capital on hand.

With respect to the contemplated preferred stock, Glavin recommended an adequate sinking fund or mandatory retirement provision, limitations on the amount of preferred stock and funded indebtedness of the corporation, limitations on the dividends of junior stocks, restrictions on the sale of the Pan American and Crown Central shares held by Atapco, and certain other terms which are normally contained in a good-quality preferred stock. Jacob Blaustein objected to the proposed limitations relating to the funded indebtedness and the disposition of the Pan American and Crown Central shares. He was of the opinion that these two limitations were not important as Atapco had no intention of selling either the Pan American or Crown Central shares and there was no need for such a debt limitation. Although Glavin thought the proposed preferred stock would be salable, he felt that the inclusion of the two limitations would make the issue more attractive.

On December 26, 1951, the directors and stockholders of Atapco approved amendments to its charter providing for an authorized capital of 300,000 shares of class A first preferred stock with a $10 par value, 300,000 shares of class B first preferred stock with a $10 par value, 1 million shares of second preferred stock with a $10 par value, and 200,000 shares of common stock without par value. The amendments also provided for the exchange of 16 shares of class B first preferred stock, 32 shares of second preferred stock, and 10 shares of the new common stock for each share of common stock outstanding. On December 27, 1951, the articles of amendment were filed with and approved by the State Tax Commission.

The directors of Atapco approved the new stock certificates and authorized the issuance of the new shares pursuant to the articles of amendment on December 27, 1951, and the new shares were duly issued to the stockholders.

On December 27, 1951, immediately after the change in capital structure, the stockholders of Atapco and their respective holdings were as follows:

Stockholders	Class B first preferred	Second preferred	Common
Jacob Blaustein, trustee	88,000	176,000	55,000
Henrietta Blaustein	25,600	51,200	16,000
Jacob Blaustein	57,552	115,104	35,970
Fanny B. Thalheimer	62,672	125,344	39,170
Ruth B. Rosenberg	62,672	125,344	39,170
	296,496	592,992	185,310

The holders of class B first preferred shares were entitled to cumulative dividends at the rate of 5 percent, payable quarterly. The shares were redeemable in whole or in part, at the option of the corporation, for a sum equal to all unpaid dividends accumulated to date plus $10.30 per share if redeemed on or before January 1, 1955; $10.20 per share if redeemed on or before January 1, 1958; $10.10 per share if redeemed on or before January 1, 1961; and $10 per share if redeemed later. On default in the payment of four consecutive quarterly dividends, the holders of the first preferred shares were entitled to elect one-third of the board of directors. As long as any of these shares were outstanding, the corporation required the consent of holders of two-thirds of the shares in order to permit the aggregate of the issued first preferred stock to exceed 300,000 shares; to authorize or issue any class of stock on a parity with or having priority over the first preferred stock; to pay dividends or make distributions in redemption with respect to any subordinate stock while there were unpaid accumulated dividends on the first preferred stock; or to pay any dividends or make any distributions in redemption if the aggregate of all dividends and distributions authorized from December 30, 1950, to the date of the proposed dividend or distribution exceeded the earned surplus arising during that period. Any holder of class B first preferred shares could convert them into class A first preferred shares on a share-for-share basis. The terms of the class A stock were similar to those of the class B stock, except that each year the corporation was obligated to redeem 7 percent of the aggregate number of issued class A shares at par value plus all accumulated unpaid dividends. In the event of a default in discharging this obligation, the corporation was prohibited from paying dividends or making distributions in redemption with respect to any subordinate stock. The holders of the second preferred stock were entitled to cumulative dividends at the rate of 6 percent, payable semiannually. They could not vote under any circumstances except as otherwise provided by law. The second preferred shares were redeemable at the option of the corporation at par plus all unpaid dividends accrued to the date of redemption.

Although petitioners made no effort prior to the recapitalization on December 27, 1951, to sell the class B first preferred shares, Glavin was advised by Steinmann on December 28, 1951, the day following the recapitalization, that members of the Blaustein family wished to sell part of the shares issued, and he was asked to take charge of the offering. In a letter dated December 28, 1951, from Steinmann to Glavin, Steinmann stated:

> "Our clients proposed to convert not less than a million and a half and probably up to two million dollars of Second Preferred stock and First Preferred stock, and would like you to handle the sale of not less than a million and a half and up to two million dollars of First Preferred stock.
>
> "This is a formal authorization to offer this stock at par plus accumulated dividends. You are to receive compensation in the event of the sale equivalent to $1\frac{1}{2}\%$ of the amount of the sale. . . ."

In a letter under date of January 2, 1952, Glavin replied:

> "I believe two things are necessary before we make a positive step. First, I would like to know when you will decide how much you are going to sell. You speak of not less than $1,500,000 nor more than $2,000,000. It might not be good sales approach to talk to people on a variable amount, as it might give the atmosphere of uncertainty about our ability to sell it.
>
> "The other thing I should have is a basic memorandum describing American Trading, so that we will have all of the basic facts about the Company and its operations. Either as a part of such a memorandum, or to be used with it, should be some up-to-date financial statements as well as a ten-year record of earnings in reasonable detail. You have talked about preparing such a memorandum in your office and I would be delighted to have you do so if you are still so inclined. The other alternative would be for us to take a crack at a presentation memorandum and send it down to you for filling in the blanks and correcting the errors. I am perfectly clear that we should have all this information in presentable form before calling on a prospective buyer rather than going in half prepared and then trying to get answers to questions raised. . . ."

The presentation memorandum discussed by Glavin in the foregoing letter was particularly necessary before offering the class B first preferred shares because Atapco was an unusual company and investors were not familiar with its management. From January to April 1952 Glavin and two of his associates at First Boston, together with Steinmann, worked on a presentation memorandum to be used in approaching possible purchasers of the class B first preferred shares. The memorandum was completed in early April.

First Boston began to offer the petitioners' shares after the presentation memorandum was completed. None of the shares of Henrietta Blaustein or Jacob Blaustein, trustee, which shares comprised 38 percent of the class B first preferred, was offered for sale. All potential buyers were to be approved by Jacob Blaustein before they could be approached by First Boston. Atapco was engaged in litigation with the Standard Oil Company of Indiana and Blaustein did not want the shares to get into the hands of the latter corporation directly or indirectly. First Boston confined its sales efforts to a limited number of prospects because a wider solicitation might have constituted a public offering requiring registration under the Securities Act.

On October 17, 1952, petitioners entered into contracts with Massachusetts Mutual Life Insurance Company, Phoenix Mutual Life Insurance Company, the Lincoln National Life Insurance Company, Central Life Assurance Company, the Stein Roe & Farnham Fund Incorporated, and Milius Shoe Company, hereinafter sometimes referred to as the purchasers. Under these contracts petitioners agreed to sell and deliver and the purchaser agreed to buy and pay for an aggregate of 180,000 shares of Atapco class B first preferred stock at a price of $10 per share plus accrued dividends from September 1, 1952. Also on October 17, 1952, petitioners executed an indemnity agreement under which each of the petitioners agreed and undertook to indemnify and hold the purchasers harmless from any liability for or on account of any tax penalty or interest assessed or claimed against the purchasers or their assignees in respect of the issue of class A first preferred stock of Atapco upon conversion of shares of class B first preferred.

On October 17, 1952, the class B first preferred shares were held as follows:

	Class B first preferred
Jacob Blaustein, trustee	88,000
Henrietta Blaustein	25,600
Jacob Blaustein	57,552
Fanny B. Thalheimer	62,672
Ruth B. Rosenberg	62,672

On October 23, 1952, petitioners delivered to the purchasers 180,000 shares of class B first preferred stock under the terms of the contracts and they received from each purchaser the [aliquot portion of the purchase price]. . . .

Atapco's charter was amended on October 17, 1952, to include additional protective provisions relating to the class A first preferred stock. The amendments required Atapco to obtain the consent of holders of two-thirds of the outstanding shares of that stock before incurring a funded debt which, together with the par value of the outstanding class A and class B first preferred stock, exceeded $10 million, and before selling or otherwise disposing of more than 10 percent of its shares in Pan American or Crown Central. At the time of the offering, insurance companies were generally uninterested in issues of preferred stock and were largely investing in bonds. The changes in the charter were recommended by Glavin in order to make the first preferred a more attractive investment. Glavin had previously been informed by Massachusetts Mutual and Lincoln National that they desired such protective provisions. Glavin felt it better to satisfy this group of highly desirable investors than enter into any extensive solicitation that might be deemed a public offering under the Securities Act.

The purchasers of the 180,000 class B first preferred shares exercised their option to convert them into class A first preferred shares on October 23, 1952, which was the same day that petitioners delivered the 180,000 shares of class B first preferred stock to the purchasers.

The petitioners paid $27,000 to First Boston as compensation for its services on their behalf in placing the 180,000 shares of class B first preferred stock. Of the $27,000 Jacob Blaustein paid $8,510.40, and Ruth B. Rosenberg and Fanny B. Thalheimer each paid $9,244.80. The petitioners also paid $7,751.11 for legal services and related disbursements in connection with the sales. Of the $7,751.11 Jacob Blaustein paid $2,443.15, and Ruth B. Rosenberg and Fanny B. Thalheimer each paid $2,653.98. The respondent has treated those payments as amounts deductible by the petitioners.

The earned surplus of Atapco appears on its corporate income tax return as $1,086,294.34 at the end of 1950. During 1950, $4,406,681.29 was "transferred to capital stock." In 1951 the amount at the end of the period was $686,791.25 which was the remainder following a reduction of earned surplus of $2,163,005 for "recapitalization." The earned surplus at the end of 1952 was not less than $2 million.

In 1951 Atapco was aware that the Commissioner was examining its records with respect to the possibility of a surtax under section [531] . . . for 1948. However, a conferee recommended that no deficiency be asserted for 1948. Subsequently a deficiency was asserted under section [531] for the years 1951, 1952, and 1953. The case is pending before this Court, American Trading and Production Corporation, Docket No. 76554.

Between the years 1952 and 1958 Atapco's business continued to expand, two additional tankers were acquired and a third renovated. In 1958 Jacob Blaustein and other executives of Atapco consulted Glavin with reference to methods of refinancing its outstanding obligations. It was finally decided to issue long-term notes which would be privately placed through First Boston. The amount of the proposed issue required Atapco to obtain the prior consent of the holders of the class A first preferred shares. It was Glavin's recommendation that the class A first preferred shares be redeemed. On December 2, 1958, 41,800 shares of class A first preferred stock were outstanding, Atapco having redeemed each year, in accordance with the provisions of its charter, 7 percent of the 180,000 class A first preferred shares originally outstanding. The remaining shares were redeemed on December 30, 1958.

On February 10, 1959, First Boston, as agent for Atapco, sold $7,500,000 of 5¼-

percent sinking fund notes due December 1, 1973. Two-thirds of the notes were bought by five holders of the class A first preferred stock. These were Massachusetts Mutual Life Insurance Company, Phoenix Mutual Life Insurance Company, the Lincoln National Life Insurance Company, Central Life Assurance Company, and the Stein Roe & Farnham Fund Incorporated. Several other insurance companies also acquired portions of the notes because of the favorable response by the large institutions which had previously invested in the class A first preferred stock.

The petitioners' holding period for the class B first preferred shares sold by them on October 23, 1952, pursuant to the contracts of October 17, 1952, was more than 6 months. None of these shares was stock in trade of a holder thereof, or property of a kind properly includible in inventory if on hand at the close of the taxable year, or property held primarily for sale to customers in the ordinary course of a trade or business. The petitioners reported the following long-term capital gains after deducting the basis for the shares and the expenses of the sales and paid the following taxes:

	Gain	*Tax*
Ruth B. Rosenberg	$583,203.17	$151,632.84
Fanny B. Thalheimer	583,203.17	151,632.84
Jacob Blaustein	537,071.45	139,638.58

The Commissioner determined that the amounts received by petitioners from the sale of the class B first preferred shares of Atapco were taxable as dividends under sections [61] and [301]. . . .

Opinion

The instant case involves the siphoning off of the earnings and profits of a closely held corporation by a process which has come to be known as a "preferred stock bailout." After the earnings and profits have been capitalized the mechanics of the bailout varies with the preferred stock being distributed either as a stock dividend as in Chamberlin v. Commissioner, 207 F.2d 462 (C.A. 6, 1953), reversing 18 T.C. 164 (1952), or as in this case as part of a recapitalization. The distribution is followed by a sale of the stock, the purchasers usually being large corporate investors. The preferred shares are then redeemed by the issuing corporation within a reasonably short period of time so that the original shareholder's equity is only temporarily diluted.

In *Chamberlin* a corporation wanted to distribute its large accumulated earnings and profits but did not wish to declare a cash dividend. It settled on a plan whereby a pro rata dividend of cumulative preferred stock was issued to the common shareholders, common being the only class outstanding. Pursuant to a prearranged plan substantially all of the preferred shares were sold to two insurance companies which had formulated the terms of the issue. They provided that the shares would be redeemed over an 8-year period and also imposed restrictions on the corporation's assuming obligations, changing the capitalization, or paying dividends on the common stock. This Court held that such a preferred stock dividend when received was the equivalent of a cash dividend constituting ordinary taxable income. The Sixth

Circuit reversed and held that the stock dividend was nontaxable following Strassburger v. Commissioner, 318 U.S. 604 (1943).

In the case before us the Commissioner takes the position that the taxable event was the sale of the class B first preferred shares. However, he determined that the proceeds were not long-term capital gains but were taxable as dividends under sections [61] and [301]. . . . The issue here though not identical to that presented in *Chamberlin,* is related due to the similar purpose in carrying out the transaction.

The theory of the Commissioner in arriving at his determination is that Atapco sold the first preferred shares directly to the corporate investors with the petitioners being mere conduits through whom the shares passed and the proceeds of the sales were then distributed to petitioners.

Petitioners argue that there was no prearranged plan between Atapco and the corporate investors as in *Chamberlin*. They contend that the negotiations to sell the first preferred shares were not commenced until after the recapitalization and were conducted entirely between the corporate investors and themselves.

The evidence substantiates petitioner's contention that there were no negotiations prior to the stock distribution, however we do not think that the form of the transaction is controlling as the Court of Appeals in *Chamberlin* apparently did.

> "The incidence of taxation depends upon the substance of a transaction. The tax consequences which arise from gains from a sale of property are not finally to be determined solely by the means employed to transfer legal title. Rather, the transaction must be viewed as a whole, and each step, from the commencement of negotiations to the consummation of the sale, is relevant. A sale by one person cannot be transformed for tax purposes into a sale by another by using the latter as a conduit through which to pass title. To permit the true nature of a transaction to be disguised by mere formalisms, which exist solely to alter tax liabilities, would seriously impair the effective administration of the tax policies of Congress." Commissioner v. Court Holding Co., 324 U.S. 331, 334 (1945).

Our conclusion after viewing the substance of the transaction as a whole is that it was a predetermined plan with Atapco and the petitioners acting in concert to bail out the large amount of earnings and profits which had accumulated in the corporation for petitioners' personal use and to avoid the imposition of a surtax under section [531].

The testimony that the preferred stock was issued in order to place Atapco shares in the hands of high-grade institutional investors and thereby establish the credit of the corporation with such investors and facilitate its later financing through such sources is not convincing. We think such a consideration was merely ancillary to the prime purpose of providing a route whereby petitioners could extract the earnings and profits from the corporation.

There is no doubt that the first preferred shares were designed to accomplish this preconceived plan. The class B first preferred shares initially distributed permitted the shareholders who had planned to hold the stock to do so without a mandatory yearly redemption, a feature of the class A first preferred. Such yearly redemptions would have been a dividend to those shareholders under 115(g), I.R.C. 1939.* At the same time the conversion privilege allowed petitioners to sell their shares to the corporate investors which petitioners knew would immediately convert them to the class A shares as evidenced by the indemnity agreement executed by petitioners in connection with the sale of the class B shares to the corporate investors. A further consideration in utilizing this form was that it precluded any contention that the sale was an assignment of income by petitioners, Helvering v. Horst, 311 U.S. 112 (1940), Hort v. Commissioner, 313 U.S. 28 (1941), a theory predicated upon the fact that the yearly redemptions of the class A first preferred shares would have been dividends to petitioners. See sec. 115(g), I.R.C. 1939.

In *Chamberlin,* the Court of Appeals in commenting on the distribution of shares with a mandatory redemption provision similar to the shares in this case, stated at page 471 that:

> "Redemption features are well known and often used in corporate financing. If the . . . [redemption provision] was a reasonable one, not violative of the general principles of bona fide corporate financing, and acceptable to experienced bona fide investors familiar with investment fundamentals and the opportunities afforded by the investment market we fail to see how a court can properly classify the issue, by reason of the redemption feature, as lacking in good faith or as not being what it purports to be. . . . In our opinion, the redemption feature, qualified as it was with respect to premiums, amounts subject to redemption in each year, and the length of time the stock would be outstanding, together with the acceptance of the stock as an investment issue, did not destroy the bona fide quality of the issue. . . ."

Similarly, petitioners defend the mandatory redemption provision of the class A shares as necessary, because institutional investors desire to reconsider their positions from time to time and such a provision enables them to do so periodically. We think such a contention has little significance insofar as the substance of the transaction is concerned. Assertions of such business reasons might be appropriate if the corporate purpose was to sell the shares to raise additional capital but that is not the situation here. As we view it, the purpose was to siphon off the corporate earnings and profits and the importance which we attach to the redemption provision is that it enabled petitioners to accomplish the plan without a permanent impairment of their ownership and control of the corporation.

Continuing with respect to the form of the transaction, petitioners claim that there were no negotiations to sell prior to the recapitalization in this case. While this is a fact to be considered, the controlling factor in ascertaining whether the sale was made by the corporation, as we see it, is the extent of the corporate activity throughout the entire transaction.

In Commissioner v. Court Holding Co., supra, the corporation negotiated the sale of an apartment house; however, prior to the sale the asset was transferred in the form of a liquidating dividend to the shareholders who made the formal con-

---

*Section 115(g)(1) is set forth in footnote 1 in *Chandler,* page 238 supra. Section 302 is the 1954 Code counterpart, especially subsections (a), (b)(1) and (d). — Ed.

veyance to the purchasers. This procedure was designed to avoid the imposition of large income tax on the corporation. The Supreme Court held that it would treat the sale as if made by the corporation.

Conversely, in United States v. Cumberland Public Service Co., 338 U.S. 451, 453 (1950), a case similar to *Court Holding Co.,* the Supreme Court held that the sale was made by the shareholders after finding that "the liquidation and dissolution genuinely ended the corporation's activities and existence" and "at no time did the corporation plan to make the sale itself."

In a footnote in *Cumberland* at page 454, the Court said:

> "What we said in the *Court Holding Co.* case was an approval of the action of the Tax Court in looking beyond the papers executed by the corporation and shareholders in order to determine whether the sale there had actually been made by the corporation. We were but emphasizing the established principle that in resolving such questions as who made a sale, fact finding tribunals in tax cases can consider motives, intent, and conduct in addition to what appears in written instruments used by parties to control rights as among themselves. See, e.g., Helvering v. Clifford, 309 U.S. 331, 335-337, 60 S. Ct. 554, 556-557, 84 L. Ed. 788; Commissioner of Internal Revenue v. Tower, 327 U.S. 280, 66 S. Ct. 532, 90 L. Ed. 670, 164 A.L.R. 1135."

The motive and intent of the transaction here was to bail out the corporate earnings and profits. The corporation was closely held and its conduct was always subject to the petitioners' dictates. Proof that Atapco was a pawn of petitioners' always ready to comply with their command is the fact that the corporate charter was amended to include certain protective provisions with respect to the first preferred shares when it became evident that petitioners could more easily dispose of the stock if such provisions were included in the charter. We believe that when a closely held corporation, manipulated by its shareholders, distributes shares to such shareholders with the knowledge that they will immediately be sold as part of a scheme to avoid taxes and the corporation then plays an active role in the subsequent disposal, the sale in substance is made by the corporation with the distribution to and sale by the shareholders being a transitory step with no independent significance. See United States v. Lynch, 192 F.2d 718 (C.A. 9, 1951), certiorari denied 343 U.S. 934 (1952).

In the course of its reversing opinion in *Chamberlin* the Sixth Circuit said at page 471 that:

> "A non-taxable stock dividend does not become a taxable cash dividend upon its sale by the recipient. On the contrary, it is a sale of a capital asset. . . .
>
> ". . . although the stockholder *acquired* money in the final analysis, he did not *receive* either money or property *from* the corporation. Sec. 115(a), Internal Revenue Code, in dealing with taxable dividends, defines a dividend as 'any distribution *made by a corporation* to its shareholders, whether in money or in other property . . . out of its earnings or profits. . . .' [Emphasis added.] The money he received was received from the insurance companies. It was not a 'distribution' by the corporation declaring the dividend, as required by the statute."

We are of the opinion that Congress under section 115, I.R.C. 1939, clearly intended to tax such distributions out of earnings and profits at ordinary income rates. The fact that the money did not physically pass between Atapco and the petitioners should not be the sole determinant. We believe the question to be answered is whether the net effect of the transaction was the realization of a dividend by the shareholders made by the corporation out of its earnings and profits.

The courts have had little difficulty in finding that a shareholder realizes a dividend when the corporation discharges his indebtedness even though there has been no physical flow of money or property between the corporation and the shareholder. See Duffin v. Lucas, 55 F.2d 786 (C.A. 6, 1930), where the court held that when a corporation paid an indebtedness of a shareholder "it was analogous to and more or less equivalent to a regular earned and declared dividend and taxable as such" even "though it never came to his hands directly" from the corporation. See also United States v. Joliet & Chicago R. Co., 315 U.S. 44 (1942); Commissioner v. Western Union Telegraph Co., 141 F.2d 774 (C.A. 2, 1944).

The net effect of the transaction in this case shows the realization of a dividend by petitioners. We think that to look only to the form of the transaction and ignore the substance gives credence to the circuitous method employed to achieve the dividend distribution. "A given result at the end of a straight path is not made a different result because reached by a devious path." Minnesota Tea Co. v. Helvering, 302 U.S. 609 (1938). Accordingly, we sustain the Commissioner's determination.

Reviewed by the Court.

Decisions will be entered for the respondent.

2. *Under §§305, 306, and 307*

REVENUE PROCEDURE 66-34
1966-2 Cum. Bull. 1232

[The Internal Revenue Service has announced a policy which it will follow in connection with ruling requests involving convertible preferred stock.]

. . . A ruling will usually be issued to the effect that preferred stock that is convertible into common stock which is received in a reorganization by exchanging shareholders who will own no common stock after the reorganization will not be "section 306 stock", within the meaning of section 306(c) of the Code, provided the convertible preferred stock will be widely-held or it is represented that there will not be any conversion of the convertible preferred stock pursuant to a concerted plan which will result in both preferred and common stock being held by an exchanging shareholder. In all other cases, opinion will be reserved as to what part, if any, of the convertible preferred stock will constitute "section 306 stock." . . .

[Apparently convertible preferred stock that meets the foregoing tests will not be deemed "section 306 stock" even if it is redeemable. If it fails those tests, however, a redeemable feature in, or the prospect of redemption of, the convertible preferred stock (or certain other "section 306 stock") will prevent the issuance of a favorable ruling under section 306(b)(4) except that:]

A ruling will usually be issued under section 306(b)(4) of the Code to the effect that a distribution of "section 306 stock" (other than a distribution under section 305 of the Code) and the disposition or redemption of the "section 306 stock" is not pursuant to a plan of tax avoidance if the stock of the issuing corporation is widely held and

(a) the "section 306 stock" is not by its terms redeemable for at least five years from the date of issuance; and

(b) it is represented that there will be no redemption of the "section 306 stock", by tender or otherwise, within the five-year period.

A ruling will usually be issued under section 306(b)(4) of the Code to the effect that a distribution of "section 306 stock" (other than a distribution under section 305 of the Code) and the disposition of the "section 306 stock", other than by redemption and other than in anticipation of a redemption, is not pursuant to a plan of tax avoidance if the stock of the issuing corporation is widely held and

(a) the "section 306 stock" is by its terms redeemable within five years from the date of issuance, or

(b) the "section 306 stock" is not redeemable within five years from the date of issuance but the issuing corporation will not represent that there will be no redemption (as a result of a change in the terms of the stock, an invitation for tenders or otherwise) within five years from the date of issuance. . . .

NOTE

The Internal Revenue Service will not ordinarily issue an advance ruling on the question whether the distribution, disposition or redemption of "section 306 stock" in a *closely held corporation* is in pursuance to a plan within the meaning of §306(b)(4). Rev. Proc. 69-6, 1969-1 Cum. Bull. 396, 397.

REVENUE RULING 66-332
1966-2 Cum. Bull. 108

Advice has been requested whether, under the circumstances set forth below, the class A stock and preferred stock are "section 306 stock" within the meaning of section 306(c) of the Internal Revenue Code of 1954.

A corporation had outstanding $100 par value common stock. Pursuant to a plan of reorganization (recapitalization) under section 368(a)(1)(E) of the Code the common stock was reclassified as class A stock and each shareholder of the corporation could continue to hold his class A stock or exchange, over a 30-day period, all or part of the class A stock for units consisting of one share of $100 par value new preferred stock and one share of $1 par value new class B stock. The exchange ratio was one share of class A stock for each unit of one share of preferred stock and one share of class B stock.

The preferred stock is entitled to a cumulative dividend of $7 per share before any dividend is paid on either class A or class B stock. The class A stock is entitled to a cumulative dividend of $7 per share before any dividend is paid on class B stock. After all cumulative dividends on the preferred stock and the class A stock have been paid, the class A and class B stock share equally in all further dividends. The preferred stock is entitled to a preference on any distribution of assets in the amount of its par value. After this preference has been satisfied the class A stock is entitled to a preference on any distribution in the amount of one and one-half times the amount of its par value and thereafter the class A and class B stock share equally in any further distribution of assets. The class A and class B stock both have voting rights. The preferred stock is nonvoting except in case of a dividend arrearage.

During the 30-day exchange period certain shareholders of the corporation exchanged all of their shares of class A stock for units of preferred and class B stock. Other shareholders exchanged only portions of their class A stock for units of preferred and class B stock. Still other shareholders exchanged none of their class A stock for units of preferred and class B stock.

The recapitalization is a reorganization under section 368(a)(1)(E) of the Code and the exchanges are nontaxable under section 354(a)(1) of the Code.

Section 306(c)(1)(B) of the Code provides, in part and in, effect, that "section 306 stock" in any stock, except common stock, which is received by a shareholder in pursuance of a plan of reorganization under section 368 of the Code with respect to the receipt of which gain or loss to the shareholder was to any extent not recognized by reason of section 354 of the Code, provided the effect of the transaction is substantially the same as the receipt of a stock dividend.

The effect of the transaction to those shareholders of the corporation who exchanged all of their class A stock for units of preferred and class B stock is substantially the same as the exchange of their old common stock for shares of class B stock and the receipt of a stock dividend in shares of preferred stock.

The shareholders who exchanged only a portion of their class A stock for units of preferred and class B stock, still own class A stock which is preferred both as to dividends and distributions over the class B stock. Therefore, the class A stock is not common stock as that term is used in section 306(c)(1)(B) of the Code. Thus, the effect of the transaction as to them is substantially the same as the exchange of their old common stock for shares of class B stock and the receipt of a stock dividend in shares of class A stock and other preferred stock.

The shareholders who retained all of their class A stock own no shares of class B stock. The effect of the transaction as to them is substantially the same as the exchange of their old common stock for participating class A preferred stock. Had cash been received in lieu of the class A stock, such cash would not have been treated as a dividend. See section 1.306-3(d) of the Income Tax Regulations. Therefore, the retention of class A stock by these shareholders is not substantially the same as their having received a stock dividend.

Accordingly, (1) the preferred stock is "section 306 stock" in the hands of those shareholders who exchanged all of their class A stock for units of preferred and class B stock, (2) the class A stock retained as well as the preferred stock is "section 306 stock" in the hands of those shareholders who exchanged only a portion of their class A stock for units of preferred and class B stock, and (3) the class A stock retained by those shareholders who exchanged none of their class A stock for units of preferred and class B stock is not "section 306 stock."

NOTE

See D. B. Carlson, Taxation of "Taxable" Stock Rights: The Strange Persistence of Palmer v. Commissioner, 23 Tax L. Rev. 129 (1968); P. Metzer, The Impact of Section 306 Upon Convertible Preferred Stock Issued in a Corporate Reorganization, 116 U. Pa. L. Rev. 755 (1968); S. Solomon, How to Deal with Section 306, 1968 So. Calif. Tax Inst. 167; M. Chirelstein, Optional Redemptions and Optional Dividends: Taxing the Repurchase of Common Shares, 78 Yale L.J. 739 (1969).

C. *STOCK DIVIDEND vs. COMPENSATION —* §§305, 267, 61, AND 421

COMMISSIONER v. FENDER SALES, INC.
338 F.2d 924 (9th Cir.), cert. denied, 382 U.S. 813 (1965)

Before Pope and Barnes, Circuit Judges, and Thompson, District Judge.

Thompson, District Judge. These are petitions by the Commissioner of Internal Revenue for review of decisions of the Tax Court of the United States of which this Court has jurisdiction under Section 7482 of the Internal Revenue Code of 1954 (26 U.S.C. §7482.) The Tax Court held neither the corporate taxpayer, Fender Sales, Inc., nor the individual stockholder-taxpayers, Donald D. and Jean Randall, and C. Leo and Esther Fender, liable for a deficiency of income taxes on account of the transactions set forth in the following statement of the case, as made in petitioner's opening brief and concurred in by respondents.

The taxpayer Fender Sales, Inc. was incorporated in 1953 as a California corporation. It was authorized to issue 2,500 shares of common stock with a par value of $100 per share. At the commencement of the events material to this case, only 100 shares were outstanding, 50 of which were held by the taxpayer Donald D. Randall, and the other 50 by the taxpayer C. Leo Fender. Randall and Fender were also employees of Fender Sales and as such, were entitled to receive, as compensation for their services, $15,000 a year plus amounts equal to four per cent and one per cent, respectively, of annual sales.

Fender Sales was the exclusive sales agent for Fender Electric Instrument Co., Inc., a corporation owned entirely by C. Leo Fender.

Although Fender Sales has always been financially solvent, from its inception it has been plagued by the shortage of cash. This financial predicament was brought about primarily because it had to pay for its purchases upon receipt of the merchandise while it was often required to finance the dealers who purchased merchandise from it. Accordingly, in 1955, Fender Sales found it necessary to seek bank financing. Originally the bank did not ask for security for its loan, but later it required the subordination of other liabilities and personal guarantees from the corporate officers. In addition it became concerned about accrued (but unpaid) officers' salary liabilities that appeared on Fender Sales' balance sheet; it felt that these liabilities could represent potential priority claims over the bank's claim. To remedy this, the bank suggested that these liabilities be capitalized.

In each case of its fiscal years ending May 31, 1954, 1955 and 1956, Fender Sales, which used the accrual method of accounting for federal income tax purposes, accrued $30,000 on its books of account as representing officers' salaries payable, but unpaid, in the amount of $15,000 a year each to Randall and Fender. In each of those years, Fender Sales deducted the $30,000 on its federal income tax return. Accordingly, as of August 6, 1956, Fender Sales owed Randall and Fender each $45,000 for salaries payable for the fiscal years ended May 31, 1954 through 1956.

On or about August 6, 1956, Randall and Fender, in order to comply with the bank's suggestion, offered to discharge Fender Sales' liability for salaries due and payable to them by accepting from Fender Sales an additional share of $100 par value common stock for each $100 of salary debt. On August 6, 1956, the board of directors of Fender Sales, consisting of Mr. and Mrs. Randall and Mr. and Mrs. Fender resolved to accept the offers by Randall and Fender. After obtaining a permit from the Commissioner of Corporations of the State of California, Fender Sales, on December 3, 1956, issued to Randall and to Fender 450 shares each of its $100 par value common stock in discharge and cancellation of its indebtedness of $45,000 owing to each of them. As a result of this issuance of stock, Sales' capital stock account was increased from $10,000 to $100,000 and its $90,000 liability for salaries owed to Randall and Fender was discharged and cancelled.

During the fiscal year ended May 31, 1957, Fender Sales accrued on its books of account $30,000 which represented officers' salaries payable, but unpaid, of $15,000 each to Randall and Fender. Fender Sales deducted this amount of $30,000 on its federal income tax return for the fiscal year ended May 31, 1957.

On or about February 3, 1958, when Fender Sales was still indebted to Randall and Fender for $15,000 each for salary for the fiscal year ended May 31, 1957, Randall and Fender offered to discharge Fender Sales' liability for salaries due and payable to them by accepting from Fender Sales an additional share of $100 par value common stock for each $100 of salary debt. On February 3, 1958, the Board of Directors of Fender Sales resolved to accept the offers by Randall and Fender. On May 9, 1958, Fender Sales issued to Randall and Fender 150 shares each of its $100 par value common stock in discharge and cancellation of its indebtedness of $15,000 owing to each of these individuals. On the same date, it issued to Randall and Fender 350 shares each of its $100 par value common stock as a stock dividend. As a result, Fender Sales' capital stock account was increased from $100,000 to $200,000, its earned surplus account was decreased $70,000, and its $30,000 liability for salaries owed to Randall and Fender was discharged and cancelled.

On their federal income tax returns for the years 1956 and 1958, Fender and his wife did not report any amount as taxable income resulting from Fender's receipt of 450 shares of Fender Sales' stock on December 3, 1956, and 150 shares of Fender Sales' stock on May 9, 1958. On their federal income tax returns for the year 1956 and on their joint federal income tax returns for the year 1958, Randall and his wife did not report any amount as taxable income resulting from Randall's receipt of 450 shares of Fender Sales' stock on December 3, 1956, and 150 shares of Fender Sales' stock on May 9, 1958. On its corporate federal income tax returns for the fiscal years ended May 31, 1957 and May 31, 1958, Fender Sales did not report any amount as taxable income resulting from the discharge and cancellation on December 3, 1956 and May 9, 1958 of its indebtednesses for officers' salaries payable to Fender and Randall.

The Commissioner determined that the receipt of the stock constituted taxable salary income to Fender and Randall and, alternatively, that if it did not constitute taxable income to them, Fender Sales realized taxable income upon the cancellation of the salary indebtedness. The Tax Court held, however, that the cancellation of the indebtedness and issuance of the stock did not result in taxable income either to Fender and Randall or to Fender Sales. From that holding the Commissioner has sought review by this Court.

It is implicit in the foregoing fact statement and is conceded by respondents that the shares of Fender Sales, Inc. issued to each of the shareholders, Fender and Randall, had a fair market value of $100 per share (par value).

Tax Liability of Fender and Randall

Cases numbered 19075 to 19079, inclusive, present petitions by the Commissioner to review decisions by the Tax Court that the individuals, Donald D. Randall and his wife, Jean Randall, and C. Leo Fender and his wife, Esther Fender, incurred no income tax liability arising from the transactions related in the statement of facts. The complete rationale of the Tax Court decision is found in the following quotation:

> "Fender and Randall were the sole shareholders of Sales regardless of whether they each owned 50 shares or 1,000 shares. Their wealth was no more increased by the issuance of additional shares than if the corporation had caused its stock to be split 20 for 1. The issuance of such additional shares to Fender and Randall did not constitute income to them within the meaning of the 16th Amendment to the Constitution regardless of whether it represented a stock dividend or represented compensation for services. Eisner v. Macomber [252 U.S. 189, 40 S. Ct. 189, 64 L. Ed. 521], supra. . . ."

We disagree, and reverse the decision of the Tax Court in these cases.

The stockholder-employees received and accepted capital stock in discharge of the delinquent obligations of the corporation to them for salaries. If these were not equal stockholders to whom the corporation owed equal sums for unpaid salaries, there would be no semblance of a basis for dispute. The law and regulations plainly tax "all income from whatever source derived" (26 U.S.C. §61), and provide: ". . . if a corporation transfers its own stock to an employee . . . as compensation for services, the fair market value of the stock at the time of transfer shall be included in the gross income of the employee." Regulations, §1.61-2(d)(4). Here the parties agree the fair market value of the stock of Fender Sales, Inc. equalled its par value, and the additional stock issued is, in any event, presumptively equal in value to the liquidated obligations discharged. Regulations, §1.61-2(d).

Respondents say this case is different because the taxpayers were stockholders as well as employees and the equal (50-50) stock ownership by Fender and Randall remained equal after the additional stock was issued; and that they, therefore, "received nothing which they did not already possess, i.e., the entire capital stock of Fender Sales, Inc."

But the corporation was a substantially different corporation after the transactions than before. After the transactions on August 6, 1956, for example, the net worth of the company (excluding capital stock as a liability) was increased by $90,000, resulting from the cancellation of the accrued salary indebtedness. The fact is clear that the interests of Fender and Randall in Fender Sales, Inc. were substantially enhanced in value and that they did, in effect, receive something of value constituting taxable income under the Sixteenth Amendment to the Constitution. In this context, Eisner v. Macomber (1920), 252 U.S. 189, 40 S. Ct. 189, 64 L. Ed. 521, is not even apposite, let alone controlling. True, a stock dividend is just a piece of paper and, when issued proportionately to all stockholders, represents nothing of value and does not result in the realization of taxable income. But this is only because the basic net worth of the corporation, excluding capital stock as a liability, has not been changed. The stockholders have retained an equal interest in the same investment. In our situation, the stockholders have retained an equal interest in a substantially different investment. The *Eisner* opinion was explicit in pointing out that a stock dividend is "paper certificates that evidence an *antecedent* increase in the value of the stockholder's capital interest" (not, as here, a contemporaneous quid pro quo increase thereof), and "merely bookkeeping that does not affect the aggregate assets of the corporation or its outstanding liabilities" (not, as here, a $90,000 reduction in debts of Fender Sales, Inc. in August, 1956). The obvious differences between the economic interests represented by an unsecured debt as compared with stock ownership need no elaboration.

We interpret Lidgerwood Manufacturing Co. v. Commissioner (2 CCA 1956), 229 F.2d 241, as supporting our conclusions. In *Lidgerwood,* the debts which were cancelled arose from loans, and, if paid would not have represented taxable income to the stockholder. In that case, a sole stockholder cancelled debts, receiving capital stock in exchange, to enable the corporation to obtain bank loans. The debts cancelled were uncollectible and the stockholder-taxpayer claimed bad debt deductions on its income tax returns. The Court rejected the taxpayer's contention that nothing had been received by virtue of the issuance of the additional stock and, denying the bad debt deduction, said:

> "The petitioner contends that since the debts were assumed to be uncollectible, the cancellation of worthless debts and the issuance of stock therefor were meaningless formalities. We disagree. When a creditor cancels a debt in return for stock, he gives up the right to repayment, however

prosperous the debtor may become, and he acquires a right to dividends from future prosperity. If he owns less than all of the debtor's stock, the issuance of additional shares increases his share of possible dividends. If, as here, the creditor owns all the debtor's stock, his share is not increased but he has retained his 100 per cent right to future dividends, and, if the cancelled debts had any value whatever, to that extent he has increased his capital investment. It is not entirely clear what the Tax Court meant by its assumption that the debts were 'uncollectible.' Although the petitioner had contended that the subsidiaries were insolvent both before and after the cancellations, no finding of insolvency was made. But even on the assumption that the debtors were insolvent after as well as before the cancellations, wiping out the debts was a valuable contribution to the financial structure of the subsidiaries. It enabled them to obtain bank loans, to continue in business and subsequently to prosper."

Finally, Respondents say, in substance — break the transaction down to its component parts, none of them is a taxable event, therefore in the aggregate, they cannot generate a tax liability. The argument is: First, the receipt by equal stockholders of equal additional shares of capital stock, without more, is nontaxable; second, the forgiveness by a stockholder of the corporation's debt to him is, without more, a contribution to the capital of the corporation which is expressly excluded from the corporation's gross income. Therefore, a combination of the two cannot impose income tax liability on anyone. The answer is that the argument is a complete non-sequitur. The first statement deals with the tax liability of the individual stockholders and the second with the tax liability of the corporation.

To be persuasive with respect to the tax liability of the individual stockholders, Respondents' contentions should be: First, the acquisition of additional stock in equal proportionate shares is not a taxable event; second, the cancellation of a debt which, if collected, would represent taxable income is not a taxable event; therefore, the two in combination cannot generate tax liability. This Court does not accept the second premise. We are not prepared to hold that the voluntary surrender or forgiveness by a taxpayer of a receivable which, if collected, would represent taxable income, is, in all circumstances, a non-taxable event. We believe the authorities are opposed to such a conclusion.

In Helvering v. Horst, 1940, 311 U.S. 112, 61 S. Ct. 144, 85 L. Ed. 75, the Supreme Court held that the income received on payment of coupons clipped from coupon bonds and given by a father to his son was taxable to the father, and said, in part:

"Admittedly not all economic gain of the taxpayer is taxable income. From the beginning the revenue laws have been interpreted as defining 'realization' of income as the taxable event rather than the acquisition of the right to receive it. And 'realization' is not deemed to occur until the income is paid. But the decisions and regulations have consistently recognized that receipt in cash or property is not the only characteristic of realization of income to a taxpayer on the cash receipts basis. Where the taxpayer does not receive payment of income in money or property realization may occur when the last step is taken by which he obtains the fruition of the economic gain which has already accrued to him. Old Colony Trust Co. v. Commissioner, 279 U.S. 716 [49 S. Ct. 499, 73 L. Ed. 918]; Corliss v. Bowers, 281 U.S. 376, 378 [50 S. Ct. 336, 74 L. Ed. 916]. Cf. Burnet v. Wells, 289 U.S. 670 [53 S. Ct. 761, 77 L. Ed. 1439] . . . .

"Underlying the reasoning in these cases is the thought that income is 'realized' by the assignor because he, who owns or controls the source of the income, also controls the disposition of that which he could have received himself and diverts the payment from himself to others as the means of procuring the satisfaction of his wants. The taxpayer has equally enjoyed the fruits of his labor or investment and obtained the satisfaction of his desires whether he collects and uses the income to procure those satisfactions, or whether he disposes of his right to collect it as the means of procuring them. Cf. Burnet v. Wells, supra. . . .

"The dominant purpose of the revenue laws is the taxation of income to those who earn or otherwise create the right to receive it and enjoy the benefit of it when paid. See Corliss v. Bower, supra [281 U.S. 378, 50 S. Ct. 336]. . . . The tax laid by the 1934 Revenue Act upon income 'derived from . . . wages, or compensation for personal service, of whatever kind and in whatever form paid . . . ; also from interest . . . ' therefore cannot fairly be interpreted as not applying to income derived from interest of compensation when he who is entitled to receive it makes use of his power to dispose of it in procuring satisfactions which he would otherwise procure only by the use of the money when received."

In *Lidgerwood* (supra), the case in which the taxpayer sought a bad debt deduction in addition to the capital stock received for the cancelled obligation, the Court succinctly said: "If the debtor has received a contribution to capital, the creditor must have made the contribution. Consistency requires that both parties treat it alike."

In Helvering v. Horst, the coupons were actually paid in the year of the gift, and Respondents point to this as a distinguishing feature, claiming the salaries due from Fender Sales, Inc. were never "paid". But, in *Horst,* the Supreme Court relied on the broader concept of "realization of income" rather than a restricted notion of actual payment for its conclusions, and we think it necessary and logical, in the just administration of the tax laws, that the Courts continue to recognize that a taxpayer may realize the income represented by an account receivable by exercising his rights of control and disposition of it for his economic benefit in ways other than receipt of payment in money. In Commissioner of Internal Revenue v. Lester, 1961, 366 U.S. 299, 304, 81 S. Ct. 1343, 1346, 6 L. Ed. 2d 306, the Supreme Court approvingly quoted from *Horst:* "The power to dispose of income is the equivalent of ownership of it." We add, the exercise of the power to dispose of income is the equivalent of the realization of it. Fortunately, under the agreed facts of this case, we have no problem respecting the taxable value of the income thus realized and no problem respecting the tax year in which the income is reportable.

Randall and Fender, when they voluntarily elected to exercise their dominion and control over the choses in action against Fender Sales, Inc. for unpaid salaries by extinguishing them for the benefit of the corporation, of which they were sole owners, thereby augmenting the intrinsic worth of the capital stock they held, more surely "realized" for their own benefit the value of the obligations discharged than did Horst in his gift of interest coupons to his son.

In summary, we hold that the discharge by a corporation of its salary obligations to any employee (stockholder or not) by the issuance of the corporation's capital stock to the employee is a payment and realization of income by the employee in the amount of the fair market value of the stock. The transaction is controlled by Section 61 of the Internal Revenue Code and Section 1.61-2 of the Regulations. We disagree with the conclusions in Josephson v. Commission, 6 T.C.M. 788 and Daggit v. Commissioner, 23 T.C. 31, cited by Respondents.

The decisions of the Tax Court in cases numbered 19075 to 19079, inclusive, are reversed.

Tax Liability of Fender Sales, Inc.

Case No. 19074 presents a petition to review the determination by the Tax Court that the corporation, Fender Sales, Inc., incurred no income tax liability by reason of the related transactions.

Although the Commissioner argued for assessing tax liability against the corporation, this was only as an alternative should the individuals be held not liable. The Commissioner's brief states: "For the reasons already shown, we believe that Fender and Randall are taxable on the amounts of the accrued salaries and that Fender Sales is not. We do not contend that both are taxable on the same amounts." Whether viewed as payments for stock of the corporation or as the forgiveness by the shareholders of debts owed to them by the corporation, the transactions were nontaxable payments or contributions to capital from the point of view of the corporation's tax liability. 26 U.S.C. §118; I.R.C. 1032(a); Reg. 1.1032-1; Reg. 1.61-12(a). . . .

The petition in Case No. 19074 should be dismissed.

BARNES, Circuit Judge (dissenting in part and concurring in part). I respectfully dissent. I would affirm the Tax Court in respect to the nonliability of the individual taxpayers, i.e., cases 19075 to 19079, inclusive.

I deduce the matter that concerns my brothers is the loophole in present laws which allows a corporation whose stock is owned equally by two principals to take deductions in certain years for accrued salaries payable, never incur actual expenses for such deductions, and then have the liabilities written off without any tax recognition because the item is treated as a capital contribution by the shareholders. If on a balancing of all factors, this method of corporate tax liability reduction is a loophole that should be plugged, then it should be done by legislative action, not by judicial fiat. The majority opinion seeks to remedy the supposed leak by attaching liability to the *individuals* involved by extending the dominion and control cases, represented by Helvering v. Horst, 311 U.S. 112, 61 S. Ct. 144, 85 L. Ed. 75 (1940).

This majority opinion is the first I have encountered which recognizes a realization of income by shareholders upon an increase in corporate net worth, *where no dividend has been declared or capital gain yet realized* by the shareholders. Shareholders' interests in corporations change every day. The net worth of corporations is in a constant state of flux. Surely, when it increases, the shareholders are not *yet* deemed to have made a taxable gain. Rather the increase in corporate net worth is merely a paper increase of the shareholders' equity, not taxable until such time as the shareholders realize the increase by virtue of a dividend, or the sale or exchange of the security investment above cost. Then, and only then, have the courts traditionally recognized "a taxable event."

The use of the *Horst* line of cases as authority for recognizing the creation of a taxable event for the individuals in the case at bar is to me misleading. The evasionary device attacked in *Horst* and its progeny was different from the present situation. Those cases involved assignments of income rights to others prior to the point of realization of the income by the taxpayer himself. Such an anticipatory device by a taxpayer with complete control over the income was clearly a loophole in our tax laws that required plugging. Otherwise a taxpayer could assign his earnings directly to his creditors or family and claim there was never any income realization on his part. The case at bar does not involve a flagrant example of this potential loophole. The taxpayers here have no benefits *realized* by the issuance of additional stock for the cancellation of a corporate debt; their income has not been *diverted* to anyone else for their own personal benefit. They did not exert any power to dispose of their alleged "income" in a manner equivalent to ownership, and will not do so until the ordinary taxable event occurs — the sale of their stock.

The *Lidgerwood* case, cited, is in my opinion not controlling on the facts of this case. In fact the opinion seems to overlook the corporate nature of the stockholder in that case. The bad debt deduction was disallowed the parent-stockholder, but the cancellation was treated not as income to the parent *or its creditor subsidiaries;* rather it was properly treated as a capital contribution. To the extent the *Lidgerwood* case is relevant to the facts before us, it supports the conclusion that the taxpayers have not yet realized income by the receipt of additional shares of stock (while maintaining their identical proportional interests) for a debt cancellation.

> "This court and others have held that cancellation of a debt owed by a corporate debtor to a stockholder of the debtor does not constitute taxable income to the debtor but is a capital contribution by the creditor. For many years the Treasury Regulations have so provided. . . . If the debtor has received a contribution to capital, the creditor must have made the contribution. Consistency requires that both parties treat it alike. *Whether the creditor's investment will result in profit or loss to the investor cannot be determined forthwith. Loss, if any is eventually realized, occurs when the investment is closed out; that is, when the shares of stock of the debtor are sold or become worthless.*" (Emphasis supplied.) Lidgerwood Mfg. Co. v. Commissioner, 229 F.2d 241, at 242-43 (2d Cir. 1956).

Another approach to the problem, which to me supports the decision of the Tax Court, is as follows:

The two equal owners of the corporation are cash basis taxpayers. They each work on behalf of the corporation for three years without drawing a salary. Thus each has no current employment income subject to tax. However, the full time services each renders to the corporation are of some value; and are here valued at $15,000 per year. These services have their effect on the corporate performance. Consequently, these gratuitous services result, at the end of three years, in a corporate net worth presumably $90,000 greater than it would have been without their services. If at any time one or both of the individual owners decides to sell his investment, he will be taxed in effect for his gratuitous services because the proceeds from any sale would presumably be $45,000 greater than they would have been had he not contributed his services. He has not taken advantage of any tax loophole that does not already exist. Rather, he has just chosen not to take a current salary which would be taxed at ordinary income rates, and has instead increased the value of his investment to be taxed at a subsequent time at capital gain rates. I contend that, from the individual's standpoint, this is exactly what has occurred in the case at bar.

As to the corporation tax liability (case No. 19074), I would affirm.

Under the Internal Revenue Code and regulations, the corporation did not realize income on account of its issuance of capital stock to Fender and Randall, and did not realize income on account of the cancellation of the salary indebtedness to Fender and Randall. From the point of view of the corporation, any consideration received by it upon an original issue of its corporate stock, whether more or less than the actual or the stated value thereof, is a receipt of capital, not income. Merten's "Law of Federal Income Taxation," Vol. 7, p. 67; I.R.C. 1032(a); Reg. 1.1032-1.

Also, should we treat the capital stock issued as valueless and view the transactions as the gratuitous forgiveness of the salary obligations of the corporation by the respective stockholder-employees, still the corporation would not thereby have realized taxable income. It is established both by regulation and court decision that the gratuitous forgiveness by a shareholder of a debt owed to him by the corporation represents a contribution to the capital of the corporation and is not taxable income. Regulation 1.61-12(a). . . . Under the Internal Revenue Code, a contribution to the capital of a corporate taxpayer is expressly excluded from the definition of reportable gross income. 26 U.S.C. §118. In this case, the corporate obligations which were cancelled were unpaid salary obligations to the shareholders which had been deducted as operating expenses by the corporate taxpayer in its annual accrual-accounting income tax returns and which, if paid, would have represented taxable income to the shareholder-employees. In dealing with a corporation's possible tax liability arising from the gratuitous forgiveness of a debt by a shareholder, the law makes no distinction on the basis of how the obligation arose, that is, whether or not it arose out of a transaction which had permitted the corporation, in an earlier tax year, to deduct the charge from reportable gross income, or whether or not the obligation, if paid, would have constituted reportable income to the shareholder-taxpayer. The forgiveness of the debt by the shareholder is, in either case, from the viewpoint of the corporate taxpayer, a contribution to capital, and not a taxable event. In Helvering v. American Dental Co., 318 U.S. 322, 63 S. Ct. 577, 87 L. Ed. 785 (1943), the Supreme Court held the forgiveness of interest on notes and of rentals due by nonstockholder creditors to be gifts and capital contributions to a corporation, though "the motives leading to the cancellation were those of business or even selfish." Also, in Commissioner v. Auto Strop Safety Razor Co., 74 F.2d 226 (2d Cir. 1934), the court, under regulations like those now prevailing, held the voluntary cancellation by the sole stockholder of a subsidiary corporation of over two million dollars in debts, a portion of which represented expense items previously deducted, such as royalties and interest, to be a nontaxable contribution to the capital of the subsidiary corporation, and said: "When the indebtedness was canceled, whether or not it was a contribution to the capital of the debtor depends upon considerations entirely foreign to the question of the payment of income taxes in some previous year."

I believe a word or two of further explanation is required. The amounts now being treated as contributions to capital have previously been deducted by the corporation on its accrual-method tax returns. Had the individual taxpayers merely loaned money to the corporation and now cancelled the indebtedness, the cancellation would clearly be a contribution to capital, and such contribution should not be treated as taxable income to the corporation. However, the case at bar involves an indebtedness in the nature of accrued salaries which, unlike the hypothetical taxpayer loans, have once been deducted from income in prior years, consequently lessening the corporation's tax liability. Where sums have been deducted as expenses in previous years under an accrual method of accounting, and are now forgiven and are no longer corporate liabilities, the corporation ordinarily must add back the amount of the cancellation to its current income. If it need not, a flagrant loophole is created whereby expense deductions are taken without expenses ever being incurred or paid out. I refer to the language in Helvering v. Jane Holding Corp., 109 F.2d 933 (8th Cir. 1940).

> "The above cases recognize the principle that an obligation, once deducted but not paid, represents income when, because of subsequent circumstances, it is cancelled or it may be determined with reasonable certainty that it will never be enforced. None of the cases attach any importance to the means by which the cancellation is effected. That is immaterial, the controlling factors being the previous deductions offsetting income otherwise taxable and the subsequent release of the indebtedness before payment.
>
> "The Trust filed all of its returns for prior years on the cash basis and never reported as taxable income the interest accrued and deducted by the Corporation. The Trust, through the trustees, has, at all times since its creation, been in a position to determine and dictate the policies of the Corporation. It has chosen to earmark the payments which it received from the Corporation as payments on account of principal and at the same time, throughout the entire period, these payments have been in effect deducted as interest accrued in the Corporation's returns. To now permit this accrued liability, after the forgiveness thereof, to be called surplus and addition to capital without taxing the income actually received by the Corporation would result in an unjustifiable avoidance of tax."

While I agree with Judge Thompson's ultimate conclusion that the company has not realized income by the cancellation of the accrued salaries obligation, I do believe to properly justify that conclusion requires some discussion of the conflicting line of cases dealing with shareholder cancellations of indebtedness where the indebtedness has previously been deducted by the corporation as an operating expense.

Regulation §1.61-12(a) addresses itself directly to the problem of the cancellation of an indebtedness by a shareholder of a corporation. *Generally,* it maintains that the gratuitous forgiveness of a debt constitutes a contribution to capital, the corporation thus realizing no income. The leading precedent for this line of reasoning is Helvering v. American Dental Co., supra. In that case, the Commissioner had increased the taxpayer's reported income by the sum of the items of the cancelled indebtedness which had served to offset income in like amounts in prior years. But the Supreme Court held that the gratuitous cancellation of rent and interest due should be deemed a gift and not income.

The leading precedent for the opposing point of view, recognizing income to the taxpayer relieved of an indebtedness, is the later case of Commissioner v. Jacobson, 336 U.S. 28, 69 S. Ct. 358, 93 L. Ed. 477 (1949), which taxed the difference between the face amount of the taxpayer's personal indebtedness as the maker of secured bonds issued at face value, and a lesser amount paid by him for their repurchase. There was no evidence that there had been a transfer of something for nothing: the seller received the maximum price attainable.

Neither of these cases serves as exact precedent for the situation we have here; the cancellation of accrued salaries which have been deducted by the debtor-corporation in prior years. The leading exponents of the conflicting points of view in the accrued salary cases are Helvering v. Jane Holding Corp., supra, in favor of income recognition, and Carroll-McCreary Co. v. Commissioner, 124 F.2d 303 (2d Cir. 1941), holding no realization of income from the gratuitous cancellation of debts for unpaid salaries owing to officer-shareholders. The *Jane* case preceded the decision in *American Dental Co.,* supra, and the trend of the case law since the latter decision has been to follow *Carroll-McCreary* and hold no income is recognized if there was no consideration given as inducement for the cancellation. The cases have interpreted "gratuitous" forgiveness of a debt as simply meaning that no consideration was paid by the corporation for release of the debt. The prior deduction of the debt as a corporate expense has been held immaterial to the question of whether a nontaxable capital contribution was effected by the debt release. . . .

In the absence of evidence of consideration passing from Fender Sales, Inc., to the individual shareholders for cancellation of the accrued salaries indebtedness, the above case law supports the conclusion that the corporation did not realize income by the release of the accrued salaries liability, though the corporation had already taken the amount as deduction for expense of doing business.

Any potential loophole that is created by attaching no tax liability to the individuals or the corporation is a product of the legislature's failure to compel the corporation to make an income recognition when their accrued deductions are cancelled. This is an error which the legislature should be called upon to reconsider. It should not be corrected by committing a second error in the present case to offset the first.

NOTE

1. Why was §267(a)(2) inapplicable to the deductions claimed by Fender Sales, Inc. for salaries accrued but unpaid? Should §267 be amended to cover such a case? If so, how?

2. Does the *Fender Sales* majority or dissent present the more persuasive case as to the taxability of the individuals? Why? Is the majority's position consonant with the premise underlying §305? What would be the dissenting judge's position if the shareholders had had unequal share interests but the stock-for-salary distribution had been 50-50? What should it be? See the Commissioner's view in Rev. Rul. 67-402, 1967-2 Cum. Bull. 135.

3. If the dissenting judge is right in his position that the individuals had no income on the stock distribution, is he right that the termination of the corporate liability was a tax-free contribution to capital? In a tax sense, did the shareholders have "property" to contribute? How would you have decided the *Fender Sales* issue involving the corporate taxpayer? Why?

4. Ordinarily, when employees are not the sole and equal shareholders, as they were in *Fender Sales,* it is not questioned that they have ordinary income on receipt of their employer's stock in compensation for their services. If they receive the stock pursuant to their exercise of an option granted by their employer, they normally have ordinary income measured by the difference between the option price and the fair market value of the stock on the date of exercise. Commissioner v. Lo-Bue, 351 U.S. 243 (1956); Treas. Reg. §§1.61-15; 1.421-6. Sections 421-425 provide special opportunities for avoiding the result in *LoBue,* opportunities for deferring the income until the stock is sold and converting it into long-term capital gain. Attention to those sections and care in following their requirements produce handsome rewards for corporate executives (and, perhaps, for the tax lawyers who guide them). However, the "bargain" element in a "qualified" stock option (§422(b)) or a "restricted" stock option (§424(b)) is now an item of "tax preference" (§57(a)(6)), subject to the "minimum tax" values of §56. Revenue Ruling 68-86, page 458 infra, is an example of tax lawyers' ingenuity which succeeded without special legislation. Some would say it is also an example of Treasury obtuseness.

5. An employee of Corporation A is given an option to purchase 20 per cent of the corporation's shares. Thereafter Corporation A and Corporation B agree to a plan of reorganization in which the shares of A will be exchanged for voting stock of B (a "B" reorganization). The employee transfers his option to purchase A stock to B in exchange for voting stock of B. Must the employee recognize income? If so, when? What other facts should you know? Compare LeVant v. Commissioner, 376 F.2d 434 (7th Cir. 1967).

REVENUE RULING 68-86
1968-1 Cum. Bull. 184

Advice has been requested as to the time income is realized, and as to the amount of income realized, for Federal income tax purposes, by an employee under the circumstances described below.

An agreement between a corporation and an employee provides that the employee is to receive as compensation a base salary plus an annual bonus established by the board of directors of the corporation. The employee has the right to elect, prior to January 1 of each year, to have all or part of any bonus which may be awarded to him for that year paid to him in restricted stock of the corporation. The election for that year can be neither modified nor revoked thereafter.

The certificates of restricted stock paid to the employee pursuant to his election are stamped with a legend stating that the shares represented by such certificates shall not be sold, assigned, transferred, discounted, or pledged as collateral for a loan, without the prior written consent of the salary committee of the board of directors. Those restrictions continue in effect during the employee's employment with the corporation, and lapse a specific number of years after the effective date of termination of such employment for whatever cause. However, the corporation's salary committee will approve a release from the restrictions in the case of hardship which in the sole judgment of the committee justifies such action.

The foregoing restrictions, as evidenced by the legend stamped on the certificates of stock, have a significant effect on the value of the stock. Thus, under section 1.61-2(d)(5) of the Income Tax Regulations, the time and amount of compensation paid the employee in the form of such stock are determined by application of the rules prescribed by section 1.421-6(d)(2) of the regulations. Under the provisions of that section of the regulations, compensation is realized when the restrictions on the stock lapse, or when the stock is sold or exchanged in an arm's-length transaction, whichever occurs earlier. The amount of such compensation is the lesser of (1) the fair market value of the stock (determined without regard to the restrictions) at the time of its acquisition, or (2) either the fair market value of the stock at the time the restrictions lapse, or the consideration received upon the sale or exchange, whichever is applicable.

Accordingly, the election by the employee in the instant case, prior to January 1 of a given year, to have all or part of any bonus awarded him for that year paid to him in stock of his employer corporation that is subject to restrictions which have a significant effect on its value, will result in the realization of compensation by the employee at the time the restrictions on the stock lapse, or the stock is sold in an arm's-length transaction, whichever event occurs earlier.

NOTE

1. If the taxpayer in Rev. Rul. 68-86 had had the right to make his election after January 1, would the result have been different? Why? Should application of a "constructive receipt" doctrine be dependent upon such delicate timing? Why?

2. Section 83, added to the Code by the Tax Reform Act of 1969, substantially changed the law reflected in Rev. Rul. 68-86, supra. For a critical discussion of the prior history of the tax treatment of "restricted stock" see Blum, Restricted Stock Arrangements Reconsidered, 46 Taxes 598 (1968).

RESTRICTED PROPERTY*

. . . [U]nder the old law, if property is transferred as compensation for services and such property is subject to a restriction which has a significant effect on its value, the income tax didn't apply until such time as the restriction lapsed or the property was sold or exchanged. At this time the taxpayer has to include as part of his income the lesser of (1) the fair market value of the property at the time of acquisition or (2) the fair market value of the property at the time the restriction lapsed or the property is sold or exchanged, whichever is applicable, less the taxpayer's basis in the property.

The employer would have been entitled to a deduction at the same time and in the same amount as the taxpayer was deemed to receive as income with respect to the transaction. This permitted both tax deferral and realization of capital gains where the property increased in value.

On October 28, 1968, the Internal Revenue Service proposed regulations which would have treated the transfer of restricted property after June 30, 1969 as an open transaction until the restriction lapsed or the property was sold or exchanged. Taxes would then have been incurred at ordinary income rates on the fair market value of the property at such time. The employer would then have been entitled to deduct an equivalent amount. These regulations were shelved when work was begun on the Tax Reform Act of 1969.

Now, with respect to the 1969 Act, the House Bill provided that a person who received compensation in the form of property, such as stock, which is subject to a restriction, generally is to be taxed on the value of the property at the time of its receipt unless his interest is subject to a substantial risk of forfeiture. In this latter case, he is to be taxed on the value of the property at the time the risk of forfeiture is removed. A person's rights are subject to a "substantial risk of forfeiture" if they are conditioned upon the full performance of substantial services by any individual. The restrictions on the property are not taken into account in determining its value except in the case of a restriction which by its terms will never lapse.

*Excerpted from R. S. Taft, Compensation Problems, in A Practitioner's Guide to the Tax Reform Act of 1969 (Practising Law Inst. 1970), at 63. Reprinted by permission. — ED.

The Senate Bill generally followed the House version but added certain elements as follows: (a) Employees receiving restricted property subject to substantial risk of forfeiture could elect to pay the tax thereon in year of receipt based on the unrestricted value of the property at that time. If an election is made and the employee subsequently forfeits the restricted property, he would not be eligible for a tax refund of the tax previously paid on the property. (b) If restricted property subject to a substantial risk of forfeiture is exchanged in a tax-free exchange for other stock or property subject to substantially the same restrictions, the exchange will not trigger application of tax. (c) Employers would get deductions on pay-out of restricted property in non-exempt trusts.

Joint conference followed the Senate version, and this became law on December 30, 1969. . . .

NOTE

See J. Sobeloff, Payment of Compensation in the Form of Restricted Property: Problems of Employer and Employee — The Rules of New Code Section 83, 28 N.Y.U. Inst. on Fed. Tax. 1041 (1970).

III. RECAPITALIZATIONS AND CERTAIN INVESTOR EXCHANGES

A. *RECAPITALIZATION* — §§368(a)(1)(E), 354, 356

BAZLEY v. COMMISSIONER
331 U.S. 737 (1947), aff'g 155 F.2d 237 (3d Cir. 1946)

Mr. Justice FRANKFURTER delivered the opinion of the Court. The proper construction of provisions of the Internal Revenue Code relating to corporate reorganizations is involved in both these cases. Their importance to the Treasury as well as to corporate enterprise led us to grant certiorari, 329 U.S. 695, 329 U.S. 701. While there are differences in detail to which we shall refer, the two cases may be disposed of in one opinion.

In the *Bazley* case, No. 287, the Commissioner of Internal Revenue assessed an income tax deficiency against the taxpayer for the year 1939. Its validity depends on the legal significance of the recapitalization in that year of a family corporation in which the taxpayer and his wife owned all but one of the Company's one thousand shares. These had a par value of $100. Under the plan of reorganization the taxpayer, his wife, and the holder of the additional share were to turn in their old shares and receive in exchange for each old share five new shares of no par value, but of a stated value of $60, and new debenture bonds, having a total face value of $400,000, payable in ten years but callable at any time. Accordingly, the taxpayer received 3,990 shares of the new stock for the 798 shares of his old holding and debentures in the amount of $319,200. At the time of these transactions the earned surplus of the corporation was $855,783.82.

The Commissioner charged to the taxpayer as income the full value of the debentures. The Tax Court affirmed the Commissioner's determination, against the taxpayer's contention that as a "recapitalization" the transaction was a tax-free "reorganization" and that the debentures were "securities in a corporation a party to a reorganization," "exchanged solely for stock or securities in such corporation" "in pursuance of the plan of reorganization," and as such no gain is recognized for income tax purposes. . . . [Sections 368(a)(1)(E) and 354(a)(1)].* The Tax Court found that the recapitalization had "no legitimate corporate business purpose" and was therefore not a "reorganization" within the statute. The distribution of debentures, it concluded, was a disguised dividend, taxable as earned income under [§§61(a), 301 and 302]. . . . The Circuit Court of Appeals for the Third Circuit, sitting en banc, affirmed, two judges dissenting. . . .

Unless a transaction is a reorganization contemplated by §[368], any exchange of "stock or securities" in connection with such transaction, cannot be "in pursuance of the plan of reorganization" under §[354(a)(1)]. While §[368(a)(1)] informs us that "reorganization" means, among other things, "a recapitalization," it does not inform us what "recapitalization" means. "Recapitalization" in connection with the income tax has been part of the revenue laws since 1921. . . . Congress has never defined it and the Treasury Regulations shed only limited light. Treas. Reg. [368-2(e)]. One thing is certain. Congress did not incorporate some technical concept, whether that of accountants or of other specialists, into §[368] assuming that there is agreement among specialists as to the meaning of recapitalization. And so, recapitalization as used in §[368(a)(1)(E)] must draw its meaning from its function in that section. It is one of the forms of reorganization which obtains the privileges afforded by §[354(a)(1)]. Therefore, "recapitalization" must be construed with reference to the presuppositions and purpose of [the reorganization provisions]. It was not the purpose of the reorganization provision to exempt from payment of a tax what as a practical matter is realized gain. Normally, a distribution by a corporation, whatever form it takes, is a definite and rather unambiguous event. It furnishes the proper occasion for the determination and taxation of gain. But there are circumstances where a formal distribution, directly or through exchange of securities, represents merely a new form of the previous participation in an enterprise, involving no change of substance in the rights and relations of the interested parties one to another or to the corporate assets. As to these, Congress has said that they are not to be deemed significant occasions for determining taxable gain.

These considerations underlie §[368] and they should dominate the scope to be given to the various sections, all of which converge toward a common purpose. Application of the language of such a revenue provision is not an exercise in framing

---

*The 1939 Code under which this case was litigated had no counterparts to §§354(a)(2) and 356(d). — ED.

abstract definitions. In a series of cases this Court has withheld the benefits of the reorganization provision in situations which might have satisfied provisions of the section treated as inert language, because they were not reorganizations of the kind with which [the reorganization provisions], in [their] purpose and particulars, concern [themselves]. See Pinellas Ice & Cold Storage Co. v. Commissioner, 287 U.S. 462; Gregory v. Helvering, 293 U.S. 465; LeTulle v. Scofield, 308 U.S. 415.

Congress has not attempted a definition of what is recapitalization and we shall follow its example. The search for relevant meaning is often satisfied not by a futile attempt at abstract definition but by pricking a line through concrete applications. Meaning frequently is built up by assured recognition of what does not come within a concept the content of which is in controversy. Since a recapitalization within the scope of [the reorganization provisions] is an aspect of reorganization, nothing can be a recapitalization for this purpose unless it partakes of those characteristics of a reorganization which underlie the purpose of Congress in postponing the tax liability.

No doubt there was a recapitalization of the Bazley corporation in the sense that the symbols that represented its capital were changed, so that the fiscal basis of its operations would appear very differently on its books. But the form of a transaction as reflected by correct corporate accounting opens questions as to the proper application of a taxing statute; it does not close them. Corporate accounting may represent that correspondence between change in the form of capital structure and essential identity in fact which is of the essence of a transaction relieved from taxation as a reorganization. What is controlling is that a new arrangement intrinsically partake of the elements of reorganization which underlie the Congressional exemption and not merely give the appearance of it to accomplish a distribution of earnings. In the case of a corporation which has undistributed earnings, the creation of new corporate obligations which are transferred to stockholders in relation to their former holdings, so as to produce, for all practical purposes, the same result as a distribution of cash earnings of equivalent value, cannot obtain tax immunity because cast in the form of a recapitalization-reorganization. The governing legal rule can hardly be stated more narrowly. To attempt to do so would only challenge astuteness in evading it. And so it is hard to escape the conclusion that whether in a particular case a paper recapitalization is no more than an admissible attempt to avoid the consequences of an outright distribution of earnings turns on details of corporate affairs, judgment on which must be left to the Tax Court. See Dobson v. Commissioner, 320 U.S. 489.

What have we here? No doubt, if the Bazley corporation had issued the debentures to Bazley and his wife without any recapitalization, it would have made a taxable distribution. Instead, these debentures were issued as part of a family arrangement, the only additional ingredient being an unrelated modification of the capital account. The debentures were found to be worth at least their principal amount, and they were virtually cash because they were callable at the will of the corporation which in this case was the will of the taxpayer. One does not have to pursue the motives behind actions, even in the more ascertainable forms of purpose, to find, as did the Tax Court, that the whole arrangement took this form instead of an outright distribution of cash or debentures, because the latter would undoubtedly have been taxable income whereas what was done could, with a show of reason, claim the shelter of the immunity of a recapitalization-reorganization.

The Commissioner, the Tax Court and the Circuit Court of Appeals agree that nothing was accomplished that would not have been accomplished by an outright debenture dividend. And since we find no misconception of law on the part of the Tax Court and the Circuit Court of Appeals, whatever may have been their choice of phrasing, their application of the law to the facts of this case must stand. A "reorganization" which is merely a vehicle, however elaborate or elegant, for conveying earnings from accumulations to the stockholders is not a reorganization under [the reorganization provisions]. This disposes of the case as a matter of law, since the facts as found by the Tax Court bring them within it. And even if this transaction were deemed a reorganization, the facts would equally sustain the imposition of the tax on the debentures under §[356(a)(1) and (2)]. Commissioner v. Estate of Bedford, 325 U.S. 283.

In the *Adams* case, No. 209, the taxpayer owned all but a few of the 5914 shares of stock outstanding out of an authorized 6000, par value $100. By a plan of reorganization, the authorized capital was reduced by half, to $295,700, divided into 5914 shares of no par value but having a stated value of $50 per share. The 5914 old shares were cancelled and the corporation issued in exchange therefor 5914 shares of the new no-par common stock and 6 per cent 20 year debenture bonds in the principal amount of $295,700. The exchange was made on the basis of one new share of stock and one $50 bond for each old share. The old capital account was debited in the sum of $591,400, a new no-par capital account was credited with $295,700, and the balance of $295,700 was credited to a "Debenture Payable" account. The corporation at this time had accumulated earnings available for distribution in a sum not less than $164,514.82, and this account was left unchanged. At the time of the exchange, the debentures had a value not less than $164,208.82.

The Commissioner determined an income tax deficiency by treating the debenture bonds as a distribution of the corporation's accumulated earnings. The Tax Court sustained the Commissioner's determination, 5 T.C. 351, and the Circuit Court of Appeals affirmed. 155 F.2d 246. The case is governed by our treatment of the *Bazley* case. The finding by the Tax Court that the reorganization had no purpose other than to achieve the distribution of the earnings, is unaffected by the bookkeeping detail of leaving the surplus account unaffected. See §[316(a)], and Commissioner v. Wheeler, 324 U.S. 542, 546.

Other claims raised have been considered but their rejection does not call for discussion.

Judgments affirmed.

Mr. Justice Douglas and Mr. Justice Burton dissent in both cases for the reasons stated in the joint dissent of Judges Maris and Goodrich in the court below. Bazley v. Commissioner, 155 F.2d 237, 244.

B. *EXERCISE OF CONVERSION PRIVILEGES*

In Rev. Rul. 57-535, 1957-2 Cum. Bull. 513, the Commissioner ruled that there is no realization in a transaction in which a security, convertible by its terms, is converted into another. The transaction is treated as a transformation, not an "exchange" or "disposition." Since no "closed transaction" has occurred, there is no "realization;" and so no nonrecognition provision, such as §354 or §1031 or §1036 (see infra this page), is needed to defer taxation.

C. *DEBT REFUNDING*

The exchange of bonds for other bonds of the same issuer which differ only in immaterial details (e.g., extended maturity) does not produce a "realization." Such "refunding" does not constitute an "exchange" or "other disposition." See West Missouri Power Co., 18 T.C. 105 (1952), acq. 1952-2 Cum. Bull. 3; Rev. Rul. 56-435, 1956-2 Cum. Bull. 506. See Treas. Reg. §1.1001-1(a) for the materiality necessary for a "closed transaction."

What distinguishes a "refunding" or "conversion" from a "sale," "exchange," or "other disposition"? What should the law be? Why?

D. *EXCHANGE OF INVESTOR INTEREST*

1. *For Assets — §1031*

Normally, a corporate investor who exchanges his appreciated (or depreciated) corporate stock or debt for assets (other than for stock or securities) has recognized gain (or loss). Chapter 2, page 123 supra, deals with many of the exchange transactions in which the issuing corporation exchanges its assets for the investor's interest.

If an investor transfers his corporate interest to a person other than the issuing corporation and receives assets (other than stock or securities) in exchange, his gain is recognized. A few provisions (e.g., §§267, 1091) provide for nonrecognition of his loss. Section 1031, a nonrecognition provision applicable to the exchange of business and investment assets, is made expressly inapplicable to an exchange involving stock or securities. Why?

2. *For Stock or Securities — §§1031, 1036*

Section 1036 provides for nonrecognition (and §1031(d) for carryover of basis) where common stock is exchanged for common stock in the same corporation and where preferred stock is exchanged for preferred stock in the same corporation. Note that a "reorganization" is not a prerequisite for this provision to operate, as it is for §354.

Why is §1036 in the Code? Why is it limited to stock "in the same corporation"? Why does it not cover an exchange of common for preferred (or vice versa) in the same corporation? Does §1036 cover an exchange between investors only? Between an investor and his corporation only? Between investors as well as between the investor and his corporation? See Treas. Reg. §1.1036-1.

Is §1036 applicable to an exchange of Class A (voting) common stock for Class B (non-voting) common stock in the same corporation? Why? Is it applicable to an exchange of a 6 per cent, participating, cumulative, non-voting preferred stock for an 8 per cent, non-participating, non-cumulative, voting preferred stock in the same corporation? Why?

IV. THE STATUTE IN PERSPECTIVE

A. *BEFORE SPECIAL STATUTORY TREATMENT*

MARR v. UNITED STATES
268 U.S. 536 (1925), aff'g 58 Ct. Cl. 658

Mr. Justice Brandeis delivered the opinion of the Court. Prior to March 1, 1913, Marr and wife purchased 339 shares of the preferred and 425 shares of the common stock of the General Motors Company of New Jersey for $76,400. In 1916, they received in exchange for this stock 451 shares of the preferred and 2,125 shares of the common stock of the General Motors Corporation of Delaware which (including a small cash payment) had the aggregate market value of $400,866.57. The difference between the cost of their stock in the New Jersey corporation and the value of the stock in the Delaware corporation was $324,466.57. The Treasury Department ruled that this difference was gain or income under the Act of September 8, 1916, c. 463, Title I, §§1 and 2, 39 Stat. 756, 757;* and assessed, on that account, an additional income tax for 1916 which amounted, with interest, to $24,944.12. That sum Marr paid under protest. He then appealed to the Commissioner of Internal Revenue by filing a claim for a refund; and, upon the disallowance of that claim, brought this suit in the Court of Claims to recover the amount. Judgment was entered for the United States. 58 Ct. Cl. 658. The case is here on appeal under §242 of the Judicial Code.

The exchange of securities was effected in this way. The New Jersey corporation had outstanding $15,000,000 of 7 per cent. preferred stock and $15,000,000 of the common stock, all shares being of the par value of $100. It had accumulated from profits a large surplus. The actual value of the common stock was then $842.50 a share. Its officers caused to be organized the Delaware corporation, with an authorized capital of $20,000,000 in 6 per cent. non-voting preferred stock and $82,600,000 in common stock, all shares being of the par value of $100. The Delaware corporation made to stockholders in the New Jersey corporation the following offer for exchange

*Section 61(a) of the 1954 Code. — Ed.

of securities: For every share of common stock of the New Jersey corporation, five shares of common stock of the Delaware corporation. For every share of the preferred stock of the New Jersey corporation, one and one-third shares of preferred stock of the Delaware corporation. In lieu of a certificate for fractional shares of stock in the Delaware corporation payment was to be made in cash at the rate of $100 a share for its preferred and at the rate of $150 a share for its common stock. On this basis all the common stock of the New Jersey corporation was exchanged and all the preferred stock except a few shares. These few were redeemed in cash. For acquiring the stock of the New Jersey corporation only $75,000,000 of the common stock of the Delaware corporation was needed. The remaining $7,600,000 of the authorized common stock was either sold or held for sale as additional capital should be desired. The Delaware corporation, having thus become the owner of all the outstanding stock of the New Jersey corporation, took a transfer of its assets and assumed its liabilities. The latter was then dissolved.

It is clear that all new securities issued in excess of an amount equal to the capitalization of the New Jersey corporation represented income earned by it; that the new securities received by the Marrs in excess of the cost of the securities of the New Jersey corporation theretofore held were financially the equivalent of $324,466.57 in cash; and that Congress intended to tax as income of stockholders such gains when so distributed. The serious question for decision is whether it had power to do so. Marr contends that, since the new corporation was organized to take over the assets and continue the business of the old, and his capital remained invested in the same business enterprise, the additional securities distributed were in legal effect a stock dividend; and that under the rule of Eisner v. Macomber, 252 U.S. 189, applied in Weiss v. Stearn, 265 U.S. 242, he was not taxable thereon as income, because he still held the whole investment. The Government insists that identity of the business enterprise is not conclusive; that gain in value resulting from profits is taxable as income, not only when it is represented by an interest in a different business enterprise or property, but also when it is represented by an essentially different interest in the same business enterprise or property; that, in the case at bar, the gain actually made is represented by securities with essentially different characteristics in an essentially different corporation; and that, consequently, the additional value of the new securities, although they are still held by the Marrs, is income under the rule applied in United States v. Phellis, 257 U.S. 156; Rockefeller v. United States, 257 U.S. 176; and Cullinan v. Walker, 262 U.S. 134. In our opinion the Government is right.

In each of the five cases named, as in the case at bar, the business enterprise actually conducted remained exactly the same. In United States v. Phellis, in Rockefeller v. United States and in Cullinan v. Walker, where the additional value in new securities distributed was held to be taxable as income, there had been changes of corporate identity. That is, the corporate property, or a part thereof, was no longer held and operated by the same corporation; and, after the distribution, the stockholders no longer owned merely the same proportional interest of the same character in the same corporation. In Eisner v. Macomber and in Weiss v. Stearn, where the additional value in new securities was held not to be taxable, the identity was deemed to have been preserved. In Eisner v. Macomber the identity was literally maintained. There was no new corporate entity. The same interest in the same corporation was represented after the distribution by more shares of precisely the same character. It was as if the par value of the stock had been reduced, and three shares of reduced par value stock had been issued in place of every two old shares. That is, there was an exchange of certificates but not of interests. In Weiss v. Stearn a new corporation had, in fact, been organized to take over the assets and business of the old. Technically there was a new entity; but the corporate identity was deemed to have been substantially maintained because the new corporation was organized under the laws of the same State, with presumably the same powers as the old. There was also no change in the character of securities issued. By reason of these facts, the proportional interest of the stockholder after the distribution of the new securities was deemed to be exactly the same as if the par value of the stock in the old corporation had been reduced, and five shares of reduced par value stock had been issued in place of every two shares of the old stock. Thus, in Weiss v. Stearn, as in Eisner v. Macomber, the transaction was considered, in essence, an exchange of certificates representing the same interest, not an exchange of interests.

In the case at bar, the new corporation is essentially different from the old. A corporation organized under the laws of Delaware does not have the same rights and powers as one organized under the laws of New Jersey. Because of these inherent differences in rights and powers, both the preferred and the common stock of the old corporation is an essentially different thing from stock of the same general kind in the new. But there are also adventitious differences, substantial in character. A 6 per cent. non-voting preferred stock is an essentially different thing from a 7 per cent. voting preferred stock. A common stock subject to the priority of $20,000,000 preferred and a $1,200,000 annual dividend charge is an essentially different thing from a common stock subject only to $15,000,000 preferred and a $1,050,000 annual dividend charge. The case at bar is not one in which after the distribution the stockholders have the same proportional interest of the same kind in essentially the same corporation.

Affirmed.

The separate opinion of Mr. Justice VAN DEVANTER, Mr. Justice McREYNOLDS, Mr. Justice SUTHERLAND and Mr. Justice BUTLER. We think this cause falls within the doctrine of Weiss v. Stearn, 265 U.S. 242, and that the judgment below should be reversed. The practical result of the things done was but the reorganization of a going concern. The business and assets were not materially changed, and the stockholder received nothing actually severed from his original capital interest — nothing differing in substance from what he already had.

Weiss v. Stearn did not turn upon the relatively unimportant circumstance that the new and old corporations were organized under the laws of the same State, but upon the approved definition of income from capital as something severed therefrom and received by the taxpayer for his separate use and benefit. Here stockholders got nothing from the old business or assets except new statements of their undivided interests, and this, as we carefully pointed out, is not enough to create taxable income.

B. *BUSINESS PURPOSE*

HELVERING v. GREGORY
*69 F.2d 809 (2d Cir. 1934), aff'd, 293 U.S. 465 (1935)**

Before L. Hand, Swan, and Augustus N. Hand, Circuit Judges.

L. Hand, Circuit Judge. This is an appeal (petition to review), by the Commissioner of Internal Revenue from an order of the Board of Tax Appeals expunging a deficiency in income taxes for the year 1928. The facts were as follows: The taxpayer owned all the shares of the United Mortgage Corporation, among whose assets were some of the shares of another company, the Monitor Securities Corporation. In 1928 it became possible to sell the Monitor shares at a large profit, but if this had been done directly, the United Mortgage Corporation would have been obliged to pay a normal tax on the resulting gain, and the taxpayer, if she wished to touch her profit, must do so in the form of a dividend, on which a surtax would have been assessed against her personally. To reduce these taxes as much as possible, the following plan was conceived and put through: The taxpayer incorporated in Delaware a new company, organized ad hoc, and called the Averill Corporation, to which the United Mortgage Corporation transferred all its shares in the Monitor Securities Corporation, under an agreement by which the Averill Corporation issued all its shares to the taxpayer. Being so possessed of all the Averill shares, she wound up the Averill company three days later, receiving as a liquidating dividend the Monitor shares, which she thereupon sold. It is not disputed that all these steps were part of one purpose to reduce taxes, and that the Averill Corporation, which was in existence for only a few days, conducted no business and was intended to conduct none, except to act as conduit for the Monitor shares in the way we have described. The taxpayer's return for the year 1928 was made on the theory that the transfer of the Monitor shares to the Averill Corporation was a "reorganization" under section 112(i)(1)(B) of the Revenue Act of 1928† (26 USCA §2112(i)(1)(B)), being "a transfer by a corporation of . . . a part of its assets to another corporation" in such circumstances that immediately thereafter "the transferor or its stockholders or both are in control of the corporation to which the assets are transferred." Since the transfer was a reorganization, she claimed to come within section [354(a)(1)] . . . ,‡ and that her "gain" should not be "recognized," because the Averill shares were "distributed, in pursuance of a plan of reorganization." The Monitor shares she asserted to have been received as a single liquidating dividend of the Averill Corporation, and that as such she was only taxable for them under section [331] . . . and upon their value less the cost properly allocated to the Averill shares. That cost she determined as that proportion of the original cost of her shares in the United Mortgage Corporation,

*Page 471 infra. — Ed.
†Cf. §368(a)(1)(D) of the 1954 Code. — Ed.
‡Cf. §354(b) of the 1954 Code. —Ed.

which the Monitor shares bore to the whole assets of the United Mortgage Corporation. This difference she returned, and paid the tax calculated upon it. The Commissioner assessed a deficiency taxed upon the theory that the transfer of the Monitor shares to the Averill Corporation was not a true "reorganization" within section 112(i)(1)(B), 26 USCA §2112(i)(1)(B), being intended only to avoid taxes. He treated as nullities that transfer, the transfer of the Averill shares to the taxpayer, and the winding up of the Averill Corporation ending in the receipt by her of the Monitor shares; and he ruled that the whole transaction was merely the declaration of a dividend by the United Mortgage Corporation consisting of the Monitor shares in specie, on which the taxpayer must pay a surtax calculated at their full value. The taxpayer appealed and the Board held that the Averill Corporation had been in fact organized and was indubitably a corporation, that the United Mortgage Corporation had with equal certainty transferred to it the Monitor shares, and that the taxpayer had got the Averill shares as part of the transaction. All these transactions being real, their purpose was irrelevant, and section 112(i)(1)(B) was applicable, especially since it was part of a statute of such small mesh as the Revenue Act of 1928; the finer the reticulation, the less room for inference. The Board therefore expunged the deficiency, and the Commissioner appealed.

We agree with the Board and the taxpayer that a transaction, otherwise within an exception of the tax law, does not lose its immunity, because it is actuated by a desire to avoid, or, if one choose, to evade, taxation. Any one may so arrange his affairs that his taxes shall be as low as possible; he is not bound to choose that pattern which will best pay the Treasury; there is not even a patriotic duty to increase one's taxes. . . . Therefore, if what was done here, was what was intended by section 112(i)(1)(B), it is of no consequence that it was all an elaborate scheme to get rid of income taxes, as it certainly was. Nevertheless, it does not follow that Congress meant to cover such a transaction, not even though the facts answer the dictionary definitions of each term used in the statutory definition. It is quite true, as the Board has very well said, that as the articulation of a statute increases, the room for interpretation must contract; but the meaning of a sentence may be more than that of the separate words, as a melody is more than the notes, and no degree of particularity can ever obviate recourse to the setting in which all appear, and which all collectively create. The purpose of the section is plain enough; men engaged in enterprises — industrial, commercial, financial, or any other — might wish to consolidate, or divide, to add to, or subtract from, their holdings. Such transactions were not to be considered as "realizing" any profit, because the collective interests still remained in solution. But the underlying presupposition is plain that the readjustment shall be undertaken for reasons germane to the conduct of the venture in hand, not as an ephemeral incident, egregious to its prosecution. To dodge the shareholders' taxes is not one of the transactions contemplated as corporate "reorganizations."

This accords both with the history of the section, and with its interpretation by the courts, though the exact point has not hitherto arisen. It first appeared in the Act of 1924, §203(h)(1)(B), 26 USCA §934(h)(1)(B), and as the committee reports show (Senate Reports 398), was intended as supplementary to section 112(g), 26 USCA §2112(g), then section 203(c), 26 USCA §934(c); both in combination changed the law as laid down in U.S. v. Phellis, 257 U.S. 156, 42 S. Ct. 63, 66 L. Ed. 180, and Rockefeller v. U.S., 257 U.S. 176, 42 Sup. Ct. 68, 66 L. Ed. 186. In the House Report (No. 179, 68th Congress 1st Sess.), and in the Senate Report (No. 398), the purpose was stated to be to exempt "from tax the gain from exchanges made in connection with a reorganization in order that ordinary business transactions will not be prevented." . . . Moreover, we regard Pinellas Ice & Cold Storage Co. v. Com'r, 287 U.S. 462, 53 S. Ct. 257, 77 L. Ed. 428, and our own decision in Cortland Specialty Co. v. Com'r, 60 F.(2d) 937, as pertinent, if not authoritative. In each the question was of the applicability of a precursor of section 112(i)(1)(A) of 1928, 26 USCA §2112(i)(1)(A), to the sale of all the assets of one company to another, which gave in exchange, cash and short time notes. The taxpayer's argument was that this was a "merger or consolidation," because the buyer acquired "all the property of another corporation," the seller, that being one statutory definition of "merger or consolidation." That assumed, the exemption was urged to fall within section 112(g) as here. It might have been enough to hold that short time notes were not "securities," within section 112(g); but both courts went further and declared that the transaction was not a "merger or consolidation," but a sale, though literally it fell within the words of section 112(i)(1)(A). This they did, because its plain purpose was to cover only a situation in which after the transaction there continued some community of interest between the companies, other than holding such notes. The violence done the literal interpretation of the words is no less than what we do here. Moreover, the act itself gives evidence that, on occasion anyway, the purpose of a transaction should be the guide; thus in section 115(g), 26 USCA §2115(g),* the cancellation of shares is to be treated as a dividend — though otherwise it would not be such — if it is "essentially equivalent to the distribution of a taxable dividend"; again in section 112(c)(2), 26 USCA §2112(c)(2),† a distribution is in part taxable as a dividend, if it "has the effect of the distribution of a taxable dividend."

We do not indeed agree fully with the way in which the Commissioner treated the transaction; we cannot treat as inoperative the transfer of the Monitor shares by the United Mortgage Corporation, the issue by the Averill Corporation of its own shares to the taxpayer, and her acquisition of the Monitor shares by winding up that company. The Averill Corporation had a juristic personality, whatever the purpose of its organization; the transfer passed title to the Monitor shares and the taxpayer became a shareholder in the transferee. All these steps were real, and their only defect was that they were not what the statute means by a "reorganization," because the transactions were no part of the conduct of the business of either or both companies; so viewed they were a sham, though all the proceedings had their usual effect. But the result is the same whether the tax be calculated as the Commissioner calculated it, or upon the value of the Averill shares as a dividend, and the only question that can arise is whether the deficiency must be expunged, though right in result, if it was computed by a method, partly wrong. Although this is argued with some warmth,

*Cf. §§302(a) and 317(b) of the 1954 Code. — ED.
†Cf. §356(a)(2) of the 1954 Code. — ED.

it is plain that the taxpayer may not avoid her just taxes because the reasoning of the assessing officials has not been entirely our own.

Order reversed; deficiency assessed.

GREGORY v. HELVERING
293 U.S. 465 (1935), aff'g 69 F.2d 809 (2d Cir. 1934)

Mr. Justice SUTHERLAND delivered the opinion of the Court. Petitioner in 1928 was the owner of all the stock of United Mortgage Corporation. That corporation held among its assets 1,000 shares of the Monitor Securities Corporation. For the sole purpose of procuring a transfer of these shares to herself in order to sell them for her individual profit, and, at the same time, diminish the amount of income tax which would result from a direct transfer by way of dividend, she sought to bring about a "reorganization" under §112(g) of the Revenue Act of 1928, c. 852, 45 Stat. 791, 818, set forth later in this opinion. To that end, she caused the Averill Corporation to be organized under the laws of Delaware on September 18, 1928. Three days later, the United Mortgage Corporation transferred to the Averill Corporation the 1,000 shares of Monitor stock, for which all the shares of the Averill Corporation were issued to the petitioner. On September 24, the Averill Corporation was dissolved, and liquidated by distributing all its assets, namely, the Monitor shares, to the petitioner. No other business was ever transacted, or intended to be transacted, by that company. Petitioner immediately sold the Monitor for $133,333.33. She returned for taxation as capital net gain the sum of $76,007.88, based upon an apportioned cost of $57,325.45. Further details are unnecessary. It is not disputed that if the interposition of the so-called reorganization was ineffective, petitioner became liable for a much larger tax as a result of the transaction.

The Commissioner of Internal Revenue, being of opinion that the reorganization attempted was without substance and must be disregarded, held that petitioner was liable for a tax as though the United corporation had paid her a dividend consisting of the amount realized from the sale of the Monitor shares. In a proceeding before the Board of Tax Appeals, that body rejected the commissioner's view and upheld that of petitioner. 27 B.T.A. 223. Upon a review of the latter decision, the circuit court of appeals sustained the commissioner and reversed the board, holding that there had been no "reorganization" within the meaning of the statute. 69 F.(2d) 809. Petitioner applied to this court for a writ of certiorari, which the government, considering the question one of importance, did not oppose. We granted the writ.

Section 112 of the Revenue Act of 1928 deals with the subject of gain or loss resulting from the sale or exchange of property. Such gain or loss is to be recognized in computing the tax, except as provided in that section. The provisions of the section, so far as they are pertinent to the question here presented, follow:

"Sec. 112. (g) *Distribution of stock on reorganization.*—If there is distributed, in pursuance of a plan of reorganization, to a shareholder in a corporation a party to the reorganization, stock or securities in such corporation or in another corporation a party to the reorganization, without the surrender by such shareholder of stock or securities in such a corporation, no gain to the distributee from the receipt of such stock or securities shall be recognized. . . .

"(i) *Definition of reorganization.* — As used in this section . . .

"(1) The term 'reorganization' means . . . (B) a transfer by a corporation of all or a part of its assets to another corporation if immediately after the transfer the transferor or its stockholders or both are in control of the corporation to which the assets are transferred, . . ."

It is earnestly contended on behalf of the taxpayer that since every element required by the foregoing subdivision (B) is to be found in what was done, a statutory reorganization was effected; and that the motive of the taxpayer thereby to escape payment of a tax will not alter the result or make unlawful what the statute allows. It is quite true that if a reorganization in reality was effected within the meaning of subdivision (B), the ulterior purpose mentioned will be disregarded. The legal right of a taxpayer to decrease the amount of what otherwise would be his taxes, or altogether avoid them, by means which the law permits, cannot be doubted. United States v. Isham, 17 Wall. 496, 506; Superior Oil Co. v. Mississippi, 280 U.S. 390, 395-6; Jones v. Helvering, 63 App. D.C. 204; 71 F.(2d) 214, 217. But the question for determination is whether what was done, apart from the tax motive, was the thing which the statute intended. The reasoning of the court below in justification of a negative answer leaves little to be said.

When subdivision (B) speaks of a transfer of assets by one corporation to another, it means a transfer made "in pursuance of a plan or reorganization" [§112(g)] of corporate business; and not a transfer of assets by one corporation to another in pursuance of a plan having no relation to the business of either, as plainly is the case here. Putting aside, then, the question of motive in respect of taxation altogether, and fixing the character of the proceeding by what actually occurred, what do we find? Simply an operation having no business or corporate purpose — a mere device which put on the form of a corporate reorganization as a disguise for concealing its real character, and the sole object and accomplishment of which was the consummation of a preconceived plan, not to reorganize a business or any part of a business, but to transfer a parcel of corporate shares to the petitioner. No doubt, a new and valid corporation was created. But that corporation was nothing more than a contrivance to the end last described. It was brought into existence for no other purpose; it performed, as it was intended from the beginning it should perform, no other function. When that limited function had been exercised, it immediately was put to death.

In these circumstances, the facts speak for themselves and are susceptible of but one interpretation. The whole undertaking, though conducted according to the terms of subdivision (B), was in fact an elaborate and devious form of conveyance masquerading as a corporate reorganization, and nothing else. The rule which excludes from consideration the motive of tax avoidance is not pertinent to the situation, because the transaction upon its face lies outside the plain intent of the statute. To hold otherwise would be to exalt artifice above reality and to deprive the statutory provision in question of all serious purpose.

Judgment affirmed.

NOTE

The Court of Appeals said that "the result is the same whether the tax be calculated as the Commissioner calculated it, or upon the value of the Averill shares as a dividend. . . ." (page 470 supra). The Commissioner, according to that court, argued that "the whole transaction was merely the declaration of a dividend by the United Mortgage Corporation consisting of the Monitor shares in specie. . . ." (page 469 supra). The Supreme Court, however, thought that the Commissioner claimed the transaction should be taxed "as though the United [C]orporation had paid her a dividend consisting of the amount realized from the sale of the Monitor shares." Might there be any difference in result?

The Supreme Court says (page 472 supra) that a "plan of reorganization" does not exist where the transfer has "no relation to the business of either" corporation. If the transfer has some relation to the business of the parent, must there be a non-tax reason for the particular method of disposition chosen in order to avoid the result in *Gregory*? Why?

Should the result in a "reorganization" case depend on the purpose or motive of the transaction? How might the Supreme Court have reached the result it did without reference to the parties' tax as opposed to non-tax objectives?

GRANITE TRUST CO. v. UNITED STATES
238 F.2d 670 (1st Cir. 1956)

Before MAGRUDER, Chief Judge, and WOODBURY and HARTIGAN, Circuit Judges.

MAGRUDER, Chief Judge. . . . In 1928 the Building Corporation was organized by Granite Trust Company for the purpose of acquiring land and constructing an office building thereon to be occupied by the bank. The land and building cost over $1,000,000 and were financed through the purchase by the taxpayer bank of all the stock of the Building Corporation. The Building Corporation rented a portion of the premises to Howard D. Johnson Company for a rental of approximately $13,700 per year. This last-named corporation was in 1943 wholly owned by Howard D. Johnson, an individual. Neither Howard D. Johnson Company, nor Johnson, owned any stock in Granite Trust Company, and no shareholder or officer of Howard D. Johnson Company was a director in, or otherwise connected with, Granite Trust Company, though both Howard D. Johnson Company, and Johnson, were depositors in the taxpayer bank.

Beginning at least as early as 1936, the amount at which the stock of the Building

Corporation was carried upon the taxpayer's books was subjected to continuous criticism by various banking authorities. As a result, the taxpayer wrote down the value of the stock on its books, but nevertheless the examining authorities continued to press for further annual reductions.

At some time prior to October, 1943, the taxpayer's management commenced the formulation of a plan to bring this issue to a close by the expedient of having Granite Trust Company purchase the real estate from the Building Corporation for $550,000, a fair current appraisal, after which the subsidiary Building Corporation was to be liquidated. The practical problem in the execution of this plan resulted from the fact that the distribution in the liquidation of the subsidiary corporation was expected to amount to something between $65 and $66 per share upon the shares of common stock in the Building Corporation for which the taxpayer had paid $100 per share. In thus contributing to the simplification of the corporate structure of the taxpayer as a holding company, an end deemed desirable by the Congress, Granite Trust Company naturally wanted to be assured that its prospective loss to be realized upon the liquidation of its subsidiary would lawfully be "recognized" at once so as to be available as a tax deduction.

In order that this forthcoming loss upon its investment might not be denied recognition by §[332] . . . , the taxpayer, on advice of counsel, proceeded to divest itself of some of its shares of common stock in the Building Corporation by means of several purported sales and of a gift, the facts concerning which are as follows:

As of December 1, 1943, the outstanding capital stock of the Building Corporation, all owned by the taxpayer, consisted of 2,250 shares of preferred stock and 5,000 shares of common stock, the latter being the sole voting stock. On December 6, 1943, the taxpayer sold to, or went through the form of selling to, Howard D. Johnson Company 1,025 shares of common stock of the Building Corporation, that being 20.5 per cent of the outstanding voting stock. Howard D. Johnson Company paid $65.50 per share, a total of $67,137.50, and delivered to the taxpayer its check for this amount, which was charged to the deposit account of Howard D. Johnson Company on December 6, 1943, and credited to the general funds of the taxpayer. On the same day the taxpayer surrendered to the Building Corporation certificates covering 1,025 shares of common stock, and the Building Corporation issued to Howard D. Johnson Company a new certificate for that number of shares, which certificate was held by Howard D. Johnson Company until it was surrendered on December 17, 1943, in the course of the final liquidation of the Building Corporation.

At a meeting of the Building Corporation stockholders held on December 10, 1943, the taxpayer submitted a written offer to purchase the real estate for $550,000. The stockholders voted to accept this offer, and at the same meeting the following vote was taken:

> "That if and when this Corporation shall receive $550,000, adjusted as
> provided in the vote with regard to the sale of the Corporation's real estate,
> this Corporation shall be completely liquidated, and after payment or pro-
> vision for payment of all debts of, claims against and obligations of this

Corporation, all of its remaining assets shall be distributed at such time or times to stockholders of record at such date or dates, and under and subject to such circumstances as the Board of Directors may determine, to the stockholders of the Corporation pro rata in accordance with the respective priorities of the outstanding shares of the Corporation, provided, however, that such liquidation and distribution shall be made and shall be entirely completed prior to December 30, 1943."

At the date of the foregoing corporate action by the Building Corporation, namely, December 10, 1943, Granite Trust Company was the legal and equitable holder of 3,975 shares (79.5 per cent) of the then outstanding 5,000 shares of common stock. Howard D. Johnson Company, which as above stated held a certificate for 1,025 shares of common stock, waived notice of the stockholders' meeting and did not attend. Taxpayer's 3,975 shares were the only shares represented and acting at the meeting.

Thereafter, on December 13, 1943, the taxpayer sold, or went through the form of selling, ten shares each of the common stock in the Building Corporation to Howard D. Johnson individually and to one Ralph E. Richmond, for a price of $65.50 per share. On the same day the taxpayer donated to the Greater Boston United War Fund two shares of the common stock of the Building Corporation. Johnson and Richmond duly paid by check for the shares they bought, and the taxpayer delivered to them and to the United War Fund certificates sufficient to cover the shares sold or donated, which certificates were held by Johnson, Richmond, and the United War Fund until surrendered by them on December 17 in the course of the final liquidation of the Building Corporation.

At no time after the making of the above sales and gift did the taxpayer acquire any additional common stock in the Building Corporation.

On December 15, 1943, the real estate was conveyed to the taxpayer by the Building Corporation, and the taxpayer paid the Building Corporation the price of $550,000, appropriately adjusted for local taxes, rentals and insurance. The real estate was thereby brought on to the taxpayer's books at a cost equivalent to current fair market value, thus satisfying the banking authorities.

On December 17, 1943, the Building Corporation called for retirement at par of its outstanding preferred stock and paid the taxpayer therefor the sum of $225,000. On the same day the Building Corporation paid a final liquidating distribution in the amount of $65.77 per share with respect to each share of its outstanding common stock, and all holders surrendered their certificates for such outstanding shares. The taxpayer, as the owner of 3,953 shares of common stock, received $259,988.81. The owners of the other 1,047 shares of the Building Corporation common stock received, respectively: Howard D. Johnson Company, $67,414.25; Howard D. Johnson, $657.70; Ralph E. Richmond, $657.70; Greater Boston United War Fund, $131.54. Each payee received and retained these amounts.

On December 30, 1943, a final meeting of the Building Corporation stockholders was held, there being represented at the meeting the taxpayer, Howard D. Johnson

Company, Howard D. Johnson, Ralph E. Richmond, and Greater Boston United War Fund. Dissolution was voted, with authority to the corporation's directors and officers to take all steps necessary or advisable to that end.

The taxpayer concedes that it would not have made the sales described above had it not been for §[332]. . . . While the taxpayer maintains that the gift to the United War Fund was but part of the total gift to that organization for the year 1943, it seems clear, because this was the only case where shares of stock rather than cash were distributed to the charity, that at least the specific object given at this time was dictated by §[332].

The precise issue before us is whether or not to give effect for tax purposes to the aforesaid sales and gift by the taxpayer. If the answer is in the affirmative, there is no doubt that the liquidation distribution of the property of the Building Corporation was not in "complete liquidation" within the very special meaning of that phrase in §[332] . . . , and, accordingly, the taxpayer may recognize the loss on its investment.

Although there is no dispute that the transactions in form at least purport to be sales and a gift, the Commissioner nevertheless maintains that we should not accord them that significance. The Commissioner's argument is in two parts: The first proposition derives from the basic finding of the district court that the taxpayer effected the liquidation "in such manner as to achieve a tax reduction" and that this was "without legal or moral justification." The Commissioner attempts to bolster this argument by his traditional corporation reorganization analysis to the effect that, so long as the "end-result" of the transactions involved complies with the "criteria of the statute," intermediary steps (in this case the sales and gift) should be ignored as if they were nonexistent. His reasoning is that, if the final outcome is complete liquidation of a subsidiary corporation which at the outset was wholly owned by the taxpayer, the entire procedure comes within the intendment of the statute and "[c]ircuitous steps to avoid Section [332]" occurring prior to the ultimate liquidation should be disregarded.

The Commissioner's second proposition is that there were *in fact* no valid sales or gift of stock made by the taxpayer. This argument rests on the taxpayer's admission that the transfers were motivated solely by tax considerations and were made in a friendly atmosphere to friendly people who knew of the decision to liquidate the corporation before the end of the year. As the Commissioner points out, the liquidation took place shortly after the transfers, and the transferees then received back the money they had paid in, plus a small profit. Therefore, the Commissioner argues, relying heavily on Gregory v. Helvering, 1935, 293 U.S. 465, 55 S. Ct. 266, 79 L. Ed. 596, that "the stock transfers in question had no independent purpose or meaning — either for the transferor or the transferees — but constituted merely a transitory and circuitous routing of legal title for the purpose of avoiding taxes, within the meaning of Gregory v. Helvering, supra. It was not expected or intended by any of the parties that the transferees should become true stockholders. Legal title passed; but beneficial ownership surely never passed. The transferees who paid money for their stock knew that the subsidiary would be liquidated in a few days and that they would get their money back — as in fact they did, with additional amounts to pay them for their cooperation in serving as conduits of title." The gift of stock to the United War Fund is dismissed as "nothing more than a gift of the cash." . . .

Our conclusion is that the Commissioner's arguments must be rejected, and that the taxpayer should be permitted to "recognize" the loss on its investment, which it undoubtedly realized upon the liquidation of the Building Corporation.

Initially we may note, without ruling upon it, one legal argument made by the Commissioner having to do with the efficacy of the purported sale of 1,025 shares of stock to Howard D. Johnson Company on December 6, 1943. The Commissioner contends that, to satisfy the first condition of nonrecognition prescribed in §[332], it is not necessary to have a formal plan of liquidation, evidenced by a corporate resolution, but it is sufficient if there is a "definitive determination" to achieve dissolution. It is claimed by the Commissioner that such a definitive determination existed here by November 10, 1943, and, therefore, that the sale of stock to Howard D. Johnson Company which took place on December 6, 1943 (before the formal adoption of the plan of liquidation) occurred *after* the "adoption of the plan of liquidation" within the meaning of §[332]. In this view the taxpayer owned 100 per cent of the subsidiary's stock on the date the plan of liquidation was adopted, from which it would follow, on the basis of the first condition of §[332], that the loss should not be "recognized."

We need not consider the foregoing legal argument on its merits, because the subsequent actions by the taxpayer — the sales to Johnson individually and to Richmond on December 13, 1943, and the gift of stock on the same day to the United War Fund — of themselves, if valid, successfully accomplished the taxpayer's purpose of avoiding the nonrecognition provisions of §[332] under the second condition contained in that subsection. This second condition prescribes, in a sort of backhanded way, that gain or loss shall be recognized if, at any time on or after the date of adoption of the plan of liquidation and prior to the date of the receipt of the property distributed in final liquidation, the receiving corporation is the owner of a greater percentage of any class of stock of the corporation being liquidated than the percentage of such stock owned by it at the time of the receipt of the property — which means that this condition precedent to the nonrecognition of a realized gain or loss is not satisfied if, in the described period, the receiving corporation has made an effective disposition of any of the shares of stock held in the subsidiary corporation, without making any countervailing acquisitions of such stock.

Turning then to the basic contentions of the Commissioner, not much need be said with reference to the proposition that the tax motive for the sales and gift rendered the transactions "immoral" and thus vitiated them. Again and again the courts have pointed out that a "purpose to minimize or avoid taxation is not an illicit motive." Sawtell v. Commissioner, 1 Cir., 1936, 82 F.2d 221, 222. The *Gregory* case itself makes this clear, Gregory v. Helvering, supra, 293 U.S. at page 469, 55 S. Ct. at page 267. . . .

As for the Commissioner's "end-result" argument, the very terms of §[332] make it evident that it is not an "end-result" provision, but rather one which prescribes specific conditions for the nonrecognition of realized gains or losses, conditions which, if not strictly met, make the section inapplicable. In fact, the Commissioner's own regulations (Reg. [§1.332-2]) emphasize the rigid requirements of the section and make no allowance for the type of "step transaction" theory advanced in this case.

The legislative history of §[332] likewise tends to support the position of the taxpayer. That history indicates that Congress was primarily concerned with providing a means of facilitating the simplification of corporate structures pursuant to the general policy enunciated in the Public Utility Holding Company Act of 1935, 49 Stat. 803, 15 U.S.C.A. §79 et seq. See Seidman's Legislative History of Federal Income Tax Laws 240-43 (1938); Helvering v. Credit Alliance Corp., 1942, 316 U.S. 107, 112, 62 S. Ct. 989, 86 L. Ed. 1307. This fact, while perhaps not conclusive as to the proper interpretation of §[332], nevertheless does lend a favorable background to the taxpayer's contention that the subsection, as a relief measure, was "not designed as a strait jacket into which corporations should be forced at the penalty of forfeiture of losses on liquidation of subsidiaries."

The more specific and more important bit of legislative history is found in the Report of the Senate Finance Committee at the time that §112(b)(6) [of the 1939 Code] was reenacted, with amendments, as §332 of the Internal Revenue Code of 1954. At this time, when Congress was engaged in a comprehensive reexamination of the Internal Revenue Code, the well-known case of Commissioner of Internal Revenue v. Day & Zimmermann, Inc., 3 Cir., 1945, 151 F.2d 517, had been decided in favor of the taxpayer, and it reasonably could be supposed that Congress, had it disapproved of the decision in that case, would have overturned its conclusion by making over §[332] into an "end-result" provision. In the *Day & Zimmermann* case, the taxpayer, admittedly in order to avoid the nonrecognition provisions of §[332] had sold at public auction a sufficient number of shares of a wholly owned subsidiary corporation to reduce its holdings below 80 per cent. These shares were bought, after general bidding, by the treasurer of the taxpayer, who, after receiving cash dividends in the subsequent liquidation of the companies, reported his gain and paid income tax thereon. The Third Circuit held that §[332] did not apply to the liquidation, emphasizing that the treasurer had paid a fair price for the shares, had used his own money, had not been directed by anyone to bid, and that there had been no showing of any understanding existing between him and the corporation by which the latter was to retain any sort of interest in the securities or in the proceeds therefrom. . . . Commissioner of Internal Revenue v. Day & Zimmermann, Inc., is not to be distinguished, as the Commissioner suggests, on the ground that the sale of stock was at public auction, without specific negotiation between the treasurer and the taxpayer. The significant thing in the case is its ultimate rationale that the purported sales of stock to the treasurer were in fact sales, notwithstanding the tax motive which prompted the corporation to enter into the transaction; from which it would seem to be irrelevant how the transfer was arranged, or whether or not it occurred at a public auction or exchange, so long as the beneficial as well as legal title was intended to pass and did pass. . . .

We come then to the Commissioner's second major contention, resting on Gregory v. Helvering, supra, that the sales of stock by the corporation should be ignored on the ground that they were not bona fide, and that the taxpayer therefore retained "beneficial ownership". The Commissioner characterizes the transfers as artificial, unessential, transitory phases of a completed tax avoidance scheme which should be disregarded.

In answer to this contention, it is first necessary to determine precisely what the *Gregory* case held. Judge Learned Hand, in Chisholm v. Commissioner, 2 Cir., 1935, 79 F.2d 14, 15, 101 A.L.R. 200, certiorari denied 1935, 296 U.S. 641, 56 S. Ct. 174, 80 L. Ed. 456, analyzed the case as follows:

> "*The question always is whether the transaction under scrutiny is in fact what it appears to be in form;* a marriage may be a joke; a contract may be intended only to deceive others; an agreement may have a collateral defeasance. In such cases the transaction as a whole is different from its appearance. . . . In Gregory v. Helvering, supra, 293 U.S. 465, 55 S. Ct. 266 . . . the incorporators adopted the usual form for creating business corporations; but their intent, or purpose, was merely to draught the papers, in fact not to create corporations as the court understood that word. That was the purpose which defeated their exemption, not the accompanying purpose to escape taxation; that purpose was legally neutral. Had they really meant to conduct a business by means of the two reorganized companies, they would have escaped whatever other aim they might have had, whether to avoid taxes, or to regenerate the world." [Italics added.]

In the present case the question is whether or not there actually were sales. Why the parties may wish to enter into a sale is one thing, but that is irrelevant under the *Gregory* case so long as the consummated agreement was no different from what it purported to be.

Even the Commissioner concedes that "[l]egal title" passed to the several transferees on December 13, 1943, but he asserts that "beneficial ownership" never passed. We find no basis on which to vitiate the purported sales, for the record is absolutely devoid of any evidence indicating an understanding by the parties to the transfers that any interest in the stock transferred was to be retained by the taxpayer. If Johnson or Richmond had gone bankrupt, or the assets of both had been attached by creditors, on the day after the sales to them, we do not see how the conclusion could be escaped that their Building Corporation stock would have been included in their respective assets; and if Johnson or Richmond had died, surely the holdings of stock of each would have passed to his executors or administrators, or legatees.

In addition to what we have said, there are persuasive reasons of a general nature which lend weight to the taxpayer's position. To strike down these sales on the alleged defect that they took place between friends and for tax motives would only tend to promote duplicity and result in extensive litigation as taxpayers led courts into hairsplitting investigations to decide when a sale was not a sale. It is no answer to argue that, under Gregory v. Helvering, there is an inescapable judicial duty to examine into the actuality of purported corporate reorganizations, for that was a special sort of transaction, whose bona fides could readily be ascertained by inquiring whether the ephemeral new corporation was in fact transacting business, or whether there was in fact a continuance of the proprietary interests under an altered corporate form. See Lewis v. Commissioner, 1 Cir., 1949, 176 F.2d 646.

What we have said so far is related chiefly to the validity of the sales. When we turn to the gift on December 13, 1943, to the United War Fund, the taxpayer is on even firmer ground. The Commissioner says that the gift was nothing more than a gift of cash, that the charity "was, at most, a passive transferee, without independent purpose, which held legal title to two shares for four days." This assertion rests, when examined closely, on the simple fact that the purpose for the gift was a tax avoidance one. But this does not disqualify it as an effective gift, transferring title. A gift certainly may have a tax motive. See Commissioner of Internal Revenue v. Newman, 2 Cir., 1947, 159 F.2d 848; Sawtell v. Commissioner, supra, 82 F.2d at page 222. Charitable contributions of low-cost securities are an every-day type of transfer motivated by tax purposes. The gift to the United War Fund, being valid, transferred two shares from the taxpayer after the adoption of the plan of liquidation, and alone sufficed to put the liquidation beyond the reach of the nonrecognition provisions of §[332].

In short, though the facts in this case show a tax avoidance, they also show legal transactions not fictitious or so lacking in substance as to be anything different from what they purported to be, and we believe they must be given effect in the administration of §[332] as well as for all other purposes. . . .

A judgment will be entered vacating the judgment of the District Court and remanding the case to that court with direction to enter judgment for the sum of $57,801.32, with interest.

C. STEP TRANSACTIONS

HELVERING v. ELKHORN COAL CO.
95 F.2d 732 (4th Cir. 1937), cert. denied, 305 U.S. 605 (1938)

Before PARKER and NORTHCOTT, Circuit Judges, and HENRY H. WATKINS, District Judge.

PARKER, Circuit Judge. This is a petition to review a decision of the Board of Tax Appeals holding profit realized by the Elkhorn Coal & Coke Company upon a transfer of certain mining properties to the Mill Creek Coal & Coke Company to be nontaxable. The ground of the decision was that the transfer was made pursuant to a plan of reorganization within the meaning of section [368(a)(1)(C)]. . . . The facts were stipulated and are set forth at length in the findings of the Board which are reported with its opinion in Elkhorn Coal Co. v. Com'r, 34 B.T.A. 845. Those material to the question presented by the petition are in substance as follows:

Prior to December 18, 1925, the Elkhorn Coal & Coke Company, to which we shall hereafter refer as the old company, owned certain coal mining properties in West Virginia and certain stocks in other mining companies engaged in business in that state. It was closely associated with the Mill Creek Coal & Coke Company, which owned neighboring property; and a majority of the directorate of both corporations consisted of the same persons. Early in December, 1925, a plan was formed whereby the old company was to transfer its mine, mining plant, and mining equipment at Maybeury, W. Va., to the Mill Creek Company in exchange for 1,000 shares of the capital stock of that company. This exchange was accomplished on December 31, 1925, at which time, it is stipulated, the stock received by the old company had a fair market value of $550,000 which is in excess of the deficiency asserted by the Commissioner. There is no contention that the transfer by the old company was to a corporation controlled by it or by its stockholders and therefore within the nonrecognition provision of section [368(a)(1)(D)] of the act; but the argument of the taxpayer is that the transfer was of all the properties of one corporation for the stock of another, and therefore within the nonrecognition provision of section [368(a)(1)(C)].

The contention that the transfer in question was of all the properties of the old company depends upon the legal conclusion to be drawn from certain evidentiary facts relating to the prior organization of another corporation and the transfer to it of all the property of the old company which was not to be transferred to the Mill Creek Company. These facts, which were found by the Board and are undisputed, are as follows: At the time that the transfer to the Mill Creek Company was decided upon, the officers of the old company caused another corporation to be organized under the name of the Elkhorn Coal Company, which we shall refer to hereafter as the new company, and on December 18, 1925, transferred to it, in exchange for 6,100 shares of its stock, all of the property of the old company which was not to be transferred to the Mill Creek Company except certain accounts, which were transferred to the new company on December 28, 1931, in consideration of its assuming the liabilities of the old company. The 6,100 shares of stock in the new company were promptly distributed by the old company as a dividend to its stockholders. This left the old company owning only the property which was to be transferred to the Mill Creek Company under the plan and which was transferred to that company on December 31st, as mentioned in the preceding paragraph. Following that transfer and the receipt by the old company of the 1,000 shares of the stock of the Mill Creek Company pursuant thereto, the new company proceeded to place itself in the same position relative to the stockholders of the old company that the old company had occupied, and then to wind up its affairs. It accomplished that result in the following manner: On January 22, 1926, it exchanged 1,440 shares of its capital stock for the 7,540 shares of the outstanding capital stock of the old company, making the exchange with the stockholders of that company. This gave those who had been stockholders in the old company the same interest in the new company that they had had in the old, and gave to the new company the ownership of all of the stock in the old. The 1,000 shares of stock received from the Mill Creek Company were then transferred to the new company and the old company was dissolved. No business whatever was done by the old company after the transfer of assets to the Mill Creek Company on December 31st; and no reason appears for the organization of the new company except to provide a transferee to take over and hold the assets which were not to be transferred to the Mill Creek Company so that the transfer to that company when made would be a transfer of all the assets of the old company.

The Board was of opinion that all of these transactions were carried through pursuant to prearranged plan, saying: "We do not doubt that before a single step was taken a plan had been formulated for regrouping the corporate assets"; and "The stipulated facts justify the inference that one of the motives which the stockholders of Elkhorn had in organizing the new corporation and causing the three corporations to adopt the several steps or plans of reorganization which were adopted and carried out, was to make the transfer of the mining properties from Elkhorn to Mill Creek without resulting tax liability to Elkhorn or to themselves." The Board thought, however, with five members dissenting, that because the transfers from the old company to the new were genuine and were separate and distinct from the transfer to the Mill Creek Company, the latter must be treated as a transfer of substantially all of the properties of the corporation within the meaning of the reorganization statute, summing up its conclusions as follows: "In our opinion, the facts show affirmatively that the transfer to Mill Creek was completely separate and distinct from the earlier transfer by Elkhorn to the new corporation. The transfer made on December 18 was complete within itself, regardless of what Elkhorn planned to do later, or did subsequently do. It was not a sham or a device intended to obscure the character of the transaction of December 31. The stipulated facts do not suggest other than a bona fide business move. The transfer made on December 31 was also complete within itself, and was made for reasons germane to the business of both corporations. This transfer falls within the terms of [§368(a)(1)(C)] . . . , whether or not Elkhorn was dissolved."

While we are bound by the Board's findings of evidentiary facts, we are not bound by the foregoing conclusion set forth in the opinion and embodying a mixed question of law and fact. As said by the Supreme Court in the recent case of Helvering v. Tex-Penn Oil Co., 300 U.S. 481, 57 S. Ct. 569, 574, 81 L. Ed. 755: "The ultimate finding is a conclusion of law or at least a determination of a mixed question of law and fact. It is to be distinguished from the findings of primary, evidentiary, or circumstantial facts. It is subject to judicial review and, on such review, the court may substitute its judgment for that of the Board."

A careful consideration of the evidentiary facts discloses no purpose which could have been served by the creation of the new company and the transfer of the assets to it, except to strip the old company of all of its properties which were not to be transferred to the Mill Creek Company, in anticipation of that transfer. The creation of the new company and its acquisition of the assets of the old was not a corporate reorganization, therefore, within the meaning of the statute or within any fair meaning of the term "reorganization." It did not involve any real transfer of assets by the business enterprise or any rearranging of corporate structure, but at most a mere shifting of charters, having no apparent purpose except the avoidance of taxes on the transfer to the Mill Creek Company which was in contemplation. To use in part the language of the Supreme Court in Gregory v.

Helvering, 293 U.S. 465, 469, 55 S. Ct. 266, 267, 79 L. Ed. 596, 97 A.L.R. 1355, it was "simply an operation having no business or corporate purpose — a mere device which put on the form of a corporate reorganization as a disguise for concealing its real character, and the sole object and accomplishment of which was the consummation of a preconceived plan, not to reorganize a business or any part of a business," but to give to the intended transfer to the Mill Creek Company the appearance of a transfer of all the corporate assets so as to bring it within the nonrecognition provision of section [368(a)(1)(C)].

Under such circumstances we think that the decision in Gregory v. Helvering, supra, is controlling. In that case, for the purpose of avoiding taxes on a liquidating dividend of shares of stock held by a corporation, a subsidiary was organized within the terms of the reorganization statute and the shares were transferred to it. The stock of the subsidiary was then delivered to the sole stockholder of the original corporation and shortly thereafter the subsidiary was dissolved and the shares which had been transferred to it were delivered to the stockholder. The court held that although the organization of the subsidiary came within the letter of the reorganization statute, such corporate manipulation would be ignored when it fulfilled no proper corporate function and was not in reality a reorganization within the meaning of the statute. The court said: "In these circumstances, the facts speak for themselves and are susceptible of but one interpretation. The whole undertaking, though conducted according to the terms of [§368(a)(1)(D)], was in fact an elaborate and devious form of conveyance masquerading as a corporate reorganization, and nothing else. The rule which excludes from consideration the motive of tax avoidance is not pertinent to the situation, because the transaction upon its face lies outside the plain intent of the statute. To hold otherwise would be to exalt artifice above reality and to deprive the statutory provision in question of all serious purpose."

We do not see how that case can be distinguished from this. If the property which was to be transferred to Mill Creek had been transferred to a new company created for the purpose and had been by that company transferred to Mill Creek, no one would contend that there was a distinction; and certainly there is no difference in principle between creating a subsidiary to take and convey the property to the intended transferee and creating a subsidiary to take over the other assets and having the old company make the transfer. In either case, the apparent reorganization is a mere artifice; and it can make no difference which of the affiliated corporations makes the transfer of assets which it is desired to bring within the nonrecognition provisions of the statute.

It is suggested in the opinion of the Board that the case before us is analogous to that which would have been presented if the old company, prior to the transfer to Mill Creek, had distributed to its stockholders all of the assets except those destined for such transfer; but the distinction is obvious. In the case supposed, the business enterprise would have definitely divested itself of the property distributed. Here it did not divest itself of the property at all, but merely made certain changes in the legal papers under which it enjoyed corporate existence. No rule is better settled than that in tax matters we must look to substance and not to form; and no one who looks to substance can see in the mere change of charters, which is all that we have here, any reason for permitting a transfer of a part of the corporate assets to escape the taxation to which it is subject under the statute.

Congress has seen fit to grant nonrecognition of profit in sale or exchange of assets only under certain conditions, one of which is that one corporation shall transfer "substantially all" of its properties for stock in another. If nonrecognition of profit can be secured by the plan adopted in this case, the exemption is broadened to cover all transfers of assets for stock, whether "substantially all" or not, if only the transferor will go to the slight trouble and expense of getting a new charter for his corporation and making the transfer of assets to the new corporation thus created in such way as to leave in the old only the assets to be transferred at the time the transfer is to be made. We do not think the statutory exemption may be thus broadened by such an artifice.

Having reached this conclusion, it is unnecessary to decide whether the unity of the plan under which the transfer was made brings it, without a unifying contract, within the principles laid down in Starr v. Commissioner (C.C.A. 4th) 82 F.(2d) 964, 968, wherein we said: "Where transfers are made pursuant to such a plan of reorganization, they are ordinarily parts of one transaction and should be so treated in application of the well-settled principle that, in applying income tax laws, the substance, and not the form, of the transaction shall control. First Seattle D. H. Nat. Bank v. Commissioner (C.C.A. 9th) 77 F.(2d) 45; Prairie Oil & Gas Co. v. Motter (C.C.A. 10th) 66 F.(2d) 309; Howard v. Commissioner (C.C.A. 6th) 56 F.(2d) 781; American Security & Trust Co. v. Tait (D.C.) 5 F. Supp. 337. This is demanded also by the principle, equally well settled, that a single transaction may not be broken up into various elements to avoid a tax. Ahles Realty Corporation v. Commissioner (C.C.A. 2d) 71 F.(2d) 150, 151; West Texas Refining & Development Co. v. Commissioner (C.C.A. 10th) 68 F.(2d) 77, 79, 80; Prairie Oil & Gas Co. v. Motter, supra (C.C.A. 10th) 66 F.(2d) 309, 311; Tulsa Tribune Co. v. Commissioner (C.C.A. 10th) 58 F.(2d) 937."

For the reasons stated, the decision of the Board will be reversed, and the cause will be remanded to it for further proceedings in accordance with this opinion.

Reversed.

HENRY H. WATKINS, District Judge (dissenting). I am unable to concur in the foregoing opinion. The reasons therefor will be briefly stated. The prevailing opinion recites the facts at some length but seems to lose sight of the emphasis that should be placed upon certain determinative and uncontradicted findings of the Board of Tax Appeals. Prior to December, 1925, when the transactions in question took place, Elkhorn Coal & Coke Company and Mill Creek Coal & Coke Company, both organized under the laws of West Virginia, had been actively engaged in coal mining operations; the former since its organization in 1889, and the latter since its organization in 1891. One of the Elkhorn Company's mines was located in McDowell county, W. Va.; the other at Maybeury in that state. Mill Creek's mines were located at Maybeury, adjacent to the property of Elkhorn. Owners of a controlling interest in Mill Creek, and the officers of the two companies were largely the same. In December, 1925, it was decided that it would be in the interest of economy to have all of the Maybeury properties owned by the two companies under one management, and for this purpose the reorganization plans outlined in the prevailing opinion were perfected. No claim is made that the transactions between Elkhorn Coal & Coke Company and Elkhorn Coal Company are taxable. The contention is that the transaction between Elkhorn Coal & Coke Company and Mill Creek Coal & Coke Company is taxable. Admittedly, if this transaction is isolated from the antecedent transactions, it was a transfer of all of the assets then owned by the one company to the other in exchange for stock. It is argued, however, that the antecedent transactions, which included the organization of the Elkhorn Coal Company, and the transfer to it by the original company of approximately 80 per cent. of its properties in exchange for stock, and the ultimate liquidation of the original company, showed that the whole transaction was a mere device to permit the sale of the Maybeury mines without incurring the liability for income and profits tax. In this connection we call attention to the fact that the very purpose of the statute in question was to permit, through corporate reorganization, an exchange of corporate stock without tax liability at the time, permitting the holder of the stock to await its sale before incurring such liability. Two facts should be borne in mind in determining the questions at issue; first, that the Elkhorn Coal & Coke Company received nothing but stock and in turn transferred to its stockholders nothing but stock in exchange for its properties; second, that the primary purpose of the plan of reorganization related to a more economical operation of the mining properties which had previously been carried on for many years, and which have since been carried on for approximately twelve years. The case is in striking contrast with that of Gregory v. Helvering, 293 U.S. 465, 55 S. Ct. 266, 267, 79 L. Ed. 596, 97 A.L.R. 1355, and, so far from regarding that case as requiring a reversal of the decision of the Board of Tax Appeals, I am convinced that it furnishes ample authority for sustaining the Board. In the *Gregory* Case, the court said that if a reorganization is in reality effected within the meaning of the statute, its ultimate purpose will be disregarded since the legal right of the taxpayer to decrease the amount of what would otherwise be his taxes, or altogether avoid them by means which the law permits, cannot be doubted. The court held, however, that: "When [§368(a)(1)(D)] speaks of a transfer of assets by one corporation to another, it means a transfer made 'in pursuance of a plan of reorganization' . . . *of corporate business;* and not a transfer of assets by one corporation to another in pursuance of a plan having *no relation to the business of either,* as plainly is the case here." (Italics ours.) It was further held that that case involved "Simply an operation having no business or corporate purpose — a mere device which put on the form of a corporate reorganization as a disguise for concealing its real character, and the sole object and accomplishment of which was the consummation of a preconceived plan, not to reorganize a business or any part of a business, but to transfer a parcel of corporate shares to the petitioner. No doubt, a new and valid corporation was created. But that corporation was nothing more than a contrivance to the end last described. It was brought into existence for no other purpose; it performed, as it was intended from the beginning it should perform, no other function. When that limited function had been exercised, it immediately was put to death." In that case, Mrs.

Gregory was the owner of all of the stock of the United Mortgage Corporation, which held among its assets 1,000 shares of the Monitor Securities Corporation. For the sole purpose of procuring a transfer of these shares to herself in order to sell them, as she did immediately sell them for her individual profit, and at the same time to diminish the amount of income tax which would have resulted from direct transfer by way of dividend, she organized the Averill Corporation of which likewise she was the sole owner, and had the United Mortgage Corporation transfer to it the 1,000 shares of Monitor stock in exchange for all the corporate shares of the Averill Corporation. Having been organized on September 18, 1928, and transacted the business for which it was brought into life, the Averill Corporation was six days later, on September 24th, dissolved by distributing all of its assets, namely the Monitor shares, to Mrs. Gregory. No other business was ever transacted or intended to be transacted. Contrast these facts with those above set out in the instant case, where the new corporation immediately entered into the active business of mining and has ever since discharged the mining functions for which it was chartered, and in which also the Mill Creek Company, in which other shares were acquired, was then fulfilling, and is still fulfilling, its corporate business of mining. There was no sham or pretense about the whole matter. It seems to me that the case comes more nearly under the decision of the Fifth Circuit Court of Appeals, David Gross v. Commissioner of Internal Revenue, 88 F.(2d) 567, which reverses David Gross, 34 B.T.A. 395; the last-mentioned case being one of those relied upon by the dissenting members of the Board of Tax Appeals in the *Elkhorn* Case.

On Rehearing.

PARKER, Circuit Judge. The rehearing granted in this case and careful consideration of the briefs filed and arguments made thereon have served only to strengthen the majority of the court in the opinion heretofore expressed; and we see no basis whatever for the contention that our former opinion was based on a ground not considered by the Board of Tax Appeals. The question before the Board was whether the transfer to Mill Creek was of all the assets of the old company . . . .

It was not intended by what was said in the original opinion, to the effect that the transfer of assets from the old company to the new did not constitute a bona fide reorganization, to suggest that the transfer was a taxable transaction, but to point out that the creation of the new company and the transfer of the assets to it was a mere shifting of charters having no purpose other than to give to the later transfer to Mill Creek the appearance of a transfer of all the corporate assets so as to bring that transfer within the non-recognition provisions of section [368(a)(1)]. . . . The transfer to the new company was non-taxable whether it was a real reorganization or a mere shifting of charters, which would of course come within the terms of the reorganization statute. It is only in relation to the subsequent transfer to Mill Creek that it becomes important to determine whether the organization of the new company and its taking over of the assets was a genuine reorganization. If there was no real reorganization and transfer, but a mere shifting of charters, the subsequent transfer to Mill Creek was not within the terms of the nonrecognition provision of the statute.

We are confirmed in our original opinion by the recent decision of the Supreme Court in Minnesota Tea Co. v. Helvering, 58 S. Ct. 393, 395, 82 L. Ed. In that case there was a reorganization in which stockholders paid the debts of a corporation from the cash distributed to them in the course of the reorganization. The question was whether the corporation was taxable on the amount of the debts thus paid on the theory that the cash used for that purpose was in reality received by the corporation, or whether it was nontaxable on the theory that the distribution to the stockholders was within the nonrecognition provisions of the statute. In holding the corporation taxable thereon the court said: "The conclusion is inescapable, as the court below very clearly pointed out, that by this roundabout process petitioner received the same benefit 'as though it had retained that amount from distribution and applied it to the payment of such indebtedness.' Payment of indebtedness, and not distribution of dividends, was, from the beginning, the aim of the understanding with the stockholders and was the end accomplished by carrying that understanding into effect. *A given result at the end of a straight path is not made a different result because reached by following a devious path.* The preliminary distribution to the stockholders was a meaningless and unnecessary incident in the transmission of the fund to the creditors, all along intended to come to their hands, so transparently artificial that further discussion would be a needless waste of time." (Italics ours.)

In the case at bar, the "aim" of the incorporation of the new company and the transfer made to it, was that the transfer to Mill Creek should appear to be a transfer of all of the assets of the company; and this was the end accomplished, and the only end accomplished so far as the record shows, by the incorporation and transfer. The incorporation of the new company and the transfer to it was a "meaningless and unnecessary incident." It is true that the new company was incorporated under the laws of a different state from the old; but it does not appear that any corporate purpose was served by this change of jurisdictions and certainly the integrity of the existing business was not affected by the change. Cf. Braden Steel Corp. v. Commissioner, 10 Cir., 78 F.2d 808, 810. It is said that the transfer to Mill Creek had a real corporate purpose. This is true, but it was taxable unless constituting a transfer of all the assets of the corporation. The incorporation of and transfer to the new company, which had no proper corporate purpose, were resorted to in order to give the transfer to Mill Creek the appearance of being a transfer of all the assets of the transferor and hence not taxable. All that was done by the complicated corporate maneuvering employed was the transfer of a part of the assets of the old company to Mill Creek in exchange for 1,000 shares of its stock, leaving the business of the old company in the hands of the old stockholders, with a new charter, but otherwise unaffected. This result is "not a different result because reached by following a devious path."

And we think it clear that the incorporation of the new company and the transfer made to it were but parts of a single plan under which the transfer was made to Mill Creek and that they should be treated as parts of one transaction.

When this is done, there is no room for the contention that all of the assets of the corporation were transferred to Mill Creek. Even though there was no unifying contract, the unity of the plan brings the case within the rule applied in Starr v. Commissioner, 4 Cir., 82 F.2d 964.

For the reasons stated here and in our former opinion, the decision of the Board of Tax Appeals will be reversed.

Reversed.

HENRY H. WATKINS, District Judge, dissents.

D. *CONTINUITY OF BUSINESS ENTERPRISE*

BENTSEN v. PHINNEY
199 F. Supp. 363 (S.D. Tex. 1961)

GARZA, District Judge. This is a suit for refund of federal income taxes paid by plaintiffs to defendant.

All of the facts have been stipulated, and the case has been submitted to the Court on written briefs and on oral argument.

A brief summary of the stipulated facts is as follows:

Plaintiff taxpayers were shareholders of Rio Development Company, a Texas corporation, which in 1955 was engaged in the land development business in the Rio Grande Valley, along with two other corporations, Bentsen Brothers, Inc., and Bentsen Loan & Investment Company.

The shareholders in such three corporations were all members of the families of Lloyd M. Bentsen, Sr., and Elmer C. Bentsen.

On March 7, 1955, the three corporations transferred all of their respective properties, subject to their liabilities, to the newly formed Consolidated American Life Insurance Company. For the sake of brevity and consistency, the former will be referred to as the "Transferor Corporations", and the latter will be referred to as the "Insurance Company".

Immediately thereafter, the stockholders of the three transferor corporations surrendered all of their stock in the three transferor corporations for cancellation. The three transferor corporations were liquidated and dissolved, and the Insurance Company issued all of its voting stock directly to the former stockholders of the three transferor corporations which had been dissolved, to Bentsen Development Company, a partnership, and to Lloyd M. Bentsen, Sr., individually. Bentsen Development Company, a partnership, and Lloyd M. Bentsen, Sr., individually, had also transferred their assets to the Insurance Company.

It is stipulated that prior to the transaction, the transferor corporations were going concerns in the land development business in the Rio Grande Valley of Texas. The Insurance Company was a going concern created to carry on the corporate business of selling life insurance.

It has been stipulated that there were business reasons and purposes for the transaction.

It is the exchange by the plaintiff taxpayers of their stock in Rio Development Company for Insurance Company stock that was the specific event out of which this refund suit arose.

It has been stipulated that there was continuity of corporate activity as between the Rio Development Company and the Insurance Company, the only change being that the type of business carried on was changed from the land development business to the insurance business.

The net result of the transactions involved in this case was that all and the same assets which had been owned by the transferor corporations, were, after the transaction, owned by the Insurance Company. The same individuals who had owned stock in the transferor corporations now owned the stock of the Insurance Company.

It has also been stipulated that prior to the consummation of the corporate transaction involved here, the Commissioner of Internal Revenue was requested to rule in advance on the federal income tax consequences of the transaction, and that the said Commissioner on two separate occasions ruled that in his opinion an exchange of stock in the Insurance Company for the land development companies' or transferor corporations' stock, was taxable because the Insurance Company engaged in a different business from the three land development corporations.

Although the plaintiff taxpayers disagreed with the Commissioner's ruling, in their respective 1955 income tax returns they reported the exchange of their Rio Development Company stock for Insurance Company stock as a taxable event and paid a tax thereon.

Thereafter the necessary procedural steps were taken to bring this refund suit before the Court for a decision as to the income tax consequences of such exchange of stock by the taxpayers.

The question for the Court to decide is: Was such corporate transaction a corporate "reorganization", as the term "reorganization" is defined in Section 368(a)(1), Internal Revenue Code of 1954, even though Rio Development Company engaged in the land development business and thereafter the new Insurance Company engaged in the insurance business?

The plaintiff taxpayers contend there was a corporate reorganization. The Government, defendant in this cause, maintains that there was not a corporate reorganization under Section 368(a)(1) of the Internal Revenue Code of 1954, because there was not a continuity of business enterprise before and after the reorganization; and that this is a prerequisite as set out in the Treasury Regulations.

This case is governed by [§§368(a)(1)(C) and (D) and 354(a)(1)]. . . .

It is conceded that the 1939 Internal Revenue Code was the same in this respect as the 1954 Code, and that the corresponding Treasury Regulations issued under the 1939 Code are similar to the corresponding Treasury Regulations issued under the 1954 Code.

The Treasury Regulation states: "Requisite to a reorganization under the Code, are a continuity of business enterprise under the modified corporate form."[1]

---

[1]Treasury Regulation 118, Section 39.112(g)-1(b) under the 1939 Code; and Section 1.368-1(b) under the 1954 Code.

The Government contends that since there was a lack of "continuity of the business enterprise", there was not a reorganization as contemplated under the statutes.

The question for this Court to decide is the meaning of "continuity of business enterprise", and whether or not it exists in this case.

The Government takes the position that "continuity of business enterprise" means that the new corporation must engage in the same identical or similar business. Stated in another manner, the Government maintains it is necessary that there must be an identity of type of business before and after the reorganization.

The plaintiff taxpayers have cited to the Court the case of Becher v. Commissioner, 221 F.2d 252 (2d Cir. 1955) affirming 22 T.C. 932 (1954), which the Government has tried to distinguish. In this case the taxpayer owned all the stock in a corporation engaged in the sponge rubber and canvas-product manufacturing business. The new corporation engaged in the business of manufacturing upholstered furniture. In that case, the Government took the position that there had been a reorganization and that a cash distribution to the shareholders of the old corporation was taxable as "boot" and was ordinary income to the shareholders. The Government prevailed in that case, and the Court, at 221 F.2d 252, said: ". . . but the Tax Court here correctly held that a business purpose does not require an identity of business before and after the reorganization. . . ."

Other cases cited are Pebble Springs Distilling Co. v. Commissioner, 231 F.2d 288 (7th Cir. 1956), cert. denied 352 U.S. 836, 77 S. Ct. 56, 1 L. Ed. 2d 55, affirming 23 T.C. 196 (1954). There the old corporation had the power to carry on both a whiskey distilling business and a real estate business, but it engaged solely in the real estate business.

Another case cited to the Court is Morley Cypress Trust v. Commissioner, 3 T.C. 84 (1944). In that case the old corporation owned land held for timber and the land was conveyed to a new corporation engaged in the oil business.

The Government tries to distinguish these last two cases by saying that in the *Pebble Springs Distilling Co.* case the new corporation could engage in the whiskey distilling business if it had wanted to, and that in the *Morley Cypress Trust* case, after the problem of continuity of business enterprise had been presented, the required continuity could have been found because both the old and the new corporations were actively engaged in exploiting the natural resources of the same land.

The Government also contends that under Texas law an insurance company cannot engage in any business other than that of insurance.

The *Morley Cypress Trust* case cited above, this Court believes, is the case most like the case before the Court. In the *Morley Cypress Trust* case the land was held for timber. In this case it was held for development. In the *Morley* case land was conveyed to a new oil corporation for use in the oil business. In this case, land (plus proceeds from the sale of land) was conveyed to a new corporation to furnish the means to capitalize a new insurance business.

The Government contends that the corresponding Treasury Regulation issued under the 1939 Code was in existence when the 1954 Code was enacted and Congress did not see fit to make any changes; that Treasury Regulations have the force of law when the Code section which they interpret is reenacted after they have once been promulgated, and cites Roberts v. Commissioner, 9 Cir., 176 F.2d 221, 10 A.L.R.2d 186.

The Government has been unable to present the Court with any decision in which the meaning of "continuity of business enterprise" as used in the Treasury Regulations, has been interpreted. Since no Court had upheld the contention made by the Government as to the interpretation to be given said words in the Regulations, it is unfair to say that Congress had an opportunity to make a change in passing the 1954 Code. Congress was not apprised of the meaning that the Government wishes to give to said language in the Regulations, and therefore the rule expressed in Roberts v. Commissioner, supra, is not controlling here.

This Court finds that no court has passed on the question of whether "continuity of business enterprise", as used in the Regulations, means that the new corporation must engage in the identical type of business or a similar business; and it is, therefore, held that this Court is not bound by any Treasury Regulation since it is the province of the Court to decide whether the Treasury Regulation means what the Government contends it means; and whether or not if it means what the Government contends, said regulation is one that could be promulgated under the appropriate sections of the Internal Revenue Code.

This Court finds that "continuity of business enterprise", as used in the Regulations, does not mean that the new corporation must engage in either the same type of business as the old or a similar business, for if this be the requirement, then said Regulation is without authority.

To qualify as a "reorganization" under the applicable statutes, the new corporation does not have to engage in an identical or similar type of business. All that is required is that there must be continuity of the business activity.

This Court therefore finds that there was a reorganization under the applicable sections of the Internal Revenue Code.

Under the facts stipulated in this case, it is found that there was a continuity of the business activity and all requisites having been complied with, the plaintiff taxpayers have a right to a refund of the income taxes paid on the exchange of stock. The amounts to be refunded by the Government are to be those as stated in the Stipulation. . . .

REVENUE RULING 63-29
1963-1 Cum. Bull. 77

Advice has been requested whether the transaction described below qualifies as a reorganization under section 368(a)(1)(C) of the Internal Revenue Code of 1954.

M corporation and N corporation were respectively engaged in the manufacture of children's toys and in the distribution of steel and allied products. At some time in the past, M corporation sold a substantial part of its operating assets for cash and notes to a third party and more recently sold all but a small part of the remaining operating assets for cash, also to a third party. Thereafter, for valid business reasons, it acquired all of the property of N corporation solely in exchange for its voting stock. N corporation distributed the M stock received to its shareholders and then dissolved. M corporation used the assets resulting from the sale of its operating assets to expand the operations of the steel distributing business acquired from N corporation.

Section 368(a)(1)(C) of the Code states that the term "reorganization" means the acquisition by one corporation, in exchange solely for all or part of its voting stock, of substantially all the properties of another corporation.

Section 1.368-1(b) of the Income Tax Regulations specifies that a reorganization, to satisfy the requirements of the Code, must result in a continuity of the business enterprise under modified corporate form. This requirement will not be satisfied unless the surviving corporation is organized to engage in a business enterprise. See, for example, Standard Realization Company v. Commissioner, 10 T.C. 708 (1948), acquiescence, C.B. 1948-2, 3. However, the surviving corporation need not continue the activities conducted by its predecessors. See Donald L. Bentsen et al. v. Phinney, 199 Fed. Supp. 363 (1961); and Ernest F. Becher v. Commissioner, 221 Fed. (2d) 252 (1955). See also Pebble Springs Distilling Co. v. Commissioner, 231 Fed. (2d) 288 (1956), certiorari denied, 352 U.S. 836 (1956); WAGE, Inc. v. Commissioner, 19 T.C. 249 (1952); and Morley Cypress Trust, Schedule "B" et al. v. Commissioner, 3 T.C. 84, (1944), Acquiescence, C.B. 1944, 20.

Since M corporation engaged in the steel distribution business after the merger, the requirement that the reorganization result in a continuity of the business enterprise within the meaning of section 1.368-1(b) of the regulations was satisfied in the instant case, even though the toy business formerly conducted by M corporation was discontinued.

Accordingly, it is held that the acquisition by M corporation of all of the properties of N corporation solely in exchange for its voting stock constitutes a reorganization as defined in section 368(a)(1)(C) of the Code.

In view of these conclusions, reconsideration has been given to Revenue Ruling 56-330, C.B. 1956-2, 204, which held, in part, that the required continuity of the business enterprise was lacking where the successor corporation in a transaction otherwise qualifying as a reorganization engaged in a new business enterprise entirely different from that conducted by its predecessors. The conclusions reached in the instant case are equally applicable to the question involved in Revenue Ruling 56-330.

Accordingly, Revenue Ruling 56-330 is revoked.

NOTE

In Rev. Proc. 64-31, 1964-2 Cum. Bull. 947, 949-950, the Internal Revenue Service reaffirmed an earlier announced position that it would not issue advance rulings on the question whether §368 is applicable to the acquisition by an investment company of stock or assets of another investment company where, as a result of the acquisition, the shareholders of either or both companies achieve a substantially wider diversification of the investment assets underlying the stock holdings. In 1969 the Service issued a superseding Revenue Procedure which listed the areas in which advance rulings would and would not be issued. The new Procedure makes no reference to this issue under §368. Rev. Proc. 69-6, 1969-1 Cum. Bull. 396. Why do you think the Service had been unwilling to rule in this area, and why do you think it has apparently changed its mind? Do you think the Service's seeming willingness to rule implies agreement or disagreement with the applicability of §368?

V. CORPORATE FUSION — MERGERS AND OTHER AMALGAMATIONS

A. *INTRODUCTION AND HISTORY*

Before cases like Marr v. United States, 268 U.S. 536 (1925), page 415 supra, reached the Supreme Court, Congress in 1918 adopted its first nonrecognition provision and did so in circumstances limited to corporate reorganizations. Primitive in retrospect, §202(b) of the Revenue Act of 1918 provided that "when in connection with the reorganization, merger, or consolidation of a corporation a person receives in place of stock or securities owned by him new stock or securities of no greater aggregate par or face value, no gain or loss shall be deemed to occur from the exchange, and the new stock or securities received shall be treated as taking the place of the stock, securities, or property exchanged." According to the Senate Finance Committee which proposed the section, it was "to negative the assertion of tax in the case of certain purely paper transaction." Seidman's Legislative History 1938-1861 899 (1938); R. and G. Blakey, The Federal Income Tax 175 (1940).

The federal income tax law has contained reorganization-nonrecognition provisions continuously since 1918. They have become more complex and have taken crucial turns at different times. Study of some of the cases which dealt with the statute as it was during the years prior to those covered by present law is essential to a full understanding of present law and to the continuing administrative and judicial attitudes toward particular types of problems.

B. *STATUTORY "CLOSE-ORDER DRILL" — §§368, 354, 356, 357, 358, 361, 362, 332, AND 334(b)*

It will be helpful, even before reading cases involving earlier statutory provisions, to gain familiarity with the pattern and interrelationship of the relevant sections of the 1954 Code.

a. Start with §368(a). It defines the various reorganizations. It is not a section which fixes tax consequences or determines recognition. Subsection (a)(1) lists and defines six types of "reorganization," from (A) to (F). Tax lawyers, familiar with the definitions, use a shorthand reference system in identifying a particular type of reorganization. They refer to an "A reorganization," or just an "A," if they mean one defined in §368(a)(1)(A), and to a "B," if they mean one defined in §368(a)(1)(B), and so forth. This book will use that shorthand.

(i) An "A" reorganization is a statutory merger or consolidation of two or more corporations. By "statutory" the Code means a merger or consolidation effected pursuant to state or federal statutory law.

(ii) A "B" reorganization contemplates one corporation's acquisition, in exchange for a portion of its voting stock, of "control" of another corporation. When the reorganization is completed the acquiring corporation will be the parent and the acquired corporation will be a subsidiary (although not necessarily a 100 per cent owned subsidiary). The former shareholders of the subsidiary corporation will now own voting shares in the parent.

(iii) A "C" reorganization is sometimes referred to as a "de facto" merger, in contrast with the "de jure" merger embraced in the "A" reorganization. In general, a "C" reorganization contemplates one corporation's transfer of "substantially all of its properties" to another corporation in exchange for a portion of the latter's voting stock. In an "A" reorganization the corporation which merges into the surviving corporation ceases to exist. Under the current definition of a "C" there is no requirement that the transferor corporation liquidate, although frequently it does so. The "A" reorganization does not require that the transferee pay for the assets received with voting stock, as the "C" does.

(iv) A "D" reorganization requires the transfer of a portion of one corporation's assets to another in circumstances in which the transferor or its shareholders are immediately thereafter "in control" of the transferee corporation. Ordinarily, the transferee issues stock to the transferor, and the transferor then liquidates, distributing to its shareholders the stock received from the transferee corporation. The last clause of §368(a)(1)(D) requires a distribution that meets particular statutory patterns. Essentially, a "D" contemplates the division of one corporation into two or more or the substitution of one for another, in either case with substantial continuity of control.

(v) An "E" reorganization is a "recapitalization," studied earlier in this chapter, page 460 supra.

(vi) An "F" reorganization on its face involves very little, a "mere change in identity, form or place of organization." Thought for years to be unimportant, an unnecessary provision, it has recently taken on a vigor and force of significant and as yet unmeasured proportion. See page 622 infra.

b. Section 368(a)(2) sets forth modifications and amplifications of the sometimes stark and restrictive definitional rules in §368(a). Read the section carefully. Its full impact will become clearer as you work through the development of the case law.

c. The provisions that determine the tax consequences of "reorganization" refer to those who are "a party to a reorganization." Section 368(b) defines a "party." It, too, will become clearer in significance as you study the case law, but it is important now to keep in mind the necessity for determining who is a "party."

d. "Control" is a frequent requirement for particular tax consequences in reorganization. It is defined in §368(c), as it was for purposes of §351. See Chapter 3, page 290 supra.

e. With the definitions of §368 in mind, move to §354(a)(1), a section which provides tax consequences for corporate investors who exchange "stock or securities in a corporation a party to a reorganization . . . in pursuance of the plan of reorganization. . . ." Note the reference to "reorganization," defined in §368(a)(1), and to "a party," defined in §368(b). Note, too, the requirement for a "plan," a term not defined by statute, and for "stock or securities," similarly undefined. Since the term "securities" presumably means something other than "stock," it is taken to mean corporate debt, but not all corporate debt. Case and administrative law flesh out the meaning somewhat painstakingly, somewhat irritatingly. If §354(a)(1) covers, the investor's gain or loss is not recognized. If §354(a)(1) does not cover because the consideration received by the investor is not exclusively stock or securities, or because the securities received are as described in §354(a)(2), §354(a)(3) remits the taxpayer to §356. Section 356(a) describes the tax treatment when "boot" is received, taxing the gain to the extent of the "boot" as capital gain if §356(a)(1) applies, and as a dividend if §356(a)(2) applies. Despite the presence of "boot," loss is not recognized. Section 356(c).

f. If §354 or §356 applies to the investor transaction, his basis for the consideration received on the exchange is determined under §358, much as it is in the case of an investor in a §351 transaction.

g. Section 355 is applicable to corporate proliferations — spin-offs, split-offs and split-ups. It is not dependent on a "reorganization," defined in §368(a)(1), but frequently operates on a "D" reorganization. Read the provisions of §355 now, and the accompanying "boot" provisions in §356(b), but their full impact must await the cases that begin with page 583 infra. Mark for inquiry later the fact that the "boot" taxable under §356(a) is limited to "gain." No such limitation encumbers §356(b).

h. Corporations are transferors of assets in "A," "C," and "D" reorganizations. Recognition of their gain or loss is determined by §361. Note the special "boot" provision in §361(b), applicable if property not permitted by §361(a) is received. It works quite differently from §356, the "boot" provision applicable to investors. Section 357 determines the tax effect of an assumption of indebtedness.

The transferor corporation's basis for the consideration (usually stock or securities) it receives for its assets is determined under §358, the section generally applicable to investors receiving stock or securities in a reorganization exchange.

i. The corporate transferee in an "A," "C" or "D" reorganization has no gain or loss on the issuance of its stock. Section 1032. Its basis for the assets received is determined under §362(b). Section 362(b) also determines the basis to the acquiring corporation of the stock which it acquires in a "B" reorganization in exchange for its own voting stock.

j. Normally, an intercorporate liquidation (subsidiary into parent) is not technically a "reorganization" as defined in §368(a)(1). An intercorporate liquidation of a controlled subsidiary covered by §332 results in the nonrecognition of the parent's gain or loss in its stock investment. Section 332 is treated with reorganizations because the effect of an intercorporate liquidation is substantially the same as a merger, and sometimes such a liquidation can be effected as an "A" reorganization. If §332 provides for nonrecognition of the parent's gain or loss, the assets which the parent receives from the subsidiary will take their basis under §334(b)(1). Section 336 denies recognition of gain or loss to the subsidiary with respect to assets distributed to its parent in retirement of its stock. Section 332(c) does the same with respect to the appreciation in assets distributed to its parent in satisfaction of indebtedness. See Chapter 1, page 19 supra.

The foregoing generalized summary of the Code provisions applicable to corporate amalgamation is only that. It is no substitute for detailed analysis, close reading of the relevant Regulations and an understanding of how they came to be (and what they may become), which your study of the case law may help to provide. As you deal with specific and seemingly narrow statutory issues, take the time necessary to reflect and consider the general perspective in which courts view reorganizations; pages 465-493 supra.

C. *THE STATUTORY ISSUES*

1. *Continuity of Interest*

a. INTEREST ACQUIRED

PINELLAS ICE & COLD STORAGE CO. v. COMMISSIONER
57 F.2d 188 (5th Cir. 1932), aff'd, 287 U.S. 462 (1933)

[The factual statement set forth below is taken from the opinion of Mr. Justice McReynolds, speaking for the Supreme Court in its affirmance of this case, 287 U.S. 462 (1933).* Excerpts from Judge Foster's opinion, speaking for the Court of Appeals, follow the factual statement.]

"Petitioner, a Florida corporation, made and sold ice at St. Petersburg. Substantially the same stockholders owned the Citizens Ice and Cold Storage Company, engaged in like business at the same place. In February, 1926, Lewis, general manager of both companies, began negotiations for the sale of their properties to the National Public Service Corporation. Their directors and stockholders were anxious to sell, distribute the assets and dissolve the corporations. The prospective vendee desired to acquire the properties of both companies, but not of one without the other.

"In October, 1926, agreement was reached and the vendor's directors again approved the plan for distribution and dissolution. In November, 1926, petitioner and the National Corporation entered into a formal written contract conditioned upon a like one by the Citizens Company. This referred to petitioner as 'vendor' and the

*Page 500 infra. — Ed.

National Corporation as 'purchaser.' The former agreed to sell, the latter to purchase the physical property, plants, etc., 'together with the goodwill of the business, free and clear of all defects, liens, encumbrances, taxes and assessments for the sum of $1,400,000, payable as hereinafter provided.' The specified date and place for consummation were eleven A.M., December 15, 1926, and 165 Broadway, New York City, when 'the vendor shall deliver to the purchaser instruments of conveyance and transfer by general warranty in form satisfactory to the purchaser of the property set forth. . . . The purchaser shall pay to the vendor the sum of $400,000.00 in cash.' The balance of the purchase price ($1,000,000.00) shall be paid $500,000.00 on or before January 31, 1927; $250,000.00 on or before March 1, 1927; $250,000.00 on or before April 1st, 1927. Also, the deferred installments of the purchaser price shall be evidenced by the purchaser's 6% notes, secured either by notes or bonds of the Florida West Coast Ice Company, thereafter to be organized to take title, or other satisfactory collateral; or by 6% notes of such Florida company secured by first lien on the property conveyed, or other satisfactory collateral.

"The vendor agreed to procure undertakings by E. T. Lewis and Leon D. Lewis not to engage in manufacturing or selling ice in Pinellas County, Florida, for ten years.

"The $400,000 cash payment was necessary for discharge of debts, liens, encumbrances, etc. The Florida Company, incorporated December 6, 1926, took title to the property and executed the purchase notes secured as agreed. These were paid at or before maturity except the one for $100,000, held until November, 1927, because of flaw in a title. As the notes were paid petitioner immediately distributed the proceeds to its stockholders according to the plan.

"The property conveyed to the Florida Company included all of petitioner's assets except a few vacant lots worth not more than $10,000, some accounts — $3,000 face value — also a small amount of cash. Assets, not exceeding 1% of the whole, were transferred to the Citizens Holding Corporation as trustee for petitioner's stockholders — 99% of all vendor's property went to the Florida Company. The plan of the whole arrangement as carried out was accepted by petitioner's officers and stockholders prior to November 4, 1926.

"The Commissioner of Internal Revenue determined that the petitioner derived taxable gain exceeding $500,000 and assessed it accordingly under the Act of 1926. The Board of Tax Appeals and the Circuit Court of Appeals approved this action.

"The facts are not in controversy. The gain is admitted; but it is said this was definitely exempted from taxation by §203, Revenue Act of 1926.

"The Act, approved February 26, 1926, c. 27, 44 Stat. 9, 11, 12, —

'Sec. 202. (a) Except as hereinafter provided in this section, the gain from the sale or other disposition of property shall be the excess of the amount realized therefrom over the basis provided in subdivision (a) or (b) of section 204, and the loss shall be the excess of such basis over the amount realized.

'(b) . . . .

'(c) The amount realized from the sale or other disposition of property shall be the sum of any money received plus the fair market value of the property (other than money) received.

'(d) In the case of a sale or exchange, the extent to which the gain or loss determined under this section shall be recognized for the purposes of this title, shall be determined under the provisions of section 203.

'(e) . . . .

'(Sec. 203. (a) Upon the sale or exchange of property the entire amount of the gain or loss, determined under section 202, shall be recognized, except as hereinafter provided in this section.

'(b)(1) and (2) . . . .

'(3) No gain or loss shall be recognized if a corporation a party to a reorganization exchanges property, in pursuance of the plan of reorganization, solely for stock or securities in another corporation a party to the reorganization.

'(4) and (5) . . . .

'(c) and (d) . . . .

'(e) If an exchange would be within the provisions of paragraph (3) of subdivision (b) if it were not for the fact that the property received in exchange consists not only of stock or securities permitted by such paragraph to be received without the recognition of gain, but also of other property or money, then —

'(1) If the corporation receiving such other property or money distributes it in pursuance of the plan of reorganization, no gain to the corporation shall be recognized from the exchange, but

'(2) If the corporation receiving such other property or money does not distribute it in pursuance of the plan of reorganization, the gain, if any, to the corporation shall be recognized, but in an amount not in excess of the sum of such money and the fair market value of such other property so received, which is not so distributed. . . .

'(h) As used in this section and sections 201 and 204 —

'(1) The term "reorganization" means (A) a merger or consolidation (including the acquisition by one corporation of at least a majority of the voting stock and at least a majority of the total number of shares of all other classes of stock of another corporation, or substantially all the properties of another corporation), or (B) a transfer by a corporation of all or a part of its assets to another corporation if immediately after the transfer the transferor or its stockholders or both are in control of the corporation to which the assets are transferred, or (C) a recapitalization, or (D) a mere change in identity, form, or place of organization, however effected.

'(2) The term "a party to a reorganization" includes a corporation resulting from a reorganization and includes both corporations in the case of an acquisition by one corporation of at least a majority of the voting stock and at least a majority of the total number of shares of all other classes of stock of another corporation.'

"All of §203(b) is in the margin.* . . ."

---

*Sec. 203(a) Upon the sale or exchange of property the entire amount of the gain or loss, determined under section 202, shall be recognized, except as hereinafter provided in this section.

(b)(1) No gain or loss shall be recognized if property held for productive use in trade or business or for investment (not including stock in trade or other property held primarily for sale, nor stocks, bonds, notes, choses in action, certificates of trust or beneficial interest, or other securities or evidences of indebtedness or interest) is exchanged solely for property of a like kind to be held either for productive use in trade or business or for investment, or if

Before BRYAN, FOSTER, and WALKER, Circuit Judges.

FOSTER, Circuit Judge. . . . Relying on the provisions of section 203, paragraphs (b)(3), (e)(1) and (h)(1)(A) . . . , it is contended by petitioner: That there was a reorganization to which petitioner and the West Coast Company were parties; that the notes were securities of the new company; that there was an exchange of the property of petitioner for cash and securities; that this was distributed in pursuance of a plan of reorganization; and that therefore no gain to the corporation should be recognized.

Apparently there are no decisions in point, and it would be useless to review the cases cited by either side.

Section 203* appeared first in the 1924 Revenue Act (26 USCA §934). . . . Prior thereto the profit resulting from all exchanges of property was taxable. It is evident that in enacting section 203 Congress intended to exempt from consideration for either profit or loss transfers of property which were really exchanges of capital assets, and, to a certain extent, to brush aside technicalities in so construing them. It is equally clear that there was no intention to exempt profit arising from an outright sale of property, or an exchange of property, between corporations where there was in fact no reorganization.

There is no doubt that the written agreement of November 4, 1926, for the disposition of petitioner's property to a new corporation, contemplated an outright sale and not an exchange or a reorganization. The conveyance of the property on December 17, 1926, was in form a sale and not an exchange. This is not seriously disputed by petitioner, but it is contended that under the definition of paragraph

---

common stock in a corporation is exchanged solely for common stock in the same corporation, or if preferred stock in a corporation is exchanged solely for preferred stock in the same corporation.

(2) No gain or loss shall be recognized if stock or securities in a corporation a party to a reorganization are, in pursuance of the plan of reorganization, exchanged solely for stock or securities in such corporation or in another corporation a party to the reorganization.

(3) No gain or loss shall be recognized if a corporation a party to a reorganization exchanges property, in pursuance of the plan of reorganization, solely for stock or securities in another corporation a party to the reorganization.

(4) No gain or loss shall be recognized if property is transferred to a corporation by one or more persons solely in exchange for stock or securities in such corporation, and immediately after the exchange such person or persons are in control of the corporation; but in the case of an exchange by two or more persons this paragraph shall apply only if the amount of the stock and securities received by each is substantially in proportion to his interest in the property prior to the exchange.

(5) If property (as a result of its destruction in whole or in part, theft or seizure, or an exercise of the power of requisition or condemnation, or the threat or imminence thereof) is compulsorily or involuntarily converted into property similar or related in service or use to the property so converted, or into money which is forthwith in good faith, under regulations prescribed by the Commissioner with the approval of the Secretary, expended in the acquisition of other property similar or related in service or use to the property so converted, or in the acquisition of control of a corporation owning such other property, or in the establishment of a replacement fund, no gain or loss shall be recognized. If any part of the money is not so expended, the gain, if any, shall be recognized, but in an amount not in excess of the money which is not so expended.

*The precursor, inter alia, to §§354 and 361 of the 1954 Code. — ED.

(h)(1)(A)* the mere acquisition by the Florida West Coast Ice Company of substantially all the property of petitioner was a reorganization. . . .

As applied to corporations, the terms "merger" and "consolidation" have well known legal meanings. While the result is practically the same in either event, there is this difference. In a merger one corporation absorbs the other and remains in existence while the other is dissolved. In a consolidation a new corporation is created and the consolidating corporations are extinguished. In either event, the resulting corporation acquires all the property, rights, and franchises of the dissolved corporations, and their stockholders become its stockholders. . . .

It must be assumed that in adopting paragraph (h) Congress intended to use the words "merger" and "consolidation" in their ordinary and accepted meanings. Giving the matter in parenthesis the most liberal construction, it is only when there is an acquisition of substantially all the property of another corporation in connection with a merger or consolidation that a reorganization takes place. Clause (B) of the paragraph removes any doubt as to the intention of Congress on this point.

It follows that there was no reorganization, and consequently no party to a reorganization, in connection with the disposition of petitioner's property. It is unnecessary to pass upon petitioner's other contentions.

The record presents no reversible error. The petition is denied.

PINELLAS ICE & COLD STORAGE CO. v. COMMISSIONER
287 U.S. 462 (1933)

Mr. Justice McReynolds delivered the opinion of the Court. . . . Counsel for the petitioner maintain —

The record discloses a "reorganization" to which petitioner was party and a preliminary plan strictly pursued. The Florida West Coast Ice Company acquired substantially all of petitioner's property in exchange for cash and securities which were promptly distributed to the latter's stockholders. Consequently, under §203, the admitted gain was not taxable.

The Board of Tax Appeals held that the transaction in question amounted to a sale of petitioner's property for money and not an exchange for securities within the true meaning of the statute. It, accordingly and as we think properly, upheld the Commissioner's action.

The "vendor" agreed "to sell" and "the purchaser" agreed "to purchase" certain described property for a definite sum of money. Part of this sum was paid in cash; for the balance the purchaser executed three promissory notes, secured by the deposit of mortgage bonds, payable, with interest, in about forty-five, seventy-five, and one hundred and five days, respectively. These notes — mere evidence of obligation to pay the purchase price — were not securities within the intendment of the act and were properly regarded as the equivalent of cash. It would require clear language to lead us to conclude that Congress intended to grant exemption to one who sells property

*Cf. §368(a)(1)(C) of the 1954 Code. — Ed.

and for the purchase price accepts well-secured, short-term notes, (all payable within four months), when another who makes a like sale and receives cash certainly would be taxed. We can discover no good basis in reason for the contrary view and its acceptance would make evasion of taxation very easy. In substance the petitioner sold for the equivalent of cash; the gain must be recognized.

The court below held that the facts disclosed failed to show a "reorganization" within the statutory definition. And, in the circumstances, we approve that conclusion. But the construction which the court seems to have placed upon clause A, paragraph (h)(1), §203, we think is too narrow. It conflicts with established practice of the tax officers and if passed without comment may produce perplexity.

The court said — "It must be assumed that in adopting paragraph (h) Congress intended to use the words 'merger' and 'consolidation' in their ordinary and accepted meanings. Giving the matter in parenthesis the most liberal construction, it is only when there is an acquisition of substantially all the property of another corporation in connection with a merger or consolidation that a reorganization takes place. Clause (B) of the paragraph removes any doubt as to the intention of Congress on this point."

The paragraph in question directs — "The term 'reorganization' means (A) a merger or consolidation (including the acquisition by one corporation of at least a majority of the voting stock and at least a majority of the total number of shares of all other classes of stock of another corporation, or substantially all the properties of another corporation)." The words within the parenthesis may not be disregarded. They expand the meaning of "merger" or "consolidation" so as to include some things which partake of the nature of a merger or consolidation but are beyond the ordinary and commonly accepted meaning of those words — so as to embrace circumstances difficult to delimit but which in strictness cannot be designated as either merger or consolidation. But the mere purchase for money of the assets of one Company by another is beyond the evident purpose of the provision, and has no real semblance to a merger or consolidation. Certainly, we think that to be within the exemption the seller must acquire an interest in the affairs of the purchasing company more definite than that incident to ownership of its short-term purchase-money notes. This general view is adopted and well sustained in Cortland Specialty Co. v. Commissioner of Internal Revenue, 60 F.(2d) 937, 939, 940. It harmonizes with the underlying purpose of the provisions in respect of exemptions and gives some effect to all the words employed.

The judgment of the court below is
Affirmed.

NOTE

See E. Griswold, "Securities" and "Continuity of Interest," A Suggestion for the Reexamination of Two Concepts in the Reorganization Provisions of the Tax Laws, 58 Harv. L. Rev. 705 (1945).

CORTLAND SPECIALTY CO. v. COMMISSIONER
60 F.2d 937 (2d Cir. 1932), cert. denied, 288 U.S. 599 (1933)

[As in *Pinellas,* the principal issue was seen to be whether a corporation's transfer of substantially all its properties to another corporation for cash and notes payable within 14 months was a "reorganization" within the meaning of §203 of the Revenue Act of 1926. Like the Fifth Circuit in *Pinellas,* the Second Circuit concluded (at 940) that a transfer of assets, to constitute a reorganization, must smack of "merger" or "consolidation," and those concepts imply "a continuance of interest on the part of the transferor in the properties transferred."

If the Supreme Court had reviewed *Cortland* it would probably have affirmed on grounds like those employed in *Pinellas,* rejecting the notice of required nexus to "merger" or "consolidation." As the concluding paragraph in the Supreme Court's opinion in *Pinellas* indicates, however, a second ground for decision was employed by the Second Circuit in *Cortland,* this one very much to the Supreme Court's liking, as indicated by its statements in *Pinellas* and in later cases. As seen by the Second Circuit, this secondary issue was posed: Even if the transfer of assets for cash and short term notes had been made pursuant to a "plan of reorganization," did the payment that *Cortland* received in exchange have to include some "stock or securities," and if so, had they been included in this case?]

Before L. HAND, AUGUSTUS N. HAND, and CHASE, Circuit Judges.

AUGUSTUS N. HAND, Circuit Judge. . . . Furthermore the Cortland Company cannot come within the exception to the general rule that gains realized from exchanges of property represent taxable income unless section 203(e) and section 203(e)(1)* apply. Under those clauses, even if the transfer to Deyo was an exchange in pursuance of a "plan of reorganization," the property received by Cortland had to include *some* "stock or securities" (section 203(e)), or the exemption could not be had. As no stock was issued against the transfer, the conditions for an exemption were not fulfilled unless the notes, all payable within fourteen months of the date of the transfer, and all unsecured, can be considered "securities" under section 203(e). Inasmuch as a transfer made entirely for cash would not be enough, it cannot be supposed that anything so near to cash as these notes payable in so short a time and doubtless readily marketable would meet the legislative requirements.

The very reason that section 203(e) requires that some of the property received in exchange should be *"stock or securities"* is to deprive a mere sale for cash of the benefits of an exemption and to require an amalgamation of the existing interests. There can be no justice or propriety in taxing one corporation who transfers its properties for cash and in relieving another that takes part of its pay in short time notes. The situation might be different had the "securities," though not in stock, created such obligations as to give creditors or others some assured participation in the properties of the transferee corporation. The word "securities" was used so as not to de-

---

*Cf. §361(b) of the 1954 Code. — ED.

feat the exemption in cases where the interest of the transferor was carried over to the new corporation in some form. . . .

The orders of the Board of Tax Appeals are affirmed.

NOTE

Suppose the "notes" were payable in five years, or ten years. Would it make any difference if they were redeemable at the issuer's option? At any time? If there were a plan for their redemption? If there were or were not a ready market in the "securities" of the issuer?

The Supreme Court regarded the Court of Appeals' construction of §203(h) (1)(A) as "too narrow." Why? Was it "too narrow," in your judgment? Why? What function would clause (A) serve if the Court of Appeals' construction had been accepted? The effects of the Supreme Court's view that the parenthetical clause had independent significance were far-reaching, as later cases show. As you read the cases consider whether the Supreme Court's construction was helpful or harmful in the evolution of the law of reorganization.

JOHN A. NELSON CO. v. HELVERING
296 U.S. 374 (1935), rev'g 75 F.2d 696 (7th Cir. 1935)

Mr. Justice McReynolds delivered the opinion of the Court. The petitioner contests a deficiency income assessment made on account of alleged gains during 1926. It claims that the transaction out of which the assessment arose was reorganization within the statute. Section 203, Revenue Act, 1926, c. 27, 44 Stat. 9, 11, is relied upon. The pertinent parts are in the margin of the opinion in Helvering v. Minnesota Tea Co., post, p. 378.*

In 1926, under an agreement with petitioner, the Elliott-Fisher Corporation organized a new corporation with 12,500 shares non-voting preferred stock and 30,000 shares of common stock. It purchased the latter for $2,000,000 cash. This new corporation then acquired substantially all of petitioner's property, except $100,000, in return for $2,000,000 cash and the entire issue of preferred stock.† Part of this cash was used to retire petitioner's own preferred shares, and the remainder and the preferred stock of the new company went to its stockholders. It retained its franchise and $100,000, and continued to be liable for certain obligations. The preferred stock so distributed, except in case of default, had no voice in the control of the issuing corporation.

The Commissioner, Board of Tax Appeals and the court all concluded there was no reorganization. This, we think, was error.

---

*Page 506 infra. — Ed.

†Taxpayer actually received 14,060 shares of preferred with a par value of $100 each, the added shares representing profits earned by taxpayer between the date of agreement and the date of transfer. — Ed.

The court below thought the facts showed "that the transaction essentially constituted a sale of the greater part of petitioner's assets for cash and the preferred stock in the new corporation, leaving the Elliott-Fisher Company in entire control of the new corporation by virtue of its ownership of the common stock."

"The controlling facts leading to this conclusion are that petitioner continued its corporate existence and its franchise and retained a portion of its assets; that it acquired no controlling interest in the corporation to which it delivered the greater portion of its assets; that there was no continuity of interest from the old corporation to the new; that the control of the property conveyed passed to a stranger, in the management of which petitioner retained no voice.

"It follows that the transaction was not part of a strict merger or consolidation or part of something that partakes of the nature of a merger or consolidation involving a continuance of essentially the same interests through a new modified corporate structure. Mere acquisition by one corporation of a majority of the stock or all the assets of another corporation does not of itself constitute a reorganization, where such acquisition takes the form of a purchase and sale and does not result in or bear some material resemblance to a merger or consolidation."

True, the mere acquisition of the assets of one corporation by another does not amount to reorganization within the statutory definition. Pinellas Ice Co. v. Commissioner, 287 U.S. 462, so affirmed. But where, as here, the seller acquires a definite and substantial interest in the affairs of the purchasing corporation, a wholly different situation arises. The owner of preferred stock is not without substantial interest in the affairs of the issuing corporation, although denied voting rights. The statute does not require participation in the management of the purchaser; nor does it demand that the conveying corporation be dissolved. A controlling interest in the transferee corporation is not made a requisite by §203(h)(1)(A). This must not be confused with par. (h)(2).

Finally, as has been pointed out in the *Minnesota Tea* case, supra, par. (h)(1)(B) was not intended to modify the provisions of par. (h)(1)(A). It describes a class. Whether some overlapping is possible is not presently important.

The judgment below must be
Reversed.

HELVERING v. MINNESOTA TEA CO.
296 U.S. 378 (1935), aff'g 76 F.2d 797 (8th Cir. 1935)

Mr. Justice McReynolds delivered the opinion of the Court. . . . Respondent, a Minnesota corporation with three stockholders, assailed a deficiency assessment for 1928 income tax, and prevailed below. The Commissioner seeks reversal. He claims the transaction out of which the assessment arose was not a reorganization within §112, par. (i)(1)(A), Revenue Act, 1928, c. 852, 45 Stat. 791: "The term 'reorganization' means (A) a merger or consolidation (including the acquisition by one corporation of at least a majority of the voting stock and at least a majority of the total number of shares of all other classes of stock of another corporation, or substantially all the properties of another corporation)." The Circuit Court of Appeals held otherwise and remanded the cause for determination by the Board whether the whole of the cash received by the Minnesota Tea Company was in fact distributed as required by the act. We granted certiorari because of alleged conflicting opinions.

The petition also stated that, as the taxpayer made an earlier conveyance of certain assets, the later one, here in question, of what remained to the Grand Union Company did not result in acquisition by one corporation of substantially all property of another. This point was not raised prior to the petition for certiorari and, in the circumstances, we do not consider it.

Statutory provisions presently helpful are in the margin.*

*Revenue Act, 1918, c. 18, 40 Stat. 1060.

Sec. 202. (b) When property is exchanged for other property, the property received in exchange shall for the purpose of determining gain or loss be treated as the equivalent of cash to the amount of its fair market value, if any; but when in connection with the reorganization, merger, or consolidation of a corporation a person receives in place of stock or securities owned by him new stock or securities of no greater aggregate par or face value, no gain or loss shall be deemed to occur from the exchange, and the new stock or securities received shall be treated as taking the place of the stock, securities, or property exchanged.

Revenue Act, 1921, c. 136, 42 Stat. 230.

Sec. 202. (c) For the purposes of this title, on an exchange of property, real, personal or mixed, for any other such property, no gain or loss shall be recognized unless the property received in exchange has a readily realizable market value; but even if the property received in exchange has a readily realizable market value, no gain or loss shall be recognized —

(2) When in the reorganization of one or more corporations a person receives in place of any stock or securities owned by him, stock or securities in a corporation a party to or resulting from such reorganization. The word "reorganization," as used in this paragraph, includes a merger or consolidation (including the acquisition by one corporation of at least a majority of the voting stock and at least a majority of the total number of shares of all other classes of stock of another corporation, or of substantially all the properties of another corporation), recapitalization, or mere change in identity, form, or place of organization of a corporation.

Revenue Act, 1924, c. 234, 43 Stat. 256.

Sec. 203. (a) Upon the sale or exchange of property the entire amount of the gain or loss, determined under section 202, shall be recognized, except as hereinafter provided in this section.

(b)(2) No gain or loss shall be recognized if stock or securities in a corporation a party to a reorganization are, in pursuance of the plan of reorganization, exchanged solely for stock or securities in such corporation or in another corporation a party to the reorganization.

(3) No gain or loss shall be recognized if a corporation a party to a reorganization exchanges property, in pursuance of the plan of reorganization, solely for stock or securities in another corporation a party to the reorganization.

(4) No gain or loss shall be recognized if property is transferred to a corporation by one or more persons solely in exchange for stock or securities in such corporation, and immediately after the exchange such person or persons are in control of the corporation; but in the case of an exchange by two or more persons this paragraph shall apply only if the amount of the stock and securities received by each is substantially in proportion to his interest in the property prior to the exchange.

(e) If an exchange would be within the provisions of paragraph (3) of subdivision (b) if it were not for the fact that the property received in exchange consists not only of stock or securities permitted by such paragraph to be received without the recognition of gain, but also of other property or money, then —

(1) If the corporation receiving such other property or money distributes it in pursuance of the plan of reorganization, no gain to the corporation shall be recognized from the exchange, but

(2) If the corporation receiving such other property or money does not distribute it in pursuance of the plan of reorganization, the gain, if any, to the corporation shall be recognized, but in an amount not in excess of the sum of such money and the fair market value of such other property so received, which is not so distributed.

July 14, 1928, respondent caused Peterson Investment Company to be organized and transferred to the latter real estate, investments and miscellaneous assets in exchange for the transferee's entire capital stock. The shares thus obtained were immediately distributed among the three stockholders. August 23, 1928 it transferred all remaining assets to Grand Union Company in exchange for voting trust certificates, representing 18,000* shares of the transferee's common stock, and $426,842.52 cash. It retained the certificates; but immediately distributed the money among the stockholders, who agreed to pay $106,471.73 of its outstanding debts. Although of opinion that there had been reorganization, the Commissioner treated as taxable gain the amount of the assumed debts upon the view that this amount of the cash received by the company was really appropriated to the payment of its debts.

The matter went before the Board of Tax Appeals upon the question whether the Commissioner ruled rightly in respect of this taxable gain. Both parties proceeded upon the view that there had been reorganization. Of its own motion, the Board questioned and denied the existence of one. It then ruled that the corporation had realized taxable gain amounting to the difference between cost of the property transferred and the cash received plus the value of the 18,000 shares — $712,195.90.

The Circuit Court of Appeals found there was reorganization within the statute and reversed the Board. It concluded that the words "the acquisition by one corporation of . . . substantially all the property of another corporation" plainly include the transaction under consideration. Also that Clause (B), §112(i)(1), first introduced by Revenue Act of 1924, and continued in later statutes, did not narrow the scope of Clause (A). Further, that reorganization was not dependent upon

---

(h) As used in this section and sections 201 and 204 —

(1) The term "reorganization" means (A) a merger or consolidation (including the acquisition by one corporation of at least a majority of the voting stock and at least a majority of the total number of shares of all other classes of stock of another corporation, or substantially all the properties of another corporation), or (B) a transfer by a corporation of all or a part of its assets to another corporation if immediately after the transfer the transferor or its stockholders or both are in control of the corporation to which the assets are transferred, or (C) a recapitalization, or (D) a mere change in identity, form, or place of organization, however effected.

(2) The term "a party to a reorganization" includes a corporation resulting from a reorganization and includes both corporations in the case of an acquisition by one corporation of at least a majority of the voting stock and at least a majority of the total number of shares of all other classes of stock of another corporation.

Revenue Act, 1926, c. 27, 44 Stat. 12 (26 U.S.C.A. §112 note).

Section 203(a), (b)(2), (b)(3), (b)(4), (e), (e)(1), (e)(2), (h), (h)(1), and (h)(2) repeat the words of Section 203(a), (b)(2), (b)(3), (b)(4), (e), (e)(1), (e)(2), (h), (h)(1) and (h)(2) of the Act of 1924.

Revenue Act, 1928, c. 852, 45 Stat. 816 (26 U.S.C.A. §112 note.)

Section 112(a), (b)(3), (b)(4), (b)(5), (d), (d)(1), (d)(2), (i), (i)(1) and (i)(2) repeat the words of Section 203(a), (b)(2), (b)(3), (b)(4), (e), (e)(1), (e)(2), (h), (h)(1) and (h)(2) of the Act of 1924.

Revenue Act, 1932, c. 209, 47 Stat. 196 (26 U.S.C.A. §112 and note.)

Section 112(a), (b)(3), (b)(4), (b)(5), (d), (d)(1), (d)(2), (i), (i)(1) and (i)(2) repeat the words of Section 203(a), (b)(2), (b)(3), (b)(4), (e), (e)(1), (e)(2), (h), (h)(1) and (h)(2) of the Act of 1924. [Footnote by the Court.]

*The 18,000 shares amounted to 7½ per cent of Grand Union's outstanding stock. — ED.

dissolution by the conveying corporation. And finally, that its conclusions find support in Treasury regulations long in force.

These conclusions we think are correct.

The Commissioner maintains that the statute presents two definitions of reorganization by transfer of assets. One, Clause (B), requires that the transferor obtain control of the transferee. The other, Clause (A), is part of the definition of merger or consolidation, and must be narrowly interpreted so as to necessitate something nearly akin to technical merger or consolidation. These clauses have separate legislative histories and were intended to be mutually exclusive. Consequently, he says, Clause (A) must be restricted to prevent overlapping and negation of the condition in Clause (B). Also, the transaction here involved substantially changed the relation of the taxpayer to its assets; a large amount of cash passed between the parties; there are many attributes of a sale; what was done did not sufficiently resemble merger or consolidation as commonly understood.

With painstaking care, the opinion of the court below gives the history of Clauses (A) and (B), §112(i)(1). We need not repeat the story. Clause (A) first appeared in the Act of 1921; (B) was added by the 1924 Act. We find nothing in the history or words employed which indicates an intention to modify the evident meaning of (A) by what appears in (B). Both can have effect, and if one does somewhat overlap the other the taxpayer should not be denied, for that reason, what one paragraph clearly grants him. Treasury regulations long enforced support the taxpayer's position, as the opinion below plainly points out.

Pinellas Ice Co. v. Commissioner, 287 U.S. 462, 470, considered the language of §203(h)(1)(A), Act of 1926, which became §112(i)(1)(A), Act of 1928, and held that a sale for money or short-term notes was not within its intendment. We approved the conclusion of the Commissioner, Board of Tax Appeals and Court of Appeals that the transaction there involved was in reality a sale for the equivalent of money — not an exchange for securities. But we disapproved the following assumption and observations of the court: "That in adopting paragraph (h) Congress intended to use the words 'merger' and 'consolidation' in their ordinary and accepted meanings. Giving the matter in parenthesis the most liberal construction, it is only when there is an acquisition of substantially all the property of another corporation in connection with a merger or consolidation that a reorganization takes place. Clause (B) of the paragraph removes any doubt as to the intention of Congress on this point." And we said: "The words within the parenthesis may not be disregarded. They expand the meaning of 'merger' or 'consolidation' so as to include some things which partake of the nature of a merger or consolidation but are beyond the ordinary and commonly accepted meaning of those words — so as to embrace circumstances difficult to delimit but which in strictness cannot be designated as either merger or consolidation. But the mere purchase for money of the assets of one Company by another is beyond the evident purpose of the provision, and has no real semblance to a merger or consolidation. Certainly, we think that to be within the exemption the seller must acquire an interest in the affairs of the purchasing company more definite than that incident to ownership of its short-term purchase-money notes." And we now add that this interest must be definite and material; it must represent a substantial part of the value of the thing transferred. This much is necessary in order that the result accomplished may genuinely partake of the nature of merger or consolidation.

Gregory v. Helvering, 293 U.S. 465, revealed a sham — a mere device intended to obscure the character of the transaction. We, of course, disregarded the mask and dealt with realities. The present record discloses no such situation; nothing suggests other than a bona fide business move.

The transaction here was no sale, but partook of the nature of a reorganization in that the seller acquired a definite and substantial interest in the purchaser.

True it is that the relationship of the taxpayer to the assets conveyed was substantially changed, but this is not inhibited by the statute. Also, a large part of the consideration was cash. This, we think, is permissible so long as the taxpayer received an interest in the affairs of the transferee which represented a material part of the value of the transferred assets.

Finally, it is said the transferror was not dissolved and therefore the transaction does not adequately resemble consolidation. But dissolution is not prescribed and we are unable to see that such action is essential to the end in view.

The challenged judgment is

Affirmed. . . .

NOTE

After *Pinellas, Cortland,* and *Minnesota Tea,* the transferor corporation or its shareholders had to acquire a "definite and substantial interest" in the transferee corporation, representing a "material part of the value of the transferred assets," in order that the transfer qualify as a reorganization. In terms of tax planning, counseling or litigating, did these developments contribute materially to certainty? Given the ends which the courts indicate the reorganization provisions are designed to serve, how likely were the Supreme Court's formulations to contribute to their attainment? Why?

HELVERING v. WATTS
296 U.S. 387 (1935), aff'g 75 F.2d 981 (2d Cir. 1935)

Mr. Justice McReynolds delivered the opinion of the Court. These causes involved deficiency assessments for income tax against the three respondents for the year 1924.

They were the sole stockholders of United States Ferro Alloys Corporation — herein Ferro Alloys — and the causes, alike in all essential particulars, were dealt with below in one opinion.

The respondents maintain that they exchanged all stock of Ferro Alloys for shares of Vanadium Corporation of America and bonds of Ferro Alloys guaranteed by Vanadium; that these two corporations were parties to a reorganization, and that under §203(b)(2), Revenue Act, 1924, no taxable gain resulted. The Commissioner insists that the transaction was a sale of all the stock of the Ferro Alloys and therefore taxable gain resulted. The applicable statutory provision is §203, Revenue Act, 1924, the pertinent parts of which are in the margin of the opinion in Helvering v. Minnesota Tea Co. [page 505 supra].

In December, 1924, respondents owned all the stock of Ferro Alloys Corporation. They exchanged this with the Vanadium Corporation for stock of the latter valued at $30 per share and for $1,161,184.50 mortgage bonds of Ferro Alloys guaranteed by Vanadium. Ferro Alloys continued to conduct business until its dissolution in 1928. Article 1574 of Treasury Regulations 65 provided that under the Act of 1924 no gain or loss shall be recognized to the shareholders from the exchange of stock made in connection with the reorganization, if two or more corporations reorganize, for example, by either the sale of the stock of B to A, or the acquisition by A of a majority of the total number of shares of all other classes of stock of B.

The transaction here involved is within the description of reorganization recognized by the Treasury Regulation above quoted. And if the regulation can be taken as properly interpreting the statute, the challenged judgment must be affirmed.

The court below recites the history of the Treasury Regulation above quoted and concludes that, in view of the reenactment of the paragraph to which it refers without change, Congress intended to approve the regulation as written.

The Commissioner here maintains that the definition of reorganization found in §203(h)(1)(A), Revenue Act, 1924, should be limited to transactions which partake of the nature of mergers or consolidations and that here the Vanadium merely made an investment in Ferro Alloys stock and obtained only the rights of a stockholder therein. It is also urged that an exchange of stocks for bonds results in a substantial change of position and that such bonds are "other property" within the meaning of the statute and as such subject to tax. Much of the argument presented is the same as the one considered in the *Minnesota Tea Company* case, and it need not be again followed in detail. The bonds, we think, were securities within the definition and cannot be regarded as cash, as were the short term notes referred to in Pinellas Ice Co. v. Commissioner, 287 U.S. 462.

The judgment of the court below must be
Affirmed.

LeTULLE v. SCOFIELD
308 U.S. 415 (1940), aff'g 103 F.2d 20 (5th Cir. 1939)

Mr. Justice ROBERTS delivered the opinion of the court. We took this case because the petition for certiorari alleged that the Circuit Court of Appeals had based its decision on a point not presented or argued by the litigants, which the petitioner had never had an opportunity to meet by the production of evidence.

The Gulf Coast Irrigation Company was the owner of irrigation properties. Petitioner was its sole stockholder. He personally owned certain lands and other irrigation properties. November 4, 1931, the Irrigation Company, the Gulf Coast Water Company, and the petitioner, entered into an agreement which recited that the petitioner owned all of the stock of the Irrigation Company; described the company's properties, and stated that, prior to conveyance to be made pursuant to the contract, the Irrigation Company would be the owner of certain other lands and irrigation properties. These other lands and properties were those which the petitioner individually owned. The contract called for a conveyance of all the properties owned, and to be owned, by the Irrigation Company for $50,000 in cash and $750,000 in bonds of the Water Company, payable serially over the period January 1, 1933, to January 1, 1944. The petitioner joined in this agreement as a guarantor of the title of the Irrigation Company and for the purpose of covenanting that he would not personally enter into the irrigation business within a fixed area during a specified period after the execution of the contract. Three days later, at a special meeting of stockholders of the Irrigation Company, the proposed reorganization was approved, the minutes stating that the taxpayer, "desiring also to reorganize his interest in the properties," had consented to be a party to the reorganization. The capital stock of the Irrigation Company was increased and thereupon the taxpayer subscribed for the new stock and paid for it by conveyance of his individual properties.

The contract between the two corporations was carried out November 18, with the result that the Water Company became owner of all the properties then owned by the Irrigation Company including the property theretofore owned by the petitioner individually. Subsequently all of its assets, including the bonds received from the Water Company, were distributed to the petitioner. The company was then dissolved. The petitioner and his wife filed a tax return as members of a community in which they reported no gain as a result of the receipt of the liquidating dividend from the Irrigation Company. The latter reported no gain for the taxable year in virtue of its receipt of bonds and cash from the Water Company. The Commissioner of Internal Revenue assessed additional taxes against the community, as individual taxpayers, by reason of the receipt of the liquidating dividend, and against the petitioner as transferee of the Irrigation Company's assets in virtue of the gain realized by the company on the sale of its property. The tax was paid and claims for refund were filed. Petitioner's wife having died he brought suit individually and as her executor and representative in the community property against the respondent to recover the amount of the additional taxes so assessed. He alleged that the transaction constituted a tax-exempt reorganization as defined by the Revenue Act.[1] The respondent traversed the allegations of the complaints and the causes were consolidated and tried by the District Court without a jury. The respondent's contention that the transaction amounted merely to a sale of assets by the petitioner and the Irrigation Company and did not fall within the statutory definition of a tax-free reorganization was overruled by the District Court and judgment was entered for the petitioner.

The respondent appealed, asserting error on the part of the District Court in matters not now material and also assigning as error the court's holding that the transaction constituted a nontaxable reorganization.

The Circuit Court of Appeals concluded that, as the Water Company acquired substantially all the properties of the Irrigation Company, there was a merger of the

---

[1]§112(i) of the Revenue Act of 1928, c. 852, 45 Stat. 791, 818.

latter within the literal language of the statute, but held that, in the light of the construction this Court has put upon the statute, the transaction would not be a reorganization unless the transferor retained a definite and substantial interest in the affairs of the transferee. It thought this requirement was satisfied by the taking of the bonds of the Water Company, and, therefore, agreed with the District Court that a reorganization had been consummated. It added, however, "We find a reason for reversing the judgment which has not been argued." Adverting to the fact that the transfer of the petitioner's individual properties to the Irrigation Company was for the purpose of including them in the latter's assets to be transferred in the proposed reorganization, the court said the statute did not extend to the reorganization of an individual's business or affairs, and the transaction was a reorganization within the meaning of the Revenue Act as respects the corporation's assets owned on November 4, 1931, but not as respects the petitioner's individual properties included in the sale. It concluded: "Only so much of the consideration as represents the price of the properties and business of the Irrigation Company is entitled to be protected from taxation as arising from a reorganization. It does not appear what the proper apportionment is. The burden was upon LeTulle to show not only that he had been illegally taxed, but how much of what was collected from him was illegal. The latter he did not do. The evidence does not support the judgment for the full amount paid by him. It is accordingly reversed, that further proceedings may be had consistent herewith."[2]

The petitioner sought certiorari asserting that the Circuit Court of Appeals had departed from the usual and accepted course of judicial proceedings by deciding the cause upon a ground not presented or argued and hence had deprived the petitioner of his day in court. The respondent, though he had contended below that the transaction in question did not amount to a tax-free statutory reorganization, did not file a cross petition asking for a review of that part of the judgment exempting from taxation gain to the Irrigation Company arising from the transfer of its assets owned by it on and prior to November 4, 1931, and the part of the liquidating dividend attributable thereto.

We find it unnecessary to consider petitioner's contention that the Circuit Court of Appeals erred in deciding the case on a ground not raised by the pleadings, not before the trial court, not suggested or argued in the Circuit Court of Appeals, and one as to which the petitioner had never had the opportunity to present his evidence, since we are of opinion that the transaction did not amount to a reorganization and that, therefore, the petitioner cannot complain, as the judgment must be affirmed on the ground that no tax-free reorganization was effected within the meaning of the statute.

Section 112(i) provides, so far as material:

"(1) The term 'reorganization' means (A) a merger or consolidation (including the acquisition by one corporation of at least a majority of the voting stock and at least a majority of the total number of shares of all other classes of stock of another corporation, or substantially all the properties of another corporation) . . ."

[2]103 F.2d 20.

As the court below properly stated, the section is not to be read literally, as denominating the transfer of all the assets of one company for what amounts to a cash consideration given by the other a reorganization. We have held that where the consideration consists of cash and short term notes the transfer does not amount to a reorganization within the true meaning of the statute, but is a sale upon which gain or loss must be reckoned.[3] We have said that the statute was not satisfied unless the transferor retained a substantial stake in the enterprise and such a stake was thought to be retained where a large proportion of the consideration was in common stock of the transferee,[4] or where the transferor took cash and the entire issue of preferred stock of the transferee corporation.[5] And, where the consideration is represented by a substantial proportion of stock, and the balance in bonds, the total consideration received is exempt from tax under §112(b)(4) and 112(g).[6]

In applying our decision in the *Pinellas* case the courts have generally held that receipt of long term bonds as distinguished from short term notes constitutes the retention of an interest in the purchasing corporation. There has naturally been some difficulty in classifying the securities involved in various cases.

We are of opinion that the term of the obligations is not material. Where the consideration is wholly in the transferee's bonds, or part cash and part such bonds, we think it cannot be said that the transferor retains any proprietary interest in the enterprise. On the contrary, he becomes a creditor of the transferee; and we do not think that the fact referred to by the Circuit Court of Appeals, that the bonds were secured solely by the assets transferred and that, upon default, the bondholder would retake only the property sold, changes his status from that of a creditor to one having a proprietary stake, within the purview of the statute.

We conclude that the Circuit Court of Appeals was in error in holding that, as respects any of the property transferred to the Water Company, the transaction was other than a sale or exchange upon which gain or loss must be reckoned in accordance with the provisions of the revenue act dealing with the recognition of gain or loss upon a sale or exchange.

Had the respondent sought and been granted certiorari the petitioner's tax liability would, in the view we have expressed, be substantially increased over the amount found due by the Circuit Court of Appeals. Since the respondent has not drawn into question so much of the judgment as exempts from taxation gain to the Irrigation Company arising from transfer of its assets owned by it on and prior to November 4, 1931, and the part of the liquidating dividend attributable thereto, we cannot afford him relief from that portion of the judgment which was adverse to him.

A respondent or an appellee may urge any matter appearing in the record in support of a judgment, but he may not attack it even on grounds asserted in the court below, in an effort to have this Court reverse it, when he himself has not sought review of the whole judgment, or of that portion which is adverse to him.

The judgment of the Circuit Court of Appeals is affirmed and the cause is re-

[3]Pinellas Ice & Cold Storage Co. v. Commissioner, 287 U.S. 462.
[4]Helvering v. Minnesota Tea Co., 296 U.S. 378.
[5]Nelson Co. v. Helvering, 296 U.S. 374.
[6]45 Stat. 816, 818. See Helvering v. Watts, 296 U.S. 387.

manded to the District Court with directions to proceed in accordance with the opinion and mandate of the Circuit Court of Appeals.

Affirmed.

NOTE

The taxpayers in *LeTulle* received $50,000 cash and $750,000 in bonds redeemable over 11 years; in *Watts* the taxpayers received 32 shares of common stock, with a stipulated value of $960, and mortgage bonds of approximately $1,160,232; and in *Nelson* the taxpayer received two million dollars cash and 14,060 shares of non-voting preferred stock, valued at $1,406,000. Is there a sufficient difference, in terms of the concept of "reorganization," to justify the treatment of the taxpayers in *LeTulle?* In any event, who has a more significant interest in the corporate assets: the owner of ten-year, fixed-interest bonds or the owner, e.g., of non-voting, non-cumulative preferred stock?

ROEBLING v. COMMISSIONER
143 F.2d 810 (3d Cir. 1944), cert. denied, 323 U.S. 773 (1944)

Before Jones and McLaughlin, Circuit Judges, and Kalodner, District Judge.

Kalodner, District Judge. This appeal presents three questions: (1) Whether the transaction hereafter stated between a lessor corporation and a lessee corporation constituted a "statutory merger," within the meaning of Sec. [368(a)(1)(A)]; (2) whether the doctrine of "continuity of interest" as enunciated in LeTulle v. Scofield, 308 U.S. 415, 60 S. Ct. 313, 84 L. Ed. 355, applies to a "statutory merger," and (3) whether under the facts a "continuity of interest" actually existed.

Taxability on gain resulting to the petitioner on the exchange of stock in the lessor corporation for bonds of the lessee corporation under the provisions of Sec. 112(b)(3) of the Revenue Act of 1938[2] depends on the disposition of the issues above stated.*

The facts are all stipulated. Summarized they are as follows: . . .

On December 5, 1935, petitioner acquired by gift 166 shares of the stock of South Jersey Gas, Electric and Traction Co. (hereinafter referred to as South Jersey). This stock had been acquired by petitioner's donor on March 12, 1914, at a cost of $16,600.

---

[2]"Sec. 112. Recognition of gain or loss

"(a) General rule. Upon the sale or exchange of property the entire amount of the gain or loss, determined under section 111, shall be recognized, except as hereinafter provided in this section.

"(b) Exchanges solely in kind . . .

"(3) Stock for stock on reorganization. No gain or loss shall be recognized if stock or securities in a corporation a party to a reorganization are, in pursuance of the plan of reorganization, exchanged solely for stock or securities in such corporation or in another corporation a party to the reorganization."

*Cf. §354(a) of the 1954 Code. — Ed.

South Jersey was a corporation organized on August 31, 1900, under the laws of the State of New Jersey, for the purpose of furnishing electricity and gas for public and private use in that state.

In June, 1903, South Jersey had leased all its franchises, plants and operating equipment to Public Service Corporation of New Jersey for 900 years. The lessee was to pay rent which beginning December 1, 1908, amounted to $480,000 per annum. In addition the lessee agreed to pay the interest charges on the lessor's bonded indebtedness, all taxes, insurance and such sums as were necessary to maintain, repair, improve and extend the leased properties. *All replacements and additions became the property of South Jersey subject to the terms of the lease.*

The lease further provided that *upon default of the terms of the lease* for a period 30 days, after notice, *South Jersey could terminate the lease, reenter and reacquire the property and additions and extensions thereto.*

Under the terms of the lease South Jersey could enter upon the leased property for the purpose of inspecting it and determining its condition and the character of the management and whether the covenants of the lease were being complied with.

In July, 1924, this lease was assigned by Public Service Corporation of New Jersey to Public Service Electric and Gas Company which assumed the obligations thereof.

From December 1, 1908, to June 1, 1937, the net rentals received by South Jersey, the lessor company, were distributed to its stockholders at the rate of 8% per annum on the par value of its stock. South Jersey had outstanding 60,000 shares of capital stock of $100 par value, of which Public Service Electric and Gas Company, the assignee of the lease, held 1,705 shares, and Public Service Corporation of New Jersey, the original lessee, held 15,773 shares. The remaining 42,521 shares were held by other interests. Public Service Corporation of New Jersey held substantially all the voting stock of Public Service Electric and Gas Company.

Public Service Electric and Gas Company as a part of its unified electrical system held and operated under long-term leases the properties of many other utility companies. For more than ten years Public Service and its parent, Public Service Corporation of New Jersey, had engaged in a systematic effort to acquire the fee to these properties, and by 1927 had acquired more than two-thirds of the stock of certain of these lessor companies. A projected merger of the lessee companies into Public Service Electric Gas through the exchange of stock in the lessor companies for 6% cumulative preferred stock of Electric and Gas callable in three years was enjoined by the Chancery Court of New Jersey as unfair to the minority stockholders of those companies. Outwater v. Public Service Corporation, 103 N.J. Eq. 461, 143 A. 729.

On May 10, 1937, the directors of South Jersey and of Public Service Electric and Gas Company adopted a "Plan of Reorganization" under which it was proposed that the former company be merged into the latter in accordance with the statutes of New Jersey. This plan provided that the stockholders of South Jersey (other than Public Service Electric and Gas Company) should exchange, dollar for dollar, their stock in South Jersey for 8% one hundred years first mortgage bonds of Public Service Electric and Gas Company. These bonds were to be issued under a prior mortgage of Public Service Electric and Gas Company dated August 1, 1924, and under a supplemental indenture later to be executed. It was expressly provided in the "Agreement of

Merger" executed on the same day: "The capital stock of the Public Service Electric and Gas Company . . . will not be changed by reason of this agreement." Also, the stock of South Jersey held by Public Service Electric and Gas Company was not to participate in the exchange but was to be delivered up and cancelled.

The "Agreement of Merger" was accepted by the stockholders of South Jersey and of Public Service Electric and Gas Company, and approved by the Board of Public Utilities Commissioners of the State of New Jersey and by the Federal Power Commission. The "Agreement of Merger" with the certificates of the secretaries of the constituent companies as to the confirmatory votes of the stockholders, and the certificates of approval of the Public Utility Commissioners of New Jersey and of the Federal Power Commission was filed with the Secretary of State of New Jersey on November 17, 1938.

The "Agreement of Merger" was consummated pursuant to its provisions. In accordance therewith the taxpayer received in exchange for his 166 shares of stock in South Jersey, $16,600, principal amount of 8% bonds which on November 25, 1938, had a fair market value of $34,777.

The Commissioner determined that the difference between the basis of the taxpayer's stock in South Jersey and the fair market value of the bonds received in exchange therefor must be recognized as taxable income in 1938 and he asserted a deficiency which the Tax Court sustained, so far as it was based upon this item.

The issues presented here arise by reason of taxpayer's contention (1) that the merger of South Jersey into Public Service Electric and Gas Co. was a "true statutory merger" under the laws of the state of New Jersey and therefore the exchange of stock for bonds was not a taxable event under [the reorganization provisions]; (2) that since there was a "true statutory merger" the "continuity of interest" doctrine in the LeTulle v. Scofield case is inapplicable and (3) that in any event a "continuity of interest" actually existed in the instant case.

As to the taxpayer's first two contentions, which may be considered together: The admitted fact that the merger of the two corporations was a "true statutory merger" under the New Jersey law is not dispositive of the question as to whether there was a "statutory merger" here within the meaning of Sec. [368(a)(1)(A)]. It is well-settled that a State law cannot alter the essential characteristics required to enable a taxpayer to obtain exemption under the provisions of a Federal Revenue Act.

We so held in Commissioner of Internal Revenue v. Gilmore's Estate, 3 Cir., 130 F.2d 791. Indeed that case is completely dispositive of the taxpayer's first two contentions. In *Gilmore's Estate* we found that though there was, in that case, a "true statutory merger" under the identical laws of New Jersey involved here, (1) such "true statutory merger" is insufficient without more to qualify as a "reorganization" under the Revenue Act, and (2) that a "continuity of interest" as enunciated in numerous decisions of the Supreme Court of the United States and the pertinent Treasury Regulation 101[4] must still be present to establish a true reorganization. In *Gilmore's Estate* we said, on page 794:

---

[4]Treasury Regulation 101, Article 112(g)(1) reads as follows:

"The purpose of the reorganization provisions of the Internal Revenue Code is to except from the general rule certain specifically described exchanges incident to such readjustments

"It is now settled that whether a transaction qualifies as a reorganization under the various Revenue Acts *does not turn alone upon compliance with the literal language of the statute.* The judicial interpretation has determined that something more may be needed and that, indeed, under some circumstances, something less will do. Our concern in this case is the 'something more' since we have concluded that there was a literal compliance. . . .

"The reorganization provisions were enacted to free from the imposition of an income tax purely 'paper profits or losses' wherein there is no realization of gain or loss in the business sense *but merely the recasting of the same interests in a different form,* the tax being postponed to a future date when a more tangible gain or loss is realized. . . ." (emphasis supplied)

. . . In Helvering v. Alabama Asphaltic Limestone Co., 1942, 315 U.S. 179, at page 182, 62 S. Ct. 540, at page 542, 86 L. Ed. 775, the Supreme Court of the United States succinctly stated the rule as follows:

"From the *Pinellas* case, Pinellas, Ice & Cold Storage Co. v. Commissioner of Internal Revenue, 287 U.S. 462, 53 S. Ct. 257, 77 L. Ed. 428, to the *LeTulle* case, LeTulle v. Scofield, 308 U.S. 415, 60 S. Ct. 313, 84 L. Ed. 355, it has been recognized that a transaction may not qualify as a 'reorganization' under the various revenue acts though the literal language of the statute is satisfied. See Paul, Studies in Federal Taxation (3d Series), p. 91 et seq. The *Pinellas* case introduced the continuity of interest theory to eliminate those transactions which had 'no real semblance to a merger or consolidation' (287 U.S. page 470, 53 S. Ct. [257,] 77 L. Ed. 428) and to avoid a construction which 'would make evasion of taxation very easy.' . . ."

That Sec. [368] has made "the continuity of interest test . . . much stricter" was held in Helvering v. Southwest Corporation, 315 U.S. 194-198, 62 S. Ct. 546, 550, 86 L. Ed. 789. Said the Court, page 198 of 315 U.S., at page 550 of 62 S. Ct.:

"Under the statute involved in Helvering v. Alabama Asphaltic Limestone Co., 315 U.S. 179, 62 S. Ct. 540, 86 L. Ed. 775, decided this day, there would have been a 'reorganization' here. For the creditors of the old company had acquired substantially the entire proprietary interest of the old stockholders. See Helvering v. Minnesota Tea Co., 296 U.S. 378, 56 S. Ct. 269, 80 L. Ed. 284. But clause (B) of §112(g)(1)* of the 1934 Act [26 U.S.C.A. Int. Rev. Acts, page 695] effects an important change as respects transactions whereby one corporation acquires substantially all of the assets of another. See S. Rep. No. 558, 73d Cong., 2d Sess., Committee Reports, Revenue Acts 1913-1938, pp. 598-599. *The continuity of interest test is made much stricter.* See Paul, Studies in Federal Taxation (3rd Series), pp. 36-41. . . ."[5] (Emphasis supplied)

---

of corporate structures, made in one of the particular ways specified in the Code, as are required by business exigencies, and which effect only a readjustment of continuing interests in property under modified corporate forms. Requisite to a reorganization under the Code are a continuity of the business enterprise under the modified corporate form, and a continuity of interest therein on the part of those persons who were the owners of the enterprise prior to the reorganization. . . . Both the terms of the specifications and their underlying assumptions and purposes must be satisfied in order to entitle the taxpayer to the benefit of the exception from the general rule."

*Cf. §368(a)(1)(B) of the 1954 Code. — Ed.

[5]Following is an excerpt from the Committee Report referred to in Helvering v. Southwest Corporation:

In view of the cases cited we cannot subscribe to the taxpayer's contention that under Sec. [368(a)(1)(A)] of the Revenue Act of 1938 the requirements of New Jersey law supersede the "continuity of interest" test as applied in LeTulle v. Scofield and the numerous other decisions.

The taxpayer's remaining contention that the requisite "continuity of interest" is present under the peculiar facts in this case is premised on a rather novel theory. He urges that "prior to the merger, the stockholders of South Jersey had *no proprietary interest* in its properties in any real sense", and that in sanctioning the merger "the decision of the New Jersey courts recognized that the stock in the lessor companies was substantially equivalent to a perpetual 8% bond."

This contention places the taxpayer in an anomalous position. Whereas the "continuity of interest" principle is predicated on the existence of a proprietary right which must be carried over into the reorganized corporation, the taxpayer at one and the same time asserts that a "continuity of interest" existed in the reorganized company, even though there was *no* proprietary interest by the stockholders in the merged corporation to be carried over into the reorganized corporation.

It is unnecessary, however, to further explore this contention because two things are so clear that he who runs may read. First, the stockholders in South Jersey had a definite and clearly fixed proprietary interest in its property. The lease provided that all replacements and additions to the leased property were to be the property of South Jersey and subject to the terms and conditions of the lease. Further, on the expiration of the lease all the property subject to its terms was to be returned to South Jersey. South Jersey owned the property under lease even though that lease was for a 900-year term. The lease further provided that upon default of its terms South Jersey could terminate the lease and *re-enter and re-acquire the property and additions and extensions thereto.*

In view of the incontrovertible facts the taxpayer's argument that the stockholders in South Jersey had *no* proprietary interest is without basis.

Finally, it is equally clear that when the stockholders of South Jersey exchanged their stock in that corporation for the long-term bonds of Public Service Electric and Gas Company, they surrendered their proprietary interest and simply became creditors of Public Service. They no longer owned any of the former property of South Jersey

---

"Your committee is in complete agreement with the purposes of the House bill which aim at tax-avoidance schemes in this connection. However, some modifications are recommended in order to bring about a more uniform application of the provisions in all 48 of the States. Not all of the States have adopted statutes providing for mergers or consolidations; and, moreover, a corporation of one State can not ordinarily merge with a corporation of another State. The committee believes that it is desirable to permit reorganizations in such cases with restrictions designed to prevent tax avoidance. Consequently, the committee recommends the insertion in the House bill of an addition to the definition of the term 'reorganization' as follows:

" '(B) the acquisition by one corporation in exchange solely for its voting stock: of at least 80 per centum of the voting stock and at least 80 per centum of the total number of shares of all other classes of stock of another corporation; or of substantially all the properties of another corporation;'

"The committee believes that these transactions, when carried out as prescribed in this amendment, are in themselves sufficiently similar to mergers and consolidations as to be entitled to similar treatment."

and they had no proprietary interest in the property of Public Service. The Tax Court succinctly described the situation when it stated:

". . . *It follows that no continuing stake in the merged enterprise was retained by South Jersey or its stockholders, and hence that the requisite continuity of interest is not furnished either by the proprietary interests acquired by the merged corporation, nor by the bondholders' status conferred upon the former shareholders.*" (emphasis supplied)

Taxpayer urges that the substance of the transaction here is close to that involved in Commissioner of Internal Revenue v. Neustadt's Trust et al., 2 Cir., 131 F.2d 528. That is not so. In the *Neustadt's Trust* case the taxpayers merely exchanged their holdings of long-term debenture bonds for an equivalent face amount of short-term debenture bonds and both the Tax Court and the United States Circuit Court of Appeals for the Second Circuit ruled that the transaction was part of a "recapitalization" where no transfer of assets and no change of capital stock occurred.

For the reasons stated the decision of the Tax Court of the United States is affirmed.

NOTE

Judge Kalodner thought that the taxpayer's interest was less remote before the merger than after. Is the right to income from a corporation which owns and operates the assets more remote from the assets than the expectancy of income from a corporation which, for 900 years, has only a right to income from the assets? What relevance do questions like these have to the meaning of "reorganization"?

How would each of the cases in this section be decided under the 1954 Code? Why?

REVENUE PROCEDURE 66-34
1966-2 Cum. Bull. 1232

[The Internal Revenue Service has announced an "operating rule" which will guide it in issuing rulings where the "continuity of interest" requirement of Treas. Reg. §1.368-1(b) is involved.]

. . . The "continuity of interest" requirement of section 1.368-1(b) of the Income Tax Regulations is satisfied if there is a continuing interest through stock ownership in the acquiring or transferee corporation (or a corporation in "control" thereof within the meaning of section 368(c) of the Code) on the part of the former shareholders of the acquired or transferor corporation which is equal in value, as of the effective date of the reorganization, to at least 50 percent of the value of all of the formerly outstanding stock of the acquired or transferor corporation as of the same date. It is not necessary that each shareholder of the acquired or transferor corporation receive in the exchange stock of the acquiring or transferee corporation or a corporation in "control" thereof, which is equal in value to at least 50 percent of the value of his former stock interest in the acquired or transferor corporation, so long as one or more of the shareholders of the acquired or transferor corporation have a continuing interest through stock ownership in the acquiring or transferee corporation (or a corporation in "control" thereof) which is, in the aggregate, equal in value to at least 50 percent of the value of all of the formerly outstanding stock of the acquired or transferor corporation. Sales, redemptions, and other dispositions of stock occurring prior or subsequent to the exchange which are part of the plan of reorganization will be considered in determining whether there is a 50 percent continuing interest through stock ownership as of the effective date of the reorganization. . . .

REVENUE RULING 66-224
1966-2 Cum. Bull. 114

Corporation X was merged under state law into corporation Y. Corporation X had four stockholders (A, B, C, D), each of whom owned 25 percent of its stock. Corporation Y paid A and B each $50,000 in cash for their stock of corporation X, and C and D each received corporation Y stock with a value of $50,000 in exchange for their stock of corporation X. There are no other facts present that should be taken into account in determining whether the continuity of interest requirement of section 1.368-1(b) of the Income Tax regulations has been satisfied, such as sales, redemptions or other dispositions of stock prior to or subsequent to the exchange which were part of the plan of reorganization.

Held, the continuity of interest requirement of Section 1.368-1(b) of the regulations has been satisfied. It would also be satisfied if the facts were the same except corporation Y paid each stockholder $25,000 in cash and each stockholder received corporation Y stock with a value of $25,000.

NOTE

What is the focus of the "continuity of interest" doctrine: continuity of enterprise, continuity of asset interest, or something else?

See R. Beghe, Consideration in Tax-Free Asset Acquisitions, 26 N.Y.U. Inst. on Fed. Tax. 881 (1968); H. Malzeke, Current IRS Procedure for Issuing Rulings in Reorganization Cases: How It Operates, 27 J. Taxation 336 (1967).

b. INTEREST SURRENDERED

HELVERING v. ALABAMA ASPHALTIC LIMESTONE CO.
315 U.S. 179 (1942), aff'g 119 F.2d 819 (5th Cir. 1941)

Mr. Justice DOUGLAS delivered the opinion of the Court. Respondent, in 1931, acquired all the assets of Alabama Rock Asphalt, Inc., pursuant to a reorganization plan consummated with the aid of the bankruptcy court. In computing its depreciation and depletion allowances for the year 1934, respondent treated its assets as having the same basis which they had in the hands of the old corporation. The Commissioner determined a deficiency, computed on the price paid at the bankruptcy sale.[1] The Board of Tax Appeals rejected the position of the Commissioner. 41 B.T.A. 324. The Circuit Court of Appeals affirmed. 119 F.2d 819. We granted the petition for certiorari because of the conflict between that decision[2] and Commissioner v. Palm Springs Holding Corp., 119 F.2d 846, decided by the Circuit Court of Appeals for the Ninth Circuit, and Helvering v. New President Corp., 122 F.2d 92, decided by the Circuit Court of Appeals for the Eighth Circuit.

The answer to the question[3] turns on the meaning of that part of §112(i)(1) of the Revenue Act of 1928 (45 Stat. 791, 818) which provides: "The term 'reorganization' means (A) a merger or consolidation (including the acquisition by one corporation of ... substantially all the properties of another corporation). ..."

The essential facts can be stated briefly. The old corporation was a subsidiary of a corporation which was in receivership in 1929. Stockholders of the parent had financed the old corporation taking unsecured notes for their advances. Maturity of the notes was approaching and not all of the noteholders would agree to take stock for their claims. Accordingly, a creditors' committee was formed, late in 1929, and a plan of reorganization was proposed to which all the noteholders, except two, assented. The plan provided that a new corporation would be formed which would acquire all the assets of the old corporation. The stock of the new corporation, preferred and common, would be issued to the creditors in satisfaction of their claims. Pursuant to the plan, involuntary bankruptcy proceedings were instituted in 1930. The appraised value of the bankrupt corporation's assets was about $155,000. Its obligations were about $838,000, the unsecured notes with accrued interest aggregating somewhat over $793,000. The bankruptcy trustee offered the assets for sale at public auction. They were bid in by the creditors' committee for $150,000. The price was paid by $15,000 in cash, by agreements of creditors to accept stock of a new corporation in full discharge of their claims, and by an offer of the committee to meet the various costs of administration, etc. Thereafter, respondent was formed and acquired all the assets of the bankrupt corporation. It does not appear whether the acquisition was directly from the old corporation on assignment of the bid or from the committee. Pursuant to the plan, respondent issued its stock to the creditors of the old corporation — over 95% to the noteholders and the balance to small creditors. Nonassenting creditors were paid in cash. Operations were not interrupted by the reorganization and were carried on subsequently by substantially the same persons as before.

From the *Pinellas* case (287 U.S. 462) to the *LeTulle* case (308 U.S. 415) it has been recognized that a transaction may not qualify as a "reorganization" under the

[1]Petitioner now takes the position that the new basis should be measured by the market value of the assets rather than the bid price. See Bondholders Committee v. Commissioner, [315 U.S. 189 (1942)].

[2]And see Commissioner v. Kitselman, 89 F.2d 458, and Commissioner v. Newberry Lumber & Chemical Co., 94 F.2d 447, which are in accord with the decision below.

[3]If there was a "reorganization," the respondent was entitled to use the asset basis of the old corporation as provided in §113(a)(7) [362(b)].

various revenue acts though the literal language of the statute is satisfied. See Paul, Studies in Federal Taxation (3d Series), pp. 91 et seq. The *Pinellas* case introduced the continuity of interest theory to eliminate those transactions which had "no real semblance to a merger or consolidation" (287 U.S. p. 470) and to avoid a construction which "would make evasion of taxation very easy." Id. p. 469. In that case, the transferor received in exchange for its property cash and short term notes. This Court said (id. p. 470): "Certainly, we think that to be within the exemption the seller must acquire an interest in the affairs of the purchasing company more definite than that incident to ownership of its short-term purchase-money notes." In the *LeTulle* case, we held that the term of the obligation received by the seller was immaterial. "Where the consideration is wholly in the transferee's bonds, or part cash and part such bonds, we think it cannot be said that the transferor retains any proprietary interest in the enterprise." 308 U.S. pp. 420-421. On the basis of the continuity of interest theory as explained in the *LeTulle* case, it is now earnestly contended that a substantial ownership interest in the transferee company must be retained by the holders of the ownership interest in the transferor. That view has been followed by some courts. Commissioner v. Palm Springs Holding Corp., supra; Helvering v. New President Corp., supra. Under that test, there was "no reorganization" in this case, since the old stockholders were eliminated by the plan, no portion whatever of their proprietary interest being preserved for them in the new corporation. And it is clear that the fact that the creditors were for the most part stockholders of the parent company does not bridge the gap. The equity interest in the parent is one step removed from the equity interest in the subsidiary. In any event, the stockholders of the parent were not granted participation in the plan qua stockholders.

We conclude, however, that it is immaterial that the transfer shifted the ownership of the equity in the property from the stockholders to the creditors of the old corporation. Plainly, the old continuity of interest was broken. Technically that did not occur in this proceeding until the judicial sale took place. For practical purposes, however, it took place not later than the time when the creditors took steps to enforce their demands against their insolvent debtor. In this case, that was the date of the institution of bankruptcy proceedings. From that time on, they had effective command over the disposition of the property. The full priority rule of Northern Pacific Ry. Co. v. Boyd, 228 U.S. 482, applies to proceedings in bankruptcy as well as to equity receiverships. Case v. Los Angeles Lumber Products Co., 308 U.S. 106. It gives creditors, whether secured or unsecured, the right to exclude stockholders entirely from the reorganization plan when the debtor is insolvent. See In re 620 Church St. Bldg. Corp., 299 U.S. 24. When the equity owners are excluded and the old creditors become the stockholders of the new corporation, it conforms to realities to date their equity ownership from the time when they invoked the processes of the law to enforce their rights of full priority. At that time they stepped into the shoes of the old stockholders. The sale "did nothing but recognize officially what had before been true in fact." Helvering v. New Haven & S.L.R. Co., 121 F.2d 985, 987.

That conclusion involves no conflict with the principle of the *LeTulle* case. A bondholder interest in a solvent company plainly is not the equivalent of a proprietary interest, even though upon default the bondholders could retake the property transferred. The mere possibility of a proprietary interest is, of course, not its equivalent. But the determinative and controlling factors of the debtor's insolvency and an effective command by the creditors over the property were absent in the *LeTulle* case.

Nor are there any other considerations which prevent this transaction from qualifying as a "reorganization" within the meaning of the Act. The *Pinellas* case makes plain that "merger" and "consolidation" as used in the Act includes transactions which "are beyond the ordinary and commonly accepted meaning of those words." 287 U.S. p. 470. Insolvency reorganizations are within the family of financial readjustments embraced in those terms as used in this particular statute. Some contention, however, is made that this transaction did not meet the statutory standard because the properties acquired by the new corporation belonged at that time to the committee and not to the old corporation. That is true. Yet, the separate steps were integrated parts of a single scheme. Transitory phases of an arrangement frequently are disregarded under these sections of the revenue acts where they add nothing of substance to the completed affair. Gregory v. Helvering, 293 U.S. 465; Helvering v. Bashford, 302 U.S. 454. Here they were no more than intermediate procedural devices utilized to enable the new corporation to acquire all the assets of the old one pursuant to a single reorganization plan.

Affirmed.

NOTE

Before the transaction in *Alabama Asphaltic Limestone Co.*, the "equity" interest in the assets was owned by the parent corporation. The parent, in turn, was owned by the same persons who held the subsidiary's notes. Why is not the readjustment which took place a prototype "reorganization"? Of what possible relevance is the *LeTulle* line of cases to the basis of assets of a corporation after it has been taken over by creditors in an insolvency proceeding? Should the character of the pre-insolvency interest of the subsequent stockholders have any effect on these questions? Today, insolvency reorganizations are the subject of specific legislation in §§371-374. See D. Tillinghast and S. Gardner, Acquisitive Reorganizations and Chapters X and XI of the Bankruptcy Act, 26 Tax L. Rev. 663 (1971).

2. *Securities*

NEVILLE COKE & CHEMICAL CO. v. COMMISSIONER
148 F.2d 599 (3d Cir. 1945), cert. denied, 326 U.S. 726 (1945)

Before BIGGS, GOODRICH, and McALLISTER, Circuit Judges.

GOODRICH, Circuit Judge. The question for us in this case is the correctness of the Tax Court's conclusion concerning the Neville Coke & Chemical Company's tax liability for 1936. Two corporations known as the Hillman Coal & Coke Company and W. J. Rainey, Inc., had made advances of money and sold coal on credit to a corporation known as the Davison Coke & Iron Company. In 1932 the debtor corporation was in some financial difficulty and a reorganization was determined upon.

The Hillman and Rainey companies subsequently caused the formation of the tax-payer corporation as a step to facilitate reorganization of the Davison company. To the new corporation Hillman and Rainey transferred their claims against or interest in, the debtor. These consisted of "preferred accounts", first mortgage bonds, accounts receivable, notes of the debtor due in three, four and five years without interest,[2] and stock, of various classifications, in the debtor company.

The 1932 efforts not having proved sufficient to get the debtor out of its troubles, in 1935 it filed a 77B petition; a plan of reorganization was promptly approved and final decree entered on January 31, 1936. Under the plan the debtor issued new common stock and debenture bonds. Its old bonds were exchanged for debentures and the holders of certain notes, the nature of which is discussed below, got new debentures in the same face amount ($1,129,000) plus 22,580 shares of common stock in the reorganized company. . . .

. . . The relevant sections of the Revenue Act of 1936, are noted in the margin.[3] The storm center of the controversy here relates to §112(b)(3) [of the 1936 Act]. There is no gain or loss recognized if "stock or securities in a corporation . . . are . . . exchanged solely for stock or securities in such corporation. . . ." Were the notes of Davison, which the taxpayer had in its possession, and which it exchanged for debentures and shares of stock issued by the reorganized debtor, "securities" within the wording of the statute? No question has been raised as to the sufficiency of the evidence of obligations issued by the reorganized debtor to qualify under the description of "stock or securities", and the problem is limited to the consideration of what the taxpayer turned in, that is, the notes above mentioned.

What then are "securities" within the meaning of the section? The taxpayer makes a tentative argument that the word ought to be taken in its common, accepted interpretation and that interpretation includes evidence of indebtedness, but he goes on to admit that the Supreme Court has read into the term a meaning differing radically from common interpretation.

---

[2]The four and five year notes bore interest after three years.

[3]Revenue Act of 1936, c. 690, 49 Stat. 1648, 1678-1679, 1681, 26 U.S.C.A. Int. Rev. Acts, pp. 854-858.

"Sec. 111. Determination of Amount of, and Recognition of, Gain or Loss. . .

"(c) Recognition of Gain or Loss. In the case of a sale or exchange, the extent to which the gain or loss determined under this section shall be recognized for the purposes of this title, shall be determined under the provisions of section 112.

"Sec. 112. Recognition of Gain or Loss

"(a) General rule. Upon the sale or exchange of property the entire amount of the gain or loss, determined under section 111, shall be recognized, except as hereinafter provided in this section.

"(b) Exchanges solely in kind. . . .

"(3) Stock for stock on reorganization. No gain or loss shall be recognized if stock or securities in a corporation a party to a reorganization are, in pursuance of the plan of reorganization, exchanged solely for stock or securities in such corporation or in another corporation a party to the reorganization.

"(4) Same — Gain of corporation. No gain or loss shall be recognized if a corporation a party to a reorganization exchanges property, in pursuance of the plan of reorganization, solely for stock or securities in another corporation a party to the reorganization. . . .

"(g) Definition of reorganization. As used in this section and section 113 —

"(1) The term 'reorganization' means . . . (D) a recapitalization, . . ."

It is to be noted that the phrase "stock or securities" appears twice in §112(b)(3). Once it refers to what a party turns into a corporation being reorganized. The second appearance of the phrase relates to what a recipient takes from the reorganized company as a result of the transaction. We have no reason for thinking that the phrase has a different meaning in either of the two instances and the argument by the taxpayer that it does differ fails to convince us. Cf. Lloyd-Smith v. Commissioner of Internal Revenue, 2 Cir., 1941, 116 F.2d 642, certiorari denied 1941, 313 U.S. 588, 61 S. Ct. 1111, 85 L. Ed. 1543.

Most of the decisions seem to have concerned themselves with what was issued to the recipient by the reorganized corporation. In Pinellas Ice & Cold Storage Co. v. Commissioner of Internal Revenue, 1933, 287 U.S. 462, 53 S. Ct. 257, 77 L. Ed. 428, the taxpayer was given short term secured notes, maturing in 45, 75 or 105 days, respectively. The Court said that to give an exemption "the seller must acquire an interest in the affairs of the purchasing company more definite than that incident to ownership of its short-term purchase-money notes." Id., 287 U.S. at page 470, 53 S. Ct. at page 260, 77 L. Ed. 428. Was the term "security" then to depend upon the length of time between inception and maturity of the obligation? The courts talked and decided as though length of time were the test. See the discussion and authorities cited in L. & E. Stirn, Inc. v. Commissioner of Internal Revenue, 2 Cir., 1939, 107 F.2d 390. Six year bonds were held to be securities by this Court in Commissioner of Internal Revenue v. Freund, 3 Cir., 1938, 98 F.2d 201. On the other hand, when the reorganized corporation issued evidence of indebtedness, ten year notes were held to be "securities" sufficient for a tax transaction in Burnham v. Commissioner, 7· Cir., 1936, 86 F.2d 776, certiorari denied, 1937, 300 U.S. 683, 57 S. Ct. 753, 81 L. Ed. 886.

This tendency to measure legal sufficiency on a time basis was noted by the Supreme Court in LeTulle v. Scofield, Collector of Internal Revenue, 1940, 308 U.S. 415, 60 S. Ct. 313, 316, 84 L. Ed. 355. The Court there declared that "the term of the obligations is not material." It drew the distinction between a case where, after the reorganization, the transferee* retained a proprietary interest in the enterprise or simply became a creditor.

Did the notes which taxpayer held against Davison Company give it a "proprietary" interest in the enterprise or was it only a creditor? Since LeTulle v. Scofield was decided the Second Circuit has held that short term notes (six months or on demand) which, however, were secured, "were but short term obligations having the character of temporary evidence of debt," as distinguished from "the well known permanent, or semi-permanent, status of long term obligations, which are to be treated as securities within the meaning of that term in §112(b)(3) . . . ." Commissioner of Internal Revenue v. Sisto Financial Corporation, 2 Cir., 139 F.2d 253, 255. The set of facts in that case differs from those here in the length of time in which the obligation had to run before maturity. But, it is to be remembered in this connection, the time element is not the determining factor.

The Commissioner's argument is to the effect that the notes in question do not

---

*Does the court mean transferee or transferor? — Ed.

represent a stake in the business of the corporation. Their total amount was $1,129,000. $500,000 was due in three years, $250,000 in four years and $250,000 in five years. These had been received by the Hillman Company in 1932 in exchange for $500,000 demand notes and $500,000 past due promissory notes which Hillman Company had discounted for the debtor corporation. The remaining $129,000 represented three year notes received by Hillman Company and the Rainey Company in 1932 as current creditors of the debtor. It is pointed out that J. H. Hillman, Jr., of the Hillman Company, testified that the $1,000,000 loaned in 1930 was conditioned upon the debtor giving his Company its business in low volatile coal, thus indicating no intention of investing in debtor's business. The taxpayer, in its reply brief, meets this point with great vigor and considerable force. It calls to our attention the reorganization agreement of 1932 which was not a court proceeding, but an agreement between the Davison Company and its principal creditors. This document is in evidence and it is stipulated that the recital of fact therein contained may be taken as true. In that contract the debtor agreed that certain creditors of the corporation, including representatives of Rainey and Hillman should become members of the debtor's Board of Directors; stockholders of Davison surrendered prerogatives to receive cash dividends; the debtor limited its power to create new obligations. The arrangement in 1932 does indicate a stringent control on the part of the debtor corporation by its chief creditors. Most of those creditors received from the debtor promissory notes of the type held by Hillman and Rainey which were exchanged in the 1935 reorganization proceeding.

The weakness of the taxpayer's argument in this respect is that the taxpayer itself was not a party to this agreement. Provisions making certain creditors directors of the debtor company named specifically representatives of The Koppers Company, Hillman Coal & Coke Company, W. J. Rainey, Inc., and M. A. Hanna Company. The taxpayers, as the assignee of the notes given by the debtor to Hillman Company and others, did not succeed to this right of control of the debtor because it became the possessor of the promissory notes. While it is true that the taxpayer was set up by two of these creditors for the convenience of reorganization it is, nevertheless, a separate legal entity and will have to take the disadvantages as well as the advantages of such corporate arrangement. Our conclusion is that the agreement of 1932, as a consequence of which the notes were issued, was an arrangement whereby creditors of Davison became very active in its management. But they did so by virtue of the agreement and not as holders of the notes, the issuance of which was one item in the agreement.

There is one further point in this connection. It was stipulated in the reorganization agreement that the notes should contain a provision giving the holder an option to convert up to 50% of the face amount thereof in prior preferred stock, if the option was exercised within three years. Petitioner contends that this is sufficient in itself to bring the notes into the category of securities and cites E. P. Raymond v. Commissioner of Internal Revenue, 1938, 37 B.T.A. 423. There the shareholder turned in his old shares and got back an option to buy new shares in the reorganized company. The taxpayer in the instant case was a creditor who had an option to become a shareholder if it had asked for stock instead of money. The fact that it had a chance to acquire a proprietary interest in its debtor does not change it from a creditor to a security holder, we think, unless and until the option is exercised.

The taxpayer also argues that its notes were "property", and that §112(b)(4) covers his case. If that argument is correct this paragraph makes §112(b)(3) unnecessary in every case where the creditor of a corporation in reorganization is itself a corporation. One can hardly conceive of any type of interest which is not describable as "property", and thus make the language applicable. All the learning which has gone into the concept of "security" in §112(b)(3) becomes wasted effort so far as corporate creditors are concerned. Section 112(b)(4) is not applicable to this case. We note that the taxpayer, who has supported most of his points through a thorough and ably prepared reply brief, does not labor the contention of the applicability of §112(b)(4) therein. . . .

The decision of the Tax Court is affirmed.

NOTE

Should the "continuity of interest" doctrine prevent "reorganization" where the taxpayer changes the form of his investment to make cash less available and more subject to corporate risk?

As taxpayer's counsel, how would you have argued for reversal on appeal to the Supreme Court? Why? How would you have decided such an appeal? Why?

3. *Party to a Reorganization*

REVENUE RULING 63-234
1963-2 Cum. Bull. 148

Advice has been requested whether the successive exchanges of corporate stock described below constitute, separately or in concert, a reorganization as defined in section 368(a)(1)(B) of the Internal Revenue Code of 1954.

In 1960, the M corporation directly and through its subsidiaries operated a chain of retail stores. It owned 60 shares (60 percent) of the 100 outstanding shares of N corporation's voting common stock. A group of taxpayers, hereinafter referred to as the X group, owned 18 shares (18 percent) of N's voting stock, and the remaining 22 shares (22 percent) were held by other shareholders.

Among the assets of the N corporation was 50 percent of the voting stock of the O corporation. The remaining 50 percent of O's voting stock was owned by members of the X group.

For the purpose of affecting certain economies in operation and to make the filing of a consolidated income tax return possible, the above-mentioned parties adopted a plan of reorganization pursuant to which the following action was taken:

(1) The charter of the N corporation was amended to enlarge its board of directors from ten to 12 members and to provide that the two new members of the board would be elected by the owners of a newly authorized class of preferred stock.

(2) Newly created preferred stock of the N corporation was issued to the members of the X group in exchange for all their holdings of the O corporation's voting stock.

The N corporation thus acquired 100 percent of the outstanding stock of the O corporation and the holdings of the X group in the N corporation were increased to include all of that corporation's preferred stock.

(3) Immediately thereafter, the X group transferred all of its stock of the N corporation (18 percent of the common stock and 100 percent of the preferred stock) to the M corporation in exchange for the latter's voting common stock. As a result, the M corporation became the owner of 78 percent of N's common stock and 100 percent of the preferred shares.

The voting power of the N corporation preferred stock confers upon the holders of such stock the right to significant participation in the management of the affairs of the corporation. This preferred stock is therefore "voting stock" within the meaning of the reorganization provision. See I.T. 3896, C.B. 1948-1, 72. Under the principles set forth in I.T. 3896, the voting rights of the M corporation respecting the affairs of the N corporation, when properly weighted, totaled 81.67 percent of the "voting power" of all classes of "voting stock" of the N corporation. Thus, the M corporation acquired "control" of the N corporation within the meaning of section 368(c) of the Code.

Section 368(a)(1)(B) of the Code provides that, for purposes of parts I, II, and III of subchapter C of chapter 1 of subtitle A of the Code, the term "reorganization" means —

> the acquisition by one corporation, in exchange solely for all or a part of its voting stock, of stock of another corporation if, immediately after the acquisition, the acquiring corporation has control of such other corporation (whether or not such acquiring corporation had control immediately before the acquisition);

Among the requisites to a reorganization under the Code is that of continuity of interest on the part of those persons who, directly or indirectly, were the owners of the enterprise prior to the reorganization. See section 1.368-1(b) of the Income Tax Regulations.

Taking into account all the facts and circumstances, it is concluded that the two exchanges of corporate stock in the instant case were but successive steps in the execution of the single plan adopted earlier by the parties. See Whitney Corporation v. Commissioner, 105 Fed. (2d) 438 (1939), and United Light and Power Co. v. Commissioner, 105 Fed. (2d) 866 (1939), certiorari denied; 308 U.S. 574 (1939). When the component steps in the plans are combined it becomes apparent that the X group exchanged its stock in the O corporation for stock of the M corporation, which did not thereafter directly own either stock of O corporation or its assets. The receipt of N corporation preferred shares by the X group may be disregarded for purposes of the reorganization provisions of the Code since the X group's holding of such shares was "transitory and without real substance." Helvering v. Raymond I. Bashford, 302 U.S. 454 (1938), Ct. D. 1299, C.B. 1938-1, 286, at 288; see also the *United Power and Light Co.* case, supra.

Under the principles established by the Supreme Court of the United States in Herman C. Groman v. Commissioner, 302 U.S. 82 (1937), Ct. D. 1285, C.B. 1937-2, 286, and the *Bashford* case, the stock of M corporation does not provide the X group with the requisite continuity of interest in the O corporation stock transferred to the N corporation because the group had only an indirect interest in the O stock following the transaction. The rule of the *Groman* and *Bashford* cases is still applicable to reorganizations sought to be brought within the provisions of section 368(a)(1)(B). See S. Report No. 1622, Eighty-third Congress, Second Session, 51 and 273.

Accordingly, it is held that the transfer by the X group of its shares in the O corporation to the N corporation in exchange for the latter's newly issued preferred stock and the subsequent transfer of the newly acquired preferred shares of N to the M corporation in exchange for voting stock in M does not qualify, either in whole or in part, as a reorganization within the meaning of section 368(a)(1)(B) of the Code.

However, it is held that the exchange of N corporation stock owned by the X group before any of the exchanges described above for voting common stock of M corporation constitutes a reorganization within the meaning of section 368(a)(1)(B) of the Code, and that M and N corporations are each a party to such reorganization within the meaning of section 368(b)(2) of the Code.

NOTE

1. Is the result in Rev. Rul. 63-234 compelled by the decisions in Groman v. Commissioner, 302 U.S. 82 (1937), and Helvering v. Bashford, 302 U.S. 454 (1938)? Why? Is the result in Rev. Rul. 63-234 a sensible one? Why? Were the results in *Groman* and *Bashford* compelled by the statute? Were they desirable? Why?

2. What impact do the 1964 amendments to §368(a)(1)(B) and §368(a)(2)(C) have on the specific problem posed in Rev. Rul. 63-234?

3. In Rev. Rul. 63-234 the Commissioner declined to recognize the X group's holding of the N Corporation's newly issued voting preferred stock because it was "transitory and without real substance" (page 527 supra). For what purpose, however, does the ruling implicitly recognize the reality of the N Corporation's newly issued voting preferred stock? In this connection, consider the last paragraph of Rev. Rul. 63-234.

REVENUE RULING 64-73
1964-1 Cum. Bull. 142

Advice has been requested whether the transaction described below constitutes a reorganization within the meaning of section 368(a) of the Internal Revenue Code of 1954.

L corporation owns 100 percent of the outstanding stock of corporation M. M owns 100 percent of the outstanding stock of corporation N. L entered into an agreement with X, an unrelated corporation, under which L acquired all of the assets of X, solely in exchange for L voting stock. Some of the X assets were transferred from X to N, and the remaining X assets were transferred to L. Neither the assets which were transferred to N nor the assets transferred to L constituted substantially all of X's assets, but together they constituted all of X's assets.

Section 368(a)(1)(C) of the Code provides, in part, that the term reorganization means —

> "(C) the acquisition by one corporation, in exchange solely for all or a part of its voting stock (or in exchange solely for all or a part of the voting stock of a corporation which is in control of the acquiring corporation), of substantially all of the properties of another corporation . . . ."

Prior to the enactment of the 1954 Code, the described transaction would not have qualified as a reorganization, as it was believed that the ultimate lodging of some of the assets in any subsidiary of the acquiring corporation failed to satisfy the continuity-of-interest requirements of the reorganization provisions. See Herman C. Groman v. Commissioner, 302 U.S. 82 (1937), Ct. D. 1285, C.B. 1937-2, 286; and Helvering v. Raymond I. Bashford, 302 U.S. 454 (1938), Ct. D. 1299, C.B. 1938-1, 86.

The Congress, in 1954, modified the *Groman-Bashford* doctrine to provide that the placement of acquired assets in a controlled corporation would no longer destroy the continuity-of-interest requirements of section 368(a)(1)(C) reorganizations. See S. Report No. 1622, Eighty-third Congress, Second Session, at 51-52 and 273, 275.

In applying specific statutory relief to certain factual situations previously governed by the *Groman* and *Bashford* cases and section 112(g) of the Internal Revenue Code of 1939 (the predecessor of section 368(a)(1)(C) of the 1954 Code), Congress indicated its desire to remove the continuity-of-interest problem from the section 368(a)(1)(C) reorganization area. Having modified the continuity-of-interest rule where assets move to a corporation directly controlled by the parent in exchange for the parent's stock, there is no sound reason to assume the Congress intended to have the *Groman-Bashford* rule apply where the assets are caused to be transferred by the parent to a wholly-owned subsidiary of a corporation controlled by the parent corporation.

No cases involving the transfer of some of the acquired assets to remote subsidiaries in attempted section 368(a)(1)(C) reorganizations had arisen prior to the enactment of the 1954 Code. The specific statutory exceptions to the *Groman-Bashford* doctrine contained in sections 368(a)(1)(C), 368(a)(2)(C), and 368(b) are not intended to exclude a transfer of assets to a wholly-owned subsidiary of a corporation which is controlled by the parent corporation.

However, it should be noted that the Congress in 1954 did not change the definition of a reorganization contained in section 368(a)(1)(B) of the Code so as to modify the continuity-of-interest doctrine in that area. See Revenue Ruling 63-234, C.B. 1963-2, 148.

The described transaction is viewed as an acquisition by L, in exchange solely for part of its voting stock, of substantially all of the properties of X. The fact that in the instant case the plan of reorganization provides that some of the assets are to be transferred directly from X to N, rather than through L and M, does not detract from the conclusion that in substance L is to acquire substantially all the X assets. To hold otherwise would defeat the purpose of the 1954 Code change in the definition of a section 368(a)(1)(C) reorganization. The subsequent transfer of assets acquired in a reorganization under section 368(a)(1)(C) of the 1954 Code to a wholly-owned subsidiary of a corporation controlled by the acquiring corporation, even though pursuant to the plan of reorganization, will not affect the reorganization.

Accordingly, it is held that the transaction described in the instant case constitutes a reorganization as defined in section 368(a)(1)(C) of the Code.

NOTE

If the facts of Rev. Rul. 64-73 were modified to provide that X is to receive voting stock of L for the assets lodged in L and voting stock of M for the assets lodged in N, would the transaction constitute a reorganization? Why?

There is no indication in Rev. Rul. 64-73 that X was liquidated. Liquidation is not a necessary condition of a "C" reorganization. If the plan of reorganization had called for liquidation, what provision of the Code would have governed the tax consequences to the shareholders of X?

REVENUE RULING 67-326
1967-2 Cum. Bull. 143

Advice has been requested whether the nonrecognition provisions of section 361(a) of the Internal Revenue Code of 1954 apply to a transaction qualifying as a merger under applicable State law where the acquiring corporation exchanged the stock of its parent for all of the assets of an unrelated corporation and whether section 354(a) of the Code will apply to the exchange by the shareholders of the acquired corporation of all of their stock of the acquired corporation for stock of the parent of the acquiring corporation.

Corporation S is a wholly owned subsidiary of P corporation. In a transaction which qualified as a merger under the law of the State in which S and X are incorporated, S acquired from X, an unrelated corporation, all of its assets and assumed all of its liabilities in exchange for stock of P which had previously been contributed to S. Pursuant to the plan of reorganization, the shareholders of X exchanged their stock of X for stock of P.

Section 361(a) of the Code provides in part for the nonrecognition of gain or loss if a corporation a party to a reorganization exchanges property, in pursuance of a plan of reorganization, solely for stock in another corporation a party to the reorganization. In order for this section to be applicable to the exchange of assets by X for stock of P, X and P must be parties to the reorganization.

Section 354(a) of the Code provides in part for the nonrecognition of gain or loss if stock in a corporation a party to a reorganization is, in pursuance of the plan of reorganization, exchanged solely for stock in such corporation or in another corporation a party to the reorganization. In order for this section to be applicable to the exchange of X stock by the shareholders of X for stock of P, X and P must be parties to the reorganization.

Section 368(b) of the Code defines a party to a reorganization as: "(1) a corporation resulting from a reorganization, and (2) both corporations, in the case of a reorganization resulting from the acquisition by one corporation of stock or properties of another."

Section 368(b) of the Code provides that in the case of a reorganization qualifying under paragraph (1)(B) or (1)(C) of section 368(a) of the Code, if the stock exchanged for the stock or properties of another corporation is stock of a corporation which is in control of the acquiring corporation, the term "a party to a reorganization" includes the corporation so controlling the acquiring corporation. Section 368(b) of the Code does not include, however, as a party to a reorganization a corporation which is in control of the acquiring corporation in a reorganization qualifying under section 368(a)(1)(A) of the Code.*

Accordingly, although the transaction described is a statutory merger of S and X under State law, the nontaxable provisions of section 361(a) of the Code will not apply to the exchange of the assets of X for stock of P and section 354(a) will not apply to the exchange by the shareholders of X of their stock of X for stock of P.

A reorganization under section 368(a)(1)(C) of the Code is the acquisition by one corporation, in exchange solely for all or a part of its voting stock (or in exchange solely for all or a part of the voting stock of a corporation which is in control of the acquiring corporation), of substantially all of the properties of another corporation. As indicated, section 368(b) of the Code includes as a party to a reorganization described in section 368(a)(1)(C) of the Code a corporation which is in control of the acquiring corporation. Therefore, if the transaction otherwise qualifies as a reorganization as defined in section 368(a)(1)(C) of the Code, the nonrecognition provisions of sections 361(a) and 354(a) of the Code will apply to the exchanges described.

NOTE

1. Was the ruling correct in holding the transaction could not qualify as an "A," but could qualify as a "C," reorganization? Why? Can it matter to either the taxpayer or the government that the transaction is a "C," but not an "A," reorganization? Why?

2. The "Legislative Recommendation" which follows was proposed in August 1968 by the Committee on Corporate Stockholder Relationships of the Section of

---

*Section 368(b), as now amended, includes the corporation controlling the acquiring corporation as a "party to [the] reorganization." — Ed.

Taxation of the American Bar Association. Amendments changing §368(b) to include the corporation controlling the acquiring corporation as a "party to a reorganization" have already been adopted. See J. Levin, The New Subsidiary-Merger Statute and Other Current Tax Problems in Acquisitions, 47 Taxes 779 (1969). Should Congress adopt the remaining recommendations suggested by the American Bar Association? Why?

LEGISLATIVE RECOMMENDATION
Making the Parent of the Surviving or Disappearing Corporation in a Statutory Merger a Party to the Reorganization

Resolved, That the American Bar Association recommends to the Congress that the Internal Revenue Code of 1954 be amended to make the parent of the surviving or disappearing corporation in a statutory merger a party to the reorganization; and

Further resolved, That the Association proposes that this result be effected by amending its 1965 Legislative Recommendation for the amendment of Section 368 of the Internal Revenue Code of 1954; and

Further resolved, That the Legislative Recommendation appearing at pp. 32-36 of the Bulletin of the Section of Taxation, Volume XVIII, Number 4, July, 1965,* be amended by revising Section 368(a)(2)(B) of the Internal Revenue Code of 1954, as added by Sec. 1 of said Legislative Recommendation, to read as follows (revised matter in italics):

(B) Stock of Parent Corporation Received in the Exchange. — For purposes of paragraph (1)(A), (1)(B), or (1)(C), the term "stock of the acquiring corporation" shall include stock of a corporation which is in control of the acquiring corporation. If the stock exchanged includes such stock, the term "acquiring corporation" as used in this subsection and the term "a party to a reorganization" as defined in subsection (b) shall include not only the acquiring corporation but also the corporation which is in control of the acquiring corporation. *If one corporation controls another, and the principal asset of the controlled corporation is stock of the controlling corporation, the term "a party to a reorganization" includes the controlling corporation if the controlled corporation is merged into a third corporation in a reorganization qualifying under paragraph (1)(A).*†

Explanation

Summary. In Rev. Rul. 67-326, 1967-2 Cum. Bull. 143,‡ the Internal Revenue Service ruled that if the "X" corporation is merged into the "S" corporation in exchange for stock of S's parent "P", neither the exchange of assets for stock nor the distribution of such stock to the shareholders of X will be tax-free unless the transaction qualifies as a Section 368(a)(1)(C) reorganization. If the transaction is viewed

---

*The import of the 1965 recommendation will become clear as you read through this recommendation. — ED.

†See §368(b), as amended in November 1968. — ED.

‡Page 530 supra. — ED.

as a statutory merger, neither Section 361 nor Section 354 will apply because P, the surviving corporation's parent, will not be a party to the reorganization within the meaning of those sections and Section 368(b). In 1965, the Section of Taxation adopted a Legislative Recommendation which would make such mergers tax-free by providing that the parent would be a party to the Section 368(a)(1)(A) reorganization. (See Bulletin of the Section of Taxation, July 1965, p. 35, setting forth the text of proposed Section 368(a)(2)(B).)

However, the 1965 legislative proposal did not deal with the related problem which arises under existing law in cases where "P" transfers its stock to a 100% subsidiary, "S", and S is then merged into X in a statutory merger, with P receiving X stock, and the former shareholders of X receiving the transferred P stock. In Rev. Rul. 67-448, [1967-2 C.B. 144], the Internal Revenue Service held that such a transaction could qualify as a Section 368(a)(1)(B) reorganization, but not as a Section 368(a)(1)(A) or (C) reorganization. The proposed revision of the 1965 Legislative Recommendation assumes that the transaction could qualify as a Section 368(a) (1)(A) reorganization, and provides tax-free treatment at the shareholder level by making P a party to the reorganization.

Discussion. 1. Cases Where The Subsidiary Is The Surviving Corporation In The Statutory Merger: In Groman v. Commissioner, 320 U.S. 82 (1937), Helvering v. Bashford, 320 U.S. 454 (1937), and subsequent lower court decisions, the courts held that the reorganization provisions of the 1939 Code and prior Revenue Acts did not apply where the stock or assets of one corporation were acquired by another corporation and then transferred to a subsidiary of the acquiring corporation. In addition, the courts held that the reorganization provisions did not apply where an acquisition of stock or assets was made directly by a subsidiary in exchange for stock of its parent.

In large measure the *Groman-Bashford* rules have been abolished by legislative changes made in 1954 and 1964. See Sen. Rep. No. 1662 (83d Cong., 2d Sess.) pp. 273-275; Sen. Rep. No. 830 (88th Cong., 2d Sess.) pp. 82-83. As a result of these changes it is now possible for the acquiring corporation in a Section 368(a)(1)(A), (B) or (C) reorganization to transfer part or all of the acquired stock or assets to a subsidiary. It is also possible for a subsidiary to make a direct acquisition of stock or assets under Section 368(a)(1)(B) or (C) in exchange for stock of its parent. The only case of this type not covered by the 1954 or 1964 legislation is a statutory merger in which a subsidiary directly acquires the assets of another corporation in exchange for stock of the subsidiary's parent. The Committee Reports cited above do not explain the failure to make the 1954 and 1964 legislation applicable to statutory mergers of this type, but the explanation may be that the drafters simply overlooked the fact that such mergers can be effected under the laws of a number of states. In any event, there appears to be no sound policy reason for treating statutory mergers differently from (B) or (C) acquisitions.

While existing law makes it possible for a subsidiary to acquire assets directly in a Section 368(a)(1)(C) transaction, or for a parent to acquire assets in a statutory merger and then transfer them to a subsidiary, it seems desirable to provide for direct acquisitions by a subsidiary pursuant to state statutory merger laws. The merger route makes it possible for the acquiring subsidiary to offer consideration which would not be permitted in a Section 368(a)(1)(C) reorganization, and there may be cases where it is possible under state law to use a subsidiary, but impractical to use the parent, as the acquiring corporation.

For the foregoing reasons, language making the parent corporation a party to the reorganization in such cases was incorporated in a 1965 Tax Section Legislative Recommendation which dealt with a number of other aspects of Section 368. See Bulletin of the Section of Taxation, July 1965, p. 35, setting forth the text of proposed Section 368(a)(2)(B).

2. Cases Where The Subsidiary Is The Disappearing Corporation In The Merger: As previously stated, it is the Service's present position that Section 368(a)(1)(A) and (C) do not apply if a parent ("P") contributes its stock to a wholly-owned subsidiary ("S"), and S is thereafter merged into an unrelated corporation ("X"), with the former X stockholders receiving the transferred P stock and P receiving X stock in exchange for its S stock. In Rev. Rul. 67-448, supra, the Service ignored the transitory existence of S, and stated that the transaction could not constitute an (A) or (C) reorganization because no assets of X, the unrelated corporation, were transferred by it or acquired by any other corporation. Moreover, even if the merger of S into X (with X regarded as the acquiring corporation) were held to constitute a good (A) or (C) reorganization under existing law, the exchanges at the shareholder level would be subject to tax under Section 354 because P would not be a party to the reorganization. The 1965 Tax Section Legislative Recommendation discussed in part (1) above would not make P a party to the reorganization because the acquiring corporation, X, would not be controlled by P prior to the transfer. However, under the proposed revision of the 1965 Legislative Recommendation, P would be treated as a party to the merger in cases of this type.

Such mergers are authorized by the statutory merger laws of many states, and they provide a convenient way of acquiring 100% control of an outside company without terminating its corporate existence. See, e.g., Casco Products Corp. v. Commissioner, 49 T.C. No. 5 (1967).* While the Internal Revenue Service is willing to treat such a transaction as a (B) reorganization, it would be desirable in many cases to classify the transaction as an (A) reorganization in order to have greater flexibility in determining the consideration to be furnished. Cf. Casco Products Corp. v. Commissioner, supra. From a tax standpoint, treating the transaction as an (A) reorganization makes sense, since the end result, tax-wise, is equivalent to a merger of X into P, followed by a transfer of X's business to a new wholly-owned subsidiary of P. Under existing law, the latter transaction is, of course, tax-free.

The proposed amendment does not change the definition of a Section 368(a)(1)(A) reorganization because it is believed that the legislative history of the proposed changes would clearly reflect an intention to have the disappearing subsidiary recognized for tax purposes, in which case its merger into the X corporation would qualify under Section 368(a)(1)(A) so long as the regular non-statutory requirements were met.

*Page 678 infra. — ED.

3. If it seemed desirable for any reason, the proposals discussed herein could be readily separated from the remainder of the 1965 Legislative Recommendation. In that event, the proposals could be effected by revising Section 368(b) of existing law to read as follows (new matter in italics):

(b) Party to a Reorganization. — For purposes of this part, the term "a party to a reorganization" includes —

(1) a corporation resulting from a reorganization, and

(2) both corporations, in the case of a reorganization resulting from the acquisition by one corporation of stock or properties of another.

In the case of a reorganization qualifying under paragraph (1)(A), (1)(B), or (1)(C) of subsection (a), if the stock exchanged for the stock or properties is stock of a corporation which is in control of the acquiring corporation, the term "a party to a reorganization" includes the corporation so controlling the acquiring corporation. *If one corporation controls another, and the principal asset of the controlled corporation is stock of the controlling corporation, the term "a party to a reorganization" includes the controlling corporation if the controlled corporation is merged into a third corporation in a reorganization qualifying under paragraph (1)(A).* In the case of a reorganization qualifying under paragraph (1)(A), (1)(B), or (1)(C) of subsection (a) by reason of paragraph (2)(C) of subsection (a), the term "a party to a reorganization" includes the corporation controlling the corporation to which the acquired assets or stock are transferred.

NOTE

On January 12, 1971, President Nixon approved P.L. 91-693, which added subparagraph (E) to §368(a)(2) and a new sentence at the end of §368(b). The effect of these changes is to afford tax-free status to "reverse" statutory mergers occurring after December 31, 1970, in which a subsidiary corporation is merged into an unrelated corporation which survives, and the voting stock of the corporation controlling the subsidiary is exchanged for control of the surviving corporation.

4. *Solely for Voting Stock — "B" and "C" Reorganizations*

TURNBOW v. COMMISSIONER
368 U.S. 337 (1961), aff'g 286 F.2d 669 (9th Cir. 1960)

Mr. Justice WHITTAKER delivered the opinion of the Court. This case involves and turns on the proper interpretation and interaction of §§112(g)(1)(B), 112(b)(3) and 112(c)(1) of the Internal Revenue Code of 1939. Specifically the question presented is whether, in the absence of a "reorganization," as that term is defined in §112(g)(1)(B) [368(a)(1)(B)] and used in §112(b)(3) [354(a)(1)], the gain on an exchange of stock for stock *plus cash* is to be recognized in full, or, because of the provisions of §112(c)(1) [356(a)], is to be recognized only to the extent of the cash.

The facts are simple and undisputed. Petitioner owned all of the 5,000 shares of outstanding stock of International Dairy Supply Company ("International"), a Nevada corporation. In 1952, petitioner transferred all of the International stock to Foremost Dairies, Inc. ("Foremost"), a New York corporation, in exchange for 82,375 shares (a minor percentage) of Foremost's common (voting) stock of the fair market value of $15 per share or $1,235,625 *plus cash* in the amount of $3,000,000. Petitioner's basis in the International stock was $50,000, and his expenses in connection with the transfer were $21,933.06. Petitioner therefore received for his International stock property and money of a value exceeding his basis and expenses by $4,163,691.94.

In his income tax return for 1952, petitioner treated his gain as recognizable only to the extent of the cash he received. The Commissioner concluded that the whole of the gain was recognizable and accordingly proposed a deficiency. On the taxpayer's petition for redetermination, the Tax Court, following its earlier decision in Bonham v. Commissioner, 33 B.T.A. 1100, 1104,[3] and the opinion of the Seventh Circuit in Howard v. Commissioner of Internal Revenue, 238 F.2d 943, 948,[4] held that the gain was recognizable only to the extent of the cash. 32 T.C. 646. On the Commissioner's appeal, the Ninth Circuit disagreed with the Tax Court and with the Seventh Circuit's decision in the *Howard* case, supra, and reversed. 286 F.2d 669. To resolve this conflict, on a matter of importance to the proper interpretation and uniform application of the Internal Revenue laws, we granted certiorari. 366 U.S. 923.

Because of the arbitrary and technical character, and of the somewhat "hodgepodge" form, of the statutes involved, the interpretation problem presented is highly complicated; and although both parties rely upon the "plain words" of these statutes, they arrive at diametrically opposed conclusions. That plausible arguments can be and have been made in support of each conclusion must be admitted; and, as might be expected, they have hardly lightened our inescapable burden of decision.

The starting point of our analysis must be the "General rule" stated in

---

[3]The Tax Court concluded "that *but for* the cash received by petitioner . . . the exchange would have met the 'solely' requirement of section 112(g)(1)(B) and fallen within section 112(b)(3). Howard v. Commissioner, supra at 948. Therefore, under section 112(c)(1) the gain to petitioner may not be recognized in an amount in excess of [the cash received]." 32 T.C., at 652-653.

[4]In the *Howard* case, supra, the acquiring corporation obtained 80.19% of the stock of the acquired corporation by transferring to the holders, including petitioners, a part of its voting stock in exchange for their stock in the acquired corporation, and acquired the remaining 19.81% of the acquired corporation's stock from other holders for an agreed price in cash. As stated, petitioners received only stock and no cash. The Commissioner determined that the gain realized by petitioners on their exchange solely of stock for stock should be recognized under the general rule of §112(a) of the Code. The Seventh Circuit, following this Court's decision in Helvering v. Southwest Consolidated Corp., 315 U.S. 194, held "that because of the cash payment, the transaction in question fails to meet the 'solely' requirement of §112(g)(1)(B) of the 1939 Code. Hence it does not fall within the ambit of §112(b)(3)." 238 F.2d, at 947. But, turning to and relying on §112(c)(1), it also held that "*but for* the cash received [by others than petitioners] in exchange for 19.81% of the common stock of Binkley, the transaction would have met the 'solely' requirement of §112(g)(1)(B) and fallen within the scope of §112(b)(3). To the extent that 'boot' was received, gain would be recognized under our interpretation of the application of §112(c)(1). However, no cash was received by the taxpayers in question, and as a consequence thereof, no gain at the time of the transaction ever arose." 238 F.2d at 948.

§112(a)[1002]. It provides: "General rule. Upon the sale or exchange of property the entire amount of the gain or loss . . . shall be recognized, except as hereinafter provided in this section." Various exceptions, dealing with exchanges solely in kind, are stated in subsections (b)(1) through (b)(6).[5] The exception claimed to be relevant here is contained in subsection (b)(3). It provides: "Stock for stock on reorganization. No gain or loss shall be recognized if stock or securities in a corporation a party to a reorganization are, in pursuance of the plan of reorganization, exchanged solely for stock or securities in such corporation or in another corporation a party to the reorganization." By definition, contained in §112(g)(1)(B), the term "reorganization" means "the acquisition by one corporation, in exchange *solely* for all or a part of its voting stock, of at least 80 per centum of the . . . stock of another corporation."[6] (Emphasis added.) This type of reorganization is commonly called a "(B) reorganization."

There is no dispute between the parties about the fact that the transaction involved was not a "reorganization," as defined in §112(g)(1)(B), because "the acquisition by" Foremost was not "in exchange *solely* for . . . its voting stock," but was partly for such stock and partly for cash. Helvering v. Southwest Consolidated Corp., 315 U.S. 194. Nor is there any dispute that the transaction was not actually within the terms of §112(b)(3), because the exchange was not of "stock . . . in . . .

---

[5]The various exceptions, respecting exchanges solely in kind, contemplated by §112(b), are the following:

§112(b)(1): The exchange of tangible property, held for productive use or investment, "solely" for property "of a like kind." [Compare §1031.]

§112(b)(2): The exchange of stock "solely" for stock in the same corporation. [Compare §1036.]

§112(b)(3): The exchange of stock in a party to a "reorganization," as defined in §112(g) (1), "solely" for stock or securities in the same corporation or in another corporation which is a party to the reorganization. [Compare §354(a)(1).]

§112(b)(4): The exchange by a corporation, a party to a reorganization, of "property," in pursuance of the plan of reorganization, "solely" for stock or securities in another corporation which is a party to the reorganization. [Compare §361.]

§112(b)(5): The transfer of property to a controlled corporation in exchange "solely" for stock or securities of that corporation. [Compare §351.]

§112(b)(6): The receipt by a corporation of property in complete liquidation of another corporation. [Compare §332.]

See also §112(l) which provides a similar exception in respect to: The exchange of stock or securities "solely" for stock or securities of a successor corporation pursuant to a court-approved plan in debtor or insolvency proceedings. [Compare §371.]

[6]Section 112(g)(1) provides:

"(g) Definition of reorganization. As used in this section . . . —

"(1) The term 'reorganization' means (A) a statutory merger or consolidation, or (B) the acquisition by one corporation, in exchange solely for all or a part of its voting stock, of at least 80 per centum of the voting stock and at least 80 per centum of the total number of shares of all other classes of stock of another corporation, or (C) the acquisition by one corporation, in exchange solely for all or a part of its voting stock, of substantially all the properties of another corporation, but in determining whether the exchange is solely for voting stock the assumption by the acquiring corporation of a liability of the other, or the fact that property acquired is subject to a liability, shall be disregarded, or (D) a transfer by a corporation of all or a part of its assets to another corporation if immediately after the transfer the transferor or its shareholders or both are in control of the corporation to which the assets are transferred, or (E) a recapitalization, or (F) a mere change in identity, form, or place of organization, however effected." [Compare §368(a)(1).]

a party to a reorganization," "in pursuance of [a] plan of reorganization," nor "for stock . . . in another corporation [which was] a party to the reorganization."

But petitioner contends that §112(c)(1) authorizes the indulging of assumptions, contrary to the actual facts, hypothetically to supply the missing elements that are necessary to make the exchange a "reorganization," as defined in §112(g)(1)(B) and as used in §112(b)(3), and the case turns on whether that is so. Section 112(c)(1) provides:

> "Gains from exchanges not solely in kind. (1) If an exchange would be within the provisions of subsection (b)(1), (2), (3), or (5), or within the provisions of subsection (1), of this section if it were not for the fact that the property received in exchange consists not only of property permitted by such paragraph or by subsection (1) to be received without the recognition of gain, but also of other property or money, then the gain, if any, to the recipient shall be recognized, but in an amount not in excess of the sum of such money and the fair market value of such other property."

Centering upon this section, and upon the Seventh Circuit's interpretation of it in the *Howard* case, supra,[7] petitioner argues that "if it were not for the fact that the property [he] received in [the] exchange" consisted not only of voting stock — "property permitted [by §112(b)(3)] to be received [if in a corporation which is a party to a reorganization] without the recognition of gain" — but also of cash, the exchange *would have been* a "reorganization," as defined in §112(g)(1)(B), because, in that case, "the acquisition by" Foremost would have been "in exchange *solely* for . . . its voting stock"; and the exchange also *would have been* within the terms of §112(b)(3) because, in that case, the exchange would have been of "stock . . . in . . . a party to a reorganization," "in pursuance of [a] plan of reorganization," and "for stock . . . in another corporation [which was] a party to the reorganization." Petitioner then argues that inasmuch as his transaction *would have been* a "reorganization," as defined in §112(g)(1)(B) and used in §112(b)(3), and hence "would [have been] within the provisions of subsection (b) . . . (3)," "if it were not for the fact that the property [he] received" consisted "not only of" voting stock "but also of . . . money," §112(c)(1) authorizes the *assumption,* as respects the Foremost stock he received, that the exchange *was* a "reorganization," as defined in §112(g)(1)(B) and used in §112(b)(3), and hence precludes recognition of his gain "in excess of the . . . money" he received.

But we cannot agree that §112(c)(1) authorizes the assumption, contrary to the actual facts, of a "reorganization," as defined in §112(g)(1)(B) and used in §112 (b)(3). To indulge such an assumption would actually be to permit the negation of Congress' carefully composed definition and use of "reorganization" in those subsections, and to permit nonrecognition of gains on what are, in reality, only sales, the full gain from which is immediately recognized and taxed under the general rule of §112(a). To the contrary, we think that an actual "reorganization," as defined in §112(g)(1) and used in §112(b)(3), must exist before §112(c)(1) can apply thereto.

[7]See note 4.

We are also agreed that §112(c)(1) can apply only if the exchange actually consists *both of* "property permitted by [subsection (b)(1), (2), (3), or (5), or subsection (1) of §112] . . . to be received without the recognition of gain" *and* "other property or money." And we think it is clear that the "property permitted by [§112(b)(3)] . . . to be received without the recognition of gain" is "stock or securities in . . . a party to a reorganization," "in pursuance of [a] plan of reorganization," and "for stock . . . in such corporation or in another corporation [which is] a party to the reorganization." Since, as is admitted, none of the property involved in this exchange actually met that description, none of it was "property permitted by [§112(b)(3)] . . . to be received without the recognition of gain," and therefore §112(c)(1) does not apply to postpone recognition of petitioner's gain from the Foremost stock.[8]

This, of course, is not to say that §112(c)(1) is without purpose or function. It is to say only that it does not apply unless some part, at least, of the property exchanged *actually* meets the particular description contained in the applicable section or subsection of the Code. But, inasmuch as §112(g)(1)(B) defines "reorganization" to mean "the acquisition by one corporation, in exchange solely for all or a part of its voting stock, of at least 80 per centum of the . . . stock of another corporation," an exchange of stock *and* cash — approximately 30 per centum in stock and 70 per centum in cash — for "at least 80 per centum of the . . . stock of another corporation" cannot be a "reorganization," as defined in §112(g)(1)(B), nor hence of "stock . . . in . . . a party to a reorganization" as required by §112(b)(3), and thus §112(c)(1) cannot be applicable to petitioner's transaction. That holding determines this case and is all we decide.

Collaterally, petitioner argues that tax "loopholes" will be opened under other sections of the Code unless his interpretation is adopted. The Commissioner answers that "loopholes" will be opened under the sections involved and other sections only if petitioner's interpretation is adopted. Inasmuch as what we have said decides the case, we have no need or occasion to follow the parties into, or to decide, collateral questions.

Affirmed.

Mr. Justice HARLAN concurs in the result.

NOTE

Taxpayer, the owner of all Corporation B's stock, receives from Corporation A, in exchange for all of his Corporation B stock, $80,000 worth of Corporation A voting stock and $20,000 cash. Is the transaction a "B" reorganization? Why?

Taxpayer X owns 80 per cent of Corporation B's outstanding stock, and taxpayer Y owns the remaining 20 per cent. Corporation A, as part of a plan, acquires X's shares in exchange for part of its own voting stock, and it acquires Y's shares — one

---

[8]The legislative history, much of which is set forth in the opinion of the Court of Appeals, though tending to support our decision, is inconclusive, and no more can fairly be said of the Commissioner's Regulations. See Treas. Reg. 118, §§39.112(c)-1(e), 39.112(g)-4, 39.112(g)-1(c).

half for cash and one half for part of its voting stock. To what extent, if any, is the transaction tax-free to X and Y? What is the basis in Corporation A's hands of the Corporation B stock acquired from X? From Y?

To what extent is "boot" permissible in a "C" reorganization? What effect do the transferor's liabilities have in such a reorganization?

See J. Leake, Coping with the Problems Presented in a Stock-Plus-Boot "C" Reorganization, 29 J. Taxation 354 (1968); S. Toll, Transfers of Boot in Stock-for-Stock Acquisitions, 15 U.C.L.A.L. Rev. 1347 (1968); A. Vernava, The *Howard* and *Turnbow* Cases and the "Solely" Requirement of "B" Reorganizations, 20 Tax L. Rev. 387 (1965); B. Kanter, Cash in a "B" Reorganization: Effect of Cash Purchases on "Creeping" Reorganization, 19 Tax L. Rev. 441 (1964); C. Randall, Income Tax Consequences of Boot in Section 368(a)(1)(B) Stock for Stock Reorganizations, 71 Yale L.J. 1316 (1962).

REVENUE RULING 66-365
1966-2 Cum. Bull. 116

Advice has been requested whether the payment of cash by an acquiring corporation to the shareholders of the acquired corporation in lieu of issuing fractional shares to the shareholders who are entitled to receive fractional share interests violates the "solely for voting stock" requirement of section 368(a)(1)(B) and (C) of the Internal Revenue Code of 1954. Advice has also been requested concerning the tax treatment of cash received by shareholders in lieu of fractional shares in certain reorganizations defined in section 368(a)(1) of the Code.

In Mills, et al. v. Commissioner, 331 F.2d 321 (1964), reversing 39 T.C. 393 (1962), the United States Court of Appeals for the Fifth Circuit held that the "solely for voting stock" requirement of section 368(a)(1)(B) of the Code was satisfied where the acquiring corporation received all of the stock of several corporations and distributed in return for such stock, shares of its voting common stock and a small amount of cash in lieu of fractional shares. After finding that the cash given in lieu of fractional shares was simply a mathematical rounding-off for the purpose of simplifying the corporate and accounting problems which would have been caused by the actual issuance of fractional shares, the Court concluded that the receipt of the stock of the acquired corporations was for all practical purposes "solely in exchange for voting stock".

The Internal Revenue Service will follow the decision of the Court of Appeals in Mills, et al. v. Commissioner in similar factual situations. Accordingly, the "solely for voting stock" requirement of section 368(a)(1)(B) and (C) of the Code will not be violated where the cash paid by the acquiring corporation is in lieu of fractional share interests to which the shareholders are entitled, representing merely a mechanical rounding-off of the fractions in the exchange, and is not a separately bargained-for consideration. Where, however, the cash paid by the acquiring corporation is not in lieu of fractional share interests to which the shareholders are entitled or is a separately bargained-for consideration, the "solely for voting stock" requirement of section 368(a)(1)(B) and (C) of the Code will not be satisfied.

In a transaction qualifying as a reorganization under section 368(a)(1)(A) or (D) (or (C) by reason of section 368(a)(2)(B)) of the Code where the cash paid by the acquiring corporation represents a separately bargained-for consideration it will be treated as the receipt of "boot" under sections 361(b) and 356(a) of the Code. See Tenney Ross v. United States, 173 F. Supp. 793 (1959), in which the cash distributed to the shareholders of the acquired corporation pursuant to a reorganization under section 368(a)(1)(A) of the Code was held to be dividend boot under section 356(a)(2) of the Code where the cash paid did not result in a mere mechanical rounding-off of fractions but was a separately bargained-for consideration. See also Revenue Ruling 56-220, C.B. 1956-1, 191, which holds, in effect, that all of the cash paid to the shareholders of the acquired corporation was separately bargained-for consideration in the exchange. The Revenue Ruling states that the acquiring corporation did not desire to give the stockholders of the acquired corporation a large common stock ownership in itself.

In all reorganizations described in the preceding paragraphs where the cash payment made by the acquiring corporation is not bargained for, but is in lieu of fractional share interests to which the shareholders are entitled, such cash payment will be treated under section 302 of the Code as in redemption of the fractional share interests. Therefore, each shareholder's redemption will be treated as a distribution in full payment in exchange for his fractional share interest under section 302(a) of the Code provided the redemption is not essentially equivalent to a dividend. The *Mills* case is an example of the type of case in which capital gain or loss treatment will be accorded a redemption where cash is paid in lieu of fractional share interests. If the redemption is essentially equivalent to a dividend, it will be treated as a distribution under section 301 of the Code as provided in section 302(d) of the Code. All the facts and circumstances of each case will be considered in determining whether the cash distribution in lieu of the fractional shares is essentially equivalent to a dividend.

The foregoing principles are illustrated by the following example. If, in a reorganization described in section 368(a)(1)(A) of the Code, a shareholder receives stock worth $100 and cash boot of $20, the gain, if any, realized on the exchange, will be recognized under section 356(a) of the Code but not in excess of $20. If the shareholder also receives $4 and it is not bargained for but is in lieu of a fractional share interest, the $4 will be considered as the proceeds from a redemption of the fractional share interest under section 302 of the Code.

If the cash payment made by the acquiring corporation is in lieu of fractional share interests of stock which is section 306 stock, such cash payment will be treated as a distribution in redemption to which section 301 applies unless it is established to the satisfaction of the Commissioner that the distribution of cash was not in pursuance of a plan having as one of its principal purposes the avoidance of Federal income tax. See section 306(b)(4) of the Code.

Revenue Ruling 56-220, C.B. 1956-1, 191, is clarified to remove any implication that the cash paid by the acquiring corporation to the shareholders of the acquired corporation was in lieu of fractional shares, rather than bargained-for additional consideration.

NOTE

According to Rev. Rul. 66-365, cash paid in lieu of fractional shares in a reorganization of the "A," "C," or "D" variety will be regarded as "boot" if separately bargained for. If it has the effect of a dividend, taxation under §356(a)(2) may result. If the cash is not separately bargained for, however, the conception is that of a redemption of the fractional shares. If the redemption distribution has dividend equivalence, then taxation under §301 may result. What may be the practical tax difference to the shareholder? In a would-be "B" reorganization, the separate bargain for the cash will destroy the reorganization because of the "solely for voting stock" requirement. When might it have that effect in a would-be "C" reorganization?

Rev. Rul. 66-365 refers to cash that is not separately bargained for *and* not in excess of the amount representing the value of the fractional share interest. Can you conceive of a case in which cash representing only and precisely the value of the fractional shares is paid, but it is held nevertheless that there had been a "separate bargain" which destroys an otherwise qualifying "B" reorganization?

REVENUE RULING 66-112
1966-1 Cum. Bull. 68

Advice has been requested whether the transaction described below satisfies the "solely for voting stock" requirement of section 368(a)(1)(B) of the Internal Revenue Code of 1954.

The capital stock of M corporation was owned equally by X corporation and Y corporation. For good business reasons Y was interested in acquiring X's one-half interest in M. Because M was closely held it was difficult to ascertain the fair market value of the M stock. Accordingly, X and Y entered into an agreement pursuant to which X transferred its one-half interest in M to Y in exchange for 40,000 shares of Y's voting stock. In addition, the agreement accorded X the right to receive additional shares of Y's voting stock in each of the succeeding 4 years following the date of the initial exchange in which M's net income exceeded a specified amount. If M's net income in the succeeding 4 years did not exceed the specified amount, no additional shares were to be received by X. The maximum number of additional shares of Y voting stock which could be received under the plan of reorganization was 20,000 shares. The right to receive such additional shares was not assignable and such right could give rise to the receipt of only additional voting stock.

Section 368(a)(1)(B) of the Code provides that the term "reorganization" includes the acquisition by one corporation, in exchange solely for all or a part of its voting stock, of stock of another corporation if, immediately after the acquisition, the acquiring corporation has control of such other corporation (whether or not such acquiring corporation had control immediately before the acquisition).

Section 354(a)(1) of the Code provides that in general no gain or loss shall be recognized if stock or securities in a corporation a party to a reorganization are, in pursuance of a plan of reorganization, exchanged solely for stock or securities in such corporation or in another corporation a party to the reorganization.

The "control" requirement of section 368(a)(1)(B) of the Code is clearly satisfied since Y owns all of the stock of M immediately after the initial exchange. The only question remaining is whether the "solely for voting stock" requirement has been met. Whether this requirement has been met is dependent on the treatment to be accorded the contractual right of X to receive additional voting shares of Y based upon the net income of M. If such right is considered other property, the "solely for voting stock" requirement of section 368(a)(1)(B) of the Code will not have been satisfied nor will the requirements of section 354(a) of the Code have been met.

Under the facts of this case, the reorganization exchange has been fully consummated, except insofar as the contingent contractual right to receive additional voting stock of Y is concerned. This right is not assignable and it can give rise to only additional Y voting stock. Because of this and the fact that only voting stock has been and can be issued under the terms of the plan of reorganization, the initial receipt by X of 40,000 shares of Y voting stock and the later receipt by X of up to 20,000 additional shares of such stock that may be issued in the 4-year period following the initial exchange will satisfy the "solely for voting stock" requirement of section 368(a)(1)(B) of the Code.

In James C. Hamrick, 43 T.C. 21 (1964), the Tax Court held that taxpayer's contractual right to receive additional stock, contingent upon the earnings of the corporation exceeding a specified amount, is the equivalent of "stock or securities" within the meaning of section 351(a) of the Code so that the receipt of additional shares in later years pursuant to the original incorporation agreement does not result in recognizable gain to him. The Tax Court relied to a large extent on Carlberg v. United States, 281 Fed. (2d) 507 (8th Cir., 1960), in support of its conclusion, which case conflicts with the Service's position as announced in Revenue Ruling 57-586, C.B. 1957-2, 249.

The position expressed above that a reorganization exchange can be fully consummated, except insofar as the right to receive additional stock is concerned, is equally applicable to section 351 exchanges. Since the contingent contractual right in James C. Hamrick was not specifically assignable nor readily marketable and could only give rise to the receipt of additional stock by one who was a party to the transfer, both the "stock or securities" and the "control" tests of section 351(a) of the Code were satisfied. Accordingly, the Internal Revenue Service acquiesces in result only in James C. Hamrick. See page 2 of this Bulletin.

The facts involved in the present case and in James C. Hamrick are distinguishable from those in Revenue Ruling 57-586 which, contrary to *Carlberg,* holds that negotiable certificates distributed to shareholders of an acquired corporation in connection with a statutory merger, representing contingent interests in shares of the common stock of the surviving corporation to be issued in certain eventualities along with cash representing the value of dividends which would have been paid in the meantime, are considered "other property" within the meaning of section 356 of the

Code, relating to the treatment of additional consideration received in connection with reorganizations and other distributions.

In that ruling, a mere contract right only to future distributions of stock provided for in a reorganization agreement was not in question. The question was whether negotiable certificates of contingent interest were merely evidence of the existing right to receive additional common stock or whether they provided the holder of such certificates with something more. Since the issuance of these certificates created a transferable interest which contained a dividend income element, it was determined that the holder had been granted something more than a mere right to receive additional common stock. Therefore, the certificates were considered "other property" under section 356 of the Code.

In the present case the contingent contractual right to additional voting stock in the future is not assignable and can only ripen into additional voting stock. Accordingly, under the circumstances set forth above, the existence of this right will not be treated as violating the "solely for voting stock" requirement of section 368(a)(1)(B) of the Code.

The facts of every delayed stock issuance case, whether arising under section 368 or section 351 of the Code, will be carefully examined to insure that bona fide business reasons justify not issuing all of the stock immediately, and will also be examined to insure that stock issued as a bonus or compensation to the exchanging shareholders is not treated as received in the exchange.

For the effect section 483 of the Code, dealing with interest on certain deferred payments, has on delayed issuance of stock exchanges see sections 1.483-1(b)(6) Example 7, 1.483-1(e)(3) Example 2 and 1.483-2(a)(2) of the Income Tax Regulations.

Revenue Ruling 57-586, C.B. 1957-2, 249, distinguished.

REVENUE PROCEDURE 67-13
1967-1 Cum. Bull. 590

In reorganizations under sections 368(a)(1)(A), 368(a)(1)(B) and 368(a)(1)(C) of the Internal Revenue Code of 1954 where the requisite stock or property has been acquired, it is not necessary that all of the stock of the acquiring corporation or a corporation in "control" thereof, which is to be issued in exchange therefor, be issued immediately provided (1) that all of the stock will be issued within five years from the date of the transfer of assets in the case of reorganizations under sections 368(a)(1)(A) and 368(a)(1)(C) of the Code, or within five years from the date of the initial distribution in the case of reorganizations under section 368(a)(1)(B) of the Code; (2) there is a valid business reason for not issuing all of the stock immediately, such as the difficulty in determining the value of one or both of the corporations involved in the reorganization; (3) the maximum number of shares which may be issued in the exchange is stated; (4) at least fifty percent of the maximum number of shares of each class of stock which may be issued is issued in the initial distribution; (5) the agreement evidencing the right to receive stock in the future prohibits assignment (except by operation of law) or, in the alternative, if the agreement does not prohibit assignments, the right must not be evidenced by negotiable certificates of any kind and must not be readily marketable; and (6) such right can give rise to the receipt of only additional stock of the acquiring corporation or a corporation in "control" thereof, as the case may be. Stock issued as compensation royalties or any other consideration other than in exchange for stock or assets will not be considered to have been received in exchange.

REVENUE RULING 67-90

1967-1 Cum. Bull. 79

Advice has been requested whether the transaction described below satisfies the "solely for voting stock" requirement of section 368(a)(1)(B) of the Internal Revenue Code of 1954.

Corporation X and corporation Y are both publicly held corporations. The stock of each corporation is listed and actively traded on a national stock exchange. Pursuant to a plan of reorganization X will acquire all of the Y stock from the Y shareholders. On the date the plan of reorganization was adopted by X and the Y shareholders the X stock closed at $45 per share and the Y stock closed at $52 per share. After substantial arms-length negotiations the agreed plan of reorganization provides that all of the Y shareholders will exchange all of their 50,000 shares of Y voting stock for 50,000 shares of X voting stock and a contingent contractual right to receive additional X voting stock.

The contingent right to receive additional X voting stock is evidenced only by the plan of reorganization agreed to by the parties, is not evidenced by a negotiable certificate of any kind, is not readily marketable, and can give rise to the receipt of only additional X stock. All additional X stock will be issued 4 years from the date of the initial distribution. All of the stock cannot be issued immediately because the parties are unable to agree on the value of the X stock for purposes of the exchange, notwithstanding that it is listed and traded on a national stock exchange. The maximum number of additional X shares that may be issued to the Y shareholders is 50,000. The plan of reorganization provides that the Y shareholders will receive the additional X shares only if on the fourth anniversary of the initial distribution the closing market price of the X stock is less than $50 per share. If the market price is below $50 per share, X will issue sufficient additional shares (but in no event more than 50,000) so that the total market value of the shares of both the initial and fourth anniversary distributions computed on the basis of the fourth anniversary closing price will equal $2,500,000. Subject to the 50,000 additional share limitation, this formula guarantees the exchanging Y shareholders a $50 per share value for the X stock they receive pursuant to the plan of reorganization.

Section 368(a)(1)(B) of the Code provides that the term "reorganization" includes the acquisition by one corporation, exchange solely for all or a part of its voting stock, of stock of another corporation, if, immediately after the acquisition, the acquiring corporation has control of such other corporation (whether or not such acquiring corporation has control immediately before the acquisition).

Revenue Ruling 66-112, C.B. 1966-1, 68, holds that the "solely for voting stock" requirement of section 368(a)(1)(B) of the Code is satisfied where the number of additional shares to be issued under the provisions of a nonassignable contractual right is determined by a formula contingent upon the future earnings of the acquired corporation. In this case the number of additional shares is contingent upon the future market price of the acquiring corporation's stock. Where the parties are unable to agree on the value of the stock of the acquiring corporation for purposes of the exchange, notwithstanding that the stock is traded on a national stock exchange, a valid business reason exists for issuing less than all of the stock immediately.

Accordingly, in the present case where the parties cannot agree on the value of the X stock, the proposed plan of reorganization satisfies the "solely for voting stock" requirement of section 368(a)(1)(B) of the Code.

The facts of every delayed stock issuance case arising under section 368 of the Code will be carefully examined to insure that bona fide business reasons justify issuing less than all of the stock immediately, and will also be examined to insure that the stock issued is issued solely in exchange for stock or assets, as the case may be, and is in fact not being issued in lieu of other consideration, such as compensation or royalties.

For the effect section 483 of the Code, dealing with interest on certain deferred payments, has on delayed issuance of stock exchanges see sections 1.483-1(b)(6), Example 7; 1.483-1(e)(3), Example 2; and 1.483-2(a)(2) of the Income Tax Regulations.

See further Revenue Procedure 66-34, C.B. 1966-2, 1232 as amplified by Revenue Procedure 67-13, page 590, this Bulletin.

NOTE

1. In William H. Bateman, 40 T.C. 408 (1963), Corporation A and Corporation B merged. Corporation A survived and changed its name to C. Each shareholder of B was entitled to two and one-fourth shares of C common and one stock purchase warrant for each share of B surrendered. Each warrant entitled the holder to purchase one share of C within ten years for a stated price. Are the warrants "stock"? Are they "securities"? Does it matter whether they are securities? Cf. §354(a)(2)(B).

Does the exchange have the effect of a distribution of a dividend? What adjustment would be made to earnings and profits? To the shareholders' basis in their stock? If the exchange does not have the effect of a distribution of a dividend at the time, what result when exercised? If the warrants are sold in the meantime to a third party? How should the distribution of warrants be treated?

What is the relevance of each of the criteria set forth in Rev. Proc. 67-13 to the statutory "voting stock" requirement? Is the Commissioner's position in Rev. Rul. 67-90 correct? See J. Murphy, Contingent Share Reorganizations, 1969 So. Calif. Tax Inst. 255; D. Tillinghast, Contingent Stock Pay-Outs in Tax-Free Reorganizations, 22 Tax Lawyer 467 (1969).

What is the relationship of the "voting stock" requirement of the "B" and "C" reorganization to the "continuity of interest" doctrine? What continuity protections are afforded the "A" reorganization? Can you rationalize the different statutory treatment of the continuity problem in the "A," the "B," and the "C" reorganization provisions? See R. Dailey, The Voting Stock Requirement of B and C Reorganizations, 26 Tax L. Rev. 725 (1971).

2. In Rev. Rul. 67-275, 1967-2 Cum. Bull. 142, the Commissioner ruled that the costs paid by an acquiring corporation in an "A" reorganization to register with the SEC the stock it was to issue to the acquired corporation's shareholders do not constitute "boot" to the shareholders, since "the costs of registering its own stock are properly attributable to the acquiring corporation. . . ." What arguments might be made for and against that result? What would the result be if the acquiring corporation had paid the legal fees of the lawyers who advised the acquired corporation and its shareholders? Why? Would it matter whether the lawyers' advice related to the reorganization or to legal affairs of the acquired corporation and its shareholders that antedated the plan of reorganization? Why?

5. *Acquisition of Control*

a. CREEPING

BAUSCH & LOMB OPTICAL CO. v. COMMISSIONER

267 F.2d 75 (2d Cir. 1959), cert. denied, 361 U.S. 835 (1959)

Before MEDINA and HINCKS, Circuit Judges, and MATHES, District Judge.

MEDINA, Circuit Judge. Petitioner Bausch & Lomb Optical Company, a New York corporation engaged in the manufacture and sale of ophthalmic products, on March 1, 1950 owned 9923¼ shares of the stock of its subsidiary Riggs Optical Company, or 79.9488% of the 12,412 outstanding shares of Riggs. In order to effectuate certain operating economies, Bausch & Lomb decided to amalgamate Riggs with itself. To this end on April 22, 1950 Bausch & Lomb exchanged 105,508 shares of its unissued voting stock for all of the Riggs assets. An additional 433 shares of Bausch & Lomb stock went to 12 Riggs' employees.

On May 2, 1950, according to a prearranged plan, Riggs dissolved itself, distributing its only asset, Bausch & Lomb stock, pro rata to its shareholders. Bausch & Lomb thus received back 84,347 of its own shares which became treasury stock, while 21,161 shares went to the Riggs minority shareholders.

The Commissioner determined that the substance of these transactions was that Bausch & Lomb received the Riggs assets partly in exchange for its Riggs stock and partly for its own stock, and that the gain which Bausch & Lomb realized upon the Riggs "liquidation" was subject to tax. In other words, that Bausch & Lomb parted with 21,161 shares of its own voting stock, plus 9923¼ shares of its Riggs stock, for the transfer to it of all of the Riggs assets. Bausch & Lomb contends, however, that a "reorganization" was effected under Section 112(g)(1)(C) of the 1939 Internal Revenue Code,[1] and that it is therefore entitled to tax-free treatment.[2] The Tax Court sustained the Commissioner's position and held that the acquisition of the Riggs assets and the dissolution of Riggs must be viewed together, and that the surrender by Bausch & Lomb of its Riggs stock was additional consideration. The Tax Court accordingly held that the Riggs assets were not obtained "solely for all or a part of its voting stock." We agree.

Bausch & Lomb concedes that to qualify as a "C" reorganization, it could not furnish any additional consideration over and above its own stock. Helvering v. Southwest Consolidated Corp., 1942, 315 U.S. 194, 62 S. Ct. 546, 86 L. Ed. 789; Adwood Corp. v. Commissioner, 6 Cir., 1952, 200 F.2d 552, certiorari denied 346 U.S. 818, 74 S. Ct. 30, 98 L. Ed. 344; Stoddard v. Commissioner, 2 Cir., 1944, 141 F.2d 76. Moreover, Bausch & Lomb admits, as the correspondence and minutes of pertinent meetings plainly show, that the acquisition of the Riggs assets and the dissolution of Riggs were both part of the same plan. Nevertheless, Bausch & Lomb asserts that the exchange of the Riggs assets for its stock should be treated as separate and distinct from the dissolution. The argument runs to the effect that, if the two steps are viewed apart from one another, a "C" reorganization is effected.

Petitioner contends that, even if a qualification according to the literal terms of Section 112(g)(1)(C) is not found, the amalgamation was in substance a "reorganization" because it has the attributes of one, including "continuity of interest" and business purpose. This is factually not quite true for, while the amalgamation may have been for genuine business reasons, the division into two steps served only to facilitate the liquidation of Riggs. It was considered easier to distribute Bausch & Lomb stock than distribute the Riggs assets. Hence the "business purpose" of dividing the liquidation into two steps lends no support to Bausch & Lomb's contention that in substance and actuality a reorganization was achieved. Moreover, the Congress has defined in Section 112(g)(1)(C) how a reorganization thereunder may be effected, and the only question for us to decide, on this phase of the case, is whether the necessary requirements have been truly fulfilled. It is for the Congress and not for us to say whether some other alleged equivalent set of facts should receive the same tax free status.

Nor does the fact that Bausch & Lomb may well have desired to hold the 84,347 shares of its own voting shares as treasury stock change our opinion of the transaction as a whole.

---

[1] Section 112(g)(1)(C) provides: "(1) The term 'reorganization' means . . .

"(C) the acquisition by one corporation, in exchange solely for all or a part of its voting stock, of substantially all the properties of another corporation, but in determining whether the exchange is solely for voting stock the assumption by the acquiring corporation of a liability of the other, or the fact that property acquired is subject to a liability, shall be disregarded, . . ." .

[2] Section 112(b)(3) provides: "(b) *Exchanges solely in kind.* . . .

(3) Stock for stock on reorganization. No gain or loss shall be recognized if stock or securities in a corporation a party to a reorganization are, in pursuance of the plan of reorganization, exchanged solely for stock or securities in such corporation or in another corporation a party to the reorganization."

Bausch & Lomb suggests that under our present holding even if it had but a 1% interest in Riggs, the requirement that the acquisition be "solely for . . . its voting stock" could defeat Section 112(g)(1)(C) reorganization treatment. This hypothesis is a far cry from the facts disclosed in this record, and the lack of controlling interest surrounds it with a mist of unreality. In any event, it will be time to consider such a situation in all its aspects when, as and if it comes before us. We merely hold that the attempt to thwart taxation in this case by carrying out the liquidation process in two steps instead of one fell short of meeting the requirements of a "C" reorganization. See Gregory v. Helvering, 1935, 293 U.S. 465, 55 S. Ct. 266, 79 L. Ed. 596; Helvering v. Alabama Asphaltic Limestone Co., 1942, 315 U.S. 179, 62 S. Ct. 540, 86 L. Ed. 775; Helvering v. Bashford, 1938, 302 U.S. 454, 58 S. Ct. 307, 82 L. Ed. 367; Minnesota Tea Co. v. Helvering, 1938, 302 U.S. 609, 58 S. Ct. 393, 82 L. Ed. 474.

Of course, the fact that Bausch & Lomb "could have" merged with Riggs and hence qualified the transaction as a reorganization under [section 112(g)(1)(A)] is beside the point. For reasons of its own it chose not to do so. This is clearly not an "A" reorganization.

Bausch & Lomb also claims that a tax-free liquidation was effected under Section [332] although it plainly lacked the necessary 80% of the voting stock. This belabored effort to claim ownership of the 51 shares of Riggs voting stock for which 12 of Riggs' employees had received credit on Riggs' books, so as to raise Bausch & Lomb's interest slightly above the 80% required by Section [332] has nothing whatever to commend it. As found by the Tax Court, Bausch & Lomb never was the legal or equitable owner of these shares, there was never any agreement on the part of the employees to assign them to Bausch & Lomb, and the original stock purchase agreements of the Riggs employees provided that if Riggs should be reorganized and its business acquired by another corporation, a successor corporation would have the right to assume the contract and substitute its stock in the place of the Riggs' stock originally reserved under the stock purchase agreements. New arrangements were made later, in line with the provision of the original stock purchase agreements just referred to, and the employees received certain cash payments and the 433 shares of Bausch & Lomb stock mentioned in the opening part of this opinion. We find in the facts of this case no foundation whatever for the claim that a liquidation was effected under Section [332].

Affirmed.

NOTE

Was there a way by which Bausch & Lomb might have proceeded (without recognition) to get a substituted basis? If so, what was it and why was it not used? See generally P. Trimble, Creeping Control: An Analysis of Tax Problems of the Multi-stage Acquisition, 28 J. Taxation 135 (1968). Compare Rev. Rul. 68-526, 1968-2 Cum. Bull. 156, and Rev. Rul. 69-585, 1969-2 Cum. Bull. 56.

AMERICAN POTASH & CHEMICAL CORP. v. UNITED STATES
399 F.2d 194 (Ct. Cl. 1968)

On Defendant's Motion for Summary Judgment

Before Cowen, Chief Judge, Laramore, Durfee, Davis, Collins, Skelton, and Nichols, Judges.

Laramore, Judge. . . . [The facts are set forth at pages 67-69 supra.]

II.

Section 1012 provides that the basis of property is its cost except where otherwise provided. Section 362(b) requires a carryover basis for depreciable assets received in "connection with" a transaction which qualifies as a reorganization as defined in section 368(a)(1). Defendant concludes that a C reorganization has occurred and, therefore, a carryover basis is required for the assets.

A C reorganization, in general, is a transaction whereby one corporation (the acquiring corporation) acquires substantially all of the property of another corporation (the transferor corporation) as part of an exchange in which the acquiring corporation gives solely its voting stock (or the voting stock of its parent) to the transferor corporation in exchange for the transferor corporation's assets. Under certain limited circumstances, money or other property in addition to voting stock may be exchanged.

Before a transaction can be classified as a C reorganization three basic factors must be present. These are (a) an acquiring corporation gives *stock* to another corporation, and (b) receives *in exchange* for that stock (c) substantially all of the *properties* of the transferor corporation.

Defendant argues that the taxpayer has not *purchased* Wecco's stock for cash and liquidated but has *exchanged* its stock for Wecco stock and then liquidated Wecco pursuant to its plan and intent to obtain Wecco's assets. Plaintiff, defendant continues, has therefore exchanged its stock for Wecco's assets, a transaction which qualifies as a C reorganization. Defendant contrasts a *purchase* of stock followed by a liquidation (in which the stockholders of the acquired company do not have any stock interest in the acquiring company) with an *exchange* of stock for stock followed by a liquidation (in which the stockholders of the acquired company become stockholders of the acquiring company). In the latter situation, defendant argues that there is a continuity of ownership, which, together with the basic intent to obtain assets establishes that the entire transaction was a reorganization.

Taxpayer's intent is considered in determining the existence of an overall plan to accomplish a particular result by a series of steps and in determining the existence of a plan to reorganize. The existence of either a plan to reorganize or a plan to accomplish a particular end result, however, does not necessarily mean that the particular route chosen to accomplish the desired result qualifies as a reorganization, as that term is defined in the statute.

A continuity of ownership and of interest are elements of a reorganization which must be present in addition to the specific exchange provided for by the statute.[6] See: Reg. Sec. 1.368-1(b). The existence of either one or both elements does not establish that the particular process through which continuity was achieved is a reorganization. Nor does the end result of a transaction establish the presence of a reorganization. The existence of a continuity of ownership indicates only that one element of a reorganization is present. The particular transaction must meet all of the specific requirements of the statute before we can conclude that a reorganization occurred.

A regulation under section 368 (Reg. §1.368-1(b)) explains the purpose of the specific requirements of the organization provisions. It states:

> ". . . *In order to exclude transactions not intended to be included, the specifications of the reorganization provisions of the law are precise. Both the terms* of the specifications *and the underlying assumptions and purposes* must be satisfied in order to entitle the taxpayer to the benefit of the exception from the general rule [gain or loss must be recognized on the exchange of property]." [Emphasis supplied.]

We note that defendant admits, and we agree, that the form of this transaction — a transfer of Potash stock to the shareholders of Wecco in return for stock of Wecco — resembles, and would seem to invoke the provisions of, section 368(a) (1)(B), if any reorganization provision were applicable. Without question, the basic transaction was a stock for stock exchange (B reorganization) rather than a stock for asset exchange (C reorganization). Potash transferred stock to, and received stock from, the Wecco shareholders. It did not transfer stock to the Wecco corporation in return for a transfer by the corporation of its assets.

In our view the transaction does not meet the requirements of a B reorganization but only because control of Wecco was not obtained by a series of stock for stock exchanges within a 12-month period (as is required by the applicable regulations, infra). This is an aspect of the attainment of stock control by "creeping acquisitions" rather than a single stock for stock exchange.

The creeping acquisition of control problem arose under the 1939 Code in a B reorganization when an acquiring corporation owned some stock of the corporation to be acquired but less than control. To resolve any lingering doubts about the validity of classifying successive stock for voting stock exchanges as a B reorganization, the 1954 Code specifically approved its use in the context of a B reorganization. See: S. Rep. No. 1622, 83d Cong., 2d Sess. 273 (1954).

By its regulation (Reg. §1.368-2(c)), which echoes S. Rep. No. 1622, supra, the government provided: "Such an acquisition [B reorganization] is permitted tax-free in a single transaction or in a series of transactions taking place *over a relatively short period of time such as 12 months."* [Emphasis supplied.]

The infirmity, in this case, is that the entire transaction took place over a period of 14 months, and plaintiff never obtained control within any 12-month

[6]Southwest Natural Gas Co. v. Commissioner, 189 F.2d 332 (5th Cir. 1951), cert. denied, 342 U.S. 860; Pinellas Ice & Cold Storage Co. v. Commissioner, 287 U.S. 462 (1933); LeTulle v. Scofield, 308 U.S. 415 (1940); United States v. Hendler, 303 U.S. 564 (1938).

period. Defendant has not urged that this was a B reorganization. Were this a B reorganization which was complete when the stock for stock exchange resulted in control, we would be faced with a problem which has faced many other courts, i.e., whether the post-reorganization liquidation was an integral step of the overall plan to obtain the assets and, therefore, a carryover basis is appropriate for the assets received in the process of liquidation. The liquidation is denied independent tax significance, and a carryover basis is imposed. We will discuss the post-reorganization liquidation problem in more detail at a later point. Insofar as the facts of this case are concerned, Potash did not obtain control within a 12-month period, and we find that a B reorganization did not occur.

Defendant argues that despite its form (stock for stock) the entire transaction should be tested as a C reorganization because plaintiff has stated that it intended to obtain Wecco's assets. This position is premised on our integrating and collapsing the several transactions which began with the first acquisition in 1954 and ended with the assets received in the June 1956 liquidation into a "single transaction". That "single transaction," defendant argues, is a reorganization when measured against the provisions of section 368(a)(1)(C). Plaintiff's intent, as mentioned above, is relevant to the existence of a plan to obtain the assets and is an important factor when we are faced with denying independent tax significance to a liquidation which follows a reorganization. It does not establish that a reorganization occurred, or that *stock* was, in fact, *exchanged for assets* as is required in a C reorganization.

The issue before the court is whether we can transform a stock for stock exchange which does not itself qualify as a B reorganization, into a C-type stock for asset exchange by finding that the subsequent liquidation and distribution of the assets of the acquired corporation had no tax significance and that Potash, therefore, exchanged its stock with the Wecco corporation for the Wecco assets. The issue before us is not whether a liquidation which follows a valid B reorganization is to be given independent tax significance. In this case we are faced with the more basic problem; i.e., finding if a reorganization occurred. We cannot find any decision which has transformed a non-qualifying B-type exchange into a valid C reorganization by concluding that a subsequent liquidation of the acquired corporation was without significance. Defendant has not urged that this transaction was anything other than a C reorganization. Courts have concluded, under comparable circumstances, that the property received in the post-reorganization (qualifying) liquidation was property received in connection with a transaction which separately qualified as a B reorganization.[7] Other courts have concluded that an assets transfer was a mere change in the identity or form of the corporation and, therefore, a reorganization occurred.[8] (Both of these possibilities will be explored at a later point.)

Defendant would have us create a C reorganization out of the substructure of an unqualified B-type exchange and a subsequent liquidation. We find that there was no reorganization to which we might attach the liquidation and that the

---

[7]E.g., Piedmont Financial Co., 26 B.T.A. 1221 (1932).
[8]E.g., Ahles Realty Corp. v. Commissioner, 71 F.2d 150 (2d Cir. 1934), cert. denied, 293 U.S. 611.

liquidation itself does not transform the non-qualifying B-type exchange into a valid C reorganization.

The C reorganization subsection evolved as a "practical merger" alternative and was designed to permit corporate combinations which did not meet the applicable state requirements for a merger or consolidation. The Revenue Act of 1921, 42 Stat. 227, 230, provided, in section 202(c)(2), that: "The word 'reorganization' ... includes a merger or consolidation (including the acquisition by one corporation ... of substantially all the properties of another corporation) ..." The parenthetical exception was construed as permitting combinations which were "effective mergers." See: Pinellas Ice & Cold Storage Co. v. Commissioner, 287 U.S. 462 (1933); and Cortland Specialty Co. v. Commissioner, 60 F.2d 937 (1932), cert. denied, 288 U.S. 599 (1933).

The legislative history surrounding the Revenue Act of 1934, 48 Stat. 680, 705, enactment of section 112(g)(1), reaffirmed the interpretation given the earlier statutes and concluded that the "practical merger" provision was designed to permit transactions which are "equivalent to a merger." See: S. Rep. No. 558, 73d Cong., 2d Sess. 17 (1934). This provision, basically, is the present section 368(a)(1)(C).

Corporations may choose between a stock for stock exchange or a stock for asset exchange to effect a combination. Typically, in a C reorganization the transferor corporation is divested of its assets (and usually is liquidated). A B reorganization results in the acquisition of a subsidiary.

One important reason for choosing a B rather than a C exchange is that gradual exchanges of stock may be accomplished in a B "creeping" reorganization. The acquisition of assets in a C reorganization should be accomplished in a single exchange transaction. In addition, the transferor corporation in a C reorganization must obtain stockholder approval before transferring its assets. In a B reorganization, however, each stockholder can, independently, exchange his stock for the stock offered by the acquiring corporation.

There is no evidence that Potash or Wecco could have obtained the approval of Wecco shareholders, and the presence of a dissenting majority during the first series of acquisitions would seem to imply that Potash could not have chosen a C reorganization. Potash states that it was *forced* to seek the Wecco assets by an acquisition of stock because it could not otherwise obtain the assets.

The practical merger aspect of a C reorganization precludes multiple stock for asset exchanges. A creeping asset acquisition is not permissible in a C reorganization as it would be impermissible in a statutory merger.[9]

The stock for stock exchange series in this case would have qualified as a B reorganization (a "creeping acquisition") if control had been obtained within 12 months. Were we to conclude that a C reorganization had occurred because the B reorganization was followed by a liquidation, we would approve a seriatim

---

[9]This is in distinction to the "creeping C" reorganization which may occur if the acquiring corporation is a stockholder in the corporation to be acquired, prior to the stock for asset exchange. See Bausch & Lomb Optical Company, 30 T.C. 602 (1958), aff'd, 267 F.2d 75 (2d Cir. 1959), cert. denied, 361 U.S. 835; and Goldman, The C Reorganization, 19 Tax L. Rev. 31, 69-71 (1963).

creeping acquisition of stock control which, by virtue of a subsequent liquidation, becomes a seriatim acquisition of assets. The latter is not permissible under the statute, and in addition it contradicts the basic "merger equivalence" of a C reorganization.

Defendant relies on the step-transaction doctrine to achieve a C reorganization. The application of the step-transaction analysis is an attempt to look through the form of a transaction which was designed to accomplish a particular tax consequence to the reality of the transaction. Commissioner v. Ashland Oil & Refining Corp., 99 F.2d 588 (6th Cir. 1938), cert. denied, 306 U.S. 661 (1939); Ahles Realty Corp. v. Commissioner, 71 F.2d 150 (2d Cir. 1934), cert. denied, 203 U.S. 611.

The basic rationale of this rule was first stated in Ashland Oil & Refining Corp. v. Commissioner, supra. Under this concept, as followed and extended by *Kimbell-Diamond Milling Co.,* [14 T.C. 74 (1950)], if a taxpayer who is interested primarily in acquiring a corporation's assets first purchases stock and then liquidates the acquired corporation to reach its assets, the interim, purportedly separate steps taken to accomplish the primary objective will be disregarded and the steps considered a single transaction. Objectively, in form a purchase of stock has been accomplished; in substance the transaction is considered a purchase of property. The transaction, however, is not a reorganization.

In this case we are not faced with the question of whether each of several steps in a multiple step transaction had a separate business purpose and completeness (and therefore each is to be accorded independent tax significance). The step-transaction doctrine, when applied to a purchase of stock followed by a liquidation, is a determination that some of the several steps are part of a single overall integrated transaction, and the interim transactions are denied tax significance. Admittedly the liquidation of Wecco was pursuant to the basic plan to obtain its assets. Defendant has not argued merely that the liquidation is without tax significance, but that the several steps should be amalgamated into one transaction — a stock for asset exchange. This "collapse" would have us alter the facts of the transaction and does not merely "ignore" certain aspects of the transaction for tax purposes. The explicit statutory reorganization definition — a stock for asset exchange — must, as a matter of fact, occur. The section is detailed and specific. It fixes the tax consequences of corporate combinations and should be applied with some precision. See: Commissioner v. Gordon, United States Supreme Court, Nos. 760 and 781 (decided May 20, 1968).* There is no doubt that the liquidation of Wecco was part of the single scheme to obtain assets. The existence of this plan to obtain assets, however, does not establish that the specific exchanges involved are within section 368(a)(1)(C).

Two exchanges occurred in this case — an exchange of Potash stock for Wecco stock and a later liquidation in which Wecco was dissolved and the assets were distributed to Potash. Defendant's analysis is that this was one integrated transaction and, therefore, it became an exchange of stock for assets. If this is an integrated transaction *and the stock for stock exchange were a qualifying reorganization,* at most we could conclude that the liquidation lacked separate tax significance and that

*See page 616 infra. — Ed.

the assets were received pursuant to the reorganization. This is the tax treatment of a liquidation which is an integral part of an overall transaction, some other part of which qualifies as a reorganization. Assets which are received in a liquidation that occurs subsequent and pursuant to a valid reorganization are considered assets received in connection with a reorganization, and the basis of these assets in the hands of the transferor corporation is carried over. The reorganization to which the liquidation distribution is connected, generally, is either a B reorganization — stock for stock exchange, or a D reorganization (F under the 1954 Code) — a mere change in form or identity of the corporation with a continuation of the same stockholders in the new corporation which owns the assets of the old company. At issue, in these situations, is whether the liquidation was an *independent* transaction. The actual facts of the transaction are not remolded or restructured. The tax consequences of an interim transitory step are ignored, but the facts of each step are neither disturbed nor re-cast. . . .

In Ahles Realty Corp. v. Commissioner, supra, a new corporation was created. All of the stock of the old corporation was exchanged for the stock of the new corporation, and the new company held the old company as a subsidiary. The old company was thereafter liquidated and the assets transferred to the new company. At the completion of both transactions the sole shareholder of the old company was the sole shareholder of the new corporation and all of the old company's assets were held by the new company.

The court found that there had been a reorganization, a D reorganization. A "mere change in . . . form" had been accomplished. The assets received by liquidation were received "in connection with the reorganization" and, therefore, a carryover basis was required.

The court followed what has become a pattern in these cases. A court finds that a reorganization occurred, that under the step-transaction doctrine the subsequent liquidation was a part of the overall scheme in which the reorganization was an earlier step and, therefore, the assets received upon liquidation were, for tax purposes, received "in connection with a reorganization". We are unable to follow the pattern in this case because there is no valid earlier reorganization to which we can graft the liquidation. . . .

In Piedmont Financial Co., supra, the parties stipulated that a reorganization occurred, and the court concluded that the property received in a subsequent liquidation was property acquired "in connection with a reorganization," but it was not property acquired in the course of the tax-free reorganization itself. For defendant to prevail we must conclude that the assets of Wecco were received in the reorganization itself. Assets are received *in* a reorganization where assets are exchanged for stock (C or D reorganization) or by statutory merger (A reorganization). Assets may be received *in connection with any* reorganization defined in section 368 (a)(1). . . .

These decisions are indicative of the usual step-transaction analysis applied when assets are received pursuant to a liquidation which occurs as part of an overall scheme to obtain assets through a reorganization other than a direct stock for assets exchange. The liquidation of Wecco was part of an overall plan to obtain its assets. The assets, however, were not obtained in connection with a reorganization because the only possible reorganization was the exchange of Potash stock for Wecco stock, and that, by defendant's own admission, was not a qualifying B reorganization.

Defendant contends that the liquidation should be denied any significance because it was an interim transitory step in the overall scheme. Its argument is that the liquidation and the stock for stock exchange should be combined, and that the only transaction which should be given tax significance is the one which did not in fact occur, a transfer of stock for assets. This is a misuse of the step-transaction doctrine which was promulgated to deny the independent tax validity of an interim step in a transaction which is not otherwise disturbed.

In South Bay Corporation v. Commissioner, 345 F.2d 698 (2d Cir. 1965), the court considered an argument comparable to that which defendant has structured in this case. In deciding the applicability of the step-transaction doctrine the court looked to the essential transactional purpose of the scheme and telescoped several steps thereby depriving the intermediate steps of tax significance. The court found that the overall purpose was to acquire assets and, therefore, the intermediate stock acquisition was not given finality. That, however, did not establish that a reorganization occurred. The court found that the taxpayer had purchased assets and that a reorganization had not occurred. The "reorganization" involved was a stock for stock exchange, and in defendant's view the assets were received in connection with that reorganization by a subsequent merger. The court said: ". . . [T]he *Kimbell-Diamond* line of cases may be apt guides in determining whether the specific purpose of the whole transaction is, precisely, to acquire assets, as such, and not stock, but it cannot help to resolve the question whether a set of steps resulting in a property acquisition took place by purchase or 'in connection with a reorganization.' " [345 F.2d 704].

The step-transaction approach does not resolve the question whether a reorganization occurred. It would be available to deny tax consequence to the liquidation as an interim step of a scheme to obtain assets, if the stock for stock exchange had been a qualifying reorganization.

For all of the above reasons, we conclude that the nonqualifying B type exchange cannot be deemed a valid C reorganization by virtue of a subsequent liquidation. A C reorganization requires an exchange of stock for assets which we find did not, in fact, occur. Nor is there a qualifying reorganization pursuant to which we could find that the liquidation was undertaken.

Defendant argues that, in any event, Revenue Ruling 67-274, 1967-35 C.B. 10,* is applicable and controlling. The Ruling explains the tax consequences of a transaction wherein X corporation acquires all of the outstanding stock of Y corporation in exchange solely for its voting stock, and thereafter, as part of the same plan, Y is completely liquidated and its assets are distributed to X. The Ruling states that this transaction will be considered a C reorganization rather than a B reorganization.

As explained above, where subsequent to a valid B reorganization the acquired company is liquidated, the assets received in that liquidation (if it is a part of the

---

*Rev. Rul. 67-274 is set forth at page 715 infra. — ED.

same scheme), are considered assets received in connection with a reorganization. The Ruling apparently would prefer to consider this a C reorganization rather than a B reorganization to which the liquidation is linked. It is applicable to situations where the stock for stock exchange would qualify as a reorganization and, therefore, it is not applicable to this case. Moreover, if the Ruling is intended to be applicable to stock for stock exchanges which occur during a 12-month period (a creeping acquisition) we would conclude that this approach denies the basic purpose of a C reorganization (to permit combinations which are "practical mergers"). In addition, it would permit taxpayers to circumvent the absence of any provision for a series of *stock for assets exchanges,* by simply liquidating the corporation acquired by a stock for stock exchange, and, by virtue of the Ruling, characterize the transaction as a C reorganization. We find that the Ruling is inapplicable to a stock for stock exchange which is not a qualifying B reorganization.

We do not reach the question posed by both parties, whether the rule enunciated in Mills v. Commissioner, 331 F.2d 321 (5th Cir. 1964), for application to B reorganizations, is equally applicable to a C reorganization. That rule, basically, is that cash which is paid in lieu of fractional shares does not violate the requirement that the acquiring corporation transfer *solely* its voting stock.

We turn, therefore, to consider defendant's alternative argument. . . . [The alternative argument involving the *Kimbell-Diamond* doctrine and §334(b)(2) is set forth at page 69 supra.]

On Petition for Reconsideration
402 F.2d 1000 (Ct. Cl. 1968)

Laramore, Judge. This case is before the court on Defendant's Petition for Reconsideration of our decision issued July 17, 1968 (American Potash & Chemical Corp. v. United States, Ct. Cl., 399 F.2d 194), in which we denied defendant's motion for summary judgment. Defendant has argued that plaintiff must use a carryover basis for the assets received in liquidation of its subsidiary, Wecco, because the acquisition of Wecco stock in a series of exchanges of stock for stock over a 14-month period either qualified as a C reorganization or, alternatively, because it failed to qualify under section 334.[1] We denied the motion and decided both issues in favor of plaintiff. As we said in our opinion, defendant did not urge the court to construe this transaction as a B reorganization.[2]

---

[1] At first blush it is possible to view our consideration of the step-transaction arguments in a C reorganization context as inconsistent with the disposition of the same issue in the context of section 334. In C reorganizations, the step-transaction doctrine has been applied to an exchange which qualifies as a reorganization and as part of the same transaction that qualifying exchange is followed by a liquidation of the acquired corporation. Potash's intent to acquire assets reveals its plan to obtain assets and no more; it does not establish the existence of a transaction which meets the statutory requirements for a C reorganization (or on the facts then before us, a B reorganization).

In the section 334 area, we faced the issue of whether the step-transaction argument could be presented despite the enactment of section 334. We decided that the legislative history fails to reveal any intent by Congress to pre-empt the step-transaction approach; rather by section 334(b)(2) it established a degree of certainty in the area of parent-subsidiary liquidations and established a fixed rule as to transactions occurring within a 12-month period.

[2] Defendant also states that plaintiff is not entitled to the equity of the *Kimbell-Diamond*

In this petition, however, defendant requests the court to reconsider our conclusion that a B reorganization did not occur and either grant its motion for summary judgment or vacate the opinion and remand the case for a full trial on all of the facts. We concluded in our opinion that:

> Insofar as the facts of this case are concerned as [presented by the briefs and arguments before the court], Potash did not obtain control within a 12-month period, and we find that a B reorganization did not occur.

From the facts and arguments presented to us the only apparent issue was whether the transaction qualifies as a B reorganization when the series of acquisitions seeking control occurs over a 14-month period.

Defendant submits, for the first time in this case, the argument that the 12-month rule of Treasury Regulation 1.368-2(c) is merely a guideline to determine which exchanges of a series of exchanges of stock for stock qualify as tax-free under the B reorganization provisions.[3] In our view, *all* of the individual acquisitions which form a series of stock for stock acquisitions over a period in excess of 12 months (which result in control) do not qualify as tax-free under the reorganization provisions unless the entire series is proved to have been part of a continuing offer to purchase. Defendant argues that plaintiff's admitted intent to acquire Wecco's assets reveals that there was a clear connection between all of the acquisitions and that therefore a continuing offer existed. Plaintiff's response is that two offers to purchase all of the stock are involved (which cannot be deemed a continuing offer) and, therefore, not having obtained control within 12 months, a B reorganization did not occur.

Alternatively, defendant argues that the final acquisition of 52% of the Wecco stock (whereby control was obtained) itself, qualifies as a tax-free exchange within the definition of a B reorganization and, therefore, a carryover basis for depreciation is appropriate for all of the assets later acquired by liquidation.[4] This assumes that several separate exchanges were made and that the last acquisition was not part of a continuing offer to acquire stock.

The facts surrounding the relationship between the two offers and the several exchanges, inter se, and their relationship to the later liquidation revolve around unsettled questions of fact. We, therefore, upon consideration of the arguments presented by both parties, deny defendant's request that the court either grant its motion for summary judgment or vacate its earlier opinion and we remand the case for trial and a recommended opinion pursuant to Rule 52(b) on the issue of whether a B reorganization occurred, in addition to the issues previously remanded.

---

doctrine because the transaction qualifies as a stock for stock reorganization. Defendant no longer argues that the *Kimbell-Diamond* approach is not viable, but that it is not applicable to the facts of this case.

[3]We note again that this is not a situation where a corporation *purchases* some stock and in a later, independent transaction it acquires control by a stock exchange.

[4]Neither party has addressed itself to the reasons for concluding that either a cost or carryover basis is appropriate for all of the assets received in liquidation, assuming that only 52% of the stock acquired qualifies as a tax-free reorganization exchange.

NOTE

See F. Henderson, Jr., Voting Stock in a Two-Step Asset Acquisition: The *Kimbell-Diamond* Reorganization, 25 Tax L. Rev. 375 (1970).

b. TEMPORARY

REVENUE RULING 63-260
1963-2 Cum. Bull. 147

A owned all of the stock of X which owned 70 shares of the stock of Y. A also owned the remaining 30 shares of Y stock directly. A contributed 10 shares of his Y stock to X. Immediately thereafter, X distributed all 80 shares of Y stock now held by it to A.

Held, the distribution by X does not qualify as a nontaxable distribution under the provisions of section 355 of the Internal Revenue Code of 1954, because X did not have "control" of Y within the meaning of section 368(c) of the Code immediately before the distribution except in a transitory and illusory sense.

Section 355 of the Code cannot be made to apply to a transaction in which an immediately preceding contribution to capital by the distributor corporation's shareholder is made solely to attempt to qualify the transaction as a nontaxable distribution under that section.

NOTE

1. Should §355(b)(2)(D) have wrought a different result? Why? Is Rev. Rul. 63-260 consonant with the statute? Why? What relevance does §318(a)(3)(C) have to this problem?

2. Is there an inconsistency in the approaches in Rev. Rul. 63-260 and the *Granite Trust* case (page 473 supra)? Why? What would the result have been in *Granite Trust* if the sales had been to a major stockholder? Why?

6. *Yielding Control*

Reread Granite Trust Co. v. United States, 238 F.2d 670 (1st Cir. 1956), page 473 supra.

Can the shareholders of Corporation X assure recognition of some of their stock investment loss by transferring in the aggregate only 79.9 per cent of the outstanding stock in X (which has only common outstanding) to Corporation Y in exchange for 50 per cent of Corporation Y's voting stock? Will this not constitute a "B" reorganization, and will §354(a)(1) not apply? Is the result a wise one? If not, what would you propose?

7. *"Substantially All of the Properties" — §368(a)(1)(C)*

In Rev. Proc. 66-34, 1966-2 Cum. Bull. 1232, the Internal Revenue Service announced the "operating rule" which will guide it in issuing rulings where the "substantially all" requirement of §§354(b)(1)(A), 368 (a)(1)(C) and 368(a)(2)(B) is involved. Acknowledging that its operating rule does not, as a matter of law, define the lower limits, the Service held the requirement "is satisfied if there is a transfer of assets representing at least 90 percent of the fair market value of the net assets and at least 70 percent of the fair market value of the gross assets held by the [transferor] corporation immediately prior to the transfer."

8. *Assumption of Liabilities — §357*

UNITED STATES v. HENDLER
303 U.S. 564 (1938), rev'g 91 F.2d 680 (4th Cir. 1937)

Mr. Justice BLACK delivered the opinion of the Court. The Revenue Act of 1928[1] imposed a tax upon the annual "net income" of corporations. It defined "net income" as "gross income . . . less the deductions allowed . . . ," and "gross income" as including "gains, profits and income derived from . . . trades . . . or sales, or dealings in property, . . . or gains or profits and income . . . from any source whatever."[2]

Section 112 of the Act exempts certain gains which are realized from a "reorganization" similar to, or in the nature of, a corporate merger or consolidation. Under this section, such gains are not taxed if one corporation, pursuant to a "plan of reorganization" exchanges its property "solely for *stock* or *securities,* in another corporation a party to the reorganization." But, when a corporation not only receives "stock or securities" in exchange for its property, but also receives "other property or money" in carrying out a "plan of reorganization,"

> "(1) If the corporation receiving such other property or money *distributes* it in pursuance of the plan of reorganization, no gain to the corporation shall be recognized from the exchange, but
>
> "(2) If the corporation receiving such other property or money *does not distribute* it in pursuance of the plan of reorganization, the gain, if any, to the corporation shall be recognized [taxed] . . ."

In this case, there was a merger of "reorganization" of the Borden Company and the Hendler Creamery Company, Inc., resulting in gains of more than six million dollars to the Hendler Company, Inc., a corporation of which respondent is

---

[1] Revenue Act of 1928, c. 852, 45 Stat. 791, §13.
[2] Id., §§21-22.

transferee. The Court of Appeals, believing there was an exemption under §112, affirmed the judgment of the District Court holding all Hendler gains non-taxable.

This controversy between the government and respondent involves the assumption and payment — pursuant to the plan of reorganization — by the Borden Company of $534,297.40 bonded indebtedness of the Hendler Creamery Co., Inc. We are unable to agree with the conclusion reached by the courts below that the gain to the Hendler Company, realized by the Borden Company's payment, was exempt from taxation under §112.

It was contended below and it is urged here that since the Hendler Company did not actually receive the money with which the Borden Company discharged the former's indebtedness, the Hendler Company's gain of $534,297.40 is not taxable. The transaction, however, under which the Borden Company assumed and paid the debt and obligation of the Hendler Company is to be regarded in substance as though the $534,297.40 had been paid directly to the Hendler Company. The Hendler Company was the beneficiary of the discharge of its indebtedness. Its gain was as real and substantial as if the money had been paid it and then paid over by it to its creditors. The discharge of liability by the payment of the Hendler Company's indebtedness constituted income to the Hendler Company and is to be treated as such.[6]

Section 112 provides no exemption for gains — resulting from corporate "reorganization" — neither received as "stocks or securities," nor received as "money or other property" and distributed to stockholders under the plan of reorganization. In Minnesota Tea Co. v. Helvering, 302 U.S. 609, it was said that this exemption "contemplates a distribution to stockholders, and not payment to creditors." The very statute upon which the taxpayer relies provides that "If the corporation receiving such other property or money does not distribute it in pursuance of the plan of reorganization, the gain, if any, to the corporation shall be recognized [taxed] . . ."

Since this gain or income of $534,297.40 of the Hendler Company was neither received as "stock or securities" nor distributed to its stockholders "in pursuance of the plan of reorganization" it was not exempt and is taxable gain as defined in the 1928 Act. This $534,297.40 gain to the taxpayer does not fall within the exemptions of § 112, and the judgment of the court below is

Reversed.

Mr. Justice CARDOZO and Mr. Justice REED took no part in the consideration or decision of this case.

NOTE

If Congress had permitted the *Hendler* decision to stand, what impact would the decision have had on corporate reorganizations? How would you have argued for a contrary result in *Hendler*? Why?

Reread the *Raich* case (page 350 supra) and the Comment that follows it. What effect does *Raich* have in the reorganization area? Why?

[6]Old Colony Trust Co. v. Commissioner, 279 U.S. 716, 729; Douglas v. Willcuts, 296 U.S. 1, 8, 9.

To what extent does §357 overrule *Hendler?* What is the reason for §357(c)? What is the relationship between §§357 and 368(a)(2)(B)? If X Corporation transfers substantially all its property with a basis of $60,000 which is now worth $100,000 to Y in exchange for 20 per cent of Y's stock worth $80,000, and Y assumes a liability of $20,000, what is X's basis in its Y stock? Suppose Y also gave X $1000 cash to pay for liquidating expenses?

Suppose X assumes $1,015,000 in liabilities of its transferor, but only $600,000 of the assumption is proven to be for a bona fide business purpose. How much of the liability is "other property"? See Estate of Stoll, 38 T.C. 223 (1962).

See Rev. Rul. 68-637, 1968-2 Cum. Bull. 158, in which the assumption of stock options and warrants was held to be "liabilities" and not "boot" under §368(a)(1)(C).

9. *Effect of "Boot"*

a. ON CORPORATIONS

If a transferor corporation in an "A," "C," or "D" reorganization receives "boot" (anything in addition to stock or securities in another corporation which is a party to the reorganization), §361(b) provides that no gain will be recognized to the transferor if it distributes the "boot" "in pursuance of the plan of reorganization." Why does it so provide? If the transferor retains the "boot," gain to the extent of the retained "boot" will be recognized. In what types of reorganizations might such "boot" retention occur? Despite retention of "boot," no loss is recognized. Section 361(b)(2). Why?

Section 354(a)(2) and (3) treats "securities" as "boot" in designated circumstances. Section 361 does not so provide. Should it? Why?

If a corporation receives a "boot" distribution that is taxable to it as a dividend under §356(a)(2), is it entitled to the dividends-received deduction under §243? See King Enterprises, Inc. v. United States, 418 F.2d 511 (Ct. Cl. 1969). What is the measure of a "boot" distribution received in kind? See §301(b)(1)(B).

b. ON SHAREHOLDERS

COMMISSIONER v. ESTATE OF BEDFORD
325 U.S. 283 (1945), rev'g 144 F.2d 272 (2d Cir. 1944)

Mr. Justice FRANKFURTER delivered the opinion of the Court. . . . The estate of Edward T. Bedford, who died May 21, 1931, included 3,000 shares of cumulative preferred stock (par value $100) of Abercrombie & Fitch Company. Pursuant to a plan of recapitalization respondent, as executor of the estate, in 1937 exchanged those shares for 3,500 shares of cumulative preferred stock (par value $75), 1,500 shares of common stock (par value $1), and $45,240 in cash (on the basis of $15.08 for each of the old preferred shares). The recapitalization had been proposed because the company, after charging against its surplus account stock dividends totaling $844,100, distributed in 1920, 1928, and 1930, had incurred a book deficit in that account of $399,771.87. Because of this deficit, the company, under applicable State law, was unable to pay dividends although for the fiscal year ending January 31, 1937 it had net earnings of $309,073.70.

By comparing the fair market value of the old preferred shares at the date of Bedford's death with the market value of the new stock and cash received the gain to his estate was $139,740. Admittedly the recapitalization was a reorganization, §[368(a)(1)(E)], so that only the cash received, but none of the stock is taxable. Sections [354(a)(1), 356(a)]. The sole issue is whether the cash, $45,240, is taxable as a dividend, or merely as a capital gain . . . . The Tax Court sustained the determination of the Commissioner that the cash was taxable as a dividend, 1 T.C. 478, but was reversed by the Circuit Court of Appeals. 144 F.2d 272. On a showing of importance to the administration of the Revenue Acts, we granted certiorari. 323 U.S. 707.

The precise question is whether the distribution of cash in this recapitalization "has the effect of the distribution of a taxable dividend" under §[356(a)(2)] and as such is fully taxable, or is taxable only . . . as a capital gain under §[356(a)(2)].

The history of this legislation is not illuminating. Section [356(a)(2)] originated in §203(d)(2) of the Revenue Act of 1924 . . . . But the reports of the Congressional Committees merely use the language of the section to explain it. H. Rep. No. 179, 68th Cong., 1st Sess., pp. 14-15; S. Rep. No. 398, 68th Cong., 1st Sess., pp. 15-16. Nor does the applicable Treasury Regulation add anything; it repeats substantially the Committee Reports. Treas. Reg. 94, Art. 112(g)-4. We are thrown back upon the legislative language for ascertaining the meaning which will best accord with the aims of the language, the practical administration of the law and relevant judicial construction.

Although Abercrombie & Fitch showed a book deficit in the surplus account because the earlier stock dividends had been charged against it, the parties agree that for corporate tax purposes at least earnings and profits exceeding the distributed cash had been earned at the time of the recapitalization. That cash therefore came out of earnings and profits and such a distribution would normally be considered a taxable dividend, see §[316(a)], and has so been treated by the courts in seemingly similar situations. It has been ruled in a series of cases that where the stock of one corporation was exchanged for the stock of another and cash and then distributed, such distributions out of earnings and profits had the effect of a distribution of a taxable dividend under §[356(a)(2)]. . . . The Tax Court has reached the same result, that is, has treated the distribution as a taxable dividend, in the case of the recapitalization of a single corporation. . . . We cannot distinguish the two situations and find no implication in the statute restricting §[356(a)(2)] to taxation as a dividend only in the case of an exchange of stock and assets of two corporations.

Respondent, however, claims that this distribution more nearly has the effect of a "partial liquidation" as defined in §115(i).[5] But the classifications of §115, which

---

[5]"(i). *Definition of Partial Liquidation.* — As used in this section the term 'amounts distributed in partial liquidation' means a distribution by a corporation in complete cancellation

governs "Distribution of Corporations" apart from reorganizations, were adopted for another purpose. They do not apply to a situation arising within §112 [the reorganization and non-recognition provisions]. The definition of a "partial liquidation" in §115(i) is specifically limited to use in §115. To attempt to carry it over to §112 would distort its purpose. That limitation is not true of §[316(a)] which defines "dividends" for the purpose of the whole title. Accordingly, this definition is infused into §112(c) (2) [356(a)(2)]. Under §[316(a)] a distribution out of accumulated earnings and profits is a "dividend," thus confirming the conclusion that a distribution of earnings and profits has the "effect of the distribution of a taxable dividend" under §[356(a) (2)].

Recapitalization does not alter the "effect." Although the capital of a company is reduced, the cash received is a distribution of earnings and profits and as such falls within the federal tax. That the company's treatment of its stock dividends may bring consequences under State law requiring a capital reduction does not alter the character of the transactions which bring them within the federal income tax. Recapitalization is one of the forms of reorganization under §112 . . . . It cannot therefore be urged as a reason for taking the transaction out of the requirements of §112 and forcing it into the mold of §115. The reduction of capital brings §112 into operation and does not give immunity from the requirements of §[356(a)(2)].

Treating the matter as a problem of statutory construction for our independent judgment, we hold that a distribution, pursuant to a reorganization, of earnings and profits, "has the effect of a distribution of a taxable dividend" within §[356(a)(2)]. As is true of other teasing questions of construction raised by technical provisions of Revenue Acts the matter is not wholly free from doubt. But these doubts would have to be stronger than they are to displace the informed views of the Tax Court. And if the case can be reduced to its own particular circumstances rather than turn on a generalizing principle we should feel bound to apply Dobson v. Commissioner, 320 U.S. 489, and sustain the Tax Court.

Reversed.

NOTE

1. What is Justice Frankfurter's test for determining whether a distribution "has the effect of the distribution of a dividend"? Is his test justifiable? Why? What relevance does the presence of §§302 and 346 in the Code have to a determination whether the mere presence of earnings and profits will produce a dividend in a reorganization-connected distribution? What other guides are there in deciding whether a distribution has the "effect" of a distribution of a dividend? See B. Shoulson, Boot Taxation: The Blunt Toe of the Automatic Rule, 20 Tax L. Rev. 573 (1965); J. Moore, Taxation of Distributions Made in Connection with a Corporate Reorganization, 17 Tax L. Rev. 129, 141-150 (1961).

2. If a reorganization produces *any* change in the nature of the shareholder's in-

___

or redemption of a part of its stock, or one of a series of distributions in complete cancellation or redemption of all or a portion of its stock."

terest, can it be said that the distribution has the effect of the distribution of a dividend? Cf. Idaho Power Co. v. United States, 161 F. Supp. 807 (Ct. Cl.), cert. denied, 358 U.S. 832 (1958). Is this decision persuasive? Why? Does §356(a)(2) direct the Commissioner to look at the effect of the exchange as a whole, or only at the effect of the distribution of "boot"? If there is a sufficient continuity of interest to meet the *LeTulle* line of cases, is it a tenable argument that all "boot" distributed should be treated as a dividend to the extent of earnings and profits? Why?

3. What is the result if a taxpayer exchanges, in reorganization, securities in the face amount of $1000, worth $900, for securities in the face amount of $1000, worth $950? Why? For securities in the face amount of $1200, worth $950? Why? What result if taxpayer exchanges common stock worth $1000 for preferred stock worth $500 and $500 face amount bonds worth $550? Worth $450? Why? Cf. §1036.

4. In William H. Bateman, page 546 supra, the distribution of warrants in the issuer's stock was held not to have dividend effect since no corporate assets were "distributed." Is this a persuasive basis for decision? Why? What counter-arguments would you have made as Commissioner's counsel on appeal?

5. See Note 2, page 547 supra, as to the taxability of costs paid by an acquiring corporation in an "A" reorganization.

6. Section 356(a)(2) taxes as a dividend those distributions which have "the effect of a dividend," but only to the extent of the shareholder's "gain." Why should taxation of a dividend-type distribution be limited to a shareholder's gain? Compare §§302(d), 356(b) and 356(e). Study Treas. Reg. §1.301-1(e). What is its purpose? Can it mesh with the limitation-to-gain provision of §356(a)(2)?

10. *Subsidiary's Dealings with Stock in Parent*

COMMITTEE ON CORPORATE TAXATION, TAX SECTION OF THE NEW YORK STATE BAR ASSOCIATION, SALE OR EXCHANGE BY A SUBSIDIARY CORPORATION OF ITS PARENT CORPORATION'S STOCK*

I. BASIS OF ASSETS ACQUIRED IN EXCHANGE FOR STOCK

A. Value of Stock as Basis for Assets

Where a corporation acquires property for its stock in a taxable exchange, that is, a transaction in which gain or loss is recognized to the transferor of the property, the corporation's tax basis for the property so acquired is the fair market value of stock at the time of the exchange.[1] The corporation does not inherit the transferor's basis for the assets under Section 362(a) or (b) because those provisions apply only where property is acquired in a Section 351 transaction, as a contribution to capital, or in a reorganization.

---

*Reprinted, by permission, from 47 Taxes 146 (1969). — ED.
[1]MacCallum Gauge Co., . . . 32 BTA 544 (1935), acq. XIV-1 CB 12; Rev. Rul. 56-100, 1956-1 CB 624.

The foregoing principle is of frequent practical application in transactions which do not qualify as tax-deferred "incorporations" under Section 351 or tax-deferred "reorganizations" under Section 368. Thus, for example, Section 351 may not apply because the assets do not come from persons owning at least 80 per cent of the stock of the acquiring corporation immediately after the transfer. The acquisition of assets for stock may not qualify as a "reorganization" under Section 368(a)(1)(C) because the assets come from an individual, partnership, or other noncorporate entity. Or the assets may represent less than "substantially all" the assets of a corporate transferor. Moreover, the consideration for the assets may consist of more "boot" than is permitted by Section 368(a)(2)(B). Or the "assets" acquired may consist of shares of stock acquired in an exchange which does not qualify as a "reorganization" under Section 368(a)(1)(B), for example, because the consideration moving from the acquiring corporation does not consist solely of voting stock.

B. *Acquisition of Assets by Parent Which Transfers Assets to Subsidiary*

The same principle also applies where a corporation first acquires assets in a taxable exchange and then transfers those assets to a wholly owned subsidiary,[2] either as a contribution to the subsidiary's capital or in exchange for shares of the subsidiary's stock. The parent corporation's basis for the acquired assets is the fair market value of its stock given in exchange, and that tax basis will carry over to the subsidiary under Section 362(a). The transfer of assets from parent to subsidiary would normally result in no taxable gain to the parent[3] or to the subsidiary, which would receive the assets tax free pursuant to Section 118 or 1032. The parent's basis for the subsidiary's stock would thereafter include the parent's cost basis for the assets (as provided either by Section 358(a)(1) or by Section 1016(a)(1)), and such basis would, in turn, reflect the fair market value of the parent's stock given in exchange for those assets.

C. *Acquisition of Assets Directly by Subsidiary*

Instead of the parent's acquiring assets in exchange for its stock and then transferring the assets to its subsidiary, the latter may acquire assets directly from an unaffiliated transferor in a taxable exchange for stock of the subsidiary's parent. There are two basic methods by which this may be accomplished.

The first method is for the parent corporation to issue or transfer its stock to the owner of the assets, requesting that the assets be transferred directly to the subsidiary.

---

[2]All references to subsidiary corporations in this Report are to wholly owned subsidiaries.

[3]The law is presently unsettled as to whether a contribution to the capital of a wholly owned corporation should be viewed as involving a "constructive" issuance of additional shares of stock in exchange for the contributed assets. Such a constructive issuance would require an advance ruling under Section 367 to prevent recognition of gain upon a contribution of appreciated assets to a foreign corporation. The "constructive" exchange theory was recently rejected in the Section 367 context in Werner Abegg, . . . 50 TC 145 (1968), in which the Tax Court expressly refused to follow Rev. Rul. 64-155, 1964-1 CB (Part 1) 138, and distinguished King v. United States, . . . 79 F.2d 453 (CA-4), and Commissioner v. Morgan, . . . 288 F.2d 676 (CA-3), cited as authorities in the Ruling. However, whether or not gain is realized on contributions to capital generally, the U.S. parent would normally realize no gain from such a transaction if the assets were transferred to the foreign subsidiary immediately after the parent's acquisition of those assets.

The tax consequences of this procedure appear to be identical with those (described above) which follow where the parent acquires the assets and then transfers them to the subsidiary.

The second method is for the parent to transfer its shares to the subsidiary, which in turn transfers those shares to the owner of the assets in exchange for the transfer of the assets directly to the subsidiary. Here the subsidiary may have received the parent's shares as a capital contribution or in exchange for the issuance or transfer of shares of the subsidiary's own stock to the parent.

Our Committee believes that the tax treatment of a transaction utilizing this second method should depend upon the circumstances under which the subsidiary has acquired the parent's shares. Part II of this Report discusses the tax treatment of cases in which the subsidiary acquires the parent's shares pursuant to a plan under which the subsidiary is to use those shares to purchase particular assets. Part III of this Report discusses the tax treatment of cases in which the subsidiary has acquired the parent's shares in a prior transaction for some purpose unrelated to the subsidiary's acquisition of particular assets.

II. Acquisition of Parent's Stock by Subsidiary as Step in Plan for Acquisition of Assets by Subsidiary

A. Substance of Transaction

Where the subsidiary acquires only transitory ownership of the parent's shares, pursuant to a plan by which the subsidiary is to exchange those shares for assets, the transaction is, in substance, identical with cases where (i) the parent acquires the assets and then transfers them to the subsidiary as a capital contribution or pursuant to a Section 351 exchange for shares of the subsidiary's stock, or (ii) the parent issues or transfers its stock to the owner of the assets which are transferred directly to the subsidiary. Accordingly, these cases should have the same tax consequences: the fair market value of the stock given for the assets should (a) be included in the parent's tax basis for the subsidiary's stock, and (b) determine the tax basis for the assets in the hands of the subsidiary.

The foregoing approach to such non-reorganization transactions is consistent with the position taken by the Internal Revenue Service in Rev. Rul. 64-73, 1964-1 CB (Part 1) 142, concerning a multi-party reorganization.[4] There a parent corporation L owned 100 per cent of the stock of a subsidiary M, which, in turn, owned 100 per cent of the stock of another subsidiary N. L entered into an agreement with X, an unrelated corporation, whereby X received shares of L's voting stock in consideration for the transfer of substantially all of X's assets. Some of the X assets were transferred from X to N, and the remaining X assets were transferred to L. Neither L nor N acquired direct ownership of "substantially all" of X's assets.

In holding that this transaction qualified as a reorganization, Rev. Rul. 64-73 stated in material part:

"The described transaction is *viewed* as an acquisition by L, in exchange solely for part of its voting stock, of substantially all of the properties of X. The fact that in

[4]Sec. 368(a)(2)(C).

the instant case the plan of reorganization provides that some of the assets are to be transferred directly from X to N, rather than through L and M, does not detract from the conclusion that in *substance* L is to acquire substantially all the X assets." (Italics added.)

This statement suggests that assets moving directly to a subsidiary corporation are to be treated as moving first to the subsidiary's parent, if the consideration given for the assets originates with the parent as part of a single transaction.

Additional support for this view is furnished by Rev. Rul. 57-278, 1957-1 CB 124, dealing with a three-party reorganization under Section 368(a)(1)(C). There a parent corporation issued shares of its voting stock to a new subsidiary which used those shares to acquire all of the assets of a third corporation. The Service ruled, among other things, that no gain or loss was recognized to the new subsidiary "as a result of the exchanges made pursuant to the plan of reorganization." This ruling is significant because none of the Code's nonrecognition provisions was expressly applicable to the new subsidiary. The ruling would therefore seem to imply that the assets were treated as having first been acquired by the parent and then transferred by it to the new subsidiary as a contribution to capital. So treated, both the acquisition of the assets by the parent and the subsequent receipt of the assets by the subsidiary as a contribution to capital are directly covered by nonrecognition provisions in the Code.[5]

It is also significant that the Code does not contain any express provision for determining the parent's basis for the stock of a new subsidiary after a reorganization of the type analyzed in Rev. Rul. 57-278. However, it is the understanding of our Committee that, notwithstanding this statutory omission, the policy of the Service is to rule that the parent's basis for the new subsidiary's stock will include the basis of the assets carried over from the transferor corporation. This result also implies that those assets should be treated as moving initially to the parent, which furnishes the consideration therefor.

Our Committee believes that a similar analysis should apply in those non-reorganization cases where the parent's stock originates with the parent and is transferred to the subsidiary pursuant to a plan for its use by the subsidiary solely to acquire particular assets. Where such a plan exists, the parent should be treated as having acquired the assets in exchange for its own stock and having transferred those assets to the subsidiary. This interpretation should be given uniform application without regard to the formal sequence of steps that may be taken to accomplish the purpose of the plan. Thus, the tax consequences to both parent and subsidiary should be the same —

(a) regardless of whether the assets (i) move directly from the transferor to the subsidiary, or (ii) move first to the parent, which then transfers them to the subsidiary, and

---

[5]Secs. 1032 and 118. As a policy matter, nonrecognition of gain to the subsidiary in a three-party C reorganization may be dictated at least in part by the inequity of subjecting the subsidiary to tax upon transfer of its parent's shares without permitting the subsidiary a "cost" basis for the acquired assets equal to the current fair market value of the parent's stock. See Sec. 362(b).

(b) regardless of whether the parent's shares (i) move directly from the parent to the transferor, or (ii) move first from the parent to the subsidiary, which then transfers them to the transferor of the assets.

B. *Recommendations for Revenue Ruling*

In order to clarify the federal income tax consequences of several of the more common types of transactions, other than a tax-deferred "reorganization," in which a subsidiary corporation acquires assets in exchange for stock of the subsidiary's parent, our Committee recommends the publication of a Revenue Ruling.

Such a Revenue Ruling would provide that in all cases where assets are, in substance, acquired by the parent and then transferred to the subsidiary, the fair market value of the parent's stock becomes the subsidiary's tax basis for the assets and part of the parent's basis for the subsidiary's stock. Specifically, the Revenue Ruling would make it clear that, if several steps are parts of an overall plan under which the assets end up in the subsidiary and the parent's shares end up in the hands of the original owner of the assets, the tax consequences to both parent and subsidiary will not depend upon:

(a) whether the assets (i) move directly from their original owner to the subsidiary or (ii) move first to the parent, which then transfers them to the subsidiary, or

(b) whether the parent's shares (i) move directly from the parent to the owner of the assets or (ii) move first from the parent to the subsidiary, which then transfers them to the owner of the assets.

By contrast, where a subsidiary has acquired shares of its parent's stock in a separate prior transaction, the Revenue Ruling might appropriately point out that Section 1032 does not prevent recognition of gain or loss to the subsidiary upon the receipt of money or assets in exchange for that stock. It is recommended, however, that the proposed Revenue Ruling refrain from taking any position as to the method for determining a subsidiary's tax basis for shares of its parent's stock in those cases where such shares were acquired by the subsidiary in a separate transaction as a contribution to capital or in exchange for shares of the subsidiary's own stock. As discussed below, the law in this area is not well settled. Moreover, under the approach herein, the issue will have little practical importance because a parent corporation will seldom issue shares of its stock to a subsidiary in the absence of a plan contemplating the subsidiary's transfer of that stock to a third party.[6]

III. Acquisition of Parent's Stock by Subsidiary in Separate Transactions

The tax consequences are not clear in those cases where a subsidiary acquires assets in exchange for shares of its parent's stock which were received by the subsidiary in a prior transaction unrelated to the subsidiary's acquisition of the particular

---

[6]In the absence of a plan for the subsidiary's use of the parent's stock, the issuance of that stock to the subsidiary may raise corporate law questions as to whether the parent's stock is "fully paid and non-assessable" under statutes such as McKinney's N.Y. Bus. Corp. Law Sec. 504(i) or Delaware Code, Title 8, Sec. 152.

assets. In such cases the subsidiary's ownership of the parent's stock is not transitory, with the result that the subsidiary may realize gain or loss when it exchanges that stock for assets, the amount of any such gain or loss depending in part on its tax basis for the parent's stock.

A. Inapplicability of Section 1032

Assuming that gain or loss is realized by a subsidiary upon its exchange of its parent's stock for assets, Section 1032 would not prevent such gain or loss from being "recognized" for tax purposes to the subsidiary. Section 1032 states:

"No gain or loss shall be recognized to a corporation on the receipt of money or other property in exchange for stock (including treasury stock) *of such corporation."* (Italics added.)

This statute clearly does not prevent a subsidiary from recognizing gain or loss upon receipt of money or other property in exchange for stock of another corporation, its parent. It therefore appears that gain or loss may be recognized to a subsidiary to the extent that the money or the value of other property received by it in exchange for its parent's stock is greater or less than the subsidiary's basis for the parent's stock. Accordingly, determination of the amount of that basis becomes crucial.

B. Subsidiary's Basis for Parent's Stock

Different factual patterns and legal theories may be relevant in determining the subsidiary's basis for stock of its parent.

1. *Cost Basis.* — The subsidiary's basis will clearly be cost where the subsidiary has acquired its parent's stock by purchase from an unrelated party in an arm's length transaction. Similarly, the subsidiary should have a cost basis for the parent's stock if acquired from the parent (by subscription to newly issued shares or by purchase of previously outstanding or treasury shares) for cash or other property equal in value to the current fair market value of the parent's stock when acquired by the subsidiary.

If the amount paid to the parent by the subsidiary is exactly equal to the current fair market value of the parent's stock and the subsidiary exchanges such stock for assets of equivalent value, the subsidiary should realize neither gain nor loss from the exchange, and the parent's tax basis for the subsidiary's stock should neither be increased nor decreased. If, however, the amount paid by the subsidiary to the parent is in excess of the current fair market value of the parent's stock, such excess presumably constitutes either a dividend or a distribution of capital by the subsidiary to the parent.[7]

2. *Zero Basis.* — It is not clear how the subsidiary's basis for its parent's stock should be determined where those shares have previously been acquired by the subsidiary from its parent in a separate transaction, either as a contribution to the subsidiary's capital or in exchange for additional stock of the subsidiary. Here there may

---

[7]A capital contribution by the parent to the subsidiary may occur where the subsidiary purchases the parent's stock from the parent for less than its fair market value. Such a capital contribution would be measured by the amount by which the fair market value of the parent's stock exceeds the price paid by the subsidiary.

or may not be a distinction between newly issued shares of the parent's stock and shares previously held by the parent in its treasury.[8]

On possibility is that the subsidiary is required to use a zero basis for shares of its parent's stock received as a capital contribution or in exchange for the subsidiary's own stock, at least in those cases where the subsidiary has received newly issued shares of the parent's stock. This possibility rests upon the premise that the parent has a zero basis for its own shares, and that accordingly the subsidiary inherits that basis for the shares under Section 362(a).

If this zero basis theory is correct, the subsidiary would be required to recognize gain equal to the fair market value of the assets received by it in exchange for its parent's stock. This gain would constitute either long-term or short-term capital gain, depending on whether the subsidiary owned the parent's shares for more than six months before transferring them in exchange for the assets.[10]

The zero basis approach is probably unsound, however, because it attempts to apply the principle of Section 362(a) out of the context in which that statute was enacted. That principle is properly applicable where a stockholder transfers one or more items of property owned by him to a corporation as a contribution to the latter's capital. In such a case, Section 362(a)(2) requires the transferee corporation to use the former tax basis of the property "in the hands of the transferor."

A parent corporation does not, however, own any "property" with respect to authorized but unissued shares of its own stock. The original issuance of those shares involves the creation of new property rather than a transfer of pre-existing property. Thus, until those shares are contributed to the subsidiary, there exists no "property" susceptible of having any tax basis in the hands of the parent. Accordingly, it is highly questionable whether Section 362(a)(2) should have any application in such a case.

Even if the parent's stock should be considered "property" because it becomes such in the hands of the subsidiary, Section 362(a)(2) appears to require that the property received by the transferee must have had a basis in the hands of the transferor. Authorized but unissued stock has *no basis* to the issuing corporation, but this does not mean that such stock has a *zero basis*. On the contrary, it may well mean that there is simply no basis to carry over to the subsidiary under Section 362(a)(2).

In another context the IRS has refused to attribute a zero basis to newly issued shares of a corporation's own stock merely because such stock has no basis in the hands of that corporation. This occurs where a corporation distributes newly issued shares of its stock to its preferred stockholders in discharge of preference dividends for the current year or a preceding year. Because such a distribution is taxable to stockholders,[11] it is often necessary to determine the amount taxable to a corporate shareholder under Section 301(b)(1)(B). That statute provides that the amount of a non-cash distribution by a corporation to a corporate stockholder is the lesser of (i)

---

[8]The existence of possible tax distinctions between treasury stock and newly issued stock presents the question of whether enactment of Sections 317 and 1032 in 1954 eliminated all such distinctions as they may affect the tax treatment of the issuing corporation.

[10]For possible tax consequences where the subsidiary is a foreign corporation, see the discussion under "Acquisitions by Foreign Subsidiaries" in Part IV of this Report.

[11]Section 305(b)(1).

the fair market value of the distributed property or (ii) the adjusted basis of that property "in the hands of the distributing corporation immediately before the distribution."

Instead of holding that the newly issued shares have a zero basis in the hands of the distributing corporation, Reg. Sec. 1.301-1(d) states that:

"If the property distributed consists of . . . stock of the distributing corporation treated as a property under Section 305(b) . . . , the amount of such distribution shall be . . . the fair market value of such . . . stock."

Reg. Sec. 1.301-1(d) thus indicates that where "property" consists of authorized but unissued shares not susceptible of having a basis in the hands of the issuing corporation, it is not proper to apply statutory rules — such as those in Section 301(b)(1) (B) and Section 362(a) — which would otherwise cause the tax consequences to a recipient of the property to depend on the tax basis of that property in the hands of the issuing corporation. The clear implication is that a zero basis is not to be used as the tax basis of a corporation for shares of its own authorized but unissued stock.

An additional objection to the application of Section 362 arises in those cases where the subsidiary exchanges shares of its own stock for the newly issued shares of the parent's stock. Here the carry-over basis rules of Section 362(a)(1) apply only if there is "a transaction to which Section 351 (relating to transfer of property to corporation controlled by transferor) applies."

It seems clear, however, that Section 351 does not "apply" to an issuance of the parent's newly issued shares in the sense that the operation of that statute is necessary to prevent recognition of a taxable gain that would otherwise be realized by the parent. Even before the enactment of the predecessor of Section 351 in 1921, it was clear that a corporation did not realize any taxable gain upon receipt of money or other property as the consideration for the issuance of shares of its stock.[12] Moreover, Section 1032 was enacted in 1954 solely to obviate questions which had arisen under the 1939 Code as to the circumstances in which a corporation that disposed of its own treasury shares (as contrasted with newly issued shares) might recognize gain or loss with respect to such shares.[13] Our Committee believes, therefore, that the exchange of the subsidiary's shares for newly issued shares of the parent's stock should not be considered "a transaction to which Section 351 . . . applies," as that phrase is used in Section 362(a)(1).

3. *Fair Market Value.* — The foregoing objections to the zero basis approach tend to support the view that a subsidiary which receives shares of its parent's stock as a contribution to capital should be held to acquire a tax basis for the parent's stock equal to the fair market value of such stock on the date of receipt by the subsidiary.

That view is premised on the general rule that the basis of property is its "cost," as provided by Section 1012, unless the statute provides some other rule for determining basis. In the absence of such a statutory exception, the "cost" of property acquired without consideration has been held to be its fair market value at the time

[12]See, for example, Treas. Reg. 45, Arts. 542, 563; Treas. Reg. 62, Arts. 542, 563.
[13]H.R. Rept. 1337, 83d Cong., 2d Sess. A268 (1954); S. Rept. 1622, 83d Cong., 2d Sess. 426 (1954).

of its acquisition. Thus, for example, fair market value at time of acquisition has been used as the "cost" of property received by way of gift, contribution to capital of corporations or paid-in surplus, contribution to capital of partnerships, and certain transfers to trusts.[14] While each of these instances is now controlled by a statutory provision for a carry-over basis, they nevertheless support the proposition that, in the absence of an overriding statute, a subsidiary's "cost" for its parent's stock received as a contribution to the subsidiary's capital is the fair market value of the parent's stock at the time of its acquisition by the subsidiary.

A slightly different result may obtain where the subsidiary issues its own stock in exchange for the parent's stock.[15] As noted above, the rule is well established that the "cost" of property acquired by a corporation in exchange for its stock is the fair market value of *that stock* at the time when given for the property.[16] Thus, the "cost" of the parent's shares to the subsidiary would be the value of the subsidiary's shares issued to the parent, rather than the value of the parent's shares when issued to the subsidiary. Although these two values may differ in theory, in actual practice they will often be identical.

4. *Quasi-Treasury-Stock Theory.* — The fair market value approach discussed above does not, however, completely eliminate all problems of realization and recognition of gain or loss by the subsidiary on the disposition of the parent's stock. Since the discussion in Part III of this Report assumes that the subsidiary has received the parent's stock in a transaction unrelated to the transaction in which the stock is disposed of, there may well be a fluctuation in the fair market value of the parent's stock during the period that such stock is owned by the subsidiary.

Recognition of gain or loss by the subsidiary would not occur if those shares were viewed as held by the parent until the shares are transferred by the subsidiary. In support of this approach, it can be argued that the ownership of the parent's stock by a wholly owned subsidiary is substantially equivalent, both economically and legally, to the ownership by the parent of shares of its own treasury stock.[17]

This "quasi-treasury-stock" approach receives support from numerous decisions holding that the shares of a parent corporation owned by a controlled subsidiary may not be voted, a result assured by statute in many states. Furthermore, because it is questionable whether stock of the parent in the hands of a wholly owned subsidiary is entitled to receive dividends or other distributions from the parent, it is often the

[14]As to gifts: Rice v. Eisner, . . . 16 F.2d 358 (CA-2 1926), cert. denied 273 U.S. 764 (1927); as to contributions to capital of corporations: S. Rept. 398, 68th Cong., 1st Sess. 18 (1924); as to contributions to paid-in surplus of corporations: Rosenbloom Finance Corp., . . . 24 BTA 763, 774 (1931), rev'd . . . 66 F.2d 556 (CA-3 1933), cert. denied 290 U.S. 692 (1933); as to contributions to capital of partnership: Helvering v. Walbridge, . . . 70 F.2d 683 (CA-2 1934), cert. denied 293 U.S. 594 (1934). See also Chisholm v. Commissioner, . . . 79 F.2d 14 (CA-2 1935), cert. denied 296 U.S. 641 (1935); and as to certain transfers to trusts: Bankers Trust Co., . . . 24 BTA 10 (1931), non-acq. XI-1 CB 8; Francis Francis, . . . 15 BTA 1332 (1929), non-acq. VIII-2 CB 63.

[15]This analysis would also apply if the subsidiary is considered as having constructively issued additional shares of its stock to the parent. See footnote 3.

[16]See authorities cited in footnote 1.

[17]This analysis is derived partly from a lecture delivered by Wm. Douglas Kilbourn, Jr., Professor of Law and Director of Graduate Tax Program, Boston University School of Law, November 14, 1967, at the New York University 26th Annual Institute on Federal Taxation.

practice not to make such distributions. These circumstances suggest that the "quasi-treasury-stock" theory has much to commend it.

Under that theory, no gain or loss would be realized or recognized by a subsidiary on disposition of its parent's stock, regardless of (a) whether the parent's stock was acquired by the subsidiary (i) from the parent or (ii) from an unrelated third party; (b) whether the shares acquired from the parent were (i) newly issued by the parent or (ii) previously held by the parent as treasury stock; or (c) whether such shares were acquired by the subsidiary from the parent (i) as a contribution to capital, (ii) in exchange for its own stock, or (iii) for cash.

C. Parent's Basis for Subsidiary's Stock

The parent's basis for the subsidiary's stock will depend on the circumstances under which the subsidiary obtains the shares of the parent's stock which are exchanged for the assets acquired by the subsidiary.

If assets are acquired by the parent in a non-reorganization transaction and then transferred by it to the subsidiary in a Section 351 exchange for the subsidiary's stock, the fair market value of the parent's shares given for the assets will both (i) become the basis for the assets contributed to the subsidiary and (ii) be added to the parent's basis for its stock in the subsidiary pursuant to Section 358(a)(1). These results should also follow under the recommendation made in Part II of this report where the parent requests that the assets be conveyed directly to the subsidiary, irrespective of whether the parent's shares formally pass through the subsidiary on their way to the former owner of the assets.

Moreover, these tax consequences should follow irrespective of whether the subsidiary issues additional shares of its own stock to the parent, provided that the several steps are part of a single plan. If the subsidiary does not issue additional shares of its own stock to the parent as part of a plan,[21] the parent's basis for the stock of the subsidiary should be increased by the fair market value of the parent's stock given for the assets because Section 1016(a)(1) provides that the basis of "property," that is, here the subsidiary's stock owned by the parent, is to be adjusted for "expenditures . . . properly chargeable to capital account."

The problem of determining the parent's tax basis for the subsidiary's stock becomes more complex in those instances where (a) the parent issues or transfers its stock to the subsidiary as a contribution to capital or in exchange for the subsidiary's stock and (b) the subsidiary later, in a separate transaction, uses the parent's stock to acquire assets.

1. *Zero Basis.* — The first question is whether the parent's contribution of its stock to the subsidiary will be accompanied by an increase in the parent's tax basis for the subsidiary's stock. There will be no such increase if (i) the parent's stock is considered to have a zero basis in the hands of the parent and (ii) the parent is required to use that zero basis as a substituted basis for the subsidiary's stock pursuant to Section 358(a)(1).[22]

---

[21]In this latter case, Section 358(a)(1) may not apply to the contribution to capital unless such a contribution is considered to involve a constructive issuance of the subsidiary's shares constituting a Section 351 exchange. See footnote 3.

[22]Even if a contribution to capital is not viewed as a constructive exchange subject to

This result appears erroneous, even if Section 351 were considered to "apply" to the transaction. This is because the substituted basis rule of Section 358(a)(1) is subject to an express exception found in Section 358(e), which provides:

"This section shall not apply to property acquired by a corporation by the issuance of its stock or securities as consideration in whole or in part for the transfer of the property to it."

Accordingly, the parent's basis for the subsidiary's stock cannot be a substituted basis under Section 358(a)(1) because that stock would constitute property acquired by the parent as consideration for the issuance of the parent's own stock.

Although Reg. Sec. 1.358-4 contains a cross-reference suggesting that the carryover basis rule of Section 362 might then be applicable, it would seem that Section 362 should not be used to determine the parent's basis for the subsidiary's stock inasmuch as that stock was not acquired by the parent as a contribution to *its* capital or from a person controlling the parent.[25]

2. *Fair Market Value.* — If neither Section 358(a)(1) nor Section 362(a) determines the basis of the subsidiary's stock in the hands of the parent (for the reasons set forth above), it would appear that the parent's basis for shares of the subsidiary's stock received in exchange for the parent's stock must be "cost," as required by the general rule of Section 1012. Under the long-standing interpretation of that rule, the "cost" to the parent for the subsidiary's shares would then be the fair market value of the parent's shares at the time when received by the subsidiary.

It is less clear how the parent's basis for the subsidiary's stock would be affected if no additional shares of the subsidiary's stock are received by the parent in exchange for the parent's shares. As an economic matter, the result should not turn upon whether additional shares of the subsidiary are received by the parent. The tax results should be uniform without regard to the mere formality of receipt by the parent of such additional shares. However, in view of the lack of clear authority in

---

Section 351, it might be argued that a contribution of the parent's shares to the subsidiary would not increase the parent's basis for the subsidiary's stock under Section 1016(a)(1) on the assumption that the parent had a zero basis for its own stock.

[25]If the parent were to transfer shares of its treasury stock to the subsidiary in exchange for stock of the subsidiary, it might be argued (a) that the parent's basis for the subsidiary's stock would then be determined under the substituted basis rule of Section 358(a)(1) (because there would be no "issuance" of the parent's stock to bring into play the exception to Section 358(a)(1) provided by Section 358(e)) and (b) that such basis would then be the cost of the parent's treasury stock in the hands of the parent.

Authority for this argument is furnished by Firestone Tire & Rubber Co. . . . , 2 TC 827 (1943). (Commissioner's appeal to CA-6 dismissed June 19, 1944), non-acq., 1944 CB 38, withdrawn by acq., 1945 CB 3, which held that there had been no "issuance" of stock, within the meaning of the statutory predecessor of Section 358(e), where treasury shares of the acquiring corporation were given by it in a "B" reorganization.

The Court's conclusion appears to have been dictated to some extent by the difference in tax consequences under the 1939 Code between a new issue and a transfer of treasury shares, the latter transaction resulting in recognition of gain or loss "if a corporation deals in its own shares as it might in the shares of another corporation." Reg. 118, Sec. 39.22(a)15.

The Service has taken a contrary view in a proposed amendment to Reg. Sec. 1.358-4 appearing in Vol. 33, No. 79, Federal Register 6163 (April 23, 1968), which states as follows: "The term 'issuance of stock or securities' includes any transfer of stock or securities, including stock or securities which were purchased or were acquired as a contribution to capital."

point,[27] it may be that uniform treatment can be achieved only by considering the subsidiary to have constructively issued additional shares of its stock to the parent in exchange for the contribution of the parent's shares to the capital of the subsidiary. This treatment would increase the parent's "cost" for the subsidiary's stock under the authorities cited in the preceding paragraph.

3. *Quasi-Treasury-Stock Theory.* — The tax results would be somewhat different under the "quasi-treasury-stock" theory (discussed above).

Since the "quasi-treasury-stock" approach assumes that the transaction between parent and subsidiary should not have any tax consequences until there is a disposition of the parent's stock to a third party outside the group, it can be argued that the parent's basis for the subsidiary's stock should be increased by the fair market value of the parent's stock at the time of such disposition.

This approach would present problems if the parent were to sell all or a portion of the subsidiary's stock to a third party before the subsidiary disposes of the parent's stock.[29]

4. *Carryover Basis.* — Where the parent transfers its stock to the subsidiary in exchange for shares of the subsidiary's stock, this transaction may meet all the literal requirements of a reorganization under Section 368(a)(1)(B). If these requirements are met, it can be argued that, under Section 362(b), the basis of the subsidiary's shares received by the parent is the same as the basis of those shares in the "hands" of the subsidiary immediately before their issuance or transfer to the parent.

This approach would raise several of the questions, discussed above, as to whether the subsidiary has any basis for shares of its own stock prior to their issuance or transfer to the parent. This basis, which would carry over to the parent under Section 362(b), could arguably be zero, cost (in the case of treasury shares) or fair market value.

This approach, that is, that the parent's issuance of voting stock to its wholly owned subsidiary in exchange for stock of the subsidiary constitutes a "B" reorganization, is open to the objection that the stock of the parent received by the subsidiary is not "voting stock." As noted above, in some jurisdictions such stock may not be voted while it is held by the subsidiary. In considering the term "voting stock" for the purpose of the reorganization provisions and the term "affiliated group" for the purpose of the Consolidated Return Regulations, the courts have held that stock which has conditional voting rights and is not entitled to vote generally as to the affairs of the corporation does not constitute "voting stock."

[27]Compare Edward Mallinckrodt, 38 BTA 960 (1938), with Greer v. Commissioner . . . , 230 F.2d 490 (CA-5). See Bittker & Eustice, Federal Income Taxation of Corporations and Shareholders, p. 111 (2d ed. 1966).

[29]If the parent were to sell all of the subsidiary's stock, it would seem that, if the subsidiary were capitalized with nothing but the parent's stock, the transaction should be treated as if the parent had sold its own stock, with the result that there would be no realization or recognition of gain by the parent. The result would be less clear in the case in which the parent sells only a portion of the subsidiary's stock, especially if the amount of the subsidiary's stock sold is so small that the parent retains "control" of the subsidiary. Problems of tracing, identification, and allocation of basis would arise where the subsidiary held assets other than the parent's stock.

Even if the transaction is viewed as a reorganization under Section 368(a)(1)(B), there is no statutory provision requiring a substituted basis for stock of the parent in the hands of the subsidiary. This is because the general substituted basis rule of Section 358(a)(1) is made inapplicable here by Section 358(e). Moreover, in the case where the parent transfers shares of its treasury stock, the parent might acquire a basis for the subsidiary's stock equal to the cost of the treasury stock in the hands of the parent, unless the rule of Firestone Tire & Rubber Co. is no longer good law.

D. Evaluation of Basis Theories

The foregoing analysis indicates that the law is unsettled as to the tax consequences in many cases where a subsidiary disposes of shares of its parent's stock previously acquired by the subsidiary in a separate transaction as a contribution to capital or in exchange for shares of the subsidiary's stock.

Despite the dearth of authority on the question, our Committee believes that the zero basis approach (that is, that the subsidiary has a zero basis for its parent's stock and that the parent is not entitled to reflect the transfer of its shares in computing its basis for stock of the subsidiary) is unsound on both technical and economic grounds. The gain which a zero basis would produce (when the parent's stock having a zero basis is later sold or exchanged by the subsidiary) is clearly fictitious in that it does not represent any genuine economic profit. Taxation of such a "gain" is improper because it is equivalent to taxation of a corporation on the proceeds received by it upon the issuance of its stock. Such proceeds properly represent the receipt of capital rather than profit or income.

This erroneous result cannot occur if the tax basis of the stock of parent and subsidiary in the hands of the other is fair market value at the time of receipt. Moreover, this interpretation appears technically sound in terms of the structure of the present tax statute. Thus, because the specific basis rules of both Section 358(a)(1) and Section 362(a) appear to be inapplicable, the basis of each corporation's stock held by the other should be governed by the general rule of Section 1012 that the basis of property is its "cost." The "cost" of property (including shares of another corporation) acquired by a corporation in exchange for its stock has long been held to be the fair market value of that stock at the time it is given for the property.

Although far preferable to the consequences of the zero basis theory, this result may not be completely satisfactory as a policy matter. This is because use of a cost basis reflecting fair market value at time of the subsidiary's receipt of the parent's stock will produce subsequent gain or loss to the extent of any fluctuation in the fair market value of the parent's stock during the period in which the subsidiary holds that stock. The latter gain or loss could be eliminated either by adoption of the "quasi-treasury-stock" approach or by amendment of Section 1032(a) to provide for non-recognition of all gains and losses realized by a subsidiary from sale or exchange of stock issued by its parent.[33]

The amendment would apply, not only to gains and losses of the type described

---

[33] Any such amendment of Sec. 1032(a) might well cover gains and losses realized by lower tier subsidiaries from the sale or exchange of stock of a grandparent corporation.

above, but also to gains and losses arising where a subsidiary purchases its parent's stock in the open market and later resells that stock for a higher or lower price. Accordingly, by extending Section 1032 to dealings in treasury stock conducted through a subsidiary or affiliated corporation, such an amendment would implement the present policy of Section 1032, which is to deny recognition of both gains and losses from dealings in treasury stock.

The suggested amendment of Section 1032 would also serve to obviate many of the issues discussed in this Report. Thus, the amendment would make it unnecessary to decide in each case whether the subsidiary's acquisition of its parent's stock was, in fact, part of a single transaction or plan contemplating the subsequent disposition of that stock, a question of crucial importance under the analysis set forth in Part II of this Report. Such an amendment would also make it unnecessary, in the absence of such a plan, to choose among the various legal theories, discussed in Part III of this Report, for determining the subsidiary's basis for shares of its parent's stock received from the parent as a contribution to capital or in exchange for the subsidiary's stock. Finally, the amendment would eliminate any possibility that the absence of a preconceived plan would permit recognition of loss to a subsidiary upon the sale or exchange of its parent's stock which the parent had previously purchased for a price above current market value and then transferred to the subsidiary as a contribution to capital.[34]

IV. APPLICATION OF TAX PRINCIPLES IN OTHER CONTEXTS

As noted at the outset of this Report, there are a variety of additional transactions in which a subsidiary corporation may transfer stock or securities of its parent. The principles underlying the recommendations made in Parts II and III may be helpful in clarifying the tax consequences of those transactions. Illustrations of the application of those principles to certain such transactions are set forth in this Part IV.

In the cases discussed below, the tax consequences to both parent and subsidiary will be found to turn on whether the subsidiary has (i) merely transitory ownership of the parent's shares or securities as part of a plan contemplating their later disposition by the subsidiary, or (ii) acquired genuine ownership of the parent's shares or securities in a separate transaction unrelated to the subsidiary's later disposition of those shares.

A. Effects Under Consolidated Return Regulations

Under the Consolidated Return Regulations, gain or loss recognized to a subsidiary upon the disposition of stock of its parent may affect both the taxable income of the affiliated group and the "earnings and profits" of the parent.

For example, if gain is recognized to a subsidiary upon transfer of its parent's stock to a third party outside the affiliated group, that gain will be included in the taxable income of the group. Reg. Sec. 1.1502-11(a); cf. Reg. Sec. 1.1502-12(a). In addition, such gain will increase the "earnings and profits" of the subsidiary. To the extent that this increase in "earnings and profits" is not distributed to the parent

[34]See discussion in Part IV of "Loss by Subsidiary on Sale of Parent's Treasury Stock."

as a dividend, it will increase the basis of the subsidiary's stock in the hands of the parent. Regs. Secs. 1.1502-32(b)(1)(i); 1.1502-32(e)(2).

In addition, by making certain elections, the increase in the "earnings and profits" of the subsidiary can be reflected in an equal increase in the "earnings and profits" of the parent. Regs. Secs. 1.1502-33(c)(4)(iii);[35] 1.1502-32(f)(2).

The result of these rules is that gain to the subsidiary may be reflected in the "earnings and profits" of the parent, even though no distribution is made by the subsidiary to the parent. The parent would thus be in virtually the same position as if *it* had issued or transferred its own stock directly for the asset and had been required to recognize gain contrary to the mandate of Section 1032.[36]

This anomalous result would be eliminated in the majority of cases by adoption of the recommendations made in Parts II and III of this Report.

B. Acquisitions by Foreign Subsidiaries

The principles set forth in this Report should also apply in determining the tax consequences of transactions where stock of a domestic parent corporation is used by a foreign subsidiary, that is, a subsidiary incorporated under the laws of a foreign country, under circumstances which do not receive "reorganization" treatment under Sections 367 and 368(a)(1). Thus, those principles should determine the tax effects of such transactions under Section 1491 and Subpart F, and should control the effect of such transactions on the "earnings and profits" of the foreign subsidiary.

Section 1491 imposes an excise tax of 27½ per cent on the "transfer" of stock by a domestic corporation to a foreign corporation "as paid-in surplus or as a contribution to capital." The tax is based on the excess, if any, of the value of the stock transferred over its adjusted basis in the hands of the domestic corporation. The tax can be averted under Section 1492 or 1494(b) by obtaining a ruling from the IRS that the transfer is not pursuant to "a plan having as one of its principal purposes the avoidance of Federal income taxes."

Our Committee is uncertain as to whether there can be a "transfer" of stock, within the meaning of Section 1491, where a foreign subsidiary acquires newly issued shares of its domestic parent's stock as a contribution to capital.[37] If "transfer" does not include "issuance," a further question arises as to transactions involving treasury shares. These uncertainties can be readily resolved in cases where the foreign subsidiary acquires the shares of the domestic parent pursuant to a plan whereby those shares are to be exchanged by the subsidiary. Under the approach recommended above, these steps should be treated as an acquisition of assets by the domestic parent

[35]However, the effect of these rules on groups which do *not* make the elections is presently indeterminate. Reg. Sec. 1.1502-33(c)(4)(ii).

[36]Similar results would follow where the subsidiary acquires the shares of its parent's stock by purchase for full value, either from the parent or from an unrelated third party, since such results depend solely upon whether gain is recognized to the subsidiary, regardless of how the parent's shares were acquired by the subsidiary.

[37]Although Section 1032 prevents recognition of gain or loss to the parent for income tax purposes, it presumably does not immunize the parent from the excise tax imposed by Sec. 1491.

followed by a contribution of the assets to the subsidiary. Accordingly, the foreign subsidiary would not be viewed as having acquired shares from its parent, thus obviating any question of liability for tax under Section 1491 in such cases.[39]

This approach will also determine whether gain is to be "recognized" to a foreign subsidiary upon its exchange of the parent's shares for assets. Although such a gain would seldom subject the foreign subsidiary to federal income tax, it could have important federal income tax consequences for the parent by generating both "Subpart F income"[40] and "earnings and profits" within the foreign subsidiary. Subpart F income might be taxed currently to the parent even though not actually distributed.[41] And an increase in "earnings and profits" could both (i) increase the amount taxable to the parent as a dividend upon a subsequent distribution, liquidation, or sale of stock,[42] and (ii) dilute the parent's credit for the subsidiary's foreign income taxes "deemed paid" by the parent.[43]

Under the recommended approach, however, the subsidiary would not be considered to have received its parent's stock in the many cases where the foreign subsidiary acquires only transitory ownership of the parent's stock under a plan contemplating that the subsidiary will exchange that stock for particular assets. Accordingly, in such cases, the subsidiary's exchange of the parent's stock for assets would generate neither "Subpart F income" nor additional "earnings and profits" within the subsidiary.

An important practical advantage of the use of that approach would be to reduce the number of private rulings which must be prepared by taxpayers and processed by the IRS.

C. Conversion of Debentures of Eurodollar Financing Subsidiary into Parent's Stock

Another illustration of the application of the foregoing analysis may occur in the case of Eurodollar financing arrangements. Typically, in these financings a convertible debenture of a domestic (or foreign) financing subsidiary is marketed abroad, the debentures being guaranteed by the domestic parent and convertible into the parent's stock. In some cases, upon conversion the parent itself is obligated to issue its stock directly to the holder, while in other cases the subsidiary is obligated to exchange stock of the parent with that obligation being guaranteed by the parent.

If the parent is obligated to issue its stock directly to the debenture holder on conversion, Section 1032 would prevent recognition of gain or loss to the parent. If, instead, the parent contributes stock to the subsidiary to enable the subsidiary to transfer the stock to a debenture holder who elects to convert, the tax consequences should be the same, under the approach suggested earlier in this Report.

---

[39]This analysis would not, of course, apply to those cases where there is no plan for the foreign subsidiary's subsequent disposition of the domestic parent's shares.

[40]"Subpart F income" includes "gain from the sale or exchange of stock or securities" by reason of Secs. 952, 954(c), and 553(a)(2).

[41]Sec. 951.

[42]Secs. 317 and 1248.

[43]Sec. 902.

D. Loss by Subsidiary on Sale of Parent's Treasury Stock

The recommendations made in Parts II and III of this Report may assist the IRS in giving effect to the policy of Section 1032 to prevent a corporation from recognizing a loss from the sale of its own treasury shares.[44]

This problem can be illustrated by the case of a corporation which holds treasury shares purchased by it at a price substantially above current fair market value. In an attempt to circumvent Section 1032, the corporation might transfer these high-basis treasury shares to a subsidiary as a capital contribution or in exchange for shares of the subsidiary, thus putting the subsidiary in a position to claim the parent's high basis for the treasury shares under the carry-over basis rule of Section 362(a). The subsidiary might then be able to recognize a capital loss by selling the treasury shares for their current value, since Section 1032 would not prevent the subsidiary from recognizing a loss on sale of stock of another corporation.

This obvious circumvention of Section 1032 could be prevented by applying the approach set forth above. Under that approach, no loss would be recognized to a subsidiary upon sale of shares of its parent's treasury stock transferred to the subsidiary under a plan contemplating that sale. The subsidiary would never have become the genuine owner of the shares, but would serve merely as a conduit to facilitate their sale by the parent, whose loss is disallowed by Section 1032. This analysis would harmonize with the concepts embodied in Sections 269 and 482, and particularly with decisions such as National Securities Corp. v. Commissioner.[45]

It is thus apparent that application of the principles set forth herein would serve, not only to prevent hardship to taxpayers, but also to protect the revenues.

E. Acquisition by Subsidiary in Consideration for Parent's Obligations

Much of the analysis set forth in Parts II and III of this Report is applicable where a subsidiary acquires assets from an unrelated third party who receives a bond, debenture, promissory note, or other evidence of indebtedness issued by the subsidiary's parent as part or all of the consideration for such assets.

In such cases, the parent should be treated as acquiring the assets from the third party and transferring them to the subsidiary, if the several steps are part of an overall plan or agreement under which the assets end up in the subsidiary and the parent's obligations end up in the hands of the third party. Where such a plan is found to exist, the tax consequence to both parent and subsidiary should not be affected by (a) whether the assets (i) move directly from their original owner to the subsidiary or (ii) move first to the parent, which then transfers them to the subsidiary, or (b) whether the parent's obligations (i) move directly from the parent to the owner of the assets or (ii) move first from the parent to the subsidiary, which then transfers them to the owner of the assets.

---

[44]Sec. 1032(a) provides: "No gain or loss shall be recognized to a corporation on the receipt of money or other property in exchange for stock (*including treasury stock*) of such corporation." (Italics added.)

[45]. . . 137 F.2d 600 (CA-3), cert. denied 370 U.S. 794 (1943).

The tax consequences may be different where the subsidiary has previously acquired its parent's obligations in a separate transaction unrelated to the subsidiary's use of those obligations to buy assets. Those tax consequences will ordinarily depend on (a) whether the subsidiary has acquired its parent's obligations for full value (given either to an unrelated third party or to the parent) or (b) whether those obligations were acquired from the parent for less than full value, that is, as a contribution to the subsidiary's capital or in exchange for shares of the subsidiary's stock. In case (b), questions will arise that are parallel to those, discussed in Part III of this Report, concerning (i) the subsidiary's tax basis for its parent's stock and (ii) the parent's tax basis for the subsidiary's stock.

It should be noted, however, that the tax effects of a subsidiary's use of its parent's obligations will differ in several important respects from the tax effects of a subsidiary's use of its parent's stock. Thus, the cost of assets acquired in exchange for stock is the fair market value of such stock at the time given in exchange for the assets. By contrast, the cost of assets acquired in exchange for obligations is the face amount — rather than the fair market value — of such obligations. Where the face amount of the obligations is greater than (or less than) the fair market value of such obligations, it becomes necessary to determine whether the difference between face amount and fair market value represents a discount (or premium), which would have tax consequences beyond the scope of this Report.

CONCLUSIONS

Our Committee submits that the foregoing analysis indicates the need for clarification of the federal income tax consequences of "non-reorganization" transactions in which a subsidiary sells or exchanges shares of its parent's stock.

In the great majority of transactions where the parent contributes its shares to the capital of the subsidiary, the subsidiary acquires only transitory ownership of its parent's stock pursuant to a plan contemplating the subsidiary's transfer of that stock to a third party, typically as part of the consideration for assets acquired by the subsidiary. The tax treament of these common transactions could readily be clarified by publications of a Revenue Ruling holding that the tax consequences to both parent and subsidiary will be the same as those which apply where the parent's shares are issued or transferred by the parent directly to the third party.

A major advantage of the suggested Revenue Ruling is that it would confine the difficult tax questions, discussed in Part III of this Report, to those relatively infrequent cases where a subsidiary has previously acquired shares of its parent's stock in a separate transaction that was not part of a plan for the subsidiary's disposition of that stock. Moreover, the suggested Revenue Ruling would furnish a useful precedent for analysis of related issues, as noted in Part IV of the Report.[47]

It is relatively rare for a parent to contribute shares of its stock to a subsidiary in

---

[47]Our Committee notes, however, that the approach recommended in Part II of this Report may not be appropriate where questions are presented which do not relate to the determination of gain or loss to a subsidiary or the basis of the subsidiary's stock in the hands of its parent. Our Committee feels that such situations should be dealt with on a case by case basis, with due regard for other relevant factors.

the absence of a plan for the subsidiary's disposition of that stock. Thus, the publication of the suggested Revenue Ruling would assure that questions will seldom arise as to whether the subsidiary or parent (or both) may be required to use a zero basis for the stock of the other.

In the few cases where such questions would still arise, our Committee believes that a zero basis approach should not be applied. The analysis herein indicates that the zero basis approach is not warranted by the statutory language and is also economically unsound because it would cause the eventual taxation of a "gain" representing paid-in capital rather than true profit.

NOTE

A number of bad puns press hard for recognition as one contemplates the confusion out of and into which the rules relating to fusion have evolved. It seems preferable to forego the puns for a few questions of policy which may evoke others:

". . . The reorganization rules provide for corporate continuity of basis even though a transferee corporation delivers boot in part payment for assets, provided that the transferor does what is necessary to avoid recognition under section 361(b)(1)(A). Is that the right approach, or would a step-up to the extent of the boot make sense? The reorganization rules exact a corporate tax as the price of a step-up, yet the combination of Sections 337 and 334(b)(2) makes it possible in the non-reorganization area to effect tax-free step-ups. Does it make sense . . . that these apparent inconsistencies in approach continue?

"Should a corporation's cash purchase of the assets used in business by another corporation ever be a taxable event to the seller and should it ever provide the buyer with a 'cost' basis? If so, why is a merger tax-free and why in mergers is basis continued despite the fact that, at a later date, a cash redemption of the shares held by the former shareholders of the transferor corporations will not generate a corporate tax or a step-up in basis? The difficulty in answering some of these questions suggests some of the difficulties with any corporate income tax . . . ." B. Wolfman, Book Review, 76 Yale L.J. 1036, 1045 (1967).

VI. CORPORATE FISSION — SPIN-OFFS AND OTHER CORPORATE PROLIFERATIONS

A. *INTRODUCTION AND HISTORY*

Lawyers have coined brief phrases to describe three of the most common types of corporate divisions — transactions in which some or all of the assets held by one corporation are transferred to one or more corporations, and some or all of the shareholders of the transferor become shareholders in the transferee:

Spin-off: Corporation A transfers some of its assets to Corporation B in exchange for all of the latter's authorized stock. Corporation A thereupon distributes a pro rata dividend to its shareholders consisting of the stock it receives in B. A's shareholders now own stock in both A and B. (In some cases a spin-off involves the pro rata distribution of the stock of an old subsidiary, one not formed or one who stock was not purchased as part of a plan that included distribution of the stock.)

Split-off: The transaction is very much the same as a spin-off, except that Corporation A distributes the B stock to its shareholders in redemption of a proportionate share of their stock in A. As with a spin-off, the shareholders of A now own stock in both A and B, but in the aggregate they own fewer shares (not a lower percentage) of the A stock.

Split-up: Corporation A transfers part of its assets to Corporation B in exchange for all of B's stock and transfers the remainder of its assets to Corporation C for all of its stock. A then liquidates, distributing the stock of B and C in retirement of its own outstanding stock. The shareholders now own stock in B and C in place of their stock in the defunct Corporation A.

The cases posed are prototypes, not exclusive. The principal tax issues are usually these: (1) recognition of income or loss to the shareholders on receipt of stock in the transferee corporations; (2) basis to the shareholders of the stock they receive; (3) recognition of gain or loss to the transferor corporation; and (4) basis of assets in the hands of the transferee corporations. Sections 355, 356(b) and 368(a)(1)(D) are the provisions primarily involved. Sections 351, 361 and 358 also play roles.

Gregory v. Helvering, 293 U.S. 465 (1935), page 471 supra, concerned a spin-off in which the taxpayer unsuccessfully claimed that the distribution of the transferee corporation's stock was tax-free under §112(g) of the Revenue Act of 1928 (the earliest version of the current §355(a)(1)) as part of a reorganization plan under §112(i)(1)(B) of that Act (an early version of the "D" reorganization). Why did Mrs. Gregory fail under the 1928 Act? Would she fail under current law?

In 1934 Congress repealed §112(g) of the 1928 Act as part of a legislative program to eliminate what it then thought were unwarranted tax avoidance devices. Tax-free spin-offs returned to the statute in 1951 as §112(b)(11) of the 1939 Code. With modification, the provision was continued in the 1954 Code as §355. Although earlier statutory versions required a "plan of reorganization," §355 does not. Frequently, however, a corporate division may be part of a "D" reorganization. When it is not (and even when it is), §351 may operate to avoid recognition to the transferor corporation. If there is a "D" reorganization, §361 will be operative, often along with §351.

B. *STATUTORY ISSUES*

1. *Purpose*

ESTATE OF PARSHELSKY v. COMMISSIONER
303 F.2d 14 (2d Cir. 1962)

Before LUMBARD, Chief Judge, and MEDINA and WATERMAN, Circuit Judges.

LUMBARD, Chief Judge. The principal question to be decided is whether the distribution by a corporation to its sole shareholder of the shares of a newly organized subsidiary constituted a taxable dividend under §[316(a)] . . . , or a tax-free-spin-off reorganization within §112(b)(11) of the Code, 26 U.S.C.A. §112(b)(11).[1] The Tax Court held that there was no business purpose for the exchange and thus the exchange was used principally as device for the distribution of earnings. 34 T.C. 946 (1960). We think that the Tax Court's inquiry into business purpose was too narrow since it evaluated only those reasons for the spin-off which benefited the corporation and ignored any valid shareholder non-tax-avoidance reasons which might be present. Consequently, we reverse and remand for further findings in accordance with the views expressed in this opinion.

I. Facts

Moses L. Parshelsky had been for many years, until his death, sole shareholder of Parshelsky Brothers, Inc., which operated a wholesale lumber and millwork business at Meserole Street and Morgan Avenue in Brooklyn, on property which it owned. This consisted of a one-story building with 50,000 to 60,000 square feet of floor area where the corporation stored all forms of wood trim for sale to local wholesalers and builders. Parshelsky was active in the management and conduct of the business and personally handled or supervised most of the office work.

During the Korean War inventory was difficult to procure and the unit volume of sales declined while costs increased. Due to these factors net income declined

---

[1] . . . §112(b)(11) *"Distribution of stock not in liquidation.* If there is distributed, in pursuance of a plan of reorganization, to a shareholder of a corporation which is a party to the reorganization, stock (other than preferred stock) in another corporation which is a party to the reorganization, without the surrender by such shareholder of stock, no gain to the dis- tributee from the receipt of such stock shall be recognized unless it appears that (A) any cor- poration which is a party to such reorganization was not intended to continue the active conduct of a trade or business after such reorganization, or (B) the corporation whose stock is distributed was used principally as a device for the distribution of earnings and profits to the shareholders of any corporation a party to the reorganization."

§112(g) *"Definition of reorganization.* As used in this section . . . (1) The term 'reorganiza- tion' means . . . (D) a transfer by a corporation of all or a part of its assets to another cor- poration if immediately after the transfer the transferor or its shareholders or both are in control of the corporation to which the assets are transferred . . . ."

The 1939 Code applies to this transaction since it took place before June 22, 1954. Internal Revenue Code of 1954, §§391, 393, 26 U.S.C.A. §§391, 393.

markedly. By the end of the Korean conflict, the warehouse was 40% empty, and Parshelsky engaged in some discussions relevant to renting space to outsiders.

The corporation had built up its liquid assets and was improving its net asset position. Total current assets, more than one-half of which were United States Treasury notes, remained at approximately $1,400,000 from 1950 to 1954 while current liabilities fell from $181,000 to $16,000. In each of these tax years the corporation paid a tax for unreasonably accumulating its earnings.[4] Parshelsky was advised by his attorney that, notwithstanding this surtax, his high personal tax rates made it advantageous not to distribute the corporate earnings.

Because of the decline in net profits and because in 1953 he was 79 years old, Parshelsky became concerned about the disposition of the business after his death. His will provided that certain of his key employees could purchase Parshelsky Brothers' inventory, fixtures, equipment, and customer lists at favorable prices and could use the real estate at a favorable rental. Although he hoped that his employees would carry on the business, he did not want his name to be connected with it.

After consultation with his attorney and his accountant Parshelsky caused a new corporation, Parshelsky Realties, Inc. (Realties), to be organized late in 1953. On January 4, 1954, Parshelsky Brothers transferred the real estate to Realties in exchange for all of the latter's capital stock which was immediately distributed to Parshelsky, the sole shareholder of Parshelsky Brothers. Simultaneously with the carrying out of this exchange, Realties leased the real estate back to Parshelsky Brothers for five years at an annual rental of $42,000 with an option to renew for an additional five years. The lease gave Parshelsky Brothers, the lessee, the right to sublease for its own account up to 50% of the floor space.

At trial Parshelsky's attorney testified that there were several reasons why Parshelsky did not want the real estate, worth $360,000, to remain in the Parshelsky Brothers' corporation. First, Parshelsky did not want the valuable real estate to remain subject to the hazards of the wholesale lumber and millwork business. Second, he wanted to put "the operating company [Parshelsky Brothers] in a position where it had a very much better chance of survival in operation when he relieved his employees who might take over the inventory of the problem of having to deal with the building." Third, he wanted his "successor in interest to continue to own and operate . . . this real estate regardless of whether Parshelsky Brothers survived, because he believed that it ought to be a very profitable thing." Finally, he wanted the real estate to be readily available to his executors as a separate asset of his estate.

Parshelsky retained all the stock in both Parshelsky Brothers and Realties until his death on March 13, 1955. In his will he made a number of specific bequests, most of which were to miscellaneous charities; he created a trust fund with a principal of $200,000 for the benefit of his only surviving relative, his brother Abraham, for life; and he left the residue of his estate and the remainder of his brother's trust fund to charity.

---

[4]Internal Revenue Code of 1939, §102, . . . (substantially similar to Internal Revenue Code of 1954, §§531-537) . . . .

The government did not claim that the spin-off decreased this tax. See Internal Revenue Code of 1954, §1551 . . . .

Parshelsky treated the receipt of Realties' stock as a tax-free corporate reorganization under 1939 Code §112(b)(11) and thus reported no income therefrom. The Commissioner, on the other hand, has taken the view that §112(b)(11) does not apply because of the absence of a "business purpose," has treated the distribution of the Realties stock as a $360,000 dividend, and thus has asserted a $311,637.89 deficiency against the Estate of Moses L. Parshelsky for the calendar year 1954. . . . [A] single judge of the Tax Court upheld the deficiency on the ground that since there was no corporate business purpose for the reorganization, the transaction was a device for the distribution of earnings and profits. 34 T.C. 946 (1960). The full Tax Court reviewed this decision without a dissent. The taxpayer appeals. . . .

We find that the distinction between corporate and shareholder benefit does not accord with the purpose of Congress in enacting §112(b)(11). We hold that while corporate benefit is relevant to the application of the tax-free spin-off provision, shareholders' personal non-tax-avoidance reasons must also be considered.

II. Corporate and Shareholder Business Purpose

Because the first provision for tax-free spin-offs did not contain restrictions like those of §112(b)(11)(A) and (B),[6] a literal reading of the statute made it subject to abuse. By having an existing corporation transfer liquid assets to a new corporation, the stock of which would then be distributed to the existing corporation's shareholders who would liquidate the new corporation, the assets when liquidated would be taxed at capital gains rather than dividend rates. In the case of Gregory v. Helvering, 203 U.S. 465, 55 S. Ct. 266, 79 L. Ed. 596 (1935), the Supreme Court held that such a scheme was not a tax-free spin-off. The *Gregory* case has been accepted as laying down a general principle of tax law, that in order to fit within a specified provision of the Internal Revenue Code a transaction must not only comply strictly with the explicit requirements of the section, but it must also have a "business purpose" that falls within the spirit of the section.[7]

Many of the earlier cases in applying the business-purpose test to reorganizations gave credence only to those non-tax-avoidance purposes which benefited the corpora-

---

[6]Revenue Act of 1924, §203(c).

For the history of tax-free spin-offs, see generally, Spangler v. Commissioner, 18 T.C. 976, 987 (1952); Mintz, Divisive Corporate Reorganizations, Split-Ups and Split-Offs, 6 Tax L. Rev. 365 (1951) . . . .

[7]. . . The taxpayer argued that the two specific provisos of §112(b)(11), the "active business" and the "device" restrictions, have occupied the field so that the "business-purpose" method of statutory interpretation does not apply. The legislative history of the 1951 Act makes it clear that Congress was very concerned with tax evasion schemes of the Gregory type when it enacted §112(b)(11). Representative Camp, the sponsor of the bill in the House, stated that if the bill was passed spin-offs would be "subject to the general limitations embodied in the *Gregory* case and subsequent decisions based thereon." 96 Cong. Rec., Part 14, 1980 (1950). Therefore, to the extent that §112(b)(11)'s two provisos are not as broad as the judicial safeguard of statutory interpretation, Congress did not intend to shackle the courts. See American Law Institute, Federal Income, Estate and Gift Tax Project, Income Tax Problems of Corporations and Shareholders 138 (October 31, 1958) (hereinafter cited as A.L.I. 1958 Tax Project); Bittker, [Federal Income Taxation of Corporations and Shareholders], at 399-400; Michaelson, ["Business Purpose" and Tax-Free Reorganization, 61 Yale L.J. 14], at 21 n.32. The courts have assumed that the "device" restriction requires inquiry into business purpose. See, e.g., Bondy v. Commissioner, 269 F.2d 463 (4 Cir. 1959).

tions involved. This required a separation of the corporate reasons for the reorganization from those of the shareholders. Most of the more recent cases have rejected this approach in favor of an evaluation of all the non-tax-avoidance motives of both the corporations and shareholders involved. However, the regulations apparently lend support to the so-called "corporate-benefit test." Regs. 118, §39.112(g)-2(g).*

The rationale for this distinction between corporate purposes and shareholder purposes is not explicitly elucidated in the cases which adopted it. Partly it may rest upon a misconception of the business-purpose test, that is, an assumption that the words "business purpose" have independent significance relating to the business of the corporation rather than merely being a shorthand expression for the *Gregory*-type statutory interpretation process. Partly, however, it probably rests upon an interpretation of early legislative history of the tax-free reorganization provisions. They were enacted because Congress thought it unwise to tax "purely paper transactions," S. Rept. No. 617, 65th Cong., 3d Sess. 5 (1918); accord, H.R. Rept. No. 1337, 83rd Cong., 2d Sess. 34 (1954), that are "merely changes in form and not in substance," H.R. Rept. No. 704, 73rd Cong., 2d Sess. 13 (1934); Statement of the Changes Made in the Revenue Act of 1921 by H.R. 6715 and the Reasons Therefor (1924) 10, 13 (Gregg Statement), and because Congress thought that normal business readjustments should not be impeded by the imposition of an income tax. See H.R. Rept. No. 179, 68th Cong., 1st Sess. 13 (1924); Sen. Rept. No. 398, 68th Cong., 1st Sess. 14-15 (1924); Statement of the Changes Made in the Revenue Act of 1921 by H.R. 6715 and the Reasons Therefor (1924) 6 (Gregg Statement). The latter statement is susceptible of the interpretation that corporate business reasons are necessary to the existence of the non-taxable reorganization. However, considered both in light of the later legislative history, and the situations in which spin-off reorganizations occur, these statements can be interpreted as admitting both corporate and shareholder non-tax-avoidance reasons.[11]

Congress enacted §112(b)(11) so that businesses could be broken up "into a greater number of enterprises when undertaken for legitimate business purposes." Sen. Rept. No. 781, 82nd Cong., 1st Sess. 58 (1951), U.S. Code Congressional and Administrative News 1951, pp. 1969, 2029. Shortly thereafter Congressional committees reported that the tax-free treatment for reorganizations was "to provide for nonrecognition of gain or loss in cases which involve a mere rearrangement of the corporate structure or other shifts in the form of the corporate enterprise which do not involve any distribution of corporate assets to shareholders." H.R. Rept. No. 1337, 83d Cong., 2d Sess. 34 (1954); accord, Sen. Rept. No. 1662, 83rd Cong., 2d Sess. 42 (1954), U.S. Code Congressional and Administrative News 1954, pp. 4025, 4629.

Furthermore, since most spin-offs, including the one involved in this case, concern closely-held corporations, it is not only difficult but often purely formalistic to distinguish between corporate and personal benefit. The separate legal entity of cor-

---

*Treas. Reg. §1.368-2(g) requires that the transaction "be undertaken for reasons germane to the continuance of the business of a corporation a party to the reorganization." Cf. Treas. Reg. §1.368-1(c). — ED.

[11]See A.L.I. 1958 Tax Project, supra note 7, at 137-39, 147-49; see also Surrey, Income Tax Problems of Corporations and Shareholders: American Law Institute Tax Project — American Bar Association Committee Study on Legislature Revision, 14 Tax L. Rev. 1, 12-13 (1958).

porations cannot obscure the fact that they are operated by their shareholders in the manner most likely to benefit themselves. Lewis v. Commissioner, 176 F.2d 646, 649 (1 Cir. 1949), aff'g 10 T.C. 1080, 1086 (1948); Bazley v. Commissioner, 155 F.2d 237, 245 (3 Cir. 1946) (dissent), aff'd 331 U.S. 737, 67 S. Ct. 1489, 91 L. Ed. 1782 (1947). The benefits to the corporation and to the shareholders are virtually indistinguishable. Consequently, the courts have uniformly held transactions such as reallocations of ownership interests between different groups of shareholders to be tax-free reorganizations. See e.g., Wolf Envelope Co. v. Commissioner, 17 T.C. 471 (1951), appeal dismissed, 197 F.2d 864 (6 Cir. 1952) . . . :

We find, therefore, that the Tax Court erred in this case when it examined only those reasons for the reorganization "relating to the business being carried on by the corporation, or relating otherwise to the corporation's organization or functioning" and refused to examine those "arising from and serving only the personal or noncorporate-business interests of the shareholders." 34 T.C. at 951. The Tax Court thought it to be the very antithesis of acceptable business purpose for the reorganization to deprive the corporation of such a valuable asset as the real estate upon which the business was being conducted, and to burden it with an annual rental charge of $42,000. However, all spin-offs necessarily leave the original corporation with less assets than they had to begin with.

III. Evaluation of the Spin-off's Corporate and Shareholder Reasons and Tax-Avoidance Probabilities

In enacting §112(b)(11) Congress meant to grant tax-free treatment to those spin-offs which were designed to serve valid non-tax-avoidance corporate or shareholder purposes but not to those which were effected for tax-avoidance. The principal likelihood of tax avoidance at the time of the spin-off was that Parshelsky might have transferred ordinary income into capital gain. Normally when a corporation distributes assets to its shareholders or sells the assets and distributes their proceeds, a dividend results and the shareholders pay ordinary income tax. However, if the corporation is permitted to transfer the assets to a new corporation and distribute the new corporation's stock to its shareholders in a tax-free spin-off, the shareholders could completely liquidate the new corporation or sell its stock, thus realizing capital gain rather than ordinary income. Because of these tax-avoidance possibilities, Congress intended to limit tax exemption to those spin-offs where the taxpayer had corporate or shareholder purposes such as would motivate a reasonable businessman to effect a spin-off. Therefore, the court must first ascertain the taxpayer's corporate and shareholder purposes and then evaluate their validity on such an objective basis.

Parshelsky's executors argue that one reason for the spin-off was to remove the valuable real estate from the hazards of the declining wholesale business. However, after the reorganization Parshelsky Brothers retained in excess of $750,000 in Treasury notes and cash, and the corporation's current liabilities had declined to approximately $16,000. In short, these facts lend little support to this argument of the executors. Moreover, the real estate could have been safeguarded from the creditors of the wholesale business merely by having Parshelsky Brothers transfer the wholesale business to a subsidiary corporation and retain the real estate. In light of the tax-avoidance possibilities which a spin-off often provides, there must be non-tax reasons not only for the separation of the two businesses but also for direct ownership of both by the shareholders. The fact that creation of a subsidiary corporation would necessarily bring with it either the intercorporate dividend tax or the additional tax on corporations filing a consolidated return is not by itself sufficient to justify split ownership at the shareholder level.

A second reason advanced by the executors is that the employees who might take over the wholesale business after Parshelsky's death would not have to deal with the real estate and thus would have a better chance of survival. This might be true if employees who were to buy the stock of a corporation could not afford to pay for real estate as well as operating assets, as was the situation in Wilkins v. United States, 188 F. Supp. 91 (S.D. Ill. 1960). However, in this case the plan specifically elucidated in Parshelsky's will was to sell certain assets to the employees but not to sell the stock, because Parshelsky did not want the name Parshelsky Brothers, Inc., to be carried on. Therefore, the purpose of permitting the employees to purchase the operating assets while leasing the real estate could have been accomplished by leaving all the assets in Parshelsky Brothers and permitting that corporation to act as lessor to the employees. In fact, that is the plan originally envisaged by Parshelsky's will drawn nearly three years before the spin-off was effected.

The validity of the third reason, that Parshelsky wanted his successors to continue to own the real estate regardless of the fate of the wholesale business because he considered it a good investment, is minimized by the fact that Parshelsky Brothers could have retained both the real estate and the wholesale business, selling or liquidating the latter if it proved unsuccessful.

The final reason, that Parshelsky wanted the real estate to be readily available to his executors as a separate asset of his estate, has more weight. Parshelsky left his residuary estate to the Moses L. Parshelsky Foundation, a charitable institution, which would channel the assets to various charities. To the extent that Parshelsky wanted the real estate and operating business to go to different legatees, his aim appears to be within the legislative purpose of the spin-off provision.[19] In order to carry out this non-tax-avoidance purpose the ownership of the real estate and operating assets would have to be separated at the shareholder level.

The court must determine whether, in light of all the facts, this transaction falls within Congress' purpose in enacting §112(b)(11), i.e., to grant tax-free treatment to those spin-offs the principal purpose of which was to effectuate valid corporate or shareholder non-tax-avoidance purposes but not to those the principal purpose of which was tax-avoidance.[20] Since the Tax Court held that shareholder non-tax-avoid-

---

[19]If the stock in the single pre-spin-off corporation had been left to two legatees, they could accomplish the same result by separating the real estate and operating businesses into two corporations, each legatee taking one corporation tax free. . . .

[20]Although many opinions, including this court's and the Supreme Court's *Gregory* opinions purport to ignore any tax-avoidance motives, it is evident that they did take cognizance of them in evaluating the validity of the taxpayer's asserted "business purpose." See Rice, [Judicial Techniques in Combatting Tax Avoidance, 51 Mich. L. Rev. 1021], at 1033-38; Spear,

ance purposes could not be considered in determining whether a spin-off was within §112(b)(11), it failed to evaluate all the relevant facts. We believe that such examination of the shareholders' reasons and the evaluation of their validity is the duty of the fact-finder. Such evaluation "must be based ultimately on the application of the fact-finding tribunal's experience with the mainsprings of human conduct to the totality of the facts of each case. The nontechnical nature of . . . [this examination], the close relationship of it to the data of practical human experience, and the multiplicity of relevant factual elements, with their various combinations, creating the necessity of ascribing the proper force to each, confirm us in our conclusion that primary weight in this area must be given to the conclusions of the trier of fact." Commissioner v. Duberstein, 363 U.S. 278, 80 S. Ct. 1190, 4 L. Ed. 2d 1218 (1960). Therefore, we remand to the Tax Court.

IV. Active Business Requirement

Although the Commissioner conceded that the transaction met all "the requirements for a non-taxable reorganization except for the absence of a valid business purpose under the rule of Gregory v. Helvering," 34 T.C. at 950, the Tax Court appeared to place some reliance upon its finding that Realties "was not intended to engage in the active conduct of any separate related business such as in the example given in the Commissioner's regulations." 34 T.C. at 953. This finding apparently refers to §112(b)(11)(A) which requires that each corporate party to the reorganization was intended to continue "the active conduct of a trade or business after such reorganization." We think that on remand the Tax Court should reconsider this finding.

Probably the Tax Court's view of what constitutes an active business for §112 (b)(11) is colored by the successor provision, §355 of the Internal Revenue Code of 1954, 26 U.S.C.A. §355. The regulations under §355, provide that the active conduct of a trade or business does not include "the ownership and operation of land or buildings all or substantially all of which are used and occupied by the owner in the operation of a trade or business." Treas. Reg. 1.355-1(c)(2); see also Treas. Reg. 1.355-1(d)(2). However, §355 of the 1954 Code departs radically from §112(b)(11) of the 1939 Code in many respects. That they may use the term "active conduct of a trade or business" with different shades of emphasis is clear beyond challenge. The regulations under §112(b)(11) do not include the limitations of the §355 regulations. See Treas. Reg. 118, §39.112(b)(11). It is clear that acting as lessor of real property which is rented to others can constitute a trade or business. E.g., Pinchot v. Commissioner, 113 F.2d 718 (2 Cir. 1940); Gilford v. Commissioner, 201 F.2d 735 (2 Cir. 1953); Lagriede v. Commissioner, 23 T.C. 508 (1954); Elek v. Commissioner, 30 T.C. 731 (1958). Absent the limitations of the §355 regulations, acting as lessor to a related corporation can also constitute an active trade or business within the meaning of §112(b)(11). See Wilkins v. United States, 188 F. Supp. 91 (S.D. Ill. 1960); Bondy v. Commissioner, 269 F.2d 463, 465 (4 Cir. 1959). . . .

["Corporate Business Purpose" in Reorganization, 3 Tax L. Rev. 225 (1947)], Bittker, [Federal Income Taxation of Corporations and Shareholders], at 15. . . .

The decision of the Tax Court is reversed and remanded for further proceedings not inconsistent with this opinion.

PARSHELSKY v. COMMISSIONER
22 CCH Tax Ct. Mem. 911 (1963)

Memorandum Findings of Fact and Opinion

OPPER, Judge: This case is before us on mandate from the United States Court of Appeals for the Second Circuit . . . .

The case was remanded to us for an "examination of the shareholders' reasons and the evaluation of their validity" (p. 21). . . .

Decedent wanted the real estate left so that it would be readily available to his executors as a separate asset for the ultimate benefit of his previously-created charitable foundation.

Decedent's action in removing the real estate from Brothers was intended to and did put Schwartz and other employees on notice that if they continued the occupancy of the premises they would be required to meet the rental obligations of such lease. Meanwhile, Realties, under the direction of decedent, Baker, and Bachrach, had taken over from Brothers all power to control and manage the property covered by the lease.

Decedent wanted to be in the position where he or his successors could make a move with respect to the operating business, which was growing less profitable, that would not interfere with continued ownership of the real estate property.

During the period that decedent was contemplating transfer of the real estate from Brothers to Realties (October-December 1953), there was no discussion with respect to the possible tax consequences that might result from such transfer. Nor was there any discussion with respect to avoiding tax on account of unreasonable accumulation of surplus under section [531]. . . .

Organization of Realties, the transfer thereto of the real estate formerly owned by Brothers, and distribution to decedent of Realties' stock served a legitimate personal business purpose of decedent connected with the administration, conservation, and ultimate disposition of his estate. Decedent had non-tax-avoidance reasons for the "spin-off" reorganization. . . .

Decision will be entered under Rule 50.

NOTE

Does *Parshelsky* require a reason not only for the segregation of assets but also for the distribution of corporate control of these assets to the shareholders? Cf. *Gregory* (page 471 supra).

In view of the outer parenthetical in §355(a)(1)(B), what circumstances might demonstrate that the transaction was used as a device for the siphoning of earnings and profits? What do you think led to the outer and inner parentheticals? Treas. Reg. §1.355-1(b)(1) provides that the post-distribution sale, though not negotiated or agreed upon before the distribution, "will be evidence that the transaction was used principally as . . . a device" to siphon earnings and profits. Is that a proper interpretation of the statute? Why?

2. *"Active Conduct of a Trade or Business"*

ELLIOTT v. COMMISSIONER
32 T.C. 283 (1959)

DRENNEN, Judge: . . . The only issue for determination is whether the distribution of all the stock of Centrifix Management Corporation, a wholly owned subsidiary, hereinafter referred to as Management, by Centrifix Corporation, hereinafter referred to as Centrifix, to Randall T. Elliott, the principal stockholder of Centrifix, on December 15, 1954, was taxable as a long-term capital gain to Elliott or qualified as a nontaxable "split-off" under section 355, I.R.C. 1954.

Findings of Fact

. . . At all times material hereto, Centrifix was an Ohio corporation formed in 1926. . . . Centrifix was organized to engineer and develop apparatus for the purification and separation of liquids and gases, and at all times material hereto was engaged in said business.

Management was incorporated under the laws of Ohio on April 22, 1950, as a wholly owned subsidiary corporation of Centrifix. At all times material hereto it had authorized capital of 150 shares of no-par common stock having a stated value of $100 per share.

In 1946, Centrifix acquired property at 3029 Prospect Avenue, Cleveland, Ohio, consisting of an old 2-story house with caretakers quarters and a carriage house in the rear. Centrifix occupied approximately one-half of the available space in the house and carriage house as an office and shop for its engineering business and made available for rent to various tenants the balance of the property. Centrifix continued to use part of this property in its business and rented the balance of the property until it was sold in 1950.

In 1950, Centrifix sold the property at 3029 Prospect Avenue and acquired property at 3608 Payne Avenue, Cleveland, Ohio. When the new property on Payne Avenue was acquired, it was transferred to Management in exchange for all of the stock of Management in a transaction that was tax free under section [351]. . . .

During the period from April 27, 1950, to December 15, 1954, Management owned and operated the Payne Avenue property. The property consisted of land and a 3-story brick loft building having a total area of 28,144 square feet, of which Centrifix leased 14,468 square feet, Tetrad Company, unrelated, leased approximately 5,200 square feet, and the balance was unoccupied but was available for rental to third parties.

On December 15, 1954, Randall T. Elliott surrendered to Centrifix the 1,852¾ shares of cumulative preferred stock of Centrifix which he owned, in exchange for which Centrifix transferred to Elliott 150 shares being all of the authorized common stock of Management, and canceled an indebtedness of $5,241.48 which had been owing from Elliott to Centrifix. No other consideration was involved in this transaction. . . . At the same time Elliott agreed to the cancellation of cumulative past-due dividends on the preferred stock in the amount of $242,894.75.

On December 15, 1954, the 150 shares of no-par-value common stock of Management distributed in the above transaction to Elliott had a fair market value of $78,837.34, and the adjusted basis of 1,852¾ shares of Centrifix cumulative preferred stock in the hands of Elliott was $750. . . . As of December 15, 1954, and December 31, 1954, Centrifix had no accumulated earnings and profits.

In their 1954 return, petitioners reported no gain or loss on the above transaction.

During that part of the year 1946 after Centrifix acquired the Prospect Avenue property, and through that part of the year 1950, prior to the time said property was sold, Centrifix realized gross rental income from the Prospect Avenue property, gross income from all sources, net income from all sources, and reported net taxable income for each of the years 1946 through 1950 as follows:

Period covered	Gross rental income	Gross income[1]	Net income[1]	Net taxable income
1946	$380.90	$150.120.18	$ 2,461.26	($ 707.39)
1947	591.00	253,193.64	20,927.09	24,609.37
1948	780.00	238,280.53	13,516.60	17,424.16
1949	780.00	243,344.39	16,765.13	20,152.71
1950[2]	325.00	324,253.26	19,932.20	26,176.20

[1]All sources.
[2]5 months.

The gross rental value of the entire Prospect Avenue property would have been between $1,700 and $1,800 per year during the period it was owned by Centrifix, if rented on a commercial basis. Centrifix made no allocation of expenses in connection with the Prospect Avenue property and it could not be determined from its books whether the rental portion of the property produced a net income or a net loss.

During the period April 22, 1950, to December 31, 1954, Management realized gross rental income and net income as follows:

Period covered	Gross rental income	Net income
1950	$ 7,257.17	$ 484.37
1951	14,682.44	1,884.79
1952	17,080.00	1,840.43
1953	19,292.00	3,034.64
1954	19,179.00[1]	3,757.60
	32.50[2]	

[1]Not including $217.47 from other sources.
[2]Discount earned.

Opinion

. . . The only issue is whether the distribution by Centrifix of all the stock of its wholly owned subsidiary, Management, to its principal stockholder, Elliott, qualifies as a nontaxable distribution under section 355, I.R.C. 1954. . . .

. . . Respondent agreed in the opening statement of his counsel that the transaction was not used principally as a distribution of earnings and profits of either corporation. Both parties are in agreement that all requirements of section 355(a) are satisfied, except the requirement of subsection (b) relating to the active conduct of businesses.

Respondent does not question the fact that Management had been engaged in the real estate rental business from the date the Payne Avenue property was conveyed to it in April of 1950 to the date of distribution of its stock to Elliott on December 15, 1954, a period of less than 5 years, but does contend that such business had not been actively conducted by either Centrifix or Management prior to April of 1950, so that the 5-year active conduct of business requirement of subsection (b) was not satisfied. Respondent, therefore, determined that the distribution, to the extent that it exceeded basis, was taxable to Elliott as a capital gain, Centrifix having had no earnings or profits at the time of the distribution.

Petitioners contend that all the requirements of subsection (b), including the 5-year active conduct of the real estate rental business, were satisfied. So we are concerned only with whether the requirements of subsection (b) relating to active conduct of businesses are satisfied.

Subsection (b) of section 355 subjects the nonrecognition of gain or loss to a shareholder provided in subsection (a) to certain conditions. One of those conditions is that the distributing corporation and the controlled corporation are engaged immediately after the distribution in the active conduct of a trade or business. A corporation may be regarded as engaged in the active conduct of a trade or business only if, inter alia, "such trade or business has been actively conducted throughout the 5-year period ending on the date of the distribution." See sec. 355(b)(2)(B). Respondent concedes that Management was engaged in the real estate rental business immediately after the distribution, but argues that it was not actively engaged in that business for a total of 5 years prior to the distribution.

Management was not incorporated until April 22, 1950. The Payne Avenue property was acquired by Centrifix at some time during 1950 and was transferred to Management in exchange for its stock. This stock was distributed to Elliott on December 15, 1954. Obviously, Management did not actively conduct and could not have actively conducted any business for 5 years prior to the distribution since it had been in existence for less than 5 years prior to December 15, 1954. Thus, the 5-year requirement of section 355(b)(2)(B) is not satisfied by the activities of Management alone, and cannot be satisfied under any circumstances in this case unless Centrifix actively conducted the same business for a period of at least 4½ months prior to the transfer of the Payne Avenue property to Management, and unless such a period of operation by Centrifix can be added to the period that Management conducted the business in order to satisfy the above requirement. We will assume for the purpose of further discussion that two such periods may be added together.

The issue then becomes whether Centrifix actively conducted a real estate rental business within the meaning of section 355(b) for a period of time prior to the formation of Management in 1950.

. . . Centrifix purchased an old house with a carriage house in the rear located on Prospect Avenue in Cleveland, Ohio, in 1946. Centrifix occupied about half the space in this property as its office and shop and rented the balance of the property to various tenants from the time it was acquired until it was sold in 1950. The gross rentals received did not exceed $780 per year in any of these years, which sum represented about 40 per cent of the rental value of the entire property, based on an 8 per cent gross return on the cost of the property. No allocation was made on the books of the company of that portion of the expenses attributable to the rented portion of the property, and there is no evidence with respect to the net income or loss attributable to that portion of the property.

. . . The gross rental income represented a very small part of the total gross income of Centrifix. There is no evidence of any specific activity on the part of the management of Centrifix in renting this property and no evidence that Centrifix ever engaged in any other real estate rental activities.

When the Prospect Avenue property was sold in 1950 and the new Payne Avenue property acquired, the new property was put in the name of the newly formed subsidiary corporation, Management, which thereafter leased about one-half of the new property to Centrifix, and the balance to other tenants. Management did not engage in any other business activities and Centrifix continued in the engineering business.

On this evidence we are not convinced that prior to 1950 Centrifix could be considered to have been actively conducting the same business subsequently conducted by Management within the meaning of section 355(b). What constitutes a trade or business is not defined in section 355 or anywhere else in the Internal Revenue Code. This Court held in John D. Fackler, 45 B.T.A. 708 (1941), affd. 133 F.2d 509 (C.A. 6), that where the owner of depreciable property devotes it to rental purposes and exclusively to the production of taxable income, the property is used by him in a trade or business and depreciation is allowable thereon. Since the *Fackler* case, we have also held that a single piece of rental property constitutes property used in a trade or business so as to be excluded from the definition of "capital assets" regardless of whether taxpayer was engaged in any other trade or business, Leland Hazard, 7 T.C. 372 (1946), and in Anders I. Lagreide, 23 T.C. 508 (1954), that real estate devoted to rental purposes constitutes use of the property in trade or business for purposes of determining operating loss carrybacks regardless of whether it is the only property so used, without too much inquiry into the activity of the taxpayer in renting and managing the property. . . . However, the *Fackler, Hazard,* and *Lagreide* cases are not authority for holding that the incidental rental of that portion of real estate used in a trade or business which is not needed for the principal business constitutes the active conduct of a rental business within the meaning of section 355(b). . . . By this we do not mean to imply that rental of a substantial part of property occupied in part by the owner for the conduct of its principal business cannot qualify as the active conduct of a trade or business within the meaning of section 355(b). But in section

355, we are concerned with the *active conduct of a trade or business,* and we must examine that phraseology in the light of the purpose for which it is used in this particular section of the Code. Bazley v. Commissioner, 331 U.S. 737, 740.

This provision was a part of section 353 of the Revenue Act of 1954 as originally introduced in the House of Representatives (H.R. 8300, 83d Cong., 2d Sess.). That section had no requirement relative to the active conduct of a trade or business either before or after the distribution. The Senate Finance Committee rewrote this provision as section 355 of its version of the bill, to introduce the requirement of active conduct of a trade or business both before and after the distribution, the stated purpose for the 5-year predistribution active conduct of a trade or business requirement being to provide a safeguard against avoidance not contained in the present law. See S. Rept. No. 1622, 83d Cong., 2d Sess., p. 50. The Senate thereby chose the 5-year active conduct of a trade or business limitation as one method of safeguarding against tax avoidance rather than a 10-year post-distribution penalty provision contained in the House version of the bill. The House accepted the Senate version but with the understanding that a trade or business which had been actively conducted throughout the 5-year period described would meet the requirements even though such trade or business underwent change during the 5-year period, such as an addition of new or the dropping of old products, changes in production capacity, and the like, provided the changes were not of such a character as to constitute the acquisition of a new or different business. See H. Rept. No. 2543, 83d Cong., 2d Sess., pp. 37-38.

This requirement in section 355(b) therefore necessitates an examination of the activities of the parent and subsidiary corporations in each of the two or more businesses conducted to determine whether this requirement is satisfied in each individual case. We do not think a mere passive receipt of income from the use of property which is used in the principal trade or business and which is only incidental to, or an incidental use of a part of property used primarily in, the principal business would constitute the active conduct of a trade or business within the meaning of section 355(b) of the Code, whether or not such use of property might constitute a trade or business within the meaning of other sections of the Code.

The Commissioner of Internal Revenue has defined a trade or business for purposes of section 355, in section 1.355-1(c), Income Tax Regs., as consisting of a "specific existing group of activities being carried on for the purpose of earning income or profit from only such group of activities, and the activities included in such group must include every operation which forms a part of, or a step in, the process of earning income or profit from such group. Such group of activities ordinarily must include the collection of income and payment of expenses." . . .

In this case the evidence does not support a conclusion that Centrifix was ever actively conducting a real estate rental business within the meaning of section 355, I.R.C. 1954. . . .

Why Centrifix did not hold the stock of Management for 4 or 5 additional months to complete the 5-year period prior to distributing Management's stock is not our concern. The fact is that Management had not been actively conducting its trade or business for a period of 5 years at the time of distribution, and we cannot find that Centrifix was actively conducting the same business within the meaning of section 355 prior to the formation of Management. The transaction therefore failed to qualify as a tax-free distribution under section 355, and the distribution was taxable as determined by respondent. . . .

Decision will be entered for the respondent.

NOTE

Would the House proposal in 1954 (page 597 supra) have been a better approach to permitting business readjustments on a tax-free basis while taxing bail-outs? Why? Note the attempt in Treas. Reg. §1.355-4 to give content and some measure of certainty to the phrase "active conduct of a trade or business." Would the House's idea of a bail-out period have been preferable? Do the Regulations under §355 provide standards adequate to the Congressional objectives referred to by the Second Circuit in *Parshelsky?*

In 1968 X incorporates Y Corporation to conduct his wholesale and his retail plumbing fixture businesses which he has conducted as an individual since 1960. He soon finds it impracticable to run both businesses under one corporate roof. Must he wait five years from incorporation to spin off one of the businesses on a tax-free basis? Why? See §355(b)(2)(C).

In W. E. Gabriel Fabrication Co., 42 T.C. 545 (1964), the taxpayer and his brother, owners of 70 per cent of A Corporation, had a falling out and wanted to separate business interests without waiting the 14 months necessary for the expiration of five years. Corporation A therefore "loaned" taxpayer the assets which, 14 months later, were transferred to a new subsidiary and split off to taxpayer. The Tax Court held the distribution tax-free under §355, and the Commissioner has acquiesced (1965-2 Cum. Bull. 5).

How are earnings and profits to be allocated between distributing and controlled corporation in a tax-free corporate division under §355? See §312(i) and Treas. Reg. §1.312-10.

COADY v. COMMISSIONER
33 T.C. 771 (1960), aff'd per curiam, 289 F.2d 490 (6th Cir. 1961)

Opinion

TIETJENS, Judge: . . . The issue for decision is whether the transfer by the Christopher Construction Company of a portion of its assets to E. P. Coady and Co. in exchange for all of the Coady Company's stock, and the subsequent distribution by the Christopher Company of such Coady stock to petitioner in exchange for his Christopher stock, constituted a distribution of stock qualifying for tax-free treatment on the shareholder level under the provisions of section 355 of the 1954 Internal Revenue Code. . . .

Christopher Construction Co., an Ohio corporation, is now engaged, and for more than 5 years prior to November 15, 1954, was engaged, in the active conduct of a construction business primarily in and around Columbus, Ohio. In an average year the Christopher Company undertook approximately 6 construction contracts, no one of which lasted for more than 2 years. Its gross receipts varied between $1,500,000 and $2,000,000 per year.

At its central office, located at 16 East Broad Street in Columbus, the Christopher Company kept its books of account, paid its employees, prepared bids for its jobs, and, excepting minor amounts of tools and supplies, made its purchases. In addition, it maintained temporary field offices at each jobsite. It also maintained a central repair and storage depot for its equipment. Equipment in use on particular jobs was kept at the jobsite until work was terminated. Then, it would either be returned to the central depot or moved to another jobsite.

At all times material hereto, the stock of the Christopher Company was owned by M. Christopher and the petitioner. For a number of years, petitioner owned 35 per cent of that stock and Christopher owned 65 per cent. However, on April 19, 1954, petitioner purchased 15 per cent of the total stock from Christopher. From that date until November 15, 1954, each owned 50 per cent of the company's stock.

Sometime prior to November 15, 1954, differences arose between the petitioner and Christopher. As a result, they entered into an agreement for the division of the Christopher Company into two separate enterprises. Pursuant to that agreement, the Christopher Company, on November 15, 1954, organized E. P. Coady and Co., to which it transferred the following assets, approximating one half the Christopher Company's total assets:

A contract for the construction of a sewage disposal plant at Columbus, Ohio, dated June 1, 1954.
A part of its equipment.
A part of its cash, and certain other items.

In consideration for the receipt of these assets, E. P. Coady and Co. transferred all of its stock to the Christopher Company. The Christopher Company retained the following assets, which were of the same type as those transferred to E. P. Coady and Co.:

A contract for a sewage treatment plant in Charleston, West Virginia.
A part of its equipment.
A part of its cash.

Immediately thereafter, the Christopher Company distributed to the petitioner all of the stock of E. P. Coady and Co. held by it in exchange for all of the stock of the Christopher Company held by petitioner. The fair market value of the stock of E. P. Coady and Co. received by petitioner was $140,000. His basis in the Christopher Company stock surrendered was $72,500.

Since the distribution, both E. P. Coady and Co. and the Christopher Company have been actively engaged in the construction business.

On their 1954 Federal income tax return, petitioner and his wife reported no gain or loss on the exchange of the Christopher Company stock for the stock of E. P. Coady and Co.

Respondent determined that petitioner realized a capital gain on that exchange in the amount of $67,500, 50 per cent of which was taxable in 1954.

Petitioner contends that the distribution to him of the E. P. Coady and Co. stock qualified for tax-free treatment under the provisions of section 355 of the 1954 Code, arguing that it was received pursuant to a distribution of a controlled corporation's stock within the meaning of that section.

Respondent on the other hand maintains petitioner's receipt of the Coady stock did not fall within those distributions favored by section 355, inasmuch as the 5-year active business requirements of 355(b) were not met. More particularly he argues that section 355 does not apply to the separation of a "single business"; and, inasmuch as the Christopher Company was engaged in only one trade or business (construction contracting), the gain realized by petitioner upon receipt of the Coady stock was taxable. As authority for his position respondent points to [Treas. Reg. §1.355-1(a)] . . . which expressly provides that section 355 does not apply to the division of a single business.

Conceding that the Christopher Company was engaged in a "single business" immediately prior to the instant transaction, petitioner contends that the regulations, insofar as they limit the applicability of section 355 to divisions of only those corporations which have conducted two or more separate and distinct businesses for a 5-year period, are without support in the law, are without justification, are unreasonable and arbitrary, and therefore are invalid.

Thus, the issue is narrowed to the question of whether the challenged portion of the regulations constitutes a valid construction of the statute, or whether it is unreasonable and plainly inconsistent therewith. Though this appears to be a case of first impression, the question has not gone without comment.[3]

Section 355 of the 1954 Code represents the latest of a series of legislative enactments designed to deal with the tax effect upon shareholders of various corporate separations. Where the 1939 Code contained three sections, 112(b)(3), 112(b)(11), and 112(g)(1)(D), which controlled the tax impact of these exchanges, present law groups the statutory requirements into two sections, 355 and 368(c). A careful reading of section 355, as well as the Finance Committee report[4] which accompanied its enactment, reveals no language, express or implied, denying tax-free treatment at the shareholder level to a transaction, otherwise qualifying under section 355, on the grounds that it represents the division or separation of a "single" trade or business.

In general, section 355(a) prescribes the form in which a qualifying transaction must be cast, providing that a divisive distribution will not give rise to taxable gain or loss if: (1) The distributing corporation distributes stock or securities of a corporation of which it has, immediately prior to the distribution, 80 per cent control as

---

[3]See: Young, "Corporate Separations: Some Revenue Rulings Under Section 355," 71 Harv. L. Rev. 843, 850-853 (1958); Mintz, "Corporate Separations," 36 Taxes 882, 885-886 (1958); Brodsky, "Corporate Separations," N.Y.U. 16th Inst. on Fed. Tax. 393, 397-403 (1958); Note, "Divisive Reorganizations," 67 Yale L.J. 38, 44-50 (1957); Dean, "Spin-Offs," N.Y.U. 15th Inst. on Fed. Tax. 571, 576-578 (1957); Lyons, "Some Problems in Corporate Separations Under the 1954 Code," 12 Tax L. Rev. 15 (1957); Friedman, "Divisive Corporate Reorganizations Under the 1954 Code," 10 Tax L. Rev. 487, 493 (1955).

[4]S. Rept. No. 1622, 83d Cong., 2d Sess. (1954), pp. 50-51.

defined in section 368(c); (2) the distribution is not principally a device for distributing earnings and profits of either the distributing or controlled corporations; (3) the 5-year active business requirements of 355(b) are satisfied; and (4) the distributing corporation distributes either all its stock and securities in the controlled corporation, or so much thereof as constitutes control, as defined in 368(c), and retention of the balance is shown not to be in pursuance of a plan having as one of its principal purposes tax avoidance. The distribution itself must be either to a shareholder with respect to its stock, or a security holder with respect to its securities. With respect to a distribution of stock, the distribution need not be on a pro rata basis; the shareholder need not surrender stock in the distributing corporation; and the distribution need not have been made in pursuance of a plan of reorganization. However, subsection (a) contains no language which would require that the distributing corporation be engaged in more than one trade or business prior to the distribution.

The active business requirements of 355(b)(1) prohibit the tax-free separation of a corporation into active and inactive entities. Section 355(b)(1)(A) extends the provisions of 355(a) only to those divisive distributions where the distributing corporation and the controlled corporation are engaged immediately after the distribution in the active conduct of a trade or business. In the case of those distributions which involve liquidation of the transferor, 355(b)(1)(B) requires that immediately before the distribution the transferor have no assets other than stock or securities in the controlled corporations, and that immediately thereafter each of the controlled corporations is engaged in the active conduct of a trade or business. Neither 355(b)(1)(A) nor (B) concerns itself with the existence of a plurality of businesses per se; rather both speak in terms of a plurality of corporate entities engaged in the active conduct of *a* trade or business, a distinction we believe to be vital in light of provisions of 355(b)(2).

Section 355(b)(2) details the rules for determining whether a corporation is engaged in the active conduct of a trade or business, and provides that a corporation shall be treated as so engaged, if, and only if: (1) It is engaged in the active conduct of a trade or business, or substantially all its assets consist of stock and securities of a corporation controlled by it immediately after the distribution which is so engaged; (2) such trade or business has been actively conducted throughout the 5-year period ending on the date of the distribution; (3) such trade or business was not acquired within that 5-year period in a transaction in which gain or loss was recognized; and (4) control of a corporation, which at the time of acquisition of control was conducting such trade or business, was not acquired within that 5-year period, or, if acquired within that period, was acquired by reason of a transaction in which no gain or loss was recognized, or by reason of such transactions combined with acquisitions made before the beginning of that 5-year period. Again we note the statute avoids the use of the plural when referring to "trade or business," but rather provides that: "[A] corporation shall be treated as engaged in the active conduct of *a* trade or business if and only if . . . it is engaged in the active conduct of *a* trade or business . . . [and] such trade or business has been actively conducted through the 5-year period ending on the date of the distribution." (Emphasis supplied.)

Respondent maintains that a reading of 355(b)(2)(B) in conjunction with the requirement of 355(b)(1) that both "the distributing corporation, *and* the controlled corporation . . . , [be] engaged immediately after the distribution in the active conduct of a trade or business" (emphasis supplied) indicates Congress intended the provisions of the statute to apply only where, immediately after the distribution, there exist two separate and distinct businesses, one operated by the distributing corporation and one operated by the controlled corporation, both of which were actively conducted for the 5-year period immediately preceding the distribution. In our judgment the statute does not support this construction.

As noted, the only reference to plurality appears in section 355(b)(1), and deals with corporate entities, not businesses. Recognizing the divisive nature of the transaction, subsection (b)(1) contemplates that where there was only one corporate entity prior to the various transfers, immediately subsequent thereto, there will be two or more *corporations*. In order to insure that a tax-free separation will involve the separation only of those assets attributable to the carrying on of an active trade or business, and further to prevent the tax-free division of an active corporation into active and inactive entities, (b)(1) further provides that each of the surviving corporations must be engaged in the active conduct of *a* trade or business.

A careful reading of the definition of the active conduct of a trade or business contained in subsection (b)(2) indicates that its function is also to prevent the tax-free separation of *active* and *inactive* assets into *active* and *inactive* corporate entities. This is apparent from the use of the adjective "such," meaning before-mentioned, to modify "trade or business" in subsection (b)(2)(B), thus providing that the trade or business, required by (b)(2)(B) to have had a 5-year active history prior to the distribution, is the same trade or business which (b)(2)(A) requires to be actively conducted immediately after the distribution. Nowhere in (b)(2) do we find, as respondent suggests we should, language denying the benefits of section 355 to the division of a single trade or business.

Nor can respondent derive support for his position by reading subsections (b)(1) and (b)(2) together, inasmuch as the plurality resulting therefrom is occasioned, not by any requirement that there be a multiplicity of businesses, but rather by the divisive nature of the transaction itself: i.e., one corporation becoming two or more corporations. Moreover, from the fact that the statute requires, immediately after the distribution, that the surviving corporations each be engaged in the conduct of a trade or business with an active 5-year history, we do not think it inevitably follows that each such trade or business necessarily must have been conducted on an individual basis throughout the 5-year period. As long as the trade or business which has been divided has been actively conducted for 5 years preceding the distribution, and the resulting businesses (each of which in this case, happens to be half of the original whole) are actively conducted after the division, we are of the opinion that the active business requirements of the statute have been complied with.

Respondent argues his construction of section 355 is confirmed by the report of the Senate Committee on Finance which accompanied the 1954 Internal Revenue Code. He refers us to that portion of the report which provides:

"Present law contemplates that a tax-free separation shall involve only the separation of assets attributable to the carrying on of an active business. Under the House bill, it is immaterial whether the assets are those used in an active business but if investment assets, for example, are separated into a new corporation, any amount received in respect of such an inactive corporation, whether by a distribution from it or by a sale of its stock, would be treated as ordinary income for a period of 10 years from the date of its creation. Your committee returns to existing law in not permitting the tax free separation of an existing corporation into active and inactive entities. It is not believed that the business need for this kind of transaction is sufficiently great to permit a person in a position to afford a 10-year delay in receiving income to do so at capital gain rather than dividend rates. Your committee requires that *both* the business retained by the distributing company and the business of the corporation the stock of which is distributed must have been actively conducted for the 5 years preceding the distribution, a safeguard against avoidance not contained in existing law." [Emphasis supplied.]

He argues that use of the term "both," with reference to the business retained by the distributing corporation and that operated by the controlled corporation, indicates that Congress intended there be in operation and existence during the 5 years preceding the distribution two or more separate and distinct businesses. We do not agree.

A reading of the quoted section of the report in its entirety reveals that the committee was addressing itself to the nature and the use of the particular assets which were transferred (active v. inactive), rather than to any distinction between one or more businesses. This is obvious when the entire paragraph is considered in the light of its topic sentence. The committee notes that under present law only assets attributable to the carrying on of an active trade or business may be separated tax free. After acknowledging a departure from this requirement in the House bill, the committee disapproves of the position taken by the House, and indicates it is returning to existing law by not permitting the tax-free separation of a corporation into active and inactive entities, and strengthens this provision by requiring that *both* the business retained by the distributing corporation and that of the controlled corporation must have been actively conducted for 5 years preceding the distribution. The excerpt makes no mention of trades or businesses per se. . . .

There being no language, either in the statute or committee report, which denies tax-free treatment under section 355 to a transaction solely on the grounds that it represents an attempt to divide a single trade or business, the Commissioner's regulations which impose such a restriction are invalid, and cannot be sustained. Commissioner v. Acker, 361 U.S. 87 (1959). . . .

Inasmuch as the parties treat the distribution as otherwise qualifying under section 355 for tax-free treatment, and inasmuch as we have found that portion of the regulations denying application of section 355 to the division of a single business to be invalid, we conclude that petitioner properly treated the distribution to him of the stock of E. P. Coady and Co. as a nontaxable transaction.

No evidence having been introduced with respect to the addition to tax under section 294(d)(2) of the 1939 Code, it is sustained subject to our holding on the above issue.

Reviewed by the Court.

Decision will be entered under Rule 50.

PIERCE, J., dissents.

HARRON, J., dissenting: The petitioner claims that no gain is to be recognized from the distribution of all of the Coady corporation stock in exchange for all of his Christopher corporation stock. In order to obtain such tax-free treatment of the exchange, he relies upon the provisions of section 355 of the 1954 Code. The provisions of section 355 provide exceptions to the rule recognizing gain or loss. In considering whether the transaction in dispute is entitled to the nonrecognition provisions of section 355, we must inquire whether the transaction before us is the kind of transaction that Congress intended to relieve of tax. Cf. Commissioner v. Gregory, 69 F.2d 809, affd. 293 U.S. 465; and Bazley v. Commissioner, 331 U.S. 737. . . .

Section 355 requires that two tests shall be met to obtain tax-free treatment: (1) The transaction must not be "principally . . . a device for the distribution of the earnings and profits of the distributing corporation." (2) The transaction must satisfy "the requirements of subsection (b) (relating to *active businesses*)." (Emphasis added.) Subsection (b) states the requirements as to "active businesses." It is required by (b)(1)(A) that subsection (a) shall apply only if the distributing corporation, and the controlled corporation, are engaged immediately after the distribution "in the active conduct of a trade or business." That is to say, immediately after the distribution, *both* the distributing corporation and the controlled corporation must be engaged in the active conduct of a trade or business. The punctuation of (b)(1)(A) has meaning. The words, "and the controlled corporation" are set off by commas; the verb, "is engaged," has two singular subjects, "the distributing corporation," and "the controlled corporation." The statute then defines the phrase "active conduct of a trade or business" (subsec. (b)(2)). The definition specifies that the trade or business which is actively conducted immediately after the distribution (referred to in subsection (a) and subsection (b)(1)) must be a trade or business which has been actively conducted throughout a 5-year period ending on the date of distribution. I believe there can be no doubt that since it is required by subsection (b)(1)(A) that *both* the distributing corporation and the controlled corporation must be engaged immediately after the distribution in the active conduct of a trade or business, the meaning of subsection (b)(2)(B) is that *both* the distributing corporation and the controlled corporation must actively conduct a business, respectively, which had been conducted for 5 years prior to the date of the distribution; each corporation must carry on a business after the distribution which had been carried on for 5 years before the distribution. I disagree with the conclusion that the statute does not so require. . . .

. . . Furthermore, I strongly disagree with the view that the purpose of the active business requirements of section 355(b)(1) is limited to the prohibition of a tax-free separation of a corporation into active and inactive entities, and to the prevention of "the tax-free separation of *active* and *inactive* assets into *active* and *inactive* corporate entities." Of course, such results are not allowed by section 355, but that kind of separation is not involved here and the point is not relevant to the issue in this case.

The error which I believe is made here in the construction of subsection (b) of section 355 is found in the failure to agree that the definition of the phrase "active conduct of a trade or business" contained in (b)(2) has reference to "a corporation"; that by reference to (b)(1), "a corporation" must refer to both the distributing corporation and the controlled corporation; and that the first sentence of (b)(2) deals with "a corporation" as a matter of convenience in drafting the definition so as not to engage in repetitions of the words "the distributing corporation" and "the controlled corporation." In this context, I think it is entirely clear that the word "such" in (b)(2)(B) refers back to the active conduct of a trade or business by "a corporation," be the corporation either the distributing corporation or the controlled corporation. . . .

. . . I respectfully dissent.

ATKINS, J., dissenting: I think the majority opinion errs in holding that section 1.355-1 of the Income Tax Regulations under the Internal Revenue Code of 1954 is invalid in providing that section 355 does not apply to the division of a single business.

The Supreme Court has many times held that Treasury regulations must be sustained unless unreasonable and plainly inconsistent with the revenue statutes, and that they constitute contemporaneous constructions by those charged with administration of these statutes which should not be overruled except for weighty reasons. Commissioner v. South Texas Lumber Co., 333 U.S. 496. It has also been stated by the Supreme Court that the practical interpretation of an ambiguous or doubtful statute that has been acted upon by officials charged with its administration will not be disturbed except for weighty reasons. Brewster v. Gage, 280 U.S. 327, and cases therein cited.

Section 355 is not clear. It might be susceptible to different interpretations. However, it seems that the interpretation adopted in the regulations is not unreasonable and plainly inconsistent with the statute, specifically section 355(b)(2)(B). This is particularly true if the legislative history of the statutory provision is taken into consideration. See section 353 of the House bill (H.R. 8300), which required that a corporation would be treated as an "inactive corporation" unless separate books and records had been maintained for the business transferred to it. This clearly contemplated the separation of distinct businesses. See H. Rept. No. 1337, 83d Cong., 2d Sess., p. A124. The law as finally adopted did not incorporate this particular requirement that separate books should be kept, but in S. Rept. No. 1622, 83d Cong., 2d Sess., p. 50, it is stated that the changes made by the Senate in existing law correspond substantially to those made in the House bill and, as shown in the quotation from the Senate report, contained in the majority opinion, it was the intention that "both the business retained by the distributing company and the business of the corporation the stock of which is distributed must have been actively conducted for the 5 years preceding the distribution, a safeguard against avoidance not contained in existing law." . . .

TURNER, HARRON, OPPER, and TRAIN, JJ., agree with this dissent.

NOTE

1. Did the Commissioner's solicitude for the revenue lead him to adopt a wholly unreasonable regulation? What potential for tax avoidance did the Commissioner perceive in the *Coady* situation? In Rev. Rul. 64-147, 1964-1 Cum. Bull. 136, the Commissioner announced that he would follow the Sixth Circuit's decision in *Coady* and the Fifth Circuit's similar decision in United States v. W. W. Marett, 325 F.2d 28 (1963), and that he would give consideration to a modification of Treas. Reg. §1.355-1(a) to the extent that it holds §355 of the Code inapplicable to the division of a single business.

2. In Estate of Lockwood v. Commissioner, 350 F.2d 712 (8th Cir. 1965), the issue was whether the five-year rule was satisfied when a "D" reorganization separated the Maine sales organization from the midwestern-based parent only three years after the Maine business was actively conducted. The court held that, under *Coady,* the question is whether the two corporations existing after the distribution are doing the same type of work and using the same type of assets as before in the original business, without reference to geographic area. Section 355(b)(2) was held satisfied.

3. Suppose a restaurant chain opens a new restaurant location, deducts the initial operating losses incurred in establishing the new location, reduces its earnings and profits by its losses and then separately incorporates the new restaurant and distributes the stock to its shareholders. Is the distribution tax-free? Why?

REVENUE RULING 59-400
1959-2 Cum. Bull. 114

Advice has been requested whether a distribution of stock by a corporation engaged in the hotel and real estate business qualifies under the nontaxable provisions of section 355 of the Internal Revenue Code of 1954.

M corporation was engaged in two businesses, operating a hotel and renting improved real estate (both commercial and residential). The hotel business was started upon organization in 1920 and has been actively conducted up to the present time. In 1934, M corporation also entered into the rental real estate business when it purchased property, constructed a garage and automobile agency facilities thereon and rented it to a dealer. In the intervening years, it acquired other rental properties which it has continued to operate. In 1954, the hotel had a fair market value of 550x dollars and a net book value of 350x dollars. The rental properties had a fair market value of 305x dollars and a net book value of 167x dollars.

During the five-year period commencing with 1954, the operation of the hotel business resulted in earnings, after taxes, of 240x dollars, and the operation of the real estate business resulted in earnings of approximately 75x dollars. In 1958, a new rental office building was built for 400x dollars, some 175x dollars thereof being provided by loans from banks. At the beginning of 1959, the hotel business was placed in a new corporation N, and the stock thereof distributed to the shareholders of M on a pro rata basis. N corporation received the hotel, plus certain receivables and other hotel business assets. M corporation retained the real estate liabilities and assets, which at that time had a net book value of 372x dollars and a fair market value of 705x dollars.

Section 355 of the Code states, in part, that in order for a distribution of stock to qualify under the nontaxable provisions of such section, each of the corporations involved must be engaged in a trade or business which has been actively conducted throughout the five-year period ending on the date of distribution, and that the transaction must not be used principally as a device to distribute the earnings and profits of either corporation.

The purpose behind the five-year limitation of section 355 is to prevent the corporate earnings of one business from being drawn off for such a period and put into a new business and thereby, through the creation of a marketable enterprise, convert what would normally have been dividends, into capital assets that are readily saleable by the shareholders.

It is the position of the Internal Revenue Service that where a corporation which is devoted to one type of business also engages in the rental business, and substantial acquisitions of new rental property are made within the five-year period preceding the separation of these businesses, a "spin-off" transaction will not qualify under section 355 unless it can be shown that the property acquisitions were substantially financed out of the earnings of the rental business and not out of the earnings of the other business.

From the facts presented herein, it is readily apparent that there has been a very substantial increase in the rental properties subsequent to 1954, primarily as a result of the addition of the large office building in 1958. Further, it is also apparent that, viewing the transaction most favorably to the taxpayer, earnings properly attributable to the hotel business, in the amount of approximately 150x dollars, have been employed in increasing the real estate business. In view of this substantial financing out of the earnings of the hotel business, it is held that the distribution of the stock of N corporation to the shareholders of M corporation will not qualify as a nontaxable distribution under section 355 of the Code.

NOTE

1. How were corporate earnings here "drawn-off . . . and put into a new business"? Note the form in which the reorganization was structured; what purpose was sought to be achieved by this structure? Is this properly a §355 problem, or should this transaction be approached under §312(i)? See Treas. Reg. §1.312-10(a). Is this a "proper case" for "such other method as may be appropriate under the facts and circumstances . . ."? Even if all the earnings and profits produced by the hotel properties are allocated to N Corporation, will that assure proper tax treatment when the M stock is sold or M is liquidated? Since it is held that the distribution of

N stock does not qualify as a non-taxable distribution under §355, what are the consequences to M, N and their shareholders?

2. In James Armour, Inc., 43 T.C. 295 (1964), X and Y were sole shareholders of A Corporation, engaged in the construction business, and B Corporation, which owned and leased to A the equipment necessary for the latter's business. B transferred its operating assets to A for cash and accounts receivable equal to fair market value. B then distributed all its assets, including an office building, in redemption of its stock. The stockholders immediately leased the office building to A, which also took over the employees of B. The court held that this was a "D" reorganization and that the property distributed to B's shareholders was "boot" and a dividend to the extent of B's earnings and profits; an actual exchange of stock was unnecessary since X and Y owned 100 per cent of both corporations. What if X had sold Y 15 per cent of his interest in B?

The court further found that "substantially all the assets" were transferred under §354(b)(1)(A), even though they were only 51 per cent of the total assets, since all the operating assets were transferred to A. Does the statute warrant this interpretation? Compare Rev. Proc. 66-34, 1966-2 Cum. Bull. 1232, page 560 supra, and Moffatt v. Commissioner, 363 F.2d 262 (9th Cir. 1966), page 643 infra.

3. *"Device" for Siphoning Earnings and Profits*

COMMISSIONER v. MORRIS TRUST
367 F.2d 794 (4th Cir. 1966)

Before HAYNSWORTH, Chief Judge, J. Spencer BELL, Circuit Judge, and STANLEY, District Judge.

HAYNSWORTH, Chief Judge. Its nubility impaired by the existence of an insurance department it had operated for many years, a state bank divested itself of that business before merging with a national bank. The divestiture was in the form of a traditional "spin-off," but, because it was a preliminary step to the merger of the banks, the Commissioner treated their receipt of stock of the insurance company as ordinary income to the stockholders of the state bank. We agree with the Tax Court, that gain to the stockholders of the state bank was not recognizable under §355 of the 1954 Code.

In 1960, a merger agreement was negotiated by the directors of American Commercial Bank, a North Carolina corporation with its principal office in Charlotte, and Security National Bank of Greensboro, a national bank. American was the product of an earlier merger of American Trust Company and a national bank, the Commercial National Bank of Charlotte. This time, however, though American was slightly larger than Security, it was found desirable to operate the merged institutions under Security's national charter, after changing the name to North Carolina National Bank. It was contemplated that the merged institution would open branches in other cities.

For many years, American had operated an insurance department. This was a substantial impediment to the accomplishment of the merger, for a national bank is prohibited from operating an insurance department except in towns having a population of not more than 5000 inhabitants. To avoid a violation of the national banking laws, therefore, and to accomplish the merger under Security's national charter, it was prerequisite that American rid itself of its insurance business.

The required step to make it nubile was accomplished by American's organization of a new corporation, American Commercial Agency, Inc., to which American transferred its insurance business assets in exchange for Agency's stock which was immediately distributed to American's stockholders. At the same time, American paid a cash dividend fully taxable to its stockholders. The merger of the two banks was then accomplished.

Though American's spin-off of its insurance business was a "D" reorganization, as defined in §368(a)(1), provided the distribution of Agency's stock qualified for non-recognition of gain under §355, the Commissioner contended that the active business requirements of §355(b)(1)(A) were not met, since American's banking business was not continued in unaltered corporate form. He also finds an inherent incompatibility in substantially simultaneous divisive and amalgamating reorganizations.

Section 355(b)(1)(A) requires that both the distributing corporation and the controlled corporation be "engaged immediately after the distribution in the active conduct of a trade or business." There was literal compliance with that requirement, for the spin-off, including the distribution of Agency's stock to American's stockholders, preceded the merger. The Commissioner asks that we look at both steps together, contending that North Carolina National Bank was not the distributing corporation and that its subsequent conduct of American's banking business does not satisfy the requirement.

A brief look at an earlier history may clarify the problem.

Initially, the active business requirement was one of several judicial innovations designed to limit nonrecognition of gain to the implicit, but unelucidated, intention of earlier Congresses.

Nonrecognition of gain in "spin-offs" was introduced by the Revenue Act of 1924. Its §203(b)(3), as earlier Revenue Acts, provided for nonrecognition of gain at the corporate level when one corporate party to a reorganization exchanged property solely for stock or securities of another, but it added a provision in subsection (c) extending the nonrecognition of gain to a stockholder of a corporate party to a reorganization who received stock of another party without surrendering any of his old stock. Thus, with respect to the nonrecognition of gain, treatment previously extended to "split-offs" was extended to the economically indistinguishable "spin-off."

The only limitation upon those provisions extending nonrecognition to spin-offs was contained in §203(h) and (i) defining reorganizations. The definition required that immediately after the transfer, the transferor or its stockholders or both be in control of the corporation to which the assets had been transferred, and "control" was defined as being the ownership of not less than eighty per cent of the voting stock and eighty per cent of the total number of shares of all other classes of stock.

With no restriction other than the requirement of control of the transferee, these provisions were a fertile source of tax avoidance schemes. By spinning-off liquid assets or all productive assets, they provided the means by which ordinary distributions of earnings could be cast in the form of a reorganization within their literal language.

The renowned case of Gregory v. Helvering, 293 U.S. 465, 55 S. Ct. 266, 79 L. Ed. 596, brought the problem to the Supreme Court. [The recitation of the *Gregory* facts is omitted.]*

The Supreme Court found the transaction quite foreign to the congressional purpose. It limited the statute's definition of a reorganization to a reorganization of a corporate business or businesses motivated by a business purpose. It was never intended that Averill engage in any business, and it had not. Its creation, the distribution of its stock and its liquidation, the court concluded, was only a masquerade for the distribution of an ordinary dividend, as, of course, it was.

In similar vein, it was held that the interposition of new corporations of fleeting duration, though the transactions were literally within the congressional definition of a reorganization and the language of a nonrecognition section, would not avail in the achievement of the tax avoidance purpose when it was only a mask for a transaction which was essentially and substantively the payment of a liquidating dividend, a sale for cash, or a taxable exchange.

Such cases exposed a number of fundamental principles which limited the application of the nonrecognition of gain sections of the reorganization provisions of the Code. Mertens defines them in terms of permanence, which encompasses the concepts of business purpose and a purpose to continue an active business in altered corporate form. As concomitants to the primary principle and supplements of it, there were other requirements that the transferor, or its stockholders, retain a common stock interest and that a substantial part of the value of the properties transferred be represented by equity securities.

Underlying such judicially developed rules limiting the scope of the nonrecognition provisions of the Code, was an acceptance of a general congressional purpose to facilitate the reorganization of businesses, not to exalt economically meaningless formalisms and diversions through corporate structures hastily created and as hastily demolished. Continuation of a business in altered corporate form was to be encouraged, but immunization of taxable transactions through the interposition of short-lived, empty, corporate entities was never intended and ought not to be allowed.

While these judicial principles were evolving and before the Supreme Court declared itself in Gregory v. Helvering, an alarmed Congress withdrew nonrecognition of gain to a stockholder receiving securities in a spin-off. It did so by omitting from the Revenue Act of 1934, a provision comparable to §203(c) of the Revenue Act of 1924.

Nonrecognition of gain to the stockholder in spin-off situations, however, was again extended by §317(a) of the Revenue Act of 1951, amending the 1939 Code by

*See page 471 supra. — ED.

adding §112(b)(11). This time, the judicially developed restrictions upon the application of the earlier statutes were partially codified. Nonrecognition of gain was extended "unless it appears that (A) any corporation which is a party to such reorganization was not intended to continue the active conduct of a trade or business after such reorganization, or (B) the corporation whose stock is distributed was used principally as a device for the distribution of earnings and profits to the shareholders of any corporation a party to the reorganization."

If this transaction were governed by the 1939 Code, as amended in 1951, the Commissioner would have had the support of a literal reading of the A limitation, for it was not intended that American, in its then corporate form, should continue the active conduct of the banking business. From the prior history, however, it would appear that the intention of the A limitation was to withhold the statute's benefits from schemes of the Gregory v. Helvering type. It effectively reached those situations in which one of the parties to the reorganization was left only with liquid assets not intended for use in the acquisition of an active business or in which the early demise of one of the parties was contemplated, particularly, if its only office was a conduit for the transmission of title. The B limitation was an additional precaution intended to encompass any other possible use of the device for the masquerading of a dividend distribution.

The 1954 Code was the product of a careful attempt to codify the judicial limiting principles in a more particularized form. The congressional particularization extended the principles in some areas, as in the requirement that a business, to be considered an active one, must have been conducted for a period of at least five years ending on the distribution date and must not have been acquired in a taxable transaction during the five-year period.[10] In other areas, it relaxed and ameliorated them, as in its express sanction of non-prorata distributions.[11] While there are such particularized variations, the 1954 Code is a legislative re-expression of generally established principles developed in response to definite classes of abuses which had manifested themselves many years earlier. The perversions of the general congressional purpose and the principles the courts had developed to thwart them, as revealed in the earlier cases, are still an enlightening history with which an interpretation of the reorganization sections of the 1954 Code should be approached.

Section 355(b) requires that the distributing corporation be engaged in the active conduct of a trade or business "immediately after the distribution." This is in contrast to the provisions of the 1951 Act, which, as we have noted, required an intention that the parent, as well as the other corporate parties to the reorganization, continue the conduct of an active business.[12] It is in marked contrast to §355(b)'s highly particularized requirements respecting the duration of the active business prior to the reorganization and the methods by which it was acquired. These contrasts suggest a literal reading of the post-reorganization requirement and a holding

---

[10]Section 355(b)(2).

[11]Section 355(a)(2) . . . .

[12]See, also, the Senate Finance Committee Report explaining §317 of the Revenue Act of 1951. Sen. Rep. No. 781, 82d Cong., 1st Sess. (1951), U.S. Code Congressional and Administrative News, p. 1969.

that the Congress intended to restrict it to the situation existing "immediately after the distribution."

Such a reading is quite consistent with the prior history. It quite adequately meets the problem posed by the Gregory v. Helvering situation in which, immediately after the distribution, one of the corporations held only liquid or investment assets. It sufficiently serves the requirements of permanence and of continuity, for as long as an active business is being conducted immediately after the distribution, there is no substantial opportunity for the stockholders to sever their interest in the business except through a separable, taxable transaction. If the corporation proceeds to withdraw assets from the conduct of the active business and to abandon it, the Commissioner has recourse to the back-up provisions of §355(a)(1)(B) and to the limitations of the underlying principles. At the same time, the limitation, so construed, will not inhibit continued stockholder conduct of the active business through altered corporate form and with further changes in corporate structure, the very thing the reorganization sections were intended to facilitate.

Applied, to this case, there is no violation of any of the underlying limiting principles. There was no empty formalism, no utilization of empty corporate structures, no attempt to recast a taxable transaction in nontaxable form and no withdrawal of liquid assets. There is no question but that American's insurance and banking businesses met all of the active business requirements of §355(b)(2). It was intended that both businesses be continued indefinitely, and each has been. American's merger with Security, in no sense, was a discontinuance of American's banking business, which opened the day after the merger with the same employees, the same depositors and customers. There was clearly the requisite continuity of stockholder interest, for American's former stockholders remained in 100% control of the insurance company, while, in the merger, they received 54.385% of the common stock of North Carolina National Bank, the remainder going to Security's former stockholders. There was a strong business purpose for both the spin-off and the merger, and tax avoidance by American's stockholders was neither a predominant nor a subordinate purpose. In short, though both of the transactions be viewed together, there were none of the evils or misuses which the limiting principles and the statutory limitations were designed to exclude.

We are thus led to the conclusion that this carefully drawn statute should not be read more broadly than it was written to deny nonrecognition of gain to reorganizations of real businesses of the type which Congress clearly intended to facilitate by according to them nonrecognition of present gain.

The Commissioner, indeed, concedes that American's stockholders would have realized no gain had American not been merged into Security after, but substantially contemporaneously with, Agency's spin-off. Insofar as it is contended that §355 (b)(1)(A) requires the distributing corporation to continue the conduct of an active business, recognition of gain to American's stockholders on their receipt of Agency's stock would depend upon the economically irrelevant technicality of the identity of the surviving corporation in the merger. Had American been the survivor, it would in every literal and substantive sense have continued the conduct of its banking business.

Surely, the Congress which drafted these comprehensive provisions did not intend the incidence of taxation to turn upon so insubstantial a technicality. Its differentiation on the basis of the economic substance of transactions is too evident to permit such a conclusion.

This, too, the Commissioner seems to recognize, at least conditionally, for he says that gain to the stockholders would have been recognized even if American had been the surviving corporation. This would necessitate our reading into §355(b)(1)(A) an implicit requirement that the distributing corporation, without undergoing any reorganization whatever, whether or not it resulted in a change in its corporate identity, continue the conduct of its active business.

We cannot read this broader limitation into the statute for the same reasons we cannot read into it the narrower one of maintenance of the same corporate identity. The congressional limitation of the post-distribution active business requirement to the situation existing "immediately after the distribution" was deliberate. Consistent with the general statutory scheme, it is quite inconsistent with the Commissioner's contention.

The requirement of §368(a)(1)(D) that the transferor or its stockholders be in control of the spun-off corporation immediately after the transfer is of no assistance to the Commissioner. It is directed solely to control of the transferee, and was fully met here. It contains no requirement of continuing control of the transferor. Though a subsequent sale of the transferor's stock, under some circumstances, might form the basis of a contention that the transaction was the equivalent of a dividend within the meaning of §355(a)(1)(B) and the underlying principles, the control requirements imply no limitation upon subsequent reorganizations of the transferor.

There is no distinction in the statute between subsequent amalgamating reorganizations in which the stockholders of the spin-off transferor would own 80% or more of the relevant classes of stock of the reorganized transferor, and those in which they would not. The statute draws no line between major and minor amalgamations in prospect at the time of the spin-off. Nothing of the sort is suggested by the detailed control-active business requirements in the five-year predistribution period, for there the distinction is between taxable and nontaxable acquisitions, and a tax free exchange within the five-year period does not violate the active business-control requirement whether it was a major or a minor acquisition. Reorganizations in which no gain or loss is recognized, sanctioned by the statute's control provision when occurring in the five years preceding the spin-off, are not prohibited in the post-distribution period. . . .

Nor can we find elsewhere in the Code any support for the Commissioner's suggestion of incompatibility between substantially contemporaneous divisive and amalgamating reorganizations. The 1954 Code contains no inkling of it; nor does its immediate legislative history. The difficulties encountered under the 1924 Code and its successors, in dealing with formalistic distortions of taxable transactions into the spin-off shape, contain no implication of any such incompatibility. Section 317 of the Revenue Act of 1951 and the Senate Committee Report, to which we have referred, did require an intention that the distributing corporation continue the conduct of its active business, but that transitory requirement is of slight relevance to an interpretation of the very different provisions of the 1954 Code and is devoid of any implication of incompatibility. If that provision, during the years it was in effect, would have resulted in recognition of gain in a spin-off if the distributing corporation later, but substantially simultaneously, was a party to a merger in which it lost its identity, a question we do not decide, it would not inhibit successive reorganizations if the merger preceded the spin-off.

The Congress intended to encourage six types of reorganizations. They are defined in §368 and designated by the letters "A" through "F." The "A" merger, the "B" exchange of stock for stock and the "C" exchange of stock for substantially all of the properties of another are all amalgamating reorganizations. The "D" reorganization is the divisive spin-off, while the "E" and "F" reorganizations, recapitalizations and reincorporations, are neither amalgamating nor divisive. All are sanctioned equally, however. Recognition of gain is withheld from each and successively so. Merger may follow merger, and an "A" reorganization by which Y is merged into X corporation may proceed substantially simultaneously with a "C" reorganization by which X acquires substantially all of the properties of Z and with an "F" reorganization by which X is reincorporated in another state. The "D" reorganization has no lesser standing. It is on the same plane as the others and, provided all of the "D" requirements are met, is as available as the others in successive reorganizations. . . .

. . . After the merger, North Carolina National Bank was as much American as Security. It was not one or the other, except in the sense of the most technical of legalisms; it was both, and with respect to the Charlotte operation, old American's business, it was almost entirely American. North Carolina National Bank's business in the Charlotte area after the merger was American's business conducted by American's employees in American's banking houses for the service of American's customers. Probably the only change immediately noticeable was the new name.

. . . [I]t is important to the result that, as in every merger, there was substantive continuity of each constituent and its business. In framing the 1954 Code, the Congress was concerned with substance, not formalisms. Its approach was that of the courts in the Gregory v. Helvering series of cases. Ours must be the same. The technicalities of corporate structure cannot obscure the continuity of American's business, its employees, its customers, its locations or the substantive fact that North Carolina National Bank was both American and Security.

A decision of the Sixth Circuit[16] appears to be at odds with our conclusion. In *Curtis,* it appears that one corporation was merged into another after spinning-off a warehouse building which was an unwanted asset because the negotiators could not agree upon its value. The Court of Appeals for the Sixth Circuit affirmed a District Court judgment holding that the value of the warehouse company shares was taxable as ordinary income to the stockholders of the first corporation.

A possible distinction may lie between the spin-off of an asset unwanted by the acquiring corporation in an "A" reorganization solely because of disagreement as to its value and the preliminary spin-off of an active business which the acquiring

---

[16]Curtis v. United States, 6 Cir., 336 F.2d 714.

corporation is prohibited by law from operating. We cannot stand upon so nebulous a distinction, however. We simply take a different view. The reliance in *Curtis* upon the Report of the Senate Committee explaining §317 of the Revenue Act of 1951, quite dissimilar to the 1954 Code, reinforces our appraisal of the relevant materials. . . .

For the reasons which we have canvassed, we think the Tax Court, which had before it the opinion of the District Court in *Curtis,* though not that of the affirming Court of Appeals, correctly decided that American's stockholders realized no recognizable taxable gain upon their receipt in the "D" reorganization of the stock of Agency.

Affirmed.

NOTE

1. What is it about the transactions in *Morris Trust* and *Curtis* (cited in the *Morris Trust* opinion at page 614 supra) that gave the Commissioner concern? What is the significance of the inner and outer parenthetical clauses in §355(a)(1)(B)? If you were Government counsel in *Morris Trust* what argument might you have advanced, based on the inner parenthetical clause? As the taxpayer's counsel, how might you have responded? What decision should a court reach with respect to the applicability of the inner parenthetical clause in cases like *Morris Trust* and *Curtis?* Why? In Rev. Rul. 68-303, 1968-2 Cum. Bull. 148, the Commissioner indicated that he would no longer attack the "spin-away" transaction sustained under §355 in *Morris Trust.*

2. Is §355 drafted as you think appropriate? In this connection consider the history of the spin-off provisions as summarized in *Morris Trust.* What is the relevance of the "active conduct of a trade or business"? Does it reflect the best way to deal with the underlying congressional concern? Why? See E. Brown, An Approach to Subchapter C, 3 Tax Revision Compendium 1619, 1621-1627 (1959).

3. In Rev. Rul. 64-102, 1964-1 Cum. Bull. 136, the issue was whether a non-pro rata distribution of stock in a subsidiary in exchange for all of certain minority shareholders' stock in the parent was a "device," when shortly before the distribution the parent transferred a sizable amount of cash to the subsidiary in order to equalize the value of the subsidiary's and parent's stock. What result would you expect? Why? Cf. H. Grady Lester, 40 T.C. 947 (1963), where the distributing corporation transferred $200,000 to the controlled corporation. Of that sum $140,000 was used to purchase starting inventory, and the remaining $60,000 was needed to begin business immediately. The court held this was not "principally" a "device," and the Commissioner has acquiesced. 1964-2 Cum. Bull. 6.

4. *Distribution of "Control" Stock*

COMMISSIONER v. GORDON
391 U.S. 83 (1968), rev'g 382 F.2d 499 (2d Cir. 1967),
aff'g 382 F.2d 485 (9th Cir. 1967)

Mr. Justice HARLAN delivered the opinion of the Court.

These cases, involving the interpretation of §355 of the Internal Revenue Code of 1954, have an appropriately complex history.

American Telephone and Telegraph Company (hereafter A.T. & T.) conducts its local communications business through corporate subsidiaries. Prior to July 1, 1961, communications services in California, Oregon, Washington, and Idaho were provided by Pacific Telephone and Telegraph Company (hereafter Pacific). A.T. & T. held about 90% of the common stock of Pacific at all relevant times. The remainder was widely distributed.

Early in 1961, it was decided to divide Pacific into two separate corporate subsidiaries of A.T. & T. The plan was to create a new corporation, Pacific Northwest Bell Telephone Company (hereafter Northwest) to conduct telephone business in Oregon, Washington, and Idaho, leaving the conduct of the California business in the hands of Pacific. To this end, Pacific would transfer all its assets and liabilities in the first three States to Northwest, in return for Northwest common stock and debt paper. Then, Pacific would transfer sufficient Northwest stock to Pacific shareholders to pass control of Northwest to the parent company, A.T. & T.

Pacific had, however, objectives other than fission. It wanted to generate cash to pay off existing liabilities and meet needs for capital, but not to have excess cash left over. It also feared that a simple distribution of the Northwest stock would encounter obstacles under California corporation law.[1] Consequently, the "Plan for Reorganization" submitted to Pacific's shareholders on February 27, 1961, had two special features. It provided that only about 56% of the Northwest common stock would be offered to Pacific shareholders immediately after the creation of Northwest. It also provided that, instead of simply distributing Northwest stock pro rata to shareholders, Pacific would distribute to its shareholders transferable rights entitling their holders to purchase Northwest common from Pacific at an amount to be specified by Pacific's Board of Directors, but expected to be below the fair market value of the Northwest common.

In its February 27 statement to shareholders, Pacific said that it was seeking a ruling from the Internal Revenue Service "with respect to the tax status of the rights to purchase which will be issued in connection with the offerings of capital stock of the New Company to shareholders of the Company . . . ." The statement warned,

---

[1] The record indicates that Pacific's attorneys had advised that if Pacific distributed the Northwest shares without payment of consideration by Pacific's shareholders, the distribution would have to be charged to earned surplus; the attorneys further advised that Pacific had insufficient earned surplus for this purpose, and that if this difficulty were avoided by creation of a reduction surplus, the reduction surplus would, under California law, have to be used first to redeem Pacific's preferred shares.

however, that "[t]axable income to the holders of such shares may result with respect to such rights."

The plan was approved by Pacific's shareholders on March 24, 1961. Pacific transferred its assets and liabilities in Oregon, Washington, and Idaho to Northwest, and ceased business in those States on June 30, 1961. On September 29, 1961, Pacific issued to its common stockholders one right for each outstanding share of Pacific stock. These rights were exercisable until October 20, 1961. Six rights plus a payment of $16 were required to purchase one share of Northwest common. The rights issued in 1961 were sufficient to transfer some 57.3% of the Northwest stock.

By September 29, 1961, the Internal Revenue Service had ruled that shareholders who sold rights would realize ordinary income in the amount of the sales price, and that shareholders who exercised rights would realize ordinary income in the amount of the difference between $16 paid in and the fair market value, measured as of the date of exercise, of the Northwest common received. The prospectus accompanying the distributed rights informed Pacific shareholders of this ruling.

On June 12, 1963, the remaining 43% of the Northwest stock was offered to Pacific shareholders. This second offering was structured much as the first had been, except that eight rights plus $16 were required to purchase one share of Northwest.

The Gordons, respondents in No. 760, and the Baans, petitioners in No. 781, were minority shareholders of Pacific as of September 29, 1961. In the rights distribution that occurred that day the Gordons received 1,540 rights under the plan. They exercised 1,536 of the rights on October 5, 1961, paying $4,096 to obtain 256 shares of Northwest, at a price of $16 plus six rights per share. The average price of Northwest stock on the American Stock Exchange was $26 per share on October 5. On the same day, the Gordons sold the four odd rights for $6.36. The Baans received 600 rights on September 29, 1961. They exercised them all on October 11, 1961, receiving 100 shares of Northwest in return for their 600 rights and $1,600. On October 11, the agreed fair market value of one Northwest share was $26.94.

In their federal income tax returns for 1961, neither the Gordons nor the Baans reported any income upon the receipt of the rights or upon exercising them to obtain Northwest stock at less than its fair market value. The Gordons also did not report any income on the sale of the four rights. The Commissioner asserted deficiencies against both sets of taxpayers. He contended, in a joint proceeding in the Tax Court, that taxpayers received ordinary income in the amount of the difference between the sum they paid in exercising their rights and the fair market value of the Northwest stock received. He contended further that the Gordons realized ordinary income in the amount of $6.36, the sales price, upon the sale of their four odd rights.

The Tax Court upheld taxpayers' contention that the 1961 distribution of Northwest stock met the requirements of §355 of the Code, with the result that no gain or loss should be recognized on the receipt by them or their exercise of the rights. The Tax Court held, however, that the Gordons' sale of the four odd rights resulted in ordinary income to them. The Commissioner appealed the *Baan* case to the Court of Appeals for the Ninth Circuit, and the *Gordon* case to the Court of Appeals for the Second Circuit; in the latter, the Gordons cross-appealed. The Ninth Circuit reversed the Tax Court, holding that the spread between $16 and fair market value was taxable as ordinary income to the Baans. The Second Circuit disagreed, sustaining the Tax Court on this point in the *Gordon* case. The Second Circuit went on to hold that the amount received by the Gordons for the four odd rights was taxable as a capital gain rather than as ordinary income, reversing the Tax Court on this point.

Because of the conflict, we granted certiorari. 389 U.S. 1033, 1034. We affirm the decision of the Court of Appeals for the Ninth Circuit, and reverse the decision of the Court of Appeals for the Second Circuit on both points.

Under §§301 and 316 of the code, subject to specific exceptions and qualifications provided in the code, any distribution of property by a corporation to its shareholders out of accumulated earnings and profits is a dividend taxable to the shareholders as ordinary income. Every distribution of corporate property, again except as otherwise specifically provided, "is made out of earnings and profits to the extent thereof." It is here agreed that on September 28, 1961, Pacific's accumulated earnings and profits were larger in extent than the total amount the Commissioner here contends was a dividend — the difference between the fair market value of all Northwest stock sold in 1961 and the total amount, at $16 per share, paid in by purchasers.

Whether the actual dividend occurs at the moment when valuable rights are distributed or at the moment when their value is realized through sale or exercise, it is clear that when a corporation sells corporate property to stockholders or their assignees at less than its fair market value, thus diminishing the net worth of the corporation, it is engaging in a "distribution of property" as that term is used in §316.[4] Such a sale thus results in a dividend to shareholders unless some specific exception or qualification applies. In particular, it is here agreed that the spread was taxable to the present taxpayers unless the distribution of Northwest stock by Pacific met the requirements for nonrecognition stated in §355, or §354, or §346(b) of the code.[5]

---

[4]See, e.g., Choate v. Commissioner, 129 F.2d 684 (C.A. 2d Cir.). In Palmer v. Commissioner, 302 U.S. 63, 69, this Court said, "While a sale of corporate assets to stockholders is, in a literal sense, a distribution of its property, such a transaction does not necessarily fall within the statutory definition of a dividend. For a sale to stockholders may not result in any diminution of its net worth and in that case cannot result in any distribution of its profits.

"On the other hand such a sale, if for substantially less than the value of the property sold, may be as effective a means of distributing profits among stockholders as the formal declaration of a dividend."

In *Palmer,* rights were distributed entitling shareholders to purchase from the corporation shares of stock in another corporation. Finding that the sales price represented the reasonable value of the shares at the time the corporation committed itself to sell them, this Court found no dividend. It held that the mere issue of rights was not a dividend. It has not, however, been authoritatively settled whether an issue of rights to purchase at less than fair market value itself constitutes a dividend, or the dividend occurs only on the actual purchase. In the present case this need not be decided.

[5]It is important to begin from this premise. In our view, the Court of Appeals for the Second Circuit erred in its approach to the §355 problem because it assumed, at the outset, that the Commissioner essentially sought to tax a transaction that brought no "income" to Pacific shareholders. Whether the shareholders received income, however, cannot in practice be determined in the abstract, before looking at §355.

Any common shareholder in some sense "owns" a fraction of the assets of the corporation in which he holds stock, including those assets that reflect accumulated corporate earnings. Earnings are not taxed to the shareholder when they accrue to the corporation, but instead when they are passed to shareholders individually through dividends. Consequently it does not help to note, as the Second Circuit here did, that the distribution of Northwest stock

Since the Tax Court concluded that the requirements of §355 had been met, it did not reach taxpayers' alternative contentions. . . .

Section 355 provides that certain distributions of securities of corporations controlled by the distributing corporation do not result in recognized gain or loss to the distributee shareholders. The requirements of the section are detailed and specific, and must be applied with precision. It is no doubt true, as the Second Circuit emphasized, that the general purpose of the section was to distinguish corporate fission from the distribution of earnings and profits. However, although a court may have reference to this purpose when there is a genuine question as to the meaning of one of the requirements Congress has imposed, a court is not free to disregard requirements simply because it considers them redundant, or unsuited to achieving the general purpose in a particular case. Congress has abundant power to provide that a corporation wishing to spin off a subsidiary must, however bona fide its intentions, conform the details of a distribution to a particular set of rules.

The Commissioner contends that the 1961 distribution of Northwest stock failed to qualify under §355 in several respects.[7] We need, however, reach only one. Section 355(a)(1)(D) requires that, in order to qualify for nonrecognition of gain or loss to shareholders, the distribution must be such that

"as part of the distribution, the distributing corporation distributes —

"(i) all of the stock and securities in the controlled corporation held by it immediately before the distribution, or

"(ii) an amount of stock in the controlled corporation constituting control within the meaning of section 368(c), and . . . ."

Section 368(c) provides in relevant part that

"the term 'control' means the ownership of stock possessing at least 80 percent of the total combined voting power of all classes of stock entitled to vote and at least 80 percent of the total number of shares of all other classes of stock of the corporation."[8]

---

merely changed the form of ownership that Pacific's shareholders enjoyed and did not increase their wealth. This is only very roughly true at best, but in the rough sense in which it is here true, it is true of any dividend. The question is not whether a shareholder ends up with "more" but whether the change in the form of his ownership represents a transfer to him, by the corporation, of assets reflecting its accumulated earnings and profits.

There may be a genuine theoretical difference between a change in form representing a mere corporate fission, separating what the shareholder owns into two smaller but essentially similar parts, and a change in form representing a dividend, separating what a shareholder owns qua shareholder from what he owns as an individual. This difference, however, must be defined by objectively workable tests, such as Congress supplied in §355. Neither the Second Circuit nor the taxpayers have suggested any other way of identifying a true fission.

[7]The Commissioner contends, first, that Pacific did not distribute "solely stock or securities" as required by §355(a)(1)(A), because it distributed rights rather than stock. He contends, second, that Pacific did not distribute the Northwest stock "to a shareholder, with respect to its stock" as required by §355(a)(1)(A)(i), because it did not distribute the stock to shareholders but sold it to holders of transferable rights, for cash consideration. He contends, third, that Northwest did not meet the quantity requirements of §355(a)(1)(D) because it parted with only 57% of the stock in 1961.

Any one of these arguments, if established, would support the result the Commissioner seeks. The Court of Appeals for the Second Circuit perforce rejected all three. The Court of Appeals for the Ninth Circuit accepted all three. We reach only the last.

[8]In the Tax Court, the Commissioner did not argue that Pacific had failed to meet the requirement that it distribute at least 80% of the Northwest stock, but rested upon his other

On September 28, 1961, the day before the first rights distribution, Pacific owned all of the common stock of Northwest, the only class of securities that company had issued. The 1961 rights offering contemplated transferring, and succeeded in transferring, about 57% of the Northwest common to Pacific shareholders. It therefore could not be clearer that this 1961 distribution did not transfer "all" of the stock of Northwest held by Pacific prior to it, and did not transfer "control" as that term is defined in §368(c).

Nevertheless, taxpayers contend, and the Second Circuit agreed, that the requirements of subsection (a)(1)(D) were here met because Pacific distributed the remaining 43% of the Northwest stock in 1963. The court said that the purpose of the subsection "in no way requires a single distribution." The court apparently concluded that so long as it appears, at the time the issue arises, that the parent corporation has in fact distributed all of the stock of the subsidiary, the requirements of §(a)(1)(D)(i) have been satisfied.

We are forced to disagree. The code requires that "the distribution" divest the controlling corporation of all of, or 80% control of, the controlled corporation. Clearly, if an initial transfer of less than a controlling interest in the controlled corporation is to be treated for tax purposes as a mere first step in the divestiture of control, it must at least be identifiable as such at the time it is made. Absent other specific directions from Congress, code provisions must be interpreted so as to conform to the basic premise of annual tax accounting. It would be wholly inconsistent with this premise to hold that the essential character of a transaction, and its tax impact, should remain not only undeterminable but unfixed for an indefinite and unlimited period in the future, awaiting events that might or might not happen. This requirement that the character of a transaction be determinable does not mean that the entire divestiture must necessarily occur within a single tax year. It does, however, mean that if one transaction is to be characterized as a "first step" there must be a binding commitment to take the later steps.[11]

Here, it was little more than a fortuity that, by the time suit was brought alleging a deficiency in taxpayers' 1961 returns, Pacific had distributed the remainder of the

---

arguments against applying §355. When the Tax Court rejected these arguments, the Commissioner raised the 80% question, as well as his other arguments in both Courts of Appeals. Both considered the point on the merits, dividing on it as on the others. Since the general issue of the applicability of §355 has been in the case since its inception, taxpayers do not contend that the 80% question is not properly before this Court. Since the record leaves no disputed issue of fact with respect to this question, we find it proper to decide it here without reference to a tryer of fact.

[11]The Commissioner contends that a multistep divestiture presents special problems in preventing bailouts of earnings and profits. The Second Circuit, recognizing such potential problems, held that they can be dealt with under §(a)(1)(B), which provides that nonrecognition shall result only when it appears that "the transaction was not used principally as a device for the distribution of the earnings and profits of the distributing corporation or the controlled corporation or both . . . ."

Congress may, of course, have chosen not to leave problems created by multistep divestitures to specific adjudication under this "device" subsection, but to require *both* a unitary divestiture *and* satisfaction of the "device" requirement. Whether §(a)(1)(D) would prohibit or limit a divestiture of control committed from the outset but spread over a series of steps is a problem we need not reach.

stock. The plan for reorganization submitted to shareholders in 1961 promised that 56% of that stock would be distributed immediately. The plan went on,

> "It is expected that within about three years after acquiring the stock of the New Company, the Company by one or more offerings will offer for sale the balance of such stock, following the procedures described in the preceding paragraph. The proceeds from such sales will be used by the Company to repay advances then outstanding and for general corporate purposes including expenditures for extensions, additions and improvements to its telephone plant.
>
> "The prices at which the shares of the New Company will be offered pursuant to the offerings referred to . . . will be determined by the Board of Directors of the Company at the time of each offering."

It was further stated that such subsequent distributions would occur "[a]t a time or times related to its [Pacific's] need for new capital." Although there is other language in the plan that might be interpreted to prevent Pacific management from dealing with the Northwest stock in any way inconsistent with eventual sale to Pacific shareholders, there is obviously no promise to sell any particular amount of stock, at any particular time, at any particular price. If the 1961 distribution played a part in what later proved to be a total divestiture of the Northwest stock, it was not, in 1961, either a total divestiture or a step in a plan of total divestiture.

Accordingly, we hold that the taxpayers, having exercised rights to purchase shares of Northwest from Pacific in 1961, must recognize ordinary income in that year in the amount of the difference between $16 per share and the fair market value of a share of Northwest common at the moment the rights were exercised.

The second question presented by the petition in No. 760, whether the $6.36 received by taxpayers Gordon upon the sale of four rights was taxable as ordinary income, as a capital gain, or not at all, does not require extended discussion in light of our view upon the first question. Since receipt and exercise of the rights would have produced ordinary income, receipt and sale of the rights, constituting merely an alternative route to realization, also produced income taxable at ordinary rates. Helvering v. Horst, 311 U.S. 112; Gibson v. Commissioner, 133 F.2d 308.

The judgment of the Court of Appeals for the Second Circuit is reversed. The judgment of the Court of Appeals for the Ninth Circuit is affirmed. . . .

It is so ordered.

Mr. Justice MARSHALL took no part in the consideration or decision of these cases.

NOTE

On remand, see Gordon v. Commissioner, 424 F.2d 378 (2d Cir. 1970), aff'g 51 T.C. 1032 (1969).

See also R. Jacobs, Supreme Court Further Restricts the Step Transaction Doctrine, 29 J. Taxation 2 (1968); Comment, 42 Temp. L.Q. 185 (1969); Recent

Case, 37 U. Cin. L. Rev. 820 (1968); Recent Decision, 43 St. John's L. Rev. 287 (1968).

See generally C. Whitman, III, Draining the Serbonian Bog: A New Approach to Corporate Separations Under the 1954 Code, 81 Harv. L. Rev. 1194 (1968).

VII. CORPORATE SUBSTITUTION — REINCORPORATIONS, "F" REORGANIZATIONS AND RELATED PROBLEMS

HELLER v. COMMISSIONER
2 T.C. 371 (1943), aff'd, 147 F.2d 376 (9th Cir. 1945),
cert. denied, 325 U.S. 868 (1945)

MELLOTT, Judge: . . . [Heller, Bruce & Co., a Delaware corporation ("Heller Delaware") was in the investment banking business. Because it was thought preferable to operate as a California corporation, a Heller, Bruce & Co. ("Heller California") was organized under California law on December 6, 1937. Nine days later, the taxpayer (the president and a shareholder in Heller Delaware) and the other two shareholders and officers of Heller Delaware contributed cash to Heller California, for which the latter issued its stock. The taxpayer had borrowed the amount of cash he used for the transaction from a bank on the same day. On the next day Heller California bought the assets of Heller Delaware, paying for them in part with the cash its shareholders contributed and in part with the proceeds of a bank loan. Heller Delaware had been indebted to the bank for the same amount borrowed by Heller California, and the former's collateral was applied to the latter's loan. Heller Delaware used part of the purchase price it received to pay off its debt to the bank, this transaction occurring the same day as the loan to Heller California and its purchase from Heller Delaware. Four days later Heller Delaware distributed the balance of its cash to its shareholders as a liquidating distribution, and it dissolved. Heller California's shareholders, officers and directors were identical to Heller Delaware's, and the business conducted by the latter continued. The amount which the taxpayer received in liquidation of Heller Delaware was less than the basis of his stock, and so he claimed a loss which the Commissioner disallowed.]

Respondent contends that petitioner did not sustain a deductible loss in 1937 by reason of the series of steps set out in our findings; that they were part of one transaction, the substance of which was an exchange of stock in the Delaware corporation for stock in the California corporation pursuant to a plan of reorganization; and that no gain or loss is recognizable because of the provisions of section [354(a)(1)].
. . .

[Section 368(a)(1)] . . . provides that the term "reorganization" comprehends "[D] a transfer by a corporation of all or a part of its assets to another corporation if immediately after the transfer the transferor or its stockholders or both are in control of the corporation to which the assets are transferred, . . . or [F] a mere change in identity, form, or place of organization, however effected." Immediately after the transfer of the assets of the Delaware corporation to the California corporation, petitioner and the other stockholders of the transferor were in control of the California corporation. The plan also contemplated a mere change in the place of organization of the Delaware corporation. Clearly, therefore, there was a statutory reorganization, and the plan pursuant to which it was executed was a plan of reorganization, even though it was not in writing. Hortense A. Menefee, 46 B.T.A. 865.

Petitioner contends that even if there were a statutory reorganization there was no exchange of stock for stock pursuant to a plan of reorganization as required by the provisions of section [354(a)(1)] . . . and that he is, therefore, entitled to the claimed capital loss deduction. He argues that he bought the stock of the California corporation for cash, which he paid to the corporation before he received anything from the Delaware corporation; that the stock was issued to him in accordance with the permit of the California Commissioner of Corporations; that he ultimately received cash upon the liquidation of the Delaware corporation but prior to that time his investment in the California corporation had been completed; that he, on December 15, 1937, and for some time thereafter, had an investment in both corporations; and that the existence of a reorganization is not sufficient to establish tax exempt status unless there is an actual exchange of stock or securities for stock or securities.

Petitioner cites and relies upon Minnie C. Brackett, administratrix (1930), 19 B.T.A. 1154; affd., 57 Fed. (2d) 1072; James E. Wells (1933), 29 B.T.A. 222; William H. Mullins (1928), 14 B.T.A. 426; and Henry M. Robinson (1930), 21 B.T.A. 677. He also quotes from Commissioner v. Gilmore, 130 Fed. (2d) 791, in which the court affirmed the holding of the Board (Anna V. Gilmore, 44 B.T.A. 881) that a reorganization (merger of two companies) was not a mere device for liquidating one of the corporations and hence to be disregarded for tax purposes under the rationale of Gregory v. Helvering, 293 U.S. 465, and similar cases. (Cf. Commissioner v. Kann, 130 Fed. (2d) 797, decided at the same time.) The *Brackett* and *Mullins* cases, supra, tend to support petitioner's contention that each step taken pursuant to a plan is to be treated as a separate transaction. That view is no longer held. "For income tax purposes, the component steps of a single transaction cannot be treated separately. . . . Effect is to be given to the substance rather than to the form. . . . In determining the substance of a transaction it is proper to consider the situation as it existed at the beginning and end of the series of steps as well as the object sought to be accomplished, the means employed, and the relation between the various steps. Commissioner v. Schumacher Wall Board Corporation, 93 Fed. (2d) 79; Republic Steel Corporation v. United States, 40 Fed. Supp. 1017, and cases cited.

Petitioner and two others, the stockholders and directors of the Delaware corporation, decided to have the business, assets, and liabilities of that company taken over by a new California corporation. The desired end was accomplished by a series of steps, all of which were planned in advance. When the plan was completed the former stockholders and directors of the Delaware corporation were in control of the new California corporation, and it had acquired the assets, business, and liabilities of its predecessor. The net result was that petitioner and the other two stockholders had substituted their interest in the Delaware corporation for substantially the same interest in the California corporation. The nonrecognition of gain or loss provisions of the statute are "intended to apply to cases where a corporation in form transfers its property, but in substance it or its stockholders retain the same or practically the same interest after the transfer." . . .

The result achieved under the plan could have been accomplished by having the California corporation acquire the assets of the Delaware corporation for its stock, and by having the latter distribute the stock to its stockholders in complete liquidation. Petitioner and his associates apparently chose the longer route, hoping that they might thereby become entitled to a loss deduction. However, as the Supreme Court pointed out in Minnesota Tea Co. v. Helvering, 302 U.S. 609, 613, "a given result at the end of a straight path is not made a different result because reached by following a devious path." The effect of all the steps taken was that petitioner made an exchange of stock of one corporation for stock of another pursuant to a plan of reorganization. No gain or loss can be recognized for tax purposes on such a transaction. The fact that petitioner, by putting up some additional cash, acquired a slightly greater interest in the California corporation than he had in the Delaware corporation is of no particular significance. When he disposes of his shares of California corporation stock, his gain or loss will be measured by the difference between the amount realized and the cost of his Delaware stock plus the additional cash invested in the stock of the California corporation. . . .

NOTE

Was there a "business purpose" for the reorganization in *Heller,* or is "business purpose" not always a prerequisite?

COMMISSIONER v. MORGAN
288 F.2d 676 (3d Cir. 1961), cert. denied, 368 U.S. 836 (1962)

Before KALODNER, STALEY and HASTIE, Circuit Judges.

STALEY, Circuit Judge. This petition for review requires us to determine whether distributions made to a shareholder pursuant to a corporate liquidation are taxable as dividend income under subsection [356(a)(2)] or as a long term capital gain under . . . [§331] . . . .

For many years Wellington Fund, Inc. ("Fund"), a mutual fund, had separate contracts with Wellington Corporation ("transferor") for investment advisory services, and with W. L. Morgan & Company ("transferee") for the national promotion and distribution of the Fund's securities. These contracts constituted the principal if not exclusive business of the transferor and transferee. In 1952, the Fund terminated its contract with transferor and immediately thereafter entered into a contract with transferee for identical services.

Transferor was then liquidated, and the assets that it had utilized in performing the contract with the Fund were conveyed to the transferee. In addition, the following distributions were made to the taxpayer, transferor's sole stockholder:

May 27, 1952	Cash	$100,000.00
June 1, 1952	United States Treasury Bonds	48,906.25
Sept. 18, 1952	Cash	65,244.74
		$214,150.99

In his 1952 tax return, the taxpayer reported $212,150.99 ($214,150.99 distribution less cost of his stock) as a long term capital gain under . . . [§331]. The Commissioner, however, determined a deficiency on the ground that the distribution was taxable as dividend income under the related provisions of subsections [354(a), 356(a)]. The Tax Court held that even assuming all the other conditions had been met, the distribution could not qualify as dividend income because there had not been an actual exchange of stock between taxpayer and transferee. The Commissioner here maintains that in substance and effect an exchange of stock was made since the taxpayer owned all the stock in both transferor and transferee.

In order to sustain the Commissioner, it must be shown that (1) there was a distribution of property or money ("boot") in addition to an exchange of stock all made in pursuance of a plan of reorganization, and (2) that such boot has the effect of a taxable dividend, i.e., it is not in excess of the taxpayer's share of the undistributed earnings and profits of the corporation accumulated after February 28, 1913.[5]

We think that a chronological statement of the facts in the record, uncontradicted, largely stipulated and as found by the Tax Court, leads irresistibly to the conclusion that the distributions here were made in pursuance of a plan of reorganization [under §368(a)(1)(D)].

At all times relevant, taxpayer was president and board chairman as well as sole stockholder of both transferor and transferee, which were organized in 1929 and 1931 respectively. Another board member was Joseph E. Welch, who was also a principal executive officer in transferor, transferee, and the Fund. The taxpayer was also president of the Fund and chairman of its board. The ten other members of the board consisted of four executive officers in the transferor and transferee, the father of taxpayer's wife who died in 1941, business associates with taxpayer in other enterprises, and two others with whom he had no apparent business relationship. Four out of five and five out of seven executive officers of transferor and transferee respectively served on the Fund's board.

For the fiscal year ended May 31, 1951, transferor reported an income of $305,-175.96. However, no dividends were paid that year. During late 1951 and early 1952, an internal revenue agent on several occasions met with transferor's representatives and discussed the imposition of a surtax under section [531] . . . for an allegedly improper accumulation of surplus. On February 11, 1952, a conference was held between the agent's group chief and transferor's representatives without any agreement being reached.

At the Fund's board meeting held on February 27, 1952, taxpayer raised the question of transferring the contract from transferor to transferee. It was the consensus of the board that the contract with transferor should be terminated and one calling

[5]The parties stipulated that the distributions did not exceed such earnings.

for similar services be entered into with transferee which was to change its name to include the word "Wellington." Minutes of that meeting, signed by the Fund's secretary, who was a vice president in both transferor and transferee, contained the following:

> "... and it was the sense of the meeting that the present contract between the Fund and Wellington Corporation should not be renewed but that the activities of Wellington Corporation and W. L. Morgan & Co. should be combined into one company for greater efficiency and the Investment Advisory Contract be made with this company."

At that meeting, taxpayer also presented a form of proposed investment services contract with transferee, apparently identical in all essential respects with the contract then in effect between the Fund and transferor.

At a special meeting of transferor's board attended by taxpayer and Welch, held on March 3, 1952, to discuss termination of its contract with the Fund, taxpayer stated that when a new contract with transferee was approved by the Fund, all of transferor's employees would be placed on transferee's payroll.

In soliciting the Fund's shareholders for approval of the change, a proxy dated March 7, 1952, prepared under order of the Fund's board and distributed over the name of its secretary, who was a vice president in both transferor and transferee, contained the following:

> "Investment Advisory Agreement with The Wellington Company
>
> "For greater efficiency and corporate simplification and economy, the Directors of Wellington Corporation, the investment advisor for Wellington Fund, Inc., and the Directors of W. L. Morgan & Co., the sponsor and national distributor for the Fund, have resolved that their activities should be combined into one company to be called The Wellington Company. Under this arrangement, the general management, investment management and research services and distribution activities will be conducted in the future by separate departments of one corporation rather than by two corporations as heretofore. This arrangement involves no changes in investment or management policies or practices. The Executive Committee, Investment Committee and the entire statistical and research staff and all employees of the investment advisor will become associated with The Wellington Company with the same duties and responsibilities as heretofore. *The name of W. L. Morgan & Co. will be changed to The Wellington Company, and the present Wellington Corporation will be dissolved."* (Emphasis supplied.)

The shareholders met on April 9, 1952, at 3:00 P.M. and approved the contract with transferee. At 4:00 P.M. on that same date, transferee's board at a special meeting resolved that transferee would assume the obligation transferor had toward its employees under a profit-sharing plan. The minutes of that meeting also indicate that transferee had already decided to change its name to include the word "Wellington."

On April 10, 1952, the contract with transferor was terminated and on April 12, 1952, one calling for similar services was entered into with transferee.

In the meantime, transferee took over the transferor's furniture and other equipment, research data, and all of transferor's employees together with the employees' profits sharing plan.

On May 27, 1952, after unsuccessfully attempting to secure new business, transferor's board, pursuant to taxpayer's written consent, resolved to liquidate.

Upon completion of the arrangements outlined above, the transferee had a new corporate division devoted to investment counselling. Without hiatus an intact capability to perform the contract with the Fund was transplanted from transferor to transferee. Taxpayer continued to be the sole stockholder of transferee. Also, the transferor, as taxpayer himself testified, could perform no investment advisory services without the use of transferee's personnel.

It is clear to us that these actions constituted the carrying out of a plan of reorganization under subsection [368(a)(1)(D)].

The taxpayer contends there was no reorganization since the contract with the Fund, the transferor's most valuable asset, was not transferred. This, of course, is without merit. We need not articulate the obvious answer which the facts compel, for the subsection involved requires only that part of the assets be transferred. . . .*

As we noted earlier, the Tax Court held that there must be an actual physical exchange of stock before the distribution here could be taxable as dividend income. With this conclusion we cannot agree, for it is contrary to the purposes that Congress meant to serve in enacting subsections [354(a) and 356(a)(2)].

Subsection [356(a)(2)] was enacted to reach and tax as ordinary income gain realized by a stockholder from a corporate reorganization to the extent that such gain constitutes undistributed earnings. It appeared as subsection 203(d)(2) of the Revenue Act of 1924, 26 U.S.C.A. (Rev. Act of 1924). The Senate Finance Committee Report[7] accompanying the 1924 Act and commenting on that subsection stated:

> "The committee approves certain amendments to the income tax law contained in the House bill to stop the methods of avoidance which are now being commonly availed of by taxpayers.
> "(1) The provisions of the reorganization section of the present law have been rewritten to prevent the use of the section to escape proper taxation . . . by distributing as capital gain what are in effect dividends out of earnings."

If the transferor's assets had been transferred to a newly formed corporation in exchange for stock, there is no question that the boot would have been taxable as dividend income. That an existing corporation in which the taxpayer was the sole shareholder was used instead of a newly formed one cannot alter the true nature of the transaction. Here, the issuance of new stock would have been a meaningless gesture since the stock the taxpayer already held represented the total value of all the assets except for the boot.

Liddon v. Commissioner, 6 Cir., 230 F.2d 304, certiorari denied 1956, 352 U.S.

---

*This case arose under the 1939 Code, which had no provisions corresponding to Subsection (b) of §354. — ED.

[7] S. Rep. No. 398, 68th Cong., 1st Sess. p. 7 (1939-1 Cum. Bull. (Part 2) 266, 271).

824, 77 S. Ct. 34, 1 L. Ed. 2d 48, which involved similar facts, fully supports our conclusion. There, the taxpayers, husband and wife, owned eighty per cent of the stock in a corporation engaged in selling and servicing automobiles under a franchise dealer contract with General Motors Corporation, while one Davis owned the other twenty per cent. Davis' offer to sell his stock to the taxpayers for book value was refused. Thereafter, taxpayers established a new corporation in which they owned all but one share of stock and secured a new franchise contract. The new corporation then agreed to a plan whereby it would purchase the old corporation's assets and accept an employees' retirement fund. Taxpayers invested an additional twenty thousand dollars in personal funds in the new corporation. Thereafter Davis' stock was purchased by the old corporation, which was then dissolved, and $150,000 in cash and notes distributed to the taxpayers, which the Commissioner contended, and the Tax Court agreed, should be taxed as ordinary income and not as capital gain. In affirming on this point, Judge Stewart, now Justice Stewart, approved and summarized the Tax Court's reasoning, 230 F.2d at pages 306-307:

> "Moreover, since at the beginning of the series of transactions the petitioners held stock in the old corporation, and at the end they held stock in the new corporation, plus 'money-to-boot,' the court reasoned that, although there was not a direct exchange of stock in the old corporation for stock in the new, plus 'other property or money,' that was the net effect of what was done. Accordingly, the court concluded that the case was governed by sections 112 (b)(3) and 112(c) of the 1939 Code."

Taxpayer cites Emma Cramer, 1953, 20 T.C. 679, and Trianon Hotel Co., 1958, 30 T.C. 156, which are inapplicable since in neither of these cases did the court conclude that there was a reorganization as was the case both here and in *Liddon*.

The decision of the Tax Court will be reversed and the cause remanded for further proceedings not inconsistent with this opinion.

HASTIE, Circuit Judge (dissenting). The question here is whether the gain element in the sum of $214,150.99 received by the taxpayer in 1952 in exchange for his stock in Wellington Corp., upon total liquidation of that corporation, is taxable as long term capital gain under Section [331] . . . or whether it may be taxed as ordinary income in the nature of a dividend received in the course of a reorganization under Section [356(a)(2)].

This court now holds that the taxpayer's gain is taxable as ordinary income. In so doing it recognizes that the result it reaches can be achieved only by fitting the transactions in this case within the situation described in Section[s] [354(a)(1) and 356(a)(2),] i.e., where "stock or securities in a corporation a party to a reorganization are . . . exchanged . . . for stock or securities . . . in another corporation a party to the reorganization" and, in addition to stock thus received, the stockholder also receives "other property or money". In the words of the majority opinion, "it must be shown that (1) there was a distribution of property or money ('boot') in addition to an exchange of stock all made in pursuance of a plan of reorganization, and (2) that such boot has the effect of a taxable dividend . . . ." I agree that the plain language of the statute requires that there be an exchange of stock. . . .

Having thus stated what the statute requires, the court also recognizes that the series of transactions in this case involved no actual acquisition of stock by the taxpayer either through an ordinary exchange or, as in Liddon v. Commissioner, 6 Cir., 1956, 230 F.2d 304, upon which the court relies, through the creation of a new corporation during a reorganization with the taxpayer as an original stockholder. It is argued, however, that in this case no transfer of stock of a corporation to the taxpayer is the legal equivalent of an actual stock transfer merely because the taxpayer already was and long had been sole stockholder of that corporation. I can see no logical basis for thus finding an exchange of stock within the statutory requirement without any demonstration that something happened in this case which was equivalent to a transfer of stock to the taxpayer.

There may be one situation in which it is properly arguable that the equivalent of a stock transfer has occurred pursuant to a reorganization though technically there was no transfer. Assume a case which is like the present one in that an individual owns all the stock of both a liquidating corporation and a second corporation which assumes the functions of the liquidating corporation, but with the additional fact that the worth of the second corporation is substantially increased in a reorganization by an intercorporate transfer of valuable assets of the liquidating corporation. The reorganization deprives the individual of his stock in the first corporation and in return enhances the value of his ownership of the transferee corporation. Such added worth of the second corporation might be the basis for the issuance of new certificates, but it would be pointless to issue new certificates to one who already is the sole stockholder. Therefore, for purposes of Section [356(a)] it is arguable that such a case should be treated as one in which there has been an exchange of stock for stock without requiring the formality of a new stock issue.

But on the record here there was no substantial increase in the worth of the second corporation through any transfer of assets by the liquidating corporation. The only intercorporate transfers of assets in this case are described as follows in the unchallenged findings of the Tax Court:

> "Subsequent to the adoption of the liquidating resolution, the Corporation sold its office furniture and equipment to the Company for a price set by the Company's firm of accountants as the fair market value thereof. We have no issue as to gain or loss on this sale. The Corporation also transferred to the Company possession of, access to, and the right to make use of certain investment statistical and research material, if not title thereto, without consideration of any kind."

As a sale for fair value, the transfer of office furniture and equipment did not enrich the transferee corporation. While statistical and research data may have substantial utility, it is not claimed that in the circumstances of this case the transfer of data substantially increased the worth of the transferee corporation. Of course, the re-employment of employees of the liquidating company by the transferee company, which the majority emphasizes, is not a transfer of assets and does not increase corporate worth.

One other item deserves mention in this connection. It is the contract long held by the liquidating corporation to render investment advisory services to Wellington Fund, Inc. Its duration paralleled that of the present transferee corporation's separate contract with the Fund for promotional services. The Tax Court found that the Fund made a business decision to attempt to reduce its costs and gain other advantages by contracting with a single corporation for both advisory and promotional services. Accordingly, the Fund cancelled its contract with its longtime adviser and two days later entered into a similar contract with the company which theretofore had done only promotional work for it.

This action of the Fund ruined the business of the original advisory corporation and caused its liquidation. It also conferred a very substantial economic advantage on the transferee corporation. But that is not enough to make the Fund's action significant for present purposes. Our concern is with property transfers between a liquidating corporation and a transferee corporation within and pursuant to a plan of reorganization. There was here no assignment of contract rights between such corporations. Nor is it found as a fact that they or their sole stockholder either could or did use the Fund as an instrumentality to do their bidding. True, their sole stockholder was also President and Chairman of the Board of the Fund. But the Tax Court found that he, his family and his close business associates owned only .003 percent of the stock of the Fund. It has already been pointed out that the Fund derived a business advantage of its own from shifting its contractual arrangement for advisory services. Moreover, under the Tax Court's findings, the decision to liquidate was not made until after the shifting of the Fund's contract and only after a search for other business to replace the cancelled contract had proved unsuccessful. It seems worthwhile to spell this matter out in some detail because in my view it involves the only doubtful point in this case, even though on this point I do not disagree with the majority opinion which apparently concedes that the conduct of the Fund in cancelling one contract and entering into another did not constitute a transfer of assets between the two service companies and was not a step in a reorganization.

In these circumstances, I do not see how it can be said in any meaningful way that there was in this case even a conceptual exchange of stock, and, of course, there was not a real one.[1] Therefore, Section [356(a)] is inapplicable and the decision of the Tax Court should be affirmed.

NOTE

Was the investment advisory contract an "asset" of the transferor? Was this asset "transferred" to the transferee? How would the result be affected if the contract was

---

[1]Although I can find no Section [354(a)(1)] exchange of stock here to prevent treatment of the present distribution as one made in liquidation under Section [331,] I recognize that the taxpayer is accomplishing a type of "bail-out" of accumulated corporate earnings while the same business continues in another corporation under his ownership and control. If this discloses a "loophole" in the statutory taxing scheme which should be closed, resort should be to Congress for appropriate action. In this connection see the discussion of a proposed amendment to Section 356(a)(2)(B)(ii) in Revised Report on Corporate Distributions and Adjustments, transmitted to the House Committee on Ways and Means by the Advisory Group on Subchapter C, at 66-67 (1958).

an "asset" but was found not to have been "transferred"? Does "acquired" mean "acquired from the transferor"?

After these transactions, what was taxpayer's basis in his W. L. Morgan & Co. stock?

In Rev. Rul. 70-240, 1970-1 Cum. Bull. 81, the Commissioner held that a corporation's sale of its operating assets to another corporation under common control with the transferor, followed by liquidation of the transferor and distribution to the sole shareholder, resulted in a "D" reorganization and a dividend.

GALLAGHER v. COMMISSIONER
39 T.C. 144 (1962)

Respondent has determined deficiencies in income tax in these consolidated cases as follows:

Docket No.	Petitioner	1955	1956
87610	Gallagher	$ 16,884.90	$ 2,214.10
87611	Bush	178,236.52	10,346.56
87612	Grant	13,174.61	207.43
87667	Cuffe	126,933.87	15,877.91

The issues remaining for determination are (1) whether a series of distributions received in liquidation of a corporation should be treated as taxable dividends or distributions of earnings and profits incidental to a reorganization within the meaning of sections 354, 356, and 368 of the Internal Revenue Code of 1954 and, if either, (2) whether the amount taxed as ordinary income should be reduced by the capital contribution to the original corporation or the capital contributed to a new corporation formed to conduct the business of the original corporation.

Findings of Fact

. . . West Coast Terminals, Inc., a Delaware corporation with its principal business office in San Francisco, California (hereinafter called Delaware), was organized on May 13, 1946. Delaware was at all material times until its dissolution, hereinafter described, engaged in the general stevedoring and terminal business, which consisted of providing under contract the services (including labor and equipment) required to load, unload, and handle cargo carried on vessels, including both loading and unloading of vessels and both loading and unloading of freight cars, trucks, and other vehicles for the purpose of transferring cargo to or from vessels. The business was conducted principally at various points on San Francisco Bay, at the port of Stockton, at the port of Los Angeles, at Long Beach harbor, all in California, and at Portland, Oregon. . . .

William J. Bush (hereinafter called Bush) . . . , was president and a director and stockholder of Delaware, holding 391 shares of its stock at all material times until its dissolution. Bush was the chief executive officer of Delaware and devoted full time to its management, including the supervision of its stevedoring and terminal operations, the supervision of its financial affairs, and the supervision of relations with the ship operators who were its customers or potential customers.

Joseph C. Gallagher (hereinafter called Gallagher) . . . , was vice president and general manager and a director and stockholder of Delaware, holding 58 shares of its stock, at all material times until its dissolution. Gallagher was the second highest executive officer of Delaware and devoted full time to participation in its management, including participation in the supervision of its stevedoring and terminal operations, the supervision of its financial affairs, and the supervision of relations with the ship operators who were its customers or potential customers.

George H. Grant (hereinafter called Grant) . . . , was a director and stockholder of Delaware, holding 57 shares of its stock at all material times until its dissolution. Grant was a member of the board of directors having general control of the management of Delaware and, in addition, assisted in its relations with the ship operators who were its customers or potential customers.

Thomas E. Cuffe (hereinafter called Cuffe) . . . , was a director and stockholder of Delaware, holding 267 shares of its stock, at all material times until its dissolution. Cuffe was a member of the board of directors having general control of the management of Delaware and, in addition, assisted in its relations with the ship operators who were its customers or potential customers and was himself president of one of the ship operators who were customers of Delaware, namely, Pacific Far East Lines, Inc. . . .

The nine shareholders of Delaware consisted of two groups, as shown by the following schedule:

Stockholders	Percentage of stock	Shares of stock
Bush	30.24	391
Cuffe	20.65	267
Gallagher	4.49	58
Grant	4.41	57
Burkman	2.16	28
Total	61.95	801
Sexton (an estate)	20.65	267
Seid (an estate)	5.80	75
Lyon (a widow)	5.80	75
Seidenspinner (a widow)	5.80	75
Total	38.05	492
Grand total	100.00	1,293

The first group consisted of active executives and directors, as follows: Bush, Cuffe, Gallagher, and Grant, who were all directors of Delaware and two of whom were officers, and D. R. Burkman (hereinafter called Burkman), who was district manager in direct charge of all operations of Delaware in southern California, including Los Angeles and Long Beach harbor. The second group consisted of the remaining shareholders of record . . . (hereinafter referred to as the estates and widows), all of whom were . . . shareholders who had acquired their stock through the death of persons formerly active in Delaware. . . . The estates and widows were inactive and of no assistance to Delaware, and several members of this group wished to liquidate their interest because of the low yield and speculative nature of the business.

Article 40 of the by-laws of Delaware provided that each stockholder desiring to sell his shares —

> "must upon each occasion first offer for sale said shares to the other stockholders of record. The other stockholders of record shall be entitled to purchase said shares so offered on a pro rata basis dependent on the percentage of stock issued and outstanding and which is owned by the respective purchasing stockholders. The stock shall be sold to the stockholders who desire to acquire the same at a price equal to the prevailing book value of said stock as determined by the books of account of the corporation. . . ."

The minutes of a meeting of the board of directors of Delaware on May 31, 1955, state in part as follows:

> "The President stated that he and certain other of the shareholders of [Delaware], together with other persons, were planning to organize a California corporation for the purpose of offering to purchase the operating assets and goodwill of [Delaware]. The President then presented to the meeting a Plan of Complete Liquidation of [Delaware] involving the sale of the operating assets of [Delaware] as aforesaid, to be followed by the dissolution and liquidation of [Delaware]. . . ."

A special meeting of the stockholders of Delaware was held on June 14, 1955. The minutes of this meeting state in part as follows:

> . . . "*Resolved,* that the Plan of Complete Liquidation of . . . [Delaware] submitted to this meeting and hereby ordered to be made a part of the records of this meeting, be and same is hereby adopted;
>
> "*Resolved,* that, when and if . . . [Delaware] shall receive an offer to purchase the operating assets of . . . [Delaware], including its goodwill and the assignment of its operating contracts, then the President or Vice-President and Secretary are authorized and empowered to sell such assets at any price which in their judgment is deemed advisable; provided, however, that such price shall not be less than the book value thereof as of May 31, 1955, or as of the time of sale, whichever is less;
>
> . . . "The Chairman stated that the assets to be sold comprised equipment and prepaid insurance having April 30, 1955 book values of $86,760.26 and $10,754.71 respectively."

The plan of liquidation of Delaware provided in part as follows:

"2. Immediately upon adoption of the Plan, the shareholders voting for its adoption shall adopt appropriate resolutions authorizing the appropriate officers of . . . [Delaware] to take all necessary steps to sell and transfer the operating assets of . . . [Delaware], including its goodwill, and to assign its operating contracts. The sales price of such assets shall be not less than the book value thereof as of May 31, 1955, or as of the time of sale, whichever is less. It is understood and contemplated that such assets may be sold to a corporation some of the shareholders of which are also shareholders and/or officers of . . . [Delaware] . . . .

"5. If and when the operating assets of . . . [Delaware] have been sold as contemplated by Section 1 hereof, the officers and directors in so far as possible shall reduce all other assets of . . . [Delaware] to cash and upon compliance with the applicable laws of the State of Delaware may from time to time make one or more pro rata distributions in cash to the shareholders of . . . [Delaware] . . . .

"6. On or before, but not later than, May 1, 1956, all known assets of . . . [Delaware], except such assets as may be retained to meet claims against . . . [Delaware] which it shall not have been possible to discharge prior to that date, shall be distributed pro rata to the shareholders of . . . [Delaware] in complete liquidation of . . . [Delaware]. If any of . . . [Delaware's] assets shall not have been reduced to cash prior to the date of such distribution, which shall take place on May 1, 1956, if not earlier, undivided interests in such assets shall be distributed to the shareholders or such assets shall be otherwise divided ratably among the shareholders of . . . [Delaware]. Such distribution of all of the assets of . . . [Delaware] shall be in complete cancellation of all outstanding shares of . . . [Delaware]."

. . . On June 17, 1955, there was incorporated West Coast Terminals Co. of California, a California corporation (hereinafter referred to as California). California had only one class of stock. It issued this capital stock on July 15, 1955, and received full payment therefor in cash in the aggregate amount of $300,000.

Certain employees, important in the operation of the business and who had not owned any stock in Delaware, became stockholders in California. . . .

The capital stock of California at all material times has been owned, by petitioners and others, as shown by the following schedule:

Stockholders	*Percentage of stock*	*Shares of stock*
Bush, W. J.	30	900
Gallagher, J. C.	21	630
Cuffe, T. E.	10	300
Grant, G. H.	6⅔	200
Burkman, D. R.	5	150
Total	72⅔	2,180
Kurtz, M. O.	5	150
Johnson, A. E.	4⅔	140
Johnson, O.	4⅔	140
Kavanaugh, L. B.	4⅔	140
Linden, N. R.	4⅔	140
Cervelli, G. F.	1⅚	55
O'Leary, J.	1⅚	55
Total	27⅓	820
Grand total	100.00	3,000

On July 18, 1955, Delaware effected a sale of all of its operating assets and pre-paid expenses and an assignment of its current trade contracts to California. The consideration for the above purchase was a check dated July 18, 1955, for the book value of the property in the amount of $100,264.56, said to be the fair market value of the properties. Nothing was paid for the partially performed contracts with customers beyond the purchaser's assumption of the obligations of these contracts. The opening balance sheet of California on July 18, 1955, was set up on the books as follows:

Assets:
Tangible Property ... $100,264.56
Cash ... 199,735.44

Total ... $300,000.00

Liabilities ... 0
Capital Contributed ... $300,000.00
Retained Earnings ... 0

Total ... $300,000.00

In all cases the assignment of the contracts was agreed to by the third party involved, except in the case of the United States Government, which required that a new contract in the form of a novation be entered into. In securing these assignments, the customers were informed that the same key personnel would be with California and that Bush and Gallagher would control the company. ...

After July 18, 1955, Delaware completely terminated its business, retaining only the personnel and office facilities necessary to effect an orderly liquidation. After July 18, 1955, the principal assets remaining to be converted to cash by Delaware were its accounts receivable. On July 21, 1955, Delaware was issued a document entitled "Certificate of Dissolution" by the State of Delaware.

By May 3, 1956, Delaware had made a series of distributions of all remaining assets to its shareholders pro rata . . . . After these distributions, Delaware had no remaining assets and all of its outstanding shares of stock were surrendered and canceled.

Delaware's total accumulated earnings and profits since its organization did not exceed $949,221, and petitioner's respective shares thereof did not exceed the following:

Bush	$287,044.30
Cuffe	196,014.14
Gallagher	42,620.02
Grant	41,860.65

Petitioners' respective shares of Delaware capital and the individual adjusted basis for Federal income tax purposes were as follows:

	Capital	Basis
Bush	$39,100	$59,209.36
Cuffe	26,700	26,700.00
Gallagher	5,800	15,206.00
Grant	5,700	14,943.82

As of May 31, 1955, Delaware had retained earnings of $838,329.80 and capital contributed in the amount of $156,000. . . .

The business of the two corporations required only a small amount of operating assets. . . .

The principal business of California was substantially the same as that of Delaware. When California commenced operations in 1955, the use of a name similar to that of Delaware was convenient for the purpose of indicating the same personnel of directors and executives, but was not necessary.

. . . About eight customers accounted for 75 percent of Delaware's business. One of these customers was the United States Army, which accounted for more than 40 percent of Delaware's business. . . . At the beginning of 1956, California lost the Army contract. . . .

Throughout the 4 fiscal years immediately preceding May 31, 1955, the earned surplus was invested in assets required by business needs. The cash in the business was enough to meet approximately 1 week's operating expenses. Bush had sought counsel as to Delaware's dividend policy with respect to the accumulated earnings tax for each of the fiscal years during 1953 through 1955 and was advised that it was not necessary to have a dividend in either 1953, 1954, or 1955 as long as the first distribution in dissolution was made before August 15, 1955. Adams opposed any dividends and wanted Delaware to build its net worth to reduce the risk of borrowing.

The following were some of the corporate business reasons for liquidating Delaware: To eliminate the inactive estates and widows, representing 38 percent of the outstanding stock, from the business; to permit Gallagher to acquire more stock so that Bush and Gallagher could control the business; to bring into stock ownership seven or eight executives who had helped in making a success of Delaware; to limit Cuffe's ownership of the business. Cuffe had previously withdrawn his account in San Francisco and stated his intention of going into the stevedoring business. The liquidation was intended to limit the possibility of Cuffe's 20.65 percent being combined with the estates and widows to control the business.

The dissolution of Delaware, incorporation of California, and transfer of the assets were all part of a single plan formulated by petitioners upon the advice of their attorney and tax counsel to effect the stated ends and achieve favorable tax results. . . .

None of the shareholders of Delaware and none of the shareholders of California occupied a relationship to any other shareholder of either Delaware or California, either by reason of being a member of a family or of owning any interest in any partnership, estate, trust, or corporation or for any other reason which would make applicable the constructive ownership rules of section 318 of the Internal Revenue Code of 1954 . . . . All of the stock of each petitioner here involved had been held for more than 6 months before January 1, 1955.

Petitioners, in their individual returns, treated the liquidating distributions of Delaware as part or full payment in exchange for their stock and reported the amounts received in excess of the adjusted basis as long-term capital gains. Respondent, in his deficiency notices, "determined that the amount[s] . . . received . . . from [Delaware] . . . [are] taxable in full as dividend income."

Opinion

Opper, Judge: Respondent's position consists of two alternative contentions which are so mutually exclusive as to make it desirable to consider them separately. His first argument, as stated in his brief, is "predicated basically on the thesis that the facts show that a complete [or partial] liquidation did not in substance occur." He therefore insists that the amount received by the individuals consisted of a dividend within the purview of section 301 of the 1954 Code. Although he does not specifically refer to section 302, the implication appears to be that the redemption, which he does not dispute, was essentially equivalent to a dividend under section 302(b)(1), see Neff v. United States, 305 F.2d 455 (Ct. Cl. 1962), vacating and withdrawing 301 F.2d 330 (Ct. Cl. 1962), and hence is not to be treated as a capital transaction under section 302(a), but as a dividend under section 301(c)(1), with ordinary income consequences. His alternative argument is that this was a reorganization within the meaning of section 368, that presumably the proceeds of the redemptions constituted "boot," and, accordingly, under section 356, are, at least to some extent, to be treated as ordinary income.

There can be no doubt that the stock of Delaware was redeemed and, if that were all there was to it, we might look to section 302, and then to section 301, for guidance in settling the ordinary-income problem. But the redemption was only one step in what was undoubtedly a liquidation-reincorporation operation, see David T. Grubbs, 39 T.C. 42 (1962), as respondent himself suggests in his second alternative.

As to the first proposition, we are accordingly able to resort to the step-transaction theory and to view the entire series of transactions as interrelated and inextricable. . . . Respondent does not, in fact, suggest anything to the contrary, but merely contends that some of the steps actually taken can be disregarded.[12] But, at least in such a situation as this, we cannot justify the inclusion of some and the exclusion of other essential steps. . . .

The concept of a continuation of the existing business through a section 331 liquidation, coupled with an intercorporate transfer, falls into the general area of corporate reorganizations, so that it is in the so-called reorganization sections, if anywhere, that we should expect it to be dealt with.

The fact that the assets of a business are transferred to a new corporation does not by itself change the effect of the liquidation of the original corporation. If, for example, the assets had been transferred to another corporation in which the old shareholders had no interest, even though the business continued, Fowler Hosiery Co., 36 T.C. 201 (1961), affd. 301 F.2d 394 (C.A. 7, 1962); or if they had been transferred to another corporation, but the old corporation's business had not been continued, it seems clear respondent would have had no possible ground for contending that the liquidating distribution, even though partly composed of accumulated earnings, could be taxed as an ordinary dividend. Hellmich v. Hellman, 276 U.S. 233 (1928). So that it is only the continuance of the business in a new corporation, preponderantly owned by the shareholders of the old, upon which respondent can rely for his first contention.

But, generally speaking, it is exactly where the same enterprise is in essence wholly or partly continued even after some more or less radical change in its organization or conduct that it is the purpose of the so-called "reorganization" section of the law to operate.[15] The basic approach of the complicated series of enactments incorporated in the 1954 Code appears to be that all such situations are to be tested by the "reorganization" portion of the statute, and that it was intended that if a transaction of a similar kind does not fall within them, but lies in the general area of arrangements which may, in effect, constitute the continuation of an existing business, it shall be treated as a transaction giving rise to gain or loss and not as a distribution.[16]

[12]"Furthermore, the 27⅓ [%] stock interest purchased in the new corporation by third parties should be disregarded and reorganization treatment applied to the step transaction. This step can be disregarded since without it the dominant purpose — to withdraw corporate earnings while continuing the equity interest in substantial part — was fully achieved."

[15][Treas. Reg. §1.368-1(b).]

[16]S. Rept. No. 1622, to accompany H.R. 8300 (Pub. L. 591), 83d Cong., 2d Sess., pp. 43, 230 (1954):

"Your committee has also structurally revised the first three parts of the subchapter. Under your committee's bill, part I of the subchapter contains rules primarily devoted to the treatment of current distributions by a corporation, *and does not contain rules with respect to distributions pursuant to a recapitalization or other type of reorganization.* Part II, as under the

Respondent's first contention includes the insistence that we should ignore the liquidation of Delaware and test these transactions solely as a redemption. Yet he makes no reference in his brief to section 302 which is the primary redemption section. It is not clear whether for this proposition he relies on the rationale of such cases as Bazley v. Commissioner, 331 U.S. 737 (1947), rehearing denied and prior opinion amended 332 U.S. 752 (1947); see also Gregory v. Helvering, 293 U.S. 465 (1935), although there it was a "recapitalization," not a liquidation, that was held not to fall within the statute. In *Bazley,* the Supreme Court found that a transaction which literally complied with the reorganization provisions was not to be accorded reorganization treatment because it was primarily a vehicle for the distribution of undistributed earnings. *Gregory* similarly denied the benefits of the reorganization provisions to a plan which met the literal definition of the Code because the plan had no relation to the business of either corporation.

Respondent would have us hold here that the liquidation of Delaware was not a liquidation, although it literally complied with all the terms, because the transaction is alleged to have been primarily a vehicle for the distribution of undistributed earnings. But, unlike the reorganization sections which were involved in *Bazley* and similar cases, liquidation is usually accompanied by some kind of distribution which may well include accumulated earnings of the liquidating corporation. Hellmich v. Hellman, supra. That this is recognized by the statutory provisions themselves seems to us to permit of no uncertainty. Even though respondent from time to time refers to the section relating to complete liquidation,[19] no definition of this term appears in the statute nor in the regulations. A complete liquidation of a corporation can apparently exist only where the definition of partial liquidation does not apply, since otherwise there would be no purpose in distinguishing between complete and partial liquidation as defined in section 346(a)(1); although, of course, there may be situations in which, since the result would be the same, it is unnecessary to determine whether the liquidation is complete or partial.

Instead, it appears that what actually occurred here must be treated as a partial liquidation since it falls squarely within the definition of such a transaction which does appear in the statute.[20] It is difficult to find any ground for holding that this was not in every respect a partial liquidation to which section 331(a)(2) would expressly apply. . . .

We think it follows that the distributions made by Delaware are governed by the rules established by section 346. There was unquestionably a series of distributions

---

House bill, contains rules relating primarily to liquidations. Part III relates only to reorganizations and *includes their effects on the shareholders.*

. . . "Part I of subchapter C provides rules relating to the tax treatment to shareholders of corporate distributions of property. While your committee continues the treatment provided in the House bill under which part I has no application at the corporate level to distributions of property in complete or partial liquidation, your committee's bill, unlike the House bill, does not include in part I rules for distributions made in connection with corporate reorganizations. Under your committee's bill, distributions and exchange made in connection with reorganization transactions are treated, in general, in part III." [Emphasis added.]

[19]Sec. 331. . . .
[20]Sec. 346. . . .

in complete redemption of all of Delaware's stock pursuant to a plan. Although these distributions completely liquidated Delaware, the transaction literally falls within section 346(a)(1).

The conclusion that the redemption of Delaware's stock in the course of its liquidation is not to be considered as an ordinary dividend is fortified by an examination of the provisions of section 346. From the language of section 346(a), it would appear that a distribution in redemption of all of the stock of the corporation pursuant to a plan can never be essentially equivalent to a dividend as referred to in section 302(b)(1). This is because Congress found it necessary to include that condition in section 346(a)(2), which refers to the redemption of a part of the stock of the corporation, but omitted it in section 346(a)(1). We cannot assume that this was without significance.

Furthermore, "Section 302 does not apply to that portion of any distribution which qualifies as a distribution in partial liquidation under section 346." Sec. 1.302-1(a), Income Tax Regs. Not only this, but we have been referred to no authority, either under the 1954 Code or under the less restrictive language of the preceding revenue acts, in which a liquidation-reincorporation has been held to give rise to ordinary income, except where that result could be accomplished by applying the provisions relating to reorganizations. Cf. Richard H. Survaunt, 5 T.C. 665 (1945), affirmed on this issue 162 F.2d 753 (C.A. 8, 1947); Estate of John B. Lewis, 6 T.C. 455 (1946), affd. 176 F.2d 646 (C.A. 1, 1949).

Of course, this does not eliminate respondent's second argument contending for the existence of a reorganization and accompanying "boot." With the limited exception of special situations specifically provided for by statute, see, e.g., sections 333, 341, this would be the only time a series of redemptions of all the stock of a corporation pursuant to a plan, or distributions in complete liquidation of a corporation, would receive treatment as a distribution to which section 301 applies. When the redemption, whether in complete or partial liquidation, is in pursuance of a plan of reorganization, as defined by section 368, and section 356 regarding "boot" comes into play, it is apparent that the dividend provisions of section 301 must apply.

The difficulty is that this series of steps does not amount to a statutory reorganization. Although several cases have found reorganization upon similar facts under subsection (D) relating to intercorporate transfers of assets with retention of "control," see, e.g., Heller v. Commissioner, 147 F.2d 376 (C.A. 9, 1945), affirming 2 T.C. 371 (1943), certiorari denied 325 U.S. 868; William M. Liddon, 22 T.C. 1220 (1954), affirmed on this issue 230 F.2d 304 (C.A. 6, 1956), certiorari denied 352 U.S. 824; Pebble Springs Distilling Co., 23 T.C. 196 (1954), affd. 231 F.2d 288 (C.A. 7, 1956), certiorari denied 352 U.S. 836, see also Richard H. Survaunt, supra; those cases differ from the instant case in one important respect. Respondent specifically renounces subsection (D). This may be because only 72⅔ percent of California's stock was owned by former shareholders of Delaware. In this respect, if no other, the present case is unlike David T. Grubbs, supra. "Since the [shareholders of the transferor] owned less than 80 percent of the stock of the new corporations, the acquisition of the assets of the [transferor] is precluded from being a tax-free reorganization within the meaning of section [368(a)(1)(D)]." Austin Transit, Inc., 20 T.C. 849, 856 (1953).

The step-transaction approach makes it possible to view this arrangement as an acquisition of Delaware's assets by California in exchange for California's voting stock to petitioners. But then we must consider that there was also a payment of cash to the retiring 38 percent owned by the estates and widows. Possibly, this is the reason respondent has not attempted to apply subsection (C), relating to the acquisition of assets, "in exchange *solely* for . . . voting stock." (Emphasis added.) . . .

The remaining arguments for reorganization treatment are even less persuasive. Respondent's own regulation under section 368, section 1.368-1, 2, Income Tax Regs., disposes of respondent's contention on brief that "Reorganization treatment can be ascribed . . . without literal satisfaction of the requirements of Sec. 368." Furthermore, "there was not that reshuffling of a capital structure, *within the framework of an existing corporation,* contemplated by the term 'recapitalization'," as now described in subsection (E). . . . (Emphasis added.) And the shift that occurred in the proprietary interest of the two corporations was hardly the "*mere* change in identity, form, or place of organization" (emphasis added) required by subsection (F). . . .

We rest the conclusion that there was no reorganization here on the form and content of the reorganization sections, not on the ground that there was no business purpose. . . .

Section 1.331-1(c), Income Tax Regs., does not interfere with our ultimate conclusion. This regulation adopts the holding of Richard H. Survaunt, supra. In *Survaunt,* a transaction in which the original corporation was liquidated and the shareholders and directors transferred the assets to a new corporation in exchange for stock was found to be a reorganization under the intercorporate transfer of assets provision of subsection (D) when petitioners failed to prove the absence of a business purpose. The regulation describes similar facts and the . . . language invokes section 356 to cover the distribution of "boot" in pursuance of a plan of reorganization. Since we cannot conclude that the facts in the instant case constitute a reorganization, the reference to section 356 will not support respondent's position.

Section 1.331-1(c), Income Tax Regs., also cites section 301 as authority. This may be explained as further description of section 356. See section 356(a)(2). Respondent, however, takes the position that the regulation may require dividend treatment in any case of liquidation-reincorporation. It is argued that Congress did not intend a liquidation followed by a reincorporation of the business into a corporation with similar equity interests to be a liquidation within the meaning of section 331, with the result that section 331(b) should not apply. As we have already concluded, however, Congress accorded ordinary income treatment to liquidations only, if at all, in reorganization situations. . . .

We accordingly think petitioners correctly treated the cash and property received from Delaware as a payment in exchange for the Delaware stock redeemed by them. To take account of uncontested adjustments,

Decisions will be entered under Rule 50.

Reviewed by the Court.

WITHEY, J., concurs in the result.

PIERCE, J., dissenting: [The opinion of Judge PIERCE, in which Judges RAUM and ATKINS joined, is omitted.]

NOTE

1. See Berghash v. Commissioner, 361 F.2d 257 (2d Cir. 1966). What was the basis of the Commissioner's first argument? See Treas. Reg. §1.301-1(l). Would this approach lead to dividend treatment of all the shareholders of Delaware? Of all who continued in California? By what factors did the Commissioner determine that there was "in substance a separate transaction"? What is the Commissioner's authority for disregarding the "net effect" here, while disregarding the separate steps in *Morgan?* Where might you look to determine, under §356(a)(2), whether a "boot" distribution "has the effect of the distribution of a dividend"? Consider the relevance of §302(b).

Is Treas. Reg. §1.301-1(l) valid in light of the provisions of §356(a), which limit taxation of the "boot" to the "gain" realized? Why is the limitation to "gain" found in §356(a) but not in §356(b) or 356(e)? Should §356(a) be limited to "gain"? Why? Cf. §302(d). See Notes 1, 2, and 6, pages 564-565 *supra.*

2. Assume that X, a real estate corporation 86 per cent owned by individual A, adopts a plan of complete liquidation under §337. Within twelve months the following transactions occur:

1) X sells investment securities at a gain of $8,000,000;

2) Members of A's family form Z Corporation, contributing $20,000;

3) A sells Z land for $420,000, Z giving A its note for $140,000 and A's family promising to pay $280,000, for which Z issues another $280,000 in stock to A's family;

4) X sells Z three of its six pieces of real estate, accounting for 35 per cent of X's rental income but all of X's shopping center properties, for which Z gives a ten-year, 4 per cent note totaling $890,000;

5) X distributes all its remaining assets, real estate and Z's notes, to its shareholders, principally A, and dissolves.

As Commissioner, what would you claim were the tax consequences to X? To A? To Z? See Book Production Industries, Inc., 24 CCH Tax Ct. Mem. 339 (1965). See also Retail Properties, Inc., 23 CCH Tax Ct. Mem. 1463 (1964), where taxpayer corporation owned five parcels of land. After the adoption of a plan of liquidation, one parcel was sold to an unrelated party. The remainder was conveyed to L, a wholly owned subsidiary, in exchange for cash, notes and the assumption of mortgage liabilities. Taxpayer then distributed all its assets and dissolved. The court found a "D" reorganization, not a §337 liquidation. The control requirement was met, since taxpayer or its shareholders owned 80 per cent of the stock of L after the transfer, and there is no necessity that control be acquired as a result of the transfer.

3. Suppose the transferee shareholder group in *Gallagher* had ended up with 80 per cent of California; what result for each of them? If, instead, the Delaware Corporation had redeemed the stock of those whose interests were eliminated or re-

duced and the new or increased interests had acquired stock in Delaware, and then California had been organized and had taken over the Delaware assets with its stock going proportionately to the Delaware stockholders, what result would you expect? Why? Should the result in that case be different from the result in *Gallagher?* Under the existing statute? Under an ideal statute? Why? See Note, 25 Tax L. Rev. 282 (1970); N. Lane, The Reincorporation Game: Have the Ground Rules Really Changed? 77 Harv. L. Rev. 1218 (1964).

MOFFATT v. COMMISSIONER
363 F.2d 262 (9th Cir. 1966), cert. denied, 386 U.S. 1016 (1967)

Before BARNES and KOELSCH, Circuit Judges, and CRAIG, District Judge.

BARNES, Circuit Judge: . . . One basic question involving the corporate tax provisions of the Internal Revenue Code of 1954 is presented for our consideration. We must determine whether distributions by the corporation, Moffatt & Nichol, Inc., to its shareholders (petitioners) were liquidating distributions under Sections 331(a)(2) and 346, and therefore taxable as capital gains, or were distributions incident to a plan of reorganization under Sections 354 and 368, and therefore taxable as dividends under Section 356. Taxpayers challenge the decision of the Tax Court on the grounds . . . (2) that the steps taken, even if viewed as interrelated, did not satisfy the statutory reorganization requirements of Sections 354 and 368.

From the date of its incorporation in 1947 until approximately October 1957, Moffatt & Nichol, Inc. was primarily engaged in consulting engineering. Its principal place of business was located in Long Beach, California. During those years the company's stock was owned by taxpayers John G. Moffatt (45%), Frank E. Nichol (45%) and George G. Murray (10%). In addition to its principal activity, the company (hereinafter sometimes referred to as "Inc.") also participated in various joint ventures and was licensed as a building contractor, although it did not actually engage in any building activities. Although the shareholders were Inc.'s key employees, more than sixty other people were employed, about one-third of whom were considered of professional standing. The company prospered greatly during this decade, and though its taxable income declined in 1957 from the preceding year's figure, the 1957 income had still more than quadrupled the 1953 figure. Despite its prosperity, however, only one dividend ($30,000 in 1955) had been paid from the company's inception.

On April 12, 1957, Henry E. Howard, a certified public accountant, was engaged by Inc. to review the company's tax problems. Howard attended a conference with Inc.'s counsel on April 30, 1957, and afterwards prepared a memorandum concerning those tax matters discussed. This memorandum read in part as follows:

May 6, 1957

"Introductory Statement. At the conference held in your office Tuesday last, certain proposals were discussed relating to the tax problems of the

above corporation and its principal stockholders. Several tentative solutions were set forth. Briefly: [1] Liquidation of the corporation. [2] Sale by principal shareholders of a portion of their holdings. [3] Purchase of real estate by stockholders and subsequent sales. [4] Tax planning for existing corporation. . . . [6] Problems of principal stockholders relating to bad debt loss resulting in capital loss carryovers.

I

"*Liquidation of Corporation.* While we appreciate that this would provide the principal stockholders with the sought-after capital gains, it would present other problems which could very well offset the advantages obtained. The principal disadvantage would be the amount of taxes required to be paid in the year of liquidation. This corporation is reporting profits on a hybrid-accrual method. If this method is adhered to consistently it is doubtful that a change will be made by the commissioner [I.R.C. 446(c)], however if the corporation ceases operations and liquidates it is probable that all earned income both recorded and unrecorded will immediately become subject to corporate tax rates and also be subject to liquidating dividends. [Rev. Rul. 1953-255.]

. . . "An alternative may be found in the delaying of liquidation with a transfer of operations. Under this plan the existing corporation would remain in existence for a period of time, its only activity being completion of present projects and collection of outstanding accounts. This would be accompanied by the formation of a new organization to take on new contracts. The effect would be to defer the payment of the taxes mentioned before and also to cover the possibility of additional nonbusiness bad debts in the hands of the individuals which may occur in future years. This plan of course would require a division of labor and other costs with the resulting increase of time and cost in record keeping. The period for which liquidation could be delayed would be determined by application of section 531, which would probably be about one year after the plan became effective."

This possible approach to the tax problems of Inc. and its key employees reflected the fact that Moffatt and Nichol had each suffered substantial nonbusiness bad debt losses in 1954, 1956 and 1957, and both anticipated future bad debt losses on outstanding loans to one Powers. The above proposal sought primarily to provide ample capital gains against which the capital losses could be offset.

In substance, the above plan of Howard was adopted by Inc.'s management. A new entity, Moffatt & Nichol, Engineers (hereinafter referred to as Engineers), was incorporated on July 22, 1957, with the same principal place of business as Inc. On October 10, 1957, the stock was authorized to be issued to Moffatt (40%), Nichol (40%), Murray (10%), and 10% to Bobisch, a structural engineer, who for some time had been negotiating to purchase a proprietary interest in the consulting engineering operation. When Bobisch, on March 7, 1958, terminated his employment with Engineers, his ten per cent was bought by and distributed equally to Moffatt and Nichol, giving each the identical share that he possessed in the ownership of Inc. Engineers' stock was not actually issued until September 2, 1958.

Moffatt, Nichol and Murray obtained loans in the aggregate amount of $22,500 from Inc. on their notes, in order to pay for their Engineers stock. Payment for the stock was made on October 1, 1957, by having Inc. issue its check for $22,500 to Engineers. The obligations of Moffatt, Nichol and Murray on their notes were discharged on December 23, 1957, through deductions from their salaries by Engineers which were applied for that purpose.

As a consequence of Engineers formation as of October 1, 1957, all employees of Inc., including all officers, were transferred to the books of Engineers. Inc.'s pending contracts were not assigned to Engineers, but the work in process was delegated to the new company which in turn was duly compensated for its efforts. Engineers operated in the same physical premises that Inc. had used since its inception. It also used the same equipment which, for accounting purposes, it leased from Inc. at the depreciation rate plus ten per cent. All new contracts entered into after October 1, 1957, were undertaken in Engineers' name.

The findings of the Tax Court, supported by the evidence in the record, summarize the effects of this transformation:

> "Subsequent to October 1, 1957, Moffatt and Nichol, Inc. had no paid employees, no equipment, and no facilities for conducting an engineering business. Moffatt and Nichol, Inc. had made available to Engineers all of the equipment and facilities necessary to carry on the engineering business it had previously conducted. Its assets consisted, in addition, of cash and liquid items (including accounts receivable), land and building plans relating to such land. Cash necessary for the operation of the consulting engineering business was made available to Engineers by means of loans, and accounts receivable were ultimately transferred to Engineers, all as hereinafter set forth. The land, hereinafter described, had never in fact been used in the business.
>
> "Moffatt and Nichol, Inc. had to remain in existence after October 1, 1957, in order to 'phase out' outstanding Government contracts in its hands at the time. These contracts were nonassignable. The primary activity of Moffatt and Nichol, Inc., subsequent to the October 1957 transfer, was the collection of accounts in respect of contracts in its name for which work had been done by it (prior to the transfer) and by Engineers (subsequent to the transfer)." (Tr. 169-70.)

Subsequent to the transfer of the engineering operations to Engineers, loans in the amount of $89,000 were made to Engineers by Inc. Finally, on December 23, 1958, Inc.'s board of directors drafted a formal resolution to wind up its company's affairs. In this regard, Inc. distributed to its shareholders promissory notes, cash, automobiles, office furniture, and other equipment. On January 2, 1960, Engineers purchased the notes and the equipment (with the single exception of one automobile) from the taxpayers. Much of the cash was also transferred by the stockholders to Engineers in exchange for notes.

As a result of this series of transactions, Moffat and Nichol each reported long-term capital gain in respect of liquidating dividends of Inc. totaling $88,162.89 for the taxable years 1958 and 1959. Substantial capital losses were offset by each taxpayer against these reported gains. The Tax Court, however, held that the distributions in liquidation by Inc. were "boot" incident to a corporate reorganization (§368(a)(1) (D)), and as such were taxable as ordinary income under Section 356 of the Internal Revenue Code of 1954.

From the above statement of facts, as found by the Tax Court, we find the Tax Court correct in its conclusion that the individual steps taken, beginning with the formation of Engineers, were interrelated parts of an integrated plan of reorganization. The proposal contained in the Howard memorandum, adopted with only minor deviation, unquestionably sought to continue the corporate operations, while siphoning off substantial earnings at capital gains rates. The net effect of the steps taken was merely to change the name of the corporation. Inc. remained in existence, for all practical purposes, for the sole purpose of collecting the amounts due on pending contracts which were delegated to Engineers for completion. The evidence thus clearly supports the finding of one integrated transformation.

There remains for our consideration, however, the question of whether the interrelated steps described above constitute a plan of reorganization within the purview of Section 368 of the Internal Revenue Code. It was the determination of the Tax Court that this integrated plan qualified as a reorganization under subsection "D" of Section 368. . . .

The findings alluded to above clearly disclose that the transactions in question were pursuant to an integrated plan and did not involve an exchange of stock for stock. This leaves as the only Section 354 requirement that must be met for the transaction to qualify as a type "D" reorganization under Section 368 that the new corporation acquired "substantially all" of the assets of the old corporation.

The taxpayers in the present case strenuously contend that not substantially all of Inc.'s assets were transferred to Engineers, and a 368(a)(1)(D) reorganization therefore did not occur. The taxpayers rely primarily on the fact that a large portion of the book assets of Inc. (35.48%) was in the form of land investment and building plans (held for a proposed building construction) which never came into the ownership of Engineers. We find substance to taxpayers' contention when we apply a straight percentage of book assets test to determine what constitutes "substantially all." Commissioner v. First Nat. Bank, 104 F.2d 865 (3d Cir. 1939), is frequently cited for the proposition that 86 per cent total net worth is "substantially all." Arctic Ice Machine Co. v. Commissioner, 23 B.T.A. 1223 (1931), similarly is cited for the proposition that 68 per cent is insufficient.

We are of the opinion, however, that a sounder view is espoused by Rev. Rul. 57-518, 1957-2 C.B. 253, to the effect that no particular or specific percentage should be controlling. Rather, the ruling advises that "the nature of the properties retained by the transferor, the purpose of retention, and the amount thereof" are all to be considered. In the present case the Tax Court made the following finding which we deem dispositive of taxpayers' contention when viewed in the light of the more flexible rule:

"In one form or another the new company had the use and benefit of all the assets relating to the operation of the business, whether by 'loans', 'rentals' of equipment followed ultimately by sale thereof, or otherwise. And it finally wound up with all the assets that were necessary or appropriate to the conduct of the business. There remained in the hands of the stockholders only certain nonoperating assets that were not required in the business, and even these assets [as resources] were 'pledged' [Tr. 171; Ex. PP] by Moffatt and Nichol, Inc. to the new corporation." (Tr. 197-98.)

In the setting of a service organization such as a consulting engineering operation, the retention of physical nonoperating assets such as land should not cloud the fact that the essential tangible and intangible assets of one corporation have been transferred to another corporation. That is what occurred here. The skilled employees, the most essential asset of any service organization, were all transferred to Engineers. Similarly, almost the entire lot of operating assets was also transferred. We would ignore the real character and substance of a transaction to hold in this case, as the petitioners urge, that the retention of a substantial portion of the company's dollar assets, unnecessary and unused in the business, is sufficient to defeat the operation of Section 368(a)(1)(D) without making any further inquiry as to the nature of those retained assets and the purpose behind their retention.

In support of affirmance the Commissioner contends the same result is reached by application of 26 U.S.C. §368(a)(1)(F) which applies whenever there is a "mere change in identity, form, or place of organization, however effected."

Considering these additional factors, and dispensing with the solitary and technical percentage theory, we find, in accordance with the position taken by the Tax Court, that Inc. transferred *substantially* all of its assets to Engineers. We therefore find that the transactions in question did constitute a type "D" reorganization.

The decisions of the Tax Court are affirmed.

CRAIG, District Judge [dissenting] . . . . The Commissioner first contends that "substantially all of the assets" means "substantially all of the operative assets". I cannot agree. If Congress intended to limit the transfer to "operative assets" it would have said so. Congress did not, and the Court should not read into the Code that which is not there. . . .

Petitioners cite numerous cases which indicate that "substantially all of the properties" under the 1939 Code was interpreted as meaning at least 80% if not more of the properties, including intangibles such as accounts receivable. . . . In Halliburton v. Commissioner, 9 Cir., 78 F.2d 265 (1935), the Court held that the term "property" in the tax law includes "money", unless otherwise expressly provided by Congress. There is no way of knowing precisely why Congress adopted the new terminology of "assets" over the old "properties", but the effect was certainly not to narrow the scope of the phrase. Therefore, were the Court to conclude, and it should not, that the building and the land were the only assets which were not transferred to the new company, this would constitute a transfer of only 64.52% of the assets, which is not "substantially all of the assets". It is not necessary to decide where the demarcation line of "substantially all" may lie, but it should be held that it is certainly somewhere above 64.52%.

In appraising the evidence as to whether there was a "substantial transfer", the respondent seeks to place a value on "intangibles", which may also be described as "good will". This suggestion arises from the nature of Engineers' business. . . .

While Congress may be presumed to have exercised its taxing power to the fullest, that presumption does not authorize this Court to supply additional language to the act. Moreover, if we were to disregard the record in this case and assign a "thin air" value to good will, or intangibles, or whatever name may be applied, even to the extent of $180,000.00, we would still have under 80% of the assets transferred.

It has been suggested that a loan should be treated as a "transfer of assets" within the meaning of the statute. The two terms are wholly and completely incompatible. A transfer of assets under any interpretation denotes an investment with the attendant risks. A loan carries with it an obligation to repay with a fixed rate of interest. . . .

The Respondent contends that an historical analysis of Congressional action produces the startling conclusion that Congress intended "substantially all" in Section 354 to mean 50%. This conclusion is reached by inferring that a proposed Section 357 (H.R. 8300), which was never enacted, was incorporated in Section 354. This is unrealistic and untenable. If Congress says "substantially all", it means just that, and not 50%. . . .

NOTE

1. Assume that Inc. had formed Engineers and had transferred to it the assets which Engineers had received in *Moffatt* and that Engineers had issued its stock to Inc. in exchange therefor. Assume further that Inc. had distributed the shares of Engineers to the Inc. shareholders in exchange for a pro rata portion of the outstanding Inc. shares. A corporate division would thus have been effected, with Inc.'s owning non-business and liquid assets and Engineers' owning the business assets. Would the transaction have been tax-free under §368(a)(1)(C) and §354(a)(1), setting up the format for a future sale of the Inc. stock as a capital gain? Does the *Moffatt* notion of "substantially all" effectively defeat the "active business" requirement of §355? Might the Commissioner be able to defeat the result implied above by asserting that, since the transaction is (looks like?) both a "C" and a "D" reorganization, it must, under §368(a)(2)(A), be treated as a "D," and, therefore, according to §354(b)(1), Inc. would have had to distribute all its properties (something not done in this hypothetical)? What argument should the taxpayer make in opposition? How should a court resolve the problem? Why?

2. Is the Commissioner's *Moffatt* position as to the meaning of "substantially all" consistent with his position in Rev. Proc. 66-34, 1966-2 Cum. Bull. 1232, page 560 supra? Compare James Armour, Inc., 43 T.C. 295 (1964), Note 2, page 608 supra. See E. Surkin, The Reincorporation Quandary Under Sections 368(a)(1)(D) and 354(b)(1): Comments on Moffatt v. Comm., 53 Cornell L. Rev. 575 (1968); M. Whittaker, Liquidation and Reincorporation, 1966 So. Calif. Tax Inst. 191.

DAVANT v. COMMISSIONER
366 F.2d 874 (5th Cir. 1966), cert. denied, 386 U.S. 1022 (1967)

Before RIVES and BELL, Circuit Judges, and FULTON, District Judge.

RIVES, Circuit Judge: The petitioners are persons who claim that the income from the sale of their stock in the South Texas Rice Warehouse Company should be taxed solely as a capital gain. The Tax Court found that a corporate reorganization had taken place and held that at least part of petitioners' income should be taxed as a dividend constituting ordinary income. The government took a cross appeal contending that the Tax Court should have held that a greater portion of petitioners' income was ordinary income. Since we agree with the government, we affirm in part and reverse in part.

South Texas Rice Warehouse Co.[2] was incorporated under the laws of the State of Texas in 1936. The principal business of Warehouse consisted of drying, cleaning, and storing rice. Warehouse's principal source of rice was land owned by a brother corporation, South Texas Water Co.[4]

Water was incorporated under the laws of the State of Texas in 1934. Water had two principal businesses. It owned land which it rented to a partnership, South Texas Rice Farms,[5] and it owned and operated an irrigation canal system used to irrigate the ricelands that it leased to Farms.

The principal business of Farms was releasing the land rented from Water to tenant farmers on a sharecrop arrangement. Generally, the tenant retained 50% of the rice produced and Farms received the other 50% as payment for the land provided.

The riceland which was leased by Farms from Water was irrigated by Water and the rice which Farms received from its tenants was put through Warehouse's dryer and stored by Warehouse. Water's lessees generally put their rice through Warehouse's dryer, and then stored their rice in Warehouse's facilities.

Warehouse and Water were each owned in equal proportions by four families. The partners in Farms were the same persons who were the stockholders of Warehouse and Water and their respective interests were in substantially the same proportions as their stock ownership in the two corporations. The books and records of these three enterprises, while separately prepared, were all kept in the same office.

In 1960 a number of the stockholders consulted an attorney, Homer L. Bruce, Esq., about the possibility of transferring Warehouse's operating assets to Water for $700,000 and then liquidating Warehouse. This attorney had represented Warehouse, Water, and their stockholders for many years.

In the attorney's opinion, section 337 would allow the individuals to obtain capital gains treatment for any income they might receive in the transaction they

[2]Hereafter, Warehouse.
[4]Hereafter, Water.
[5]Hereafter, Farms.

contemplated.[8] However, Mr. Bruce advised against such a course of conduct. He told them that in a situation where such a sale and distribution was made when the stockholders of the two corporations were identical it was probable that the Internal Revenue Service would take the position that the stockholders had received a dividend taxable at ordinary rates and not a capital gain.

Mr. Bruce then suggested an alternate course of conduct which he believed would have the desired effect of having any gains taxed at the capital rather than the ordinary rate. The suggestion was that if the stockholders made a sale of their stock to a person not connected with them or their corporations at a fair price which would allow that person to make a reasonable profit, then that person could sell Warehouse's operating assets to Water and liquidate Warehouse without endangering the original stockholders' capital gains treatment.

Homer L. Bruce, Jr., a practicing attorney and the son of petitioners' attorney, was suggested by one of the stockholders as an appropriate person to buy their stock. Both Water and Warehouse had a corporate account with the Bank of the Southwest[9] and the Bank had for many years been represented by Mr. Bruce's law firm.

Mr. Bruce contacted A. M. Ball, a vice-president of the Bank. He told Mr. Ball that his son wished to buy Warehouse for $914,200 and wished to borrow the necessary funds from the Bank. The stock of Warehouse was to be the collateral for the $914,200 note of Bruce, Jr. It was understood that Water would then buy the assets of Warehouse for $700,000, and that this money plus part of the approximately $230,000 which Warehouse had in its bank account would be used, after Warehouse was liquidated, to repay the loan. This procedure allowed Bruce, Jr. to receive $15,583.30 for his part in the transaction, and allowed the Bank to receive what the parties designated as one day's interest on its $914,200 loan or $152.37.

Homer L. Bruce, Jr. was not present during his father's discussions with Mr. Ball nor did Bruce, Jr. participate in the discussions which determined that $914,200 should be the purchase price for the Warehouse stock and $700,000 the purchase price of Warehouse's operating assets to be paid by Water. No appraisals were made of the properties of Warehouse during 1960, although the Tax Court later found their fair market value to be at least the $700,000 paid for them by Water. The Bank loaned Bruce, Jr. $914,200, yet was never furnished a statement of his finances nor an appraisal or statement on Warehouse.

Mr. Ball, who approved the $914,200 loan, had no authority to approve loans in excess of $25,000 without prior approval of the Bank's discount committee. This particular transaction was not approved by the discount committee until after it was entirely a fait accompli.

On August 26, 1960 the stockholders of Warehouse, Mr. Ball, Mr. Bruce and his son met at the Bank. In accordance with a detailed instruction sheet, the respective parties went through the motions of making a loan, selling stock, electing new corporate officials, selling Warehouse's assets, liquidating Warehouse, and repaying the

[8]While the attorney spoke in terms of section 337, he, of course, meant sections 337 and 331.

[9]Hereafter, Bank.

loan. Thanks to the careful prearrangement of all the details, the parties were able to act out their respective roles in approximately one hour.[11]

In terms of the actual physical carrying on of Warehouse's business, absolutely no disruption was occasioned by the paper transfer to Water. Every part of the business was carried on as before with the sole change being that it was necessary to keep one less set of books at the office. August 26 came during the busy rice drying season, but for those physically involved in carrying on Warehouse's business affairs, August 26, 1960 came and went like any other day — the dryers kept right on drying.

Petitioners take the position that the sale of their stock in Warehouse to Bruce, Jr. was a bona fide sale and that they properly reported their profits as the gain from the sale of a capital asset held over six months. The Commissioner argues that the transaction involved in this case is a corporate reorganization and that to the extent of the earnings and profits of both Warehouse and Water the gain reported here must be considered as a dividend taxable as ordinary income. The Tax Court held that the instant transaction constituted a corporate reorganization coming under section 368(a)(1)(D) of the Internal Revenue Code of 1954. However, the Tax Court also held that the gain was taxable as a dividend only to the extent of Warehouse's earnings and profits. . . .

In order to effectuate the intent of Congress the dividend, liquidation, redemption and reorganization sections of the Code must be examined and viewed as a functional whole. The basic framework by which Congress sought to tax corporate distributions is contained in sections 301(a), 301(c) and 316. Distributions of corporate funds to stockholders made with respect to their stockholdings must be included in their gross income to the extent that those distributions are made out of the corporation's earnings and profits. Such distributions are termed by the Code as dividends and are taxed as ordinary income.

All of the steps taken by taxpayer in this case with regard to the $200,000 worth of earnings and profits generated by Warehouse and the $700,000 worth of earnings and profits generated by Water were for the sole purpose of turning what otherwise would be a dividend taxed at the ordinary income rate into a gain made on the sale or exchange of a capital asset taxed at the much lower capital gains rate.

First, petitioners tell us that all they have done is sell their entire stock interest in Warehouse in a bona fide sale to an outside party. The sale of all of one's stock in a corporation, thus terminating a taxpayer's proprietary interest in a corporation and its assets, is probably one of the most common forms of capital sales. But the Tax Court held, "The facts in this case show that Homer L. Bruce, Jr., was not a purchaser of the stock in any real sense but merely a conduit through which funds passed from Water Co. to Warehouse and from Warehouse to petitioners." In this Court petitioners stress the fact that there was never a binding, written obligation on Water to buy Warehouse's assets or on Bruce, Jr. to sell them. Like the Tax Court, in view of all the circumstances, we can attach very little importance to the absence of any written obligations.

---

[11]In addition to the instruction sheet, all of the necessary documents had been prepared in advance. These documents included the necessary papers for Warehouse's "sale" of its operating assets to Water.

For the purposes of the personal income tax provisions, courts have never been shackled to mere paper subterfuges. It is hard to imagine a transaction more devoid of substance than the purported "sale" to Bruce, Jr. . . . Congress has provided in great detail what the tax consequences of a reorganization or partial or complete liquidation of a corporation should be. The tax consequences of this transaction must be judged by those standards because to allow the "sale" to Bruce, Jr. to divert our attention from the tax policies enacted by Congress would be to exalt form above all other criteria. He served no function other than to divert our attention and avoid tax. Stated another way, his presence served no legitimate nontax-avoidance business purpose. . . .

The petitioners insist that, even if we recognize that Bruce, Jr. was merely their agent and impute his acts to them, they are entitled to capital gains treatment. They stress that they did no more than completely liquidate Warehouse corporation, which entitled them to a capital gain under section 331. The sale to Water of Warehouse's operating assets should not be treated as a taxable event, the petitioners argue, because of section 337. The "general rule" pronounced by section 337 is that if a corporation adopts a plan of complete liquidation and distributes all of its assets in complete liquidation within 12 months after the date the plan was adopted, no recognition of gain or loss shall be recognized on the sale of its property made during those 12 months.

Section 331 provides that when a corporation is completely liquidated section 301 is inapplicable and the gain shall be treated as if derived from a sale or exchange of the stock. In short, the gain is to be treated as a capital gain. It would appear at first blush that petitioners have carefully fitted themselves directly within the statutory wording. But in the landmark case of Gregory v. Helvering, 293 U.S. 465 (1935) the Supreme Court refused to give effect to a corporate transaction which complied precisely with the formal requirements for a nontaxable corporate reorganization, on the ground that the transaction had served no function other than that of a contrivance to bail out corporate earnings at capital gains tax rates. That is precisely the charge made here. Let us examine what legitimate purposes might be served by the transactions here under consideration. Three distinct and separate things occurred.

First, $700,000 in earnings and profits possessed by Water were passed through Warehouse to petitioners. Second, $200,000 in earnings and profits from Warehouse were distributed to petitioners. Third, the operating assets of Warehouse were combined with Water and were from that point on owned and controlled through Water. Only one business nontax-avoidance purpose can be found to support any of these events: petitioners wished to eliminate one of the corporate shells and thereafter control all of the properties under one roof. This motive legitimately explains why petitioners transferred the operating assets of Warehouse to Water. But it does not explain either of the first two steps. Under the reorganization provisions of the Code petitioners could have transferred all of Warehouse's assets, including its earnings and profits, to Water without paying any tax. Thus the payment of $200,000 from Warehouse to petitioners cannot be explained as necessary in order to place both businesses under the same roof. Likewise, there was no need for petitioners to cast the transfer of Warehouse's operating assets in the form of a sale. The businesses could be combined under one roof without the $700,000 from Water ever coming over to Warehouse. It is apparent that no functional relationship exists between either the $200,000 coming to petitioners from Warehouse or the $700,000 coming to petitioners from Water and the transfer of Warehouse's assets to Water. Petitioners make no attempt to provide a nontax-avoidance purpose for their actions, but instead argue that these events cannot be a reorganization because they do not come under the literal language of the reorganization provisions. They then reason they must be a complete liquidation since they do come under the literal language of the complete liquidation provisions. As Justice Frankfurter once put it, "The syllogism is perfect. But this is a bit of verbal logic from which the meaning of things has evaporated."[20]

Clearly, this liquidation cannot come within the intention of Congress in enacting the complete liquidation provisions. Those provisions contemplate that operating assets will no longer be used by the stockholders to carry on the business as a corporation. It has long been recognized that taxpayers cannot liquidate a corporation with the intention of immediately reincorporating it in order to hold back liquid assets and cash for the purpose of getting capital gains treatment or to obtain a stepped-up basis for the operating assets or to wipe out old earnings and profits or other tax attributes. Such a liquidation reincorporation transaction does not qualify for section 331 treatment. . . . Applying the concept that we must look at petitioners' plan as a whole to the extent that the parts are functionally related, and not at its constituent parts individually, for the purpose of determining whether section 331 applies, we conclude that section 331 does not apply in this case.

Petitioners never intended to give up the corporate form of doing business. At all times relevant their intention was to transfer Warehouse's operating assets to Water. Water and Warehouse were owned by identical shareholders with identical distribution of shares. At no time did the petitioners' interest in the operating assets change. Most of the reported cases involve situations where the stockholders create a new corporate shell to receive the assets, but we see no difference between a liquidation followed by a transfer to a new corporate shell and a liquidation followed by a transfer to an already existing corporate shell.

Since this interchange of events cannot be viewed as a complete liquidation, we must now decide, for the purposes of the federal tax code, what it is. In the Tax Court the Government contended that this was a 368(a)(1)(D) or (F) reorganization.

A section 368(a)(1)(F) reorganization is defined as "a mere change in identity, form, or place of organization, however effected." Since the Tax Court held that this transaction was a (D) reorganization, it apparently believed that it was unnecessary to decide the (F) question. In the past, type (F) reorganizations have overlapped with type (A), (C) and (D) reorganizations. For this reason this provision has received almost no administrative or judicial attention. It is true that a substantial shift in the proprietary interest in a corporation accompanying a reorganization can hardly be characterized as a mere change in identity or form. Helvering v. Southwest Consolidated Corp., 315 U.S. 194 (1942).

[20]Phelps Dodge Corp. v. NLRB, 313 U.S. 177, 191 (1941).

The term "mere change in identity [or] form" obviously refers to a situation which represents a mere change in *form* as opposed to a change in substance. Whatever the outer limits of section 368(a)(1)(F), it can clearly be applied where the corporate enterprise continues uninterrupted, except for a distribution of some liquid assets or cash. Under such circumstances, there is a change of corporate vehicles but not a change in substance. If Water had no assets of its own prior to the transfer of Warehouse's operating assets to it, could we say that Water was any more than the alter ego of Warehouse? The answer is no. The fact that Water already had other assets that were vertically integrated with Warehouse's assets does not change the fact that Water was Warehouse's alter ego. Viewed in this way, it can make no practical difference whether the operating assets were held by Water or Warehouse, and a shift between them is a mere change in identity or form. At least where there is a complete identity of shareholders and their proprietary interests, as here, we hold that the type of transaction involved is a type (F) reorganization.

In the alternative, we also hold that the Tax Court correctly held that these events constituted a 368(a)(1)(D) reorganization. The (D) question is more complex than the (F) question. . . . In this case, it is clear that the petitioners have satisfied part one of the type (D) definition. Warehouse is a "corporation" and it transferred "a part of its assets to another corporation," Water. Since both corporations were owned identically by petitioners the "control" requisite was fulfilled.

Petitioners argue that the provision cannot apply to them because in part two Congress specifically required that "stock or securities" of the transferee corporation be passed to petitioners. They, of course, point out that they received no new stock in Water as a part of their transaction. We cannot agree that this statutory requirement must be taken literally, especially where it would prevent the effectuation of the tax policies of Congress.

The (D) reorganization provisions have never been confined to a strictly literal application. It will be noted that section 368(a)(1)(D) requires that the transferor be "a corporation." But it has been consistently held that a proper interpretation and application does not prevent from coming under the aegis of 368(a)(1)(D) a transfer made by "persons" who have received assets from a corporation with the intention of transferring them to another corporation. . . .

Nor in ascertaining the intention of Congress should we ignore the function intended for part two of the type (D) definition. Section 368 is not an operative provision but merely defines what Congress meant by the term reorganization. The operative provisions for a 368(a)(1)(D) reorganization are those which Congress has cited, sections 354, 355 and 356. These latter three sections determine what will be the tax consequences of a type (D) reorganization. . . .

In sections 354, 355 and 356 Congress has provided for the tax consequences of holding out cash or liquid assets in a 368(a)(1)(D) reorganization. Congress has drawn these provisions to cover the normal procedure for a taxpayer legitimately wishing to take advantage of the taxfree reorganization provisions. It is only natural then that Congress would speak in terms of stock transferred in the course of a reorganization. The exchange of stock in the course of a legitimate reorganization was the specific case most likely to occur to the mind and the most logical way to draw the statute. The fact that Congress drew the statute to fit the most common form of the problem does not mean that it had any intention of allowing the two evils most inherent in a reorganization scheme to persist. . . .

Moreover, since the operative sections were cast in terms of stock transfers, it was only normal that in referring to those sections in 368(a)(1)(D) . . . Congress referred to "stock or securities" "distributed in a transaction which qualifies under section 354, 355, or 356." Congress thus did not intend to place any special emphasis on the idea that stock *must* be transferred, rather Congress only intended to use this convenient terminology in referring to the operating provisions of the Code.

Petitioners' major argument against the application of 368(a)(1)(D) and 354, 356 thus rests on the weak foundation that Congress required stock to pass before a reorganization under section 368(a)(1)(D) could be found. Section 354 when coupled with section 356 requires that cash or liquid assets received by stockholders as part of a reorganization be taxed as a dividend. In Commissioner of Internal Revenue v. Morgan, 288 F.2d 676 (3 Cir. 1966), the taxpayer also claimed that Congress' clear intent could be avoided by a transaction where no new stock passed.

. . . Applying the rationale of *Morgan* to the instant case requires the same result. The same stockholders owned all of the stock of both Water and Warehouse. Before the transaction the operating assets' value of Warehouse was reflected in the value of its stock. Similarly, the operating assets' value of Water was reflected in the value of its stock. The stockholders had both stocks and their combined certificates reflected the value of their combined operating assets. After the transaction petitioners only had the stock of Water, but it then reflected the value of the combined operating assets of Water and Warehouse. Therefore, the appreciation of the value of Water's stock certificates caused by the transfer of Warehouse's operating assets to Water was the equivalent of issuing $700,000 worth of new or additional stock to Water's stockholders.[26] "*Here, the issuance of new stock would have been a meaningless gesture* . . . ." Commissioner of Internal Revenue v. Morgan, supra; accord, Liddon v. Commissioner, 230 F.2d 304 (6 Cir. 1956), cert. den., 352 U.S. 824, 77 S. Ct. 34 (1956). To require the actual transfer of stock certificates where such a transfer would be a meaningless gesture would be to make the reorganization provisions optional with the taxpayer, a result which Congress clearly did not intend. . . .

We come now to the last leg of our journey; the question of whether the earnings and profits of Warehouse and Water should be combined in determining whether the full $900,000 cash received by petitioners should be treated as a dividend. We hold that the $700,000 coming indirectly from Water and the $200,000 coming from Warehouse must be tested against their combined earnings and profits. Whether we reach this result by means of calling this transaction a type (D) or type (F)

[26]It follows logically from what we have said that the basis formerly belonging to petitioners' Warehouse stock must now be added to the basis of their Water stock. Had the assets of Warehouse been transferred to Water for Water's stock, as they would have been if this transaction had actually been cast as a reorganization, the Water stock would have received the basis of petitioners' Warehouse stock when Warehouse was liquidated. See Treasury Reg. 1.358-1. A different result should not be obtained just because petitioners received no new stock but merely allowed their existing stock to appreciate in value. Cf. Treasury Reg. 1.302-2 (c).

reorganization, or a dividend declared simultaneously with a reorganization, makes no difference. But, in order to avoid future confusion, we think it appropriate to explain our three separate rationales.

Taking in inverse order the separate methods of reaching our conclusion, we hold that the $700,000 petitioners received from Water and the $200,000 petitioners received from Warehouse were dividends under section 301, declared incident to a reorganization. See Bazley v. Commissioner, 331 U.S. 737, 67 S. Ct. 1489 (1947). In *Bazley,* a corporation attempted to transfer liquid assets to a taxpayer, claiming they were a part of a reorganization under what is now section 368(a)(1)(E) which provides for recapitalizations. The Supreme Court characterized the modification of the capital account which constituted the reorganization-recapitalization as "unrelated" to the transfer of the liquid assets which the Court held to be a dividend under what is now section 301.

The same characterization is apt in the instant case. Three separate events took place. The distribution of $700,000 which had been generated incident to the earnings and profits of Water has no rational connection with the reorganization involving Warehouse. It was not necessary to pass this money through Warehouse and Bruce, Jr. in order to accomplish the reorganization. Everything that we said about Bruce, Jr. may be said about Warehouse in regard to the $700,000. Warehouse, under the circumstances of this case, was in no real sense a seller of assets to Water but merely a conduit through which funds passed from Water to Water's stockholders. Since both Warehouse and Water were owned in exactly the same way by the same stockholders, after the funds ended their circuitous route through Warehouse and Bruce, Jr., we see that they were a distribution "with respect to its stock" as required by section 301. The effect was precisely the same as if Water had passed them up directly to its stockholders.

The fact that we held that the transfer of Warehouse's assets and the "sale"-liquidation of Warehouse's stock should be viewed as an integrated transaction does not mean that we are being inconsistent when we separate the distribution of Water's cash to its stockholders. We are merely recognizing that two distinct and functionally unrelated types of transactions were carried on simultaneously — one was a dividend and the other a reorganization. The Code does the same thing in section 356. It recognizes that a series of complicated events may occur which are legitimately a reorganization. These are not taxed. Simultaneously, a taxpayer may receive boot having the effect of a dividend. The dividend's only relation to the reorganization is that it occurred at the same time. The boot where appropriate is taxed as a dividend.

Water, if it chose, could have declared the $700,000 as a dividend before the reorganization with Warehouse ever took place. Or Water could have waited and a week, a month or a year later distributed this dividend. Had it chosen any of these courses, the reorganization involving Warehouse would not have been affected in the slightest. We, therefore, hold that the $700,000 received by petitioners from Water is a distribution governed by sections 301(a), 301(c) and 316. The same reasoning demonstrates that $200,000 coming from Warehouse was a dividend since it was functionally unrelated to the reorganization. We, therefore, hold that the $200,000 received by petitioner from Warehouse is a distribution governed by sections 301(a), 301(c) and 316.

Even if the $700,000 received from Water were not a dividend under sections 301(c) and 316, it would be boot under section 356. Section 356 tells us that, when a taxpayer as part of a reorganization receives not only stock but liquid assets or cash to boot, that boot shall be taxed as a dividend to the extent of the earnings and profits of the distributing corporation. The Tax Court believed the words "of the corporation" referred only to Warehouse and, therefore, held that the $900,000 received should be taxed only to the extent of Warehouse's earnings and profits since it was the only distributing corporation.

We cannot agree with this narrow construction in a case where there is complete identity of ownership of both corporations. Water and Warehouse were but different pockets in the same pair of trousers worn by petitioners. It would be illogical to say that $700,000 would be used to measure how much of the $900,000 distribution had the effect of a dividend if Water were merger into Warehouse and only $200,000 should be used to measure how much of the $900,000 distribution had the effect of a dividend just because Warehouse was merged into Water.

Where there is complete identity of stockholders, the use of the earnings and profits of both corporations is the only logical way to test which distributions have the effect of a dividend. Before the reorganization the petitioners had two pockets with $900,000 in cash divided between them. After the reorganization the petitioners had removed all that cash from both pockets, and it should not matter that before removing it completely they took it out of the right pocket and put it in the left.

The statute in speaking of "the corporation" means the corporation controlled by the stockholders receiving the distribution. Where there is complete identity, as here, the stockholders control both corporations and it is virtually impossible to tell which corporation is in reality "the corporation" distributing the cash. We have two corporations each one of which is distributing cash; therefore, we must look at the earnings and profits of both corporations to see if the distribution is essentially equivalent to a dividend or has the effect of a dividend.

The Tax Court was correct that section 356(a)(2) in using the term "the corporation" meant the distributing corporation. However, the Tax Court erred when it failed to see that in this case there were two distributing corporations, each of which was a party to this reorganization. As we said in connection with our holding for purposes of applying section 301, Warehouse was a conduit for Water's distribution of $700,000 and thus, in determining which corporation was the distributing corporation for purposes of 356(a)(2), we must look through Warehouse and reach Water. . . .

It would not benefit petitioners even if they prevailed on their argument that "the corporation" means only the last distributing corporation. Section 482 permits the Commissioner to "allocate" such tax attributes as are here involved between two corporations "owned" "by the same interests" if "such" "allocation is necessary in order to prevent evasion of taxes." No clearer evasion of taxes can be imagined than converting what would be a dividend taxable at ordinary rates into a capital gain by merely passing it through another corporate shell. We hold that under section 356 and/or section 482 the effect of distributing the $700,000 and the $200,000 must be tested by the combined earnings and profits of both Warehouse and Water.

We need pause for only a moment at the door of 368(a)(1)(F). The effect of a type (F) reorganization is largely unchartered ground; we hold that the funds passed to stockholders in a type (F) reorganization must be tested by the standards laid down under sections 301 and 316. As we showed earlier, that would result in the $900,000 being tested by the earnings and profits of both Warehouse and Water.

Since the Tax Court did not find what Water's earnings and profits were at the time relevant for determining the effect of its distribution of $700,000, we must remand this case. The opinion of the Tax Court is affirmed in part and reversed in part, and the case is remanded for further proceedings not inconsistent with this opinion.

Affirmed in part and reversed in part.

NOTE

Suppose the ownership of Water and Warehouse had not been exactly the same. Might this still have been a "D" reorganization? Would it have been proper to combine the earnings and profits of Water and Warehouse? Suppose there were a 5 per cent stockholder in Warehouse who had no interest in Water. What accounting would be made for his basis in his Warehouse stock? What effect would his situation have on the other stockholders?

Suppose Warehouse had an accumulated deficit. Would this have been set off against the earnings and profits of Water?

On the assumption that the court properly measured earnings and profits in *Davant,* does it follow that there is a dividend to the extent of all ratable earnings and profits? What is the significance of the formulae in §356(a)(2) which limits taxation to *gain?* Why is there no such limitation in §356(b)? Should the difference in language be ignored? See Note 1, page 642 supra.

Did *Davant* present an "F" reorganization? Why?

See, generally, R. Hjorth, Liquidations and Reincorporations — Before and After *Davant,* 42 Wash. L. Rev. 737 (1967).

REEF CORP. v. COMMISSIONER
368 F.2d 125 (5th Cir. 1966), cert. denied, 386 U.S. 1018 (1967)

Before RIVES and BELL, Circuit Judges and FULTON, District Judge.

BELL, Circuit Judge. [The Court, dealing with a complex set of facts, decided unanimously that, in effect: (1) Reef Fields Gasoline Corporation (Reef Fields) first redeemed all the stock of a shareholder group owning 48 per cent of its outstanding shares; (2) Reef Fields transferred about 80 per cent of its assets to a new corporation (new Reef) wholly owned by the controlling (52 per cent) shareholder group of Reef Fields; (3) the transfer of assets was pursuant to a plan of reorganization under

§368(a)(1)(D); (4) the assets transferred met the "substantially all" requirement of §354(b)(1)(A); and (5) there was a "distribution" sufficient to meet the requirements of §354(b)(1)(B). The Court then considered whether the "D" reorganization might also constitute an "F" reorganization. If an "F" reorganization had occurred, Reef Fields would not have been entitled to file a return for the "short period" from the beginning of its taxable year on July 1, 1958, to April 27, 1959, the date of its dissolution, and the Commissioner's deficiency notice, sent to new Reef as successor in name only, would be valid to cover the entire period, July 1, 1958, to June 30, 1959.]

. . . The Commissioner, by way of a cross-appeal, contends that the Tax Court erred in not holding that the transaction which is the subject matter of the litigation constituted a corporate reorganization under §368(a)(1)(F) of the Internal Revenue Code of 1954, as amended. Additional taxes would be due under such a holding. We . . . reverse on the cross-appeal. . . .

Reef Fields, which filed its income tax returns on an accrual basis and whose fiscal year ran from July 1 to June 30, filed an income tax return for the short taxable period July 1, 1958 to the date of dissolution, April 27, 1959. . . . The Commissioner disallowed the return on the basis that new Reef was the successor in name to Reef Fields and thus the return should have been for the full fiscal year. This position, rejected by the Tax Court, was based on the premise that the transaction resulted in a reorganization under §368(a)(1)(F).

Reef Corporation (new Reef), the petitioner, which had adopted the accrual method and the July 1 to June 30 fiscal year, filed an income tax return covering the short period December 15, 1958, the date of its incorporation, to June 30, 1959. . . .

. . . The Commissioner contends on his appeal that the Tax Court erred in holding that the transaction did not constitute a reorganization under §368(a)(1)(F), and in thus holding that the notice of deficiency to petitioner as the successor in name to Reef Fields Gasoline Corporation for a full fiscal year was invalid. . . .

. . . It is his contention that the Tax Court erred in failing to hold that the transaction resulted in a corporate reorganization within the scope of §368(a)(1)(F). His position is that no more took place than a mere change in identity, form, or place of organization of Reef Fields. Judges Rives and Fulton are of the view that this contention should be sustained. This means that the notice of deficiency sent to petitioner as the successor in name to Reef Fields will be validated and a remand will be necessary so that the Tax Court may consider the Commissioner's position under that deficiency notice.

The Commissioner sent two statutory notes of deficiency as a protective measure. One notice, addressed to "Reef Corporation (successor in name to Reef Fields Corporation)", was based on the position that new Reef, although a new corporate entity, was the same taxable entity as Reef Fields. The deficiency under this notice was claimed to be $111,894.40. The other notice, addressed to "Reef Corporation", treated new Reef as a new taxable entity to file a return covering the short taxable period but the depreciation and interest deductions were disallowed, as stated, and the additional tax due was claimed to be $70,695.18.*

---

*The depreciation and interest deductions were claimed on the theory that there had not

The Tax Court rejected the Commissioner's position with respect to §368(a) (1)(F), and thus the deficiency notice to petitioner as successor in name to Reef Fields was invalid. As noted, the Tax Court did adopt the Commissioner's alternative position that the transaction resulted in a corporate reorganization under §368(a) (1)(D), and concluded that the assets transferred by Reef Fields to new Reef had a substituted basis for depreciation and not a stepped-up basis.

The reasoning which supports the conclusion of Judges Rives and Fulton that this is a §368(a)(1)(F) reorganization follows.

In concluding that the instant case was not a type (F) reorganization, the Tax Court interpreted the Supreme Court's last sentence in Helvering v. Southwest Consolidated Corporation, 1942, 315 U.S. 194, 202, 203, 62 S. Ct. 546, 86 L. Ed. 789, as holding §368(a)(1)(F) is "inapplicable when there is a shift in proprietary interest." *Southwest Consolidated* was decided under the 1939 Internal Revenue Code, and we think that the complete revision of the Code in 1954 compels a different result under the instant circumstances from that reached in *Southwest Consolidated*. Further, this case is distinguishable on its facts from *Southwest Consolidated*.

A.

The intricate and confusing facts of this case have been carefully explained. Distilled to their pure substance, two distinct and unrelated events transpired. First, the holders of 48% of the stock in Reef Fields had their stockholdings completely redeemed. Second, new Reef was formed and the assets of Reef Fields were transferred to new Reef. The business enterprise continued without interruption during both the redemption and the change in corporate vehicles.

Much confusion flows from the fact that the corporate reorganization took place simultaneously with the stock redemption. But taking the Code as a standard, these two elements were functionally unrelated. Reef Fields could have completely redeemed the stock of 48% of its shareholders without changing the state of its incorporation. A complete redemption is not a characteristic of a reorganization. Congress clearly indicated this when it defined reorganization in section 368. Section 368(a) (1)(A) speaks of a "merger or consolidation" which looks to the joining of two or more corporations. Section 368(a)(1)(B) and (C) look to one corporation acquiring the assets of another or control of another corporation solely for its voting stock. Section 368(a)(1)(D) looks to the consolidation of two or more corporations or the division of two or more going businesses into separate corporations. Only sections 368(a)(1)(E) and (F) look to adjustments within a corporation. But none of these provisions focuses on a complete redemption as a characteristic of a reorganization. Congress did not have redemption of stock as a primary purpose of any of the forms of a reorganization. That subject came under consideration when it undertook to enact specific legislation on complete and partial redemptions, section 302.

The boot provision, section 356, is adequate to cover a complete redemption when it occurs incident to a reorganization whose primary purpose conforms to the intent

---

been a reorganization but a sale of assets by Reef Fields to new Reef, with a step-up in basis and part of the purchase price represented by interest-bearing debt. — ED.

of section 354 or 355. But section 356 was principally designed to cover dividends incident to a reorganization. When the primary characteristics of the reorganization conform to those described by 368(a)(1)(F), we should parse the occurrences into their functional elements. The reorganizational characteristics present in the instant case do not conform to those generally intended to be covered by section 354 and therefore we should not be blinded by the 356 boot provision. To effectuate the intention of Congress manifested in the Code, we must separate this transaction into its two distinctly separate functional parts. The test of whether events should be viewed separately or together as part of a single plan is not temporal but is functional. See Davant v. Commissioner of Internal Revenue, 5 Cir. 1966, 366 F.2d 874. Applying this test to the instant case, it is clear that the redemption and the change of corporate vehicles must be viewed as separate and distinct occurrences. Cf. Bazley v. Commissioner of Internal Revenue, 1947, 331 U.S. 737, 67 S. Ct. 1489, 91 L. Ed. 1782, 173 A.L.R. 905.

B.

In 1954 Congress completely overhauled the sections of the Code detailing the tax consequences of many types of corporate transactions. Grouped together by Congress were the sections dealing with corporate distributions and adjustments, including the sections dealing with partial liquidations, stock redemptions (complete or partial), and corporate reorganizations. As we said in Davant v. Commissioner of Internal Revenue, 5 Cir. 1966, 366 F.2d 874 at 879: "In order to effectuate the intent of Congress the dividend, liquidation, redemption and reorganization sections of the Code must be examined and viewed as a functional whole."

Prior to 1954 Congress had not specifically provided for the tax treatment of partial liquidations or redemptions. This problem had been handled by judicial decisions which caused "considerable confusion" and in some cases resulted in "unwarranted" taxes and in others allowed taxpayers to "avoid" proper taxation. To correct this situation, Congress enacted a comprehensive set of rules governing the complete and partial redemptions of a stockholder's interest in a corporation. Section 302.

In the instant case the only way to protect the statutory intent of Congress is to test the redemption of stock by the provisions of section 302. A similar result as to the stockholders comes from applying sections 368, 354 and 356. But this method may not always reach the same result and in the instant case would cause an improper result with regard to the corporation. Since the reorganization and the redemption are functionally unrelated in this case, the redemption should be tested by the standard Congress has laid down in section 302.

Prior to 1954 Congress had not specifically provided which tax attributes should be carried over to the surviving or new corporation remaining after a reorganization. . . .

These adjustments had been left to judicial interpretation. . . . Thus, in 1954, in order to correct the existing problems created by unrealistic and conflicting judicial decisions, Congress enacted a comprehensive set of rules governing the carry-over of tax attributes from one corporation to another as a result of a reorganization. Section 381.

In section 381 Congress made a rational distinction between reorganizations that constitute a mere change in form and those that integrate two previously separate and independent enterprises. Where two or more separate businesses are unified into a single enterprise under a 368(a)(1)(D), 354 reorganization, Congress recognized that the resulting new enterprise should be allowed to change certain of its accounting procedures. See for example section 381(b). But Congress also realized that when the business enterprise is carried on as before, with no change in its substance, this is not a proper time to allow the business to change its accounting procedures. See for example 381(b).[12] Thus for the first time, in 1954 it became important to determine whether a reorganization was considered a (D) type or an (F) type reorganization.[13]

Virtually all (F) reorganizations also qualify as (D) reorganizations.[14] When a transaction qualifies as both an (F) and a (D) reorganization, if the new entity were governed by the less stringent continuity rules of (D) reorganizations, provided by section 381, the (F) rules would become a dead letter. The (F) rules are stricter than the (D) rules because a mere change of corporate charter or state of incorporation is not the proper occasion for wholesale accounting method changes that would not have been permitted if no reorganization had taken place.

Only those reorganizations which reflect a substantial change in the corporate operation should be viewed as *solely* (D) reorganizations qualifying for the more liberal rules. Where there is no substantial change in the corporate operation, (F) should be applied since it invokes the stricter rules.

In the instant case there has been no substantial change in the operation of the corporate business. It is carried on just as before but in a new corporate vehicle. This is not a 354 "integration of two or more separate businesses into a unified business enterprise," which Congress considered when it adopted the more liberal rules applicable to a (D) reorganization.

What characteristics of reorganization are present in this case? The only characteristics of a corporate reorganization are the changes in name and state of incorporation. Those are primarily the characteristics of an (F), not a (D), reorganization. The redemption is not a characteristic of a reorganization, as is demonstrated by the fact that a redemption standing alone would not allow a corporation to make wholesale changes in its method of accounting.

If a corporation did no more than completely redeem the stock interest belonging to 48% of its shareholders, it could not under the Code make wholesale account-

---

[12]Section 381(b) excludes type (F) reorganizations from the liberal treatment accorded type (D) reorganizations.

[13]Whether a reorganization is only a (D) type or also qualifies as an (F) type reorganization is also important in applying section 1244. Section 1244(d)(2) applies different rules to an (F) type reorganization than are applied to an (A), a (C) or a (D) reorganization.

[14]In its revision of the Code, the House Committee "deleted as unnecessary" section 368 (a)(1)(F). 1954 U.S. Code Cong. & Admn. News at 4253. The Senate Committee restored that provision (1954 U.S. Code Cong. & Admin. News (Senate Rep.) 4621, 4911), however, noting that "section 354 provides rules for exchanges by shareholders and security holders in reorganizations described in sections 368(a)(1)(A), (B), (C), (E), and (F)." 1954 U.S. Code Cong. & Admn. News at 4903. Thus, the fact that the instant reorganization qualifies under 354 does not mean that it is not also an (F) type reorganization.

ing method changes. Likewise, if a corporation did no more than change its name and state of incorporation, it could not under the Code make wholesale accounting method changes. Combining these two events, neither of which would be sufficient alone, will not permit a corporation to make wholesale accounting method changes. Nothing in the Internal Revenue Code of 1954 contemplates such a result.

. . . The Tax Court's position might have more force if the change in proprietary interests were to new persons and less than 50% of the former stockholders' interest in the old corporation remained in the new corporation. Then the change begins to look like a sale of the assets to a new and legally separate entity followed by a bona fide liquidation. . . . But just how much of a complete redemption would be required to avoid the impact of section 381? Would 1% be enough? Sufficient continuity of interest has been found where 67% or 69% of the old corporation's stockholders control the new corporation. Reilly Oil Co. v. Commissioner of Internal Revenue, 5 Cir. 1951, 189 F.2d 382; Western Mass. Theaters v. Commissioner of Internal Revenue, 1 Cir. 1956, 236 F.2d 186. Changes of less than 50%, as we have here, or for that matter any change not sufficient to prevent the finding of a reorganization should not be sufficient to prevent the operation of section 381. The corporate enterprise went on as before, no new blood was injected and all that took place was a redemption followed by a change in name.

We hold, therefore, that the changes made in the Code in 1954 make the *Southwest Consolidated* decision inapplicable here. We hold also that under the 1954 Code this transaction constituted both a 368(a)(1)(D) and a 368(a)(1)(F) reorganization. . . .

BELL, Circuit Judge, dissenting in part: I respectfully dissent from [the latter part] of the majority opinion. I do not think that the transaction in question constituted a corporate reorganization within the meaning of §368(a)(1)(F). That section has been construed by the Supreme Court as being inapplicable where there is a shift in proprietary interest. Helvering v. Southwest Consolidated Corporation, 1942, 315 U.S. 194, 62 S. Ct. 546, 86 L. Ed. 789. 3 Mertens, Law of Federal Income Taxation, §20.94. Here there was a clear and substantial change in proprietary interest. [One] group was eliminated.

This is to be distinguished from the situation where only minor and technical differences between the original and surviving corporation will justify classification as a reorganization under §368(a)(1)(F). See, for example, Davant v. Commissioner of Internal Revenue, 5 Cir., 1966, 366 F.2d 874, involving two corporations having precisely the same stockholders and proprietary interests. The assets of one corporation were conveyed to the other. And the court held the result to be a §368(a)(1)(F) corporate reorganization. The court concluded that whether the assets were held by one or the other corporations made no practical difference and that the shift of the assets between them in view of the complete identity of stockholders and their proprietary interest, resulted in a mere change in identity or form. There was a change in corporate vehicles but not in substance. . . .

There is nothing in §381 of the Code, 26 U.S.C.A. §381, or elsewhere, to overrule the specific holding of Helvering v. Southwest Consolidated Corporation, supra, and it is our duty, as was the case with the Tax Court, to follow that decision in the absence of more specific congressional direction. My view is that this was not an appropriate case for the application of §368(a)(1)(F).

NOTE

Is it likely that Congress intended to equate the absence of "a substantial change in the corporate operation" with "a mere change in identity, form, or place of organization"? Is it likely that Congress contemplated an "F" reorganization where 48 per cent of the equity interest is redeemed? See R. Hertzog, The Reincorporation Problem in Subchapter C: A Question of Semantics? 9 Wm. & Mary L. Rev. 928 (1968).

STAUFFER ESTATE v. COMMISSIONER
403 F.2d 611 (9th Cir. 1968)

Before JONES,* BARNES, and HAMLEY, Circuit Judges.

BARNES, Circuit Judge: The issue before us is whether §381 of the Internal Revenue Code . . . , carryovers in certain corporate acquisitions, permits a loss sustained by the transferee corporation after a corporate reorganization to be carried back to a premerger taxable year of one of three transferor corporations. The Commissioner takes the position, sustained by the Tax Court below, that the reorganization falls within the definition of a statutory merger, . . . §368(a)(1)(A), and therefore the carryback of net operating loss, . . . §172, is proscribed. Treas. Reg. §1.381(c)(1)-1(b), example (2). The taxpayer contends that the reorganization is one defined by §368(a)(1)(F), "a mere change in identity, form, or place of organization," and that such a loss carryback is proper under §381(b)-1(a) in accordance with §172(b).

The facts were stipulated in the Tax Court. At all times relevant to the proceedings below, Bernard H. Stauffer was the sole owner of three corporations, Stauffer Reducing, Inc., of California (Stauffer California), Stauffer Reducing, Inc., an Illinois corporation (Stauffer Illinois), and Stauffer Reducing, Inc., of New York (Stauffer New York). Each of the three companies was engaged in the business of selling and promoting mechanical weight and posture control devices which were manufactured by the California and Illinois corporations. The officers and directors of each of the companies were the same, board meetings of each of the three companies were always held at the home office of Stauffer California in Los Angeles, and the books of the three corporations were kept in Los Angeles. Each corporation filed a separate income tax return.

In 1958 Mr. Stauffer decided to relocate the Stauffer operations in New Mexico, and in pursuit of this end a shell corporation, Stauffer Laboratories, Inc., of New Mexico (Stauffer New Mexico) was incorporated in 1959. A formal merger agree-

*Hon. Warren L. Jones, Senior Circuit Judge, Fifth Circuit, sitting by assignment.

ment was approved by Mr. Stauffer in his capacity as sole stockholder of each of the four corporations, whereby the California, Illinois and New York corporations were to merge into Stauffer New Mexico. By the terms of the agreement, the stated capital, paid-in surplus and retained earnings of Stauffer New Mexico were to equal the sums of the respective items of the three transferor corporations; all property of whatever kind owned by the three constituent corporations was to be vested in the New Mexico concern; and the liabilities and obligations of each of the three transferring corporations were to become the responsibilities of Stauffer New Mexico. On the effective date of the merger the separate existences of each of the three constituent corporations were to cease. On October 1, 1959, the merger was consummated by the filing of the merger agreement with the secretaries of state in each of the four respective states.

Prior to the consummation of the merger, Mr. Stauffer sought and obtained from the Internal Revenue Service a ruling that the contemplated venture constituted a "statutory merger" within the terms of §368(a)(1)(A). In accordance with this ruling, it was required of each of the transferor corporations to file a closing income tax return as of the last day of their existence, September 30, 1959. §381(b)(1). As each of the three corporations reported their income on the fiscal year basis, February 1, to January 31, their respective closing tax returns were to have reflected their income over the eight month period, February 1, 1959, to September 30, 1959. On December 15, 1959, requests on behalf of each of the transferor corporations were filed for an extension of time within which to file their closing returns. Along with these requests were tendered the amounts of $300,000 in the name of Stauffer California, $200,000 in the name of Stauffer Illinois, and $7,500 in the name of Stauffer New York. The three corporations never filed separate returns. At the close of its fiscal year, January 31, 1960, Stauffer New Mexico filed a single tax return reporting the income of the California, Illinois and New York corporations from February 1, 1959, to September 30, 1959, as well as reporting its income from the date of the merger, October 1, 1959, to January 31, 1960. Accompanying the tax return was the following explanation of the single return in lieu of the three returns due on behalf of the transferring corporations as of September 30, 1959:

> "Taxpayer [Stauffer New Mexico] has been advised by counsel that inasmuch as the reincorporation of California, Illinois, and New York in the State of New Mexico involved no change in the existing stockholders or change in the assets of the corporation involved, but was intended to effectuate relocation of the corporate domiciles in the State of New Mexico, the reorganization is within the scope of section 368(a)(1)(F) and section 381(b); that under the authority of Rev. Rul. 57-276 (1957-1 C.B. 126), a single return must therefore be filed by Stauffer Laboratories, Inc., for the fiscal year commencing February 1, 1959, and ending January 31, 1960, claiming only a single surtax exemption, and combining the operations of all the corporations for the entire fiscal year, and that separate closing returns for New York, Illinois, and California should not be filed."

The Commissioner contested neither Stauffer New Mexico's characterization of the merger as an "F" reorganization nor the filing of the single tax return. The computed tax was $356,701, and applying the previous sums tendered in the names of Stauffer California, Stauffer Illinois, and Stauffer New York, Stauffer New Mexico claimed, and was paid a refund.

The contemplated relocation in New Mexico of the physical assets of the Stauffer enterprises did not take place. The business was operated precisely as it had been previously. There was no change in officers, directors or shareholders. Beginning in the latter part of 1959, publicity unfavorable to the mechanized weight control industry began to take its toll of Stauffer's sales volume. Increased competition in the industry caused further decreases in Stauffer's share of the market. In its tax return for the fiscal year ended January 31, 1961, Stauffer New Mexico reported a net operating loss of $3,366,052. On April 10, 1961, the corporation filed an Application for Tentative Carryback Adjustment, requesting a refund of $1,481,653 paid in taxes by Stauffer California for the year ended January 31, 1958, and of $263,194 of the taxes paid by that same company for the year ended January 31, 1959. The application stated that Stauffer New Mexico was "a continuing corporation pursuant to a reorganization under IRC Section 368(a)(1)(F)." The carryback adjustment (known as the "quickie" refund) authorized the secretary or his delegate to make such a refund to the taxpayer within 90 days of his application therefor. 26 U.S.C. §6411. The application was approved and the adjustment paid, with interest. Following the close of the fiscal year on January 31, 1961, Stauffer New Mexico was dissolved. The business was carried on by Mr. Stauffer as a sole proprietorship. Consequently, although the "quickie" refund was paid by checks drawn to Stauffer New Mexico, the checks were negotiated by Mr. Stauffer, as trustee in dissolution and former sole stockholder of the dissolved corporation.

In June, 1963, the Commissioner assessed deficiencies against Stauffer New York in the amount of $6,943.95 for the period February 1, 1959, to September 30, 1959, against Stauffer Illinois in the amount of $340,822.82 for the same period, and against Stauffer California in the amount of $412,021.19 for the same period. In addition, the income tax of Stauffer California for the years ended January 31, 1958, and January 31, 1959, were determined to be deficient in amounts equal to the loss carryback refund adjustments paid to Stauffer New Mexico, $1,481,653 and $213,472, respectively. Liability for the deficiencies was attributed to petitioner as the transferee of the assets of Stauffer New Mexico which in turn was transferee of the assets of each of the corporations whose income taxes had been assessed deficient. From judgments of the Tax Court adverse to petitioner on each of the assessed deficiencies, Bonnie H. Stauffer, Executrix of the Estate of Bernard H. Stauffer, appeals. Our jurisdiction to review the judgment of the Tax Court rests on 26 U.S.C. §7482.

In §368 Congress defined the term "corporate reorganization" for purposes of providing for the tax-free exchange of corporate enterprises. In §368(a)(1) six types of corporate transactions are defined as beneficiaries of tax-free treatment: (A) a statutory merger or consolidation; (B) and (C) acquisitions by one corporation of the controlling voting stock or substantially all the assets of another corporation; (D) transfers to certain controlled corporations; (E) a recapitalization; or (F) "a mere change in identity, form or place of organization, however effected." The proposition underlying the tax-free corporate exchange is "that the new enterprise, the new corporate structure, and the new property are substantially continuations of the old still unliquidated." Treas. Reg. §1.1002-1(c). Continuity of investment lies at the heart of the tax-free exchange. This much may be said for each of the definitions (A) through (F) in §368(a)(1). However, §368(a)(1) is a definit[ional] section, inoperative in and of itself. It takes on significance when considered in light of other sections of the code.[4] That section of the code with which we are here concerned as it and §368(a)(1) interrelate is §381, providing that the operating loss carryover, earnings and profits, and other tax attributes of a transferor corporation are passed on to the transferee or acquiring corporation, subject to the limitations set forth in §382(b).

We deal here with the question of whether the transaction heretofore described, is an "F" reorganization within the definition of that term in §368(a)(1). If an "F" reorganization took place, §381(b) provides:

> "*Operating rules.* — Except in the case of an acquisition in connection with a reorganization described in subparagraph (F) of section 368 (a)(1) — ...
>
> "(3) The corporation acquiring property in a distribution or transfer described in subsection (a) shall not be entitled to carry back a net operating loss for a taxable year ending after the date of distribution or transfer to a taxable year of the distributor or transferor corporation."

Assuming an "F" reorganization was effected, Stauffer New Mexico was entitled to carry back its net operating loss to the taxable years of its transferor corporations.[5]

The "F" reorganization is defined in §368(a)(1) as "a mere change in identity, form or place of organization, however effected," and is not further defined in the regulations. There is a dearth of administrative and judicial attention to this section of the Code. There is no case law dealing with the problem before us. The "F" reorganization first appeared in the Revenue Act of 1921, §202(c)(2), as a "mere change in identity, form, or place of organization of a corporation." In 1924 the reenactment of the Revenue Act left the section unchanged except for the deletion of the words "of a corporation." In 1954 the House proposed the repeal of §368(a)(1)(F) because the corporate alterations it permitted could be accomplished through other types of reorganizations. See generally, Bittker & Eustice, Federal Income Taxation of Corporations and Shareholders, 548 (2d ed. 1966); ... The proposal was rejected, however, and the "F" reorganization was carried over to the 1954 code. 1 Hearings Before the Senate Committee on Finance on the Internal Revenue Code of 1954, 83rd Cong., 2d Sess., at 403, 539 (1954).

The cases in which the "F" reorganization has been brought into litigation revolve principally around the reorganization-liquidation problem, wherein the shareholders of the liquidated transferor corporation in an "A", "C" or "D" type reorganization seek to treat the increment realized on the redemption of their shares as capital gains. ... §§331, 337. In such cases, the Commissioner has advocated that the transferee

---

[4]See §§354, 361, 356, 357, 358, 362(b) and 381.

[5]Whether a carryback as to only *one* of the transferor corporations is permissible is another question, discussed, infra.

corporation has in effect consummated but a "mere" reincorporation under §368(a)(1)(F) and therefore the liquidation distribution payments to the shareholders of the transferor corporation are in fact dividends, taxable at ordinary rates. . . .

From the foregoing cases evolve two principles which form the basis of the controversy in the case before us. The Commissioner contends, with the exception of the holding in Davant v. Commissioner, [366 F.2d 874 (5th Cir. 1966)], that these cases stand for the rule that an "F" reorganization is restricted in number of participating corporations to one. That is, section (F) of 368(a)(1) applies only to the reorganization of a single corporation, and a multi-corporate merger defeats the right of the surviving transferee corporation to carry back losses under §381(b). It is asserted that the acquiring corporation cannot be treated, for tax purposes, as standing in the shoes of all of the pre-merger transferor corporations. Treas. Reg. §1.381(b)-1(a)(2). The taxpayer replies that to the contrary, . . . continuity of ownership and continuity of business enterprise are the only indicia of an "F" reorganization, regardless of the number of merging transferor corporations.

We are wary of an easy solution which predicates its reasoning on literal compliance with the Code provisions and the rules resulting therefrom. "[L]iteral compliance with the reorganization provisions is not enough; a transaction will be governed by the statutory provisions *only if it comes within their presuppositions* as well as their language." Bittker & Eustice, supra, at 505. (Emphasis added.) The proposition underlying the continuity of interest rationale as applied to the statutory definition of corporate reorganization is to deny tax-free status to the transaction which is in fact a "sale" although it complies with the literal definition of a reorganization. . . . The rationale behind the continuity of business enterprise requirement is to prevent the liquidation transaction taxable as ordinary income from disguising itself as a capital gains distribution. . . . [S]ee Treas. Reg. §1.368-1(b). The liquidation transaction sought to be denied the tax-free privilege is one in which business activity terminates, as opposed to the continuity existing in a liquidation-reorganization transaction. Bearing these underlying purposes in mind, the taxpayer's argument falls short of attributing to the "F" reorganization characteristics which are indicative of a congressional intent other than that which is attributable to the other reorganization definitions in §368(a)(1).

The six reorganizations defined in 368(a)(1) are not necessarily mutually exclusive. At least it seems undisputed that an "F" reorganization may also qualify under one of the other reorganization definitions, and the Commissioner of Internal Revenue has so ruled.

The Commissioner's position, that the "F" reorganization is restricted to but one participant, likewise presents problems. In Davant v. Commissioner . . . , the Fifth Circuit had under consideration a liquidation-reorganization transaction. There, two corporations, "Water" and "Warehouse," were both owned in equal proportions by four families who sought to transfer the operating assets of Warehouse to Water and then liquidate Warehouse. In an effort to preserve the capital gains treatment of the Warehouse stock, a plan was carried out whereby the Warehouse stock was sold to a person not connected with the families or the corporations who in turn sold the Warehouse assets to Water at a price which allowed the individual to make a reasonable profit. Warehouse was then liquidated, without disruption of its business activities. The families reported the gain realized on the transfer of their Water stock as capital gains. The Commissioner assessed deficiencies, arguing that the reported gain to the extent of the earnings and profits of both Water and Warehouse must be taxed as ordinary income, the profit being nothing more than a dividend paid in the course of a corporate reorganization.

The Tax Court held that the transaction constituted a §368(a)(1)(D) reorganization, rejecting the Commissioner's argument that the reorganization was also a section (F) reorganization, but holding that the gain was taxable as a dividend only to the extent of Warehouse's earnings and profits. On appeal, the Commissioner sought to have the gain realized from Water's earnings and profits taxed as dividends. In concluding that following the transaction the stockholders owned only stock in Water but that the certificates reflected the combined assets of both Water and Warehouse and therefore the earnings and profits of Water were taxable as dividends to the extent of the gain realized by the transfer of the Warehouse assets, the Fifth Circuit Court held that the transaction was *both* a "D" and an "F" reorganization. In discussing a section 368(a)(1)(F) reorganization, the court said it could not cover "a substantial shift in the proprietary interest in a corporation accompanying a reorganization," citing Helvering v. Southwest Consol. Corp., 315 U.S. 194 (1942), but would include "a mere change in *form* as opposed to a change in substance." If the corporate enterprise continues uninterrupted, except for a distribution of some liquid assets or cash, §368(a)(1)(F) can be applied. The court states there was, in *Davant,*

> "[A] change of corporate vehicles but not a change of substance. If Water had no assets of its own prior to the transfer of Warehouse's operating assets to it, could we say that Water was any more than the alter ego of Warehouse? The answer is no. The fact that Water already had other assets that were vertically integrated with Warehouse's assets does not change the fact that Water was Warehouse's alter ego. Viewed in this way, it can make no practical difference whether the operating assets were held by Water or Warehouse, and a shift between them is a mere change in identity or form. *At least where there is a complete identity of shareholders and their proprietary interests, as here, we hold that the type of transaction involved is a type "F" reorganization."*

366 F.2d at 884 (emphasis added). The Commissioner does not favor the *Davant* case. He argues that the Court therein rested its decision on the fact that the reorganization was of the "D" type; that the finding that there also occurred an "F" reorganization was "unnecessary to its decision." But, the finding that the reorganization was a "D" type was likewise unnecessary to the decision. As stated by the court, "Whether we reach this result [that the combined earnings and profits of the two companies are to be taxed as dividends to the extent of the gain realized] by means of calling the transaction a type (D) or type (F) reorganization . . . makes no difference." 366 F.2d at 888. But, says the Commissioner, *Davant* "was in an entirely different context than this case." "Section 381 was not before the Fifth Circuit and,

unfortunately, the legislative evidence presented to the Tax Court and this court was not presented to it." But the Commissioner does not take issue with the "F" reorganization finding in the *Davant* factual context. In effect, he says that an "F" reorganization is one thing when the issue is treatment of gain and another when the issue is loss carryback. The Commissioner's varying position is illustrative of the taxpayer's paradox herein.

Had Stauffer Illinois and Stauffer New York merged into Stauffer California, the latter could have carried back a post-merger loss *to one of its own* pre-merger taxable years. Regs. §1.381(c)(1)-1(b). Or, had Stauffer Illinois and Stauffer New York merged into Stauffer California followed by the acquisition of Stauffer California by Stauffer New Mexico as a subsidiary, a loss sustained by Stauffer California could have been carried back to a pre-acquisition taxable year of Stauffer California. Id. Or, had Stauffer California reincorporated into Stauffer New Mexico and thereafter consummated a merger with Stauffer New York and Stauffer Illinois, a loss sustained by Stauffer New Mexico could have been carried back to a taxable year of Stauffer California. Id. This condition of circumstances has led the petitioner herein to exclaim that she "[H]as been victimized by the old shell game. . . . [T]he pea, i.e., the loss carryback, must be found under one shell or another. . . ."

We do not see how the definitive principles of an "F" reorganization can change from one case to another; from one context to another, dependent upon which position the Commissioner of Internal Revenue prefers. While the factual situation which gives rise to a determination in a given case will invariably differ, the standards by which the determination is to be made cannot. An "F" reorganization is just that, and tax consequences flow from that determination, not vice versa.

Nor are we persuaded that a different result should have been obtained in *Davant* because of the "legislative evidence" which was not presented to that court but which is before us. The principle we derive from *Davant* is that a shift in operating assets from the transferor corporation to its alter ego wherein the identity of the proprietary interests remains intact and the business enterprise of the transferor corporation continues unimpaired results in an "F" reorganization. There is a change of corporate vehicles but not a change in the substance of the transferor corporation. In *Davant* the change was reflected by the disappearance of the Warehouse stock; the substance of the two pre-merger corporations did not change; the assets of Warehouse were merely reflected in the books of Water and in the increment in the Water stock. In the instant case, the only change that took place was that Stauffer New Mexico reported the combined income of the three pre-merger corporations in one tax return; the individual books of the constituent enterprises were kept as they had been before the merger; the enterprises continued to operate in the same manner and at the same locations as before the merger; the change was one of corporate vehicles only. The Regulations, §1.381(b)-1(a)(2), state that in an "F" reorganization the acquiring corporation is to be treated "just as the transferor corporation would have been treated if there had been no reorganization." Thus, the identity of pre- and post-merger entities is so complete that for tax purposes the latter is the former. That Stauffer New Mexico stood in the shoes of each of the three constituent corporations cannot be here denied; it was the alter ego of each of the three pre-merger entities.

The Commissioner seeks to defeat such a construction of the facts of this case by arguing in terms of the alleged undesirability and unworkability of the tax consequences of such a construction. He contends that if the transaction herein is an "F" reorganization the following anomaly results: §381(b) would permit Stauffer New Mexico to carry back its post-merger loss to a pre-merger taxable year of the transferor corporations, while §381(c)(1)(A), which does not exempt the "F" reorganization, would prevent a carryback of a net operating loss of the transferor corporations to a pre-merger year of Stauffer New Mexico. Thus, the Commissioner argues that if Congress had intended the "F" provision to encompass more than a single enterprise it logically would have provided the same exception in §381(c)(1) (A) as it provided in §381(b). We believe this argument fails for two reasons. First, and most important, Stauffer New Mexico had no pre-merger taxable year to which *any* loss could have been carried back. This fact strongly indicates that Stauffer New Mexico is nothing more than the alter ego of the three constituent corporations, and further evidences the degree to which it stands in the shoes of the pre-merger corporations. Secondly, we reject the adoption of the negative inversion of §381(c)(1)(A) suggested in the Commissioner's brief. (Op. Br. p. 28). Reading §381(c)(1)(A) *as written,* it provides that the pre-merger net operating loss of the transferor corporation may be carried *forward* to a post-merger year of the transferee corporation. Together with §381(b) whereby the transferee corporation may carry back a post-merger loss to a pre-merger taxable year of a transferor corporation, it provides the transferee in an "F" reorganization with a most favorable treatment of losses. With tax advantages such as these available to the "F" reorganization, we fail to see an anomaly in the denial of the carryback of the transferor's pre-merger net operating loss to a pre-merger taxable year of the transferee. As the Commissioner states, §381 (c)(1)(A) applies to *all* corporate reorganizations. And that section necessarily applies to multi-corporate reorganizations and can have no intention of encompassing a uni-corporate reorganization, for in a reorganization of the latter type, under the "F" definition, the transferee corporation would, in every instance, be but a shell corporation organized to reincorporate the transferor and would, consequently, have no pre-merger taxable years to which to carry back a pre-merger net operating loss of the transferor. Consequently, the Commissioner's argument in support of uni-corporate intention on the part of Congress in the enactment of §381(c)(1)(A) carries little convincing weight. Indeed, assuming that the inverse of §381(c)(1)(A), as stated by the Commissioner, is a correct statement of the law, and further assuming that Congress sought to limit the "F" reorganization to a single corporation, it surely would have excepted the "F" reorganization from the multi-corporate provisions in §381(c)(1)(A).

The Commissioner next contends that to permit multi-corporate "F" reorganizations would "make Section 381(b)(1) unworkable and would run counter to the most elementary principles of taxation." We must assume, for purposes of this argument (says the Commissioner) that two of the pre-merger Stauffer companies filed tax returns reporting different fiscal years (contrary to the facts of this case). This assumption in hand, it can then be seen that under §381(b)(1), the taxable years of the transferor corporations do not end on the date of the merger, but their income is reported by the transferee corporation at the close of its fiscal year. Consequently, serious questions arise as to how the transferee corporation will treat the varying fiscal year accountabilities of the constituent corporations. The Commissioner would have us dismiss as "pure happenstance" the fact that the three pre-merger Stauffer companies employed the identical fiscal year accounting methods.

We find the government's argument in this respect to be all the more indicative of the complete identity existent between the three constituent corporations and Stauffer New Mexico. The latter corporation, being the alter ego of the transferor corporations, merely assumed their accounting procedures without change. We do not view this as pure happenstance, but as a further indicium of identity consistent with an "F" reorganization. We do not here decide whether different accounting methods by the transferor corporations would disrupt the requisite continuity of the "F" reorganization. But Congress apparently did not regard this as of great significance. (See §381(c)(4), providing for the post-merger combination of varying accounting procedures.)

Having concluded that the merger here in question constituted an "F" reorganization under §368(a)(1), we turn to the problem of determining the loss which Stauffer New Mexico is entitled to carry back and of determining to which of the three pre-merger corporations the loss may be carried. As discussed, supra, had the merger been effected in a number of other ways, the loss sustained by Stauffer New Mexico, to the extent that it represented the loss of Stauffer California, could have been carried back to a pre-merger taxable year of Stauffer California. *But for* the simultaneous merger of the three corporations, the loss carryback would have been undeniably allowed. This, the Commissioner admits.

Gregory v. Helvering, 293 U.S. 465, 79 L. Ed. 587, 55 S. Ct. 256 (1935) teaches that mere compliance with the Code provisions resulting in a tax advantage will be sanctioned by the courts only when there is, independent of the tax consequences, engagement in a business or corporate purpose intended by the statute utilized. The Tax Court found, in the case before us, that the merger of the three Stauffer corporations was motivated solely by legitimate business purposes, the consolidation of the operational facilities under one roof. Indeed, no losses occurred until after the reorganization took place. Hence, we are not confronted with purposeful tax avoidance executed in compliance with the Code provisions.

In Libson Shops, Inc. v. Koehler, 353 U.S. 382, 1 L. Ed. 2d 924, 77 S. Ct. 990 (1957), the court had before it a case in which 16 separate corporations engaged in a related business enterprise were all owned by the same interests. Three of the corporations had sustained continued losses, and in an effort to offset the profits of the prosperous corporations against the losses incurred by these three corporations, a merger was effected. Thereafter, the losses were carried forward to a taxable year of the transferee corporation. The court used the "but for" rationale, stating, "had there been no merger, these businesses would have had no opportunity to carry over their losses." 353 U.S. at 388. Distinguished by the court was the case of Newmarket Mfg. Co. v. United States, 233 F.2d 493 (1st Cir. 1956), where, in an "F" type reorganization (although occurring before the enactment of the 1954 Code) a single corporation reincorporated in another state, with the court remarking, "[B]ut for the [Newmarket] merger, the old corporation itself would have been entitled to a carryback." 353 U.S. at 388. See also Casco Products Corp., 49 T.C. No. 5; and Dunlap & Associates Inc., 47 T.C. 542 (1967).

In the case before us, the Commissioner has failed "to sustain the contention that the effectuation of this statutory merger . . . defeats the carry-back deduction which would otherwise have been available," under the afore-recited hypothetical situations. Newmarket Mfg. Co. v. United States, supra, 233 F.2d at 497. The only *fact* which the Commissioner relies upon to defeat the carry-back is that the three corporations merged *at the same time.* Under the hypothesis stated, supra, the Stauffer transferee would have been entitled to carry back that portion of the loss attributable to Stauffer California's operations to a pre-merger year of that same corporation. Accordingly, that portion of the losses of Stauffer New Mexico attributable to the operations of Stauffer California, $2,184,689 may be carried back to a pre-merger taxable year of Stauffer California.

Had the operational facilities of the three pre-merger corporations been dismantled and transported to the State of New Mexico we would have a different situation. Then, the financial status of Stauffer New Mexico would have reflected a single operational concern. In such a case, there would be no means by which a loss could be pro-rated among the pre-merger identities, and the combined losses of what was in fact the consolidation of three companies could not have been set off against the pre-merger income of but one of those companies, for this would have resulted in a windfall to the transferee. The losses of the Illinois and New York corporations could not have been carried back to, or offset by, prior taxable years of the California corporation before the merger, and to permit their combined losses to be so offset after the merger, would accord to the transferee a benefit which would not have been available prior to the merger. However, we emphasize that this is but a problem of tax accountability and does not reflect on our conclusion that the herein transaction was an "F" reorganization.

Lastly, the taxpayer contends that because the refund was paid to Stauffer New Mexico the Commissioner must proceed against that corporation for recovery of the refund and not against Stauffer California, the tax of which was assessed as deficient because of the refund payment. She claims that Stauffer New Mexico is a stranger to this proceeding. Our conclusion that the reorganization was of the "F" type disposes of this argument.[8]

As the loss attributable to Stauffer California is not in excess of the refund heretofore paid from the taxable years 1958-59 of Stauffer California, the refund will stand. It was proper for Stauffer New Mexico as the "F" reorganization transferee of the California, Illinois, and New York corporations to consolidate their income for the period February 1, 1959, to September 30, 1959, in its tax return for the fiscal year February 1, 1959, to January 31, 1960. Rev. Rul. 57-276 (1957-1 C.B. 126).

---

[8]At oral argument, it was stipulated as follows: "that if the Court decides that the transaction constituted an "F" reorganization, the Court need not reach the issue concerning whether there was a deficiency with respect to the taxes of Stauffer California."

The judgments of the Tax Court upholding the deficiency assessments by the Commissioner are reversed.[9]

REVENUE RULING 69-185
1969-1 Cum. Bull. 108

The Internal Revenue Service will not follow the decisions of the Court of Appeals for the Ninth Circuit in Estate of Bernard H. Stauffer v. Commissioner, 403 F.2d 611 (1968), and Associated Machine v. Commissioner, 403 F.2d 622 (1968), nor that portion of the decision of the Court of Appeals for the Fifth Circuit in J. E. Davant, et al. v. Commissioner, 366 F.2d 874 (1966), certiorari denied, 386 U.S. 1022 (1967), dealing with the question whether a combination of two or more commonly owned operating corporations may qualify as a reorganization within the meaning of section 368(a)(1)(F) of the Internal Revenue Code of 1954.

Estate of Stauffer involved the consolidation under the applicable State laws of three corporations into a new corporation. Each of the transferor corporations had previously conducted an active business in a separate State. All four corporations were owned by the same sole shareholder.

The consolidation was effected on October 1, 1959. The three transferor corporations, which reported their income on a January 31 fiscal year basis, did not file final returns for the period from February 1, 1959, to September 30, 1959. Instead, the transferee corporation, which also used a January 31 fiscal year, included the pre-consolidation income of the transferor corporations in its return filed for the year ended January 31, 1960. Since the transferee corporation had incurred substantial losses during the 4-month period following its organization and consolidation (October 1, 1959, to January 31, 1960), the effect of filing a single return covering the period from February 1, 1959, to January 31, 1960, was to offset post-consolidation losses against pre-consolidation gains without regard to the source of the gains and losses. The pre-consolidation gains were sufficient, however, to produce some taxable income for fiscal year 1960.

In addition to incurring losses during the four months of fiscal year 1960 following consolidation, the transferee corporation incurred losses during fiscal year 1961, resulting in a net operating loss for that year. Although the books of the transferee corporation indicated that the net operating loss was attributable to the operation of each of the businesses that had previously been carried on by the three transferor corporations, the transferee corporation sought to carry back the net operating loss to pre-consolidation taxable years of only one of the transferor corporations.

The Tax Court of the United States, in a reviewed opinion, unanimously accepted the Service's position that the consolidation constituted a "statutory merger or consolidation" within the meaning of section 368(a)(1)(A) of the Code but did not constitute "a mere change in identity, form, or place of organization" within the meaning of section 368(a)(1)(F) of the Code. Estate of Bernard H. Stauffer v. Com-

---

[9]Cf. Associated Machine v. C. I. R., 403 F.2d 622 (9th Cir. 1968), decided this day.

missioner, 48 T.C. 277 (1967). The court held that an "F" reorganization does not extend to a multicorporate combination where each corporation has been conducting a separate business but is restricted to the reorganization of a single corporation. In reaching this conclusion the Tax Court overruled its prior decision in Pridemark Inc., et al. v. Commissioner, 42 T.C. 510 (1964), acquiescence on another issue C.B. 1966-1, 3, reversed, 345 F.2d 35 (4th Cir. 1965). This action by the court was consistent with the Service's position before the Tax Court in *Stauffer* that the decision in *Pridemark* regarding the application of section 368(a)(1)(F) of the Code was erroneous.

The result of the Tax Court's decision in *Stauffer* would have been, first, to require each of the transferor corporations to file final returns covering the period from February 1, 1959, to September 30, 1959. This requirement would have had the corollary effect of requiring the transferee corporation to file a short-period return covering the period from October 1, 1959, to January 31, 1960, the end of its first taxable year. Sections 381(b)(1) and 443 of the Code. The holding of the Tax Court that the transaction did not constitute an "F" reorganization would also have had the effect of precluding the transferee corporation from carrying back its net operating loss to prior taxable years of any of the transferor corporations. Section 381(b)(3) of the Code.

The Court of Appeals for the Ninth Circuit reversed the Tax Court's decision in *Stauffer* and held that under the specific facts presented consolidation of the three operating companies into a new corporation constituted an "F" reorganization. The court reached the same conclusion in a companion case, Associated Machine v. Commissioner, 403 F.2d 622 (1968), reversing 48 T.C. 318 (1967), which involved the merger under the applicable state laws of one operating company into a second commonly owned operating company. As in *Stauffer*, the transferee corporation in *Associated Machine* sought to carry back a net operating loss incurred in a year subsequent to the merger to a prior taxable year of the transferor corporation.

Both decisions of the Court of Appeals for the Ninth Circuit rely in large part on the decision of the Court of Appeals for the Fifth Circuit in J. E. Davant, et al. v. Commissioner, 366 F.2d 874 (1966), certiorari denied, 386 U.S. 1022 (1967). In *Davant*, the Court of Appeals held that the acquisition by one operating company of substantially all of the assets of a second such company, both of which were owned by the same shareholders, constituted a reorganization within the meaning of subparagraphs "D" and "F" of section 368(a)(1) of the Code. In proceedings before the Tax Court, the Service argued that the transaction was both a "D" and "F" reorganization. The Tax Court accepted the Service's argument regarding the applicability of section 368(a)(1)(D) of the Code but did not rule on the assertion that the transaction also met the definition of an "F" reorganization. South Texas Rice Warehouse Company, et al. v. Commissioner, 43 T.C. 540 (1965).

On the appeal of *South Texas Rice Warehouse Company* to the Court of Appeals for the Fifth Circuit, sub nom. J. E. Davant, et al. v. Commissioner, the Service abandoned the position that the transaction constituted an "F" reorganization. Instead the Service relied solely on the application of section 368(a)(1)(D) of the Code. Similarly, in opposing the taxpayer's petition for a writ of certiorari before the Supreme Court of the United States, the Service relied on the characterization of the transaction as a "D" reorganization. In proceedings before the Court of Appeals for the Ninth Circuit in *Stauffer,* the Service urged the court not to follow that portion of the decision of the Court of Appeals for the Fifth Circuit in *Davant* applying section 368(a)(1)(F) of the Code to an amalgamating reorganization.

A reorganization is defined in section 368(a)(1)(F) of the Code as "a mere change in identity, form, or place of organization, however effected".

Section 381(b) of the Code provides in part:

"(b) *Operating rules.* — Except in the case of an acquisition in connection with a reorganization described in subparagraph (F) of section 368(a)(1) —

"(1) The taxable year of the distributor or transferor corporation shall end on the date of distribution or transfer.

"(3) The corporation acquiring property in a distribution or transfer described in subsection (a) shall not be entitled to carry back a net operating loss for a taxable year ending after the date of distribution or transfer to a taxable year of the distributor or transferor corporation."

The definition of an "F" reorganization is by its terms more limited than the other reorganization definitions contained in section 368(a)(1) of the Code. It is the Service's position that the history and function of section 368(a)(1)(F) of the Code preclude its application to amalgamations of multiple operating corporations. Only by attributing this restricted scope to the definition of an "F" reorganization is it possible to give meaning to the exception in section 381(b) of the Code, with respect to the filing of final returns and the carryback of net operating losses, and to the absence of an exception for an "F" reorganization in section 381(c)(1) of the Code, which imposes restrictions on the carryover of net operating losses of a transferor corporation to taxable years of the transferee corporation in amalgamating reorganizations and certain liquidations described in section 332 of the Code.

If an "F" reorganization may encompass an amalgamation of multiple business enterprises, it is anomalous for Congress to have provided an exception in section 381(b) of the Code to the requirement of filing final returns and to have permitted the carryback of net operating losses in the case of such a reorganization without granting similar treatment of all amalgamating transactions encompassed by section 381(a) of the Code. Similarly, the absence of an exception for an "F" reorganization in section 381(c)(1) of the Code is anomalous unless Congress intended section 368 (a)(1)(F) of the Code to be limited to the reorganization of a single business enterprise, in which case the transferee corporation merely continues the taxable year of the transferor corporation and takes into account the net operating loss carryovers of the transferor corporation and any losses of the transferor corporation incurred earlier in the year as if there had been no reorganization. Compare section 1.381(b)-1 (a)(1) and (2) of the Income Tax Regulations with section 1.381(c)(1)-1(b), example 2, of the regulations. The dichotomy between amalgamating reorganizations and the reorganization of a single business is demonstrated in the explanation of section 381(b)(3) of the Code contained in Senate Report No. 1622, Eighty-third Congress, 2d Session, at page 276.

Accordingly, the Service will not follow as precedent in the disposition of similar cases the decisions of the Court of Appeals for the Ninth Circuit in *Stauffer* and *Associated Machine,* nor that portion of the decision of the Court of Appeals for the Fifth Circuit in *Davant,* holding that a transaction resulting in the combination of two or more operating corporations constitutes an "F" reorganization.

REVENUE RULING 66-284

1966-2 Cum. Bull. 115

In determining the applicability of Revenue Ruling 57-276, C.B. 1957-1, 126, relating to the requirements for filing Federal income tax returns in cases involving certain reorganizations described in section 368(a)(1) of the Internal Revenue Code of 1954, advice has been requested whether the statutory merger described below qualifies as a reorganization within the meaning of section 368(a)(1)(F) of the Code.

For a valid business purpose, X Corporation, a publicly held State A Corporation, desired to reincorporate in State B. Accordingly, X organized a new X Corporation in State B and then merged itself into new X pursuant to the laws of States A and B.

Shareholders owning less than one percent of the outstanding shares of old X voted against the plan of merger. These dissenting shareholders elected to have their shares appraised under State law and they received payment representing the fair value of their shares. All other shareholders participated in the merger and received one share of new X stock for each share of old X stock surrendered.

Pursuant to the plan of merger, new X received the assets and assumed the liabilities of old X and continued the same business without interruption.

Section 368(a)(1)(F) of the Code provides, in part, that a mere change in place of organization is a reorganization. Revenue Ruling 58-422, C.B. 1958-2, 145, states, in part, that section 368(a)(1)(F) of the Code is applicable to all reorganizations where there is no change in existing shareholders or in the assets of the corporation involved. A question has been raised whether the instant transaction, which qualifies as a reorganization described in section 368(a)(1)(A) of the Code, also qualifies as a reorganization described in section 368(a)(1)(F) of the Code in view of the action taken by the dissenting shareholders.

Where, as in the instant case, a plan of merger is designed only to effect a change in the corporation's place of organization, the Internal Revenue Service considers the failure of dissenting shareholders owning a total of less than 1 percent of the outstanding shares to participate in the plan of merger to be such a de minimis change in the corporation's shareholders and its assets as not to disqualify the merger as a reorganization under section 368(a)(1)(F) of the Code. Accordingly, pursuant to the provisions of section 381(b) of the Code, old X Corporation is not required to file a Federal income tax return for that portion of the taxable year prior to the effective date of the reorganization, but that portion of the taxable year prior to the effective date of the reorganization and that portion of the taxable year after such effective date constitute a single taxable year for new X Corporation. See Revenue Ruling 57-276, supra.

Revenue Ruling 58-422, C.B. 1958-2, 145, amplified.

NOTE

How do you explain the Commissioner's litigating position in *Reef* (page 658 supra) in light of his position in Rev. Rul. 66-284?

Compare the result of the finding of an "F" reorganization in *Davant* (page 649 supra) with that in *Stauffer* (page 664 supra). Should the finding have been made in both cases? In one, but not in the other? In neither? Why?

Should a court be less willing to find an "F" reorganization when pressed by the taxpayer (who has structured the transaction) than when pressed by the Commissioner? Why?

See R. Pugh, The F Reorganization: Reveille for a Sleeping Giant? 24 Tax L. Rev. 437 (1969); M. Grossberg, Type F Reorganizations in the Fifth Circuit: The Mouse That Roared, 5 Houston L. Rev. 926 (1968); R. Hjorth, Liquidations and Reincorporations — Before and After *Davant,* 42 Wash. L. Rev. 737 (1967); C. MacLean, Problems of Reincorporations and Related Proposals of the Subchapter C Advisory Group, 13 Tax L. Rev. 407 (1958).

CASCO PRODUCTS CORP. v. COMMISSIONER
49 T.C. 32 (1967)

TANNENWALD, Judge: Respondent determined deficiencies in petitioner's income tax for the taxable years ended February 28, 1959 and February 29, 1960 and the taxable period March 1, 1960 to December 31, 1960 in the amounts of $247,870.91, $399,861.84, and $245,540.69, respectively. The essential issue involved is the extent to which petitioner should be permitted to carry back its 1961 net operating loss as an offset against prior earnings of its predecessor.

Findings of Fact

All of the facts have been stipulated and are incorporated herein by this reference.

The Casco Products Corporation (hereinafter referred to as "Old Casco") was organized in 1928 as a Connecticut corporation. It filed its returns for the fiscal years ended February 28, 1959 and February 29, 1960 and, having validly elected to change its fiscal year, for the period March 1, 1960 to December 31, 1960 with the district director of internal revenue, Hartford, Connecticut.

On June 9, 1960, Standard Kollsman Industries Inc., by a public tender, offered to purchase all of the issued and outstanding shares of Old Casco. On July 12, 1960, it acquired by a single purchase 310,483 shares out of a total of 511,356 shares issued and outstanding at that time. On the same date, Standard Kollsman extended its previous offer to purchase the remaining shares. By February 28, 1961, it had acquired a total of 464,515 shares. Difficulties had been and continued to be encountered in acquiring the remaining shares, which were owned by dissident shareholders.

The parties have stipulated that "for the sole purpose of providing a legal technique by which Standard Kollsman could become owner of 100% of the outstanding stock" of Old Casco, Standard Kollsman on February 28, 1961 formed SKO, Inc. as a Connecticut corporation. SKO, Inc. issued 25 shares of no-par stock to Standard Kollsman for $1,000 and thus became the wholly-owned subsidiary of Standard Kollsman.

On March 2, 1961, Old Casco and SKO, Inc. entered into an agreement to merge Old Casco into SKO, Inc. under the laws of Connecticut.

The merger agreement provided, inter alia:

"At the time the merger becomes effective, (a) all shares of common stock, without par value, of Casco which are owned by SKO shall be cancelled and shall not receive any distribution with respect to such shares, and all rights attaching to such shares shall terminate; (b) all shares of common stock, without par value, of Casco which are owned by [Standard Kollsman] shall be cancelled and shall not receive any distribution with respect to such shares, and all rights attaching to such shares shall terminate; (c) there shall be distributed the sum of $10.15 in cash on each of the issued and outstanding shares of common stock, without par value, of Casco owned by persons other than SKO and [Standard Kollsman], and all shares of common stock, without par value, of Casco owned by persons other than SKO and [Standard Kollsman] shall be cancelled and shall not be converted into any securities of SKO, and all rights attaching to such shares shall terminate."

The merger agreement was approved at duly constituted meetings of the directors and shareholders of both corporations. At the meeting of the shareholders of Old Casco on March 16, 1961, several of the minority shareholders filed formal objections to the merger. These shareholders were informed that their sole right was to be paid in cash for their shares. Despite these objections, Standard Kollsman voted its shares in Old Casco for the merger. Because only a two-thirds majority was necessary, the approximately 91 percent interest held by Standard Kollsman provided sufficient votes to pass the merger resolution. Accordingly, on March 16, 1961, Old Casco was merged into SKO, Inc., which then changed its name to The Casco Products Corporation (hereinafter "New Casco").

SKO, Inc. conducted no business before the merger, except to incorporate and to agree to the merger. New Casco continued business in exactly the same manner as had Old Casco. It had the same programs and activities, the same customers (except for normal variations), the same employees, the same bank accounts, etc. Except for the $1,000 capital invested by Standard Kollsman in SKO, Inc., the assets of Old Casco immediately before the merger were the same as the assets of New Casco immediately after the merger. At all times relevant, including the time of filing of the petition herein, New Casco continued to have its principal place of business in Bridgeport, Connecticut, at the same location used by Old Casco prior to the merger.

New Casco filed its income tax return for the calendar year 1961 with the district director of internal revenue, Hartford, Connecticut, disclosing a net operating loss of approximately $1,500,000. New Casco then filed applications for tentative allowance of a loss carryback against the income shown on the returns filed by Old Casco for the fiscal years ended February 28, 1959 and February 29, 1960 and the fiscal period March 1, 1960 to December 31, 1960. The applications were tentatively allowed.

The December 31, 1960 return was the last return filed by Old Casco. No return was filed by Old Casco for the period January 1, 1961 to March 16, 1961, the date of the merger.

Respondent subsequently issued a deficiency notice disallowing the loss carryback in its entirety. Respondent did not allocate any portion of the 1961 loss to the period prior to the merger on the ground that petitioner had not shown that a portion of the loss was so allocable.

Opinion

The factual situation against which the decision herein must be made is extremely narrow. Standard Kollsman set out in 1960 to become the sole shareholder of Old Casco. Pursuant to a public tender, it succeeded in acquiring approximately 91 percent thereof through voluntary sales by existing shareholders. Having found that its public tender could not entirely accomplish its purpose, Standard Kollsman resorted to the legal technique of a merger, permitted under Connecticut law, to force out the remaining shareholders of Old Casco. As its instrument, it formed New Casco and acquired 100 percent of its issued and outstanding stock. By virtue of that ownership and its ownership of 91 percent of the shares of Old Casco, it accomplished a merger of Old Casco into New Casco, pursuant to which its shares in Old Casco were cancelled without payment and the shares of the remaining shareholders were to be paid for in cash. Simultaneously with the merger becoming effective, the obligation to make such cash payment devolved upon New Casco.[1]

Against this factual background, petitioner makes these arguments: First, it asserts that the loss carryback is allowable under section 172 on the ground that no reorganization took place and that realistically there was a legal identity between Old Casco and New Casco. Alternatively, petitioner argues that, if a reorganization did in fact occur, it was an "F" reorganization under section 368(a)(1) and that therefore the loss carryback is allowable under section 381(b).

Respondent counters with the arguments that, given the presence of business purpose, continuity of business enterprise, and continuity of proprietary interest, petitioner's use of the reorganization form requires that the transaction be treated as a reorganization; that it cannot be an "F" reorganization because of the 9 percent shift in proprietary interest between Old Casco and New Casco; and that consequently the loss carryback was properly disallowed under section 381(b).

Thus, both parties invite us to engage in an interpretative exercise as to the scope of section 368(a)(1)(F) and the relationship between sections 381(b) and 172. We decline the invitation to attempt to navigate these treacherous shoals. See Reef Corporation v. Commissioner, 368 F.2d 125 (C.A. 5, 1966), certiorari denied 386 U.S. 1018, affirming in part and reversing as to the "F" reorganization issue a Memo-

---

[1]It is not clear under Connecticut law whether this obligation first became that of Old Casco and was then assumed by New Casco or whether it originally arose as an obligation of New Casco, but resolution of this esoteric question of local law is unnecessary to our decision.

randum Opinion of this Court; Estate of Bernard H. Stauffer, 48 T.C. 277 (1967), on appeal (C.A. 9, Sept. 5, 1967); Associated Machine, 48 T.C. 318 (1967), on appeal (C.A. 9, Sept. 15, 1967); Dunlap & Associates, 47 T.C. 542 (1967). Instead, we take a different tack.

There is no question, and indeed, respondent so concedes, that if Old Casco had redeemed the shares of the minority shareholders and had continued in business the loss carryback would have clearly been available. As we see it, the circumstances herein should not produce a different result. To hold otherwise would be to exalt form over substance and to accord an unjustifiable vitality to the merger format which was admittedly adopted only as a "legal technique."

In this case, Standard Kollsman sought to become the sole shareholder of Old Casco. Its voluntary efforts having failed as to 9 percent of the shares, it resorted to a "squeeze-out" technique via the merger route, as permitted by Connecticut law. It formed a new corporation (New Casco) under the same state law[3] to conduct the same business at the same location with the same employees. In fact, upon the accomplishment of the merger, the New Casco was identical in all respects to the Old Casco with a single exception. That exception was that, although there were no new shareholders, 9 percent of the holders of Old Casco shares did not hold any shares in New Casco.

Taxwise, New Casco was merely a meaningless detour along the highway of redemption of the minority interests in Old Casco. The merger itself, although in form a reorganization, had as its sole purpose the accomplishment of the redemption — an objective which Standard Kollsman had not been able to achieve through its original program of voluntary acquisition of all of the Old Casco shares. On this basis, we think that the instant case falls squarely within the ambit of the principles which we laid down in Utilities & Industries Corporation, 41 T.C. 888 (1964), reversed on this issue sub nom. The South Bay Corporation v. Commissioner, 345 F.2d 698 (C.A. 2, 1965). That case involved a question of the basis of certain assets acquired by the taxpayer through the purchase-of-stock – merger route rather than by direct purchase of the assets themselves. Since the taxpayer had not shown its inability to accomplish its objective by such direct purchase, we held that the mergers had to be treated as reorganizations because they were not so integrated or interdependent as to have been *solely for the purpose* of acquiring assets. The Second Circuit Court of Appeals reversed us on the ground that we imposed too strict a test. We need not now decide the extent to which we will adopt the broader approach of the Court of Appeals, for it is clear that the instant situation falls within our stricter test. Cf. Long Island Water Corporation, 36 T.C. 377 (1961); Kimbell-Diamond Milling Co., 14 T.C. 74 (1950), affirmed per curiam 187 F.2d 718 (C.A. 5, 1951). Here, New Casco was formed and the merger route utilized for the sole purpose of redeeming the

---

[3]Where incorporation takes place in another state, different corporation laws imposing different rights and obligations apply. Often such incorporation is accomplished in a state such as Delaware in order to obtain the greater flexibility provided by its laws. Under these circumstances, an independent significance may attach to the merger so as to require it to be treated as a true reorganization. Cf. Reef Corporation v. Commissioner, 368 F.2d 125 (C.A. 5, 1966) (Texas to Delaware); Dunlap & Associates, Inc., 47 T.C. 542 (1967) (New York to Delaware).

minority shares. This course was followed because Standard Kollsman had no alternative way of accomplishing its objective of sole ownership of Old Casco; its efforts to do so via the stock acquisition route had been tried and had failed. Under these circumstances, the merger was a reorganization in form only and should consequently be ignored as such. What took place was a redemption of 9 percent of the Old Casco shares and no more.[4] Under the limited circumstances of this case, we hold that New Casco was simply a continuation of Old Casco and the loss carryback should have been allowed.

In view of our holding, we do not reach the question whether, if there had been a reorganization which did not qualify under section 368(a)(1)(F), petitioner would nevertheless have been entitled to carry back that portion of the 1961 loss allocated to the period prior to the effective date of the merger.

Reviewed by the Court.

Decision will be entered for the petitioner.

RAUM, Judge, dissenting: I cannot agree that the merger of Old Casco into New Casco was only "in form a reorganization" and that New Casco was "merely a meaningless detour." New Casco was not a corporation with transitory life; it was not a mere stopping place en route to an ultimate destination; it was itself the end product of the transactions before us, and indeed is the petitioner herein. Old Casco was a corporation existing for a number of years and the deficiencies in controversy were determined with respect to *its* tax years, not those of New Casco. Both Old Casco and New Casco were separate, distinct viable corporations. One was merged into the other in order to squeeze out a 9 percent minority stockholder interest. Such merger was a corporate reorganization, and section 381(b)(3) forbids the carryback of a post reorganization net loss to a taxable year of the predecessor corporation unless the transaction is a reorganization "described in subparagraph (F) of section 368(a)(1)." I can see no escape from the necessity of determining whether this reorganization fell within (F).

The question whether the elimination of a 9 percent adverse minority interest may be ignored or regarded as de minimis in order to satisfy the requirement of (F) that there is a "mere change in identity, form, or place of organization" is a teasing and difficult one. And I can understand why one might wish to avoid it. But it cannot be sidestepped here and must be faced. In failing to address itself to the issue thus presented and argued by the parties, I think the majority erred. I express no opinion on the question itself at this time until it is considered by the Court.

WITHEY, ATKINS, SCOTT and FEATHERSTON, JJ., agree with this dissenting opinion.

SCOTT, Judge, dissenting: I respectfully disagree with the holding of the majority that the merger of Old Casco into New Casco was a reorganization in form only and should be ignored. The reorganization was in accordance with provisions of the laws of Connecticut whereby the holders of 91 percent of the stock of Old Casco were able to accomplish their objective of becoming 100 percent stockholders of a new corpo-

---

[4]The fact that Standard Kollsman did not seek to acquire 100 percent ownership of Old Casco by causing that corporation to attempt voluntary redemption of the minority shares is not significant. To have endeavored so to do would have constituted a meaningless ritual in view of the unsuccessful efforts to acquire such shares directly.

ration which owned the operating assets and conducted the business previously conducted by Old Casco. Corporate reorganizations provided for by State laws often effect little substantive change in the equitable ownership of a corporation or the nature of the corporate business. However, the Federal tax consequences of any reorganization are controlled by the specific provisions of the Internal Revenue Code.

In my opinion the case should have been decided by a determination of whether the reorganization here involved was "a mere change in identity, form, or place of organization," so as to constitute a reorganization within the meaning of section 368(a)(1)(F).

RAUM, WITHEY and ATKINS, JJ., agree with this dissenting opinion.

NOTE

Was the court majority in *Casco* justified in failing to decide whether the transaction was an "F" reorganization? Why do you think it did not wish to decide? Was the transaction an "F" reorganization? See R. Pugh, The F Reorganization: Reveille for a Sleeping Giant? 24 Tax L. Rev. 437 (1969); J. Kasner, The "F"-Reorganization Enigma: What is a "Mere Change in Form or Place"? 29 J. Taxation 210 (1968).

VIII. CARRYOVERS — §§381, 382, 172, 269

A. *EARNINGS AND PROFITS*

COMMISSIONER v. SANSOME
60 F.2d 931 (2d Cir. 1932), cert. denied, 287 U.S. 667 (1932)

Before L. HAND, AUGUSTUS N. HAND, and CHASE, Circuit Judges.

L. HAND, Circuit Judge. Sansome, the taxpayer, on January 1, 1921, bought some shares of stock, having $100 par value, in a New Jersey company, which on April 1, 1921, sold out all its assets to another company of the same state. The new company assumed all existing liabilities, and issued its shares to the shareholders of the old, without change in the proportion of their holdings, though the number of new shares was increased five times, and they were without par value. The new charter differed only in that the company could manufacture other products besides silk, to which the charter of the old company had been confined. There was no other change in the "financial structure," as the phrase is.

The old company had carried upon its books a large surplus and undivided profits, which we may assume to have been altogether earned before January 1, 1921, and which the new company carried over at the same figure upon its books for the year, 1921, but somewhat reduced because of losses in 1922. The business made no profit, and the company was dissolved in 1923. During this year Sansome received payments upon his shares in liquidation which the Commissioner included in his returns as dividends for the year 1923, for the distribution of that year did not exhaust the surplus and undivided profits which still remained. Sansome protested; he wished to use these dividends to compute the "gain" upon his investment; that is, to take all liquidating dividends first to amortize his cost, or "base," and return any overplus as profit in the year, 1924, when the last payment was made. The question is whether section 201 of the Revenue Act of 1921 (42 Stat. 228) justified the Commissioner's position. The Board held that as the companies were separate juristic persons, the later one had distributed nothing "out of *its* earnings or profits."

Section 201 of 1921 differed from the same section in the Act of 1918 (40 Stat. 1059), which expressly provided that all liquidation dividends should be taken as in exchange for shares, and that the gain should be computed by the formula which Sansome wished to use; and the Act of 1924, §201(c), 26 USCA §932(c), restored the law to its original form. The change of 1921 must have been deliberate and we cannot disregard it; it is also unequivocal, only distributions not allocated to profits by subdivision b may be used to reduce the subtrahend for computing the gain derived, or the loss sustained. This means that the shareholder is to be taxed upon the dividends as such so far as they represent profits, calculated under the preceding subdivision and that what is left shall be treated as amortizing his cost. The rule would work in some cases to the taxpayer's advantage and in others not; he escapes normal taxes pro tanto, provided he has enough income in later years to use as a deduction the loss calculated upon the reduced payments. . . .

Nor is there doubt as to the constitutionality of the section. When Sansome bought the old shares, the profits had indeed been already earned; yet he might be taxed upon ordinary dividends paid out of them. . . . He could not successfully assert that such dividends must be computed as part of his gain on the transaction, but must be content with a corresponding allowance when he sold. If so, Congress might insist that a dividend in liquidation should be treated like any other, for while this may violate ordinary usage, once we conceive of income as the change from undivided profits to an immediately available dividend, the rest follows. The taxpayer gets his quid pro quo in the closing transaction. Though it is a chance whether the final resultant will be favorable nor not, the dice are not loaded against him. Thus, there was income to tax as much as though the company continued its life; and it was not an unfair method.

All this the Board accepted, but held with Sansome, because it treated the company as new and independent, and the liquidating dividends as distributed out of capital, not "out of its earnings or profits," of which there were none. Under the Act of 1916, which had not yet developed the elaborate definition of the later statutes, greater corporate differences have been considered not to break the identity of the older company. . . . In Marr v. U.S., 268 U.S. 536, 45 S. Ct. 575, 69 L. Ed. 1079, still greater differences did indeed change the result, but for our purposes the decision is irrelevant, for the facts were wide of those at bar. . . .

However, we prefer to dispose of the case as a matter of statutory construction, quite independently of decisions made in analogous, though not parallel, situations.

It seems to us that section 202(c)(2) (42 Stat. 230) should be read as a gloss upon section 201. That section provides for cases of corporate "reorganization" which shall not result in any "gain or loss" to the shareholder participating in them, and it defines them with some particularity. He must wait until he has disposed of the new shares, and use his original cost as the "base" to subtract from what he gets upon the sale. Such a change in the form of the shares is "an exchange of property," not "a sale or other disposition" of them. Section 201 was passed, in some measure at least, to fix what should come into the computation of "gain or loss"; it allowed all payments except those cut out by subdivision c. It appears to us extremely unlikely that what was not "recognized" as a sale or disposition for the purpose of fixing gain or loss, should be "recognized" as changing accumulated profits into capital in a section which so far overlapped the later. That in substance declared that some corporate transactions should not break the continuity of the corporate life, a troublesome question that the courts had beclouded by recourse to such vague alternatives as "form" and "substance," anodynes for the pains of reasoning. The effort was at least to narrow the limits of judicial inspiration, and we cannot think that the same issue was left at large in the earlier section. Hence we hold that a corporate reorganization which results in no "gain or loss" under section 202(c)(2) (42 Stat. 230) does not toll the company's life as continued venture under section 201, and that what were "earnings or profits" of the original, or subsidiary, company remain, for purposes of distribution, "earnings or profits" of the successor, or parent, in liquidation. As the transaction — "reorganization" — between the companies at bar fell plainly within section 202(c)(2), it seems to us that the Board was wrong.

Order reversed; cause remanded for further proceedings in accord with the foregoing.

NOTE

What kind of reorganization was involved in *Sansome?* Would Judge Hand's reasoning apply equally to an amalgamating merger of two ongoing businesses? With the same shareholder interest? With differing shareholder interests? Would he have applied it so? Compare *Stauffer,* page 664 supra, *Davant,* page 649 supra, and Note, page 658 supra.

UNITED STATES v. SNIDER
224 F.2d 165 (1st Cir. 1955)

Before MAGRUDER, Chief Judge, and WOODBURY and HARTIGAN, Circuit Judges.

HARTIGAN, Circuit Judge. . . . The plaintiffs sued to recover an alleged over payment of taxes for the calendar year 1950, stating in their complaint that $3,909.01 of a $9,000 dividend paid to the plaintiff, Abraham Snider, by the Hotel Kenmore Corp. in 1950 had been erroneously reported by them as taxable income whereas in fact it was not taxable income being a distribution of the capital of the Hotel Kenmore Corp. rather than a distribution of earnings and profits.

The stipulated facts deal mainly with the tax-free reorganization of a Massachusetts real estate trust, which owned and operated two Boston hotels, the Hotel Braemore and Hotel Kenmore, into two corporations, the Hotel Braemore Corp. and the Hotel Kenmore Corp. The dividend, the nature of which is the principal issue in this case, was declared by the Hotel Kenmore Corp.

The plaintiff, Abraham Snider, owned 25 shares of the 100 shares outstanding of the Massachusetts real estate trust which had been organized in 1922. In 1947 the stockholders of the trust agreed that it would be preferable that the hotel properties be owned and operated by two corporations rather than a real estate trust. At this time the trust had a deficit of about $327,000. The Hotel Braemore Corp. was organized on May 29, 1947. The real estate trust transferred the Hotel Braemore property to this Hotel Braemore Corp. in exchange for all the outstanding stock of the latter corporation except for four shares which had previously been issued to the trust for a nominal sum. Also on May 29, 1947 the Hotel Kenmore Corp. was organized and this corporation issued all its outstanding stock to the four stockholders of the real estate trust in exchange for their trust stock except for four shares which had been issued to these four stockholders for a nominal sum. The Hotel Kenmore Corp. then liquidated the real estate trust and transferred all its assets to itself. Thus the Hotel Kenmore Corp. acquired ownership of the Hotel Kenmore and through its ownership of the stock of the Hotel Braemore Corp., the Hotel Braemore. The new corporations were apparently more successful than the real estate trust, although there was no change in any material manner in the operation of the business, and profits were earned by the Hotel Kenmore Corp. in the fiscal years ending March 31, 1948, 1949, 1950 and 1951 of about $140,000. On December 8, 1950 a cash dividend of $36,000 was paid to the stockholders of the Hotel Kenmore Corp., the plaintiff Abraham Snider, receiving $9,000. The Hotel Kenmore Corp. had available for distribution in 1950 as current earnings and profits a little over $20,000 and there is no question that approximately $5,100 of the $9,000 received by the plaintiff was clearly dividend income attributable to current earnings and profits and taxable to the plaintiffs.

The issue in this case is whether any portion of this $36,000 distribution to stockholders of the Hotel Kenmore Corp. may be offset by the 1947 deficit of the Massachusetts real estate trust (which deficit is greater than the earnings and profits accumulated by the Hotel Kenmore Corp. since 1947) despite the fact that the real estate trust was terminated in 1947 following the tax-free reorganization of the ownership of the hotel properties. The sections of the Internal Revenue Code of 1939 involved are Sec. 115(a), (b) and (d), 26 U.S.C. 1952 ed. §115, the pertinent parts of which provide as follows:

"§115. *Distributions by corporations — (a) Definition of dividend.*

"The term 'dividend' when used in this chapter . . . means any distribution made by a corporation to its shareholders, whether in money or in other property, (1) out of its earnings or profits accumulated after February 28, 1913, or (2) out of the earnings or profits of the taxable year (computed as of the close of the taxable year without diminution by reason of any distributions made during the taxable year), without regard to the amount of the earnings and profits at the time the distribution was made. . . .

"*(b) Source of distributions.*

"For the purposes of this chapter every distribution is made out of earnings or profits to the extent thereof, and from the most recently accumulated earnings or profits. . . .

"*(d) Other distributions from capital.*

"If any distribution made by a corporation to its shareholders is not out of increase in value of property accrued before March 1, 1913, and is not a dividend, then the amount of such distribution shall be applied against and reduce the adjusted basis of the stock provided in section 113, and if in excess of such basis, such excess shall be taxable in the same manner as a gain from the sale or exchange of property. . . ."*

In applying this statute to the facts in the instant case it is apparent that whether or not the $3,909.01 in question is a "dividend" and taxable depends on whether at the date of distribution there existed any assets which could be attributed to "earnings and profits accumulated after February 28, 1913," as the other source of dividends — "the earnings and profits of the taxable year" — had been already exhausted. It would be logical to assume that the earnings and profits of the Hotel Kenmore Corp. would have no relation to the earnings and profits of the trust, they being two separate entities. However, it was decided in Commissioner of Internal Revenue v. Sansome, 2 Cir., 1932, 60 F.2d 931, 933, . . . that a corporate reorganization which did not result in the gain or loss in the value of the corporate stock being recognized for tax purposes "does not toll the company's life as continued venture . . . and that what were 'earnings or profits' of the original, or subsidiary, company remain, for purposes of distribution, 'earnings or profits' of the successor, or parent, in liquidation." In that case the original enterprise was a corporation which had large accumulated earnings and profits. Its assets were conveyed to a new corporation, the stock of the new corporation being issued to the shareholders of the old corporation. The new corporation made no profits, and payments in distribution of its assets were made to the taxpayer who treated such payments as return of capital and not as income, maintaining that the distributions could not have been dividends as the corporation had never had any earnings and profits. The court, however, held that the first corporation's earnings and profits were attributable to the second corporation and consequently the second corporation's cash distribution was a taxable dividend to the extent of such earnings and profits.

It would appear to follow from the reasoning used in the *Sansome* case that the plaintiffs are entitled to recover, for logic would seem to require that if the prior business organization's profits and losses must be attributed to the successor corporation following a tax-free reorganization, similarly the prior enterprise's deficits should be attributed to the successor corporation. However, the Supreme Court in Commssioner of Internal Revenue v. Phipps, 1949, 336 U.S. 410, 69 S. Ct. 616, 93 L. Ed. 771, dealt with this problem as it affected parent and subsidiary corporations and it is

*Cf. §§316 and 301 of the 1954 Code. — Ed.

clear from its opinion that subtracting the deficit of a subsidiary business from the accumulated earnings and profits of the parent corporation is not a corollary to the carrying over of the subsidiary's earnings and profits to the parent. The Court stated in 336 U.S. at page 417, 69 S. Ct. at page 620 "that the *Sansome* rule is grounded not on a theory of continuity of the corporate enterprise but on the necessity to prevent escape of earnings and profits from taxation." See Commissioner of Internal Revenue v. Munter, 1947, 331 U.S. 210, 215, 67 S. Ct. 1175, 91 L. Ed. 1441.

In the *Phipps* case, a parent corporation had large accumulated earnings and profits but it owned several subsidiary corporations possessing deficits. By means of a tax-free reorganization the parent acquired the assets of its subsidiaries and later made pro rata cash distributions to its preferred stockholders. The Court held that the deficits of the subsidiaries could not be used to reduce the accumulated earnings and profits of the parent and consequently the cash distribution was in the nature of a taxable dividend.

In the instant case the district court said that the *Phipps* opinion did not repudiate the entire doctrine of continuity of venture that had been advanced in the *Sansome* case but that it superimposed on the *Sansome* rule the further principle that it is inconsistent with the idea of a tax-free reorganization that the Government should lose by the process. The district court further said that the *Phipps* opinion did not hold that the Government should gain through this process and consequently in the instant case the taxpayer would be allowed to utilize the deficit of the defunct real estate trust in determining the taxability of cash distributions made by its corporate successor.

The plaintiff contends in support of the district court's decision that there is a crucial distinction between the situation presented in the instant case and that which was presented in the *Phipps* case. In the instant case the transferee, Hotel Kenmore Corp., had no accumulated earnings and profits at the time of the reorganization while in the *Phipps* case the parent corporation did possess accumulated earnings and profits at the date of the tax-free reorganization. Any distributions made by the parent corporation in the *Phipps* case would have undoubtedly been dividends and therefore taxable to the recipient if the reorganization had not taken place. The result in the *Phipps* case was necessary in order to prevent corporations which had earnings and profits from distributing these earnings and profits so as to avoid taxation merely by acquiring the assets of a business possessing a deficit. In the instant case, however, where there were no accumulated earnings and profits at the date of the reorganization of the ownership of the Hotel Braemore and Hotel Kenmore, the taxpayer could not have obtained a tax advantage through a reorganization. In other words, if the taxpayer's business had continued in its trust form and there had been no reorganization, the $3,909.01 distribution clearly would not have qualified as a dividend under the 1939 Internal Revenue Code and therefore would not have been taxable to the plaintiffs.

There is language in the *Phipps* opinion which tends to support the plaintiff's contention. At page 420 of 336 U.S., at page 621 of 69 S. Ct. it is said ". . . the effect of the *Sansome* rule is simply this; a distribution of assets that would have been taxable as dividends absent the reorganization or liquidation does not lose that character by virtue of a tax-free transaction." At page 421 of 336 U.S., at page 622 of 69 S. Ct.: "There has been judicially superimposed by the *Sansome* rule, with the subsequent explicit ratification of Congress, the doctrine that tax-free reorganizations shall not disturb the status of earnings and profits otherwise available for distribution."

Thus, the Supreme Court seems to emphasize the possession by one of the business entities involved in the tax-free reorganization of accumulated earnings and profits at the time of the reorganization. The nonexistence of such earnings and profits in the instant case clearly distinguishes it from the *Phipps* case. We consequently hold that a logical application of the *Sansome* rule, even as that rule has been defined by the Supreme Court in the *Phipps* case, compels us to conclude that in determining whether distributions made to its stockholders by the Hotel Kenmore Corp. are dividends, the deficit of its real estate trust predecessor must be taken into account.

The judgment of the district court is affirmed.

NOTE

1. Do §381(a) and (c)(2) modify or codify the law as you glean it from *Sansome, Phipps* and *Snider*? How would the following distributions be treated under current law?

(a) B merges into C on the last day of their taxable years in an "A" reorganization. B has an accumulated deficit of $50,000; C has accumulated earnings and profits of $10,000. In the year following the consummation of the merger C breaks even. During that year C distributes the $10,000.

(b) B merges into C as above. B had accumulated earnings and profits of $50,000. C had neither a deficit nor accumulated earnings and profits. In the year following the merger C broke even and on the last day of the year distributed $10,000.

(c) B merges into C as above. B had a deficit of $50,000. C had neither a deficit nor accumulated earnings and profits. In the year following merger C earned over $10,000 after all corporate taxes. In the second year following merger C broke even and distributed $10,000.

2. In Dunning v. United States, 353 F.2d 940 (8th Cir. 1965), cert. denied, 384 U.S. 986 (1966), a bankrupt corporation was reorganized in 1935 under what is now Chapter 10 of the Bankruptcy Act. The common stock was wiped out, and the preferred stock and the indebtedness were adjusted downward. There was a pre-reorganization deficit of almost $1,500,000. The court held that the pre-reorganization deficit could not be offset against subsequent earnings of the successor corporation, although the court stated there might be a different result in a less drastic reorganization. What should the result be? Why?

3. See C. Nesson, Earnings and Profits Discontinuities Under the 1954 Code, 77 Harv. L. Rev. 450 (1964); D. Halperin, Carryovers of Earnings and Profits, 18 Tax L. Rev. 289 (1963); R. Testa, "Earnings and Profits" After Bankruptcy Reorganiza-

tion, 18 Tax L. Rev. 573 (1963). As to the law prior to §381, see R. Rice, Transfers of Earnings and Deficits in Tax-free Reorganizations: The *Sansome-Phipps* Rule, 5 Tax L. Rev. 523 (1950).

B. *NET OPERATING LOSSES*

LIBSON SHOPS, INC. v. KOEHLER
353 U.S. 382 (1957), aff'g 229 F.2d 220 (8th Cir. 1957)

Mr. Justice BURTON delivered the opinion of the Court. The issue before us is whether, under §§23(s) and 122 of the Internal Revenue Code of 1939, as amended, a corporation resulting from a merger of 17 separate incorporated businesses, which had filed separate income tax returns, may carry over and deduct the pre-merger net operating losses of three of its constituent corporations from the post-merger income attributable to the other businesses. We hold that such a carry-over and deduction is not permissible.

Petitioner, Libson Shops, Inc., was incorporated on January 2, 1946, under the laws of Missouri, as Libson Shops Management Corporation, to provide management services for corporations selling women's apparel at retail. Its articles of incorporation also permitted it to sell apparel. At about the same time, the same interests incorporated 16 separate corporations to sell women's apparel at retail at separate locations. Twelve were incorporated and went into business in Missouri; four in Illinois. Each of these 16 sales corporations was operated separately and filed separate income tax returns. Petitioner's sole activity was to provide management services for them. The outstanding stock of all 17 corporations was owned, directly or indirectly, by the same individuals in the same proportions.

On August 1, 1949, the 16 sales corporations were merged into petitioner under the laws of Missouri and Illinois. New shares of petitioner's stock were issued, pro rata, in exchange for the stock of the sales corporations. By virtue of the merger agreement, petitioner's name was changed, the amount and par value of its stock revised, and its corporate purposes expanded. Following the merger, petitioner conducted the entire business as a single enterprise. Thus, the effect of the merger was to convert 16 retail businesses and one managing agency, reporting their incomes separately, into a single enterprise filing one income tax return.

Prior to the merger, three of the sales corporations showed net operating losses. . . . In the year following the merger, each of the retail units formerly operated by these three corporations continued to sustain a net operating loss. . . .

Section 23(s) authorizes a "net operating loss deduction computed under section 122."[1] Section 122 prescribes three basic rules for this calculation. Its pertinent parts

---

[1] As originally added to the 1939 Code by the Revenue Act of 1939 . . . , §122 provided for the computation and carry-over of net operating losses without expressly relating them to a given taxpayer. Section 153(a) of the Revenue Act of 1942 . . . amended §122(b) not only to allow carry-backs for the first time, but also to provide, as to both carry-backs and carry-overs, that it was only the net operating losses of "the taxpayer" which could be so utilized.

provide generally (1) that a "net operating loss" is the excess of the taxpayer's deductions over its gross income (§122(a)); (2) that, if the taxpayer has a net operating loss, the loss may be used as a "net operating loss carry-back" to the two prior years (§122(b)(1)(A)) and, if not exhausted by that carry-back, the remainder may be used as a "net operating loss carry-over" to the three succeeding years (§122(b)(2)(C)); and (3) that the aggregate of the net operating loss carry-backs and carry-overs applicable to a given taxable year is the "net operating loss deduction" for the purposes of §23(s) (§122(c)).

We are concerned here with a claim to carry over an operating loss to the immediately succeeding taxable year. The particular provision on which petitioner's case rests is as follows: "If for any taxable year beginning after December 31, 1947, and before January 1, 1950, *the taxpayer* has a net operating loss, such net operating loss shall be a net operating loss carry-over for each of the three succeeding taxable years. . . ." (Emphasis supplied.) §122(b)(2)(C), 64 Stat. 937, 938, 65 Stat. 505, 26 U.S.C. §122(b)(2)(C). The controversy centers on the meaning of "the taxpayer."[2] The contentions of the parties require us to decide whether it can be said that petitioner, a combination of 16 sales businesses, is "the taxpayer" having the pre-merger losses of three of those businesses.

In support of its denial of the carry-over, the Government argues that this statutory privilege is not available unless the corporation claiming it is the same taxable entity as that which sustained the loss. In reliance on New Colonial Co. v. Helvering, 292 U.S. 435, . . . the Government argues that separately chartered corporations are not the same taxable entity. Petitioner, on the other hand, relying on Helvering v. Metropolitan Edison Co., 306 U.S. 522, . . . argues that a corporation resulting from a statutory merger is treated as the same taxable entity as its constituents to whose legal attributes it has succeeded by operation of state law. However, we find it unnecessary to discuss this issue since an alternative argument made by the Government is dispositive of this case. The Government contends that the carry-over privilege is not available unless there is a continuity of business enterprise. It argues that the prior year's loss can be offset against the current year's income only to the extent that this income is derived from the operation of substantially the same business which produced the loss. Only to that extent is the same "taxpayer" involved.

The requirement of a continuity of business enterprise as applied to this case is in accord with the legislative history of the carry-over and carry-back provisions. Those provisions were enacted to ameliorate the unduly drastic consequences of taxing income strictly on an annual basis. They were designed to permit a taxpayer to set off its lean years against its lush years, and to strike something like an average taxable income computed over a period longer than one year. There is, however, no indication in their legislative history that these provisions were designed to permit the averaging of the pre-merger losses of one business with the post-merger income of some other business which had been operated and taxed separately before the

---

[2]These words have been omitted from the new provisions of the Internal Revenue Code of 1954 relating to carry-backs and carry-overs after corporate acquisitions of assets of another corporation. See §§381, 382. [See also §172, the successor to §§23(s) and 122. — Ed.]

merger. What history there is suggests that Congress primarily was concerned with the fluctuating income of a single business.[6]

This distinction is recognized by the very cases on which petitioner relies. In Stanton Brewery, Inc. v. Commissioner, 176 F.2d 573, 577, the Court of Appeals stressed the fact that the merging corporations there involved carried on "essentially a *continuing enterprise,* entitled to all . . . benefits [of the carryover provisions] in ameliorating otherwise harsh tax consequences of fluctuating profits or expanding business." (Emphasis supplied.) And in Newmarket Manufacturing Co. v. United States, 233 F.2d 493, 497, the court expressly distinguished the case before it from the instant case on the ground that there "one single business" was involved in the merger, while in this case there were "several businesses."[7]

This difference is not merely a matter of form. In the *Newmarket* case, supra, a corporation desiring to change the state of its domicile caused the organization of a new corporation and merged into it. The new corporation sought to carry back its post-merger losses to the pre-merger income of the old corporation. But for the merger, the old corporation itself would have been entitled to a carry-back. In the present case, the 16 sales corporations, prior to the merger, chose to file separate income tax returns rather than to pool their income and losses by filing a consolidated return. Petitioner is attempting to carry over the pre-merger losses of three business units which continued to have losses after the merger. Had there been no merger, these businesses would have had no opportunity to carry over their losses. If petitioner is permitted to take a carry-over, the 16 sales businesses have acquired by merger an opportunity that they elected to forego when they chose not to file a consolidated return.

We do not imply that a question of tax evasion or avoidance is involved. Section [269(a)] . . . does contain provisions which may vitiate a tax deduction that was made possible by the acquisition of corporate property for the "principal purpose" of

---

[6]The House Committee on Ways and Means, reporting on §122 as it was originally added to the 1939 Code by the Revenue Act of 1939, c. 247, 53 Stat. 862, 867-868, stated that — "The bill, together with the committee amendments, permits taxpayers to carry over net operating business losses for a period of 2 years. Prior to the Revenue Act of 1932, such 2-year carry-over was allowed. No net loss has ever been allowed for a greater period than 2 years. In the Revenue Act of 1932, the 2-year net loss carry-over was reduced to 1 year and in the National Industrial Recovery Act the net loss carry-over was entirely eliminated. As a result of the elimination of this carry-over, *a business* with alternating profit and loss is required to pay higher taxes over a period of years than *a business* with stable profits, although the average income of the two firms is equal. New enterprises and the capital-goods industries are especially subject to wide fluctuations in earnings. It is, therefore, believed that the allowance of a net operating business loss carry-over will greatly aid business and stimulate new enterprises." (Emphasis supplied.) H.R. Rep. No. 855, 76th Cong., 1st Sess. 9.

[7]Koppers Co. v. United States, 133 Ct. Cl. 22, 134 F. Supp. 290, also involves a situation in which the corporation resulting from the merger carried on essentially the same taxable enterprise as before, since the merged corporations had been filing consolidated tax returns. E. & J. Gallo Winery v. Commissioner, 227 F.2d 699, is inconclusive on this point since the opinion does not disclose whether or not a continuing enterprise was involved. Cf. §382(a) of the Internal Revenue Code of 1954 relating to the purchase of a corporation and change in its trade or business. Under circumstances there defined, that section precludes a carry-over by the *same* corporation, unless it continues to engage in "substantially the same" trade or business as before the change in ownership. §382(a)(1)(C).

tax evasion or avoidance. And that section is inapplicable here since there was no finding that tax evasion or avoidance was the "principal purpose" of the merger. The fact that §[269(a)] is inapplicable does not mean that petitioner is automatically entitled to a carry-over. The availability of this privilege depends on the proper interpretation to be given to the carry-over provisions. We find nothing in those provisions which suggests that they should be construed to give a "windfall" to a taxpayer who happens to have merged with other corporations. The purpose of these provisions is not to give a merged taxpayer a tax advantage over others who have not merged. We conclude that petitioner is not entitled to a carry-over since the income against which the offset is claimed was not produced by substantially the same businesses which incurred the losses."

The Judgment of the Court of Appeals is
Affirmed.

Mr. Justice DOUGLAS dissents.

Mr. Justice WHITTAKER took no part in the consideration or decision of this case.

FRANK IX & SONS v. COMMISSIONER
375 F.2d 867 (3d Cir. 1967),
cert. denied, 389 U.S. 900 (1967)

FREEDMAN, Circuit Judge: Petitioner attacks the Tax Court's disallowance of net operating loss carryover deductions on losses which it incurred prior to a reorganization.

The Ix family, through a number of corporations, was engaged in the manufacture and sale of woven synthetic fibers. Separate corporations operated separate mills which manufactured the same types and styles of cloth within the multi-corporation structure. A central office was maintained for accounting, bookkeeping, inventory control and yarn purchasing. There was also provided a central sales force as well as complete technical and production and control staffs. Orders were solicited and returned to a central office in New York where the production and control department determined on the basis of work load and availability of skilled operators which corporation would manufacture the cloth.

In 1952 Frank Ix & Sons, Inc., borrowed $3,000,000 from a bank to make loans to a number of Ix family corporations. To secure the bank indebtedness it pledged as collateral all the capital stock which it owned in the other Ix family corporations and the promissory notes which it received from them for their participation in the loan. One of the conditions of the bank's loan was the maintenance in specified amounts of the working capital of the family corporations.

One of the Ix family corporations operated a mill in Cornelius, North Carolina.

---

[9]We do not pass on situations like those presented in Northway Securities Co. v. Commissioner, 23 B.T.A. 532; Alprosa Watch Corp. v. Commissioner, 11 T.C. 240; A. B. & Container Corp. v. Commissioner, 14 T.C. 842; WAGE, Inc. v. Commissioner, 19 T.C. 249. In these cases a *single* corporate taxpayer changed the character of its business and the taxable income of one of its enterprises was reduced by the deductions or credits of another.

Because of the similarity in names of the various Ix corporations and the change in the corporate name of the petitioner, we shall refer to this entity as "Cornelius Ix." Cornelius Ix received $2,550,000 from Frank Ix & Sons, Inc., the major share of the bank loan. In accordance with the bank's requirement, Cornelius Ix agreed that it would maintain its working capital in the amount of $2,800,000. More than a year and a half later, when Cornelius Ix's working capital had fallen nearly a million dollars below the stipulated requirement, a plan of reorganization was adopted with the bank's approval by which there were transferred to Cornelius Ix all of the assets of another Ix family corporation which operated a mill in Charlottesville, Virginia, and which we shall for convenience refer to as "Charlottesville Ix." Both corporations were engaged in the manufacture and sale of woven synthetic fibers, and their common stock was owned in the same proportions by Ix family members. Pursuant to the plan of reorganization Charlottesville Ix transferred all its assets to Cornelius Ix, in return for which Charlottesville Ix received new common stock of Cornelius Ix on the basis of thirteen shares of Cornelius Ix for each outstanding share of Charlottesville Ix. Charlottesville Ix then distributed these shares to its stockholders in complete liquidation and was dissolved. The plan of reorganization was fully consummated on September 30, 1953, and Cornelius Ix changed its name to Frank Ix & Sons Virginia Corporation, the petitioner. It is conceded that the transaction constituted a valid, tax-free "D reorganization" . . . . After the reorganization the same persons held the common stock in the new corporation in the same proportions as their pre-reorganization holdings in Cornelius Ix and Charlottesville Ix.

Cornelius Ix had operated its mill at a loss before the reorganization for the years ending March 31, 1952 and March 31, 1953. After the reorganization, petitioner operated both the mill in Cornelius, North Carolina and the mill in Charlottesville, Virginia, maintaining separate records for each of them, until July 22, 1954, when it shut down the North Carolina mill, which had continued to operate at a loss. The Charlottesville, Virginia mill had realized taxable net income in the years prior to the reorganization and continued to operate at a profit thereafter. For the year ending March 31, 1954, the first fiscal year after the reorganization, petitioner showed a net loss from the operation of the Cornelius mill for the period from September 30, 1953 to the end of the fiscal year, and sustained a net operating loss for the full fiscal year.

What is before us now is the determination by the Commissioner of deficiencies resulting from petitioner's deduction on its 1957, 1958 and 1959 income tax returns of net operating losses sustained by Cornelius Ix for the fiscal year ending March 31, 1953,[1] and by Cornelius Ix and petitioner for the fiscal year ending March 31, 1954. The action of the Commissioner was upheld by the Tax Court on the ground that the deductibility of the net operating loss carryovers was determined by the 1939 Code, under which the deduction was barred by the doctrine of Libson Shops, Inc. v. Koehler, 353 U.S. 382 (1957). Frank Ix & Sons Virginia Corporation (N.J.) v. C.I.R., 45 T.C. 533 (1966).

---

[1]The net operating loss for the fiscal year ending March 31, 1953 was carried over only in part to the years here involved. Petitioner utilized a portion of it in earlier returns which the Commissioner did not challenge.

In the Tax Court petitioner's argument for the deductions rested on two grounds. One was that the *Libson Shops* doctrine was inapplicable to the transaction because Cornelius Ix, which acquired the assets of Charlottesville Ix, was a loss corporation, which made the situation radically different from that with which the *Libson Shops* doctrine dealt. The second contention was that in any event the "continuity of business enterprise" requirement of the *Libson Shops* doctrine had been met.

These two contentions lead us back to the *Libson Shops* case, which the Supreme Court decided in 1957 under the 1939 Code. There a number of individuals directly or indirectly owned in the same proportions the stock of seventeen corporations. One of the corporations provided management services for the remaining sixteen corporations, each one of which, separately operated, was engaged in the retail sale of women's apparel. Each corporation filed a separate income tax return. In a tax-free reorganization the sixteen operating corporations, three of which had been sustaining losses and thirteen of which had been profitable, were merged into the management corporation. The Commissioner disallowed the deduction by the surviving corporation from its net income derived from the thirteen profitable units of the losses carried over from former years of the three unprofitable corporations. The Supreme Court found it unnecessary to decide the Commissioner's primary contention that the surviving corporation was not the same "taxpayer" as that which had sustained the losses in the prior years.[2] Instead the Court disallowed the deduction on the ground that the losses, and the profits from which they were sought to be deducted, were not produced by "substantially the same businesses." The Court thus chose to decide the case on the basis of economic substance rather than on the more technical question whether the surviving corporation was the same "taxpayer" as the constituent units which had sustained the losses.

The *Libson Shops* case has given rise to a flood of discussion and much dispute regarding its application in particular circumstances.[3] The facts in the present case however, fall so remarkably close to the circumstances which existed in *Libson Shops* and we therefore stand so close to the center of the doctrine that there is no need to consider its application in the more remote areas in which its repercussions may be felt. The decisive fact in *Libson Shops* was that a number of individuals had chosen to cast their investment into seventeen separate corporations and thus to spread the risk of their undertaking among separate business units and to enjoy the benefits of separate incorporation and separate tax returns for each of them. Thus, by their own choice they made each corporation a separate business unit as well as a separate taxpayer. The Court therefore determined that they could not disregard this choice in order to enjoy the deduction of a net operating loss carryover of one taxpayer – business unit from the profits of another, separate taxpayer – business unit by a formal

[2]Sections 23(s) and 122(b)(C) of the 1939 Code authorized a net operating loss carryover for three years "if for any taxable year beginning after December 31, 1947, and before January 1, 1950, *the taxpayer* has a net operating loss. . . ." (Emphasis added.)

[3]See, e.g., Comment, Loss Carryover — The Viability of the *Libson Shops* Doctrine under the 1954 Code, 61 Northwest. L. Rev. 555 (1966); Tarleau & Hodes, *Libson Shops* and the 1954 Code, 20 Southwest. L.J. 258 (1966); Harris, *Libson Shops* and Related Cases, N.Y.U. 21st Inst. on Fed. Tax 1307 (1963); Comment, Loss Carryovers and the *Libson Shops* Doctrine, 32 U. Chicago L. Rev. 508 (1965).

act of corporate merger. The court believed that such a deduction was forbidden by the policy underlying the allowance of net operating loss carryovers, which was to protect a single business from the hazards of fluctuating income. The establishment of the seventeen separate business units was a choice in the opposite direction; within each individual unit the loss carryover provision applied, but the investors could not enjoy that benefit and also reap the contradictory advantage, by merger, of enjoying the loss carryover advantage beyond the boundaries of the individual unit.

In the present case, as in *Libson Shops,* individuals chose to cast their investment into separate corporate units, each of which was a separate economic entity as well as a separate legal entity, and the assets which produced the income against which earlier losses were sought to be applied were different from the assets which produced the losses. If the separate businesses had not been combined there would have been no right to utilize the net operating loss carryover from the unprofitable corporation to reduce the taxable income of the profitable corporation. Whatever differences exist between the factual circumstances in the present case and in *Libson Shops* are not of decisive significance. The fact that what occurred here was not an "A reorganization", a statutory merger, but instead a "D reorganization", a transfer of assets for stock, is a factual difference without any legal distinction. The policy of *Libson Shops,* where indeed there was a retention of one hundred per cent control, cannot be diminished because the "D reorganization" involved here was subject to a statutory requirement of eighty per cent retention of control of the transferee corporation by the owners of the transferor corporation.

Petitioner earnestly contends that the fact that here the loss corporation acquired in reorganization the assets of the profitable corporation significantly distinguishes this case from *Libson Shops,* where the central service corporation absorbed by merger the remaining sixteen corporations including the three loss corporations.

Shortly after the Supreme Court decided *Libson Shops* the view was advanced that the decision might have been different had the loss corporations survived. For there would then not be present the implication that the transaction was without a business purpose, which is so clearly evident when a loss corporation is acquired by a profitable corporation, a transaction which ordinarily has no economic advantage except for the net operating loss carryover which the absorbing corporation, as a result of taking over the shell, can apply against its net taxable income. On the other hand, if the loss corporation is the survivor in the reorganization, it is to be looked upon as the business enterprise which continues, and this prevents regarding it as an empty shell acquired by another merely for the purpose of enjoying its accumulated net losses. In addition, where the loss corporation is the survivor, the identity of the corporation which had sustained the original losses and the corporation which is carrying them forward to the tax year for deduction is the same, and this satisfies the requirement, which *Libson Shops* had emphasized, that the deduction must be taken by the same taxpayer which had suffered the original loss.[4]

These distinctions, however, are too artificial for application in dealing with economic realities. It is easy enough for those planning a reorganization to turn the shell

[4] See Levine & Petta, *Libson Shops:* A Study in Semantics, 36 Taxes 445, 449 (1958).

on end and make it the surviving corporation if this difference will have substantial tax advantages. The courts to which the question has been presented therefore have rejected the distinction. Allied Central Stores, Inc. v. C. I. R., 339 F.2d 503 (2 Cir. 1964), cert. denied, 381 U.S. 903 (1965); see Julius Garfinckel & Co., Inc. v. C. I. R., 335 F.2d 744 (2 Cir. 1964), cert. denied, 379 U.S. 962 (1965). We agree with this view, especially where, as in this case, the corporations involved were originally owned by the same individuals, whose proportionate interest in each corporation was the same. The conclusion is compelled by the underlying policy of *Libson Shops* that losses incurred by a business unit should not be applied against profits which come from other assets which the shareholders had originally decided to operate separately, even though each unit is owned by the same group of shareholders. . . .

Petitioner invokes Revenue Ruling 63-40,[7] which permits the carryover of a net operating loss where a corporation which is sustaining losses in its business acquires from unrelated sellers the assets of another business which it then carries on. This change in activity by the same corporation presents a situation which the Supreme Court in *Libson Shops* expressly noted was not reached by its opinion.[8] The Revenue Ruling is inapplicable where a group of shareholders choose originally the benefits of separate incorporation. It merely recognizes the general principle acknowledged by the Second Circuit in Norden-Ketay Corp. v. C. I. R., 319 F.2d 902, 906 (2 Cir. 1963): "It may well be that shareholders who sustain a loss and then are wise enough to liquidate an uneconomic enterprise and embark on a different and profitable field of endeavor through the same corporation are equally entitled to offset the earlier losses as those who see an unprofitable corporation through the lean years into the good ones in the same activity.". . .

Section 172(a) of the 1954 Code is a general provision authorizing the deduction of net operating losses which are carried over from former years; it is similar to the provision of §23(s) of the 1939 Code. The 1954 Code, however, contains new provisions in §381 and §382 which deal with carryovers in certain corporate acquisitions and special limitations on net operating loss carryovers. Section 381, to the extent it is relevant here, provides that a corporation which acquires the assets of another corporation in certain tax-free transactions, such as a "D reorganization" shall succeed to the net operating loss carryover of the acquired corporation. §381(a)(2), (c)(1). Section 382 establishes two limitations on the carryover of a net operating loss: (1) it completely disallows any loss carryover where there has been a change of fifty percentage points or more in the ownership of the total fair market value of the outstanding stock of the corporation among any one or more of the ten persons who own the greatest percentage of the stock, and where the corporation has not continued to carry on substantially the same trade or business as that conducted before the change in ownership (§382(a)); and (2) it imposes a proportionate reduction in the amount of the net operating loss carryover permitted where in a reorganization such as a "D reorganization" the shareholders of the loss corporation immediately after the reorganization own less than twenty per cent of the fair

[7]1963-1 Cum. Bull. 46. [See Note 2, page 699 infra. — ED.]
[8]See 353 U.S. at 390, n.9; C. I. R. v. Virginia Metal Products, Inc., 290 F.2d 675, 677 (3 Cir. 1961), cert. denied, 368 U.S. 889 (1961); Julius Garfinckel & Co., Inc. v. C. I. R., supra.

market value of the outstanding stock of the acquiring corporation (§382(b)), a proportionate limitation which does not apply, however, if the transferor corporation and the acquiring corporation are owned substantially by the same persons in the same proportions. (§382(b)(3)).[9]

Petitioner argues that the maze of provisions in §381 and §382 which provide for the survival of a loss carryover in the hands of a transferee corporation and place limitations upon it, are inapplicable under their terms where it is the loss corporation which survives. From this it claims that it enjoys the right to the deduction of the net operating loss carryover under the simple authority of §172(a), which, with §§381 and 382 inapplicable, is accordingly without limitation.[10] The result of their contention would be that a loss corporation absorbing by reorganization a profitable corporation would enjoy without any limitation the right under §172(a) to deduct net operating loss carryovers. Although the language of §382 does not indubitably lead to petitioner's construction of its meaning,[11] we are not required to decide the question. For by the express terms of the Code,[12] neither §381 nor §382 is applicable to the present case because they are effective only where the plan of reorganization is adopted on or after June 22, 1954. Petitioner argues, however, that since under its view §§381 and 382 would by their terms be inapplicable where the loss corporation survives and thus §172(a) would be operative without limitation, it is true a fortiori where §§381 and 382 are inapplicable because of their effective dates. In effect, this argument if accepted would mean that petitioner would obtain the benefit of whatever plan the 1954 Code envisages even though essential portions of the plan had not yet come into effect.

The law which existed on September 30, 1953 when the plan of reorganization was consummated was the 1939 Code. Its §23(s) was substantially reincorporated in the 1954 Code as §172(a). In these circumstances we see no reason why the taxpayer should be freed from the judicially created *Libson Shops* doctrine before the restrictions of §381 and §382 went into effect even if they should be considered to be congressional substitutes for the *Libson Shops* doctrine. If they were such substitutes, the fact that Congress held them in abeyance until June 22, 1954 in order to permit taxpayers to complete pending transactions in reliance on the former law,[13] can result in no less than the continued validity of the *Libson Shops* doctrine until they went into effect. In saying this we do not mean to indicate what our view would be in the case of a plan of reorganization adopted after June 22, 1954 which would bring into the problem the extent to which §§381 and 382 are substitutes for the *Libson Shops* doctrine and their applicability where an acquisition is made by a loss corporation by way of merger or other reorganization. . . .

The decision of the Tax Court will be affirmed.

---

[9]The provisions of §§381 and 382 are discussed at length in Net Operating Loss Carryovers and Corporate Adjustments: Retaining an Advantageous Tax History under *Libson Shops* and Sections 269, 381 and 382, 69 Yale L.J. 1201, 1238-67 (1960).

[10]Section 269, which deals with attempts to avoid tax, concededly is not here involved.

[11]Thus, §382(b)(1) applies "If . . . the transferor corporation or the acquiring corporation" has the net operating loss.

[12]Sections 393(b)(1) and 394.

[13]Senate Committee Report accompanying H.R. 8300, 1954-3 U.S. Code Cong. & Admin. News, p. 4925.

NOTE

1. In Rev. Rul. 58-603, 1958-2 Cum. Bull. 147, and Rev. Rul. 59-395, 1959-2 Cum. Bull. 475, the Service ruled that the *Libson Shops* doctrine would not be relied upon under the 1954 Code in cases to which §381(a) applied. In Rev. Rul. 66-214, 1966-2 Cum. Bull. 98, it construed its prior rulings to bar the application of the *Libson Shops* doctrine to the carryover of a net operating loss in the case of an "A" reorganization (statutory merger) in which the surviving corporation, no longer engaged in its pre-merger business, sought to set off its earlier loss against the profits of the business previously conducted by the constituent corporation whose identity had not survived reorganization. This was a liberalization of the Service's prior rulings, since §381(a) does not speak to the surviving corporation's own loss carryover. What does? Compare §382(b) in this respect.

2. Although the facts in *Libson Shops* involved a reorganization, in Rev. Rul. 63-40, 1963-1 Cum. Bull. 46, the Service indicated clearly that in some non-reorganization cases under the 1954 Code it would apply the doctrine of that case to deny a corporation the use of its own loss carryover. This application would be made, presumably, where the facts of a given case did not invoke the bar of §382(a). Excerpts from Rev. Rul. 63-40 are set forth below. Consider the principle the Service follows in distinguishing those non-reorganization cases in which it will apply a *Libson Shops* doctrine from those in which it will not:

"Advice has been requested whether either the rationale of the decision in Libson Shops, Inc. v. Koehler, 353 U.S. 382 (1957), Ct. D. 1809, C.B. 1957-2, 891, . . . prevent[s] the use of a net operating loss carryover under the circumstances described below.

"1. The M corporation was organized in 1947 by three individuals who owned an equal number of shares of its authorized and outstanding stock. From the date of its incorporation until the early part of 1958 it was engaged in the fabrication and sale, through distributors, of household light steel products. The business was successful during its early years of operation. However, commencing in 1953 it sustained losses in each of its taxable years and over the period ending December 31, 1957, had accumulated substantial net operating losses.

"In 1958 M corporation purchased for cash, at fair market value, all of the assets of N corporation, which had a history of successful operation of drive-in restaurants. M and N were unrelated corporations and none of the shareholders of M corporation owned, directly or indirectly, any stock of N corporation. The funds for the cash purchase were derived in part from M corporation's own business assets and in part from an equal contribution to its capital of cash by its three stockholders. Shortly thereafter, M corporation discontinued its former business activity, sold the assets connected therewith, and engaged exclusively in the business of operating the chain of drive-in restaurants formerly operated by the N corporation.

"Under the facts presented, . . . the sole question raised is whether the rationale of the *Libson Shops* decision bars the allowance of the net operating loss deduction attributable to losses incurred prior to the acquisition of the new business activity for M corporation's taxable year ended December 31, 1958.

"In cases, like the one discussed above, arising under section 122 of the Internal Revenue Code of 1939 or section 172 of the 1954 Code in which losses have been incurred by a single corporation and there has been little or no change in the stock ownership of the corporation during or after the period in which the losses were incurred, the Internal Revenue Service will not rely on the rationale of the *Libson Shops* decision to bar the corporation from using losses previously incurred by it solely because such losses are attributable to a discontinued corporate activity. Accordingly since there was no change in stock ownership in M corporation either before the discontinuance of its former business activity or after the commencement of its new business activity, a net operating loss deduction is allowable for its taxable year ended December 31, 1958.

"However, if there is more than a minor change in stock ownership of a loss corporation which acquires a new business enterprise, the Service may continue to contest the deductibility of the carryover of the corporation's prior losses against income of the new business enterprise. See, for example, as involving substantial changes in stock ownership, Mill Ridge Coal Co. v. Patterson, 264 Fed. (2d) 713 (1959), certiorari denied, 361 U.S. 816 (1959); A. C. Willingham v. United States, 289 Fed. (2d) 283 (1961), certiorari denied, 368 U.S. 828 (1961); Commissioner v. Virginia Metal Products, Inc., 290 Fed. (2d) 675 (1961), certiorari denied, 368 U.S. 889 (1961); J. G. Dudley Co., Inc. v. Commissioner, 298 Fed. (2d) 750 (1962); and Huyler's v. Commissioner, 38 T.C. 773 (1962). Compare Kolker Bros., Inc. v. Commissioner, 35 T.C. 299 (1960), nonacquiescence at page 5 of this Bulletin, where part of the funds used by the corporation to purchase assets of a new business activity were borrowed from some nonstockholders who several months after the purchase acquired about 46 percent of the corporation's stock in exchange for the indebtedness owed them.

"For a discussion of the Service position with respect to the application of *Libson Shops* to a merger or other transaction described in section 381(a) of the Code, see Revenue Ruling 58-603, C.B. 1958-2, 147. Further Service views concerning the application of *Libson Shops* are set out in Revenue Ruling 59-395, C.B. 1959-2, 475.

"2. Advice has also been requested whether the Service would apply different treatment to a case involving the same facts as are set out in the foregoing except for a difference in the method of acquisition by M corporation of the assets of N corporation. In this second case M corporation first attempted in extended negotiations to purchase the assets of N corporation, but the shareholders of N corporation were unwilling to consummate the transaction except by way of the sale of their stock to M corporation. M corporation purchased the stock of N corporation for cash, at fair market value, solely for the purpose of acquiring its assets to earn a profit with those assets and *immediately* liquidated that corporation under such circumstances that the basis of the assets to M corporation will be determined by the amount it paid for the stock of N corporation.

"Under the facts of this second case, . . . the conclusion reached with respect to the first case is equally applicable here.

"No opinion is expressed as to other cases where the facts show that the purchase price is payable over a substantial period of time (whether or not specifically payable only out of earnings of the business) or exceeds fair market value or where other circumstances may justify the application of section 269 of the Code. . . ."*

MAXWELL HARDWARE v. COMMISSIONER
343 F.2d 713 (9th Cir. 1965)

Before HAMLEY and MERRILL, Circuit Judges, and THOMPSON, District Judge.

THOMPSON, District Judge: This is a petition for review of a decision of the Tax Court of the United States, jurisdiction of which is conferred on this Court under Title 26, U.S.C. §7482. The Tax Court disallowed to Petitioner, Maxwell Hardware Company, a corporation, net operating loss carryover deductions taken for its tax years ending January 31, 1957 to 1960, inclusive.

In summary, the facts are that Maxwell Hardware had sustained approximately $1,000,000 of losses in a hardware business. It entered into an agreement with two partners, Beckett and Federighi, who were engaged in numerous real estate development activities as partners and controlling stockholders of corporations, whereby a real estate department was established in Maxwell Hardware to develop a subdivision, the funds therefor being furnished by the two partners through purchases of nonvoting preferred stock in the corporation for an amount which was approximately two-fifths of the then value of the common stock of the corporation. The real estate department was accounted for independently of the other corporate business. The agreement provided that the real estate department should not be discontinued for a period of six years, that the preferred stockholders should not sell their stock for this period, and thereafter, if the department were discontinued at the option of either the corporation or preferred stockholders, the preferred stock should be redeemed by distribution in kind of ninety per cent of the department's assets to the preferred stockholders. A voting trust agreement was established to restrict the control of the common stockholders over the corporation for a period of five years. The voting trust agreement did not, however, transfer such control to the new investors. The hardware business was discontinued and the real estate business (Bay-O-Vista Subdivisions) operated at a profit. The net operating losses which had been previously sustained by the hardware business were deducted as loss carryovers from the real

*Rev. Rul. 63-40 was modified in part by T.I.R. 773, page 706 infra. — ED.

estate profits. The agreement between the corporation and the new preferred stock-holders was entered into on October 18, 1954, and was therefore governed by the provisions of Internal Revenue Code of 1954.

The transactions and events giving rise to this dispute are complicated and extensive. The Fndings of Fact and Opinion of the Tax Court are published (Arthur T. Beckett v. Commissioner, 41 T.C. 386). . . . With one exception, the findings of the Tax Court have not been contested on this appeal. Petitioner complains that the finding that the "primary purpose of Beckett and Federighi in entering into the agreement of October 18, 1954 with Maxwell Hardware was to enable the profits which they anticipated would be made in the development of the Bay-O-Vista Subdivision to be offset by net operating losses which had been sustained by Maxwell Hardware in prior years" is contrary to the evidence. We think the finding to be amply sustained by substantial evidence and not subject to review by this Court. . . .

. . . The common issue of fact consolidated for trial was whether the income of the real estate department of Maxwell Hardware Company should have been returned by Maxwell Hardware Company or by the partnership of Beckett and Federighi, and derivatively, by the partners individually. The Government contended that the transactions were a sham, and that the operation of the real estate business under the corporate cloak was pure subterfuge, without factual substance.

The Tax Court, relying upon substantial evidence, resolved this issue in favor of the bona fides of the transactions in the sense that they were not sham, that there was a genuine business purpose for using a corporation for the real estate development enterprise, and that the resulting transactions were corporate actions of Maxwell Hardware, not actions of Beckett and Federighi carried on under a corporate name. The Tax Court held that the subdivision income was properly returned as the income of Maxwell Hardware Company. This conclusion is not excepted to by either party on this appeal and constitutes the foundation for our consideration of the case. . . .

Applicability of the *Libson Shops* Doctrine

The Tax Court relied upon the decision of the Supreme Court in Libson Shops, Inc. v. Koehler, 1957, 353 U.S. 382, 77 S. Ct. 990, 1 L. Ed. 2d 924. In that case, the transactions generating the tax liability occurred prior to the effective date of the 1954 Code. The issue there was "whether under §§23(s) and 122 of the Internal Revenue Code of 1939, as amended, a corporation resulting from a merger of 17 separate incorporated businesses, which had filed separate income tax returns, may carry over and deduct the pre-merger net operating losses of three of its constituent corporations from the post-merger income attributable to the other businesses." (Idem. 382, 77 S. Ct. 990). The Supreme Court denied the loss carryover deduction, saying: "We conclude that petitioner is not entitled to a carry-over since the income against which the offset is claimed was not produced by substantially the same businesses which incurred the losses." (Idem. 390, 77 S. Ct. 994). The Commissioner, the Tax Court and Petitioner all agree that if *Libson Shops* had arisen under the 1954 Code, the same decision could not have been made inasmuch as Section 381 of the

1954 Code would expressly allow the net operating loss carryover and the limitations of Section 382 would be inapplicable.

Whenever a Court adopts a rule of decision to sustain a conclusion, interpreting statutory law then applicable, and the legislative authority amends or changes the statutory law to the effect that the same decision could not be reached if the new statute were applied to the same facts, the case is not controlling precedent for judicial interpretation of the new law. By enacting the 1954 Code, Congress destroyed the precedential value of the rule of decision of *Libson Shops;* that is, that for a loss carryover deduction to be allowed, the income against which the offset was claimed must have been produced by substantially the same businesses which incurred the losses. This is not now the law. It seems to us irrelevant that *Libson Shops* was decided in 1957, long after the enactment of the 1954 Code. The Supreme Court, in *Libson Shops,* decided the case by deliberately interpreting and applying the Internal Revenue Code of 1939, as amended, and, while noting a minor change in the 1954 Code (Idem. 385, 77 S. Ct. 992, footnote 2), did not comment upon or consider how the case should be decided if the 1954 Code were applicable.

Sections 172 and 382 Limitations

Recognizing the frailty of *Libson Shops* as a precedent for decision in this case, the Government suggests alternative bases to sustain the Tax Court. One is the contention that Section 172, which establishes the net operating loss carryover deduction does not apply to Maxwell Hardware. The argument is that, viewed realistically, the transactions amounted to placing "two separately owned business entities under a single corporate roof", and that the net operating loss carryover deduction inures only to the business entity which generated it. As a matter of statutory interpretation, we find nothing in §172 which justifies such a conclusion. We cannot disregard the finding of the Tax Court that Maxwell Hardware Company, a corporation, is the taxable entity in this case and that it is the entity which suffered the losses as well as generated the subsequent income sought to be taxed. . . .

With respect to the limitations applicable to the deductibility of net operating loss carryovers, the Government says that the deduction is disqualified in this case by the special limitation provisions of Section 382(a).

The Tax Court found Section 382(a) to be inapplicable, and we agree. The conditions of subsection (C) have been fulfilled, i.e., Maxwell Hardware did not continue to "carry on a trade or business substantially the same as that conducted before any change in the percentage ownership of the fair market value" of the stock. It is also clear, however, that these complicated transactions did not result in persons, as defined, owning fifty percentage points more of the total fair market value of the outstanding stock of such corporation than theretofore. The Tax Court found that the stock acquired by Beckett and Federighi was "non-voting stock which is limited and preferred as to dividends" [26 U.S.C. §382(c)], and said: "It is clear that the issuance of the preferred stock to Beckett and Federighi does not come within any of these provisions." (T.C. 417). Its concise statement of the problem remaining is (T.C. 417): "The problem is whether by specifying the various circumstances in section 382 in which net operating loss deductions would be disallowed in whole or in part where a change in stock ownership has occurred followed by a change in corporate business, Congress intended to provide that in all other instances the loss corporation would be entitled to deduct its net operating loss carryover from earnings from a different business enterprise unless such deduction fell within the prohibition of section 269." We disagree with the Tax Court's negative answer to this inquiry. We conclude from the legislative history that it was the clearly expressed intention of Congress to attempt to bring some order out of chaos, and, in effect, to countenance "trafficking" in operating loss carryovers except as affected by the special limitations of Section 382 and the general limitations of Section 381. (Other Code sections, such as Section 269, are disregarded in this discussion and will be hereinafter considered separately.)

By adopting Section 172(a), Congress created a net operating loss deduction, applicable to taxpayers generally. In Section 381, Congress dealt specifically with the transfer of a variety of deductions, including net operating loss carryovers [Sec. 381(c)(1)] in cases of corporate reorganizations and acquisitions; and in Section 382, Congress provided special limitations by careful and specific definition upon the right to take a net operating loss carryover deduction where there had been a change in ownership of the corporate stock and a change in the corporation's trade or business. Section 172 is a substantial revision of Section 122 of the 1939 Code. . . . We cannot ascribe to a Congress which, after years of thorough and careful committee consideration aided by the solicited advice of the finest students of taxation, has adopted a fully integrated revenue code, the intention that its provisions should be lightly disregarded by the courts. . . . The Reports respecting Section 382 even more clearly demonstrate Congressional intent to substitute statutory rules for judge-made law. It is quite unlikely that the stated purposes of certainty, consistency and objectivity are to be achieved if each court considering a loss carryover problem adds a gloss of judicial exceptions reflecting what a particular judge or group of judges thinks Congress should have done, rather than what it did. An expression like "trafficking in loss carryovers" is a question-begging epithet which clouds reason. A dispassionate consideration of the 1954 Code must lead to the conclusion, we believe, that Congress has deliberately sanctioned such so-called "trafficking" in those situations where it is not expressly abjured.

This is not to say that the language of the 1954 Code is to be given a sterile, mechanical, literal application. The courts must give sense and vitality to that language, but this must be done within the framework of the Code to achieve the Congressional design.

Applicability of Section 269

As a second alternate basis for affirmance, the Government invokes the applicability of Title 26, U.S.C. §269. Subsections (a) and (b) of this Section were carried forward from Section 129 of the 1939 Code. Subsection (c), providing a presumption of wrongful purpose in certain circumstances was added by the 1954 Code. . . .

The new presumption is of no interest here as the Tax Court found that the

Maxwell Hardware acquisition by Beckett and Federighi was made for the avoidance of Federal income tax by securing the benefit of the net operating loss deduction. Just as Section 382(a) requires more than proof of a substantial change in the trade or business conducted to disqualify the deduction, so does Section 269 require more than proof of a purpose to evade or avoid taxes. The additional requirement is the acquisition directly or indirectly of control of a corporation, specifically, the ownership of stock possessing at least fifty per cent of the voting power or at least fifty per cent of the total value of shares of all classes. The purchase by Beckett and Federighi of preferred shares for $200,000 of a corporation whose common shares were found to have a fair market value of $500,000 on its face did not satisfy the requirement of acquisition of fifty per cent of the total value of the shares outstanding, and there is nothing in this record which would justify a conclusion that the true fair value of the preferred shares at the date of acquisition exceeded the amount paid therefor.

Invoking Section 269, the Government argues that the complex transaction between Maxwell Hardware and Beckett and Federighi, viewed realistically, resulted in the indirect acquisition by Beckett and Federighi of fifty per cent of the total combined voting power of the corporation. An integral component of the entire transaction was the voting trust agreement which, although not mentioned in the basic agreement of October 18, 1954, bore even date therewith. The agreement created an irrevocable voting trust of all the common shares of Maxwell Hardware until January 31, 1961 and invested the trustee, The San Francisco Bank, with all voting rights, limiting its authority only in respect of the selection of the Board of Directors. The agreement required the trustee to vote for T. P. Coates, an officer of the Bank, and John M. Bryan, as two members of the three man board. The trustee's selection of the third member was unfettered. The agreement accomplished a relinquishment by the common stockholders of their voting control; but the condition for the invoking of Section 269 is the acquisition by persons (here, Beckett and Federighi) of fifty per cent voting control. This is an integrated voting trust agreement which controlled the trustee's powers and responsibilities. It cannot fairly be construed as an acquisition by Beckett and Federighi of any voting control.

True, the evidence proved and the Tax Court found that it was understood that Federighi would be the third director of Maxwell Hardware (T.C. 399), and that there was an oral agreement that Bryan would not be vetoed on any reasonable business investment he wished to make on behalf of Maxwell Hardware. Such evidence was probative and relevant on the issue of sham, an issue which has been permanently resolved against the Government, and on the issue under Section 269 of purpose to evade or avoid, an issue which has been conclusively determined against Petitioner, Maxwell Hardware. Such evidence, however, does not, in our view, justify an inference, as the Government asserts, that fifty per cent voting control was thereby acquired by Beckett and Federighi. A voting trust agreement is too valuable a vehicle for the effectuation of innumerable commercial transactions to be thus lightly impugned; and the eagerness of the Commissioner to collect taxes, a duty imposed on him by law, should not lead the courts arbitrarily to disregard established and useful forms of business relationships. The voting trust agreement invested the voting control in the trustee, not in Beckett or Federighi. If the evidence were such as to justify a finding that under all the circumstances, either the trustee bank of T. P. Coates, a designated director, was under the domination and control of Beckett and Federighi, the case would be different. There is no such evidence. The Tax Court correctly said: "We think it clear that the provisions of Section 269 are not applicable here because of the absence of the type of acquisition provided for therein." (T.C. 414.) . . .

Summary

This decision is reached in a straightjacket. We are bound by the Tax Court finding that the Maxwell Hardware transaction was a bona fide business transaction creating substantial, and not illusory, business relationships. We are concerned only with the tax liability of Maxwell Hardware, which, the Tax Court found, properly reported as its income the profit from the subdivision business. We are faced only with the problem of whether the net operating loss deduction generated by the hardware business may be taken against the income from its subdivision business. . . .

Libson Shops, decided under the 1939 Act, is no longer law. It has been superseded by the 1954 Internal Revenue Code which, in Section 382, dealt specifically and differently with the concept of continuity of business enterprise upon which the *Libson Shops* decision was based.

. . . We cannot, within the statutory framework applying a fair and reasonable interpretation to the language used, disallow to Maxwell Hardware the net operating loss deduction.

The decision of the Tax Court is reversed.

TECHNICAL INFORMATION RELEASE 773
7 CCH 1965 Stand. Fed. Tax Rep. ¶6751

The United States Internal Revenue Service . . . announced that it will not follow the decision of the United States Court of Appeals for the Ninth Circuit in the case of Maxwell Hardware Co. v. Commissioner, 343 F.2d 713 (1965).

In that case, the circuit court held that the Supreme Court's decision in Libson Shops, Inc. v. Koehler, 353 U.S. 382 (1957) has no precedential value under the 1954 Code, and that the net operating loss carryovers involved therein were not subject to disallowance under sections 172, 269 or 382. The court, by way of dictum, stated that the Commissioner might have successfully applied section 482 in this case.

It is the position of the Revenue Service that in cases similar to *Maxwell Hardware,* sections 269 and 382, as well as section 482, are applicable in dealing with the carryover of losses. The Revenue Service believes that the foregoing statutory provisions must be construed to effectuate congressional intent in combating "trafficking in loss carryovers". Moreover, the Service also believes that the loss carryover in cases similar to *Maxwell Hardware* should be denied under the rationale of the *Libson Shops* decision since to permit a loss carryover in such cases would run counter to the legislative objectives of the carryover privilege.

The cornerstone of the *Libson Shops* decision was a searching examination of the purposes of the carryover privilege. Thus, in approaching the question of whether the taxpayer was entitled to a loss carryover, the Supreme Court held that the loss carryover provision was not automatic and that the "availability of . . . [the loss carryover] privilege depends on the proper interpretation to be given to the carryover provisions". The Service believes that this fundamental type of statutory analysis was not made obsolete by the enactment in 1954 of provisions limiting or denying loss carryovers in certain situations involving abuses that were specifically brought to the attention of Congress. It is the view of the Service that the basic approach of the Supreme Court in *Libson Shops* retains vitality under the 1954 Code in interpreting the application of section 172.

Accordingly, the Service will apply *Libson Shops* in any loss carryover case under the 1954 Code, not contemplated by the announcement in Revenue Ruling 58-603, C.B. 1958-2, 147,* where there has been both a 50 percent or more shift in the benefits of a loss carryover (whether direct or indirect and including transactions having the effect of shifting the benefit of the loss by shifting assets, stock, profit interests or other valuable rights) and a change in business as defined in section 382(a) and the regulations thereunder. The Service will not rely on *Libson Shops* under the 1954 Code in any loss carryover case where there has been less than a 50 percent change in the beneficial ownership of the loss or where there has been no change in business as defined in section 382(a) and the regulations thereunder. However, the Service will continue to rely on sections 269 and 482, where appropriate, in dealing with the carryover of losses. Revenue Ruling 63-40, C.B. 1963-1, 46† will be modified to the extent inconsistent herewith. . . .

COMMONWEALTH CONTAINER CORP. v. COMMISSIONER
393 F.2d 269 (3d Cir. 1968)

Before BIGGS, KALODNER and FREEDMAN, Circuit Judges.

BIGGS, Circuit Judge: The taxpayer, Commonwealth Container Corporation, appeals from a decision of the Tax Court of the United States holding that there were deficiencies in income taxes for the year 1961 in the sum of $28,474.52 and for the year 1962 in the sum of $21,460.75. Jurisdiction is based on 26 U.S.C. §7482. The only issue presented is what part of the net operating loss carryover of Tri-City Container Corp., which merged into Commonwealth on or about June 21, 1961, may be included in Commonwealth's net operating loss deduction for the years 1961 and 1962.

Simply stated the facts are as follows. The Tri-City Corporation was a New York corporation engaged in the manufacture of corrugated paperboard and containers. From its organization in 1955 up to the date of its merger with the taxpayer, Commonwealth Container, it had 180 outstanding shares owned as follows:

*See Note 1, page 699 supra. — ED.
†See Note 2, page 699 supra. — ED.

Shareholder	Number of Shares
Paul Densen	85½
Abbot Greene	85½
Irwin Densen	9
Total	180

Sometime prior to the merger of Tri-City with the taxpayer, Paul Densen and Abbot Greene each transferred 10 shares of their stock to trusts for their children so that immediately prior to the merger the stock of Tri-City was owned as follows:

Shareholder	Number of Shares	Percentage of Total
Paul Densen	75½	41.94
Abbot Greene	75½	41.94
Irwin Densen	9	5.00
Various parties as trustees of 4 trusts holding 5 shares for each trust	20	11.02
Total	180	100.00[1]

[1]Discrepancies between the totals and figures shown in this and other included charts are due to the rounding off of some of the figures.

The taxpayer is a New Jersey corporation which is also engaged in the corrugated paperboard container business. It was organized by Paul and Irwin Densen and Abbot Greene in 1951. Prior to the merger of taxpayer with Tri-City on June 21, 1961, taxpayer's stock was owned as follows:

Shareholder	Number of Shares	Percentage of Total
Paul Densen	356	29.66
Abbot Greene	356	29.66
Irwin Densen	60	5.00
Elmer Hertzmark	300	25.00
Various parties as trustees of 4 trusts, holding 32 shares for each trust	128	10.68
Total	1200	100.00

[Post-Merger Stock Ownership]

For some years prior to 1960 the taxpayer had operated at a profit while Tri-City had operated at a loss. The shareholders of both companies decided to merge the companies and the original plan of reorganization called for a transfer of the assets and business of Tri-City to the taxpayer in exchange for 300 shares of the latter's common stock. This plan was abandoned when taxpayer was unable to obtain a favorable ruling from the Internal Revenue Service that no gain or loss would be recognized by the stockholders of either party to the reorganization. Subsequently, in March, 1961, a new plan was adopted whereby each share of the 180 outstanding common shares of Tri-City was exchanged for and converted into one share of the common stock of the taxpayer. Immediately after the merger, on June 21, 1961, the taxpayer's outstanding common stock was owned as follows:

Shareholder	*Number of Shares*	*Percentage of Total*
Paul Densen	431½	31.20
Abbot Greene	431½	31.20
Elmer Hertzmark	300	31.74
Irwin Densen	69	5.00
Various parties as trustees of 4 trusts, holding 37 shares each	148	10.72
Total	1380	100.00

About six months after the merger, Hertzmark and taxpayer dissolved their old employment agreement, under which Hertzmark had purchased his stock in Commonwealth, by entering into a new agreement. The new agreement continued the earlier restrictions on alienation of Hertzmark's stock but added that in computing the value of his shares any value attributable to the assets and business of taxpayer's Tri-City division was to be excluded, and that his stock was to be equal to .25 per cent of the value of all of taxpayer's issued and outstanding stock after deducting any value attributable to the Tri-City division.

After Commonwealth was informed by a revenue agent that it may not have issued a sufficient number of shares in exchange for the Tri-City stock in order to be able to deduct Tri-City's full operating loss carryover from Commonwealth's income, Commonwealth, sometime after September 25, 1964, issued an additional 120 shares (which were dated October 19, 1961, the date on the certificates of the 180 shares which had been issued) to Paul, Irwin, Abbot and the trusts for Paul's and Abbot's children. These 120 shares increased the total of taxpayer's outstanding common stock to 1500 shares, which were then held as follows:

Shareholder	*Number of Shares*	*Percentage of Total*
Paul Densen	481⅚	32.12
Abbot Greene	481⅚	32.12
Elmer Hertzmark	300	20.00
Irwin Densen	75	5.00
Various parties as trustees of 4 trusts, holding 40⅓ shares for each trust	161⅓	10.76
Total	1500	100.00

After trial, the Tax Court determined that the taxpayer was entitled to deduct only 65 percent of Tri-City's premerger net operating losses because it failed to meet the criterion of section 382(b) of the Code. First, the court held that the shareholders of the loss corporation did not own 20 percent of the fair market value of taxpayer's outstanding stock "as a result of owning stock of the loss corporation" as required by Section 382(b)(1)(B) because they received only 180 out of taxpayer's 1,380 shares for their share of Tri-City. Second, it held that the taxpayer and the loss corporation were not owned "substantially by the same persons in the same proportion" as required by Section 382(b)(3) because Hertzmark owned 25 percent of the taxpayer but had no interest in Tri-City.

These conclusions were based on the assumption that each share of the taxpayer's stock owned by Hertzmark was equal in value to each share held by the other stockholders. Because taxpayer has not shown that Hertzmark's shares differed in value from those held by the other shareholders of Commonwealth, see footnote 6 in the Tax Court's opinion, 48 T.C. 483, we will affirm the judgment of the Tax Court on Chief Judge Drennen's exhaustive opinion.

KALODNER, Circuit Judge, would affirm for the reasons stated in the Tax Court's opinion.

[Judge Drennen's opinion, excerpted from Commonwealth Container Corporation, 48 T.C. 483 (1967) follows:]

DRENNEN, Judge: . . . The principal issue is whether the amount of the net operating loss carryover of Tri-City, acquired by petitioner as the result of a merger with Tri-City, which petitioner may include in its net operating loss deduction is limited by section 382(b) of the Code.

Section 381(a)(2) and (c)(1) of the Code provides that in the case of the acquisition of assets of a corporation by another corporation in a section 368(a)(1) (A), (C), (D), or (F) reorganization to which section 361 applies the acquiring corporation shall succeed to and take into account the net operating loss carryover of the transferor corporation. If no other statutes were involved it would appear that petitioner was entitled to take into account for years subsequent to the merger the entire amount of Tri-City's operating loss carryover.

However, section 382(b)(1) provides that if, in a reorganization specified in section 381(a)(2), the transferor corporation or the acquiring corporation has a net operating loss which is a net operating loss carryover to the first taxable year of the acquiring corporation ending after the date of the transfer, and the stockholders (immediately before the reorganization) of the loss corporation, as the result of owning stock of the loss corporation, own (immediately after the reorganization) less than 20 percent of the fair market value of the stock of the acquiring corporation, the total net operating loss carryover of the loss corporation, which the acquiring corporation may utilize, shall be limited as determined under paragraph (2). Succinctly stated, paragraph (2) reduces the total net operating loss carryover by 5 percent for each percentage point below 20 percent of the fair market value of the stock of the acquiring corporation acquired by the stockholders of the loss corporation as a result of the reorganization. If the limitation of section 382(b) is applicable petitioner would be entitled to include in its net operating loss deduction only 65 percent of Tri-City's net operating loss carryover.[6]

Whether section 382(b) is applicable depends, except as might otherwise be affected by section 382(c), upon whether the fair market value of Hertzmark's stock of petitioner must be included in the 20-percent computation.

Petitioner argues first that inasmuch as the stockholders of Tri-City had a controlling interest in petitioner both before and after the merger, there was the requisite continuity of interest in the operating loss carryover which Congress sought to require in order to make the entire operating loss carryover available to the acquiring corporation. We agree that in enacting section 381(c)(1) Congress sought to liberalize the carryover of operating losses in certain corporate reorganizations but we must also recognize that in section 382(b) Congress established an objective test to determine whether all or only a part of the operating loss carryover would be available to the acquiring corporation in such a reorganization; and that the test is based upon the percentage of interest in the acquiring corporation the stockholders of the loss corporation *receive as a result of the reorganization.* To interpret the statute otherwise would require reading the phrase "as the result of owning stock of the loss corporation" completely out of the statute; and this we are not justified in doing. Hanover Bank v. Commissioner, 369 U.S. 672; Frank W. Verito, 43 T.C. 429.

There was no counterpart of sections 381 and 382 in the 1939 Code and the "trafficking in loss corporations," while extensive, was a rather uncertain venture under the Court-made rules applied in disallowing operating loss carryovers to successor corporations or businesses. In adopting sections 381 and 382 of the 1954 Code, Congress apparently intended to liberalize and make more certain the availability of the net operating carryover to successor corporations and businesses, provided there was not a substantial change in ownership of a closely held corporation. In the House version of H.R. 8300, 83d Cong., 2d Sess. (See H. Rept. No. 1337, p. A-135, et seq.) the carryover was made available to the acquiring corporation, limited only if there was a change of at least 50 percentage points in the ownership of stock by any 1 or more of the 10 largest stockholders during a 2-year period as a result of a purchase or redemption of stock, in which event there would be a percentage reduction in the amount of the loss carryover available. The Senate bill, however, modified the limitation provision, eliminating the carryover entirely if there was a 50-percent or more change in ownership of the stock and a substantial change in the trade or business conducted, and providing for the reduction in the amount of the carryover available unless the acquiring corporation gave up at least

[6]Assuming the fair market value of each share of petitioner's stock is the same. Neither party argues that the percentage of the fair market value of petitioner's outstanding stock represented by Hertzmark's stock was any different than the percentage of the total outstanding shares of petitioner's stock represented by Hertzmark's shares, although petitioner does argue that because of the employment agreement Hertzmark's shares should be ignored for purposes of the computation under sec. 382(b) and the application of sec. 382(b)(3). There is no evidence in the record from which we could determine the fair market value of any of petitioner's stock and we have not been asked to do so. Neither does either party make any reference to the preferred stock of petitioner which was outstanding at the time of the merger.

a 20-percent interest to the stockholders of the corporation with the net operating loss carryover. The Senate Finance Committee report (see S. Rept. No. 1622, 83d Cong., 2d Sess., pp. 284, 286), specifically states that the "stockholders of the corporation with the net operating loss carryover must own, as a result of owning stock in the loss corporation immediately before the reorganization, 20 percent or more of the fair market value of the outstanding stock of the acquiring corporation or the reduction in paragraph (2) will apply."

The Senate version of section 382 was accepted by the Conference Committee and became the law. While it seems quite likely that the clause "as a result of owning stock of the loss corporation" was inserted by Congress to prevent avoidance of the limitation by the stockholders of the loss corporation temporarily buying stock of the acquiring corporation immediately before the reorganization, rather than the situation we have here where they already owned the stock of the acquiring corporation, nevertheless there is no ambiguity in the words used in the statute, and if they are applied literally here, the reduction provided in section 382 must be applied. . . . While the stockholders of Tri-City (the loss corporation) owned 1,080 of the 1,380 shares of petitioner outstanding immediately after the merger, or over 78 percent, they received only 180 shares, or about 13 percent, of the shares of petitioner's common stock as a result of the merger.

Section 1.382(b)-1(a)(2), Income Tax Regs., provides as follows:

"The ownership of at least 20 percent of the fair market value of the stock of the acquiring corporation after the reorganization must result from the ownership of stock in the loss corporation immediately before the reorganization. Thus, if stockholders of a transferor-loss corporation before the reorganization also own stock of the acquiring corporation at such time, such stock of the acquiring corporation is not considered as owned after the reorganization by such stockholders as a result of owning stock in the loss corporation in determining whether the 20-percent requirement is satisfied. Moreover, the stockholders (immediately before the reorganization) of a transferor-loss corporation shall not be regarded as owning, immediately after the reorganization, any stock of the acquiring corporation which is not distributed to such stockholders pursuant to the plan of reorganization."

We think this is a reasonable interpretation of the statute.

We cannot ignore the clear language of the statute, and unless there is some other reason why the reduction provided in section 382(b)(1) and (2) should not be applied, we must sustain respondent's position that only 65 percent of the Tri-City net operating loss carryover is available to petitioner.

Petitioner argues, albeit without much conviction, that the issuance of the additional 120 shares of petitioner's stock to the former stockholders of Tri-City sometime after September of 1964, thus bringing the interest they received as a result of the merger up to exactly 20 percent of petitioner's stock, should avoid the application of section 382(b). It may be that because the Densens and Greenes controlled both corporations prior to the merger, the merger agreement could just as well have provided for the issuance of 300 shares of petitioner's stock in exchange for the Tri-City stock, but the fact remains that it did not do so. The merger agreement under which the merger was accomplished provided for the issuance of 1 share of petitioner's stock for each share of Tri-City stock and only 180 shares of petitioner's stock were issued in effecting the merger. Section 382(b)(1)(B) provides specifically that if the stockholders of the loss corporation "own (immediately after the reorganization) less than 20 percent" of the fair market value of the stock of the acquiring corporation, as a result of the reorganization, the reductions provided in paragraph (2) of subsection (b) shall be applied. The stockholders of Tri-City did not own the additional 120 shares of petitioner *immediately after the reorganization,* and those shares cannot be used in computing the amount of the reduction in the operating loss carryover.

Petitioner also contends that the reduction provided under section 382(b)(1) and (2) is not required because of the exception provided in paragraph (3) of subsection (b). Paragraph (3) provides that the limitation in subsection (b) shall not apply "if the transferor corporation and the acquiring corporation are owned substantially by the same persons in the same proportion."

We find no guide either in the legislative history of this provision or in any decided case as to just what was meant by the word "substantially" as used in this paragraph, or just what this provision was intended to cover. We surmise that it was inserted to avoid application of the mechanical test provided in paragraph (2) where both corporations involved in a reorganization were for all practical purposes owned by the same persons in the same proportions before the reorganization so that it would make little difference how much stock of the acquiring corporation was issued to the transferor corporation or its stockholders under the plan of reorganization, because the same persons who suffered the losses would be getting the benefit of the carryover in the same proportions as the losses were incurred. Such was the situation in James Armour, Inc., 43 T.C. 295, where this Court recognized that a transaction wherein one corporation transferred certain of its assets to another corporation without receiving shares of the transferee nevertheless qualified as a section 368(a)(1)(D) reorganization, saying:

> "However, the petitioners already owned all the stock of Excavating and it was not necessary that further stock be issued in order that they might retain their same proprietary interest in the assets received by Excavating. The issuance of further stock would have been a meaningless gesture, and we cannot conclude that the statute requires such a vain act. . . ."

But the situation is not the same here because before the merger Hertzmark had no proprietary interest in the corporation which sustained the loss but immediately after the merger he had a 21.74 percent interest in the corporation which seeks to utilize the loss carryover for tax purposes. Before the merger Hertzmark had no interest in Tri-City but had a 25 percent interest in petitioner. Also before the merger Paul Densen and Abbot Greene each had a 41.94 percent interest in Tri-City but only a 29.66 percent interest in petitioner; and immediately after the merger they each had a 31.20 percent interest in petitioner.

"Substantially" is a relative term and, in the absence of a statutory definition thereof, we must consider it in the context in which it is used and give it a meaning which we think will be consonant with the purpose of Congress in enacting the particular statute in which the term is used.

In his regulations dealing with this provision, sec. 1.382(b)-1(d)(2), Income Tax Regs., respondent does not attempt to define the term specifically but does state that the transferor corporation and the acquiring corporation will be considered as owned substantially by the same persons only if the same persons own substantially all the stock of the corporations in substantially the same proportion. He then illustrates the rule by several examples. In example (1), A and B each own 50 percent of the fair market value of the stock of the transferor corporation, in a reorganization to which section 381(a) applies, and A owns 52 percent and B owns 48 percent of the fair market value of the stock of the acquiring corporation. The exception provided in section 382(b)(3) is said to apply. But in example (2), where A and B each own 50 percent of the transferor corporation but A owns 60 percent and B owns 40 percent of the acquiring corporation, the exception is said not to apply. If example (2) in the regulations is a correct illustration of the meaning of section 382(b)(3), then the exception provided in that section would not be applicable here because there was a deviation of more than 20 percent in the ownership of the stock of Tri-City and petitioner.

Petitioner argues that because of the percentage of ownership the Densen and Greene families had in both corporations, and the restrictions attached to the stock held by Hertzmark, the Densens and Greenes had substantial control of both corporations and this should satisfy the requirements of section 382(b)(3). The fallacy in this argument is that section 382(b)(3) does not deal with "control," but rather with common and proportionate ownership of the proprietary interests in both corporations. In this context we cannot conclude that both petitioner and Tri-City were owned substantially by the same persons in the same proportions within the meaning of this section so as to make the exception applicable.

Petitioner contends that because the stockholders of Tri-City had control of petitioner before the merger and could have terminated Hertzmark's employment at any time and forced him to sell his stock to petitioner or to them, this in effect gave them an option to acquire Hertzmark's stock at any time and was tantamount to ownership of his stock for purposes of this section; at least, they argue, the Hertzmark stock should not be considered in determining whether the section is applicable. We do not view the situation that way. There obviously was a sound business reason for selling the stock to Hertzmark in the first place. He paid what would appear to have been a computed value for it and while he continued to hold it he had all the incidents and attributes of full ownership of the stock. It would also appear that petitioner's other stockholders had no intentions of terminating Hertzmark's employment and forcing a sale of his stock because soon after the merger petitioner and Hertzmark entered into a new employment agreement which specifically recognized his ownership of the stock and provided for a continuance of his 25-percent interest in the assets and business of petitioner, exclusive of the Tri-City division. While this might indicate that an effort was being made to provide a

100-percent continuity of interest in the same persons in the assets and business of Tri-City after the merger, the operating loss carryover that is available to petitioner will be a deduction against the entire income of petitioner, not just the income from the Tri-City division.

While we have some doubt that the purpose of imposing the limitation or reduction provided for in section 382(b)(1) and (2) was to limit the availability of the carryover in situations such as that before us, where there was no purchase of stock to obtain the full tax advantage of the loss carryover, it would nevertheless be second-guessing Congress on our part to ignore a part of the language used by Congress for that reason alone. An effort was made by Congress in enacting sections 381 and 382 to bring some order out of the chaos in this area of the law and to liberalize the carryover of operating losses where the owners of the corporation which suffered the losses had a continuing proprietary interest in those losses or the business that produced them. A mechanical formula was adopted to accomplish that result, which appears to be quite fair to the taxpayers. An exception was provided where the mechanical requirement could not be met but where there was no real change in ownership of the business that produced the loss. Our best judgment is that the exception should be, and was intended to be, rather narrowly confined and applied to avoid the uncertainties of the past.

We conclude that the total net operating loss carryover from prior taxable years of Tri-City to the first taxable year of petitioner ending after the date of the merger shall, subject to the conditions and limitations specified in section 381(b) and (c), be reduced by 35 percent, so that petitioner, in computing its net operating loss deduction, may take into account 65 percent of Tri-City's net operating loss carryover.

Decision will be entered under Rule 50.

REVENUE RULING 67-274
1967-2 Cum. Bull. 141

. . . Pursuant to a plan of reorganization, corporation Y acquired all of the outstanding stock of corporation X from the X shareholders in exchange solely for voting stock of Y. Thereafter X was completely liquidated as part of the same plan and all of its assets were transferred to Y which assumed all of the liabilities of X. Y continued to conduct the business previously conducted by X. The former shareholders of X continued to hold 16 percent of the fair market value of all the outstanding stock of Y.

Section 368(a)(1)(B) of the Code provides in part that a reorganization is the acquisition by one corporation, in exchange solely for all or a part of its voting stock, of stock of another corporation if, immediately after the acquisition, the acquiring corporation has control (as defined in section 368(c) of the Code) of such other corporation. Section 368(a)(1)(C) of the Code provides in part that a reorganization is the acquisition by one corporation, in exchange solely for all or a part of its voting stock, of substantially all of the properties of another corporation, but in determining whether the exchange is solely for stock the assumption by the acquiring corporation of a liability of the other, or the fact that property acquired is subject to a liability, is disregarded.

Under the circumstances of this case the acquisition of X stock by Y and the liquidation of X by Y are part of the overall plan of reorganization and the two steps may not be considered independently of each other for Federal income tax purposes. See Revenue Ruling 54-96, C.B. 1954-1, 111, as modified by Revenue Ruling 56-100, C.B. 1956-1, 624. The substance of the transaction is an acquisition of assets to which section 368(a)(1)(B) of the Code does not apply.

Accordingly, the acquisition by Y of the outstanding stock of X will not constitute a reorganization within the meaning of section 368(a)(1)(B) of the Code but will be considered an acquisition of the assets of X which in this case is a reorganization described in section 368(a)(1)(C) of the Code. Moreover, since the transaction is one to which section 381(a)(2) of the Code applies, the provisions of section 382(b) of the Code and the regulations thereunder relating to the limitation on the carryover of a net operating loss where a change of ownership occurs as a result of a reorganization are also applicable. See section 1.382(b)-1(a)(6) of the Income Tax Regulations.

NOTE

1. Why is it significant to determine whether the transaction in Rev. Rul. 67-274 is a "B" or a "C" reorganization? How would the last paragraph of the ruling have been written if the Commissioner had determined it was a "B" reorganization?

2. Is the ruling correct? Would the Court of Claims agree with you? See American Potash & Chemical Corp. v. United States, page 550 supra. Does the Court of Claims distinguish the ruling from the case before it in adequate fashion?

REVENUE RULING 67-186
1967-1 Cum. Bull. 81

. . . A corporation conducted a lumber business until the sale of its operating assets during its taxable year ended July 31, 1959. The corporation incurred a net operating loss from the lumber business in the year of the sale of its assets. Since the sale of its operating assets, the corporation's sole source of income has been from investments in stocks and securities purchased after the sale of its operating assets. At the close of the taxable year ended July 31, 1962, shareholders of the corporation owned a percentage of the total fair market value of the corporation which was at least 50 percentage points more than such persons owned at either the beginning of such taxable year or the prior taxable year within the meaning of section 382(a) of the Code.

Section 1.382(a)-1(h)(4) of the Income Tax Regulations states that for purposes of section 382(a) of the Code the holding, purchase, or sale for investment purposes of stock, securities or similar property shall not be considered a trade or business unless such activities historically have been the primary activities of the corporation.

Section 1.382(a)-1(h)(6) of the regulations states that a corporation has not continued to carry on a trade or business substantially the same as that conducted before any increase in the ownership of its stock if the corporation is not carrying on an active trade or business at the time of such increase in ownership.

Since the investment activities were not historically the primary activities of this corporation prior to the change in ownership, such activity is not considered for purposes of section 382 of the Code to constitute carrying on a trade or business.

Therefore, when this corporation ceased its lumber business and engaged in investment activity, for purposes of section 382(a) of the Code the corporation is not regarded as having continued to carry on a trade or business substantially the same as that conducted by it before the change of ownership.

Accordingly, in the instant case the corporation is not entitled to avail itself of net operating loss carryovers from taxable years prior to such change in ownership.

COMMISSIONER v. BRITISH MOTOR CAR DISTRIBUTORS, LTD.
278 F.2d 392 (9th Cir. 1960)

Before Pope, Hamlin and Merrill, Circuit Judges.

Merrill, Circuit Judge. The taxpayer corporation incurred losses while engaged in the business of selling home appliances. It disposed of all its assets and the corporate shares were then sold to new owners, who used the corporation to operate a previously going automobile business. The question here presented is whether the taxpayer is entitled to carry over the losses incurred in the old business, where it is clear that the principal purpose of the acquisition of the taxpayer by the new owners was to avoid taxes. The Tax Court, five judges dissenting, ruled in the affirmative, 31 T.C. 437 (November 26, 1958), and the Commissioner has appealed. We here hold that carryover of the loss is forbidden under §[269(a)]. . . . The judgment of the Tax Court accordingly must be reversed.

Empire Home Equipment Company, Inc., was incorporated under the laws of California on November 13, 1948. Empire engaged in the business of selling home appliances at wholesale and retail. During its fiscal years ending in 1949, 1950 and 1951, Empire incurred net operating losses in the sum of $374,406.57. In December, 1949, Empire's lease of its premises at 40 Drumm Street in San Francisco was cancelled. Unamortized leasehold improvements were written off by January, 1950. In February, 1950, its merchandise inventory was liquidated in bulk at a considerable loss. All of its furniture and fixtures were sold by February 20, 1950. On April 1, 1950, its accounts receivable were sold. On its tax return for the fiscal year ending October 31, 1951, Empire reported its assets as "Nil."

British Motor Car Company was a partnership consisting of Kjell H. Qvale, who had an 85 per cent interest, and his wife, who had a 15 per cent interest. The partnership had existed from about May 1, 1948, and engaged, in San Francisco, in the business of importing, distributing and selling foreign automobiles and parts. On September 11, 1951, the partnership submitted an offer to counsel for the Empire Home Equipment Company, in which the former offered to buy the outstanding stock of the corporation from its then owners for $21,250.00, upon the conditions, inter alia, that the corporation would increase its authorized capital and change its name. The offer was accepted. On November 2, 1951, Empire changed its name to British Motor Car Distributors, Ltd. On November 30, 1951, the partnership acquired all the outstanding shares of stock and immediately thereafter transferred its net assets (exclusive of the acquired shares) to the corporation in exchange for an additional 15,923 shares of stock. It is not claimed that there was any business purpose in the acquisition.

In the tax years ending October 31, 1952, and October 31, 1953, the corporation operated profitably in the automobile business. In its income and excess profits tax returns for those years, it carried forward the net operating losses that it had sustained in the appliance business in its fiscal years ending in 1949, 1950 and 1951.

The Commissioner disallowed the claimed deductions and gave notice of deficiency. The corporation then petitioned the Tax Court for a redetermination.

The Tax Court, in its construction of §[269(a)], adhered to its view as expressed in T. V. D. Company, 27 T.C. 879, 886,[2] following the dictum in Alprosa Watch Company, 11 T.C. 240, to the effect that "it is manifest from the unambiguous terms of §129* that it applies only to an acquiring corporation." The court points out that here the corporation is seeking to make use of its own previous loss; that it is the corporation, and not its new stockholders, which is securing the benefit of the deduction. *Alprosa Watch* is quoted to the effect that §129(a) "would seem to prohibit the use of a deduction, credit or allowance only by the acquiring person or corporation and not their use by the corporation whose control was acquired."

We do not read the language of the section, "securing the benefit of a deduction," as applying only to the actual taking of such deduction by the taxpayer. We should be closing our eyes to the realities of the situation were we to refuse to recognize that the persons who have acquired the corporation did so to secure *for themselves* a very real tax benefit to be realized by them *through* the acquired corporation and which they could not otherwise have realized.

This is not, as the corporation protests, a disregard of its corporate entity. Since §[269(a)] is expressly concerned with the persons acquiring control of a corporation, we must recognize such persons as, *themselves*, having a significant existence or entity apart from the corporation they have acquired. To ignore such independent entity simply because such persons are also the stockholders of their acquisition is to ignore the clear demands of §[269(a)]. It is not the fact that they are stockholders which subjects them to scrutiny. Rather, it is the fact that they are the persons specified by the section: those who have acquired control of the corporation. They may not

---

[2]This case involved an attempt to *tax income* to an acquired corporation which had been merged into the acquirer. No question of disallowance of losses was before the Court. In W.A.G.E., Inc., 1952, 19 T.C. 249, and in A.B. & Container Corporation, 1950, 14 T.C. 842, also referred to by the Tax Court, business purpose was expressly found.

*Section 129 is the 1939 Code predecessor to §269. — Ed.

escape the scrutiny which the section demands by attempting to merge their identity with that of their acquisition.

Section [269(a)] contemplates that it shall not be limited to corporate acquirers. While Clause (2) is specifically limited to corporate acquirers, Clause (1) deals with "persons" as acquirers. That Clause (1) is to include noncorporate acquirers could not be more clearly implied. Nor do we find any sound reason, if this device for tax avoidance is to be struck down, for doing the job only when the tax avoider is a corporation. Legislative history indicates that a much broader construction was intended.[3]

To limit the effect of §[269(a)] to cases in which the taxpayer is seeking to deduct as its own a loss incurred by another would seem to limit Clause (1) to corporate acquirers. Who but a corporation could claim as its *own* a loss which had been incurred by an acquired corporation? Certainly an individual could not do so. The construction here contended for by the taxpayer corporation would then clearly frustrate legislative purpose.

Such construction is not the necessary result of the language used. To construe "benefit" as limited to the taking of the deduction; or "deduction" as limited to one claimed by the acquirer is to read something into the section which is not expressly there and which serves to prevent its application in an area clearly intended to have been included.

The corporation contends, as stated by the Tax Court, that the benefit to the stockholders (as distinguished from that to the corporate taxpayer) is too tenuous to bring the section into play. Tenuous or not, it is the benefit which actuated these persons in acquiring this corporation and is thus the very benefit with which this section is concerned. It is not for the courts to judge whether the benefit to the acquiring persons is sufficiently direct or substantial to be worth acquiring. That

---

[3]H.R. No. 871, 78th Congress, First Session (1944 Cum. Bull. 901, 938):

"This section is designed to put an end promptly to any market for, or dealings in, interests in corporations or property which have as their objective the reduction through artifice of the income or excess profits tax liability.

"The crux of the devices which have come to the attention of your committee has been some form of acquisition on or after the effective date of the Second Revenue Act of 1940, but the devices take many forms. Thus, the acquisition may be an acquisition of the shares of a corporation, or it may be an acquisition which follows by operation of law in the case of a corporation resulting from a statutory merger or consolidation. The person, or persons, making the acquisition likewise vary, as do the forms or methods of utilization under which tax avoidance is sought. Likewise, the tax benefits sought may be one or more of several deductions or credits, including the utilization of excess profits credits, carry-overs and carry-backs of losses or unused excess profits credits, and anticipated expense of other deductions. In the light of these considerations, the section has not confined itself to a description of any particular methods for carrying out such tax avoidance schemes but has included within its scope these devices in whatever form they may appear. For similar reasons, the scope of the terms used in the section is to be found in the objective of the section, namely, to prevent the tax liability from being reduced through the distortion or perversion effected through tax avoidance devices."

The taxpayer corporation contends that the Conference Report, H. Rep. 1079, 78th Congress, Second Session (1944 Cum. Bull. 1069) shows a narrowing of the intendment of the section. However, reference to Sen. Rep. 627, 78th Congress, First Session (1944 Cum. Bull. 973, 1016-1018) clearly shows that restriction on the sweep of the house bill was confined to the elimination of overlaps with existing sections and the formulation of a standard for "control" and that the spirit of the measure was left unaffected.

judgment was made by the acquirers. The judicial problem is whether the securing of the benefit was the principal purpose of the acquisition. If it was, the allowance of the deduction is forbidden. See: Mill Ridge Coal Co. v. Patterson, 5 Cir., 1959, 264 F.2d 713; Tarleau, Acquisition of Loss Companies, 1953, 31 Taxes, The Tax Magazine, 1050.

Judgment reversed. The deductions claimed by the taxpayer are disallowed and judgment is entered for the Commissioner.

ZANESVILLE INVESTMENT CO. v. COMMISSIONER
335 F.2d 507 (6th Cir. 1964)

Before PHILLIPS, Circuit Judge, McALLISTER, Senior Circuit Judge, and LEVIN, District Judge.

LEVIN, District Judge. The question presented for decision is whether Section 269 of the Internal Revenue Code of 1954 or some judicially enunciated principle of law prevents the offsetting in a consolidated return of cash operating losses and losses realized on the sale of physical assets sustained after affiliation by one corporate member of an affiliated group with the post-affiliation profits of another corporate member thereof, where it could be anticipated that such operating losses would be incurred.

The cases principally relied on by the Government[2] are not apposite, as they all concern situations where a taxpayer was attempting to utilize built-in tax losses (i.e., losses which had economically accrued prior to the affiliation but which had not as yet been realized in a tax sense), whereas the taxpayer in this case is attempting to offset actual cash losses incurred both economically and taxwise after the affiliation.

Since the Government cites no authority in point and independent research discloses none, it will be necessary to review the history of Section 269 and the consolidated returns provisions to determine whether the interpretation sought by the Commissioner is correct. The facts of this case are as follows:

During the period 1951 through August 31, 1955, a coal mine corporation (Muskingum Coal Company), which in prior years had been highly profitable (almost four million dollars of net income in the period 1945 to 1950), sustained operating losses of about $730,000 in an attempt to develop a new mine opening to replace the prior mine opening which had been exhausted. These losses had been financed in part by loans from the taxpayer and its wholly-owned subsidiary, Earl J. Jones Enterprises, Inc., totaling $320,268.68, during the period from September 1953 to August 1955, of which $42,930.79 was repaid. Enterprises was profitably engaged in operating a newspaper.

In September 1955, Muskingum was in the process of attempting to solve its

---

[2] R. P. Collins & Co., Inc. v. United States, 303 F.2d 142 (1st Cir. 1962); Elko Realty Co. v. Commissioner, 29 T.C. 1012, affirmed per curiam, 260 F.2d 949 (3rd Cir. 1958); J. D. & A. B. Spreckels Co. v. Commissioner, 41 B.T.A. 370 (1940).

problems through a new type of mechanization, but encountered continuing difficulty. Muskingum did not have adequate funds either to finance the purchase of such equipment or absorb the operating losses that almost certainly would continue to be sustained before profitable operations might be expected.

At this juncture, on September 1, 1955, Earl J. Jones, the sole stockholder[3] of Muskingum since 1945, transferred all the stock thereof to the taxpayer (of which, since 1948, he was also the sole stockholder).

The Tax Court found (38 T.C. at p. 414) that the principal purpose of the transfer to the taxpayer of the stock of Muskingum (the losing coal mine business) was to utilize Muskingum's "anticipated" losses on a consolidated return to be filed with the other members of the affiliated group, including the profitable newspaper publisher (Enterprises) and that this was interdicted under the provisions of Section 269 of the Internal Revenue Code of 1954 and the principle enunciated in J. D. & A. B. Spreckels Co., 41 B.T.A. 370 (1940).

The taxpayer, Enterprises, and Muskingum filed consolidated returns for 1955 and 1956. Muskingum sustained an operating loss of $176,806 during the period September 1 to December 31, 1955, and an operating loss of $369,950 during the period January 1 to July 10, 1956. In July 1956 Muskingum sold its mine properties at a net loss of about $480,000 and later filed a petition in bankruptcy. Enterprises' taxable income in 1955 was $175,283.61 and during the first seven months of 1956 was $102,496.46. Enterprises operated profitably also in subsequent periods.

Both prior and subsequent to affiliation, Muskingum's operations were extensive, its sales were at an annual rate in excess of two million dollars, and it employed several hundred persons throughout the period in question. Muskingum attempted to sell its properties between October 1955 and June 1956, and various transactions were discussed, negotiated, and, in two cases, documented; but none was consummated. Had any been consummated, Muskingum's properties would have been disposed of at a tax gain rather than a loss.

It is not disputed that Muskingum and the other members of the affiliated group that were financing it were engaged in a good faith but unsuccessful attempt to overcome the engineering problems and thereby render operations at the second mine opening economically profitable. In this connection, the taxpayer and Enterprises made further advances of $161,359.28 to Muskingum in the post-affiliation period, of which $44,966.59 was repaid. The total investment in physical assets, in an attempt to bring in the second mine opening, was $1,026,610.30, of which $247,309.01 was spent in the post-affiliation period. It would thus appear that approximately $247,000 of the $480,000 net loss realized on the sale of Muskingum's properties was paid for in cash after affiliation. The Government has not contended that such loss was incurred in an economic sense prior to affiliation.

. . . Most of the cases that have arisen under Section 269 and its predecessor, Section 129, have dealt with the sale by one control group to another of a corporation with, typically, a net-operating loss carryover, and the efforts of the new control

---

[3]Less than one per cent of the stock was held by others.

group to utilize this carryover by funneling otherwise taxable income to a point of alleged confluence with the carryover.[4]

Until this case, the Commissioner made no attempt in the approximately twenty years since enactment of Section 129 (now Section 269), so far as the reported cases indicate, to deny a taxpayer the right to offset an out-of-pocket dollar loss incurred after affiliation with post-affiliation income.[5] We do not believe that Section 269 requires such a result.

An examination of the Senate Finance Committee report accompanying the Revenue Act of 1943, which enacted Section 129 of the I.R.C. of 1939, reveals that the statutory language cannot be mechanically interpreted and that all acquisitions that result in tax saving are not prohibited. The test, according to the Senate Finance Committee, is: ". . . whether the transaction or a particular factor thereof 'distorts the liability of the particular taxpayer' when the 'essential nature' of the transaction or factor is examined in the light of the *'legislative plan'* which the deduction or credit is intended to effectuate." 1944 Cum. Bull., p. 1017. (Emphasis added.)

This legislative explanation found its way into [Treas. Reg. §1.269-2(b)]. . . .

In deciding whether the essential nature of the transaction before this court violates the "legislative plan," the fact that the Tax Court's decision is the first[5] in the heavily litigated tax field where a court was asked to deny a taxpayer the right to use real post-affiliation losses, incurred and paid in cash after affiliation, against post-affiliation income suggests that the legislative plan may not be violated by allowing the deduction. . . .

But here, the loss was incurred by one entity, and the profit was realized by another. What is the legislative plan in this regard?

Congress first required[7] and now permits[8] certain affiliated corporations to file consolidated returns and to offset the losses of one against the profits of another. The consolidated return regulations forbid the use of pre-affiliation losses of one entity against pre- or post-affiliation consolidated income (Reg. 1.1502-31(b)(3)) but have never suggested that post-affiliation losses may not be utilized against post-affiliation consolidated income. In fact, these regulations specifically permit the use of post-affiliation losses against post-affiliation consolidated income (Reg. 1.1502-31(b)).

All the cases cited by the Government where consolidation was denied involved situations where the taxpayer sought to take advantage of the realization after affiliation of losses which in an economic sense had occurred prior to the affiliation. . . .

---

[4]In each of the following cases cited by the Government, there was a change in the stock-holding group after the occurrence of the operating losses and before the income sought to be offset against the same was earned. . . .

[5]In R. P. Collins & Co., Inc. [303 F.2d 142], discussed later in this opinion, the out-of-pocket dollar loss incurred after affiliation was not allowed because a majority of the court felt that it was tainted — being in respect to the built-in loss, the obtaining of which was the primary purpose of the acquisition, and hence within the proscription of Section 269. . . .

[7]Internal Revenue Regulations 41, Article 77; Sec. 1331 of the Internal Revenue Act of 1921; Sec. 240 of the Internal Revenue Act of 1918.

[8]Section 240 of the Internal Revenue Act of 1921; Sec. 1501 et seq. of the 1954 I.R.C.

... *Collins* [see footnote 5] is not authority for the proposition here advanced by the Government because even the majority would not have disallowed the post-affiliation operating loss if it stood by itself, as it does in this case, and only denied the post-affiliation operating loss because it was thought to be tainted as in respect to the built-in loss the use of which, as we have seen, Section 269 was designed to prevent. The fact that the dissenting judge in *Collins* would have allowed the post-affiliation operating loss and the two majority judges denied it only because it was tainted ("They are tarred by the same brush," 303 F.2d at p. 146), as incidental to the built-in loss, tends to support the taxpayer's view that post-affiliation operating losses standing by themselves are not within the coverage of Section 269. . . .

. . . [H]ad Earl Jones dissolved all three corporations he could have utilized the Muskingum losses against the publishing company's profits; or if he had dissolved Muskingum and contributed its property to the taxpayer or to Enterprises he could have accomplished a similar result.

In Revenue Ruling 63-40, 1963-1 Cum. Bull. 46, the Internal Revenue Service stated its view that where there is no change in the control group, Section 269 was not applicable to the addition of a new profitable business to a loss corporation, which had discontinued the money losing business, even if the means by which this was accomplished was the purchase by the loss corporation of the stock of the money-making business and the transfer of its assets in liquidation to its new stockholder. Compare Kolker Brothers, Inc., 35 T.C. 299 (1960).

Section 382 of the Internal Revenue Code of 1954 expressly permits the use of historical losses against the income of other businesses where either there has not been a change in the control group (as defined therein) or there has not been a substantial change in the trade or business conducted before the change in control.[12] One would think that if the same control group could, after the loss, add new income (Revenue Ruling 63-40, supra), there would be no objection to the offsetting of a future loss against future income. The latter case, which is the case before this court, would appear to be a stronger one for the taxpayer. . . .

. . . [O]ne is left with the definite impression that there is no legislative plan to deny the utilization of post-affiliation losses against post-affiliation income and one suspects that one of the basic reasons why taxpayers consolidated corporations and paid the two per cent penalty that prior to the enactment of the Revenue Act of 1964 was payable on consolidated taxable income, was to be able to offset the losses of one corporation against the profits of another. Inherent in the concept of consolidation is the offsetting of loss against income. . . .

We have seen that the principal purpose of Section 269 was to deny those losses, credits, deductions, etc., which could only be obtained by acquiring (generally, by buying) a corporation which, because of its own history, had obtained such benefits and which benefits the acquiring person could not otherwise obtain.

[12]Compare Commissioner of Internal Revenue v. Goodwyn Crockery Company, 315 F.2d 110 (6th Cir. 1963), where this court held that the net operating losses could be utilized against future income even though there was a change in the control group because it was found that there was no substantial change in the trade or business conducted.

The regulations and the courts included within the scope of Section 269 the organization of a corporation as an "acquisition," on the ground that the stockholders are the underlying persons obtaining the benefit. Regulation 1.269-3(b)(2). James Realty Company v. United States, 280 F.2d 394 (8th Cir. 1960); Coastal Oil Storage Co. v. Commissioner of Internal Revenue, 242 F.2d 396 (4th Cir. 1957). . . .

In this case, it may well be, as the Tax Court found, that the taxpayer desired to offset anticipated losses against income; but there is no evidence that such objective is violative of the legislative plan which permits just that in an effort to counter-balance profits with losses. The over-all purpose of Section 269 was to prevent distortion of a taxpayer's income resulting from the utilization of *someone else's loss* or a *built-in but unrealized loss* or, as found by the court in Coastal Oil Storage Co. v. Commissioner of Internal Revenue, supra, through the utilization of the corporate veil to acquire a benefit (the multiplying of surtax exemptions through the organization of so-called "multiple corporations") which otherwise was unobtainable; but there is no indication that Section 269 was designed to prohibit the utilization of future losses against future income merely because a corporate rather than a partnership or individual proprietorship form of business enterprise was involved. . . .

In view of this court's decision, it is unnecessary to consider taxpayer's alternative arguments that there was no acquisition because Earl J. Jones (the underlying controlling person) owned the stock of Muskingum many years before the prohibited purpose could come to mind,[14] or that a loss deduction should be allowed alternatively at least to the extent of the loss realized on the sale of the physical assets in July 1956; the Government does not contend that this is a built-in loss (Regulation 1.1502-31 (b)(9)). Likewise, taxpayer's alternative theory seeking the allowance of bad debt deductions under Section 166(a)(1) need not be reached.

This case is remanded to the Tax Court for the entry of a judgment not inconsistent with this opinion.

Reversed.

NOTE

Compare *Zanesville Investment* and Herculite Protective Fabrics Corp. v. Commissioner, 387 F.2d 475 (3d Cir. 1968), with R. P. Collins & Co., Inc. v. United States, 303 F.2d 142 (1st Cir. 1962); Luke v. Commissioner, 351 F.2d 568 (7th Cir. 1965); and Borge v. Commissioner, 405 F.2d 673 (2d Cir. 1968). See D. Schechter, Climate Is Improving for Deduction of Post-Acquisition Losses, 31 J. Taxation 202 (1969).

[14]The taxpayer relies on the dictum in Thomas E. Snyder Sons v. Commissioner of Internal Revenue, 288 F.2d 36 (7th Cir. 1961), that if the individual there concerned had (as did Earl J. Jones) acquired the stock in the loss corporation prior to the earliest date that he could have had any purpose to evade or avoid taxes, the Tax Court's decision in *Snyder* "could not stand.". . .

REVENUE RULING 67-202
1967-1 Cum. Bull. 73

Advice has been requested whether under section 269 of the Internal Revenue Code of 1954 the carryover of net operating losses will be disallowed under the circumstances presented below.

A, an individual, in January 1961, purchased all of the stock of unrelated corporations X and Y, each of which was actively engaged in a business. In the 5-year period preceding the acquisition, both corporations operated at a profit. During 1961 and 1962 the corporations were operated separately and both corporations showed a small profit. During 1963, 1964, and 1965, both corporations incurred substantial losses. In 1964, the Federal Government initiated procedures to condemn a portion of Y's land. In February 1966, in anticipation of the large gain to be realized from the condemnation, A contributed his X stock to Y. Five days later X was liquidated into Y so that the losses of both businesses could be used to partially offset Y's gain.

Section 269 of the Code provides in part, as follows:

"(a) *In general.* — If —

"(1) Any person or persons acquire, . . . directly or indirectly, control of a corporation, or

"(2) Any corporation acquires, . . . directly or indirectly, property of another corporation, not controlled, directly or indirectly, immediately before such acquisition, by such acquiring corporation or its stockholders, . . . and the principal purpose for which such acquisition was made is evasion or avoidance of Federal income tax by securing the benefit of a deduction, credit, or other allowance which such person or corporation would not otherwise enjoy, then the Secretary or his delegate may disallow such deduction, credit, or other allowance. For purposes of paragraphs (1) and (2), control means the ownership of stock possessing at least 50 percent of the total combined voting power of all classes of stock entitled to vote or at least 50 percent of the total value of shares of all classes of stock of the corporation."

While Y, as a matter of form, acquired control of X, the transitory control lacked substance since it was merely the initial step of a prearranged plan to liquidate X into Y. Thus, the "essential nature of the transaction" involved in the present case was the indirect acquisition by Y of the X property. See section 1.269-2(b) of the Income Tax Regulations. Accordingly, since section 269(a)(1) of the Code pertains only to the acquisition of control of a corporation and not to the acquisition of its assets, the section is not applicable to the described transaction. Moreover, section 269(a)(2) of the Code is not applicable since A owned all of the stock of each corporation prior to the acquisition of X's property by Y.

The net operating losses in this type of case will carry over under section 381 of the Code provided the transaction qualifies as a reorganization under section 368(a)(1) of the Code. Thus, the taxpayer here would have to demonstrate that corporations X and Y were combined for a valid business purpose and not merely in order to secure the benefits of the net operating loss carryovers. See section 1.368-1 of the Income Tax Regulations.

NOTE

Net operating loss carryovers have been the subject of a substantial number of law review articles. In addition to those cited in the preceding cases, see, e.g., M. Kramer, Loss Carryovers Following "A", "B", or "C" Reorganizations; Consolidated Returns, 26 N.Y.U. Inst. on Fed. Tax. 921 (1968); M. Asimow, Detriment and Benefit of Net Operating Losses: A Unifying Theory, 24 Tax L. Rev. 1 (1968); J. Pennell, Does the *Libson Shops* Doctrine Still Apply? 25 J. Taxation 336 (1966); E. Kaufman, Application of a Loss Carryover of One Business Against Profits From Another Business; *Libson Shops,* and Sections 381, 382 and 269, 24 N.Y.U. Inst. on Fed. Tax. 1199 (1966); S. Hagendorf, *Zanesville* Allows Tax Avoidance Through Use of Post-Acquisition Operating Losses, 21 J. Taxation 262 (1964); A. Feder, The Application of Section 269 to Corporations Having Net Operating Loss Carryovers and Potential Losses, 21 N.Y.U. Inst. on Fed. Tax. 1277 (1963); Comment, Net Operating Loss Carryovers and Corporate Adjustments; Retaining an Advantageous Tax History Under *Libson Shops* and Sections 269, 381 and 382, 69 Yale L.J. 1201 (1960); N. Sinrich, *Libson Shops* — An Argument Against Its Application Under the 1954 Code, 13 Tax L. Rev. 167 (1958). See also B. Bittker and J. Eustice, Federal Income Taxation of Corporations and Shareholders 629-670 (2d ed. 1966).

IX. FOREIGN CORPORATIONS — §§367, 1491, 1492

ABEGG v. COMMISSIONER
429 F.2d 1209 (2d Cir. 1970), cert. denied sub nom.
Cresta Corp., 400 U.S. 1008 (1971)

Before WATERMAN, FRIENDLY and HAYS, Circuit Judges.

FRIENDLY, Circuit Judge: These two appeals from a decision of the Tax Court, 50 T.C. 145, one by the taxpayer and the other by the Commissioner, concern a series of transactions in which Werner Abegg, a Swiss citizen, liquidated one wholly-owned personal holding company and transferred all its assets, plus other securities in substantial amount, to another personal holding company. Although the appeals relate to different tax years and present independent legal issues, there is a sufficient identity in the dramatis personae to make it convenient to state all the facts at the outset.

I. The Facts

Hevaloid Corporation was organized under the laws of Delaware in 1938. All its issued stock, 250 shares, was held by Abegg. It owned industrial patents and machinery which it leased to various American corporations. In 1955 the patents expired and it sold the machinery. In 1956 and 1957 it was a personal holding company; its assets consisted exclusively of cash, securities, receivables, and rights in a motion picture "Guest in the House." In 1957, Robert A. Cavin, a close associate and business adviser of Abegg for many years, was its president.

On March 28, 1957, Hevaloid adopted a plan of complete liquidation and dissolution. A certificate of dissolution was filed on April 18. During April and May it sold stock in four publicly owned corporations for $1,671,341, which it deposited in the New York Trust Company. These sales represented a gain of $932,701. Hevaloid reported them in its 1957 income tax return but claimed that the gain was not to be recognized under I.R.C. §337. On May 1 and 2 it drew checks to Abegg on its account at New York Trust Company aggregating $1,660,936. On May 7 it delivered to Laird & Co., a New York brokerage firm, for Abegg's account, certificates and stock powers for 7,470 shares of Brazos River Gas Company, 2,720 shares of Medallion Petroleum Limited, and 13,692 shares of Producing Properties, Inc. On May 23 it directed Laird & Co. to transfer from the account of Hevaloid to the account of Abegg 1,945 shares of Magma Copper Company and 2,600 shares of Signal Oil and Gas Company; on the same day it also transferred to Abegg its interest in a loan receivable from Perosa Corporation and in the motion picture. The final step in its liquidation was taken in December 1957 by drawing to Abegg a $32,156 check on another bank. Abegg deposited all these checks in his account at Bankers Trust Company.

Cresta Corporation, S.A., originally known as Suvretta Corporation, S.A., was incorporated in Panama in 1941 but remained inactive. On May 7, 1957, it issued 1,000 shares of stock to Abegg in return for cash and other assets, as follows: On May 7, 1957, Abegg issued to it a $1,500,000 check on his account at Bankers Trust Company, $250,000 of which was considered a demand loan and $1,250,000 as part payment for stock. On May 24, Laird & Co., on Abegg's instruction, transferred to Cresta in further payment the five securities that Hevaloid had ordered it to transfer to him earlier that month. The fair market value of each security exceeded its adjusted basis; the aggregate excess was $262,520. The same day Abegg transferred stock of Illinois Central R.R., Olin Mathiesen Chemical Corporation, additional common shares and a note of Brazos River Gas Company, preferred stock and bonds of Producing Properties, Inc., 1,000 shares of Perosa Corporation, which were regarded as valueless, and 3,000 shares of Meridan Corporation, a Rhode Island corporation in which he owned 50% of the stock and Cavin 10%. Meridan had a net worth of $2,510,673 as of December 31, 1957. Nearly sixty per cent of this represented a piano business in Michigan; it also had an interest in an operating company in Chicago and later acquired one in a company in Tacoma, Washington. On June 8 Abegg transferred to Cresta the interest in "Guest in the House" and in the debt from Perosa Corporation which Hevaloid had assigned.

The directors of Cresta, including Abegg and Cavin, met on February 6, 1958, in New York and resolved to qualify to do business in that state, to accept cash and securities from Abegg as contributions to capital, and to borrow an additional $250,000 from him on open account. Abegg drew a check for $400,000 and on February 26, 1958, contributed stock as follows:

	Adjusted Basis	Fair Market Value
50,680 shares		
Brazos River Gas Co.	$ 55,850	$101,360
4,250 shares		
General American Oil Co.	91,653	110,578
12,650 shares		
Magma Copper Co.	1,300,971	449,075
	$1,448,474	$661,013

Cavin was Cresta's sole employee in its fiscal years ending February 28, 1958 and 1959 and February 29, 1960. He maintained watch over its holdings, especially those in Meridan, and investigated at least a dozen opportunities for investing Cresta's funds with a view to acquiring the stock or assets of a going business, although no acquisitions were made. In these years Cresta paid salaries to Cavin aggregating $46,750, and also some $50,000 in legal, accounting, travel and other business expenses.[1] Cresta filed income tax returns as a personal holding company.

Only a few further facts need be stated: Abegg was not engaged in trade or business within the United States. In 1957 he was in the country only from January 1 to March 27. He was here more than 90 days in 1958. At the time when the Commissioner sent a notice of deficiency to Cresta as Hevaloid's transferee, Abegg had net assets in the United States more than sufficient to pay the tax allegedly owing from Hevaloid.

II. Cresta's Appeal

Viewed alone the liquidation of Hevaloid meets the requirements of I.R.C. §337(a). The Commissioner does not dispute this, nor its corollary that if §337 is applied, the $932,701 gain realized by Hevaloid on the sale of securities and Abegg's gain on the liquidation would escape United States taxation altogether. Hevaloid would not be taxable because of §337(a). Abegg would not be taxable on the gain from the liquidation of Hevaloid because as a nonresident alien, not engaged in trade or business within the United States, who was present in the United States for fewer than 90 days in 1957 he was subject to United States taxation only on capital

---

[1]An issue that was litigated before the Tax Court but is not before us is whether, as Cresta claimed, it was engaged in a trade or business within the United States, so as to be entitled to these deductions under IRC §882, or, as the Commissioner contended, was not so engaged and was therefore subject to the 30% tax on gross income imposed by IRC §881(a). The Tax Court decided in favor of the Commissioner. Cresta did not seek review of that decision and relies on it for one of its arguments on the appeal it has taken.

gains from sales or exchanges of personal property in the United States while he was present here,[3] and Hevaloid's liquidating distributions were carried out during his absence.

On February 19, 1962, the Commissioner mailed to Cresta as transferee a notice of deficiency reading as follows:

> The reported liquidation of Hevaloid Corporation, the transfer of assets to W. Abegg and the retransfer of such assets by him to Cresta Corporation, S.A. were in substance, component steps in a reorganization within the meaning of section 368(a) of the Internal Revenue Code of 1954. Accordingly, the benefits of section 337 of the Internal Revenue Code of 1954 are not applicable and the capital gains realized on the sale of assets as shown in the 1957 return of Hevaloid Corporation, are includible in gross income.
>
> Since, in substance, Hevaloid Corporation in the course of the reorganization transferred assets to Cresta Corporation S.A., a foreign corporation and did not secure clearance under section 367 of the Internal Revenue Code of 1954 prior to the transfer, Hevaloid Corporation is denied the benefits of section 361(a) of the Internal Revenue Code of 1954. The gains realized on the transfer as computed in Exhibit A are recognized.

The gains from Hevaloid's sales of securities amounted, as previously indicated, to $932,701; the gains from the transfers to Cresta of property which Abegg had received from Hevaloid were $262,519 with respect to securities stated above, plus $4,725 with respect to "Guest in the House." The Tax Court sustained the Commissioner.

Cresta does not dispute that if the result of the 1957 transactions had been achieved by a straightforward reorganization under §368(a)(1)(D), the gains realized by Hevaloid on sales of securities would not come under the non-recognition shelter of §337 and the gains realized on transfers of appreciated securities would likewise be taxable since they would qualify for non-recognition only by virtue of §§351 and 354(a)(1), and that protection was lost by failure to obtain a ruling under §367. It nevertheless contested the determination of deficiency on three grounds. It claimed that the reorganization provisions are not applicable to corporations that are mere personal holding companies; that if that position were rejected, the judicially created "liquidation-reincorporation" doctrine on which the Commissioner relied should not be applied when what has come to be a personal holding company as a result of the cessation of an active business distributes liquid assets to its sole stockholder; and, in any event, that, since the transfer from Hevaloid to Cresta was routed through Abegg and he was financially able to pay any tax owed by Hevaloid, Cresta was not liable as a transferee. The Tax Court rejected all three contentions. Although Cresta's arguments are not without force, we agree with the Tax Court.

Cresta concedes, as it must, that no case directly holds the reorganization provi-

---

[3]I.R.C. §871. The section was extensively amended by Pub. L. No. 89-809, Title I, §103 (a)(1), 80 Stat. 1547 (1966), and now taxes nonresident aliens on capital gains not effectively connected with the conduct of a trade or business in this country only if the alien was present in this country for 183 days or more during the taxable year. See S. Rep. No. 1707, 89th Cong., 2d Sess., reprinted in 1966 U.S. Code Cong. & Adm. News 4446, 4467-70.

sions inapplicable to personal holding companies, and indeed the one case cited that considered the question is to the contrary. Estate of Elise W. Hill, 10 T.C. 1090 (1948). Cresta nevertheless points to language in the Regulations and in judicial decisions referring to the need for a "business purpose" for the reorganization[5] or for a "continuation of the business enterprise."[6] Relying in part on the Tax Court's ruling that it was not engaged in a trade or business for purposes of I.R.C. §882, see fn. 1, Cresta contends that the activities of a mere holding company are not enough of a "business" to satisfy these requirements. However, the language Cresta cites was not remotely addressed to the issue here under consideration, and we see no warrant for ruling that a personal holding company may not take advantage of the reorganization provisions if their requirements are otherwise met. Certainly it would be hard to require a personal holding company or its shareholders to recognize gain when the company undergoes "a statutory merger or consolidation," "a recapitalization," or "a mere change in identity, form or place of organization" within I.R.C. §368(A), (E), and (F), and there would be little virtue in permitting them to take a loss at will by such a transaction. Thus we think it plain that reorganizations of personal holding companies fall within "the plain intent of the statute," Gregory v. Helvering, supra, 293 U.S. at 470, and should be treated accordingly. Indeed, the examples in §1.381(c)(14)-1(c) of the Regulations explicitly assume that a personal holding company may result from a reorganization.

Cresta's second argument, relating to the judge-made "liquidation reincorporation" doctrine,[7] is more appealing, but not appealing enough. The doctrine indeed has its elements of curiosity. Building on statutory provisions intended for the benefit of taxpayers, over which the Treasury has vigilantly stood guard, it forces their consequences on taxpayers who want nothing of them. See Hewitt and Cuddihy, The Liquidation Reincorporation Problem, a Running Tax Battle, 12-13 (1969). However, the tax avoidance purposes that can be served by "the liquidation of a corporation followed by a transfer of part or all of the assets to a newly-organized corporation owned by the same shareholders" are so numerous and serious, see Bittker & Eustice, Federal Income Taxation of Corporations and Shareholders, 569-70

---

[5]Helvering v. Gregory, 69 F.2d 809, 811 (2 Cir. 1934), aff'd, 293 U.S. 465 (1935): "the underlying presupposition is plain that the readjustment shall be undertaken for reasons germane to the conduct of the venture in hand, not as an ephemeral incident, egregious to its prosecution." The requirement also appears, less elegantly, in §1.368-2(g) of the Regulations.

[6]Lewis v. C.I.R., 176 F.2d 646 (1 Cir. 1949). See also Regs. §1.368-1(b).

[7]The House draft of the 1954 Code, H.R. 8300, 83d Cong., 2d Sess., §357 (1954), attempted to deal with the problem in a manner that would not have helped the Commissioner in this case, since the proposed statute would have applied only when the distributee transferred more than 50% of the assets received on liquidation other than money and stock and securities (except stock or securities of the distributing corporation). This was deleted by the Senate without explanation. The House Managers attributed the deletion to "certain technical problems," and explained their acquiescence on the grounds "that, at the present time, the possibility of tax avoidance in this area is not sufficiently serious to require a special statutory provision" and that any such possibility "can appropriately be disposed of by judicial decision or by regulation within the framework of the other provisions of the bill." H.R. Rep. No. 2543, 83d Cong., 2d Sess. 41 (1954), reprinted in 1954 U.S. Code Cong. & Adm. News 5280, 5301. We do not regard any of this to be significant.

(2d ed. 1966), that the doctrine had to be created. In any event it is too late to question its vitality and Cresta does not do so.

It is true enough that the vice of liquidation-reincorporation appears most clearly when a company engaged in active business purports to liquidate but the shareholders then put the operating assets back into a new corporation. Although as a practical matter incorporation is a necessity for the business, the shareholders by a mere sleight of hand would have withdrawn earnings and profits on payment only of a capital gains tax and would have achieved a stepped-up basis for appreciated assets if the liquidation-reincorporation doctrine did not prevent. There seems to be no similar necessity for stockholders who have received only liquid assets on liquidation to transfer them to a new corporation. However, Abegg evidently decided it was to his advantage that the management of certain of his liquid assets in the United States which the Delaware corporation had come to own as a result of cessation of its active business, as well as other assets transferred by him, should not be conducted by him, but rather by a Panamanian corporation qualified in New York, which should seek out opportunities for acquiring active businesses. As has been said, "The 'reincorporation' problem arises when taxpayers seek to combine the benefits of a complete liquidation (i.e., capital gain or loss on the distribution, a new basis for the assets, and elimination of corporate earnings and profits), with the 'reorganization' advantages of continued operation of the business in corporate form." Bittker & Eustice, supra, at 572. That is precisely what happened here, see Hewitt and Cuddihy, supra, at 95-103; it was Abegg's decision to put the cash and securities derived from the liquidation of Hevaloid back into Cresta, rather than retain them in his own accounts with attendant freedom from United States taxes.

Cresta's argument that Hevaloid had already liquidated when it ceased its active business and thus could not liquidate again is mostly a play upon words. Like many other terms, liquidation does not mean in tax language what it may in ordinary speech. The Regulations, §1.332-2(c), instruct that "A status of liquidation exists when the corporation ceases to be a going concern and its activities are merely for the purpose of winding up its affairs, paying its debts, and distributing any remaining balance to its stockholders." Hevaloid did not attain that status until the spring of 1957. We do not regard Pridemark, Inc. v. C.I.R., 345 F.2d 35 (4 Cir. 1965), relied on by Cresta, as conflicting in any way with the result reached here. The Commissioner in that case apparently did not argue that a "D" reorganization had occurred, but only that no "complete" liquidation had occurred within the meaning of §337, or alternatively that the liquidation and subsequent incorporation there constituted an "F" reorganization. See 345 F.2d at 41. The court rejected the first contention on the ground that the liquidation of the old company was intended to be complete and final, and the starting up of the new company was a later idea, hit upon only after the owners had been unsuccessful in other lines of business. The second contention was rejected on the ground that the shifts in officers and shareholder interests, along with the operating scale of the new company, were simply too much to be called a "mere change in identity, form, or place of organization." It is apparent that neither basis of the decision is applicable here. . . . [Transferee liability issue omitted.]

III. The Commissioner's Appeal

The Commissioner also determined a deficiency with respect to Abegg's contributions to Cresta of 50,680 appreciated shares of Brazos River Gas Co. and of 4,250 appreciated shares of General American Oil Co. on February 26, 1958. He started from the fact that Abegg was present in the United States for more than 90 days in 1958, and from I.R.C. §871(a)(2)(B) and (b) which subject a nonresident alien so present to tax on "sales and exchanges of capital assets effected at any time during such year" in excess of losses from such sales and exchanges. He acknowledged that if Cresta had been a United States corporation, the contribution on his view would be protected by §351, which provides for nonrecognition of gain or loss "if property is transferred to a corporation by one or more persons solely in exchange for stock in such corporation and immediately after the exchange such person or persons are in control (as defined in section 368(c)) of the corporation." But here again, the Commissioner contended, §367 reared its ugly head in Abegg's path. For, as stated in fn. 4, §367 mandates that "in determining the extent to which gain shall be recognized in the case of any of the exchanges described" in various sections including §351, "a foreign corporation shall not be considered a corporation" unless before such exchange a ruling has been obtained that the exchange is not in pursuance of a plan having federal income tax avoidance as a principal purpose, and it is stipulated that this was not done here.

In answer to the argument that since Abegg received nothing in exchange and thus realized no gain within the meaning of §1001(b), the Commissioner contended that issuance of stock by a corporation to a 100% shareholder is a meaningless ritual. He cited cases, notably C.I.R. v. Morgan, 288 F.2d 676 (3 Cir.), cert. denied, 368 U.S. 836(1961), and Davant v. C.I.R., 366 F.2d 874, 884-87 (5 Cir. 1966), cert. denied, 386 U.S. 1022 (1967), which applied the liquidation-reincorporation doctrine to find a "D" reorganization although the transfer was from one owned corporation to another and there was no "distribution" of stock of the latter. He also relied on the holding in King. v. United States, 10 F. Supp. 206 (D. Md.), aff'd, 79 F.2d 453 (4 Cir. 1935), that a corporation which received property from its sole shareholder without consideration took the latter's basis under §204(a)(8) of the Revenue Act of 1926, relating to property acquired by a corporation "by the issuance of stock or securities" in a transaction where the seller's gain or loss was not recognized.[9] In answer to the point that the aggregate effect of the three security transfers on February 26, 1958, was a loss of $787,461, the Commissioner responded, in line with Rev. Rul. 67-192, 1967-2 Cum. Bull. 140, that §367 cancels only the nonrecognition of gain provided by §351 but leaves intact that section's provision for nonrecognition of loss.

---

[9]Abegg seeks to distinguish *King* on the basis that the shares in question were contributed within 30 days of the issuance of stock for other shares owned by the organizer and the delay apparently was accidental. Congress solved the problem that gave rise to the *King* case and also to Rosenbloom Finance Corp., 24 B.T.A. 763 (1931), rev'd 66 F.2d 556 (3 Cir.), cert. denied, 290 U.S. 692 (1933), by enacting §113(8) of the Revenue Act of 1932, now I.R.C. §362, which provided that a corporation takes the transferor's basis for property acquired "by the issuance of its stock or securities in connection with a transaction described in section 112(b)(5)" *or* "as paid-in surplus or as a contribution to capital."

Not reaching the last point, the Tax Court found determinative the absence of any stock issuance in exchange. It refused to follow Rev. Rul. 64-155, 1964-1 Cum. Bull. (Part 1) 138, in which the Commissioner took the same position he urges here, and it distinguished King v. United States, supra, 10 F. Supp. 206, and C.I.R. v. Morgan, supra, 288 F.2d 676, on which that ruling had relied. The Commissioner vigorously challenges this holding. He cites the report of the Senate Finance Committee which explained the importance of §112(k) of the Revenue Act of 1932, the progenitor of §367, in preventing tax avoidance by a procedure whereby a taxpayer with large unrealized profits in securities would transfer them to a foreign corporation in exchange for its stock without recognition of gain under the predecessor §351, would have the foreign corporation sell the securities in a foreign country imposing no tax on the gain, would cause the foreign corporation to invest the proceeds in the stock of a new American subsidiary, and would then have the foreign corporation distribute the latter's stock in a tax-free reorganization. S. Rep. No. 665, 72d Cong., 1st Sess., pp. 26-27, 1939-1 Cum. Bull. (Part 2) 496, 515.[10] The Commissioner argues that the tax avoidance potential would be equally great where a sole shareholder contributed appreciated securities to an existing foreign corporation, possibly with only a nominal capitalization.

That is very likely so, but the 1932 Congress took steps to deal expressly with that problem so far as United States citizens were concerned. By §901 of the Revenue Act of 1932, now carried forward as I.R.C. §1491, it imposed on "the transfer of stock or securities by a citizen or resident of the United States, or by a domestic corporation or partnership, or by a trust which is not a foreign trust, to a foreign corporation as paid-in surplus or as a contribution to capital, or to a foreign trust, or to a foreign partnership, an excise tax equal to 25 per centum of the excess of (1) the value of the stock or securities so transferred over (2) its adjusted basis in the hands of the transferor . . ."; §902(b) made this tax inapplicable "if prior to the transfer it has been established to the satisfaction of the Commissioner that such transfer is not in pursuance of a plan having as one of its principal purposes the avoidance of Federal income taxes."[11] See Sen. Rep. No. 665, 72d Cong., 1st Sess., pp. 55-56, 1939-1 Cum. Bull. (Part 2) 496, 536. If the combination of §112(k) and 112(b)(5), the predecessor of I.R.C. 351, reached a contribution to the capital or paid-in surplus of a foreign corporation, §901 was unnecessary, since Congress obviously did not mean that in the absence of an advance ruling by the Commissioner such a contribution by a United States citizen should be subjected both to income taxation on any excess of value over basis and to excise taxation on the same amount, whereas an exchange in the literal sense should be subjected only to the former. Hence, unless §901 is to be a deadletter, §112(k) must be read as not reaching a contribution to the capital of a foreign corporation by a United States citizen taxpayer covered by §901.[12] But it would be anoma-

[10]For another example, wherein the appreciated securities are owned by a United States corporation, see Section 367 and Tax Avoidance: An Analysis of the Section 367 Guidelines, 25 Tax L. Rev. 429, 432 (1970).

[11]These two sections of the 1932 Act became I.R.C. §§1491 and 1492(2) except that the rate was increased to 27½%.

[12]The Commissioner conceded at argument that if we should sustain his position as to

lous to hold that although the combination of §112(k) and §112(b)(5) of the 1932 Act, now I.R.C. §351, did not reach the important subject of contributions of appreciated assets to capital or paid-in surplus by a United States citizen to a foreign corporation, which Congress felt obliged to cover separately in §901, it did reach contributions of such assets as capital or paid-in surplus by nonresident aliens. While the alternative, distinguishing among transfers by nonresident aliens to wholly-owned foreign corporations on the basis of whether they take stock back, is also anomalous, it is less so. Indeed, the real anomaly may be in a nonresident alien's being caught in the net at all, when he could have avoided the problem altogether by selling the securities abroad and transferring the proceeds. If there are significant avenues of tax avoidance in respect of the contribution by nonresident aliens of appreciated assets to capital or surplus of foreign corporations in the United States, the Commissioner has not brought them to our attention.

To put the matter in another way, since the legislative history shows that §367 was aimed primarily at tax avoidance by United States taxpayers, nonresident aliens should not be subjected to it in a situation where, as regards United States citizens, Congress thought it necessary to make a special although similar provision. Counsel for a nonresident alien reading §901 of the 1932 Act or §1491 of the 1954 Code would be abundantly justified in thinking that Congress meant to require advance approval of contributions to the capital or paid-in surplus of a foreign corporation only when these were made by the persons there described. It may well be, as the Commissioner suggests, that §901, like the change in §113(8) of the 1932 Act, see fn. 9, represented an unnecessary overreaction to the decision of the Board of Tax Appeals with respect to contributions to capital or surplus in the *Rosenbloom* case, and that if Congress had only remained silent, the courts would have handled the problem. But Congress did what it did, and a taxpayer is justified in assuming that it cast its net no further. Agreeing with the Commissioner that the problem is considerably more difficult than the Tax Court thought, we thus believe it reached the right result.

On both appeals the judgment of the Tax Court is affirmed. No costs.

NOTE

On January 12, 1971, the President approved legislation modifying §367 to provide that in the case of transfers made after December 31, 1970, an advance ruling must be obtained under §367 to insure tax-free treatment of a capital contribution by a United States shareholder to a controlled foreign corporation, even though no stock is received for the contribution. As to the impact of §367 on §351 generally, see Chapter 3, pages 397-401 supra. The law was changed further to provide that in the case of an "F" reorganization (involving mere change in form), the §367 ruling may be obtained either before *or after* the transaction in the case of transfers made after December 31, 1967.

---

the coverage of §367, it would be necessary to issue a ruling, which he undertook to do, that the same transaction was not to be subjected both to income and to excise tax.

REVENUE PROCEDURE 68-23
1968-1 Cum. Bull. 821

Section 1. Purpose.

The purpose of this Revenue Procedure is to set forth guidelines for taxpayers and their representatives in connection with requests for advance rulings required under section 367 of the Internal Revenue Code of 1954 in respect of certain types of transactions involving foreign corporations.

Sec. 2. Background.

.01 Section 367 of the Code provides as follows:

"In determining the extent to which gain shall be recognized in the case of any of the exchanges described in sections 332, 351, 354, 355, 356, or 361, a foreign corporation shall not be considered as a corporation unless, before such exchange, it has been established to the satisfaction of the Secretary or his delegate that such exchange is not in pursuance of a plan having as one of its principal purposes the avoidance of Federal income taxes. For purposes of this section, any distribution described in section 355 (or so much of section 356 as relates to section 355) shall be treated as an exchange whether or not it is an exchange."

.02 Whether an exchange or distribution described in sections 332, 351, 354, 355, 356, or 361, of the Code involving a foreign corporation is pursuant to a plan, one of the principal purposes of which is the avoidance of Federal income tax, depends upon all the facts and circumstances of each case. This Revenue Procedure describes certain guidelines which will be used by the Service in considering requests for rulings under section 367 of the Code. However, this Revenue Procedure in no way affects the requirement that before a taxpayer may claim that any of the nonrecognition provisions relating to an exchange enumerated in section 367 of the Code will apply to a transaction the taxpayer must obtain a ruling under section 367 of the Code, before such exchange, to the effect that the proposed transaction is not in pursuance of a plan one of the principal purposes of which is the avoidance of Federal income tax. See section 1.367-1 of the Income Tax Regulations and Revenue Procedure 67-1, C.B. 1967-1, 544, for requirements and procedures in obtaining such a ruling. In reviewing each request for ruling to determine whether a favorable section 367 ruling should be issued under the guidelines, the Service reserves the right to issue an adverse ruling if, based on all the facts and circumstances of a case, it is determined that the taxpayer has not established that tax avoidance is not one of the principal purposes of the transaction. Similarly, a taxpayer shall be free to establish that based on all the facts and circumstances of the taxpayer's case a favorable ruling under section 367 of the Code should be issued, notwithstanding a contrary statement or implication contained in the guidelines. For the effect on a transaction in respect of which the Service issues a ruling under section 367 of the Code, see Revenue Procedure 67-1 and for the effect on a transaction in respect of which a ruling under section 367 of the Code is not obtained from the Service before an exchange, see Revenue Ruling 64-177, C.B. 1964-1 (Part I), 141.

.03   The transactions referred to in this Revenue Procedure are not all inclusive of transactions for which an advance ruling may be required under section 367 of the Code.

Sec. 3.   Transactions Which Ordinarily Receive Favorable Consideration Under Section 367 of the Code.

.01   Section 332 of the Code. Complete liquidation of subsidiaries.

(1)   Where a foreign corporation is liquidated into a domestic parent corporation and the latter agrees to include in its gross income as a dividend deemed paid in money for its taxable year in which the distribution in liquidation occurs the portion of the accumulated earnings and profits, if any, of the foreign corporation for all taxable years of such foreign corporation properly attributable to such domestic parent corporation's stock in such foreign corporation. (See Sec. 4 below.) In such cases, the foreign tax credit provisions (sections 78, and 901 through 905 of the Code) will be applied as if immediately before the liquidation such earnings and profits were distributed as a dividend by the foreign corporation to the domestic parent corporation.

(2)   Where a domestic corporation is liquidated into a foreign parent corporation and the domestic corporation agrees to include in its gross income for its taxable year in which the distribution in liquidation occurs an appropriate amount to reflect realization of income or gain in respect of those transferred assets the transfer of which by a taxpayer to a foreign corporation in an exchange described in section 351 of the Code would not be accorded a favorable ruling under section 367 of the Code. (See Sec. 3.02(1) below.) If income or gain is required to be taken into gross income under this paragraph, the character of the income or gain shall be determined, and adjustments in basis made, as though the assets transferred by the domestic corporation were acquired by the acquiring foreign corporation from the transferor domestic corporation in a taxable exchange.

(3)   Where a foreign corporation is liquidated into another foreign corporation. . . .

.03   Section 354 of the Code (Exchanges of stock and securities in certain reorganizations); section 355 of the Code (Distribution of stock and securities of a controlled corporation); section 356 of the Code (Receipt of additional consideration); and section 361 of the Code (Nonrecognition of gain or loss to corporations).

(1)   This category encompasses all exchanges described in sections 354, 355, 356, or 361 of the Code which relate to the acquisition of all or part of the assets or stock of one corporation by another corporation in a transaction in which one or more of the parties to the reorganization or other transaction is a foreign coporation. For this purpose, therefore, asset acquisitions include corporate divisions and reincorporations as well as so-called practical mergers. The guidelines for issuing rulings in these cases will differ depending upon whether the acquiring corporation, the acquired corporation, or both are foreign corporations.

(a)   Where assets of a domestic corporation are acquired by a foreign corporation, and the domestic corporate transferor agrees to include in its gross income for its taxable year in which the transfer occurs an appropriate amount to reflect realization of income or gain in respect of those transferred assets the transfer of which by a domestic taxpayer to a foreign corporation in an exchange described in section 351 of the Code would not be accorded a favorable ruling under section 367 of the Code. (See Sec. 3.02(1) above.) If income or gain is required to be taken into gross income under this paragraph, the character of the income or gain shall be determined, and adjustments in basis made, as though the assets transferred by the domestic corporation were acquired by the acquiring foreign corporation from the transferor domestic corporation in a taxable exchange.

(b) Where assets of a foreign corporation are acquired by a domestic corporation and stock of the acquired foreign corporation is exchanged (or treated as exchanged under section 355 of the Code) for stock of the domestic corporation incident to the plan of reorganization if the shareholders of the foreign corporation agree to include in their gross income, as gain from the sale of a noncapital asset (in the case of a foreign investment company as defined in section 1246 of the Code) or as a dividend deemed paid in money for their taxable year in which the exchange of stock occurs, the portion of the earnings and profits, if any, of the foreign corporation properly attributable under section 1246 or 1248 of the Code to such shareholders' stock in such foreign corporation which would have been includible in their gross income under section 1246 or 1248 of the Code if at the time of such acquisition the stock of such foreign corporation was exchanged in a taxable exchange. In addition, if 20 percent or more of the outstanding stock of the foreign corporation is owned by a domestic corporation, such domestic corporation must agree to include in its gross income, as gain from the sale of a noncapital asset (in the case of a foreign investment company as defined in section 1246 of the Code) or as a dividend deemed paid in money for its taxable year in which the exchange of stock occurs, its portion of the accumulated earnings and profits, if any, of the foreign corporation for all taxable years of such corporation properly attributable to the stock which such domestic corporation owns in such foreign corporation. (See Sec. 4 below.) In cases described in this subparagraph in which shareholders agree to include earnings and profits in gross income as a dividend deemed paid in money, the foreign tax credit provisions (sections 78, and 901 through 905 of the Code) will be applied as if immediately before the acquisition such earnings and profits were distributed as a dividend. The 20 percent principle may be illustrated by the following example:

> Domestic corporation X owns more than 20% of the outstanding stock of foreign corporation Y (which is not a foreign investment company). A favorable section 367 ruling will be issued in connection with the reincorporation of Y into a newly organized domestic corporation Z only if domestic corporation X agrees to include in its gross income as a dividend deemed paid in money for its taxable years in which the exchange of stock occurs its portion of the accumulated earnings and profits, if any, of Y for all taxable years of Y properly attributable to the stock which X owns in Y. This is because, after reincorporation of Y as a domestic corporation, the gross amount of dividends paid by Y will be subject to United States income tax

in the hands of domestic corporation X only after being reduced by the dividends received deduction contained in section 243 of the Code.

(c) Where assets of a foreign corporation are acquired by another foreign corporation and stock of the acquired foreign corporation is exchanged (or treated as exchanged under section 355) for stock of the acquiring foreign corporation incident to the plan of reorganization, if in the event that the acquired foreign corporation is a controlled foreign corporation (as defined in section 957(a) of the Code) at the time of the exchange of stock or at any time within five years prior thereto, the shareholders of such corporation agree to include in their gross income, as a dividend deemed paid in money for their taxable year in which the exchange of stock occurs, the portion of the earnings and profits, if any, of the acquired foreign corporation properly attributable under section 1248 of the Code to such shareholders' stock in such corporation which would have been includible in their gross income under section 1248 of the Code if at the time of such acquisition the stock of such corporation was exchanged in a taxable exchange. In cases described in this subparagraph in which shareholders agree to include earnings and profits in gross income as a dividend deemed paid in money, the foreign tax credit provisions (sections 78, and 901 through 905 of the Code) will be applied as if immediately before the acquisition such earnings and profits were distributed as a dividend.

(d) Where the stock of a domestic corporation is acquired in exchange for stock of a foreign corporation and immediately after the exchange the shareholders of the acquired domestic corporation do not own directly or indirectly, within the meaning of section 958 of the Code, more than 50 percent of the total combined voting power of all classes of stock entitled to vote of the acquiring foreign corporation, unless the assets of the acquired domestic corporation consist principally of stock or securities. For the effect of section 367 of the Code in cases in which stock of a domestic corporation is acquired by a foreign corporation and where, immediately after the exchange, shareholders of the domestic corporation are in control (as defined in section 368(c) of the Code) of the acquiring foreign corporation, see Sec. 3.02(a)(1)(iii) above.

(e) Where the stock of a foreign corporation is acquired by a domestic corporation.

(f) Where stock of a foreign corporation is acquired in exchange for stock of another foreign corporation and immediately after the exchange (1) the acquiring foreign corporation is controlled (within the meaning of section 954(d)(3) of the Code) by a person or persons who immediately prior to such exchange controlled the acquired foreign corporation, and (2) the acquired foreign corporation meets the requirements of subsections 954(c)(4)(A)(i) and (ii) of the Code. Moreover, when the acquiring foreign corporation is not a controlled foreign corporation (as defined in section 957(a) of the Code) the preceding sentence shall apply only if the shareholders of the acquired foreign corporation agree to include in their gross income as a dividend deemed paid in money for their taxable year in which the exchange of stock occurs, the portion of the earnings and profits, if any, of the acquired foreign corporation properly attributable under section 1248 of the Code to such shareholders' stock in such acquired foreign corporation which would have been includible in their income under section 1248 of the Code if at the time of such acquisition the stock of such acquired foreign corporation was exchanged in a taxable exchange.

(g) Where stock of a foreign corporation is acquired in exchange for stock of another foreign corporation and immediately after the exchange the shareholders of the acquired corporation do not own directly or indirectly, within the meaning of section 958 of the Code, more than 50 percent of the total combined voting power of all classes of stock entitled to vote of the acquiring foreign corporation. Moreover, when the acquiring foreign corporation is not a controlled foreign corporation (as defined in section 957(a) of the Code) the preceding sentence shall apply only if the shareholders of the acquired foreign corporation agree to include in their gross income as a dividend deemed paid in money for their taxable year in which the exchange of stock occurs, the portion of the earnings and profits, if any, of the acquired foreign corporation properly attributable under section 1248 of the Code to such shareholders' stock in such acquired foreign corporation which would have been includible in their income under section 1248 of the Code if at the time of such acquisition the stock of such acquired foreign corporation was exchanged in a taxable exchange. For the effect of section 367 of the Code in cases in which stock of a foreign corporation is acquired by another foreign corporation and immediately after the exchange shareholders of the acquired foreign corporation are in control (as defined in section 368(c) of the Code) of the acquiring foreign corporation see Sec. 3.02(1)(a)(iii) above.

(h) A favorable ruling generally will be issued for all exchanges involving the mere recapitalization of a foreign corporation.

Sec. 4. *Earnings and Profits.*

.01 Earnings and profits of a foreign corporation which are to be taken into the gross income of a domestic parent corporation or the United States shareholders of a foreign corporation under circumstances set forth in this Revenue Procedure, are determined (1) for taxable years beginning before January 1, 1963, in accordance with the criteria contained in Revenue Ruling 63-6, C.B. 1963-1, 126; and (2) for taxable years beginning after December 31, 1962, in accordance with the rules contained in subsections 1248(c) and (d) of the Code and the regulations thereunder. However, in determining the earnings and profits of a foreign corporation includible in the income of a domestic parent corporation under Sec. 3.01(1) above (relating to complete liquidation of subsidiaries) or in the income of a domestic corporate shareholder owning 20% or more of the outstanding stock of the foreign corporation under Sec. 3.03(1)(b) above (relating to the acquisition by a domestic corporation of assets of a foreign corporation), the exclusions set forth in section 1248(d)(4) of the Code ("United States Income") apply but the exclusions set forth in section 1248 (d)(2) of the Code ("Gain Realized From The Sale Or Exchange Of Property In Pursuance Of A Plan Of Complete Liquidation") and section 1248(d)(3) of the Code ("Less Developed Country Corporations") do not apply. But with respect to the exclusion in section 1248(d)(3) of the Code, see Sec. 4.02(1) below. For taxable years beginning after December 31, 1962, the earnings and profits described in section 1248(c)(2) of the Code are taken into gross income in transactions described in

Sec. 3.03(1)(c) above (relating to an acquisition of assets of a foreign corporation by another foreign corporation) and Sec. 3.03(1)(f) and (g) above (relating to an acquisition of stock of a foreign corporation by another foreign corporation) in which the acquiring corporation is not a controlled foreign corporation. For purposes of determining the portion of the earnings and profits of a foreign corporation properly attributable to stock in such foreign corporation owned by a U.S. person and the manner in which such portion is includible in the gross income of a United States person, the rules of subsections 1248(a) and (b) of the Code and the regulations thereunder generally apply. See sections 1.1248-2 and 1.1248-3 of the regulations. In applying the provisions of this paragraph, the rules of sections 1248(e) through (g) of the Code are also to be followed.

.02   Special provisions for the purpose of this Revenue Procedure —

(1) Earnings and profits of less developed country corporations. — Where earnings and profits accumulated by a foreign corporation during taxable years in which such corporation meets the requirements of section 955(c) of the Code, or would have met such requirements if the Revenue Act of 1962 had then been in effect, are required to be included as a dividend in the gross income of a domestic corporation owing 20 percent or more of the outstanding stock of the foreign corporation such earnings and profits are taxed as capital gain to the domestic corporation if it so elects in its request for ruling and the ten-year stock ownership requirement of section 1248(d)(3) of the Code is met with respect to its stock in the foreign corporation at the time of the transaction described in Sec. 3.01(1) above (relating to complete liquidation of subsidiaries) or the transaction described in Sec. 3.03(1)(b) above (where assets of a foreign corporation are acquired by a domestic corporation).

(2) Earnings and profits of foreign investment companies. — Where earnings and profits accumulated by a foreign investment company (as defined in section 1246(b) of the Code) are required to be taken into gross income of shareholders of such a company, such earnings and profits are treated as (i) gain from the sale of a noncapital asset in the case of earnings and profits accumulated in taxable years beginning after December 31, 1962, and (ii) a dividend deemed paid in money in the case of earnings and profits accumulated in taxable years beginning before January 1, 1963.

(3) Earnings and profits of corporations organized in U.S. possessions. — Earnings and profits accumulated by a corporation created or organized in, or under the laws of, the Commonwealth of Puerto Rico, or a possession of the United States, during taxable years in which such corporation meets the requirements of section 957(c) of the Code, or would have met such requirements if the Revenue Act of 1962 had then been in effect, are not required to be taken into gross income under these guidelines.

(4) A corporation which during its first taxable year beginning after December 31, 1962 meets the requirements of section 955(c) or section 957(c) of the Code will be conclusively presumed to have met such requirements during taxable years beginning prior to January 1, 1963.

Sec. 5.   Other Principles and Requirements.

.01   If a proposed transaction is not carried out in accordance with a plan submitted in respect of which a favorable ruling is issued by the Service under section 367 of the Code, such favorable ruling will not make the transaction tax free. See section 1.367-1 of the regulations. If a change in plans is proposed the taxpayer may apply for a supplemental ruling that the change has no effect upon the original ruling and it remains in full force and effect.

.02 In cases in which a favorable ruling is issued under section 367 of the Code, appropriate adjustments to bases, earnings and profits, carryovers, and carrybacks, and other similar adjustments may be required. In addition, in appropriate cases not specifically mentioned in the guidelines but involving an exchange of stock of a foreign corporation within the ambit of section 367, the shareholders participating in such exchange may be required to include in their gross income, as a dividend deemed paid in money for their taxable year in which such exchange occurs, the portion of the earnings and profits, if any, of the foreign corporation properly attributable under section 1248 of the Code to such shareholders' stock in such foreign corporation which would have been includible in their gross income under section 1248 of the Code if at the time of such exchange the stock of such foreign corporation was exchanged in a taxable transaction. The preceding sentence is intended to insure that the tax under section 1248 of the Code will be imposed in any case in which failure to impose such tax may result in the permanent avoidance of such section 1248 tax in respect of post-1962 earnings and profits of a foreign corporation. . . .

NOTE

1. See Rev. Proc. 69-12, 1969-1 Cum. Bull. 401, for the administrative procedure available to protest adverse determinations under §367. See also Note, The Availability and Reviewability of Rulings of the Internal Revenue Service, 113 U. Pa. L. Rev. 81 (1964). Cf. Texas-Canadian Oil Corp., Ltd., 44 B.T.A. 913 (1941). See also Note, page 401 supra.

2. If an exchange of stock is tax-free under §1036, no ruling under §367 is necessary even though the transaction constitutes an "E" reorganization. Rev. Rul. 64-156, 1964-1 (Part 1) Cum. Bull. 139. Should a ruling be required under §367 when a foreign corporation transfers stock to a domestic corporation pursuant to a plan of reorganization that meets the requirements of both a "B" reorganization and §351? See Rev. Rul. 70-433, 1970-34 I.R.B., 11.

3. The Commissioner holds that, absent an advance ruling under §1492(2), the excise tax imposed by §1491 applies when a domestic parent corporation sells stock of a wholly owned foreign subsidiary to a controlled foreign corporation for cash. Rev. Rul. 70-111, 1970-1 Cum. Bull. 185. Cf. Rev. Rul. 69-450, 1969-2 Cum. Bull. 168. What purpose does §1491 serve in the tax system?

PART II

5 | Partnerships

I. INTRODUCTION AND HISTORY

Prior to the enactment of the Internal Revenue Code of 1954 the taxation of partnerships was a very confusing and uncertain area. The statutory framework was thin. If left most of the law of partnership taxation to be worked out either in the courts or within the administrative processes of the Treasury. The 1954 enactment was an attempt to eliminate the inconsistency and uncertainty of the prior law. Although passage of Subchapter K in 1954 did mark the end of much uncertainty, it imposed upon taxpayers the burden of understanding an intricate system of partnership taxation which required the keeping of detailed records whereby entries as to a single piece of property might differ with respect to each individual partner. And, of course, new uncertainties replaced some of the older ones.

The scheme of Subchapter K retained the structure of prior law whereby the partnership is used only as an accounting entity. It pays no taxes. The partners pay tax individually. Using the partnership as an accounting entity requires that partnership net income be computed and reported. This is done, except for certain modifications required in §703, in the same manner as for an individual. From this calculation the partner takes his distributive share of the income and losses of the partnership into his individual income tax return. A partner must include his distributive share of his partnership's income on his own return even though the partnership makes no distribution of its income.

In certain instances the concept of the partnership as only an accounting unit gives way to a view that the partnership is an entity distinct from the individual partners. This occurs, for example, when the partner is considered an employee, creditor or third party transacting business with the partnership (§707). In those cases the partnership is not considered only as a conduit through which income and losses flow, but rather as an entity with which the partner does business, and the tax consequences are gauged accordingly. Similarly, when the partner leaves the partnership the transaction might be viewed as one in which the partnership distributes assets to him or as one in which the partner is dealing in an interest in a separate entity (§§736 and 741). In most instances the determination of the way the partner is acting in regard to the partnership will affect the tax consequences of the transaction. Subchapter K uses both approaches and in many instances allows the partners to choose between them, thus permitting the partners themselves to determine on which of them the tax burdens will fall. It is because of the flexible nature of the taxation of partnerships that it is such a difficult area and of such importance for the tax counsellor.

In most cases taxpayers may transfer appreciated assets to a partnership in exchange for (or to build up) an interest in the partnership without recognition of gain (§721). In many respects the transaction is treated like one of incorporation under §351. In a very important respect, however, §721 has broader scope. Tax-free incorporation requires that the transferors be in "control." There is no such requirement for §721 to be operative.

"Partnership" and "partner" are defined by the Code in two separate places, and not exactly the same way in each place. See §§761(a) and (b) and 7701 (a)(2).

See generally J. Pennell and J. O'Byrne, Federal Income Taxation of Partners and Partnerships (1971); A. J. B. Aronsohn, Partnerships and Income Taxes (rev. ed. 1970); D. Westfall, Corporate Analogues in Partnership Taxation, 80 Harv. L. Rev. 765 (1967); A. Willis, Handbook of Partnership Taxation (1957); Anderson and Coffee, Proposed Revision of Partner and Partnership Taxation: Analysis of the Report of the Advisory Group on Subchapter K, 15 Tax L. Rev. 285 (1960); B. Wolfman, Level for Determining Character of Partnership Income — "Entity" v. "Conduit" Principle in Partnership Taxation, 19 N.Y.U. Inst. on Fed. Tax. 287 (1961).

II. STATUTORY ISSUES — §§701-771

A. *CONTRIBUTIONS — "PROPERTY" vs. "SERVICES"*

UNITED STATES v. FRAZELL
335 F.2d 487 (5th Cir. 1964), rehearing denied, 339 F.2d 885 (5th Cir. 1964),
cert. denied, 380 U.S. 961 (1965)

Before TUTTLE, Chief Judge, and HUTCHESON and GEWIN, Circuit Judges.

TUTTLE, Chief Judge. . . . On February 9, 1951, William Frazell, a geologist, entered into a contract with the N. H. Wheless Oil Company, a partnership, and W. C. Woolf, under which Frazell was to check certain areas to determine whether potentially productive oil and gas properties might be procured there. He was to recommend those properties he found suitable to Wheless and Woolf, and upon their joint approval, he was to attempt to acquire such properties, taking title thereto in the names of Wheless and Woolf in equal shares. In return for these services, Frazell was to receive "a monthly salary or drawing account," plus expenses, and specified interests in the property acquired. It was agreed, however, "that Frazell shall not be entitled to, nor shall he be considered as owning, any interest in said properties until such time as Wheless and Woolf shall have recovered their full costs and expenses of said properties" including the amounts paid out to Frazell. . . .

The arrangement proved successful, and it was evident in the early part of 1955 that Wheless and Woolf would fully recover their costs and expenses by the end of November of that year. In April 1955, the 1951 contract was terminated, and by contract dated April 20, 1955, all the properties acquired under the earlier arrangement were transferred to the W.W.F. Corporation, a Delaware corporation formed specifically to acquire these properties in return for the issuance of debentures to Wheless and Woolf and of stock to Wheless, Woolf, and Frazell. Frazell received 6,500 shares of W.W.F. stock (13% of the total issued), having a fair market value of $91,000.00, but he included no part of this amount in his 1955 income tax return. The Commissioner ruled that the $91,000.00 should have been included in income and assessed a deficiency, which Frazell paid under protest and seeks to recover here.

Frazell contends that he received the W.W.F. stock in a tax-free exchange within the terms of section 351(a), Internal Revenue Code of 1954. That section provides:

> "No gain or loss shall be recognized if property is transferred to a corporation by one or more persons solely in exchange for stock or securities in such corporation and immediately after the exchange such person or persons are in control . . . of the corporation. For purposes of this section, stock or securities issued for services shall not be considered as issued in return for property."

The district court agreed that section 351(a) is applicable in this case. This was said to follow from that court's finding that the 1951 contract created a "joint venture" among the three participants. 213 F. Supp. at 468. We take no issue with the trial court's finding of fact in this matter, but it does not follow from the categorization of the 1951 arrangement as a "joint venture" that the April 1955 transactions resulted in no taxable income to Frazell.

It is fundamental that "compensation for services" is taxable as ordinary income under the Internal Revenue Code of 1954. I.R.C. 1954 §61(a)(1). This principle applies whether the one compensated for his services is an employee receiving a salary, fees, or commission (ibid.), one receiving corporate securities (I.R.C. 1954 §351(a)), or a "service partner" receiving an interest in the partnership. (I.R.C. 1954 §721; Treas. Reg. §1.721-1(b)(1).)

The regulation pertaining to partnerships provides that

> "the value of an interest in such partnership capital so transferred to a partner as compensation for services constitutes income to the partner under section 61. The amount of such income is the fair market value of the interest in capital so transferred . . . at the time the transfer is made for past services. . . . The time when such income is realized depends on all the facts and circumstances, including any substantial restrictions or conditions on the compensated partner's right to withdraw or otherwise dispose of such interest."

This rule would have been directly applicable had the 1951 contract continued in effect through November 1955, the date on which Wheless and Woolf would have fully recovered their costs in the venture. The contract made it clear that Frazell would "not have the right to dispose of any rights which may accrue to him" before those costs were recovered. 213 F. Supp. at 472. But after November, he would have received a largely unrestricted[1] interest in about 13% of the partnership properties. That this interest was primarily, if not entirely, in return for Frazell's services to the enterprise is undisputed. Thus, so much of the interest Frazell was to receive in November 1955 as could be attributed to his services for the oil venture would have been ordinary income to him in the year of receipt.

The applicable rule is in no way changed by Frazell's contention that his interest in the enterprise was a "carried interest." . . . Even if Frazell is taken to have had some sort of interest in the properties in question from their first acquisition, his interest would not have become possessory until November 1955. Under Treasury Regulation §1.721-1(b)(1), the value of that interest would have been taxable to him at that time. . . .

The fact that the contract was terminated prior to November 1955 should have no effect on the tax consequences of Frazell's arrangements. The transactions of April 1955 may be viewed in either of two ways: (1) If Frazell's partnership interest became possessory immediately upon the termination of the 1951 contract, so much of that interest received as compensation for services was taxable to him under the rule of Treasury Regulation §1.721(b)(1). Thereafter, the transfer of his interest for W.W.F. stock was tax-free under section 351(a). (2) If the $91,000.00 of W.W.F. stock was given in substitution for the partnership interest originally contemplated, so much of that stock received in compensation for services was taxable to Frazell under section 351(a). As either view of the 1955 transactions results in ordinary income to Frazell there is no reason for us to split hairs and choose between them.

This is not to say that the full $91,000.00 is ordinary income. The trial court found that, just as Wheless and Woolf contributed large amounts of capital, "Frazell supplied to the venture a very valuable oil map which was his private property." . . . Indeed the record shows that prior to entering into the 1951 contract Frazell had acquired several maps which apparently proved very helpful to the work of the venture. Among the reasons given by Mr. Wheless for desiring to employ Frazell was that "he had accumulated maps, geological data and various information that was valuable to the arrangement that it would have taken a long time for someone else just moving into the territory to accumulate." And Frazell himself testified that he "had contributed considerable information and maps which resulted in the discovery and production of oil. . . ." Although it is clear that the greater part of the 13% interest received by Frazell was received as compensation for services, the court's finding and the cited testimony suggest that some part of that interest might have been received in return for "property;" namely, the maps. That part of the property Frazell received in 1955 attributable to his contribution of maps is not taxable in 1955 no matter whether we view the interest received as a partnership interest vesting on the termination of the 1951 contract (I.R.C. 1954 §721) or as shares of W.W.F. stock given in substitution therefor. (I.R.C. 1954 §315(a)). See Treas. Reg. §1.351-1(2), example 3; . . . Such part of $91,000.00 as exceeds the value of the maps as determined by the trial court is properly taxable to Frazell as ordinary income.

[1] Even after Wheless and Woolf recovered their costs, the contract gave them a right of first refusal should Frazell desire to dispose of any of his interests in the properties in question.

Reversed and remanded.

HUTCHESON, Circuit Judge (dissenting). [Opinion omitted.]

NOTE

1. Chief Judge Tuttle's opinion quotes extensively from Treas. Reg. §1.721-1(b)(1). Does a reading of the whole section support the language of the opinion in this case? Which partner in this case gave up his right to be repaid his contribution to the partnership? On the facts of the case Wheless and Woolf were at all times to be repaid their capital contributions before Frazell could participate in the earnings of the venture. Would the case have been decided differently if the three partners had waited until November 1955 to incorporate, when Wheless and Woolf were expected to recover "their costs"?

Do the *Frazell* case and the Regulation under §721 require a "services partner" always to recognize ordinary income when he gains an interest in the capital accounts of the partnership without his having made a pro rata contribution?

2. Treasury Regulation §1.721-1(b)(1) deals with the problems of how the services partner is to evaluate his partnership interest in capital and when he must take that interest into ordinary income. As to when the services partner must take his interest into income, see Lehman v. Commissioner, 19 T.C. 659 (1953), which held that the partner must recognize as income any credits to his account when the credit was due him, not when the entries were recorded on the books of the partnership. What impact does §83, added by the Tax Reform Act of 1969, have on the question of the timing and amount of income of a partner who receives a "restricted" interest in a partnership in return for services? How should the penultimate sentence in Treas. Reg. §1.721-1 (b)(1) be changed in light of §83?

3. The *Frazell* case has created uncertainty as to the tax consequences to the services partner on the formation of the partnership. Prior to the decision it was fairly clear that if the services partner was credited with a capital account and that account resulted from transferring the credit from another partner's capital account, the services partner must recognize ordinary income. Lehman v. Commissioner, supra; cf. Farris v. Commissioner, 222 F.2d 320 (10th Cir. 1955). Both of the cited cases support the validity of Treas. Reg. §1.721-1(b)(1). However, *Frazell* seems to go farther than either the Regulations or the cited cases. In *Frazell* there is no indication that Frazell's capital account was transferred from either of his other partners. Both Wheless and Woolf were to be fully repaid their capital contributions before Frazell could share in any profits. His capital interest would not accrue until after all original contributions had been paid back. Suppose partner A contributes $100,000 to the venture and his capital account is credited for that amount. Partner B, the services partner, contributes nothing to the business, but nevertheless he is credited with a $100,000 contribution. When and to what extent does B have income? See Treas. Reg. §1.721-1(b)(1). See also J. Hewitt, How to Avoid the Common Tax Problems in Forming or Dissolving a Partnership, 24 J. Taxation 294 (1966); E. Weiss-

man, Problems in Transferring a Partnership Interest as Compensation for Services, 25 J. Taxation 162 (1966).

4. For the tax consequences to a partner when making a contribution of property to the partnership, see §721. This provision parallels the corporate rule contained in §351, except that, under §721, appreciation will go unrecognized even if property is contributed after formation of the partnership by one not in control. See Treas. Reg. §1.721-1(a). The basis of the partnership interest is the same as the adjusted basis of the property contributed and any money contributed, less any liabilities assumed, by the other partners (§§772 and 752(b), and Treas. Reg. §1.722-1). The adjusted basis of the contributed property is carried over and is the basis of the property in the hands of the partnership (§723).

5. Because the basis of contributed property is carried over when the property is in the hands of the partnership, inequities among partners as to how much depreciation a partner may take may be created. This situation occurs when partner A contributes depreciable property with a value and adjusted basis of $10,000, while partner B contributes depreciable property worth $10,000 with an adjusted basis of $5000. Is not partner A contributing a greater tax benefit to the enterprise than partner B? Section 704(c) permits the partners to agree as to how the depreciation allowance should be allocated between them. This provision also applies to allocation of gain or loss on the sale of property contributed. Therefore in the example above A and B may agree that any gain realized on the sale of the property with an adjusted basis below its value will be recognized by B alone.

A and B would also likely agree that twice as much of the depreciation deduction should be allocated to A, since he contributed property with twice the depreciable basis. While these two pieces of property are maintained, A would take two-thirds of the deduction, B one-third. If B's contribution were sold for $10,000 when its depreciable basis had been reduced to $4000, B would be charged with recognition of $5000 of the $6000 capital gain, whereas the $1000 remainder would be equally divided, since B would have made up for his original disparate contribution. Any property now purchased with the proceeds from this sale would be depreciated equally.

What limitation is imposed on such allocations? See §704(b)(2) and Treas. Reg. §1.704-1(b)(2). May the partners allocate between themselves as they see fit the interest from tax-free bonds contributed to the partnership? See §704(c)(1) and (2).

ORRISCH v. COMMISSIONER
55 T.C. 395 (1970)

Featherston, Judge: Respondent determined deficiencies in petitioners' income tax for 1966 and 1967 in the respective amounts of $2,814.19 and $3,018.11. The only issue for decision is whether an amendment to a partnership agreement allocating to petitioners the entire amount of the depreciation deduction allowable on two buildings owned by the partnership was made for the principal purpose of the avoidance of tax within the meaning of section 704(b).

Findings of Fact

Stanley C. Orrisch (hereinafter sometimes referred to as Orrisch) and Gerta E. Orrisch were husband and wife until a judgment of divorce was entered by the Superior Court of San Mateo County, California, on May 22, 1969. They filed joint Federal income tax returns for 1966 and 1967 with the district director of internal revenue, San Francisco, California. At the time they filed their petition, they were legal residents of Burlingame, California.

In May of 1963, Domonick J. and Elaine J. Crisafi (hereinafter the Crisafis) and petitioners formed a partnership to purchase and operate two apartment houses, one located at 1255 Taylor Street, San Francisco, and the other at 600 Ansel Road, Burlingame, California. The cost of the Taylor Street property was $229,011.08, and of the Ansel Road property was $155,974.90. The purchase of each property was financed principally by a secured loan. Petitioners and the Crisafis initially contributed to the partnership cash in the amounts of $26,500 and $12,500, respectively. During 1964 and 1965 petitioners and the Crisafis each contributed additional cash in the amounts of $8,800. Under the partnership agreement, which was not in writing, they agreed to share equally the profits and losses from the venture.

During each of the years 1963, 1964, and 1965, the partnership suffered losses, attributable in part to the acceleration of depreciation — the deduction was computed on the basis of 150 percent of straight line depreciation. The amounts of the depreciation deductions, the reported loss for each of the three years as reflected in the partnership returns, and the amounts of each partner's share of the losses are as follows:

Year	Depreciation Deducted	Total Loss	Each partner's share of the losses — 50 percent of the total loss
1963	$ 9,886.20	$ 9,716.14	$4,858.07
1964	21,051.95	17,812.33	8,906.17*
1965	19,894.24	18,952.59	9,476.30*

*The amounts of the losses allocated to the Crisafis for 1964 and 1965 were actually $8,906.*16* and $9,476.*29*, respectively.

Petitioners and the Crisafis respectively reported in their individual income tax returns for these years the partnership losses allocated to them.

Petitioners enjoyed substantial amounts of income from several sources, the principal one being a nautical equipment sales and repair business. In their joint income tax returns for 1963, 1964, and 1965, petitioners reported taxable income in the respective amounts of $10,462.70, $5,898.85, and $50,332, together with taxes thereon in the amounts of $2,320.30, $1,059.80, and $12,834.

The Crisafis were also engaged in other business endeavors, principally an insurance brokerage business. They owned other real property, however, from which they realized losses, attributable largely to substantial depreciation deductions. In their joint income tax returns for 1963, 1964, and 1965, they reported no net taxable income.

Early in 1966, petitioners and the Crisafis orally agreed that, for 1966 and subsequent years, the entire amount of the partnership's depreciation deductions would be specially allocated to petitioners, and that the gain or loss from the partnership's business, computed without regard to any deduction for depreciation, would be divided equally. They further agreed that, in the event the partnership property was sold at a gain, the specially allocated depreciation would be "charged back" to petitioner's capital account and petitioners would pay the tax on the gain attributable thereto.

The operating results of the partnership for 1966 and 1967 as reflected in the partnership returns were as follows:

Year	Depreciation Deducted	Loss (including depreciation)	Gain [(or Loss)] without regard to depreciation
1966	$18,412.00	$19,396.00	($984.00)
1967	17,180.75	16,560.78	619.97

The partnership returns for these years show that, taking into account the special arrangement as to depreciation, losses in the amounts of $18,904 and $16,870.76 were allocated to petitioners for 1966 and 1967, respectively, and petitioners claimed these amounts as deductions in their joint income tax returns for those years. The partnership returns reported distributions to the Crisafis in the form of a $492 loss for 1966 and a $309.98 gain for 1967. The Crisafis joint income tax returns reflected that they had no net taxable income for either 1966 or 1967.

The net capital contributions, allocations of profits, losses and depreciation, and ending balances of the capital accounts, of the Orrisch-Crisafi partnership from May 1963 through December 31, 1967, were as follows:

	Petitioners'	Crisafis'
Excess of capital contributions over withdrawals during 1963	$ 26,655.55	$12,655.54
Allocation of 1963 loss	(4,858.07)	(4,858.07)
Balance 12/31/63	$ 21,797.48	$ 7,797.47
Excess of capital contributions over withdrawals during 1964	$ 4,537.50	$ 3,537.50
Allocation of 1964 loss	(8,906.17)	(8,906.16)
Balance 12/31/64	$ 17,428.81	$ 2,428.81
Excess of capital contributions over withdrawals during 1965	$ 4,337.50	$ 5,337.50
Allocation of 1965 loss	(9,476.30)	(9,476.29)
Balance 12/31/65	$ 12,290.01	$(1,709.98)

	Petitioners'	Crisafis'
Excess of capital contributions over withdrawals during 1966	$ 2,610.00	$ 6,018.00
Allocation of 1966 loss before depreciation	(492.00)	(492.00)
Allocation of depreciation	(18,412.00)	-0-
Balance 12/31/66	$ (4,003.99)	$ 3,816.02
Excess of withdrawals over capital contributions during 1967	$ (4,312.36)	$(3,720.35)
Allocation of 1967 profit before depreciation	309.99	309.98
Allocation of depreciation	(17,180.75)	-0-
Balance 12/31/67	$(25,187.11)	$ 405.65

In May of 1968, before petitioners Stanley C. Orrisch and Greta E. Orrisch were divorced, they entered into a Marital Property Settlement Agreement which, as part of paragraph 8, contained the following:

(c) The parties recognize that each of said parcels of real property is encumbered by loans and requires certain maintenance, upkeep and repair and certain other expenses for the operation thereof. The parties further understand that at the present time neither of said parcels of real property produces sufficient cash flow to meet loan payments and the other expenses above referred to. For this reason, husband agrees that from the date of this agreement forward, so long as they shall own or hold either or both of said parcels of real property, he (as between the parties hereto) shall be responsible for providing from time to time any money required to meet said loan payments or expenses. Husband further agrees to hold wife free and harmless of and from any losses or claims in connection with either or both of said parcels of real property. Upon the sale or disposition of either or both of said parcels of real property, the parties hereto will equally divide the profits or proceeds of such sale or disposition, provided that from such profits or proceeds husband shall be first reimbursed for such moneys as he may have advanced for the parties' joint benefit for either or both of said parcels of real property as hereinabove provided.

(d) In consideration of the foregoing, wife agrees that she will not deduct on her Federal and State income tax returns any depreciation allowable by reason of the ownership of the said 2 parcels of real property. Wife makes no representation or warranty as to the propriety of husband's taking on his income tax returns the depreciation that would be otherwise allowable to her. Husband is informed and advised that this would be proper by reason of the burdens of the ownership assumed by him under this paragraph. Upon the sale or other disposition of either or both of said parcels of real property, each party hereto shall be responsible for reporting on his or her respective income tax returns one-half of the capital gain or loss, if any, realized from such sale or disposition.

By an agreement dated May 12, 1969, the foregoing provisions were modified as follows:

> (c) The parties recognize that each of said parcels of real property is encumbered by loans and requires certain maintenance, upkeep and repair and certain other expenses for the operation thereof. The parties further understand that at the present time neither of said parcels of real property produces sufficient cash flow to meet loan payments and other expenses above referred to. Commencing with the calendar year 1969, the parties hereto shall contribute equally to their collective share of the money required to meet said loan payments or expenses. Except as otherwise provided herein, the parties shall each report on their federal and state income tax returns one-half of their collective share of the income and one-half of their collective share of the deductions, including (but not limited to) depreciation, arising from or related to said property. Upon the sale or other disposition of either or both of said parcels of real property, each party shall be responsible for reporting on his or her respective income tax returns his or her share of the gain or loss, if any, realized from such sale or disposition, and for purposes of computing the same, all depreciation taken by Husband with respect to said property in the calendar year 1968 shall only reduce the basis of Husband in said property and not the basis of Wife.

In the notice of deficiency, respondent determined that the special allocation of the depreciation deduction provided by the amendment to the partnership agreement "was made with the principal purpose of avoidance of income taxes" and should, therefore, be disregarded. Partnership losses for 1966 and 1967, adjusted to reflect a correction of the amount of depreciation allowable, were allocated equally between the partners.

Ultimate Finding of Fact

The principal purpose of the special allocation to petitioners of all of the deductions for depreciation taken by the Orrisch-Crisafi partnership for 1966 and 1967 was the avoidance of income tax.

Opinion

The only issue presented for decision is whether tax effect can be given the agreement between petitioners and the Crisafis that, beginning with 1966, all the partnership's depreciation deductions were to be allocated to petitioners for their use in computing their individual income tax liabilities. In our view, the answer must be in the negative, and the amounts of each of the partners' deductions for the depreciation of partnership property must be determined in accordance with the ratio used generally in computing their distributive shares of the partnership's profits and losses.

Among the important innovations of the 1954 Code are limited provisions for flexibility in arrangements for the sharing of income, losses, and deductions arising from business activities conducted through partnerships. The authority for special allocations of such items appears in section 704(a), which provides that a partner's share of any item of income, gain, loss, deduction, or credit shall be determined by the partnership agreement.[3] That rule is coupled with a limitation in section 704(b), however, which states that a special allocation of an item will be disregarded if its "principal purpose" is the avoidance or evasion of Federal income tax. . . . In case a special allocation is disregarded, the partner's share of the item is to be determined in accordance with the ratio by which the partners divide the general profits or losses of the partnership. Sec. 1.704-1(b)(2), Income Tax Regs.

The report of the Senate Committee on Finance accompanying the bill finally enacted as the 1954 Code (S. Rept. No. 1622, to accompany H.R. 8300 (Pub. L. 591), 83d Cong., 2d Sess., p. 379 (1954)) explained the tax avoidance restriction prescribed by section 704(b) as follows:

> Subsection (b) . . . provides that if the principal purpose of any provision in the partnership agreement dealing with a partner's distributive share of a particular item is to avoid or evade the Federal income tax, the partner's distributive share of that item shall be redetermined in accordance with his distributive share of partnership income or loss described in section 702(a)(9) [i.e., the ratio used by the partners for dividing general profits or losses]. . . .
>
> Where, however, a provision in a partnership agreement for a special allocation of certain items has substantial economic effect and is not merely a device for reducing the taxes of certain partners without actually affecting their shares of partnership income, then such a provision will be recognized for tax purposes. . . .

This reference to "substantial economic effect" did not appear in the House Ways and Means Committee Report (H. Rept. No. 1337, to accompany H.R. 8300 (Pub. L. 591), 83d Cong., 2d Sess., p. A223 (1954)) discussing section 704(b), and was apparently added in the Senate Finance Committee to allay fears that special allocations of income or deductions would be denied effect in every case where the allocation resulted in a reduction in the income tax liabilities of one or more of the partners. The statement is an affirmation that special allocations are ordinarily to be recognized if they have business validity apart from their tax consequences. Driscoll, Tax Problems of Partnerships — Special Allocation of Specific Items, 1958 So. Calif. Tax Inst. 421, 426.

In resolving the question whether the principal purpose of a provision in a partnership agreement is the avoidance or evasion of Federal income tax, all the facts and circumstances in relation to the provision must be taken into account. Section 1.704-1(b)(2), Income Tax Regs., lists the following as relevant circumstances to be considered:

> Whether the partnership or a partner individually has a business purpose for the allocation; whether the allocation has "substantial economic effect", that is, whether the allocation may actually affect the dollar amount

---

[3]Section 761(c) defines the term "partnership agreement" . . .

of the partners' shares of the total partnership income or loss independently of tax consequences; whether related items of income gain, loss, deduction, or credit from the same source are subject to the same allocation; whether the allocation was made without recognition of normal business factors and only after the amount of the specially allocated item could reasonably be estimated; the duration of the allocation; and the overall tax consequences of the allocation. . . .

Applying these standards, we do not think the special allocation of depreciation in the present case can be given effect.

The evidence is persuasive that the special allocation of depreciation was adopted for a tax avoidance rather than a business purpose. Depreciation was the only item which was adjusted by the parties; both the income from the buildings and the expenses incurred in their operation, maintenance, and repair were allocated to the partners equally. Since the deduction for depreciation does not vary from year to year with the fortunes of the business, the parties obviously knew what the tax effect of the special allocation would be at the time they adopted it. Furthermore, as shown by our Findings, petitioners had large amounts of income which would be offset by the additional deduction for depreciation; the Crisafis, in contrast, had no taxable income from which to subtract the partnership depreciation deductions, and, due to depreciation deductions which they were obtaining with respect to other housing projects, could expect to have no taxable income in the near future. On the other hand, the insulation of the Crisafis from at least part of a potential capital gains tax was an obvious tax advantage. The inference is unmistakably clear that the agreement did not reflect normal business considerations but was designed primarily to minimize the overall tax liabilities of the partners.

Petitioners urge that the special allocation of the depreciation deduction was adopted in order to equalize the capital accounts of the partners, correcting a disparity ($14,000) in the amounts initially contributed to the partnership by them ($26,500) and the Crisafis ($12,500). But the evidence does not support this contention. Under the special allocation agreement, petitioners were to be entitled, in computing their individual income tax liabilities, to deduct the full amount of the depreciation realized on the partnership property. For 1966, as an example, petitioners were allocated a sum ($18,904) equal to the depreciation on the partnership property ($18,412) plus one-half of the net loss computed without regard to depreciation ($492). The other one-half of the net loss was, of course, allocated to the Crisafis. Petitioners' allocation ($18,904) was then applied to reduce their capital account. The depreciation specially allocated to petitioners ($18,412) in 1966 alone exceeded the amount of the disparity in the contributions. Indeed, at the end of 1967, petitioners' capital account showed a deficit of $25,187.11 compared with a positive balance of $405.65 in the Crisafis' account. By the time the partnership's properties are fully depreciated, the amount of the reduction in petitioners' capital account will approximate the remaining basis for the buildings as of the end of 1967. The Crisafis' capital account will be adjusted only for contributions, withdrawals, gain or loss, without regard to depreciation, and similar adjustments for these factors will also be made in petitioners' capital account. Thus, rather than correcting an imbalance in the capital accounts of the partners, the special allocation of depreciation will create a vastly greater imbalance than existed at the end of 1966. In the light of these facts, we find it incredible that equalization of the capital accounts was the objective of the special allocation.[5]

Petitioners rely primarily on the argument that the allocation has "substantial economic effect" in that it is reflected in the capital accounts of the partners. Referring to the material quoted above from the report of the Senate Committee on Finance, they contend that this alone is sufficient to show that the special allocation served a business rather than a tax avoidance purpose.

According to the regulations, an allocation has economic effect if it "may actually affect the dollar amount of the partners' shares of the total partnership income or loss independently of tax consequences."[6] The agreement in this case provided not only for the allocation of depreciation to petitioners but also for gain on the sale of the partnership property to be "charged back" to them. The charge back would cause the gain, for tax purposes, to be allocated on the books entirely to petitioners to the extent of the special allocation of depreciation, and their capital account would be correspondingly increased. The remainder of the gain, if any, would be shared equally by the partners. If the gain on the sale were to equal or exceed the depreciation specially allocated to petitioners, the increase in their capital account caused by the charge back would exactly equal the depreciation deductions previously allowed to them, and the proceeds of the sale of the property would be divided equally. In such circumstances, the only effect of the allocation would be a trade of tax consequences, i.e., the Crisafis would relinquish a current depreciation deduction in exchange for exoneration from all or part of the capital gains tax when the property is sold, and petitioners would enjoy a larger current depreciation deduction but would assume a larger ultimate capital gains tax liability. Quite clearly, if the property is sold at a gain, the special allocation will affect only the tax liabilities of the partners and will have no other economic effect.

To find any economic effect of the special allocation agreement aside from its

---

[5]We recognize that petitioners had more money invested in the partnership than the Crisafis and that it is reasonable for the partners to endeavor to equalize their investments, since each one was to share equally in the profits and losses of the enterprise. However, we do not think that sec. 704(a) permits the partners' prospective tax benefits to be used as the medium for equalizing their investments, and it is apparent that the economic burden of the depreciation (which is reflected by the allowance for depreciation) was not intended to be the medium used.

This case is to be distinguished from situations where one partner contributed property and the other cash; in such cases sec. 704(c) may allow a special allocation of income and expenses in order to reflect the tax consequences inherent in the original contributions.

[6]This language of sec. 1.704-1(b)(2), Income Tax Regs., listing "substantial economic effect" as one of the factors to be considered in determining the principal purpose of a special allocation, is somewhat similar to the material quoted in the text from S. Rept. No. 1622, to accompany H.R. 8300 (Pub. L. 591), 83d Cong., 2d Sess., p. 379 (1954). But the latter is broader. It is an explanation of the "principal purpose" test of sec. 704(b), and contemplates that a special allocation will be given effect only if it has business validity apart from its tax consequences. Driscoll, Tax Problems of Partnerships — Special Allocation of Specific Items, 1958 So. Calif. Tax Inst. 421, 429 fn. 17; Willis, Handbook of Partnership Taxation (1957) at 141.

tax consequences, we must, therefore, look to see who is to bear the economic burden of the depreciation if the buildings should be sold for a sum less than their original cost. There is not one syllable of evidence bearing directly on this crucial point. We have noted, however, that when the buildings are fully depreciated, petitioners' capital account will have a deficit, or there will be a disparity in the capital accounts, approximately equal to the undepreciated basis of the buildings as of the beginning of 1966.[7] Under normal accounting procedures, if the building were sold at a gain less than the amount of such disparity petitioners would either be required to contribute to the partnership a sum equal to the remaining deficit in their capital account after the gain on the sale had been added back or would be entitled to receive a proportionately smaller share of the partnership assets on liquidation. Based on the record as a whole, we do not think the partners ever agreed to such an arrangement. On dissolution, we think the partners contemplated an equal division of the partnership assets which would be adjusted only for disparities in cash contributions or withdrawals.[8] Certainly there is no evidence to show otherwise. That being true, the special allocation does not "actually affect the dollar amount of the partners' shares of the total partnership income or loss independently of tax consequences" within the meaning of the regulation referred to above.

Our interpretation of the partnership agreement is supported by an analysis of a somewhat similar agreement, quoted in material part in our Findings, which petitioners made as part of a marital property settlement agreement in 1968. Under this agreement, Orrisch was entitled to deduct all the depreciation for 1968 in computing his income tax liability, and his wife was to deduct none; but on the sale of the property they were to first reimburse Orrisch for "such moneys as he may have advanced," and then divide the balance of the "profits or proceeds" of the sale equally, each party to report one-half of the capital gain or loss on his income tax return. In the 1969 amendment to this agreement the unequal allocation of the depreciation deduction was discontinued, and a provision similar to the partnership "charge back" was added, i.e., while the proceeds of the sale were to be divided equally, only Orrisch's basis was to be reduced by the depreciation allowed for 1968 so that he would pay taxes on a larger portion of the gain realized on the sale. Significantly, in both this agreement and the partnership agreement, as we interpret it, each party's share of the sales proceeds was determined independently from his share of the depreciation deduction.

In the light of all the evidence we have found as an ultimate fact that the "principal purpose" of the special allocation agreement was tax avoidance within the meaning of section 704(b). Accordingly, the deduction for depreciation for 1966 and 1967 must be allocated between the parties in the same manner as other deductions.

Decision will be entered for the respondent.

---

[7]This assumes, of course, that all partnership withdrawals and capital contributions will be equal.

[8]We note that, in the course of Orrisch's testimony, petitioners' counsel made a distinction between entries in the taxpayers' capital accounts which reflect actual cash transactions and those relating to the special allocation which are "paper entries relating to depreciation."

B. *"ENTITY" vs. "CONDUIT"*

REVENUE RULING 67-188
1967-1 Cum. Bull. 216

Advice has been requested relative to the treatment of a distributive share of a partnership's loss, resulting from the foreclosure of a mortgage on a hotel acquired and held by the partnership, by a general partner who is engaged as a real estate dealer for his individual account.

The taxpayer, engaged as a real estate dealer for his individual account, is a general partner in a partnership which was formed to acquire, own, operate, lease, and manage a hotel. The hotel property was purchased subject to existing mortgages which were not assumed by the purchaser. The hotel property was purchased subject also to a lease and was operated by various lessees until foreclosed by a second mortgagee some five years after the partnership had acquired it. Under the laws of the State in which the hotel was located, the foreclosure sale was not subject to a period of redemption.

The partnership agreement provided, in part, that the net profits of the partnership would be divided among the partners and the net losses would be borne by them, pro rata, in proportion to their respective original contributions to the capital of the partnership.

The taxpayer in his individual capacity during the year the mortgage on the hotel property was foreclosed had no transactions involving property described in section 1231 of the Internal Revenue Code of 1954.

Section 1231 of the Code provides that a taxpayer's recognized gains and losses from the disposition (including involuntary conversion) of "property used in the trade or business," as defined in section 1231(b) of the Code, and from the involuntary conversion of capital assets held for more than six months shall be treated as long-term capital gains and losses if the total gains exceed the total losses. If the total gains do not exceed the total losses, all such gains and losses are treated as ordinary gains and losses. Section 1231 of the Code, to the extent here pertinent, applies to recognized gains and losses from the sale, exchange, or involuntary conversion of property held for more than six months and used in the taxpayer's trade or business, which is either real property or is of a character subject to the allowance for depreciation under section 167 of the Code (even though fully depreciated), and which is not property of a kind which would properly be includible in the inventory of the taxpayer if on hand at the close of the taxable year, or property held by the taxpayer primarily for sale to customers in the ordinary course of business. See section 1.1231-1 (c) of the Income Tax Regulations.

Since the real and depreciable property comprising the hotel was held by the partnership for more than six months, was used in the partnership business, and was not inventory or property held by the partnership primarily for sale to customers, it qualifies as property described in section 1231 of the Code. The partnership had no other property described in section 1231 of the Code.

Section 165(a) of the Code provides, in part, that there shall be allowed as a deduction any loss sustained during the taxable year and not compensated for by insurance or otherwise.

Section 702 of the Code provides, in substance, that, in determining his income tax, each partner shall take into account separately his distributive share of the partnership's gains and losses from sales and exchanges of capital assets and from property described in section 1231 of the Code, as well as other items of income, gain, loss, deduction, or credit, to the extent provided by the Code and by regulations prescribed by the Secretary of the Treasury or his delegate. The character of any such item included in a partner's distributive share shall be determined as if the item were realized by the partner directly from the source from which realized by the partnership or incurred in the same manner as incurred by the partnership. For example, a partner's distributive share of gain from the sale of depreciable property used in the trade or business of the partnership shall be considered as gain from the sale of such depreciable property in the hands of the partner. See section 1.702-1(b) of the regulations.

Section 1.702-1(a)(3) of the regulations provides, in effect, that each partner, in determining his income tax, shall take into account separately, as part of his gains and losses from sales or exchanges of property described in section 1231 of the Code, his distributive share of the combined net amount of such gains and losses of the partnership. Each partner must also take into account separately his distributive share of any partnership item which, if separately taken into account by any partner, would result in an income tax liability for that partner different from that which would result if that partner did not take the item into account separately. See section 1.702-1(a)(8)(ii) of the regulations. . . .

Since the hotel property involved here qualifies as property described in section 1231 of the Code, the partnership's loss resulting from foreclosure thereof is a partnership loss under section 1231 of the Code, each partner's distributive share of which must be taken into account separately by him. Accordingly, each partner's distributive share of such loss must be considered a loss from the sale of property described in section 1231 of the Code in the hands of the partner.

Accordingly, the taxpayer's share of the partnership's loss resulting from the foreclosure of the mortgage on the hotel, is to be treated as an ordinary loss to the taxpayer under section 1231 of the Code, inasmuch as he had no gains for the taxable year from the disposition of property of the type described in that section.

The taxpayer's distributive share of partnership loss will be allowed only to the extent of the adjusted basis of his interest in the partnership at the end of the partnership year in which such loss occurred. See section 704(d) of the Code.

NOTE

1. Given the facts stated, the result to the individual taxpayer in Rev. Rul. 67-188 is the same as it would have been if the property had been inventory in the partner-

ship's hands. Although the ruling serves a didactic purpose as a doctrinal text would, it is not clear why the Commissioner issued it. What would the result have been if the taxpayer had had §1231 gains individually during the year in question? What would the result have been if, having had such gains, the property had been inventory to the partnership?

2. Section 6031 requires that the partnership file a return for its taxable year. This is required even though the partnership is not a taxable entity. However, the partnership must compute its "taxable income." This is done in the same manner as for an individual except that certain deductions such as the standard deduction, the personal exemption deduction and others listed in §703(a) are not allowed. In computing its income the partnership must state separately the different items described in §702(a)(1)-(9) (see §703(a)(1)). It is from these computations that the individual partner is required to compute his partnership income, gains and losses.

3. Section 702(a) requires the partner, in determining his income tax, to take into account his distributive share of the partnership income. The gross income of the partner must include his distributive share of the gross income of the partnership (§702(b)). The distributive share of the partner is determined by the provisions of §704. Thus in computing his income tax the partner must report items of net income and gain whether or not property is distributed. Treas. Reg. §1.702-1(a).

4. The character of the income taken into account by each partner remains the same as it was to the partnership (§702(b)). Thus, as was indicated in Rev. Rul. 67-188, §1231 losses to the partnership are §1231 losses to the partner. The Commissioner has also held that a partner may take into account in his distributive share of partnership income as capital gain his share of the partnership's long-term capital gain even though the partner has a holding period for his partnership interest of not more than six months. Rev. Rul. 68-79, 1968-1 Cum. Bull. 310. In a like manner, the Commissioner has ruled that under the provisions of §703(b) an individual partner may not elect to defer gain under §1033 unless the election is made by the partnership. And for the §1033 election to be effective, the partnership, and not an individual partner, must replace the involuntarily converted property. Mihran Demirjian, 54 T.C. 1691 (1970); Rev. Rul. 66-191, 1966-2 Cum. Bull. 300. Cf. Rev. Rul. 70-144, 1970-1 Cum. Bull. 170. See also Rev. Rul. 68-139, 1968-1 Cum. Bull. 311 (election to expense intangible drilling costs under §263(c) and Treas. Reg. §1.612-4 must be made by the partnership); L. L. Stone v. United States, 61-1 U.S. Tax Cas. ¶9486 (D.C. Colo. 1961) (individual partner could not report gain from the sale of assets on the installment method since the partnership did not so elect). See B. Wolfman, Level for Determining Character of Partnership Income — "Entity" v. "Conduit" Principle in Partnership Taxation, 19 N.Y.U. Inst. on Fed. Tax. 287 (1961).

5. Since the partner must include in his income his distributive share of partnership profits, whether distributed or not, he is not required to report it when it is distributed. This is accomplished by providing that no gain is recognized unless the money distributed by a partnership exceeds his basis in his partnership interest (§731 (a)(1)). The basis of the partnership interest will have been increased by the amount of the distributive share he has already reported (§705(a)). Subsequent to

distribution, the basis of the partnership interest is reduced by the amount of money distributed (§733). The basis of the partnership interest will therefore include only the partner's distributive share which has been reported but which has not also been distributed. What is the effect of a distribution of property other than money? See §731(a)(1). As to the basis in the hands of the partner of property other than money, see §732. As to how long a partner must hold distributed property before selling it and receiving capital gains treatment, see §735(b). As to whether ground rents are inventory items for purposes of §735(a)(2), requiring a five-year holding period, see J. Thomas Requard, 25 CCH Tax Ct. Mem. 732 (1966).

ARMSTRONG v. PHINNEY
394 F.2d 661 (5th Cir. 1968)

Before COLEMAN, AINSWORTH and DYER, Circuit Judges.

DYER, Circuit Judge: Appealing from an adverse judgment[1] in the court below, taxpayer, Tobin Armstrong, presents a novel question for our determination: Under the Internal Revenue Code of 1954 is it legally possible for a partner to be an employee of his partnership for purposes of section 119 of the Code? In granting the government's motion for summary judgment, the District Court answered this question in the negative. We disagree and reverse.

Taxpayer is the manager of the 50,000 acre Armstrong ranch located in Armstrong, Texas. Beef cattle are raised and some of the land contains certain mineral deposits. The ranch is owned by a partnership in which taxpayer has a five percent interest. In addition to his share of the partnership profits and a fixed salary for his services as manager of the ranch, the partnership provides taxpayer certain other emoluments which are the subject of this controversy. The partnership provides a home at the ranch for taxpayer and his family, most of the groceries, utilities and insurance for the house, maid service and provides for the entertainment of business guests at the ranch. Taxpayer did not include the value of these emoluments in his gross income for the years 1960, 1961 or 1962. The Internal Revenue Service determined that these items should have been included and therefore increased his taxable income by approximately $6,000[3] for each year involved. Taxpayer paid the assessed deficiencies, filed a refund claim, and no action having been taken thereon within the requisite period taxpayer brought this suit seeking to recover the paid deficiencies on the ground that he is an employee of the ranch and that, as such, he comes within the provisions of section 119 of the Internal Revenue Code of 1954 and is therefore entitled to exclude the value of the items in question from his gross income. Taxpayer filed an affidavit in support of his allegations and his deposition was taken. Each side moved for a summary judgment. The court granted the government's motion without an opinion and this appeal ensued.

The case law interpreting the 1939 Internal Revenue Code held that a partner

---

[1]On cross motions for summary judgment, the District Court entered a final judgment in favor of the District Director.

[3]Both sides agree that $6,000 correctly represents the yearly value of the items in question.

could not be an employee of his partnership under any circumstances, and that therefore no partner could take advantage of the "living expense" exclusion promulgated in the regulations and rulings under the 1939 Code.[5] Commissioner v. Robinson, 3 Cir. 1959, 273 F.2d 503; United States v. Briggs, 10 Cir. 1956, 238 F.2d 53; Commissioner v. Moran, 8 Cir. 1956, 236 F.2d 595; Commissioner v. Doak, 4 Cir. 1956, 234 F.2d 704.* The earlier cases, *Doak* and *Moran,* followed with little discussion by the later cases, were grounded on the theory, present throughout the 1939 Code, that a partnership and its partners are one inseparable legal unit. However, in 1954 Congress rejected this "aggregate theory" in favor of the "entity theory" in cases where "a partner sells property to, or performs services for the partnership." H.R. Rep. No. 1337, 83d Cong., 2d Sess. 67 (1954). Under the entity approach "the transaction is to be treated in the same manner as though the partner were an outsider dealing with the partnership." Id. This solution to the problem of the characterization of a partner's dealings with his partnership was codified as section 707(a) of the 1954 Code, 26 U.S.C.A. §707(a).

Considering the legislative history and the language of the statute itself, it was manifestly the intention of Congress to provide that in any situation not covered by section 707(b)-(c), where a partner sells to or purchases from the partnership or renders services to the partnership and is not acting in his capacity as a partner, he is considered to be "an outsider" or "one who is not a partner." The terms "outsider" and "one who is not a partner" are not defined by Congress; neither is the relationship between section 707 and other sections of the Code explained. However, we have found nothing to indicate that Congress intended that this section is not to relate to section 119.[8] Consequently, it is now possible for a partner to stand in any one of a number of relationships with his partnership, including those of creditor-debtor, vendor-vendee, *and* employee-employer. Therefore, in this case the government is not entitled to a judgment as a matter of law.[9]

Our reversal of the District Court is not dispositive of the issues upon which rest taxpayers ultimate right of recovery. On the record before us we cannot

---

[5]The provisions of section 119 were first codified in the 1954 Code. However, that section brings forward the Commissioner's basic policy under the 1939 Code. See Treas. Reg. 45, Art. 33 (1919); Treas. Reg. 118, §39.22(a)-3 (1939).

*But see, Wegener v. Commissioner, 5 Cir. 1941, 119 F.2d 49, cert. denied, 314 U.S. 643; Sverdrup v. Commissioner, 1950, 14 T.C. 859; Toy v. Commissioner, 1942, P-H Memo. T.C. ¶42.452.

[8]We are convinced that section 119 is not a provision where "the concept of the partnership as a collection of individuals is more appropriate," H. Conference Rep. No. 2543, 83d Cong., 2d Sess. 59 (1954), where Congress indicated that the "aggregate" approach is still to be used. This language from the legislative history, cited by the government, has a direct and logical connection with the provisions such as 26 U.S.C.A. §§701, 702. However, it is clear that this statement was not designed to prevent the use of the entity approach in cases such as the one sub judice. Cf., Burde v. Commissioner, 2 Cir. 1965, 352 F.2d 995, 1000; Weller v. Brownell, M.D. Pa. 1965, 240 F. Supp. 201, 210; Foster v. United States, D. Conn. 1963, 221 F. Supp. 288, 294-95.

[9]The only case presenting the question of whether under the 1954 Code a partner can stand in an employee-employer relationship with his partnership for purposes of the section 119 exclusion is Wilson v. United States, Ct. Cls. 1967, 376 F.2d 280, which held that such a relationship could not exist, relying on the 1939 Code cases discussed earlier in this opinion. However, the Court in *Wilson* did not consider the applicability or the effect of section 707, and does not, therefore, affect our consideration of the question before us.

resolve these issues, nor do we express any opinion on the final outcome of the case. Among the questions which must be answered are whether taxpayer is, in fact, an employee of the partnership; whether meals and lodging are provided for the convenience of the employer; whether living at the ranch is a condition of taxpayer's employment; whether taxpayer's wife and children are also employees and, if not, how much of the $6,000 must be allocated to their meals and lodging. These questions are not meant to be exhaustive, but are merely intended to give an indication of the nature of the inquiry into the merits which must be held on remand.[10]

Reversed and remanded.

NOTE

Is the decision in this case properly a function of "entity" vs. "conduit" theory? Does §707 provide the answer to the issue posed? What considerations would you think relevant in deciding the applicability of §119 to a partner? How would you have decided this case? Why? See Comment, A Partner Can Be the Employee of a Partnership, Says CA-5, 29 J. Taxation 48 (1968). See Burde v. Commissioner, 352 F.2d 995 (2d Cir. 1965), cert. denied, 383 U.S. 966 (1966), as to partners and §1235.

C. *GUARANTEED PAYMENTS; LOSSES; FISCAL YEAR*

FALCONER v. COMMISSIONER
40 T.C. 1011 (1963)

DAWSON, Judge: Respondent determined deficiencies in the petitioners' income taxes as follows:

Year	Deficiency
1957	$ 397.07
1958	1,114.85

---

[10] It should be noted in passing that we have considered and reject the government's contention, first raised on oral argument, that section 707(c) governs this case and prevents any exclusion from gross income under section 119 by taxpayer. There is no evidence in the record that the emoluments were "determined without regard to the income of the partnership," or that they consisted of "payments" rather than lodging and meals furnished in kind. Furthermore, even should evidence be produced on remand showing that these two requirements for the application of section 707(c) are present, such evidence would not affect the result in this case. Under section 707(c) such "payments to a partner for services . . . *shall* be considered as made to one who is not a member of the partnership . . . for the purpose of section 61(a) . . . ." (Emphasis added.) Section 61(a) defines gross income as "all income from whatever source derived," but with the proviso "except as otherwise provided in this subtitle." 26 U.S.C.A. §61(a). Thus section 61(a) incorporates the other sections of the subtitle, including section 119, and requires that the other provisions of the subtitle be considered and utilized in determining gross income. Cf., Foster v. United States, supra.

The issues for decision are:

(1) Whether amounts received by petitioner F. A. Falconer during the calendar years 1957 and 1958 from a partnership were guaranteed payments under the provisions of section 707(c), I.R.C. 1954, and taxable income to petitioners under section 61(a)(1).

(2) Whether amounts received by petitioner F. A. Falconer during the taxable year 1958 from a corporation are income to him in that year.

(3) Whether the petitioner F. A. Falconer is entitled to a deduction during taxable year 1958 as his share of the partnership's net operating loss. . . .

[Taxpayers are on the] calendar year basis and on the cash basis of accounting. . . .

On or about September 1, 1957, F. A. Falconer (hereinafter referred to as petitioner) entered into a partnership agreement with Stella Breazeale (sometimes hereinafter referred to as petitioner's partner) to operate an employment agency, doing business under the name of Acme Employment Service (sometimes referred to herein as the partnership). The partnership agreement, dated November 5, 1957, provided in pertinent part, as follows: . . .

> "6. As compensation for services to be rendered by the partners, each is to be paid as a salary the sum of $150.00 per week, such salaries to be paid on such date of the week as may be mutually agreed. . . . The salaries so paid insofar as the partners are concerned shall be considered as a part of the operating expense of the business.
>
> "7. It is recognized by the partners that Breazeale has advanced certain sums of money to the partnership and may advance additional sums before the business has attained a sufficient volume of business and attained successful operation so as to pay the operating costs and expenses. It is agreed when the income of the business is sufficient to meet the cost of operations, any and all excess of such income shall be paid monthly to Breazeale until she has been repaid in full all of such advances.
>
> "The ownership of the partnership business shall be on the basis of 50% by Falconer and 50% by Breazeale, and after all advances referred to in the preceding paragraph have been paid to Breazeale, the share of the net profits shall be paid to Falconer as to 50% and paid to Breazeale as to 50%; the division of the net profits and the payment of the same to the respective partners shall be at such time or times as the partners may from time to time mutually agree. In the event of losses accruing to the partnership, each partner shall contribute his or her 50% portion of such loss or losses so that each partner shall bear his or her just portion of such loss and thus avoid the necessity of either partner having to suffer the entire loss. Neither partner shall draw from the business more than his or her respective portion of the net profits without the written consent of the other. . . ."

The partnership continued in business until May 12, 1958, at which time it was dissolved and was succeeded by a corporation organized under the laws of the State of Texas. It adopted the name of Acme Employment Service, Inc. (sometimes hereinafter referred to as the corporation).

A partnership income tax return of petitioner and Stella Breazeale, doing business as the Acme Employment Service, was initially filed for the partnership for the period commencing September 1, 1957, and ending April 30, 1958, with the district director of internal revenue at Dallas, Tex. This return shows income in the amount of $6,434.80, operating expenses totaling $13,436.62, and a net loss of $7,001.82. It is labeled "First and Final Return."

After filing the first partnership income tax return, an unsigned partnership income tax return of petitioner and Stella Breazeale, doing business as the Acme Employment Service, for the period commencing January 1, 1958, and ending December 31, 1958, was filed with the district director of internal revenue at Dallas, Tex. A loss of $7,292.62 was shown on the return. By letter dated July 10, 1959, addressed to petitioner and Stella Breazeale, the district director advised them that the partnership income tax return had not been executed and requested them to execute a declaration which should have been signed on the return. The declaration was not executed and returned to the district director.

Subsequent to the filing of both of these partnership income tax returns, still another unsigned partnership return of petitioner and Stella Breazeale, doing business as the Acme Employment Service, covering the period commencing September 1, 1957, and ending June 30, 1958, was filed with the district director of internal revenue at Dallas, Tex. A loss of $7,292.62 was shown on this return. Attached thereto is a schedule designated "Withdrawals Made by F. A. Falconer." Such unexecuted return is identical with the return described in the preceding paragraph except that the period in the former return was interlined and another period substituted therefor. Such partnership income tax return has likewise not been executed.

During the calendar year 1957 the petitioner received weekly payments from the partnership under the terms of the partnership agreement aggregating $2,550, which sum was not reported by petitioners as income on their individual income tax return for such year or any other year.

During the period commencing September 1, 1957, and ending June 30, 1958, the petitioner received weekly payments aggregating $6,450, no part of which was reported by petitioners as income on their individual income tax return for the calendar year 1957, the calendar year 1958, or any other year.

Of such sum of $6,450, petitioner received income from the partnership under the terms of the partnership agreement in the amount of $2,850 from January 1, 1958, through May 10, 1958. From May 17, 1958, through June 28, 1958, petitioner received $1,050 from the corporation as salary, totaling $3,900 during the calendar year 1958, none of which was reported by petitioner in their income tax return for such year. The schedule attached to the last mentioned partnership return reflects the amounts paid by the partnership and the successor corporation and the dates such payments were made.

Petitioner made no contributions to the capital of the partnership. Stella Breazeale contributed all the capital of $19,775. Petitioner executed on May 12, 1958, which was the date the partnership dissolved, a demand promissory note, payable to the order of Stella Breazeale, in the principal sum of $9,862.50.

During the calendar year 1958 the petitioners claimed on their individual income tax return a loss of $3,646.31 from the operation of such partnership.

In his statutory notice of deficiency dated February 28, 1962, the respondent gave the following explanations for his adjustments:

"*1957.* (a) It is determined that the weekly payments aggregating $2,550.00, which you received from the partnership Acme Employment Service in 1957, and which were not reported on your return, constituted taxable income under the internal revenue laws. Adjusted gross income is being increased accordingly.

"*1958.* (a) It is determined that the weekly payments, aggregating $6,450.00, which you received from the partnership, Acme Employment Service and/or its successors, during the period September 1, 1957, through June 30, 1958, which were not reported on your returns, were taxable income to you for the calendar year 1958 under internal revenue laws. Accordingly, your 1958 income is being increased by $6,450.00.

"(b) It is determined that, under the internal revenue laws, you are not entitled to a deduction for any part of the loss of $3,646.31 alleged to have been incurred from the operation of the partnership, Acme Employment Service, in the years 1957 and 1958."

Issue 1. Guaranteed Payments

It is the petitioner's contention that the payments, totaling $5,400, which he received from the partnership in 1957 and 1958 were loaned to him by his partner, Stella Breazeale, and, therefore, created a debt to her, as evidenced by the demand promissory note executed on the date the partnership was dissolved. Respondent, on the other hand, argues that the amounts received constitute guaranteed salary payments under the provisions of section 707(c). We agree with the respondent.

Section 707(c) has no counterpart in the Internal Revenue Code of 1939. It initially appeared in the Internal Revenue Code of 1954. Since we have been unable to locate in our research any court decisions pertaining directly to the issue here presented, we approach the problem as one of first impression. . . . The legislative history of section 707(c) reveals that it was specifically intended to require ordinary income treatment to the partner receiving guaranteed salary payments and to give a deduction at the partnership level.[3]

---

[3] S. Rept. No. 1622 to accompany H.R. 8300, 83d Cong., 2d Sess., p. 387 (1954), contains the following explanation:

"Subsection (c) provides a rule with respect to guaranteed payments to members of a partnership. A partner who renders services to the partnership for a fixed salary, payable without regard to partnership income, shall be treated, to the extent of such amount, as one who is not a partner, and the partnership shall be allowed a deduction for a business expense. The amount of such payment shall be included in the partner's gross income, and shall not be considered a distributive share of partnership income or gain. A partner who is guaranteed a minimum annual amount for his services shall be treated as receiving a fixed payment in that amount."

The touchstone for determining "guaranteed payments" is whether they are payable without regard to partnership income. And, in determining whether in a particular case an amount paid by a partnership to a partner is a "drawing" or a "guaranteed payment," the substance of the transaction, rather than its form, must govern. See sec. 1.707-1(a), Income Tax Regs. These are both factual matters to be judged from all the circumstances.

We are convinced that the facts of this case clearly place the payments made to petitioner within the ambit of the term "guaranteed payments" as used in section 707(c). Paragraph 6 of the partnership agreement provided that each partner was to receive a salary of $150 per week from the partnership as compensation for services rendered; that the amount of the *compensation* agreed to was subject to change only by mutual agreement of the partners; and that such *salaries* were to be considered a part of the operating expenses of the business. . . . There is no doubt in our minds that these weekly salary payments were made "without regard to the income of the partnership." The partnership was being operated at a loss and, consequently, it was necessary to make the guaranteed salary payments out of the capital Stella Breazeale had contributed. Petitioner's mere characterization of the payments in the partnership returns as "withdrawals" is not persuasive when viewed in connection with the precise provisions of the partnership agreement. This leads us inescapably to the conclusion that the amounts received by petitioner from the partnership under the terms of the agreement are guaranteed payments without regard to the income of the partnership and, as such, are includable in his gross income.

Under the provisions of section 706(a) such payments are characterized as ordinary income to the recipient for his taxable year within or with which ends the partnership taxable year in which the partnership deducted the payments. Hence, the taxable year of the partnership must be first determined.

In view of these rules and the facts herein, this partnership could only adopt a calendar year basis. Since the petitioner reported his income on a calendar year basis during 1957 and 1958, and was a principal partner by virtue of owning a 50-percent interest in the partnership, the partnership was precluded from adopting a fiscal year basis without the prior approval of the Secretary of the Treasury or his delegate. The record not only fails to reveal such approval, but there is no evidence that such approval was ever sought. Thus, the only recourse remaining to the partnership was the adoption of a calendar year which under the specific language of section 1.706-1(b)(1)(ii), Income Tax Regs., does not require the prior approval of the Commissioner. . . . It then follows that the payments, totaling $2,550, made to petitioner during the partnership's taxable year ending December 31, 1957, were includable in his taxable income for the calendar year 1957. Since the partnership's existence terminated[7] upon its dissolution on May 12, 1958, the partnership taxable year was closed on that date.[8] As a result thereof, the guaranteed payments of $2,850 made by the partnership during the taxable year beginning January 1, 1958,

[7]Sec. 708. . . .
[8]Sec. 706. . . .

and ending May 12, 1958, were includable in petitioner's taxable income for the calendar year 1958.

Petitioner stresses that the "withdrawals by F. A. Falconer, constituted a loan to him and not income." We find no merit in this position. His attempt to cast the relationship between himself and Stella Breazeale as that of debtor and creditor is wholly inconsistent with the express terms of the partnership agreement and contrary to all outward manifestations of their intent. Nor are we swayed by the fact that the petitioner executed a demand note for $9,862.50 to Stella Breazeale on the day the partnership was terminated. We do not even know for what purpose the note was given. The petitioner, who has the burden of proof, offered no evidence regarding it. Consequently, any conclusions we might try to draw with respect to the note and the purpose for it would be purely speculative. Even if we assume, as petitioner would have us do, that the note represented the "withdrawals" by the petitioner from the partnership and "his part of the expenses" paid from the capital account, it cannot serve to convert what was paid as salaries into something else. Certainly the character of such payments cannot be changed retroactively into a loan.

Issue 2. Corporate Salary

The parties have stipulated that from "May 17, 1958, through June 28, 1958, petitioner received $1,050.00 from the corporation as salary, . . . none of which was reported in the income tax return of petitioners for such year." Because the payments were "salary," they are clearly includable in his gross income for 1958. See sec. 61(a)(1) . . . .

Issue 3. Net Operating Loss

At the outset of our discussion on this issue we observe that only the partnership return signed by the petitioner can be used for determining any partnership loss. The two later unsigned partnership returns are of no avail.[9]

From the inception of the partnership through its dissolution, the petitioner made no contributions to capital. By the provisions of section 704(d), a partner may deduct currently his portion of distributable losses only to the extent of the adjusted basis of his interest in the partnership. Stated differently, a partner in any accounting year may deduct all of his portion of partnership loss *only* if he has sufficient "capital" retained in the partnership. Thus a determination of the basis of petitioner's partnership interest becomes necessary. Section 705 sets forth the basis of a partner's interest. Insofar as pertinent here, section 705(a)(2)(A) provides that the adjusted basis of a partner's interest in a partnership shall be the basis of such interest determined under section 722 decreased (but not below zero) by the sum of his distributive share for the taxable years and prior taxable years of losses of the partnership. Since petitioner contributed neither money nor property to the partnership, the basis of his interest was zero. As previously noted, the petitioner's

[9]See section 6063, which requires that a partnership return must be signed by one of its partners.

distributive share of the partnership loss is limited by section 704(d) to his adjusted basis, which was also zero, in determining the amount allowable as a deduction under section 702(a)(9). Accordingly, we conclude that none of the loss of the partnership is deductible by petitioner in either 1957 or 1958. . . .

NOTE

1. When the court says that "the character of such payments [made to Falconer] cannot be changed . . . into a loan," is it disregarding the clear language of §761(c)? See Commissioner v. Jackson Investment Co., page 802 infra. Is there any indication given in the facts of the case that the note Falconer executed would not be paid? If he does pay the note what tax benefit will he be entitled to?

2. The "guaranteed payments" provision of §707(c) applies not only to payments for services but also to payments for the use of capital. If a partner is guaranteed a percentage return on his capital invested in the partnership, will §707(c) apply? What if a partner is guaranteed a 4 per cent return on his invested capital but otherwise is still entitled to share in the net profits of the business? In a case where the profit participation was less than the guaranteed minimum payment, the Commissioner ruled that only the difference between the distributive share and the minimum guarantee is a "guaranteed payment" for purposes of §707(c), notwithstanding provisions to the contrary in the partnership agreement. Therefore only that difference may be deducted as an expense under §162(a). Rev. Rul. 66-95, 1966-1 Cum. Bull. 169.

3. If the court in *Falconer* had been willing to recognize the bona fides of the note executed by the taxpayer, what would the basis in his partnership interest be? See §§752(a) and 722. Even disregarding the issue of the validity of the note, did not Falconer assume half the liabilities of the partnership in paragraph 7 of the Partnership Agreement? Therefore, under the cited provisions, did he not have a sufficient basis in his partnership interest to deduct the loss the court disallowed under §704(d)? Compare Rev. Rul. 68-629, 1968-2 Cum. Bull. 154.

4. Section 704(d) has its greatest effect in tax planning. In *Falconer* and in United States v. Frazell, page 746 supra, the business enterprises begun as partnerships eventually were converted into corporate form. This was more than likely done in order that in the early history of the business, when losses will be sustained, the investors are able to take those losses into their individual returns. However, after a business becomes successful it will be incorporated, and earnings will be taken out in salaries. However, §704(d) limits how effectively this device may be used. The case of Curtis W. Kingbay v. Commissioner, 46 T.C. 147 (1966), illustrates this. Taxpayer was a limited partner with a small capital contribution, which therefore limited the amount of losses which he could report as his distributive share. The one general partner was a corporation owned by a limited partner. The partnership owned property subject to mortgages on which only the corporate general partner was liable. Because of the §704(d) ceiling and the fact that the partnership was suffering losses, the limited partners argued that the corporation was a "dummy" and

that, therefore, no one partner was liable for the mortgage debt of the partnership. As a result, all the partners would be liable in the same proportion as they shared the profits. Under §752(a) this would increase the basis of the partnership interest of the limited partner. And, therefore, the distributive share of the losses could be reported in the individual partner's returns. The court held, however, that the form of the transaction would not be disregarded, for the taxpayer could show no valid reason for doing so.

5. The court in *Falconer* had to decide what the partnership's taxable year was. As it pointed out, the taxable year had to be a calendar year unless the Commissioner approved the adoption of a fiscal year. Since the Commissioner did not give such approval, the partnership's taxable year had to be a calendar year. Section 706(b)(1) requires such a holding, since the partnership must adopt the taxable year of its principal partners if the Commissioner has not approved otherwise. The Commissioner is not empowered to approve a taxable year of the partnership different from that of the principal partners unless the partnership can show a "business purpose" for so doing. The business purpose rule of §706(b) is not satisfied where the reason put forth is the partnership's desire to show a full year's operation in its first accounting period and to make it convenient for the partners to complete their individual returns. Rev. Rul. 60-182, 1960-1 Cum. Bull. 264.

The decision as to the partnership's taxable year is important, because this is used in determining in what year the individual partner must report his distributive share of the partnership's income and losses and any §707(c) "guaranteed payments" he has received. Section 706(a) provides that the inclusions required by §§702 and 707(c) must be reported by the partner in his taxable year for the taxable year of the partnership ending within or with the partner's taxable year. Thus if the partnership's taxable year ends on January 31, 1968, the partner on a calendar year does not report his income for that year until after the calendar year 1968 is over. Therefore, income earned for the most part during 1967 is taxed as 1968 income. The individual partner will be able thereby to postpone the payment of his taxes. The strict provisions of §706(b) were inserted in order to prevent such postponements. When will the advantage be converted into a disadvantage whereby income is "bunched up" and possibly greater taxes will be paid? See §706(c)(2). See also G. Horn, Taxable Years of Partners and Partnerships, 19 N.Y.U. Inst. on Fed. Tax. 297 (1961).

D. *"SALE" vs. "LIQUIDATION"; BASIS; TERMINATION; HOLDING PERIOD*

REVENUE RULING 66-264
1966-2 Cum. Bull. 248

As a result of litigation among equal partners of a five-man partnership, the court ordered all assets of the partnership to be sold at a judicial sale. Three of the five partners bought all of the assets and continued operation of the business. Each of the other two partners received a share of the sale proceeds in liquidation of his 20 per cent interest. Under the provisions of section 708(b) of the Internal Revenue Code of 1954, the partnership did not terminate.

Held, for Federal income tax purposes the transaction will not be treated as a sale of partnership assets to the three remaining partners, but will be considered as a sale or a liquidation of the partnership interests of the two withdrawing partners depending upon the facts and circumstances of the particular case.

MUSHRO v. COMMISSIONER
50 T.C. 43 (1968), non-acq. 1970-38 I.R.B. 5

FAY, Judge: . . . Certain issues raised in the pleadings were disposed of by concessions of the parties. The issues left for decision are (1) what are the tax bases of the interests which petitioners Victor G. Mushro and Louis A. Mushro held in the Algiers Motel partnership and (2) what is the total tax basis of the assets which the Algiers Motel partnership sold during its final taxable year.

Findings of Fact

. . . Victor G. Mushro (hereinafter referred to as Victor) and Luella Mushro are husband and wife. . . .

Louis A. Mushro (hereinafter referred to as Louis) and Anita A. Mushro are husband and wife. . . .

Because Luella Mushro and Anita Mushro are parties to these proceedings only by virtue of filing joint returns with their husbands, only the latter are hereinafter referred to as petitioners.

On September 1, 1953, Lawrence A. Mushro (hereinafter referred to as Lawrence), Victor, and Louis created a partnership called Algiers Motel (hereinafter referred to as the partnership). The partnership was in the business of owning and operating a motel in Detroit, Michigan. Victor, Louis, and Lawrence were brothers.

During the summer of 1956, the three partners agreed to enter into a buy-sell contract to be effective if one of them should die. They agreed that the estate of a deceased partner was to receive cash instead of an interest in the partnership. The cash was to be obtained from the proceeds of an insurance policy which each partner was to take out on his own life.

On June 16, 1956, Lawrence applied to the Crown Life Insurance Company (hereinafter referred to as insurance company) for a $125,000 ten-year term insurance policy on his life. Soon thereafter, the insurance company issued a policy. The policy number was 725,008. The beneficiary was Lawrence's wife, Pauline Mushro (hereinafter referred to as Pauline).

Later in the summer of 1956, the three partners engaged a lawyer to draw up a formal partnership agreement and a buy-sell contract. When the lawyer completed the job, Lawrence refused to sign the documents. He objected to the buy-sell agreement because it provided that the partnership was to be the beneficiary of the insurance policies on the lives of the partners. Lawrence insisted that Pauline was to be the beneficiary of the policy on his life. He was afraid that if the partnership was the beneficiary, and if he were the first to die, his brother might make it difficult for his estate to get its money under the buy-sell contract. The fear arose because of animosity between his brothers and his wife.

Because of Lawrence's objection to the buy-sell contract, Victor and Louis agreed to have it rewritten. They also decided to wait until a later time to sign the partnership agreement.

Early in September 1956, the lawyer submitted a new buy-sell contract and resubmitted the formal partnership agreement to the three partners. On September 5, 1956, the partners executed both documents.

The formal partnership agreement provided, inter alia, that the three partners were to share gains, losses, and capital equally and that Victor was to be the managing partner. The agreement also contained the following:

> "The partners further agree that they shall purchase insurance contracts for the payment of the proceeds of the policy to the beneficiary or estate of a deceased partner and that each of the partners agree to execute a partnership agreement as to said business life insurance. . . .
>
> "Upon the death or withdrawal of any of the partners, the co-partnership shall cease as to him, but shall continue as to the survivors or continuing partners in accordance with the terms of this agreement."

The relevant portions of the buy-sell contract were as follows:

> "*Whereas,* the partners desire to arrange for the sale to the partnership of the interests of any deceased partner in the partnership, and
>
> "*Whereas,* the partners believe it to be for their best interests and for the best interest of the partnership that the interest of a deceased partner be acquired by the partnership, and
>
> "*Whereas,* the partnership has arranged to provide the funds needed to acquire the interests of a deceased partner through life insurance policies on the lives of the partners.
>
> "*It Is Therefore Agreed:* . . .
>
> "2. The partnership shall be the owner of, and shall pay the premiums on all of the policies listed in Schedule 'A'. The partnership shall charge the account of each partner with a part of the premiums on all the policies proportionate to his interest in the partnership.
>
> "3. The policy or policies on the life of each partner shall be payable as a death claim to the beneficiary or beneficiaries designated in the policies by such partner. Each partner shall have the right to designate and to change the beneficiary of the policy or policies on his life, and to specify the method

of paying the insurance to said beneficiary and the other partners agree to join in any request for that purpose.

"Upon the death of a partner, the proceeds of the policy or policies, on his life shall, when approved for payment by the insurance company constitute payment in behalf of the surviving partners for so much of the partnership interest of the decedent as can be purchased with said insurance proceeds. . . .

"If the valuation of a decedent's interest in the partnership . . . is less than the amount of said insurance proceeds, the decedent's beneficiaries shall, nevertheless, retain the full amount of the insurance proceeds, and the excess shall be deemed as additional payment for the decedent's interest in the good will of the partnership.

"4. At the death of the partner, the surviving partners

"A. Shall be the sole owners of the partnership business and all the assets employed therein, both tangible and intangible, including the good will and the right to use the firm name;

"B. Shall assume full liability for and save the estate of the decedent harmless against all partnership debts and obligations; and

"C. Shall pay to the executor or administrators of the decedent the amount, if any, by which the value of the decedent's interest in the partnership . . . exceeds the amount of the proceeds of said policy or policies, if any, on decedent's life. . . ."

Because the buy-sell contract as finally written provided that the partnership was to own insurance policies on the lives of the partners, it became necessary to replace policy No. 725,008 which Lawrence owned on his life. On January 3, 1957, therefore, the partnership applied to insurance company for a $125,000 ten-year term insurance policy on Lawrence's life. On January 18, 1957, insurance company cancelled policy No. 725,008 as originally written and reissued it to the partnership. The reissued policy was the same as the original one, except that the partnership, rather than Lawrence, owned it.

On June 25, 1958, the partnership applied to insurance company to reduce the sum insured of policy No. 725,008 from $125,000 to $100,000. Insurance company complied with the request, thereby reducing the premium on the policy.

On November 5, 1960, Lawrence died as a result of injuries sustained in an automobile accident. On November 21, 1960, Pauline filed a claim with insurance company for the sum insured under policy No. 725,008.

Insurance company was reluctant to pay the sum insured to Pauline because it believed the partnership had a greater right to the money. It therefore requested Pauline and the partnership to agree with each other as to who should receive the money.

On December 15, 1960, the partnership dissolved. Victor, Louis, Pauline, and John B. Kiefer, co-executor with Pauline of Lawrence's estate, signed a dissolution agreement. The agreement provided, inter alia, that the sum insured under policy No. 725,008 belonged to Pauline. It further provided that the sum insured exceeded the value of Lawrence's interest in the partnership at the date of his death and that Pauline was entitled to the excess as payment for goodwill. The agreement also contained the following:

> "*Whereas* on the [5]th day of November, 1960, the aforesaid Lawrence Mushro died and thereupon the proceeds of the Crown Life Assurance [Insurance?] Company policy became due and payable to Pauline M. Mushro and . . . the proceeds thereof were to constitute payment on behalf of the surviving partners, parties of the first part, [in purchase] of the interest of Lawrence Mushro . . . in the partnership business owned by the first parties and said Lawrence Mushro, and . . .
>
> "*Whereas* . . . the proceeds of the insurance shall be applied in like manner as if said funds were paid by said first parties to [Pauline] in full payment of all right, title and interest of Lawrence Mushro (now deceased) in his share and interest in the partnership and the assets and good-will thereof . . .
>
> "*Now Therefore,* . . . The first parties herein agree to assume all of the obligations, debts, and liabilities, of the partnership firm known as the Algiers Motel and further agrees [sic] to save harmless the [party] of the second part [Pauline] . . ."

On December 23, 1960, the partnership formally assigned all its right, title, and interest in the proceeds of policy No. 725,008 to Pauline. Insurance company thereupon paid $99,613.81 to Pauline. On January 10, 1961, Pauline wrote insurance company claiming an additional $468 under the policy. On January 19, 1961, insurance company replied that it did not owe the claimed amount because it represented unpaid premiums for the policy year in which Lawrence died. Soon thereafter, the partnership paid the disputed amount to Pauline. Victor and Louis felt that the partnership should pay the final premium because it had paid all the others.

On January 27, 1961, Victor filed a "Certificate of Discontinuance of Co-Partnership" on behalf of the partnership with the Wayne County Clerk in Detroit. On the same day, Victor and Louis filed a "Certificate of Co-Partnership" with the Wayne County Clerk evidencing the creation of a new Algiers Motel partnership (hereinafter referred to as new partnership). The partners of new partnership were Victor and Louis.

On July 10, 1961, new partnership sold all its assets for $300,000. Part of the $300,000 was a land contract and chattel note in the face amount of $202,950. New partnership sold the land contract and note on August 24, 1961, for $174,559.45.

In September 1961, new partnership filed a final Federal income tax return. It covered the period beginning September 1, 1960, and ending August 24, 1961. The return reflected new partnership's sale of its assets. It also included new partnership's election under section 754 to utilize the optional basis-adjustment provisions of subchapter K. Pursuant to the election, new partnership increased the total basis of its assets by $63,850.63. The return included the following explanation of the basis adjustment:

FINAL RETURN

ALGIERS MOTEL

SCHEDULE OF COMPUTATION OF ADJUSTMENT TO BASIS OF PARTNERSHIP
ASSETS AS OF NOVEMBER 5, 1960

DATE OF DEATH OF LAWRENCE MUSHRO, PARTNER

Assets	Book Value	*Appraisal Value*
Fixed Assets	$187,006.56	$386,500.00
Current Assets	2,921.18	2,921.18
Goodwill	10,000.00	
TOTAL ASSETS	$199,927.74	$389,421.18

Liabilities	Book Value	*Appraisal Value*
Mortgage note on Land and Building	$ 92,077.48	$ 92,077.48
Mortgage note on Swimming Pool	4,828.50	4,828.50
Accounts Payable	4,083.71	4,083.71
Accrued Expenses	5,888.52	5,888.52
TOTAL LIABILITIES	$106,878.21	$106,878.21

Investment	Book Value	*Appraisal Value*
33.9% — Victor Mushro	$ 31,515.84	$ 95,782.07
32.4% — Louis Mushro	30,167.34	91,543.92
33.7% — Lawrence Mushro (deceased)	31,366.35	95,216.98
100.0% — TOTAL INVESTMENT	$ 93,049.53	$282,542.97
TOTAL LIABILITIES AND INVESTMENT	$199,927.74	$389,421.18

Per Code Sec. 743, Para. 3978, Regulations 1.743-1:
Lawrence Mushro's adjusted share of interest in
partnership property:

Fair Market Value of Lawrence Mushro interest at date of death		$ 95,216.98
Add, Share of liabilities (⅓ of $106,878.21) ..		35,626.07
Total		$130,843.05

Widow's share of the adjusted basis of partnership property:

Book value of husband's investment at date of death	$ 31,366.35	
Add: Share of liabilities (⅓ of $106,878.21) ..	35,626.07	
Total widow's share		66,992.42

Balance, equals amount to be added to the basis of partnership property	$ 63,850.63

As used in the above table, "book value" means tax basis.

On October 24, 1961, new partnership dissolved. On the same day, it distributed all its assets to Victor and Louis.

On their Federal income tax returns for 1961, petitioners reported their proportionate shares of the gain which new partnership reported from the sale of its assets. Neither petitioner, however, reported income from the dissolution of new partnership. Part of the reason for this was that each petitioner increased the basis of his interest in new partnership by $47,608.49. The increase for each petitioner was equal to one-half the value of Lawrence's interest in the partnership on the date of his death, exclusive of partnership goodwill.

In his statutory notice of deficiency, respondent increased the amount of gain reportable by each petitioner as his share of new partnership's gain from the sale of its assets. The ground for the increase was that new partnership was not entitled to increase the basis of its assets. Furthermore, respondent included in the income of each petitioner a gain from the dissolution of new partnership. The ground for the inclusion was that neither partner was entitled to increase the basis of his interest in new partnership.

Opinion

There are two issues for decision. First, did new partnership properly increase the basis of assets subsequent to Lawrence's death? Second, did petitioners properly increase the bases of their interests in new partnership subsequent to Lawrence's death?

To resolve these issues, we must first decide what happened to Lawrence's interest in the partnership when he died. Viewing the record as a whole, we think the realities of the situation are that either petitioners or new partnership received the proceeds of the insurance policy [on] Lawrence's life and then paid them to Pauline in exchange for Lawrence's interest in the partnership. It is true that Pauline was the named beneficiary of the life insurance policy. The policy was written this way, however, solely as a security device. Petitioners proved to our satisfaction that the three partners intended either the surviving partners or the partnership to receive the insurance proceeds and pay them to the deceased partner's beneficiary in exchange for his interest. The original buy-sell agreement was written in terms of this intention. Petitioners further proved that Lawrence, after seeing the original agreement, insisted that its terms be changed to circumvent any reluctance in his brothers to pay the policy proceeds to his wife if he were the first to die. Thus, for security reasons only, the terms of the buy-sell agreement were changed and Pauline was named the beneficiary of the insurance policy on Lawrence's life. Under the circumstances here presented, we feel constrained to heed the realities of the situation as reflected by the proved intent of the partners, not the labels which they were forced by the exigencies of life to apply to the realities of their transaction. Cf. Orr Mills, 30 T.C. 150 (1958), acq. 1958-2 Cum. Bull. 7.

In reaching this view of what happened to Lawrence's interest in the partnership when he died, we are not unmindful of the holding in Paul Legallet, 41 B.T.A. 294 (1940). Some of the facts in that case are similar to those in the case at bar. In *Legallet,* the Court found the realities of the situation to be that the beneficiary named in the insurance policy received the proceeds thereof when the partner-insured died. There is, however, a vital difference between *Legallet* and the case at bar. In *Legallet,* the reason the partners' wives were the beneficiaries of the insurance policies was to make it possible for the wife of the first partner to die to receive, in effect, an annuity for life. In the opinion in that case, we said:

> "In conference the question arose as to how the insurance on the policies then held would be paid to the wife of O'Neill. O'Neill wanted her to be certain to have fixed installments during her entire life. As then written, the policies provided a lump sum payment to the surviving partner and the agent suggested that a change was necessary if O'Neill wanted the insurance payable covering her entire life. The policies were changed as suggested by the agent." [41 B.T.A. at 297.]

When the partners in *Legallet* named their wives beneficiaries of the life insurance policies, they were carrying out their basic intent — to provide an annuity to the wife of the first partner to die. It follows that in *Legallet* the partners did not intend, in their buy-sell agreement, for anyone other than their wives to receive the proceeds of the insurance policies. In the case at bar, however, the partners' real intent was to have either the surviving partners or the partnership receive the insurance proceeds. When the partners named their wives beneficiaries of the policies, they were not carrying out their real intent; they were only creating a security device to satisfy Lawrence.

Having decided that Pauline did not in reality receive the proceeds of the insurance policy on Lawrence's life, it is now necessary to decide who — as between petitioners and new partnership — did receive them. Viewing the record as a whole, we find the realities of the situation to be that petitioners received the insurance proceeds. Although the record contains evidence going both ways, the greater weight of the evidence supports this view. While many paragraphs of the buy-sell contract are worded in terms of the partnership buying the deceased partner's share, paragraph 4.C. is as follows:

> "4. At the death of the partner, the surviving partners . . .
> "C. Shall pay to the executor or administrators of the decedent the amount, if any, by which the value of the decedent's interest in the partnership . . . exceeds the amount of the proceeds of said policy or policies, if any, on decedent's life. . . ."

This provision is strong evidence that the three partners actually intended the surviving partners to buy the deceased partner's interest. It also suggests that the references elsewhere in the contract to the partnership as the buyer are merely shorthand for saying that the surviving partners are the buyers. Furthermore, the language of the dissolution agreement consistently portrays the surviving partners, not the partnership, as the buyers. All in all, we think the partners intended to create a buy-sell agreement between themselves, not between the partnership and each of them.

It is now possible to decide whether the basis adjustments in issue were proper. We look first at the adjustment which each petitioner made to the basis of his interest in new partnership. Petitioners argue that these adjustments are supportable under section 705(a)(1)(B). We do not agree with this theory. Under our interpretation of the facts, new partnership did not, in reality, receive the insurance proceeds. It follows that section 705(a)(1)(B) is inapplicable to the facts of this case.

While we do not agree with petitioners' theory in regard to their basis adjustments, we think the adjustments themselves are supportable. We hold above that in reality petitioners bought Lawrence's interest in the partnership with the insurance proceeds. It follows that each petitioner had a cost basis pursuant to section 1012 for half of Lawrence's interest. See section 742 and Income Tax Regs. section 1.742-1. Because the interest which each petitioner acquired by purchase merged with his prior interest, each was entitled to increase the basis of his whole interest by the cost of the newly-acquired addition. Thus, we conclude that each petitioner is entitled, under section 1012, to increase the basis of his interest in new partnership by at least $47,608.49.

Looking at new partnership's basis adjustment, we hold that it too is supportable. New partnership made its adjustment pursuant to section 743(b)(1). Section 743(b) (1) provides for, inter alia, an adjustment to the basis of partnership assets with respect to persons who purchase an interest in a partnership. Because we hold that in reality petitioners purchased Lawrence's interest in the partnership, an adjustment under section 743(b)(1) is necessary and proper. We therefore hold that new partnership is entitled to increase the total basis of its assets by at least $63,850.63.

In summary, we hold that new partnership's basis adjustment was proper and that petitioners' basis adjustments were proper.

Reviewed by the Court.

Decisions will be entered under Rule 50.

[Concurring Opinion]

SIMPSON, Judge, concurring: I agree with the ultimate conclusions of the Court in this case, but I am not convinced by the attempt to distinguish *Legallet*. Of course, the evidence in the two cases is different, but in my view, the inferences to be drawn from the evidence are not significantly different. However, since the Court today does draw different inferences, its decision does in effect overrule *Legallet*, and I would say so.

NOTE

1. Suppose partners A, B, C, and D contributed property of equal value to the partnership, which presently has an adjusted basis of $100,000. Since the time the partnership was formed those assets appreciated in value, and they are now worth $400,000. At this time partner C wants to sell his partnership interest to partner B, who pays partner C $100,000. Is there any way that partner B can have the basis of the partnership assets adjusted so as to reflect his payment of $100,000 for partner C's interest? Section 743(b) permits partner B to increase the basis of the assets to

$125,000 as to him, but only if the partnership so elects under §754. What would the result be to B if all the partnership assets were sold and no §754 election were in effect? See Ford v. Commissioner, 6 T.C. 499 (1946), and §743(a). What if such an election were in effect? Similar adjustments are permitted in the case of the death of a partner. Section 755 provides rules for allocating such adjustments among the different properties of the partnership. For similar provisions for adjusting the basis of partnership property when the partnership distributes property to a partner in liquidation, see §734. See generally W. Hill, Bases of Partnership Interest, 15 N.Y.U. Inst. on Fed. Tax. 57 (1957).

2. Why do you think the Commissioner has non-acquiesced in *Mushro?*

FOXMAN v. COMMISSIONER
41 T.C. 535 (1964)

The Commissioner determined deficiencies in income tax for 1958 . . . against David A. and Dorothy A. Foxman, Horace W. and Judith Grenell, and Norman B. and Laura Jacobowitz, respectively. . . .

The principal issue common to all three cases is whether an agreement dated May 21, 1957, between petitioner Jacobowitz and petitioners Foxman and Grenell resulted in a "sale" of Jacobowitz's interest in a partnership to the two remaining partners under section 741, I.R.C. 1954, or whether the transaction must be considered a "liquidation" of Jacobowitz's partnership interest under sections 736 and 761(d). A second issue is whether $16,790 received by Jacobowitz represents his share of the partnership earnings for the period March 1-May 21, 1957, in accordance with the partnership agreement, as modified by the foregoing agreement of May 21, 1957, pursuant to section 761(c). The third issue, involving only Foxman and Grenell, is whether the partnership "terminated" on June 2, 1958, under section 708, by reason of a certain transaction, so as to render them accountable in their 1958 returns for their respective shares of distributive partnership income during the period March 1-June 2, 1958. . . .

Prior to 1954, Abbey Record Manufacturing Co. was a partnership composed of petitioner Jacobowitz and two associates named Zayde and Brody, engaged in the business of custom manufacturing of phonograph records. The enterprise had been founded about 1948, with Jacobowitz as the active principal. Prior to 1954 the partnership, hereinafter referred to as Abbey, manufactured primarily 10-inch 78 r.p.m records on contract for various companies. Petitioner Grenell purchased the interests of Zayde and Brody on December 31, 1953, and became an equal partner with Jacobowitz on January 2, 1954. Early in 1954 the partners agreed to enter the business of manufacturing 12-inch long playing records, known as LPs. Petitioner Foxman, who had been a consultant to the business when it was originally formed in 1948, was hired as a salaried employee in June 1954 to provide the necessary technical assistance for the changeover in machinery and production methods. Thereafter, as a result of certain agreements dated February 1, 1955, and January 26, 1956, Foxman, Grenell, and Jacobowitz became equal partners in Abbey, each with a one-third interest.

Abbey kept its accounts and filed its Federal income tax returns on an accrual basis of accounting and on the basis of a fiscal year ending February 28.

A related venture commenced by Jacobowitz, Foxman, and Grenell, individually, was represented by Sound Plastics, Inc., a corporation in which each owned one-third of the stock; it was engaged in the business of manufacturing "biscuits" or vinyl forms used in the making of records.

During the early period of the changeover to LPs, Abbey faced many problems in production and quality control. However, with Foxman and Jacobowitz in charge of production and with Grenell responsible for much of the selling, Abbey's fortunes were on the upswing. Its net income for the fiscal year ending February 29, 1956, was approximately $108,000, and for the fiscal year ending February 28, 1957, was approximately $218,000. Grenell, who acted as consultant and repertory director for two mail-order record companies, Music Treasures of the World and Children's Record Guild, was able to get these companies as customers of Abbey and they accounted for approximately 50-75 percent of Abbey's business.

The Agreement of May 21, 1957

Notwithstanding Abbey's success there was considerable disharmony among and between the partners. As a result there were discussions during the spring of 1956 relating to the withdrawal of Jacobowitz from Abbey. These negotiations did not lead to any agreement and the partners continued to work and to quarrel. Early in 1957, Foxman and Grenell decided to resolve the conflict by continuing the partnership without Jacobowitz and discussions were resumed again in March 1957. It was at about this time that Foxman offered Jacobowitz $225,000 in cash, an automobile which was in Abbey's name, and Foxman's and Grenell's interest in Sound Plastics, Inc., for Jacobowitz's interest in Abbey. Jacobowitz prepared a draft of an option agreement providing for Foxman's purchase of his one-third interest in the partnership and sent it to Foxman. Foxman never signed the option agreement. During the latter part of March or early April 1957, the negotiations of the three partners led to a tentative agreement whereby Jacobowitz's partnership interest would be purchased for $225,000 plus the aforementioned auto and stock in Sound Plastics, Inc. Jacobowitz, who did not trust either Foxman or Grenell, initially desired cash. Foxman and Grenell explored the possibilities of a $200,000 bank loan from the First National Bank of Jersey City, hereinafter referred to as First National, and informed First National of their tentative agreement to buy Jacobowitz's interest for $225,000; they had further discussions with First National concerning a possible loan on May 1, 1957, and on May 3, 1957. First National indicated, on the basis of an examination of the financial assets of Abbey, that it would consider a loan of approximately only $50,000.

The negotiations of the three partners culminated in an agreement dated May 21, 1957, for the "sale" of Jacobowitz's partnership interest; the terms of this agreement were essentially the same terms as the terms of the option agreement which Foxman did not execute.

Relevant portions of the May 21, 1957, agreement are as follows:

"Agreement, made this 21st day of May 1957, between Norman B.

Jacobowitz, hereinafter referred to as the 'First Party', and Horace W. Grenell, and David A. Foxman, individually, jointly and severally, hereinafter referred to as the 'Second Parties' and Abbey Record Mfg. Co., hereinafter referred to as the 'Third Party', Witnesseth:

"Whereas, the parties hereto are equal owners and the sole partners of Abbey Record Mfg. Co., a partnership, hereinafter referred to as 'Abbey', and are also the sole stockholders, officers and directors of Sound Plastics Inc., a corporation organized under the laws of the State of New York; and

"Whereas, the first party is desirous of selling, conveying, transferring and assigning all of his right, title and interest in and to his one-third share and interest in the said Abbey to the second parties; and

"Whereas, the second parties are desirous of conveying, transferring and assigning all of their right, title and interest in and to their combined two-thirds shares and interest in Sound Plastics, Inc. to the first party;

"Now, Therefore, It Is Mutually Agreed As Follows:

"*First:* The second parties hereby purchase all the right, title, share and interest of the first party in Abbey and the first party does hereby sell, transfer, convey and assign all of his right, title, interest and share in Abbey and in the moneys in banks, trade names, accounts due, or to become due, and in all other assets of any kind whatsoever, belonging to said Abbey, for and in consideration of the following:

"A) The payment of the sum of Two Hundred Forty Two Thousand Five Hundred & Fifty ($242,550.00) Dollars, payable as follows:

"$67,500.00, on the signing of this agreement, the receipt of which is hereby acknowledged:

"$67,500.00 on January 2nd, 1958;

"$90,000.00 in eighteen (18) equal monthly installments of $5,000.00 each, commencing on February 1st, 1958 and continuing on the first day of each and every consecutive month thereafter for seventeen (17) months;

"$17,550.00, for services as a consultant, payable in seventy-eight (78) equal weekly installments of $225.00 each, commencing on February 1st, 1958 and continuing weekly on the same day of each and every consecutive week thereafter for seventy-seven (77) weeks.

"The balance set forth hereinabove is represented by a series of non-interest bearing promissory notes, bearing even date herewith, and contain an acceleration clause and a grace period of ten (10) days.

"Said balance is further secured by a chattel mortgage, bearing even date herewith and contains a provision that same shall be cancelled and discharged upon the payment of the sum of $67,500.00 on or before January 2nd, 1958.

"The right is hereby granted to the second parties to prepay all or part of the balance due to the first party. If prepayment is made of both of the sums of $67,500.00 and $90,000.00 set forth above, prior to February 1st, 1958, there shall be no further liability for the balance of $17,550.00 or any of the payments of $225.00 weekly required thereunder. If such prepayment is made after February 1st, 1958, the first party shall be entitled to retain payments made to date of payment of the full sums of $67,500.00 and $90,000.00 (plus any weekly payments as aforesaid to date of payment) and there shall be no further liability for any remaining weekly payments.

"B) In addition to the payments required under paragraph 'A' hereof, the second parties hereby transfer, convey and assign all of their right, title and interest in Sound Plastics, Inc. to the first party. Simultaneously herewith, the second parties have delivered duly executed transfers of certificates of stock, together with their resignations as officers and directors of said Sound Plastics, Inc. Receipt thereof by the first party is hereby acknowledged.

"C) In addition to the payments required under paragraph 'A' hereof and the transfer of stock referred to in paragraph 'B' hereof, the second parties hereby transfer, convey and assign all of their right, title and interest in and to one, 1956 Chrysler New Yorker Sedan, as evidenced by the transfer of registration thereof, duly executed herewith, the receipt of which by the first party is hereby acknowledged. . . .

"*Fourth:* All parties do hereby agree that the true and accurate status of Abbey and Sound Plastics, Inc. as to liabilities and assets are reflected in the balance sheets attached hereto and made a part hereof and represent the true condition of the companies as of March 1, 1957. *First party shall not be entitled to any further share of profits that may accrue since March 1, 1957 and may retain any sums received therefrom to date hereof.* [Italicized words inserted by hand.] . . ."

Paragraph Twelfth of the agreement provides that "The first party [Jacobowitz] hereby retires from the partnership." The part of the agreement designating payment of $17,550 in weekly installments of $225 per week found in paragraph "First: A)" was embodied in a separate document also dated May 21, 1957; it was signed by Abbey, Foxman, and Grenell, respectively.

The chattel mortgage mentioned in "First: A)" of the agreement, in describing the translation provided for in the agreement of May 21, 1957, started in part: "the party of the second part [Jacobowitz] has sold, transferred, assigned and conveyed all his right, title and interest as a partner . . . to the parties of the first part [Foxman and Grenell, individually and trading as Abbey]."

Samuel Feldman, a New York City attorney who represented Foxman and Grenell, drafted the agreement of May 21, 1957; at Feldman's suggestion, Abbey was added as a party to the agreement. An earlier draft of the proposed agreement did not include Abbey as a party. During the negotiations leading to the May 21, 1957, agreement, the words "retirement" or "liquidation of a partner's interest" were not mentioned. There was no specific undertaking by the third party (Abbey) any place in the instrument. A sale of a partnership interest was the only transaction ever discussed.

Jacobowitz unsuccessfully tried to obtain guarantees of payment of the notes he held from the wives of Foxman and Grenell; he was also unsuccessful in trying to obtain the homes of Foxman and Grenell as security on the notes.

The first $67,500 payment due on the signing of the agreement was made by cashier's check. On the promissory note due January 2, 1958, the name of Abbey appears as maker; the signatures of Foxman and Grenell appear on the face of the note as signatories in behalf of Abbey and on the back of it as indorsers. The 18 promissory notes, each in the amount of $5,000, also bear the signatures of Foxman and Grenell on the face of the instrument as signatories in behalf of Abbey, the maker, and on the back of the instrument as indorsers.

Payments to Jacobowitz pursuant to the May 21, 1957, agreement were timely made. Foxman and Grenell made an election to prepay pursuant to "First: A)" of the May 21, 1957, agreement, and Jacobowitz returned the series of 18 promissory notes of Abbey, in the amount of $5,000 each, and the promissory note of Abbey in the amount of $17,550 payable in 78 weekly installments of $225. Jacobowitz was paid this $90,000 amount by check with Abbey's name appearing as drawer and the names of Foxman and Grenell appearing as signatories in behalf of Abbey; they did not indorse this check. Payments made to Jacobowitz for his interest were charged to Abbey's account. The parties did not contemplate any performance of services by Jacobowitz in order for him to receive the $17,550 under the May 21, 1957, agreement; this amount was considered by the parties either as a penalty or in lieu of interest if Foxman and Grenell failed to pay the $90,000 amount prior to February 1, 1958. . . .

On May 21, 1957, Foxman and Grenell entered into an agreement providing for a continuation of the Abbey partnership which recited that Abbey had purchased the interest of Jacobowitz in Abbey. . . .

The reported earnings of Abbey for the fiscal year ending February 28, 1958, without reduction for alleged payments to partners, were $303,221.52.

In its tax return for the fiscal year ending February 28, 1958, Abbey treated the sum of $159,656.09 as a distribution of partnership earnings to Jacobowitz in the nature of a guaranteed payment under section 736 of the Internal Revenue Code of 1954. This amount was computed as follows:

Cash payments	$225,000.00
Value of automobile	2,812.82
Share of Jacobowitz's liabilities	32,455.18
Total partnership payments	260,268.00
Less Jacobowitz's share of partnership property	100,611.91
Balance	159,656.09

Jacobowitz, on the other hand, treated the transaction as a sale in his return for 1957, reporting a long-term capital gain in the amount of $164,356.09.

The $16,790 Item

Jacobowitz received $16,790 from Abbey during the period March 1, 1957, to May 21, 1957; the books and records of Abbey show that $2,790 was debited to an account entitled "Salaries-Partners," and $14,000 was debited to his drawing account. Abbey had earnings before partners' salaries of $39,807.43, $38,164.32, and $27,478.26 for the months of March, April, and May 1957, respectively. This $16,790 amount was reported by Jacobowitz on his 1957 income tax return as ordinary income, and was subtracted from the partnership income for its fiscal year ending February 28, 1958, in determining the distributive shares of Foxman and Grenell.

The handwritten insertion in Paragraph Fourth of the May 21, 1957, agreement was made at Jacobowitz's suggestion so that he could keep the foregoing $16,790 received by him during the period March 1 to May 21, 1957; it was also a waiver of his right to the balance of his share of Abbey's earnings during that period, and thus constituted a modification of the partnership agreement in respect of his distributive share of earnings for that period.

The May 29-June 2, 1958, Transfer of the Record Manufacturing Business to Abbey Record Manufacturing Co., Inc.

For some time prior to May 9, 1958, Richard D. Gittlin, in behalf of himself and two brothers, A. S. Gittlin and B. Morton Gittlin, had been negotiating with Foxman and Grenell to acquire a one-half interest in the Abbey enterprise. These negotiations culminated in an agreement executed May 9, 1958, by Foxman, Grenell, and the Gittlins. The agreement contemplated the payment of $300,022.98 by the Gittlins who would emerge as the owners of 50 percent of the stock and debentures of a corporation named Abbey Record Manufacturing Co., Inc., which was to succeed to the entire business and assets of the partnership; the remaining 50 percent of the stock and debentures was to be owned by Foxman and Grenell individually. The corporation had been organized on April 11, 1955, with Foxman, Grenell, and an employee of the partnership named Ben Goldman, each owning five shares of stock. The corporation had remained dormant since its incorporation and had no assets of any consequence prior to the transaction here under consideration. The agreement of May 9, 1958, contemplated that the 15 outstanding shares would be cancelled and new shares and debentures issued in accordance with the agreement. The agreement provided in form for a sale of the fixed assets of the partnership to the Gittlins for $300,022.98, such fixed assets to be transferred by them, in turn, to the corporation. . . .

On May 29, 1958, Abbey transferred its fixed assets to R. D. Gittlin for $300,022.98, $300,000 of which was in the form of three promissory notes; and R. D. Gittlin, at about the same time, transferred the identical fixed assets to the corporation for 500 shares of its capital stock and $200,000 6-percent 10-year debentures. Also, on May 29, 1958, Abbey transferred its remaining assets, subject to its liabilities, to the corporation in return for 500 shares of the latter's capital stock and $200,000 6-percent 10-year debentures, all of which were distributed to Foxman and Grenell in equal amounts. The original 15 shares of stock which had been issued on April 13, 1955, to Foxman, Grenell, and Ben Goldman, were canceled.

Abbey reported a capital gain of $201,550.40 in a partnership return filed by it for the fiscal year ending February 28, 1959, in respect of the foregoing "sale" of its assets to the Gittlins. . . .

In a letter agreement dated May 29, 1958, Foxman and Grenell, purporting to act "individually and as partners trading as Abbey Record Mfg. Co.," agreed to pay $15,000 to a man named Lawrence Jasie for his services in bringing about the foregoing transaction with the Gittlins. . . .

In connection with the transfer of assets to the corporation, Abbey closed out its then existing asset and liability accounts. Abbey, upon receiving the aforementioned notes from the Gittlins in exchange for its fixed assets, recorded their receipt in an entry in its journal. Abbey also set up a liability account, Accrued Commissions Payable, in the amount of $15,000 to accrue the commission due to Lawrence Jasie. . . .

The three aforementioned $100,000 notes issued by the Gittlins bore interest at 5 percent and were payable to the order of Foxman and Grenell, trading as Abbey; the notes were due on July 15, 1958, September 2, 1958, and January 15, 1959, respectively. On May 29, 1958, Foxman and Grenell discounted the $100,000 note due on July 15, 1958, and shared equally the $99,995.74 proceeds of the discounted note. Foxman and Grenell redeposited $20,000, in total, to their capital accounts. The remaining $200,000 notes were retained by Abbey until paid; the final payment was received on or about January 15, 1959.

Abbey's sole business activity was the manufacture of phonograph records; prior to June 2, 1958, it never owned any real estate or mortgages. After the transfer of assets to the corporation on May 29, 1958, Abbey did not engage in the manufacture of phonograph records, and did not have any sales income or any expenses from the manufacture of phonograph records.

Upon the advice of an accountant, in an effort to prevent the termination of the partnership, Foxman and Grenell began to look for some income-producing property for Abbey prior to June 2, 1958. In furtherance of that objective Abbey purchased a 6-percent mortgage in the face amount of $5,000 on July 28, 1958, and thereafter, on September 16, 1958, it purchased real estate for about $6,500 or $7,000 from the wife of one of the partners in the accountant's firm. The real estate was in a "very low-income housing area," and consisted of land and a frame residential building containing several apartments. The return filed on behalf of Abbey for the fiscal year ending February 28, 1959, showed rents of $485 from this property, but a net loss of $62.11 after deducting expenses and depreciation. Neither the foregoing mortgage nor the real estate was related in any way to Abbey's previous record manufacturing business. Subsequent to June 2, 1958, Abbey received not only the foregoing rent but also interest on the mortgage and interest on the Gittlin notes. Foxman and Grenell had no intention of terminating Abbey during 1958.

On January 13, 1959, an agreement was entered into between Foxman and Grenell whereby Grenell purchased Foxman's interest in Abbey, his 250 shares of stock in the corporation, his $100,000 6-percent 10-year debentures of the corporation, and his 220 shares of stock in Arco Recording Corporation, which had been organized to handle sales for the corporation. In return, Foxman received $65,000, an automobile belonging to the corporation, and the assumption by Grenell of Foxman's deficit in his capital account in Abbey in the amount of $1,200. Various distributions had previously been made by Abbey to Foxman and Grenell.

At the time of the sale by Foxman there was outstanding the $10,000 liability to Jasie and Abbey had among its assets the then unmatured third Gittlin $100,000 note and the mortgage and property purchased after June 2, 1958.

On January 13, 1959, there was filed with the State of New Jersey a "Cancellation of Business Name, Form 868" which noted the dissolution of Abbey.

On April 11, 1959, the Gittlins sold their 50-percent stock interest in the corporation and the $200,000 face value debentures to Grenell for $410,000. On April 11, 1959, the corporation sold its assets to National Aircraft Corporation for $750,000 cash. . . .

Opinion

RAUM, Judge: 1. *Tax consequences of termination of Jacobowitz's interest in Abbey; the agreement of May 21, 1957.* — On May 21, 1957, Jacobowitz's status as a partner in Abbey came to an end pursuant to an agreement executed on that day. The first issue before us is whether Jacobowitz thus made a "sale" of his partnership interest to Foxman and Grenell within section 741 of the 1954 Code, as contended by him, or whether the payments to him required by the agreement are to be regarded as "made in liquidation" of his interest within section 736, as contended by Foxman and Grenell. Jacobowitz treated the transaction as constituting a "sale," and reported a capital gain thereon in his return for 1957. Foxman and Grenell, on the other hand, treated the payments as having been "made in liquidation"[4] of Jacobowitz's interest under section 736, with the result that a substantial portion thereof reduced their distributive shares of partnership income for the fiscal year ending February 28, 1958.

The Commissioner, in order to protect the revenues, took inconsistent positions. In Jacobowitz's case, his determination proceeded upon the assumption that there was a section 736 "liquidation," with the result that payments thereunder were charged to Jacobowitz for the partnership fiscal year ending February 28, 1958, thus not only attributing to Jacobowitz additional income for his calendar year 1958 but also treating it as ordinary income rather than capital gain. In the cases of Foxman and Grenell, the Commissioner adopted Jacobowitz's position that there was a section 741 "sale" on May 21, 1957, to Foxman and Grenell, thus disallowing the deductions in respect thereof from the partnership's income for its fiscal year ending February 28, 1958; as a consequence, there was a corresponding increase in the distributive partnership income of Foxman and Grenell for that fiscal year which was reflected in the deficiencies determined for the calendar year 1958 in respect of each of them.

As is obvious, the real controversy herein is not between the various petitioners and the Government,[5] but rather between Jacobowitz and his two former partners. We hold, in favor of Jacobowitz, that the May 21, 1957, transaction was a "sale" under section 741.

The provisions of sections 736 and 741 of the 1954 Code have no counterpart in prior law. They are contained in "Subchapter K" which for the first time, in 1954, undertook to deal comprehensively with the income tax problems of partners and partnerships.

That a partnership interest may be "sold" to one or more members of the partnership within section 741 is not disputed by any of the parties. . . . Regulations, section 1.741-1(b). . . . And it is clear that in such circumstances, sections 736 and 761(d), do

---

[4]"Liquidation" of a partner's interest is defined in section 761(d) as follows: . . .
[5]The Government has undertaken, on brief for the first time, to support Jacobowitz's position.

not apply. See regulations, sec. 1.736-1(a)(1)(i). . . . Did Jacobowitz *sell* his interest to Foxman and Grenell, or did he merely enter into an arrangement to receive "payments . . . in liquidation of [his] . . . interest" from the partnership? We think the record establishes that he sold his interest.

At first blush, one may indeed wonder why Congress provided for such drastically different tax consequences, depending upon whether the amounts received by the withdrawing partner are to be classified as the proceeds of a "sale" or as "payments . . . in liquidation" of his interest.[7] For, there may be very little, if any, difference in ultimate economic effect between a "sale" of a partnership interest to the remaining partners and a "liquidation" of that interest. In the case of a sale the remaining partners may well obtain part or all of the needed cash to pay the purchase price from the partnership assets, funds borrowed by the partnership or future earnings of the partnership. See A.L.I., Federal Income Taxation of Partners and Partnerships 176 (1957). Yet the practical difference between such transaction and one in which the withdrawing partner agrees merely to receive payments in liquidation directly from the partnership itself would hardly be a meaningful one in most circumstances.[8] Why then the enormous disparity in tax burden, turning upon what for practical purposes is merely the difference between Tweedledum and Tweedledee, and what criteria are we to apply in our effort to discover that difference in a particular case? The answer to the first part of this question is to be found in the legislative history of subchapter K, and it goes far towards supplying the answer to the second part.

In its report on the bill which became the 1954 Code the House Ways and Means Committee stated that the then "existing tax treatment of partners and partnerships is among the most confused in the entire tax field"; that "partners . . . cannot form, operate, or dissolve a partnership with any assurance as to tax consequences"; that the proposed statutory provisions [subchapter K] represented the "first comprehensive statutory treatment of partners and partnerships in the history of the income tax laws"; and that the "principal objectives have been simplicity, flexibility, and equity as between the partners." H. Rept. No. 1337, 83d Cong., 2d Sess., p. 65. Like thoughts were expressed in virtually identical language by the Senate Finance Committee. S. Rept. No. 1622, 83d Cong., 2d Sess., p. 89.

[7]If the transaction were a "sale" under section 741, Jacobowitz's gain would be taxed as capital gain (there being no section 751 problem in respect of unrealized receivables or inventory items which have appreciated substantially in value), and would be reportable in 1957 rather than in 1958. On the other hand, if the transaction were a section 736 "liquidation," the amounts received by him (to the extent that they were not for his "interest . . . in partnership property" pursuant to section 736(b)(1)) would be taxable as ordinary income and would be reportable by him in 1958, rather than in 1957. The tax liabilities of the remaining partners, Foxman and Grenell, would be affected accordingly, depending upon whether section 736 or 741 governed the transaction.

[8]The only difference suggested by counsel for Foxman and Grenell, for the first time in their reply brief, is that in the event of bankruptcy of the partnership the liability to the withdrawing partner might be subject to a different order of priority depending upon whether there is involved the liability of the partnership itself, as in the case of a "liquidation," or the liability of the purchasing partners, as in the case of a "sale." However, it stretches credulity to the breaking point to assume that any such consideration motivated the parties in determining to enter into a "sale" rather than a "liquidation," or vice versa, where the only immediate matter of economic consequence was the substantial difference in tax liability depending upon which course was followed.

Although there can be little doubt that the attempt to achieve "simplicity" has resulted in utter failure, the new legislation was intended to and in fact did bring into play an element of "flexibility." Tax law in respect of partners may often involve a delicate mechanism, for a ruling in favor of one partner may automatically produce adverse consequences to the others. Accordingly, one of the underlying philosophic objectives of the 1954 Code was to permit the partners themselves to determine their tax burdens inter sese to a certain extent, and this is what the committee reports meant when they referred to "flexibility." The theory was that the partners would take their prospective tax liabilities into account in bargaining with one another.[10] . . .

Recurring to the problem immediately before us, this policy of "flexibility" is particularly pertinent in determining the tax consequences of the withdrawal of a partner. Where the practical differences between a "sale" and a "liquidation" are, at most, slight, if they exist at all, and where the tax consequences to the partners can vary greatly, it is in accord with the purpose of the statutory provisions to allow the partners themselves, through arm's-length negotiations, to determine whether to take the "sale" route or the "liquidation" route, thereby allocating the tax burden among themselves. And in this case the record leaves no doubt that they intended to and in fact did adopt the "sale" route.

The agreement of May 21, 1957, indicates a clear intention on the part of Jacobowitz to sell, and Foxman and Grenell to purchase, Jacobowitz's partnership interest. The second "whereas" clause refers to Jacobowitz as "selling" his interest and part "First" of the agreement explicitly states not only that the "second parties [Foxman and Grenell] hereby purchase . . . the . . . interest of . . . [Jacobowitz] . . . in Abbey," but also that "the first party [Jacobowitz] does here sell" his interest in Abbey. Thus, Foxman and Grenell obligated themselves *individually* to purchase Jacobowitz's interest. Nowhere in the agreement was there any obligation on the part of Abbey to compensate Jacobowitz for withdrawing from the partnership. Indeed, a portion of the consideration received by him was the Sound Plastics stock, not a partnership asset at all. That stock was owned by Foxman and Grenell as individuals and their undertaking to turn it over to Jacobowitz as part of the consideration for Jacobowitz's partnership interest reinforces the conclusion that *they as individuals* were buying his interest, and that the transaction represented a "sale" of his interest to them rather than a "liquidation" of that interest by the partnership. Moreover, the chattel mortgage referred to in part "First" of the agreement of May 21, 1957, states that Jacobowitz "has sold . . . his . . . interest as a partner."

In addition to the foregoing, we are satisfied from the evidence before us that Foxman and Grenell knew that Jacobowitz was interested only in a sale of his partnership interest. The record convincingly establishes that the bargaining between them was consistently upon the basis of a proposed sale. And the agreement

---

[10]Whether this was a realistic assumption in view of the large number of small partnerships that may not have the benefit of the highly specialized tax advice required, or whether, in view of the almost incomprehensible character of some of the provisions in subchapter K, the parties could with confidence allocate the tax burden among themselves — these are matters on which we express no opinion. The point is that Congress did intend to provide a certain amount of "flexibility" in this respect.

of May 21, 1957, which represents the culmination of that bargaining, reflects that understanding with unambiguous precision. The subsequent position of Foxman and Grenell, disavowing a "sale," indicates nothing more than an attempt at hindsight tax planning to the disadvantage of Jacobowitz. . . .

Nor is their position measurably stronger by reason of the fact that Jacobowitz was given promissory notes signed in behalf of Abbey. These notes were endorsed by Foxman and Grenell individually, and the liability of Abbey thereon was merely in the nature of security for their primary obligation under the agreement of May 21, 1957. The fact that they utilized partnership resources to discharge their own individual liability in such manner can hardly convert into a section 736 "liquidation" what would otherwise qualify as a section 741 "sale." . . . While we do not suggest that it is never possible to look behind the words of an agreement in dealing with problems like the one before us, the considerations which Foxman and Grenell urge us to take into account here are at best of an ambiguous character and are in any event consistent with the words used. We hold that the Commissioner's determination in respect of this issue was in error in Jacobowitz's case but was correct in the cases involving Foxman and Grenell. . . .

2. *The $16,790 received by Jacobowitz from Abbey.* — During the period March 1, 1957, to May 21, 1957, inclusive, Jacobowitz received a total of $16,790 from Abbey, and reported it as ordinary income in his 1957 return. The Commissioner treated this item as reportable by Jacobowitz in 1958, but made a corresponding inconsistent adjustment in the cases of Foxman and Grenell by ruling that this amount was improperly subtracted from the partnership income for its fiscal year ending February 28, 1958, in computing the distributive shares of Foxman and Grenell. Jacobowitz now contends that this item represented merely a withdrawal of capital. We hold that Jacobowitz correctly reported this amount as ordinary income in his 1957 return, and that it was properly taken into account by Foxman and Grenell in the computation of their distributive shares of partnership income in their 1958 returns.

Section 702(a) requires a partner to take into account his distributive share of the partnership's taxable income in determining his income tax. Section 704(a) provides that a partner's distributive share of income shall be determined by the partnership agreement. Under section 761(c) a partnership agreement "includes any modifications of the partnership agreement made prior to, or at, the time prescribed by law for the filing of the partnership return for the taxable year (not including extensions) which are agreed to by all the partners, or which are adopted in such other manner as may be provided by the partnership agreement." The effect of such modification is that it relates back to the beginning of the taxable year in which the modification occurs. Thus the partners may, by agreement, adjust among themselves their interests in earnings and are taxable accordingly. . . .

Prior to May 21, 1957, the partners shared profits equally. In paragraph Fourth of the agreement of May 21, 1957, the following handwritten provision was inserted at the request of Jacobowitz: "First party [Jacobowitz] shall not be entitled to any further share of profits that may accrue since March 1, 1957 and may retain any sums received therefrom to date hereof." Absent this modification of the partners' agreement to share net profits equally, Jacobowitz would have had to include in his taxable income for his taxable year ending December 31, 1957, one-third of Abbey's earnings during the period March 1, 1957, to May 21, 1957,[16] since the taxable year of Abbey closed on May 21, 1957, under section 706(c)(2)(A)(i) with respect to Jacobowitz, who sold his entire interest in Abbey at that time, although it did not close at that time, pursuant to section 706(c)(1), in respect of the remaining partners.

The language "may retain any sums received therefrom to date hereof" plainly refers to the $16,790, which, the record shows, consists in part of "salary" and in part of "drawings." Jacobowitz's own testimony bears this out. He testified that it was his intention that the $16,790 represented moneys coming out of profits and pursuant to this reported it as ordinary income in his 1957 return. The option letter prepared by Jacobowitz also indicates that this amount was intended to be a charge against profits; it stated, in part: "Pending final settlement, you [Jacobowitz] will continue to draw $225.00 per week. If we consummate the agreement, you [Jacobowitz] relinquish all rights to profits and drawings from March 1, 1957, except those you have already received."

We are satisfied that the $16,790 reflects Jacobowitz's share of Abbey profits for the period March 1, 1957, to May 21, 1957, and was ordinary income to him for his taxable year ending December 31, 1957; Foxman and Grenell are entitled to have Abbey's income for the year ending February 28, 1958, reduced by that amount in computing their respective shares of Abbey profits for that fiscal year.

3. *Whether Abbey "terminated" on June 2, 1958* — By amendments to the Commissioner's pleadings a number of additional issues are raised, all of them depending in the first instance upon a new major issue as to whether Abbey "terminated" on June 2, 1958, within the meaning of section 708. These new matters do not involve Jacobowitz; they relate solely to Foxman's and Grenell's cases.

Abbey was on a fiscal year ending February 28, and Foxman and Grenell each reported in his 1958 return his distributive share of Abbey's income for its fiscal year ending February 28, 1958, as reflected in the partnership return for that fiscal year. The first two issues in these cases, dealt with above, relate to a revision of Abbey's reportable income and the distributive shares of the partners for Abbey's fiscal year ending February 28, 1958. The third issue, now under consideration, relates to Abbey's income realized *after* February 28, 1958. A "final" return was filed on Abbey's behalf purportedly for the fiscal year ending February 28, 1959, and Foxman and Grenell reported in their own returns for the calendar year 1959 their respective distributive shares of the income shown on that partnership return. The Commissioner, on the other hand, has taken the position in his amended pleadings that Abbey "terminated" on June 2, 1958, with the consequence that Foxman and Grenell were charged in 1958 with their distributive shares of Abbey's income for the short taxable year March 1, 1958, to June 2, 1958, in addition to their distributive shares for the full fiscal year ending February 28, 1958. Important subsidiary issues are also raised in this respect by the Commissioner involving the determination of the partnership's income for that short period. These subsidiary issues include the question

[16]Abbey had earnings, before partners' salaries in the amounts of $39,807.43, $38,164.32, and $27,478.26 for the months of March, April, and May 1957, respectively.

whether the transfer of Abbey's assets to the corporation was non-recognizable under section 351, the amount of gain realized if the transfer were recognizable, the amount of partnership income otherwise realized by Abbey during the period March 1-June 2, 1958, which in turn depends in part upon a proposed revision by the Commissioner of the depreciation allowance claimed on Abbey's behalf. We hold that Abbey did not terminate on June 2, 1958, as urged by the Commissioner. The subsidiary issues in this connection therefore become moot.

Upon consummation of the so-called Gittlin transaction on June 2, 1958, all of Abbey's assets had been transferred to the corporation, and the stock and debentures allocable to Abbey had been distributed to Foxman and Grenell. Also, the first of the three $100,000 Gittlin notes had been discounted and the proceeds distributed to Foxman and Grenell. Nevertheless, Foxman and Grenell promptly redeposited an aggregate of $20,000 of such proceeds to their capital accounts in Abbey, and Abbey continued to own the two remaining $100,000 Gittlin notes, one due on September 2, 1958, and the other on January 15, 1959. Moreover, there were still outstanding the two Jasie notes in the amounts of $5,000 each, due July 1, 1959, and January 2, 1960. The evidence further shows that in an effort to prevent the termination of Abbey, Foxman and Grenell began looking for income-producing property prior to June 2, 1958, to be purchased in behalf of Abbey. Two such items were in fact purchased by Abbey, a mortgage in July and rental property in September of 1958. While it is true that these items were of comparatively minor character in contrast to the enterprise previously carried on by Abbey, the fact that they were actually acquired by Abbey cannot be ignored. Abbey did receive interest on the Gittlin notes after June 2, 1958, as well as interest on the mortgage and rents from the real estate. It continued to be liable on the Jasie notes. Its affairs were not wound up on June 2, 1958. Cf. Income Tax Regs., sec. 1.708-1(b)(1)(iii). . . . We hold that the Commissioner has failed to establish that Abbey "terminated" on June 2, 1958. . . .

FOXMAN v. COMMISSIONER
352 F.2d 466 (3d Cir. 1965), aff'g 41 T.C. 535

Before McLaughlin, Hastie and Smith, Circuit Judges.

William F. Smith, Circuit Judge.

This matter is before the Court on petitions to review decisions of the Tax Court, 41 T.C. 535, in three related cases consolidated for the purpose of hearing. The petitions of Foxman and Grenell challenge the decision as erroneous only as it relates to them. The petition of the Commissioner seeks a review of the decision as it relates to Jacobowitz only if it is determined by us that the Tax Court erred in the other two cases. . . .

In its partnership return for the fiscal year ending February 28, 1958, the Company treated the sum of $159,656.09, the consideration received by Jacobowitz less the value of his interest in partnership property, as a guaranteed payment made in liquidation of a retiring partner's interest under §736(a)(2) of the Internal Revenue Code of 1954, Title 26 U.S.C.A. This treatment resulted in a substantial reduction of the distributive shares of Foxman and Grenell and consequently a proportionate decrease in their possible tax liability. In his income tax return Jacobowitz treated the sum of $164,356.09, the consideration less the value of his partnership interest, as a long term capital gain realized upon the sale of his interest. This, of course, resulted in a tax advantage favorable to him. The Commissioner determined deficiencies against each of the taxpayers in amounts not relevant to the issue before us and each filed separate petitions for redetermination.

The critical issue before the Tax Court was raised by the antithetical positions maintained by Foxman and Grenell on one side and Jacobowitz on the other. The former, relying on §736(a)(2), supra, contended that the transaction, evidenced by the contract, constituted a liquidation of a retiring partner's interest and that the consideration paid was accorded correct treatment in the partnership return. The latter contended that the transaction constituted a sale of his partnership interest and, under §741 of the Code, 26 U.S.C.A., the profit realized was correctly treated in his return as a capital gain. The Tax Court rejected the position of Foxman and Grenell and held that the deficiency determinations as to them were not erroneous; it sustained the position of Jacobowitz and held that the deficiency determination as to him was erroneous. The petitioners Foxman and Grenell challenge that decision as erroneous and not in accord with the law.

It appears from the evidence, which the Tax Court apparently found credible, that the negotiations which led to the consummation of the contract of May 21, 1957, related to a contemplated sale of Jacobowitz's partnership interest to Foxman and Grenell. The option offered to Foxman and Grenell early in May of 1957, referred to a sale and the execution of "a bill of sale" upon completion of the agreement. The relevant provisions of the contract were couched in terms of "purchase" and "sale." The contract was signed by Foxman and Grenell, individually, and by them on behalf of the Company, although the Company assumed no liability thereunder. The obligation to purchase Jacobowitz's interest was solely that of Foxman and Grenell. The chattel mortgage on the partnership assets was given to secure payment.

Notwithstanding these facts and the lack of any ambiguity in the contract, Foxman and Grenell argue that the factors unequivocally determinative of the substance of the transaction were: the initial payment of $67,500 by a cashier's check issued in exchange for a check drawn on the account of the Company; the second payment in a similar amount by check drawn on the Company's account; the execution of notes in the name of the Company as maker; and, the prepayment of the notes by cashier's check charged against the Company's account.

This argument unduly emphasizes form in preference to substance. While form may be relevant "[t]he incidence of taxation depends upon the substance of a transaction." Commissioner of Internal Revenue v. Court Holding Co., 324 U.S. 331, 334, 65 S. Ct. 707, 708, 89 L. Ed. 981 (1945); United States v. Cumberland Pub. Serv. Co., 338 U.S. 451, 455, 70 S. Ct. 280, 94 L. Ed. 251 (1950). The "transaction must be viewed as a whole, and each step, from the commencement of negotiations" to con-

summation, is relevant. Ibid. Where, as here, there has been a transfer and an acquisition of property pursuant to a contract, the nature of the transaction does not
depend solely on the means employed to effect payment. Ibid.

It is apparent from the opinion of the Tax Court that careful consideration was
given to the factors relied upon by Foxman and Grenell. It is therein stated, 41 T.C.
at page 553:

> "These notes were endorsed by Foxman and Grenell individually, and the
> liability of [the Company] thereon was merely in the nature of security for
> their primary obligation under the agreement of May 21, 1957. The fact that
> they utilized partnership resources to discharge their own individual liability
> in such manner can hardly convert into a section 736 'liquidation' what
> would otherwise qualify as a section 741 'sale'."
>
> ". . . the payments received by Jacobowitz were in discharge of their
> [Foxman's and Grenell's] obligation under the agreement, and not that of
> [the Company]. It was they who procured those payments in their own be-
> half from the assets of the partnership which they controlled. The use of
> [the Company] to make payment was wholly within their discretion and of
> no concern to Jacobowitz; his only interest was payment."

We are of the opinion that the quoted statements represent a fair appraisal of
the true significance of the notes and the means employed to effect payment.

When the members of the partnership decided that Jacobowitz would withdraw
in the interest of harmony they had a choice of means by which his withdrawal
could be effected. They could have agreed inter se on either liquidation or sale. On a
consideration of the plain language of the contract, the negotiations which preceded
its consummation, the intent of the parties as reflected by their conduct, and the circumstances surrounding the transaction, the Tax Court found that the transaction
was in substance a sale and not a liquidation of a retiring partner's interest. This
finding is amply supported by the evidence in the record. The partners having employed the sale method to achieve their objective, Foxman and Grenell cannot avoid
the tax consequences by a hindsight application of principles they now find advantageous to them and disadvantageous to Jacobowitz.

The issue before the Tax Court was essentially one of fact and its decision thereon may not be reversed in the absence of a showing that its findings were not supported by substantial evidence or that its decision was not in accord with the law.
Cleveland v. C. I. R., 335 F.2d 473, 477 (3rd Cir. 1964), and the cases therein cited.
There has been no such showing in this case.

The decisions of the Tax Court will be affirmed.

NOTE

See C. Lewis, Tax Aspects of Sale or Termination of a Partnership Interest, 45
Taxes 324 (1967); R. Swihart, Tax Problems Raised by Liquidations of Partnership
Interests, 44 Texas L. Rev. 1209 (1966); Comment, Careful Phrasing of Partnership
Agreement a Must, 28 J. Taxation 42 (1968); Comment, 52 Geo. L.J. 651 (1964).

REVENUE RULING 67-65
1967-1 Cum. Bull. 168

Advice has been requested whether the surviving partner in a two-man partnership who purchased the deceased partner's interest from his estate, acquired the assets represented thereby through a distribution within the meaning of section 735(b) of the Internal Revenue Code of 1954, so that in computing his holding period for assets attributable to the partnership interest purchased by him from the deceased partner's estate, he may include the period those assets were held in the partnership.

D and E were equal partners in a two-man partnership engaged in the wholesale produce business. Upon D's death, E purchased, pursuant to a buy and sell agreement, and through the use of his own funds, the decedent's interest in the partnership from his estate. Thereafter, the business was continued by E as a sole proprietorship.

Section 708(b)(1)(A) of the Code provides that a partnership shall terminate when the operations of the partnership are discontinued and no part of any business, financial operation or venture of the partnership continues to be carried on by any of its partners in a partnership.

Section 1.708-1(b)(1)(i) of the Income Tax Regulations implements section 708(b)(1)(A) of the Code with an example which states that on November 20, 1956, A and B, each of whom is a 20-percent partner in partnership ABC, sell their interests to C, who is a 60-percent partner. Since the business is no longer carried on by any of its partners in a partnership, the ABC partnership is terminated as of November 20, 1956.

Accordingly, in the instant case, the sale of D's partnership interest to E resulted in termination of the partnership under section 708(b)(1)(A) of the Code since the business is no longer carried on by any of its partners in a partnership.

Section 735(b) of the Code provides that in determining the period for which a partner has held property received in a distribution from a partnership there shall be included the holding period of the partnership, as determined under section 1223, with respect to such property.

Although it is recognized that one partner in a two-man partnership may sell his partnership interest to his partner (sec. 1.741-1(b) of the regulations), such a transaction is viewed as though one partner acquired by purchase, the assets attributable to the partnership interest sold by the other partner. No distribution of property by the partnership occurred with respect to such assets. However, the purchasing partner is considered to have received as a distribution in kind, through liquidation of his partnership interest, those assets attributable to his own former interest in the partnership.

Accordingly, section 735(b) of the Code is applicable with respect to the assets attributable to E's partnership interest. Hence, his holding period for those assets include the holding period of the partnership. However, section 735(b) of the Code is not applicable with respect to the assets attributable to the partnership interest purchased from D's estate. Therefore, E's holding period for those assets does not include the holding period of the partnership, and runs from the date of his purchase of D's partnership interest. See Edwin E. McCaulsen v. Commissioner, 45 T.C. 588 (1966).

NOTE

1. Why in both *Foxman* (page 780 supra) and Rev. Rul. 67-65 is it important to determine whether or not the partnership terminates? See §§708, 706(c) and (a).

2. "Sale" under §741 has been found to exist even where the selling partner gave to the buying partners a covenant not to compete and contacted clients to persuade them to remain with the partnership. Atkinson v. Commissioner, 23 CCH Tax Ct. Mem. 834 (1964); similarly a "sale" under §741 was held to have occurred despite the fact that the purchase price was 25 per cent of gross fees billed the taxpayer's former clients for three years subsequent to taxpayer's withdrawal—simply a method of valuing the interest. Wheeling v. Commissioner, 23 CCH Tax Ct. Mem. 778 (1964). Normally, a sale of a partnership interest under §741 qualifies for capital gains treatment. Rev. Rul. 59-109, 1959-1 Cum. Bull. 168. Section 751 provides otherwise in cases in which the partnership owns "unrealized receivables" or "inventory items."

3. Although a transaction is characterized as a liquidation, capital gains treatment may still be available to the retiring partner (§§736(b) and 731(a)). For an instance where a retiring partner received no assets on dissolution of the partnership, but still was entitled to only a capital loss, see Stilwell v. Commissioner, 46 T.C. 247 (1966). This case involved the dissolution of a two-man partnership where all assets of the partnership were transferred to one partner who also assumed all the partnership liabilities. The court found that this was a liquidation, and the issue was the proper treatment of the retiring partner's loss. The court held it was a capital loss in spite of the fact that no property was actually distributed to the retiring partner. The assumption of the liabilities was a distribution within the meaning of §731(a), which follows from the basis adjustment provisions of §752(a) and (b). Therefore §731(a), in conjunction with §741, requires a finding that the loss was capital rather than ordinary.

4. How can the death of a partner in a two-man partnership be prevented from terminating the partnership? See §§706(c) and 708. For a case in accord with Rev. Rul. 67-65, supra, see McCauslen v. Commissioner, 45 T.C. 588 (1966). See Treas. Reg. §1.708-1(b)(1)(i). See also P. Little, Partnership Terminations and Reorganizations, 13 N.Y.U. Inst. on Fed. Tax. 897 (1955).

5. The normal rule on dissolution of a partnership is that no gain will be recognized by the partners if no money is distributed in dissolution (§§736(b) and 731(a)(1)). Therefore, on both formation and dissolution the partners need not recognize gain. Assume that A owns appreciated X Corporation stock and B owns appreciated Y Corporation stock. Both A and B wish to diversify their stock holdings, but in order to do so they must sell some of the stock they own, recognize their gains, and then be able to buy stock in other companies; or they could swap their

stock with each other. In either event they would have taxable transactions. Could they avoid this result by contributing their stock to the AB partnership and then dissolving the partnership so that each would get an equal amount of X Corporation and Y Corporation stock? Will the distribution be tax-free under §731? See Treas. Reg. §1.731-1(c)(3) and Rev. Rul. 57-200, 1957-1 Cum. Bull. 205. See also R. Skeehan, Transfer of a Partnership Interest: Problems on Admission of New Partner and Withdrawal of Old Partner, 28 N.Y.U. Inst. on Fed. Tax. 541 (1970).

In Rev. Rul. 57-200, A and B, individuals, owned a one-half interest in Corporations X and Y. The partnership had been in existence for a number of years. Desiring to sever their business relationship, A and B contributed their stock in the X and Y Corporations to the partnership. The partnership was dissolved with A receiving certain assets and all stock in the X Corporation, while B received certain assets and the stock in the Y Corporation. The Commissioner ruled that the contribution of the stock to the partnership and the subsequent dissolution constituted a single taxable exchange of the stock between the partners. Therefore §731 does not apply to that extent, and the partners must recognize gain or loss as if they had exchanged the assets. On what authority would the Commissioner argue this case if it reached court? In holding that §731 was inapplicable to the liquidating distribution, did the Commissioner assume that §721 had been applicable to the transfers into the partnership? Should he have held that §721 was inapplicable? If so, on what ground?

REVENUE RULING 68-215
1968-1 Cum. Bull. 312

Advice has been requested whether the estate of a decedent, under the circumstances described below, is required to include in its first return the decedent's distributive share of partnership taxable income for the partnership taxable year in which he died.

A, a member of the M partnership, died on September 15, 1964. Both A and the M partnership report income on the cash receipts and disbursements method of accounting and use a calendar year accounting period. A's distributive share of the taxable income of M partnership for the period January 1, 1964, through September 15, 1964 (the date of his death) is 50x dollars of which 20x dollars was distributed to A prior to his death.

The partnership agreement provides that upon the death of a partner, his estate is entitled to receive his share of profits of the partnership realized and remaining undistributed at the time of his death, and any guaranteed amounts payable in lieu of amounts earned while the decedent was a partner but not realized by the partnership at time of his death.

At the time of A's death, three rights existed with respect to his partnership interest as follows: (1) the right to undistributed amounts of his share of profits earned and realized by the partnership before calendar year 1964; (2) the right to undistributed amounts of his share of profits earned and realized by the partnership from the beginning of 1964 to the date of A's death; and (3) the right to guaranteed payments of designated amounts in lieu of amounts earned while the decedent was a partner but not realized by the partnership at the time of A's death.

Under the terms of his will, A bequeathed to each of five beneficiaries an equal portion of the right which he had at the date of his death to receive undistributed amounts of his share of the profits earned and realized by the partnership from the beginning of 1964 to the date of his death. He also bequeathed to those beneficiaries in equal shares any guaranteed amounts to which he had a right under the terms of the partnership agreement. Pursuant to the terms of the will, on December 1, 1964, the executor of the estate assigned to each beneficiary a one-fifth interest in these two rights.

The bequest to the five beneficiaries specifically excluded A's right to undistributed amounts of his share of profits earned and realized by the partnership before calendar year 1964.

The estate reports income on the cash receipts and disbursements method of accounting and uses a fiscal year accounting period ending February 28.

Section 706(c)(1) of the Internal Revenue Code of 1954 provides the general rule that, except in the case of a termination of a partnership, the taxable year of a partnership shall not close as the result of the death of a partner.

Section 1.706-1(c)(3)(i) of the Income Tax Regulations provides, in part, that when a partner dies, the partnership taxable year shall not close with respect to such partner prior to the end of the partnership taxable year.

Section 1.706-1(c)(3)(ii) of the regulations provides, in part, that the last return of a decedent partner shall include only his share of partnership taxable income for any partnership taxable year or years ending within or with the last taxable year for such decedent partner. The distributive share of partnership taxable income for a partnership taxable year ending after the decedent's last taxable year is includible by his estate or other successor in interest in the return filed for the taxable year within or with which the taxable year of the partnership ends.

Section 1.706-1(c)(3)(v) of the regulations provides that to the extent that any part of a distributive share of partnership income of the estate or other successor in interest of a deceased partner is attributable to the decedent for the period ending with the date of his death, such part of the distributive share is income in respect to the decedent under section 691 of the Code. Similarly section 1.753-1(b) of the regulations provides that when a partner dies, the entire portion of the distributive share which is attributable to the period ending with the date of his death and which is taxable to his estate or other successor is income in respect of a decedent under section 691 of the Code.

Although section 691 of the Code and the regulations thereunder provide special rules for the reporting of income in respect of a decedent, those rules do not govern the time for reporting a deceased partner's distributive share of partnership income for the partnership's taxable year in which the decedent died. Instead, section 706 of the Code and the regulations thereunder are applicable, as provided in section 1.706-1(c) of the regulations. Under section 1.706-1(c)(3)(ii) of the regulations a deceased partner's distributive share of partnership income for the partnership's taxable year in which the decedent died is includible in the gross income of the estate or other successor in interest in its taxable year within or with which the taxable year of the partnership ends, even though there may not have been a distribution by the partnership of the amounts involved.

A's estate became successor in interest upon his death and, as such, it became the owner of the partnership interest held by the decedent. As successor in interest and owner of the partnership interest, A's estate acquired the right to receive the payments specified in the partnership agreement. Since the estate did not assign to the five beneficiaries the right to receive undistributed amounts of his share of profits earned and realized by the partnership before 1964, the estate remained the successor in interest to the entire partnership interest of the decedent as of the end of the partnership taxable year ending December 31, 1964.

Accordingly, the estate of the decedent is required to include in its gross income in its first taxable year, 50x dollars, the amount of the distributive share of partnership taxable income for the partnership taxable year ending December 31, 1964.

NOTE

See S. Bauman, Income in Respect of a Deceased Partner, 1963 So. Calif. Tax Inst. 383.

E. *GOODWILL*

SMITH v. COMMISSIONER
313 F.2d 16 (10th Cir. 1963)

Before PICKETT, BREITENSTEIN and HILL, Circuit Judges.

HILL, Circuit Judge. . . . The facts necessary for our disposition of the case are not in dispute. In January, 1947, V. Zay Smith (petitioner) and three other individuals formed a partnership known as Geophoto Services (Geophoto) for the purpose of engaging in the business of evaluating geological structures based upon aerial photography, which was to be used in the search for petroleum and petroleum reserves. Petitioner, at the time of World War II, was a geologist and, from his experience as a photo intelligence officer in the Navy, conceived the idea of using aerial photography for evaluating geological structures in the search for oil and petroleum.

The original partnership agreement was for a period of five years. Immediately prior to its expiration and on December 31, 1952, the articles of partnership were revised to provide a means of expelling one of the partners.[2]

[2]Paragraph 25 of the revised articles provided:
"If a majority of the partners at any time decide . . . that some other partner (hereinafter referred to as specified partners) [should] cease to be a member of the partnership, then . . . , the

The partnership prospered during the next four years of the 5 year period of the partnership agreement, with petitioner receiving substantial net income for his share. In January, 1957, the other three partners voted to expel petitioner as a partner in Geophoto. In accordance with paragraph 25 of the revised articles, petitioner received the consideration agreed upon therein.[4] The total amount of $77,000.00 was paid to petitioner in the form of a check for $72,740.71 and an automobile of an agreed upon value of $4,259.29. It was stipulated, however, that the book value of petitioner's interest in the partnership on the date in question was $53,264.61, thereby leaving a payment to him of $2,045.45 as salary and a payment of $21,689.94 as a "premium", for a total payment over and above his partnership interest of $23,735.39.

In their income tax return for the year 1957, petitioners reported the excess over and above his partnership interest in the amount of $23,735.39 as a capital gain — this figure includes the salary payment of $2,045.45. The Commissioner of Internal Revenue determined that the entire excess of $23,735.39 was ordinary income and, accordingly, made a deficiency assessment of $6,992.20 in their income tax for 1957.

. . . The Commissioner's position before the Tax Court was that the $23,735.39 payment to petitioner was in liquidation of his interest in the partnership and, accordingly, it was taxable as ordinary income under Section 736(a). . . . Specifically, the Commissioner contended that the $2,045.45 salary payment should be taxed as a guaranteed payment under paragraph (2) of subsection (a) and the remainder as a distributive share of partnership income under paragraph (1) thereof.

Petitioners argued that the questioned amount was a payment for "good will" and should be treated as a capital gain under section 736(b) of the Act, 26 U.S.C. §736(b). Specifically, they urged that paragraph (2)(B) of subsection (b) applied. Beyond any question, the $2,045.45 was ordinary income and no further discussion of that item is necessary.

The Tax Court rejected petitioners' contention and, in holding that the questioned amount should be treated as ordinary income, acknowledged this was a case of first impression. The provisions of Section 736 first became embodied in the tax

---

said majority, by their unanimous vote, and upon tender to the specified partner of the consideration agreed to in this paragraph 25 may expel the specified partner. . . . The amount to be paid to the specified partner on his expulsion as the agreed consideration for his said interest is the then book value of his interest in the partnership as carried on the books of the partnership plus a premium equal to forty (40%) percent of so much of such book value as does not exceed $50,000.00, plus 15 (15%) percent of so much of said book value as exceeds $50,000.00, but does not exceed $80,000.00, plus seven and one-half (7½) percent of so much of said book value as exceeds $80,000.00, but does not exceed $100,000.00 (no premium to be payable on account of any part of the book value over $100,000.00). . . ."

[4]Such consideration may be summarized as follows:

1. Total net worth of the partnership as of Dec. 31, 1956.	$215,873.34
2. Petitioner's ¼ share	53,968.34
3. Premium — 40% of $50,000.00	20,000.00
15% on capital over $50,000.00	595.25
4. Additional premium to increase amount to even figure	390.96
5. Salary from 1-1-57 to 1-21-57	2,045.45
Total	$ 77,000.00

law by the enactment of the 1954 Internal Revenue Code. This was the first time the Congress attempted to specifically cover by statute the tax situation arising when a partnership interest is in fact liquidated by payments from the partnership to the retiring or withdrawing partner. The situation here is not that of a partner selling his interest to another partner or a third party. If that was the situation, the government concedes, and we agree, that Section 741 . . . would be applicable, as contended by the taxpayer. We agree with the Tax Court that under the facts Section 736 provides the proper tax treatment.

From a careful reading of Section 736 and consideration of the Senate Finance Report[7] made at the time the new legislation was before the Congress, the intended scope of such Section appears clear. Paragraph (2)(B) of subsection (b) exempts from ordinary income treatment payments made for good will only when the partnership agreement so provides specifically and does not permit an intent to compensate for good will to be drawn from the surrounding circumstances as the taxpayer here urges us to do. In fact, the partnership agreement here specifically states ". . . In determining the value or the book value of a deceased or retiring partner's interest, no value shall be assigned to good will, . . ."

. . . [W]e think the payment in question should be treated as ordinary income rather than capital gain since the articles of partnership do not specifically provide that the payment is for good will. If intent is to be determined by something other than the plain language of the partnership agreement, uncertainty and confusion will becloud the issue and the efforts of Congress to clarify a complex situation will go for naught. Important, also, is the fact that this result treats fairly both the expelled partner and the remaining partners as the tax consequences are determined in advance by the contract to which they all agreed.

The decision of the Tax Court is Affirmed.

NOTE

1. Are the partners free to characterize whatever amount they wish as "goodwill"? See Rev. Rul. 57-480, 1957-2 Cum. Bull. 47, and Rev. Rul. 60-301, 1960-2 Cum. Bull. 15.

2. In Butler v. Commissioner, 46 T.C. 280 (1966), the Tax Court held that a taxpayer-accountant who practiced as a sole proprietorship could sell an interest in his goodwill to an employee on the formation of a partnership with the employee. Since goodwill is a capital asset, he is entitled to capital gains treatment. The government argued that a professional person cannot, on formation of a partnership, sell goodwill since he retains an interest in the partnership. Therefore, the payment was really for a relinquishment of rights to receive ordinary income in the future or a present payment for future services. The court rejected this argument. How would you have decided the case? Why?

[7] 3 U.S. Cong. & Adm. News (1954) p. 5037 . . . .

F. *THE "AGREEMENT"*

COMMISSIONER v. JACKSON INVESTMENT CO.
346 F.2d 187 (9th Cir. 1965)

Before BARNES, DUNIWAY and ELY, Circuit Judges.

BARNES, Circuit Judge: . . . The amounts in controversy involve distributions made by respondents, Jackson Investment Company and West Shore Company, partners in George W. Carter Company, to a retiring partner, Ethel M. Carter. Petitioner concluded that the distributions were not deductible expenses, and, consequently, assessed deficiencies against Jackson in the aggregate amount of $9,848.18 and against West Shore in the aggregate amount of $15,577.85. The Tax Court, however, rendered a decision adverse to the Commissioner. . . .

The question presented for our consideration involves the construction of Section 736. . . .

The intended purpose of this provision was to permit the participants themselves to determine whether the retiring partner or the remaining partners would bear the tax burdens for payments in liquidation of a retiring partner's interest. Thus, under the general approach of subsection (a), the tax burden is borne by the retiring partner — he recognizes the payments as taxable income, and the remaining partners are allowed a commensurate deduction from partnership income. Under subsection (b), the general rule conceives an approach of nonrecognition of ordinary income to the retiring partner, but places the tax burden on the partnership by denying a deduction from income for the payments. This latter subsection, however, adopts a special rule — (b)(2)(B) — in an express effort to assist the participants to decide inter sese upon the allocation of the tax burden. This special rule lies at the heart of the present controversy. Under this rule, payments for the good will of the partnership are deductible by the partnership (and hence recognizable as ordinary income to the retiring partner) "except to the extent that the partnership agreement provides for a payment with respect to good will." If the partnership agreement provides for a payment with respect to good will, the tax burden is allocated to the partnership — no deduction is allowed and the retiring partner need not recognize the payments as ordinary income. In the present case, petitioner contends that this exception under Section 736(b)(2)(B) applies, and thus the deductions taken by the partnership should be disallowed. We must determine, therefore, whether the parties intended to place the tax burden on the partnership by expressly incorporating into the partnership agreement a provision for payment to the retiring partner with respect to good will.

It is undisputed that the original Partnership Agreement did not contain a provision for partnership good will or a payment therefor upon the withdrawal of a partner. On May 7, 1956, however, the three partners executed an instrument entitled "Amendment of Limited Partnership Agreement of George W. Carter Co." . . . This instrument provided for Ethel Carter's retirement, and bound the partnership to compensate Ethel in the amount of $60,000.00 in consideration for her withdrawal. After the necessary adjustment of the figures, it was determined that $19,650.00 of the amount was in return for Ethel's "15% interest in the fair market value of all the net assets of the partnership." The other $40,350.00, the amount in controversy here, was referred to as "a guaranteed payment, or a payment for good will." . . . The $40,350.00 was paid by the partnership in three annual parts, and deductions were made for good will expense in the partnership net income for each of the years. It is these deductions that petitioner challenges.

The decision of the Tax Court (six judges dissenting), concluded that the document entitled "Amendment of Limited Partnership Agreement of George W. Carter Co." was not a part of the partnership agreement, and therefore, the exception of Section 736(b)(2)(B) was not applicable. As a result, the court held that the amounts in question were legitimate deductions from the partnership income under the terms of Section 736(a)(2). The court founded its conclusion on the fact that the "Amendment" was solely designed to effect a withdrawal of one of the partners; it was not at all concerned with any continued role for Ethel in the partnership affairs.

We cannot agree with the interpretation of the majority of the Tax Court. We find this view unduly interferes with the clear objective of the statute, i.e., to permit and enable the partners to allocate the tax burdens as they choose, and with a minimum of uncertainty and difficulty. If a partnership agreement such as the one involved here, had no provision regarding the withdrawal of a partner, and the partners negotiated to compensate the retiring partner with payments that could be treated by the recipient at capital gain rates, the statutory scheme should not be read to frustrate the parties' efforts. An amendment to the partnership agreement which incorporates the plan of withdrawal and which designates the amount payable as being in consideration for the partnership good will seems clearly to be an attempt to utilize Section 736(b)(2)(B), affording capital gain rates to the retiring partner but precluding an expense deduction for the partnership. Simply because the subject matter of the amendment deals only with the liquidation of one partner's interest, we should not thwart whatever may be the clear intent of the parties by holding the amendment is not part of the partnership agreement. The Internal Revenue Code of 1954 expressly touches upon modifications of partnership agreements, and it gives no support to the thesis that an amendment dealing with the withdrawal of a partner cannot be considered a part of the partnership agreement. Section 761(c). . . .

We hold, therefore, in harmony with the intent of the parties to the partnership, that the "Amendment of Limited Partnership Agreement of George W. Carter Co." was a modification of the partnership agreement within the meaning of Section 761(c). As such, the requirement of a provision in the partnership agreement as specified in Section 736(b)(2)(B) is satisfied.

There remains, however, an additional requirement to call into operation Section 736(b)(2)(B), viz., that the provision for payment in the partnership agreement be *with respect to good will.* As noted above, the payment of the $40,350.00 was inartistically described in the Amendment as a "guaranteed payment, or a payment for good will." The "guaranteed payment" terminology seems to expressly incorporate Section 736(a)(2), which would permit an expense deduction to the partnership, while recognizing the payments as ordinary income to the retiring partner. The "good will" language, on the other hand, would appear directed to Section 736(b) (2)(B), which results in the opposite tax consequences. In resolving this conflict, we feel the most helpful guide is to pay deference to what we may determine was the revealed intent of the parties. An examination of the entire amendment leads us to conclude that, notwithstanding the use of the words "guaranteed payment," the parties intended to invoke Section 736(b)(2)(B), not Section 736(a)(2). The Amendment expressly states the following (which we find impossible to harmonize with the majority opinion of the Tax Court or the arguments advanced by respondents in their brief):

> "It is recognized by all the parties hereto that the prior agreements among the partners do not provide for any payment to any partner *in respect to good will* in the event of the retirement or withdrawal of a partner, but George W. Carter Company will nevertheless make a payment to Ethel M. Carter *in respect to good will* as herein provided in consideration of her entering into this agreement and her consent to retire from the partnership upon the terms herein expressed." (Tr. 66.) (Emphasis added.)

The meaning of this language as well as the words chosen to express it leads to the conclusion that the $40,350.00 was to be a payment "in respect to good will," with the parties intending to be governed by the tax consequences of Section 736(b)(2)(B). The concluding paragraph of Judge Raum's dissenting opinion in the Tax Court, joined in by five other judges, expresses in our judgment sound reasoning, and we incorporate it here as a summary statement of our viewpoint:

> "To fail to give effect to the plain language thus used by the parties is, I think, to defeat the very purpose of the pertinent partnership provisions of the statute, namely, to permit the partners themselves to fix their tax liabilities inter sese. Although the May 7, 1956, agreement may be inartistically drawn, and indeed may even contain some internal inconsistencies, the plain and obvious import of its provisions in respect of the present problem was to amend the partnership agreement so as to provide specifically for a goodwill payment. This is the kind of thing that section 736(b)(2)(B) dealt with when it allowed the partners to fix the tax consequences of goodwill payments to a withdrawing partner. And this is what the partners clearly attempted to do here, however crude may have been their effort. I would give further effect to that effort, and would not add further complications to an already overcomplicated statute." (41 T.C. at 685.)

The decision of the Tax Court is reversed, and the matter is remanded to that court for further proceedings consistent with this opinion.

NOTE

See H. Mette, Partnership Practice: Some Observations and Recommendations as to the Agreement, 10 Tax Counselor's Quarterly 477 (1966).

G. *UNREALIZED RECEIVABLES*

SWIREN v. COMMISSIONER
183 F.2d 656 (7th Cir. 1950),
cert. denied, 340 U.S. 912 (1951)

Before MAJOR, Chief Judge, and KERNER and DUFFY, Circuit Judges.

DUFFY, Circuit Judge. This is a petition to review and set aside a decision of the Tax Court which affirmed the Commissioner's determination that the gain realized by taxpayer upon the sale of a partnership interest was taxable as ordinary income rather than gain on the sale of a capital asset.

Taxpayer is an attorney at law who was admitted to practice in Illinois in 1927. His first place of employment was with the law firm of Levinson, Becker, Frank, Glenn and Barnes. The firm was nationally known, and the members thereof were of prominence in the legal profession. One became a U.S. Circuit Judge, another a U.S. District Judge, and another a U.S. Senator. Mr. Levinson, the author of the Kellogg Peace Pact, was very prominent in corporate financing and reorganization matters. Since 1912 the names of Levinson, Becker had been the first two names in the law firm.

On January 1, 1932, Mr. Becker purchased the interests of Levinson, Glenn and Schwartz. Levinson retained an office with the firm and for two or three years thereafter was paid an annual salary of $15,000, and for four years thereafter $9,000 annually, and he in turn permitted the firm to retain his name. Becker fixed the value of the firm at $100,000 although this sum was substantially greater than the aggregate of all of the assets of the firm, including accounts receivable and accrued but uncollected fees. Taxpayer on January 1, 1932, purchased from Becker a 10% interest in the firm and paid $10,000 therefor. The firm was thereafter known as Levinson, Becker, Gilbert, Peebles and Swiren.

In 1934, Gilbert withdrew from the firm and taxpayer purchased another 10% interest, paying $14,750 therefor. Again the amount paid was substantially in excess of 10% of the aggregate of all the physical assets, the accounts receivable and the fees earned but unpaid. Thereafter taxpayer made purchases from other partners of portions of their capital interest in the partnership until by 1944 he had a 30% interest for an aggregate cash investment of $33,500. During the same period taxpayer had received a partial return (amounting to $14,897.74) of his total cash investment. When taxpayer sold his interest in the partnership in October, 1944, his net capital investment amounted to $18,602.26.

A short time prior to the dissolution of the partnership taxpayer prepared a statement setting forth his idea of the value of his partnership interest and the value of the partnership assets. The eight items listed totaled $151,021. Two of these items were "billed fees (excluding entirely all fees billed prior to January 1, 1944), $12,800" and "unbilled fees (exclusive of Midland), $106,093." After deducting a junior partnership share, the balance shown on the statement was $145,621, and taxpayer's 30% interest amounted to $43,686.30.

Taxpayer negotiated exclusively with Becker, telling him he believed his interest in the partnership was worth $45,000 to $50,000. No discussion was had as to the value of any of the items appearing in the memorandum. Several days later Becker offered taxpayer $40,000 for his interest, which offer was accepted. In addition to the cash consideration taxpayer received some office equipment having a book value of $506.18.

The written agreement for the sale of taxpayer's interest in the partnership was executed on December 13, 1944. Taxpayer sold and assigned "all of his . . . share and interest in the Firm, excepting only and excluding the Midland fee."[2] The agreement recited, "Max Swiren's share and interest in the Firm sold and assigned hereby shall include his share and interest in the name and good will of the Firm, all furniture, fixtures, library, cash, fees earned whether or not billed, and accounts receivable, excluding, however, the Midland fee." It was also agreed that as a basis for accounting the partnership be terminated as at October 31, 1944, and that the partners participate in income and expenses up to that date.

Taxpayer prepared his income tax return for the year 1944 on a cash receipts basis, and reported therein as ordinary income the fees of $29,917.26 he had received from the partnership during that calendar year. However, he listed the sum which he received from the sale of his partnership interest as a capital gain and did not include it among the figures comprising his ordinary income.

The Tax Court, adopting the Commissioner's determination, recognized that taxpayer had a proprietorship interest in the partnership, and permitted him to recover "the full amount of his unrecovered capital outlay" in acquiring his partnership interest. However, the balance of the money received by taxpayer for the sale of his interest in the partnership was taxed to him as ordinary income. This was despite the fact that he sold his partnership interest as a whole.

When the Commissioner made his determination in this case the persistent view of the Bureau had been that the sale of a partnership interest was a sale of the selling partner's interest in each specific partnership asset. However, later acknowledging that "the overwhelming weight of authority is contrary to the position heretofore taken by the Bureau" the general counsel announced on May 15, 1950,[4] ". . . the sale of a partnership interest should be treated as the sale of a capital asset under the provisions of section [1221]. . . . The application of this rule should, of course, be limited

---

[2]Taxpayer had been appointed as attorney for the trustee of Midland United Company, then in reorganization, upon the express direction of the court that he personally and not his law firm act as such attorney. As any award of fees would be and was made to taxpayer personally, such fees were regarded as a special item and not a firm asset. No issue was raised either by the Commissioner or the Tax Court with respect to the tax treatment of this item.

[4]G.C.M. 26379, published in the Internal Revenue Bulletin, May 15, 1950, 5 CCH Sec. 6123.

to those cases in which the transaction in substance and effect, as distinguished from form and appearance, is essentially the sale of a partnership interest." . . .

From . . . United States v. Shapiro [178 F.2d 459 (8th Cir. 1949)] we quote as noteworthy this language from Judge Sanborn's opinion, 178 F.2d page 461: "The denial, on October 10, 1949, of the petitions for certiorari in the cases of Commissioner of Internal Revenue v. Smith, 5 Cir., 173 F.2d 470, and Long v. Commissioner, 5 Cir., 173 F.2d 471, indicates to us that the Supreme Court is not disposed to disturb the rulings of the Courts of Appeals of the Second, Third, Fifth, and Sixth Circuits and of the Tax Court to the effect that the sale of an interest in a partnership is the sale of a capital asset, regardless of the nature of the partnership properties. Uniformity in the construction of tax laws is important. The District Court was entirely justified in entering judgment for the taxpayer."

In this connection we have given due weight to the factor that under Illinois law a partnership interest, such as taxpayer sold, is property distinct and separate from the partnership or underlying assets. Ill. Rev. Stat. (1949), c. 106-½, Ill. Uniform Partnership Act, Secs. 24, 25 and 26. For example, Sec. 26 of the act provides: "Interest of partner. A partner's interest in the partnership is his share of the profits and surplus, and the same is personal property." . . .

The Commissioner here attempts to segregate partnership accounts receivable and unbilled fees for work in process and arbitrarily label both past earnings. The Commissioner argues that fees billed but uncollected, together with potential fees for work in process but not ready for billing or collection were taxpayer's "distributive share of partnership earnings" and therefore not a part of his partnership interest. We cannot agree.

When taxpayer purchased his interest in the firm he became entitled to his proportionate share of all fees collected by such partnership, and a portion of such fees had on the date of his purchase been billed but uncollected and other fees were for work then in process. Such fees when collected were ordinary income and those receiving them, including taxpayer, paid a tax thereon for ordinary income.

Taxpayer was on a cash receipts basis, as was the partnership. Uncollected fees for work in process not yet completed had not been transformed on the date of taxpayer's sale of his interest into gross income. . . .

In various of the cases heretofore cited, listed among the partnership assets were such items as accounts receivable, rents receivable and unfinished work which in due course would yield gross income to the partnership. Nevertheless the various Courts of Appeals and also the Tax Court treated the partnership interest as a whole, without regard to the nature of the underlying assets, and held the interest to be a capital asset. . . .

The Commissioner and the Tax Court, while correct in part in regarding as a capital asset taxpayer's unrecovered net investment and allowing recovery therefor in full amount, failed to recognize that, as a matter of law, taxpayer's partnership interest as a whole was a capital asset within [1221] of the Internal Revenue Code, with the gain attending the sale thereof taxable as a capital gain, and not otherwise.

The decision of the Tax Court is reversed and the case remanded to it for further proceedings consistent with this opinion.

KERNER, Circuit Judge, Dissenting. . . . In United States v. Shapiro, 8 Cir., 178 F.2d 459, four parties purchased an apartment building and jointly operated the property for rental purposes, and in addition purchased jointly a few bonds issued by another apartment operator, and thereafter, Shapiro, one of the partners, sold his interest in the building. The District Court, 83 F. Supp. 375, concluded that the sale of Shapiro's one-fourth interest in the apartment building was "the sale of a capital asset resulting in a long-term capital gain." The Court of Appeals affirmed. But since the case did not involve uncollected earnings, I am not convinced that the case must be viewed as supporting petitioner's contention in this case.

It cannot be gainsaid that fees earned for services performed constitute ordinary income, and that upon petitioner's withdrawal from the partnership, he had the right to receive his distributive share of the uncollected fees, or past earnings, of the partnership. Had he remained a partner, his share of the fees would have been taxable as ordinary income to him when collected. . . . The courts have said that the sale of a right to receive ordinary income is not the sale of a capital asset. This is so even if the sale is of something which may be termed "property." In such a situation the sale price simply replaces the future income, but the sale price does not convert the ordinary income into capital gain. Hort v. Commissioner, 313 U.S. 28, 61 S. Ct. 757, 85 L. Ed. 1168. The rule is illustrated by a decision holding that when a dividend on corporate stock has been declared, a sale of the dividend rights prior to the time the dividend is payable results in ordinary income and not capital gain. Rhodes' Estate v. Commissioner, 6 Cir., 131 F.2d 50.

I have not been convinced that petitioner's share of the uncollected fees was a part of his proprietary interest in the partnership, hence I cannot say that the finding and conclusion of the Tax Court is clearly erroneous. On the contrary, I believe the evidence adequately supports the finding that petitioner upon his withdrawal from the partnership received an amount which covered both his proprietary interest and his interest in the uncollected fees, that is, capital gain and ordinary income, and since the Tax Court made an allocation between the two which is not questioned by petitioner, I would affirm the decision.

YOURMAN v. UNITED STATES
277 F. Supp. 818 (S.D. Cal. 1967)

Pre-Trial Conference Order

KUNZEL, District Judge: Following Pre-trial Proceedings, pursuant to Rule 16 of the Federal Rules of Civil Procedure, It Is Ordered:

I. The above two actions are for refunds of Federal Income Taxes for the calendar year 1955.

Miles and Minnie Yourman seek to recover a refund of $52,908.45 plus interest as provided by law.

Allen M. and Marguerite Yourman seek to recover a refund of $52,405.99 plus interest as provided by law.

These actions are at issue in accordance with plaintiffs' Complaints and defendant's Answers.

II. This Court has jurisdiction over these proceedings by virtue of Section 1346(a)(1) of Title 28, United States Code.

Venue is appropriate under the provisions of Section 1402(a)(1) of Title 28, United States Code, as the plaintiffs reside within the Southern Judicial District of California. These actions were consolidated for trial by Order of this Court dated November 24, 1965.

III. The following facts are admitted and require no proof:

1. Miles and Minnie Yourman timely filed their 1955 Joint Federal Income Tax Return paying thereon the sum of $16,900.73.

2. On October 21, 1960, the District Director of Internal Revenue, Los Angeles, made an additional assessment against the plaintiffs, Miles and Minnie Yourman, in the amount of $41,705.63 plus interest thereon of $11,202.82 (the sum of $52,908.45).

3. Said assessment was based principally upon the determination that the non pro-rata distribution of Anderson and Yourman partnership assets to the plaintiff, Miles Yourman, as a result of the dissolution of the Anderson and Yourman partnership, constituted a taxable event to Miles Yourman under the provisions of Sections 751 and 752 of the 1954 Internal Revenue Code. The balance of the assessment was attributable to an increase in capital gains in the amount of $100.00, which the plaintiffs concede is not at issue in these proceedings.

4. The assessment of $52,908.45 was satisfied by an advance payment of $41,705.63 on October 9, 1960 and a final payment of $11,202.82 on April 10, 1961.

5. On August 15, 1962, Miles and Minnie Yourman filed a Claim for Refund. On September 24, 1963, a Waiver of Notification of Disallowance of the Claim for Refund was filed. On September 17, 1965, timely suits for refund were filed.

6. Allen and Marguerite Yourman timely filed their 1955 Joint Federal Income Tax Return paying the sum of $14,146.44 thereon.

7. On October 21, 1960, the District Director of Internal Revenue, Los Angeles, made an additional assessment against the plaintiffs, Allen and Marguerite Yourman, in the amount of $41,309.57 plus interest thereon of $11,096.42 (the sum of $52,405.99).

8. Said assessment was based upon the determination that the non pro-rata distribution of Anderson and Yourman partnership assets to the plaintiff, Allen Yourman, as a result of the dissolution of the Anderson and Yourman partnership, constituted a taxable event to Allen Yourman under the provisions of Sections 751 and 752 of the 1954 Internal Revenue Code.

9. These assessments were satisfied by an advance payment of $41,309.57 on October 7, 1960 and a final payment of $11,096.42 on April 10, 1961.

10. On August 15, 1962, Allen and Marguerite Yourman filed a Claim for Refund. On September 24, 1963 a Waiver of Notification of Disallowance of the Claim for Refund was filed. On September 17, 1965, timely suits for refund were filed.

11. On or about June 1, 1939, Allen M. Yourman, Miles Yourman and William N. Anderson formed a partnership known as Anderson and Yourman.

12. From June 1, 1939, until approximately 1950, the principal economic activity of the Anderson and Yourman partnership was the growing of agricultural crops

on land owned by the partnership. From 1950 until the date of dissolution, the partnership's principal economic activity was the processing and feeding of cattle.

13. At all times material hereto, the Anderson and Yourman partnership maintained its principal office in Calexico.

14. At all times material hereto, the Anderson and Yourman partnership maintained its books and records and prepared its partnership income tax returns on the cash basis. Its tax and accounting order consisted of a fiscal year beginning on June 1 and ending on May 31.

15. At all times material hereto, the partners of the Anderson and Yourman partnership agreed to share profits and losses as follows:

William N. Anderson	1/3rd
Miles Yourman	1/3rd
Allen Yourman	1/3rd

16. Sometime prior to July 31, 1955, the partners of the Anderson and Yourman partnership met and agreed to dissolve the partnership. Pursuant thereto the partners executed a document entitled, "Agreement of Dissolution of Partnership."

17. As of August 1, 1955, the Anderson and Yourman partnership was dissolved and its business terminated.

18. As of August 1, 1955, the Anderson and Yourman partnership consisted of the following assets and liabilities at the following fair market values:

Assets	Fair Market Values
Cash	$ 5,803.59
Unrealized Receivables	61,666.69
Other Receivables	48.00
Inventory	210,959.70
Depreciable property	112,704.84
Land	416,400.00
Liabilities	180,132.81

19. As of August 1, 1955, the Anderson and Yourman partners' pro-rata interests in the Anderson and Yourman assets and liabilities at the fair market values described in paragraph 18 were as follows:

Asset	Total	William Anderson	Miles Yourman	Allen Yourman
Cash	$ 5,803.59	$ 1,934.53	$ 1,934.53	$ 1,934.53
Unrealized Receivables	61,666.69	20,555.57	20,555.56	20,555.56
Other Receivables	48.00	16.00	16.00	16.00
Inventory	210,959.70	70,319.90	70,319.90	70,319.90
Depreciable property	112,704.84	37,568.28	37,568.28	37,568.28
Land	416,400.00	138,800.00	138,800.00	138,800.00
Liabilities	180,132.81	60,044.27	60,044.27	60,044.27

20. During 1955, pursuant to the dissolution agreement of August 1, 1955, the following partnership assets were distributed to the partners and the following partnership liabilities were assumed by the partners:

Assets Distributed	Total	William Anderson	Miles Yourman	Allen Yourman
Cash	$ 5,803.59	$ 1,934.53	$ 1,934.53	$ 1,934.53
Unrealized Receivables	61,666.69	61,666.69	None	None
Other Receivables	48.00	16.00	16.00	16.00
Inventory Items	210,959.70	156,183.08	27,530.81	27,245.81
Depreciable property	112,704.84	110,539.84	1,082.50	1,082.50
Land	416,400.00	42,000.00	187,200.00	187,200.00
Liabilities Assumed	180,132.81	163,189.93	8,471.44	8,471.44

21. The distributions of (1) unrealized receivables, (2) inventory items, (3) depreciable property and (4) land, as set forth in paragraph 10, constituted non pro-rata distributions of the Anderson and Yourman partnership assets.

22. The assumption of Anderson and Yourman liabilities in the amount of $180,132.81 constituted a non pro-rata assumption of Anderson and Yourman partnership liabilities.

23. The Anderson and Yourman partnership unrealized receivables of $61,666.69 constituted unrealized receivables as defined under Section 751(c) of the 1954 Internal Revenue Code.

24. The inventory items distributed by the Anderson and Yourman partnership to its partners in dissolution of the partnership consisted of the following inventory items having the following fair market values on the date of distribution:

Inventory Items	Total Fair Market Value	William Anderson	Miles Yourman	Allen Yourman
Straw Hay	$104,377.63	$ 69,511.01	$17,575.81	$17,290.81
724 Tons Oat Hay	19,910.00	....	9,955.00	9,555.00
30 Tons Molasses	712.50	712.50	....	....
13,184 Sacks	1,977.60	1,977.60	....	....
660.55 Tons Barley	31,706.40	31,706.40	....	....
475 Tons Straw	6,650.00	6,650.00	....	....
Cotton Bolls (Waste)	450.00	450.00	....	....
9 Tons Salt	126.00	126.00	....	....
3300 Lbs. Stilbestro	108.90	108.90	....	....
14.5 Tons Mineral	1,232.50	1,232.50	....	....
5500 Lbs. Orange Pulp	132.00	132.00	....	....
39½ Tons Rice Bran	1,876.25	1,876.25	....	....
513.93 Tons Mexican Feed	26,981.33	26,981.33	....	....
12.25 Tons Cotton Seed Meal ..	784.00	784.00	....	....
1 Ton Cotton Seed Meal Mex...	50.00	50.00	....	....
10 Tons Wheat Bran	418.00	418.00	....	....

Inventory Items	Total Fair Market Value	William Anderson	Miles Yourman	Allen Yourman
3450 Sacks (Pablo's Feed Mills).	517.50	517.50	....	....
174.84 Tons Cotton Seed Hulls	2,519.44	2,519.44	....	....
50 Tons Cotton Seed Hulls	1,100.00	1,100.00	....	....
Cattle Medicine	33.65	103.00*	....	....
280 Tons Milo	9,296.00	9,296.00	....	....
Totals	$210,959.70	$156,183.08	$27,530.81	$27,245.81

*This figure should probably read $33.65. — Ed.

25. All of the inventory items referred to above, totalling $210,959.70, were purchased by the Anderson and Yourman partnership from third parties having no interest in the Anderson and Yourman partnership.

26. The fair market value of each item of inventory on the date of distribution was no greater than the price at which each said item had been purchased by the partnership.

27. Prior to the date of distribution of said items of inventory, the Anderson and Yourman partnership had expensed the cost of each item of inventory; so that immediately prior to the date of distribution, the adjusted basis to the partnership of each item of inventory was zero.

28. The Anderson and Yourman partnership inventory having a fair market value on the date of distribution of $210,959.70 constituted "inventory items" as defined under Section 751(d)(2) of the 1954 Internal Revenue Code.

29. The Anderson and Yourman partnership timely filed its final partnership Federal Income Tax Return covering accounting for the period June 1, 1955 through July 31, 1955. Thereon, it reported income from its business operations in the amount of $119,289.66.

30. No gain or loss to the Anderson and Yourman partnership from the distribution of partnership assets in dissolution of the partnership was reported on said partnership's final Federal Income Tax Return.

31. No gain or loss to the Anderson and Yourman partnership from the assumption of partnership liabilities in dissolution of the partnership was reported on the partnership's final Income Tax Return.

32. No gain or loss from the distribution of Anderson and Yourman partnership assets in dissolution of the partnership was reported by Miles and Minnie Yourman on their timely filed 1955 Federal Income Tax Return.

33. No gain or loss from the assumption of Anderson and Yourman partnership liabilities in dissolution of the partnership was reported by Miles and Minnie Yourman on their timely filed 1955 Federal Income Tax Return.

34. No gain or loss from the distribution of Anderson and Yourman partnership assets in dissolution of the partnership was reported by Allen and Marguerite Yourman on their timely filed 1955 Federal Income Tax Return.

35. No gain or loss from the assumption of Anderson and Yourman partner-

ship liabilities in dissolution of the partnership was reported by Allen and Marguerite Yourman on their timely filed 1955 Federal Income Tax Return.

36. The Anderson and Yourman partnership capital account of Miles Yourman on July 31, 1955 had a credit balance of $590.50.

37. The Anderson and Yourman partnership capital account of Allen Yourman on July 31, 1955 had a credit balance of $590.50.

IV. There are no reservations by the parties concerning the admissability into evidence of the facts cited in paragraphs II and III.

V. There are no facts which though not admitted are to be contested by evidence to the contrary.

VI. The parties hereby agree and stipulate that there are no genuine and material issues of fact to be litigated in these proceedings.

VII. No exhibits will be offered by the parties, as the relevant and material facts of the cases have been agreed upon and stipulated to in paragraphs II and III.

VIII. The following issues of law, and no others, remain to be litigated:

1. Whether the Anderson and Yourman partnership inventory items described in Part III, paragraph 24 of this Order, constitute inventory items which have appreciated substantially in value within the meaning of Section 751(a) of the 1954 Internal Revenue Code.

2. Whether Section 751(d) of the Code defines the term "inventory items which have appreciated substantially in value" as stated in Section 751(a) of the Code.

3. Whether the distribution of Anderson and Yourman partnership assets and the assumption of Anderson and Yourman partnership liabilities, as set forth in Part III, paragraph 20 of this Order, constitute distributions to be treated as a "sale or exchange" within the meaning of Section 751(b)(1)(B) of the Code and thus taxable to the plaintiffs under the provisions of Section 751(a) of the Code or are said distributions taxable to the plaintiffs, if at all, under the provisions of Section 731(a) of the Code.

IX. The parties having agreed and stipulated that there are no genuine and material issues of fact and having specified the issues of law before this Court, this order shall supplement the pleadings and govern any further proceedings in these consolidated cases, unless modified to prevent manifest injustice.

Memorandum of Decision

In these consolidated actions plaintiffs seek a refund of taxes paid to the United States. The court has jurisdiction by virtue of 28 U.S.C. §1346(a)(1).

The cases have been submitted for decision on the stipulated facts contained in the pre-trial conference order filed May 1, 1967. Counsel for both parties agree that this is a case of first impression.

Plaintiffs Miles and Allen Yourman each held a one-third interest in a partnership with William Anderson as the third member.

The partnership was dissolved in 1955 via a non-pro-rata distribution of partnership assets. Certain unrealized receivables and inventory items were distributed to Anderson. Plaintiffs received certain capital assets; principally land. The fair market value of what each partner received was equal to the cost of acquisition. However, the inventory items which Anderson received had been completely expensed so that the basis was zero.

Taxes were assessed against plaintiffs on the basis that the non-pro-rata distribution of the partnership assets to plaintiffs constituted a taxable event under the provisions of 26 U.S.C. §751 (1954).

Plaintiffs contend section 751 does not apply for the reason that language contained in section 751(b)(1)(B) limits the application of the section to a situation where a partnership continues in existence after a distribution to some or all of the partners. The section reads, in part, as follows: ". . . be considered as a sale or exchange of such property between the distributee and the partnership (as constituted after the distribution)."

The purpose expressed by Congress for the adoption of section 751 was "to prevent the conversion of potential ordinary income into capital gain by virtue of transfers of partnership interest." 3 U.S. Code Cong. & Ad. News 1954, p. 4097.

There is no credible reason for giving the language the meaning plaintiffs contend. The only logical interpretation to be given to the language in view of express congressional purpose is that it refers to the facts as they exist after the distribution. A dissolved partnership, as well as a partnership which continues to exist, are "as constituted after the distribution."

Mertens' Law of Federal Income Taxation agrees that section 751 applies to a non-pro-rata distribution whether or not the partnership remains in existence.

> "The rules of section 751(b), as thus described, are applicable both to liquidating and current distributions. In a current distribution of cash or property, section 751(b) is applicable to the extent that a distributee partner has surrendered all or a part of his interest in unrealized receivables or inventory, or conversely has acquired part of the interest of the other partners in such property. In a liquidating distribution, section 751(b) is applicable unless each of the partners receives his pro-rata share of unrealized receivables and substantially appreciated inventory items.
>
> "In general, section 751(b) applies wherever a distribution to one or more partners amounts in substance to an 'exchange' between the distributee partner and the remaining partners[9] of non capital and capital assets. If the distribution is made in such a way that each partner retains his pro-rata share of unrealized receivables and inventory, the collapsible partnership rules will not be invoked. . . ."

With respect to footnote 9, the following is stated at page 102 of Chapter 1, Subchapter K, Section 751.3.

"9. In the case of a *termination of a partnership,* (emphasis added) the exchange may take place between the various distributee partners." "Code Commentary-Sections 701-End," Chap. 1, Subchapter K, Section 751.3 p. 98.

Plaintiffs further contend that if section 751 applies to the distribution, the partnership inventory should not be taken into account for the reason that the inventory items at the time of distribution had not appreciated substantially in value as required by section 751(d). This section provides as follows:

"(d) *Inventory Items Which Have Appreciated Substantially In Value.* —

"(1) *Substantial Appreciation.* — Inventory items of the partnership shall be considered to have appreciated substantially in value if their fair market value exceeds —

"(A) 120 percent of the adjusted basis to the partnership of such property, and

"(B) 10 percent of the fair market value of all partnership property, other than money.

"(2) *Inventory Items.* — For purposes of this subchapter the term 'inventory items' means —

"(A) property of the partnership of the kind described in section 1221(1),

"(B) any other property of the partnership which, on sale or exchange by the partnership, would be considered property other than a capital asset and other than property described in section 1231, and

"(C) any other property held by the partnership which, if held by the selling or distributee partner, would be considered property of the type described in subparagraph (A) or (B)."

Plaintiffs' position in this regard is that there must be appreciation in fact as opposed to a bookkeeping appreciation.

It is stipulated that the fair market value of the inventory at the time of distribution was $210,959.70, and that the adjusted basis of the inventory on the books was zero. The stipulation further indicates that the fair market value of the inventory was in excess of ten percent of the fair market value of all the partnership property.

There would seem to be no logical reason for differentiating between an "actual appreciation" and a "bookkeeping appreciation" caused by having expensed the inventory for tax purposes. If the inventory had been sold by the partnership, the result of such sale would have been that the partners would have each been required to pay ordinary income tax on the sales price less the cost basis on the books which here was zero. If the congressional purpose for the enactment of section 751 is to be observed, the distribution here should be treated no differently than a *sale* by the partnership, and the result should be the same.

Judgment shall be for defendant.

This memorandum shall constitute the findings of fact and conclusions of law. Counsel for defendant shall prepare, serve and lodge a judgment in accordance herewith.

NOTE

1. Section 751 adopts the argument made by the government in Swiren v. Commissioner, page 805 supra. Wolcott v. Commissioner, 39 T.C. 538 (1962), held that "unrealized receivables" include payments for architectural contracts which the firm owned but for which the work was not completed. Roth v. Commissioner,

321 F.2d 607 (9th Cir. 1963), held that "unrealized receivables" include future profits to be earned under a contract for distribution of motion pictures. Glazer v. Commissioner, 44 T.C. 541 (1965), held that contracts for sale of houses which were 80 per cent complete were "unrealized receivables" within §751. What of the value of contingent fees for a lawyer's work in negligence cases? Cf. Estate of Nemerov, 15 CCH Tax Ct. Mem. 855 (1956). See D. Alexander, Collapsible Partnerships, 19 N.Y.U. Inst. on Fed. Tax. 257 (1961).

2. When the recapture provisions of §§1245 and 1250 were enacted in 1962 and 1964, respectively, the definition of "unrealized receivables" was expanded to include §1245 property and §1250 property, but only to the extent of the amount which would have been treated as gain if the property had been sold by the partnership at its fair market value at the time of the transaction.

3. In liquidation of his interest a partner receives a distribution in kind of his proportionate share of partnership assets which would be considered "inventory items which have appreciated in value" under §751(d). Does the distribution of the inventory result in recognition to the recipient? To the remaining partners? Why? See Rev. Rul. 57-68, 1957-1 Cum. Bull. 207.

4. See C. Lewis, Tax Aspects of Sale or Termination of a Partnership Interest, 45 Taxes 324 (1967).

6 | "Small Business" Corporations

I. SUBCHAPTER S — §§1371-1379

Subchapter S was added to the Code in 1958. Amendments have been made since then, and proposals for thorough overhaul are pending. Those proposals are summarized at the conclusion of this part of the chapter. The following excerpt from the Report of the Senate Finance Committee* describes the purpose of Subchapter S and its general scheme:

Section 68 — Election of certain small-business corporations
In 1954, . . . the Senate passed, but the Congress did not enact, a provision which would, at the election of the stockholders, permit corporations to forego the payment of any tax and require their shareholders to report the corporate income (whether or not distributed) as their own for tax purposes.

Your committee believes that the enactment of a provision of this type is desirable because it permits businesses to select the form of business organization desired, without the necessity of taking into account major differences in tax consequence. In this respect, a provision to tax the income at the shareholder, rather than the corporate, level will complement the provision enacted in 1954 premitting proprietorships and partnerships to be taxed like corporations. Also, permitting shareholders to report their proportionate share of the corporate income, in lieu of a corporate tax, will be a substantial aid to small business. It will be primarily beneficial to those individuals who have marginal tax rates below the 52-percent corporate rate (or 30-percent rate in the case of the smaller corporations) where the earnings are left in the business. Where the earnings are distributed (and are in excess of what may properly be classified as salary payments), the benefit will extend to individuals with somewhat higher rates since in this case a "double" tax is removed. The provision will also be of substantial benefit to small corporations realizing losses for a period of years where there is no way of offsetting these losses against taxable income at the corporate level, but the shareholders involved have other income which can be offset against these losses. In this connection is should be noted that the President's Cabinet Committee on Small Business and the President in his budget message this

*S. Rep. No. 1983, 85th Cong., 2d Sess. 68, 1958-3 Cum. Bull. 1008.

last January recommended a general provision of this type for the benefit of small business.

To permit shareholders in small-business corporations, in lieu of payment of the corporate tax, to elect to be taxed directly on the corporation's earnings, your committee has added a new subchapter (subch. S, secs. 1371-1377) to the code. Where the tax treatment provided by this subchapter is elected, the shareholders include in their own income for tax purposes the current taxable income of the corporation, both the portion which is distributed and that which is not. Neither type of income in this case is eligible for a dividend received credit or exclusion, since it has been subject to no tax at the corporate level. Generally, this income is treated as ordinary income to the shareholder without the retention of any special characteristics it might have had in the hands of the corporation. This rule has been adopted so that this provision can operate in as simple a manner as possible. Long-term capital gains, however, are an exception to this general rule. In the case of these long-term capital gains the character carries over to the shareholder level.

Where a shareholder has been taxed on corporate earnings which were not at that time distributed, and then the corporation in a subsequent year distributes these earnings to such shareholders no further tax is required from the shareholder at that time, since these earnings have already been taxed to him in a prior year. Once all such earnings have been distributed, if further distributions are then made, and the corporation had earnings and profits before it elected this special tax treatment, then such distributions are to be taxed to the shareholders in the same manner as ordinary dividends from corporations.

Under this provision the net operating losses of the corporation currently also are passed through to the shareholder. Thus, at the corporate level where this special treatment is elected, there is no carryover or carryback of operating losses to or from a year with respect to which this special treatment has been elected. At the individual level these "distributed" corporate losses are to be treated in the same manner as any loss which the individual might have from a proprietorship; that is, they first offset income of the individual, in that year (whether or not derived from another business) and then any excess of these losses may be carried back and offset against the individual's income in prior years and, if any losses still remain, they may be carried forward and offset against his income in subsequent years.

Where this special treatment has been elected the basis of a shareholder's stock is increased for any of the corporate earnings taxed to him which are not then distributed, although this basis is subsequently reduced if these taxpaid corporate earnings are distributed. The basis of the stock of a shareholder is also reduced for any corporate losses which are passed through to him. The losses that he may take, however, are limited to the basis he has for the stock. Thus, his basis for the stock cannot be reduced below zero.

The right to elect the treatment provided under this new subchapter is limited to what are defined as small business corporations. These corporations must be domestic corporations which are not eligible to file a consolidated return with any other corporation. Also, they must not have more than 10 shareholders, their shareholders must all be individuals (or an estate), no nonresident aliens may be shareholders, and the corporation may not have more than one class of stock.

An election may be made to apply the tax treatment provided by this new subchapter only if all of the shareholders consent to this election. For this purpose the shareholders are those of record as of the first day of the taxable year in question, or if the election is made after that time, shareholders of record when the election is made. An election to come under this provision must be made in a two months interval, either in the first month before the beginning of the taxable year for which the election is to be made or in the first month of that year. (A longer period of time, up to 90 days after the date of enactment of this bill, is allowed for the first taxable year beginning after December 31, 1957.) Once this provision is elected it is effective not only for the taxable year but also for all subsequent years although this election may be terminated.

The election to the tax treatment provided by this subchapter can be terminated in any one of several ways. First, the election is terminated if a new person becomes a shareholder of the corporation and he does not consent to the election. Second, the election can be terminated if all of the shareholders consent to its revocation. A revocation, however, is effective only with respect to subsequent years unless it is made in the first month of the taxable year. Third, the election as to the treatment under this new subchapter is to be terminated if the corporation ceases to qualify as a small-business corporation; that is, if the corporation no longer meets the requirements of a small business corporation, such as having not more than 10 shareholders or having no nonresident alien as a shareholder. Fourth, the election to be taxed under this new subchapter terminates if the corporation derives more than 80 percent of its gross receipts from sources outside the United States and, fifth, the election terminates if more than 20 percent of the corporation's gross receipts are derived from interest, dividends, rents, royalties, or other forms of passive income.

In order to prevent a corporation from electing in and out of the application of the provisions of this new subchapter, a limitation has been added providing that if a corporation has made an election under this subchapter, and if this election has been terminated or revoked, the corporation (or any successor) is not to be eligible to elect this treatment until its fifth year after the beginning of the year in which the determination or revocation is effective. However, the Secretary or his delegate is given the authority to make exceptions to this limitation. . . .

The foregoing Senate Finance Committee Report refers to §§1371-1377. In 1966 Congress added §1378. As you study the materials relating to Subchapter S, consider the problems that might have moved Congress to make the addition, and see S. Rep. No. 1007, 89th Cong., 2d Sess., 1966-1 Cum. Bull. 527. See also E. Cohen, Tax Planning With Subchapter S in 1967: Problems and Prospects, 53 Va. L. Rev. 1161 (1967). In 1969 Congress added §1379, which limited the tax benefits under "qualified" retirement plans available to Subchapter S "shareholder-employees" essentially to those benefits available to "owner-employees" under Subchapter D (§§401-407).

As you examine Subchapter S, consider the criteria for deciding whether the preferable business format for your clients is a partnership, a Subchapter S corporation, or a standard corporation. See generally B. Bittker and J. Eustice, Federal Income Taxation of Corporations and Shareholders 709-739 (2d ed. 1966); P. Austin, Income and Losses of Subchapter S Corporation: Impact on Corporation and Stockholder, 28 N.Y.U. Inst. on Fed. Tax. 493 (1970); I. Grant et al., The Relative Tax Advantages of Partnership and Subchapter S Corporations, 1969 So. Calif. Tax Inst. 409; A. Dixon et al., Partnerships and Subchapter S: A Comparison of Tax Advantages, A Panel Discussion, 25 N.Y.U. Inst. on Fed. Tax. 151 (1967); S. Roberts and H. Alpert, Subchapter S: Semantic and Procedural Traps in Its Use; Analysis of Dangers, 10 J. Taxation 2 (1959).

REVENUE RULING 63-226
1963-2 Cum. Bull. 341

Advice has been requested whether a corporation, which otherwise qualifies as a small business corporation, meets the requirement of section 137(a)(4) of the Internal Revenue Code of 1954 where there is agreement between the shareholders which requires shareholders who are not actively engaged in the business to grant irrevocable proxies to an active shareholder to vote their shares.

In the instant case a partnership, consisting of eight active partners and two limited partners, was incorporated. Voting common stock was the only class of stock authorized and issued. The stock was issued to the former partners of the partnership in accordance with their pro rata interest in the partnership.

All of the shareholders of the corporation entered into an agreement which provides that any shareholder who at any time is not actively engaged in the business of the corporation will grant an irrevocable proxy to one or more active shareholders to vote his shares of stock.

This required the former limited partners, who are now inactive shareholders, to grant irrevocable proxies to vote their shares to active shareholders. The specific issue is whether this requirement results in the corporation's having more than one class of stock.

One of the requirements which a corporation must meet in order to qualify as a "small business corporation" is that it must not have more than one class of stock. Section 1371(a)(4) of the Code.

In connection with the requirement that the corporation not have more than one class of stock, section 1.1371-1(g) of the Income Tax Regulations provides, in part, as follows:

". . . If the outstanding shares of stock of the corporation are not identical with respect to the rights and interests which they convey in the control, profits, and assets of the corporation, then the corporation is considered to have more than one class of stock. Thus, a difference as to voting rights, dividend rights, or liquidation preferences of outstanding stock will disqualify a corporation. . . ."

Because of the restrictions placed upon the inactive shareholders under the agreement in the instant case, it is held that their rights and interests in the control of the corporation are not identical with the rights and interests of the active shareholders. Furthermore, in the event that the outstanding stock of a corporation is subject to any other type of voting control device or arrangement, such as a pooling or voting agreement or a charter provision granting certain shares a veto power or the like, which has the effect of modifying the voting rights of part of the stock so that particular shares possess disproportionate voting power as compared to the dividend rights or liquidation rights of those shares and as compared to the voting, dividend and liquidation rights of the other shares of stock of the corporation outstanding, the corporation will be deemed to have more than one class of stock. Accordingly, the corporation does not qualify as a small business corporation.

NOTE

See M. Weinstein, Stockholder Agreements and Subchapter S Corporations, 19 Tax L. Rev. 391 (1964).

GAMMAN v. COMMISSIONER
46 T.C. 1 (1966)

DRENNEN, Judge: . . . All issues . . . have been agreed upon by the parties except one, common to all docket numbers, which is whether Century House, Inc., a corporation in which Gamman and Reese were equal owners of all the outstanding stock, qualified as a "small business corporation" under subchapter S (secs. 1371-1377), I.R.C. 1954, the underlying issue being whether purported loans to the corporation by the stockholders constituted a second class of stock. . . .

In 1959 plans were under discussion to hold a World's Fair in Seattle. The discussions indicated that the fair would open in the spring of 1961 and continue throughout the warm weather seasons of both 1961 and 1962. One concern was whether there were adequate lodging facilities in Seattle for the anticipated tourists. This gave Gamman, Reese, and William L. Hiller the idea of building a motel near the proposed site of the fair. A contract to purchase land for this purpose was entered into in April 1959. Century House was incorporated under the laws of the State of Washington as the vehicle to build and operate this motel.

The articles of incorporation for Century House were filed with the secretary of state of Washington on October 15, 1959, and were general in nature. The authorized capital stock of the corporation was 500 shares of stock having no-par value, and the amount of paid-in capital with which the corporation was to begin business was stated to be $500. The articles of incorporation had not been amended prior to the end of the years here involved and the corporation was not authorized to issue a second class of stock.

On October 21, 1959, each of the three original stockholders, Gamman, Reese, and Hiller, paid $200 to the corporation for capital stock and also advanced the corporation $5,333.33 in return for demand notes bearing 6-percent interest. Each of the three stockholders also advanced to the corporation $2,500 in cash on November 13, 1959, and $1,500 in cash on December 11, 1959, and received in return demand notes of the corporation in like amounts bearing 6-percent interest. By the close of 1959 the advances of the stockholders totaled $28,000.

In January 1960 the corporation bought the stock owned by Hiller for $200 and paid off his advances without interest. Since that time Gamman and Reese each owned one-half of the outstanding stock of Century House and were its principal officers and directors.

The expense of organizing the corporation was $1,404.05. On October 21, 1959, Century House acquired the land for the motel for $114,400 under a real estate contract which provided for $20,000 to be paid in cash by closing and the balance to be paid on or before November 1, 1962. The sellers agreed that if buyer obtained a first mortgage construction loan for building an apartment motel on the property they would subordinate their real estate contract to the construction loan and take a second mortagage on the property as security for the unpaid balance of the purchase price. All three original stockholders and their wives guaranteed performance of the real estate contract and the second mortgage. Soon thereafter construction of a motel was commenced on the property with funds advanced by the stockholders.

On February 25, 1960, Century House received a construction loan from Securities Mortgage Co. in the amount of $412,000, secured by a first mortgage on the property. A commitment for a take-out loan in the amount of $400,000 had been arranged with a life insurance company for permanent financing of the project. However, this proved to be insufficient in amount and the loan was never consummated. On January 12, 1961, Century House borrowed $175,000 from an outside lender, secured by a third mortgage on the property, on which petitioners became personally liable. On January 1, 1962, Century House borrowed $95,000 from Securities Mortgage Co. to partially refinance the construction loan. The petitioners were personally liable on this loan and it was secured by mortgages on their personal residences.

On January 16, 1962, Century House borrowed $600,000 from Fidelity Savings & Loan Association which was used to pay off the construction loan and the second mortgage. This loan, which was intended to be the permanent financing of the project, was secured by a first mortgage on the property and, in accordance with the standard policy of the lender in lending money to closely held corporations, the petitioners were personally liable for payment of the loan. The loan was conditioned upon the borrower adding a restaurant, laundry, and bar to the motel, which was done by the end of 1962.

Petitioners originally intended and hoped to obtain 100-percent permanent financing of the project from outside sources, and hoped to recover their advances to the corporation from such financing and the anticipated profits from operation of the motel. When petitioners first conceived the idea of building the motel construction funds were readily available in the Seattle area at a reasonable cost and, because of the usual increment in value of property after it was improved and anticipated high earnings from operations during the fair, some builders were able to finance their housing projects to the extent of 100 percent of cost. Petitioners originally hoped to operate the motel profitably for the 2 years the fair was supposed to be in operation and then sell out at a profit. The motel was opened for business in February 1961. However, plans for the fair were changed and it did not open in 1961 as intended, but opened in 1962 and stayed open for only 6 months, and did not attract the tourist trade that was hoped for. In addition, numerous other people in Seattle had the same idea as petitioners and there was a surplus of new housing facilities built with the result that the cost of construction increased, and the money market for tourists' housing facilities changed, and money for construction and permanent loans became scarce. As a result of the above circumstances the cost of constructing the motel was greater than anticipated, petitioners were unable to obtain the outside financing they had hoped for, Century House operated at a loss during the years 1961 and 1962, and petitioners had to advance more of their own funds to the corporation to keep it going.

At various times during the years 1960, 1961, and 1962, and continuing thereafter, Gamman and Reese advanced rather sizable amounts of cash to Century House in approximately equal amounts. The total of the amounts advanced by them at the end of 1960 was $68,066.67, at the end of 1961 was $165,670.80, and at the end of 1962 was $252,343.80. These advances to the corporation were evidenced by 6-percent demand notes. No interest had been paid on the notes and no efforts had been made by petitioners to force payment of the obligations up to the time of the trial herein. From time to time new notes of a similar character were issued to petitioners in return for old notes to avoid the statute of limitations barring collection of the old notes; and petitioners waived the interest due on the notes. The advances were carried on the books of Century House as long-term liabilities. Capital stock was shown on the balance sheet as $400 until 1964.

By the end of 1962 the balance sheet of Century House reflected current assets in the amount of $36,609.53; fixed assets, including land, buildings, furniture and fixtures, and linens, having an original cost of $1,062,342.54; and other assets in the amount of $9,147.24. The balance sheet also reflected current liabilities totaling $242,315.05; long-term liabilities totaling $845,149.54, of which $245,228.20 was due to Gamman and Reese; capital stock, less treasury stock, in the amount of $400; and a deficit in the earnings account of $183,366.21.

In July 1963 Century House was able to obtain another long-term loan of $200,000 from Fidelity Savings & Loan Association, which was guaranteed by the Small Business Administration after petitioners established to the satisfaction of the Small Business Administration that they were unable to obtain financing from other sources at a reasonable rate of interest. Petitioners were personally liable for this loan and agreed they would receive no payment for their advances until the loan was paid, and that the corporation would not pay dividends or salaries to Gamman and Reese.

In December 1964 Century House was recapitalized and a substantial portion of the advances made by the stockholders was converted into additional stock, bonds, and paid-in capital of the corporation.

On January 25, 1961, Century House, with the consent of all its stockholders, filed the election authorized by section 1372(a) of the Code not to be subject to the taxes imposed by that chapter. Petitioners claimed their prorata shares of the operating losses of Century House for the years 1961 and 1962 as deductions on their individual income tax returns for the years 1961 and 1962. Respondent has disallowed these deductions claimed by petitioners on the ground that petitioners' advances to the corporation constituted a second class of stock, as a result of which Century House did not qualify as a small business corporation under section 1371(a) of the Code.

Opinion

The one basic issue for decision is whether Century House qualified as an electing small business corporation under subchapter S of the Code during the years 1961 and 1962.

Section 1371 defines the term "small business corporation" as a domestic corporation which is not a member of an affiliated group and which does not (1) have more than 10 shareholders; (2) have as a shareholder a person (other than an estate) who is not an individual; (3) have a nonresident alien as a shareholder; and (4) have more than one class of stock. It is not questioned that Century House met all the requirements for qualification as an electing small business corporation for the years 1961 and 1962, except the last, i.e., that it not have more than one class of stock. Respondent claims that the advances to the corporation by the shareholders were actually advances of equity capital rather than loans and constituted a second class of stock. Respondent's argument is based on section 1.1371-1(g), Income Tax Regs., which provides in material part as follows:

> "A corporation having more than one class of stock does not qualify as a small business corporation. . . . If the outstanding shares of stock of the corporation are not identical with respect to the rights and interest which they convey in the control, profits, and assets of the corporation, then the corporation is considered to have more than one class of stock. Thus, a difference as to voting rights, dividend rights, or liquidation preferences of outstanding stock will disqualify a corporation. . . . If an instrument purporting to be a debt obligation is actually stock, it will constitute a second class of stock."

Respondent argues that the promissory notes issued to the shareholders in return for their advances to the corporation actually constituted a 6-percent preferred nonvoting stock — a second class of stock.

Petitioners argue that the advances made by the stockholders were intended to be loans and did not constitute equity capital, and hence the notes evidencing the advances were not actually stock; and, further, that the last sentence of respondent's regulations quoted above is invalid.

The statute itself provides only that the corporation must not have more than one class of stock; while respondent's regulation provides that "If an instrument purporting to be a debt obligation is actually stock, it will constitute a second class of stock." There is no explanation in the regulation of what is meant by the term "actually stock"; but respondent's argument on brief is based on the premise that if the advances reflected by the notes were, in fact, invested capital, the notes are actually stock. Formally, Century House did not have more than one class of stock; it was authorized to issue only one class of stock and that is all it actually issued. The above-quoted sentence of respondent's regulation, as applied in his argument on brief, therefore appears to enlarge the scope of the statutory provision by providing that if an instrument in the form of a debt obligation actually represents equity capital, it constitutes a second class of stock and it disqualifies the corporation under subchapter S. Thus, the first question presented is whether this interpretation of the statutory provision falls within the scope of the Commissioner's authority.

The Commissioner is authorized under section 7805 of the 1954 Code to prescribe all needful rules and regulations for the enforcement of the tax laws. Such regulations, insofar as consistent with expressed statutory provisions, have the force and effect of law. Maryland Casualty Co. v. United States, 251 U.S. 342. However, the power of the Commissioner to prescribe regulations for the administration of the Federal tax laws is not the power to make law but is only the power to carry into effect the will of Congress as expressed by the statute. Manhattan Co. v. Commissioner, 297 U.S. 129. A regulation may not alter or amend the revenue law, Morrill v. Jones, 106 U.S. 466; nor extend a statute or modify its provisions, Campbell v. Galeno Chemical Co., 281 U.S. 599; nor may it take away any rights and privileges which the Congress has given, Russell Manufacturing Co. v. United States, 175 F. Supp. 159 (Ct. Cl. 1959); nor can it impose or add a condition which Congress did not impose, unless such condition is necessary to make effective the conditions imposed by Congress, Philadelphia Electric Co. v. United States, 117 F. Supp. 424 (Ct. Cl. 1954). We must determine whether the additional provision contained in the last sentence of respondent's regulation is a reasonable interpretation of the statutory requirement that the corporation have only one class of stock, and is consistent with the purpose and intent of Congress in enacting that provision of the statute.

Subchapter S (Code secs. 1371-1377) became a part of the Code for the first time as section 64 of the Technical Amendments Act of 1958, H.R. 8381, 85th Cong., 2d Sess. The provisions were not included in the bill as it originally passed the House of Representatives, but were added by the Senate Finance Committee. See S. Rept. No. 1983, 85th Cong., 2d Sess., p. 88, 1958-3 C.B. 1009. So far as we can determine from the committee reports the object of the provisions was to permit businesses to select the form of business organization desired, without the necessity of taking into account major differences in tax consequences. The provisions were a counterpart to the provisions enacted in the 1954 Code (sec. 1361), which permitted proprietorships and partnerships to elect to be taxed like corporations, and were designed to permit electing corporations to forgo the payment of tax and require their shareholders to report the corporate income (whether or not distributed) as their own for tax purposes. One of the specific objectives was to permit the shareholders to deduct the operating losses of the corporation against other income, which would not ordinarily be available to the corporation itself in the loss year (Code sec. 1374). See S. Rept. No. 1983, 85th Cong., 2d Sess., pp. 87-89, 1958-3 C.B. 922, pp. 1008-1010.

We find very little said in the legislative history of subchapter S regarding the requirement that, in order to qualify, a corporation must not have more than one class of stock. It would appear that it was so provided to conform to the general design to give relief from double taxation to the shareholders of small corporations which were essentially comparable to partnerships and proprietorships, where the earnings are taxed to the owners rather than to the business organizations (although there seems to be nothing in the law to make it inapplicable to a large corporation having only a few stockholders and only one class of stock); and to avoid the complexities involved in passing the earnings of a corporation through to its stockholders where the stock of the corporation is held by a widely diversified group of stockholders with different rights. See S. Rept. No. 830, 88th Cong., 2d Sess., p. 146, 1964-1 C.B. (Part 2) 650.

While we agree that the statutory language and the above objectives permit inquiry into whether an electing corporation has, in fact, more than one class of stock, we find nothing in the law itself, the committee reports, or the assumed purpose of the legislation that would justify holding, arbitrarily and per se, that all instruments which purport to be debt obligations but which in fact represent equity capital, must be treated as a second class of stock for purposes of section 1371. Consequently, we think the last sentence of the regulation, if given the connotation argued by respondent in this case, is too broad and places a restriction on the stockholders of electing corporations which was not intended by Congress. Congress obviously anticipated that stockholders of electing corporations could advance funds to corporations in the form of loans without disqualifying the corporation for subchapter S status, because it specifically made provision in section 1376 for adjustment of a shareholder's basis in any indebtedness owing him by the electing corporation for operating losses of the corporation made available to the shareholder as a deduction. But under the regulation, applied as it is by respondent in this case, if the note or evidence of indebtedness is "actually stock," the corporation is automatically disqualified under subchapter S regardless of the terms of the note or the practical effect thereof. We think this is tantamount to an extension or modification of the law and goes beyond the Commissioner's powers. Where a regulation is an amendment or modification of the statute and therefore beyond the power of the Commissioner to make, courts must refrain from giving it effect. Louisville Gas and Electric Co. v. United States, 148 Ct. Cl. 671 (1960). We think such is the situation here.

But we must still determine, independent of the regulation, whether the notes issued by Century House to petitioners must, because of the purported rights and interest they gave petitioners in the income and assets of the corporation, be considered to be a second class of stock for purposes of subchapter S. Respondent relies on the so-called thin capitalization cases, such as O. H. Kruse Grains & Milling v.

Commissioner, 279 F.2d 123; Rowan v. United States, 219 F.2d 51; Nassau Lens Co. v. Commissioner, 308 F.2d 39; Gilbert v. Commissioner, 248 F.2d 399; and 2554-58 Creston Corp., 40 T.C. 932, to conclude that the purported loans by petitioners to Century House were in reality contributions of additional capital, and that, as a corollary, the notes received by petitioners as evidence thereof were in substance stock, although in form they were debt obligations. Respondent then relies on the formal terms of the instruments to conclude that they gave petitioners rights in the income and assets of the corporation having priority over the rights petitioners had as stockholders, and therefore the notes were a second class of stock.

We think that if we are to determine the character of the instruments by reference to the substance of the underlying transactions, we must also look to the realities of the situation to determine whether the instruments, even though they might represent equity capital, actually gave the holders thereof any rights and interests in the corporation different from that owned by the holders of the nominal stock. We do not think they did under the circumstances here present, because the advances were made and the notes were held by the stockholders in direct proportion to their stockholdings. Not only were the terms of the notes waived or ignored by petitioners as note holders, but whatever preferences the notes gave them in the income and assets of the corporation, if enforced, were preferences only over themselves as stockholders.

The notes purported to give petitioners the right to periodic payments of a fixed amount of interest; but they waived this right. The notes also purported to give them the right to have their advances repaid on demand, but they made no such demand. The notes gave the holders no right to vote or have any voice in the management of the corporation. It is rather obvious that petitioners placed little, if any, reliance on the rights and preferences granted them by the notes in making their advances to the corporation. It is likely that in the event of bankruptcy of the corporation a bankruptcy court would have subordinated their claims to those of common creditors. See Pepper v. Litton, 308 U.S. 295. Petitioners were simply advancing the corporation additional funds as it needed them for acquisition of capital assets and working capital. These advances were placed at the risk of the business just the same as the amounts petitioners paid for the capital stock. But by the same token, we think the notes would have to be considered a nullity insofar as they purported to give petitioners any rights and interests in the income and assets of the corporation different from the rights and interests they had as owners of all the capital stock of the corporation. Under the circumstances here present we do not believe the notes can be considered true debt obligations, nor can they be considered to be a second class of stock. The advances for which the notes were given were simply contributions of additional capital which were in reality reflected in the value of the common stock already held by petitioners.

In the discussion above we have considered that the advances made by petitioners were actually equity capital placed at the risk of the business. Without launching into an extended discussion of the evidence, we think it is pretty obvious from the record as a whole that these advances were placed at the risk of the business and in that sense represented equity capital. Petitioners argue that the intent of the parties with respect to the advances is the most important criterion in this determination, and that their evidence is uncontradicted that both they and the corporation at all times intended their advances to be recovered out of the permanent third-party financing of the construction and the anticipated quick profits the corporation would realize from the fair. While we agree that the intent of the parties is an important factor to be considered, see Rowan v. United States, supra, that factor alone is not decisive; and furthermore the intent of the parties cannot always be determined from their statements and their book entries alone, but must be borne out by the economic realities of the situation. As said in Bazley v. Commissioner, 331 U.S. 737, 741, "the form of a transaction as reflected by correct corporate accounting opens questions as to the proper application of a taxing statute; it does not close them." "[T]he significant factor [is] . . . whether the funds were advanced with reasonable expectations of repayment regardless of the success of the venture or were placed at the risk of the business," Gilbert v. Commissioner, supra.

It seems pretty obvious here that regardless of the intentions, hopes, and expectations of petitioners at the time they started this venture that they would get their advances back in a short time, it very rapidly become apparent that these hopes would not be realized. They must have realized that they could not recover their advances in a short time unless the corporation could obtain outside financing in an amount that would cover not only 100 percent of the cost of the land, the building, and the furniture and fixtures, but would also provide some funds for operating expenses, because the organization expenses alone far exceeded the designated capital of the corporation. It was quite evident by 1961 that this could not be accomplished. The ratio of the corporation's long-term liabilities to its nominal capital at the end of 1960 was about 1,100 to 1; but petitioners had to continue pumping their own money into the project. The ratio of petitioners' unpaid advances to their capital contributions was about 170 to 1 at the end of 1960. It is clear that outside investors would not have made the same loans to the corporation on the same terms petitioners did; Century House had difficulty raising the necessary cash on secured notes at maximum rates of interest. So we must conclude that in economic substance the advances by petitioners constituted risk capital rather than loans. But for the reasons heretofore stated we have concluded that the notes representing those advances did not constitute a second class of stock and that Century House did not have more than one class of stock within the meaning of section 1371.

Respondent claims that because of the interplay of sections 1376 and 1232 of the Code, petitioners will gain an unintended tax advantage if the corporation is recognized as a subchapter S corporation because they might recover amounts previously deducted as ordinary losses (the operating losses of the corporation which are passed through) at capital gains rates. Without going into the details of why this result might be reached, we point out that if this is a loophole it is a legislative oversight and should be more appropriately plugged by congressional action rather than by judicial legislation. This purported tax advantage has been recognized by the writers of tax articles ever since enactment of subchapter S. See Anthoine, "Federal Tax Legislation of 1958: The Corporate Election and Collapsible Amendment," 58 Col. L. Rev. 1146; Caplin, "Subchapter S and Its Effect on the Capitalization of Corporations," 13 Vand. L. Rev. 185. Nothing has been done about it. We also observe that there are tax disadvantages in the area of operating losses of subchapter S corporations, as well as the supposed advantage mentioned above, because if the operating losses of the corporation exceed the basis of the stockholders in both their stock and indebtedness, any excess of operating losses will apparently be lost forever. Further, we note that this is the only purportedly unintended tax advantage arising out of this situation which respondent has called to our attention.

Finally, respondent argues that to hold for petitioners on this issue would be contrary to our decision in Catalina Homes, Inc., T.C. Memo. 1964-225, and to the decision of the U.S. District Court for the Middle District of Alabama in Henderson v. United States, 245 F. Supp. 782, on appeal (C.A. 5). An examination of the briefs filed with this Court in Catalina Homes, Inc., supra, reveals that the applicability and validity of respondent's regulations was assumed by the parties, or at least was not argued, and the Memorandum Opinion of the Court does not pass on that issue. Neither does the published opinion of the court in Henderson v. United States, supra. Both opinions concern themselves only with whether advances by stockholders were in fact loans or equity capital; and we do not consider that either of them rules on the applicability or the validity of the last sentence of respondent's regulation discussed above. Consequently, we do not think those cases are controlling here. We know of no other court decision which has passed on this question. We believe it is a question of fact in each case whether advances by stockholders in the form of loans, which in economic substance are equity capital, constitute a second class of stock, and that this must be decided in each case independent of the last sentence of respondent's regulation.

We wish to emphasize that our consideration is limited to the facts and circumstances as they existed during the years before us and we make no judgment with respect to the qualification of the corporation in subsequent years if the facts and circumstances are different. It appears that one of the recognized advantages or disadvantages of the provisions of subchapter S is that the status of an electing corporation may be voluntarily or involuntarily changed from a qualified corporation to an unqualified corporation at any time, so we see no need to extend our consideration of the status of Century House beyond the years here involved. We also observe that while we have given lip service to the so-called thin capitalization doctrine we have some doubt as to its applicability in determining whether a corporation has more than one class of stock for purposes of subchapter S. That doctrine was promulgated by the courts to prevent the avoidance of the double tax in the normal corporation situation by distributing corporate earnings to the stockholders in the form of interest or repayments of loans. The underlying purpose of subchapter S appears to be to avoid this double tax on corporate earnings and we see little in the way of unintended tax advantages that might be gained by having the stockholders advance funds in the form of loans rather than capital where, as here, the corporation has no accumulated earnings and profits. . . .

Reviewed by the Court.

[Two separate concurring opinions and the dissenting opinion of RAUM, J., in which four other judges joined, are omitted.]

STINNETT v. COMMISSIONER
54 T.C. 221 (1970)

QUEALY, Judge: . . . The issues for decision are: (1) Whether International Meadows, Inc., had more than one class of stock within the meaning of section 1371(a) of the Internal Revenue Code of 1954 thereby rendering its election to be taxed as a small business corporation invalid; [second issue omitted].

Findings of Fact

Issue 1. Qualification Under Section 1371(a)

Some of the facts were stipulated and they are so found. The stipulation of facts and the exhibits attached thereto are incorporated herein by this reference. . . .

In early 1962 petitioners James L. Stinnett, Jr., Robert E. Brown, Louis H. Heath, and Harold L. Roberts formed a partnership known as J. B. J. Co. for the purpose of operating a golf driving range in El Segundo, Calif. Prior to this time on October 6, 1961, J. B. J. Co., which at that time was composed of Stinnett, Brown, and Heath, executed a lease with the Standard Oil Co. of California (hereinafter referred to as Standard Oil). Under this lease J. B. J. Co. leased a certain tract in El Segundo, Calif., for 3 years for use as a golf driving range.

Petitioners Brown and Stinnett had spent 2 years and 9 months in attempts to obtain this lease from Standard Oil. During this period Brown and Stinnett engaged in surveys and projections in order to evaluate the possibilities of success for a driving range in the El Segundo area. In undertaking these surveys Brown and Stinnett incurred expenses which were unreimbursed.

When Brown and Stinnett realized that the lease from Standard Oil was forthcoming, they determined that they would need additional capital. They then contacted a mutual friend, petitioner Heath, who consented to join the venture.

Brown and Stinnett each contributed $10,000 and Heath contributed $20,000. Brown and Stinnett were each to have a 35-percent interest in the partnership and Heath was to have 30 percent. In addition Heath was to manage the business and receive a salary. The reason for the discrepancy in the partnership percentage division was the aforenoted time and funds that Brown and Stinnett had expended in promoting the venture.

In the early part of 1962 petitioner Harold L. Roberts, another friend, joined the partnership. Roberts contributed about $53,000. As of May 31, 1962, the partners' percentages for sharing profits and losses were:

	Percent
Robert E. Brown	27
James L. Stinnett	27
Louis H. Heath	23
Harold L. Roberts	23

The partners' capital accounts were:

Robert E. Brown	$ 8,504.35
James L. Stinnett	8,504.35
Louis H. Heath	18,753.62
Harold L. Roberts	52,252.17

On April 6, 1962, International Meadows, Inc. (hereinafter referred to as the corporation), was formed under the laws of the State of California for the purpose of operating the golf driving range that had been operated by J. B. J. Co. Article four of the articles of incorporation provided:

> This corporation is authorized to issue only one class of shares of stock; the total number of said shares shall be One Hundred (100) of a par value of One ($1.00) Dollar per share; and the aggregate par value of all shares having a par value is One Hundred (100.00) Dollars.

On May 25, 1962, the corporation obtained from the commissioner of corporations of the State of California a permit to sell and issue 100 shares of its common stock for $1 per share. The stock was issued and held of record as follows:

	Shares
Robert E. Brown	27
James L. Stinnett	27
Louis H. Heath	23
Harold L. Roberts	23

On May 31, 1962, J. B. J. transferred all of its assets and liabilities to the corporation. In return for the transfer each partner was to receive a promissory note equal to the amount of his capital account as of May 31, 1962. Such notes were ultimately issued on November 28, 1962, payable in 58 monthly installments without interest.

The notes were executed on behalf of the corporation by James L. Stinnet. The notes were identical except for the identity of the payee and the amount payable. The note given to petitioner Heath provided:

NOTE

EL SEGUNDO, CALIFORNIA

$16,307.50

November 28, 1962

For Value received, International Meadows, Inc., a corporation, promises to pay to Louis H. Heath and/or Mary S. Heath or order at El Segundo, California, the sum of Sixteen Thousand Three Hundred Seven and 50/100th Dollars without interest, payable in fifty-eight monthly installments, fifty-seven installments of $281.16 and one final installment of $281.38. First installment to be payable January 1, 1963.

_____

President

_____

Secretary-Treasurer

On June 14, 1962, the corporation timely elected under the provisions of section 1372 to be taxed as a small business corporation.

On or about July 15, 1962, Louis H. Heath transferred three shares of stock to Harold L. Roberts. At the same time Heath also transferred to Roberts $2,446.12 of the debt owed him by the corporation. This explains the deviation between Roberts' capital account as of May 31, 1962, and the amount of the note ($54,698.29) made payable to him. Roberts gave Heath approximately $6,000 in return for the transfer of the stock and the indebtedness.

The petitioners claim, and the respondent does not seriously dispute, that Brown, Stinnett, Heath, and Roberts fully expected the notes to be repaid over the term of the lease. However, due to problems encountered in starting up the business and to its failure to come up to expectations, the corporation did not have the funds to make payments on the notes.

As of December 31, 1964, the corporation was also indebted to a bank in the sum of $18,500 in addition to certain other liabilities.

In December of 1962 James L. Stinnett, Jr., and Robert E. Brown each transferred four shares of stock of the corporation to James E. Thomas, as an inducement to Thomas to make a loan to the corporation. In November and December of 1962 Thomas made advances to the corporation of $20,000 at 6-percent interest. As of October 1967 the unpaid balance of the loan was $15,681.22 and interest had been paid up to that date.

For the taxable years in issue the corporation did not (a) have more than 10 shareholders, (b) have as a shareholder a person who is not an individual, (c) have a nonresident alien as a shareholder, and (d) have any passive investment income as that term is defined by section 1372(e)(5).

For the taxable years 1963 and 1964 each of the petitioners deducted their distributable share of the net operating loss of the corporation as follows:

	1963	1964	Total
Stinnett	$ 8,529.29	$ 6,854.55	$15,383.84
Thomas	2,966.72	2,384.19	5,350.91
Brown	8,529.29	6,854.55	15,383.84
Heath	7,416.78	5,964.08	13,380.86
Roberts	9,641.80	7,748.94	17,390.74
International Meadows	37,083.88	29,806.31[2]	66,890.19

[2]There is a discrepancy between the amount of loss distributable according to the corporation's return for 1963, i.e., $29,802.41, and the total amount deducted by all shareholders, i.e., $29,806.31. This small discrepancy is not explained in the record.

In his notice of deficiency, respondent disallowed the deduction by the individual petitioners of their respective shares of the net operating losses of the corporation for the taxable years 1963 and 1964. In support of these adjustments, the respondent took the position that the corporation did not qualify as a small business corporation under section 1371(a) of the 1954 Code. . . .

Opinion

Issue 1. Qualification under Section 1371(a)

The corporation sustained losses during the years in question which were reflected in the individual income tax returns filed by the various petitioners on the assumption that the corporation was a "small business corporation" as defined in section 1371(a) and had made a valid election to be taxed in accordance with the provisions of subchapter S. The respondent has disallowed those deductions on the ground that the corporation was not a small business corporation as defined in section 1371(a). That section provides:

(a) Small Business Corporation — For purposes of this subchapter, the term "small business corporation" means a domestic corporation which is not a member of an affiliated group (as defined in section 1504) and which does not —

(1) have more than 10 shareholders;

(2) have as a shareholder a person (other than an estate) who is not an individual;

(3) have a nonresident alien as a shareholder; and

(4) have more than one class of stock.

In the stipulation of facts, the respondent concedes that the corporation meets the first three requirements for qualification under section 1371(a) but contends that the corporation had outstanding more than one class of stock. In support of this position, the respondent argues that certain advances to the corporation by the petitioners evidenced by installment notes gave rise to an "equity" interest which was, in substance and reality, redeemable preferred stock. As a result, the corporation had outstanding two classes of stock.

We have here a case in which four individuals joined together in a partnership to establish and operate a recreation facility on leased land. Each contributed an agreed amount to the capital of the partnership in order to finance the leasehold improvements. Each was to receive a share of the profits from the venture in percentages which varied, and appear not to have been dependent upon their respective capital contributions.

Within a relatively short period thereafter, the assets and liabilities of the partnership were transferred to a newly formed corporation which issued its common stock to the former partners in proportion to their share in the profits of the partnership. In addition, the corporation issued to each a non-interest-bearing note payable in installments for the amount of the capital contributed by each to the partnership. The installment payments on these notes were designed to liquidate the obligations over the term of the lease, thereby intending that the cash flow resulting from the amortization of the leasehold improvements and from profits would provide sufficient funds to pay off the notes.

The corporation had only a nominal capitalization wholly inadequate for the needs of the business. The notes were non-interest-bearing and were subordinated in fact, if not by their terms, to the other indebtedness of the corporation. Because of the circumstances, the respondent contends that for tax purposes the so-called "debt" represented by these notes should be regarded as "equity" capital. From this premise, the respondent concludes that the corporation had outstanding two classes of stock. While the respondent's premise may be well taken, were we concerned with treatment of payments of principal or interest on account of these notes under general tax law, it is not determinative of the issue in this case. Even accepting the respondent's argument, we would not have two classes of stock, one class being represented by the common stock, and the other being represented by the notes.

The notes did not entitle the holders to any right to vote or to participate in the decision-making process. The notes did not entitle the holders to participate in any of the earnings or growth of the business, being limited solely to the repayment of the "debt" itself without interest. While the notes were subordinated and subject to all of the risks of the business, nevertheless it would be wholly unrealistic to treat these notes *standing* alone as another class of stock. The notes represented an "equity" interest only so long as coupled with the ownership of the common stock.

The obvious purpose of the notes was to provide that distributions by the corporation out of its "cash flow" would be applied first in repayment of the original capital shares of the former partners. Those amounts were disproportionate to their respective interests in the profits as represented by the common stock. Thus if we are to regard the notes as "equity," we either have an equity interest or capital advance which does not affect the character of the stock under section 1371, or we have three separate classes of stock.[4]

Faced with this choice, it is our opinion that regardless whether the notes in question be considered as "debt" or as "equity" under other provisions of the internal revenue laws, for purposes of section 1371 such notes do not change the character of the common stock so as to give rise to more than one class of stock.

[4]At the outset the interests of Robert E. Brown and James L. Stinnett represented by stock and that represented by the notes were proportionate each to the other, but disproportionate to the interests of Louis H. Heath and Harold L. Roberts, and the respective interests of the latter were also disproportionate each to the other, as shown by the following comparison:

	Proportionate right to vote and share in earnings	Proportionate distributions on account of notes
Class one:		
Robert E. Brown	27/100	8,504.35
		88,014.49
James L. Stinnett	27/100	8,504.35
		88,014.49
Class two:		
Louis H. Heath	23/100	18,753.62
		88,014.49
Class three:		
Harold L. Roberts	23/100	52,252.17
		88,014.49

An instrument which upon its face consitutes evidence of indebtedness and does not carry with it rights or privileges commonly attributed to stock is generally deemed to be an "equity" interest by coupling the debt with a formal stock interest held by the same or a related person. That is the essence of the so-called thin-capitalization doctrine. . . . In recognition of this, this Court concluded in W. C. Gamman, 46 T.C. 1 (1966), that where the debt was in the same proportion as the stock, there was not a second class of stock.

Following our decision in the *Gamman* case, the Commissioner amended regulations section 1.137-1(g) to provide, in part, as follows:

> Obligations which purport to represent debt but which actually represent equity capital will *generally* constitute a second class of stock. However, if such purported debt obligations are owned solely by the owners of the nominal stock of the corporation in substantially the same proportion as they own such nominal stock, such purported debt obligations will be treated as contributions to capital rather than a second class of stock. But, if an issuance, redemption, sale, or other transfer of nominal stock, or of purported debt obligations which actually represent equity capital, results in a change in a shareholder's proportionate share of nominal stock or his proportionate share of such purported debt, a new determination shall be made as to whether the corporation has more than one class of stock as of the time of such change. [Emphasis supplied.]

We do not regard as controlling with respect to the question whether there is more than one class of stock within the meaning of section 1371(a) the fact that "debt" characterized as "equity" capital may be disproportionate to the respective common stock interests of the stockholders. Accordingly, we must hold the regulation invalid as applied to this case. To hold otherwise not only would serve largely to defeat the purpose for which Congress enacted subchapter S, but would be inconsistent with the underlying scheme of the statute as exemplified by section 1376(b)(2).

Section 1376(b)(2) treats debt owing to stockholders as a secondary equity interest, in any event. That section provides:

> (b) Reduction in Basis of Stock and Indebtedness for Shareholder's Portion of Corporation Net Operating Loss —
> (1) Reduction in Basis of Stock. — The basis of shareholder's stock in an electing small business corporation shall be reduced (but not below zero) by an amount equal to the amount of his portion of the corporation's net operating loss for any taxable year attributable to such stock (as determined under section 1374(c)).
> (2) Reduction in Basis of Indebtedness. — The basis of any indebtedness of an electing small business corporation to a shareholder of such corporation shall be reduced (but not below zero) by an amount equal to the amount of the shareholder's portion of the corporation's net operating loss for any taxable year (as determined under section 1374(c)), but only to the extent that such amount exceeds the adusted basis of the stock of such corporation held by the shareholder.

Not only is this a clear indication that the statute contemplates that the stockholders of a subchapter S corporation would make advances or lend money to the corporation, but for the purpose of reflecting losses deducted by the stockholders in their returns, any resulting debt is treated as a part of the stockholder's "investment." The losses which are charged to that investment can only be attributable to the interest of the stockholder represented by the common stock.

If we look to the effect of section 1376(b)(2), it thus becomes apparent that for purposes of subchapter S, the statute treats debt owing to a stockholder, whether or not regarded as equity for other purposes, as a part of that stockholder's equity interest in the corporation. Debt owing to a nonstockholder is treated differently.

It is not contemplated that all rights and interests of the stockholders of a subchapter S corporation will be equal. Even if the stockholder advances were initially in proportion to their respective stock interests, disproportionate rights could result on account of the limitation on the deductibility of losses which is dependent on the stockholder's basis for both the stock and debt.

In a case where the subchapter S corporation operates at a loss, the only effect of the mixed investment of stock and debt as between stockholders is to produce a different limitation — disproportionate to their respective stock interests — in the amount of loss each can deduct. A similar disproportion results if each acquires his stock at different times or at a different cost.

Where there are profits, application of the income in payment of the debt in lieu of the distribution of a dividend has the effect of increasing the basis — also the limitation of deduction of any future losses — of the stockholders who must report the income, and of reducing the overall investment of the stockholder who receives payment on the debt. No foreseeable tax benefit results to either. Such a capital structure merely provides a means whereby a participant who does not have the capital resources is able to reinvest the aftertax earnings of the business and thereby repay funds advanced by other participants. [S]uch obviously was the intent in the case before the Court.

Since this type of transaction was clearly contemplated by the terms of the statute itself, and is the normal result of the operation of section 1376, it is only reasonable to assume that the Congress did not intend that debt owing to a stockholder of a subchapter S corporation would result in more than one class of stock under the thin-capitalization doctrine. That is not to say that an instrument called a "note" may not by its very terms be something else. However, where the instrument is a simple installment note, without any incidents commonly attributed to stock, it does not give rise to more than one class of stock within the meaning of section 1371 merely because the debt creates disproportionate rights among the stockholders to the assets of the corporation.

We do not have to decide whether the notes involved in this case might nevertheless be treated as "equity" for other purposes. We are not here concerned with the treatment of interest paid on those notes. In fact, no interest was paid. Nor are we concerned with characterizing the transaction to determine whether petitioners might have a bad debt loss in the event of worthlessness. We are not even concerned with the question whether such debt may not be treated differently under other provisions of the tax laws, even in the case of a corporation which has elected to be taxed under subchapter S. For example, there might be situations in which earnings accumulated prior to qualification under subchapter S are sought to be distributed to a stockholder-creditor of the corporation in the "guise" [of] repayment of debt.

All we are called upon to decide is whether the corporation (International Meadows) had outstanding more than "one class" of stock within the meaning of section 1371 of the Code. In the corporate or formal sense, clearly the corporation did not. There can be no question that under the laws of the State of California the corporation had outstanding 100 shares of common stock and nothing more. The only real question is whether in the "tax sense" — in order to carry out the legislative intent — we are required to disregard the form of the incorporation in order to reach a different conclusion.

The statute does not prescribe any rules which we may look to for guidance. The underlying rationale of the thin-capitalization doctrine seems to be, however, going back to Gregory v. Helvering, 293 U.S. 465, that the court will disregard the form of the transaction where it is to some degree lacking in substance *and* a failure to do so would serve to frustrate the purpose of the taxing statute. As we have pointed out, this is not that type of case. In fact, the only result of a contrary holding on this case would be to defeat an election which the Congress clearly intended to be of benefit to the small and frequently "thinly capitalized" business. . . .

Reviewed by the Court.

Decisions will be entered under Rule 50.

NOTE

See P. DiQuinzio, Refinancing and/or Sales or Acquisitions of Subchapter S Corporations, 28 N.Y.U. Inst. on Fed. Tax. 269 (1970); L. Bravenec, The One Class of Stock Requirement of Subchapter S — A Round Peg in a Pentagonal Hole, 6 Hous. L. Rev. 215 (1968); T. White, III, Recurring and New Problems Under Subchapter S, 27 N.Y.U. Inst. on Fed. Tax. 755 (1969).

DUARTE v. COMMISSIONER
44 T.C. 193 (1965)

PIERCE, Judge: Respondent determined a deficiency in income tax against petitioners in the amount of $5,970.45 for the taxable year 1959.

The issues for decision are:

(1) Whether the principal petitioner's purported transfers to his two children of 50 percent of his stock in a wholly owned business corporation, which he then elected to have taxed as a subchapter S corporation under sections 1371-1377 of the 1954 Code, were bona fide and economically real; or whether the transfers were in form only and lacked economic substance, so as to make all of the taxable income of the corporation attributable to said petitioner.

(2) If said transfers were in substance what they purported to be in form, should an increased portion of the taxable income of the corporation be allocated to said petitioner in order to reflect the value of his services in accordance with section 1375(c) of the 1954 Code?

Findings of Fact

... Petitioner has been the president of Graham Accounting & Statistical Corp. (hereinafter called Graham Corp.) since its incorporation under the laws of New York in January of 1956. From 1940 to 1956 the business had been operated by petitioner as a sole proprietorship; and at the time of incorporation of Graham Corp. all of the 100 shares of capital stock of the corporation were issued to petitioner.

Graham Corp. furnished temporary office help to other businesses in the New York area. It kept a file of available bookkeepers, stenographers, and other office help; and when called upon to do so, would furnish businesses with temporary office help by the hour, day, week, or longer periods of time. It paid the wages of the help it sent out, and charged the businesses an amount to cover wages, taxes, overhead costs, and profit. The advantage to a business that availed itself of the Graham Corp. services, was that it did not need to carry employees for a full year in order to handle busy seasons. Graham Corp. also provided businesses with other services such as the preparation of payroll tax returns and other tax reports.

Petitioner has two children — a son, Henry Duarte, Jr., who was born on June 7, 1942, and was about 15 years of age in the taxable year here involved; and a son, William P. F. Duarte, who was born on December 18, 1949, and was about 8 years of age at that time. On May 11, 1958, petitioner endorsed his stock certificate for 100 shares of Graham Corp. (being all the shares of said corporation) as follows: "For Value Received I hereby sell, assign, and transfer unto H. D. Duarte, Sr. (50 shares), Henry Duarte, Jr. (25 shares) & Wm. P. F. Duarte (25 shares) Shares of the Capital Stock represented by the within Certificate. . . ." Petitioner's stock certificate for the 100 shares was then turned back to the corporation and on May 12, 1958, the corporation issued a certificate for 50 shares to petitioner, a certificate for 25 shares to Henry D. Duarte, Jr., and a certificate for 25 shares to William P. F. Duarte. On the new stock certificates issued to petitioner's children, the names of the owners were designated at "Henry Duarte, Jr." on one certificate, and as "William P. F. Duarte" on the other certificate. At a subsequent date in 1959 the certificates were amended by inserting on the face of each certificate the additional words "To Dorothy Duarte as Custodian for" before the name theretofore shown on each certificate, and also by adding the words "Under the New York Uniform Gifts to Minors Act" after the name on each certificate.

The New York Uniform Gifts to Minors Act became effective on July 1, 1959, and it repealed the Gifts of Securities to Minors Law which had theretofore been in effect. The above-mentioned purported transfers of stock by petitioner to his children in May 1958 did not meet the requirements of the Gifts of Securities to Minors Law, because the certificates were not at that time registered in the name of a custodian.[1]

---

[1]Ch. 35, sec. 265, art. 8-A, N.Y. Laws 1956.
Sec. 265(a). Securities, if in registered form, shall be registered in the donor's name or

Petitioner filed a gift tax return for the year 1958 reflecting the purported transfer of 25 shares of stock to each of his children; but there was no reportable gift tax liability.

In January 1959 Graham Corp. filed its election in accordance with section 1372(a) of the Internal Revenue Code of 1954 to be taxed as a small business corporation and the corporation then qualified for tax treatment as what is sometimes called a subchapter S corporation or a tax option corporation. Subsequently, on January 5, 1959, a resolution was passed by the board of directors of Graham Corp. reducing petitioner's salary from the $30,000 he had been receiving annually in 1956, 1957, and 1958, to $15,600. Petitioner actually received for his services $15,200 in 1959, $14,800 in 1960, and $15,600 in 1961.

Petitioner filed on behalf of the corporation a small business corporation return (Form 1120-S) for the calendar year 1959 with the district director of internal revenue, New York, N.Y., and also similar returns for the years 1960 and 1961. The following summary shows the amounts reported on said returns as having been distributed to petitioner's children during each of the years 1959, 1960, and 1961:

| Year | Date of distribution | Amount of dividend distributions | | | Total undistributed taxable income | Total taxable income per 1120-S |
		Petitioner Henry Duarte	Henry, Jr.	William P. F.		
1959	Dec. 18, 1959	$ 8,000.00	....	....	\} $1,982.54	$ 17,982.54
	Dec. 28, 1959	....	$ 4,000.00	$ 4,000.00		
1960	Dec. 1, 1960	8,000.00	4,000.00	4,000.00	5,509.43	21,509.43
1961	Dec. 31, 1961	30,686.92	[1]15,343.46	[1]15,343.46	....	61,373.83
	Totals	46,686.92	23,343.46	23,343.46	7,491.97	100,865.80

[1]Schedule K of the 1961 return shows, in column 5, dividends of $15,360.38 distributed to each of the two children, of which $16.92 was deemed a "nondividend distribution" per column 10 — or a net of $15,343.46 to each child.

The above summary reveals that a total of $23,343.46 was distributed as dividends to petitioner's son Henry during the years 1959, 1960, and 1961; and that a like amount was distributed as dividends to his son William for the same year. In fact, neither the designated custodian of these children, nor the children themselves, received any of these amounts.

As regards the years 1959 here involved, the above summary reveals that on December 28 of that year $4,000 was distributed to each of petitioner's children; but here again, no portion of such amount was received by either of the children. No custodian account for Henry Duarte, Jr., was opened until December 29, 1961; and no account of this type was opened for William P. F. Duarte until January 30, 1962. Although an income tax return for the year 1959 was filed for each of the children,

in the name of any adult member of the minor's family or in the name of any guardian of the minor, followed by the words "as custodian, for ———————— (name of minor), a minor under article eight-a of the personal property law of New York", and the securities shall be delivered to the person in whose name they are thus registered as custodian. . . .

these returns were actually prepared and signed by petitioner, and petitioner paid all of the reported tax liability out of his personal checking account.

Petitioner during the year 1959 exercised complete dominion and control over the operations of Graham Corp. and the dividends purportedly distributed to his children.

Respondent, in his notice of deficiency herein, determined that "the entire amount of the small business corporation income is distributable to you [petitioner] and none is distributable to your sons, Henry E. [sic] Duarte, Jr. and William P. F. Duarte."

Ultimate Finding of Fact

The purported transfers of stock by petitioner to his two minor children had no economic reality; and petitioner was the true economic owner of all of the stock of the Graham Corp. during the taxable year here involved.

Opinion

Respondent contends that the transfer by petitioner of 50 percent of his stock to his children was not bona fide and lacked economic reality. We agree with respondent.

If there were not legal limitations, it would be easy for a small family business to incorporate, elect to be taxed as a subchapter S corporation, and then divide the stock among members of the family with a resulting division and splitting of the income. But in addition to general legal principles limiting the effectiveness of such a plan when it lacks economic substance, the provisions of the Internal Revenue Code of 1954 also regulate the splitting of income among members of a family. Section 1375(c) of the Internal Revenue Code of 1954 provides that:

> *"Sec. 1375. Special Rules Applicable to Distributions of Electing Small Business Corporations.*
>
> "(c) Treatment of Family Groups. — Any dividend received by a shareholder from an electing small business corporation (including any amount treated as a dividend under section 1373(b)) may be apportioned or allocated by the Secretary or his delegate between or among shareholders of such corporation who are members of such shareholder's family (as defined in section 704(e)(3)), if he determines that such apportionment or allocation is necessary in order to reflect the value of services rendered to the corporation by such shareholders."

Also Income Tax Regulations, sec. 1.1373-1, provide:

> "Sec. 1.1373-1 Corporation undistributed taxable income taxed to shareholders.
>
> "(a)(2) ... A donee or purchaser of stock in the corporation is not considered a shareholder unless such stock is acquired in a bona fide transaction and the donee or purchaser is the real owner of such stock. The circumstances, not only as of the time of the purported transfer but also during the periods preceding and following it, will be taken into consideration in de-

termining the bona fides of the transfer. Transactions between members of a family will be closely scrutinized."

The above provisions make it clear that if a transaction between members of a family is not bona fide, its effectiveness as an income-splitting device will be frustrated.

We have often held in considering various types of transactions that if a transaction is complete in form but lacks reality, it will not be recognized as effective for income tax purposes. See Gregory v. Helvering, 293 U.S. 465; Knetsch v. United States, 364 U.S. 361. This has become a major principle of income tax law.

Respondent determined that the stock transfers between petitioner and his children were not bona fide; and the burden of proving that there was substance to the transfers was on the petitioner. See Roy C. Acuff, 35 T.C. 162, 172, aff'd. 296 F.2d 725 (C.A. 6, 1961). The only witness for the petitioner was the petitioner himself; and the only exhibits received in evidence were the income tax returns of the corporation and of the petitioners, and the stock certificates involved. And after seeing and hearing petitioner testify and after considering and weighing all the evidence, we are convinced that petitioner has not carried his burden of proof.

The mere form of the stock certificates is not sufficient in itself to establish the realism of the transfers. There is no evidence that either the custodian who was named in the certificates as amended, or the children themselves, exercised any influence at all in the operation of the corporation; and to the contrary, the evidence reveals that the petitioner, following the transfers, continued to completely control the policies and operation of the corporation. As we have hereinbefore found as a fact, the children did not receive any of the $4,000 which the corporation reported as having been distributed to each of them in the taxable year involved. No bank account or book account was established for either of the children in said year; and petitioner was unable to satisfactorily explain what happened to this money.

We have heretofore found as an ultimate fact, and we here hold, that the purported transfers of stock by petitioner to his two minor children had no economic reality; and that petitioner was the true economic owner of all the stock of the Graham Corp. during the taxable year involved. We decide this first issue for the respondent.

Since we have held for respondent on the first issue, it is unnecessary for us to consider the alternative second issue.

Decision will be entered for the respondent.

NOTE

See J. McCoy, Assignment of Income: Possibilities Under Subchapter S, 23 Tax L. Rev. 213 (1968).

FEINGOLD v. COMMISSIONER
49 T.C. 461 (1968)

SIMPSON, Judge: The respondent determined deficiencies in the petitioner's income tax for the calendar year 1961 in the amount of $1,509.91 and for the calendar year 1962 of $3,937.45. The principal question in this case is whether an election by a small business corporation under subchapter S of the Internal Revenue Code of 1954 terminated by reason of its having derived more than 20 percent of its gross receipts from "rents". If such election was not terminated, there is also a question as to the amount of loss sustained by the corporation in 1962 and deductible by the petitioners in their returns for that year.

Findings of Fact

Some of the facts have been stipulated and those facts are so found.

The petitioners Max and Gertrude Feingold are husband and wife, who maintain their legal residence at Rockaway Beach, New York, at the time the petition was filed in this case. . . .

In 1961, the petitioners formed the Germac Realty Corporation (Germac) under the laws of the State of New York. During 1961 and 1962, they owned all of its outstanding stock and were its only officers. Max was president and Gertrude was secretary-treasurer. Germac filed its corporate tax returns for 1961 and 1962 with the district director of internal revenue, Brooklyn, New York. Germac filed a timely election to be taxed as a small business corporation under subchapter S for the years 1961 and following.

During the years 1961 and 1962, Germac operated a colony of 95 rental bungalows located in a 3-block area near the beach in Far Rockaway, New York. These bungalows were rented from Memorial Day to Labor Day to vacationers and their families, for whom the colony's major attraction was its proximity to the beach. During the rest of the year, the colony was closed and repairs were made during that time. Most of the bungalows were single-family units, although a few held two families. They were furnished with tables, chairs, refrigerators, stoves, beds, mattresses, and mattress covers. Germac paid the taxes on the property and performed the repairs. Max, who had had experience in renting bungalows prior to 1961, supervised Germac's operations.

In 1960 or 1961, Max and Germac paved, fenced, and provided lighting for a patio on the premises measuring 30 by 115 feet. This patio was provided as a common recreation area for the tenants and was restricted to their use. Here, during the day, children played ball, and tenants played cards and bingo, with tables, chairs, and cards provided by Germac. It occasionally gave parties for the children, providing hats and small prizes.

Two or three times during the summer of each of the years 1961 and 1962, Germac sponsored parties for the tenants. Max, who was usually on the premises and who saw the tenants frequently, notified them when a party was to be given. At each of these parties, approximately $25 of food and beverages was provided by Germac; sometimes Max bought the refreshments himself, but at other times, he gave one of the tenants money with instructions to buy "whatever you think that the people would want." Occasionally, the food and beverages were paid for by a check drawn on Germac's bank account, but usually Max paid cash out of his own pocket. At times, the tenants who attended these parties bought additional refreshments with their own money.

For 1961, the first year of Germac's operations, it reported gross income of $49,212.00, consisting entirely of rentals from the bungalows, and reported a loss of $9,929.73. For 1962, it reported gross income of $49,587.42, of which $49,274.50 constituted rentals from the bungalows and $312.92 was "other income". It reported a loss in that year of $15,290.59.

Opinion

The issue in this case is whether net operating losses sustained by Germac during the years 1961 and 1962 are deductible from the income of its shareholders, the petitioners, under section 1374. Under that section, the shareholders of an electing small business corporation are allowed to deduct the losses of the corporation. Since Germac made a timely election under section 1372 to be taxed as a small business corporation under subchapter S, the only question is whether that election terminated under section 1372(e)(5) because 100 per cent of the corporation's receipts in 1961 and more than 99 per cent of the its receipts in 1962 were derived from the rental of vacation bungalows.

Section 1372(e)(5), as applicable to the years in controversy, provided:

"*Sec. 1372. Election by Small Business Corporation.*

"(e) Termination. — . . .

"(5) Personal holding company income. — An election under subsection (a) made by a small business corporation shall terminate if, for any taxable year of the corporation for which the election is in effect, such corporation has gross receipts more than 20 per cent of which is derived from royalties, rents, dividends, interest, annuities, and sales or exchanges of stock or securities (gross receipts from such sales or exchanges being taken into account for purposes of this paragraph only to the extent of gains therefrom). Such termination shall be effective for the taxable year of the corporation in which it has gross receipts of such amount, and for all succeeding taxable years of the corporation."[2]

---

[2]In 1966, this paragraph was amended to read as follows:

"(5) *Passive investment income.* —

"(A) Except as provided in subparagraph (B), an election under subsection (a) made by a small business corporation shall terminate if, for any taxable year of the corporation for which the election is in effect, such corporation has gross receipts more than 20 per cent of which is passive investment income. Such termination shall be effective for the taxable year of the corporation in which it has gross receipts of such amount, and for all succeeding taxable years of the corporation.

"(B) Subparagraph (A) shall not apply with respect to a taxable year in which a small business corporation has gross receipts more than 20 per cent of which is passive investment income, if —

"(i) such taxable year is the first taxable year in which the corporation commenced the active conduct of any trade or business or the next succeeding taxable year; and

"(ii) the amount of passive investment income for such taxable year is less than $3,000.

"(C) For purposes of this paragraph, the term 'passive investment income' means gross receipts derived from royalties, rents, dividends, interest, annuities, and sales or exchanges of stock or securities (gross receipts from such sales or exchanges being taken into account for purposes of this paragraph only to the extent of gains therefrom)." [Act of April 14, 1966, Pub. L. 89-389, 80 Stat. 111, 114-115.]

The purpose of this provision has been defined as follows:

> "When the 'passthrough' type of tax treatment was provided for corporations, Congress decided to limit the availability of this treatment to small businesses *actively engaged in trades or businesses.* Therefore, it denied this treatment to corporations with large amounts of *passive income.* . . . [Emphasis added. S. Rept. No. 1007, 89th Cong., 2d Sess., p. 8 (1966), 1966-1 C.B. 532; H. Rept. No. 1238, 89th Cong., 2d Sess., p. 8 (1966)]"

Shortly after the enactment of subchapter S, the question arose whether section 1372(e)(5) would prevent a corporation engaged in the operation of a hotel or motel, where the major source of receipts was "rent" paid by guests for their rooms, from making an effective subchapter S election. This question was answered by section 1.1372-4(b)(5)(iv), Income Tax Regs., which provides:

> "(iv) *Rents.* The term 'rents' as used in section 1372(e)(5) means amounts received for the use of, or right to use, property (whether real or personal) of the corporation, whether or not such amounts constitute 50 per cent or more of the gross income of the corporation for the taxable year. The term 'rents' does not include payments for the use or occupancy of rooms or other space where significant services are also rendered to the occupant, such as for the use of occupancy of rooms or other quarters in hotels, boarding houses, or apartment houses furnishing hotel services, or in tourist homes, motor courts, or motels. Generally, services are considered rendered to the occupant if they are primarily for his convenience and are other than those usually or customarily rendered in connection with the rental of rooms or other space for occupancy only. The supplying of maid service, for example, constitutes such services; whereas the furnishing of heat and light, the cleaning of public entrances, exits, stairways and lobbies, the collection of trash, etc., are not considered as services rendered to the occupant. Payments for the use or occupancy of entire private residences or living quarters in duplex or multiple housing units, of offices in an office building, etc., are generally 'rents' under section 1372(e)(5). Payments for the parking of automobiles ordinarily do not constitute rents. Payments for the warehousing of goods or for the use of personal property do not constitute rents if significant services are rendered in connection with such payments."

In this case, no issue has been raised as to the correctness or validity of the regulations. The case turns on how they are to be interpreted and applied.

Germac's receipts indisputably arose from tenants' payments for the use of or right to use its property — the bungalows, the furniture, and the common recreation area. However, the petitioners contend that such receipts are not rents within the regulations because Germac rendered significant services which were primarily

---

See S. Rept. No. 1007, 89th Cong., 2d Sess. (1966), 1966-1 C.B. 527, 532-33; H. Rept. No. 1238, 89th Cong., 2d Sess., p. 8 (1966), for an explanation of the purpose of this change.

for the convenience of its tenants and which were other than those usually rendered in connection with the rental of space for occupancy only.[3] In support of this contention, the petitioners state that Germac provided the following services: It provided furniture for the bungalows and a recreation area maintained by the corporation, as well as tables and cards for use in that area; it sponsored bingo games for the adults and parties for the children at which small prizes were given; and it sponsored parties for the adults, providing food and entertainment.

We have found that Germac did provide furniture, a patio, and some recreational equipment for its tenants' use, but we do not believe that this constitutes the providing of services within the meaning of the regulations, significant or otherwise. Insofar as the corporation simply offered it tenants the right to use its property, payment by the tenant for that right constitued "rent" in its classic form and as specifically defined in the regulations. There was no proof that Germac rendered any services at all to the tenants in connection with the use of the furniture or recreation equipment. As to the patio, the only evidence of corporate activity in connection therewith was that the corporation paid the light bill and taxes for the patio area. Such activity does not constitute the performance of services to the occupant within the meaning of the regulations. We need not therefore determine whether such activity would fulfill the requirement of "significance."

The petitioners rely primarily upon their contention that Germac provided recreation and entertainment to the tenants. The petitioners point to Max's testimony that the corporation held bingo games for the adults and gave small parties for the children. We find this evidence unsatisfactory to sustain the petitioners' contention. Although uncontradicted, the testimony was unsupported by any documentary evidence, and it was completely unexplained. There was no attempt to show how many such games and parties were given in 1961 and 1962, or any other year; no indication as to what the corporation or its officers did to promote or supervise these activities except for the testimony that "we run games" and "run the parties"; no showing as to whether such activities were a significant part of the tenants' activities in terms of time, effort, or enjoyment, or were a significant part of the corporation's operations in terms of money or employee's efforts. Indeed, the tense in which the question eliciting this testimony was asked and answered at trial suggests that Max may have been testifying as to the corporation's activities and practices at the time of the hearing rather than during the years in controversy. In short, although the testimony supports our bare finding that bingo games and children's parties did take place, it does not enable us to find that these activities constituted significant services rendered by the corporation to its tenants.

The petitioners also contend that Germac gave or sponsored weekend parties for the adults. Most of the evidence at trial concerned this contention, but it was all vague, and often contradictory, as to the number of parties given during the taxable

---

[3]The proper interpretation of "rents" as used in the statute and regulations is a case of first impression. The respondent has, however, published several statements of his position in the form of revenue rulings. See Rev. Rul. 65-91, 1965-1 C.B. 431; Rev. Rul. 65-83, 1965-1 C.B. 430; Rev. Rul. 65-40, 1965-1 C.B. 429; Rev. Rul. 64-232, 1964-2 C.B. 334; Rev. Rul. 61-112, 1961-1 C.B. 399.

years in controversy, the nature of those parties, and the entertainment provided. The record shows little evidence as to the role played by the corporation in sponsoring these parties and is completely silent as to the degree or nature of the participation by the tenants. Thus, when Max testified that six or seven parties were given during each summer, the respondent introduced into evidence for purposes of impeachment, without objection from the petitioners an affidavit signed by Max and Gertrude Feingold on November 4, 1966, which had been submitted to the Internal Revenue Service in an effort to settle this case. According to that affidavit, only two or three parties were given each year. The petitioners did not attempt to explain away this affidavit, although it flatly contradicts Max's testimony. We therefore have found that the corporation gave no more than two or three parties during each of the taxable years in controversy, rather than the six or seven claimed, but that it did sponsor those two or three parties.

We have also found that the corporation provided approximately $25 in cash or $25 worth of food and beverages for each of these parties. The testimony on this issue was also vague, but we base our finding as to the amount on two checks for $25 drawn by Germac, introduced in evidence, which, Max testified without contradiction, were given to tenants on separate occasions to use to buy refreshments at parties.

We find the petitioners' claim that Germac provided entertainment at the parties, either a square dance caller or a small band, to be unsupported by the evidence. Although Max testified that Bill Lemkin was hired on occasion at $40 per evening to call square dances, and identified two checks for $40 each made out to Lemkin as having been given for such services, Germac's cash ledger shows these checks to have been drawn for repairs. The petitioners did not explain or attempt to explain why the corporate records showed the expenditures to have been made for repairs, rather than entertainment. In view of the general vagueness and inconsistencies of Max's testimony, we must give greater relative weight here to the documentary evidence. Therefore, despite our reluctance to disbelieve altogether the assertion that a square dance caller was hired for some of the parties during the years in controversy, we are presented with no reliable evidence on which to make a finding to that effect.

We find the claim that the corporation hired a small band to play for the parties on occasion during 1961 and 1962 to be completely unsupported. Max could name only one musician hired for this purpose, and on cross examination, it appeared that the person thus named must have played, if at all, in years after the taxable years in controversy. As there was no other evidence on this issue, the contention is not proved.

In summary, we conclude that the total services provided by Germac do not constitute significant services within the meaning of the regulations. In applying the tests in the regulations, we are concerned only with those services which are not customarily furnished to tenants for occupancy only. Since the evidence concerning the bingo games and children's parties was insufficient to allow us to make a finding as to their significance, the petitioners' position is reduced to a claim that corporate sponsorship of two or three parties during each of the years in question for the adult tenants, for each of which the corporation, or its principal officer Max, expended $25, constitutes "significant services." However, there is no showing that such activity was significant in any sense. It was not, so far as the record shows, an important factor in inducing tenants to rent the bungalows, or in improving their vacation while they stayed; indeed, there was no evidence whatsoever as to how many tenants participated in the parties. Nor was the corporation's activity in this regard shown to be a significant part of the corporation's activity. Financially, the proved expenditures of, at most, $75 per year on such activity, was approximately 0.15 per cent of Germac's receipts in each year in controversy. There was no showing that the corporation was involved in the parties in any way other than notifying the tenants that a party was to take place and supplying a small amount of cash or refreshments, and the evidence strongly suggests that there was no other involvement. Therefore, the "services" did not represent in any way a significant part of the corporation's operations.

The regulations include no standard for interpreting the term "significant," except as can be inferred from the examples contained therein. Clearly, the services supplied by Germac were not comparable to the services furnished by the operator of a hotel or motel. In those business, guests come and go frequently, and maids service the rooms daily. From what appears of record in this case, the occupants of the bungalows neither required nor received any such frequent or extensive services. By any test of "significance," no significant services were rendered by Germac to the tenants other than those usually rendered in connection with the rental of space or other property for occupancy only, and its income from the bungalows was "rent" within the meaning of section 1.1372-4(b)(5)(iv), Income Tax Regs.

Since more than 20 per cent of Germac's gross receipts in 1961 were such "rents," Germac's election was therefore terminated for that taxable year and subsequent taxable years under section 1372(e)(5). Consequently, its shareholders may not deduct Germac's loss from their individual income on their returns for 1961 and 1962. Our holding makes it unnecessary to consider the respondent's alternative contention that the loss suffered by Germac in 1962 was less than that claimed by the petitioners on their return for 1962.

Decision will be entered for the respondent.

PRIVATE RULING
December 14, 1961*

This is in reply to your letter dated November 7, 1961 and prior correspondence concerning a request for ruling on behalf of XYZ Shopping Center, Inc. (XYZ). The question raised is whether the amounts which XYZ will realize from its tenants constitute "rents" within the meaning of section 1372(e)(5) of the Internal Revenue Code of 1954. . . .

*This is an unpublished, private ruling issued by the Internal Revenue Service. To preserve confidentiality, the names of the parties have been deleted and letter designations are substituted. — Ed.

The facts as we understand them are as follows: XYZ had acquired 33 acres of ground as a site for a shopping center. In September 1960, XYZ sold 12 of these acres to C and leased back the premises. XYZ then sublet the premises to K. K pays a fixed annual rental of $240,000.00 directly to C. The latter, in turn, pays $25,000.00 per year to XYZ.

The lease between XYZ and K calls for K to make an additional annual payment to XYZ of $13,800.00. In consideration, XYZ is to maintain for the benefit of its tenant the exterior portion of the K Store, including the surfacing and grading of the K parking area, maintenance of the lighting equipment and facilities thereon, maintenance of directional and shopping center signs, and keeping the parking area lighted, marked and clear of ice, snow and refuse.

In addition to K, there are 32 tenant units on the remaining 21 acres comprising the shopping center. XYZ's anual rental for the units other than K will be approximately $460,000.00. All of these units, with the exception of P's, will have leases providing for a minimum rental, plus a percentage of the tenant's sales. P has no fixed minimum rental obligation, but will pay 3 per cent of its sales.

XYZ is obligated under the leases to provide and maintain the following: the parking lot; lighting of all common areas; removal of snow and trash from common areas; the comfort stations; utility lines outside of the buildings; sewers; and all pedestrian and landscaped areas. XYZ is also required to make all necessary structural repairs to the buildings, maintain the roofs and do the exterior painting.

In addition to the foregoing, XYZ will be engaged in a number of other activities in connection with the operation and promotion of the business of the shopping center. In all of these activities, it is XYZ's objective to increase the business of the tenants, in order for XYZ's income, based upon a percentage of the business transacted by the tenants, to be increased likewise. The performance of these services is significant to all the tenants, including K, notwithstanding the fact that the lease between XYZ and K provides for fixed payments. Promoting the business of the K store will increase the business of the remaining tenants. These additional services to be undertaken by XYZ will be as follows:

(a) XYZ will form and activate an organization of the tenants which will undertake activities to promote the business of the shopping center. XYZ will provide a meeting place for the organization. The tenant's leases provide authority for the assessment of member tenants. XYZ will provide such additional monies as are needed to effectuate the merchandising and promotional programs agreed upon with the tenants organization; provide an adequate public relations staff and a public relations counsel; and will handle the necessary record keeping for the organization.

(b) XYZ is to provide a large scale promotional campaign of general interest to the people in the area upon the opening of the shopping center, and for some time thereafter. Additional promotional events will be held from time to time in the shopping center. A substantial portion of all expenses of these events will be provided by XYZ.

(c) XYZ will erect a large sign on the shopping center and will provide signs for some of the major tenants; traffic control signs and other identification signs will be provided; and XYZ will provide institutional advertising of the shopping center.

(d) XYZ will provide police protection for the area and coordinate with the Highway Department and Police Department insofar as studies of traffic flow and access are concerned with the shopping center.

Section 1372(e)(5) of the Code provides that the election made by a small busines corporation shall terminate if, for any taxable year of the corporation for which the election is in effect, such corporation has gross receipts more than 20 per cent of which is derived from royalties, rents, dividends, interest, annuities, and sales or exchanges of stock or securities.

The term "rents" does not include payments for the use or occupancy of rooms or other space where significant services are also rendered to the occupant. Generally, services are considered rendered to the occupant if they are primarily for his convenience and are other than those usually or customarily rendered in connection with the rental of rooms or other space for occupancy only.

Based on the foregoing, it is concluded that amounts realized by XYZ from all its tenants, under the circumstances related above, involve the rendition of significant services, and therefore do not represent rents under section 1372(e)(5) of the Code.

NOTE

See J. Pennell, Planning for the Use of Subchapter S Corporations, 47 Taxes 746 (1969).

REVENUE RULING 64-94
1964-1 Cum. Bull. 317

Advice has been requested whether an election under section 1372 of the Internal Revenue Code of 1954 is terminated with respect to the taxable year when an electing small business corporation is merged into another corporation in a statutory merger within the meaning of section 368(a)(1)(A) of the Code.

A small business corporation, as defined in section 1371(a) of the Code, made a timely election under section 1372 of the Code which was not terminated prior to the taxable year when it was merged into another corporation in a statutory merger within the meaning of section 368(a)(1)(A) of the Code. The final taxable year of the electing small business corporation ended on the date of the merger, under section 381(b)(1) of the Code, and the surviving corporation was not an electing small business corporation.

None of the events specified in section 1372(e)(1) through section 1372(e)(5) of the Code occurred in the final taxable year of the electing small business corporation which would terminate its election under section 1372 of the Code for such year, unless it is determined that the merger falls within the intendment of section 1372(e)(3) of the Code.

Section 1372(e)(3) of the Code provides, in effect, that an election under section 1372(a) of the Code made by a small business corporation shall terminate if at any time the corporation ceases to be a small business corporation as defined in section 1371(a) of the Code. Such termination shall be effective for the taxable year of the corporation in which it ceases to be a small business corporation and for all succeeding taxable years of the corporation.

Section 1372(d) of the Code provides that an election under section 1372(a) of the Code shall be effective for the taxable year of the corporation for which it is made and for all succeeding taxable years of the corporation, unless it is terminated with respect to any such taxable year under section 1372(e) of the Code.

Section 1372(e)(3) of the Code applies to a corporation which ceases to be a small business corporation by virtue of an event which does not terminate its taxable year. Where, as in the instant case, the event which causes the corporation to be disqualified as a small business corporation also terminates its taxable year, the corporation remains a small business corporation, as defined in section 1371(a), throughout the entire taxable year so terminated.

On the basis of the foregoing, it is held that the election, under section 1372 of the Code, of the small business corporation in the instant case was not terminated with respect to its final taxable year ending with the date of the merger.

BORG v. COMMISSIONER
50 T.C. 257 (1968)

FEATHERSTON, Judge: Respondent determined a deficiency in petitioners' 1962 joint Federal income tax of $3,844.18. Both parties having conceded certain issues, the sole issue remaining for decision is whether petitioners' deductible share of the net operating losses incurred by an electing small business corporation exceeds the amounts allowed by the respondent.

Findings of Fact

... Petitioners, Joe E. Borg and Ruth P. Borg, are husband and wife and resided at Tulsa, Oklahoma at the time of the filing of the petition herein. ...

Borg Compressed Steel Corporation (hereinafter referred to as Borg Steel) is an Oklahoma corporation, duly incorporated . . . on August 1, 1947, and . . . has remained engaged in the scrap processing business continuously from its incorporation until the date of trial herein.

Borg Steel had only one class of capital stock during the period involved in this case: Common capital stock. As of July 31, 1961, and throughout the year 1962, the corporation had issued an outstanding 3,000 shares of common capital stock, owned by the following persons:

Petitioner Joe E. Borg	1,347 shares
Petitioner Ruth P. Borg	1,153 shares
Monroe J. Friedman	500 shares

The petitioners' total basis in their common capital stock of Borg Steel as of July 31, 1961, was $25,000.

Borg Steel duly elected to file its United States income tax returns on the basis of a fiscal year ending on July 31, and has so filed its returns. The corporation employs the accrual method of accounting.

On August 10, 1960, Borg Steel elected to be free of tax as a small business corporation within the purview of Subchapter S of the Internal Revenue Code of 1954, commencing with its taxable year ending July 31, 1961.

For the fiscal year commencing August 1, 1960, and ending July 31, 1961, Borg Steel sustained an operating loss in the amount of $28,630.88. The petitioners claimed and were allowed a combined deduction of $23,859.07 of the corporation's operating loss on their 1961 United States income tax return as their share of the loss as electing shareholders of a Subchapter S corporation.

On July 31, 1962, there was a balance due petitioner Joe E. Borg from Borg Compressed Steel Corporation on a promissory note of the corporation for cash advanced to it in the sum of $15,153.98.

For the fiscal year commencing August 1, 1961, ending July 31, 1962, Borg Compressed Steel Corporation sustained an operating loss in the amount of $37,564.83. Petitioners claimed a deduction on their 1962 income tax return of $31,304.03 as their share of the loss as electing stockholders of a Subchapter S corporation. Respondent disallowed the loss claimed to the extent of $15,009.12. The matter in tabular form is set forth as follows:

Loss claimed:

1961 return (first year of election)	$23,859.07	
1962 return	31,304.03	
Total losses claimed 1961-1962		$55,163.10
Basis of petitioner's stock (7-31-61)	$25,000.00	
Basis of indebtedness (balance due as of 7-31-62 on promissory note for cash advanced)	15,153.98	
		$40,153.98
Amount of loss claimed in 1962 disallowed by respondent		$15,009.12

On September 2, 1958, Borg Steel executed a promissory note to The First National Bank and Trust Company of Tulsa, Tulsa, Oklahoma, (hereinafter referred to as "the Bank") in the principal amount of $190,000, payable in installments. The proceeds of the loan as evidenced by this note went to the corporation and were used by the corporation in the operation of its business. As security for the loan the corporation gave the Bank a mortgage on substantially all of its equipment and machinery and the life insurance policies of the corporation on its officers.

On September 1, 1961, there was $67,500 due on the note given by Borg Steel to the Bank dated September 2, 1958. On that date the corporation executed a new promissory note to the Bank in the principal amount of $135,000; $67,500 of the new note was used by Borg Steel to pay the balance due on the note dated September 2, 1958, and the remaining balance was received and used by the corporation in the operation of its business. As security for the loan the corporation gave the Bank a mortgage on substantially all of its equipment and machinery and the life insurance policies of the corporation on its officers.

In order for Borg Steel to obtain the loans from the Bank, petitioners were required to pledge their personal assets and to endorse the notes. . . .

On July 31, 1962, there was a balance due to the Bank of $105,000 on the note dated September 1, 1961.

The loans as evidenced by the notes dated September 2, 1958, and September 1, 1961, were paid in full. All payments were made by Borg Steel. The petitioners were not required to make any payments.

The notes executed by Borg Steel to the Bank were carried on its books and records as notes payable to the Bank. The corporation's balance sheet for its fiscal year ending July 31, 1962, did not show any indebtedness due the petitioners Joe E. Borg or Ruth P. Borg as a result of their endorsements of the notes to the Bank.

During the fiscal years ending July 31, 1960, July 31, 1961, and July 31, 1962, the petitioner, Joe E. Borg, was employed by Borg Steel under a written employment contract dated January 17, 1953, on the basis of an annual salary of $36,000 per year, plus a bonus arrangement. This salary arrangement had been in effect since 1955 and in view of the services rendered as the principal officer of the corporation, the salary was reasonable in amount.

Because of the financial condition of Borg Steel, the petitioner, Joe E. Borg, was not paid any salary from the corporation for the fiscal year July 31, 1960 and July 31, 1961. He drew the sum of $24,000 in salary from the corporation for the fiscal year ending July 31, 1962. . . .

Borg Steel did not accrue on its accounting records the unpaid salary of petitioner Joe E. Borg for the fiscal years ending July 31, 1960, July 31, 1961, and July 31, 1962. The petitioners, who reported their income on a cash basis, did not report the unpaid salary due Joe E. Borg from the corporation on their United States income tax returns filed for the years 1960, 1961, and 1962.

At the annual meeting of the Board of Directors of Borg Steel, held at Tulsa, Oklahoma on June 25, 1960, a resolution was adopted "that the Corporation do, and the Officers of the Corporation are hereby authorized and directed to execute and deliver to Joe E. Borg a Demand Note of the Corporation in the sum of $36,000.00, with interest at six per cent per annum from date, as evidence of the indebtedness of the Corporation for said salary due and owing and not as payment." Pursuant thereto, the corporation did, on July 31, 1960, execute and deliver to Joe E. Borg its promissory note payable to him on demand, in the sum of $36,000, bearing the following legend: "This Promissory Note given and accepted as evidence of the indebtedness of the Corporation for salary due only and not as payment."

Similar resolutions and notes were made for 1961 and 1962 for the amount of compensation due petitioner.

Ultimate Findings of Fact

On July 31, 1962, petitioners' adjusted basis in the capital stock of Borg Steel was $1,140.93.

On July 31, 1962 petitioners' adjusted basis of the indebtedness due them by Borg Steel was $15,153.98.

The sum of the adjusted basis of petitioners' stock in Borg Steel and the adjusted basis of indebtedness of the corporation to petitioners was only sufficient to entitle petitioners to deduct for the taxable year 1962 the amount of $16,294.91 as their pro rata share of the corporation's net operating loss within the purview of section 1374(c).

Opinion

Petitioners owned stock in Borg Compressed Steel Corporation which had elected in 1961 as a small business corporation under section 1372(a) not to be subject to income taxes. In its fiscal year ending July 31, 1961, Borg Steel incurred a net operating loss of $28,630.88 which was allowed as a deduction to the shareholders, including the petitioners. In its fiscal year ending July 31, 1962, Borg Steel incurred a further net operating loss of $37,564.83. The question presented is what portion of this 1962 net operating loss petitioners are entitled to deduct in computing their individual income tax liabilities for the calendar year 1962.

Code section 1374(b) provides that a shareholder of a corporation which has elected to be taxed under Subchapter S of the Code shall be allowed as a deduction his portion of the corporation's net operating loss. Section 1374(c)(2) limits a shareholder's pro rata share of such a corporation's net operating loss to the sum of (A) the adjusted basis of the shareholder's stock in such corporation, and (B) the adjusted basis of "any indebtedness of the corporation to the shareholder, determined as of the close of the taxable year." Thus the answer to the question as to the amount of Borg Steel's loss that may be deducted by petitioners depends upon their adjusted basis for their stock and certain indebtedness of the corporation to them.

During the period here involved Borg Steel had 3,000 shares of capital stock outstanding of which 2,500 shares with a cost basis of $25,000 were owned by petitioners. Borg Steel owed petitioner Joe E. Borg $15,153.98 on a promissory note for a cash loan. In addition, Borg Steel owed petitioner Joe E. Borg $84,000 on notes evidencing liability for salary unpaid for the years ended July 31, 1960, 1961, and 1962. Borg Steel also owed a balance of $105,000 on a note to The First National Bank and Trust Company of Tulsa, endorsed by both petitioners and secured by assets of Borg Steel as well as the personal assets of petitioners.

Petitioners claimed and were allowed for 1961, their combined pro rata share, i.e., $23,859.07, of the net operating loss incurred by Borg Steel in its fiscal year 1961. In its fiscal year 1962 Borg Steel incurred a net operating loss of $37,564.83 and petitioners here contend that for 1962 they are entitled to deduct their full pro rata share of this loss, i.e., $31,304.03. They argue that the adjusted basis for Borg Steel's indebtedness to them must be computed by including the $84,000 in notes for unpaid salary and the $105,000 note to the Bank bearing their endorsements and secured, in part, by their property. Inclusion of the amount of either indebtedness would entitle petitioners to the disputed deduction.

Respondent contends that petitioners' 1962 deduction for Borg Steel's net operating loss should be limited under section 1374(c)(2) to $16,294.91 and the remainder should be disallowed. Petitioner's basis of $25,000 for their stock, both parties agree, must be reduced by the $23,859.07 deduction allowed petitioners for 1961, see Code section 1376(b)(1), leaving an adjusted basis of $1,140.93 for the stock. See Code section 1016(a)(18). Respondent contends that the remainder of $1,140.93, added to the $15,153.98 representing petitioner Joe E. Borg's cash loan (a total of $16,294.91) constitutes petitioners' total adjusted basis for their stock and the corporate indebtedness to them. Respondent would allow no basis for either the unpaid salary notes or the Bank note in applying the "adjusted basis" limitation prescribed by section 1374(c)(2). We agree with respondent.

The salary notes arose under a written employment contract calling for Borg Steel to pay petitioner Joe E. Borg a salary of $36,000 per annum. Because of the corporation's unfavorable financial condition, he was paid no salary for the fiscal years ending July 31, 1960 and 1961. For the fiscal year ending July 31, 1962, he was paid $24,000. The corporation each year gave petitioner Joe E. Borg a note for his unpaid salary but made a notation on each note that it was given and accepted only as evidence of indebtedness for salary due and not as payment of such salary. Petitioners, as cash basis taxpayers, did not report any part of the unpaid salary as income in their returns for 1960, 1961, and 1962, consistent with our decisions in Virginia W. Stettinius Dudley, 32 T.C. 564 (1959), affirmed per curiam 279 F.2d 219 (C.A. 2, 1960); Jay A. Williams, 28 T.C. 1000 (1957) and Robert J. Dial, 24 T.C. 117 (1955). Although Borg Steel reported under the accrual method, it claimed no deductions for its liability for such unpaid salary consistent with Code section 267.

The term "adjusted basis" is not specially defined for the purposes of the section 1374(c) limitations on the deduction of net operating losses. We, therefore, look to the general Code provisions on basis. . . .

Section 1012 provides the general rule that the "basis of property shall be the cost of such property." Petitioners cite Income Tax Reg. 1.1012-1(a), which defines "cost" to mean the "amount paid" for property "in cash or other property." Relying on this regulation, petitioners argue that Joe E. Borg's services constitute "other property" which had value equal to the notes, and that the notes, therefore, had a basis equal to their face amounts.

But "cost" for the purposes of the Code ordinarily means cost to the taxpayer. Detroit Edison Co. v. Commissioner, 319 U.S. 98 (1943). Where a taxpayer has not previously reported, recognized, or even *realized* income, it cannot be said that he has a basis for a note evidencing his right to receive such income at some time in the future. That petitioner Joe E. Borg performed valuable services for Borg Steel is undeniable; however, the performance of services, involving neither the realization of taxable income nor a capital outlay, is not the kind of cost that would be shown in a cash receipts and disbursements system of income accounting. See, e.g., Pounds v. United States, 372 F.2d 342, 351-352 (C.A. 5, 1967); Alsop v. Commissioner, 290 F.2d

726 (C.A. 2, 1961), affirming on other grounds 34 T.C. 606 (1960); Ernest W. Brown, Inc., 28 T.C. 682 (1957), affd. per curiam 258 F.2d 829 (C.A. 2, 1958). Since the services performed by petitioner Joe E. Borg had no cost within the meaning of section 1012, his notes for unpaid salary had a basis of zero and, therefore, added nothing to the adjusted basis for indebtedness for the purpose of computing the section 1374(c)(2) limitation on net operating loss deductions.

We find further support for our conclusion in the fact that allowing petitioners a deduction for the 1962 net operating loss by treating the salary claim as indebtedness with a basis equal to the face amounts of the notes for purposes of the section 1374(c)(2) limitation would apparently require a double inclusion of the salary in petitioners' income in the year when paid, once a salary received under Code section 61, and again on account of the recovery of sums due on the notes in excess of their basis. See Joe M. Smith, 40 T.C. 872, 878-879 (1967). We do not think Congress intended Subchapter S of the Code to produce such a result.

As to the Bank loan guaranteed by petitioners, section 1374(c)(2)(B) allows a shareholder in an electing small business corporation to deduct a corporate net operating loss to the extent of the adjusted basis of "any indebtedness of the corporation *to the shareholder*." In William H. Perry, 47 T.C. 159 (1966), affd., [392 F.2d 458] (C.A. 8, 1968), we held that until a shareholder who had guaranteed a corporate debt was called upon to pay on the guaranty, no debt existed for the purpose of section 1374(c)(2)(B). Petitioners' second argument presents similar facts.

In 1958, Borg Steel needed additional funds and as a separate entity it sought a loan from the Bank. The loan was refused. As a condition to making the loan, the Bank insisted that petitioners pledge and mortgage all of their oil and gas interests and other personal assets, assign individual life insurance policies and execute a personal endorsement on the note which in fact, petitioners contend, consistuted petitioners co-makers of the note and imposed upon them primary liability for payment thereof. Petitioners argument that as "a matter of law and by its express terms this obligation is more than the ordinary 'endorsement'; it is more than a guarantee; it is more than an unconditional and absolute guarantee of payment; it is in fact an agreement 'to be bound by all the provisions hereof and to assume and perform all the obligations therein contained *in like manner as the makers thereof*.'" On this ground petitioners would have us distinguish William H. Perry, supra.

Petitioners misconstrue our decision in *Perry*. The basis for our decision was not that the taxpayers' liability was secondary. Rather, it was that, under Missouri law, a guarantor does not have a debt due from the debtor until the guarantor performs on his contract of guaranty. "The statutory language clearly refers to a debt of the corporation which runs to the shareholder. There is nothing in the statutory wording, nor the regulations, nor the committee reports which warrants an inference that a shareholder's contract of guaranty with corporate creditors is tantamount to an 'indebtedness of the corporation to [him].'" William H. Perry, supra, at 163. . . .

Borg Steel owed nothing to petitioners by reason of their endorsement, and it would continue to owe nothing to them until and unless they paid part or all of the obligation. "While the sum of money may be payable upon a contingency, yet in such case it becomes a debt only when the contingency has happened, the term 'debt' being opposed to 'liability' when used in the sense of an inchoate or contingent debt." Gilman v. Commissioner, 53 F.2d 47, 50 (C.A. 8, 1931). Accord, United States v. Virgin, 230 F.2d 880 (C.A. 5, 1956); Brown-Rogers-Dixon Co. v. Commissioner, 122 F.2d 347 (C.A. 4, 1941). It follows that the sums borrowed by the corporation from the Bank did not give rise to "indebtedness of the corporation to the shareholder" and cannot be used in computing petitioners' allowable portion of the corporate net operating loss.

In view of certain concessions made by respondent,

Decision will be entered under Rule 50.

TAX REFORM STUDIES AND PROPOSALS — U.S. TREASURY DEPARTMENT*

Subchapter S

General Explanation

Background and Purpose

At present subchapter S of the Internal Revenue Code allows small corporations, those with 10 or fewer shareholders, to elect not to pay the regular corporate income tax and instead to have the income or loss of the corporation taxed directly to the shareholders. This results, in a general way, in a pattern of taxation similar to that of partnerships. Subchapter S is now being used by more than 200,000 corporations which number is constantly increasing. However, because of the hybrid nature of the entity — not quite a corporation and not quite a partnership — the governing rules have been complex. As a result they are frequently misunderstood in ways which lead to unintended hardships. On the other hand, certain taxpayers have made use of the these provisions to obtain tax benefits which are inconsistent with the partnership nature of the entity for tax purposes.

As a result of a joint study undertaken by the Treasury Department and the Committee on Partnerships of the American Bar Association Section on Taxation, a legislative proposal has been developed which will alleviate these problems. The aim has been to tax subchapter S corporations as much like partnerships as is possible in view of their hybrid nature, and in so doing remove those undesirable restrictions and complications which have been barriers to those who are aware of them and traps for those who are not. At the same time, the unwarranted advantages of subchapter S as compared to the partnership form would be eliminated.

Details of Proposal

Under the current law, the amount and the timing of the taxation of the electing corporation's income to the shareholders vary depending on whether the income is distributed and when such distributions are made. In order to conform more closely to the partnership rules which are more widely understood by taxpayers, the proposal

*Joint Publication, House Comm. on Ways and Means and Senate Comm. on Finance, 91st Cong., 1st Sess. 271 (Comm. Print 1969).

would allocate corporate income to shareholders on a day-by-day, share-by-share basis and include it in the shareholder's income for his taxable year during which or with which the corporation's year ends regardless of whether it is distributed. Cash distributions to the extent they do not exceed amounts so taxed for past years or for the current year would not be subject to tax. Moreover, tax free income received by electing corporations would retain its tax free character when distributed to shareholders rather than being converted to dividends as under existing law. Furthermore, corporate capital losses in excess of capital gains for the first time will pass through to shareholders to be used on their individual returns.

The following additional liberalizations will apply to the use of subchapter S —

> Under present law electing corporations may not have more than 20 percent of their gross receipts from passive sources such as rents, interest, and dividends. The proposal would remove this restriction.
>
> Under present law only individuals and estates may own shares in electing corporations. The proposal would permit voting trusts and trusts all the income of which is taxed to the grantor to own shares. Furthermore, transitory ownership by ineligible shareholders will not automatically be disqualifying.
>
> Under present law subchapter S corporations may have only one class of stock. Therefore, a determination by the Internal Revenue Service that an interest which the shareholders designated as debt actually represented equity and a second class of stock would lead to disqualification. This would, in general, no longer be true under the proposal. Moreover, although substantial restrictions remain on the use of stock with different rights to profits, distributions on liquidation, etc., stock which differs as to voting rights only will be permitted.
>
> The proposal also addresses the problem of inadvertent termination of a subchapter S election. Under present law each new shareholder of an electing corporation must consent to the election within a specified time. Failure to do so terminates the election. The proposal would continue the election in this case unless a new shareholder affirmatively objects to the election.

Despite the changes described above, an election may still be inadvertently terminated. To alleviate the hardship that now arises in this situation the proposal contains a series of liberalizing changes. One would provide that termination will be prospective only, rather than retroactive to the beginning of the year in which the event causing termination takes place, as under existing law. Another change would permit distributions of income which had been taxed to the shareholders but not yet distributed to be made within a specified period following termination. In other situations the proposal would permit a shareholder to repay distributions to the corporation and recover the tax paid thereon. The latter two procedures would apply to terminations occurring or discovered after the date of enactment of this legislation. There is also a provision permitting retroactive consent by the Commissioner to a new election for periods after the situation causing the termination has been cured, when the fact of termination is not discovered until a later date.

On the other hand, unintended benefits available to some taxpayers under subchapter S would be eliminated —

Under present law, shareholders can defer taxation of up to 11 months' income by electing a fiscal year for the corporation. For example, if a fiscal year ending January 31 is selected, income earned by the corporation between February 1 and December 31, 1968, will be taxed to the shareholders as 1969 income if it is not distributed in 1968 since the corporation's year ends during the shareholder's taxable year comprising the calendar year 1969. The proposal, subject to transition rules which would preserve existing fiscal years as long as a majority of the stock does not change hands, would require all electing corporations to use the calendar year as their taxable year unless their shareholders are on a different taxable year or they have a business purpose for selecting a fiscal year. This conforms to the partnership rule.

Contributions to qualified pension plans for 10 percent shareholders which exceed the limitations under H.R. 10 for partners or sole proprietors (10 percent of earned income or $2,500 whichever is greater) will be treated as if paid to such shareholder and will be taxable to him. With this change it would no longer be necessary to deny the benefits of subchapter S to corporations with more than 20 percent of their income from passive sources, such as interest and rents.

It is now claimed to be possible for shareholders to avoid self-employment tax or the restrictions on social security benefits while continuing to work by simply not paying themselves a salary and withdrawing the profits as "dividends." It is proposed to eliminate this practice.

Use of subchapter S by dealers in property in order to obtain capital gains will be curtailed by denying capital gain treatment to shareholders who would have had ordinary income had they sold the property individually. This change is particularly necessary if real estate corporations are to be allowed to use subchapter S.

Effect of Proposal

It is expected that the changes in subchapter S will make this procedure more useful to those businesses for whom it was intended. However, it is not expected that the amendments will result in any significant effect on revenue. . . .

NOTE

See P. DiQuinzio, Refinancing and/or Sales or Acquisitions of Subchapter S Corporations, 28 N.Y.U. Inst. on Fed. Tax. 269 (1970).

II. SECTION 1244

Section 1244 of the Code was enacted as part of the Small Business Tax Revision Act of 1958. Its purpose is described in H.R. No. 2198, 85th Cong., 1st Sess., 1959-2 Cum. Bull. 711, as follows:

This section provides ordinary loss rather than capital loss treatment on the sale or exchange of small-business stock. This treatment is available only in the case of an individual and only if he is the original holder of the stock.

This provision is designed to encourage the flow of new funds into small business. The encouragement in this case takes the form of reducing the risk of a loss for these new funds. The ordinary loss treatment which the bill accords shareholders in small corporations in effect is already available to proprietors and partners. They report directly the earnings from these business ventures and thus ordinary losses realized by a proprietorship or partnership presently constitute ordinary losses to the proprietor or partner. As a result, from the standpoint of risk taking, this bill places shareholders in small corporations on a more nearly equal basis with these proprietors and partners.

In accord with your committee's desire to limit the benefit of this provision to small business, the total stock offering of any corporation which is eligible for this ordinary loss treatment is limited to $500,000. Moreover, the total stock offering per corporation plus the equity capital of the corporation may not exceed $1 million. In addition, the maximum loss which a taxpayer can treat as an ordinary loss under this provision is to be $25,000 a year (or $50,000 in the case of a husband and wife filing a joint return).

Your committee also has imposed a restriction designed to limit this tax benefit to companies which are largely operating companies. Thus, the corporation, in the 5 years before the taxpayer incurs the loss on the stock must have derived more than half of its gross receipts from sources other than royalties, rents, dividends, interest, annuities, and the sale of stock or securities.

It is believed that this provision for the ordinary loss treatment for small-business stock will have no immediate effect on revenue.

See generally B. Bittker and J. Eustice, Federal Income Taxation of Corporations and Shareholders 138-144 (2d ed. 1966); R. Rubin, Section 1244 and the Stylish Stout, 12 Tul. Tax Inst. 559 (1963); F. Nicholson, Section 1244 Stock, 38 Taxes 303 (1960).

REVENUE RULING 66-67
1966-1 Cum. Bull. 191

Advice has been requested whether the minutes of a corporation's board of directors' meeting can ever qualify as a "plan" within the meaning of section 1244 (c)(1)(A) of the Internal Revenue Code of 1954 and, if so, whether the minutes described below so qualify.

A corporation was organized on January 1, 1964. The minutes of the initial board of directors' meeting show that a resolution was passed which authorized the board of directors to issue a certain amount of unsubscribed capital common stock in the corporation, in such amounts, at such times and for such terms as the board of directors may deem necessary for the business of the corporation.

Between January 1, 1964, and March 31, 1964, the board of directors caused one hundred shares of common stock in the corporation to be issued pursuant to the above-mentioned resolution.

Section 1244 of the Code provides that in certain cases a loss on "section 1244 stock" may be treated as an ordinary loss. Section 1244(c)(1)(A) of the Code provides, in part, that the term "section 1244 stock" means common stock in a domestic corporation if such corporation adopted a plan after June 30, 1958, to offer such stock for a period (ending not later than 2 years after the date such plan was adopted) specified in the plan.

Section 1.1244(c)-1(c) of the Income Tax Regulations provides, in part, as follows:

"Written plan. — (1) The common stock must be issued pursuant to a written plan adopted by the corporation after June 30, 1958, to offer only such stock during a period specified in the plan ending not later than two years after the date the plan is adopted. . . . The plan must specifically state, in terms of dollars, the maximum amount to be received by the corporation in consideration for the stock to be issued pursuant thereto."

The minutes of a board of directors' meeting can qualify as a "plan" within the meaning of section 1244(c)(1)(A) of the Code if they contain all of the required elements of a "plan" as specified in that section of the Code and the regulations thereunder.

The minutes of the board of directors' meeting in this case contained merely a resolution which authorized the directors to issue, at their discretion, a certain amount of capital common stock. The resolution failed to establish a period of time during which the stock would be offered for sale, which period would expire not later than 2 years from the date of the resolution. Further, it did not specify, in terms of dollars, the maximum amount to be received as consideration for the stock.

Accordingly, the minutes of the corporation's board of directors in this case do not qualify as a "plan" within the meaning of section 1244(c)(1)(A) of the Code and section 1.1244(c)-1(c) of the regulations.

EGER v. COMMISSIONER
393 F.2d 243 (2d Cir. 1968)

Before FRIENDLY and SMITH, Circuit Judges, and GIGNOUX, District Judge.

SMITH, Circuit Judge: This is a petition to review, pursuant to section 7482 of the Internal Revenue Code of 1954, a decision of the Tax Court, Theodore Tannenwald, Jr., Judge, T.C. Memo 1966-192, assessing income tax liabilities against the petitioner for the years 1958, 1959 and 1960. The Tax Court held that the taxpayer was not entitled in 1961 to a deduction from regular income for her loss on the sale or exchange of stock issued by Windmill Food Stores of Hewlett, Inc. (herein Hewlett) under section 1244 of the Code. Since the deduction was held invalid, the net operating loss it was alleged to have created in 1961 could not be carried back to the tax years in issue. We hold that the loss qualified as an ordinary loss under section 1244 and reverse and remand for determination of the Commissioner's alternative contentions.

In 1958, Hewlett was organized. Petitioner was the sole stockholder and paid $40,000 for her 40 shares pursuant to a corporate motion and resolution of March 31, 1959[2] which provided that on April 6, 1959 the petitioner was to pay $40,000 for 40 shares of Hewlett issued pursuant to section 1244 of the Code. Early in 1961, Hewlett filed a petition in bankruptcy under Chapter XI of the Bankruptcy Act together with a plan of reorganization which was approved by the referee and confirmed. At that point the petitioner was owed $62,000 by Hewlett. Petitioner waived any right to payment she might have under the plan. In March of 1961, petitioner entered into an agreement with Pick 'N Save, Inc., under which the latter agreed to buy and the petitioner agreed to sell her 40 shares in Hewlett. The purchase price was $100,000 plus the value of certain security deposits, other items, and the value of Hewlett's inventory on the date of closing less credits for certain secured liabilities. All payments on account of the purchase price were to be deposited in escrow for one year after the closing for the purpose of paying any claims of Hewlett's creditors for moneys due and owing at the day of closing. At closing, the petitioner was to deliver an executed release of all obligations due it from Hewlett. On April 13, the plan of arrangement was confirmed. The next day, Hewlett reaffirmed its obligations to the petitioner on its indebtedness to her, in a resolution which stated that the petitioner would accept as full payment of her claims any sum paid by Pick 'N Save left with the escrowee after the other creditors had been paid. On the same day, petitioner's sale of stock to Pick 'N Save was closed. After payment of Hewlett's other creditors, the escrowee had $30,000 left for payment to the petitioner.

Petitioner claims that the $30,000 was received as final payment on Hewlett's indebtedness to her, that her stock in Hewlett was worthless in 1961, and that she was therefore entitled to a regular loss under 1244 of the Code. The government contends that the stock in question was not 1244 stock so that all she was entitled to was a capital loss. Or, alternatively, if the stock is 1244 stock, the $30,000 received from Pick 'N Save was received for it, so that the regular loss available is only $10,000, and

[2]The Tax Court found

The minutes of the first meeting of the Board of Directors of Hewlett, held on March 31, 1959, were on a standard form with blank spaces designed to be filled with the missing details. They contained the following:

The Secretary then presented to the meeting a written proposal from Fred Eger and Sofie Eger *to this Corporation.*

Upon motion duly made, seconded and carried, the said proposal was ordered filed with the Secretary, and he was requested to spread the same at length upon the minutes, said proposal being as follows: That Fred and Sofie Eger will purchase stock of the Windmill Food Stores of Hewlett, Inc. and that they will do so provided that the said common stock is issued pursuant to the terms and provisions of Section 1244 of the Internal Revenue Code. Upon motion duly made and seconded and carried it was Resolved that the corporation accepts the offer and conditions of the offer of Fred and Sofie Eger to purchase common stock of the corporation and that it be issued pursuant to Section 1244 of the Internal Revenue Code. [Emphasis added.]

The italicized portion was from the form and the non-italicized portion was typed in.

that an unresolved question of fact remains as to the year in which the $10,000 loss was incurred. The Tax Court held for the government, relying on a finding that the stock in question was not 1244 stock.

The Tax Court's holding that the Hewlett stock was not 1244 stock was based upon a factual finding that the stock was not issued pursuant to a *written plan* as required by the Statute and Regulation 1.1244(c)-1(c). See Bruce v. United States, [279 F. Supp. 686] (S.D. Tex. 1967); Morgan v. Commissioner, 46 T.C. 878, 888-890 (1966); Spillers v. Commissioner, 26 T.C.M. 1069, 1073-74 (1967); Warner v. Commissioner, 48 T.C. 49 (1967). We disagree. The corporate minutes are a sufficient writing under the circumstances here to meet the requirement of the statute.[3] The regulations were not adopted until a time subsequent to the stock issue here, and we cannot charge the taxpayer with knowledge of their provisions.

The purpose of 1244 was to encourage the formation of small business units found to be socially and economically desirable in spite of the high risk shown by the high percentage of failure of such units in their formative years, by granting favorable tax treatment to losses incurred by investors in the formation of the small business units. At least during the period prior to the adoption of regulations spelling out under the authorization in the statute to promulgate such regulations, the details required of the plan, we think that fidelity to the purpose of the statute calls for liberal application of its language. Here the very formation of the corporation and issue of its stock was expressed to be in conformity with and limited to the conditions required by section 1244, the amount and period of time actually involved were within the statutory limitations, and the contemplated loss occurred.

The Commissioner relies on the Tax Court decisions in Shapiro v. Commissioner, 25 T.C.M. 654 (1966); Morgan v. Commissioner, supra; Warner v. Commissioner, supra, and Spillers v. Commissioner, supra. These cases, even if correctly decided, are clearly distinguishable. In *Shapiro* there was apparently no proof that the stockholder-directors had 1244 in mind or knew of its requirements, nor was there any proof of the value of the property exchanged for the stock in order to establish its basis. *Morgan* involved two payments into the corporation, one of which failed to qualify because made before any plan was adopted or entered in the minutes, the second because made after the corporate purpose had failed, in order to complete corporate liquidation and hopefully salvage something by 1244 treatment of the deficit, not for the bona fide purchase of stock. In *Warner* there was no reference to sec. 1244 in the minutes and the plan for stock purchase contemplated periodic stock purchases (over an indefinite period of time which might well extend beyond two years) from a trust whose rate of purchase depended on trust receipts from a percentage of salary payments by and for employees of another corporation. In *Spillers* there was no reference to sec. 1244 in the corporate minutes concerning the purchase of stock, and a stock voting agreement of the same date contemplated possible future issues, uncertain in time and amount. In Bruce v. United States,

---

[3]Compare the sufficiency of corporate minutes to satisfy the written memorandum requirements of the Statute of Frauds. 2 Corbin Contracts, Sec. 508. Lamkin v. Baldwin & Lamkin Mfg. Co., 72 Conn. 57, 43 A. 593, 596 (1899); Preis v. Eversharp Inc., 154 F. Supp. 98 (E.D.N.Y. 1957).

supra, the first purchase was prior to the adoption of the minutes relied on, and in none of the resolutions was there any reference to sec. 1244 or its requisites except for one which, as in *Morgan,* was after dissolution had been determined on and was held not a bona fide purchase.

Subsequent to oral argument, the Commissioner has called our attention to the case of Spiegel v. Commissioner, [49 T.C. 527 (1968)], denying deduction for lack of a written plan. However, there were in that case no corporate minutes referring to the adoption of a sec. 1244 plan, such as existed here, and even then Judge Dawson recognized that the court was "indeed faced with a close question." The taxpayer complied with the terms and the spirit of the statute as it stood when the stock was issued. There was no attempt to delay election of the form the transaction should take, or create a hedge against the future. The purpose of the plan requirement, to give unequivocal evidence of the taxpayer's commitment to investment in the covered type of small business enterprise, is met here. She is entitled to the benefit of the deduction under the statute.

The decision is reversed and remanded to the Tax Court for further proceedings not inconsistent with this opinion.

NOTE

See M. Smith and D. Tannenbaum, Second Circuit Defines Components of a Well Written Plan Under Section 1244, 29 J. Taxation 66 (1968).

7 | The Accumulated Earnings Tax — §§531-537

Individuals with incomes taxable at very high marginal rates may be willing to leave their corporate earnings in corporate solution if they can avoid taxation at the ordinary rates applicable to dividends. This would be true especially if they might withdraw the earnings at some later time at capital gains rates (e.g., under §331 or §346) or free of the income tax at death, as a result of §§1014 and 302(a), 303, 331 or 346. To discourage corporate accumulations to avoid the individual income tax, Congress has, since 1913, applied special techniques.

From 1913 to 1916, shareholders were taxed individually on their ratable share of undistributed corporate income if the corporation was "formed or fraudulently availed of" to help the shareholders avoid individual taxation. From 1916 to 1921, the individual tax could be imposed even without the showing of a fraudulent purpose. The Supreme Court sustained this tax on the shareholders against charges of unconstitutionality in Helvering v. National Grocery Co., 304 U.S. 282 (1938).

In 1921 Congress changed its approach substantially to that found in the present Code, §§531-537, in which is imposed an added tax on the undistributed earnings of the corporation if it is formed or availed of for the purpose of avoiding the income tax on its shareholders. A number of statutory amendments were made in 1954, but the basic pattern and thrust adopted in 1921 remain.

Section 531 discourages some corporate accumulations, but with the credits provided by §535(c) and a top rate of 38½ per cent, the effect of §531 on the conduct of corporations and shareholders is not dramatic. In some cases, a shareholder in the 70 per cent bracket may find it worth having his corporation incur the ordinary corporate tax under §11 and a tax under §531, too, rather than have it pay dividends. See, generally, B. Bittker and J. Eustice, Federal Income Taxation of Corporations and Shareholders 209-238 (2d ed. 1966).

LATCHIS THEATRES v. COMMISSIONER
214 F.2d 834 (1st Cir. 1954)

Before MAGRUDER, Chief Judge, and WOODBURY and HARTIGAN, Circuit Judges.

MAGRUDER, Chief Judge. The Commissioner of Internal Revenue gave notices to Latchis Theatres of Keene, Inc., and to Latchis Theatres of Claremont, Inc., two closely related New Hampshire corporations having a common ownership, of de-

864

ficiencies in their respective surtaxes for the year 1946, under §[531 et seq.*]. Upon petitions by the two corporations for redetermination of deficiencies, the Tax Court of the United States . . . rendered a decision in the case of Latchis Theatres of Keene, Inc., that there was a deficiency of $4,577.60 in its §[531] surtax for the year 1946, and a decision in the case of Latchis Theatres of Claremont, Inc., that there was a deficiency of $2,118.64 in its §[531] surtax for the same year. . . .

. . . [T]his particular corporate surtax has been somewhat stiffened by amendment. Formerly it was provided that the fact that corporate profits are permitted to accumulate beyond the reasonable needs of the business shall be prima facie evidence of a purpose to escape the surtax. In the Revenue Act of 1938, 26 U.S.C.A. Int. Rev. Acts, page 1039, and ever since then, it has been provided that the fact that the corporate profits have been permitted to accumulate beyond the reasonable needs of the business "shall be determinative of the purpose to avoid surtax upon shareholders unless the corporation by the clear preponderance of the evidence shall prove to the contrary." . . . The report of the Senate Committee on Finance[2] made this explanation of the change: "Under existing law, an unreasonable accumulation is merely prima facie evidence of purpose to avoid surtax upon shareholders. Consequently, it has been argued that the only effect of an unreasonable accumulation is to shift to the taxpayer the burden of going forward with the evidence relating to purpose. Under the amendment, however, it is clear that an unreasonable accumulation puts upon the taxpayer the burden of proving by the clear preponderance of all the evidence submitted that it did not have the purpose of avoidance."

The two petitioning corporations in the present case were incorporated in 1931 under the laws of New Hampshire. They have been engaged since that time in the operation of motion picture and vaudeville theatres in New Hampshire. During 1946 Latchis Theatres of Keene, Inc., operated two theatres in Keene and one in Milford; and Latchis Theatres of Claremont, Inc., operated one theatre in Claremont. Over 90 per cent of the capital stock of the two petitioners was held in equal shares by four Latchis brothers, Spero, Peter, John, and Emmanuel. The buildings in which petitioners operated these theatres were owned by D. Latchis, Inc., another New Hampshire corporation the stock of which was held in the same proportions by the Latchis brothers. In this family group of corporations there were also D. Latchis & Sons, Inc., a Vermont corporation which operated theatres in that state, and a realty company, the Latchis Corporation, which owned the buildings in which the Vermont theatres were located. In addition, the four brothers held the stock of Metropolitan Realty Corporation, and two of the brothers owned as equal partners the Latchis Hotel in Brattleboro, Vt.

The affairs of the petitioners were conducted informally. Minutes of meetings of the stockholders or directors were not kept regularly. At the hearing before the Tax Court, there was oral testimony by two of the brothers, Peter and John, testimony which we think the Tax Court accurately characterized as "too vague, general, inferential and indefinite in important respects". Of course, the Tax Court was

---

*Section 102 of the 1939 Code, under which this case was litigated, had no counterpart to Sections 534 and 535(c) of the 1954 Code. — Ed.

[2]S. Rep. No. 1567, 75th Cong., 3d Sess., Cum. Bull. 1939-1, Pt. 2, 790-91.

not obliged to accept as true the testimony by these two stockholders as to the purpose of the accumulations. Helvering v. National Grocery Co., 1938, 304 U.S. 282, 295, 58 S. Ct. 932, 82 L. Ed. 1346.

Neither of petitioners has ever declared a dividend since its formation in 1931. At the end of 1945 Latchis Theatres of Keene, Inc., had an earned surplus of $52,671.97. For the year 1946, it reported a net income after taxes of $16,645.82 which in its entirety was added to surplus, making the earned surplus at the end of 1946, $69,317.79. Latchis Theatres of Claremont, Inc., had an earned surplus at the end of 1945 of $20,426.09. For the year 1946 it reported a net income after taxes of $7,704.13, which was added in its entirety to surplus, making the figure of this petitioner for earned surplus at the end of 1946, $28,130.22.

The Tax Court's ultimate findings of fact were as follows:

"Each petitioner in 1946 permitted its earnings or profits to accumulate beyond the reasonable needs of its business.

"Each petitioner was availed of during 1946 for the purpose of preventing the imposition of the surtax upon its shareholders through the medium of permitting its earnings or profits to accumulate instead of being divided or distributed."

Petitioners' attack is centered on the first of these two findings. If we cannot say that the Tax Court was "clearly erroneous" in finding that each petitioner in 1946 permitted its corporate profits to accumulate beyond the reasonable needs of its business, then . . . that fact is "determinative" of the existence of the forbidden purpose, for it is not contended that, notwithstanding an accumulation beyond the reasonable needs of the business (if this finding is warranted), petitioners have nevertheless as a matter of law proved by the "clear preponderance of the evidence" that this unnecessary accumulation was for some purpose other than that of avoiding the surtax upon shareholders.

We shall not set out the facts in greater detail, for they are fully and convincingly analyzed in the opinion by Judge Murdock, speaking for the majority of the Tax Court. Particularly, we agree with the following extract from Judge Murdock's opinion:

"The members of the Latchis family, operating as a closely knit group, developed rather extensive business interests of which the two petitioner corporations were but a part. The record indicates that the individuals used the various organizations and particularly the funds of those organizations, including the funds of the petitioners, to suit their own convenience, now to start or aid one activity, again to start or aid another. Apparently, the petitioners were on the receiving end in their early days, until they had gotten started successfully, and then idle funds of the petitioners, even in excess of accumulated earnings, were used at the will of the individuals for any purpose of any part of the various businesses which they were conducting. Those purposes, so far as this record shows, were not germane to the business of the petitioners except as they may have enabled the individuals to build up and strengthen their business domain generally. The Latchis family could have put all of their properties in one corporation and operated all of their businesses through that corporation. Then the arguments they make here that the earnings of one activity can be retained to aid or develop another phase of the business would have more force. But they chose, instead, to divide their holdings and business activities among a number of separate corporations in order to limit liabilities and perhaps to obtain other benefits. They must be judged by what they did in this respect rather than by what they might have done. Attention must be focused upon the petitioners. The accumulation of the 1946 earnings of the petitioners, on top of the earnings and capital which they already had, can not be justified by various needs and purposes of other interests of the Latchis family businesses." . . .

. . . [A]fter a review of the entire record, we are not "left with the definite and firm conviction that a mistake has been committed" by the Tax Court in its crucial findings in the case at bar. United States v. United States Gypsum Co., 1948, 333 U.S. 364, 395, 68 S. Ct. 525, 92 L. Ed. 746.

The decisions of the Tax Court are affirmed.

PELTON STEEL CASTING CO. v. COMMISSIONER
251 F.2d 278 (7th Cir. 1958), cert. denied, 356 U.S. 958 (1958)

Before FINNEGAN, SCHNACKENBERG and PARKINSON, Circuit Judges.

FINNEGAN, Circuit Judge. Section [531] . . . imposed a surtax on corporations improperly accumulating surplus. The respondent Commissioner decided that Pelton Steel Casting Co., petitioner, was availed of in 1946 for the purpose of preventing the imposition of such surtax upon its shareholders by accumulating the corporate earnings and profits instead of dividing or distributing them. That determination of the Commissioner covered fiscal years ending November 30, 1945 and November 30, 1946; penalty tax for 1945 was $12,214.22 and for 1946, $69,746.66. The Commissioner conceded there was no deficiency for the year 1945. We have before us for review the Tax Court's lengthy opinion, reported as Pelton Steel Casting Co. v. Commissioner of Internal Revenue, 1957, 28 T.C. 153, approving the 1946 penalty tax, and resting in considerable part on stipulated facts. Detailing of the operative facts is obviated by their presentation in the opinion issued by the Tax Court, and for that reason we merely describe the factual situation.

During its fiscal year 1946 Pelton had earnings and profits of $209,731.58 and its common stock was held, in these proportions, by: Ehne — 60%, Fawick — 20% and, Slichter — 20%. When Ehne and Fawick informed Slichter of their mutual desire to sell Pelton, Slichter decided to avert an outside sale. After Slichter consulted a banker and lawyer the three stockholders agreed on November 11, 1946, that the corporation would buy up and redeem 80% of the common stock held by Ehne and Fawick at their price of $1,200,000 (this being 80% of $1,500,000, the selling price of the Pelton assets when offered to outsiders). Under the plan Ehne and Fawick were to receive $800,000 in cash and $400,000 in Pelton preferred stock.

That cash flowed from two sources: (1) $300,000 was Pelton's own money and, (2) $500,000 was borrowed by Pelton on a 10-year agreement, dated April 17, 1947, under which an insurance company covered $300,000 to mature in the last six years, and Pelton's bank covered $200,000 to mature during the first four years. This loan, secured by a mortgage on Pelton's plant, was made May 31, 1947, the date when Slichter became the sole common stockholder as the result of the sale-redemption arrangement of 80% of the outstanding common stock held by Ehne and Fawick. Ehne's preferred stock, newly issued to him under the above plan, was immediately purchased by Slichter who gave Ehne a 20-year installment note.

Financiers planning Pelton's purchase of the common stock advised against declaration and payment of dividends during 1946. Again, to repeat for emphasis, it is the Tax Court's opinion which contains recitals of pertinent facts and reproduces the relevant financial statements. On the other hand, this record clearly establishes Pelton as a closely held corporation whose three director-stockholders did not receive 1946 dividends.

An interesting sidelight here comes from the Tax Court opinion:

"The respective amounts of the personal income tax actually paid by A. J. Ehne for 1946 and the estimated amount of tax for which he would have been liable had all of the 1946 earnings and profits ($209,731.58) been distributed in the form of a dividend in that year and had his 60 per cent thereof (some $126,000) in addition to his other income for that year ($47,063.93, per his tax return) been taxed to him at ordinary income rates, are as follows:

Actual	*Estimated*	*Estimated difference*
$22,786.73	$124,955.96	$102,169.23

The tax paid by A. J. Ehne in 1947 on the $603,571 gain realized under the plan on the retirement of his interest in petitioner under the elective alternative tax rates in effect was approximately $150,000. . . ."

The inference, of course, is that instead of dividing all or a portion of the 1946 earnings and profits, totaling $209,731.58, Ehne, Fawick and Slichter countenanced that accumulation and then plowed these earnings into redemption of the common stock. Such an inference is within respectable bounds of reasoning on the evidence before us. On the other hand, Pelton strives to cancel out that inference, and indeed any violation of §[531] pressing on us, as it did the Tax Court, Slichter's undiminished efforts to preserve Pelton's independent existence. In short, the evidence shows that Slichter envisaged Ehne and Fawick selling Pelton to a corporate cannibal; consequently, complete control through the reorganization plan, already described, of Pelton by Slichter loomed up as the only salvation. That reorganization was rejected by the Tax Court on the grounds that it was not promoted for a valid business purpose.

Clearly the batch of ideas sponsored on Pelton's behalf fails in hurdling this passage in §[531] as amended: "There shall be levied, collected and paid for each taxable year . . . upon the net income of every corporation . . . if such corporation . . .

is . . . *availed* of for the *purpose of preventing* the imposition of the surtax upon its shareholders . . . *through the medium of permitting earnings or profits to accumulate* instead of being divided or distributed. . . ." Obviously, the fact an accumulation existed, in Pelton's case, is uncontroverted, and its appeal simply urges that the accumulation was not the type or class penalized by §[531 et seq.].

Regardless of how Pelton's propositions raised in this appeal are analyzed they recur to the basic theme of "reasonable business needs." . . .

Dill Manufacturing Co. v. Commissioner, 1939, 39 BTA 1023 and Gazette Publishing Co. v. Self, D.C. Ark. 1952, 103 F. Supp. 779 are the two main props erected by Pelton's counsel when contending that the reorganization plan was a valid business purpose outside the ambit of §[531]. But reliance on those two cases is misplaced by overlooking the fact that the Pelton plan required, and had, unanimous stockholder approval. The actuality of the consummated plan could only be reached, and was achieved, by the favorable vote of Ehne, alone, or in combination with Fawick. Both *Dill* and *Gazette* are instances where the majority of stockholders bought out a minority, and to that extent *Pelton, Dill* and *Gazette* are all cases where the majority (at bar Ehne, Fawick and Slichter) of stockholders acted, but only in *Pelton* did a minority stockholder remain in the corporation, after the majority sold out and all three men enjoy the tax benefit of the planned action. . . .

Slichter's testimony in the Tax Court demonstrates that Ehne, especially, and Fawick wanted to sell Pelton. Representing 80% of the outstanding capital, as these two men did, they could have ended the independent existence of Pelton. All Slichter's action and motivation indicates is a vague sort of moral obligation toward faithful employees and some understandable pride in perpetuating Pelton as a separate entity. Ransoming Pelton was apparently far from the evidenced state of mind attributable to Ehne or Fawick.

Section [531], containing as it did penalty provisions, was intended as a deterrent. Its aim was to prevent the corporation from being used as a device for avoiding surtax on individual incomes. The singular feature, frequently and conveniently overlooked, is that the penalty tax may be avoided by distributing earnings. See e.g. Carey, Accumulations Beyond The Reasonable Needs Of The Business: The Dilemma Of Section 102(c), 60 Harv. L. Rev. 1282 (1947). The record is utterly devoid of countervailing evidence either palliating or eradicating the situation interdicted . . . , indeed we are satisfied Pelton was "availed of" during the taxable year.

The judgment of the Tax Court is
Affirmed.

NOTE

See W. O'Neill, The Accumulated Earnings Tax — Effects of Stock Redemptions, 46 Taxes 172 (1968); G. Maxfield, Recent Cases Forecast More Liberal Trend in Allowing Accumulations to Redeem Stock, 25 J. Taxation 43 (1966); D. Herwitz, Stock Redemptions and the Accumulated Earnings Tax, 74 Harv. L. Rev. 866 (1961).

The Tax Reform Act of 1969 provided special "relief" in two redemption situations. See §537(b). Is this "relief" wise tax policy? The provisions of §537(b) are summarized tersely in A. Gannet, Accumulations for Certain Redemption Purposes Now Free of 531 Threat, 32 J. Taxation 267 (1970).

REVENUE RULING 67-64
1967-1 Cum. Bull. 150

Advice has been requested whether, in justifying the reasonable needs of its business pursuant to section 537 of the Internal Revenue Code of 1954, a corporation may include a fund equal to its depreciation reserves escalated for the economic factor of increased replacement costs.

A corporation is engaged in the manufacturing business and has operated successfully since its inception. Over the years, the corporation has expanded its plant facilities and has made replacements of machinery and equipment. The expenditures with respect to such expansion and replacements were normal for a successful business. The corporation contends that, in justifying the reasonable needs of its business, it should be permitted to include a fund equal to its depreciation reserves escalated for the economic factor of increased costs of replacement regardless of whether it has any specific or definite plans to use the funds in its business.

Section 537 of the Code provides that the term "reasonable needs of the business" includes the reasonably anticipated needs of the business. Section 1.537-1(b) of the Income Tax Regulations provides that in order for a corporation to justify an accumulation of earnings and profits for reasonably anticipated future needs, there must be an indication that the future needs of the business require such accumulation, *and the corporation must have specific, definite, and feasible plans for the use of such accumulation.* Where the future needs of the business are uncertain or vague, where the plans for the future use of an accumulation are not specific, definite, and feasible, or where execution of such a plan is postponed indefinitely, an accumulation cannot be justified on the grounds of reasonably anticipated needs of the business. These regulations express the legislative intent as stated in Senate Report 1622, 83d Congress, 2d Session, 69, and House Report 1337, 83d Congress, 2d Session, A172-A173.

Although the reserve for depreciation itself may be considered and given appropriate weight as a part of the facts and circumstances in considering the reasonable needs of the business, the concept that a noncash deduction for depreciation based on historic costs requires the setting aside for an indefinite period a cash fund adjusted for economic fluctuations in order to provide for total replacement of plant assets is not within the meaning of the term "reasonable needs of the business."

Accordingly, a corporation may not include a fund equal to its depreciation reserves escalated for the economic factor of increased replacement costs in justifying the reasonable needs of its business pursuant to section 537 of the Code. However, the reserve for depreciation itself may be considered and given appropriate weight as a part of the facts and circumstances in each case.

NOTE

1. Taxpayers have attempted to justify accumulations on the basis of working capital requirements, operating cycles, ratios of current assets to current liabilities and the like. Courts have made efforts to apply rules of thumb for such cases. See Apollo Industries, Inc. v. Commissioner, 358 F.2d 867 (1st Cir. 1966), rev'g 44 T.C. 1 (1965); Bardahl Manufacturing Corp., 24 CCH Tax Ct. Mem. 1030 (1965). See also J. Trethewey, Justifying Retention of Cash to Meet Working Capital Needs: The Problem of Section 531, 27 N.Y.U. Inst. on Fed. Tax. 737 (1969).

2. See generally N. Luria, The Accumulated Earnings Tax, 76 Yale L.J. 793 (1967); R. Levitan, Defensive Planning to Avoid the 531 Tax — Some Techniques to Use, 26 J. Taxation 88 (1967); P. Faber, Practitioner's Guide to Defending a 531 Case: Theory and Practice, 27 J. Taxation 274 (1967).

NEMOURS CORP. v. COMMISSIONER
38 T.C. 585 (1962)

The Commissioner originally determined a deficiency in petitioner's income tax for the taxable year 1956 in the amount of $745,302.63 on the theory that petitioner was subject to the personal holding company tax. The Commissioner withdrew this issue at the trial and, by amendment to his answer, determined a deficiency in the amount of $286,281.17 on the theory that petitioner was subject to the accumulated earnings tax in 1956. The correctness of the latter determination is the only issue presented. If the Court should hold for petitioner on this issue, petitioner claims an overpayment of tax in the amount of $73,826.91.

Findings of Fact.

The facts stipulated by the parties are incorporated herein by this reference.

Petitioner, a corporation organized under the laws of the State of Delaware on December 27, 1924, has its principal office in Suite 1090, DuPont Building, Wilmington, Delaware, and filed its 1956 corporate income tax return with the district director of internal revenue, Wilmington, Delaware.

During the taxable year 1956, petitioner kept its books and accounting records on a cash receipts and disbursements method of accounting, and its taxable period was the calendar year. . . . [At the time of incorporation in 1924, Paulina duPont Dean and J. Simpson Dean transferred to petitioner securities, real estate, and cash in exchange for petitioner's no-par stock.]

. . . [By] December 31, 1956, petitioner's outstanding no-par common stock in the total amount of 36,172 shares was owned as follows: Paulina duPont Dean, 26,923 shares; J. Simpson Dean, 5,249 shares; trusts for the benefit of the three Dean children, 4,000 shares.

At all times here material J. Simpson Dean was president, treasurer, and a director of petitioner, and Paulina duPont Dean was vice president and a director.

During the taxable years 1934 to 1955, inclusive, petitioner was a personal holding company within the pertinent provisions of the applicable revenue acts, Internal Revenue Codes, and regulations thereunder, and petitioner filed its returns and paid its taxes as such.

Among the assets transferred by and on behalf of Paulina duPont Dean to petitioner on its organization in 1924 were 333 shares of Delaware Realty and Investment Company no-par common stock. As a result of stock splits and stock dividends, petitioner owned 33,300 shares of Delaware Realty and Investment Company no-par common stock as of December 31, 1956, and such stock produced dividend income to petitioner in 1956 in the total amount of $1,273,725. The total cost basis of such stock on petitioner's books was $33,333.33. . . . [This stock was valued at $1,200.00 per share for loan purposes. See footnote 5 infra.]

On or about April 4, 1956, J. Simpson Dean, hereinafter for convenience sometimes referred to as Dean, was presented with a plan by tax counsel to remove petitioner from its status as a personal holding company under the revenue laws. The plan contemplated the acquisition by petitioner of income from oil and gas production to the end that such gross income from oil and gas sources would exceed 20 percent of its gross income from all sources [and would thus relieve petitioner from personal holding company liability]. The plan appealed to Dean, not only because of the substantial tax saving which it envisioned for petitioner, but also because it offered petitioner an opportunity to earn and retain a sufficient amount to be able to discharge its existing indebtedness (then amounting to $1,260,000) at the Wilmington Trust Company. Dean also considered the purchase of oil and gas properties by petitioner a form of insurance for his and his wife's estate taxes because such assets could be readily sold by petitioner and converted into cash with which the corporation could redeem all or part of their stock in the event of death. . . .

When Dean introduced oil and gas operations into petitioner's corporate activities in 1956, he considered the possibility of having petitioner acquire other gas and oil interests in the future. However, no specific plans were formulated along these lines, nor was anything relating to such possible future acquisitions recorded in a formal corporate resolution in 1956.

In the years following 1956, petitioner acquired other producing oil and gas properties as more particularly set forth in the paragraphs that immediately follow. It acquired no such additional properties until 1959.

The balance sheets of petitioner reflect the capitalized book cost of its oil and gas properties and equipment as of the end of each of the years 1956 through 1961, as follows:

Dec. 31, 1956	$2,790,064.35	Dec. 31, 1959	$4,290,468.12
Dec. 31, 1957	2,812,607.27	Dec. 31, 1960	5,080,755.97
Dec. 31, 1958	2,854,601.55	Dec. 31, 1961	5,319,831.54

During the period 1957 to 1960, inclusive, petitioner's cash expenditures in its oil and gas operations for intangible drilling costs and for other purposes which were not capitalized were as follows:

Year	Intangible drilling costs	Other cash expenditures	Total cash expenditures not capitalized
1957	$ 68,222.44	$123,988.34	$192,210.78
1958	49,418.45	125,464.31	174,882.76
1959	103,893.18	283,259.77	387,152.95
1960	238,932.05	300,229.90	539,161.95

[From 1959 to 1961, petitioner acquired a number of additional oil and gas production interests and leases. In some instances the acquisitions were financed with borrowed funds. In one instance petitioner issued shares of its no-par common stock for stock of a corporation which owned leases and whose stock had been held by the Dean children.]

Petitioner's gross receipts for the years 1956 to 1960, inclusive, from its oil and gas properties (including the receipts in 1956 and 1957 from the Midstates oil production payment) were as follows:

1956	$1,011,127.63
1957	731,868.85
1958	532,971.91
1959	978,118.88
1960	874,198.06

Prior to 1956 (while petitioner was a personal holding company under the applicable revenue laws), petitioner's dividend policy was correlated with the income tax rate of petitioner's principal stockholders, J. Simpson Dean and Paulina duPont Dean. The Deans caused petitioner to declare only sufficient dividends in each year as would produce the smallest overall tax payment for them and for petitioner. Under the statute as a personal holding company petitioner's tax ceiling was set at 85 percent. Since each year the Deans had income from sources other than petitioner which fluctuated in amount, they had petitioner declare a balancing dividend with the result that their own top bracket would not exceed 85 percent. Thus, dividends declared by petitioner fluctuated from year to year according to the outside income of the Deans. An exception to this policy occurred in 1954 when the Deans made a gift of 4,000 shares of petitioner's stock to two trusts created by them in 1937 for the benefit of their three children. To put the trusts in cash the Deans caused petitioner to pay a larger dividend in 1954 and thereby brought their individual tax rate up to 89 percent. Part of the dividend went to the trusts and because the trusts were in a lower tax bracket they retained sufficient funds to pay certain insurance premiums, thereby sparing the Deans the need of giving cash to the trusts and paying gift taxes on such cash transfers.

In 1956, when the Deans no longer considered petitioner a personal holding company, petitioner's dividend policy changed. At first Dean was of the opinion that petitioner should declare no dividend in 1956. However, it was ultimately decided that petitioner declare and pay a dividend of $2 per share or a total of $72,344 on its 36,172 outstanding shares for the year 1956. . . .

As of December 31, 1956, the Deans were indebted to petitioner in the total amount of $2,563,098.07 on non-interest-bearing demand notes. Since 1929 they had been borrowing from petitioner from time to time on such notes and, in addition thereto, since 1938 they had been borrowing from petitioner on open account. On December 31, 1952, the advances to the Deans on open account were transferred to non-interest-bearing demand notes in the amounts of their open account balances. Advances were made in 1953 to Paulina duPont Dean only, which after repayments showed a net amount owing by her on December 31, 1953, of $42,275 for which she gave a non-interest-bearing demand note. Further advances and repayments on open account were made during the year 1954 to both of the Deans, with full repayment of the net amounts then owing by December 31, 1954. During the year 1955 additional advances and repayments were made to the Deans, the principal advances being $250,000 to each on March 15, 1955, with which to pay gift taxes on the gifts of petitioner's stock made by them in 1954 to trusts for the benefit of their children. On December 31, 1955, Dean gave a non-interest-bearing demand note to petitioner in the amount of $133,431.85 covering the balance owed by him on open account, and his wife gave a similar note in the amount of $373,039.95 covering her balance. During 1956 advances were made to Paulina duPont Dean only in the total amount of $462,137.24. Partial repayment was made from time to time throughout the year, and on December 31, 1956, the outstanding balance in the amount of $399,403.01 was fully repaid. The Deans did not borrow additional funds from petitioner on non-interest-bearing demand notes during 1956. . . .

At times (while petitioner was a personal holding company) when the Deans wanted to borrow funds from petitioner and petitioner lacked the necessary cash, Dean caused petitioner to borrow money at prevailing interest rates from the Wilmington Trust Company (in which he was a director), with the prearranged purpose of then borrowing the same funds from petitioner on non-interest-bearing notes. Thus, for example, on March 15, 1955, petitioner borrowed $500,000 from the bank at an interest rate of 3 percent per annum and on the same day advanced such funds to the Deans on open account so that the Deans had cash with which to pay gift taxes owed by them. The Deans did not pay interest to petitioner on their borrowings from petitioner when the corporation was a personal holding company because in their view such interest payments would have involved only cross balancing tax deductions for them and additional income for petitioner, as well as potentially increased taxable dividends from petitioner to them.

On December 31, 1955, petitioner was indebted to the Wilmington Trust Company on demand notes signed between November of 1947 and March of 1955 in an aggregate amount of $1,260,000. By letter dated October 3, 1956, the bank wrote to Dean indicating that in view of the "change in the money market," the bank wanted payments on petitioner's outstanding indebtedness "with no specific amounts mentioned or times mentioned, but frankly as large and as rapidly as possible." On December 21, 1956, petitioner made a payment of $400,000 to the bank, leaving a balance owing as of December 31, 1956, of $860,000. The bank held 10,000 shares of Delaware Realty and Investment Company stock in 1956 as security for petitioner's indebtedness. In the regular course of making periodic appraisals of all collateral held by the loan department, the bank determined that the asset value per share of such Delaware Realty and Investment Company no-par common stock on December 29, 1955, was $1,367.77 and that 75 percent of the asset value per share was $1,025.83. On December 28, 1956, the bank determined that the asset value per share of such stock was $1,179.74 and that 75 percent of the asset value per share was $884.81.

The $990,740.93 indebtedness which petitioner incurred on June 11, 1956, in connection with the purchase of an oil production payment had been reduced to $111,105.62 as of December 31, 1956.

The $2,800,000 indebtedness which petitioner incurred on August 8, 1956, in connection with the purchase of working interests in 18 gas condensate wells had been reduced to $2,254,000 as of December 31, 1956.

Petitioner's comparative balance sheets as of December 31, 1955 and 1956, as shown on its Federal income tax returns for such years, were as follows:

	Dec. 31 —	
Assets	*1955*	*1956*
Cash	$ 528,767.17	$ 228,070.67
Notes and accounts receivable	2,688,421.01	2,721,057.18
Prepaid expenses	....	2,511.83
Other investments — securities	[1]34,868.56	[1]33,366.66
Buildings and other depreciable assets	67,115.22	255,163.88
Depletable assets	....	2,641,870.02
Land	94.33	94.33
Livestock	6,602.73	3,292.68
Total assets	3,325,869.02	5,885,427.25
Liabilities		
Accounts payable	2,278.06	63,438.12
Bonds, notes and mortgages payable (maturing less than 1 year from date of balance sheet)	1,260,000.00	3,225,105.62
Accrued expense Federal income tax	413,209.06	73,826.91
Capital stock — common stock	3,454,092.09	3,454,092.09
Earned surplus — deficit	[2](1,803,710.19)	[2](931,035.49)
Total liabilities	3,325,869.02	5,885,427.25

[1]This figure includes a book cost of $33,333.33 for 33,300 shares of Delaware Realty and Investment Company, which, however, paid dividends to petitioner in the amounts of $1,372,293 and $1,273,725 in 1955 and 1956, respectively; such stock in fact had a fair market value that was substantially in excess of the book cost reflected in these balance sheets.

[2]Deficit.

Condensed profit and loss statements of petitioner for the years [1954] to 1956, inclusive, were as follows . . . .

Income	1954	1955	1956
Dividends received	$1,093,905.00	$1,372,293.00	$1,273,725.00
Interest received	....	....	....
Farm income	15,931.05	21,581.25	29,133.00
Sale of capital assets	1,101.38	....	1,294.41
Gross income from gas and oil production payments	....	....	896,229.05
Gross income from gas and oil sales ..	....	....	114,898.58
Total	1,110,937.43	1,393,874.25	2,315,280.04

Expense			
Real estate	194.17	198.74	....
Interest	20,166.94	36,991.59	107,072.32
Office expense	37,687.63	40,243.28	56,315.27
Salaries (J. S. Dean)	30,000.00	30,000.00	36,660.00
Farm expense	99,984.73	115,298.68	102,766.49
Bad debts	....	....	....
Taxes	....	....	757.50
Depletion — Gas and oil production payments	....	....	882,398.05
Expenses — Gas and oil sales	....	....	78,320.40
Pension plan	....	....	29,497.65
Total	188,033.47	222,732.29	1,293,787.68
Net income before taxes	922,903.96	1,171,141.96	1,021,492.36
Taxes	200,991.38	[1]409,736.26	
Net income after taxes	721,912.58	761,405.70	1,021,492.36
Capital stock outstanding (common shares)	36,172	36,172	36,172
Earnings per share before taxes	$25.52	$32.38	$28.24
Earnings per share after taxes	$19.95	$21.04	$28.24
Total dividends paid	$699,928.20	$699,928.20	$72,344.00
Dividends paid per share	$19.35	$19.35	$2.00

[1]Taxes for 1955 and 1956 are adjusted "as corrected by allowable claims."

Petitioner's accumulated earnings and profits as of December 31, 1955 and 1956, as adjusted by stipulation of the parties, were $1,088,950.15 and $1,626,868.87, respectively. If petitioner's increase of accumulated earnings and profits during the taxable year 1956 had been distributed as dividends, there would have resulted a substantial increase in the Federal income taxes due and payable by J. Simpson Dean and Paulina duPont Dean.

Petitioner was not a mere holding or investment company as of December 31, 1956.

The reasonable needs of petitioner's business (including the reasonably anticipated needs of such business) did not require the accumulation of any of the corporation's earnings and profits for the taxable year 1956.

Opinion.

RAUM, Judge: The nature of the controversy herein has undergone a complete change since the Commissioner initially sent a deficiency notice to petitioner. The major portion of the $745,302.63 deficiency originally determined by the Commissioner was based on the factual determination that petitioner, which filed its returns and paid its taxes as a personal holding company under the applicable revenue laws each year from 1934 through 1955, remained a personal holding company during the taxable year 1956 and was subject to the personal holding company tax. In its petition filed with this Court, petitioner alleged that the Commissioner erred in this determination. Shortly before the trial of this case the Commissioner amended his answer to the petition to allege for the first time that, in the alternative, if petitioner was not a personal holding company in 1956, then it was subject to the accumulated earnings tax for such year, and an alternative, reduced deficiency in the amount of $286,281.17 was claimed. The Commissioner's new theory was necessarily stated as an alternative contention because section 532(b)(1) of the 1954 Code (as did predecessor revenue acts throughout the time petitioner was a personal holding company) provides that the accumulated earnings tax is not applicable to a personal holding company. Hence, it had to be assumed (contrary to the deficiency notice) for purposes of the accumulated earnings tax allegation that petitioner no longer remained a personal holding company in 1956. At the trial the Commissioner entirely abandoned the personal holding company issue, leaving the applicability of the accumulated earnings tax to petitioner in 1956 the only question for decision.

As an accumulated earnings tax dispute, this case has several unusual features. First of all because this issue was raised by the Commissioner for the first time in an amended answer to the petition, under the rules of practice of this Court it is the Commissioner and not the petitioner who has the burden of proof regarding the applicability of this special tax, that is, whether petitioner in 1956 was "availed of for the purpose of avoiding the income tax with respect to its shareholders . . . by permitting earnings and profits to accumulate instead of being divided or distributed." Sec. 532(a), I.R.C. 1954. In particular, the Commissioner has the burden in respect of the question whether petitioner permitted earnings and profits to accumulate in 1956 beyond the reasonable needs of its business, a matter upon which he presumably would have the burden in these circumstances in any event since he had not sent the notification provided for in section 534. But it must be noted from the outset that section 533 permits the Commissioner (even in the unusual circumstances of this case) to shift the burden of proof to petitioner on the ultimate question of the purpose of the accumulation by proving that the earnings and profits of petitioner were in fact permitted to accumulate beyond the reasonable needs of the business in 1956 or that petitioner was in fact a mere holding or investment company during the taxable year.

Aside from burden-of-proof responsibilities, there is a second unusual factor which sets this case apart from prior cases considered by this Court involving the accumulated earnings tax. This factor is the continuous history of the petitioner as a personal holding company under the revenue laws for over 20 years immediately preceding the taxable year in issue. During this period petitioner was subject to the added personal holding company tax but as already noted was not also subject to the accumulated earnings tax. Thus, the petitioner's business history during the years prior to the taxable year in controversy, a matter generally of considerable importance in an accumulated earnings tax case, is of limited relevance in the instant case. As a personal holding company from 1934 through 1955, for example, petitioner's dividend policy of gearing its distributions to the tax bracket of its shareholders and its loan policy of advancing in excess of $2,500,000 to its principal shareholders on personal loans without interest cannot be viewed in the same light for purposes of decision of the present issue as if petitioner had been other than a personal holding company during this period and had experienced a similar history. While at the Commissioner's request we have made extended findings of fact concerning the petitioner's business and financial history while it remained a personal holding company, we think such findings are of limited usefulness except as a general background to petitioner's changed status during the taxable year in issue.

We do not mean to imply that petitioner's former status as a personal holding company in any sense exempts petitioner from the application of the accumulated earnings tax after it no longer comes within the statutory definition of a personal holding company. On the contrary, in the framework of the 1954 Code both the accumulated earnings and personal holding company taxes are contained within subchapter G which is entitled "Corporations Used to Avoid Income Tax on Shareholders," and thus petitioner's extended history as a personal holding company, if anything, makes it suspect in terms of other means, such as accumulating surplus, for avoiding shareholder taxes. We do think, however, in fairness to petitioner that while the corporation was paying its taxes as a personal holding company, petitioner and especially petitioner's principal shareholders, the Deans, had the right to treat and use the corporation as a personal holding company for all purposes and that petitioner's conduct during this period (when the accumulated earnings tax did not apply) should not necessarily prejudice its position once it becomes an ordinary operating corporation under the revenue laws.

We turn then to the issue of the applicability of the accumulated earnings tax to petitioner in 1956. After carefully studying all of the evidence of record and the arguments of counsel, we have concluded that petitioner in 1956 was availed of for the purpose of avoiding the income tax with respect to its shareholders by permitting its earnings and profits to accumulate instead of being distributed and that, therefore, it is subject to the accumulated earnings tax imposed by section 531.

Although the question is not free from doubt, we have made a finding that petitioner was not a "mere holding or investment company" (as the phrase is used in section 533(b), supra) as of December 31, 1956. We think that petitioner's purchase of working interests in 18 gas condensate wells in 1956 constitutes sufficient nonholding or noninvestment company activity to take petitioner out of the "mere holding or investment company" category as used in the statute and the applicable regulations. Sec. 1.533-1(c), Income Tax Regs. In this regard, we reject the Commissioner's argument on brief that petitioner's purchase of oil and gas interests in 1956, because "for the admitted specific purpose of removing petitioner from a personal holding company classification, is incompatible with business status and is legally inadequate to remove petitioner from a holding and investment company status." By conceding that petitioner was no longer a personal holding company in 1956, the Commissioner has recognized the validity of the oil and gas interest purchases. We therefore find it difficult to follow the Commissioner's reasoning that such investments (for whatever purpose) were something less than they purported to be. To be sure, petitioner's working interests in gas condensate wells in 1956 were managed and operated by its agent, Hudson Gas and Oil Company. However, we think this agency arrangement and the gradual takeover of operations by petitioner were consistent with prudent business practice and in not way detract from petitioner's actual entry into the gas condensate business in the taxable year. We think that the scope of this business[3] was of such magnitude that petitioner cannot properly be described as a mere holding or investment company as of the close of the taxable year.[4]

As noted above in our discussion of the burden of proof, section 533(a) provides that the fact that the earnings and profits of a corporation are permitted to accumulate beyond the reasonable needs of the business shall be considered determinative of the purpose to avoid the income tax with respect to shareholders, unless the corporation by the preponderance of the evidence shall prove to the contrary. We think on the record before us that the Commissioner has successfully proved that petitioner's earnings and profits were permitted to accumulate beyond the reasonable needs of the business (including the reasonably anticipated needs of the business as provided in section 537) and that the petitioner has failed to

---

[3]The Commissioner relies on language in John Provence #1 Well, 37 T.C. 376, [affirmed sub nom. John Provence #1 Well v. Commissioner, 321 F.2d 840 (3d Cir. 1963)], to argue that petitioner's working interests in the wells represented mere investments and not business activities. However, the working interests sold in that case, unlike those purchased by petitioner, did not include any managerial rights. Since the absence of a transfer of managerial functions was an important factor in reaching the conclusion that the working interests in Provence were akin to corporate stock, we think that case is distinguishable.

[4]Petitioner does not argue that its purchase of an oil production payment in 1956 constituted sufficient business activity to remove it from the "mere holding or investment company" category, and therefore we express no opinion on the question whether this phase of petitioner's total activities constituted anything more than an investment or holding of property for the production of income.

offer a preponderance of evidence to show that such accumulation was not for the interdicted purpose of avoiding shareholder taxes.

As of the start of the taxable year 1956, the parties have stipulated that petitioner's adjusted accumulated earnings and profits amounted to $1,088,950.15. The Commissioner has argued that no further accumulations were necessary for petitioner's business needs in 1956. The petitioner has tried to show that such needs justified the retention of the additional $537,918.72 earnings and profits which it is agreed were accumulated during the taxable year. We think that the Commissioner has proved his case.

In 1956 petitioner's chief income-producing asset continued to be its 33,300 shares of Delaware Realty and Investment Company stock.[5] While its dividend income from such stock in 1956 was slightly less than it had been in 1955, still such income alone, amounting to $1,273,725, was nearly sufficient to pay all of petitioner's operating expenses during the taxable year.[6] In addition, petitioner received over $1 million in gross income from the oil and gas interests it acquired in 1956. By removing itself from the personal holding company classification, petitioner eliminated a Federal income tax expense of in excess of $800,000 in 1956. Thus, although petitioner's net income before taxes in 1956 was almost $150,000 under what it had been in 1955, its net income after taxes was $1,021,492.36 in 1956 as compared to $761,405.70 in 1955. As a result, petitioner's earnings per share after taxes increased from $21.04 in 1955 to $28.24 in 1956.

From these facts it is difficult to understand why, when petitioner was able to pay a dividend of $19.35 per share in 1955, it paid only $2 per share with increased net earnings in 1956. The answer of petitioner's president, J. Simpson Dean, in testimony at the trial was that petitioner's indebtedness incurred in connection with the purchase of its working interests in gas wells, together with its indebtedness on demand notes to the Wilmington Trust Company, was of such magnitude in relation to its cash position at the end of 1956 that a $2 dividend was determined to be all that was "reasonably safe" in the circumstances. If petitioner in fact had no choice but to pay any dividend declared in 1956 in cash, such

---

[5]The Delaware Realty and Investment Company stock was carried on petitioner's books at a cost value of $33,333.33, or approximately $1 a share. We think it clear on this record that the fair market value of such stock was substantially higher. Moreover, we are not at all persuaded by Dean's testimony that "Delaware Realty and Investment Company [stock] had no market, and I have my own ideas about what it would have sold for in a free market if you were ready to sell it to a willing buyer." Such testimony is equally consistent with a deliberate determination by the owners of such stock to keep it off the market and we are by no means convinced that if any such stock were offered for sale there would be any real difficulty in disposing of it at a fair price. In view of the fact, as shown by the evidence, that Delaware Realty's income stemmed largely from its extensive holdings of stock in E. I. duPont de Nemours and Company (partly owned directly and partly through holdings in Christiana Securities Company, which in turn owned large amounts of duPont stock), we have little doubt that a ready market for Delaware Realty stock could be found if only the effort were made. In regard to the actual value of this stock, it is noteworthy that shares of Delaware Realty were given a value ranging from $884.81 to $1,330 per share for collateral purposes in 1956 by institutions which held such stock as security for loans made to petitioner.

[6]Petitioner's total operating expenses in 1956, including a depletion allowance for its newly acquired gas and oil interests in the amount of $882,398.05, amounted to $1,293,787.68.

reasoning might perhaps[7] be persuasive. However, this was not the case. Petitioner held non-interest-bearing notes in the total amount of $2,563,098.07 from its principal stockholders, the Deans, and in these circumstances a sizable dividend might have been declared by discharging a substantial portion of these notes without reducing the corporation's cash or general quick assets position.

At the trial when petitioner's counsel asked J. Simpson Dean whether such a method of paying a noncash dividend had been considered in 1956, his answer was as follows: "You could not give much consideration to that because if Mrs. Dean and I had gotten let's say a dividend not in cash from Nemours, we could not get the money to pay the tax on what we got. So it, it could be thought of, but not actually considered. It was not practical or feasible." Such an answer, obviously given in complete candor, furnishes no basis to the corporation for retaining earnings. The inconvenience of a noncash dividend to shareholders, while admittedly a matter of practical concern to the shareholders, can hardly justify a corporation which has more than sufficient accumulated earnings and profits but relatively little cash (in relation to its business needs) from declaring an appropriate dividend in terms of its current earnings. Certainly the cash requirements of the shareholders do not constitute a "business need" of the corporation insofar as the retention of earnings under the statute is concerned. Dean's answer to petitioner's counsel's question can only be viewed as a frank admission that no corporate business reason existed for not paying a dividend in 1956 in the notes of the principal shareholders and that the true reason for not following such a course was to avoid the resulting tax on the shareholders.

In Whitney Chain & Mfg. Co., 3 T.C. 1109, affirmed per curiam, 149 F.2d 936 (C.A. 2), a similar situation existed. In that case, a major portion of the corporation's assets was tied up in corporate stock for which there was no ready market and in the form of non-interest-bearing loans to shareholders.[8] The corporation in that case was considering expanding, and it argued that its lack of quick assets fully justified the accumulations involved. This Court's answer to such argument is particularly relevant here (3 T.C. at 1119):

"We think these contentions would acquire force if, in fact there was no way to liquidate the assets. However, there is a ready answer to both of these propositions, which might be expected to have occurred to a directorate of the caliber of petitioner's. If the $70,000 retained by the petitioner was, in

---

[7]We use the qualifying word "perhaps," because the record strongly indicates that, at least as to petitioner's indebtedness in respect of its oil and gas interests, it was anticipated that such indebtedness would be paid off out of the oil and gas revenues and that no cash accumulation of current earnings was necessary for that purpose.

[8]While on brief petitioner argues that similarly there was no market in 1956 for its Delaware Realty and Investment Company stock, we do not accept petitioner's contention in this regard nor the corollary contention that such stock did not have a fair market value. See footnote 5, supra. In addition, in *Whitney Chain* the major portion of the non-interest-bearing notes had benefited a predecessor in interest of the then present shareholders who had assumed the debts involved. In the instant case all of such loans were made directly to the present principal shareholders, the Deans. As a result, the facts in these key respects in the present case are not as strong for petitioner as they were in *Whitney Chain*.

fact, needed in the business, a complete distribution could have been made on the condition that the stockholders apply the amount of the distribution to the reduction of their indebtedness; or a dividend in kind, payable by the cancellation of the debts of the stockholders to the extent of the $70,000 retained; or a dividend payable in the stock of Hanson-Whitney might have been made, to the extent of the earnings retained. Had any one of these courses been pursued, the petitioner would have been in no worse position, as regards the financing of the proposed expansion, and yet would have avoided any further accumulation of earnings."

Moreover, in *Whitney Chain,* this Court concluded that a predominantly independent board of directors could not have been ignorant of the ready means available by which a dividend might have been paid and that the board's failure to follow such a course was indicative of a purpose to reduce the surtax burden of the shareholders. In the present case, where petitioner's board of directors was made up of and controlled by the very shareholders (the Deans) who received the tax benefits of a minimum dividend, the same conclusion follows with even greater force. Cf. Kerr-Cochran, Inc. v. Commissioner, 253 F.2d 121, 128 (C.A. 8), affirming a Memorandum Opinion of this Court.

Apart from petitioner's cash position at the end of 1956, the only other reason suggested for petitioner's failure to distribute its current earnings was that petitioner intended to expand its oil and gas activities and in fact did expand such interests in subsequent years and that such expansion plans constituted a reasonable need of the business in 1956 (or, at least, a reasonably anticipated need of the business in such year) for which an accumulation of earnings was required. While there is some indication in the record that Dean, as petitioner's president, did consider the possibility of causing petitioner to acquire other oil and gas properties subsequent to 1956, it appears that no plans were made along such lines during the taxable year. The testimony that we heard showed that petitioner's officers in 1956 were concerned mainly with obtaining sufficient gross income from oil and gas sources to remove petitioner from the personal holding company classification in that year and in subsequent years, and that expansion beyond this goal — while it may possibly have been in Dean's mind — was vague and indefinite. Such nebulous expansion "plans" do not justify the retention of earnings by petitioner over and above the earnings already accumulated prior to the taxable year. Cf. Barrow Manufacturing Company v. Commissioner, 294 F.2d 79, 80-81 (C.A. 5), affirming a Memorandum Opinion of this Court, certiorari denied 369 U.S. 817; American Metal Products Corporation v. Commissioner, 287 F.2d 860, 864-865 (C.A. 8), affirming 34 T.C. 89; Dixie, Inc. v. Commissioner, 277 F.2d 526 (C.A. 2), affirming 31 T.C. 415, certiorari denied 364 U.S. 827; I. A. Dress Co. v. Commissioner, 273 F.2d 543 (C.A. 2), affirming 32 T.C. 93, certiorari denied 362 U.S. 976; Smoot Sand & Gravel Corp. v. Commissioner, 241 F.2d 197, 202 (C.A. 4), reversing on other grounds a Memorandum Opinion of this Court, certiorari denied 354 U.S. 922. Moreover, it must be recalled that the oil and gas interests acquired in 1956 were obtained with borrowed funds rather than out of petitioner's own assets, and it seems plain that any possible future acquisitions could similarly be financed by borrowing. Indeed, the record affirmatively shows that such future purchases were in fact made primarily with borrowed funds. In our judgment, the explanation that petitioner's earnings were retained for this purpose is spurious.

We conclude, on the record as a whole, that the Commissioner has proved that the earnings and profits of petitioner in 1956 were allowed to accumulate beyond the reasonable needs of the business. Under the statute the accumulated earnings tax is thereby applicable, the petitioner having failed to prove by a preponderance of the evidence that the earnings and profits in fact accumulated in 1956 were not for the purpose of avoiding the income tax with respect to its shareholders.

Decision will be entered under Rule 50.

NEMOURS CORP. v. COMMISSIONER
325 F.2d 559 (3d Cir. 1963), aff'g 38 T.C. 585 (1962)

Before STALEY and GANEY, Circuit Judges, and NEALON, District Judge.

PER CURIAM: The taxpayer in the above matter sought a review of the Commissioner of Internal Revenue's determination that there existed a deficiency in its income tax for the taxable year 1956, on the theory that it was subject to the personal holding company tax. During the trial, the Commissioner, after he had amended his answer to the petition, abandoned his former claim and determined that the taxpayer was deficient in a lesser amount on the ground that it was subject to the accumulated earnings tax under §§531 and 532 of the Internal Revenue Code of 1954, 26 U.S.C.A. §§531 and 532. The Tax Court found that the taxpayer was liable for the tax.

The taxpayer claims here that the Tax Court erred in finding that the Commissioner met his burden of proof. There is no question that the burden of proof (i.e., the duty to produce evidence and the risk of non-persuasion) was on him since no notice of a deficiency based on the imposition of the accumulated earnings tax was sent to the taxpayer by the Commissioner. See §534 of the Internal Revenue Code of 1954, 26 U.S.C.A. §534. The fact that Rule 32 of the Tax Court likewise placed the burden of proof on the Commissioner did not increase the obligation. From our view of the record it seems clear that the Commissioner performed his duty to produce the requisite evidence. Most of the basic facts concerning the financial history of the taxpayer were stipulated upon in the Tax Court. These were supplemented and explained by agents of the Internal Revenue Service. In addition, the Commissioner elicited testimony from the president of the taxpayer, which was unfavorable to the taxpayer from an objective point of view.

The taxpayer asserts here that the evidence is insufficient to support a finding that the reasonable needs of its business (including the reasonably anticipated needs of such business) did not require the accumulation of any of the corporation's earnings and profits for the taxable year 1956. It is the duty of the Tax Court, not that of this Court, to determine whether or not there has been an unreasonable accumulation of earnings and profits by a taxpayer. Applying the rule announced by the Supreme Court in Commissioner v. Duberstein, 363 U.S. 278, 291 (1960), we cannot say that the Tax Court's finding of an unreasonable accumulation by the taxpayer is clearly erroneous.

The taxpayer next contends that the Commissioner's burden of proof, in addition to requiring a demonstration that it was unreasonable for it to retain and use its 1956 earnings and profits of $537,918.72 for any of the payments of installments on certain loans made by it, or in anticipation of the increased cash needed for the development and operation of oil and gas well properties, necessitated a showing that its retention and use of those earnings and profits was for the deliberate purpose of avoiding the tax on its stockholders. This contention is contrary to the plain terms of §533(a) of the 1954 Code. Moreover, the Tax Court, at page 605 of its opinion (38 T.C. 585), concludes: "Under the statute the accumulated earnings tax is thereby applicable, the petitioner having failed to prove by a preponderance of the evidence that the earnings and profits in fact accumulated in 1956 were not for the purpose of avoiding the income tax with respect to its shareholders." The evaluation of the evidence is not clearly erroneous. And, although the Tax Court did not specifically include in its findings of fact that the accumulation in question was for the purpose of avoiding income tax with respect to the shareholders of the taxpayer, it made reference in its opinion that in view of the testimony of taxpayer's president the true reason why the remaining portion of the 1956 accumulation was not distributed "was to avoid the resulting tax on the shareholders." 38 T.C., at 603.

The decision of the Tax Court will be affirmed.

NOTE

Treas. Reg. §1.537-2(b)(2) indicates that accumulation for expansion or to acquire a business constitutes an accumulation "for the reasonable needs of the business." Under the 1939 Code it was thought that "a radical change of business" would not be a justifiable basis for accumulation for *the* business. See Treas. Reg. 118, §39.102-3(b). The Commissioner's position under the 1954 Code appears to be more lenient, with Treas. Reg. §1.537-3(a) providing that the corporation's business "is not merely that which it has previously carried on but includes, in general, any line of business which it may undertake." See Comment, The Accumulated Earnings Tax and the Problem of Diversification, 64 Mich. L. Rev. 1135 (1966).

The provision in §537(a)(1) to the effect that the term "reasonable needs of the business" includes its "reasonably anticipated needs" was not in the 1939 Code, but was added in 1954 as a liberalization. See S. Rep. No. 1622, 83d Cong., 2d Sess. 318.

In Rev. Rul. 70-301, 1970-1 Cum. Bull. 139, the Service ruled that an accumulation to meet an asserted tax deficiency for prior years under §531 was an accumulation "for the reasonable needs of the business." For another example of a case justifying an accumulation to deal with a *contingent* liability, see William C. Atwater & Co., 10 T.C. 218 (1948), a case relied upon in Rev. Rul. 70-301.

UNITED STATES v. DONRUSS CO.
393 U.S. 297 (1969), rev'g 384 F.2d 292 (6th Cir. 1967)

Mr. Justice MARSHALL delivered the opinion of the Court. This case involves the application of §§531-537 of the Internal Revenue Code of 1954, which impose a surtax on corporations "formed or availed of for the purpose of avoiding the income tax with respect to . . . [their] shareholders . . . by permitting earnings and profits to accumulate instead of being divided or distributed."

Respondent is a corporation engaged in the manufacture and sale of bubble gum and candy and in the operation of a farm. Since 1954, all of respondent's outstanding stock has been owned by Don B. Wiener. In each of the tax years from 1955 to 1961, respondent operated profitably, increasing its undistributed earnings from $1,021,-288.58 to $1,679,315.37. The company did not make loans to Wiener or provide him with benefits other than a salary, nor did it make investments unrelated to its business, but no dividends were declared during the entire period.

Wiener gave several reasons for respondent's accumulation policy; among them were capital and inventory requirements, increasing costs, and the risks inherent in the particular business and in the general economy. Wiener also expressed a general desire to expand and a more specific desire to invest in respondent's major distributor, the Tom Huston Peanut Company. There were no definite plans during the tax years in question, but in 1964 respondent purchased 10,000 shares in Tom Huston at a cost of $380,000.

The Commissioner of Internal Revenue assessed accumulated earnings taxes against respondent for the years 1960 and 1961. Respondent paid the tax and brought this refund suit. At the conclusion of the trial, the Government specifically requested that the jury be instructed that:

> "[I]t is not necessary that avoidance of shareholder's tax be the sole purpose for the unreasonable accumulation of earnings; it is sufficient if it is one of the purposes for the company's accumulation policy."

The instruction was refused and the court instructed the jury in the terms of the statute that tax avoidance had to be "the purpose" of the accumulations. The jury, in response to interrogatories, found that respondent had accumulated earnings beyond the reasonable needs of its business, but that it had not retained its earnings for the purpose of avoiding income tax on Wiener. Judgment was entered for respondent and the Government appealed.

The Court of Appeals reversed and remanded for a new trial, holding that "the jury might well have been led to believe that tax avoidance must be the sole purpose behind an accumulation in order to impose the accumulated earnings tax." Donruss Co. v. United States, 384 F.2d 292, 298 (C.A. 6th Cir. 1967). The Court of Appeals rejected the Government's proposed instruction and held that the tax applied only if tax avoidance was the "dominant, controlling, or impelling motive" for the accumulation. Ibid. We granted the Government's petition for certiorari to resolve a conflict among the circuits[1] over the degree of "purpose" necessary for the application of the accumulated earnings tax, and because of the importance of that question in the administration of the tax. 390 U.S. 1023 (1968).

I.

The accumulated earnings tax is established by §§531-537 of the Internal Revenue Code of 1954. Section 531 imposes the tax. Section 532 defines the corporations to which the tax shall apply. That section provides:

"The accumulated earnings tax imposed by section 531 shall apply to every corporation . . . formed or availed of for the purpose of avoiding the income tax with respect to its shareholders or the shareholders of any other corporation, by permitting earnings and profits to accumulate instead of being divided or distributed."

Section 533(a) provides that:

"For purposes of section 532, the fact that the earnings and profits of a corporation are permitted to accumulate beyond the reasonable needs of the business shall be determinative of the purpose to avoid the income tax with respect to shareholders, unless the corporation by the preponderance of the evidence shall prove to the contrary."

In cases before the Tax Court, §534 allows the taxpayer in certain instances to shift to the Commissioner the burden of proving accumulation beyond the reasonable needs of the business. Section 535 defines "accumulated taxable income." It also provides for a credit for that portion of the earnings and profits retained for the reasonable needs of the business, with a minimum lifetime credit of $100,000. Finally, §537 provides that "reasonable needs of the business" include "reasonably anticipated" needs.

The dispute before us is a narrow one. The Government contends that in order to rebut the presumption contained in §533(a), the taxpayer must establish by the preponderance of the evidence that tax avoidance with respect to shareholders was not "one of the purposes" for the accumulation of earnings beyond the reasonable

---

[1]The court below adopted the view of the First Circuit. See Young Motor Co. v. Commissioner, 281 F.2d 488, 491 (1960); see also Apollo Industries, Inc. v. Commissioner, 358 F.2d 867, 875-876 (1966). The Second Circuit has rejected "the view that the prevention of the imposition of surtaxes must have been shown to have been the dominant factor behind the accumulations." Trico Prods. Corp. v. Commissioner, 137 F.2d 424, 426, cert. denied, 320 U.S. 799 (1943). See also United States v. Duke Laboratories, Inc., 337 F.2d 280 (1964). The Fifth Circuit has also rejected the position that tax avoidance must be the "primary or dominant" purpose of the accumulation. Barrow Mfg. Co. v. Commissioner, 294 F.2d 79, 82 (1961), cert. denied, 369 U.S. 817 (1962). The Eighth and Tenth Circuits have taken what appears to be an intermediate position, holding that imposition of the tax is proper if tax avoidance is one of the "determining purposes." Kerr-Cochran, Inc. v. Commissioner, 253 F.2d 121, 123 (C.A. 8th Cir. 1958); World Pub. Co. v. United States, 169 F.2d 186, 189 (C.A. 10th Cir. 1948), cert. denied, 335 U.S. 911 (1949). The Sixth Circuit has adhered to its view in Shaw-Walker Co. v. Commissioner, 390 F.2d 205 (1968). A petition for certiorari in that case is now pending in this Court.

needs of the business. Respondent argues that it may rebut that presumption by demonstrating that tax avoidance was not the "dominant, controlling, or impelling" reason for the accumulation. Neither party questions the trial court's instructions on the issue of whether the accumulation was beyond the reasonable needs of the business, and respondent does not challenge the jury's finding that its accumulation was indeed unreasonable. We intimate no opinion about the standards governing reasonableness of corporate accumulations.

We conclude from an examination of the language, the purpose, and the legislative history of the statute that the Government's construction is the correct one. Accordingly, we reverse the judgment of the court below and remand the case for a new trial on the issue of whether avoidance of shareholder tax was one of the purposes of respondent's accumulations.

II.

Both parties argue that the language of the statute supports their conclusion. Respondent argues that Congress could have used the article "a" in §§532 and 533 if it had intended to adopt the Government's test. Instead, argues respondent, Congress used the article "the" in the operative part of the statute, thus indicating that tax avoidance must at least be the dominant motive for the accumulation.[4] The Government argues that respondent's construction gives an unduly narrow effect to the word "the." Instead, contends the Government, this Court should focus on the entire phrase "availed of for the purpose." Any language of limitation should logically modify "availed of" rather than "purpose" and no such language is present. The Government further argues that Congress has dealt with similar problems in other sections of the Code and has used terms such as "principal purpose," §§269(a), 357(b)(1), and "used principally," §355(a)(1)(B). Similar terms could have been used in §§532(a) and 533(a), but were not. Finally, the Government points to the fact that prior to adoption of §102 of the Revenue Act of 1938 (52 Stat. 483) the forerunner of §532(a) used the words "the purpose," while the evidentiary section used the words "a purpose," thus indicating that tax avoidance need only be one purpose. Respondent replies that the change from "a" to "the" in the evidentiary section supports its conclusion. Respondent also contends that the statute before the change was consistent with its construction.

We find both parties' arguments inconclusive. The phrase "availed of for the purpose" is inherently vague, and there is no indication in the legislative history that Congress intended to attach any particular significance to the use of the article "the." Nor do we find the change in the evidentiary section from "a" to "the" at all helpful. That change came as part of a significant revision in the operation of the section, and there is no indication that it was other than a mere change in phraseology.[5] Indeed, the Report of the Senate Finance Committee accompanying the bill

---

[4]The First Circuit in Young Motor Co. v. Commissioner, 281 F.2d 488 (1960), in part based its conclusion that tax avoidance must be the "primary or dominant purpose" on the use of "the" rather than "a."

[5]No change was made in that part of the statute providing that "[t]he fact that any corporation is a mere holding or investment company shall be prima facie evidence of *a* purpose" to avoid tax. Revenue Act of 1938, §102(b), 52 Stat. 483 (emphasis added).

that was to become the Revenue Act of 1938, insofar as it sheds any light on the question, supports the view of the Government. "The proposal is to strengthen [the evidentiary] section by requiring the taxpayer by a clear preponderance of the evidence to prove the absence of *any* purpose to avoid surtaxes upon shareholders . . . ." S. Rep. No. 1567, 75th Cong., 3d Sess., 5 (1938) (emphasis added). Since the language of the statute does not provide an answer to the question before us,[6] we have examined in detail the relevant legislative history. That history leads us to conclude that the test proposed by the Government is consistent with the intent of Congress and is necessary to effectuate the purpose of the accumulated earnings tax.

III.

The accumulated earnings tax is one congressional attempt to deter use of a corporate entity to avoid personal income taxes. The purpose of the tax "is to compel the company to distribute any profits not needed for the conduct of its business so that, when so distributed, individual stockholders will become liable" for taxes on the dividends received, Helvering v. Chicago Stock Yards Co., 318 U.S. 693, 699 (1943). The tax originated in the Tariff Act of 1913, 38 Stat. 114, the first personal income tax statute following ratification of the Sixteenth Amendment. That Act imposed a tax on the shareholders of any corporation "formed or fraudulently availed of for the purpose of preventing the imposition of such tax through the medium of permitting such gains and profits to accumulate instead of being divided or distributed . . . ." §II(A)(2), 38 Stat. 166. The same section provided that accumulation beyond the reasonable needs of the business "shall be prima facie evidence of a fraudulent purpose to escape such tax . . . ." 38 Stat. 167.

In its first years of operation, difficulties in proving a fraudulent purpose made the tax largely ineffective. To meet this problem, Congress deleted the word "fraudulently." Revenue Act of 1918, §220, 40 Stat. 1072; see S. Rep. No. 617, 65th Cong., 3d Sess., 5 (1918).[7]

During the next few years, numerous complaints were made about the ineffectiveness of the accumulated earnings tax. Various attempts were made to strengthen the tax during the 1920's and 1930's, but the statute remained essentially the same until 1934. See Joint Committee on the Economic Report, The Taxation of Corporate Surplus Accumulations, 82d Cong., 2d Sess., 200-205 (Comm. Print 1952). In 1934, Congress dealt with one of the more flagrant examples of that ineffectiveness, the personal holding company. Personal holding companies were exempted from the general accumulated earnings tax and were subjected to a tax on undistributed income, regardless of the purpose of that accumulation. Revenue Act of 1934, §§102, 351, 48 Stat. 702, 751. The reason for the change was that, "[b]y making partial distribution of profits and by showing some need for the accumulation of the re-

---

[6]The Regulations shed no light on the problem. See Treas. Reg. §§1.531-1.537, 26 CFR §§1.531-1.537.

[7]Another major change was made in the Revenue Act of 1921, 42 Stat. 227. Section 220 of that Act shifted the incidence of the accumulated earnings tax from the shareholders to the corporation itself. 42 Stat. 247. The change was prompted by the decision in Eisner v. Macomber, 252 U.S. 189 (1920). See H.R. Rep. No. 350, 67th Cong., 1st Sess., 12-13 (1921).

maining profits, the taxpayer makes it difficult to prove a purpose to avoid taxes." H.R. Rep. No. 704, 73d Cong., 2d Sess., 11 (1934).

Again in 1936, Congress attempted to solve the continuing problem of undistributed corporate earnings. "The difficulty of proving such [tax avoidance] purpose . . . has rendered . . . [the accumulated earnings tax] more or less ineffective." H.R. Rep. No. 2475, 74th Cong., 2d Sess., 5 (1936). However, Congress did not change the requirement that "purpose" must be proved. Rather, it attempted the alternative method of imposing an undistributed profits surtax on most corporations. Revenue Act of 1936, §14, 49 Stat. 1655. The tax on personal holding companies and the general accumulated earnings tax were retained.[8]

The problem continued to be acute and several proposals were made by and to Congress in 1938. The House Ways and Means Committee proposed a surtax on all closely held operating companies. Only minor changes were proposed by the Committee in the accumulated earnings tax. See H.R. Rep. No. 1860, 75th Cong., 3d Sess. (1938). The House rejected all but the changes in the accumulated earnings tax. The Senate approached the problem of retained corporate earnings in a different way. Labeling the House Committee's recommendation a "drastic" remedy, the Senate Finance Committee recommended "dealing with this problem where it should be dealt with — namely, in section 102, relating to corporations improperly accumulating surplus. The proposal is to strengthen this section by requiring the taxpayer by a clear preponderance of the evidence to prove the absence of any purpose to avoid surtaxes upon shareholders after it has been determined that the earnings and profits have been unreasonably accumulated." S. Rep. No. 1567, 75th Cong., 3d Sess., 5 (1938). The change was thought to make it clear that the burden of proving intent, rather than the lesser burden of producing evidence on the question, was to be on the taxpayer. Id., at 16. The Senate proposal was enacted. Revenue Act of 1938, §102, 52 Stat. 483. The Committee felt that a "reasonable enforcement of this revised section will reduce tax avoidance . . . ." S. Rep. No. 1567, supra, at 5.

Only insignificant changes were made in the accumulated earnings tax from 1938 to 1954. Discussion of the problem continued, however, and numerous proposals were made to alter the tax. See, e.g., Joint Committee on the Economic Report, The Taxation of Corporate Surplus Accumulations, 82d Cong., 2d Sess. (Comm. Print 1952). Congress took cognizance of these complaints and incorporated many of them in the Internal Revenue Code of 1954, but no change was made in the required degree of tax avoidance purpose.[9] Rather, the changes, which were generally favorable to the taxpayer, demonstrated congressional disaffection with the effect of the tax and its emphasis on intent. Congress' reaction to the complaints

---

[8]Tax avoidance and evasion were a major subject of congressional concern in 1937. See, e.g., H.R. Rep. No. 1546, 75th Cong., 1st Sess. (1937). Congress addressed itself to another aspect of the problem by establishing a separate method for the taxation of foreign personal holding companies, again without regard to corporate intent. Revenue Act of 1937, §201, 50 Stat. 818.

[9]Congress was urged to adopt a test of purpose similar to that proposed by respondent in the present case. See, e.g., Hearings before the House Committee on Ways and Means Pertaining to the General Revision of the Internal Revenue Code, 83d Cong., 1st Sess., pt. 3, p. 2142 (1953).

was to emphasize the reasonable needs of the business as a proper purpose for corporate accumulations[11] and to make it easier for the taxpayer to prove those needs.[12] As the House Ways and Means Committee said, "Your committee believes it is necessary to retain the penalty tax on unreasonable accumulations as a safeguard against tax avoidance. However, several amendments have been adopted to minimize the threat to corporations accumulating funds for legitimate business purposes . . . ." H.R. Rep. No. 1337, 83d Cong., 2d Sess., 52 (1954).

As this brief summary indicates, the legislative history of the accumulated earnings tax demonstrates a continuing concern with the use of the corporate form to avoid income tax on a corporation's shareholders. Numerous methods were employed to prevent this practice, all of which proved unsatisfactory in one way or another. Two conclusions can be drawn from Congress' efforts. First, Congress recognized the tremendous difficulty of ascertaining the purpose of corporate accumulations. Second, it saw that accumulation was often necessary for legitimate and reasonable business purposes. It appears clear to us that the congressional response to these facts has been to emphasize unreasonable accumulation as the most significant factor in the incidence of the tax. The reasonableness of an accumulation, while subject to honest difference of opinion, is a much more objective inquiry, and is susceptible of more effective scrutiny, than are the vagaries of corporate motive.

Respondent would have us adopt a test that requires that tax avoidance purpose need be dominant, impelling, or controlling. It seems to us that such a test would exacerbate the problems that Congress was trying to avoid. Rarely is there one motive, or even one dominant motive, for corporate decisions. Numerous factors contribute to the action ultimately decided upon. Respondent's test would allow taxpayers to escape the tax when it is proved that at least one other motive was equal to tax avoidance. We doubt that such a determination can be made with any accuracy, and it is certainly one which will depend almost exclusively on the interested testimony of corporate management. Respondent's test would thus go a long way toward destroying the presumption that Congress created to meet this very problem. As Judge Learned Hand said of the much weaker presumption contained in the Revenue Act of 1921, §220, 42 Stat. 247, "[a] statute which stands on the footing of the participants' state of mind may need the support of presumption, indeed be practically unenforceable without it . . . ." United Business Corp. v. Commissioner, 62 F.2d 754, 755 (C.A. 2d Cir. 1933). And, "[t]he utility of . . . [that] presumption . . . is well nigh destroyed if . . . [it] is saddled with requirement of proof of 'the primary or dominant purpose' of the accumulation." Barrow Mfg. Co. v. Commissioner, 294 F.2d 79, 82 (C.A. 5th Cir. 1961), cert. denied, 369 U.S. 817 (1962).

The cases cited by respondent do not convince us to the contrary. For the most part, they lack detailed analysis of the precise problem. Perhaps the leading case for

---

[11]Section 535(c) provided a credit for such accumulations.

[12]Section 534 allowed the taxpayer to shift to the Commissioner in certain instances the burden of proving unreasonable accumulation. Section 537 included anticipated needs as reasonable needs of the business. In addition to those changes, §533(a) omitted the requirement that the taxpayer negate the existence of tax avoidance purpose by a "clear preponderance of the evidence," and substituted a "preponderance" test.

respondent's position is Young Motor Co. v. Commissioner, 281 F.2d 488 (C.A. 1st Cir. 1960). That case relied in part upon the use of the article "the" instead of "a." We have previously rejected that argument. The case also relied, as did the court below, on certain cases from the gift and estate tax areas.[13] We find those cases inapposite. They deal with areas of the Code whose language, purpose, and legislative history are entirely different from those of the accumulated earnings tax. See Commissioner v. Duberstein, 363 U.S. 278, 284 (1960).

Finally, we cannot subscribe to respondent's suggestion that our holding would make purpose totally irrelevant. It still serves to isolate those cases in which tax avoidance motives did not contribute to the decision to accumulate. Obviously in such a case imposition of the tax would be futile. In addition, "purpose" means more than mere knowledge, undoubtedly present in nearly every case. It is still open to the taxpayer to show that even though knowledge of the tax consequences was present, that knowledge did not contribute to the decision to accumulate earnings.

Reversed and remanded.

Mr. Justice HARLAN, whom Mr. Justice DOUGLAS and Mr. Justice STEWART join, concurring in part and dissenting in part. I agree with the Court that the Court of Appeals erred in framing its remand order in this case. However, I would modify the order in a different way, which I find more in harmony with the statutory scheme than the one the Court has chosen.

Section 532 of the Internal Revenue Code of 1954 states in relevant part:

> "The accumulated earnings tax imposed by section 531 shall apply to every corporation . . . formed or availed of for the purpose of avoiding the income tax with respect to its shareholders . . . , by permitting earnings and profits to accumulate instead of being divided or distributed."

Section 533(a) provides:

> "For purposes of section 532, the fact that the earnings and profits of a corporation are permitted to accumulate beyond the reasonable needs of the business shall be determinative of the purpose to avoid the income tax with respect to shareholders, unless the corporation by the preponderance of the evidence shall prove to the contrary."

Our task is to decide what jury instruction with respect to the definition of "purpose" comports best with Congress' intent as revealed by this statutory language and the underlying legislative history.

I am in accord with much of the Court's opinion. I too find that the successive changes in the wording of the statute, even when read together with the legislative history, do not help in our inquiry. I too find that the legislative history reveals a progressive congressional intention to rely more and more heavily upon a comparatively objective criterion: whether the accumulated earnings were in excess of the corporation's reasonable business needs. Nevertheless, it is apparent from the

---

[13]Commissioner v. Duberstein, 363 U.S. 278 (1960); Allen v. Trust Co. of Georgia, 326 U.S. 630 (1946); City Bank Farmers Trust Co. v. McGowan, 323 U.S. 594 (1945); United States v. Wells, 283 U.S. 102 (1931).

language of §533(a), and from the legislative materials, that Congress chose still to give the taxpayer a "last clear chance" to prove that, despite the unreasonableness of the accumulation by business standards, the accumulation was not due to the proscribed purpose. My difficulty with the instruction approved by the Court is that in most instances it will effectively deny to the taxpayer the "last clear chance" which Congress clearly meant to afford and substitute a very fuzzy chance indeed.

I reach this conclusion on what I regard as common-sense grounds. In practice, the accumulated-earnings provisions are applied only to closely held corporations, controlled by relatively few shareholders.[1] As the Court admits, the shareholders almost always will have been advised that accumulation of corporate earnings will result in individual tax savings. That fact will be before the jury. In accord with the Court's decision, the jury will be instructed that "it is sufficient if [avoidance of shareholders' tax] is *one* of the purposes of the company's accumulation policy." (Emphasis supplied.)

Under these circumstances, the jury is very likely to believe that it must find the forbidden purpose and impose the tax whenever the Government shows that the taxpayer has accumulated earnings with knowledge of the resultant tax saving, irrespective of any contrary evidence put forward by the taxpayer. The approved instruction simply tells the jury that the taxpayer must have had a "purpose" to avoid individual taxes. In everyday speech, we commonly say that a person has a "purpose" to do something when he acts with knowledge that the thing will inevitably result. Even were the jury legally knowledgeable, it might reach the same conclusion, for, assuming that the word "purpose" as used in §532 is synonymous with "intention,"[2] there is ample authority for the proposition that an actor will be deemed to have an "intention" to cause consequences of an act if "the actor . . . believes that the consequences are substantially certain to result from [the act]."[3] To confront the taxpayer with this likelihood that its evidence of another purpose will be entirely disregarded is inconsistent with the provision of §533(a) which explicitly affords the taxpayer an opportunity to avoid the tax by showing "by the preponderance of the evidence" that it had a "contrary" purpose.

The Court, while conceding that the shareholders will know of the expected tax saving "in nearly every case," see ante, at 309, reasons that the taxpayer will have its opportunity because "[i]t is still open to the taxpayer to show that even though knowledge of the tax consequences was present, that knowledge did not contribute to the decision to accumulate earnings." Ibid. If, as appears from the Court's opinion, this exegesis is not to be a part of the jury instruction, then the Court is simply engaging in wishful thinking. If by chance the explication is to be included in the instruction, then the jury will be told to impose the tax only if it finds that a desire to avoid tax "contribute[d] to the decision to accumulate earnings." Such an instruction would at least inform the jury that the tax consequence must actually

---

[1]See S. Rep. No. 1622, 83d Cong., 2d Sess., 69 (1954); B. Bittker & J. Eustice, Federal Income Taxation of Corporations and Shareholders 213-214 (2d ed. 1966).

[2]"Purpose" is listed as a synonym for "intention" in Black's Law Dictionary, at 948 (4th ed. 1968). Many courts have used the two words interchangeably in construing §§532 and 533(a). . . .

[3]Restatement (Second), Torts §8A (1965). . . .

have been in the shareholders' minds when they decided to accumulate. However, once the shareholders are shown to have had knowledge of the tax saving, it still will be extraordinarily difficult for the taxpayer to convince the jury that the knowledge did not play some part, however slight, in the decision. Again, it seems to me that such an instruction would not give proper scope to the congressional intention that the taxpayer have a chance to prove "by the preponderance of the evidence" that it had a "contrary" purpose. I would therefore adopt an instruction less loaded against the taxpayer.

The Court of Appeals for the Sixth Circuit decided, and respondent argues, that the tax should apply only if the jury finds that tax avoidance was the "dominant, controlling, or impelling motive" for the accumulation. I agree with the Court that such an instruction would be improper. It apparently would require the Government to show that tax avoidance was stronger than any other motive, and perhaps that it was stronger than all other motives put together. This would largely negate the statutory presumption of improper purpose contained in §533(a). In my view, it would also result in nonimposition of tax in cases where Congress meant there to be liability, for I think that Congress must at least have intended that the tax should apply whenever the taxpayer would have distributed, instead of accumulating, corporate earnings had there been no possibility of a tax saving.

These considerations suggest what I believe to be the best rule: the jury should be instructed to impose the tax if it finds that the taxpayer would not have accumulated earnings but for its knowledge that a tax saving would result. This "but for cause" test would be consistent with the statutory language. It would allow the Government to succeed if it could show, with the aid of the §533(a) presumption, that without the spur of tax avoidance the taxpayer would not have accumulated the earnings, thus giving effect to the presumption and fulfilling Congress' desire to penalize those with a "purpose" to avoid the tax. It would permit the taxpayer to escape the tax if it could convince the jury that for other, perhaps irrational, reasons it would have accumulated even had no tax saving been possible, thus affording the opportunity for proof of a "contrary" purpose which Congress intended to provide. In addition, I believe that this instruction would be relatively easy for a jury to understand and apply. For all of these reasons, I consider it preferable to the standard adopted by the Court.

NOTE

See D. Altman and A. Muchin, Supreme Court's *Donruss* Decision Calls for a Shift in Tactics in 531 Area, 30 J. Taxation 202 (1969).

CHATHAM CORP. v. COMMISSIONER
48 T.C. 145 (1967)

TANNENWALD, Judge: This case involves a determination by respondent that petitioner is subject to the accumulated earnings tax under section 531 for the fiscal years ending June 30, 1961, 1962, 1963, and 1964. Respondent sent a notice to petitioner in accordance with section 534(b) and petitioner submitted a timely statement purporting to comply with the requirements of section 534(c). At the call of the case for trial on February 17, 1967, petitioner moved for a ruling that the burden of proof with respect to the grounds set forth in its statement rests upon respondent as provided in section 534(a). Decision was reserved by the judge before whom the case was originally calendared and trial was continued to be heard by him at a future date.

In denying a similar motion in Shaw-Walker Co., 39 T.C. 293 (1962), we stated: "It may be that a ruling on the burden-of-proof question as a preliminary matter would in some instances serve the convenience of the petitioner, but we think that the interests of both parties as well as that of the Court will best be served by allowing this question to be disposed of at or after trial."

In *Shaw-Walker,* the motion was submitted to the judge of the motions calendar in advance of trial. By way of contrast, the motion herein has been submitted to the judge before whom the case is to be tried. Nothing in *Shaw-Walker* precludes a ruling in such a situation. On the contrary, the above-quoted language specifically recognizes that an advance ruling might issue under appropriate circumstances.

Petitioner's statement, consisting of 49 pages, sets forth two grounds, with supporting facts, for retaining its earnings and profits: (a) to finance the expansion of the market for its products by five enumerated means and (b) to provide reserves for the diversification of its business through the development of new products and the acquisition of business enterprises. The amount of funds required for (a) is projected in great detail year by year from 1959 to 1970. With respect to (b), efforts to develop new products are set forth and more than twenty-five instances of negotiations relating to prospective acquisitions, during the period commencing in the fiscal year 1960, are listed, many of which were pursued simultaneously and were not considered alternative possibilities. Several had price tags attached thereto. The nature of the plans for expansion of markets and six instances of negotiations for acquisition are described in great detail. Names of other business concerns and individuals involved are given in practically every instance. The aggregate of the anticipated expenditures for market expansion, acquisitions to which price tags were attached, and development of new products exceeded the maximum of petitioner's apparent accumulated earnings during the years in question.

Respondent asserts that petitioner's statement is insufficient. He makes no claim that the *factual elements* in the statement are false. Essentially, his arguments are directed to questioning the judgment of petitioner's management. If such judgment was clearly erroneous, we might properly characterize the statement as sham. But such is not the case herein, with the result that we think respondent's assertions are more appropriate to the substantive issues which will be involved in a trial. Nor do we agree with respondent that the fact that all but one of the negotiations failed is necessarily fatal.

Under the circumstances, we are not called upon at this point to determine whether the grounds and facts in the statement are true. That will come after trial. Petitioner's grounds are specific and not in the conclusory language of the statute and the supporting facts are substantial, material, definite, and clear. We conclude that the statement is sufficient to shift the burden of proof to respondent with respect to the grounds stated therein. Compare John P. Scripps Newspapers, 44 T.C. 453 (1965), J. Gordon Turnbull, Inc., 41 T.C. 358 (1963), affd. [373 F.2d 87 (C.A. 5, 1967)], and American Metal Products Corporation, 34 T.C. 89 (1960), affd. 287 F.2d 860 (C.A. 8, 1961), with Wellman Operating Corporation, 33 T.C. 162 (1959), I. A. Dress Co., 32 T.C. 93 (1959), affd. 273 F.2d 543 (C.A. 2, 1960), certiorari denied 362 U.S. 976, and Dixie, Inc., 31 T.C. 415 (1958), affd. 277 F.2d 526 (C.A. 2, 1960), certiorari denied 364 U.S. 827.

Petitioner's motion is granted.

NOTE

See L. Goldfein, Tax Court in *Chatham Corporation* Clarifies Timing of Shift of Burden in 531 Cases, 27 J. Taxation 2 (1967).

RHOMBAR CO. v. COMMISSIONER
386 F.2d 510 (2d Cir. 1967)

Before FRIENDLY, KAUFMAN and ANDERSON, Circuit Judges.

KAUFMAN, Circuit Judge: This petition to review a decision of the Tax Court, Atkins, J., reported at 47 T.C. 75 (1967), holding Rhombar Co., Inc. liable for the accumulated earnings tax imposed by Section 531 of the Internal Revenue Code of 1954 for the taxable years ending January 31, 1960, 1961, and 1962,[1] presents what may be the first instance in which a taxpayer's counsel has had the "abnormally strong nervous system"[2] necessary to risk his entire accumulated earnings tax case on the burden of proof issue under §534. The Tax Court held that Rhombar had the burden of proving it was not a "mere holding or investment company" within the meaning of §533(b), and that it had failed to introduce any evidence to support its position; accordingly, it held against taxpayer. We affirm the decision of the Tax Court.

The facts are fully set out in the Tax Court's opinion, and we need recite them here only briefly. Rhombar Co. is a closely held corporation owned almost entirely by the family of Herbert M. Rothschild. Before 1952 it engaged in the furniture distribution business under the name of John Stuart Inc. In that year it sold all its business assets, including the right to use the John Stuart corporate name, to John Widdicomb Co., Inc. (New York) [Widdicomb], another closely held corporation in which the Rothschilds had, after the sale, a controlling interest.[3] Since that time

---

[1]The Tax Court found deficiencies of $17,257.53, $17,618.46, and $18,325.78 for the 3 years here at issue. Other issues were presented to the Tax Court, but they are not before us on this appeal.

[2]Bittker & Eustice, Federal Income Taxation of Corporations and Shareholders (2d ed.) 234.

[3]Before the agreement of sale was entered into, the Rothschilds owned 50 per cent of the outstanding stock of Widdicomb. Afterwards, they possessed 66 per cent of the voting power.

Widdicomb has operated Rhombar's former business and has adopted Rhombar's old name, John Stuart Inc. Rhombar, on the other hand, has not re-entered the furniture business; instead it has steadily accumulated its income, which is derived entirely from dividends, interest, and capital gains from the sales of securities and from installment payments it receives from Widdicomb. As a result its surplus had more than doubled, rising to over $2,000,000, but only de minimis dividends of $700 annually were paid.[4]

I.

The accumulated earnings tax is imposed on corporations "formed or availed of for the purpose of avoiding the income tax with respect to its shareholders . . . by permitting earnings and profits to accumulate instead of being divided or distributed." Code, §532(a). In this connection, two statutory presumptions have long been spelled out in the Code. The first of these, found in §533(a), provides that "the fact that the earnings and profits of a corporation are permitted to accumulate beyond the reasonable needs of the business shall be determinative of the purpose to avoid the income tax with respect to shareholders, unless the corporation by the preponderance of the evidence shall prove to the contrary." The second, contained in §533(b) states: "The fact that any corporation is a mere holding or investment company shall be prima facie evidence of the purpose to avoid the income tax with respect to shareholders." Accordingly, the forbidden purpose of avoiding income tax may be established by either of these statutory presumptions.

Ordinarily, the burden of proving that the Commissioner's determination is wrong rests on the taxpayer, because the Commissioner's deficiency assessment is considered presumptively correct.[5] But Congress recognized this rule might have "several undesirable consequences"[6] when the Commissioner sought to assess an accumulated earnings tax. As a result, in 1954 it enacted §534.[7] This section sets forth

---

[4]For the fiscal years ending January 31, 1954 through 1963, Rhombar's net income before taxes ranged from a high of $468,549.53 in 1961-62, to a low of $49,827.58 in 1962-63. Surplus increased from $1,167,648.74 to $2,382,494.55, and the fair market value of its investments was considerably higher.

[5]Tax Court Rule 32: Helvering v. Taylor, 293 U.S. 507 (1935).

[6]The Senate Finance Committee Report on the Internal Revenue Code of 1954, S. Rep. No. 1622, 83d Cong., 2d Sess. (1954), reprinted in 3 U.S. Code Cong. & Admin. News 4621, 4702 (1954), states:

"Your committee agrees with the House that this imposition of the burden of proof on the taxpayer has had several undesirable consequences. The poor record of the Government in the litigated cases in this area indicates that deficiencies have been asserted in many cases which were not adequately screened or analyzed. At the same time taxpayers were put to substantial expense and effort in proving that the accumulation was for the reasonable needs of the business. Moreover, the complaints of taxpayers that the tax is used as a threat by revenue agents to induce settlement on other issues appear to have a connection with the burden of proof which the taxpayer is required to assume. It also appears probable that many small taxpayers may have yielded to a proposed deficiency because of the expense and difficulty of litigating their case under the present rules."

[7] . . . If Congress hoped that these provisions would make a material difference in tax litigation it has been frustrated, for the Tax Court will not rule in advance on the adequacy of taxpayers' statements. See, e.g., Shaw-Walker Co., 39 T.C. 293 (1962). As a result, taxpayers are rarely certain that the burden of proof has been shifted to the Commissioner. Thus, rather than risking all on the burden of proof issue, they continue to introduce evidence just as they

the procedures, followed by the Commissioner and the taxpayer in this case, for switching the burden of proof. The Commissioner notified Rhombar on July 23, 1964 that he proposed to issue a statutory notice of deficiency based on the accumulated earnings tax. In response, on September 3, 1964, Rhombar submitted to the Commissioner a 13-page statement setting forth in detail a recitation of its efforts since it sold its business to Widdicomb to acquire another furniture company. The statement claimed that "the reasonable needs of the business of Rhombar required it to set aside and maintain a reserve at least equal to its entire net worth and to build up such reserve out of its earnings and profits, as soon as feasible, to a minimum of at least $3,500,000 in order to finance an acquisition program (adopted in 1952 under circumstances more fully described below) or purchasing interests in businesses engaged in the manufacture of furniture and/or furniture manufacturing facilities. At no time during the years at issue had Rhombar accumulated sufficient amounts for this purpose." Accordingly, Rhombar claimed it had not accumulated its earnings beyond its reasonable business needs.

It appears, therefore, that under §534, the burden of proof under §533(a) (accumulation beyond reasonable needs of business) was shifted to the Commissioner if Rhombar's statement contained "sufficient" facts.[8] Rhombar makes the novel claim — rejected by the Tax Court — that the statement submitted to the Commissioner under §534 also shifted the burden of proof to the Commissioner with respect to §533(b) (mere holding or investment company).

Reference to the language of §534 should be sufficient to refute Rhombar's argument. It provides that when a notice of deficiency is based on the allegation that "the earnings and profits have been permitted to accumulate beyond the reasonable needs of the business," the burden of proof "with respect to such allegation" shall be shifted if the taxpayer submits an appropriate statement showing the facts and grounds on which he relies to establish that earnings and profits "have not been permitted to accumulate beyond the reasonable needs of the business." Thus, §534 echoes the exact language of §533(a), but does not give the slightest indication that it is applicable to §533(b). The maxim expressio unius est exclusio alterius is not without relevancy under these circumstances.

Moreover, this is not a situation in which a straight-forward reading of the Code does violence to the Congressional purpose. Sections 533(a) and 533(b) are alternative presumptions which can be used to prove the ultimate objective of tax avoidance. In fact, when first enacted in the Income Tax Act of 1913, they were explicitly treated in the disjunctive.[9] And, the Revenue Act of 1938 increased the strength of the presumption to be given an accumulation beyond the reasonable needs of the business, but left unchanged the force of the presumption that a holding or invest-

---

did before §534 was enacted. See Mertens, Law of Federal Income Taxation, Code Commentary, §534.1. For a criticism of the Tax Court's policy, see Holzman, Burden of Proof in Accumulated Earnings Tax Cases and Its Development in the Second Circuit Court of Appeals, 11 Buff. L. Rev. 328, 362-63 (1962).

[8]The Tax Court expressly did not decide whether the statement was sufficient to shift the burden of proof.

[9]38 Stat. 114, 166.

ment company was a tax avoidance device.[10] Thus, when §534 was enacted in 1954, Congress was well aware of the distinction between §533(a) and §533(b). That §534 affects only §533(a) is not surprising nor inconsistent, for the Committee Reports indicate that Congress was concerned in the main with the difficulty taxpayers faced in proving that their accumulations were not in excess of the reasonable needs of their businesses. The Reports are barren of any indication that Congress had any concern with the distinctly different problems taxpayers faced when proving that they engaged in activities beyond "holding property and collecting the income therefrom or investing therein,"[11] i.e., that they were not mere holding or investment companies.

Rhombar contends, however, that the credit provisions of §535 support its argument that the burden of proving it was a mere holding or investment company rested on the Commissioner. Section 535, like §534, was added to the Internal Revenue Code in 1954. It provides, inter alia, a credit for that portion of a corporation's earnings and profits which were accumulated for the reasonable needs of the business. The tax is thus imposed only on that portion of the accumulation which exceeds the reasonable needs of the business. Specifically, the statute provides, "in the case of a corporation *other than a mere holding or investment company* the accumulated earnings credit is (A) an amount equal to such part of the earnings and profits for the taxable year as are retained for the reasonable needs of the business . . . ." Code, §535(c)(1) (emphasis added). For most corporations this credit is potentially unlimited in amount, but in the case of mere holding or investment companies, credit is limited by §535(c)(3) to a maximum of $100,000.

It is conceded that if a proper §534 statement had been submitted, the Commissioner had the burden of proving the amount of the credit to which the taxpayer was entitled, i.e., the amount of the accumulation retained for reasonable business needs. Rhombar argues from this that if the credit is to be limited because a taxpayer is a mere holding or investment company, the burden of proving this must be on the Commissioner "since it is a necessary part of the [Commissioner's] admitted burden of proving the amount of the credit to which a taxpayer is entitled under §535(c)(1)."

The difficulty with this contention is that a basic maxim of tax law interpretation is that rarely are there occasions when each provision of the Code can be interpreted as if existing in a vacuum. In any event, it is hardly likely that Congress intended that §534 and §535, enacted at the same time, would work at cross purposes. Indeed, to permit the credit section to overpower or submerge and dilute the burden of proof section would be to permit the tail to wag the dog.

The question of the reasonable needs of the business about which §534 speaks is not relevant to §533(b) for, as Congress was informed by a former Secretary of the Treasury, "it is questionable whether any investment company could have a surplus beyond the reasonable needs of its business, since its sole business was to invest."[12] Thus, the most intelligible reading of the italicized words in §535(c)(1) on which

---

[10]52 Stat. 447, 483.
[11]Treas. Regs. 1.533-1(c).
[12]Secretary of the Treasury Mellon, 65 Cong. Record, Part 7, p. 7355 (1924).

taxpayer relies is that they constitute a recognition of the truth of the Secretary's remark.

Accordingly, we believe the Tax Court was correct in holding that §534 statements do not shift the burden of proof with respect to §533(b).

II.

Rhombar makes the interesting argument that, in any event, the Tax Court erred in not considering, for the purpose of determining whether it was a mere holding or investment company, the allegations in its §534 statement. But the short answer to this is that Rhombar never sought to place the statement in evidence or to establish any of the facts contained therein by competent testimony. Tax Court Rule 31(f) states clearly, "Ex parte affidavits, statements in briefs, and unadmitted allegations in pleadings do not constitute evidence." Rhombar seeks to excuse its failure to comply with this rule by asserting that the Commissioner was in possession of the statement for 18 months before trial, but made no effort to controvert its allegations. This argument has superficial appeal only. If Rhombar was laboring under the impression that the Commissioner was conceding the truth of the facts alleged in the statement by not controverting them, then it would have been simple enough to at least tie this down by seeking a stipulation from the Commissioner consenting to the introduction of the statement in evidence, thus making it competent evidence. Then, if the Commissioner withheld his consent, Rhombar would have been required to call a witness to testify to the matters alleged in the statement. This procedure is not a mere exercise in technicalities, for, in that event, the Commissioner would not have been deprived of the opportunity to cross-examine as to the validity of the allegations of the statement.

Rhombar attempts to circumvent this weakness in its argument by claiming that Congress intended to modify the usual rules of evidence by making §534 statements substitutes for testimony at trial. But, the statute and the legislative history are totally devoid of even a suggestion that Congress intended to change so settled a rule of evidence. We have not been cited to nor have we found any indication either that §534 statements do more than shift the burden of proof, or that a statement, without testimonial authentication or stipulation consenting to its admission in evidence, can be used as a substitute for competent evidence. To accept taxpayer's position would mean that we agree that rules of evidence, whether contained in a Tax Court rule (Rule 31(f)) or applicable to ordinary trials in a district court, could be easily circumvented in instances where the opposing side had knowledge of a party's claim before trial (which is not rare in this day of extensive pre-trial discovery) but did not assume the burden of disproving the claims even before the claims were established by competent evidence.

III.

Finally, at argument of this appeal, Rhombar maintained that it was "taken by surprise" by the Commissioner's reliance on §533(b) in the Tax Court. It is not without significance that no such claim was made or even hinted at in the taxpayer's motion in the Tax Court to vacate the opinion or in its supporting memorandum.[13] Certainly, if taxpayer felt aggrieved over the Commissioner's position and the Tax Court's reliance on §533(b), it is reasonable to expect such a claim to have been asserted at that time. Thus, we find it difficult to conclude that the claim of surprise is anything but a resourceful afterthought. In any event, we believe that the Commissioner gave taxpayer reasonable notice that he was relying on §533(b). The Commissioner's 10-page answer in the Tax Court was sufficient to put Rhombar on notice that the Commissioner was relying on §533(b). For example, it stated that after the sale of its business assets to Widdicomb, "Petitioner continued in existence as an investment company," and pointedly stated, "Petitioner is a holding or investment company." Moreover, it is of some interest that the taxpayer, in its reply, explicitly referred to and denied both these allegations, thus showing an awareness of the Commissioner's claim. And, it strains one's credulity to accept taxpayer's suggestion that the failure of the Commissioner to charge it with being a "mere" holding company instead of just a holding company was misleading in some fashion. Our examination of the Tax Court record furthermore convinces us that Rhombar knew that the thrust of §533(b) was in issue. Counsel for the Commissioner began his brief opening statement by referring to "the holding company, the investment company which resulted out of John Stuart, Inc., which it before us here as Rhombar Co., Inc. . . ." And the basic arguments in the Tax Court were over Rhombar's claim that it was a holding company, but not a "mere" holding company, and over its interpretation of §535.

It appears to us that Rhombar deliberately chose to rest its hopes in the Tax Court on its §535 argument — that Congress intended §534 statements to shift to the Commissioner the burden of proving that taxpayer was a mere holding or investment company — which the Tax Court rejected, and which we have rejected in part I of this opinion. Competent tax counsel, having followed this strategy in the Tax Court, is not entitled to have the slate wiped clean and to start all over in this Court.

The decision of the Tax Court is affirmed.

NOTE

See R. Monyek, The Growing Problem of Accumulated Earnings: Section 531 Today, 47 Taxes 761 (1969); Comment, A 534 Statement: Its Use in Court Remains Limited, 28 J. Taxation 105 (1968). For a worthwhile dialogue, although it antedates *Donruss* and *Rhombar,* see S. H. Levy et al., Corporate Accumulations: How to Meet the Problems of Section 531: A Panel Discussion of Techniques and Issues, 23 N.Y.U. Inst. on Fed. Tax. 745 (1965).

If you are troubled by the fact that corporate accumulations may defeat the income tax on shareholders, what statutory approach would you suggest to meet the problem? Why?

[13]These concerned themselves only with taxpayer's interpretation of §535.

8 | Personal Holding Companies — §§541-547

In 1934 Congress confronted the fact that, despite the accumulated earnings tax, many wealthy individuals were able to utilize corporations to house their investments and maintain a combined corporate and individual income tax rate far below the effective rate that would have been applicable to their income if "incorporated pocket books" had not been employed. To deal with the problem Congress imposed a high rate of corporate tax on the undistributed income of "personal holding companies." Contrary to the approach taken in §531, the special corporate tax on the undistributed income of personal holding companies was not made dependent upon a subjective test which looked to the purpose of the accumulation. Standards intended to be entirely objective were established. Defects found in the 1934 legislation were addressed in 1937, when the personal holding company tax was strengthened by amendment. In 1964 Congress made a major overhaul, designed to bring the law into phase with the reality of some modern business and investment practices and to streamline procedures, but without changing the basic purpose of the law. As to the 1934 legislation, see H.R. Rep. No. 704, 73d Cong., 2d Sess., 1939-1 Cum. Bull. (Part 2) 554, 562; as to the 1937 legislation, see H.R. Rep. No. 1546, 75th Cong., 1st Sess., 1939-1 Cum. Bull. (Part 2) 704, 705. Although the legislation that emerged in 1964 is not precisely as recommended by the Senate Finance Committee, and there have been minor changes in the law since 1964, the following excerpt from the report of the Senate Finance Committee in 1964 explains the basic thrust of the personal holding company tax provisions as they appear today:

REPORT OF THE SENATE COMMITTEE ON FINANCE
S. Rep. No. 830, 88th Cong., 2d Sess., 1964-1 Cum. Bull. 505, 608

(a) *Present law.* — Under present law, a domestic personal holding company is taxed on its "undistributed personal holding company income" at a rate of 75 percent on the first $2,000 and 85 percent on the balance. This is in addition to the regular corporate income tax. In general terms, a personal holding company is a closely held corporation, most of whose income is derived from certain specified forms of passive income. The tax applies only where 50 percent or more in value of the outstanding stock of the corporation is owned directly or indirectly by five or fewer individuals. In addition, at least 80 percent of the corporation's gross income must be from what is defined as "personal holding company income."

In general terms, personal holding company income consists of income from what are considered to be passive forms of investment. Thus, it includes dividends, interest, and annuities. It also includes most royalties although mineral, oil, or gas royalties are included only where these royalties do not represent 50 percent or more of the company's gross income or where there are not trade or business deductions (other than compensation for personal services rendered by shareholders) equal to 15 percent or more of the company's gross income. Copyright royalties also are classified as personal holding company income if they represent less than 50 percent of the company's gross income or the business deductions (other than compensation for personal services rendered by shareholders) represent less than 50 percent of gross income or if other personal holding company income constitutes more than 10 percent of gross income. Thus, where these mineral, oil, gas, or copyright royalties represent the principal business of the company, this type of income is not classified as personal holding company income, if there also is evidence, in the form of sufficient business deductions, that the company is actively engaged in business. Rents also are classified as personal holding company income unless they represent 50 percent or more of the company's gross income. Other forms of income which are classified as personal holding company income includes income from stock, security, and commodity transactions (except in the case of dealers, producers, etc.), income from estates and trusts, income from personal service contracts where 25 percent or more of the stock of the corporation is owned directly or indirectly by the individual performing the services, and income from the right to use property of the corporation where 25 percent or more of the stock of the corporation is owned directly or indirectly by the person eligible to use the property. This latter category of income, however, is treated as personal holding company income only where 10 percent or more of its income (without regard to this latter category or rents) is personal holding company income.

(*b*) *General reasons for provisions.* — Congress first imposed this tax on personal holding companies in 1934 in order to prevent the avoidance of the individual upper bracket surtax rates, by leaving what is essentially investment-type income in a corporate organization, subject to the lower corporate income tax. As indicated by the Administration, ways around the present personal holding company provisions have been found in several arrangements which permit the use of holding companies to avoid the individual income tax with respect to what is essentially investment-type income without the company involved being classified as a "personal holding company."

The principal avoidance devices involve the use of rental income, income from mineral operations, and certain capital gains which are not classified as personal holding company income as means of sheltering other investment income in such a manner that 80 percent or more of the company's gross income does not come within the technical definition of personal holding company income. In view of this, a number of modifications are made in the personal holding company provisions designed primarily to minimize the extent to which these special categories of income can be used to shelter clearly passive income. More detailed reasons for each of the various modifications provided by the bill are set forth in the explanation given below with respect to each of the modifications.

(c) *General explanation of provisions.* — The bill makes a series of modifications in the application of the personal holding company tax in the case of domestic corporations. However, except in the case of the dividends paid deduction in a liquidation, no change is made in the case of foreign personal holding companies. Most of the modifications described below are designed to eliminate various means by which holding companies have been avoiding classification as personal holding companies, although other problems are also dealt with.

(c)(i) *Tax rate of 70 percent.* — In view of the fact that this bill decreases the maximum tax rate applicable to individuals from 91 to 70 percent, your committee agrees with the House that the rates applicable to personal holding companies also should be lowered from the present rate of 75 percent on the first $2,000, and 85 percent on the excess, to what will be the new top individual income tax rate. Moreover, there appears to be no particular purpose for continuing the graduation in the personal holding company tax rate from 75 percent on the first $2,000 to 85 percent on the balance. In view of this, the bill provides that the personal holding company tax is to be 70 percent of the undistributed personal holding company income.

(c)(ii) *Decrease in 80-percent test.* — As previously indicated, one of the tests under present law provides that a company, to be a personal holding company, must derive 80 percent or more of its gross income from certain specified types of passive income, called personal holding company income. The bill decreases this 80-percent test to 60 percent. The decrease in this percentage is made because too many holding companies which are essentially holding companies of passive income have avoided the classification as such by holding their "personal holding company income" just slightly below the 80-percent limit. The more realistic 60-percent limit together with other modifications described below will make the avoidance of this classification much more difficult for holding companies generally.

(c)(iii) *Adjusted ordinary gross income requirement.* — Under present law the 80-percent requirement referred to above is applied to the gross income of the corporation; i.e., if the gross income derived from certain specified passive sources equals 80 percent of the total gross income of the corporation, the corporation is classed as a personal holding company. This has made it possible for corporations to avoid personal holding company classification by seeking out types of income not characterized as passive, or of a personal holding company type, which give rise to a proportionately large amount of gross income even though leaving little, if any, income after the deductions attributable to this income. In this manner, various types of income have been used to shelter investment income and remove the company from the classification of a personal holding company. Rents, where they constitute more than 50 percent of the gross income of the corporation, are an example of a type of income used to shelter passive income, such as dividends. Mineral, oil, and gas income are the other principal examples of income which have been so used.

To overcome this problem, the bill adjusts downward the income from certain sources to the extent of certain specified deductions attributable to these types of income. Thus, the corporation will be a personal holding company if 60 per cent of "adjusted" gross income consists of certain passive income. The adjustments are as follows:

1. In the case of gross income from rents, the deductions for depreciation and amortization, property taxes, interest, and rents paid to the extent attributable to the rental income received, are to be deducted from gross income.

2. In the case of mineral, oil, and gas royalties and also in the case of working interests in oil or gas wells, the deductions attributable to these royalties or working interests for depreciation, amortization and depletion, property and severance taxes, interests and rents paid are to be deducted in computing this adjusted gross income. It should be clearly understood that although income from working interests in an oil and gas well for purposes of the 60-percent limitation are reduced by the deductions referred to above such income is itself never classified as personal holding company income.

3. Interest from U.S. Government bonds held for sale by a dealer who is making a primary market for these obligations and interest on condemnation awards, judgments and tax refunds also are to be excluded in arriving at adjusted gross income for this purpose. This adjustment serves a different purpose from the first two deductions in that it merely excludes from the base on which personal holding company income is computed this particular type of interest income which in reality is not passive in nature.

In applying the 60-percent test, not only is the total gross income adjusted downward by the amount of the deductions (or interest) referred to in the cases specified above, but also in determining the rental income and mineral, oil and gas income for purposes of this test, this income also is reduced by the specified reductions.

(c)(iv) *Capital gains.* — Under present law capital gains (other than capital gains attributable to stock, securities, or commodities) are not treated as personal holding company income. All capital gains, however, are included in the gross income of the company for purposes of the 80-percent test. As in the case of the deductions referred to above, some companies have timed the realization of their capital gains income in such a manner as to keep their personal holding company income below the 80 percent. The bill avoids this problem by excluding all capital gains from the gross income in determining whether the 60-percent test is met. Thus, the test under the bill is based on adjusted ordinary gross income.

(c)(v) *Rental income.* — Under present law rental income is classified as personal holding company income only if it represents less than 50 percent of total gross income. This is based on the concept that where rental income represents the major activity, the activity involved is more likely to be of an active rather than passive character. The House bill retains this 50-percent test (applying it, however, to adjusted income from rents and to adjusted ordinary gross income) but adds a second test providing that rental income may be characterized as passive, or personal holding company income even where it represents 50 percent or more of the adjusted ordinary gross income if, apart from the rental income, more than 10 percent of the ordinary gross income (gross income excluding capital gains) of the company is personal holding company income. For this purpose, income derived from the use of corporate property by shareholders is not viewed as personal holding company income, but income from copyright royalties and the adjusted income from mineral, oil, and gas royalties is included for this purpose as personal holding company income.

Your committee has accepted the House changes in the 50-percent test with one modification. Your committee has made an amendment to this test with regard to rentals of tangible personal property retained by the lessee for three years or less. Under the amendment, in the case of such property, the income is not to be reduced by depreciation attributable to it for purposes of the 50-percent test and also for purposes of computing ordinary gross income. However, in the case of the provision in the House bill that the personal holding company income (apart from rent) may not exceed 10 percent of the ordinary gross income, your committee's amendments provide that the personal holding company income for this purpose may be reduced by dividends paid during the year, by dividends paid in the next year which are treated as if paid in the year in question, and by consent dividends. Your committee believes that this prevents the 10-percent rule from working harshly where the personal holding company income other than rents may exceed 10 percent of ordinary gross income, perhaps by only a small amount but under the House bill, nevertheless, result in the entire amount of rental income being classified as personal holding company income. Your committee's amendment in effect permits taxpayers to meet the 10-percent test after dividend payments (or amounts treated as paid in dividends). At the same time it gives assurance that the personal holding company income (apart from rent) sheltered in the company may not exceed 10 percent of its ordinary gross income.

The fact that rental income, both in applying the 60-percent test and also in applying the 50-percent provision to the rental income itself, is determined on the basis of reducing rental income by depreciation, amortization, property taxes, interest, and rents paid has already been noted above. However, as previously indicated, tangible personal property rented for three years or less is not reduced by depreciation attributable to it for purposes of these tests, under your committee's amendments.

(c)(vi) *Mineral, oil, and gas royalties.* — Under present law mineral, oil, and gas royalties are considered to be personal holding company income unless they represent 50 percent or more of the gross income of the company and unless the trade or business expense deductions (other than compensation for personal services rendered by shareholders) represent 15 percent or more of the gross income of the company. Thus, under present law, as in the case of rental income, mineral, oil, or gas royalties are treated as personal holding company income unless they represent the bulk of the company's income. However, in this case there also must be business expenses — indicating the active character of the business — constituting 15 percent or more of the gross income.

The bill retains these two tests but applies them on the basis of the adjusted ordinary gross income, thereby reducing, for this purpose, the income considered to be in these categories by depreciation, depletion, property and severance taxes, interest, and rent paid.

In addition, the bill adds another test which must be met in such cases for the mineral, oil, or gas royalty income to escape characterization as personal holding company income. The personal holding company income of the company, apart from this category of income (but including as such income that from copyright royalties and from rents), must not represent more than 10 percent of the ordinary gross income of the company. Thus, the personal holding company type income which mineral, oil, or gas royalty income may shelter even where this income represents the bulk of the income of the company must be relatively small; namely, less than 10 percent of ordinary gross income. Your committee has also added an amendment making it clear that income from mineral, oil, and gas royalties includes production payments and overriding royalties.

(c)(vii) *Copyright royalties.* — Under present law, copyright royalties also are considered to be personal holding company income unless they represent 50 percent or more of the total gross income. An additional test which must be met in order to escape such classification is that the personal holding company income, apart from the copyright royalty income, must not exceed 10 percent of the company's gross income and the trade or business expense deductions (other than those for compensation for personal services rendered by shareholders or for royalties paid to shareholders) must represent 50 percent or more of the company's gross income. This provision is modified by the bill in that the requirement that deductions equal at least 50 percent of gross income is changed to provide that they must equal 25 percent of ordinary gross income reduced by royalties paid and by depreciation deductions with respect to the copyrights.

(c)(viii) *Produced film rents.* — Under present law payments received from the distribution and exhibition of motion picture films are treated as rentals. As a result, under present law, a corporation may be formed by an individual who owns a motion picture negative and have its earnings treated as rents for purposes of the personal holding company tax. Since in such a case more than 50 percent of its gross income would be considered to be from rents, there would be no personal holding company tax payable in this case.

To meet this problem, the bill provides that payments received from the use of, or the right to use, films generally will be characterized as copyright royalty income. Thus, such income will be classified as personal holding company income unless 50 percent or more of the company's ordinary income is from this source, not more than 10 percent of the company's ordinary gross income is personal holding company income, and the deductions properly allocable to this film income represent 25 percent or more of the gross income from this source reduced by royalties paid and depreciation taken.

The bill, however, retains what is essentially the treatment of present law for "produced film rents." Produced film rents are rents arising from an interest in a film acquired before the production of the film was substantially complete. It was thought that less severe tests should be applied in such cases because the participation in the production of the film in itself indicates an active business enterprise in this case. For produced film rent to escape characterization as personal holding company income, as under present law, these rents need constitute only 50 percent or more of the ordinary gross income of the company.

(*c*)(*ix*) *Other types of income characterized as personal holding company income.* — Compensation for the use of property by a shareholder, amounts received under a personal service contract, and income from estates and trusts continue to be classified as personal holding company income essentially to the same extent as under present law, except for the fact that capital gain income is not classified as part of gross income in applying the 10-percent test in the case of the use of corporate property by shareholders.

(*c*)(*x*) *Personal finance companies.* — Present law provides that certain types of companies are not to be classified as personal holding companies. These include, for example, banks, life insurance companies, and surety companies. Also excluded from such classification are certain types of personal finance companies. Under present law, there are four different types of personal finance companies which are excluded from the personal holding company category. These categories in general terms are as follows:

1. Licensed personal finance companies, 80 percent of whose gross income is interest from loans if at least 60 percent of their gross income is received from loans classified as "small loans" by State law (or $500 if there is no State law limit) and if the interest is not payable in advance and computed only on unpaid balances. In addition, loans to a person who is a 10-percent shareholder must not exceed $5,000 in principal amount. These frequently are known as "Russell Sage" type personal finance companies.

2. Other lending companies engaged in the small loan or consumer finance business, 80 percent of whose gross income consists of interest or similar charges on loans to individuals and income from 80-percent-owned subsidiaries which in turn themselves meet this test. In addition, at least 60 percent of the company's income must be from interest or similar charges made in accordance with small loan or consumer finance laws to individuals where the loans do not exceed the State specification for small loans (or if there is no such limit, $1,500) and if the trade or business expenses of the company represent 15 percent or more of the company's gross income. These companies also must not have loans outstanding to shareholders, with a 10-percent interest or more, which exceed $5,000.

3. A loan or investment company (such as a Morris Plan bank), a substantial part of whose business consists of receiving funds not subject to check and evidenced by certificates of indebtedness or investment, and making loans and discounts. Here also loans to a person who is a 10-percent shareholder may not exceed $5,000 in principal amount.

4. A finance company actively engaged in purchasing or discounting accounts or notes receivable, or installment obligations, or in making loans secured by

any of these or by tangible personal property, if at least 80 percent of its gross income is derived from such business. In addition, at least 60 percent of such a company's gross income must be derived from certain categories of income. These categories, in general, relate to business or factoring-type loans: such as purchasing or discounting accounts or notes receivable, or installment obligations arising out of the sale of goods or services by the borrower in his business; making loans for not more than 36 months to businesses where the amounts are secured by accounts or notes receivable or installment obligations of the type described above, or secured by warehouse receipts, bills of lading, inventories, chattel mortgages on property used in the borrower's trade or business, etc. In the case of these companies, the trade or business expense deductions must represent at least 15 percent of the gross income of the company, and loans to those who are 10-percent shareholders in such company must not exceed $5,000 in principal amount.

In the interest of simplification, the House substituted one exclusion for the four now provided these categories of lending or finance companies. At the same time, it saw no need for purposes of the personal holding company provision to restrict the type of loans which these companies could make. It was suggested that this was properly a matter of regulation by State law governing these lending or finance businesses and that in any event the personal holding provisions do not apply to widely held corporations. In these latter cases only State law governs the type of loans which can be made.

In view of these considerations the House bill substituted for all four of the categories described above, one definition of a lending or finance company which is to be excluded from personal holding company tax treatment. This definition provided is designed first to assure that 60 percent of the company's income is from the active, regular conduct of a lending or finance business, and second that its personal holding company income[1] plus interest from U.S. obligations as a dealer in these obligations is not more than 20 percent of the company's ordinary income. These two limitations, and the restriction described below relating to business expense deductions, are designed to give assurance that the company is actively engaged in the lending or finance business and that not more than 20 percent of its remaining income is personal holding company income.

Your committee has modified the requirement that not more than 20 percent of the company's ordinary income may constitute personal holding company income. The House bill permits a company engaged in the small loan business to satisfy the 20-percent test by excluding income which it receives from subsidiaries in the lending or finance business. Your committee's bill would extend this treatment to finance companies. Finally, a technical amendment makes it clear that income received for furnishing services and facilities to a lending or finance company is not to be treated as personal holding company income to members of the same

---

[1]For this purpose personal holding company income is computed without regard to income from subsidiaries qualifying under this exemption as lending businesses, but including gross income from rents, royalties, produced film rents, and compensation for use of corporate property by shareholders.

affiliated group which meet the requirement of the exemption for the lending and finance companies, whether they are exempt from the personal holding company tax under the same or another provision.

In addition to 60- and 20-percent tests, the company must have certain business deductions described below, which are directly attributable to its lending or finance business equal to 15 percent of the ordinary gross income up to $500,000 plus 5 percent of the ordinary gross income between $500,000 and $1 million. This provision gives further assurance, as evidenced by the deductions of the company, that it is actively engaged in the lending or finance business. A fourth limitation applicable under present law in the case of all of the categories of lending companies denies the right to make loans to persons who are 10-percent shareholders to the extent of more than $5,000 a year in principal amounts.

The lending or finance business for purposes of this provision is defined as including the business of making loans and purchasing or discounting accounts receivable, notes, or installment obligations receivable, notes or installment obligations. It does not include, however, the making of loans or purchasing or discounting accounts receivable, notes or installment obligations if the remaining period to maturity on the loan or paper exceeds 60 months. It also does not include the making of loans evidenced by indebtedness issued in a series under a trust indenture and in registered form or with interest coupons attached. Your committee has amended the definition of a lending or finance business to make it clear that this includes the income from rendering services or making facilities available to another member of the same affiliated group which is also in the lending or finance business. This is provided because as a matter of economical operations, one company frequently hires the necessary personnel, acquires the appropriate facilities, and in accordance with the requirements of banks, borrows all of the money for the group. Then all of the corporations in the group pay a service charge for these services to the company performing them.

Business deductions for purposes of the 15-percent or 5-percent test include only those trade or business expense deductions which are deductible only by reason of section 162 or section 404 (other than compensation for personal services rendered by shareholders or members of their family), and depreciation deductions and deductions for real property taxes to the extent that the property to which they relate is used in the regular conduct of the lending or finance business. Trade or business expense deductions which are allowable specifically under other sections, such as the deduction for interest expense which is also allowable under section 163, are not included for purposes of the 15-percent or 5-percent test.

(c)(xi) *Liquidating dividends.* — Under present law, the 75- or 85-percent tax (70 percent under the bill) on personal holding companies applies only to the undistributed personal holding company income. Thus, this tax is applied after dividend distributions are taken into account. Included among the amounts treated as dividends eligible for the dividends paid deduction are distributions in liquidation to the extent of the accumulated earnings and profits. As a result, in the year of the liquidation of a personal holding company there is no income subject to personal holding company tax for that year. Despite the fact that the distributions are treated as dividends to the personal holding company, its stockholders in that year receive this income and report it at capital gains rates.

Thus, under present law, a company which is a personal holding company may nevertheless avoid both the personal holding company tax and the ordinary income treatment to its shareholders with respect to the personal holding company income the year in which it liquidates.

A problem is also presented in the case of corporations where a subsidiary is liquidated and both the parent and the subsidiary corporation are personal holding companies. In such a case, if the earnings and profits of the subsidiary exceed its undistributable personal holding company income in the year of the liquidating distribution, the parent corporation may use the excess dividend paid deduction in computing its own dividend paid deduction, thereby reducing its own undistributed personal holding company income in the taxable year and also in the 2 succeeding taxable years.

The bill meets these problems by limiting the application of section 562(b) to companies other than personal holding companies or foreign personal holding companies. However, it is provided in section 316(b) that in the case of a complete liquidation of a personal holding company within a 24-month period after the adoption of the plan of liquidation, that the term "dividend" is to include any amounts distributed in this liquidation to other than corporate shareholders to the extent of its undistributed income (before any deductions for this amount) only if the corporation involved designates amounts as dividends (and so notifies the distributee). If the corporation does so designate the distributions as dividends the individuals receiving a liquidating distribution from the personal holding company must report the amount so distributed as a dividend in the year of receipt. The bill also provides that in the case of a foreign personal holding company, the amount included in a United States shareholder's income is not to be diminished by any liquidating distributions made during the year.

An amendment is also made to the code which provides in the case of corporate distributees that where a complete liquidation of a personal holding company occurs within 24 months after the adoption of the plan of liquidation, the distribution is to be treated as a dividend for purposes of the personal holding company tax only to the extent of the corporate distributee's share of the undistributed personal holding company income for the taxable year of the distribution. Thus, the dividends paid deduction is allowed to a personal holding company only to the extent of the undistributed income for the taxable year and with respect to noncorporate distributees, only if such distributees treat such distribution as a dividend. . . .

(c)(xiv) *Deduction for amortization of indebtedness.* — In 1934, when the personal holding company provision was first adopted, Congress provided that indebtedness incurred before 1934 by a company which subsequently became a personal holding company would receive a special debt amortization deduction in computing its personal holding company tax. It was provided that to the extent that this debt was paid off, or amounts were set aside to pay off this debt, the tax base for purposes of the personal holding company tax was to be reduced by the amount of the amortization payments. Thus, these amortization payments were treated for purposes of the personal holding tax as deductions in the same manner as dividend distributions to shareholders.

The bill adds a similar provision for indebtedness incurred after December 31, 1933, and before January 1, 1964 (August 1, 1963, under the House bill), in the case of corporations which were not personal holding companies in one of the 2 most recent taxable years ending before December 31, 1963, but would have been had the new personal holding company provision been in effect at that time. . . .

NOTE

See generally B. Bittker and J. Eustice, Federal Income Taxation of Corporations and Shareholders 238-256 (2d ed. 1966); D. Lubick, Personal Holding Companies — Yesterday, Today and Tomorrow, 42 Taxes 855 (1964), page 930 infra.

O'SULLIVAN RUBBER CO. v. COMMISSIONER
120 F.2d 845 (2d Cir. 1941)

Before L. HAND, CHASE and FRANK, Circuit Judges.

FRANK, Circuit Judge. This is a petition for review of a decision of the Board of Tax Appeals, reported at 42 B.T.A. 721, which found a deficiency for 1935 in personal holding company tax of $4,198.37 and a penalty of $1,049.59.

In the disputed year petitioner was a dissolved corporation in process of liquidation. It sold its business of selling rubber heels and dissolved in 1932; since then it has not engaged in business, but has endeavored to liquidate as rapidly as possible. The original sales price, after defaults in payments, was reduced in 1935, and notes, bearing interest payable semi-annually and with serial maturities beginning in 1936, were taken for the unpaid balance of $340,000 due on the adjusted price. Prior to 1935 it had distributed in liquidation about $7 per share, but in that year, the amount available being small, it made no distribution. At least 80 per cent of its income in 1935 was derived from interest, and at least 50 per cent of its outstanding stock was owned by not more than five individuals. It came, therefore, directly within the definition of "personal holding company" in [§542(a)(1) and §542(a)(2)], unless it was not then a "corporation."

[The court held that although the taxpayer was a "dissolved corporation in process of liquidation, having sold its business and liquidating 'as rapidly as possible,'" it remained a "corporation."]

But, urges the petitioner, the personal holding surtax was enacted to remedy the evil of the "incorporated pocket book," deliberately created to reduce the personal taxes of those who created them, and, therefore, to impose the tax upon a corporation in petitioner's position is a perversion of the Congressional purpose. We may assume that the taxpayer here was not deliberately aiming to relieve its stockholders from personal taxation. It is, however, abundantly clear that Congress, in correcting an evil, is not narrowly confined to the specific instances which suggested the remedy. "Of course, all personal holding companies were not conceived in sin — many were organized for legitimate personal or business reasons; but Congress has made little distinction between the goats and the sheep."[1] In enacting the very section being applied here, Congress was attempting to foreclose the defense, available under [§531], that the accumulation of profits was responsive to a legitimate business need. See Committee on Ways and Means, 73d Cong., 2d Sess., House Report No. 704, p. 12: "The effect of this system . . . is to provide for a tax which will be automatically levied upon the holding company without any necessity for proving a purpose of avoiding surtaxes."

Cf. Committee on Finance, 73d Cong., 2d Sess., Senate Report No. 558, p. 15. It is suggestive that an earlier revenue bill, that of 1928, proposed by the House Committee on Ways and Means, contained in section 104, a definition substantially identical with [§531], but that it was stricken by the Senate because: "As in the case of all arbitrary definitions, the effect was to penalize corporations which were properly building up a surplus and to fail to recognize business necessities and sound practices." Committee on Finance, 70th Cong., 1st Sess., Senate Report No. 960, p. 12; cf. Committee on Ways and Means, 70th Cong., 1st Sess., House Report No. 2, p. 17. Having before us indisputable proof from the exactitude of [§542(a)] itself, reinforced by the Committee reports, that Congress wished to establish objective criteria for imposition of the tax, we cannot, by probing into corporate motives, undertake to relieve from the alleged harshness of a particular application of the statute. The Board of Tax Appeals, therefore, was correct in sustaining the deficiency asserted in personal holding company surtax. . . .

The decision of the Board of Tax Appeals is affirmed.

KENA, INC. v. COMMISSIONER
44 B.T.A. 217 (1941)

. . . The basic issue is whether or not the petitioner was a personal holding company. . . . The specific question is whether or not the income received by the petitioner during the taxable year was either interest or gain from the sale of stock or securities, as those terms are used in the statute.

Findings of Fact.

. . . During the taxable year Norman P. deMauriac and Alice B. deMauriac, his wife, owned all of the stock of Wydelke, Inc., a Delaware corporation. Wydelke, Inc., owned all of the stock of the petitioner and also owned other nonincome-producing stock and a book account against deMauriac. Wydelke, Inc., was merged into the petitioner on or about June 26, 1937, and filed its income and excess profits tax returns and also a personal holding company return for the taxable year.

Wydelke, Inc.'s, only source of income during the taxable year was dividends

[1] Rudick, Section 102 and Personal Holding Company Provisions of the Internal Revenue Code, 49 Yale L.J. (1939), 171, 203.

aggregating $93,572 paid to it by the petitioner. The assets of the petitioner consisted of a claim of $500 against Alice B. deMauriac and a claim against deMauriac, amounting to $395,609.26 on November 30, 1936, arising out of a contract dated December 13, 1932, between him and the petitioner. That contract was extended from time to time and, as extended, was in effect during the taxable year.

The contract recited that deMauriac had been successful in conducting stock trading accounts but was without funds and that the petitioner desired to invest its funds "with safety as to principal and an opportunity for enhancement thereof." The parties thereupon agreed that the petitioner should lend $195,227.50 in cash to deMauriac and deMauriac acknowledged the receipt of that sum "as and for a loan", under the following terms:

"1. DeMauriac promised to repay the loan on December 1, 1933.

"2. DeMauriac agreed, in consideration of the making of the loan, to pay the petitioner on December 15, 1933, 'an additional sum of money in lieu of interest, which additional sum shall be an amount equal to 80 per cent of the net profits of deMauriac in his stock trading business' for the period from December 13, 1932, to December 1, 1933."

The petitioner was permitted to have full access to deMauriac's books and records but had no power or authority over his business. The relation between the petitioner and deMauriac was stated to be that of a creditor and debtor. DeMauriac was liable for the payment of only the principal and the petitioner was not liable for any loss "either by way of sharing the same or otherwise." Provisions were made to extend the agreement to cover any future loans and to continue the life of the agreement by mutual consent.

The only income received by the petitioner during the taxable year was $124,091.65, representing the contractual percentage (reduced to 66⅔ percent by an amendment to the contract) paid to it by deMauriac. The dividends paid to Wydelke, Inc., by the petitioner were paid out of its income for the taxable year. . . .

Opinion.

Van Fossan: The respondent has pitched his entire argument on the interpretation of the word "interest" . . . . The petitioner contends that the sum received by it pursuant to the contract with deMauriac was not interest and did not represent "gains from the sale of stock or securities." If such payment is determined to be either interest or gains from the sale of stock or securities, the section automatically applies to the situation before us . . . . It is to be noted that, while counsel for petitioner contends the payment was not interest or gains from the sale of stock or securities, he does not venture to suggest an alternative characterization or name.

It is axiomatic that the language used to describe a thing does not determine its character. The contract of December 13, 1932, denominated the amount to be paid to the petitioner as "an additional sum in lieu of interest." The word "lieu" means "place or stead." It does not imply that the character of the payment was different from interest but indicates that the method of computation was not in accord with the usual method of computing interest, the percentage of profit being employed as a substitute. The contract itself must be examined to determine whether the sum so designated was actual interest or was something else.

Funk & Wagnalls New Standard Dictionary defines interest as "Payment for the use of money, or money so paid; an agreed or statutory compensation accruing to a creditor during the time that a loan or debt remains unpaid, reckoned usually as a yearly percentage of the sum owed."

In Old Colony Railroad Co. v. Commissioner, 284 U.S. 552, the Supreme Court stated: "And as respects 'interest', the usual import of the term is the amount which one has contracted to pay for the use of borrowed money. He who pays and he who receives payment of the stipulated amount conceives that the whole is interest . . . . We cannot believe that Congress used the word having in mind any concept other than the usual, ordinarily, and everyday meaning of the term . . . ."

In Elverson Corporation, 40 B.T.A. 615, we said: ". . . Interest, as generally understood, means simply the 'compensation allowed by law, or fixed by the parties for the use or forbearance of money, or as damages for its detention'; 'the compensation which is paid by the borrower of money to the lender for its use'; 'the price or rate of premium per unit of time, paid by the borrower of money to the lender for its use.' 33 Corpus Juris 178; Joseph W. Bettendorf, 3 B.T.A. 378, 383; Bouvier's Law Dictionary; Webster's New International Dictionary; Anderson & Co., 6 B.T.A. 713, 716. 'The usual import of the term is the amount which one has contracted to pay for the use of borrowed money.' Old Colony Railroad Co. v. Commissioner, 284 U.S. 552, 560. Congress apparently used the word in its usual and commonly accepted sense, DeGanay v. Lederer, 250 U.S. 376, and there is nothing in the legislative history to indicate that it was to be construed otherwise. Avery v. Commissioner, 292 U.S. 210. (See Report No. 704, Ways and Means Committee, 73d Cong. 2d Sess., p. 11, and Report No. 558, Senate Finance Committee, pp. 13, 16.) . . ."

. . . The contract called the amount delivered to deMauriac a loan and deMauriac acknowledged its receipt as such. DeMauriac promised to repay the loan on a definite date, December 1, 1933. He agreed to pay to the petitioner "in lieu of interest" a sum equal to 80 percent of the net profits of his business earned during the term of the loan. The contract specifically designated the relationship between the petitioner and deMauriac as that of creditor and debtor and meticulously provided that only the principal amount should be repaid and that the petitioner should share no losses of the business.

The record convinces us that the amount originally delivered to deMauriac and the amount subsequently advanced under the extended agreement were loans of cash made by the petitioner to deMauriac. The amounts paid for the use of such borrowed money were interest thereon.

It is not essential that interest be computed at a stated rate, but only that a sum definitely ascertainable shall be paid for the use of borrowed money, pursuant to the agreement of the lender and borrower. Excpt for the usury laws of the several states, there is no limit set upon the amount of interest which may be paid under specific contract between the creditor and the debtor. . . .

The lender may forego interest if he chooses. He may agree not to charge interest or to reduce the amount of interest, provided certain events occur. That situation would exist here if deMauriac had made no profits. The possibility that no interest might be payable does not affect the character of the interest when actually paid.

Here the amount in controversy was paid for the use of the primary loan as augmented by additional loans made under the same contractual terms. Consequently, the petitioner derived at least 80 percent of its gross income from interest and is a personal holding company as defined in the statute.

In view of the above holding it is unnecessary to consider whether the amount received by petitioner represented "gains from the sale of stock or securities."*

The action of the respondent, in denying the 20 percent credit in computing the petitioner's undistributed adjusted net income subject to surtax, is sustained.

Decision will be entered for the respondent.

320 EAST 47th STREET CORP. v. COMMISSIONER
243 F.2d 894 (2d Cir. 1957)

Before Clark, Chief Judge, Medina, Circuit Judge, and Smith, District Judge.

J. Joseph Smith, District Judge. Petitioner is a New York corporation whose stock in 1950 was wholly owned by two individuals. In that year the petitioner reported a gross income of $26,871.85. $6,000 of this was received as rental income from a corporation whose shareholders were the same individuals as petitioner's sole shareholders. $20,728.81 was that part of an award denominated "interest" for the condemnation of petitioner's property by the City of New York in 1948, paid in 1950. The balance, $143.04, was miscellaneous income. After receipt of the award, taxpayer acquired another piece of real property at 215 East 58th Street, New York City. Grosfeld House, Inc., whose shareholders are identical with those of petitioner, commenced occupancy of the premises in October 1950, paying $6,000 as rental during that year. The Commissioner determined that the $20,728.81 item was personal holding company income and that the petitioner was subject to the personal holding company tax imposed by Section 500 of the 1939 Code, 53 Stat. 104, as amended, 26 U.S.C. Section 500.† The petitioner brought suit in the Tax Court contending that the Commissioner's determination as to the $20,728.81 interest item was erroneous, and in the alternative that the $6,000 rental income was not personal holding company income within the meaning of Section 502(g),‡ that accordingly

---

*Since the 1964 amendments, gains from stock or securities transactions are not personal holding company income. — Ed.

†This corresponds with the current §541. — Ed.

‡Section 502(g), which corresponds generally with the current §543(a)(2), provided as follows:

"(g) RENTS. — Rents, unless constituting 50 per centum or more of the gross income. For the purposes of this subsection the term 'rents' means compensation, however designated, for the use of, or right to use, property, and the interest on debts owed to the corporation, to the extent such debts represent the price for which real property held primarily for sale to customers in the ordinary course of its trade or business was sold or exchanged by the corporation; but does not include amounts constituting personal holding company income under subsection (f)." — Ed.

less than 80% of its gross income was personal holding company income, and therefore the petitioner was not subject to the tax imposed by Section 500. The Tax Court held that both items of income were personal holding company income as defined in Section 502(a)* and (g), and from this decision the petitioner has brought this appeal. The inclusion of these items within the definition of personal holding company income presents novel questions which must be treated separately.

The Tax Court found that so much of the condemnation award denominated "interest" received by the petitioner was "interest" within the meaning of Section 502(a) of the 1939 Code. . . . [T]he basic question on the first point of this appeal is whether the term "interest," as generally understood, Old Colony R. Co. v. Com'r, 284 U.S. 552, 560, 52 S. Ct. 211, 76 L. Ed. 484, is limited to compensation for use of money voluntarily loaned or whether it also includes compensation for money withheld from the taxpayer without his consent. Only one case has dealt with this problem in the personal holding company area, Vertex Investment Co., 47 B.T.A. 252. There the taxpayer settled with the estate of its deceased president in a suit to recover sums apropriated by the president to his personal use. Part of the settlement was based on interest running from the date of appropriation by the deceased president. The Tax Board reasoned that such compensation was interest within the meaning of Section 502(a) even though it might be strictly regarded as "damages for detention of money." However the decision of the Board finally rested on the grounds that the corporation had ratified the "appropriation" as a "loan" and thus the compensation for the use of money was held to be interest on the basis. The terms used in [the personal holding company provisions have the same meaning as in the regular income tax provisions] . . . and in that area the meaning of "interest" has been more extensively determined. Neither the *Old Colony R. Co.* case, supra, nor Deputy v. du Pont, 308 U.S. 488, 60 S. Ct. 363, 84 L. Ed. 416 appear to be helpful since they deal with the significance of "interest" as opposed to other types of obligations arising from the voluntary use of money. This is especially true in light of the distinction drawn by the Court in the *du Pont* case between such interest and interest for the detention or use of money, at page 498, footnote 11. Of more help is Kieselbach v. Com'r, 317 U.S. 399, 63 S. Ct. 303, 87 L. Ed. 358, where the interest on a condemnation award was held to be income as opposed to part of the compensation for the property itself. While the Court, 317 U.S. at page 405, 63 S. Ct. at page 306, refused to express an opinion on whether or not such income would be "interest" within the meaning of Section [61] . . . , it did analogize such payments to the interest received on a purchase money lien, 317 U.S. at page 403, 63 S. Ct. at page 305. Johnson & Co. v. U.S., 2 Cir., 1945, 149 F.2d 851, carried the *Kieselbach* rationale to its ultimate conclusion by holding that even though the compensation award, plus the interest, is less than the taxpayer's basis, the "interest" received was ordinary income and not part of the sale price. If then the so-called "interest" is not part of the sale price, but is ordinary income, how is it to be characterized under the personal holding company income provisions? . . . And in United States Trust Co. of New York v. Anderson,

---

*This corresponds generally with the current §543(a)(1). — Ed.

2 Cir., 1933, 65 F.2d 575, 89 A.L.R. 994, and American Viscose Corp. v. Com'r, 3 Cir., 1932, 56 F.2d 1033, the courts experienced no difficulty in characterizing as "interest," interest received on land condemnation and tax refunds, respectively, in determining whether such interest payments came within the exemption of Section [103(a)] .... While these ... cases are persuasive in determining the meaning of "interest" in Section 502(a) in 1950, they have added significance in that they reflect the accepted meaning of "interest" in 1934 when the Personal Holding Company surtax was originated.

House Report 704 (73rd Congress, 2nd Sess.) found that many wealthy taxpayers were avoiding the surtax on individual income by transferring their securities to corporations formed for that purpose and allowing the income from such securities to accumulate in these corporations subject only to the lower corporate tax rates. To combat this device The Revenue Act of 1934, 48 Stat. 680, imposed a surtax on the undistributed adjusted net income of all corporations having no more than five shareholders if at least 80% of such corporation's gross income was derived from "royalties, dividends, interest, annuities, and ... gains from the sale of stocks or securities." ... From the inception of this section the terms used were given the same meaning as in the income tax chapter.... Interest received in a land condemnation proceeding would appear to be as much a target of this enactment as dividends or other forms of interest, since such "interest" payments would have been taxable as ordinary income if paid to the individual. United States Trust Co. of New York v. Anderson, supra. Had such payments been channeled to a corporation, the individual surtax would have been successfully avoided prior to 1934, as would the surtax on dividends and other interest similarly channeled. The fact that petitioner was not formed for the purpose of tax avoidance, and that barring this unusual receipt of income it apparently would not have been a personal holding company within the meaning of Section 501 can have no effect on this issue. O'Sullivan Rubber Co. v. Com'r, 2 Cir., 1941, 120 F.2d 845. We conclude that the amounts required to be paid under state law denominated as interest on the condemnation award from the date of the taking to the date of payment are within the meaning of interest in 502(a) and includible within personal holding company income.*

But petitioner contends that even if the condemnation interest is personal holding company income it is still not subject to the surtax because less than 80% of its gross income is holding company income. It argues that the $6,000 rental income was erroneously held to be includible under subsection (g), but should be included under subsection (f)† and thus be eligible for the exemption provided

---

*The Revenue Act of 1964 excluded interest on condemnation awards from the personal holding company tax base (§543(b)(2)(C)(ii)). Section (c)(iii) of the Senate Finance Committee report, page 903 supra, indicates the change was made because "this particular type of interest income ... is not passive in nature." — ED.

†Section 502(f), which corresponds generally with the current §543(a)(6), provided as follows:

"(f) USE OF CORPORATION PROPERTY BY SHAREHOLDERS. — Amounts received as compensation (however designated and from whomsoever received) for the use of, or right to use, property of the corporation in any case, where, at any time during the taxable year, 25 per centum or more in value of the outstanding stock of the corporation is

for by Section 223 of the 1950 Revenue Act, 64 Stat. 947, as amended by the Act of August 11, 1955, 69 Stat. 693, 26 U.S.C.A. Section 502 note.† Subsection (f) of Section 502 defines as personal holding company income compensation received for the use of corporate property by a holder of 25% or more of that corporation's stock "whether such right is obtained directly from the corporation or by means of a sublease or other arrangement." Such compensation is specifically excluded from subsection (g) inclusion. The sole question on this leg of the appeal is whether rental income, received from a lessee corporation, whose shareholders are identical with those of the lessor corporation comes with "other arrangement" of Section 502(f). The Tax Court in Minnesota Mortuaries, Inc., 4 T.C. 280, held that such income was not includible under (f), reasoning that a lease to a corporation, no matter by whom owned, cannot give "the use of, or the right to use" to an individual. Randolph Products Co. v. Manning, 3 Cir., 1949, 176 F.2d 190 and Walnut Street Co. v. Glenn, D.C.W.D. Ky. 1948, 83 F. Supp. 945, in including within (f) rent received from a partnership made up of the shareholders of the lessor corporation, reasoned that the partnership was not an entity and so the use of the property was in the individual shareholders.

As noted above the tax imposed by Section 500 was created by Section 351 of the Revenue Act of 1934 to reach for taxation purposes the income from securities shielded from the individual surtax by a corporate entity. In determining whether the corporation was a personal holding company income from rent was not taken into consideration in the 1934 and 1936 Acts. This proved to be a loophole whereby the entire tax could be avoided. A taxpayer could transfer his securities to a corporation. Under the 1934 and 1936 Acts the income would be subject to the surtax of Section 351, presuming that all other prerequisites were met. However if the taxpayer also transferred to the same corporation assets, such as houses or yachts, which he would then rent from the corporation, the entire surtax on the corporation would be avoided, if the income from such rentals constituted more than 20% of the corporation's gross income. By this device the income from securities was shielded from both the individual surtax of Chapter 1 and the corporate surtax of Section 351. (H. Rept. 1546 and S. Rept. 1242, 75th Congress, 1st Sess.) To remedy this situation subsection (f) was created in the 1937 amendment, 50 Stat. 813, to the 1936 Act. The wording of this subsection is broad. The rental may be received from anyone; the individual need not actually use the property, so long as he has the right to use; the stock ownership may be direct or indirect; the right to use may be obtained directly or by means of a sublease or other arrangement. Subsections (f) and (g) were enacted at the same time and, except for the exclusion of (f) income in (g), are overlapping. That is to say, barring (f), rental received from an individual stockholder would have been includible under (g). But (f)

---

owned, directly or indirectly, by or for an individual entitled to the use of the property, whether such right is obtained directly from the corporation or by means of a sublease or other arrangement." — Ed.

†Section 223 of the Revenue Act of 1950 provides that §502(f) shall not apply to rents received during taxable years ending after December 31, 1945, and before January 1, 1950, if the rents were received for use by the lessee, in the operation of a bona fide commercial, industrial or mining enterprise, of property of the taxpayer. — Ed.

does not have the 50% test that (g) does. Quite clearly the protection afforded real estate operating companies by the 50% test in (g) was not thought appropriate for (f) where the lessee would be the shareholder of the lessor corporation. (Cf. H. Rept. 1546, 75th Congress, 1st Sess.; S. Rept. 558, 73rd Congress, 2nd Sess.) Thus, after the 1937 Amendment, rent received by the lessor corporation for the use by a shareholder of the lessor's property was not, under (f), subject to the 50% exemption. There would appear to be no reason to attribute to Congress an intent to allow this provision to be frustrated by the mere creation of a second corporation which would pay the rent instead of the individual shareholder. While it is true that under New Colonial Ice Co. v. Helvering, 1934, 292 U.S. 435, 54 S. Ct. 788, 78 L. Ed. 1348, the corporation is an entity for the purpose of the imposition of taxes, the two sole shareholders of a corporation indirectly do have the use of its leased property. Thus to construe the rents paid by the lessee corporation as includible under subsection (f) does not require that "individual" be construed to include corporations, as supposed in the Minnesota Mortuaries, Inc., *Randolph Products,* and *Walnut Street Co.* cases, but merely to hold that such a device is one of the "other arrangements" of the subsection.

However, the exemption of the 1950 Act as amended applies to the rents received by the taxpayer here, since they were received for the use by the shareholders of the property through Grosfeld House, Inc. in a bona fide commercial or industrial enterprise. The application of 502(f) was found to work a hardship on shareholders in corporations which had become closely held and which had rented most of their assets for use in the operation of businesses to the individuals holding the stock in the corporation, thus unwittingly making the corporations personal holding companies and subject to the penalty tax. The Congress therefore in 1950 for a period later extended to include 1950, limited the application of 502(f) "to eliminate . . . rents for the use of a corporation's property by persons holding 25 percent or more of the stock of the company where the property is used by such persons '. . . in the operation of a bona fide commercial, industrial or mining enterprise . . .'" Senate Report No. 2374, 81st Congress, 2nd Session.

Literally if we consider the language of the statutory exception, Sec. 223 of the 1950 Act, P.L. 814, 81st Congress, extended by P.L. 370, 84th Congress, 1st Session, that 502(f) "shall not apply," it may be argued that the rent is holding company income since there is no provision that the remainder of 502 shall not apply. It would follow, that the 50% provision of (g) would apply, and that since the $6,000 is less than 50% of the gross income, it would be considered as holding company income. The reference to rental of "most of" the assets is said to point in that direction. 2 U.S. Code Cong. Serv. 81st Cong. 2nd Session, p. 3120. However, if the proportion of assets rented were the test, this taxpayer would be exempt. Here *all* of the assets were rented to the shareholders for bona fide industrial or commercial use. The timing of the compensation award and purchase of the new building was such that the rent was for a portion only of the tax year, and since it was less than the interest portion of the award, did not meet the 50% test of (g) if that test is applicable. However, the language of the Committees in discussing the proposal in 1950 and in 1955 points to an intention to exclude such rent from holding company income, not merely from subsection (f). The Committee Report on Section 223, which appears at 2 U.S. Code Cong. Serv. 81st Cong. p. 3239, is as follows:

> "Section 223. Personal Holding Company Income.
>
> "This section excludes from the definition of domestic personal holding company income for a limited period (taxable years ending after December 31, 1945, and before January 1, 1950) rents received by a corporation for the use of its property by a stockholder if the rents were received for the use of property by the lessee in the operation of a bona fide commercial, industrial, or mining enterprise. The revenue effect is negligible."

This intent to exclude the rent, from shareholders for commercial, etc. use, from personal holding income entirely, not merely from 502(f), is reiterated in the report of the House Committee on Ways and Means on the Act of 1955 which extended the exception to cover the period in suit. This language was adopted by the Senate Committee on Finance. 2 U.S. Code Cong. & Admin. News, 84th Cong. 1st Session, pp. 3036, 3037. While the approach to the problem was changed in the 1954 Code, due to the danger of loopholes in the temporary measure, it would appear that this taxpayer in the year in question, fell within the class for which relief was intended.

It was the plain intention of the Congress for the period in question to exempt from personal holding company income rents from shareholders in the situation of these two individuals, who leased taxpayer's property through a wholly owned corporation through which they used it to carry on a bona fide commercial or industrial enterprise.

Exclusion of the $6,000 from personal holding company income brings the percentage of such income below 80% of its gross income, and requires a judgment in favor of petitioner.

Reversed and remanded for proceedings consistent with this opinion.

[Concurring opinion of Judge Medina is omitted.]

NOTE

1. In Rev. Rul. 65-259, 1965-2 Cum. Bull. 174, the Service announced its intention to follow the holding in *320 East 47th Street* after June 30, 1965, and no longer to follow the contrary holding in Minnesota Mortuaries, Inc., 4 T.C. 280 (1944). See G. Bass, Will Leases Between Related Corporations Create a Personal Holding Company Trap? 26 J. Taxation 93 (1967).

2. In June 1968 the Committee on Corporate Stockholder Relationships of the Section of Taxation of the American Bar Association gave consideration to proposing the following "Legislative Recommendation" for treating compensation for the use of corporation property by the shareholders just as all other rental income is treated for personal holding company tax purposes. Should Congress adopt the proposal? Why?

LEGISLATIVE RECOMMENDATION REPEALING
SECTION 543(a)(6)

Resolved, that the American Bar Association recommends to the Congress that the Internal Revenue Code of 1954 be amended so as to treat for personal holding company purposes compensation for the use of corporation property by shareholders in the same manner as all rental income; and

Further resolved, that the Association proposes that this result be achieved by repealing section 543(a)(6) of the Internal Revenue Code of 1954; and

Further resolved, that the Section of Taxation is directed to urge the repeal of section 543(a)(6), effective for taxable years beginning after the effective date of the enactment of the repeal, upon the proper committees of Congress.

Explanation

Summary. The proposed repeal of section 543(a)(6) will treat for purposes of personal holding company classification, compensation for the use of corporation property by shareholders in the same manner as all rental income. Prior to the Revenue Act of 1964, rental income could, if it constituted 50 percent or more of gross income, shelter the other income of the corporation from the personal holding company tax, and a special provision was thus necessary to prevent a corporation from building up its rental income by leasing property to shareholders. The 1964 amendments to section 543(a)(2) prevent rental income from being used to shelter any appreciable amount of other passive income from the personal holding company tax. Accordingly, there is not further need for a special provision relating to rental income from property used by shareholders.

Moreover, the proposed repeal of section 543(a)(6) and the resulting treatment of all rental income under section 543(a)(2) would eliminate an unnecessary distinction under present law whereby a corporation with rental income under section 543(a)(2) may, under certain circumstances, avoid personal holding company classification by distributing most of its other passive income, whereas a corporation whose rental income falls into section 543(a)(6) as income from the use of corporation property by a shareholder may not take advantage of a distribution of its other passive income to avoid personal holding company classification.

Discussion. Prior to the Revenue Act of 1937 rents were not included in personal holding income, the apparent intention being to exclude bona fide real estate or rental companies from personal holding company classification as they were regarded as business enterprises rather than investment companies or incorporated pocketbooks.

The Revenue Act of 1937 included rents, unless constituting 50 percent or more of gross income, in personal holding company income. The Revenue Act of 1937 also included in personal holding company income rent received from 25 percent or more shareholders without regard to the 50 percent rule. This special treatment of rents received from 25 percent or more shareholders was explained in the House Ways and Means Committee Report, H. Rept. No. 1546, 75th Cong., 1st Sess., 1939-1 (Part 2) C.B. 704, 707, as follows:

> "Subsection (f) includes in personal holding company income amounts received as compensation for the use of, or the right to use, the property of the corporation. However, this rule only applies where during the taxable year of the corporation, 25 per cent or more in value of its outstanding stock is owned, directly or indirectly, by an individual leasing or otherwise entitled to the use of the property. It makes no difference whether the right to use the property is obtained by the individual directly from the corporation or by means of a sublease or other arrangement. Since under existing law, this type of compensation is not now included for the purpose of determining whether the corporation meets the 80-per cent test, the taxpayer may fix such compensation in an amount sufficient to bring its other investment income below the 80-per cent test. It has been shown to the committee that this device has been employed by taxpayers who had incorporated their yachts, city residences, or country houses and had paid sufficient rent to give the corporations enough income from their service to take them out of present section 351. By including this type of income in the definition of personal holding company income, your committee removes this method of tax avoidance."

It is thus apparent that rents from 25 percent or more stockholders were included without regard to the 50 percent rule because Congress felt that the amount of this type of rental income could be easily manipulated by the shareholders to produce the desired result.

A temporary change in this provision occurred in The Revenue Act of 1950, section 223, which amended the predecessor of section 543(a)(6) (section 502(f) of the 1939 Code) by providing that this section shall not apply to rents received during taxable years ending after December 31, 1945, and before January 1, 1950, for the use of the property by the lessee in the operation of a bona fide commerical, industrial, or mining enterprise. In 1954 a relief provision appeared in section 543(a)(6) which excluded from personal holding company income rent from 25 percent or more shareholders if the passive income other than all rental income did not exceed 10 percent of gross income. And until 1964, section 543(a)(2) and its predecessor remained virtually unchanged.

Thus until 1964, section 543(a)(6) was useful in preventing a corporation from avoiding personal holding company classification by building up its gross rents to 50 percent or more of gross income by leasing property to its shareholders.

The 1964 amendments to section 543(a)(2) prevent rental income from being used to shelter any appreciable amount of other passive income from the personal holding company tax. This is accomplished by providing, in general, that, in order not to constitute personal holding company income, rental income must satisfy two tests. First, "adjusted income from rents" (defined in section 543(b)(3) as the gross income from rents less depreciation, property taxes, interest and rent properly allocable thereto) must constitute 50 percent or more of the "adjusted ordinary gross income" (i.e. ordinary gross income adjusted as provided in section 543(b)(2)), that is, the 50 percent test is now measured by "net" rents rather than "gross" rents. Second, personal holding company income other than rents (including as rents, for this purpose, rents from 25 percent or more shareholders), less dividends paid or deemed paid as consent dividends, must be 10 percent or less of "ordinary gross income" as defined in section 543(b)(1). Thus, in general, there is a 50 percent test based on net income and a 10 percent test based on gross income. If the rental income falls into section 543(a)(6) as income from the use of corporation property by a shareholder, the dividend escape valve in connection with the 10 percent test is unavailable, and the corporation cannot avoid personal holding company status by distributing dividends in sufficient amount to reduce the non-rental personal holding company income to 10 percent of "ordinary gross income."

Thus, the repeal of section 543(a)(6) and the inclusion of all rents under section 543(a)(2) would allow no appreciably greater manipulation of rents in order to avoid personal holding company classification than now exists. For the 10 percent test of section 543(a)(2) is identical to the present 10 percent test of section 543(a)(6). And, in fact, the 50 percent test of section 543(a)(2) creates an additional burden not contained in section 543(a)(6), since at present this latter section does not apply to rents from 25 percent or more shareholders if the 10 percent test is met, regardless of whether the adjusted income (that is, the net income) from such rents meets the 50 percent test, so that rents from 25 percent or more shareholders may very likely not constitute personal holding company income if the 10 percent test is met, although these rents would constitute personal holding company income if governed by section 543(a)(2) if the additional 50 percent test is not met. See Regulations section 1.543-1(b)(9) (not reflecting the 1964 amendments) and 320 E. 47th St. Corp. v. Commissioner, 243 F.2d 894 (2d Cir. 1957),* to the effect that rents from 25 percent or more shareholders to which section 543(a)(6) is inapplicable is not then tested under section 543(a)(2) and is thus not personal holding company income.

Moreover, the repeal of section 543(a)(6) would eliminate the inequities which are presently engendered by that section. The dividend escape valve of section 543(a)(2), whereby non-rental personal holding company income may be distributed in order to satisfy the 10 percent rule, is unavailable in section 543(a)(6), a difference which appears to serve no purpose in light of the fact that the distribution pro tanto unshelters the corporate income.

In addition, section 543, read literally, requires inclusion in personal holding company income of the gross rents from 25 percent or more shareholders, whereas section 543(a)(2) requires inclusion only of net rents. Thus, it may be more difficult for a corporation with rents from 25 percent or more shareholders than a corporation with outside rents (which do not meet the 50 percent test) to escape being classified as a personal holding company by reason of the fact that personal holding company income is at least 60 percent of "adjusted ordinary gross income" under section 542(a)(1).

*Page 915 supra. — Ed.

These differences between section 543(a)(6) and section 543(a)(2) are magnified by Revenue Ruling 65-259, 1965-2 C.B. 174, which held that rental income derived from a corporate lessee any one of whose shareholders directly or indirectly owns 25 percent or more in value of the outstanding stock of the lessor corporation constitutes income for the use of corporation property by a shareholder under section 543(a)(6). For under this ruling, not only is the determination of section 543(a)(6) rents made complex and uncertain, but also section 543(a)(6) will cover many corporate arrangements which are motivated primarily by bona fide business considerations, thus causing a corporation to be a personal holding company in many situations where it would not be a personal holding company if section 543(a)(2) applied and where no manipulation of rents could occur to avoid the tests of section 543(a)(2).

It is recognized that the repeal of section 543(a)(6) would allow net rents from 25 percent or more shareholders to be added to other net rents in determining whether the 50 percent test of section 543(a)(2) is met. However, to the extent that 50 percent of "adjusted ordinary gross income" exceeds other net rents, the shareholder would have to pay rent to the corporation in a sufficient amount so that the net rent therefrom equals twice such excess, in order to manipulate the rental income so as to satisfy the 50 percent test. The shareholder would thus have to pay rent which would yield the corporation a profit subject to corporate tax, unlike pre-1964 law where the 50 percent test could be satisfied by gross rents yielding little or no profit, and would thus have little incentive to engage in such manipulation. This problem, then, is of minor significance and, on balance, would appear to be greatly outweighed by the desirability of eliminating the complexities and uncertainties brought about by the attempt to maintain a distinction between the two types of rents.

Accordingly, because section 543(a)(6) is no longer necessary to carry out its original purpose to prevent manipulation of rents from 25 percent or more shareholders in order to avoid personal holding company classification, which is now adequately effectuated under the conditions of section 543(a)(2), and, further, because this section creates unnecessary difficulties of interpretation and unnecessary differences from section 543(a)(2) in the treatment of rent received from shareholders in bona fide business arrangements, section 543(a)(6) should be repealed.

While certain tax-motivated arrangements may exist whereby corporations own property leased to shareholders for their personal use, these arrangements are related to the conversion of nondeductible personal expenses into deductible corporate expenses and are not pertinent to a consideration of the personal holding company provisions.

AFFILIATED ENTERPRISES, INC. v. COMMISSIONER
140 F.2d 647 (10th Cir. 1944)

Before PHILLIPS and MURRAH, Circuit Judges, and VAUGHT, District Judge.
MURRAH, Circuit Judge. The question presented by this appeal is whether

80 per cent of the taxpayer's income for the taxable year 1937 was derived from "royalties" or "other like property", and consequently taxable as personal holding company income. . . . The answer depends on whether the principles announced by this court in a former case involving the taxpayer's income for the taxable years 1934, 1935 and 1936 is applicable to and controlling of the instant facts. Commissioner v. Affiliated Enterprises, Inc., 10 Cir., 123 F.2d 665, certiorari denied 315 U.S. 812, 62 S. Ct. 796, 86 L. Ed. 1211. The Tax Court held the facts here insufficiently different on principle to warrant a contrary result, and that accordingly the taxpayer fell within the statutory definition of a personal holding company for the taxable year 1937. By this appeal, the taxpayer does not attack the former holding as applied to those facts, but does contend that these facts, when applied to the principles announced there, requires a different result.

Affiliated Enterprises, Inc. (taxpayer and herein called Affiliated), was organized in 1933 to promote the sale of a plan or scheme called "Bank Night" to theater owners throughout the country. The plan was designed to stimulate theater business by encouraging attendance in the following manner: Any person over sixteen years of age who registered in the lobby of a theater using the plan was given a number. These numbers were placed in a box, and on an appointed night a number was drawn from the box on the stage of the theater, and the holder of the number drawn, if present, received a sum of money which had been placed in a special account in a local bank. "Bank Night" was advertised by means of cards, posters, and film trailers which Affiliated sold to the theater owners. The plan was immediately successful, and was used extensively throughout the country. Between 1933 and 1938, Affiliated made repeated attempts to obtain a patent on the "means for conducting prize drawings", but it was denied on the grounds that the art was not patentable. It did succeed however in securing copyrights on certain film trailers and instruction sheets which described the system, and the name "Bank Night" was registered as a trade-mark name in most of the states.

The plan was originally sold to theater owners thorughout the country under a written agreement labelled "Bank Night License Agreement", which recited that Affiliated was the owner of the copyrighted and trade-marked name "Bank Night", and of certain copyrights and patents pending, together with other accessories such as cards, posters, registers, film trailers, record books, and instruction sheets used in the operation of "Bank Night". The theater operator was called a licensee, and the agreement recited that the licensee desired to acquire a limited license to use the "Bank Night" system in his theater. The licensee acknowledged Affiliated's ownership of the trade-marks, copyrights, patents pending, and further acknowledged that it was purchasing only the right to use that which Affiliated owned, and agreed to pay damages of $100 per day if it used the system or any modification thereof after the termination of the license agreement. Affiliated reserved the right to defend in the name of the licensee any attack upon the right to exercise the license or any phase thereof, and it paid legal retainers throughout the country to thirty or more attorneys for the purpose of defending various attacks upon the system. By the terms of the license agreement, the theater owners agreed to pay a stipulated fee of from $5 to $10 per week for the right to use the system. Affiliated also sold the theater owners all of the accessories and equipment used in the operation of the plan, but more than 80 per cent of its income for the taxable years 1934, 1935 and 1936 was derived directly from the sale of "Bank Night License Agreements."

On December 3, 1936, this court in Affiliated Enterprises, Inc., v. Gantz, 86 F.2d 597, 599, held that the trade-mark registration of the term "Bank Night" afforded Affiliated no protection of the plan or system employed. It further held that Affiliated had no property right in the plan or system called "Bank Night"; that it was "too closely akin [to a lottery]" to "have the protection . . . of a court of equity." On December 18, 1936, the First Circuit in Affiliated Enterprises, Inc., v. Gruber, 86 F.2d 958, likewise held that Affiliated had no property right in the plan or system capable of protection in a court of equity.[2] Thereafter, the Commissioner determined that Affiliated fell within the statutory definition of a personal holding company with respect to its tax liability for the taxable years 1934, 1935 and 1936, and assessed a deficiency accordingly. On redetermination, the Board of Tax Appeals (now the Tax Court) held that since Affiliated had no property right in its idea or system which it could protect, or "on which it could give licenses to others", the income from the sale of the license agreements was not royalty or "other like property", and consequently Affiliated was not a personal holding company within the meaning of the Act. Affiliated Enterprises v. Commissioner, 42 B.T.A. 390. The Board thought that the income was in reality derived from a sales promotion scheme, which those purchasing same believed worth the payment of the fee charged under the written agreement.

On appeal (123 F.2d 665, 667), this court held that the test was not whether the system was patentable or capable of protection in a court of equity, but rather "whether the idea is new or novel and has value." The court stated, "it is apparent from the record that respondent [Affiliated] in its dealings with theater operators treated the transaction as one involving the payment of royalty for the use of a creative, novel idea possessing utility"; that since the parties at the time of the transaction "certainly thought they were dealing with reference to an idea subject to protection by patent or copyright, and that the transaction involved royalty payments", the income derived from the sale of the contracts constituted royalty or other like property for income tax purposes.

Whether Affiliated falls within the arbitrary statutory definition of a personal holding company for the taxable year 1937 depends upon the peculiar facts applicable for that year, and not upon its taxable status in any other year. See Mertens Law of Federal Income Taxation, Vol. 7, Sec. 39.01, p. 70. With the beginning of the year 1937, the *Gantz* and *Gruber* cases had been given wide publicity by means of trade journals and general newspaper comments. Theater owners and managers were given to understand that Affiliated could no longer claim any exclusive right to the use of the "Bank Night" system, and Affiliated also realized that it had nothing to sell capable of protection as a patentable or copyrightable idea. It was faced with the necessity of changing its "mode of operation" if it were to stay in business. Consequently, to meet this exigency, it devised what it called a "Bank

---

[2]Affiliated discontinued operations in 1938 when a fraud order was issued against it by the Post Office Department on the grounds that its system constituted a lottery.

Night Theater Service", which, by means of a manual published early in 1937, it advertised a comprehensive and complete theater service designed to give the independent theater owner specialized advice for the operation of a theater in the most efficient and economical manner. The "Bank Night Theater Service" was advertised through the manual to the theater owners as a "Department of Affiliated Enterprises, Inc., owner of the trade-name, trade-mark, copyrights and/or patents pertaining to Bank Night". Twenty-two items[3] were listed as subjects for specialized advice and counsel. Included in the service offered was the "Bank Night" plan as a "business stimulator", but no exclusive rights in the "Bank Night" idea was claimed, and the accessories and supplies used in connection with the system were furnished without extra cost to the purchasers of the service.

Of the total gross income of the taxpayer for the year 1937, 58.32 per cent was realized from the sale of written "License Agreements" identical to those used in prior years, some of which were sold in 1936 prior to the *Gantz* and *Gruber* decisions, and others in 1937. With respect to this income, Affiliated concedes that it is controlled by the earlier decision of this court, and that it is to be classified as royalty or other like property for the purposes of this case. But 41.30 per cent of the total gross income of Affiliated for the year 1937 was realized from the sale of the "Bank Night Theater Service" to theater operators who did not sign any contract or agreement, but orally agreed to pay a stipulated amount for the service, with the privilege of termination at will. In other words, 41.30 per cent of the taxpayer's income was derived from sources which cannot be said to be attributable to any written agreements wherein the parties by contract "treated the transaction as one involving the payment of royalty for the use of a creative, novel idea possessing utility." The parties did not treat the idea as one subject to protection by patent, copyright, or otherwise. The Commissioner concedes of course that if the 41.30 per cent of the taxpayer's income was realized for services rendered, having no relation to royalties or other like property, it does not come within the statutory definition of a personal holding company for the taxable year 1937.

To hold that the income derived from the oral contracts constituted royalties or other like property is pushing the rule announced in the earlier case beyond the practical and common sense interpretation accorded that term. It follows that Affiliated does not fall within the statutory definition of a personal holding company for the taxable year 1937, and the order of the Tax Court is accordingly reversed.

VAUGHT, District Judge (dissenting). [Opinion omitted.]

GENERAL MANAGEMENT CORP. v. COMMISSIONER
135 F.2d 882 (7th Cir. 1943), cert. denied, 320 U.S. 757 (1943)

Before KERNER, MINTON, Circuit Judges, and LINDLEY, District Judge.
LINDLEY, District Judge. Petitioner questions a decision of the Tax Court de-

---

[3]Electrical survey, power costs, heating analysis, accounting, advertising and exploitation, architecture, business stimulators, discounts, decorating, electricity, equipment, financing, insurance, laboratories, library, heating and cooling, modernization, physical operation, projection and sound, purchasing advice, valuation, and summary.

claring it a personal holding company in the taxable year 1938, for the reason that more than 80 per cent of its gross income for that year constituted "personal service corporate income" within the meaning of Section [543(a)(7)]. . . . The propriety of the decision depends wholly upon whether a contract with United Printers and Publishers, Inc., hereafter referred to as United, from which it derived $24,000, was a "personal service contract" which "designated" the person who was to perform the services. . . .

Petitioner is a corporation which has, for a number of years, been engaged actively in rehabilitating financially embarrassed business concerns. Grant Gillam owned 100 of its total capital issue of 200 shares; his sister, S. Margaret Gillam, 80 and Marguerite Miller, 20. From 1932 to 1938 petitioner served United, first, at the request of a creditor bankers' committee and, finally, under a contract made in February, 1937, after the bank loans had been retired, wherein it was provided, amongst other matters, that petitioner should render certain services, including specifically those of Gillam, for $2,000 per month. The agreement designated Gillam as comptroller, provided that he should "continue to supervise the physical operations of United, its divisions and subsidiaries" and gave to him full authority over the expenditure and borrowing of money. It provided further that, if he should die or become incapacitated and no one could be obtained to take his place satisfactory to United, the latter might terminate the contract. In addition to the services to be performed by Gillam, petitioner agreed also to furnish budgets, audits, cost accounts and various reports. In pursuance of this employment, petitioner received in 1938, $24,000 as compensation.

Under Section [543(a)(7)] personal service income includes amounts received under contracts under which the corporation is to furnish personal service, provided 25 per cent or more in value of the outstanding stock of the corporation is owned by an individual designated as the one to perform such service. Inasmuch as Gillam owned 50 per cent of the corporate stock, the question narrows to whether he is "designated by the contract as the one to perform such service."

Gillam, as the principal stockholder of petitioner, had for some years been a doctor of financially embarrassed corporations and other business set-ups. He had had wide experience in solutions of problems of management, production, finance and rejuvenation of sick industrial enterprises. Beginning with 1932, as the active agent of petitioner, he had rendered curative administrative service to United, visiting and surveying its plants, its operating divisions and its production, directing its activities, its fiscal and financial policies, acting not only as "comptroller" but also as supervisory administrative head and exercising and making available his discretionary executive talents. Successful results ensuing from his service culminated in 1937 in retirement of United's bank loans, ridding it of supervision by the representatives of bank creditors, whose pressure had brought petitioner into the picture as financial director.

The bank loans having been satisfied, United voluntarily contracted with petitioner to continue to render similar service. This agreement specifically provided for discharge of supervisory functions by Gillam, saying that he should "continue" as comptroller and supervise the physical and financial operations of United, its various divisions and subsidiaries. No money was to be borrowed or paid except as approved by him. Thus he continued as the administrative, financial, fiscal and supervisory head of United. His was the voice of discretionary control. In case of his death, United was to have the option of rescission of the contract. Obviously, the evidence supported the finding that United's desire to avail itself of his constructive discretionary and advisory capacities was the inspiring motive leading to execution of the contract.

In addition to Gillam's designated services under the contract, petitioner, through employees other than Gillam, made projected budgets of United's cash needs, audited its accounts, prepared its income tax returns and made up statements of costs, balance sheets and similar reports. In actual preparation of none of these did Gillam participate. In consequence, petitioner insists, as he was not designated to perform all services rendered United, the income received from United is not within the statute. But the labor supplied by persons other than Gillam consisted, obviously, of preparation of the mechanical tools necessary to efficient discharge of his functions as administrative and controlling head. Such budgets, statements, and reports are some of the implements by which an executive or administrative agent works his way to a definite determination of corporate policy. In their preparation, discretion is not involved but, rather, physical compilation and few if any directors of policies are capable of exercising a wise discretion without their employment. They are the trowel of the mason, the plane of the carpenter, the nurse assisting the physician. The contract designated Gillam as the only agency endowed with discretion, and was made optionally contingent upon his continued ability to act. Under it, anyone included in the personnel of petitioner or found outside might supply the working tools. Their source was a factor of no importance. Clearly the court was justified in finding from this evidence that discretionary service designated to be performed by Gillam was the inspiring motive for his designation and that the makers of the tools utilized supplied only incidental aid necessary to achievement of the desired purpose, — administrative supervision by Gillam.

The value of labor supplied in preparing reports, audits and accounts may be an element proper to be considered in determining the question but where, as here, the evidence amply justifies the ultimate conclusion of fact that such additional service amounted to mere supply of the implements needed in performance of the administrative duties of Gillam, we think that the tax court properly refused to give determinative weight to that factor.

Petitioner insists that the contract was not the type of agreement intended by Section [543(a)(7)]. But we think the statute speaks clearly and covers the kind of service contract here involved.

Inasmuch as it results from inclusion of $24,000 as a part of the personal service income that more than 80 per cent of the gross income of petitioner is personal service income, the decision is affirmed.

MINTON, Circuit Judge (dissenting). [Opinion omitted.]

DONALD C. LUBICK, PERSONAL HOLDING COMPANIES — YESTERDAY, TODAY AND TOMORROW
42 Taxes 855 (1964)*

It has been recognized from the earliest income tax acts under the Sixteenth Amendment that the existence of corporate income tax rates lower than individual income tax rates requires special provisions to prevent avoidance of taxes on individual incomes. Otherwise individuals would be able through incorporation of their investments, or in some cases, their personal talents, to divert income from themselves (where it would be taxed at high marginal rates) to a separate corporate entity subject to lower tax. A special tax or rate of tax on all undistributed corporate profits might, of course, alter the balance sufficiently to obviate the need for the penalty taxes on unreasonable accumulations and personal holding companies. Indeed it has been said that such a tax in the 1936 Act was more effective in preventing corporate accumulations to avoid personal tax than measures tailored for that purpose.[1] The merits and implications of such a measure, however, involve a broad reconsideration of the whole system of taxation of corporations and shareholders beyond the scope of this paper.

This paper will examine the personal holding company provisions of the Code within the scope, then, of the present relationship of corporate and personal income taxes. First one must keep in mind the mathematics of the advantages of incorporation in the absence of provisions to prevent avoidance of tax by shareholders, in order to evaluate the necessity for various of the personal holding company provisions. Assuming 1965 corporate rates of 22 per cent of the first $25,000 of corporate income and 48 per cent of the excess and a marginal individual rate of 70 per cent on income over $100,000 ($200,000 for a joint return), the advantages of incorporation of investment are striking if the personal holding company tax is avoided.

Illustration 1: A portfolio of $3,000,000 of common stocks yielding 4 per cent is placed in corporation X by its sole shareholder, A, whose income is subject to the 70 per cent top marginal rate. Absent personal holding company provisions and Section 531 penalty tax on accumulated earnings, the tax improvement to A by incorporation is as follows:

Taxation without incorporation		*Taxation with corporation*	
Dividend income	$120,000	Dividend income	$120,000
X Individual rate	.70	Less intercorporate dividend deduction — 85 per cent ...	102,000
		Taxable income	$ 18,000
Tax	$ 84,000	Tax at 22 per cent	$ 3,960

---

*Reprinted by permission. Mr. Lubick, a partner in the Buffalo, N.Y., law firm of Hodgson, Russ, Andrews, Woods and Goodyear, was the Treasury Department's Tax Legislative Counsel during the pendency and passage of the Revenue Act of 1964. — Ed.

[1]Rudick, "Section 102 and Personal Holding Company Provisions of the Internal Revenue Code (1939)," 49 Yale Law Journal 171, 174.

If A liquidates corporation X before his death, there is an additional capital gains tax of $29,010, but this is avoidable by holding until death.[2]

The net after taxes without the capital gains tax is over $116,000, which is what A would retain after taxes from a portfolio in excess of $9,500,000. The net after taxes including the capital gains tax is about $87,000. To retain the equivalent without a corporation would require a portfolio of $7,250,000.

If the dividend income is taxable to the corporation at a marginal rate of 48 per cent because it has $25,000 of other income, the corporate tax would be $8,640, and the capital gains tax on liquidation before death would be $27,840. The equivalent retention from stocks held in individual name would require a portfolio of close to $7,000,000.

The situation with interest income, absent the 85 per cent intercorporate deduction, is not so dramatic, but nevertheless advantageous:

Illustration 2: A portfolio of bonds of $625,000 yielding 4% is placed in corporation X by its sole shareholder, A, whose income is subject to the top marginal rate. Absent personal holding company provisions and Section 531, the tax improvement by incorporation is as follows:

Taxation without incorporation		*Taxation with corporation*	
Interest income	$25,000	Interest income	$25,000
X Individual rate	.70	X Normal tax	.22
Tax	$17,500		$ 5,500

The net after taxes of $19,500 would require a portfolio of $1,625,000 held in A's name as an individual. If A liquidates corporation X before his death, there is an additional capital gains tax of $4,875, reducing the saving to $7,125 plus net additional income earned through deferral of capital gains tax. The net after taxes of $14,625 would require a portfolio of over $1,000,000 held individually.

If the interest income is taxable to the corporation at a marginal rate of 48 per cent, the corporate tax would be $12,000, still a current saving of $5,500. $3,250 would be eliminated by a capital gains tax on liquidation (offset by the advantage of deferral). Even paying corporate tax of 48 per cent and capital gains tax on the balance, the net to A through use of a corporation would be the equivalent of the yield individually to him from an $812,500 portfolio rather than $625,000.

If A were able to keep his investment income in multiple corporations to avoid a 48 per cent corporate rate, similar computations would show an advantage based upon a 28 per cent corporate rate[3] and income from a portfolio of unlimited size could escape top marginal individual tax rates.

The need is therefore clearly demonstrated that additional statutory provisions are required to prevent avoidance of individual rates through incorporation. Our

---

[2]Enactment of the 1963 presidential recommendations to deal generally with multiple surtax exemptions and capital gains escaping income taxation at death, or at least enactment of a carry-over basis, would have incidentally reduced the usefulness of many holding companies.

[3]See Section 1562(b). (Unless otherwise stated, section references are to the Internal Revenue Code of 1954.)

present corporate income tax recognizes the corporation as a separate taxpaying business entity, without taxation of shareholders prior to distribution, but to the extent that use of the corporation is without business justification, it should not insulate shareholders from taxation. The separateness of the corporation is recognized in the closely held corporate business situation, as much as the widely held situation, even though the mechanical problems of currently taxing corporate income to the shareholders are nowhere near so formidable as in a widely held corporation. The line has thus been drawn between income retained for the conduct of active business through a corporation, recognized as not improper merely because of the number of shareholders, and hence subject to no tax but the corporate normal and surtax, and that accumulated merely for investment where business considerations do not call for the use of corporate form or retention by the corporation. The objective is to draw a statute that will strike at the latter tax avoidance situations without interfering with legitimate business operations.

Is an Unreasonable Accumulations Provision Sufficient?

The initial approach to tax avoidance through incorporation was along the lines of present Section 531, imposing a penalty on account of corporate accumulations of surplus for the purpose of avoiding surtax on shareholders. The earlier statutes taxed the unreasonable accumulations to the shareholders, but since 1921 the penalty tax has been at the corporate level.

During consideration of the 1964 Act it was suggested that more reliance on Section 531 might be an adequate substitute for strengthening the personal holding company provisions. Both the Treasury and Congressional experts who considered this idea rejected it.

There are a number of reasons why Section 531 is not adequate to do the job required of the personal holding company provisions.

First there is the arithmetic of Section 531 rates. The accumulated earnings tax is $27\frac{1}{2}$ per cent of the accumulated taxable income up to $100,000 plus $38\frac{1}{2}$ per cent of the excess.

Using the $27\frac{1}{2}$ per cent rate, applicable to accumulations based on several million dollars of investment, and assuming the rate is not revised upward which, as indicated below, is probably not justifiable, a top bracket shareholder could be ahead by keeping his investment in corporate solution even with the payment of an accumulated earnings tax. For example, $100 subject to corporate tax of 48 per cent leaves $52 subject to $27\frac{1}{2}$ per cent accumulated earnings tax, or $14.30. The total tax is $62.30 which is almost $8 below the top marginal rate. If the balance of $37.70 were subjected to a capital gains tax, the total taxes would rise to $71.725, but the probability of escape of capital gains tax at death or at least the advantage of deferral until liquidation would make the individual better off.

The foregoing example is based on a 48 per cent corporate rate and a $27\frac{1}{2}$ per cent accumulated earnings tax. If the income were subject to only a 22 per cent or 28 per cent corporate tax (because corporate income does not exceed $25,000), or a 7.2 per cent corporate tax on dividend income (or even 3.3 per cent if less than $25,000), obviously the accumulated earnings tax at any feasible rate becomes an insufficient deterrent to corporate shelter. Add to that the factor that the 27½ per cent accumulated earnings tax will not apply to the first $100,000 of accumulations (and that multiple $100,000 accumulation credits may be available) or that it may not apply at all if some business purpose can be established for nondistribution and it is clear why Section 531 is an ineffectual deterrent regardless of rate.

Second, the personal holding company provisions had their origin in the shortcomings of the accumulated earnings tax. The House Committee Report under the 1934 Act (H. Rept. No. 704, 73d Cong., 2d Sess., 1939-1 CB (Part 2) 554, 562) stated that:

"It is true that section 104 of the existing income-tax laws puts a 50 per cent penalty on this accumulation of profits to avoid surtaxes, but, nevertheless, there seems no doubt that this form of avoidance is still practiced to a large extent. By making partial distribution of profits and by showing some need for the accumulation of the remaining profits, the taxpayer makes it difficult to prove a purpose to avoid taxes."[4]

The Congress found that to deal with the extreme cases of avoidance an automatic mechanical penalty tax was needed. The accumulated earnings tax was continued for those cases where avoidance could not be automatically inferred from the high percentage of income of the kind not normally required to be received in corporate form (dividends and interest) or where the income accumulated was from the conduct of an active business, but its retention not needed by the business.

Thus Congress decided that to raise the accumulated earnings tax rate would not be an appropriate solution since that tax was needed for many situations other than incorporated pocketbooks and the like. For instance in the operating corporation which accumulates its earnings and profits from its operating business, Section 531 was still needed to apply to the income from active operations properly derived in corporate form without any tax avoidance motive, but thereafter retained in corporate solution to avoid individual taxes. In the personal holding company situation the very use of the corporate form in deriving the income is the avoidance device. Thus a raise in rate would be unduly severe in many cases where the income itself is legitimately derived in corporate form, though it ought to be distributed,[5] especially since this requires subjective judgment.

---

[4]For example, the retention of corporate earnings to amortize corporate indebtedness has always been recognized as a ground to avoid the accumulated earnings tax. See Treas. Reg. Sec. 1.537-2. Thus the Treasury presented cases to Congress in 1963 whereby rental real estate was purchased subject to large indebtedness (as is customary in conducting a real estate business). The gross rentals were sufficiently large under the pre-1964 law to preclude personal holding company liability and the indebtedness was amortized by the net income from the rentals and the dividends from sheltered securities which had been taxed only at intercorporate dividend rates. The net income being required to amortize the indebtedness, Section 531 did not apply and hence the purchase of the real estate could be financed out of retained earnings at practically no tax cost. The 1964 Act by limiting the dividends which can be sheltered by rentals will curtail this practice. Those corporations which had relied on prior law and had counted on earnings to amortize their real estate indebtedness will be permitted to do so without penalty taxes through a special deduction in arriving at undistributed personal holding company income for amounts used to amortize pre-1964 indebtedness. Sec. 545(c).

[5]See, Rudick, "Effect of the Corporate Income Tax on Management Policies," 2 Howard Law Journal 232, 238-253 (1956).

The problem becomes one of determining clear cases where the need to derive income in corporate form is so slight that the statute is justified in making receipt of such income in corporate form, or at least receipt and retention, prohibitively costly without permitting inquiry into motive. This paper will briefly review the development of the present structure of the personal holding company tax to show how the present provisions originated, evaluate how well they work and indicate some areas to consider for improvement.

Rate of Tax

The personal holding company tax under the 1964 Act is 70 per cent of the undistributed personal holding company income of a personal holding company. Personal holding companies are those companies which, with certain exceptions, meet two objective tests, one with respect to closely held stock ownership and the other with respect to a high percentage of income derived from passive investments or certain other activities where derivation of income in corporate form is indicative of tax avoidance.

The rates under the 1934 Act when the personal holding company provisions were first introduced were 30 per cent of the first $10,000 of undistributed adjusted net income and 40 per cent of the excess; the 1935 Act changed them to a schedule running from 20 per cent of the first $2,000 of undistributed adjusted net income to 60 per cent of such income over $1,000,000; the 1936 Act ran the scale from 8 per cent to 48 per cent; and the 1937 Act introduced a rate of 65 per cent applicable to the first $2,000 of such income and 75 per cent on the excess. The 65 per cent and 75 per cent figures of the 1937 Act were raised by 10 per cent for 1940 and were set at 75 per cent and 85 per cent by the 1942 Act. The 1964 Act lowered the rate to 70 per cent of all undistributed personal holding company income to conform to the top individual surtax rate.

Although income subjected to the 70 per cent personal holding company tax rate, if the corporation also has taxable income subject to corporate tax, will be taxed by at least a few percentage points in excess of the top marginal individual rate,[6] there is no point to achieving exact correlation. Statistics of Income for 1958-9 (the latest computation with respect to personal holding companies) showed 6,285 returns with schedule PH attached and total personal holding company tax receipts of $559,000 from 305 corporations. This confirms the point that the personal holding company tax does not and, is not designed to, raise revenue directly; rather it is intended to force distributions which will be taxable to shareholders at their individual rates. Even a corporation which becomes subject to personal holding company tax can avoid it subsequently through the deficiency dividend procedure.[7] Therefore, the 70 per cent rate is adequate for its purpose to be sufficiently high to compel distributions, and so long as the personal holding company tax remains a tax on the

[6]Since taxable income permits the deduction for intercorporate dividends while undistributed personal holding company income, to which the personal holding company tax applies, does not, the difference in over-all effective rates would be slight where dividends constitute the bulk of the income and the shareholder's marginal rate is 70 per cent.
[7]Sec. 547.

corporation (as distinguished from taxing personal holding company income directly to shareholders as in the case of foreign personal holding companies), there is no reason, nor is it feasible, to complicate it to extract only the exact tax payable as if distributions had been made.

Stock Ownership

In order to be a personal holding company, Section 542(a)(2) provides that:

"At any time during the last half of the taxable year more than 50 per cent in value of its outstanding stock is owned, directly or indirectly, by or for not more than 5 individuals."

This has been the provision since the 1934 Act, except that since 1954 certain exempt organizations and charitable trusts have been treated as individuals to prevent avoidance of the stock ownership rules through a donor controlled foundation.[8] Thus if there are nine or fewer individual stockholders, more than 50 per cent of the stock will be owned by five or fewer individuals. If there are ten or more individuals owning stock or a stockholder is a corporation, trust, estate or partnership, the attribution rules of Section 544 must be applied. In addition, under that section certain convertible securities are treated as stock. These rules have remained unchanged in substance since 1937.

The stock ownership test seems to have worked satisfactorily in the personal holding company area. Aside from some general criticism of the complexity of the attribution rules of the Code,[9] there has been no particular movement by either the Treasury or taxpayers to change the rules.

It is unlikely that a corporation with more than nine equal stockholders after application of attribution rules would be able to operate an investment company to accumulate income in avoidance of shareholder taxes. The requirement of diverse ownership among so many families would make it difficult to manage a corporation with the unity of accumulation purpose required. Nor does it seem appropriate to ease the stock ownership requirement, certainly so long as a corporation must be so essentially passive in order to meet the gross income test.

Gross Income

Even if a corporation meets the stock ownership test, as most corporations do, it will not be a personal holding company unless at least 60 per cent of its adjusted ordinary gross income is personal holding company income. Personal holding company income is defined in detail and embraces various kinds of normally passive investment income and some special items of personal service income.

Originally under the 1934 Act a corporation was not a personal holding company unless at least 80 per cent of its gross income was derived from royalties, dividends, interest, annuities or except for a regular dealer, gains from the sale of stock

[8]Query whether this can be avoided by transfers to multiple foundations created by the same donor. See, Greenfield, "Personal Holding Company Dangers and How to Meet Them," (1955) Proceedings New York University 13th Annual Institute on Federal Taxation 823, 837.

[9]See, Ringel, Surrey, and Warren, "Attribution of Stock Ownership in the Internal Revenue Code," (1958) 72 Harvard Law Review 209.

or securities. The 1937 Act continued the 80 per cent requirement, adding a number of categories of personal holding company income, and provided that once caught as a personal holding company for any year under the 80 per cent test, the gross income test was reduced to 70 per cent for subsequent years until the stock ownership requirement was not met for the last half of a taxable year or three consecutive years followed with less than 70 per cent personal holding company income. The additional 70 per cent test for a corporation once tainted was eliminated by the 1954 Act and the 1964 Act retains a single percentage regardless of prior personal holding company status.

The 1964 change in the percentage test is significant in two respects: the reduction of the percentage of personal holding company income from 80 per cent to 60 per cent and the use of "adjusted ordinary gross income" as the base rather than "gross income." Personal holding company income still includes dividends, interest, royalties and annuities; the principal changes are to eliminate capital gains altogether and to make adjustments in gross rents and gross mineral, oil and gas royalties to eliminate deductions for depreciation, depletion, property taxes, interest and rent paid.

The 60 Per Cent Test

The old percentage test was liberal and easy to avoid. A corporation had to have nonpersonal holding company income only slightly more than 20 per cent of its gross income to shelter the balance of its portfolio income. Thus numerous cases were discovered of dividends being sheltered by fairly inactive businesses which produced little or no profit but enough gross income to shelter up to four times as much personal holding company income. One of the more startling cases was the telephone answering service which predictably produced gross income of about $100,000 a year but had equally predictable expenses somewhat in excess of that. It was acquired for a nominal investment because it was not capable of producing any real profit; yet it was able to shelter gross income of up to $400,000 from dividends taxable at intercorporate dividend rates and from a portfolio at a 4 per cent yield of $10,000,000.

Even at the new 60 per cent test a nominal investment in a telephone answering service with $100,000 of gross income can shelter up to $150,000 of dividend income from $3,750,000 of portfolio.

Quite obviously in situations like the telephone answering service, even the 60 per cent test is unduly liberal. What about the 60 per cent test in other situations? Suppose a genuine manufacturing operation which has a bad year. Its gross receipts are not its gross income;[10] if its cost of goods sold approaches its gross receipts, and if it has other income from interest and dividends, it may be caught as a personal

---

[10]Treas. Reg. Sec. 1.542-2 points out that gross income is not necessarily synonymous with gross receipts. It refers to Section 61 and the regulations thereunder for a definition of gross income. The most serious difficulties in defining gross income arise in cases involving reimbursement for expenses and computation of cost of goods sold. See Maloney, "What is a Personal Holding Company?" (1951) Proceedings New York University 9th Annual Institute on Federal Taxation 745, 747 et seq.; Levine, "Gross Income in the Personal Holding Company," (1954) 9 Tax Law Review 453.

holding company. This, of course, was possible under the 80 per cent test; under the 60 per cent test the area of danger is increased. If the other income is rents or royalties, the proportion of adjusted ordinary gross income might change to qualify the rents or royalties as nonpersonal holding company income (more than 50 per cent of adjusted ordinary gross income) and this would automatically satisfy the requirement of more than 40 per cent nonpersonal holding company income. Where the other income is all interest or dividends, or interest or dividends mixed with rentals, or rentals and royalties mixed, the decline in nonpersonal holding company income could conceivably change the normal percentage ratios so that the corporation becomes a personal holding company.

How serious is the problem? Is it so likely to arise as to call the 60 per cent test into question? If the over-all operation of the corporation is at a loss (disregarding the dividends received deduction), there would be no undistributed personal holding company income and hence no problem. If there is over-all income but a loss from operations, the corporation can avoid tax by making a distribution of its personal holding company income equal to its over-all profit (disregarding the intercorporate dividend deduction). If there is a small profit from operations, but not enough *gross* income to equal 40 per cent of adjusted ordinary gross, a larger distribution would be needed. It is unlikely that any such distributions would strain corporate resources. Since portfolio investments usually are capitalized at 20 to 25 times earnings and investments in businesses which are uncertain enough to have fluctuations producing this problem are hardly ever capitalized at more than six times average earnings, any corporation facing the problem would have an unusually large investment portfolio in relation to its capital investment in operating assets. Not only could it likely make the distribution required without strain, but one would suspect the large portfolio investment is good evidence that the corporation was at least partially used to avoid tax at the shareholder level.

If the income extrinsic to the primary business operation is rental or royalty, it could be separately incorporated as a subsidiary so as always to avoid personal holding company income classification under the 50 per cent test.

The conclusion is, therefore, that the 60 per cent test sets a minimum fair percentage allowing most of the gross income to be portfolio income and an overwhelming proportion of the capital investment to be portfolio type and will not interfere with normal conduct of business operations.

Use of Adjusted Ordinary Gross Income

The 60 per cent is applied to adjusted ordinary gross income; the old 80 per cent test applied to gross income. The first difference is that capital gains are eliminated entirely from both sides of the equation.

The 1934 Act included in the tainted income for the 80 per cent test gains from the sale of stock or securities (except in the case of regular dealers). The 1937 Act added gains from future transactions in commodities unless part of bona fide hedging operations by producers or handlers of the commodity which were necessary to the conduct of the business. Presumably these inclusions were based on the notion that this is the sort of income likely to be derived by incorporated pocketbooks and they were originally included at a time when corporate capital gains did not receive different treatment from corporate ordinary income. Although these capital gains continued until the 1964 Act to be considered as personal holding company income in classifying a corporation as a personal holding company, the alternative tax introduced in 1942 for corporations applied in lieu of personal holding company tax as well as corporate normal tax and surtax. Since 1954 undistributed personal holding company income has been reduced by the excess of net long-term capital gain over net short-term capital loss so that capital gains are never subjected to the penalty tax even if not distributed.

Since capital gains other than from security and commodity future transactions were not personal holding company income, a capital gain could be realized on some other asset, such as Section 1231 real estate, which would raise the percentage of nonpersonal holding company income to permit shelter of portfolio investment. By spreading such a capital gain over many years under the installment method, a long-term shelter without business risk was possible.[11]

By excluding capital gains altogether from the gross income test under the 1964 Act, capital gains from the sale of Section 1231 property on the installment method can no longer be used as part of the active income side of the ledger to shelter personal holding company income for many years following a sale; neither will a casual sale of stock or securities at a large capital gain be treated as personal holding company income to throw a corporation into personal holding company status. Because long-term capital gains are taxed at the same maximum rate to corporations and individuals, they do not raise a problem of corporate shelter. It is fair that neither benefit nor burden results from this special type of income.

The second difference which the use of adjusted ordinary gross income introduces is the requirement of adjustments to both the over-all income to which the 60 per cent test applies and the items which are included as personal holding company income.

The adjustments apply to reduce gross income from rents, mineral income and, in limited situations, interest income. Gross rents are reduced by depreciation (with an exception designed to cover rentals from short-term leases of cars and other equipment),[12] property taxes, interest paid allocable to the property leased and rent paid. Similarly mineral, oil and gas royalty gross income is reduced by deductions for depreciation and depletion, property and severance taxes, interest and rent. The same reductions apply to income from working interests in an oil or gas well even though such income is not personal holding company income in any case. There is eliminated from adjusted ordinary gross income and hence personal holding company income, interest received on a condemnation award, judgment or tax refund and certain interest received by dealers who make a primary market in United States Government Bonds.

[11]See for example Case IV, Exhibit 11 submitted by Secretary Dillon to the Ways and Means Committee, February 6, 1963, Hearings Before the Ways and Means Committee on President's 1963 Tax Message, Part 1, 356.

[12]Sec. 543(b)(2)(A)(i). In this situation depreciation is apt to be an unusually high percentage of gross income and the degree of risk and activity so high, that it is unlikely to serve as a shelter, at least not with the same ease as real estate.

The adjustments were intended to make the measurement of the percentage of personal holding company income as applied to total income a more accurate measure of the activity of the corporation — to determine whether in fact it was simply a shelter for investment type income or truly engaged in an active business enterprise.

For example, evidence was adduced that working interests in oil and gas wells were being used to shelter dividend and interest income. The working interests had been purchased with a knowledge of the oil and gas in place so the income was predictable with little risk. Of course, the extraction activity was carried on by an agent. Since the income from a working interest is not royalty income, but non-personal holding company income, only slightly over 20 per cent of gross was needed to shelter large dividend investment income.[13] It was thought than an analogy to manufacturing or mercantile corporations would require reductions from gross income to be equivalent to the reduction from gross receipts by the cost of goods sold. In essence, depletion and property and severance taxes represent the cost of producing the oil and gas for sale. Certainly these costs are at least as, and usually much more, predictable than those of the manufacturing company and hence there is no reason why a corporation whose income is derived from working interests needs to maintain relatively greater passive reserves in the form of investment portfolio than a manufacturing company.

The adjustments to rents and royalties have a similar justification. Depreciation in the case of a real estate corporation is the cost of the property sold to produce its gross receipts. The adjustments also prevent a corporation from avoiding personal holding company status through inflating its gross income to a point where gross rentals are more than 50 per cent of total gross income. Wash items, such as rent paid under a sublease arrangement whereby the holding company simply acts as an intervening lessee to inflate its gross rentals, are eliminated. Thus, a much greater proportion of rental activity to total income is required to meet the 50 per cent test if rentals or royalties are to be treated as nonpersonal holding company income.

It should be noted, however, that for a corporation which has less than 50 per cent of its income from rentals or royalties, the "adjusted ordinary gross income" concept makes it easier to meet the over-all 60 per cent test. A corporation which has some incidental rental income will be charged only with adjusted rentals as personal holding company income, and while the denominator of the fraction:

$$\frac{\text{personal holding company income}}{\text{adjusted ordinary gross income}}$$

is smaller, the equivalent decrease in the numerator more than offsets this. For example, using the old measuring rod of gross income, a corporation with $35,000 of gross operating income, $25,000 of dividends and $40,000 of gross rentals would have $65,000 personal holding company income out of $100,000 gross income. Under

---

[13]See, for example, the testimony on behalf of Broseco Corp. and the colloquy with Senator Douglas, Hearings Before Sen. Finance Committee, 88th Cong., 1st Sess., on H.R. 8363, part 5, pp. 2109 ff.

the 1964 Act, if the adjusted rentals are $20,000 the personal holding company income is $45,000 and the adjusted ordinary gross income is $80,000, so that the personal holding company income falls below 60 per cent.

The adjustments to interest can also constitute a liberalization. By and large they eliminate interest items not usually in the control of the recipient and hence have been eliminated from both parts of the fraction in measuring personal holding company status.

The Criteria Used to Classify Items as Personal Holding Company Income

In defining what is personal holding company income Congress has generally sought to classify those sorts of income which are not derived from the active conduct of a business and which do not involve risks requiring incorporation. There is in the usual case no non-tax reason why they ought not to be received directly by the shareholder rather than his corporation. Hence dividends, interest, royalties (other than mineral, oil or gas royalties and copyright royalties), and annuities are clearly personal holding company income[14] and have been since the 1934 Act.

[14]Some justification exists for an amendment to exclude dividends from controlled operating subsidiaries from being considered as personal holding company income. It might be appropriate to accomplish this by permitting an electing affiliated group (perhaps as defined in new Section 243(b)(5)) even though not filing a consolidated return, to file a consolidated personal holding company return under the conditions of Section 542(b). That section denies the privilege of consolidation for personal holding company purposes if any member of the affiliated group derives 10 per cent or more of its adjusted ordinary gross income from outside sources and if 80 per cent of such amount is personal holding company income. For this purpose dividends of the common parent from a nonpersonal holding company which it controls (more than 50 per cent) are not personal holding company income. The restriction on personal holding company income derived from outside sources is to prevent the owner of an operating business from separately incorporating his portfolio and avoiding personal holding company status through consolidation without subjecting the portfolio to the risks of the operating business. This is good evidence that there is no need to use the corporate form for holding the portfolio. If all of the personal holding company income — dividends, interest, rent or royalties — is derived from intercorporate transactions within an affiliated group, the accumulated earnings tax should be relied upon to curb abuse. Personal holding company status should not arise merely because income is shifted among members of the same corporate group.

Incidentally, the 80 per cent requirement of Section 542(b)(2)(B) should probably have been changed to 60 per cent in keeping with the basic change in the gross income test. For example, a taxpayer with a personal holding company which met the former 80 per cent test but not the new 60 per cent test could avoid the new test by acquiring an operating subsidiary and filing a consolidated return. The portfolio investment in the personal holding company will not be at the risk of the operating business and although both corporations will have more than 10 per cent of their income from outside sources, in neither will 80 per cent of that amount be personal holding company income. True the owners to avoid personal holding company status must acquire additional operating income (if not already available), but not by placing their portfolio at the risk of such operating business. The 10 per cent test of Section 542(b)(2)(A) could be liberalized so long as the test of Section 542(b)(2)(B) is set at 60 per cent and if the intercorporate dividends (Section 542(b)(4)) are excluded from adjusted ordinary gross income for this purpose. In that way aside from intercorporate dividends, no member of the affiliated group could be a personal holding company and the effect would be merely to prevent intercorporate transactions within the same group from causing personal holding company liability. See Committee Reports accompanying the Internal Revenue Code of 1954, House Rept. No. 1337, 83d Cong., 2d Sess., p. 55; Sen. Rept. No. 1622, 83d Cong., 2d Sess., p. 73.

Income from personal services of a taxpayer should not be insulated from personal taxation by purely formal corporate intervention. The same is true in cases where income is shunted to a corporation from its shareholder for use of corporate property, where there is evidence that the arrangement is purely a shelter for portfolio investment.

Rentals from real property involve an area where there are legitimate reasons for incorporation to limit liability, yet this sort of income can in many cases be derived from investment requiring no operational talent and with no need to maintain a large portfolio for working capital. Hence, there are rules which permit accumulation in the corporate shelter if the bulk of the income is from that activity and if the rentals are not used to shelter other passive income. Mineral, oil and gas royalties have been analogized to rentals with more dubious justification.

Finally some sorts of income are personal holding company income unless in addition to constituting the bulk of the corporate income, and not being used to shelter other passive income, there are sufficient expenses incurred to indicate activity, for example, copyright royalties.

Since the personal holding company provisions are designed to force distributions in the clearest cases of avoidance, leaving to the subjective tests of Section 531 the cases which require a more flexible treatment, mechanical rules are required. A test such as that in Section 954(c)(3) excluding rents derived in the active conduct of a trade or business would not work in the personal holding company area because of its uncertainty. Taxpayers need to know as much as possible within the taxable year where they stand because the penalty tax is so severe and it is neither in their interest nor that of the government to encourage litigation to define what is "active."

In a number of situations what is passive income to most taxpayers is clearly properly attributable to an active business which ought not to be deprived of its ability to operate in corporate form merely because it is closely held. Hence, instead of excepting interest and dividends derived from the active conduct of a trade or business, the statute preserves certainty by excepting certain corporations — banks, insurance companies, finance companies, etc. — which derive income from interest and dividends. In such cases the interest and dividends are clearly related to the principal business activity and not simply sheltered income for the shareholders. To qualify for exemption as a finance company, a subjective test of "active business" must be met, but it is reinforced by requiring that the finance company have certain minimum business expenses as evidence of activity and by permitting the finance company to receive only limited passive income of other sorts so that the operating income from interest cannot shelter other personal holding company income.

Kinds of Personal Holding Income

Section 543(a) now lists the items of adjusted ordinary gross income which constitute personal holding company income. Those other than rentals may be briefly summarized.

Paragraph 1 specifies dividends, interest, royalties (other than mineral, oil or gas royalties or copyright royalties) as personal holding company income. Those corporations receiving interest as part of an active business such as banks and finance companies are excepted from classification as personal holding companies as noted above. Certain special kinds of interest are excluded in determining adjusted ordinary gross income as well as personal holding company income, also as noted above.

Paragraph 2 deals with rents and deserves more extended treatment below.

Paragraph 3 includes mineral, oil and gas royalties. The 1937 Act added an exception to eliminate such royalties from personal holding company income if they constituted at least 50 per cent of gross income and if trade or business expenses under Section 23(a) of the 1939 Code (Section 162, 1954 Code) other than compensation for services of shareholders constituted at least 15 per cent of gross income.

The 1964 Act modifies the tests to qualify as excepted mineral, oil and gas royalties. The 50 per cent test applies to the ratio of adjusted mineral, oil and gas royalties to adjusted ordinary gross income; there is a new requirement that other personal holding company income including rents not exceed 10 per cent of ordinary gross income; and the Section 162 deductions usable in measuring the 15 per cent minimum business expenses to show activity are those allowable only under Section 162 (thus excluding interest, taxes and depreciation).

The 15 per cent business expense test is not a particularly sensible one as drafted originally and as continued since it does not require the expenses to be related to the production of the royalty income.[15] Hence, it has little value as an indicium that the royalties are derived from a business activity. The 10 per cent test added in 1964, however, helps insure that mineral, oil and gas royalties may not shelter an excessive amount of other passive income. The 10 per cent test applies absolutely to mineral, oil and gas royalties — if the other passive income exceeds the 10 per cent amount, all the mineral, oil and gas royalties become personal holding company income, even if the other passive income in excess of the 10 per cent is distributed. Such a distribution would avoid the personal holding company taint in the case of rents. There is, however, no particular need for an escape hatch in this area, since the need to maintain large portfolio reserves does not exist. In the rental area there is some need for reserves because of financing arrangements, requirements to maintain the property, etc.

Subparagraph 4 contains an exception to permit copyright royalties received by music publishers to be classified as nonpersonal holding company income. As added in 1959 copyright royalties do not constitute personal holding company income if they are 50 per cent or more of gross income, the Section 162 deductions (other than compensation and royalties paid to shareholders) constitute at least 50 per cent of gross income and the sheltered income is not more than 10 per cent of gross income.[16] This paragraph was slightly modified in the 1964 Act to perfect the tests originally designed.[17]

---

[15]See Paul, "The Background of the Revenue Act of 1937," 5 University of Chicago Law Review 41, 63 (1937).

[16]Certain dividends from subsidiaries which themselves derive income from copyright royalties which qualify under paragraph 4 as derived in an active business are not treated

The 1964 Act added a new category of personal holding company income —
produced film rents where less than 50 per cent of ordinary gross income. Prior to
1964 all film rentals were classified along with ordinary rentals — not personal holding company income if total rentals were at least 50 per cent of gross income. The
1964 Act added a provision that purchased film rentals — amounts received from
the distribution and exhibition of a film negative acquired after substantial completion — are to be treated as copyright royalties. Purchased film rentals are thus subjected to the more stringent tests limiting other sheltered personal holding company
income to 10 per cent of ordinary gross and requiring substantial related business
expense deductions. On the other hand, produced film rentals — where the interest
in the film was acquired before substantial completion — were separated from ordinary rentals and left as nonpersonal holding company income if at least 50 per cent
of ordinary gross income.

The small likelihood of a purchased film rental being used as a shelter would
not seem to justify the distinction from produced film rentals. It would have been
better to put all film rentals under paragraph 2 which applies to rentals generally,
or failing that, to preserve the pre-1964 treatment of paragraph 5 for all film rentals.

Paragraph 6 originated in the 1937 Act. It treats as personal holding company
income amounts received for the use of property of a corporation from a 25 per cent
or greater stockholder. The abuse was the incorporated yacht. A shareholder would
incorporate his portfolio and along with it, his yacht or country residence and pay
rental for the use of the yacht or residence to the corporation. The rental would thus
shelter dividends and interest from the portfolio.

The statute applies whether the shareholder obtains the right to use the property
directly or by sublease or other arrangement. This language has been construed to
apply to all sorts of indirect use of the property. Thus if a corporation leases property to another corporation and both are owned by the same shareholder, the shareholder has been held to be using the property through his lessee corporation and the
rental would be personal holding company income to the lessor.[18] The saving feature in the situation of the bona fide business lease between related corporations is
provided by a 1954 amendment which prevents application of the paragraph unless
the corporation has other nonrental personal holding company income in excess of
10 per cent of gross income (now "ordinary gross income"). Thus if there is no
sheltered income, Section 543(a)(6) will not be a problem. However, if there is
dividend or interest income over 10 per cent of ordinary gross income, a distribution
of the passive income alone will not help.

In addition, in determining undistributed personal holding company income,
the base to which the personal holding company tax applies, business expenses

---

as personal holding company income to the parent for this 10 per cent test, but copyright
royalties for the use of works created by more than 10 per cent shareholders are so treated.

[17]The Section 162 deductions must constitute 25 per cent of ordinary gross income minus
royalties paid and depreciation with respect to royalties, instead of 50 per cent of gross
income, but only exclusively Section 162 deductions count. See Section 543(a)(4)(C).

[18]320 East 47th St. Corp. v. Commissioner, 57-1 USTC ¶9576, 243 F.2d 894, (CA-2 1957).
Contra Minnesota Mortuaries, Inc., CCH Dec. 14,209, 4 TC 280 (1944), acq. 1945 CB 5.

and depreciation allocable to the operation of corporate property[19] may not exceed the rental from the property unless the taxpayer establishes that the rent received was the highest available, that the property was held in the course of business carried on bona fide for profit and that either there was reasonable expectation that operation of the property would result in a profit or that the property was necessary to the conduct of the business.[20] Thus excessive deductions cannot shelter dividend income from tax, even where the classification of the rental from property used by the shareholder as personal holding company income is not a serious hurdle to the corporation because the rentals do not produce net income.

Paragraph 7 was also added by the 1937 Act to deal with the incorporated talent device. If the corporation is to furnish personal services under a contract and if the services are required to be performed by a 25 per cent or more stockholder (directly or indirectly) either by the terms of the contract or by designation of someone other than the corporation furnishing the services, the payments are personal holding company income. The provision was originally aimed at actors, cartoonists and the like who incorporated their services to avoid high individual rates and to obtain capital gains rates on liquidation. It can also apply, however, to corporations performing services of all kinds, such as engineering and technical services, where the party performing the services is designated by the purchaser.[21] Should professional service corporations succeed in establishing taxability as corporations, many of them might find this section troublesome where the client or patient seeks the services of a particular corporate employee lawyer or physician.

Paragraph 8 includes as personal holding company income amounts to be taken up as a corporate beneficiary of an estate or trust. It has been carried from the Revenue Act of 1937, where it was added to preclude the argument that gross income from a trust or estate was not personal holding company income. Sections 652(b) and 661(b) of the 1954 Code would now preserve the character of income distributed to the beneficiary, although the trust instrument can allocate the classes of trust income among the beneficiaries. The instrument creating a trust with both individual and corporate beneficiaries and which has some operating income could still allocate the operating income to a corporate beneficiary, which in essence is the same as a passive investor receiving dividends. Hence the provision is still necessary, and in fact ought to be expanded to include the similar situation of a corporation which is a limited partner.

The 1964 Act eliminated two kinds of personal holding company income which before 1964 had been so regarded in applying the 80 per cent test: gains from the sale of stock or securities and commodities futures. The rationale has been stated above. The elimination of all capital gains in applying the 60 per cent income test of personal holding company status is fair since capital gains income gains no advantage by receipt in the corporate entity. Since it is usually sporadic

[19]This applies to any corporate property, not just that leased to 25 per cent or more shareholders.

[20]Sec. 545(b)(8).

[21]General Management Corp. v. Commissioner, 43-1 USTC ¶9447, 135 F.2d 882, (CA-7); Rev. Rul. 54-34, 1954-1 CB 175 (insurance agency).

and hence less predictable, the tighter tests applicable to rents and the permissible percentage of personal holding company income should be relied upon to accomplish their aim of classifying the appropriate corporations as personal holding companies, rather than the haphazard receipt of capital gains not in themselves used to avoid individual taxes.

Rents

The original personal holding company provisions of the 1934 Act did not include rents as personal holding company income. Thus by generating gross rents which constituted over 20 per cent of gross income, it was easy to avoid personal holding company status.

A rent roll is comparatively easy to acquire to avoid personal holding company status. Most taxpayers would hesitate to invest in an unfamiliar mercantile business simply to avoid personal holding company status. This is not true of real estate, since most business persons have some experience with it. In view of the availability of mortgage financing, a large investment is not needed. Also the owner can readily and safely employ agents to manage the property for him. This is not easy in the case of a mercantile operation. Thus the most serious avoidance of personal holding company status has been through rentals.

The 1937 Act recognized this by classifying rentals as personal holding company income unless they constituted 50 per cent or more of gross income. The purpose of the 50 per cent rule was to permit a bona fide real estate operation to be conducted in corporate form. The 50 per cent rule, however, did not prevent the widespread use of gross rents to shelter portfolio income. The evidence submitted by the Treasury Department showed that this practice was widespread even among taxpayers with comparatively low incomes.[22]

During the consideration of H.R. 8363 it was suggested that the statute should differentiate between active rentals and passive rentals, the former being treated in all respects as nonpersonal holding company income and the latter in all respects as personal holding company income.

This was rejected for several reasons. First, it is impossible to define active rentals in a meaningful way to preserve the required degree of certainty in this area. Gearing it to a ratio of Section 162 deductions to gross income is not satisfactory. A net lease of $1,000,000 per year can easily be revised to provide for rental of $1,100,000 with a provision that the lessor will provide services up to $100,000 per year. There are so many kinds of rental property that any percentage measure of activity is too crude a yardstick.

Second, by and large, the risks inherent in rental property do not require the same portfolio reserves as other business. The ease of acquiring rent rolls with a small investment and of acquiring management makes even an active rental business a different animal from the ordinary operating business. There is no need to allow rentals to shelter an equivalent amount of dividend and interest income. The 1964 Act prevents the use of rentals to shelter dividends and interest

[22]H. Rept. No. 1546, 75th Cong., 1st Sess., (1937), 1939-1 CB (Part 2) 704, 707.

in excess of 10 per cent of gross income. A return of 15 per cent in gross rentals on original investment (a conservative figure) and a return of 4 per cent on portfolio means that if the 50 per cent test is met, close to 30 per cent of capital can be invested in assets producing personal holding company income without classification as a personal holding company under the 10 per cent test. This would seem a sufficient reserve in any case.

The 1964 Act changed the 50 per cent test to require that the adjusted rents be at least 50 per cent of the adjusted ordinary gross income. As indicated above, this is helpful to the non-real estate corporation, but it requires a real estate corporation to use a more realistic measure to show a preponderance of real estate activity. Second, the 1964 Act added a new test, that the other personal holding company income (including for this purpose all copyright royalties and the adjusted income from mineral, oil and gas royalties, but not compensation from a shareholder for use of corporate property) in excess of 10 per cent of gross income be distributed. If both tests are met, the rentals are not personal holding company income and the corporation is not a personal holding company. If either is failed the rents become personal holding company income and if the cause of failure is the 10 per cent test, the combination of at least 50 per cent rentals and 10 per cent other personal holding company income will make the corporation a personal holding company. Thus a real estate corporation cannot use rentals to shelter more than a modest amount of portfolio income; however, if rentals drop unexpectedly so that the portfolio income exceeds the 10 per cent, the corporation can purge itself by a distribution within two and one-half months after the close of its taxable year not of all its income, but only the amount necessary to meet the test. Thus the required distribution, as long as the 50 per cent test has been met, will never be more than a portion of the nonrental personal holding company income.

The new rental provisions should work successfully in curbing the principal abuse in the personal holding company area, the real estate corporation sheltering portfolio income. At the same time the introduction of the pay-out concept to eliminate personal holding company status where a distribution of excessive portfolio income is made should avoid hardship to bona fide operating corporations.

The 50 per cent side of the rental test can lead to anomalous results in some situations, however. It is possible that a corporation by increasing its active business can become a personal holding company. Suppose a corporation with adjusted rentals of $50,000, dividends of $20,000 and mercantile income of $30,000. Assuming distributions which keep dividend income to no more than 10 per cent of gross income, the rentals are not personal holding company income and the corporation clearly is not a personal holding company. If the mercantile income increases to $40,000, however, the rentals cease to equal 50 per cent of adjusted ordinary gross income and, when added to the dividends, make the personal holding company income exceed 60 per cent of adjusted ordinary gross income. Thus by increasing its active income, the corporation has become a personal holding company. This result could be prevented and at the same time the rules as to rentals could be simplified by substituting a single test for the present dual test applied to rentals. Under such a test rentals would not be personal holding company income unless the corporation had other undistributed personal holding company income in excess of 20 or 25 per cent of adjusted ordinary gross income. This would allow rentals from a highly passive net lease to be non-personal holding company income, but that is true under the 50 per cent test. The chief object of including rentals in personal holding company income is to prevent their use as a shelter for other passive income. The suggested single test would accomplish that result more simply than present law and perhaps more effectively since the allowable percentage of undistributed income would be based upon adjusted ordinary gross, rather than ordinary gross income without adjustment.

Over-all Evaluation

The personal holding company rules as refined over 30 years of experience have evolved from a simple, but ineffective set of provisions to prevent tax avoidance, to a complex melange as each taxpayer parry has been met with legislative riposte. Undoubtedly the 1964 changes will not eliminate all unwarranted tax avoidance, but they seem to have dampened considerably the chief avenues of escape. As indicated above more basic reforms such as eliminating the stepped-up basis at death and multiple surtax exemptions would take a major share of the profit out of the use of the holding company as a pure tax minimization device.

Some refinement here and there as has been indicated in this paper at various places might help simplify in places and plug small leaks in others. Nevertheless, the provisions should work well without undue deterrence to properly motivated business activities. Extremely liberal transition provisions, to facilitate liquidation of pre-existing corporations affected by the new rules, and permitting continuance to amortize pre-existing debts, will more than prevent hardship to those who have had the advantage of conducting affairs right up to the line for many years.

It may be worth exploration of the idea of extending the new pay-out concept for excess passive income in the rental area to the basic 60 per cent test itself — that is, if passive income in excess of 10 per cent of adjusted ordinary gross income has been distributed (in the current year, or perhaps on the average over three years) the corporation which fails the gross income test in a particular year would not be affected adversely. With such a rule the 60 per cent test itself could be lowered. On the other hand introduction of new complexities should await a period of experience with the 1964 provisions.

Another idea which might be explored is the one suggested 25 years ago by Harry Rudick[23] that the undistributed income of a personal holding company be taxed directly to its shareholders currently. This would permit a consolidation of the personal holding company and foreign personal holding company provisions, eliminate the deficiency dividend provisions and adjust the penalty to the appropriate one for each stockholder. The historic constitutional fear of disregarding the corporate entity would seem to be no longer a serious problem in the light of the 1962 Act. On the other hand, such a solution would introduce new problems of basis and treatment of distributions. At the same time subchapter S privileges

[23]Cited at footnote 1, at [page 930 supra].

could be extended to corporations receiving personal holding company income. This could be done if no deductions were permitted for pensions and other employee fringe benefits to owner-managers of such corporations and if certain technical provisions to prevent one shot abuses through pass through of losses and capital gains were adopted.

One can expect a settling period as far as personal holding companies are concerned. Here and there Congress will move to correct an unintended hardship and the Treasury may at the same time, induce the elimination of an unintended loophole. By and large, however, the first major changes since 1937 will require a considerable period of experience before radical overhaul is in order.

NOTE

1. Usually a shareholder who owns a personal holding company has come into that situation unwittingly. It is rare, but not entirely uncommon, that a shareholder will own a personal holding company as a matter of choice. The following describes a situation in which a shareholder might choose to have his corporation become a personal holding company.

At age 65 the sole shareholder of a manufacturing corporation decides to accept a $1 million offer for the business. The basis of his stock is $200,000. The corporation's aggregate basis for its assets is $800,000. The shareholder wishes to avoid all further active business dealings and to invest his money exclusively in income-producing marketable securities. A sale of stock, or a corporate sale of assets followed by liquidation under §337, will produce a taxable capital gain of $800,000. A corporate sale of assets, with gain recognized at the corporate level, will produce a capital gain of only $200,000 and no shareholder gain if the corporation stays alive. If the latter approach is adopted the corporation will have substantially more after-tax funds for investment than otherwise. If it invests in marketable stocks and bonds alone, it will be a personal holding company. Nevertheless, if it invests in bonds that are tax-exempt under §103, it will not have to distribute the interest income to avoid §541. If it invests in stocks whose dividends are subject to the §243 dividends received deduction, distribution of the net (after-tax) dividend income will be required. The corporate tax will be very small, however, and the shareholder will receive substantially all the income he would have received if he had invested in stocks directly and personally. (The personal holding company will avoid investing in corporate bonds because the interest income would be fully taxable to the corporation, and distribution would be required to avoid the §541 tax.) Because no sum equivalent to the individual capital gains tax was paid, there will be more for the corporation to invest than the shareholder would have had if he had sold the corporation's stock or had employed §337. If he keeps the personal holding company alive until his death, his estate can effect liquidation of the corporation under §331 without incurring any tax at the shareholder level because of the step-up in the basis of the stock provided by §1014.

2. See generally K. Liles, A New Look at Personal Holding Company Problems: The New Rules of the 1964 Act, 24 N.Y.U. Inst. on Fed. Tax. 863 (1966); A. Feder, Relieving the Impact of the Revenue Act of 1964 on "New" Personal Holding Companies, 23 N.Y.U. Inst. on Fed. Tax. 723 (1965); M. Shapiro, Personal Holding Companies and the Revenue Act of 1964, 63 Mich. L. Rev. 421 (1965).

9 | The Corporate Identity – Special Problems

I. CORPORATION VEL NON — §7701(a)(3); TREAS. REG. §§301.7701-1 TO 301.7701-4

A corporation is a corporation is a corporation, but what constitutes a corporation for federal income tax purposes is not always clear. The Code does not define "corporation," but §7701(a)(3) tells us that it "includes associations, joint stock companies, and insurance companies." In their effort to explain what "partnership" includes, §§7701(a)(2) and 761(a) provide that "partnership" does not include a trust, estate or corporation. "Trust" and "estate" are undefined. The fact that "corporation" includes "associations" evidences the Congressional intent to have the term "corporation" embrace groups which may not bear the label of, or be recognized for non-tax purposes as, corporations.

Generally, there is no difficulty in determining whether an organization is a trust, estate, partnership or corporation. In most cases the characterization applicable under state law, as selected by the parties, will be apt for tax purposes. That is not always the case, however, and where it is not the stakes may be high. More often than not, where the issue is raised the question is whether a trust under state law is to be treated as a corporation under the Code, or whether a partnership is to be so treated. Recently, the question has also been raised whether corporations organized under state laws applicable only to professionals (e.g., lawyers and doctors) might be treated as taxpayers other than corporations, i.e., as partnerships or individual proprietors.

When the Commissioner seeks to treat a trust or partnership as a corporation, his purpose is usually to impose the corporate tax under §11(a), particularly after the entity has distributed its earnings and the individual income tax on the "dividend" will also accrue, or perhaps to prevent the pass-through of losses. When the taxpayers urge corporate status and the Commissioner resists, the taxpayers are usually seeking special tax benefits (like those available under "qualified" pension and profit sharing plans) which are available to "employees" of corporations (even when they are also the shareholders), but are not available to "partners" (even partners who work for the partnership). See generally B. Bittker and J. Eustice, Federal Income Taxation of Corporations and Shareholders 27-41 (2d ed. 1966).

MORRISSEY v. COMMISSIONER
296 U.S. 344 (1935), aff'g 74 F.2d 803 (9th Cir. 1935)

Mr. Chief Justice HUGHES delivered the opinion of the Court. Petitioners, the trustees of an express trust, contest income taxes for the years 1924 to 1926, inclusive, upon the ground that the trust has been illegally treated as an "association." . . . We granted certiorari because of a conflict of decisions as to the distinction between an "association" and a "pure trust," the decisions being described in one of the cases as "seemingly in a hopeless state of confusion." Coleman-Gilbert Associates v. Commissioner, 76 F.(2d) 191, 193.

The facts were stipulated. In the year 1921 petitioners made a declaration of trust of real estate in Los Angeles. They were to be designated in "their collective capacity" as "Western Avenue Golf Club." The trustees were authorized to add to their number and to choose their successors; to purchase, encumber, sell, lease and operate the "described or other lands"; to construct and operate golf courses, club houses, etc.; to receive the rents, profits and income; to make loans and investments; to make regulations; and generally to manage the trust estate as if the trustees were its absolute owners. The trustees were declared to be without powers to bind the beneficiaries personally by "any act, neglect or default," and the beneficiaries and all persons dealing with the trustees were required to look for payment or indemnity to the trust property. The beneficial interests were to be evidenced solely by transferable certificates for shares which were divided into 2,000 preferred shares of the par value of $100 each, and 2,000 common shares of no par value, and the rights of the respective shareholders in the surplus, profits, and capital assets were defined. "Share ledgers" showing the names and addresses of shareholders were to be kept.

The trustees might convene the shareholders in meeting for the purpose of making reports or considering recommendations, but the votes of the shareholders were to be advisory only. The death of a trustee or of a beneficiary was not to end the trust, which was to continue for twenty-five years unless sooner terminated by the trustees.

During the years 1921 and 1922, the trustees sold beneficial interests and paid commissions on the sales. About 42 acres (of the 155 acres described by the declaration of trust) were plotted into lots which were sold during the years 1921 to 1923, most of the sales being on the installment basis. On the remaining property a golf course and club house were constructed, and in 1923 this property with the improvements was conveyed to Western Avenue Golf Club, Inc., a California corporation, in exchange for its stock. Under a lease from the corporation, petitioners continued the operation of the golf course until January 12, 1924. After that date petitioners' activities were confined to collections of installments of principal and interest on contracts of purchase, the receipt of interest on bank balances and of fees on assignments by holders of purchase contracts, the execution of conveyances to purchasers, the receipt of dividends from the incorporated club, and the distribution of moneys to the holders of beneficial interests. On December 31, 1923, the total number of outstanding beneficial interests was 3016, held by 920 persons; by December 31, 1926, the number of interests had been gradually decreased to 2172, held by 275 persons. The holdings by the trustees ranged approximately from 16 to 29 per cent.

Petitioners contend that they are trustees "of property held in trust," within [§641(a)], and are taxable accordingly and not as an "association." They urge that, to constitute an association, the applicable test requires "a quasi-corporate organization in which the beneficiaries, whether or not certificate holders, have some voice in the management and some control over the trustees and have an opportunity to exercise such control through the right to vote at meetings"; and that, in any event, the activities in which petitioners were engaged, during the tax years under consideration, did not constitute "a carrying on of business" within the rule applied by this Court.

The Government insists that the distinction between associations and the trusts taxed under [§641(a)] is between "business trusts on the one side" and other trusts "which are engaged merely in collecting the income and conserving the property against the day when it is to be distributed to the beneficiaries"; that Congress intended that all "business trusts" should be taxed as associations.

[Section 7701(a)(3) provides:]

"The term 'corporation' includes associations, joint-stock companies, and insurance companies." . . .

"Association" implies associates. It implies the entering into a joint enterprise, and, as the applicable regulation imports, an enterprise for the transaction of business. This is not the characteristic of an ordinary trust — whether created by will, deed, or declaration — by which particular property is conveyed to a trustee or is to be held by the settlor, on specified trusts, for the benefit of named or described persons. Such beneficiaries do not ordinarily, and, as mere cestuis que trustent, plan a common effort or enter into a combination for the conduct of a business enterprise. Undoubtedly the terms of an association may make the taking or acquiring of shares of interests sufficient to constitute participation, and may leave the management, or even control of the enterprise, to designated persons. But the nature and purpose of the cooperative undertaking will differentiate it from an ordinary trust. In what are called "business trusts" the object is not to hold and conserve particular property, with incidental powers, as in the traditional type of trusts, but to provide a medium for the conduct of a business and sharing its gains. Thus a trust may be created as a convenient method by which persons become associated for dealings in real estate, the development of tracts of land, the construction of improvements, and the purchase, management and sale of properties; or for dealings in securities or other personal property; or for the production, or manufacture, and sale of commodities; or for commerce, or other sorts of business; where those who become beneficially interested, either by joining in the plan at the outset, or by later participation according to the terms of the arrangement, seek to share the advantages of a union of their interests in the common enterprise.

The Government contends that such an organized community of effort for the doing of business presents the essential features of an association. Petitioners stress the significance of, and the limitations said to be implied in, the provisions classifying associations with corporations.

The inclusion of associations with corporations implies resemblance; but it is resemblance and not identity. The resemblance points to features distinguishing associations from partnerships as well as from ordinary trusts. As we have seen, the classification cannot be said to require organization under a statute, or with statutory privileges. The term embraces associations as they may exist at common law. Hecht v. Malley, 265 U.S. 144 (1924). We have already referred to the definitions, quoted in that case, showing the ordinary meaning of the term as applicable to a body of persons united without a charter "but upon the methods and forms used by incorporated bodies for the prosecution of some common enterprise." These definitions, while helpful, are not to be pressed so far as to make mere formal procedure a controlling test. The provision itself negatives such a construction. Thus unincorporated joint-stock companies have generally been regarded as bearing the closest resemblance to corporations. But, in the revenue acts, associations are mentioned separately and are not to be treated as limited to "joint-stock companies," although belonging to the same group. While the use of corporate forms may furnish persuasive evidence of the existence of an association, the absence of particular forms, or of the usual terminology of corporations, cannot be regarded as decisive. Thus an association may not have "directors" or "officers," but the "trustees" may function "in much the same manner as the directors in a corporation" for the purpose of carrying on the enterprise. The regulatory provisions of the trust instrument may take the place of "bylaws." And as there may be, under the reasoning in the *Hecht* case, an absence of control by beneficiaries such as is commonly exercised by stockholders in a business corporation, it cannot be considered to be essential to the existence of an association that those beneficially interested should hold meetings or elect their representatives. Again, while the faculty of transferring the interests of members without affecting the continuity of the enterprise may be deemed to be characteristic, the test of an association is not to be found in the mere formal evidence of interests or in a particular method of transfer.

What, then, are the salient features of a trust — when created and maintained as a medium for the carrying on of a business enterprise and sharing its gains — which may be regarded as making it analogous to a corporate organization? A corporation, as an entity, holds the title to the property embarked in the corporate undertaking. Trustees, as a continuing body with provision for succession, may afford a corresponding advantage during the existence of the trust. Corporate organization furnishes the opportunity for a centralized management through representatives of the members of the corporation. The designation of trustees, who are charged with the conduct of an enterprise — who act "in much the same manner as directors" — may provide a similar scheme, with corresponding effectiveness. Whether the trustees are named in the trust instrument with power to select successors, so as to constitute a self-perpetuating body, or are selected by, or with the advice of, those beneficially interested in the undertaking, centralization of management analogous to that of corporate activities may be achieved. An enterprise carried on by means of a trust may be secure from termination or interruption by the death of owners of beneficial interests and in this respect their interests are distinguished from those of partners and are akin to the interests of members of a corporation. And the trust type of organization facilitates, as does corporate organization, the transfer of beneficial interests without affecting the continuity of the enterprise, and also the introduction of large numbers of participants. The trust method also permits the limitation of the personal liability of participants to the property embarked in the undertaking.

It is no answer to say that these advantages flow from the very nature of trusts. For the question has arisen because of the use and adaptation of the trust mechanism. The suggestion ignores the postulate that we are considering those trusts which have the distinctive feature of being created to enable the participants to carry on a business and divide the gains which accrue from their common undertaking, — trusts that thus satisfy the primary conception of association and have the attributes to which we have referred, distinguishing them from partnerships. In such a case, we think that these attributes make the trust sufficiently analogous to corporate organization to justify the conclusion that Congress intended that the income of the enterprise should be taxed in the same manner as that of corporations.

Applying these principles to the instant case, we are of the opinion that the trust constituted an association. The trust was created for the development of a tract of land through the construction and operation of golf courses, club houses, etc. and the conduct of incidental businesses, with broad powers for the purchase, operation and sale of properties. Provision was made for the issue of shares of beneficial interests, with described rights and priorities. There were to be preferred shares of the value of $100 each and common shares of no par value. Thus those who took beneficial interests became shareholders in the common undertaking to be conducted for their profit according to the terms of the arrangement. They were not the less associated in that undertaking because the arrangement vested the management and control in the trustees. And the contemplated development of the tract of land held at the outset, even if other properties were not acquired, involved what was essentially a business enterprise. The arrangement provided for centralized control, continuity, and limited liability, and the analogy to corporate organization was carried still further by the provision for the issue of transferable certificates . . . .

The judgment is affirmed.

UNITED STATES v. EMPEY
406 F.2d 157 (10th Cir. 1969), aff'g 272 F. Supp. 851 (D. Colo. 1967)

Before PHILLIPS, HILL and SETH, Circuit Judges.

ORIE L. PHILLIPS, Circuit Judge. Empey brought this action to recover a refund of federal income taxes paid for the year ending December 31, 1965. From a judgment for Empey, the United States has appealed.

The material facts are not in dispute.

On December 29, 1961, a corporation was created, pursuant to the general corporation laws of Colorado,[1] under the name Drexler, Wald, Sobol and Coffee Professional Company,[2] to carry on the practice of law.

Rule 265 of the Colorado Rules of Civil Procedure, effective December 5, 1961, (Colo. R. Civ. P. 265, 1965 Perm. Cum. Supp. to Colo. Rev. Stat. Ann. 1963, pp. 27-29) authorizes lawyers to organize professional service corporations under the Colorado Corporation Code and thereafter operate them for the practice of law, provided they organize and operate such corporations in accordance with the provisions of such Rule.[3]

It will be observed that Rule 265 provides that the articles of incorporation of a professional service corporation formed for the practice of law "shall contain provisions complying with," inter alia, "the following requirements":

The corporation shall be organized solely for the purpose of carrying on the practice of law only through persons qualified to practice law in the State of Colorado;

The corporation may exercise the powers and privileges conferred on it by the Colorado corporation laws, only in furtherance of such purpose;

---

[1] Colorado Corporation Code, 2 Colo. Rev. Stat. Ann. 1963, Articles 1-10, inclusive.

[2] Hereinafter called the Corporation.

[3] The pertinent parts of such Rule read:

"265. *Professional Service Corporations* . . . . Lawyers may form professional service corporations for the practice of law under the Colorado Corporation Code, providing that such corporations are organized and operated in accordance with the provisions of this Rule. The articles of incorporation of such corporations shall contain provisions complying with the following requirements:

"A. The name of the corporation shall contain the words 'professional company' or 'professional corporation' or abbreviations thereof, ...

"B. The corporation shall be organized solely for the purpose of conducting the practice of law only through persons qualified to practice law in the State of Colorado.

"C. The corporation may exercise the powers and privileges conferred upon corporations by the laws of Colorado only in furtherance of and subject to its corporate purpose.

"D. All shareholders of the corporation shall be persons duly licensed by the Supreme Court of the State of Colorado to practice law in the State of Colorado, and who at all times own their shares in their own right. They shall be individuals who . . . are actively engaged in the practice of law in the offices of the corporation.

"E. Provisions shall be made requiring any shareholder who ceases to be eligible to be a shareholder to dispose of all his shares forthwith either to the corporation or to any person having the qualifications described in paragraph D above.

"F. The president shall be a shareholder and a director, and to the extent possible all other directors and officers shall be persons having the qualifications described in paragraph D above. . . .

"G. The articles of incorporation shall provide and all shareholders of the corporation shall agree (a) that all shareholders of the corporation shall be jointly and severally liable for all acts, errors and omissions of the employees of the corporation, . . . except during periods of time when the corporation shall maintain in good standing lawyers' professional liability insurance which shall meet the following minimum standards:

"1. The insurance shall insure the corporation against liability imposed upon the corporation by law for damages resulting from any claim made against the corporation arising out of the performance of professional services for others by attorneys employed by the corporation in their capacities as lawyers.

"2. Such policy shall insure the corporation against liability imposed upon it by law for damages arising out of the acts, errors and omissions of all nonprofessional employees."

All shareholders shall be duly licensed to practice law in Colorado and actively engaged in the practice of law;

A shareholder who ceases to be eligible to hold shares in the corporation shall forthwith dispose of his stock, either to the corporation or to a person eligible to be a shareholder;

The shareholders shall be jointly and severally liable for all acts, errors and omissions of employees of the corporation, except during periods of time when the corporation maintains a lawyers' professional liability insurance policy meeting the requirements set forth in Paragraph G of Part I of such Rule.

At all times here material, the Corporation has carried professional liability insurance in full conformity with the provisions of Paragraph G of Part I of such Rule.

The Corporation was organized and thereafter operated in full compliance with Rule 265. The Corporation, its shareholders, and its lawyer employees in carrying on the practice of law through the Corporation have not violated the Canons of Professional Ethics applicable to lawyers.[4]

On January 3, 1962, the Corporation issued its stock, as follows: Drexler — 30 shares, Wald — 30 shares, Sobol — 30 shares, Coffee — 10 shares. The stock was issued in exchange for furniture, fixtures, equipment and cash. The amount of stock allotted each was based on his seniority status and the volume of his practice.

Prior to the creation of the Corporation, Sobol and Drexler were partners and Wald and Coffee were sole practitioners. However, they all occupied the same suite of offices.

Prior to October 3, 1962, Circular No. 230 of the United States Treasury Department[5] prohibited employees of professional service corporations from representing clients before such Department. On October 3, 1962, the circular was amended, so as to permit such employees to represent clients before the Treasury Department.[6]

Since the principal practice of the shareholders of the Corporation had to do with tax matters, it did not become active until after the promulgation of such amendment.

On November 1, 1962, the Corporation elected officers, adopted by-laws and a seal, and changed its corporate name to Drexler and Wald Professional Company. Wald and Drexler were elected president and vice-president, respectively, and remained such at all times here material. Sobol was elected treasurer and Coffee was elected secretary. In August 1963, the offices of treasurer and secretary were combined and Sobol became secretary-treasurer of the Corporation. At all times here material, Drexler, Wald and Sobol have been the directors of the Corporation.

On November 1, 1962, the Corporation began the active practice of law and each shareholder entered into an employment contract with the Corporation, identical, except as to the amount of monthly salary. Nonshareholder lawyer employees entered into like contracts with the Corporation at the beginning of their employment with it. The salary of each employee was determined by taking the "norm of" his "prior years' earnings, . . . averaging it," and thereby arriving at a starting salary.

[4]See Opinion 303 of American Bar Association's Committee on Professional Ethics, 48 A.B.A.J. 159 (1962).

[5]1962-2 C.B. 394, 31 C.F.R. §10.4(d) (1959).

[6]1962-2 C.B. 394.

On November 1, 1962, the shareholders of the Corporation entered into a stock redemption contract, which provided, inter alia:

"2. *Retirement or Death*. Each shareholder, and his estate, shall have the option of selling all of his shares to the Professional Company at any time. On redemption of stock, the price of the shares which are surrendered to the Professional Company shall be, except as is provided in Paragraph 3 hereinbelow, the book value thereof as of the last day of the month preceding the month in which the redemption is made and the payment therefor shall be made in cash on receipt of shares. Since this corporation has no good will, book value shall include no good will. All shareholders of the corporation shall be persons duly licensed by the Supreme Court of the State of Colorado to practice law in the State of Colorado. They shall also be individuals who, except for time spent for illness, accident, time spent in the armed services, on vacations, and on leaves of absence not to exceed one year, are actively engaged in the practice of law in the offices of the corporation. All shares of any shareholder who ceases to be eligible to be a shareholder of this corporation shall be redeemed immediately in accordance with the provisions of this paragraph.

"3. *Free Transferability of Shares*. A shareholder may transfer all or any portion of his shares to any person qualified by the Articles of Incorporation to be a shareholder; provided, however, that the shareholder desiring to transfer all or any portion of his shares first shall advise the Professional Company of the proposed transfer and the price offered for the shares. Prior to any such sale, the Professional Company shall have the option to redeem the said shares at the same price offered by the proposed transferee. If said option is not exercised by the Professional Company within ten (10) days after notice to it of the proposed sale, the shareholder shall be free to sell his said shares to said transferee."[7]

The employment contracts referred to above contained provisions giving the Corporation substantial control over its lawyer employees' work, including the assigning of clients, fixing work deadlines, determining working hours, and reviewing and modifying work product.

Most of the Corporation's business comes to it by referrals from lawyers or accountants. Usually, the referrer sends his client's matter to a lawyer employee of the Corporation whom the referrer has used before, or with whom he is acquainted.

[7]The Articles of Incorporation in part provided:
"SECOND: The corporation shall have perpetual existence. . . .
"FOURTH: All shareholders of the corporation shall be persons duly licensed by the Supreme Court of the State of Colorado to practice law in the State of Colorado. They shall also be individuals who, except for time spent for illness, accident, time spent in the armed services, on vacations, and on leaves of absence not to exceed one year, are actively engaged in the practice of law in the offices of the corporation. All shares of any shareholder who ceases to be eligible to be a shareholder of this corporation shall be called immediately in accordance with the provisions of Article FIFTH (c), or the ownership thereof shall otherwise immediately be vested in persons qualified to be shareholders."

Since to some extent the lawyer employees of the Corporation specialize in different fields of tax law, in a routine case the lawyer employee either decides he shall handle the matter himself, or if the matter falls within the specialty of another lawyer employee, decides to pass it on to the latter. However, if the case is unusual or not routine, it is usually referred to the board of directors, which selects the lawyer employee who shall handle the case.

Sometimes a matter is referred to the Corporation generally, and not to a particular lawyer employee. In such instances, if it is a routine case, it is assigned to a particular lawyer employee by Sobol, the office manager. If it is a matter that is unusual or not routine, the executive committee, composed of Wald and Sobol, determines to whom the matter shall be assigned.[8]

If the case is a routine one, the lawyer employee who handles it usually fixes the fee to be paid by the client, but if the case is a large one, or the person to whom the service is rendered is a "major client," the board of directors usually fixes the fee.

The board of directors fixes deadlines and guidelines, fixes working hours, and determines the amount of bonuses to be paid particular lawyer employees, based on the amount of income generated by the efforts of the lawyer employee. The board of directors also determines whether employment tendered by a particular client shall be rejected, because in their opinion the client is undesirable.

The Corporation has obtained short-term loans to provide working capital from time to time in its own name, without any shareholder endorsement, guaranty or liability. It has entered into a 10-year lease of its law offices at a basic annual rental in excess of $8,800, without individual guaranty or liability on the part of the shareholders.

The name of the Corporation appears on the letterhead of the stationery used by its officers and lawyer employees. The Corporation's name appears on its office doors, in the building directory, and in its listing in the Martindale-Hubbell Law Directory. It maintains a corporate bank account. In courts where so authorized, it signs pleadings in its corporate name. It has obtained an employer identification number from the Internal Revenue Service; has regularly filed employer-employee tax returns and paid the tax thereon; has made all corporate reports required by state or federal laws; and has filed corporate tax returns, both state and federal, and paid the taxes assessed thereon. It has established an employee profit sharing plan and trust and makes annual contributions thereto. It carries for its employees Blue Cross and Blue Shield insurance, health and accident insurance, and group life insurance. It also carries professional liability insurance. It has a large investment in books, office furniture, fixtures, and equipment. It holds stockholders' and directors' meetings.

In August 1963, Coffee left the employment of the Corporation and his stock was redeemed by the Corporation and held as treasury stock.

From January 1, 1965, to November 1, 1965, Empey was employed by the Corporation as a lawyer, but did not own any stock in the Corporation. On November 1,

---

[8]A standard fee agreement entered into between the Corporation and its clients reserves the right of the Corporation to select the lawyer employee to handle the matter.

1965, he became the owner of 10 shares, or 10 per cent of the outstanding stock of the Corporation. From November 1 to December 1, 1965, Empey continued to be a lawyer employee of the Corporation.

In his federal income tax return for the calendar year 1965, Empey reported the salary he received from the Corporation for the first 10 months of the year. In addition, Empey reported 10 per cent of the net income of the Corporation for the months of November and December, 1965, although he received no part of such income by way of dividend or otherwise.

Empey timely filed a claim for a refund of the tax paid by him on the difference between his salary for the months of November and December, 1965, and 10 per cent of the Corporation's net earnings for those months. On July 20, 1966, after the Commissioner had failed to take any action on the claim within six months after it was filed, Empey commenced this action.

The applicable provisions of the Internal Revenue Code of 1954 are found in 26 U.S.C.A. §7701. . . .

The provisions of Treasury Regulations on Procedure and Administration (1954 Internal Revenue Code), §§301.7701-1 and 301.7701-2, promulgated November 15, 1960, . . . are most pertinent in the instant case . . . .

The pertinent parts of an amendment to §301.7701-2, approved January 28, 1965, and published February 3, 1965, in 30 F.R. 1116, applicable to professional service organizations' taxable years, beginning after December 31, 1964 [are provided in Treas. Reg. §301.7701-2(a)(5)].

It is fairly obvious that the purpose of the amendment of January 28, 1965, was to prevent a professional service organization from being able to qualify as a corporation for tax purposes under the Internal Revenue Code.

The issue presented is whether the Corporation, for federal income tax purposes, should be classified and taxed as a corporation, as asserted by Empey, or as a partnership, as asserted by the United States. That question in turn involves the interpretation of §7701(a)(2) and (3) of the Internal Revenue Code of 1954, which defines the terms "partnership" and "corporation" for federal income tax purposes, and Treasury Regulations 301.7701-1(1) and (2), promulgated thereunder on November 15, 1960, and, in particular, the validity of paragraph (h) of Treasury Regulation 301.-7701-2, approved January 28, 1965.

In the Internal Revenue Act of 1894, c. 349, 28 Stat. 509, 556, and in the several internal revenue acts since enacted by Congress, it has seen fit to treat corporations and partnerships differently for federal income tax purposes. The term "corporation" was first defined by Congress in the Internal Revenue Act of 1918, c. 18, 40 Stat. 1057, 1058. It defines a corporation as including "associations, joint-stock companies, and insurance companies." That Act did not define partnerships. It did define a "personal service corporation" as "a corporation whose income is to be ascribed primarily to the activities of the principal owners or stockholders who are themselves regularly engaged in the active conduct of the affairs of the corporation and in which capital . . . is not a material income-producing factor." (Revenue Act of 1918, c. 18, 40 Stat. 1057, 1059, §200.) It provided that such corporations were to be treated as partnerships for income tax purposes. (Revenue Act of 1918, c. 18, 40 Stat. 1057, 1070, §218(e).) However, that tax treatment was short-lived and it was eliminated by the Revenue Act of 1921, c. 136, 42 Stat. 227, 245, §218(d).

Since 1921, Congress has not seen fit to provide different treatment for personal service corporations and other corporations, and it was not until 1965 that the Treasury Department attempted any such distinction.

The Revenue Act of 1932, c. 209, 47 Stat. 169, 289, §1111, defined the term "partnership" substantially as it is defined in the Revenue Act of 1954. And since 1918 the term "corporation" and since 1932 the term "partnership" have been defined in successive Revenue Acts without substantial change, to and including the Internal Revenue Code of 1954.

The trial court held that the Regulations here involved are inconsistent with the statutory definition of corporations and partnerships and the judicial construction thereof, and constitute the exercise of a nondelegable legislative function and are therefore invalid and unenforceable.

The trial court further held that the Corporation more nearly resembled a corporation than a partnership, and even if the Regulations were valid, it would be entitled to be treated as a corporation for federal income tax purposes.

It will be observed that the statutory definition of the term "corporation" extends, rather than limits, the ordinary meaning thereof. It includes "associations, joint-stock companies, and insurance companies," as well as entities organized as corporations, while the statutory definition of the term "partnership" includes a "syndicate, group, pool, joint venture, or other *unincorporated organization*." (Italics ours.)

Prior to 1965, the Treasury Department consistently treated an entity chartered and operated in good faith as a corporation under state law, as a corporation for federal income tax purposes.[11]

Although classification as a corporation for federal income tax purposes generally results in additional income tax and possible tax disadvantages, it also can provide income tax advantages not otherwise available.[12] Thus, the employees of a corporation or an association may participate in a qualified pension and profit-sharing plan and any contribution by the employer thereto is not taxable to the employees when made, although it is deductible by the employer. Such benefits are not available to partners, because they are not employees.

In Morrissey v. Commissioner, 296 U.S. 344, 56 S. Ct. 289, 80 L. Ed. 263 (1935), the petitioners, as trustees of an express trust, contested income taxes assessed for the years 1924-1926, inclusive. The question was whether the declaration of trust created

---

[11]Professional Corporations and Associations, 75 Harv. L. Rev. 756, 785 (1962); Anderson, Tax Aspects of Professional Corporations, U.S.C. 15th Tax Inst. 309, 320-322 (1963); Bittker, Professional Associations and Federal Income Taxation, 17 Tax Law Rev. 1, 26 (1961), where the author said: ". . . until now all organizations bearing the label 'corporation' under state law have, without further inquiry, been accorded that status for federal income tax purposes, the only debate in this area having been concerned with the classification of organizations that are *not* labelled 'corporations' by state law."

[12]Eaton, Professional Corporations and Associations in Perspective, 23 Tax Law Rev. 1, 22-23 (1967).

a pure trust or an association for federal income tax purposes. In 1921, the petitioners executed a declaration of trust, transferring certain real estate described therein to designated trustees. In their collective capacity, the trustees were designated as "Western Avenue Golf Club." The trust instrument authorized the trustees to add to their number and choose their successors; to purchase, encumber, lease, or sell the described real estate or other lands; to construct and operate golf courses and club houses; to make loans and investments, and generally manage the trust estate as if the trustees were the absolute owners thereof. The trust instrument declared they were without power to bind the beneficiaries personally by "any act, neglect or default," and that persons dealing with the trust must look to the trust property for payment or indemnity. The beneficial interests in the trust were evidenced by transferable certificates, consisting of 2,000 shares of preferred stock of the par value of $100 each, and 2,000 shares of common stock of no par value.

The trust instrument provided that the death of a trustee or beneficiary should not end the trust, but that it should continue for 25 years. Beneficial interests were sold in 1921 and 1922.

About 42 acres of the 155 acres described in the trust instrument were subdivided into lots and sold in the years 1921 to 1923, mostly on installment contracts. On the remaining acreage, the trustees constructed a golf course and club house. In 1923, they transferred the golf course and club house to a California corporation in exchange for stock of the latter. They operated the golf course under lease until January 12, 1924. Thereafter, the activities of the trust were confined to collection of principal and interest on installment contracts for the purchase of lots, receipt of interest on bank balances, fees on assignment of installment contracts, making of conveyances to purchasers of lots, receipt of dividends on corporate stock, and distribution of money to owners of the beneficial interests.

The court held that the salient features of a trust, when created and maintained for carrying on a business enterprise and sharing in its gains, which may be regarded as making it analogous to a corporation are: Holding title to the property as an entity; trustees as a continuing body with provisions for succession; nontermination of the enterprise by reason of the death of the owners; transferability "of beneficial interests without affecting the continuity of the enterprise"; limitation of personal liability of the shareholders by vesting complete control in the trustees.

It will be observed that the court, in referring to transferability of beneficial interests, makes no reference to "free transferability," that is, without limitation as to who may purchase. Reference is made only to transfers "of beneficial interests without affecting the continuity of the enterprise."

The court concluded the trust was an association within the meaning of the applicable statutory definition [substantially the same as it is in the Internal Revenue Code of 1954] and taxable as a corporation. The court observed, however, that the statutory definition implies resemblance, saying, "it is resemblance and not identity."

In Pelton v. Commissioner, 7 Cir., 82 F.2d 473 (1936) the facts were these:

Between 1913 and 1920, Ora L. Pelton, Sr., and Ora L. Pelton, Jr., both of whom specialized in surgery, and S. L. Gabby, who specialized in internal medicine, practiced medicine at Elgin, Illinois. They occupied a suite of offices with a common waiting room.

On September 1, 1920, they entered into an indenture, by which they transferred to themselves as trustees property of an estimated value of $14,000, consisting of office furniture and equipment, instruments, laboratory equipment, x-ray devices and equipment, and a library. Pelton, Jr., died in 1929, leaving Pelton, Sr., and Gabby as the surviving trustees.

The indenture authorized the trustees to use the property conveyed to them in any manner they deemed advisable, to operate clinics and any business or professional pursuit allied thereto, to retain any professional assistance needed to discharge such duties, including that of the trustees in a professional capacity, to incur indebtedness and to invest and reinvest in securities.

The indenture provided the trustees would receive for their services salaries not to exceed $25,000 per year; that they had the power to divide their duties and assume appropriate titles; that they would distribute the net income annually or oftener; that "they were not to be liable in a personal capacity for the duties performed by them"; that vacancies among the trustees should be filled by the beneficiaries; that the holders of 51 per cent of the beneficial interests should have the power to modify the trust; that the trust should be designated as "The Pelton Clinic," "The Pelton Clinic, not Inc.," or "The Pelton Clinic Trust"; that it should continue for 10 years, and that the assets should then be distributed to the beneficiaries of record.

At the beginning, Pelton, Sr., had a beneficial interest of 40 per cent, or 200 units; Pelton, Jr., had 35 per cent, or 175 units; and Gabby had 25 per cent, or 125 units.

Provision was made for the distribution, upon the death of a beneficial owner, to his wife or other relatives, of any units owned by him at the time of his death.

The beneficial interests were represented by shares which were transferable, but the other beneficiaries were to have the option to purchase them at $30 per share before they were sold to outsiders. By an amendment made by the beneficiaries of January 1, 1924, the price was changed from $30 per share to book value and provision was made for the retention of $10,000, or 75 per cent, of the net income each year, to be used in acquiring fixed or other assets for the trust.

The three physicians were the sole beneficiaries during the tax years involved.

In 1924 and 1925, the trustees employed, in addition to themselves, one physician, and in 1926 and 1927, three physicians.

The issue was whether the trust constituted an association, taxable as a corporation, or whether the individual members were taxable as partners under the Revenue Acts of 1924 and 1926.

Deficiencies were assessed by the Commissioner, on the ground that the trust was an association and taxable as a corporation. The Board of Tax Appeals sustained the deficiencies and the Court of Appeals affirmed, holding that the continuity of the enterprise, centralized control, limited liability and transferability of interests were present, and that there were substantial dissimilarities to a partnership.

Following *Pelton*, members of learned professions, because of increasingly higher income taxes and the realization that pension and profit-sharing plans would result in tax benefits, began to form associations for the practice of their professions, and claimed the tax advantages that flowed therefrom. This was particularly true of medical groups, which, under state law, could not carry on the practice of medicine through a corporation.

This led the Treasury Department to change its position, so instead of asserting, as theretofore, that such organizations should be treated as corporations for federal income tax purposes, it asserted that they should be regarded as partnerships for such purposes and were not entitled to the tax benefits they sought to obtain.

The correctness of the Treasury Department's new position came before the Ninth Circuit in the case of United States v. Kintner, 9 Cir., 216 F.2d 418, in 1954. In that case, a doctor of medicine, who will hereinafter be referred to as the taxpayer, and his wife brought an action to recover a deficiency tax assessed for federal income taxes in 1948, which they had paid. From a judgment in favor of the taxpayer and his wife, the United States appealed.

The taxpayer, for many years prior to June 30, 1948, was a member of a co-partnership composed of eight physicians, who practiced medicine in Montana, under the name "Western Montana Clinic." On that date, the partnership was dissolved, and the eight physicians executed articles of association for the practice of medicine. The assets and liabilities of the partnership were taken over by the association. The articles of the association provided it should continue until the death of the last of the eight original members; that only physicians and surgeons licensed to practice medicine in Montana were eligible for membership; that the business of the association would be managed by an executive committee of five members, who would elect the officers of the association; that "only the members were to be liable to third parties for professional misconduct"; that the association would collect accounts receivable for services rendered by its members; that net earnings would be divided annually among the members in proportion to the salaries received and would be deemed compensation for services rendered by them; that the association would furnish members with the equipment needed to render professional services and pay all expenses incident to the practice of medicine and surgery by the members; that the death or retirement of a member would not result in dissolution of the association; and that on the withdrawal or death of a member, he or his estate would receive, instead of a share in the association's assets, the benefits of the pension plan, the expense of which was to be borne by the association.

The court held that the association more nearly resembled a corporation than a partnership and should be treated as a corporation for federal income tax purposes, and affirmed the judgment.

In Galt v. United States, N.D. Tex., 175 F. Supp. 360 (1959), a group of physicians executed articles of association, setting forth in substance all of the provisions that would have been set out in articles of incorporation of "an active" corporation or in its "charter issued to them under the laws of the State of Texas," had such laws permitted physicians to form corporations for the practice of medicine. The name of the association was the "Southwest Clinic Association," and it carried on the operation of the clinic substantially as it would have, had it been a corporation organized under the laws of Texas.

The court held that it was an association, taxable as a corporation.[13]

The members of the association in *Kintner* had only a qualified limitation on personal liability.

The Treasury Department did not seek review of *Kintner* by petition for certiorari, nor *Galt* by appeal. Instead, on November 15, 1960, it promulgated, under the Internal Revenue Code of 1954, Treasury Regulations 301.7701-2(a)(1), (2) and (3), with the purpose of indirectly overturning the decisions in *Kintner* and *Galt*. Indeed, that purpose was so obvious that such Regulations came to be referred to generally as the "*Kintner* Regulations." However, they are apparently directed only at unincorporated organizations.

Regulations long in effect, under §3797(a)(2) and (3) of the Internal Revenue Code of 1939, (the predecessor of §7701(a)(2) and (3) of the Internal Revenue Code of 1954) were based on the decision in Morrissey v. Commissioner, 296 U.S. 344, 56 S. Ct. 289, 80 L. Ed. 263 (1935), and decisions and rulings under the Internal Revenue Code of 1939, holding that unincorporated organizations should be taxed as corporations, if corporate characteristics were present, and not as partnerships.

The 1960 Regulations apparently were designed to make it as difficult as possible for professional groups, which formed unincorporated organizations to practice their professions, to obtain treatment of such associations as corporations for federal income tax purposes.

However, the 1960 Regulations, unlike the 1965 amendment thereto, contain no indication of a change in the long followed administrative practice of treating a corporation organized and chartered under state law as a corporation for federal income tax purposes. That was a practice that had been tacitly approved by the Congress, by its reenactment at least 11 times of the definition of the term "corporation" in substantially identical language.

Notwithstanding that the 1960 Regulations were designed to make it quite difficult for associations formed by professional groups to practice their professions, Foreman v. United States, S.D. Fla., 232 F. Supp. 134 (1964), held that an association formed by two physicians to operate an orthopedic clinic was taxable as a corporation, even though limited liability was absent from its corporate characteristics.

In the 1960 Regulations, the case law standards of continuity of life, centralization of management, limited liability and transferability of ownership interests were still used to govern, but the Treasury Department shifted its position as to the meaning of such criteria. An example was the flat position taken by the Treasury Department that an association subject to the Uniform Partnership Act of a state could never achieve such standards. Accordingly, beginning in 1961, Connecticut, Georgia, Illinois, Ohio and Pennsylvania adopted standards which permitted members of professions to form associations without being subject to the Uniform Partnership Acts of the states. Florida, Minnesota, Oklahoma, Tennessee and Wisconsin enacted statutes authorizing members of professions to carry on their practices through corporations organized under the general corporation laws of such states. They made specific

---

[13]See also, Foreman v. United States, S.D. Fla., 232 F. Supp. 134 (1964).

provisions, however, to preserve traditional professional standards and professional responsibility to patients or clients, and prohibited the ownership of shares by unlicensed persons or persons not actively employed in a professional capacity by such a corporation.

The question of whether a corporation organized to practice a learned profession under the general corporation laws of a state, which had to meet requirements like those laid down in Rule 265, supra, was entitled to be treated as a corporation for federal income tax purposes, was adjudicated for the first time in the instant case.

The findings of the trial court, which are set forth in Note 14, are supported by the evidence, which is not in conflict, and are not clearly erroneous.[14]

The trial court, in a well reasoned opinion, held that the 1965 amendment was invalid, and that the corporation was entitled to be treated as a corporation for the purposes of federal income tax. We agree with the conclusion of the trial court.

There has been no substantial change in the definition of the term "corporation" and the term "partnership" since the Revenue Act of 1932, and the definitions of those terms in the Internal Revenue Code of 1954 are identical with their definitions in the Revenue Act of 1939. The definition of a partnership, by its language, plainly refers to unincorporated organizations. To treat as a partnership for federal income tax purposes a corporation, organized and chartered under state laws as a corporation and operated as such in good faith, does violence to the statutory definitions of the terms "partnership" and "corporation," to long followed administrative practice prior to 1965, and to the decided cases dealing with analogous organizations. Moreover, Congress has not seen fit to take any legislative action to overturn such long standing practices and decisions, and the Treasury Department only undertook to do so by a greatly belated Regulation.

We conclude the 1965 Regulations are "unreasonable and plainly inconsistent with the revenue statutes,"[16] and are therefore invalid. Moreover, we think the 1965

---

[14]"1. Drexler and Wald Company has associates.

"2. Its objective is to carry on the practice of law for profit and to divide the gains therefrom.

"3. By its charter it has perpetual life and it has continuity of life within the requirements of the regulations in that death, insanity, bankruptcy, retirement, resignation or expulsion of any member will not cause or require a dissolution of the corporation.

"4. The lawful authority of the company is vested in its directors and officers and the evidence discloses that the directors and officers have exercised their powers of management although routine matters are handled by the office manager.

"5. Shareholders are liable for corporate debts except during periods of time when the corporation shall maintain lawyers' professional liability insurance in specified amounts; the Court finds that Drexler and Wald has at all times carried such insurance in the specified amounts and that the nature of the liability of the shareholders of Drexler and Wald is more similar to that of a corporate shareholder than to that of a partner.

"6. The transferability of the shareholders' interests in Drexler and Wald is restricted to transfers to lawyers who are actively engaged in the practice of law in the offices of the corporation or to the corporation.

"The Court further finds that the corporate characteristics of Drexler and Wald are such that the organization more nearly resembles a corporation than a partnership."

[16]See Commissioner v. South Texas Lumber Co., 333 U.S. 496, 501, 68 S. Ct. 695, 92 L. Ed. 831, where the court set forth the language last quoted as the test to be applied in determining the validity of Treasury Regulations.

Regulations "amount to an attempt to legislate" and are therefore invalid.[17]

The judgment is affirmed.

REVENUE RULING 70-101
1970-1 Cum. Bull. 278

The Internal Revenue Service has been requested to state its position with respect to the classification of professional service organizations formed under state professional association or corporation statutes.

In the light of recent decisions of the Federal courts, the Service generally will treat organizations of doctors, lawyers, and other professional people organized under state professional association acts as corporations for tax purposes.

The Government has not applied for certiorari in the cases of United States v. O'Neill, 410 F.2d 888 (6th Cir. 1969); Kurzner v. United States, 413 F.2d 97 (5th Cir. 1969); Empey v. United States, 406 F.2d 157 (10th Cir. 1969); and Holder v. United States, 289 F. Supp. 160 (1968), affirmed, per curiam, 412 F.2d 1189 (5th Cir. 1969). Also the Government will not further press its appeals in Wallace v. United States, 294 F. Supp. 1225 (1968). Furthermore, no appeal will be prosecuted in any other pending cases decided adversely to the Government on the same issue involving similar facts and all similar cases now in litigation or under audit are being reviewed to see if they should be conceded. However, the Government reserves the right to conclude differently in any cases reflecting special circumstances. ... [Citations omitted.]

It is held that a professional service organization will be treated as a corporation in any case arising in the same state as, and having facts similar to, the cases cited above.

A professional service organization that is organized and operated under the statutes listed below for each state will also be treated as a corporation except in those instances in which it is illegal, as a matter of state law, for the professional service organization claiming corporate status to engage in the practice of the particular profession that it is organized to engage in. [Listing of state statutes omitted.]

Furthermore, if a corporation is organized and operated as a professional service business under the general business corporation statute of its state, it will generally be recognized as a corporation.

In addition, a professional service organization that meets the requirements for corporate classification under section 301.7701-2 of the Procedure and Administration Regulations, exclusive of the 1965 amendments (section 301.7701-2(h) of the regulations) made thereto, in its organization and operation will be classified as a corporation. ...

A professional service organization must be both organized and operated as a

---

[17]The Supreme Court also has held that Treasury Regulations will be disregarded when they are contrary to the "unambiguous mandate of the statute" and when they "amount to an attempt to legislate." Helvering v. Sabine Transportation Co., 318 U.S. 306, 311, 312, 63 S. Ct. 569, 572, 87 L. Ed. 773.

corporation to be classified as such. See Jerome J. Roubik and Joan M. Roubik, et al., v. Commissioner, 53 T.C. 365, No. 36 (1969).*

Notwithstanding that a professional service organization is, in accordance with this Revenue Ruling, classified as a corporation, if it reported income as a partnership in accordance with then existing regulations for taxable years ending prior to the issuance of this Revenue Ruling, March 2, 1970, it will not be required to report income as a corporation for such prior years. Also, a professional service organization that qualifies as a corporation under this Revenue Ruling and is presently reporting income as a partnership will be permitted to continue reporting such income as a partnership for any taxable year ending on or before December 31, 1970.

The foregoing position relates solely to the issue of the tax classification of professional service organizations. Professional service organizations classifiable as corporations are subject to audit to the same extent as other corporations, and nothing contained herein is to be construed as waiving the assertion of any issues against such organizations other than that of classification.

NOTE

See L. Reich, Alternatives to the Professional Service Corporation: Partnership; Association Taxable as a Corporation; Advantages and Disadvantages of Each; Present State of the *Kintner* Regulations, 28 N.Y.U. Inst. on Fed. Tax. 1173 (1970); K. Worthy, IRS Chief Counsel Outlines What Lies Ahead for Professional Corporations, 32 J. Taxation 88 (1970); T. Troyer, Prescriptions for Professionals by Doctors Kintner and Keogh: The Current State of the Therapy, and Some Observations on Prognosis, 27 N.Y.U. Inst. on Fed. Tax. 1279 (1969); W. Thies, Professional Service Organizations: A Comment, 24 Tax L. Rev. 291 (1969); B. Bittker, Professional Service Organizations: A Reply, 24 Tax L. Rev. 300 (1969); W. Thies, Professional Service Organizations: A Rebuttal, 24 Tax L. Rev. 551 (1969); B. Bittker, Professional Service Organizations: A Critique of the Literature, 23 Tax L. Rev. 429 (1968); B. Eaton, Jr., Professional Corporations and Associations in Perspective, 23 Tax L. Rev. 1 (1967).

II. IGNORING THE CORPORATION

JACKSON v. COMMISSIONER
233 F.2d 289 (2d Cir. 1956)

Before FRANK, MEDINA and WATERMAN, Circuit Judges.

FRANK, Circuit Judge. The basic question here is whether certain corporations

---

*In *Roubik* the Commissioner successfully contended that the income of a professional service corporation was taxable directly to the shareholders as those who had earned it, applying the assignment of income doctrine. — ED.

should be disregarded with the result that transactions carried out by them should be treated as if the corporations did not exist and as if the transactions had been those of the taxpayers themselves. . . .

Taxpayers and two others, Cohn and Harris, each owned one-third of the stock of Empire Industries, Inc. (hereafter Empire). Empire owned numerous other corporations whose acquisition had been financed by loans personally guaranteed by Mr. Jackson. Attempts by Jackson to reduce this large contingent liability engendered such friction between Jackson and Cohn that it was decided to form a new corporation, Lewis of Delaware (hereafter Lewis), to which would be transferred one-third of the assets of Empire in exchange for all the capital stock of Lewis. Lewis was to be either a wholly-owned subsidiary controlled and managed by Jackson or a separate corporation owned, as well as controlled, by Jackson. The latter alternative was eventually chosen, and the taxpayers proceeded to exchange their one-third interest for all of the Lewis stock by a series of transactions involving two corporations, Dumelle Corporation (Dumelle) and Belgrade Properties, Inc. (Belgrade), wholly owned and controlled by taxpayers. Taxpayers first created Dumelle and then transferred their one-third interest in Empire to Dumelle in exchange for all of Dumelle's capital stock. Then a pre-existing corporation, Belgrade, which was wholly owned by Mrs. Jackson and had never conducted any business, purchased the Empire stock from Dumelle in exchange for $1,000 in cash and $469,000 in interest-bearing notes payable over 20 years. The final step in the overall transaction was an exchange between Belgrade and Empire — Belgrade receiving the entire capital stock of Lewis in exchange for the one-third interest in Empire which Belgrade then held. The activity of the two corporations in question was of a very limited nature. Dumelle's only activity was the receipt of Empire stock from the taxpayers and the sale of the same stock to Belgrade. Belgrade's only activity was to purchase the Empire stock from Dumelle, exchange it for Lewis stock with Empire, and to hold the Lewis stock.

The taxpayers had this purpose in creating the Dumelle Company and using the Belgrade Company: to insure that Mrs. Jackson, as owner of all the stock of Belgrade, should have, as her sole property, free of any claim of Jackson's creditors, any future increment in the value of the stock of the Lewis Company over and above its fair market value in April 1949 (that value as of that date being $1,000 more than the face amount of the note for $469,000 given by Belgrade to Dumelle). Although Belgrade was to and did become the owner of the Lewis stock, it was intended not to and did not exercise any functions with respect to the management of Lewis.

Unquestionably, the taxpayers had a personal business purpose other than (or in addition to) that of avoiding taxation. Consequently, if a taxpayer's personal purpose, in creating a corporation, controls, the Tax Court erred. But we read the pertinent Supreme Court decisions, and our own decisions interpreting the Supreme Court's views, as follows: A corporation may not be disregarded in respect of taxation if, inter alia, a bona fide intention in creating it was that the corporation itself should have some real substantial business function,[1] or if it actually engages in business;

---

[1] When there is such an intention, but the intended business functioning does not become effective, the corporation is not to be disregarded in the interval before it becomes evident

on the other hand, the corporation may be disregarded, in the absence of such an intention or activity. The intended or actual business functioning of the corporation itself, not the taxpayer's aim to be accomplished via the corporation, is the test.[2]

Reviewing previous decisions, including Higgins v. Smith, 308 U.S. 473, 477-478, 60 S. Ct. 355, 84 L. Ed. 406, the Supreme Court in Moline Properties v. Commissioner, 319 U.S. 436, 439, 63 S. Ct. 1132, 1134, 87 L. Ed. 1499 said: "The doctrine of corporate entity fills a useful purpose in business life. Whether the purpose be to gain an advantage under the law of the state of incorporation or to avoid or to comply with the demands of creditors or to serve the creator's personal or undisclosed convenience, so long as that purpose is the equivalent of business activity or is followed by the carrying on of business by the corporation, the corporation remains a separate taxable entity." In National Investors Corp. v. Hoey, 2 Cir., 144 F.2d 466, 468, a parent company wished to combine itself and several subsidiaries into a single corporation; as a preliminary step, it transferred the stock of the subsidiaries to another corporation which had no other assets or liabilities; during the time when the plan of consolidation was being formulated and submitted to the stockholders of the parent, the new company engaged in no activity except to receive and hold the stock of the subsidiary companies; the plan of consolidation was rejected by the stockholders of the parent company, and the new company was subsequently liquidated. We ruled that the corporate entity of the new company could not be disregarded up to the time when the stockholders rejected the plan of consolidation, because its use, meanwhile, as a means of achieving the consolidation and holding the transferred securities, "was a 'business' activity." We said that *Moline Properties* "merely declares that to be a separate jural person for purposes of taxation, a corporation must engage in some industrial, commercial, or other activity besides avoiding taxation: in other words, that the term 'corporation' will be interpreted to mean a corporation which does some 'business' in the ordinary meaning . . . ." In Paymer v. Commissioner, 2 Cir., 150 F.2d 334, 337, a corporation was formed with the sole intention of serving "as a blind to deter the creditors of one of the partners" who had organized it. We said that it "was at all times but a passive dummy which did nothing but take and hold the title to the real estate conveyed to it. . . . It was but a sham, to be disregarded for tax purposes." We think the instant case comes within this *Paymer* ruling.[3]

Affirmed.

---

that the corporation will not so function. See National Investors Corp. v. Hoey, 2 Cir., 144 F.2d 466.

[2] A natural person may be used to receive income which in fact is another's. So, too, a corporation, although for other purposes a jural entity distinct from its stockholders, may be used as a mere dummy to receive income which in fact is the income of the stockholders or of someone else; in such circumstances, the company will be disregarded.

[3] This conclusion is fortified by the fact that taxpayers' purpose would have been as well served if the Lewis shares had been transferred to Mrs. Jackson as her property in consideration of her giving the $470,000 note, or if they had been transferred to a trustee for Mrs. Jackson and the trustee had given the note.

We disagree with the Tax Court as to the following: We think it immaterial (1) that the transactions between the Jacksons, the Dumelle Company and the Belgrade Company were not "at arm's length," and (2) that there was no disclosure of those transactions to Harris and Cohn.

NOTE

See generally D. Watts, Tax Problems of Regard for the Corporate Entity, 20 N.Y.U. Inst. on Fed. Tax. 867 (1962).

III. STRAW CORPORATIONS

COMMISSIONER v. STATE-ADAMS CORP.
283 F.2d 395 (2d Cir. 1960), cert. denied, 365 U.S. 844 (1961)

Before CLARK, MAGRUDER, and FRIENDLY, Circuit Judges.

CLARK, Circuit Judge. Petitioner asserted deficiencies amounting to $88,558.18 in the income and excess profit taxes due from respondent corporation for the year 1951. The Tax Court held that respondent was not a corporation for tax purposes and therefore owed no tax. 32 T.C. 365. This petition for review followed.

In its corporate income tax return for 1951, respondent, following its practice since its incorporation in 1933, reported no net income. After reporting the receipt of rent in the sum of $140,000 respondent deducted $984.32 as "legal services and collection charges," and deducted the remaining $139,015.68 as "interest" paid on notes held by the shareholders. The Commissioner determined that this "interest" was in reality a dividend — a conclusion which respondent does not contest. But respondent argues that it was a mere dummy for the holding of title, and therefore its separate corporate existence should be disregarded for federal tax purposes.

Respondent was incorporated under the laws of Illinois on September 26, 1933, for the purpose of holding title to certain land at State and Adams Streets in Chicago. This "State-Adams" property was then owned by Mrs. Frances Sheldon Whitehouse as sole trustee of the "Sheldon Trust," of which she was sole income beneficiary. On Mrs. Whitehouse's death the land would be distributed to her descendants per stirpes. In 1933, Mrs. Whitehouse was 81 years of age and had six children and several minor grandchildren. Two of these children were aliens and were prohibited by Illinois law from owning real estate for more than six years. There was the further possibility that part of the ownership of the State-Adams property would become vested in minor beneficiaries. To avoid these difficulties which might arise on the death of Mrs. Whitehouse, the family attorney caused the incorporation of the respondent. Mrs. Whitehouse, as trustee of the Sheldon Trust, transferred title of the State-Adams property to the new corporation in return for all its capital stock. At the time, the property had been leased to The Fair department store for a term of 79 years, at annual rentals which increased periodically from $125,000 for 1915-20 to $140,000 for 1950-94. This lease was transferred to respondent in exchange for its promissory note payable to Mrs. Whitehouse as trustee, the interest on the note being equivalent to the amount of rent received from The Fair. At the time of incorporation, Mrs. White-house was advised by her attorney that the "new arrangement" would in no way affect the present crediting of her account "with a sum equal to the total rent from the property."

Before respondent's incorporation the rental income from The Fair was trans-mitted to the Bank of Montreal, New York, which credited the funds to Mrs. Whitehouse's account as trustee. After respondent was incorporated, The Fair made its checks payable to respondent. But pursuant to a duly authorized resolution of respondent, The Fair caused the checks to be transmitted to the Bank of Montreal and credited directly to Mrs. Whitehouse's account, as had been done previously. Upon the death of Mrs. Whitehouse in 1944, the stock in respondent and the note became the property of her six children, but the general collection process continued substantially as before. The Bank received the rentals and forwarded them directly to the accounts of the shareholders. Since the interest payments were intended to exhaust the rental income, appropriate corporate action was taken to refund the debt by notes at a higher interest rate when, under the terms of the lease, the rental income increased. At times the amount paid out as interest exceeded the amount due on the notes.

The lease under which these rental payments were made was a "net lease," under which all the usual duties of ownership and management were imposed upon the lessee. Respondent, organized to hold the title to the land and the lease, did not engage in general activities unconnected with this purpose. Thus it did not maintain an office (other than the required Illinois statutory office) for the transaction of busi-ness. It had no bank account. Its mailing address was at all times in care of the at-torneys for the Whitehouse family. It had no expenses except for the service fee charged by the Bank of Montreal, small legal fees paid to the family attorneys, and Illinois franchise taxes. Its only source of income was the rental checks which, after payment of the above expenses, were distributed by the Bank directly to the share-holders, as stated above.

Hence consistent with its purpose the only activities required of respondent were such as at once to preserve its existence and to provide for collection of the rent and its distribution to the shareholders. So at all times it executed the necessary documents to this end with the required corporate formalities. It held a stockholders' meeting in 1933 for the purpose of organization and election of directors, and another in 1947 for ratification of the lease by the then stockholders as requested by counsel for the lessee, The Fair. It held some ten directors' meetings, the directors and officers con-sisting of certain trust beneficiaries who served without compensation and of the family attorneys who were compensated for their legal services. Minutes were kept of these meetings, and these showed choice of new directors to fill vacancies, modifica-tions in some details as to the payment instructions on transfer of a note by the holder to her children, and refunding of the notes at a higher interest rate as the lease rental increased. In 1935 respondent was dissolved by the Superior Court of Illinois for failure to pay franchise taxes, but the dissolution decree was vacated in 1938 when the attorneys learned of it and paid the delinquent taxes. Respondent filed income tax returns as above stated and has carried on the present proceedings in the Tax Court and here in its corporate name. There can be no question but that respondent is and has been a valid corporation under state law.

Respondent asserts, however, that the question whether it was a bona fide corporation under state law is not dispositive of the question whether it should be recognized as a corporation for federal income tax purposes. We are referred to Moline Properties v. C. I. R., 319 U.S. 436, 439, 63 S. Ct. 1132, 1134, 87 L. Ed. 1499, where the Supreme Court stated that a corporation will be treated as a separate taxable entity so long as the purpose of incorporation "is the equivalent of business activity or is followed by the carrying on of business by the corporation." In National Investors Corp. v. Hoey, 2 Cir., 144 F.2d 466, 468, this Court, per L. Hand, J., took this statement to mean "that to be a separate jural person for purposes of taxation, a corporation must engage in some industrial, commercial, or other activity besides avoiding taxation: in other words, that the term 'corporation' will be interpreted to mean a corporation which does some 'business' in the ordinary meaning; and that escaping taxation is not 'business' in the ordinary meaning." It may be noted that in both cases decision went against the taxpayer.

We think that respondent, having full beneficial ownership of the land and collecting the rent therefrom, engaged in business under the principles above enunciated. This is not a case where the corporation was a mere nominee, powerless to act with respect to the land other than with consent of the beneficial owners. Had the corporate officers and directors determined to sell the land, or to reinvest in other property, the shareholders who had been receiving the rent could not have complained. This is not a case where income belonging to the shareholders was received in form by the corporation. The income belonged to the corporation, and was paid directly to the shareholders only because this suited the purpose for which the corporation had been established. Thus the corporation was organized for a specific purpose which required for its fulfillment a separate legal entity, more than a sham or "shell"; and over the years it carefully satisfied every legal requirement to achieve its purpose.

Respondent relies chiefly on Paymer v. C. I. R., 2 Cir., 150 F.2d 334, 336, where this Court, at the instance of the taxpayer, disregarded the separate existence of a corporation created to hold title to real estate. There title to certain real estate was conveyed by a partnership to the Westrich Realty Corp. for the purpose of concealing the true ownership from creditors. The conveyance was made "with the express understanding that the corporation is only to hold title to the property, the beneficial interest and profits to be in the individual stockholders and the management and control of the property exclusively theirs." No attempt was made even to assign the leases existing on the real estate to the corporation. Here respondent was the complete beneficial owner of the property and the lease. The difference between respondent and Westrich is the difference between a beneficial owner of income-producing property and a mere nominee for furnishing a name for the land records. In reality *Paymer* is nothing more than a restatement of the fundamental rule that income from real estate held in the name of a nominee will be taxed to the beneficial owner, not to the nominee.[1] We do not understand United States v. Brager Bldg. & Land Corp., 4 Cir., 124 F.2d 349, to involve anything more than another application of this rule.

O'Neill v. C. I. R., 2 Cir., 170 F.2d 596, certiorari denied 336 U.S. 937, 69 S. Ct. 747, 93 L. Ed. 1096, does not hold to the contrary. There an individual taxpayer created two wholly owned corporations to hold title to real estate, so that the taxpayer could deal with it without requiring his wife's signature on deeds or other documents. The corporations received some rent, and some proceeds from sale of real estate. This Court there held that the corporation was not sufficiently distinct an entity from its sole shareholder to permit advances made by the shareholder to the corporation to be treated as debts. But the corporate entity was not disregarded, because the advances were given effect as capital contributions. The question whether a corporation is to be treated as a separate taxable entity is distinct from the question whether advances made by a shareholder to that separate entity are loans or capital contributions. Nor is Jackson v. C. I. R., 2 Cir., 233 F.2d 289, in point. That case involved intermediate corporations in a holding company structure — a problem not here present. The instant case would be analogous to *Jackson* only if the shareholders of respondent formed a new corporation and transferred their stock and notes in respondent to that new corporation in exchange for its stock. The new corporation would then be comparable to the Belgrade corporation in the *Jackson* case.

Furthermore, it is to be noted that in *Jackson*, as in *O'Neill* and most of the other cases cited, the corporate entity was disregarded at the instance of the Commissioner. As is shown by this Court's decision in Gregg Co. of Del. v. C. I. R., 2 Cir., 239 F.2d 498, certiorari denied 353 U.S. 946, 77 S. Ct. 825, 1 L. Ed. 2d 856, made soon after *Jackson*, the Commissioner, to prevent unfair tax avoidance, has greater freedom and responsibility to disregard the corporate entity than a taxpayer, who normally cannot be heard to complain that a corporation which he has created, and which has served his purpose well, is a sham. In the *Gregg* case, taxpayer was a subsidiary of a New York corporation whose business operations were conducted wholly outside the United States. The parent, to eliminate the United States corporate tax on these foreign operations, decided to form a corporation in the Republic of Panama to carry on the foreign operations. In a tax-free reorganization the parent transferred its operating assets to the taxpayer in exchange for all the taxpayer's stock. The taxpayer then transferred these assets to the Panama corporation in exchange for preferred stock. Thus the taxpayer was an intermediate holding company not substantially different from the Belgrade corporation in *Jackson*. In *Jackson* the Commissioner was permitted to disregard Belgrade's corporate existence, even though that existence served the taxpayer's purpose of segregating out for the wife, as sole shareholder of Belgrade, all future profits. But in *Gregg*, 2 Cir., 239 F.2d 498, 502, when the taxpayer argued that its separate existence should be disregarded because it was a "mere conduit

---

[1]It is significant that in the *Paymer* case the court held another similar holding company, Raymep Realty Corp., Inc., taxable as a corporation because it had made a single loan, assigning its lease rights as security. While respondent stresses the absence of such circumstance here, it is obvious that this is without significance here where the corporation had no need or use of a loan to fulfill its corporate purpose.

to receive dividends," and therefore was not engaged in business activity, this Court stated: "The petitioner was originally formed in order to effectuate a tax-free reorganization, the purpose of which was found by the Tax Court to be the elimination of a corporate tax on the foreign profits of the *Gregg* operations. The reorganization was accomplished, and the petitioner served continuously as a holding company from that date forward, reporting as its corporate income the dividends it received from the corporate stock it held. Thus the petitioner has performed the functions for which it was created, and those functions are sufficient to constitute a 'business activity' for purposes of taxation."

Hence we conclude that respondent has performed the functions for which it was created, and these functions are sufficient to constitute a business activity for purposes of taxation. Higgins v. Smith, 308 U.S. 473, 477, 60 S. Ct. 355, 84 L. Ed. 406.[2] It follows that the decision of the Tax Court must be reversed and the proceedings remanded to that court for the assessment of deficiencies. It is so ordered.

J. KURTZ AND C. KOPP, TAXABILITY OF STRAW CORPORATIONS IN REAL ESTATE TRANSACTIONS*
22 Tax Lawyer 647 (1969)

One who holds record title as a nominee or agent for a beneficial owner of property is commonly referred to as a "straw." The tax consequences surrounding the use of corporate straws are in a sufficiently confused state to deter many from using them. In this article we will try to point out how this uncertainty developed, why it is unnecessary and how we believe straw corporations can be organized and handled to avoid any substantial doubt about their tax status.

Reasons for Using Straws in Real Estate

There are a number of non-tax reasons why it is frequently desirable to have title to property held by one other than the beneficial owner of the property. This practice is particularly useful where the property is real estate, primarily because of the title recording systems and financing practices unique to real estate. Some of the reasons for using a straw for real estate are:

1. To avoid mortgage liabilities. In some jurisdictions a straw is used in a mortgage transaction to limit the liability of the beneficial owner to the property.

2. To secure anonymity of ownership.

3. To simplify conveyancing. This is particularly advantageous where the property is beneficially owned by a relatively large group of individuals. In these circumstances, straw ownership permits leases or deeds to be executed by the straw rather than by each member of the large owning group and perhaps also by their spouses.

---

[2]When Congress has desired to give taxpayers the benefit of using the corporate form without paying a corporate income tax, it has known how to do so specifically and directly. Compare the election as to their taxable status given "certain small business corporations" by I.R.C. 1954, subchapter S, §§1371-77, added by Pub. L. 85-866, Tit. I, §64(a), Sept. 2, 1958, 72 Stat. 1650.

*Reprinted by permission. — ED.

4. To avoid title complications occasioned by the death of an owner. Where beneficial owners are individuals, a death of one will cloud title until the administration of his estate.

While an individual may serve as a straw, an individual straw presents these problems:

1. He is not immortal and, therefore, while he avoids title delays on the death of a beneficial owner, his own death may cause problems.

2. Although he may protect the beneficial owner from contract liability, he may incur it himself. Therefore, an individual can only be a straw for a single piece of property, since any property of which he is record holder will be subject to claims. Moreover, he must be and remain impecunious. Bachelorhood is also desirable, otherwise marital difficulties can cause considerable title problems.

These problems are eliminated if the straw is a corporation. A corporation is immortal. Separate straws can be used for each piece of property, thereby insulating each property from the liabilities of others. A corporation can be kept impecunious. Its officers can execute all documents, and officers can easily be changed if necessary.

Tax Problems — Introduction

The use of corporate straws raises troublesome and confusing tax problems.[1] The confusion and doubts seem unwarranted as a policy matter and result more from historical development than careful analysis.

The courts appear to have approached the problem of taxing straw corporations in terms of whether the corporation should be disregarded or ignored for tax purposes on the one hand, or whether it has sufficient activities to constitute a taxable entity on the other, and if it has such activities to tax it on the income from the property to which it holds title. The question properly, it seems, is not whether there is or is not a corporation for tax purposes, but rather whether an admittedly existing corporation is taxable on the income from the property in question and this, in turn, involves a factual determination as to whether the corporation is the beneficial owner of the property or only serving as a nominal titleholder.

In deciding whether a straw is a taxable entity, the courts have sometimes discussed the problem in terms of whether the real owners of the property derive any advantage from using a corporation and, if they do, the conclusion that the corporation is an entity which is taxable on the income from the property is presumed to follow. This analysis may well lead to erroneous conclusions for again the real question is not whether the use of a corporation to hold title is advantageous to the owners — presumably it always is, otherwise they would not use this form — but rather whether the corporation beneficially owns the property.

In short, the approach in the straw corporation cases should not be directed toward a determination of whether or not a particular corporation should be disregarded for tax purposes but, rather, toward a factual determination of who owns the property in question, and then taxing the income from the property to the beneficial owner.

[1]See generally, Watts, Tax Problems of Regard for the Corporate Entity, 20 N.Y.U. Inst. on Fed. Taxation 867 (1962).

To put the question in perspective, the straw corporation may be compared with an individual straw. If title to real estate is put in the name of an individual straw, there is no doubt that the real owner alone is taxable on the income from the property and not the straw. This result has nothing to do with the question whether the straw exists — he obviously does — or whether he might be paying taxes on some other income which he has, or whether he might, in fact, have income from fees which he charges for acting as a straw in this particular transaction, or whether the beneficial owner gains some non-tax advantage by using the straw. The only question is whether the straw is taxable on the income from the real estate, and this depends on whether the income is his.

Some courts have recognized the foregoing distinction. In United States v. Brager Building and Land Corp.,[2] the court held income from property taxable to a partnership where a corporation served as nominal titleholder. The court said:

> "But it is going too far to say that if a taxpayer forms a corporation for his convenience, he is thereafter estopped from disclosing the true nature of the arrangement, whenever it is of advantage to the government to recognize only the corporate form. . . . In a number of these cases . . . under circumstances quite similar to those found in the case at bar, it has been held that when a corporation has been formed merely as an agency to hold title to real estate for the convenience of the owner, and has served this purpose with little or no independent activity on its part, the property and the income therefrom should be regarded as belonging to the stockholder."[3]

Unfortunately, not all courts have adopted this analysis. The reason they have not is perhaps best explained by a look at history.

Historical Development

Although many cases dealing with straw corporations were decided prior to 1943, the logical starting point for any discussion of the subject is the Supreme Court's 1943 opinion in Moline Properties, Inc. v. Commissioner.[4] In that case, Moline Properties, Inc. sought to have its corporate existence ignored as merely fictitious for tax purposes and to have the gain on sales of real property titled in its name treated as the gain of its sole shareholder.

The facts in *Moline* were as follows: Moline Properties, Inc. was organized in 1928 at the suggestion of the second mortgagee of certain Florida realty owned by one Thompson, who was at all times Moline's sole stockholder and president. Under the mortgagee's plan, Thompson conveyed the property to the corporation, which assumed the outstanding mortgages on the property, in exchange for all but the qualifying shares of stock. Thompson then transferred the stock to a voting trustee appointed by the second mortgagee as security for an additional loan to himself.

From 1928 to 1933, the activities of the corporation consisted of the assumption of a certain obligation of Thompson to the original creditor, the defense of certain

[2] 124 F.2d 349 (4th Cir. 1941).
[3] Id. at p. 351.
[4] 319 U.S. 436 (1943).

condemnation proceedings, and the institution of a suit to remove restrictions imposed on the property by a prior deed. The expenses of the suit were paid by Thompson. In 1933, the loan which occasioned the creation of the corporation was repaid through a refinancing, and control of the corporation was returned to Thompson. In 1934, the corporation leased a portion of the property for a rental of $1,000.

The refinanced mortgage debt was paid in 1936 by means of a sale of a portion of the property titled in the corporation. The remaining property titled in the corporation's name had been sold in three parcels, one each in 1934, 1935 and 1936, the proceeds being received by Thompson and deposited in his bank account.

The corporation had no activity after the sale of the last property in 1936 but was not dissolved. It kept no books and maintained no bank account during its existence, and owned no assets other than those referred to above. The sales made in 1934 and 1935 were reported on the corporation's income tax returns, a small loss being reported in 1934 and a gain of over $5,000 being reported for 1935. Subsequently, Thompson filed a claim for refund on the corporation's behalf for 1935, and sought to report the 1935 gain on his individual return. He reported the gain on the 1936 sale.

The Supreme Court held that the corporation could not be disregarded for tax purposes in this case, and set forth the following principle which has been stated over and over again in later cases:

> "The doctrine of corporate entity fills a useful purpose in business life. Whether the purpose be to gain an advantage under the law of the state of incorporation or to avoid or to comply with the demands of creditors or to serve the creator's personal or undisclosed convenience, so long as that purpose is the equivalent of business activity or is followed by the carrying on of business by the corporation, the corporation remains a separate taxable entity."[5]

Applying the foregoing principle to the facts in the case, the Supreme Court said:

> "The petitioner corporation was created by Thompson for his advantage and had a special function from its inception. At that time it was clearly not Thompson's alter ego and his exercise of control over it was negligible. It was then as much a separate entity as if its stock had been transferred outright to third persons. The argument is made by petitioner that the force of the rule requiring its separate treatment is avoided by the fact that Thompson was coerced into creating petitioner and was completely subservient to the creditors. But this merely serves to emphasize petitioner's separate existence. . . . Business necessity, i.e., presure from creditors, made petitioner's creation advantageous to Thompson."[6]

Although the decision in this case may have been correct — after all Thompson had, for tax purposes, treated the corporation as the taxpayer by filing corporate re-

[5]Id. at pp. 438-439.
[6]Id. at pp. 439-440.

turns showing all the income and expenses of the property and paying tax — the language of the opinion is at the root of the trouble in this area.

Problems with *Moline* Approach

Evidence of the difficulties stemming from *Moline* can be seen in cases such as Paymer v. Commissioner.[7] In that case, two parcels of income-producing real estate owned by two partners were transferred respectively to two newly organized corporations in order to prevent possible attachment of the real estate by creditors of one of the partners. The partners each received half of the stock of the grantee corporations. The corporate minutes expressly stated that the corporations received the property as mere titleholders and that the full beneficial ownership and control and rights to profits remained in the two partners. The corporation had no further meetings and no office or bank accounts.

Six years after incorporation, one of the corporations (Raymep) obtained a loan from an insurance company and, as part security for the loan, executed an assignment of all of the lessor's rights in two leases on the property and expressly covenanted that it was the sole lessor.

The second corporation (Westrich) never had any activity after it took title to the real estate.

The Court of Appeals for the Second Circuit held that the second corporation was a passive dummy that could be disregarded for tax purposes but that Raymep, which engaged in the financing transaction, was not a mere dummy and should not be disregarded for tax purposes.

The court said:

> "We think that Raymep was active enough to justify holding that it did engage in business in 1938. The absence of books, records and offices and the failure to hold corporate meetings are not decisive on that question. Though Raymep was organized solely to deter creditors of one of the partners, it apparently was impossible or impracticable to use it solely for that purpose when it became necessary or desirable to secure the above mentioned loan in a substantial amount. . . .
>
> "Westrich, however, was at all times but a passive dummy which did nothing but take and hold the title to the real estate conveyed to it. It served no business purpose in connection with the property and was intended to serve only as a blind to deter the creditors of one of the partners."[8]

The *Paymer* court did not face the question of the relevance of the corporate resolutions indicating that the corporations were acting as nominal title holders. The activity of Raymep does not seem inconsistent with its role as a straw. Being the record title holder, it might well be required to execute financing documents in that capacity. The business activity test set forth in *Paymer* which is derived from *Moline* seems entirely inappropriate where the corporate records clearly indicate from the outset that the corporation is a straw and its subsequent activities are consistent with

---

[7]150 F.2d 334 (2nd Cir. 1945).
[8]Id. at pp. 336-337.

its role as a straw. To repeat an earlier example, we would not tax an individual straw on the income from property to which he held record title if he happened to execute a mortgage agreement on the property. The question properly is not whether the corporation has activity or is carrying on a business, but whether its activities or its business are those of a beneficial owner or the activities or business of a straw or agent.

The Agency Approach

Even though a number of cases have adopted an interpretation of *Moline* similar to that of the *Paymer* court,[9] another group of cases has developed the test suggested, that is, whether the corporation, admittedly in existence and having activity is acting on its own behalf or as an agent for the beneficial owners.

The foundation for the agency approach to the problem actually goes all the way back to *Moline*. In that case the Supreme Court, while setting forth the test discussed above, pointed out that there was no contract of agency nor the usual incidents of an agency relationship in the case before it. This language naturally suggested that the Court might not have taxed the income to the corporation had it been shown that the corporation was acting pursuant to an agency contract with its shareholder.

A few years after *Moline*, in National Carbide Corporation v. Commissioner of Internal Revenue,[10] the Supreme Court had the opportunity to consider a case firmly grounded on the agency theory. In that case, a parent corporation had entered into a contract with three of its subsidiaries under which the parent agreed to make available to the subsidiaries certain assets, executive management and working capital in return for which the subsidiaries agreed to turn over to the parent all of their profits from operations except a nominal amount. The Supreme Court held that ownership and control of a subsidiary does not constitute an agency relationship for tax purposes, that the contractual arrangements were entirely consistent with a corporation — sole stockholder relationship whether or not any agency relationship existed (and with other relationships as well), and that the subsidiaries were all taxable on their entire net income.

The Court went on to state, however:

"What we have said does not foreclose a true corporate agent or trustee from handling the property and income of its owner-principal without being taxable therefor . . . . If the corporation is a true agent, its relations with its principal must not be dependent upon the fact that it is owned by the principal, if such is the case. Its business purpose must be the carrying on of the normal duties of an agent."[11]

The dicta in *Moline* and *National Carbide* have been followed in several instances by the Tax Court. In two cases decided after *Moline*, but before *National Carbide*, the Tax Court held against the Commissioner on the theory that the titleholding

---

[9]See, e.g., Commissioner v. State-Adams Corporation, 283 F.2d 395 (2nd Cir. 1960); Tomlinson v. Miles, 316 F.2d 710 (5th Cir. 1963).

[10]336 U.S. 422 (1949).

[11]Id. at p. 437.

corporation was an "agent" of the beneficial owner and was, therefore, not taxable on the income received from the property held in its name. First, in Worth Steamship Corporation,[12] the Tax Court held that a corporation with record title to a steamship and an agreement to operate the ship for a joint venture owning the vessel was not taxable on the net income earned from operating the ship. The fees paid to the "agent" corporation for managing the ship's operations were reported by the corporation as its income and a tax paid thereon. In addition to a complete set of documents clearly stating that the corporation was merely holding title for the beneficial owners rather than for itself, the record in this case indicated that the beneficial owners of the vessel were not all shareholders of the titleholding corporation. One of the three joint venturers held no stock in the corporation.[13] And, in the other case — Industrial Union Oil Company[14] — the Tax Court held that a corporation which held oil leases in its name was not taxable on the income from such leases because it was specifically provided by appropriate corporate resolution that all property standing in the name of the corporation would not belong to the corporation but would be held by it as agent or trustee for the beneficial owner. In holding for the taxpayer in *Industrial Union Oil*, the court stated:

> "The respondent relies on Moline Properties, Inc. v. Commissioner, which lays down the rule, bottomed on corporate entity, that where a corporation is engaged in business it has a 'tax identity' distinct from its stockholder and gain to the corporation cannot be treated as gain to the stockholder. In the *Moline* case 'there was no actual contract of agency nor the usual incidents of agency relationship' and the Court said that 'the mere fact of the existence of a corporation with one or several stockholders, regardless of the corporation's business activities, does not make the corporation the agent of its stockholders.'
>
> "Undoubtedly, the rule laid down in the *Moline* case is thoroughly sound, but in our judgment it has no application under the facts of the case before us. . . .
>
> "The Petitioner does not contend that it was not a distinct corporate entity nor does it seek to have its corporate entity disregarded. It stands on the perfectly simple proposition that the property involved was in fact the property of Miller and the income therefrom taxable to him."[15]

The "agency" approach to the straw corporation problem is to be found continuing in the Tax Court in Caswal Corporation.[16] In that case, the Tax Court held that a corporation was not taxable on the rental income from real property titled in its name because it was acting only in a fiduciary capacity (in this case called a

[12]7 T.C. 654 (1946).
[13]The separation of ownership of the real estate and the stock of the nominal titleholder was also considered an important factor in K-C Land Company, Inc., 19 T.C.M. 183 (1960), where the Tax Court held that a titleholding corporation was not taxable on income with respect to property titled in its name.
[14]5 T.C.M. 879 (1946).
[15]Id. at pp. 881-882.
[16]19 T.C.M. 757 (1960).

"trustee" rather than an "agent" because the documents in the case described the corporation as "trustee" rather than "agent" for the beneficial owners) in collecting and remitting net rentals to its shareholders, the beneficial owners of the property.

The court's approach to the problem was as follows:

> "We need not say here . . . that the separate entity of petitioner is to be disregarded. . . . We shall assume that it was an existing and functioning corporation which was operated for the purpose of acting as fiduciary. As such, its existence separate from that of stockholders or trust beneficiaries is to be respected. But neither do we feel free to disregard the trust instrument or its effect upon the relationship of the parties. . . .
>
> "That petitioner did not actually engage in any business in its own right also seems clear. The mere collection and transmittal of the rents, with such incidental activities as negotiating with tenants and keeping the property in repair, do not on this record justify dignifying petitioner's operations an engaging in business, any more than would have been the case if an unrelated corporate fiduciary had done the same. . . . Petitioner's business, if any, was acting as fiduciary, not owning and operating an enterprise."[17]

Problems of Proof

There are, of course, considerable difficulties facing courts in applying the agency approach in certain situations. These difficulties involve making factual determinations as to whether activities performed by a corporation are performed in the capacity of beneficial owner or in the capacity of agent for the beneficial owner. Closely held corporations are controlled directly by their shareholders, just as agents are controlled by their principals. Therefore, where the shareholders of a closely held corporation argue that the corporation is in reality their agent, it is difficult to establish an agency relationship since there are few meaningful criteria available for determining the capacity in which the corporation really is acting. Many facts relied upon in support of an agency relationship are also consistent with a shareholder-corporation relationship.

The proof questions, however, only seem difficult where the stock of the corporation purporting to act as an agent as to property is owned by the beneficial owners of the property. There is little difficulty in making this determination where the beneficial owners have no interest in the stock of the corporation. That obviously is the reason that we have no problem in deciding that stock owned in street name is not owned by the brokerage firm; the beneficial owners typically have no interest in the brokerage firm and therefore the relationships are clear. This is true notwithstanding the fact that the brokerage firm may perform substantial acts in its name in connection with the stock, such as collecting dividends, voting, or selling all or part of the stock.

The ambiguous nature of the shareholder-owner-corporation-agent relationships, it is submitted, is at the heart of the problem and is the underlying reason for the courts' decisions in the cases like *Moline* and *Paymer*. A careful reading of the *Moline*

---

[17]Id. at p. 763.

case indicates that the court was not denying that a corporation could be a straw. It was more likely concerned, however, with the substantial problems of proof that would ensue if it adopted fairly liberal views as to when a corporation could be considered the agent for its shareholders. It seems to have adopted what amounts to a presumption that a corporation is the beneficial owner of property titled in its name, as against the claimed beneficial ownership of its shareholders. Some other courts, unfortunately, have misinterpreted *Moline* and seem to have made the presumption conclusive except where the corporation did absolutely nothing.

It should be pointed out, in all fairness, that most of the cases were apparently decided properly on their facts.[18] It seems appropriate that the taxpayer be faced with a substantial burden of proof where he claims that a corporation is not the beneficial owner of property titled in its name. But the burden of proof should not be insurmountable — presumption should not be conclusive against him. Where the corporate documents are clear from the beginning that the corporation is an agent and where its activities are consistent with its agent's role, the agency should be recognized. Moreover, an agent may well have activities in connection with the property, such as signing documents incident to its role as title holder.

The burden of proof problem could be more easily met by individuals wishing to use corporate straws if they used corporate straws in which they had no interest as shareholders. If the agency cases are correct, and it is believed they are, and if *Moline* and the cases following it are essentially failure of proof cases, as it is believed they are, then there is nothing in any of the cases which would imply that a corporation would be taxed with the income of property titled in its name where it is clearly acting as a straw.

Such a corporation would not be claiming that it did not exist for tax purposes or that it was a dummy, but rather that it was an existing corporation in the business of acting as a straw or agent, and, in fact, it would probably have income from fees charged for this service.

Summary and Recommendations

To summarize, the basic problem of straw corporations should not be a theoretical one of whether a corporation should be ignored for tax purposes or whether it should be viewed as a taxable entity where the shareholder-owners chose to use the corporate form to hold legal title for non-tax reasons, but rather should be one of proof of who owns the property. However, the courts — witness the recent *Miles* case[19] — still speak in terms of the shareholder's personal reasons for forming the corporation, the business activities of the corporation and whether the corporation should be disregarded or not for tax purposes. Therefore, it remains difficult for a taxpayer to feel at all secure in using a straw corporation to hold title to real

---

[18]In Commissioner v. State-Adams Corporation, 283 F.2d 395 (2nd Cir. 1960), for example, there were no specific corporate documents to indicate that the corporation was to act in the capacity of agent rather than beneficial owner. On the other hand, in Tomlinson v. Miles, 316 F.2d 710 (5th Cir. 1963), there were appropriate corporate documents but the corporation's activities were more consistent with the role of beneficial owner than of agent.

[19]Supra note 17.

estate where, as in the normal case, the corporation is admittedly formed for the personal convenience of the shareholder, and will in fact engage in business activities involving the execution of various documents for acquisitions, mortgages, leases, sales, etc.

The situation is, of course, particularly risky where the taxpayer is striving to bring his case under the *Moline* rule of having the straw corporation disregarded for tax purposes. Any corporate activity such as obtaining a loan — as in *Paymer* — can cause a court to hold that the corporation cannot be ignored for tax purposes. Moreover, any one or a combination of maintaining a corporate bank account, using corporate funds to acquire and maintain the property, executing a substantial number of leases, mortgages, sales, etc., in its name, or failing to have documentary evidence that the corporation is acting only as a nominal titleholder for the real owners, may well cause a court to treat a corporation as a separate entity for tax purposes. It is believed, however, that a taxpayer should be relatively safe in having the income or loss from real estate taxed directly to him where he transfers record title to a corporation formed to act as an *agent* for himself, the beneficial owner.

In the "agency" approach, the importance of carefully drawn documents clearly describing the limited purposes, duties and powers of the corporate agent or nominee and the control and beneficial ownership in the principal cannot be overstated. A straw corporation should be recognized as such if (1) it sets forth in its articles of incorporation that its corporate powers are limited to holding title to property on behalf of others and not itself, (2) it executes appropriate agreements and corporate resolutions spelling out clearly that the corporation's sole business is acting as agent and nominal titleholder for the beneficial owners, (3) under the terms of its agreements with the beneficial owners, the corporation has no discretionary authority to act with respect to the property titled in its name but may act only upon written direction from the beneficial owners, (4) the corporation agrees by contract to terminate the agency relationship upon notice from the beneficial owners and to retransfer legal title to such owners at their direction, (5) all income and expenses with respect to the property are paid to and out of the beneficial owners' bank account, the only funds passing through the straw corporation's bank account being the fees it receives for acting as nominal titleholder and executing specific documents on behalf of the beneficial owners, and amounts which it pays out for professional fees, etc., incurred as a result of conducting its business as an agent, and (6) all other corporate documents are consistent with the proposition that the straw corporation has no interest in, or duties or responsibilities toward, the property except to perform purely ministerial tasks at the direction of the real owners. And, as a final and important step in avoiding difficult proof problems concerning the tax status of the straw corporation as an agent, the shareholders of the straw corporation should be different from and independent of the beneficial owners of the property.

In these circumstances, the taxpayer would not argue that the corporation should be disregarded for tax purposes. He would concede that the corporation exists and, in fact, the corporation would file tax returns showing the income from nominee fees received and expenses incurred by the corporation from its business of acting as a nominal titleholder. If the factual situation conforms with the above pattern, it is believed that the profit or loss from the property should properly be taxed to the beneficial owners and not to the agent or nominee corporation.

IV. MULTIPLE CORPORATIONS — §§269, 1551, 1561-1563

COASTAL OIL STORAGE CO. v. COMMISSIONER
242 F.2d 396 (4th Cir. 1957)

Before PARKER, Chief Judge, SOBELOFF, Circuit Judge, and GILLIAM, District Judge.

PARKER, Chief Judge. These are cross appeals from the decision of the Tax Court of the United States reported in 25 T.C. 1304. The questions involved relate to the right of a corporate taxpayer to the $25,000 corporate surtax exemption and minimum excess profits credit . . . . The corporation was organized February 1, 1951. The surtax exemption and minimum excess profits credit were claimed for the months of February to June 1951. They were denied by the Tax Court for the months of April, May and June 1951 under the restrictions imposed by section 15(c) of the Tax Code but allowed for the months of February and March for the reason that the restrictions imposed by that section were not applicable in the latter months. The taxpayer appeals from the denial for the months of April, May and June, the Commissioner from the allowance for February and March, the Commissioner contending that they should be denied for those months under the provisions of section [269(a)]. . . .

Taxpayer's Appeal

Coastal Terminals, Inc. was organized in 1944 for the purpose of supplying and storing petroleum products. It constructed a terminal at North Charleston, S.C. and leased some of the storage facilities there to the office of the Quartermaster General under renegotiable contracts. On February 1, 1951 Coastal Terminals, Inc., caused the taxpayer, the Coastal Oil Storage Company, to be organized and transferred to it seven oil storage tanks, with a capacity of 150,000 barrels, for $100,000 of the capital stock of taxpayer, which was all of the capital stock that taxpayer issued, and a note for $38,706.79, which taxpayer paid off at the rate of $5,062.50 per month until it was extinguished. The reason given in the testimony before the Tax Court for the creation of taxpayer was to separate storage operations under storage contracts with the government from operations under contracts with others; but it was admitted that tax aspects of the transaction were taken into consideration and no satisfactory reason was given why the same advantages could not have been obtained by separate bookkeeping that were obtained by separate incorporation, which necessarily resolved itself into little more than separate bookkeeping. As a result of the incorporation of taxpayer, the operations at North Charleston received two $25,000 surtax exemptions and minimum excess profits credits instead of one; and the Tax Court found that taxpayer had failed to establish by a clear preponderance of the evidence that the securing of the extra exemption or credit, or both, was not a major purpose of the transfer of the property to the taxpayer. It, therefore, denied the exemption for the months of April, May and June 1951, under section 15(c) of the Tax Code,[1] the pertinent portion of which is as follows:

> "If any corporation transfers, on or after January 1, 1951, all or part of its property (other than money) to another corporation which was created for the purpose of acquiring such property or which was not actively engaged in business at the time of such acquisition, and if after such transfer the transferor corporation or its stockholders, or both, are in control of such transferee corporation during any part of the taxable year of such transferee corporation, then such transferee corporation shall not for such taxable year (except as may be otherwise determined under section [269] be allowed either the $25,000 exemption from surtax . . . or the $25,000 minimum excess profits credit . . . unless such transferee corporation shall establish by the clear preponderance of the evidence that the securing of such exemption or credit was not a major purpose of such transfer."

We agree with the Tax Court that the taxpayer failed to sustain the burden of proof imposed by the statute to "establish by the clear preponderance of the evidence that the securing of such exemption or credit was not a major purpose of such transfer". Since the keeping of separate records as to government business would have accomplished the separation of government business from other business just as well as the incorporation of a subsidiary corporation, it is difficult to see how the incorporation and transfer could have had any real purpose other than tax avoidance. At all events, we would not be justified in setting aside the finding of the Tax Court as clearly erroneous.

The Commissioner's Appeal

While admitting that the section of the Revenue Code above quoted has no application to income for the months of February and March 1951, the Commissioner contends that the taxpayer should be denied the surtax exemption and minimum excess profits credit for those months under the provisions of section [269]. . . .*

The Tax Court considered this contention of the Commissioner but held the section inapplicable, without passing on the question as to whether or not tax evasion or avoidance was the principal purpose of the transfer in question. In this we think there was error. It is clear that the parent corporation acquired complete control of taxpayer through stock ownership and the parent corporation was certainly a person within the meaning of subsection (1) of the statute. As a result of the transfer of its property in exchange for the stock, it was able to obtain through this splitting up of its corporate business the benefit of an exemption and credit which it would not other-

---

[1]This section was added by section 121(f) of the Revenue Act of 1951 and is applicable only after March 31, 1951 . . . .

[The 1954 Code successor is §1551.]

*Subsection (c) of §269 was added in 1954 and had no counterpart in the law applicable to this case. — ED.

wise have enjoyed. While the exemption is claimed by taxpayer, the sole benefit thereof would accrue to the parent corporation, the sole owner of its stock. Cf. Higgins v. Smith, 308 U.S. 473, 476, 60 S. Ct. 355, 84 L. Ed. 406. We see no reason, therefore, why subsection (1) of the section is not applicable. Subsection (2) is applicable also, since taxpayer, as a result of the transfer from the parent corporation, received property having a basis for tax purposes which would be determined by reference to its basis in the hands of the parent corporation,[2] and the transfer resulted in the securing of a surtax exemption and minimum profits credit, to which neither the taxpayer nor the parent corporation would have been entitled otherwise; for the taxpayer could not have enjoyed the benefit of the surtax exemption and excess profits tax credit but for the acquisition of the property producing the income from or against which the exemption and credit are claimed. That the section was intended to reach just such schemes for tax evasion or avoidance by the splitting up of a business enterprise clearly appears from the H. Rep. No. 871, 78th Cong. 1st Sess., p. 49, where it is said:

> "This section . . . provid[es] that in the case of acquisitions on or after October 8, 1940, of an interest in or control of corporations or property which the Commissioner finds to be principally motivated by or availed of for the avoidance of income or excess profits tax by securing the benefit of a deduction, credit, or other allowance, then the tax benefits are to be disallowed or allowed only in part in a manner consistent with the prevention of tax avoidance. This section is designed to put an end promptly to any market for, or dealings in, interests in corporations or property which have as their objective the reduction through artifice of the income or excess profits tax liability.

> "The crux of the devices which have come to the attention of your committee has been some form of acquisition on or after the effective date of the Second Revenue Act of 1940, but the devices take many forms. Thus, the acquisition may be an acquisition of the shares of a corporation, or it may be an acquisition which follows by operation of law in the case of a corporation resulting from a statutory merger or consolidation. The person, or persons, making the acquisition likewise vary, as do the forms or methods of utilization under which tax avoidance is sought. Likewise, the tax benefits sought may be one or more of several deductions or credits, including the utilization of excess profits credits, carry-overs, and carry-backs of losses or unused excess profits credits, and anticipated expense of other deductions. In the light of these considerations, the section has not confined itself to a description of any particular methods for carrying out such tax avoidance schemes but has included within its scope these devices in whatever form they may appear. *For similar reasons, the scope of the terms used in the section is to be found in the objective of the section, namely, to prevent the tax liability from being reduced through the distortion or perversion effected through tax avoidance devices. . . ."* (Italics supplied.)

[2] It is not disputed that the basis of the seven storage tanks in the hands of the taxpayer should be determined by reference to the basis in the hands of the parent corporation [under §362]. . . .

This accords with the interpretation placed upon the section by a later Congress, where in the Senate report on proposed amendments to the corporate surtax exemption provisions, it was said (S. Rep. No. 2375, 81st Cong. 2d Sess. p. 70, 2 Cum. Bull. 483, 533):

> "It is not intended, however, that the exemption of the first $25,000 of a corporation's surtax net income from the surtax shall be abused by the splitting up, directly or indirectly, of a business enterprise into two or more corporations or the forming of two or more corporations to carry on an integrated business enterprise. It is believed that sections [482 and 269] will prevent this form of tax avoidance."

The Tax Court refers to its decision in Commodores Point Terminal Corp. v. Com'r, 11 T.C. 411; but that was an entirely different case from this and is no precedent for its decision here. There a corporation had acquired a controlling interest in another corporation and the question was whether it was entitled to a dividends received credit on the stock purchased in the transaction. The Tax Court in allowing the credit pointed out that the dividends, and consequent credit, were not dependent on the taxpayer's having acquired control of the other corporation. In this case, as pointed out above, the taxpayer could not have enjoyed the exemption and credit claimed but for the acquisition of the property producing the income, which was transferred to it by the parent corporation. There, not only was there a holding that there was no purpose of tax avoidance, but the transaction was not one which involved tax avoidance. Here there can be no question but that tax avoidance necessarily resulted from the corporate splitting which was involved. . . .

Affirmed on Taxpayer's Appeal.

Reversed and Remanded for further proceedings on Commissioner's Appeal.

JAMES REALTY CO. v. UNITED STATES
280 F.2d 394 (8th Cir. 1960)

Before GARDNER, WOODROUGH, and BLACKMUN, Circuit Judges.

WOODROUGH, Circuit Judge. The taxpayer James Realty Company, a corporation, . . . received and made return of income of $24,699.05 for the period and claimed deduction under the $25,000 corporate surtax exemption and $25,000 minimum excess profits tax credit. . . .

The Commissioner disallowed the deduction and credit on the ground that the corporation was created solely for the purpose of tax avoidance and was deprived of the right to the exemption and credit by Sections [269(a) and 1551]. . . .

It appeared on the trial that Adolph Fine organized Adolph Fine, Inc., in 1944 to engage in the construction business and later in 1949 he incorporated Fine Realty, Inc., whose principal activity was to sell homes built by Adolph Fine, Inc. Both of these corporations were controlled and managed by Adolph Fine and his wife, Mildred, who owned the stock of such corporations individually or in trust for their children. Also, at all times pertinent hereto, Adolph Fine was president and treasurer,

Mildred Fine was vice president and secretary, and June Myslajek was assistant secretary to Adolph Fine, Inc.; Mildred Fine was president and treasurer, M. L. Grossman was vice president, and June Myslajek was secretary of Fine Realty, Inc.

In 1952, Adolph Fine, as an individual, owned certain undeveloped land located in the village of St. Louis Park, Minnesota, which he caused to be subdivided and platted for the purpose of home development, and named it the Jeffrey, James Fine Addition to St. Louis Park.

On November 20, 1952, Adolph Fine caused the taxpayer, James Realty Company, to be organized with an initial authorized capital of $25,000, consisting of ten shares of Class A common stock at a par value of $100 (voting) and two hundred and forty shares of Class B common stock at a par value of $100 (non-voting). According to the articles of incorporation, the purpose of the corporation was, among other things: "To acquire, improve, and develop real property; to erect dwellings of all kinds and to sell, or rent the same; also to acquire, by purchase, lease, or otherwise, and to take, own, hold, sell, exchange, transfer, lease, repair, maintain, improve, mortgage, or in any other manner deal in and with real property . . . ."

On November 24, 1952, Adolph Fine conveyed eighteen of the lots in the Jeffrey, James Fine Addition to the taxpayer corporation in exchange for two shares of its Class A common stock and thirty-four shares of its Class B common stock. The value of the lots in terms of the thirty-six shares was $200 per lot or $3,600. On the same day, Adolph Fine transferred seventeen shares of the Class B stock to his wife Mildred in trust for their sons Jeffrey and James.

Also on November 24, 1952, the taxpayer corporation, acting through its president, Adolph Fine, entered into two written contracts. The first was an agreement with Adolph Fine, Inc., by which that corporation would construct houses on the lots owned by the taxpayer James Realty Co., at cost plus 12½%. By the terms of a second contract, with Fine Realty, Inc., that corporation was made the exclusive selling agent of the homes to be constructed for taxpayer by Adolph Fine, Inc. Sales commissions were to be from 5% to 7½% depending upon financing arrangements and costs.

In August, 1953, taxpayer purchased thirty-six lots located in the neighboring West Tonka Hills Addition from Fine Realty, Inc. at a price of $650 per lot, or a total price of $23,000.

During its fiscal year ended November 30, 1953, when taxpayer reported taxable income in the amount of $24,699.05, only $355.56 of this amount was attributable to the sale of lots purchased from Fine Realty, Inc., while the remaining income was derived from sales of houses built on lots acquired from Adolph Fine.

Taxpayer was one of nine development companies formed by Adolph Fine between 1950 and 1954. All of them occupied offices owned by Adolph Fine, Inc., and were supplied with bookkeeping services by the same personnel who kept the books of Adolph Fine, Inc. . . .

The Court considered the testimony tendered by the taxpayer to show that its existence was justified by bona fide business purposes although as Mr. Fine testified, "he was aware" of the tax results of the multiple corporations he caused to be organized.

The District Court found as ultimate facts: (a) that there was no real business purpose for the creation of the taxpayer corporation and that it derived no income from independent activities of a nature different from those of Adolph Fine, Inc., and Fine Realty, Inc.; (b) that the principal purpose for the acquisition of the taxpayer corporation by Adolph Fine was tax avoidance by securing the benefit of another corporate surtax exemption and excess profits credit which he would not otherwise enjoy; (c) that taxpayer was created for the purpose of acquiring property from other corporations controlled by the same stockholders and was not actively engaged in business in August, 1953, when it acquired the thirty-six lots from Fine Realty, Inc.; (d) that at the time of the formation of the taxpayer-corporation Adolph Fine, Inc., and Fine Realty, Inc., were conducting trades or businesses substantially similar to that of the taxpayer corporation during its taxable year ended November 30, 1953; (e) and that during its taxable year ended November 30, 1953, the taxpayer did not permit earnings or profits to accumulate beyond the reasonable needs of its business.

Accordingly, the court concluded that the Commissioner properly disallowed the surtax exemption and minimum excess profits tax credit under Sections [1551 and 269(a)].

The question presented here is whether control of the taxpayer was acquired by Adolph Fine for the principal purpose of avoiding federal income and excess profits taxes by securing the benefit of another surtax exemption and excess profits tax credit which he would not otherwise enjoy so that the disallowance of the exemption and credit was proper. . . .

The determination by the District Court that Mr. Fine organized and acquired control of the taxpayer corporation for the principal purpose of tax avoidance was a finding of fact which is conclusive on this appeal if supported by substantial evidence and not clearly erroneous. Although Mr. Fine testified that in forming the taxpayer and eight other corporations he had in mind the two purposes of implementing his estate plan and of spreading and minimizing risks of loss from business reversal or tort liability and that tax saving was not the principal purpose, he admitted that he was aware of the tax consequences of the multiple corporate set up and testimony of his secretary and bookkeeper was to the effect that "she made adjusting entries" in the books of Adolph Fine, Inc., Fine Realty, Inc., and the development companies including taxpayer; that "a great deal of consideration was given to taxes" by Mr. Fine and his accountants and that "we were very careful to keep the figures under $25,000.00, the profit figures." An office memorandum from Mr. Fine made in 1957 concerning "the land status" of "the following companies" "to determine what company should own and develop" certain lands included the statement: "This will depend upon the possible profit status for the year 1957 in each of the companies." The tax returns of the various corporations formed by Mr. Fine as shown in the Exhibit B which the District Court included in its opinion shows that in 1950 the income from development and sale of homes reported by Adolph Fine, Inc. and Fine Realty, Inc. was $202,268.00 and $34,212.00. For the ensuing years 1951-1956 following the creation of the various development companies the taxable income of the two named companies dropped with but few exceptions to less than $25,000.00

and each of those companies reported less than $25,000.00. Notwithstanding Mr. Fine's testimony that avoidance of tax was not a prime consideration in splitting his home building business, there was substantial evidence to support the finding of the Court that the principal purpose was to avoid federal income or excess profit tax by securing the benefit of deductions and credits which he would not otherwise enjoy.

Appellant contends here as it did below that creation of a new corporation and obtaining its stock is not an acquisition of the control of a corporation within the meaning of Section [269(a)]. The Court in rejecting the contention said [176 F. Supp. 310]:

> "Although the legislative history and the case law under Section 129 indicate that it was aimed at the abuses of one corporation acquiring going concerns which had accrued certain tax exemptions, see J. E. Dilworth Co. v. Henslee, D.C. Tenn. 1951, 98 F. Supp. 957, 960 (dictum); Rudick, Acquisitions to Avoid Income or Excess Profits Tax: Section 129 of the Internal Revenue Code, 58 Harv. L. Rev. 196 (1944), there is no settled view that 'acquisition of control' cannot and should not include the organization of a new corporation such as was done here. See Alcorn Wholesale Co., 1951, 16 T.C. 75, 88; 7 Mertens, Federal Taxation, §38.66, n.75 (1956). The regulations promulgated under the 1939 Code provide that acquisition of control of a corporation may be accomplished by acquiring the stock of a newly organized corporation. Reg. 118, §§39.129-1(d) and 39.129-3(b)(2)."

We find no error in the Trial Court's ruling on this contention. . . .

In view of our conclusion in this case that the deduction claimed by the taxpayer was forbidden by Section [269(a)] it is not necessary for us to pass upon the application and effect of Section [1551] and we expressly refrain from doing so.

The judgment appealed from is
Affirmed.

J. LEVIN, MULTIPLE CORPORATIONS*

One of the most significant corporate changes made by the 1969 Act is in the multiple corporation area.

A. Prior Law

Under section 2 of the Code corporations pay tax at a 48% rate, but if a corporation is entitled to a $25,000 surtax exemption it pays tax at a 22% rate on its first $25,000 of taxable income and 48% only on the excess over $25,000. Thus a $25,000 surtax exemption can save a corporation $6,500, that is, 26% of $25,000.

In 1964 Congress enacted Code sections 1561 through 1564 which provide, in general, that certain groups of related corporations will be allowed only one $25,000

*Excerpted from Corporate Adjustments, in A Practitioner's Guide to the Tax Reform Act of 1969, 25 (1970). Reprinted by permission of Practising Law Institute. — ED.

surtax exemption rather than one for each corporation in the group. This rule applied to two types of related corporate groups: a parent corporation and its 80% owned subsidiaries (called a parent-subsidiary group) and a group of corporations each of which is 80% owned by one person, including stock which is attributed to such person (called a brother-sister group).

However, the 1964 Act contained a gaping exception. If a parent-subsidiary or brother-sister group filed a written election, each corporation in the group could take a $25,000 surtax election but there would be three disadvantages flowing from this election. First, each corporation in the group would pay 28% rather than 22% tax on the first $25,000 of its taxable income. In general, this merely reduced the tax saving from multiple surtax exemptions from $6,500 each to $5,000 each.

The second disadvantage to a group which made the multiple surtax election was that it could not elect to have 100% of its intercorporate dividends excluded from income under Code section 243(b). Only the usual 85% dividends received deduction would apply to (a) intercorporate dividends received in a year in which a multiple surtax election was in effect or (b) intercorporate dividends received out of earnings and profits (that is, E & P) earned during a year in which a multiple surtax election was in effect.

The third disadvantage of a multiple surtax election was that any losses suffered by a member of the group during a year in which a multiple surtax election was in effect would be separate return limitation year losses. This meant that if the group later filed a consolidated tax return, a loss suffered by one of the corporations during a year in which the group had a multiple surtax election in effect could not be offset against the profits of any other member of the group.

Despite these three disadvantages of making the multiple surtax election, it was generally still attractive for most businesses to operate through multiple corporations, to make the election and thus to pay tax at the 28% rate rather than the 48% rate on the first $25,000 of taxable income of each corporation.

There was one exception to the above stated rules. Under certain circumstances stated in Code sections 1551 and 269 where the formation of a new corporation had a tax avoidance motive, the new corporation's $25,000 surtax exemption would be disallowed regardless of the election. However, sections 1551 and 269 turn on a subjective test and the government frequently had difficulty proving its case.

B. Changes Made by the 1969 Act

The 1969 Act made a very significant change in the law of multiple corporations. Effective for years beginning after December 31, 1974, a parent-subsidiary or brother-sister group is allowed only one $25,000 surtax exemption and only one $100,000 accumulated earnings tax credit. After 1974, there will be no such thing as an election to claim multiple surtax exemptions.

These changes are phased in over a six-year period from 1969 through 1974. During this six-year period, an electing parent-subsidiary or brother-sister group is entitled to one $25,000 exemption and the amount of each exemption in excess of one is reduced by one-sixth per year. Thus, for taxable years which include December 31, 1969, a group electing multiple surtax exemptions can claim a $25,000 surtax exemption for each corporation in the group; for years which include December 31, 1970 one corporation in such a group can claim a $25,000 surtax exemption and each other corporation can claim approximately a $20,800 surtax exemption. In succeeding years the amount of the surtax exemptions in excess of one drops to $16,600 in 1971, $12,500 in 1972, $8,300 in 1973, $4,100 in 1974 and zero thereafter. Similarly the $100,000 accumulated earnings credit in excess of one drops approximately $16,600 each year until it is zero in 1975. Because these transition rules apply to years including a particular December 31, it may be advantageous for newly formed corporations to elect fiscal years ending on November 30.

During the transition period each corporation which is a member of a group electing multiple surtax exemptions pays 28% rather than 22% tax on its taxable income up to the amount of its surtax exemption.

As I mentioned earlier, if a corporation elected multiple surtax exemptions, it was not entitled to elect the 100% dividends received deduction under Code section 243(b), and was entitled to exclude only 85% of intercorporate dividends. The 1969 Act permits certain groups to elect to gradually increase their dividends received deduction from 85% to 100% over the six-year period as the benefit of their multiple surtax exemptions gradually declines from $25,000 to zero. This provision applies only to groups which had a multiple surtax election in effect on April 22, 1969. If such a group makes a proper election, its intercorporate dividends received deduction increases by 2½% per year. For such a group, dividends distributed out of E & P accumulated in 1969 and prior years are entitled to an 85% dividends received deduction; dividends distributed out of E & P accumulated in 1970 are entitled to an 87½% dividends received deduction and so on until the figure reaches 100% for E & P accumulated in 1975 and thereafter. However, with regard to E & P accumulated before 1975, this provision applies only if the dividend is paid before 1978.

Another significant change effected by the 1969 Act is a substantial broadening of the definition of a brother-sister group. Formerly a brother-sister group included only those corporations 80% owned by one person, including stock attributed to such person. Thus, if Mr. A and Mr. B were unrelated and each owned 50% of the stock of 10 corporations, the 10 corporations were not a brother-sister group and were free to claim multiple surtax exemptions without paying the 6% penalty tax, since no one person (either directly or by attribution) owned 80% of both corporations' stock.

The 1969 Act provides, with one qualification, that a brother-sister group includes all corporations which are 80% owned (directly or by attribution) by 5 or fewer persons. The qualification is that this rule applies only to those corporations in which the 5 or fewer persons own more than 50% of the stock counting each person's ownership only to the extent of his lowest percentage ownership of any corporation in the group. Thus, if Corporation X is owned 80% and 20% by A and B, respectively, and Corporation Y is owned 20% and 80% by the same two people, the two corporations would not be part of a brother-sister controlled group, since the overlapping ownership is only 40%. But if the two corporations were owned 70%-30% and 30%-70% by the two men, there would be 60% overlapping ownership and the two would be a brother-sister group. . . .

NOTE

For comment on, and analysis of, the law antedating the Tax Reform Act of 1969, see T. White, III, The New Broader Sweep of Section 1551: An Analysis of IRS' Regulations, 28 J. Taxation 100 (1968); P. Elder, Operating Problems of Multiple Corporations, 24 N.Y.U. Inst. on Fed. Tax. 1145 (1966); W. Hannam, Planning for Controlled Corporations Under the Revenue Act of 1964, 1965 So. Calif. Tax Inst. 85. See generally B. Bittker and J. Eustice, Federal Income Taxation of Corporations and Shareholders 67-79, 684-689 (2d ed. 1966).

As to current law, see J. Kringel, Coping with the 1969 Act's New Rules for Corporate Groups, 32 J. Taxation 136 (1970); J. Eustice, Corporations and Corporate Investors, 25 Tax L. Rev. 509 (1970).

V. REALLOCATION OF CORPORATE INCOME — §482

NATIONAL SECURITIES CORP. v. COMMISSIONER
137 F.2d 600 (3d Cir. 1943), cert. denied, 320 U.S. 794 (1943)

Before Biggs, Maris, and Goodrich, Circuit Judges.

Maris, Circuit Judge. The petitioner, National Securities Corporation, is the successor of the taxpayer, American Gas & Electric Securities Corporation, and is liable by reason of its merger with the taxpayer for all obligations of the latter, including federal income taxes. During its entire existence the taxpayer was a wholly owned subsidiary of American Equitable Assurance Company of New York. The taxpayer's income and expenses were recorded in separate books of account kept by it and its accounts were not commingled with those of the parent. In August and September, 1929 the parent purchased as an investment 1,000 shares of the common stock of Standard Gas and Electric Company at a cost of $140,378.06. By 1933 the parent's purchases of Standard stock had increased to a total of 3,500 shares, at a cost of $418,780.19. During 1935 reorganization of Standard was commenced under §77B of the Bankruptcy Act . . . . At the close of that year the Standard stock, for which the parent had paid an average of approximately $120 per share, had decreased in value to $6.25 per share. In January, 1936 the parent sold 2,500 shares of Standard stock in the open market at prices ranging from $7.75 to $9.125 per share. On February 13, 1936 the parent delivered its remaining 1,000 shares of Standard to the taxpayer in exchange for the latter's capital stock having a stated value of $10 per share and a market value of more than $92 per share. These shares on the date when delivered to the taxpayer had a market value of $8,562.50. On December 11, 1936 the taxpayer sold the Standard stock for $7,175.00. The proceeds of the sale were received and kept by the taxpayer. In its income tax return for

1936 the taxpayer claimed as a deductible loss $133,203.06 representing the difference between the cost of the 1,000 shares to the parent ($140,378.06) and the amount for which the taxpayer sold them ($7,175.00).

The Commissioner disallowed in its entirety the deduction claimed by the taxpayer and assessed a deficiency. At the hearing before the Board of Tax Appeals, however, he conceded that the taxpayer was entitled to that part of the claimed deduction which represented the difference between $8,562.50, the fair market value of the Standard shares when acquired by the taxpayer, and $7,175.00, the amount for which the taxpayer sold them, or $1,387.50. The Board of Tax Appeals sustained the Commissioner's action as thus modified. 1942, 46 B.T.A. 562.

The Commissioner disallowed the loss upon authority of Section [482]. . . .

The taxpayer's first contention is that since Section [482] is a general statute dealing with the allocation of gross income and deductions it cannot be controlling here because Congress has specifically provided by Sections [351 and 362(a)] that a corporation, which has acquired property from its controlling stockholder and which sells that property for an amount less than the original cost of the property to its stockholder, may deduct the difference as a loss in computing its own net income for the year of the sale.

We think, however, that the petitioner misconceives the distinct functions of these provisions of the statute. Sections [351 and 362(a)(1)] were intended to regulate the time when certain gains or losses are to be recognized for tax purposes and the cost bases to be used in determining the amounts of such gains or losses. It is true that they likewise lay down a general rule to determine which taxpayer shall take such gains or losses into account. These sections were followed in the present case by the Commissioner when he determined that no loss should be recognized upon the transfer of the Standard shares by the parent to the taxpayer and that the loss sustained by the taxpayer upon the later sale of these shares should be measured by their original cost to the parent.

Section [482] on the other hand is addressed to the wholly different problem of providing a more appropriate manner of allocating income and deductions when the application of the general rules of the statute will not clearly reflect the true income. . . . Section [482] is directed to the correction of particular situations in which the strict application of the other provisions of the act will result in a distortion of the income of affiliated organizations. In every case in which the section is applied its application will necessarily result in an apparent conflict with the literal requirements of some other provision of the act. If this were not so Section [482] would be wholly superfluous. We accordingly conclude that the application of Section [482] may not be denied because it appears to run afoul of the literal provisions of Sections [351 and 362(a)(1)] if the Commissioner's action in allocating under the provisions of Section [482] the loss involved in this case was a proper exercise of the discretion conferred upon him by the section.

By Section [482] Congress has conferred authority upon Commissioner to allocate deductions "if he determines" that such allocation "is necessary". This is a broad discretion, limited only in that the necessity must arise "in order to prevent evasion of taxes or clearly to reflect the income." G. U. R. Co. v. Commissioner, 7 Cir., 1941, 117 F.2d 187.

The Commissioner takes the position that allocation was necessary in order clearly to reflect the income. In this determination he was sustained by the Board. Our examination of the facts convinces us that this determination was neither arbitrary nor capricious. The parent made the investment in Standard stock in 1929, held on to the stock as an investment until 1936, concluded to rid its own portfolio at a time when the stock had become well nigh valueless and then, instead of selling on the market, taking its loss and marking "finis" to a most unprofitable venture, transferred the stock to its wholly owned subsidiary. It seems most reasonable to treat the loss as one which had in fact been sustained by the parent rather than by its subsidiary. The shifting of the loss to the subsidiary gives an artificial picture of its true income and one which it was unnecessary for the Commissioner to accept. The shares for which the taxpayer claims a loss of $133,203.06 had been acquired by it for its own stock having a declared value on its books of only $8,000 and a market value of only about $75,000. The Commissioner was not bound to accept the petitioner's explanation that the parent transferred the stock solely for the purpose of ridding itself of an investment which it was unwise for an insurance company to retain and not for the purpose of tax avoidance. The Commissioner was justified in finding that the taxpayer's income was not clearly reflected by its return for 1936 since the return included a loss which was in fact incurred by the parent. We conclude that the Commissioner's action was neither arbitrary nor capricious.

Finally the taxpayer contends that in fact the Commissioner did not allocate the loss as Section [482] requires but merely disallowed it to the taxpayer. As we have seen, counsel for the Commissioner at the hearing before the Board conceded that $1,387.50 of the $133,203.06 loss should be allowed to the taxpayer and the Board's decision approved this allowance. For all practical purposes this was an allocation of the remainder of the loss to the parent. For in his deficiency notice the Commissioner stated that he was disallowing the deduction to the taxpayer "by application of the provisions of Section [482]. . . ." There is clearly implicit in this disallowance of the loss to the subsidiary on the authority of Section [482] a finding that the loss has been allocated to the parent. This is true even though under the circumstances of this case such an allocation would have had no practical effect upon the parent's income tax for 1936.[3]

The decision of the Board of Tax Appeals is affirmed.

[3]Though the parent's liability for tax is not here involved it appears from the stipulation that in its income tax return for that year the parent reported $1,706,683.76 profits from the sales of stock and $1,723,376.88 losses. This resulted in a net capital loss of $16,693.12. Since Sections 23(j) and 117(d) of the Revenue Act of 1936 permit deductions arising from losses from sales or exchanges of capital assets to be taken only to the extent of $2,000 the parent could not have derived any actual tax benefit from an allocation of the losses from the sale of the Standard stock.

NOTE

Does the basis provision of §362(a) apply only when §351 bars recognition of a gain, or does it also apply when §351 bars recognition of a loss? If so, when?

W. BRAUN CO. v. COMMISSIONER
396 F.2d 264 (2d Cir. 1968)

Before MOORE, WOODBURY* and SMITH, Circuit Judges.

MOORE, Circuit Judge: This case was brought to contest an asserted deficiency of $8,665.98 in the income tax return of W. Braun Co., Inc., petitioner-appellant, for the fiscal year ended February 29, 1960. The deficiency arose because the Commissioner, acting pursuant to 26 U.S.C. §482, attributed to the petitioner all the taxable income of Braunware Products Co., Inc., a corporation wholly owned by petitioner.

Three corporations are involved. Both the ownership interest therein and the chronology of the events are important in deciding the proper tax consequences of the facts hereinafter set forth.

1. W. Braun Co., an Illinois corporation ("Braun Chicago"), was owned in equal shares by Mary Braun and her three children, Morris, Julius, and Mrs. E. C. Erenberg. "Braun Chicago was engaged in the sale at wholesale of bottles and glass products to manufacturers of pharmaceuticals and cosmetics and to others" (Op. T.C.).

2. W. Braun Co. Inc., petitioner was incorporated in New York in 1946. Two-thirds of its stock were owned by the Brauns in equal shares. The other one-third was owned equally by two persons, A. A. Friedberg and M. J. Tauger, who were unrelated to the Brauns. Petitioner had been "organized to conduct the same type of business in the northeastern part of the United States as was conducted in the midwest by Braun Chicago" (Op. T.C.) under a territorial agreement that was in effect between them. Friedberg had been hired by the Brauns to run the petitioner. Both Friedberg and Tauger were employed full time by petitioner, were vice-presidents and received the major portion of the salaries paid, Friedberg receiving various amounts ranging between $14,638 and $20,250 and Tauger between $12,615 and $20,250 for the taxable years ending, respectively, in February 1956 to 1960.

3. Braunware Products Co., Inc. ("Braunware"), was incorporated in New York in 1956. Petitioner was the sole owner of its stock and its officers and directors occupied the same positions in Braunware. Braunware's business was to sell "at wholesale cosmetic travel packages and glass containers of the same type sold by the petitioner. It conducted its business on the petitioner's premises and

---

*Of the First Circuit, sitting by designation.

used the petitioner's office, telephone and correspondence facilities" (Op. T.C.). Braunware during its first taxable year ending July 31, 1957, sustained a net operating loss of $4,772.68. It remained inactive thereafter until November 1959. As of August 1, 1959, its net assets were $5,172.32.

The business arrangements between Braun Chicago and petitioner (primarily a selling organization) called for the purchase by Braun Chicago from manufacturers of the merchandise sold by petitioner. The manufacturers shipped directly to petitioner's customers and looked to Braun Chicago for payment. Braun Chicago in turn billed petitioner at cost and petitioner billed its customers, paying Braun Chicago 2% of its net sales for its services.

In June 1959 a substantial customer of Braun Chicago, Lanolin Plus, Inc., a cosmetic manufacturer, moved its plant from Chicago to Newark, New Jersey, to wit, out of Braun Chicago's territory into petitioner's. Thus, for all practical purposes the responsibility for this account fell on petitioner's operating officers Friedberg and Tauger. As owners of a one-third interest in petitioner, they had a real financial stake in the account. Their concern with respect to the Lanolin Plus account (evidenced as early as June 11, 1959 — letter from Friedberg to Julius Braun (Exh. 17)), has been well summarized by the Tax Court as follows:

> "Both Friedberg and Tauger, while recognizing that the Lanolin Plus account was a profitable account for the petitioner to have, were concerned about the risk entailed in dealing with Lanolin Plus because of the size of the account and some of the ventures that Lanolin Plus was engaged in. They thought that the business of the petitioner, and consequently their individual interests in the petitioner, might very well be destroyed if Lanolin Plus should become insolvent, and therefore wanted to eliminate the risk of such account. Both Friedberg and Tauger expressed their concern to Morris and Julius Braun. Friedberg recommended to them that the petitioner cease making shipments to Lanolin Plus and that the sales of Lanolin Plus be handled by the petitioner's inactive subsidiary, Braunware. The other officers of the petitioner agreed to Friedberg's suggestion."

There was a factual basis for the worries of Friedberg and Tauger. While Lanolin Plus returned a modest profit in 1959, it sustained a substantial loss in 1958. A large part of its assets were intangibles (patents, etc.) and a very high proportion of its costs were advertising and other selling expenses. When petitioner acquired the account, Lanolin Plus' debt to Braun Chicago stood at $250,000, one-fifth of which was past due. It took Friedberg six months to succeed in collecting the full amount for Braun Chicago. Finally, several Dun & Bradstreet reports showed that while Lanolin Plus paid most of its bills on time, it was "slow" or in arrears with several of its creditors.

Subsequent to September 1959, the Lanolin Plus account was transferred to the 1956-incorporated Braunware. Under an agreement with Braunware, Braun Chicago received as its fee for services rendered 50% of Braunware's gross profits or approximately 10% of its net sales [petitioner's gross profit was some 20% of its net sales]. In September 1959 petitioner ceased making shipments to Lanolin Plus and in November 1959 Braunware commenced handling the account. Braunware did not have separate offices but it kept its own bank account, books, and records. Friedberg was still in charge of the account and it was agreed that petitioner would receive 2% of Braunware's net sales for the use of its facilities and Friedberg's talents. For the fiscal year ended February 29, 1960, Braunware reported net profit of $17,208.00 from which it deducted its net operating loss of $4,827.00. Petitioner's net income for the same period totalled $23,461.25. The deficiency arose because the Commissioner, acting under powers bestowed upon him by Section 482 of the Internal Revenue Code of 1954, allocated all the taxable income of Braunware to petitioner.

The congressional purpose of Section 482 was to prevent the use of controlled corporations to evade or avoid otherwise payable taxes by means of shifting profits or by other financial devices. The courts have given broad scope to the Commissioner's discretion in making such allocations. On the other hand, the exercise of this power cannot be unreasonable or arbitrary. The Tax Court and other reviewing courts have endeavored to examine carefully the relationship between the controlled corporations to ascertain whether there was a "sound business purpose" served by the use of the other corporation or whether the transaction was a mere sham to effect tax evasion. Before analyzing the facts, the precepts must be noted that a taxpayer "is not required to adopt or continue with that form of organization which results in the maximum tax upon business income" and that when a taxpayer chooses to conduct his business in a certain form, "the tax collector may not deprive him of the incidental tax benefits flowing therefrom, unless it first be found to be but a fiction or a sham." Polak's Frutal Works, Inc. v. Comm'r, 21 T.C. 953, 973-74 (1954). In final analysis, "[e]ach case must be decided on its own facts." (Id. 974.)

The facts as found by the Tax Court so far as applicable are accepted as basic. The Commissioner contends "that the purpose of the petitioner's transfer of the Lanolin Plus account to Braunware was to take advantage of the net operating loss deduction which Braunware had available and Braunware's surtax exemption" (Op. T.C.). The Tax Court held that "[w]hile there is no evidence which specifically indicates that such was the purpose, the evidence does not affirmatively establish that such was not the purpose." True, "the petitioner did not, in connection with the transfer, have the advice of an attorney or an accountant" and one of petitioner's officers and stockholders knew of the unused tax loss and surtax exemption, but business transactions conducted without the advice of attorney or accountant are not per se illegal and knowledge of the law permitting corporate surtax exemptions creates no presumption that the purpose of the transaction was the evasion of income taxes. The Tax Court also held that "petitioner has failed to show that the allocation was not necessary in order clearly to reflect the income of the petitioner, within the meaning of Section 482" (Op. T.C.).

Although the facts justified both Commissioner and Tax Court in critically analyzing the Braunware transaction in the light of the family control of these corporations, we believe that the petitioner has shown sufficiently "sound business reasons" for the Braunware transaction and that to hold otherwise would be to substitute the Commissioner's business judgment for that of petitioner's officers and directors without a factual showing of unlawful purpose.

The financial welfare of Friedberg and Tauger was dependent upon petitioner's welfare and stability. Since 1956 at least they had received moderately substantial salaries from petitioner. The Brauns were in a way absentee owners but Friedberg and Tauger were the actual owner-executives on location managing the business.

The 1959 acquisition of the Lanolin Plus account was therefore not an unmixed blessing to Friedberg and Tauger. It was not unreasonable for them to assume that Lanolin Plus would continue to run a receivable balance on petitioner's books about two-and-one-half times greater than petitioner's net worth of $102,000. Since most of this money was invested in special order merchandise, if Lanolin Plus went bankrupt because of the failure of a promotional campaign, petitioner could not hope to resell its inventory. While petitioner did have credit insurance in the amount of $75,000 (this amount was later doubled when Braunware took over the account), in the event of Lanolin Plus' insolvency, petitioner's continued existence and Friedberg's and Tauger's investment therein would be in dire jeopardy. Nor was the subsequent collection of the $250,000 Lanolin Plus indebtedness proof of its stability. The transfer to Braunware must be viewed prospectively from the date June 1959.

While the transfer of the account was mainly desired by petitioner's New York management, it also appealed to the Brauns. Braun Chicago would still supply most of the merchandise requirements of petitioner as well as Braunware. From the Brauns' point of view, one effect of the transfer of Lanolin Plus from the petitioner to Braunware was the loss of security afforded by petitioner's net worth ($102,000) compared to that of Braunware (only $5,000 as of August 1, 1959). However, they felt adequately compensated because under the agreement with Braunware, Braun Chicago received as its fee 50% of Braunware's gross profits or approximately 10% of its net sales [petitioner's gross profit was approximately 20% of net sales]. Under its agreement with petitioner Braun Chicago received only 2% of net sales as its fee, or one-fifth as much for the same service.

The Tax Court took the position that there was no reasonable business purpose behind the transfer of the Lanolin Plus account to Braunware and that the primary reason for the transaction was the evasion of income taxes (via utilization of the net operating loss carryover and the additional surtax exemption). We find this holding to be based on an overly optimistic view of the risks involved in handing the Lanolin Plus account. The court's own findings as to the motivation of the parties in transferring the account and the record evidence compel the conclusion that the transfer was for a good business reason.[2] While the Tax Court might disagree with the soundness of, or the necessity for, the decision reached by petitioner's management, their decision was nevertheless a reasonable business judgment which must be respected as such.

[2] See Johnson Bronze Co. v. Comm'r, 24 TCM 1542, 1552 (1965). Counsel for the Commissioner suggested on oral argument that the Lanolin Plus account was not any riskier than petitioner's other accounts. It was conceded, however, that there was nothing in the record to support this contention, and the size of the account alone would appear to place it in a different category from petitioner's other accounts.

The Commissioner was therefore not justified in arbitrarily allocating all of Braunware's taxable income to petitioner. Such an allocation is authorized only when there is no business purpose to the challenged transactions or corporate structure.[3] Section 482 does not give the Commissioner the power to disregard separate corporate entities if they are being used for a bona fide business purpose. The mere fact that the Lanolin Plus account could have been handled by petitioner is irrelevant.[5]

In Simon J. Murphy Co. v. Commissioner, 231 F.2d 639, 644 (6th Cir. 1956), the court stated that Section 45, the predecessor of Section 482, was aimed at:

> "circumstances involving an improper manipulation of financial accounts, an improper juggling of the accounts between the related organizations, an improper 'milking' of one business for the benefit of the other, or some similar abuse of proper financial accounting, all made possible by the control of the two businesses by the same interests. When the Commissioner determined that a transaction between the controlled parties was not 'at arm's length,' an allocation would be justified in order to reflect the true net income which would have resulted if one uncontrolled taxpayer had dealt at arm's length with another uncontrolled taxpayer. Substance has been substituted for form."

. . . In summary, in opposition to the Commissioner's unsupported finding of unlawful purpose, there are definite facts which point to an opposite conclusion, i.e., (1) Braunware was not organized for tax evasion purposes but prior to the occasion of the Lanolin Plus account transfer; (2) the financial positions of Friedberg and Tauger in petitioner were quite distinct from those of the Braun family; (3) the relocation of the Lanolin Plus plant was not part of some scheme on petitioner's part; (4) the territorial division agreement pursuant to which the Lanolin Plus account was transferred from Braun Chicago to petitioner; and (5) the admitted concern of Friedberg and Tauger with respect to the Lanolin Plus account.

To give recognition to salesmen's interests, the Tax Court in Bush Hog Manufacturing Co., 42 T.C. 713 (1964), found that the formation of six additional separate sales corporations was for "sound business reasons" and "to permit the salesmen to acquire proprietary interests in the company they worked for, . . ." Id. 727. There would seem to be as sound business reasons here for protecting the salesmen responsible for petitioner's business activities and welfare.

The Tax Court, as an alternative ground of decision, held that "petitioner has failed to show that the allocation was not necessary in order clearly to reflect the income of the petitioner . . . ." The Commissioner therefore argues that even if his allocation of income was not necessary to prevent the evasion of tax, it was necessary

---

[3] [String citation of cases omitted.] See generally, Mertens, Law of Federal Income Taxation §38.63.

[5] . . . Regulation §1.482-1(b)(3); Mertens, supra n.3 ("The identity of the businesses is to be preserved, and the Secretary or his delegate has no authority under this provision to merge them into one single business, unless the businesses are carried on and manipulated in such a way as to constitute in effect one single business, or unless the 'controlled enterprise' is a sham [citations omitted]"); but see Hamburgers York Road, Inc., 41 T.C. 821 (1964).

to reflect the "true taxable income" of petitioner. See Regulation §1.482-1(a)(6). The Tax Court, which was in agreement with this view, supported its conclusion by pointing to the fact that "the record fails to show that Braunware paid petitioner any consideration whatever for the account" and by questioning whether 2% of Braunware's net sales was adequate to reimburse petitioner for the use of its personnel and facilities when petitioner's ratio of expense to sales was much higher. Petitioner argues that as to the latter item, the Tax Court, in comparing expense ratios, failed to make any allowance for the fact that Braunware was a cash basis taxpayer while petitioner was on the accrual system — hence, Braunware's obligation to pay one-half of its gross profit to Braun Chicago and other expenses were not accrued on its books. Furthermore, payment by Braunware to petitioner for the Lanolin Plus account was not the only way by which consideration could be shown. The mutual corporate undertakings of the respective owners under some circumstances might well be adequate consideration. Be that as it may, even if both points were decided favorably to the Commissioner, petitioner has still shown that an allocation of all of Braunware's net income to it is unreasonable and arbitrary, Oil Base, Inc. v. Comm'r, 362 F.2d 212, 214 (9th Cir. 1966); Comm'r v. Chelsea Products, 197 F.2d 620, 624 (3rd Cir. 1952), because it is clear that an uncontrolled taxpayer would insist on receiving some net income after expenses before agreeing to take over the Lanolin Plus account. The Commissioner has considerable discretion as to the amount which he may allocate from one controlled taxpayer to another (see Eli Lilly & Co. v. United States, 372 F.2d 990 (Ct. Cl. 1967)), but he cannot make entirely arbitrary apportionments.

We therefore remand to the Tax Court for a determination of the proper amount of income, if any, that should be allocated to petitioner from Braunware.

Reversed and remanded.

H. MANSFIELD, THE 482 PROPOSED REGS: THE PROBLEMS WITH WHICH PRACTITIONERS WILL HAVE TO CONTEND*
28 Journal of Taxation 66 (1968)

The Internal Revenue Service is using Section 482 extensively today in new ways to achieve long-desired tax results. Consequently, it behooves taxpayers to be aware of Section 482's scope and requirements, particularly the proposed new Regulations.

Neither the statute nor the Regulations, existing or proposed, make any distinction between foreign and domestic application of Section 482, but for about a decade the primary focus of the provision, in tax planning, audits and litigation, has been directed to foreign transactions. Nevertheless, the circumstances in which Section 482 is being currently applied clearly concern domestic business even more than foreign, as the rapidly growing volume of litigation, predominantly involving domestic taxpayers, attests.

*Reprinted by permission. Mr. Mansfield is a former Chairman of the American Bar Association Section of Taxation. — Ed.

It has been frequently remarked that Section 482 is a deceptively simply provision containing only a single sentence.

"In any case of two or more organizations, trade, or businesses (whether or not incorporated, whether or not organized in the United States, and whether or not affiliated) owned or controlled directly or indirectly by the same interests, the Secretary or his delegate may distribute, apportion, or allocate gross income, deductions, credits, or allowances between or among such organizations, trades, or businesses, if he determines that such distribution, apportionment, or allocation is necessary in order to prevent evasion of taxes or clearly to reflect the income of any of such organizations, trades or businesses."

Regulations thereunder presently in effect[1] are also relatively short and simple. The simple statute remains unchanged, but additional new Regulations are now proposed, running to over ten pages of fine print in the Federal Register.[2]

Two basic conditions to the application of Section 482, i.e., whether the activities are conducted by "organizations, trades or businesses" and whether the entities are "owned or controlled directly or indirectly by the same interests. . . ." are of course, fundamental. However we will not deal with them here. We shall be concerned here with the kinds of adjustments the Service may make if the above two conditions are met, the consequences to domestic taxpayers, and the conditions for avoidance of Section 482 under present and future law.

Effects of 482 Allocations

The statute permits the Service to allocate gross income, deductions, credits, or allowances. The Regulations, current or proposed, do not greatly amplify these types of adjustments. The transactions challenged have included purchases and sales, leases, sales and lease-back arrangements, rendition of personal services (such as acting as sales agents and furnishing office assistance), loans, and rental or use of property, tangible and intangible.[3]

Use of Losses

Also of importance are the taxpayer objectives which reallocations under Section 482 have thwarted. The largest category seems to be preventing the use of otherwise wasted losses. Typically the transactions attacked will involve circumstances in which income has been shifted to or deductions shifted away from an entity with either a net operating or capital loss or in which income is shifted away from an otherwise profitable corporation to produce a carryback. The Service has recently been very successful in thwarting such arrangements.[4] In even more flagrant circum-

---

[1]Reg. 1.482-1, adopted 4/14/62 by T.D. 6595.

[2]Prop. Reg. 1.482-1, 2. For another analysis of these Regulations, see Pergament, New 482 Regs provide arm's rules, flexibility in pricing of tangible property, 25 JTAX 238 (October, 1966).

[3]See Hewitt, Section 482 — Reallocation of Income and Deductions Between Related Persons — Up to Date, 22 N.Y.U. Fed. Tax Inst. 381, 407 (1964).

[4]Borge, TCM 1967-173; South Texas Rice Warehouse Co., 43 TC 540 (1965) (partial allocation only); Charles Town, Inc., TCM 1966-15, aff'd 372 F.2d 415 (CA-4, 1967); Foster, TCM 1966-273; W. Braun Co., Inc., TCM 1967-66. See Katz, Can Section 482 be used to negate the tax effect of a bona fide corporation? in 28 JTAX 2 (January, 1968).

stances, a taxpayer sought to shift losses into a profitable enterprise and was thwarted.[5] Cases of this type are generally extreme and readily decided by the courts.

Surtax Exemptions

Another major category is the utilization of surtax exemptions. While the surtax exemption is probably an "allowance" under Section 482,[6] the principle has been stated that the Service has no power to *disallow* entirely surtax exemptions under Section 482, but is limited to *allocating* them.[7] Such a limitation is of small comfort, because the same result has been achieved by allocating all the *net income* of one entity to another. For awhile, this procedure was believed to be improper, for the statute speaks in terms of reallocating only *gross* income and deductions. That view is no longer accepted, several courts having pointed out that an allocation of net income is simply a short cut to shifting individual items of income and deductions.[8] Even if only some of the gross income is reallocated, a substantial part of the net income might be shifted from the normal tax bracket to the surtax bracket, equivalent to disallowance of part of the surtax exemptions.

In Hamburgers York Road, Inc., 41 TC 821 (1964), the Service attacked the surtax exemption of a corporation operating a newly-created shopping center department store by resorting, typically, to Sections 61, 269, 1551, and 482. A sister corporation operated a large established downtown department store. The court did not reach the question of the application of Section 61, although disregard of the entity as a sham would seem difficult since the corporation leased land and a building, owned merchandise, employed separate personnel and conducted a store business at a separate location. Because the court found that the downtown and suburban store operations were parts of a single, integrated business enterprise, that the suburban store would not have been run differently if merely a branch, that there was no substantial business purpose for separate incorporation of the suburban store, that business transactions between them were not arm's-length dealings between uncontrolled taxpayers, and finally that the "taxable income of said single integrated business enterprise" was produced by and due to the business goodwill of the downtown store, its business organization and procedures, its merchandise brands and advertising, it held that all of the suburban store's net income should be allocated to the downtown store.

This result seems extreme and unwarranted, whatever might have been the result under Sections 269 or 1551. The suburban store was a tenant under a lease, it did have inventory and employees, and it should have been allowed to make some profit on these components. The case should not turn on one commonly-controlled entity's power to milk another.[9] *Hamburgers York Road* thus involved an instance where *disallowance* of the surtax exemption was not appropriate for an adjustment

---

[5]Baldwin Bros., TCM 1965-173, aff'd 361 F.2d 668 (CA-3, 1966).

[6]See Made Rite Investment Co., 41 TC 762 (1964), aff'd 357 F.2d 647 (CA-9, 1966) (surtax exemption an "allowance" under Section 269).

[7]The Challenger, Inc., TCM 1964-338.

[8]Ballentine Motor Co., 39 TC 348 (1962), aff'd 321 F.2d 796 (CA-4, 1963); Hamburgers York Road, Inc., 41 TC 821 (1964); Johnson Bronze Co., TCM 1965-281.

[9]See V. H. Monette & Co., Inc., 45 TC 15 (1965), acq., aff'd. 374 F.2d 116 (CA-4, 1967).

under Section 482, but rather, if at all, under Sections 269 or 1551 and where an allocation of all the net income might well be questioned.

Constructive Dividends

Another major problem, and probably a growing one, is that of constructive dividends. When two corporations, A and B, are owned by the same stockholder, C, and gross income is allocated from A to B under Section 482, a question obviously arises as to the means by which the funds came to rest in the recipient corporation, A, when the income is allocated to B, the other corporation. One explanation might be that the B corporation did receive the amount of gross income and distribute it as a dividend to C, who then contributed it to the capital of A corporation. Of course, there was no declaration of a dividend or formal capital contribution and the funds did not actually pass in that manner, but these omissions have not prevented courts from ascribing the receipt of dividend income to the stockholder, C.

Cases have held that a nonarm's-length transfer of property between commonly controlled corporations may be treated as a dividend and a contribution to capital. Some cases rely on the ground that that is the only way the assets could have gotten where they did.[10] Other cases rely on the ground that the increased value of the equity of the benefited corporation to persons holding shares in both corporations constitutes a constructive dividend.[11] The two theories may have different results when outsiders have an interest in the benefited corporation or where it is insolvent.[12]

An alternative approach is to restate the balance sheets of A, the recipient of the funds, and B, the taxpayer who earned them, in a way which conforms the balance sheets to what they would have shown had the transaction been at arm's-length and had entries been made in the normal way. Thus, if A sells assets to B for less than adequate consideration, a receivable would be set up on the balance sheet of A and a payable on the balance sheet of B. There would thus be no increase in the value of B which would need to be explained by positing a constructive distribution from A to C, its shareholder, and a constructive contribution to the capital of B by C. Such an approach, which would seem to be more nearly a proper readjustment of the balance sheets of A and B than to treat the transaction as a capital contribution from B's point of view, is followed by the Service where Rev. Proc. 65-17, 1965-1 CB 833 as amended by 1966-2 CB 1211, is applicable. That Procedure provides that, except in cases of fraud, the Service will, pursuant to a closing agreement executed prior to closing action on the Section 482 allocation, permit the taxpayer to set up a receivable (bearing interest at 5% after 1964 or the date the receivable should have been set up, whichever is later) to reflect income allocated to it or deductions allocated away from it for years beginning prior to 1965 and for taxable years thereafter in which tax avoidance was not a principal purpose. Although it can be strongly argued that this is the most appropriate way of adjusting for the fact that A holds funds earned

---

[10]Offutt, III, TCM 1963-126, aff'd 336 F.2d 483 (CA-4, 1964) (alternate holding). See Knipe, TCM 1965-131, aff'd 356 F.2d 514 (CA-3, 1966).

[11]Aylsworth, TCM 1963-221; Old Dominion Plywood Corp., TCM 1966-135.

[12]See Old Dominion Plywood, supra, note 11.

by B even where Rev. Proc. 65-17 is not applied, the Service has indicated in Rev. Proc. 65-31, 1965-2 CB 1024 that in cases in which Rev. Proc. 65-17 is not applied, it will take the constructive dividend approach. Recent cases apparently do not uniformly apply this approach in Section 482 allocations[13] and the Service has not apparently proposed deficiencies to reflect the constructive distributions in all cases.[14] If the constructive distribution approach is used, cases may arise where any such distribution might more appropriately be characterized as a constructive spin-off or partial liquidation. There may even be gift tax consequences when related persons hold stock in the benefited corporation. Even when deficiencies are not proposed by the Service on a constructive distribution theory, the choice between that theory and the theory that receivables and payables should be set up would influence the computation of the earnings and profits of A, the corporation that actually earned the income. Clearly, such tax consequences resulting from an allocation under Section 482 could be much more far reaching or disastrous than the tax consequences resulting directly from the allocation.

Other Adjustments

Another possible correlative tax consequence of a Section 482 adjustment might be to establish personal holding company status for a corporation, where, for instance, amounts of rental or interest income are allocated to a corporation.[15] And allocation of amounts of gross income to a taxpayer might open up the six-year statute of limitations under Section 6501(e).[16] A non-Federal result might be to increase state income taxes where gross income or deductions are reallocated, at least in states where Federal income is used as a tax base or in states in which tax laws provide for an equivalent to Section 482.

These direct and indirect consequences of a Section 482 allocation should always be borne in mind, not only when contesting a proposed adjustment but also when planning inter-company transactions. Their existence is a powerful incentive for compliance with Section 482 requirements.

Standards for Applying 482

The statute provides that Section 482 adjustments may be made if "necessary in order to prevent evasion of taxes or clearly to reflect the income" of related businesses, and these are definitely separate, alternative tests.[17]

For some years, the argument has been made that Section 482 may not be applied if there is an adequate business purpose to justify the terms of the questioned transactions. In such a case, there could hardly be any "evasion of taxes." While there was for a short time some support for the argument, this defense has now been held to be inadequate, and an adjustment is warranted whenever necessary "clearly to

[13]Cf. Knipe, supra, note 10 with Columbian Rope Co., 42 TC 800 (1964), acq.

[14]See Local Finance Co., 48 TC No. 76 (1967).

[15]Prop. Reg. 1.482-1(d)(3), Example 3.

[16]If instead of allocating income to a taxpayer, an expense of the taxpayer is allocated away from it, neither the personal holding company problem nor the extended statute of limitations problem would arise.

[17]Central Cuba Sugar Co., 189 F.2d 214 (CA-2 1952).

reflect the income" of the related businesses, regardless of the good faith or business justification of the transaction.[18] The test relating to "tax evasion" may still have some relevance in justifying decisions allocating all of the net income of one business to another, although a number of other grounds, such as the sham theory or Section 61, also may be, and have been, utilized, and even here the test of clear reflection of income may prove to be sufficient. For post-1964 years, the "avoidance of taxes" test appears to have been incorporated into the conditions for relief under Rev. Proc. 65-17, but it remains to be seen whether the test there will be given any semblance of its statutory form.

Arm's-length Test

The Regulations (at 1.482-1(b)(1)), as now supported by the courts, provide for an arm's-length standard, saying:

"The purpose of Section 482 is to place a controlled taxpayer on a tax parity with an uncontrolled taxpayer, by determining, according to the standard of an uncontrolled taxpayer, the true taxable income from the property and business of a controlled taxpayer. . . . The standard to be applied *in every case* is that of an uncontrolled taxpayer dealing at arm's length with another uncontrolled taxpayer." (Emphasis supplied.)

However, since the existing Regulations do little more than sound variations on this broad, general principle of arm's-length dealing, the courts have struggled with the problem of applying this principle to multitudes of factual situations without any detailed guidance. Taxpayers and Revenue Agents have likewise struggled to determine when there is compliance with this principle. The Treasury's proposed Regulations are designed to amplify that principle and to diminish the struggle.

Judging the Proposed Regs

During the passage of the Revenue Act of 1962, the Treasury Department sponsored statutory rules for some Section 482 adjustments, but the Congress instead invited the Treasury to promulgate detailed Regulations as guidelines. In response to this invitation, partial proposed Regulations were issued on April 1, 1965 and complete Regulations proposed on August 2, 1966. Commissioner Cohen has stated, "The general plan of the proposed regulations is to elaborate on the application of the arm's length standard in each of five specific types of transactions. In each case the rule is first stated generally — that is, that the proper arm's length consideration will be determined with reference to all the surrounding facts and circumstances. Next, in some instances, a safe haven or prima facie rule is provided where the taxpayer is not regularly engaged in similar dealings with unrelated parties." In its announcement, the Treasury Department commented that the regulations were designed to give taxpayers "guidance as to the manner in which they may carry out transactions with their affiliates with reasonable confidence that audit of these transactions by the Internal Revenue Service will not result in increased liabilities under Section 482."

---

[18]Oil Base, Inc., TCM 1964-298, aff'd 362 F.2d 212 (CA-9, 1966); Lilly & Co., 372 F.2d 990 (Ct. Cls., 1967); Local Finance Co., 48 TC No. 76.

The proposed Regulations, when made final, will be retroactively applied.[19] They are now being used as the basis for closing current cases.[20] This is because the proposed Regulations purport to do no more than apply the existing arm's-length standard. There undoubtedly will be challenges to this viewpoint. In any event, there have been assurances that it is not Service policy to make minimal allocations under Section 482 and that adjustments will be proposed only in those cases in which there have been significant deviations from arm's-length dealing or significant shifting of income. An attitude of reasonableness is to be applied. Such a spirit will be needed in exploring these new pathways.

The proposed Regulations probably should be judged in accordance with four standards: (1) whether they result in a fair statement of the income or loss of the members of the affiliated group; (2) whether they may be easily applied by commonly controlled taxpayers in fashioning their economic interrelationships and in reporting their income; (3) whether they may be effectively applied by the IRS in auditing the returns of taxpayers and in adjusting differences between the Service and taxpayers; and (4) whether they are consistent with the language of the underlying statute. Of course, in those areas in which the proposed Regulations cannot be reconciled with the language of the statute, they will not stand the ultimate scrutiny of the courts even when the other three standards would indicate that the Regulations might be desirable. Where, however, there are several approaches consistent with the statutory language which might be taken, the approach finally chosen must be judged against the three remaining standards.

Analysis of 482 Adjustments

The proposed Regulations contain some preliminary, but important, general provisions under a new subsection (d) of Reg. 1.482-1.

There is first emphasized the authority to make any kind of adjustment which may be appropriate, determined with reference to the particular transactions or arrangements. There can be increases or decreases in gross income, or in deductions, including depreciation, and increases or decreases in the basis of assets including inventory.

There is then specifically set forth the duty of the Service to make correlative adjustments to the tax accounts of a related taxpayer when it makes an allocating adjustment to one taxpayer.[21] The objective is to clearly reflect the income of both

[19]Rev. Proc. 66-33, 1966-2 CB 1231. There is a minor exception for Prop. Reg. 1.482-2(d)(4)(ii)(a) and a further exception under Rev. Proc. 64-54, 1964-2 CB 1008, as amended, for certain allocations involving loans to or use of intangibles by controlled foreign entities and certain allocations of overhead involving controlled foreign entities. These provisions are in part based on taxpayers' reliance on cases thought to forbid the creation of income and in part on administrative convenience. Since domestic taxpayers may in their interrelationships also have relied on these cases and since the interests of administrative convenience would be served thereby it would be appropriate for the Service to consider extending the procedure to domestic taxpayers.

[20]See Cohen, How the IRS intends to administer its 482 regulations [page 1016 infra]. Refunds may be claimed by taxpayers so closing current cases if the final Regulations are more beneficial.

[21]Prop. Reg. 1.482-2(d)(2).

parties. The correlative adjustment need not actually be made unless it would affect the U.S. income tax liability of the party for any pending taxable year. In any event it shall be deemed to have been made for the purposes of determining the U.S. liability of such party for a later year or of any person for any year; examples given are an increase in a corporation's net operating loss in determining the carryover to a later year or an adjustment to a foreign corporation's earnings and profits in determining the taxability of its distributions to U.S. shareholders. The taxpayer has the right to require the making of a correlative adjustment, and the District Director must give a written statement of the correlative adjustments to a taxpayer on request even though no open year is involved.

The correlative adjustment must be an appropriate one, not merely the converse of the "primary adjustment." Thus, when additional income is allocated to a taxpayer corporation because of inadequate charges for engineering services supplied in the construction of a building, the proper correlative adjustment is not a reduction of the income of the corporation owning the building but an addition to the basis of the building when it is completed.

Since no correlative adjustment is provided for any year with respect to which a credit or refund is barred by law, thought should be given to the desirability of keeping open corresponding taxable years of controlled taxpayers (except in cases in which the mitigation provisions of Sections 1311-1315 would clearly be applicable), but probably other factors will dictate early closing. Although it is also provided that a correlative adjustment is not required for any taxable year for which a return has not been filed, such a circumstance is not likely and is probably controllable by delaying the date of the primary adjustment.

Offsetting Adjustments

Section 482 adjustments are not to be made if the net effect of reimbursement arrangements between controlled taxpayers is to offset correlative charges, as when an arrangement among commonly-controlled taxpayers is not at arm's length and does advantage one taxpayer and is intended to reimburse that taxpayer for a corresponding disadvantage suffered in another transaction. However, according to Prop. Reg. 1.482-1(d)(3), setoff will not be recognized "if its effect is to change the characterization or source of the income or deductions, or otherwise distort taxable income, in such a manner as to affect the U.S. tax liability of any member." If, for example, the offset would result in failure to reflect personal holding company status by reason of receipt of personal holding company income, then individual adjustments will be made.

Apparently offsetting adjustments will be required only if the taxpayer can establish that a *reimbursement arrangement existed* during the year under consideration. This approach seems to be a throwback to cases and the provisions contained in the present Regulations, which take the position that Section 482 authorizes the IRS to make adjustments in its discretion only and is not intended as a Section taxpayers may rely on in seeking to restate transactions they have effected.[22] Following this

[22]Reg. 1.482-1(b)(3). See Interstate Fire Insurance Co., 215 F. Supp. 586 (DC Tenn., 1963), aff'd. 339 F.2d 603 (CA-6, 1964). But see, Cooper, Section 45, 4 Tax L. Rev. 131, 162

rationale, the IRS would be under no obligation to make adjustments with respect to any series of transactions unless it was really a part of another series of transactions for which adjustments were proposed. It seems strongly arguable, however, that when the Service proposes adjustments with regard to one series of transactions it should be under a duty to make adjustments with regard to other unrelated transactions brought to its attention since it would not otherwise fully carry out the mandate of the statute to adjust accounts where necessary "clearly to reflect . . . income."

"Creation" of Income

The most controversial of all the proposed provisions is Reg. 1.482-1(d)(4), which provides that adjustments may be made between related entities even though "the ultimate income anticipated from a series of transactions may not be realized or is realized in a later period. . . . The provisions . . . apply even if the gross income contemplated from a series of transactions is never, in fact, realized by the other members." No reference is made to any need for the existence of any gross income at all, even from unrelated transactions. The controversy that has surrounded the promulgation of these provisions of the proposed Regulations has to do with whether they are in all respects authorized by the statutory language. The statute permits the allocation, distribution or apportionment of gross income, deductions, credits or allowances. One reading of this statutory language would seem to forbid adjustments with regard to admittedly non-arm's-length transactions in which the requisite adjustment would be to increase the income of one party to the transaction and to increase the deductions of the other. Such an adjustment would, so the argument would run, not be an "allocation" of income or an "allocation" of a deduction but would instead be the "creation" of income and the "creation" of a deduction. The kinds of transactions which would typically not be open to adjustment under this theory would involve the transfer of the use of money or other property, tangible or intangible, for inadequate or too much consideration when the appropriate adjustment would be to adjust the interest, rental or royalty income accounts of one party and the corresponding expense accounts of the other. Several cases might be read as so interpreting the statute.

In Smith-Bridgman & Co., 16 TC 287 (1951) acq., a subsidiary corporation lent funds interest-free to its parent, which in turn used the borrowed funds to retire some of its outstanding debentures. The subsidiary's income was increased by the Commissioner in an amount equal to 4% interest on the funds loaned. No corresponding interest deduction was allowed to the parent, its return showing a net loss. The Tax Court reversed the adjustment, stating "We think this record clearly establishes that the respondent has not distributed, apportioned, or allocated gross income, but has created or attributed income where none in fact existed." Whether the Tax Court actually meant that no adjustment could be made because to do so would create income and a deduction is in some doubt since the court went on to point out that the Commissioner had allowed no deduction to the parent.

An earlier case, Tennessee-Arkansas Gravel Co., 112 F.2d 508 (CA-6, 1940), is

---

(1949). Set-off may be permitted on a less restricted basis in the final Regulations. See article by Stanley S. Surrey [page 1019 infra].

perhaps stronger authority for this reading of the statute. The taxpayer corporation made no charge for equipment used by another, commonly-controlled corporation. The Commissioner increased the taxpayer's income by $12,000, the amount of rent that would have been payable under an earlier but rescinded lease. No adjustment was apparently made to the expense accounts of the user corporation. Although the court assumed that the user corporation had gross income equal to its total sales of $51,427.70, it disallowed the income adjustment. The Commissioner, the court said, "simply concluded that petitioner should have charged . . . rent upon the equipment for the year 1934, notwithstanding the fact that petitioner neither charged, collected or could have collected rent under its agreement . . . Section 45 [the 1939 Code equivalent of Section 482] . . . did not authorize the Commissioner to set up income where none existed. The principal purpose of the section was to clearly reflect income that did exist."

On the basis of these and other cases[23] it has been claimed by some critics that Section 482 cannot be used to "create income" in the foregoing manner. The Commissioner has expressed his agreement with these two decisions in TIR 838, 8/2/66, solely upon the basis that no correlative adjustments were made to the corporation using the money or property. The Commissioner thus has made it clear that in his view Section 482 may be used to increase the income of one member and to adjust the accounts of the other taxpayer to create what is in effect a deduction for the use of property or some other asset. Whether or not this claim will be sustained under these circumstances when correlative adjustments are made as the proposed Regulations require, remains to be seen. This position has been strongly criticized in protests filed with the Service, but it is unlikely that any change of position will result, since this part of the proposed Regulations has been twice published in the same form.

A second way of reading the statute would seem to permit allocations only on a transactional basis, that is to say, that allocations of the income ultimately arising from a series of transactions to the group as a whole could be made at the time the income does arise. The result of this approach would be to permit allocations only where property transferred among members ultimately leaves the group in a transaction giving rise to gain or loss or is otherwise ultimately used by some member of the group to generate income. The rationale of this approach is that it is only at that time that the extent of the income to be allocated becomes known. If this approach is taken, allocations might be permissible in cases like *Smith-Bridgman* and *Tennessee-Arkansas Gravel* since in such cases it can be argued that the gross income of the business which received the money or property involved without payment was in part attributable to the use of that asset. However, in proposing the deficiencies involved in those cases no attempt was made by the Commissioner to trace such an economic result, and under the proposed Regulations no showing that such an economic result in fact occurs is necessary.

The specific provisions contained in the proposed Regulations, which will be

[23]See Laster, 43 BTA 159 (1940), acq., aff'd and rev'd on other grounds, 128 F.2d 4 (CA-5, 1942); Texsum Supply Corp., 17 TC 433 (1951), acq. But see, Welworth Realty Co., 40 BTA 97 (1939); South Texas Rice Warehouse Co., 43 TC 540 (1965), aff'd 366 F.2d 890 (CA-5, 1966).

discussed later, clearly provide that when the use of money is transferred for in-adequate consideration or when the use of property is transferred for inadequate consideration, income will be allocated to the business permitting such use in an amount thought to equal or approximate a rental charge or an interest charge even though the using corporation generates no income from the asset used. In cases in which assets such as inventory are transferred (when it is probable that the assets will be retransferred outside the controlled group), the Regulations again clearly provide that allocations are to be made at the time of a transfer from one member of the group to the other whether or not the recipient of the assets later sells them at a price in excess of what it paid or whether or not the recipient sells them at all. In situations involving the transfer of inventory, the cost of the inventory of the recipi-ent is increased and this cost can be recovered only if and when permitted by the inventory accounting method of the recipient. Indeed, the proposed Regulations might be taken to indicate that an allocation, if it can be called that, of gross income can be effected even where the recipient has no gross income from any source. If the proposed Regulations do purport to go this far, they would seem, in this respect at least, to have gone beyond the authority granted by the statute.

Specific Adjustments

Specific provisions contained in the Regulations deal with loans, transfers of the use of tangible property, transfers of services, sales of tangible property and sales or transfers of the use of intangible property.

Loans and Leases

In dealing with loans and transfers of the use of tangible property, the proposed Regulations provide at 1.482-2(a)(2) that in cases in which the transferor is not engaged in the business of loaning money or in the business of leasing property, specific guidelines may be followed in determining whether the charge made for the use of the money or property is fair. In the case of loans, if the lender has borrowed amounts to put itself in a position to make the loan and if the borrowing took place at the situs of the business to which the questioned loan is made, an arm's-length interest rate will be presumed to be that actually paid by the borrower-relender unless the taxpayer established otherwise. In all other cases the arm's-length rate will be presumed to be that actually charged if that rate is between 4% and 6%. Otherwise the arm's-length rate will be 5%. The proposed Regulations (at 1.482-2 (a)(3)) recognize that trade indebtedness may remain outstanding without interest for six months or may remain outstanding beyond that time if comparable balances are as a normal matter permitted to remain outstanding for such longer times by the taxpayer or others in the industry. Where a loan is made by one in the trade or business of making loans, the arm's-length rate will be made by reference to similar loans made to others.

When the use of tangible property is transferred without an arm's-length rental charge, where the business permitting such use is not engaged in the trade or business of leasing comparable property to unrelated parties, and when the party permitting use of the tangible property has not itself leased the property, the proposed Regulations at 1.482-2(c)(2)(ii) contain a formula which will be taken to be the arm's-length rental charge unless the taxpayer can demonstrate a more reasonable charge. The formula provides that the arm's-length rental will be presumed to be the sum of the depreciation allowable to the owner of the property, a 5% return on the adjusted basis and any expenses by the party permitting use. In no event will the depreciation factor be less than the depreciation allowable if the adjusted basis of the property was 20% of the unadjusted basis. When the business permitting use is engaged in the trade or business of leasing property, an arm's-length rate will be determined by reference to rentals charged outsiders. When the business permitting use is not engaged in the business of leasing property but has itself leased the property which is subleased, the arm's-length charge will be presumed to be the rent paid by the lessee-sublessor.

One general observation can be made about the provisions dealing with loans and the use of tangible property. The formulae contained in the Regulations do provide a reasonable element of certainty in planning transactions and will facilitate the audit of returns when these types of transactions are concerned. However, it may be questioned whether the element of certainty injected into these two areas by the proposed Regulations is sufficient to outweigh the fact that in some instances the formulae themselves, if applicable, may give rise to unrealistic results and the IRS may not, although the taxpayer may, demonstrate that other rates are fairer. Situations may be easily imagined where an interest rate of between 4% and 6% or a rental calculated in accordance with the formula contained in the proposed Regulations would, in fact, transfer substantial economic benefits from one commonly controlled enterprise to another. To take a simple example, the lease of high-basis assets with a low fair market value or the lease of low-basis assets with a high fair market value might be used to effect a significant diversion of income where the formula for rental is used. In providing bright-line tests in these two areas the proposed Regulations may have under-emphasized the goal of fairly stating income and have overemphasized the elements of certainty in planning and auditing transactions. Ironically, this overemphasis has occurred in areas in which the determination of a true arm's-length rate is certainly no more difficult and probably less difficult than other areas covered by the proposed Regulations when no bright-line tests are provided.

Services

In dealing with services the proposed Regulations provide at 1.482-2(b)(3) that where the taxpayer is engaged in the business of providing services, allocations will be made on the basis of amounts actually charged to or among unrelated parties, thus including a profit element. However, where transfers of services are involved and the taxpayer is not engaged in the business of providing services, the proposed Regulations take the view that deductions, including an appropriate share of indirect costs (not including interest or capital charges) will be allocated from the party providing the services to the related taxpayer receiving them.[24] The proposed Regulations, how-

---

[24]Prop. Reg. 1.482-2(b)(3), (4) and (5). The final Regulations may be further narrowed

ever, contain a rather extended definition (at 1.482-2(b)(7)) of taxpayers that will be deemed to be in the business of providing services. Aside from a provision dealing exclusively with foreign transactions the definition appropriately enough includes situations in which the taxpayer in fact sells services to unrelated parties, in which the taxpayer sells services to another controlled taxpayer who resells them without adding significantly to their value, or in which the service is rendered to the related business in connection with the sale by it of a unique product constructed in accordance with specifications provided by the ultimate purchaser. However, the definition also states that a taxpayer will be regarded as in the business of providing services when the cost of the services should be reflected as a cost of goods sold by the controlled taxpayer receiving the benefit of the service. In view of the IRS' position, which appears to have gained some support in the courts, that an appropriate share of the general and administrative costs of a taxpayer must be included as a cost of goods sold,[25] it might well be inquired whether this last provision would not, in terms at least, mean that all taxpayers rendering general and administration services to a related manufacturing enterprise would be regarded as in the business of providing services so that an allocation of an arm's-length charge for services including a profit element would be appropriate.

Sales of Tangibles

It is well known that the provisions in the proposed Regulations dealing with the sales of tangible property were carefully and long considered prior to their promulgation. In brief, these proposed Regulations at 1.482-2(e)(2), (3) and (4) outline three methods that may be used in determining whether a price charged is fair and these methods, being of decreasing reliability, are ranked in order of use. The preferred method is the so-called "uncontrolled price method." Under this method reference is made to prices charged for the same or nearly similar property in transactions between the seller and unrelated parties, the buyer and unrelated parties or between outsiders. When there is not sufficient evidence to apply this method, the second method to be employed is the so-called "resale price method." Under this method, which may be used only if the purchaser has not significantly added to the value of the property and resells it within a reasonable period before or after the sale among the unrelated parties, the arm's-length charge is the price charged by the reseller to an outsider less an arm's-length markup. The third method which may be used only where the other two cannot is the so-called "cost plus" method where the arm's-length price is taken to equal the cost to the seller plus an appropriate gross profit determined by examining sales made by the seller or others. If the taxpayer has actually made consistent use of another method, it may be honored under the proposed Regs.

---

to permit allocation of costs, as opposed to allocation of an arm's-length charge including profit, only in cases where the services rendered are "incidental." See Surrey, supra, note 22.

[25]See Reg. 1.471-3(c)(3). Photo-Sonics, Inc., 42 TC 926 (1964), aff'd 357 F.2d 656 (CA-9, 1966) (taxpayer on prime cost method *may* be forced to change to absorption cost method). But see, Reg. 1.446-1(a); McNeil Machine & Engineering Co., Ct. Cls. Comm'r Rep. 3/29/67 (taxpayer on direct cost method, including variable factory overhead, *may not* be forced to adopt absorption method).

These methods all seem pointed towards transfers of inventory as opposed to transfers of plant and equipment although they presumably would be applicable to transfers of such other tangible property as well. The problem that under the proposed Regulations transfers of inventory give rise to income prior to the disposition of the inventory by the recipient has been discussed above. If this problem is not an insuperable one, the position taken by the proposed Regulations seems generally reasonable and well thought out. It might be said, however, that at least where the seller doesn't make like sales to outsiders, the proposed Regulations do not provide clear-cut guidelines in planning transactions and will provide ample opportunity for post hoc restatements of income by Agents in the field who might have access to economic data concerning appropriate margins or markups not available to the taxpayer at the time a transaction is planned. It would therefore seem appropriate at the very least to restrict the inquiry on audit to economic data which was known or could reasonably have been known by the taxpayer at the time an inventory pricing decision was made.

Intangible Property

In dealing with the transfer of or transfer of the use of intangible property the proposed Regulations provide the least definitive guidelines concerning the appropriateness of a charge contained anywhere in the proposed Regulations. Where one party permits another to use intangible property, Prop. Reg. 1.482-2(d)(2) states that an appropriate charge may either be a lump sum or continuing royalties, depending on circumstances which are nowhere defined in the proposed Regulations. When similar transactions on which to predicate an arm's-length charge are not available, the proposed Regulations contain no less than eleven factors which may be considered in determining the appropriateness of the charge itself.[26] When several parties have borne the cost of developing intangible property, an allocation of royalties to the party deemed to own the intangible property in the sense that it has borne the greatest share of the cost and risk of development (although it may not have been the party which actually created the intangible) will be made and the cost borne by others will merely be treated as offsets to the royalties otherwise payable unless a so-called "bona fide cost-sharing arrangement" is in effect between the parties (Prop. Reg. 1.482-2(d)(1)(ii)). To receive recognition as a "bona fide cost-sharing arrangement" after final promulgation of the Regulations, the agreement must be in writing, may not include as a party a business directly or indirectly engaged in the trade of developing intangibles for outsiders, must divide the direct and indirect costs (including the costs of using intangibles previously developed) of development among the parties in accordance with the anticipated relative benefits to be received by the parties whether or not intangible property is actually produced and must contain provisions setting forth the relative interests of the parties in the intangibles and the method of determining each party's share of the costs.[27] In view of the difficulty of determining what an arm's-length royalty for

---

[26]Prop. Reg. 1.482-2(d)(2)(iii)(a)-(l). The factor contained in Prop. Reg. 1.482-2(d)(2)(iii)(i) should not be weighed heavily, however. It states, "The next subdivision is (j). . . ."

[27]Prop. Reg. 1.482-2(d)(4).

intangible property should be it would certainly seem appropriate to permit cost-sharing on a less formal and rigid basis than that set forth in the proposed Regulations. Indeed, it might be argued that when intangibles owned by one member of a controlled group are used by another the easiest method of allocation when no charge or an inappropriate charge is actually made would be to follow the approach used in a similarly difficult area, the rendition of services, and to allocate a portion of the cost of development among users. The difficulty with this approach is that it would not take into account the costs of aborted projects and would not be useful when the costs of development had been expensed or amortized in closed periods prior to the use of the intangible by the related member.

Taxpayer's Burden of Proof

A taxpayer who is the subject of an unfavorable allocation under Section 482 faces a formidable task. In order to prevail in court he is required to show that the Service's allocation is arbitrary and capricious.[28] Not only must the *method* of allocation used by the Service be arbitrary, but the *result* must also be arbitrary.[29] If a taxpayer sues for a refund, he must show the proper allocation, if any, to establish the amount of the refund.[30] Even if the taxpayer litigates in the Tax Court and establishes that the allocation is arbitrary, the court will normally, if an allocation is indicated but little evidence exists as to its amount, make an approximate allocation which is difficult to upset on appeal.[31] This means that a taxpayer will lose his case in whole or in part, if he fails to demonstrate *the proper* allocation, when the court feels that *some* allocation is proper, even though the court may disagree with the Service's allocation. It will be a courageous taxpayer who will face litigation under Section 482 under these conditions. The burden of proof upon the taxpayer is a strong inducement to settlement.

Section 482 is a deceptively simple provision. Its sole standard of arm's-length dealing is a deceptively easy one for a Revenue Agent to apply, because of the absence of detailed technical requirements. The provision is a broad and sweeping one, overriding other provisions of the Code, such as Section 351. Furthermore, the taxpayer has an unduly heavy burden of disproving the Service's assertions. Such a situation can obviously tempt a Revenue Agent to investigate the possibility of Section 482 allocations, when related parties are involved, particularly since the Section is designed to ensure the clear reflection of income among the parties. In effect, the Section may, for such circumstances, constitute in itself an entire Code without need to resort to any other provisions. This form of tax simplification, however, is not likely to prove attractive to taxpayers who become involved in the increasing scope of Section 482.

---

[28]Aiken Drive-In Theater Corp., 281 F.2d 7 (CA-4, 1960); Spicer Theatre Inc., 346 F.2d 704 (CA-6, 1965).

[29]Dillard-Waltermire, Inc., 255 F.2d 433 (CA-5, 1958); Lilly & Co., supra, note 18.

[30]Lilly & Co., supra, note 18. See Taylor, 70 F.2d 619 (CA-2, 1934), aff'd 293 U.S. 507 (1935).

[31]See, e.g., Nat Harrison Associates, Inc., 42 TC 601 (1964), appeal to CA-5 dismissed; Ach, 42 TC 114 (1964), aff'd 358 F.2d 342 (CA-6, 1966).

S. COHEN, HOW THE IRS INTENDS TO ADMINISTER
THE NEW REGULATIONS UNDER SECTION 482*
28 Journal of Taxation 73 (1968)

The basic challenge which the Service faces in any Section 482 allocation is how to exercise the very broad and general authority given the Commissioner to allocate income between related business entities so as to prevent avoidance of tax or to clearly reflect income.

Existing [final] Regulations [1.482-1], which have been substantially unchanged since 1935, have approached the problem in a general way by providing that allocations shall be made on the basis of an arm's-length standard. In other words, in the case of transactions between controlled taxpayers, income for tax purposes is to be determined by placing the parties on a tax parity with uncontrolled parties.

General Plan

The proposed Regulations reemphasize the arm's-length standard, and provide more specific rules regarding allocations. They make clear that income generated from a series of transactions is to be divided among related parties on the same basis that it would have been divided had the intercompany transactions been at arm's-length. This is the way businessmen "divide up," in effect, the profit when unrelated parties are involved in transactions. For example, if one corporation manufactures a product at a cost of $10 and sells it to a second corporation at its fair market value of $15, and the second corporation resells the product for $18, the effect of the establishment of a price of $15 by the two corporations for the intermediate transaction is to allocate the $8 of gross income earned on the series of transactions — $5 to the first corporation and $3 to the second corporation.

The general plan of the proposed Regulations is to elaborate on the application of the arm's-length standard in each of five specific types of intercompany transactions: (1) loans, (2) services, (3) transfers of tangible property, (4) transfers of intangible property, and (5) sales of tangible property. In each case the rule is first stated generally — that is, that the proper arm's-length consideration will be determined with reference to all the surrounding facts and circumstances. Next, in some instances, a safe haven or prima facie rule is provided where the taxpayer is not regularly engaged in similar dealings with unrelated parties.

Every safe haven provision in the proposed Regulations contains language to the effect that the prescribed rate or charge will be used unless the *taxpayer* (and *not* the Government) establishes a more appropriate rate or charge. Thus, in each case the safe haven or prima facie rate or charge is designed as a shield for the taxpayer and not as a sword for the Government. Furthermore, it is not contemplated that the presence of safe haven rules will require the taxpayer to meet a burden of proof greater than he must normally meet in other tax situations. Naturally, we can anticipate that Revenue Agents will commence their audits with the safe

*Reprinted by permission. Mr. Cohen is a former Commissioner of Internal Revenue. — Ed.

haven or prima facie rate or charge in mind. In the usual case this will be favorable to the taxpayer. Nevertheless, we are emphasizing the provisions of the proposed Regulations which give the taxpayer the right to establish a more appropriate rate or charge under the general standards of arm's-length dealing. Agents are being reminded of the importance of keeping an open mind and of giving appropriate consideration to taxpayers' arguments justifying an arm's-length rate or charge other than the safe haven rate or charge.

In the areas of intercompany pricing and the determination of an arm's-length royalty with respect to the transfer of intangible property, because of widely varying business practices and circumstances we concluded that fixed rates or formulas could produce arbitrary and unreasonable results. The proposed Regulations, therefore, do not provide a safe haven rate for the determination of a royalty, or a single formula for the calculation of an arm's-length price. However, the proposed Regulations do provide guidance for taxpayers with respect to these types of transactions. They provide a list of factors to be considered in calculating an arm's-length royalty; they provide for cost-sharing arrangements for developing intangible property; and they provide a priority of pricing methods to calculate an arm's-length price.

You will note that a great deal of flexibility for the taxpayer and room for judgment for the Revenue Agent remains. This is because we know that business must be flexible in order to meet varying problems, and should not be put in a straight jacket.

Section 482 applies to a wide range of transactions and, accordingly, affects most of the large corporations in the U.S. and many small corporations as well. It is not a Section which is limited in application to instances of conscious tax avoidance or evasion.

We recognize that even under the guidelines in the proposed Regulations situations will arise where the judgment of the taxpayer, initially, and the Revenue Agent will be, subsequently, the matter in issue. We are endeavoring, therefore, to impart to all our field people the special importance of a spirit of reasonableness within the framework of the Regulations in the enforcement of Section 482. Of course, this is a two-sided coin — I hope this spirit of reasonableness will be followed by taxpayers as well as Service people.

As far as we are concerned, we intend to administer this Section in a sensible way. The proposed Regulations provide — and we intend to honor — the rule that reasonable and consistently applied methods of apportionment used to arrive at an appropriate reimbursement of costs for rendering services will not be disturbed and that arrangements made by the parties for the sharing of costs and risks of research and development on some equally reasonable basis will be acceptable. Legitimate shortcuts, such as application of pricing methods to product lines, and application of average departmental overhead rates, will be recognized.

In reviewing transactions, every reasonable effort will be made by Agents to find the prevailing price or profit in comparable uncontrolled transactions, as opposed to choosing a figure at the extreme end of a range of figures. Similarly, I hope that taxpayers will adopt such a policy in pricing their transactions in the first instance so that Agents will not have to make allocations.

It is our intention that this attitude of reasonableness will apply in reviewing transactions occuring before the issuance of these Regulations in final form as well as to future transactions. This spirit of reasonableness does not mean that we have abdicated our responsibility in the administration of Section 482. It is true that, on the one hand, as a result of the proposed Regulations and this liberal attitude toward administration, we may not raise certain issues which might have been raised in the past, and which we legally could raise. For example, in the instances specified in the proposed Regulations we will not require more than a 5% interest charge on intercompany loans. However, on the other hand, we believe that in many cases, as a result of greater certainty and definition in the proposed Regulations, we will increase efficiency in audits and encourage voluntary compliance by taxpayers.

Training of Field Personnel

We have embarked on an intensive educational program for our field people in this area. Even before the Regulations are finalized, we have been carrying on such a program. We are anticipating that final Regulations will not depart too radically from the basic approach and principal objectives of the proposed Regulations, and in the meantime, it is important to provide instructions for pending cases until the Regulations are finalized.

We recently held seminars based on the proposed Regulations and the international enforcement program in general. At these seminars the policy and thinking behind the Regulations were thoroughly explored, and we emphasized and reemphasized the spirit behind the proposed Regulations. The Service is continuing its training program. We have established the position of Regional Program Manager for the international program to provide a means for the National Office and Regional offices to be kept currently informed of developments in this important activity and as a means to insure that the program is properly and uniformly administered.

De Minimis Adjustments

Some concern has been engendered by the language in the proposed Regulations which sets forth — with some precision — the areas in which the Service may make allocations.

It is a fact that the proposed Regulations provide the standard for making allocations with respect to each of the five types of transactions described. However, the employment of Section 482 is discretionary with the Secretary or his delegate — in this case, the District Director. It is not our policy or intention to make minimal allocations under Section 482. Adjustments will be proposed only where there have been significant deviations from arm's-length dealings, or where there has been significant shifting of income.

Several taxpayers have requested that we incorporate rules in the final Regulations to eliminate so-called de minimis adjustments. For example, some taxpayers have suggested that we should announce that if the taxpayer prices within 20% of an acceptable arm's-length price we would not make an allocation. As you know, most taxpayers *net* considerably less than 20% of gross sales. To have such a de minimis rule would be to allow many taxpayers to shift all their income, and then some, to another affiliate — possibly a foreign corporation not paying U.S. tax. Obviously, we could not have such a de minimis rule, or one anywhere near that, in the area of pricing.

In the last analysis, what constitutes a de minimis adjustment depends upon the facts and circumstances of the particular case in question, and it would be very difficult to state a uniform de minimis rule. In addition, from an administrative point of view, it would appear to be unwise to publish acceptable tolerances, since such action might thereby encourage the "error" which would be tolerated. All we ask of taxpayers is that they set prices with their affiliates as if they were dealing with a stranger. It is in the Service's own best interest as well as the interest of the taxpayer that our Agents not propose frivolous or de minimis adjustments.

Closing Cases

Since we have received several inquiries on our approach in closing 482 cases prior to issuance of final Regulations, I would like to clarify our policy on this point. In view of the facts that the arm's-length standard has been the standard for many years and the proposed Regulations make no basic change in this standard, we believe that in the interest of uniformity the proposed Regulation should generally be applied to existing cases. We have, therefore, instructed our field people to close cases on the basis of the proposed Regulations. Naturally, in the event that final Regulations are more beneficial to taxpayers, they may file claims for refund.

When an examination of a return for a taxable year is substantially completed and the taxpayer has agreed to the proposed Section 482 adjustment, we are issuing instructions to agents that it will not be necessary to rework such returns to conform to the proposed Regulations in order to avoid inconvenience to taxpayers which might result from additional audits. If it appears that a case is destined for litigation, the case will be developed sufficiently so that the issues may be presented to a court within the framework of the proposed Regulations. In examinations involving Puerto Rican affiliates, we will be instructing Agents to close those cases on the basis of TIR 441, 1/11/63, if the result is more favorable than under the proposed Regs.

S. SURREY, TREASURY'S NEED TO CURB TAX AVOIDANCE IN FOREIGN BUSINESS THROUGH USE OF 482*
28 Journal of Taxation 75 (1968)

The Mandate of Section 482 is a broad one, and necessarily so, for the provision is vital to the integrity of an income tax. But we must be careful to recognize clearly the reasons for this provision, and more especially the reasons why particular taxpayers may present a situation in which a tax administrator must ask himself whether potentially a Section 482 check is in order. The salient fact is that a taxpayer

*Reprinted by permission. Mr. Surrey is a former Assistant Secretary of the Treasury for Tax Policy. — ED.

worry about the Section is almost a symbol of status, for a Section 482 worry is generally the price of possessing a tax preference.

The main corporate worriers about the rules of Section 482 in a totally U.S. domestic setting are those corporate chains which exploit the preference permitted by multiple surtax exemptions. Since they exploit that preference, they must constantly seek to distribute income and expenses among the corporate components in keeping with that mathematics.

International Application of 482

The preference analysis is also applicable to the international scene. In general, the international preference comes about because while one component, the parent, is subject to our 48% corporate rate, the other components, its foreign subsidiaries, are not subject to that rate but to the rates of tax in the foreign countries in which they are located or operate. Where those foreign rates are substantially lower or nonexistent, the preference is quite marked. A similar preference exists where a domestic Western Hemisphere Trade Corporation is used, since its tax rate is 14 percentage points below the regular U.S. corporate rate.

The factor of a tax preference in creating the potential for a Section 482 scrutiny is clearly evident in the controversies that do arise. The two major court decisions involving the inter-company pricing of goods, Eli Lilly, 372 F.2d 990 (Ct. Cl., 1967) [see O'Connor, Can intercorporate pricing arrangements avoid being upset by Section 482?, in 26 JTAX 262 (May, 1967)] and Johnson Bronze [TCM 1965-281], both concerned transactions between U.S. manufacturing companies and their Western Hemisphere Trade Corporation affiliates. Virtually all the pricing cases currently in the National Office of the Internal Revenue Service for technical advice involve either Western Hemisphere Trade Corporations or tax haven subsidiaries. If these cases are representative of the field cases, there has been far more realistic pricing of goods where no tax differential exists and, as a consequence, no Section 482 controversy.

Certainly the Western Hemisphere Trade Corporation and the tax haven situation are open invitations to temptation: if the manipulation is undetected or if a favorable "compromise price" is worked out on audit, the consequent lowering of price to the subsidiary results in after-tax savings. If the shifting is fully corrected on audit, usually any adjustment of price will simply mean a loss to the taxpayer of 6% interest (3% after tax) as the U.S. tax on the parent goes to its proper level — there is no fear of double taxation through inability to make a correlative adjustment in the Western Hemisphere case (assuming it, itself, is not subject to tax abroad) and no need for one in the tax haven case.

All this being so, the task of the Service, and indeed of any tax administration, is how to achieve a rational administration of Section 482 where there is a considerable potential area for its application, where some companies sufficiently serious in number take unwarranted advantage of the situation created by the preference, but where every company cannot and should not be carefully scrutinized and its activities second-guessed just because those who yield to temptation are mixed among the throng. One key to sensible administration in these circumstances is to provide those concerns which seek no unwarranted advantage with the standards that the Service is using to identify the others. Another key is to utilize standards that are sensibly tolerant of the very wide variety of transactions, patterns of business conduct, and investment and trade situations that are clearly present in international activities.

What 482 Regs Hope to Accomplish

This analysis leads inevitably to the provision of guidelines for the application of Section 482, as well as those Sections bearing a relationship to it, such as Sections 861 and 862 involving the allocation of expenses in determining taxable income from foreign sources. But the analysis takes us still further, for it also points to the premises on which those guidelines must be formulated. We believe that the guidelines must adhere as closely as possible to management and accounting standards developed to achieve the same goal — that of proper allocation of items among the constituent components of a business enterprise.

This adherence has two distinct advantages: (1) it will keep tax administration within the mainstream of the developments regarding these management and accounting standards. (2) The use of these management and accounting standards will provide the U.S. with a rational, consistent approach to international transactions which it can use for all of the forms which those transactions may take.

We must not forget there are two sides of the coin. Many groups focus on the side of the coin involving a parent in the United States transferring goods and services to its subsidiaries abroad. But on the other side of the coin are corporations involved in extraction or manufacture abroad and the transfer of materials or goods to the United States — they may be subsidiaries of U.S. corporations or they may involve foreign parents and their U.S. subsidiaries. These two sides of the coin underscore both the need for consistency and the care required in the formulation of appropriate rules. We have our exporters of goods and our importers of goods; we have our manufacturing industries operating at home and abroad; we have our extractive industries obtaining their raw materials at home and abroad; we have service, shipping transportation, financing, and construction industries operating across international borders; and so on. Section 482 guidelines applicable to all these activities, all of which exhibit the two sides of the coin, must be formulated in a non-discriminatory manner that permits the United States to maintain the necessary consistency of position no matter which side of the coin turns up or where it does so. Indeed, the allocation provisions, the competent authority provisions, and the nondiscrimination provision in our treaties all require this objective, even-sided approach to these guidelines.

This matter of allocation is thus not to be viewed as a typical skirmish between taxpayers and the IRS, involving only the typical parochial interests that normally color such skirmishes. On the contrary, its proper resolution is a challenge to the vision and statesmanship of those who speak of the present and coming stature of the "multinational corporation." Part of this will be an appropriate allocation of the profits of these organizations among the various countries touched by their business activities, and thereby a fair sharing among these countries of the tax revenues to be derived from those profits.

Those who are concerned with shaping the institutional character of these multinational corporations should recognize the constraints that apply in developing tax rules for this allocation. Tax disputes involve concrete cases to which a specific dollars and cents answer must be given at the end of the road. Hence accounting rules and techniques must be rephrased as tax rules in which the specific dollar results do count and in which details as well as principles must be decided by someone. The attempt to provide Section 482 guidelines is thus an effort designed to permit Government and business to think through these principles and details as broadly and thoroughly as possible, foreseeing as far as possible the issues that may arise and their ramifications. The guidelines should be designed to guide — to represent the solutions to problems achieved after careful thinking at top levels of business, the professions, and Government, rather than leaving the individual Revenue Agents to raise and solve problems on their own. This does not mean every detail must be set forth in guidelines, for intelligent discretion at the Agent level is an integral part of tax administration. But it does mean a recognition that tax allocation problems do involve many matters of substance, principle and important detail that demand a coherent and thought-through set of answers, rather than a seat-of-the-pants, "let's decide each case on its facts" approach.

We must emphasize that the guidance here sought is guidance both before and after, so to speak. It is, of course, guidance to Agents as to what to look for and what not to look for, and what to decide when issues evolve. But it is also guidance to business on how to minimize possible dispute and controversy over the tax return and how to achieve a stability in business planning and arrangements that will not be upset, maybe years later, when that inevitable IRS audit comes along.

"Mechanical Safe Haven" Test

For the past several months a group from the Treasury and the Internal Revenue Service has been concentrating on the comments presented with regard to the proposed Regulations.

The comments at the last hearing dealt mainly with the subject of inter-company pricing of goods. Part of the concern in this area may stem from the amounts that can be involved in price adjustments, the frequency of transactions involving the transfer of goods between related organizations, and the problems involved in establishing transfer prices. The concern for some companies also stems from the aspect of correlative adjustments in the tax of the foreign country applicable to a related foreign subsidiary. . . . Let me indicate why we find difficulties in some of the approaches suggested at the hearing.

A typical suggestion is that the Regulations should supply a "mechanical safe haven" in the area of the pricing of goods. Much as this solution appears as blissful to our tax administration as to the taxpayers who suggest it, we have not taken this route. The reason is that no satisfactory device has yet been suggested or worked out. The variation in profit margins from industry to industry, among companies within an industry and even among product lines within a company is much too great to permit a single percentage, or a series of percentages, as mark-ups or mark-downs in establishing transfer prices. The recognition of this problem has led other taxpayers to urge just as strongly that we do not provide a mechanical safe haven. They realize how unrepresentative that safe haven may be and they fear that in practice all territory outside the safe haven will be heavily mined for taxpayers. The "safe haven" here will, therefore, have to lie in a sensible, reasonable administration of the Regulations themselves.

"Reasonableness" Test

Another set of suggestions relates to the point of view that the only appropriate test of transfer pricing should be its "reasonableness." These comments have been phrased in a number of ways, but essentially they suggest that no Section 482 allocation be made where the price is "reasonable," or where the seller makes a "reasonable profit," or where the total profit earned by related entities is divided among them on a "reasonable basis." While the test of reasonableness has its uses in some situations, in this area it is not sufficiently precise to provide guidance — reasonable by what or by whose standards? Nor is the approach substantively accurate, since the basic arm's-length standard underlying the Section is not directly related to a reasonable profit figure for the parties involved. The arm's-length standard is designed to determine the price or charge that the parties would have arrived at assuming they had dealt with each other as independent unrelated entities — and this could mean no profit at all or indeed a loss in some cases. In essence, this suggestion for a safe haven of "reasonableness" has the same deceptive attractiveness as a mechanical safe haven. But just as in that case, its superficial appeal does not on analysis withstand its potential for real unfairness among tax-payers.

But there is a place for the concept of "reasonableness" in these Section 482 Regulations — and it lies in the way the guidelines should and will be applied. We expect these guidelines to be applied in a reasonable manner by taxpayers. They, in turn, have a right to expect a reasonable interpretation and application by the Service. The Commissioner has stressed several times in recent statements that this will be the approach of the Service.

Regs Reflect Accounting Concepts

When we turn to more substantive comments and to the other parts of the guidelines in addition to transfer pricing, we should first note that virtually no criticism was received on a conceptual basis. It is not seriously questioned that the clear reflection of income requires charges to be made for benefits received. Interest for the use of money, rent for the use of property, royalties for the use of intangibles have become such basic concepts that they are no longer seriously questioned. Some aspects of the guidelines have been criticized, however, on the ground that they are ahead of our time and that we are requiring business to meet impossible or unrealistic standards. This is not our objective and we do not feel that this is basically the case. The guidelines, and the allocation rules they contain, utilize known and accepted applications of accounting principles. We have not been referred to any instance in which the guidelines are in conflict with generally accepted accounting principles. We do, of course, recognize the limitations in these guidelines in terms of furnishing absolute or precise answers. However, as accountancy continues its development and as our management and other analytical tools become more refined, the guidelines will also benefit. Indeed, as stressed earlier, we recognize there is much to be gained by using current accounting concepts and management techniques as the foundation for these guidelines.

We can look at the relevance of the guidelines to current practices in another way. Many companies have begun to look at their foreign operations with a more realistic and objective appraisal. A foreign subsidiary can compile and attractive profit showing if it is not charged for the services it receives or the financing it obtains, or if it receives its goods at cost figures. As the Journal of one accounting firm states, the guidelines may provide an unexpected benefit to some U.S. companies by "exposing to them the true cost of their international operations, which they have not always appreciated. Companies that manage their United States operations very profitably, but are new to the international field, frequently have to pay well for their education in that field. There seems to be a tendency to conceal from oneself the cost of the education, particularly if it is embarrassingly high."

All of this underscores our desire to keep these guidelines within the mainstream of accounting principles and management techniques.

Alternative Pricing Methods

The proposed Regulations require taxpayers and Revenue Agents to test intercompany prices against the arm's-length standard of Section 482 by using one of three approaches. The first approach is the *comparable uncontrolled price method* under which the price charged to a related entity must be similar to the price charged in comparable transactions with or between independent third parties. The second approach (the *resale price method*) applicable to the situation in which the related purchaser acts as a mere distributor with respect to the goods, computes the transfer price by taking the price which such distributor charges to third parties and reducing it by the appropriate mark-up for a distributor operating under the same circumstances. The third approach is the *cost-plus method* under which the seller must charge related entities his full cost, plus an appropriate profit margin. There is, in addition, a so-called *"fourth method"* which is applicable only in situations in which a taxpayer has been using a method different from the three listed above and which the Commissioner finds is clearly more appropriate.

There appears to be a certain amount of confusion with regard to the "priority" of these methods. The priority of application rule, which calls for an application of the methods in the order they are set forth, is not intended to be an arbitrary listing of preferences among methods which might yield varying results. The fundamental arm's-length standard involves a determination of the price which would have been arrived at by independent, unrelated entities entering into the same transaction. The priority of application rule simply states the approach for obtaining the most relevant evidence to establish that price. Clearly, a price arrived at in a truly comparable third party sale is the best evidence of such a price — it is the direct way to meet the arm's-length standard. We are therefore examining the feasibility of broadening this method to allow a greater range of adjustments to comparable transactions to permit arriving at a comparable price. The resale price method and the cost-plus method are indirect ways to approach the arm's-length standard, and hence less likely to achieve that end than the direct route. The resale price method is placed ahead of the cost-plus method in the order of priority since it is felt that in the limited distributor situation to which the resale price method is applicable — where the buyer does not add significant value to the product or employ significant intangibles in its resale — a distributor profit more clearly reflects the function of the buyer-reseller and, therefore, the income of each of the parties to the transaction.

These priorities thus reflect evidentiary guides. Under the priorities, a taxpayer is protected from an arbitrary choice of method by the examining Agent, and has the assurance that the most relevant evidence will be taken into consideration in arriving at an arm's-length price. But some taxpayers apparently would like to place their bets on method three or method two and use only that approach. They may have followed that approach in establishing their prices, or they now see it as the appropriate way to support the prices used. In such situations, one would expect the examining Agent, as a sensible precaution, to check the result obtained under the methods higher in the priority scale. If the check shows a marked variation from the method chosen by the taxpayer, then an explanation would seem in order; if not, then the taxpayer's price should not be disturbed. This seems to be a sensible way to handle the three methods that are recognized as having the widest application.

There have also been comments directed at the "fourth method." This method has a limited scope under the proposed Regulations, since the method to qualify must be actually used by the taxpayer and the Commissioner must feel that it is "clearly more appropriate." Some companies have requested, in the light of their own pricing practices, that they be allowed to use a variety of methods in setting prices which they feel are not prescribed by the proposed Regulations. Some of the methods are merely variations of the specified approaches; others are based upon different premises. Where such pricing systems will yield results which are substantially the same as the prices which would have been arrived at under the Regulations, it would seem to be in the interest of both taxpayers and tax administrators to apply prices based on such systems. Of course, if such prices do in fact meet the arm's-length standard the method by which they are derived makes no difference. There is, however, a feeling among some taxpayers that the system that they follow in arriving at a price should be specifically blessed in the Regulations. This can hardly be done without allowing a proliferation of described methods, which in turn reduces the over-all guidance which these Regulations must develop in order to accomplish their avowed purpose; certainly the taxpayer whose method is left out of a long list would wonder where it stands. But, on the other hand, we are aware of the narrow focus in the proposed Regulations, and to the extent feasible will make the "fourth method" broader in its application and clarify its relation to the other three approaches.

Another set of comments relates to whether or not "marginal pricing" can be used. The guidelines are intended to achieve the following results in this area: Under the comparable uncontrolled price method, to the extent that marginal pricing is used to establish or to maintain a market, such pricing is proper under the guidelines if the buyer-reseller engages in additional expenses, such as promotional expenses or if the reduced prices are passed on to a third party. Further, if the parent company uses incremental costing in arriving at the price charged to unrelated parties, such prices may be charged to related parties in comparable circumstances. Thus, to the extent that reductions in price to third parties are based on a marginal or incremental approach, such pricing to a foreign subsidiary is allowed under the comparable uncontrolled price method. Similarly, if a foreign subsidiary of the U.S. parent could purchase goods at a certain price from third parties, the U.S. parent manufacturing company could sell at the same price under comparable circumstances.

Multi-Transactional Effect

Some comments seek to clarify the application of the guidelines where the related corporations are engaged in a number of transactions falling under Section 482, such as the transfer of goods to a subsidiary alongside the receipt of royalties from that subsidiary. We do not intend that Section 482 interfere with normal commercial transactions. That Section is designed to assist in policing the U.S. income tax system, and is not cast as a guardian with universal judisdiction. Valid business reasons may require that transactions be framed in different forms than the simplest possible accounting technique would dictate. In transactions between unrelated parties a price reduction might often be offset by an increased royalty or other charge. The proposed Regulations recognize this and provide for "set-off" computations in certain situations. This device is circumscribed in the proposed Regulations to prevent audits from becoming interminable. In addition, care must be taken to prevent unwarranted switching of sources of income and to account properly for additional foreign taxes. But we do recognize the need for flexibility in this area and are examining the Regulations with the aim of making this relief available to taxpayers to the extent feasible on a less restrictive basis.

Services and Intangibles

Other areas of the proposed Regulations are, of course, also being reviewed. Few taxpayers objected to the provisions allowing most services to be charged at cost. There is thus no question that incidental services will not have to be charged at a profit. However, there will have to be some clarification with regard to what services are, in fact, "incidental" and on our own account we are reviewing this matter. Some taxpayers have expressed concern that the "full cost" requirement in the service area would yield inappropriate results. It must be noted that all safe havens, including the service charge at cost, are secondary in order of priority to an arm's-length price. If a computer were used at only a fraction of its full capacity, a proportionate share of full cost would, in all probability, result in a very high charge to a related party. However, since many computer users are able, on an arm's-length basis, to acquire such services on a share-time or incremental basis, the appropriate arm's-length charge would be a charge based on such comparable prices. A safe haven is not binding on the taxpayer in any area and clearly would not be appropriate in a situation such as the one described. We have created safe havens to reduce uncertainty wherever possible. The taxpayer, however, is not confined to the safe havens — he can always use the arm's-length standard to support the amount of the charge.

We recognize that the valuation of intangibles and the determination of an appropriate charge for their use present extremely difficult problems. For this reason, the proposed Regulations developed a "safe haven" cost sharing arrangement in an attempt to eliminate many of the valuations which would otherwise be required. There are refinements which can be made in the comprehensive scheme outlined in the Regulations. For example, one of the principal problems remaining is the requirement that the use of previously developed intangibles be valued. We have discussed various alternatives to this extremely difficult task with industry representatives and members of the legal and accounting professions. We hope that together we can develop a satisfactory alternative which will eliminate this valuation problem. We have discussed cost sharing with representatives of foreign governments, attempting to impress upon them the need for such a system and the fact that in most cases it would result in smaller inter-company charges than would otherwise be required. There were objections to the safe haven formula for tangible property rentals contained in the proposed Regulations. The formula, which was tied to the depreciation method used by the lessor, resulted in undesirable variable rentals in many situations. We are developing a modified formula that will yield level rentals in conformity with normal commercial practices.

Correlative Foreign Tax Adjustment

These Section 482 guidelines are U.S. rules intended to minimize controversies arising under U.S. tax returns and to resolve those disputes. But these U.S. rules are being applied to international transactions and we clearly recognize that they affect entities which are under the jurisdiction of other governments. As a consequence, the correlative adjustments which are integral to Section 482 allocations are under the control of those governments. If those adjustments cannot be made, then Section 482 allocations by the United States can have consequences different from allocations affecting an entirely domestic situation.

This aspect of the application of Section 482 has led to the suggestion that no Section 482 scrutiny or adjustment need be made if the subsidiary is located in a country where the tax rate is approximately the same as that of the United States. The suggestion has support in actual practice, for as indicated earlier, Section 482 issues presumably are rarely raised by the Service in intercompany pricing cases where this circumstance exists — which leads one to conclude that the companies themselves are here more careful to prevent their pricing being suspect under Section 482. Indeed, tax motivation will here rarely be a controlling factor, for little is to be gained from the standpoint of tax saving by a departure from arm's-length pricing. This situation is the exception to the earlier observation that a Section 482 worry is the price paid for a tax preference.

We recognize that even in a situation in which no tax reduction or avoidance motive exists, the possibility of price adjustments may cause apprehension to management. Moreover, we are not unaware of the many difficulties involved in setting prices. We are aware of the fact that the proposed Regulations provide guidelines and not final answers. We understand that it can be difficult for even the best intentioned taxpayer to arrive at a price for a particular product which could not be challenged under any conditions. Under these circumstances, the apprehension for such a taxpayer with respect to a Section 482 allocation — and hence its care regarding its pricing — can lie in the fact that if a Section 482 adjustment is made, the company runs the risk of not being able to achieve a correlative adjustment in the other country, with the consequences of double taxation and a considerable tax cost.

We do not intend this result. At the same time, we must remember that the statutory standard of Section 482 is a dual one: to reflect income clearly as well as to prevent the avoidance of tax. The standard is indeed a part of the process of determining the real profitability of foreign activities, a subject mentioned earlier. In the international context the standard of "clearly reflect income" also goes beyond the allocation of income to the right company and really involves the allocation of income to the right country. It is the standard by which the United States protects its sources of revenue and its tax system from the encroachments and claims of the other countries affected by the transactions. As a consequence, the issue is more than a dispute between taxpayer and the IRS and becomes one of international accommodation. It is thus more important and more complex than domestic Section 482 issues.

For the taxpayer involved in a Section 482 allocation in a setting where the tax rate in the foreign country is around the level of the U.S. rate, the focus will be on the double taxation that will result if the correlative adjustment is not made. How can this possibility of double taxation be avoided or minimized?

A part of the approach lies in Rev. Proc. 64-54, [1964-2 CB 1008], which for taxable years through 1964 permits the foreign tax on the allocated item to be credited against the increase in U.S. tax resulting from the allocation. In effect, the United States itself is making the correlative adjustment. This international generosity can be justified on the ground that taxpayers may not in those years have had an adequate appreciation of the Section 482 rules now being applied. But any such international generosity carried into the future would simply be a complete concession by the United States that other countries may unilaterally assert any jurisdictional rules they desire and the United States will always hold its citizens harmless at the expense of our revenues. For if the United States is to relieve the double taxation that results from a failure of the foreign country to make the appropriate correlative adjustment, then what is to keep foreign countries from simply deciding not to make correlative adjustments? No sovereign country can give this blank check to the rest of the world, and we know of no country that does so. As the size and importance of international business increases, the need for each country affected by a transaction to secure its fair share of the profits produced also increases. The United States should not be called upon to forego its share of the tax on the profits generated by international business.

NOTE

The current regulations under §482 were promulgated in 1968, shortly after the articles by Messrs. Mansfield, Cohen and Surrey appeared. See T. Jenks, Treasury Regulations under Section 482, 23 Tax Lawyer 279 (1970); R. Kalish and P. Bodner, Planning to Avoid Difficulties with 482 Adjustments for Related Entities, 33 J. Taxation 2 (1970).

HUBER HOMES, INC. v. COMMISSIONER
55 T.C. 598 (1971)

Findings of Fact

The facts stipulated by the parties are incorporated herein by this reference.

Huber Homes, Inc. (sometimes referred to as "Huber Homes" or "petitioner") is an Ohio corporation, formed on April 28, 1958. . . .

The Commissioner determined deficiencies in the income tax of petitioner for the taxable year ended March 31, 1963 and the taxable period beginning March 29, 1965 and ending August 31, 1965, in the respective amounts of $25,973.15 and $79,311.41.

After concessions by both parties, the issue presented is whether the Commissioner properly "allocated" income to the petitioner, under the terms of section 482, I.R.C. 1954, in respect of its transfer of 52 houses to its wholly owned subsidiary at cost.

From its incorporation through August 31, 1965, Charles H. Huber ("Huber") owned all of the outstanding stock of petitioner. He was also chairman of its board of directors and its chief executive officer at all times involved herein. It was the successor to a Huber family enterprise that was concerned with the construction and sale of houses.

During the period from April 28, 1958 through August 31, 1965, petitioner was engaged principally in the construction and sale of single-family houses in developments. These developments were located in the metropolitan areas of Dayton, Ohio, Cincinnati, Ohio, Columbus, Ohio, and Fort Lauderdale, Florida.

Huber Heights, located a few miles outside of Dayton, Ohio, is one of the developments. At the time of the formation of Huber Homes, approximately 700 houses had already been completed in Huber Heights. Huber Homes built approximately 3,700 more houses in that area during the period from April 28, 1958 through August 31, 1965, of which approximately 3,300 were sold to the general public. The remaining houses built during that period, about 400 in number, were acquired by Huber Investment Corporation, hereinafter described.

Huber Investment Corporation ("Huber Investment") is an Ohio corporation, organized on April 10, 1959. From the date of incorporation through August 31,

1965, all of its outstanding stock was owned by petitioner. At all times involved herein Huber was the chairman of its board of directors and its chief executive officer.

Huber Investment was formed for the purpose of acquiring and holding property not directly connected with petitioner's business of building and selling single-family houses. From its incorporation until August 31, 1965, Huber Investment was engaged principally in the real estate rental business. It owned approximately 400 rental houses in Huber Heights, approximately 100 houses in Indianapolis, Indiana, and an unspecified number of houses in Columbus, Ohio, Cincinnati, Ohio, and Fort Lauderdale, Florida. The majority of the houses owned by Huber Investment on August 31, 1965, were acquired from petitioner. Huber Investment itself never built any houses.

After forming Huber Investment, with only comparatively minor exceptions, petitioner did not own, manage, or maintain any rental houses in Huber Heights. From its incorporation through the year in issue, Huber Investment sold only one of its Huber Heights homes, a single-family residence which was first rented to petitioner for use as an office and later sold to a realtor.

Petitioner and Huber Investment were operated as two separate and autonomous companies, and the books, records, and bank accounts of each were separately maintained. Each company had its own payroll and its own employees. Huber Investment's employees performed all the activities of a landlord with respect to the houses which it owned. Petitioner's employees never performed any of such activities with respect to Huber Investment's properties.

Petitioner developed the land in Huber Heights in sections, ranging in size from approximately 50 to 200 houses. As soon as a new section was opened for development, petitioner's sales department was permitted to sell the houses which were to be built there through the use of furnished and landscaped model homes. On the average, approximately 70 percent of the houses in a section were sold by the time all the houses in that section had been completed. In the late summer and fall of each year, however, petitioner would begin construction of houses beyond its immediate needs and in anticipation of sales during the following winter and spring, since it found it impractical to start construction between the beginning of November and the middle of the following April.

Based upon previous sales and upon the then current market conditions, Charles Huber, plus the sales manager, production manager, and other officers of petitioner determined, at a meeting held sometime in August, 1964, that 148 houses could be built and sold in Huber Heights from the fall of 1964 through the spring of 1965 when construction could start again. Thus, petitioner started construction on 148 houses in the late summer and early fall of 1964.

The prices at which the foregoing 148 houses and lots were offered to the public were set by petitioner on the basis of direct labor and material costs, land and land development costs, overhead, and profit. The base prices at which the houses were offered to the public varied according to the model of the particular house, ranging from $12,995 to $19,995. After the prices were established, they were made known to the public by advertising, through brochures, and in the sales office. It was petitioner's established policy never to offer any house to the public at a price below its published price.

During the period from the commencement of construction of the 148 afore-mentioned houses through the period in question, ending August 31, 1965, petitioner employed four full-time salesmen, working seven days a week, to solicit the sales of these houses. The salesmen were instructed to sell every house they could, and they were compensated on a salary plus commission basis.

Of the 148 houses started in the late summer and early fall of 1964, petitioner suc-ceeded in selling only 95 to the public. Four more houses were acquired by Huber Investment during its taxable year ended March 28, 1965. Despite petitioner's sales effort from the fall of 1964 until the early summer of 1965, the 49 houses which remained out of the original 148 could not be sold at the prices asked due to the then existing market conditions. Three other houses, constructed by petitioner at other times, were also unsold as of the early summer of 1965; one was a new style, model "Q," which had been built as a model home, and two were houses started prior to the construction of the aforementioned 148 houses. Thus, a total of 52 houses were unsold as of this time.

Petitioner transferred 38 of the 52 unsold houses and lots to Huber Investment by journal entry on July 1, 1965, approximately 8½ to 9½ months after construction on the 38 houses had begun, and approximately 2½ to 6 months after the 38 houses had been finished. It transferred another 13 of the 52 houses and lots to Huber In-vestment by journal entry on August 1, 1965, approximately 9½ to 10½ months after construction on the 13 houses had begun, and approximately 3½ to 7 months after the 13 houses had been finished. Finally, it transferred the model "Q" house and lot to Huber Investment by journal entry on August 31, 1965.

Title to the 52 houses and lots was formally transferred by petitioner to Huber Investment by deeds during August 1965.

Huber Investment acquired the aforementioned 52 houses at petitioner's actual cost of $723,003.25. On petitioner's books and records there was an "Account Re-ceivable" from its subsidiary, Huber Investment, and the debt on that inter-company open account was increased in the aggregate amount of $723,003.25 to reflect the transfer of the 52 houses at cost. During the taxable period ending August 31, 1965, the monthly balance of petitioner's "Account Receivable" from Huber Investment, as reflected on petitioner's books and records, was as follows:

March 31, 1965	$ 546,301.42
April 30, 1965	546,301.42
May 31, 1965	544,248.13
June 30, 1965	544,248.13
July 31, 1965	1,067,411.96
August 31, 1965	465,342.84

The aggregate sales price to the general public of the 52 houses was $907,807.28.

The 52 houses were transferred to Huber Investment in order that they be converted to rental properties. The decision to do so was based on the belief that the houses could not be sold to the public at the published selling prices, and that by continuing to hold the unsold houses, petitioner not only would incur interest charges and other expenses but would also sustain losses arising from vandalism and deterioration.

After their transfer, Huber Investment, with a view towards renting the houses, obtained insurance on all the 52 houses in issue, and, in addition, installed venetian blinds and curtain and drapery rods in all 52 houses except the model "Q" house, and installed stair carpeting in the eight 2-story houses that were included within the 52 houses.

The 52 houses have been rental units ever since their acquisition by Huber Investment. The rentals which it charged were usually set by model, depending upon the size of the model, with certain adjustments for "extras" such as a 2-car garage, fireplace, custom kitchen, etc. The rental price of the houses ranged from $105 to $180 per month.

In July and September 1965, the vice president in charge of the Appraisal Department of Citizens Federal Savings and Loan Association, Dayton, Ohio, Thomas J. Gilfoil, appraised each of the 52 houses and lots in issue in connection with applications for mortgage loans made by Huber Investment. He appraised the aggregate fair market value of the individual houses and lots in issue to be $852,045 as of that time. Because 38 houses and lots were transferred to Huber Investment on July 1, 1965 in a bulk transaction, and on August 1, 1965, 13 more houses and lots were also transferred in a bulk transaction, the fair market value of these houses and lots as a group was five percent less than the total of the fair market value of each individual house and lot.

During the summer of 1965, there was a resale market for houses in Huber Heights built by Huber Homes. The prices for such houses were generally lower than the prices of comparable new houses offered for sale by Huber Homes. During its taxable year ended August 31, 1966, Huber Homes sold 132 houses in Huber Heights to the general public. The model types of these houses were generally the same as those sold in previous years.

In its return for the taxable period ended August 31, 1965, Huber Homes reported a net loss of $61,882.13. This amount was carried back to its fiscal year ended March 31, 1963.

On its return for the taxable period ended August 31, 1965, Huber Investment reported gross rental income of $470,181.09 and a net loss in the amount of $56,517.99.

From the date of its incorporation through the taxable period ended August 31, 1965, Huber Investment has computed its depreciation deduction on buildings on the double-declining-balance method using a 30-year life for all single family residences.

The Commissioner determined deficiencies in the income tax of Huber Homes for its taxable year ending March 31, 1963 and the taxable period ending August 31, 1965. In his notice of deficiency he stated:

(a) It is determined that during the taxable year ended August 31, 1965 you had a profit of $205,113.85 upon transfer of houses to your wholly owned subsidiary, Huber Investment Corp. The profit is allocated to you under the provisions of section 482 of the Internal Revenue Code since it is determined that this allocation is necessary in order to prevent evasion of taxes and to clearly reflect income. Therefore, taxable income is increased $205,113.85 as shown below.

Cost of houses transferred	$723,003.25
Estimated sales prices	928,117.10
Profit	$205,113.85

This determination resulted not only in a deficiency for the taxable period ending August 31, 1965, but also a deficiency for the taxable year ending March 31, 1963, by reason of the elimination of the reported net loss for the period ending August 31, 1965, which in turn eliminated the net operating loss carryback to the year ending March 31, 1963.

The report of the Internal Revenue Service agent in respect of an audit of Huber Investment's books and records and its tax return for the taxable period beginning March 29, 1965 and ending August 31, 1965 stated, in part:

> The income of one member of a controlled group was increased by $205,113.85 . . . . The correlative adjustment to this member of the controlled group resulted in the basis of real estate being increased by $205,113.85 . . . .
> The $205,113.85 was allocated between land and buildings as follows:
>
> land $39,931.00
> buildings $165,182.85

Opinion

RAUM, Judge: During 1965 petitioner transferred, at its actual cost, 52 newly constructed houses to its wholly owned subsidiary, Huber Investment, which then rented the houses to the public. It is conceded by petitioner that at the time of the transfer the houses had a fair market value in excess of cost — though the exact amount thereof is in dispute herein. The Commissioner has determined that, pursuant to section 482, I.R.C. 1954, income should be "allocated" to petitioner to the extent of the difference between the cost of the houses and their fair market value at the time of transfer. The petitioner argues that this determination is unreasonable and arbitrary because no income was realized in respect of the transfer. . . .

The purposes of section 482, and the Commissioner's authority thereunder, were set out in Pauline W. Ach, 42 T.C. 114, 125-126, affirmed 358 F.2d 342 (C.A. 6), certiorari denied 385 U.S. 899:

> Respondent may allocate income under section 482 in order to prevent "evasion of taxes or clearly to reflect the income." The legislative history of section 482 indicates that it was designed to prevent evasion of taxes by the

arbitrary shifting of profits, the making of fictitious sales, and other such methods used to "milk" a taxable entity. Ballentine Motor Co., Inc., 39 T.C. 348, affirmed 321 F.2d 796 (C.A. 4); Seminole Flavor Co., 4 T.C. 1215, 1228. The Commissioner has considerable discretion in applying this section and his determinations must be sustained unless he has abused his discretion. We may reverse his determinations only where the taxpayer proves them to be unreasonable, arbitrary, or capricious. . . .

In order to prevent the artificial shifting of income from one related business to another, section 482 places a controlled taxpayer on a parity with an uncontrolled taxpayer, by determining according to the standard of an uncontrolled taxpayer, the true net income of a controlled taxpayer. See, e.g., Asiatic Petroleum Co.v. Commissioner, 79 F.2d 234, 236 (C.A. 2), affirming 31 B.T.A. 1152, certiorari denied 296 U.S. 645, rehearing denied 296 U.S. 664; . . . Regs. section 1.482-1(b) and 1.482-1(c). Thus, income which has been artificially diverted to one member of a controlled group but which in fact was earned by another member of the group may be "allocated" by the Commissioner under section 482 to the entity which really earned it. However, in the present case Huber Investment has not received any income — indeed, it has sustained losses — which was earned by petitioner and should be "allocated" to it. Nevertheless, the Commissioner seeks to apply section 482, relying upon Regs. section 1.482-1(a)(6), which states:

> Sec. 1.482-1. Allocation of income and deductions among taxpayers. —
> (a) *Definitions.* . . .
> (6) The term "true taxable income" means, in the case of a controlled taxpayer, the taxable income (or, as the case may be, any item or element affecting taxable income) which would have resulted to the controlled taxpayer, had it in the conduct of its affairs (or, as the case may be, in the particular contract, transaction, arrangement, or other act) dealt with the other member or members of the group at arm's length. It does not mean the income, the deductions, the credits, the allowances, or the item or element of income, deductions, credits, or allowances, resulting to the controlled taxpayer by reason of the particular contract, transaction, or arrangement, the controlled taxpayer, or the interests controlling it, chose to make (even though such contract, transaction, or arrangement be legally binding upon the parties thereto).

The Commissioner argues that had the transaction between petitioner and its subsidiary been at arm's length, additional income would have inured to petitioner in the amount of the excess of the fair market value of the houses transferred over petitioner's cost. And, if Huber Investment had dealt with its parent at arm's length it would have paid the fair market value of the houses. Hence, contends the Commissioner, in order "clearly to reflect the income" of both corporations, petitioner's income should be increased by what it would have earned in an arm's length sale and Huber Investment's basis in the houses should be increased accordingly. This approach finds at least some support in the Regulations, sections 1.482-1(a)(6), 1.482-1(d)(1), and 1(d)(4), particularly the latter.

The arm's-length standard relied upon by the Commissioner has traditionally been upheld where it has served as the basis for a reallocation of income derived from dealings with third parties — i.e., parties other than the controlled corporations which have engaged in transactions at less than arm's length. For example, in Oil Base, Inc. v. Commissioner . . . , 362 F.2d 212 (C.A. 9), the parent corporation granted its wholly owned subsidiary commissions and discounts twice as large as those allowed uncontrolled sales representatives. The Commissioner allocated portions of the subsidiary's sales income to the parent on the basis of what would have been the parent's arm's length arrangements with uncontrolled parties. The Commissioner's determination was approved. Likewise, in Eli Lilly & Co. v. United States, 372 F.2d 990 (Ct. Cl.), the Commissioner successfully charged the parent manufacturing company with portions of the profits received on sales to outsiders by its wholly owned subsidiary where the parent's sales to the subsidiary were at less than arm's length prices. In these cases, as in the other cases relied upon by the Commissioner, e.g., Dillard-Waltermire, Inc. v. Campbell, 255 F.2d 433 (C.A. 5); Grenada Industries, Inc., 17 T.C. 231, affirmed 202 F.2d 873 (C.A. 5), certiorari denied 346 U.S. 819, the determinations in issue were based on the *reallocation* of income derived from dealings with third parties. And the arm's length formula simply played a part in determining what portion of the income received by a member of the controlled group was really earned by and therefore properly allocable to another member of the group. However, we are not faced with that situation here. Huber Investment did not resell the houses transferred to it, and thereby receive a profit that was in fact attributable to petitioner but which was artificially channeled to Huber Investment by means of an intercompany sale at cost. Moreover, in contrast to his position in the foregoing cases, the Commissioner does not here contend that any of Huber Investment's gross rental income was not earned by it or that any portion of *its* income should be allocated to Huber Homes. Rather, the Commissioner is purporting to exercise his authority under section 482 to create income, i.e., to charge petitioner with the income it would have realized had its sale to Huber Investment been at arm's length. We hold that this determination is not authorized by section 482.

Essential to the application of section 482 is the distribution, apportionment, or allocation of income realized at some time by the controlled group. This was made clear in Tennessee-Arkansas Gravel Co. v. Commissioner, 112 F.2d 508 (C.A. 6), reversing a Memorandum Opinion of this Court. In that case, the taxpayer made available certain movable equipment to an affiliate, "Mississippi." During the year in issue no rental charge was made for the use of the equipment and, pursuant to section 45 of the Revenue Act of 1934 (predecessor of section 482), the Commissioner determined that the taxpayer had rental income of $12,000, the value of the use of the equipment based on arrangements made the previous year. The Court of Appeals rejected the Commissioner's position, stating (112 F.2d at 510):

> Regardless of what he [the Commissioner] may have contemplated, the undisputed fact is, that he made no distribution, apportionment or allocation of gross income between petitioner and Mississippi. He made no attempt to

allocate any portion of the $51,427.70, representing the gross income of Mississippi in 1934, to petitioner. The record clearly discloses what he did. He simply concluded that petitioner should have charged Mississippi rent upon the equipment for the year 1934, notwithstanding the fact that petitioner neither charged, collected nor could have collected rent under its agreement with Mississippi. Having so determined, the Commissioner fixed the rental to be charged at $1,000 per month based upon the rate charged by petitioner for a portion of 1933. Having so fixed the rental, he charged it to petitioner as income in the following language: "Add: . . . 2. Rent of equipment $12,000."

Section 45, supra, *did not authorize the Commissioner to set up income where none existed.* The principal purpose of the section was to clearly reflect income that did exist.

It is suggested that the law will imply that the Commissioner apportioned the $12,000 to petitioner from the gross income of Mississippi, but the law permits no inferences contrary to fact. (Emphasis supplied.)

The present case closely parallels *Tennessee-Arkansas* in that the Commissioner here, as there, did not *allocate* to the taxpayer any of the gross income of the related party to which there was a transfer at less than arm's length. Instead, here, as there, the Commissioner *created* income out of a transaction which, in the Commissioner's opinion, only *would have* produced income had the petitioner dealt with the controlled party at arm's length. Thus, it is apparent that the Commissioner here did not "distribute, apportion, or allocate gross income" within the meaning of section 482. See 7 Mertens, Law of Federal Income Taxation, sec. 38.63, p. 176; Simon J. Murphy Co. v. Commissioner . . . , 231 F.2d at 644 (dictum).[3]

The Commissioner seeks to distinguish the *Tennessee-Arkansas* case on the ground that the decision was based on the Commissioner's failure to make a correlative adjustment to the income or deductions of the related entity. We think, however, that the Sixth Circuit's decision rests on a broader ground: that the allocation under section 482 must be of income actually realized by a member of the controlled group.

Nor do we think that the Commissioner's proposed adjustment to Huber Investment's basis in the houses transferred to it sufficiently effects an allocation of Huber Investment's income to petitioner. The fact remains that even in light of this adjustment income is being attributed to petitioner that was not in fact realized by the controlled group. Compare V & M Homes, Inc., 28 T.C. 1121, affirmed 263 F.2d 837 (C.A. 6). Had petitioner retained the 148 houses and rented them itself to tenants, it could not conceivably have been charged with income to the extent that the fair market value of the houses exceeded cost, and certainly its basis for depreciation would have been only cost. Plainly, section 482 was not intended to produce a different result; it was designed merely to "unscramble" (Grenada Industries, Inc., supra, 17 T.C. at 253) a situation where income realized by the controlled group and earned

---

[3]Cf. Southern College of Optometry, Inc., 6 T.C.M. 354, 357.

by one member of the group is diverted to another group member by means of transactions not carried out at arm's length.

In E. C. Laster, 43 B.T.A. 159, acq. 1941-1 C.B. 7, modified on other grounds, 128 F.2d 4 (C.A. 5), the Board rejected the Commissioner's attempt to attribute income to a transferor of valuable oil payment rights, without charge, to its wholly owned subsidiary, the owner of the working interest. There, as in the present case, income was not realized by the transferee of the rights during the taxable year. After citing the *Tennessee-Arkansas* case, supra, the Board stated, at p. 177:

> The acquisition by the Retsal Drilling Co. of the oil payments without cost did not result in income to it or the transferor. It follows therefrom that there was no income to distribute or allocate under section 45.

In Smith-Bridgman & Co., 16 T.C. 287, acq. 1951-1 C.B. 3,[4] the petitioner, a wholly owned subsidiary of Continental, made interest-free loans to its parent. The Commissioner included in the taxpayer's gross income an amount representing a four percent interest charge in respect of its loan to its parent. The Court disapproved the Commissioner's determination (16 T.C. at 293):

> In support of his action the respondent argues that Continental, in securing these non-interest-bearing loans from petitioner, was enabled to relieve itself from paying interest on its outstanding debentures; and, furthermore, he argues, petitioner could have loaned the funds which Continental borrowed without interest to third parties at 4 per cent interest. Therefore, in order to prevent evasion of taxes and to clearly reflect the income of such related businesses, he has "allocated" to petitioner part of the income of its parent, in the exercise of the discretion conferred by section 45 of the code. The decisions involving section 45 make it clear that its principal purpose is to prevent the manipulation of or improper shifting of gross income and deductions between two or more organizations, trades, or businesses. Its application is predicated on the existence of income. The Courts have consistently refused to interpret section 45 as authorizing the creation of income out of a transaction where no income was realized by any of the commonly controlled businesses. Tennessee-Arkansas Gravel Co. v. Commissioner, 112 Fed. (2d) 508; E. C. Laster, 43 B.T.A. 159, modified on other issues, 128 Fed. (2d) 4; Epsen-Lithographers, Inc. v. O'Malley, 67 Fed. Supp. 181, cf. Hugh Smith, Inc., 8 T.C. 660, affd., 173 Fed. (2d) 224, certiorari denied, 337 U.S. 918.

The Court in *Smith-Bridgman* further noted that no correlative adjustment was made in the income of or deductions of Continental to account for the increase in the taxpayer's income. The Commissioner contends that this factor explains the decision and thereby distinguishes it from the present case. We disagree. We view this factor as no more than a possible supporting ground for the decision and not the controlling reason. It is no different in this respect from the similar situation in *Tennessee-Arkansas.*

[4]The Commissioner's acquiescence is explained in Rev. Rul. 67-79, 1967-1 C.B. 117.

Finally, in Texsun Supply Corp., 17 T.C. 433, acq. 1952-1 C.B. 4, Texsun's subsidiary sold boxes to it at its manufacturing cost, which Texsun, a cooperative supply corporation, then resold to its members. Texsun was required by its by-laws to sell to its members at cost, and it accomplished this by first selling to them at prevailing market prices and then rebating its "profits" to them at year-end. It thus realized no profit on such sales. The Commissioner attempted to "allocate" a profit to Texsun's subsidiary on the sales based on prevailing arm's length prices. The Court, citing *Smith-Bridgman & Co.,* again refused to approve the allocation.

Against the foregoing background of decided cases favorable to the petitioner, the Commissioner argues that he would be foreclosed from correcting distortions in income where goods or services are transferred to a related party at less than arm's-length prices and the goods or services are consumed rather than sold by the transferee. But if, as a consequence of such use or consumption by the transferee, income is realized within the controlled group, an entirely different question would be presented as to whether such income or a portion thereof might be allocated to the transferor under section 482. That situation, however, is not before us.

In deciding that section 482 is inapplicable here we do not reach the question whether the regulations . . . relied upon by the Commissioner are valid. They plainly contemplate a situation where one member of a controlled group sells to another at less than fair market value and where it is expected that the controlled vendee would in turn resell the product to a third party. In order properly to reflect income the profit on such resale would have to be fairly allocated between the two controlled corporations; the regulations provide that in such circumstances the allocation of its share of the profit to the original vendor need not await the year of ultimate sale but may be made immediately. We think that the regulations do not cover the present case where there was no intention to resell the 52 houses in issue, where they were converted to rental use, where they are still held for rental purposes, and where they do not appear to be productive of any net income whatever. In the circumstances we do not pass upon the validity of the regulations in situations where resale of the transferred property was contemplated regardless of when or even whether such resale in fact occurred.

The taxpayer has argued that the excess of the fair market value of the houses transferred to Huber Investment over their cost should be treated as a tax-free contribution of capital under section 118. Since we have held that section 482 is not applicable herein we need not pass upon this issue. Further, in light of the inapplicability of section 482 we need not determine the fair market value of the houses transferred to Huber Investment.

Decision will be entered under Rule 50.

NOTE

See J. Lewis, Tax Court in *Huber Homes* Holds That the IRS May Not Use 482 to Create Income, 34 J. Taxation 208 (1971).

VI. CONSOLIDATED RETURNS — §§1501-1505

ELKO REALTY CO. v. COMMISSIONER
29 T.C. 1012 (1958), aff'd per curiam, 260 F.2d 949 (3d Cir. 1958)

Train, Judge: [Taxpayer, a corporation, acquired 100 per cent of the stock of two corporations, Earl Apartments, Inc. and Spiegel Apartments, Inc., which had been operating at losses and which continued to operate at losses after the taxpayer acquired their stock. In each of the years 1951, 1952 and 1953 the taxpayer had a net profit. It filed consolidated returns in those years, however, and on those returns offset the losses of its subsidiaries against its profit. The Commissioner disallowed the deductions attributable to the subsidiaries' losses under the 1939 Code predecessor of §269, and the Tax Court sustained him, finding that the taxpayer failed to prove that the principal purpose of its acquisition of the stock of its subsidiaries was not tax avoidance. The Commissioner's alternative ground was that Earl Apartments, Inc. and Spiegel Apartments, Inc. "were not affiliates of the petitioner within the meaning of §[1504(a)] so as to permit the filing of consolidated returns in the years at issue . . . [under §1501]." (29 T.C. at 1012.) Although the court need not have dealt with the Commissioner's alternative grounds in light of its decision under §269, it did so.]

In J. D. & A. B. Spreckels Co., 41 B.T.A. 370 (1940), we laid down the rule that where the ownership of the subsidiary's stock by a parent corporation served no business purpose, as distinguished from a tax reducing purpose, the subsidiary is not an affiliate within the intent of [the consolidated return sections].

We agree with petitioner that the facts of the instant case differ in a number of respects from the facts in J. D. & A. B. Spreckels Co., supra. However, the rule of that case is applicable, regardless of distinctions of fact, where the petitioner is unable to show that a business purpose, as distinguished from a tax-reducing purpose, was served by the acquisition in question. We have already discussed at considerable length the evidence presented in this proceeding, and it is unnecessary to repeat that discussion here. After a careful examination of all the evidence, we conclude that the petitioner here has failed to show that a business purpose, as distinguished from a tax-reducing purpose, was served by its acquisition of Earl Apartments, Inc., and Spiegel Apartments, Inc.

It follows that the respondent's determination of deficiencies is, in all respects, sustained.

Decision will be entered for the respondent.

INCOME TAX DIVISION RULING 3896
1948-1 Cum. Bull. 72

Advice is requested whether certain corporations are affiliated within the meaning of section [1504(a)] of the Internal Revenue Code under the circumstances hereinafter set forth.

The parent corporation owns 100 per cent of the common stock and 55.5 per cent of the preferred stock of one of its subsidiaries. The common stock holders have the right to elect six of seven directors and have all other voting powers exclusively, except that the preferred stock holders may elect (as a class) one director and must approve (1) any change in the certificate of incorporation except an increase in common stock; (2) the disposition of the company's property by sale, merger, etc.; (3) the creation of a mortgage or lien (not including the acquisition of property subject to a lien or a renewal of an existing mortgage); (4) the issuance of bonds in excess of a certain amount; and (5) the authorization or issuance of any stock outranking the preferred stock or of any security convertible into such stock. The question has been raised whether the preferred stock is nonvoting stock which is limited and preferred as to dividends and, as such, to be disregarded in determining whether the corporations are affiliated within the meaning of section [1504(a)] of the Code, and if it is not such nonvoting stock, how the voting power of the preferred stock is to be determined. . . .

Since the preferred stock is clearly limited and preferred as to dividends, the first question to be determined is whether the stock is nonvoting stock as that term is defined in section [1504(a)] of the Code.

There are numerous court decisions with respect to what constitutes voting stock, as that term is used in section [1504(a)] of the Code. It is well established that if preferred stock carries with it the right to vote only with respect to matters pertaining to the rights of preferred stockholders, or if full voting rights are conditioned upon the happening of some event which has not occurred, such stock is nonvoting stock for the purposes of section [1504(a)] of the Code. (See Erie Lighting Co. v. Commissioner, 93 Fed. (2d), 883; Vermont Hydro-Electric Corporation v. Commissioner, 29 B.T.A., 1006, acquiescence, C.B. XIII-1, 16 (1934).) On the other hand, if preferred stock, because of dividend arrearages or the happening of some other condition, has obtained full voting rights, it has been held to be voting stock. (See Atlantic City Electric Co. et al. v. Commissioner, 288 U.S., 152, Ct. D. 637, C.B. XII-1, 281 (1933), and Pantlind Hotel Co. v. Commissioner, 23 B.T.A., 1207.) Likewise, it has been held that where, by State law, preferred stock has the privilege of voting for directors (but no other voting rights), the stock is voting stock within the meaning of section [1504(a)] of the Code. (See Rudolph Wurlitzer Co. et al. v. Commissioner, 29 B.T.A., 443, affirmed, 81 Fed. (2d), 971, certiorari denied, 298 U.S., 676.)

It remains to be determined whether the preferred stock in the instant case is voting stock because of its right as a class to elect only one of the seven directors. One possible holding is that stock is nonvoting unless it has the right to participate in the election of all directors. Such a rule must be rejected since it would require, in a case such as the instant one, a holding that both the common and preferred stocks are nonvoting if the common stock participates in the election of only six of the seven directors. Another possible conclusion is that even though the right to participate in the election of all directors is not necessary, the right to elect only one director of a total of seven directors is not sufficient to give the preferred stock any real participation in the management of the corporation, and that such preferred stock should be considered nonvoting stock for the purposes of section [1504(a)] of the Code. Such a conclusion would be based on the fact that the six directors elected by the common stock holders would so dominate the board of directors that the one director elected by the preferred stock holders would have no substantial authority. If such a theory were followed, however, it would be extremely difficult to determine when such stock becomes voting stock. If the preferred stock carried with it the right to elect three directors and the common stock four, the directors elected by the common would still be able to dominate the board, but it would not be reasonable to hold that in such a case the preferred is nonvoting stock. Likewise, it seems clear that if the preferred stock had one vote in the election of all directors and the common stock had six votes, the preferred would be considered voting stock having one-seventh of the voting power. Although those situations can be distinguished from the instant case, the basic concept, which requires a holding that the preferred stock in those situations is voting stock, is applicable here. It is the opinion of this office, therefore, that any stock which participates in the election of directors is voting stock within the intendment of section [1504(a)] of the Code.

Since, in the instant case, the preferred stock of the subsidiary company is considered voting stock for the purposes of section [1504(a)] of the Code, it is necessary to determine what percentage of such stock must be owned by the parent in order for the subsidiary to be a member of the affiliated group. The Revenue Act of 1924 provided that two or more corporations would be deemed to be affiliated if one corporation owned at least 95 per cent of the voting stock of the others. In the Revenue Act of 1926, the word "voting" was deleted and ownership of "at least 95 per centum of the stock" was required for affiliation. It was provided that the term "stock" did not include nonvoting stock which was limited and preferred as to dividends. Section 141(d) of the Revenue Act of 1928 contained similar provisions. In Anderson-Clayton Securities Corporation v. Commissioner (35 B.T.A., 795, acquiescence, C.B. 1937-2, 2), the Board of Tax Appeals (now The Tax Court of the United States), in construing section 141(d) of the Revenue Act of 1928, held that ownership of 95 per cent of the *shares* of stock of another corporation was not required for affiliation, but rather ownership of 95 per cent of the capital stock of the corporation (excluding nonvoting preferred), taking into consideration the combined *voting power* of the stock owned. In that case, the parent corporation owned 100 per cent of the preferred stock and 64 per cent of the common stock of a subsidiary. The preferred stock at that time had a voting power of 50 votes per share and the common stock had a voting power of 1 vote per share. The Board held that, since the preferred stock had a voting power of 240,000 votes and the common stock a voting power of 6,400 votes, the parent corporation owned 98.56 per cent of the voting power of the subsidiary's stock and the two corporations were affiliated. The Board said (page 800):

"... Anderson-Clayton Industries, Inc., held legal title to stock possessing more than 95 per centum of the total voting power and enjoyed a beneficial ownership of more than 95 per centum of the capital stock. ...

"... [I]t is clearly aparent that Anderson-Clayton Industries, Inc., *owned* more than 95 per cent of *the six companies*. Our conclusion is that they were affiliated with the petitioner during the taxable period."

In the Revenue Act of 1932, the right to file consolidated returns was restricted to certain railroad corporations, but the stock ownership requirements remained unchanged. The Second Revenue Act of 1940, which enacted the excess profits tax, added section 730 to the [1939 Code], which section granted the privilege of filing consolidated excess profits tax returns to affiliated groups as defined therein. Section 730(d) of the Code, as so added, defined "affiliated group" as one or more chains of includible corporations connected through stock ownership with a common parent corporation which is an includible corporation if "At least 95 per centum of each class of the stock of each of the includible corporations (except the common parent corporation) is owned directly by one or more of the other includible corporations." Nonvoting stock which was limited and preferred as to dividends was specifically excluded from the term "stock," as used therein. It would appear that Congress, in requiring ownership of 95 per cent of *each class* of the stock, intended to modify the holding in Anderson-Clayton Securities Corporation v. Commissioner, supra, that ownership of 95 per cent of the "capital stock" taken as a whole was sufficient.

The Revenue Act of 1942 made section 730 of the Code inapplicable to years beginning after December 31, 1941, and amended . . . the Code so as to extend the privilege of filing consolidated returns, for income as well as excess profits tax purposes, to any "affiliated group of corporations." The definition of an "affiliated group" in section [1504(a)] of the Code was amended to require the ownership of stock "possessing at least 95 per centum of the voting power of all classes of stock and at least 95 per centum of each class of the nonvoting stock," excluding nonvoting stock which is limited and preferred as to dividends.* It would seem that Congress, in so altering the language of . . . the Code, intended to abandon the requirement . . . that ownership of 95 per cent of *each class* of stock was necessary for affiliation and to follow the decision in the *Anderson-Clayton Securities Corporation* case which required merely the ownership of 95 per cent of the voting stock taken as a whole. However, section [1504(a)] of the Code, as amended, made explicit the requirement that 95 per cent of *each class* of nonvoting stock (which is not limited and preferred as to dividends) must be owned by the parent or one of the other includible corporations. Under the present law, therefore, it is not necessary for the parent to own 95 per cent of each class of voting stock of the subsidiary in order for the latter to be a member of the affiliated group, but it is sufficient if the parent owns 95 per cent of the voting power of all classes of voting stock taken together.

The next question, therefore, is to determine the percentage of the voting power of the stock owned by the parent corporation in the instant case. Since participation in the management of the subsidiary corporation through election of the board of directors is considered the criterion of voting power, it is believed that the common stock of the subsidiary should be held to have six-sevenths, or 85.714 per cent, of the voting power and the preferred one-seventh, or 14.286 per cent. The parent corporation owns 100 per cent of the common stock but only 55.5 per cent of the preferred stock of the subsidiary. Thus, it owns stock possessing 85.714 per cent plus 7.929 per cent (55.5 per cent of 14.286 per cent), or 93.643 per cent of the voting power of all

*The "95 per centum requirement" was reduced to "80 per cent" in 1954. — Ed.

classes of stock. In order for the subsidiary to become an includible corporation of the affiliated group, the parent corporation must own 65.01 per cent of its preferred stock, which would represent 9.287 per cent of the voting power and which, when added to 85.714 per cent of the voting power held by virtue of the common stock ownership, would give the parent "at least 95 per centum of the voting power of all classes of stock". . . .

HENRY C. BECK BUILDERS, INC. v. COMMISSIONER
41 T.C. 616 (1964)

TRAIN, Judge: Respondent determined a deficiency in income tax of petitioner Salina Management Co., Inc. (docket No. 90108), in the amount of $129,673.89 for its taxable year ended June 30, 1957.

Respondent further determined that the remaining petitioners were liable, as transferees, for Salina Management Co., Inc.'s deficiency, as follows:

Henry C. Beck Builders, Inc. (docket No. 90101)	$ 41,436.06
First National Bank in Dallas and Henry C. Beck Jr., Trustees under the will of Henry C. Beck, Deceased (docket No. 90102) ..	10,631.86
Utah Construction & Mining Co. (docket No. 90109)	52,067.92
Total	$104,135.84

The issues remaining to be decided relate to the deficiency determined against the transferor:

(1) Whether a parent corporation's intercompany profit eliminated in a prior taxable year in a consolidated income tax return is realized by the parent corporation and taxable as ordinary income upon the sale of the stock of the subsidiary to a purchaser outside the affiliation; and

(2) Whether the basis of the parent's investment in the preferred and common stock of the subsidiary-affiliate is to be reduced, on redemption or sale, by certain losses of the subsidiary which were incurred during the period of affiliation, and, if so, to what extent such basis is to be reduced.

The facts in this case have been fully stipulated and are hereby found as stipulated.

Petitioner Henry C. Beck Builders, Inc. (hereinafter sometimes referred to as Builders), is a corporation with its principal place of business in Dallas, Tex. Petitioners First National Bank in Dallas and Henry C. Beck, Jr. (hereinafter sometimes referred to as Trust), are cotrustees of a trust created under the will of Henry C. Beck, deceased, with their principal places of business in Dallas, Tex. Petitioner Utah Construction & Mining Co. (formerly Utah Construction Co., hereinafter sometimes referred to as Utah) is a Delaware corporation with its principal office in San Francisco, Calif.

Builders, Trust, and Utah are transferees of a dissolved corporation, i.e., petitioner

Salina Management Co., Inc., hereinafter sometimes referred to as Management. Its principal office was at Salina, Kans. . . .

Management was incorporated in Kansas on August 18, 1952, and completely dissolved on March 27, 1958. During this period its stock was owned as follows:

	Aug. 18, 1952, to Feb. 4, 1956	Feb. 4 to July 24, 1956	July 24, 1956, to Mar. 27, 1958
Preferred stock:			
Utah	150	150	150
Henry C. Beck Co.	150	150	0
Builders	0	0	150
Common stock:			
Utah	100	100	100
Henry C. Beck Co.	100	67½	0
Builders	0	0	67½
Trust	0	32½	32½

Salina Homes, Inc. (hereinafter sometimes referred to as Homes), was incorporated in Kansas on August 18, 1952. During the period August 18, 1952, to October 31, 1956, its 280 shares of preferred stock were owned entirely by Management and its common stock was owned as follows:

Common stock (class A)	Aug. 18, 1952, to Mar. 30, 1954	Mar. 30, 1954, to Oct. 31, 1956
Management	95	100
R. H. Hopkins	5	0

The 95 shares of Homes common stock had an original cost basis to Management of zero. The five shares of common stock originally issued to R. H. Hopkins were purchased from him by Management on March 30, 1954, for $1,750. The preferred stock was received by Management upon the incorporation of Homes in exchange for unimproved real property having a basis to Management at that time of $23,471. The preferred stock had a par value of $100, did not carry voting rights, and was limited as to dividends.

Management was organized to construct and manage a 150-dwelling-unit housing project situated near Salina, Kans., and known as the "Beck-Utah Development, Edgemere Addition to the City of Salina, Kansas," hereinafter sometimes referred to as the Project. Homes was organized to own and finance the construction of the Project.

Pursuant to an agreement of August 2, 1952, with Homes, Management constructed the Project for Homes. Construction was completed during the fiscal year ended June 30, 1953, at a cost to Management of $998,402.05. Homes paid Management $1,275,308.95 for constructing the Project. The entire amount was financed by Homes by means of a U.S. Government insured loan from the Federal National Mortgage Association and secured by the Project.

Management recorded its $276,906.90 profit from the Project's construction on its books of account and on its Federal income tax returns to the extent of $273,780.09 during its taxable year ended June 30, 1953, and $3,126.81 during its taxable year ended June 30, 1954. The entire profit was eliminated in determining consolidated net (or taxable) income on the consolidated returns filed by Management and Homes for their taxable years 1953 and 1954. In computing depreciation on the Project for its taxable years ended June 30, 1953 through 1957, Homes used a cost basis of $998,-402.05, that being Management's cost for the Project.

At all times here material Homes owned the Project, and Management performed all the requisite management services. Management's activities were confined almost exclusively to the construction and management of the Project.

On or about July 27, 1956, Homes redeemed and retired all its outstanding preferred stock for $28,000. Management reported on its June 30, 1957, return a gain of $4,529 ($28,000 received less $23,471 cost basis) on the redemption.

On or about October 31, 1956, Management sold all of the outstanding common stock of Homes to an unrelated party, Housing Service Corp. (hereinafter sometimes referred to as Housing), for $25,000. Management reported on its June 30, 1957, return a gain of $23,250 ($25,000 received less $1,750 cost basis) on the sale.

Within a few days after Housing purchased the Homes common stock from Management, Housing liquidated Homes and received its assets (principally, the Project) subject to its liabilities, including the outstanding balance of $733,516.87 on the Project construction loan.

After the sale of the Homes common stock, Management became completely inactive and was dissolved on March 27, 1958.

The following schedule reflects the taxable or net income (or loss) of Management and Homes, after elimination of all intercompany transactions and after giving effect to respondent's adjustments agreed to in connection with his audit of the 1953 and 1954 consolidated income tax returns, for each of the taxable years ended June 30, 1953 through 1957:

Taxable year	Management	Homes	Consolidated
1953	($573.86)	($25,506.02)	($26,079.88)
1954	(696.78)	19,348.92	18,652.14
1955	5,335.47	4,916.53	10,252.00
1956	168.54	(11,108.36)	(10,939.82)
1957	26,412.34	[1]1,538.63	27,950.97
Totals	30,645.71	(10,810.30)	19,835.41

[1]Homes' income from July 1 through Oct. 31, 1956, the date on which the affiliation was broken.

During Management's taxable years ended June 30, 1957, and March 27, 1958, Utah, Builders, and Trust, then constituting all of Management's shareholders, received distributions, all of which were in cash, with respect to their Management common and preferred stocks as follows:

Date	Stockholder	Amount
Feb. 28, 1957	Builders	$17,250.00
Do	Utah	23,750.00
Do	Trust	6,500.00
July 15, 1957	.... do	1,950.00
Do	Utah	6,000.00
Do	Builders	4,050.00
April 14, 1958	Utah	15,604.50
Do	Builders	15,604.40
Do	Utah	6,713.42
Do	Trust	2,181.86
Do	Builders	4,531.56
Total		104,135.84

The above-listed amounts reflect various distributions paid to the shareholders of Management for which the shareholders paid no consideration. As a result of such distributions, Management was left without assets. Immediately subsequent to the distributions made to its shareholders on February 28, 1957, Management retained as its only asset $56,635.84 in cash which was thereafter distributed to its shareholders by Management as indicated by the above schedule.

In the deficiency notice to Management, dated September 7, 1960, respondent determined that for the taxable period ended June 30, 1957, the $276,906.90 Project construction profit eliminated from the earlier returns constituted ordinary income to Management on the occasion of its sale of Homes stock to Housing. This additional income was reduced in the notice by "the excess of depreciation on the houses based on the construction price before the intercompany elimination over depreciation based on the construction price reduced by the intercompany elimination." Depreciation was allowed on the eliminated profit at the rate of $3\frac{1}{3}$ percent per year for $3\frac{3}{4}$ years, for a total of $34,613.36, leaving a net adjustment of $242,293.54 on account of this intercompany transaction.

Issue 1 — Intercompany Profit

Respondent maintains that Management's previously eliminated intercompany profit must be taxed upon Management's sale of the Homes stock, else the profit escapes taxation altogether — a result contemplated by neither the statute nor respondent's regulations. Petitioners argue that they followed the regulations and that there is no authority in either the regulations or the statute for taxing, in the year the stock of the subsidiary is sold, the previously eliminated intercompany profit.

We agree with petitioners.

Respondent agrees that Management properly eliminated from its consolidated return for the fiscal year ended June 30, 1953, the intercompany profit it received that year on the construction of the Project.[3] There is no suggestion that the $3,126.81

---

[3] Sec. 24.31(b)(1)(i), Regs. 129, substantially identical to sec. 1.1502-31(b)(1)(i), Income Tax Regs., provides:

Sec. 24.31 Bases of tax computation. — In the case of an affiliated group of corporations

eliminated from the following year's return for the same reason was not also properly so eliminated.

Although section 1502 of the Internal Revenue Code of 1954 gives respondent the power to provide by regulation for the proper determination of the tax liability of groups filing consolidated returns "both during and after the period of affiliation," respondent has not yet chosen to promulgate any regulation providing for the tax treatment he advocates in this case.

Section 1.1502-3, Income Tax Regs., states that other law will be looked to where the regulations are silent on the matter at issue. Other law does not permit inclusion in 1957 income of an item accrued in 1953 merely because the item was not taxed in 1953. Hurtz v. United States, [162 Ct. Cl. 855 (1963)]; Commissioner v. Dwyer, 203 F.2d 522 (C.A. 2, 1953) (collecting cases, at footnotes 3, 6, and 7, on the impropriety under the 1939 Code of including, in the year the Commissioner changed the taxpayer's method of reporting income, the income that had been earned in prior years); Leonard C. Kline, 15 T.C. 998 (1950) (basis from an earlier lump-sum acquisition must be properly allocated to items sold during the taxable year, even though the entire basis had previously been applied to items sold during the preceding taxable year); Policy Holders Agency, Inc., 41 T.C. 44 (1963) (unclaimed premium refunds transferred to surplus in 1958 were not includable in 1958 income because they should have been taxed in earlier years). The only exception to this rule that we regard as arguably relevant here relates to change of accounting method.

Respondent urges that elimination of intercompany profits under section 1.1502-31(b)(1)(i), Income Tax Regs., and carryover of basis under section 1.1502-38(b), Income Tax Regs., constitute a method of accounting which, under section 1.1502-31 (b)(1), Income Tax Regs.,[7] the taxpayers may change, with the Commissioner's permission. Respondent concludes from this that, when the method prescribed by the regulations fails to properly reflect income, he may compel a change of accounting method under the provisions of section 446(b).

We are not prepared at this point to agree that the foregoing constitutes a method of accounting. We are even less ready to agree that Management's method has been

which makes, or is required to make, a consolidated return for any taxable year, and except as otherwise provided in these regulations, the tax liability determined under section 24.30 shall be determined subject to the definitions and rules of computation set forth in paragraphs (a) and (b) of this section. . . .

(b) *Computations.* — In the case of affiliated corporations which make, or are required to make, a consolidated return, and except as otherwise provided in these regulations —

(1) *Net income.* — The net income of each corporation shall be computed in accordance with the provisions covering the determination of net income of separate corporations, except —

(i) There shall be eliminated unrealized profits and losses in transactions between members of the affiliated group and dividend distributions from one member of the group to another member of the group (referred to in these regulations as intercompany transactions) . . . .

[7]For the purpose of the regulations under sec. 1502, a transaction not involving a sale or exchange of a capital asset or of property subject to the provisions of sec. 1231 shall not be considered an intercompany transaction if such transaction occurs in the regular course of the trade or business of the members of the group and if such members adopt, with the consent of the Commissioner and subject to such conditions as he deems proper, a consistent acounting practice of taking into acount in the computation of consolidated taxable income the gains and losses reflected in such transactions. . . .

changed simply because there are no longer any transactions of the sort dealt with by the former "method of accounting."[9] However, even were we to agree, arguendo, with respondent's approach, at best it proves too much. The change is being made for the taxable year ending June 30, 1957; it clearly was not initiated by the taxpayer, and it involves adjustments in respect of the taxable years ending June 30, 1953, and June 30, 1954. Thus, section 481(a) specifically forbids the adjustments here at issue.[11] . . .

Respondent's citation of Ilfeld Co. v. Hernandez, 292 U.S. 62 (1934), is also not helpful. In that case the Supreme Court disallowed deduction of a corporation's loss on its investments (stock cost plus advances) in two subsidiaries with which it had filed consolidated returns. The Court determined that the regulations upon which the taxpayer there relied for its deductions were not aplicable; that other applicable regulations forbade deduction of the losses; and that the taxpayer already had the benefit in prior years of offsetting against its income the operating losses of the subsidiaries that had caused the investment losses sought to be deducted in the year before the Court. (Cf. Mary E. Burrow Trust, 39 T.C. 1080 (1963), [aff'd, 333 F.2d 66 (10th Cir. 1964)], where the same expense was allowed by statute as a deduction in the computation of two different taxes.) Here, the one occasion for including the income properly accrued in the earlier year was required by the Commissioner's regulations to be bypassed. The regulations provide that the eliminated income would reduce the basis for depreciation or sale of the Project by Homes. The additional tax due on account of this reduced depreciation during Homes' ownership of the Project was paid. There is no other occasion provided for in the regulations or the Code for taxing the previously eliminated profit. And, as indicated above, general income tax law is opposed to inclusion of the 1953 income in Management's 1957 taxable year.

This Court has already ruled in a situation where the parent corporation suffered an eliminated loss on a transfer to a subsidiary with which the parent filed a consolidated return and the parent thereafter disposes of the subsidiary during the same taxable year. . . . Fidelity National Bank & Trust Co., 14 B.T.A. 904 (1928), affd. 39 F.2d 58 (C.A. 8, 1930). . . .

The Circuit Court of Appeals, affirming, objected to the requirement of keeping intercompany transactions "open" until it was seen what happened to the affiliated status between the parties to those transactions.

Respondent's arguments in the case now before us are contrary to, and would appear to require the overruling of, Fidelity National Bank & Trust Co. . . .

[P]rinciples of consolidated returns law heretofore successfully urged upon us by respondent combine with the general annual accounting period principle to foreclose recognition, in the only year before us, of the previously eliminated intercompany profit. . . .

. . . [T]he Commissioner impliedly concedes that his consolidated returns regu-

---

[9]Since the affiliation has been broken, there is nothing that can be properly described as an intercompany transaction and so there can be no *change* in the method of treating intercompany transactions.

[11]Under sec. 7851(a)(1)(A), sec. 481 "shall apply only with respect to taxable years beginning after December 31, 1953, and ending after the date of enactment of this title, [Aug. 16, 1954]."

lations conflict with his adjustments, for he insists on the right, under section 446(b), to set aside both his regulations requiring elimination of intercompany profits and his regulations requiring a carryover of basis where there has been an intercompany transfer.

We are left with a situation where Management has taken advantage of a tax benefit (elimination of intercompany profits) offered by respondent and has successfully avoided corresponding tax detriments (lower basis for depreciation and sale) by a series of real transactions resulting in permanent transfer of Homes and the Project to an unrelated party. Essentially, respondent maintains that Management's construction profit must be taxed on the sale of Homes stock or that profit will forever escape taxation.[13]

We are not slow to look through a transaction and demand persuasive evidence of its reality or bona fides. . . . On the other hand, the doctrine that a taxpayer may arrange his affairs to minimize his taxes, so long as the form he chooses properly reflects the substance of his transactions, is well established. . . .

There is no dispute that the property was built for the amount claimed, that Homes paid a reasonable price to Management for the construction of the property, and that it really was disposed of to an independent party in an arm's-length transaction. Respondent stresses the fact that this party then liquidated Homes and presumably took the Project at a stepped-up basis under section 334(b)(2). But the purchaser was merely taking advantage of a benefit specifically provided for by the Code. What it did after its bona fide purchase should not affect the tax of the seller.

Respondent has broad power to amend his regulations. He must have known of this "loophole" before the deficiency notice was sent in this case. Revenue Ruling 60-245, 1960-2 C.B. 267, involving an almost identical set of facts, appeared 2 months before the date of the notice. Respondent there cited no provision of the Code or regulations to support his view that the parent should be taxed on the previously eliminated profit when the parent disposed of the subsidiary's stock. Respondent's reluctance to use his conceded power in this area to set forth rules of general application (see Friendly, "The Gap in Lawmaking — Judges Who Can't and Legislators Who Won't," 63 Col. L. Rev. 787, 792 et seq. (1963)) does not justify in this case a judicial improvisation to prevent a reduction of the revenue that is problematic in both nature and amount.[16]

On this issue we hold for petitioners.

[13]Management's liquidation, 1½ years after its sale of Homes stock, apparently did not qualify under the nonrecognition provisions of secs. 332 and 334. To the extent, then, that Management retained any profit from the Project construction, that profit was taxed once.

[16]In addition to the question of whether the profit should be taxed at all in 1957 there are also the questions of whether it should be taxed at ordinary rates rather than capital gain rates; whether eliminated intercompany profits of all sizes or vintages must be accounted for when the parent sells the stock; and how much of the subsidiary's stock must be sold and to whom in order to require (or permit, in the case of losses) recognition of previously eliminated profits and losses. We are reluctant to enter into this area of involved legislative and administrative policy unless compelled to do so by the controlling language of a statute or, in this case, of a "legislative" regulation.

Issue 2 — Gains on Redemption and Sale of Homes Stock

Respondent notes that Management received, during its taxable year 1957, a total of $53,000 on the redemption of Homes preferred stock and sale of its common stock. Management's aggregate basis for the two classes of stock was $25,221. The losses of which Homes could not have availed itself during the consolidated period (taxable years 1953 through 1957), had it then been filing separate returns, but which losses Management used to offset its gains, totaled (according to respondent) $42,-731.57. Respondent maintains that under section 1.1502-34, Income Tax Regs., this amount must be applied to reduce Management's basis in Homes stock — in this case to zero.

Petitioners maintain that the redemption of the Homes preferred stock is governed by section 1.1502-37(a)(1), Income Tax Regs., under the Management's basis in the Homes common stock is added to its basis in the Homes preferred for the purpose of determining recognizable gain on the redemption. This results in a gain of $2,779 — $28,000 received, minus the sum $23,471 (basis in preferred) and $1,750 (basis in common). Since Management's basis in the common stock will have been completely used in the redemption, its gain on the sale of the common will be $25,-000 — the entire receipts on that transaction. The total gain on the two transactions would then be $27,779, equal to the aggregate of the gains Management actually reported.

Alternatively, petitioners maintain that if section 1.1502-34(b), Income Tax Regs., controls, then the downward adjustment in basis (and consequent increase in gain) should not exceed $4,233.37. This is based upon the consolidated net income of the taxable years 1953 through 1956 and eliminates the taxable year 1957, the year within which both the redemption of the preferred stock and the sale of the common stock took place.

We agree with petitioners' alternate contention.

Section 1.1502-33, Income Tax Regs., prescribes the general rule, as applicable to the facts of this case, that gain or loss shall be recognized on the sale or other disposition of stock, except as otherwise provided by section 1.1502-37, and except that basis shall be determined under section 1.1502-34. Section 1.1502-37 exempts certain transactions, but not the ones here involved, from the recognition of gain or loss. Except insofar as it requires that the bases of all classes of stock be aggregated to determine gain on the redemption of any one class of stock, section 1.1502-37 does not control the computation of the gain realized. The latter function is assumed by section 1.1502-34. Petitioners maintain that since the first exception in section 1.1502-37(a)(1) . . . specifically makes section 1.1502-34 applicable, while the second exception contains no reference to section 1.1502-34, it must follow that "no adjustment is required in the case of the second exception."

We cannot agree. The general rule provided by section 1.1502-34 purports to apply to "any sale or other disposition." Consequently, it would apply to both exceptions of section 1.1502-37(a)(1), even in the absence of any clause in those sections specifically making section 1.1502-34 applicable. We are left, it appears, with the choice of determining either that section 1.1502-34 was not intended to apply to a class of cases to which it purportedly applied, despite the absence of any statement providing that it did not apply to those cases, or of deciding that the clause in section 1.1502-37(a)(1) (i), upon which petitioners here rely, is mere surplusage. We regard the clause in question as surplusage rather than as an obscure method of exempting transactions under section 1.1502-37(a)(1)(ii) from the operation of section 1.1502-34. . . .

Thus far, we agree with respondent's reading of the controlling regulations.

In the dispute regarding whether the 1957 profits and losses should be eliminated from the computation of basis, all parties rely upon section 1.1502-34(b)(2)(i) . . . . Respondent stresses the requirement that basis is to be reduced by "the sum of 'all losses of such issuing corporation sustained *during taxable years for which consolidated income tax returns were made or were required.* . . .'" A consolidated return was filed for 1957 and therefore, respondent insists, that year's results should be considered in determining basis. Petitioners point out that this provision is immediately modified to require reduction in basis only on account of such losses for consolidated return years "after such corporation became a member of the affiliated group and prior to the sale of the stock . . . ." The last such year prior to the redemption of the Homes preferred stock was the taxable year 1956.

The Homes preferred stock was redeemed within a month of the start of its 1957 taxable year. This redemption was not the occasion for the filing of a new return under section 1.1502-13 and did not otherwise bring that taxable year to a close. Section 1.1502-37(a)(1)(ii) requires aggregation of the bases of both common and preferred in determining the gain upon the redemption. At the time of the redemption, Homes' last prior taxable year was clearly its 1956 taxable year. Consequently the reduction in the bases of both classes of stock is to be determined, for purposes of the redemption, by reference to the losses and profits of Homes' taxable years 1953 through 1956. It is conceded by all parties that Management's receipts on the redemption exceeded its combined basis. All the basis for the common having been used to offset gain on the redemption of the preferred, nothing remained to the common. Consequently, even if the sale of the common in October caused the taxable year 1957 to be a prior taxable year for purposes of section 1.1502-34(b)(2)(i), that taxable year could not operate to further affect Management's basis or its gain upon the sale. Cf. Associated Telephone & Telegraph Co. v. United States, 306 F.2d 824, 825 (C.A. 2, 1962), affirming on this point on the opinion below, 199 F. Supp. 452, 469-477 (S.D.N.Y. 1961), where the court concluded that the consolidated returns regulations provided no rule requiring reduction in basis on account of net *capital* losses, that the regulations could not be construed as forbidding such reduction, and that other law (invoked via section 1.1502-3) required the reduction. Here, the applicable regulations set forth in great detail the procedure that must be followed regarding reduction of basis on account of net *operating* losses, we are dealing with that character of loss, and the language of the regulations guide us to the decision we have reached.

On this issue we agree with petitioners' alternate position.

Reviewed by the Court.

Decisions will be entered under Rule 50.

[Concurring and dissenting opinions omitted.]

NOTE

Problems such as the one posed in *Beck Builders* were addressed by the Treasury, and their solution is reflected in the current regulations, promulgated in 1966. See F. Peel, The Consolidated Return Election — The Sword of Damocles, 28 N.Y.U. Inst. on Fed. Tax. 619 (1970); T. Caps, What Every Business Lawyer and Accountant Must Know About the Law Regarding Consolidated Returns, 1969 So. Calif. Tax Inst. 191; J. Crestol, Consolidated Return Regulations and Related Tax Provisions, 26 N.Y.U. Inst. on Fed. Tax. 731 (1968); I. Salem, How to Use Net Operating Losses Effectively Under the New Consolidated Return Regulations, 26 J. Taxation 270 (1967); Note, Intercompany Accounting Under the New Consolidated Return Regulations, 116 U. Pa. L. Rev. 131 (1967). See also P. Chappell, Closing *Beck Builders* "Loophole" — The Dilemma of the Intercompany Transaction, 43 Taxes 715 (1965).

With respect to the problems of multiple corporations, reallocation of corporate income and consolidated returns generally, see J. Eustice, Tax Problems Arising from Transactions Between Affiliated or Controlled Corporations, 23 Tax L. Rev. 451 (1968).

Appendix

I. RULINGS

Tax lawyers, particularly those concerned with corporate transactions, depend heavily on the advance rulings practice of the Internal Revenue Service, authorized by §7805 of the Code. As certain as a lawyer may be that a particular exchange will be tax-free, or that "boot" in a given distribution will constitute long-term capital gain and not a dividend, he is often reluctant to advise his clients to proceed without the imprimatur of a favorable ruling.

A. ELLENTUCK, HOW AND WHEN TO GET AN ADVANCED RULING UNDER THE NEW REVISED PROCEDURES*

30 Journal of Taxation 214 (1969)

The Internal Revenue Service has just published Rev. Procs. 69-1 through 69-6, IRB 1969-1, a comprehensive set of new rules covering advanced tax rulings, determination letters and technical advice.[1] There are a number of important changes from the old rules practitioners have been following. The issuance of these new Procedures make[s] imperative a reappraisal of all the rules in this vital area of tax practice.

The advanced ruling can go far to eliminate the uncertainties inherent in tax planning. The tax advisor who has succeeded in obtaining a favorable ruling can cast his transaction with much greater assurance, since, as will be discussed below, the Service almost always considers itself bound by its own rulings. Even if the

---

*Reprinted by permission. Mr. Ellentuck is with Laventhol Krekstein Horwath & Horwath, New York City. — ED.

[1]Rev. Proc. 69-1 provides the general procedural rules for obtaining a ruling; Rev. Proc. 69-2 covers the furnishing of technical advice; Rev. Proc. 69-3 covers requests for rulings on exemptions and prohibited transactions for exempt organizations; Rev. Proc. 69-4 describes ruling requests from employee trusts; Rev. Proc. 69-5 covers rulings for master and prototype self-employed plans; and Rev. Proc. 69-6 gives the areas in which the Service will not rule. [These Revenue Procedures appear at 1969-1 Cum. Bull. 391-398.] For a complete discussion of the old procedures for obtaining a ruling, see Ellentuck, How and when to use the advanced ruling in planning tax transactions, 21 JTAX 52 (July, 1964).

Service finds a flaw in the proposed transaction, as for example when there is "boot" in a reorganization which would make it taxable, the reorganization can usually be restructured to meet the objections of the Service, and a favorable ruling can then be obtained. Business planning and negotiations can thereby be facilitated, and the possibility of conflict with the Service greatly minimized.

Alternatives

The advance or "private" ruling, as it is sometimes called, is a confidential letter issued by the National Office of Internal Revenue to a taxpayer, reciting the particular facts in his case and giving an opinion on the application of the Federal tax laws to those facts.

However, it may not be necessary to request a private ruling where an official Revenue Ruling is directly in point.[2] Many Revenue Rulings are based on private rulings to taxpayers or on technical advice to Service field offices, and in such cases identifying details and confidential information are omitted to prevent unwarranted invasions of privacy and unauthorized disclosure of information. The practitioner must consider the effect of subsequent legislation, Regulations, court decisions, rulings and procedures on the particular Revenue Ruling involved. In addition, the practitioner should not rely on that Revenue Ruling unless the facts and circumstances are substantially the same as in his proposed transaction.

An "information letter," in reply to a general question posed by the tax planner, is another alternative to consider. An information letter is a statement issued by either the National Office or by a District Director that does no more than call attention to a well established interpretation or principle of tax law without applying it to a specific set of facts. The information letter as such has no binding effect, and accordingly will not have much of value to the tax planner.

A "determination letter" is a written statement issued by a District Director in response to a written inquiry. Generally a determination letter will be issued only if the question presented is covered specifically by statute, Treasury Decision or Regulation, or by a Ruling, opinion or court decision published in the Internal Revenue Bulletin.

Specifically, District Directors issue determination letters on the qualification of employees' pension, and profit-sharing plans (including those of self-employed individuals), annuity and stock bonus plans, and on the exempt status of related trusts under these plans. They also issue determination letters as to the qualification of certain organizations for exempt status under Sections 501 and 521 and certain involuntary conversions. Determination letters are further issued by Directors on income, and gift tax matters in response to requests submitted involving completed transactions, which affect returns required to be filed in their districts. In addition, determination letters will be issued regarding estate tax returns of decedents, but not on matters involving the application of the estate tax to property or the estate of a living person.

Where virtual certainty is desired regarding the tax consequences of a proposed

[2]Section 13.09 of Rev. Proc. 69-1.

transaction, a closing agreement may be requested. Closing agreements are based on private rulings that have been signed by the Commissioner or his delegate, and in which it is indicated that a closing agreement will be entered into on the basis of the holdings in the letter ruling. Closing agreements are final and conclusive, except upon a showing of fraud, malfeasance, or misrepresentation of a material fact.[3] Generally, however, because of the permanent nature of the closing agreement the Government is understandably reluctant to enter into these agreements. They must be convinced that there is good and sufficient reason for such an agreement and that the Government will sustain no disadvantage by its consummation. In some circumstances, the Service may desire that the taxpayer requesting a ruling enter into a closing agreement and will make a closing agreement a condition to issuance of that letter ruling.

The request for technical advice, though not an alternative to the advanced ruling, should nevertheless be mentioned here. Technical advice is a memorandum issued by the National Office upon request of a District Office in connection with the examination or consideration of a taxpayer's return or claim for refund or credit. These memorandums furnish guidance as to the interpretation and proper application of Internal Revenue laws to a specific set of facts and are intended to assist Service personnel in closing cases and establishing and maintaining consistent positions in the various District Offices. The procedures for technical advice and the rights of the taxpayer in seeking technical advice will be discussed below.

"No-Ruling" Areas

The Service does not rule on every question presented to it. It will decline to rule whenever a question falls within one of its general or specific "no-ruling" areas. Most of the Service's no ruling areas are found in Rev. Procs. 69-1 and 69-6; some are specifically listed and some are merely implied.

Revenue Procedure 69-1 requires that each request for a ruling must include the names, addresses, and taxpayer identifying numbers of all interested parties involved in the transaction. Accordingly, no ruling will be issued in response to a general question or a ruling request not identifying the interested parties. Each request must also describe a transaction that is actually proposed, and rulings will not be issued regarding alternative plans or proposed transactions involving hypothetical situations.[4] In addition, the Service will not rule on any transaction to be consummated at some indefinite future time,[5] since any delay in consummating a proposed transaction increases the possibility of a change in applicable law or Service position or even in some of the facts of the transaction.

Some no ruling areas are jurisdictional. In income, profits, and gift tax matters, the National Office ordinarily will not issue an opinion on a transaction which has been completed if income tax returns for that year have already been filed; such transactions are considered to come under the jurisdiction of the District Director.[6]

[3]Section 2.06 of Rev. Proc. 69-1.
[4]Section 3.02-4 of Rev. Proc. 69-6.
[5]Section 4.02-2 of Rev. Proc. 69-6.
[6]Section 3.01 of Rev. Proc. 69-1. In estate tax matters, the National Office issues rulings with

In addition, rulings will not ordinarily be issued if the identical issue is involved in a previous return already filed for a taxable year which is still open under the statute of limitations.

The National Office will not issue rulings with respect to the replacement of involuntarily converted property, even though replacement has not been made, if the taxpayer has filed a return for the taxable year in which the property was converted.[7] However, under these circumstances a determination letter can be obtained from the District Director.[8]

Another no ruling area frequently crops up when there has been new legislation. The Service hesitates to rule on issues involving Code Sections for which final Regulations have not yet been promulgated. It will however rule if the question raised is clearly covered by the Code.[9] If the answer is not entirely free from doubt, but is "reasonably certain," a ruling will be issued only after it is established that a business emergency requires a ruling or that unusual hardship will result from failure to obtain a ruling. In such case, the ruling letter will contain a caveat stating that the ruling is without effect if Regulations, when issued, conflict with the holding; however, such a conflict is extremely unlikely. And finally, of course, no ruling will be issued if the Service is not reasonably certain of the answer.

Along similar lines, the Service will not rule where it has a matter under study, when there are conflicting court decisions, or when there has been an adverse court decision and the Service hasn't decided whether or not to acquiesce.[10]

Some general no ruling areas, arise from obvious administrative considerations on the part of the Service. No rulings can be had on transactions which lack bona fide business purposes or have as their principal purpose the reduction of Federal taxes. In addition, no rulings can be had on questions which are primarily factual, as for example the market value of property.[11]

The Service also has a number of specific no ruling areas set out in Rev. Proc. 69-6. These no ruling areas are either arbitrary or discretionary.

For example, the following are some "arbitrary" no ruling areas — questions on which the Service will not rule under any circumstances:

1. Whether compensation is reasonable under Section 162.

2. Whether a taxpayer who advances funds to a charitable organization and receives a promissory note in exchange may deduct as contributions in one taxable

---

respect to transactions affecting the estate tax of a decedent before the estate tax return is filed. It will not rule with respect to such matters after the estate tax return has been filed, nor will it rule on matters relating to the application of the estate tax to property or the estate of a living person. In employment and excise tax matters, the National Office issues rulings with respect to prospective transactions and to completed transactions either before or after the return is filed. However, the National Office will not ordinarily rule with respect to an issue, whether relative to a prospective or a completed transaction, if it knows or has reason to believe that the same or an identical issue is before any field office in an active examination or audit of the liability of the same taxpayer for the same or a prior period, or is being considered by a branch office of the Appellate Division.

[7]Section 3.01 of Rev. Proc. 69-1.
[8]Section 4.06 of Rev. Proc. 69-1.
[9]Section 3.05 of Rev. Proc. 69-1.
[10]Section 3.02-2 of Rev. Proc. 69-6.
[11]Sections 3.02-1 and 4.02-1 of Rev. Proc. 69-6.

year or in each of several years, amounts forgiven by the taxpayer in each of several years by endorsements on the note.

3. Whether an acquisition is made to evade or avoid income tax under Section 269.

4. Whether a distribution in kind by a corporation to its stockholders in complete or partial liquidation followed by a sale of the property can be deemed to have been made by the corporation under *Court Holding Company*, 324 U.S. 331 (1945).

5. The determination of earnings and profits of a corporation available for the distribution of dividends to its shareholders under Section 312. The Service had previously announced in IRS News Release 685, 7/27/64, that it would issue rulings in this area; it appears that it has reversed its position.

The following are some "discretionary" no ruling areas — questions upon which the IRS will not ordinarily rule:

1. Whether advances to thin corporations constitute loans, or are actually equity investments.

2. The tax effect of the redemption of stock for notes under Section 302 where the payments on the notes are to be made over a period in excess of 15 years from the date of the issuance of such notes. Although this had previously been phrased in terms of "a long future period," the 15-year period had long been an unpublished rule of thumb in the National Office.

3. Whether a corporation will be considered as a "collapsible corporation" under Section 341, that is, whether it was "formed or availed of" with the view of avoidance of tax to its stockholders.

4. The tax effect of a transfer under Section 351 where part of the consideration received by the transferors consists of bonds, debentures, or any other evidences of indebtedness of the transferee.

5. Whether an individual is a dealer in real estate for the purpose of determining under Section 1221 whether property held by him may be classified as a capital asset or as property held for sale to customers.

The list of no ruling areas in Rev. Proc. 69-6, is not all inclusive, and the Service may decline to rule on other questions whenever warranted by the facts or circumstances of a particular case.[12] There are several reasons why the Service will not rule in the situations set out above. Many of these questions involve factual questions to a greater or lesser degree. In addition, the Service will refuse to rule where it has an issue under study, for administrative expediency, or simply because the taxpayer is seeking to take advantage of a loophole (or so-called "tax gimmick") which is not intended.

Any practitioner contemplating an application for a ruling should carefully study the no ruling areas in Revenue Procedure 69-6. He should also ascertain whether, subsequent to that Procedure, any additional no ruling areas have been added or whether any have been withdrawn. Should there still be some question as to whether the Service will or will not rule, he can consult with the National Office of Internal Revenue in this regard.

---

[12]Section 5.01 of Rev. Proc. 69-1.

The Service has just recently barred all oral discussions with Service personnel on substantive issues prior to submission of a written ruling request.[13] However discussion as to whether the Service will rule in a particular case is still permitted. Previously, these discussions could be hypothetical, but now under Rev. Rul. 69-1 the name of the taxpayer and his identifying number must be disclosed.[14] As a practical matter this requirement should not deter such preliminary discussions, since they save time and effort for practitioners and IRS.

Initial Decision

The first step in deciding whether to request a ruling is to ascertain whether a favorable ruling can be obtained. The no ruling areas discussed above should be consulted in this regard. However, all the Service pronouncements regarding rulings are by no means negative. In recent years, the Service has issued a number of Revenue Procedures in substantive areas outlining certain rules of thumb followed by the National Office in issuing rulings.[15] These pronouncements should be carefully followed not only in deciding whether the Service would be willing to issue a favorable ruling, but also in structuring the transaction itself.

The next step as a practical matter is to estimate (1) the cost of obtaining the ruling (including such items as legal and accounting fees) and (2) the amount of "tax dollars" involved. Certainly, if the maximum deficiency that could be assessed by an examining agent (as for example if a reorganization were taxable instead of tax-free) is less than the actual cost of obtaining the ruling, a ruling request should not be considered.

The practioner must then satisfy himself as to whether the transaction is one in which clearance by the Commissioner is mandatory. In certain prospective or future transactions, the law or Regulations may require a determination of the effect of a proposed transaction for tax purposes, as in the case of a transfer coming within the provisions of Sections 1491 and 1492 (excise tax on transfers involving foreign corporations) or an exchange coming within the provisions of Section 367, explained below. The Commissioner does not have discretion here and must issue rulings in all cases under these Sections.

Section 367, mentioned above, is a noteworthy example of a provision requiring prior clearance. Its importance cannot be overemphasized. Section 367 provides that with regard to certain transfers to controlled corporations, corporate liquidations, or reorganizations, a foreign corporation will not be considered a valid corporation for Federal income tax purposes unless clearance from the Commissioner is obtained *prior to the transaction.* Clearance consists of an advanced ruling to the effect that the transaction will not be in avoidance of Federal income taxes.[16]

---

[13]See Section 12.01 of Rev. Proc. 69-1. The various branches in the Rulings Division are following this rule quite strictly.

[14]Section 12.01 of Rev. Proc. 69-1.

[15]See Rev. Proc. 66-34, 1966-2 CB 1232, amplified by Rev. Proc. 67-13, 1967-1 CB 590; Rev. Proc. 67-13, 1967-1 CB 590; and Rev. Proc. 68-23, IRB 1968-22, 3.

[16]Rev. Proc. 68-23, IRB 1968-22, gives guidelines for obtaining a favorable 367 ruling. For a complete discussion of this Procedure see 29 JTAX 158 (September, 1968), 29 JTAX 362 (December, 1968), and 30 JTAX 154 (March, 1969).

A practitioner who has determined that the cost of the ruling does not prohibit a request, and has also determined that a ruling is not mandatory, still has a decision to make as to the advisability of requesting a ruling. In order to make a proper decision in this regard, a complete understanding of the advanced rulings procedure is essential.

Withdrawing a Request

Suppose that after the practitioner submits a request for a ruling, business reasons preclude completion of the contemplated transaction. The request may be withdrawn by him at that time or at any time prior to the signing of the letter ruling.[17] Since motive is irrelevant, the request may similarly be withdrawn where the planner believes that the issued ruling will be adverse to his request.

A ruling will not be issued if the withdrawal request is timely. But the Service does reserve the right to complete its consideration of the request, and to notify the appropriate field office of any adverse conclusion without similarly notifying the ruling applicant. Ordinarily, however, the National Office will notify the field office of an adverse decision only if it believes the transaction will be completed despite the withdrawal, or if the transaction was actually completed before the withdrawal request which was made by the taxpayer.

The weight given by the practitioner to the possibility of such notification will depend on the type of case. For example, a proposed transaction may involve so many tax dollars that the taxpayer cannot take any risk of an adverse field determination. In such case the possibility of notification after withdrawal is irrelevant since the taxpayer will not, in any event, proceed without a favorable ruling.

However, since most cases do not involve a prohibitive amount of tax dollars, the possibility of notification must be carefully weighed. It will be most significant in those cases in which the taxpayer would be unwilling to complete the transaction if an adverse ruling were to be received. It will be less significant in those cases where the transaction would be consummated by the taxpayer even if an adverse ruling were to be received. It will be least significant in those cases where the same business ends of the taxpayer can be accomplished by an alternate transaction substantially different from the one proposed.

Should a Ruling Be Requested?

The practitioner faced with the ultimate question of whether to request a ruling must consider the pros and cons. The major disadvantage of a ruling request is that the transaction will be immediately placed under the scrutiny of the Service. And, an alert technician in the National Office will not only look over the issues on which rulings are requested, but will also take a look at related issues and related transactions as well.

Thus, for example, when a request is made for a ruling on a redemption of stock of a corporation under Section 302, a corporate balance sheet must be submitted. If a substantial amount of accumulated earnings is reflected on that balance

---

[17]Section 11 of Rev. Proc. 69-1. Partial withdrawal can similarly be effected by requesting withdrawal of one or more of the holdings sought in the ruling request.

sheet the National Office may well consider the applicability of Section 531. And, should it appear that Section 531 could be applicable, a caveat will be included in the ruling to the effect that the letter ruling will have no effect on Section 531's applicability.

On the other hand, an important advantage to consider is that an Internal Revenue examination of the transaction could bring out problems in the plan that have not been anticipated. If the National Office rejects a transaction, it may be possible to modify that transaction to meet the objections of the Service and obtain a favorable ruling nevertheless. If however, the transaction is completed without first seeking a ruling, the same problems raised by an examining Revenue Agent on a subsequent audit of the tax return for that year cannot, of course, be similarly remedied.

Two other comparisons are significant. First, the National Office is not empowered to settle or compromise cases since it may only resolve the legal issues involved. The determination of dollar amounts of tax liability will always be left to the Field Office. Secondly, the specialized personnel of the National Office will ordinarily have greater expertise in the particular area in which they work than the Revenue Agent whose knowledge is necessarily more generalized. The merits of the particular case and the complexity of the issues must be considered by the practitioner in determining whether either of these points constitute advantages or disadvantages in that case.

Form of the Request

Suppose now that after a thorough consideration of all the factors outlined above and the exercise of some intuition as well, the practitioner does decide to request a ruling.

His request will be made in the form of a letter addressed to the Commissioner and signed by him or the taxpayer.[18] Only one copy of the request is necessary, unless "more than one issue is presented in the request," or the request is for exemption under Section 501(c) or 501(d), or a closing agreement is requested. The request should list names, addresses and taxpayer identifying numbers of all principal parties; the District Office where each party files or will file its return or report; and furnish a description of the parties and their relationships as well as any other relevant background information.

A statement must also be included as to whether (to the best of the knowledge of the taxpayer or his representative) the identical issue is being considered by any field office of the Service in connection with an active examination or audit of a tax return already filed.

The applicant should then give a complete description of the proposed transaction, including a full and precise statement of the business reasons [therefor]. As part of the description of the transaction, if it is only one step of a larger integrated transaction, the facts and circumstances must be submitted with respect to the entire transaction.

---

[18]Section 6.01 of Rev. Proc. 69-1. This Section outlines all the requirements for the ruling request.

In addition, true copies of all contracts, wills, deeds, agreements, instruments, and other documents involved in the transaction must be submitted with the request. However, relevant facts reflected in documents submitted must also be included in the ruling request's description of the transaction, not merely incorporated by reference, and an analysis of the documents' bearing on the issues should also be included. It is wise to furnish only copies, since all documents and exhibits submitted become part of the Service file and can not be returned.

If the request is in regard to a corporate distribution, reorganization, or other similar or related transaction, the most recent corporate balance sheets should be submitted.

The application should close with a specific request for each holding desired, and a brief discussion of the grounds and authorities for such holdings. The authorities most likely to impress the Service will be the applicable Code provisions and Regulations, as well as the Service's rulings, court decisions published in the Internal Revenue Bulletin and cases in which it has acquiesced.

Since a conference may not be granted unless it is specifically asked for, it is customary to include a statement requesting a conference in the event a favorable ruling cannot be issued.[19] Of course, a power of attorney authorizing the practitioner to represent his client in the National Office must also be submitted with the request.

When the request is received in the National Office, it will be forwarded to one of two divisions and then to the appropriate branch in that division. The divisions and branches divided as to the subject matter which they handle are as follows:

Income Tax Division:
1. Corporation Tax Branch
2. Individual Income Tax Branch
3. Reorganization Branch
4. Engineering and Valuation Branch

Miscellaneous and Special Provisions Tax Division:
1. Actuarial Branch
2. Administrative Provisions Branch
3. Estate and Gift Tax Branch
4. Excise Tax Branch
5. Exempt Organizations Branch
6. Pension Trust Branch

Once located in the proper branch, the request will be assigned to a "tax law specialist" who will study the request to determine whether it is complete. If additional information is needed, the specialist or "technician" as he is sometimes called will request it from the applicant. The ruling application is then placed in a file to await later consideration.

If at such time as the request is considered the specialist arrives at a favorable conclusion, he will prepare a favorable ruling which will be reviewed, and then signed at either the Branch, Tax Ruling Division, Assistant Commissioner, or

[19]See Section 6.09 of Rev. Proc. 69-1.

Commissioner level. The level at which the ruling is signed can influence the number of Service personnel required to review it, but will in no way affect its binding nature and validity.

However, should the specialist reach an adverse conclusion, a conference will be granted the taxpayer in the National Office, provided one has been requested in the application letter. At the conference the tax law specialist will explain the grounds for the proposed adverse ruling, and the taxpayer or his representative will have the opportunity to discuss these grounds. Additional data, arguments and precedents may be raised by taxpayer at the conference; the taxpayer should subsequently follow up the conference by furnishing a memorandum covering these points for inclusion in the National Office file.

A taxpayer is entitled as a matter of right to only one conference in the National Office except when the National Office proposes to take a position less favorable than the one initially proposed, or to issue an adverse ruling but based upon grounds not previously discussed.[20] Of course, the Service can always invite additional conferences if it believes such will be helpful, and as a practical matter, additional conferences are held whenever issues are not fully covered at the initial conference.

The arguments presented at the conference on behalf of the taxpayer will be carefully considered by the Service representatives. Although, theoretically, they will not arrive at their final conclusions until the preparation and review of the ruling letter, it is likely that their final views expressed at the conference will be the ones ultimately incorporated in the ruling. If the Service representatives cannot be convinced at the conference to change their views, and the transaction cannot be modified to meet their objections, the tax adviser should seriously consider withdrawal of the application.

Alternative Procedure

The Service permits an elective procedure whereby the taxpayer may submit in addition to the complete statement of facts in his ruling request, a summary statement of the facts he considers controlling the issue.[21] Where the taxpayer's statement of controlling facts is accepted by the Service, the ruling will be based on these facts and this statement will be incorporated in the ruling letter issued.

This procedure, however, is not a *substitute* for the regular procedures for requesting a ruling. In fact, the Service reserves the right to rule on the basis of the more complete statement of facts in the ruling request letter. Moreover, even if the facts in the summary statement are accepted and incorporated in the ruling, the Service considers that the ruling is based on all the facts including those submitted in the ruling request itself.

The summary statement will give the taxpayer no substantive advantages. However, it is thought by many practitioners that this procedure will speed up to some extent the processing of a ruling inasmuch as it will (if well prepared) save the tax law specialist some effort in preparing the letter ruling. As an alternative to this procedure, some practitioners who are familiar with rulings practice will

[20]Section 7.02, Rev. Proc. 69-1.
[21]Section 5.03, Rev. Proc. 69-1.

prepare an entire letter ruling for use by the tax law specialist. Again, this practice can only be helpful if the letter is well prepared.

Length of Time

Ordinarily ruling requests are processed on a "first-in, first-out" basis: *It* can take anywhere from one day to one year (or even longer) to obtain a ruling; generally it takes three or four months.

The length of time required to obtain a ruling will vary considerably depending upon such factors as the workload of the branch or section of the branch involved, the type of case, and whether other sections, branches or divisions will also have to consider the ruling. Additional factors which affect the time lag are the difficulty of the issues involved, the level of review necessary, and whether the request must be sent to the Office of Chief Counsel for further study.

As a practical matter, timing can be crucial. One reason frequently given for completing a transaction without benefit of a tax ruling is "lack of time." In many instances, however, this urge for prompt action appears to be nothing more than a desire to finalize the transaction and promptly bind the other party. The execution of the necessary binding contracts can in no way interfere with or affect the ruling application, and can often eliminate the problem of "lack of time"; the parties can be bound promptly under an agreement perhaps conditioned on a favorable ruling.

There are of course, situations in which there is a genuine need to consummate the transaction promptly. In those situations, the practitioner can make a special request to the National Office that the ruling be expedited or even that it be issued prior to a specified date. The request must, of course, demonstrate that such expeditious treatment is clearly necessary in order to convince the Service to handle the request out of turn, thereby delaying the orderly processing of other ruling requests.

However, the Service offers no assurance that any ruling letter will be processed by the time requested.[22] This is especially true where the necessity for expeditious treatment results from deadlines unreasonably set by the parties themselves, as for example the scheduling of a closing date for a transaction or a meeting of the board of directors or shareholders without due regard to the time it may take to obtain a ruling. In addition, the possible effect of fluctuation in the market price of stocks of corporations which are parties to a reorganization will not be deemed sufficient reason for handling a request out of order.

Actually, the most effective steps to expedite the ruling request can be taken by the practitioner himself. He can submit the request as soon as the details of the proposed transaction are formulated, and make certain that the request is complete in every respect. His replies to requests for additional information should also be prompt and complete. Furthermore, the practitioner can omit or subsequently eliminate[23] from the application any nonessential issues likely to cause a delay in issuance.

---

[22]Section 6.10, Rev. Proc. 69-1.
[23]An issue can be eliminated by notifying the National Office that such issue be withdrawn from consideration.

Issuance of the Ruling

Almost all letter rulings issued by the National Office are favorable, inasmuch as objections of the IRS can normally be remedied, and if the reaction of IRS is still unfavorable, the request will usually be withdrawn. The practitioner can, if he desires, request reconsideration of an unfavorable ruling or an unfavorable issue in an otherwise favorable ruling. However, although the National Office will always reconsider once as a matter of course, there is no "right" to review, and the Service is not likely to alter its well considered initial position. Of course, if the National Office finds that the ruling is in error because of a mistake of law or fact, it will not hesitate to reverse itself.

When an adverse ruling is issued, the practitioner has a choice of abandoning the proposed transaction or consummating it despite the ruling. Should he consummate the transaction, the practitioner may be certain that the field office will also take an adverse position, since it will have received a copy of the adverse ruling and will almost always follow the conclusions of the National Office.

The practitioner who is fortunate enough to receive a favorable ruling, must study it carefully to make certain that the facts set out in the ruling letter are correct. If there are any errors, whether the fault of the applicant or the tax law specialist, the practitioner must decide whether they are sufficiently material to require correction by a request for a supplemental ruling letter.[24]

After the transaction has been consummated in reliance on a favorable ruling letter, the interested taxpayers are required to attach a copy of the ruling letter to their tax returns for the taxable year in which the transaction was consummated. It will then be the responsibility of the District Director (actually an examining Revenue Agent) to ascertain whether any ruling has been properly applied.[25] In other words, he must determine whether the representations upon which the ruling was based reflected an accurate statement of the material facts and whether the transaction was carried out substantially as proposed. If the District Director believes that the ruling was properly applied, the field office is obliged to follow that ruling unless it believes the conclusions themselves are erroneous. Almost all rulings issued by the National Office are followed by the field offices.

In the unusual case where the District Director does believe that a ruling was not properly applied or that its conclusions are in error, it will forward its findings and recommendations to the National Office for consideration prior to further action in the form of a request for technical advice.

Under the technical advice procedures, the taxpayer will be advised that a case is being forwarded for technical advice and he will be furnished with a copy of the statement by the examining Agent of the pertinent facts and the questions proposed for submission to the National Office. The taxpayer will then be given ten days (or a longer period if agreed upon) in which to indicate in writing the

---

[24]If the practitioner does request a supplemental ruling, he simply addresses a letter to the Commissioner (as in the original ruling request); refers to the letter ruling and its date, states the correct facts and explains why they should not change the result, and then requests that the original ruling letter be affirmed.

[25]Section 13.02, Rev. Proc. 69-1.

extent if any to which he is not in complete agreement with the statement of facts and specific questions presented by the District Office. Taxpayers and District Offices are encouraged to reach agreement as to the facts and specific points at issue.

If agreement cannot be reached, the taxpayer may submit a statement of his understanding as to the specific point or points at issue which statement will be forwarded to the National Office along with the request by the Revenue Agent for technical advice. The taxpayer may also submit a brief setting forth the precedents which he believes will bear on the case.

The taxpayer will also be informed of his right to a conference in the National Office in the event an adverse decision is contemplated and he will be asked to indicate whether he does desire a conference. The conference procedure for technical advice is almost identical to the conference procedure for tax rulings. Ultimately, the National Office will issue a technical advice memorandum either revoking, modifying or affirming the ruling.

Effect of Rulings

Once a taxpayer has relied on a favorable ruling and consummated his transaction, how can he be assured that the ruling will not be revoked? A ruling, except to the extent incorporated in a closing agreement, may be revoked or modified at any time "in the wise administration of the taxing statutes." A ruling can be revoked or modified with regard to all open years under the statutes (i.e., retroactively), unless the Commissioner exercises his discretionary authority under Section 7805(b) to limit the retroactive effect of the ruling. The implication is that the Commissioner has unlimited discretion to revoke with retroactive effect. Nevertheless, it is clear that this discretion may not be abused by the Commissioner.[26]

However, rulings will not be revoked retroactively with respect to the taxpayer to whom the ruling was issued or whose tax liability was directly involved, provided: (1) there has been no misstatement or omission of material facts; (2) the facts subsequently developed are not materially different from the facts on which the ruling was based; (3) there has been no change in the applicable law; (4) the ruling was originally issued with respect to a prospective or proposed transaction; and (5) the taxpayer directly involved in the ruling acted in good faith in reliance upon the ruling and the retroactive revocation would be to his detriment.[27]

The tax liability of each employee covered by a ruling relating to a pension plan of an employer is "directly involved" in that ruling. Also, the tax liability of each shareholder is directly involved in a ruling related to the reorganization of a corporation. No reliance can be placed on rulings obtained by unrelated taxpayers, although such rulings can be useful in revealing the thinking of the National Office. In this regard, refer to International Business Machines, 343 F.2d 914 (Ct. Cls., 1965).

---

[26]See International Business Machines Corporation, 343 F.2d 914 (Ct. Cls., 1965); Lesavoy Foundation, 238 F.2d 589 (CA-3, 1956); see also Goodstein, 267 F.2d 127 (CA-1, 1959); Stevens Brothers Foundation, Inc., 39 TC 93 (1962); cf. Automobile Club of Michigan, 353 U.S. 180 (1957); Lorain Avenue Clinic, 31 TC 141 (1958).

[27]See 13.05, Rev. Proc. 69-1.

First of all then in order for a taxpayer to bind the Service, he must have been the recipient of the ruling or had his liability directly involved in it. The surrounding facts and circumstances described in the ruling request must be accurate and the transaction itself must subsequently be carried out as proposed.

When the ruling is issued the transaction must still be "prospective." A business transaction ordinarily has three stages: (1) negotiations; (2) execution of the contracts; and (3) consummation. Although the negotiations have been completed and the contracts executed, the transaction will still be considered propospective. However, it will cease to be prospective when the transaction is ultimately consummated. The Service will not be bound by a ruling to a taxpayer issued after the proposed transaction has been completed.

The date of the consummation is also significant for fixing the date when reliance is considered to have taken place. Thus, the taxpayer who receives a ruling after he has completed negotiations must execute the contracts and consummate the transaction before his reliance will be effective, thus binding the Service.

Between the time the ruling is received and the time the Service can be bound by consummating the transaction, there may be a change in the applicable statute or Regulation, a change in the relevant case law, or a change in Service position (accomplished by publication in the Internal Revenue Bulletin or direct notice to the taxpayer), any of which events can revoke the ruling.

The only intervening event which will not cause prospective revocation of the ruling is an unpublished change of Service position of which the taxpayer has received no direct notice. However, even if a taxpayer has received no notice of a change of position, his reliance may not be considered by the Service to be reasonable or in good faith if he waits too long to consummate the transaction.

In any event, prompt consummation of the transaction will minimize the possibilities of prospective revocation, and is certainly well advised.

It is, however, possible for a ruling to be revoked retroactively despite the fact that all possible steps have been taken to bind the Service. A new Code Section or amended Regulation contrary to the position the Service has taken in the ruling might be promulgated with retroactive effect, automatically revoking the ruling. A controlling court decision interpreting the statute or Regulation contrary to the ruling's interpretation will similarly revoke it. The only way completely to eliminate the possibility of retroactive revocation is to obtain a closing statement.

However, the chances of having a ruling revoked retroactively are very slim indeed. As discussed above, the Service will not rule on an issue it has under study or where there are conflicting court decisions. In addition, new Code provisions or amended Regulations are rarely applied with retroactive effect, and as discussed above where no Regulation has yet been issued, a ruling will not be issued if the answer is in doubt.

Accordingly, as a practical matter, a practitioner who has obtained a ruling can safely rely on it to give his client the favorable tax treatment called for in the letter ruling.

NOTE

See Note, The Availability and Reviewability of Rulings of the Internal Revenue Service, 113 U. Pa. L. Rev. 81 (1964).

II. PROBLEMS

Some of the examination and planning type problems used at the University of Pennsylvania Law School are reproduced here in the hope that they may be useful to others as vehicles for classroom discussion and analysis as well as for study and review.

The first 14 problems were used as examination questions. Problems 1 to 11 deal primarily with the subject matter of Part I of the casebook (Chapters 1 to 4). Problems 12 and 13 relate to Part II. Problem 14 involves material covered both in Part I and in Chapter 5, Partnerships.

Problems 15 to 21 were used primarily in planning seminars. Students prepared written solutions which became the basis for discussion and analysis. See B. Wolfman, A Seminar in Counselling — Tax Conscious Planning of Corporate Transactions, 16 J. Legal Ed. 181 (1963). A number of the problems were drafted and used initially at a time when the law differed from that presently in force. The solutions offered when those problems were first used are different from the ones which are likely to be proposed today.

1.

In 1963 the Merchant Corporation directly and through subsidiaries operated a chain of retail stores. It owned 60 shares (60 per cent) of the 100 outstanding shares of Novelty Corporation's voting common stock. A group of individuals, hereinafter referred to as "Investors," owned 18 shares (18 per cent) of Novelty's voting common stock, and the remaining 22 shares (22 per cent) were held by other shareholders.

Among the assets of Novelty was 50 per cent of the voting stock of Oxymoron Corporation. The remaining 50 per cent of Oxymoron's voting stock was owned by the Investors.

For the purpose of affecting substantial economies in operation, the above-mentioned parties adopted a written plan pursuant to which the following action was taken:

(1) The charter of Novelty was amended to enlarge its Board of Directors from ten to twelve members and to provide that the two new members of the Board would be elected by the owners of a newly authorized class of voting preferred stock.

(2) All of the newly created voting preferred stock of Novelty was issued to the Investors in exchange for all their holdings of Oxymoron voting stock.

(3) Immediately thereafter, the Investors transferred all of their stock in

Novelty (18 per cent of its common and 100 per cent of its preferred) to Merchant in exchange for the latter's voting common stock. (As a result, Merchant became the owner of 78 per cent of Novelty's common stock and 100 per cent of the preferred.)

None of the corporations is "collapsible." None of the Investors is a dealer in stock or securities. The 18 per cent of Novelty's common stock and the 50 per cent of Oxymoron's voting stock had been held by the Investors for many years and had appreciated substantially in value.

You are the Commissioner of Internal Revenue and have been asked by the Investors to rule to them on the tax consequences of the foregoing. Please write your ruling, intending it for publication in the Internal Revenue Bulletin.

(After blue books are turned in, those interested in seeing Commissioner Caplin's answer may read Rev. Rul. 63-234, 1963-2 Cum. Bull. 148 [p. 526 supra].)

2.

Mr. and Mrs. Helvering each owned 50 per cent of the outstanding stock (all common) of Broadbeam Corporation, a Delaware corporation (hereinafter "Broadbeam"), which was engaged in the manufacture of oversized chairs. Mr. and Mrs. Helvering and the latter's sister, Mary Eisner, each owned one-third of the outstanding stock (all common) of Chummy Corporation, a Pennsylvania corporation (hereinafter "Chummy"), which was engaged in the manufacture of love seats.

Each of the corporations had accumulated earnings and profits of $200,000, and the assets of each, net of liabilities, had a fair market value of $400,000.

Mary Eisner wanted to sell her Chummy stock and was willing to do so for a price of $133,000. The Helverings, happy to accommodate her, consulted with counsel, who recommended a plan which he thought would be to everyone's financial advantage. Accordingly, on December 31, 1964, the following transactions occurred pursuant to counsel's advice:

(1) At 10:00 A.M., Chummy adopted a plan of complete liquidation.

(2) At 10:30 A.M., Broadbeam borrowed $200,000 from a bank on a ten-year, 6 per cent note.

(3) At 11:00 A.M., Broadbeam purchased from Chummy all of Chummy's non-cash assets, subject to all of Chummy's liabilities, for a cash price of $200,000.

(4) At noon, Chummy distributed all of its assets ($400,000 cash) in equal amounts to its three shareholders in retirement and cancellation of their Chummy stock.

The Helverings each had a basis of $50,000 in their stock in Broadbeam, and the Helverings and Mary Eisner each had a basis of $33,000 in their Chummy stock. Broadbeam and Chummy were each on a calendar year.

State and explain the federal income tax consequences of the foregoing to Mr. and Mrs. Helvering and to Mary Eisner.

3.

The Tried and True Bomb Shelter Corporation, a Pennsylvania corporation (hereinafter "T & T"), had been engaged since incorporation in 1958 in the manufacture of bomb shelters for the home. By 1961 T & T had accumulated earnings and profits of $300,000. Concerned that the bomb shelter business might fall off, diversification was decided upon. Accordingly, on June 30, 1961, T & T purchased for cash, at a price of $250,000, all outstanding stock (common only was outstanding) of the Honey-Sweet Milk Corporation, a Pennsylvania corporation (hereinafter "H-SM"). H-SM prospered. On June 30, 1963, when its accumulated earnings and profits were $400,000, H-SM issued to T & T Class "A" common (voting) stock, Class "B" common (non-voting) stock, and 6 per cent non-cumulative preferred stock in exchange for all of the common stock of H-SM theretofore outstanding in T & T's hands. The aggregate fair market value of the stock thus issued was $500,000.

On June 30, 1964, when T & T's accumulated earnings and profits were $250,000 and H-SM's were $450,000, T & T distributed pro rata to its equal shareholders, Bolt, Dolt and Dolt, Jr., all of the H-SM stock. Bolt, unrelated to Dolt or his son, Dolt, Jr., thereupon asked the Dolts to buy all of his H-SM stock. The Dolts declined but agreed to cause H-SM to purchase all of Bolt's H-SM preferred stock at its aggregate par value of $66,000. Bolt agreed, and the proposed transaction between him and H-SM was consummated.

The cost to Bolt, Dolt and Dolt, Jr., of their stock in T & T was $50,000 each. T & T and H-SM were on a June 30 fiscal year.

State and explain the federal income tax consequences to T & T, Bolt, Dolt and Dolt, Jr.

4.

Smith and Jones formed the Realty Push Corporation on January 2, 1964, by investing $100,000 each in cash and receiving 100 shares each of its $1000 par common stock (all of its authorized and issued stock). Realty Push Corporation forthwith used the bulk of its cash to purchase land and then to subdivide and improve it by adding streets, water and sewer lines. By the time the subdivision and improvements were completed the land was worth almost $400,000.

After several weeks of negotiation, on June 30, 1966, Diversified Public Corp. acquired Smith's and Jones' stock in Realty Push Corp., in exchange for which Diversified Public Corp. issued $200,000 worth of its voting preferred stock to Smith and $180,000 worth of its voting preferred stock to Jones and, in addition, paid Jones $20,000 in cash.

Prior to June 30, 1966, Realty Push Corp. had realized no income. It had a net operating loss carryover of $15,000. It was on the accrual basis, and its fiscal year ended June 30. As of the opening of business on July 1, 1966, Realty Push Corp. was completely liquidated and its assets were distributed to Diversified Public Corp., an accrual basis taxpayer on a fiscal year ending June 30. Diversified Public Corporation had accumulated earnings and profits of $5 million.

Smith's stock in Diversified Public Corp. represented approximately 1 per cent of the value of all of the outstanding stock of that corporation. On September 1, 1966, he sold to a stranger in an arm's-length transaction one-half of the stock he had received in Diversified Public Corporation, receiving therefor $115,000 in cash.

State and explain your answers to the following questions:

(a) What are the tax consequences to Smith and to Jones of the transaction between them and Diversified Public Corp.?

(b) Will Realty Push Corp.'s net operating loss carryover of $15,000 be available as a deduction against Diversified Public Corp.'s income for its fiscal year ending June 30, 1967?

(c) How should Diversified Public Corp. determine its basis for the land it receives on liquidation of Realty Push Corp.?

(d) What are the tax consequences to Smith on his sale of one-half of his Diversified Public Corp. stock?

5.

Corporation M was a manufacturer of plastic shell motor boats. Its shareholders were A, B, C and D. At December 31, 1966, this was Corporation M's summary balance sheet:

Assets		Liabilities	
Cash	$ 300,000	Accounts Payable	$ 300,000
Accounts Receivable	400,000	Accrued Payroll	100,000
Inventory	500,000		400,000
Fixed Assets	300,000		
	$1,500,000	Earned Surplus	500,000
		Common Stock	600,000
			$1,500,000

All assets are shown at their adjusted basis. The earned surplus is equivalent to the post-1913 accumulated earnings and profits. The capital stock, represented by 600,000 shares of common, $1.00 par, was held as follows: A — 240,000 shares; and B, C, and D — 120,000 shares each. Their adjusted basis for these shares in each case was $1.00 per share.

Corporation M had purchased its plastic materials from Corporation P, whose shareholders were X and Y. At December 31, 1966, this was Corporation P's summary balance sheet:

Assets		Liabilities	
Fixed Assets	100,000	Accounts Payable	$ 75,000
Accounts Receivable	50,000	Accrued Payroll	50,000
Inventory	100,000		125,000
Cash	$100,000		
	$350,000	Earned Surplus	200,000
		Common Stock	25,000
			$350,000

All assets are shown at their adjusted basis. The earned surplus is equivalent to the post-1913 accumulated earnings and profits. The capital stock, represented by

25,000 shares of common, $1.00 par, was divided equally between X and Y, each of whom had an adjusted basis for his shares of $1.00.

In 1966 the shareholders of both corporations negotiated the terms of an amalgamation which they thought would work to the business advantage of all concerned. As a result, immediately following the close of business on December 31, 1966, the following events occurred pursuant to agreement of the corporations and their shareholders:

(1) Corporation M distributed equally to its shareholders, as tenants-in-common of undivided interests, all of its assets (except for $220,000 of its accounts receivable), subject to all of its liabilities. In exchange therefor, B, C and D turned in to Corporation M all of their shares; A turned in one-half of his shares; and the shares turned in were retired and cancelled. (A was thus left with 120,000 shares, and the Corporation was left with $220,000 of receivables.)

(2) A, B, C and D contributed to Corporation P all the assets (except for the cash) which they had received from Corporation M, in exchange for which Corporation P assumed Corporation M's liabilities and issued 25,000 shares of its $1.00 par common stock to each of A, B, C and D. A, B, C and D divided the cash received from Corporation M among themselves in equal amounts.

(3) Corporation P changed its name to Corporation M, and the parties expected Corporation P to be able to enjoy the goodwill Corporation M had built up.

(4) Corporation M changed its name to the Termite-Ex Co., which A thereafter operated, deriving the necessary capital from the money it received as the $220,000 of receivables it retained were paid off.

After the foregoing transactions were consummated, the two corporations had no further business transactions with each other. A was the father of B and C. D, X and Y, all individuals, had no familial relationships with each other or with A, B or C. Except as set forth herein, the shareholders had no business or financial relationships with each other. The shareholders were on the cash basis, calendar year. The corporations were on the accrual basis, calendar year.

State and explain your answers to the following questions:

(a) What were the tax consequences of the foregoing transactions to A, B, C and D for 1966?

(b) What were the tax consequences of the foregoing transactions to Corporation M for 1966?

(c) How should Corporation P determine its basis for the assets received from A, B, C and D?

(d) How should A, B, C and D determine their basis for the shares which they have received in Corporation P?

6.

Mr. Williams had been the sole shareholder in Electrotool, Inc. since its formation in 1955. By mid-1962 the corporation had accumulated earnings and profits of $100,000, but it needed to acquire more manufacturing equipment for its growing business, and it did not have the necessary cash. As a result, on July 1, 1962, Mr.

Williams purchased machinery useful in the manufacture of electric drills and saws. He paid $100,000 in cash and then immediately contributed the equipment to Electrotool, Inc., which issued to him 100,000 additional shares of its $1.00 par common stock having a fair market value of $1.25 per share and its ten-year, 6 per cent bond in the face amount of $10,000, its fair market value.

The business continued to prosper, and on December 24, 1964, Williams gave 25 per cent of his stock in Electrotool to an irrevocable trust which his father had created many years before. Williams' father was the life tenant of the trust, and Williams' 19-year-old son was the remainderman. Williams and his father were the trustees.

The trust owned a unique machine which Electrotool could use to advantage. Although for tax purposes it had been fully depreciated by the end of 1961, it was worth $20,000 in 1965. The trust had leased the machine to a stranger, but when that lease terminated on December 31, 1965, the trust sold the machine to Electrotool for $20,000 in cash.

In mid-1966 Electrotool had excess cash of $15,000, with which it purchased marketable securities. In late 1966 Williams' father died. The trust terminated, and Williams' son, now 21 years old, received the stock in Electrotool which the trust had owned. After negotiation Electrotool purchased the son's stock for its then fair market value. Payment was made by transferring to him cash plus the marketable securities, then worth $17,500.

In November 1967 Electrotool, Inc. adopted a plan of complete liquidation and immediately thereafter sold all its machinery, tools, receivables, goodwill and inventory to a competitor corporation for a price of $400,000; $100,000 was paid in cash at the time of the sale, and the balance in equal annual installments of $100,000 each, the first to begin in 1968. The installments carried interest of 6 per cent per annum, and the obligations for the installment payments were represented by notes formally executed by the buyer corporation. On December 15, 1967, Electrotool completely liquidated, distributing all of its assets to Mr. Williams in retirement of his Electrotool stock.

Electrotool was on the accrual basis. All of the other taxpayers were on the cash basis. All taxpayers were on calendar year. Electrotool used the double declining balance method for depreciation of its machinery, and it had deducted the cost of all of its tools as a current business expense, this in closed years prior to those here in question.

State and explain the federal income tax consequences of the foregoing transactions to Mr. Williams, to his son, to the trust and to Electrotool, Inc.

7.

John operated a very successful mail-order business, selling books — encyclopedias and general reference manuals — to people who would respond to mail solicitation and newspaper advertising. He operated in unincorporated form as a sole proprietor. He worked hard, had a few clerical employees and maintained very little inventory, usually buying from the publishers just enough books to fill orders. He was on the cash basis, calendar year. At the end of 1965 his receivables amounted to $300,000, a $50,000 increase over the prior year end, and his taxable income for 1965 was $250,000. In light of his huge individual income tax liabilities, he decided to incorporate and did so on January 2, 1966. The corporation he formed, Bookish, Inc. issued to John 1000 shares of its $100 par common stock, the only stock authorized and issued. In exchange John transferred the assets, subject to the liabilities which Bookish, Inc. assumed, shown below:

Assets			*Liabilities*	
Cash		$ 20,000	Rent Payable	$ 1,000
Accounts Receivable		300,000	Wages Payable	1,000
Book Inventory		5,000	Accounts Payable	25,000
Prepaid Insurance		500	Note to Bank	50,000
Furniture	$2,000			$77,000
Less Depreciation	500	1,500		
		$327,000		

The note to the bank reflects John's borrowing of $50,000 immediately before incorporating in order to help him pay his individual income tax liabilities for 1965. The "Accounts Payable" account reflects money owed for current book purchases and advertising.

Bookish, Inc. continued the business with success. It too was on the cash basis, calendar year. By the end of 1966 its receivables were $400,000, and it had an operating income for the year of $320,000 (before deducting a salary for John). Encyclopedia Franconia, Inc. ("EF, Inc."), a very substantial competitor, then sought to acquire Bookish, Inc. The negotiations succeeded, and on July 1, 1967 the following transaction occurred: Bookish, Inc. transferred all of its assets to EF, Inc. EF, Inc. assumed all of Bookish, Inc.'s liabilities, and it issued to Bookish, Inc. shares of its common stock worth $900,000 and its ten-year, 6 per cent bonds worth $100,000. EF, Inc. also agreed to issue to Bookish, Inc. or its designees $200,000 worth of its $4.00 cumulative voting preferred stock in January 1972 if, in the interim, the profits of the acquired business averaged at least $350,000 a year. Bookish, Inc.'s stock interest in EF, Inc. came to 20 per cent of the outstanding stock. The assets acquired and the liabilities assumed by EF, Inc., as shown on the books of Bookish, Inc. on June 30, 1967, were as follows:

Assets			*Liabilities*	
Cash		$150,000	Rent Payable	$ 1,000
Accounts Receivable		400,000	Wages Payable	2,000
Book Inventory		10,000	Accounts Payable	50,000
Prepaid Insurance		1,000	Note to Bank	50,000
Furniture	$5,000			$103,000
Less Depreciation	1,000	4,000		
		$565,000		

On July 2, 1967, pursuant to plan, Bookish, Inc. completely liquidated, distributing to John in retirement of his stock in Bookish, Inc. the stock and bonds received from EF, Inc. and the contingent right to receive the EF, Inc. preferred.

State and explain the federal income tax consequences (including effect on basis) of the foregoing transactions to John and Bookish, Inc., and the basis to EF, Inc. of the accounts receivable it acquired from Bookish, Inc.

8.

On June 1, 1966, Corporation X redeemed all of the stock (both common and preferred) of one of its minority shareholders, T. Ruble Maker. The negotiated redemption price, $100,000, was paid in cash. Maker had been a disruptive force and X was well rid of him. Subsequently Maker discovered that X's management had misrepresented its profit picture to him. He thereupon brought suit against X, alleging fraud and demanding damages in the amount of $200,000. The suit was settled late in 1967 by X's delivering, and Maker's accepting, marketable securities worth $100,-000. These securities had an adjusted basis in X's hands of $75,000. Maker's aggregate adjusted basis for his stock in X (both common and preferred) was $75,000. (He had purchased the common in 1959 for $75,000 in cash, and the preferred was later issued to him as a share-for-share dividend on his common stock.) At the time Maker's stock was redeemed in 1966, the dividend arrearages on his preferred amounted to $5000.

Both X and Maker were calendar year taxpayers. At December 31, 1966, X's accumulated earnings and profits were $10 million. They were greater by the end of 1967.

State and explain the 1966 and 1967 federal income tax consequences of the foregoing events to both Maker and X.

9.

You are a lawyer on the staff of the Joint (Congressional) Committee on Internal Revenue Taxation. The Chief of Staff (your boss) asks you to draft a memorandum (1) detailing the major failings of §368 as you see them and (2) proposing a scheme which, in replacement of the present §368, will remedy the failings and achieve a rational and equitable structure for "reorganizations." He tells you not to draft statutory language at this time but to make clear what the current problems are which you wish to eliminate (why and where you find the present scheme deficient), and to be explicit in your proposals and in your reasons in support of each. It is expected that your analysis of the deficiencies in §368 will include reference not only to the statutory language but also to the current judicial and administrative resolution of controverted issues.

If your proposals for §368 require the amendment of other Code provisions, you should indicate which, how and why.

Please draft the requested memorandum. (The Chief of Staff believes firmly that his staff people do better if they think and organize before they begin writing their memoranda.)

If you are not acquainted with the Joint Committee, after the examination is over you may want to take a look at §§8000-8023, which establish the Committee and prescribe its functions.

10.

Mr. Korn and Mr. Foote decided to join business forces. Korn had a valuable patent which he had purchased and well-located real estate. Foote had cash and customer contacts. Accordingly, in 1966 they formed Korn-Foote, Inc. (hereinafter "K-F, Inc."). Korn transferred the patent and real estate for common stock (100,000 shares, $1.00 par), and Foote transferred $70,000 in cash for the same number of shares. The stock had a fair market value of $1.00 per share. The patent (worth $40,000) had an adjusted basis in Korn's hands of $20,000, and the real estate (worth $60,000), an adjusted basis of $50,000. Foote agreed to use his customer contacts for the benefit of K-F, Inc.

In 1967 Foote gave 25 per cent of his K-F stock to his wife and 25 per cent to his daughter. The business prospered. In early 1970 K-F, Inc. purchased all of Mrs. Foote's stock for $40,000. K-F paid her for the stock by delivering cash of $25,000 and $15,000 worth of A.T. & T. stock which it had purchased for $10,000 in late 1968.

State and explain:

(a) the federal income tax consequences to Korn and to Foote of the 1966 transaction;

(b) the basis to K-F, Inc. of the assets it received from its shareholders in 1966 and the federal income tax consequences to K-F, Inc. of the distribution of its shares to Korn and Foote in that year;

(c) the federal income tax consequences to Mrs. Foote of K-F's purchase of her stock in 1970; and

(d) the federal income tax consequences to K-F, Inc. of its purchase of Mrs. Foote's stock in 1970.

11.

You are commissioned by the Secretary of the Treasury to propose statutory amendments that (a) bring some certainty to the "liquidation-reincorporation" area of the law, (b) preserve the basic policies of both Section 331 and the reorganization provisions, and (c) buttress the principle that distributions out of earnings and profits of an ongoing corporate enterprise should be taxed as dividends. Without necessarily drafting statutory language, please prepare a memorandum setting forth in detail what your proposals are and why you make them.

12.

Just as Will Operator's new luxury apartment structure was nearing completion in late 1967, he incorporated, contributing the land and building and $50,000 in cash to a newly formed corporation in exchange for 100 per cent of the corporation's stock (all common). Immediately, the corporation filed a Subchapter S election, and Operator filed a consent. The corporation return for the calendar year 1967 (including only the last few months of the year) reflected no receipts but showed a loss as a result of expenses and local taxes.

In 1968 the apartments had been partially rented. A gross rental income of $250,000 was received in that year. In late December 1968 the corporation accepted

an offer for the purchase of the apartment house for a total price of $1,200,000 —
$300,000 over adjusted basis. The $300,000 sum was paid in cash in 1968, and the
balance was represented by a note and mortgage to be paid off ratably over a period
of three years, with interest payable annually at the rate of 7 per cent. The corporation distributed $300,000 to Operator in 1968.

(a) State and explain the 1967 and 1968 federal income tax consequences of the
foregoing events to the corporation and to Operator.

(b) In 1969 the corporation received a $300,000 principal payment on the mort-
gage, dividends and interest of $70,000, and municipal bond interest of $10,000, all of
which the corporation distributed immediately to Operator. State and explain the
federal income tax consequences of these facts to the corporation and to Operator.

13.

Alec Hamilton, a moneyed fellow with real estate experience, and Tom Jefferson,
a promising young architect, went into a real estate venture together in 1967. Forming a general partnership, Hamilton contributed building lots (aggregate adjusted
basis, $60,000; aggregate fair market value, $80,000) and cash of $10,000. Jefferson
contributed cash of $10,000. They agreed that Hamilton would have a 70 per cent
interest in the capital and Jefferson a 30 per cent interest, but that profits would be
split 50-50. Losses would be borne 50-50 to the extent of any reinvested profits; losses
would be borne 70 per cent by Hamilton and 30 per cent by Jefferson to the extent
that the losses impaired original capital or the original capital was insufficient. Jefferson
agreed to devote 100 per cent of his time to the venture as an architect and general
supervisor (and to stay out of politics), and to do so without salary. Hamilton agreed
to devote such minimal time to giving managerial advice as he alone might think
called for at any given time.

Construction funds aggregating $500,000 were obtained by the partnership from
a bank on the security of a first mortgage. The partners were not personally liable
on the obligation.

In 1968 Hamilton contributed to the partnership A.T. & T. stock worth $200,000
(basis of $100,000), and Jefferson contributed $85,000 worth of General Telephone
stock (basis of $40,000). The stock did not appreciate further in the partnership's
hands. In early 1969 the firm distributed $140,000 worth of the A.T. & T. stock and
$59,500 of the General Telephone stock to Hamilton, and $60,000 of the A.T. & T.
stock and $25,500 of the General Telephone stock to Jefferson.

By early 1970 the venture had done reasonably well, making a good profit on the
lots built upon and sold. Hamilton, however, did not wish to wait for the improvement and sale of the remaining lots. After a friendly negotiation, a document was
signed on April 1, 1970, under which Jefferson purchased Hamilton's interest in the
partnership for cash. The price was determined on the basis of a formula which gave
Hamilton 50 per cent of reinvested profits, 40 per cent of the appreciation in the
value of the lots and buildings-in-process, and 70 per cent of the value of the original
contributions to capital.

Assume that the partnership and the individuals are on the cash basis, calendar
year.

State and explain the federal income tax consequences to each of the partners of the events of *1967* and *1969,* and to Hamilton of the events of *1970.* In doing so state your assumption (and its significance) as to what provision, if any, was made in the partnership agreement with respect to the fact that the building lots originally contributed by Hamilton were worth more than their basis.

14.

John Rich, his son Bill, and a friend, Marvin Slick, formed a partnership on January 2, 1962, with each investing $50,000 in cash. Profits and losses were to be shared equally.

A month later the partnership invested the $150,000 cash in a corporation which it formed, taking 100 per cent of the authorized and issued common stock in exchange. The corporation immediately thereafter purchased land costing $250,000, paying $150,000 in cash and giving a purchase money mortgage to secure the balance.

The corporation then proceeded to develop the land, half of it for residential use and half as a shopping center. Construction and operating costs were provided by a construction mortgage for the full amount needed. It was intended to sell off the lots and the houses built thereon to prospective homeowners, but to keep the shopping center for its rental income.

By November 1, 1963, half the total number of houses to be built had been built, and, with the lots on which they stood, had been sold at a profit; the other half of the residential section was under construction, unsold. The shopping center was two-thirds completed but none of it yet occupied by tenants. The value of the corporation at this time was double the original cost of asset purchase and development.

The three partners began to have difficulties with each other. Slick did not get along with either John or Bill Rich. Bill Rich was anxious for some of the corporation's cash which had been generated through sales to be distributed; to date, none had been.

Since Slick could not be reconciled with the others, on November 15, 1963, he sold his interest in the partnership to Don Adams, who was unrelated by either family or business connection to any of the others. John and Bill Rich consented to the transfer of interest, and Slick reaped a substantial profit.

On December 1, 1963, the partnership distributed to Bill Rich one-sixth of its stock in the corporation in pro tanto reduction of Bill's interest in the partnership. Promptly thereafter the corporation purchased the shares held by Bill, paying him cash equal to half the amount which Slick had received from Adams for his one-third partnership interest.

None of the parties had ever had real estate interests outside of this venture.

State and explain the income tax consequences of the foregoing to Marvin Slick and Bill Rich.

15.

A large publicly held corporation (Cotton Fab) was engaged for many years in the production of cotton piece goods. About four years ago it began to lose money as a result of poor management and general business conditions in the industry. The losses were small at first, but in 1968 the corporation lost $4 million, and in 1969 it lost $11 million.

The corporation files its income tax returns on the basis of the calendar year and the accrual method of accounting. The corporation has a number of wholly owned subsidiaries which are engaged in the same type of business as the parent corporation. Consolidated income tax returns have been filed each year, beginning with the return for the year ended December 31, 1962. Returns for the year ended December 31, 1969, have not yet been filed.

On July 1, 1969, a Mr. Conwell purchased from a group of stockholders 25 per cent of the outstanding capital stock of Cotton Fab. The stock is widely held and traded over the counter, but a 25 per cent block had been owned by one group of interests from whom Mr. Conwell was able to make the purchase. The former management of the corporation was removed, Mr. Conwell was made Chairman of the Board, and he and his representatives constitute three out of seven members of the Board of Directors. The other four members of the Board are quite sympathetic with Mr. Conwell's aims and are happy to have him "run the show."

Conwell first tried efficiencies and economies in order to reverse the financial predicament of Cotton Fab and its subsidiaries. He has not been successful and expects shortly to terminate all of the cotton operation. He has just now reached this conclusion.

Last October, however, Mr. Conwell decided that the company should diversify and go into profitable business ventures, whether or not it could remain in the cotton business.

On November 1, 1969, negotiations were concluded under which Cotton Fab acquired the business of an aircraft manufacturing business.

The principals agreed on the following terms:

(1) Mr. Harbison, the owner of the aircraft manufacturing corporation, would sell to Cotton Fab or its nominee the entire aircraft manufacturing business for a total price of $4 million. (The net worth of the aircraft manufacturing company is $1.5 million at book. It has been earning $600,000 a year before income taxes.)

(2) A million dollars would be paid in cash; $200,000 would be paid by the delivery of capital stock of Cotton Fab, and the balance would be paid out of 75 per cent of the aircraft manufacturing corporation's pre-tax earnings until Cotton Fab's loss carryover was used up, and thereafter out of 75 per cent of the post-tax earnings of the operation, until the full balance of the purchase price had been paid.

(3) Cotton Fab was to be entitled to pay the $1 million down payment out of $1 million of excess cash which it would find in the aircraft company. The seller was to receive liens on the aircraft manufacturing business as security for payment of the purchase price. If the full balance of the purchase price were not paid within ten years, the debt would mature, and he would be entitled to foreclose. He would, of course, also be entitled to foreclose if any default should occur prior thereto.

(4) The seller and his representatives would continue in complete control of the aircraft manufacturing operation until they were paid in full. The seller was to remain as the chief executive officer of that operation and for his services was to continue to draw the same salary as he had previously drawn.

(5) Neither Cotton Fab nor any of its previously existing subsidiaries would have any personal liability for any portion of the purchase price beyond the initial cash payment and the Cotton Fab stock, which was to be delivered to the seller at closing. In the event of a default, the seller's remedies were to be limited to foreclosure on his security.

As indicated above, this transaction was closed on November 1, before Cotton Fab had gone out of its existing business and before it had decided to do so. It is now out of the cotton business, and its only active operation is the aircraft manufacturing business. It still owns its old manufacturing plants, however, which it now leases to others, and enjoys royalty income from the licensing of its old tradenames.

How would you have advised that the foregoing transaction be set up in order to accomplish the following:

(1) The loss carryover of Cotton Fab will be available as a deduction against the post-November 1, 1969, profits of the aircraft manufacturing operation, and no part of the acquisition transaction will result in taxable income to Cotton Fab or its subsidiaries.

(2) The buyer will be able to write up (for tax purposes) the assets of the aircraft manufacturing company to the buyer's cost of $4 million, or as close to that as possible.

(3) The seller will have no ordinary income as a result of the foregoing transaction (except for his salary) and will be entitled to report his gain on the sale of the business as long-term capital gain, the tax payable over the period when he actually receives payments from the buyer.

Your plan should be sufficiently lucid and detailed that your clients will understand each step involved. If there were time, you would be asked to follow the plan with a thorough legal memorandum, replete with your authorities, analyzing each step and explaining your conclusions in every instance. Would your conclusions be any different if

(a) Cotton Fab had no longer been in the cotton business when it acquired the aircraft company, or

(b) had decided to get out of the cotton business but had not yet done so?

Suppose the facts are as stated in the memorandum, but later this year, after Cotton Fab is out of the cotton business, it decides to buy a shoe manufacturing business on the same basis as it previously had purchased the aircraft manufacturing business. Will your plan and your conclusions with respect thereto be the same?

16.

John Whitehouse, his brother William Whitehouse, and a friend, Aaron Schmidt, are the sole and equal owners of all of the outstanding capital stock of a corporation. The corporation is engaged essentially in two operations: One operation consists of the manufacture of ladies' hosiery; the other, the operation of gasoline service stations.

Both operations have been in existence for many years. They were started on a shoestring. The capital of the corporation consists of 15,000 shares of common capital stock, $1.00 par. Each stockholder owns 5000 shares, for which he originally invested a total of $5000. As a result of favorable operations and reinvestment of the earnings in the business, the corporation today has a surplus of about $600,000. Most of the surplus is invested in fixed assets, but the corporation has about $50,000 in cash.

The stockholders would like to sell the hosiery manufacturing operation and to retain the service station operation. They, in their own mind, regard the hosiery operation and the assets devoted to it as having a fair market value of about $500,000; they believe that the service station operation (both its tangible assets and goodwill) has a fair market value of about $300,000. If they sell the hosiery operation, they would like to continue operating the service station business in corporate form if at all possible. A year ago you were consulted when the stockholders had come to this stage, and you were told to plan for this ultimate possibility.

Having planned accordingly, a purchaser now comes on the scene ready, willing and able to buy the hosiery operation for $500,000. He can finance the deal by putting up $350,000 of his own cash and by obtaining a mortgage loan on the hosiery assets themselves of $150,000.

What plan did you set up and why? How should the sale transaction be set up now so that it can be accomplished with minimum tax consequences to all parties? State your plan lucidly so that your clients will understand every step and so that agreements can be drawn on the basis of your plan.

It is significant from the tax viewpoint that the steps taken a year ago were in contemplation of a proposed sale? Does it matter that the purchaser was not at hand a year ago and just recently came upon the scene? Suppose the purchaser were at hand before any plan at all had been conceived?

17.

Two unrelated individuals wish to form a business venture in order to conduct a leather jobbing and importing business. One of the individuals, Percy Althouse, will provide $50,000 in cash. The other fellow, Hans Klugman, will contribute hides and a piece of real estate. The hides are worth $5000 and the real estate is worth $45,000. The real estate cost Mr. Klugman only $40,000, however, and the building has since been depreciated to $35,000.

It is expected that the operation will be very profitable. During its first year, however, the owners will probably not draw any compensation, and the operation may lose money, perhaps to the tune of $5000 or $10,000. During the second year, however, the operation should earn $20,000 (before salaries); during the third year, it should earn $35,000 (before salaries); and after that it is expected to earn $50,000 a year and upwards (all before salaries to owners).

The owners are each married and living happily with their wives. Each of the owners, apart from this venture, has an annual ordinary income of $10,000-$12,000; the wives have no income of their own. Klugman and Althouse each have two minor children between the ages of eight and fourteen. The children have no assets of their own and are the beneficiaries of no trusts.

How should this business venture be set up in order to provide the parties with the most equitable arrangement among themselves and also to provide them with the minimum in tax consequences? What form should the business take? How should the ownership be evidenced? In what manner should the capital be invested? Should members of the family other than Hans and Percy participate in the ownership of the venture and, if so, to what extent and in what manner? Should the form of the business association change at any time during the first five years?

Five and a half years have gone by, and we find that the leather venture has met all of its expectations. A corporation engaged in plastics manufacturing is for sale. It has lost $250,000 in operations and has a net worth at book of $20,000. Assume that the total which Hans and Percy have drawn out of their leather business as compensation over the five-year period is $30,000 each, and you can therefore compute what funds might possibly be available in the leather business, if it is to make the purchase. The leather business has never distributed dividends.

The plastics business is on its last legs. Although its current liabilities exceed its current assets, if it were to be liquidated it would be shown to have a realistic net worth of about $15,000. There is a chance that, if it is properly managed and fresh capital is infused, the plastics business itself can be made successful; but neither Percy nor Hans is very much interested in the plastics business.

The minds of the parties are not made up, except that the owners of the plastics company would like to get as much for their company as possible. They are asking $60,000. Hans and Percy would like to avail themselves of the loss carryover if they can. What would you advise? How would you set up the transaction?

Would your conclusions be any different if the owners of the plastics company were willing to take a stock interest in the leather business, in lieu of cash, for the purchase price? What percentage of the total venture would you recommend that they receive and why?

18.

Mr. Amerando and Mr. Roberts are first cousins who have been in business together for about ten years. They have been represented in their ventures by an attorney named John Lipsius.

About three years ago Amerando and Roberts began to see things differently from each other and have now reached the point of a definitive falling-out. They no longer can agree on anything as to business policy, their wives no longer speak to each other and they have engaged in petty slander. They both are intent on a separation of their business interests, and initially they both went to Mr. Lipsius to try to effect a separation. As negotiations progressed Roberts felt that there might really be something of a conflict of interest, and he decided to get his own counsel, Mr. William Brucker.

The business interests of Amerando and Roberts are conducted through three corporations. Amerando and Roberts each owns 50 per cent of the capital stock of each corporation. Only common stock is outstanding in each instance.

The first corporation, known as 30th & Johnson Street Corporation (hereinafter called "Johnson Street Corp."), owns two pieces of Philadelphia real estate, one of which it rents to the parties' second corporation, known as the Amrob Coffee Corp. (hereinafter called "Amrob"). Its other piece of property is rented to the parties' third corporation, known as Refrigeration Supply Corp.

Amrob's activities consist of the following:

(1) At three locations within the city of Philadelphia it sells non-intoxicating beverages — coffee, carbonated beverages and fruit drinks — to the public through automatic vending machines.

(2) Amrob also sells refrigeration units to various refrigeration distributors throughout the state of Pennsylvania.

(3) As mentioned before, the beverage business is conducted at three locations. The first is at one of the properties owned by Johnson Street Corp. The lease with Johnson Street Corp. was first entered into on January 1, 1948. The second establishment at which the beverage business is operated is at property leased from a third party within the city of Philadelphia. This lease was entered into on January 1, 1950. The third location is also leased from a third party, and this lease was entered into on July 1, 1954. About a third of the beverage volume and profit is derived from each location, and the assets are also equally divided among the three locations.

(4) The refrigeration business conducted by Amrob Corp. is operated out of two principal locations. One location is the second piece of real estate owned by Johnson Street Corp. This is located on Delaware Avenue in Philadelphia and is leased on a year-to-year basis to Amrob Corp.

The parties' third corporation, Refrigeration Supply Corp., has its headquarters in Pittsburgh. It sells refrigeration parts to commercial users of refrigeration equipment including, but not limited to, persons who purchase refrigerators from Amrob Corp. Its headquarters in Pittsburgh is in property which it, Refrigeration Supply Corp., owns. It is also engaged in business in Philadelphia, leasing from Johnson Street Corp. a portion of the Delaware Avenue property which Amrob Corp. uses for its refrigeration sales activities.

One of you is Mr. Lipsius who represents Amerando; the other is Mr. Brucker, who represents Roberts. The parties want to make the following deal:

(A) Amerando is to end up as sole owner of the Johnson Street Corp. or its assets. In addition to the two pieces of real estate previously mentioned, this corporation also has an accumulated surplus of cash. The real estate is free and clear of any encumbrance. Amerando is also to own the beverage business operated by Amrob and the real estate located in Pittsburgh now owned by Refrigeration Supply Corp.

(B) Roberts is to end up owning the refrigeration supply business and the refrigeration sales business but no real estate.

(C) All businesses involved here are to continue to be conducted at their existing locations.

If at all possible, the parties want to continue their business activities and real estate ownership in corporate form.

The financial facts are as follows:

(1) Johnson Street Corp. has current assets at book of $53,000, fixed assets at book of $165,000, and prepaid expenses of $2000. It has current liabilities of $33,000, and no long-term liabilities. Its outstanding capital stock consists of 70 shares of common stock, par value $100 each. The parties' cost for the stock is par.

(2) Amrob's current assets are about $100,000; its fixed assets are about $15,000; and its current liabilities are about $30,000. The outstanding capital stock (all com-

mon) has a total par value of $45,000, which represents the actual cost of the stock to the individuals. The accountants for Amrob and the parties are satisfied that the beverage business on the one hand, and the refrigeration sales business on the other, are about equal in actual value.

(3) Refrigeration Supply Corp. has current assets of $865,000 at book. Its fixed assets at book are $34,000. Its current liabilities are $350,000, and its long-term liabilities are $250,000. Its capital stock has a total par value of $60,000, which is the actual cost of the stock to the individuals.

Refrigeration Supply Corp. reports its income for tax purposes on the installment basis. As of the date on which you are consulted, the Corporation's accrued accounts receivable, after provision for uncollectible debts, amounts to $695,000. Of that amount about $350,000 represents income which has been deferred for tax purposes by reason of the installment method of accounting.

(4) Appraisals which have been obtained by independent real estate appraisers indicate that the fair market value of the real estate owned by Johnson Street Corp. and the Pittsburgh real estate, when added to the net current assets in the Johnson Street Corp., are equal in value to the business conducted by Refrigeration Supply Corp. as a going concern. In valuing the latter business for this purpose the value of the Pittsburgh real estate has, of course, been excluded.

Amerando wants to make certain that Roberts will not compete with the beverage business, and Roberts wants to make certain that Amerando will not compete with him in either the refrigeration sales business or the refrigeration supply business.

Please work out a plan for Amerando and Roberts which will accomplish what they want at the cheapest tax cost — tax-free, if you can. After setting up the plan itself, explain what the tax consequences will be and what your authority is for your conclusions. The explanation of the tax consequences and your authorities should be in the form of a thorough, well-considered legal memorandum. The plan itself should be one which will be understood by your clients and should be sufficiently lucid and detailed so that, promptly after securing your clients' approval, your law firm's corporate department can draw the necessary documents to effectuate the plan.

19.

Rocket-Whiz Corporation was organized under the laws of the state of Delaware on May 17, 1958. Its total authorized capital stock consists of 125,000 voting shares of a par value of ten cents per share, of which 116,000 shares are issued and outstanding. All of the shares are held by a number of individuals who are residents and citizens of the United States, except for 22,800 which are owned by Oceanic Inc., a foreign corporation organized under the laws of Nassau, which is not engaged in business in the United States and all of whose stockholders are nonresident aliens.

The shareholders of Rocket-Whiz paid $284,200 in cash for the 116,000 shares of stock. They also purchased for cash, at their face amount, $768,000 of subordinated notes of Rocket-Whiz which bear interest at the rate of 5 per cent per annum from June 3, 1958, and mature on July 1, 1962. These subordinated notes are payable prior to maturity at the option of the maker.

Rocket-Whiz was organized as a vehicle to acquire from Mr. Heathcliff all of the issued and outstanding stock of Rocket-Whiz Corp., a California corporation (hereinafter called "California") and its affiliated companies, Fuel Laboratories, Inc., Allie Nuclear, Inc. and Inventions Unbound, Inc., and real estate on which one of the plants of these companies is located. At the closing on June 3, 1958, Mr. Heathcliff was paid $1 million in cash and was given notes of Rocket-Whiz (Delaware) in the principal amount of $750,000, bearing interest at 5 per cent.

The parties wish to accomplish the following:

(1) The acquisition by Rocket-Whiz (Delaware) within its own corporate structure of all of the assets of the corporations previously owned by Mr. Heathcliff.

(2) The exchange by the stockholders of Rocket-Whiz of all of their stock in that corporation for 1,160,000 shares of the $1.00 par value voting stock of Venezuela Oil, Inc., a Venezuelan corporation.

The businesses conducted by the corporations previously owned by Mr. Heathcliff are all related to the production of rockets, missiles and the like.

Venezuela Oil, Inc. is a publicly held corporation whose stock is listed on the Caracas Stock Exchange and the American Stock Exchange. It is engaged principally in exploring for and producing oil and gas in Venezuela. Its operations are conducted partially on lands which it owns and partially on lands which it rents from others. Except for the operations of a Texas subsidiary mentioned below, all of these oil and gas operations are located within Venezuela. The company has been losing money — about $1.5 million in the past three years — and its Board is anxious to acquire control of Rocket-Whiz in the belief that it has a present and future earnings potential, and diversification is regarded as desirable. The Rocket-Whiz stockholders are interested in the proposed exchange because it will give them 45 per cent of the stock of Venezuela Oil which will be then outstanding, and they have hopes that perhaps the oil business may perk up. The Venezuela Oil stock has been trading of late at about $3.00 a share, generally regarded as a highly inflated value; its liquidating value is under $1.00 a share.

Venezuela Oil owns all of the capital stock of a subsidiary corporation which has been formed under the laws of Texas and which has been engaged on a small scale in the exploration and the production of oil within the state of Texas. This corporation has also been losing money, and it has a net operating loss carryover of about $200,000. Mr. Heathcliff's operation has been profitable, and the Rocket-Whiz stockholders expect the operation to continue to earn profits at the rate of $30,000 a month before taxes. The parties hope that after Venezuela Oil acquires all of the outstanding stock of Rocket-Whiz, some method can be found to enable the prior losses of Venezuela Oil and/or those of its Texas subsidiary ("Texas") to be available as a set-off against the profits of the Rocket-Whiz operation.

For political and corporate reasons unrelated to taxation, the parties would also like to terminate Venezuela Oil's status as a Venezuelan corporation and would like to have it incorporated under the laws of the state of Delaware. Venezuela law provides, however, that only Venezuelan corporations may own oil wells located within its jurisdiction.

Please outline a plan which you think may enable the parties to accomplish the foregoing objectives on a tax-free basis. If you conclude that these objectives cannot be accomplished on a tax-free basis, suggest a plan which will result in as low a tax bill as possible. State also what you can do, if anything, to make the loss carryovers available against future profits of the Rocket-Whiz operation. After setting up your plan, please follow it with a detailed legal memorandum showing your authorities and analyzing all of the legal problems which are inherent in the proposal. The plan itself should be detailed and sufficiently lucid to be understood by your clients. The plan should also be in such form as will enable the corporate lawyers in your firm to move forward immediately with the necessary agreements and corporate work.

20.

Ohio Investments, Inc. (hereinafter called "Ohio") is a corporation formed under the laws of Ohio on July 1, 1948. Until July 1, 1957, it was engaged in the manufacture of children's toys. At that time its manufacturing operation ceased and its business was sold to another company called Children's Toys, Inc., the same name by which Ohio was known prior to the date of the sale. Ohio acquired its present name immediately after the sale. Since July 1, 1957, Ohio's income has consisted primarily of rents (about 60 per cent of its gross income), and the balance consists of dividend and interest income.

As of now Ohio's balance sheet shows current assets of $290,000, investments of $4 million at market (well over cost), and fixed assets which are on the books at $1,165,000 (cost less depreciation) and which have an appraised fair market value of $1,375,000.

The current assets are cash in bank; the investments are marketable securities, government bonds, a note from Children's Toys, Inc. for an unpaid portion of the purchase price of the manufacturing business, preferred stock of Children's Toys, Inc. (part of the consideration for the sale) and a real estate mortgage. The fixed assets consist solely of real estate which is leased to Children's Toys, Inc.

The current liabilities of about $95,000 consist primarily of accrued taxes for the current and preceding year. The long-term debt of $280,000 represents a loan secured by a mortgage on the company's real estate. The outstanding capital stock consists of 435,000 shares, par value of $2.50 each. The stockholders paid par for their stock.

The principal stockholders of Ohio are John Toyson, who owns outright 155,000 shares; Bill Toyson, John's brother, who owns outright 182,000 shares; and Raymond Toyson, another brother, who owns outright 21,000 shares.

John's parents are deceased, and he has no wife, no children and no grandchildren.

One of the stockholders of the corporation is Bertha Jensen, who owns outright 400 shares. She is a sister of John, Bill and Raymond. Bertha's husband Robert is also a stockholder. He owns 400 shares outright, and Robert and Bertha own as tenants by the entireties 1062 shares outright.

Another sister, Ethel Robertson, is also a stockholder. She owns outright 400 shares.

Five years ago John created two irrevocable trusts, one for the benefit of his sister Bertha and the other for the benefit of his sister Ethel. Bertha and Ethel are the income beneficiaries of the respective trusts. The duration of each of the trusts is ten years and six months or the life of the beneficiary, whichever is longer. During the beneficiary's lifetime the latter is entitled to all of the income of the trusts. Upon termination of each of the trusts the corpus reverts to John, if living, and if not, to his estate. If the beneficiaries should die before the expiration of ten years and six months from the date of creation of the trusts, the trusts will continue until the end of that period, with the income for the period between the date of the beneficiaries' death and the date of termination of the trust to be distributed to a charitable foundation previously established by John.

John was born on December 1, 1883. Bertha was born on November 1, 1888. Ethel was born on April 1, 1890.

Except for the preferred stock previously mentioned, all of the outstanding stock of Children's Toys, Inc. is owned by the children of Bill and Raymond.

The trustees of Bertha's and Ethel's trusts would like Ohio to buy all of the capital stock of that corporation which the trusts own. John would like the corporation to buy between $450,000 and $475,000 worth of the capital stock which he owns in Ohio.

The purchase price, as to the trusts, will be paid part in cash and part in marketable securities valued at market.

As to John, the purchase price will be paid $100,000 at the time of the sale, and the balance in annual installments beginning January 1, 1950, with interest on the unpaid balance at the prime commercial Philadelphia bank rate, as that rate may be from time to time, but not in excess of 8½ per cent per annum. Ohio will have full right of prepayment without penalty. Ohio may pay John either in cash or in marketable securities valued at market.

The foregoing transaction is contingent on the assurance that the following tax consequences will result:

(1) There will be no ordinary income to anybody.

(2) The trusts will have a long-term capital gain on the sale of their stock, and no one else will have any tax consequence as a result.

(3) John will have a long-term capital gain, and he may pay his tax over the years during which he actually receives payment, and no one else will have any tax consequence as a result.

(4) There will be no tax consequence to Ohio as a result of these transactions.

(5) The basis to the trusts and to John for the securities which they will receive in part payment will be the market value of those securities at the date of receipt.

(6) John may continue as President of Ohio and as a member of its Board of Directors, and he may continue to receive a salary for his services as President and a fee for his services as a member of the Board.

To what extent can the parties accomplish their desires? How many shares of stock do you recommend that John tender? At what price per share? Please analyze the foregoing in a legal memorandum in which you first outline precisely what your plan is and then explain what the considerations are in setting up the transaction and in reaching your conclusions.

Suppose that Raymond would like Ohio to purchase all of his shares at the same time. Children of Raymond also own stock in Ohio, but they want to hold on to their shares. Raymond is not interested in remaining as an officer or director of Ohio. He does work for Children's Toys, Inc., however, and as previously mentioned, his children own stock in that corporation. If all of Raymond's stock in Ohio is sold to Ohio, would this affect the tax consequences to the Bertha and Ethel trusts and to John? Would Raymond have long-term capital gain or ordinary income? Would it make any difference if Raymond's sale occurred three or four years after the trusts and John completed their sale? Would it make any difference if the latter sale had been conceived of at the time of the earlier ones, even though the actual consummation is separated by three or four years?

Are you interested in the fact that Raymond has had a program under which he has been giving to each of his children each year $6000 worth of Ohio capital stock, and that the last such gift was made just before Christmas? Suppose Raymond had not had an annual program of gift making but he had made his first gift of Ohio stock just last year, at a time when he was thinking of the proposed sale and after his accountant had said, "You have to redeem all, or not at all."

21.

A closely held corporation has been engaged in the wholesale feed business for many years. It buys feed, warehouses it and sells it to customers. It also engages in the feed warehouse business. It owns a warehouse in which it stores its own feed as well as the feed owned by others who pay rent for the storage facilities. The company has been engaged in both operations for well over ten years.

John Haberly owns a corporation (hereinafter called "purchaser") which wants to buy the wholesale feed business. It is not at all interested in, and will not buy, the warehouse or warehousing business. It also insists that the present owners of the feed business agree not to compete with that business for five years after the sale is consummated. The U.S. Department of Agriculture must approve a sale of the assets of a feed business, and its regulations would require public hearings and all sorts of delays. To avoid the expense and delay and possible refusal of the Department, the purchaser wishes to buy only presently outstanding capital stock of the existing corporation — a transaction in which the Department of Agriculture would not be concerned.

The initial capitalization of the feed and warehouse corporation was $50,000. The corporation now has a surplus of $300,000. The proposed purchase price for the feed business is $250,000. The purchaser will expect to receive all of the fixed assets, accounts receivable, inventory and goodwill of that operation. The business has been built up, of course, through reinvestment of annual profits. The warehouse alone is worth about $150,000. The corporation has about $50,000 of cash.

The purchaser would like to deduct as an operating expense as much of the price which it is paying as possible. The sellers, on the other hand, want to receive the purchase price in cash in their individual hands and at as low a tax cost as possible.

As counsel for the purchaser, what plan would you suggest, bearing in mind, of course, what the seller's objectives are? As counsel for the sellers, what plan would you suggest, bearing in mind the purchaser's objectives as well?

If it is impossible to give the purchaser a current deduction for a portion of his price and at the same time to assure the seller that he will avoid ordinary income, then assume that the buyer is willing to give up this point and set up the transaction as favorably as you can from the buyer's point of view without the current deduction, giving him whatever other tax advantages might be available, but nevertheless keeping the seller's tax bill as low as possible.

Bear in mind, too, that the sellers would like, if at all possible, to find a purchaser for the warehouse business, and they would like, therefore, as long as possible, to keep the warehouse in the existing corporation in order to avoid incurring Pennsylvania real estate transfer taxes which would be due if that real estate had to be transferred now, even before an outside purchaser were found. What do you recommend and why?

Suppose there were no regulatory problems with the Department of Agriculture and, from that point of view, therefore, either assets or stock could be sold. But assume that the purchaser could not pay more than $50,000 down and the seller were willing to take the balance of the purchase price in three annual installments of $50,000 each, plus a final installment in the fourth year of $100,000. The purchaser does not believe that he would be able to make his first annual payment of the deferred portion of the purchase price before November or December, if the transaction is consummated on April 1, 1959 — the parties' target date. The unpaid balance of the purchase price would not bear interest, but, as you see, the total price has been jacked up from $250,000 to $300,000 because of the delay in payment.

Would these facts alter your plan? If so, set forth your revisions and your reasons therefor.

Set up your plans carefully and lucidly so that your clients will have no difficulty understanding them. Then follow with a legal memorandum analyzing each of the problems, setting forth your authorities and the reasons for your conclusions.

Index